FIELDS OF
WRITING

Second Edition

 W9-AGN-662

FIELDS OF

WRITING

READINGS ACROSS THE DISCIPLINES

Second Edition

Nancy R. Comley
QUEENS COLLEGE, CUNY

David Hamilton
UNIVERSITY OF IOWA

Carl H. Klaus
UNIVERSITY OF IOWA

Robert Scholes
BROWN UNIVERSITY

Nancy Sommers
RUTGERS UNIVERSITY

St. Martin's Press
NEW YORK

Library of Congress Catalog Card Number: 86–60644
Copyright © 1987 by St. Martin's Press, Inc.
All Rights Reserved.
Manufactured in the United States of America.
10987
fedcba
For information, write St. Martin's Press, Inc.,
175 Fifth Avenue, New York, N.Y. 10010

cover photo: Joel Gordon
cover design: Darby Downey

ISBN: 0-312-288395

ACKNOWLEDGMENTS

Ron Amundson, "The Hundredth Monkey Phenomenon," *The Skeptical Inquirer*, Vol. IX, No. 4, Summer 1985, pp. 349–356.

Maya Angelou, "Graduation," from *I Know Why the Caged Bird Sings* by Maya Angelou. Copyright © 1969 by Maya Angelou. Reprinted by permission of Random House, Inc.

Isaac Asimov, "The Case Against Man," Copyright © 1970 by Field Enterprises Inc. from SCIENCE PAST-SCIENCE FUTURE by Isaac Asimov. Reprinted by permission of Doubleday and Company, Inc.

Isaac Asimov, "My Built-In-Doubter," Copyright © 1961 by Mercury Press from FACT AND THEORY by Isaac Asimov. Reprinted by permission of Doubleday and Company, Inc.

Russell Baker, "The Cruelest Month," September 21, 1980. Copyright © 1980 by The New York Times Company. Reprinted by permission.

Diana Baumrind, "Review of Stanley Milgram's Experiments," from "Some Thoughts on the Ethics of Research: After Reading Milgram's 'Behavioral Study of Obedience'," *American Psychologist*, Vol. 19, 1964, pp. 421–423. Copyright © 1964 by the American Psychological Association. Reprinted by permission of the publisher and the author.

Bruno Bettelheim, "The Ignored Lesson of Anne Frank," Copyright © 1960 by Bruno Bettelheim and Trude Bettelheim as Trustees. Reprinted from *Surviving and Other Essays* by Bruno Bettelheim by permission of Alfred A. Knopf, Inc.

Bruno Bettelheim, "Joey: 'A Mechanical Boy'," reprinted with permission. Copyright © 1959 by Scientific American, Inc. All rights reserved.

Michael Brown, "Love Canal and the Poisoning of America," Copyright © 1979 by Michael Brown. Reprinted from LAYING WASTE: LOVE CANAL AND THE POISONING OF AMERICA by Michael Brown, by permission of Pantheon Books, a division of Random House, Inc.

Edward Hallet Carr, "The Historian and His Facts," from *What Is History?* by Edward Hallet Carr. Copyright © 1980 by Edward Hallet Carr. Reprinted by permission of Alfred A. Knopf, Inc.

Edward Hallet Carr, "The Historian and His Facts," from *What Is History?* Reprinted by permission of Macmillan, London and Basingstroke.

Rosalind Coward, "Let's Have a Meal Together," from FEMALE DESIRES. Copyright © 1985 by Rosalind Coward. Reprinted by permission of Grove Press, Inc. Reprinted by permission of Grafton Books, a division of Collins Publishing Group.

Francis Crick, "Time and Distances, Large and Small," from *Life Itself*. Copyright © 1981 by Francis Crick. Reprinted by permission of Simon & Schuster, Inc.

A.R. Damasio and D. Tranel, "Knowledge Without Awareness," from *Science*, June 21, 1985, Vol. 228, pp. 1453–1454. Copyright © 1985 by the American Association for the Advancement of Science.

Charles Darwin, "The Action of Natural Selection," from *The Essential Darwin*, edited by Robert Jastrow. Copyright © 1984 by Robert Jastrow. Reprinted by permission of Little, Brown and Company.

Acknowledgments and copyright continue at the back of the book on pages 777–780, which constitute an extension of the copyright page.

For Instructors

In putting together the second edition of *Fields of Writing*, we have once again been committed to producing a composition reader that is truly cross-curricular. Our convictions about the value of such a reader have been confirmed by the detailed reactions and suggestions of more than 100 instructors who used the first edition, virtually all of whom told us to keep the collection just as wide-ranging in its subject matter as before. So our table of contents again covers a broad array of topics, from the Egyptian pyramids to *E.T.*, from the bubonic plague of the fourteenth century to the atomic bombing of Nagasaki, from the characteristics of narcissism to the nature of mathematical proof. So, too, the table of contents again offers material drawn equally from the arts and the humanities, from the social sciences and public affairs, and from the sciences and technologies—from the major areas of the curriculum in both their academic and applied forms. Overall, then, you will find here a total of 90 selections as various in subject, form, and purpose as the different kinds of reading and writing that students are expected to carry on both in undergraduate education and in the world outside the classroom.

In organizing our collection, we have once again grouped pieces according to four broad rhetorical categories—"Reflecting," "Reporting," "Explaining," and "Arguing"—that represent essential kinds of reading and writing in virtually every academic or professional area. In every field, persons need to think about past experience (reflecting), convey information (reporting), make sense of knowledge (explaining), and debate controversial ideas and issues (arguing). Within each of these four categories, we have as before grouped the selections according to three broad curricular areas—"Arts and Humanities," "Social Sciences and Public Affairs," and "Sciences and Technologies." This combined system of organization, our reviewers tell us, has proved to be a convenient aid to discovering and assigning selections for a variety of classroom purposes.

While maintaining this rhetorical/cross-curricular system of organization, we have been stimulated by the suggestions of instructors who used the first edition to make a substantial number of changes throughout the table of contents, with the result that 50 of the 90 selections are new to this edition. These new selections, have enabled us to include pieces by some of the major scholars, thinkers, and observers who did not appear in the first edition, such as E.M. Forster,

John Kenneth Galbraith, John Hersey, Karen Horney, Carl Jung, Martin Luther King, Thomas Kuhn, Suzanne Langer, P. B. Medawar, Joyce Carol Oates, Bertrand Russell, and Alice Walker. Additional pieces by authors already appearing in the first edition have enabled us to represent several writers in depth—Isaac Asimov, Bruno Bettelheim, Stephen Jay Gould, Margaret Mead, and Lewis Thomas.

New selections have also enabled us to provide pairings or sets of topically related pieces throughout the table of contents, so that students will have numerous opportunities to read and consider different perspectives on a single issue or to explore a particular topic in depth. Wherever possible, we have placed these topically related pieces side by side, so that you can quickly find them in the table of contents. But in some instances, they necessarily appear under different rhetorical headings. So, we have also prepared a "Topical Guide to the Contents," making it possible to approach all of the selections in terms of particular subjects of study or themes of interest.

Our critical apparatus, once again, focuses on the rhetorical concepts and techniques that apply to reading and writing across the curriculum. These frameworks are discussed in our general introduction, "For Students," as well as in the more detailed introductions to each of the four main sections, "Reflecting," "Reporting," "Explaining," and "Arguing." These sectional introductions, which are illustrated with passages from the anthologized readings, define each type of writing, discuss its relevance within a broad range of fields, compare and contrast its use in differing fields and situations, as well as identify and explain methods of achieving its aims. Thus, the introductions show, for example, how description and narration are basic in reporting or how analogy, comparison and contrast, definition, and illustration are basic to explaining. All of the rhetorical aims and modes that we discuss in the critical apparatus are referenced in a "Rhetorical Index" to the collection that we have provided at the back of the book.

Concepts and terms that figure in the sectional introductions are also applied throughout the remainder of our editorial apparatus. So you will find that our headnote for each piece identifies and wherever necessary explains the professional field of its author and the rhetorical context or source of its original publication. Likewise, our questions following each selection call for reading and writing that relate form and style to purpose, subject, and academic field. Beyond these highly focused questions following each piece, you will find a more broadly based set of "Writing Suggestions" at the end of each main section. These assignments bring together two or more pieces from a particular section, relating them in terms of an academic, professional, personal, or rhetorical topic. And at the end of the collection, you will find our most spacious and challenging set of ideas for composition, "Suggestions for Writing Across the Disciplines." These assignments offer opportunities to pull together several readings and encourage the exploration of broad issues, questions, and problems that are of concern in every academic and professional field.

Because the material in this collection is intended to help students develop their reading and writing abilities, we have prepared two appendices that offer special guidance in these areas. "Reading and Rereading" explains and illustrates various approaches to reading through a detailed discussion focusing primarily on an essay by E.B. White. "Writing and Rewriting," in turn, explains and illustates the composing process through a detailed discussion of the same essay by White, including previously unpublished notes and drafts that White prepared in the process of writing the piece. These appendices, then, like the rest of this book are meant to present reading and writing not in abstract terms, but through examples that vividly demonstrate what is actually involved in each activity.

ACKNOWLEDGMENTS

Once again, we have many people to thank for helping us to make our way across the disciplines.

For their detailed reactions to the first edition of *Fields of Writing*, we are grateful to Stephen Adams, Virginia Polytechnic Institute and State University; Joanne Altieri, University of Washington; Mark C. Amodio, University of California at Berkeley; Lawrence R. Barkley, University of Redlands; Samual I. Bellman, California State Polytechnic University at Pomona; John Boe, University of California at Davis; Robert Boenig, Rutgers University; Ethel Bradford, Siena Heights College; Lori Buffum, University of Texas at San Antonio; Rosemarie Bufo, Baptist College; Stephanie Bulger, University of Utah; Charles O. Burgess, Old Dominion University; Lyall Bush, Rutgers University; Lana Cable, Russell Sage College; Wilma Clark, University of Wisconsin at Eau Claire; Marlene Clarke, University of California at Davis; Patricia C. Click, University of Virginia; Renee Lapham Collins, Siena Heights College; Linda Seidel Costic, Northeast Missouri State University; Donna Craft, Wayne State University; David Crowe, University of Minnesota; Helen Dale, University of Wisconsin at Eau Claire; Sharon Dean, Rivier College; Beverly J. DeBord, Glenville State College; Cheryl Duke, Texas Tech University; Donna Earles, Virginia Polytechnic Institute and State University; Doris S. Earnshaw, University of California at Irvine; Nancy Edwards, Bakersfield College; Wilma Evans, University of Minnesota; Ann Farmer, Whittier College; Stephanie Fay, University of California at Davis; Richard Fine, Virginia Commonwealth University; Barbara M. Goff, Rutgers University; Sandra A. Grayson, Saint Mary's College of California; Connie Jo Hale, University of Washington; Clyde Hankey, Youngstown State University; Dominick J. Hart, Eastern Kentucky University; Susan T. Hitchcock, University of Virginia; Mimi Hotchkiss, University of California at Los Angeles; Charles E. Jeffries, Glenville State College; Judith L. Johnston, Rider College; Mary G. Jones, Macomb Community College; Laurie Kaplan, Goucher College; Phyllis Karas, North Shore Community College; Lynne Kellermann, Rutgers University; Ann Kilpatrick, University of Arizona; Ann Kimmage, Plattsburgh State University; Malcolm Kiniry, University of California at Los Angeles; David J. Klooster, DePauw University; Delores LaGuardia, San Jose State University; Elizabeth Larsen, West Chester University; Thomas M. C. Lauden, Holy Cross College; Ralph M. Leary, Rutgers University; Portia Lee, University of California at Santa Barbara; Roger Lewis, George Mason University; Marie Logue, Rutgers University; Barbara A. Looney, Rutgers University; Palma Lower, California State University at Sacramento; Phillip Mahaffey, Texas Tech University; Barbara Mallonee, Loyola College; Barbara Mather, Rutgers University; Michelle S. Maycock, Virginia Polytechnic Institute and State University; Mary McCann, Siena Heights College; Lee McKenzie, University of Utah; Arthur A. Molitierno, Wright State University; Shirley Morahan, Northeast Missouri State University; Timothy Morris, Rutgers University; Diana Muir, University of California at Davis; Neil Mulhern, Rutgers University; Kathryn Neeley, University of Virginia; Gwen Nelson, Rutgers University; Elizabeth Otten, Northeast Missouri State University; Ted Otteson, University of Missouri at Kansas Cty; Susan Palo, University of California at Davis; Fred F. Paulenich, Youngstown State University; Bruce L. Pearson, University of South Carolina; Dan Propp, North Shore Community College; Lalita Prabhu, Youngstown State University; Teresa Purvis,· Ramapo College; Phyllis C. Ralph, University of Missouri at Kansas City; Lloyd Raskin, Macomb Community College; Ruth Ray, Wayne State University; Pamela Regis, Western Maryland College; W. Dean Rigby, Brigham Young University; Anca Rosu, Rutgers University; Lori Ruediger, Rivier College; Eric James Schroeder, University of California at Davis; Lisa M. Schwerdt, Purdue University; H. Lee Shannon, Wayne State University; Roger Sheffer, Mankato State University; J. D. Skaggs, University of Texas at Austin; James R. Sodon, Saint Louis Community College at Florissant Valley; Norman Stahl, Georgia State University; Marta Steele, Rider College; Patrick Story, George Mason University; Susan Strom, Rider College; Patricia Stuart, Norwich University; Audrey Fay Sullivan, West Valley College; Joanna Tapper, University of Arizona; Karen Toloui, Diablo Valley College; J. M. Valenti, University of Tampa; Whitney Vanderwerff, Elon College; Craig Werner, SUNY College at Buffalo; Julia Whitsitt, Texas Tech University; and Joan Worley, University of California at Santa Barbara.

For their knowledgeable suggestions of readings to consider for the second edition, we are grateful to Andrea Bakst; Diane Dowdey, Texas A & M University; Jim Hanlon, Shippensburg University of Pennsylvania; Nancy Jones, University of Iowa; Janine Karoly; Donald McQuade, University of California at Berkeley; Steven Moore, Rutgers University; Susan Osborn, Rutgers University; Elizabeth Robertson, Universty of Iowa; Mimi Schwartz, Stockton State College; Kurt Spellmeyer, Rutgers University; and Steven Weiland, University of Minnesota. For their expert reviews of the readings and critical apparatus in the second edition, we are grateful to Sam Dragga, Texas A & M University; Michael Finney, Youngstown State University; Linda Kitz, Cabrillo College; and Nevin K. Laib, Northern Arizona University. For her thoughtful editing of the manuscript, we are grateful to Marcia Muth. For their excellent work in bringing this book into print, we are grateful to the staff at St. Martin's Press, especially Richard Steins, Vivian McLaughlin, and Laura Starrett. Above all, we are indebted to our editor, Nancy Perry, whose contributions have, as ever, been inestimable.

N.R.C
D.H.
C.H.K.
R.S.
N.S.

Contents

REFLECTING   1

Arts and Humanities

CONTENTS

CONTENTS

CONTENTS

Social Sciences and Public Affairs

xiv

CONTENTS

xvi

CONTENTS

CONTENTS

CONTENTS

CONTENTS

CONTENTS *read*

Topical Guide to the Contents

VALUES AND BELIEFS

RACE AND RACISM

THE STATUS OF WOMEN

VIOLENCE AND WAR

LIFE AND DEATH

HEALTH, DISEASE, AND MEDICINE

SCIENTIFIC THINKING

TEACHING, LEARNING, AND SCHOOLING

SEARCHING FOR FACTS

UNDERSTANDING THE PAST

CULTURE

ART, SPORT, AND ENTERTAINMENT

For Students

Fields of Writing: Readings Across the Disciplines, second edition, is intended to help you develop the abilities in reading and writing that you will need as you move from one course to another, one field of study to another, throughout your college career. In some senses, of course, all areas of study expect the same things of you—namely, close and careful reading as well as clear and exact writing, with an attentiveness above all to information and ideas. But the particular kinds of information, ideas, and concerns that distinguish each field of study also call for somewhat different reading and writing abilities. As you might imagine, for example, a book review for a literature course requires a different form and style from a lab report in physics. So in putting together this collection, we have tried to give you a sampling of the varied fields of writing you are likely to encounter in the academic world.

Most undergraduate schools are organized around some version of the traditional division of studies into "the humanities," "the social sciences," and "the sciences." The humanities generally include fields of learning that are thought of as having a cultural orientation, such as language, literature, history, philosophy, and religion. The social sciences, which include such fields as anthropology, economics, education, political science, psychology, and sociology, deal with social institutions and the behavior of their individual members. The sciences include fields of knowledge that are concerned with the natural and physical world, such as astronomy, botany, chemistry, physics, and zoology.

These traditional divisions of study are closely affiliated with applied areas of study and work that exist not only in colleges and universities but also in the professional world outside higher education. The humanities, for example, are closely allied with the arts; the social sciences, with public affairs such as business and government; and the sciences, with technology. These basic divisions and clusterings of fields—"The Arts and Humanities," "The Social Sciences and Public Affairs," "The Sciences and Technologies"—are so broadly applicable that we have used them as one of the organizing principles in our table of contents.

Like any set of categories, these divisions are a convenient, but by no means foolproof, system of classification. Though the system can help you to understand the academic world and the broad range of academic reading and writing, it needs to be used with tact and with a recognition that it will not do perfect justice to the exact state of affairs in every specialized field at every college and university. Specialists in a particular field, such as psychology, sometimes migrate from one broad area of learning to another, from the social sciences to the sciences, for example, according to the orientation of their own research in a particular project. Or specialists from several fields may come together to work on a project or to form an interdisciplinary area of research, such as environmental studies, which involves a wide range of academic disciplines—botany, chemistry, economics, philosophy, political science, and zoology. So, the writing that results from these projects often can be categorized in more than one broad area of learning, and wherever this is so in *Fields of Writing* you will probably find that we have taken note of this alternative either in the introduction to the piece or the questions following it.

The writing we have collected here can be understood not only in terms of the area of learning that it represents, but also in terms of the particular purpose it is meant to achieve. Every piece of writing, of course, is the product of an author's personal and professional motives, so in a sense the purposes for writing are as complex and varied and ultimately mysterious as are authors themselves. But setting aside the mysteries of human nature, it is possible to define and isolate a clear-cut set of purposes for writing, which we refer to as "Reflecting," "Reporting," "Explaining," and "Arguing," one or another of which predominates in most academic and professional writing. So, we have used this set of purposes as the major organizing principle in our table of contents.

By "Reflecting," we mean a kind of writing in which authors are concerned with recalling and thinking about their past experience, for personal experience is often an especially valuable source of knowledge and learning. By "Reporting," we mean writing that is concerned primarily with conveying factual information about some particular aspect of the world, past or present. By "Explaining," we mean writing that is concerned primarily with making sense of information or shedding light on a particular subject. By "Arguing," we mean writing in which authors debate competing explanations, values, or beliefs. Like our other categories, these are a convenient, but not air-tight, system of classification. So, they need to be used tactfully, with an awareness that to some degree they are bound to overlap. Most pieces of explanation at some point will involve reporting, if only to convey the information or subject to be explained. And most pieces of argument will call for some explanation, if only to make clear the issues that are at odds with one another. But generally you will find one or another of these purposes to be dominant in any particular piece of writing, and wherever a piece seems to us to hover between two different purposes, we will mention the problem in our headnote or invite you to think about it in the questions following the selection.

We think that an awareness of these basic purposes can be especially helpful both in the process of reading and in the process of writing, no matter what academic or professional field is involved. So, we have introduced each part of our collection with an essay on "Reflecting," "Reporting," "Explaining," or "Arguing." In these essays, you will find detailed definitions and examples of each purpose, as well as explanations and illustrations of how to carry it out in differing fields and situations. Each selection within each part is accompanied by a brief headnote, explanatory footnotes where necessary, and a set of questions for you to think about in your reading and writing. At the end of each part, you will find additional reading and writing suggestions that are addressed to more than one essay. And at the end of the four parts, you will find still other suggestions that invite you to think about pieces in very broad topical frameworks which bring together a number of fields and purposes.

Following the four main parts of our anthology, you will find two special sections: "On Reading and Rereading," which will show you various ways to read and understand the pieces in this book or any other material you might encounter in your studies, and "On Writing and Rewriting," which will give you an actual example of how one writer goes through the process of composing a piece of writing. All of this supplementary material is also meant to help you develop your abilities in reading and writing. The rest is up to your instructor, your classmates, and you.

REFLECTING

REFLECTING

Here in "Reflecting," as in other parts of this collection, you will encounter writing that touches upon a wide range of topics—from the nature of colonialism to the development of modern medicine, from a sacred landmark in Oklahoma to a high school graduation in Alabama, from the sexual theory of Sigmund Freud to the personality of Albert Einstein. But you will also find that the writing in this particular section relies very heavily on personal experience. This personal element may strike you at first as being out of place in an academic textbook. But if you think about the matter, you will see that personal experience is a basic source of knowledge—as important a means of understanding the world as systematic investigation and analysis. Just think for a moment about someone you have known for a long time or about a long-remembered event in your life; then think about what you have learned from being with that person or going through that event, and you will see that personal experience is, indeed, a valuable source of knowledge. You will probably also notice that in thinking about that person or event you rely very heavily on your remembrance of things past—on your memory of particular words, or deeds, or gestures, or scenes that are especially important to you. Your memory, after all, is the storehouse of your personal knowledge, and whenever you turn to this storehouse it will give you back an image or impression of your past experience. So, you should not be surprised to find the authors in this section looking into the mirrors of their own memories. Ultimately, the activity of looking back is a hallmark of reflection because it involves writers in recalling and thinking about some aspect of their world in order to make sense of it for themselves and for others.

This essential quality of reflective writing can be seen in the following passage from George Orwell's "Shooting an Elephant":

> One day something happened which in a roundabout way was enlightening. It was a tiny incident in itself, but it gave me a better glimpse than I had had before of the real nature of imperialism—the real motives for which despotic governments act. Early one morning the sub-inspector at a police station the other end of the town rang me up on the 'phone and said that an elephant was ravaging the bazaar. Would I please come and do something about it? I did not know what I could do, but I wanted to see what was happening and I got on to a pony and started out.

This passage, which comes from the third paragraph of Orwell's essay, clearly presents him as being in a reflective frame of mind. In the opening sentence, for example, he looks back to a specific event from his personal experiences in Burma—to "One day" when "something happened." And in the midst of looking back, he also makes clear that this event is important to him because "in a roundabout way" it "was enlightening." Again in the second sentence, he looks back not only to the event, "a tiny incident in itself," but also to the understanding that he gained from the event—"a better glimpse than I had had before of the real nature of imperialism—the real motives for which despotic governments act." Having announced the general significance of this event, he then returns to looking back at the event itself, to recalling the particular things that happened that day—the phone call informing him "that an elephant was ravaging the bazaar," the request that he "come and do something about it," and his decision to get "on to a pony" in order "to see what was happening."

This alternation between recalling events and commenting on their significance is typical not only of Orwell's piece but of all the writing in this section. Sometimes, the alternation takes place within a single sentence, as in the opening of the previous passage. Sometimes, the alternation occurs between sentences or clusters of sentences, as in the following paragraph from Carl Jung's "Sigmund Freud":

> I can still recall vividly how Freud said to me, "My dear Jung, promise me never to abandon the sexual theory. That is the most essential thing of all. You see, we must make a dogma of it, an unshakable bulwark." He said that to me with great emotion, in the tone of a father saying, "And promise me this one thing, my dear son: that you will go to church every Sunday." In some astonishment I asked him, "A bulwark—against what?" To which he replied, "Against the black tide of mud"—and here he hesitated for a moment, then added—"of occultism." First of all, it was the words "bulwark" and "dogma" that alarmed me; for a dogma, that is to say, an undisputable confession of faith, is set up only when the aim is to suppress doubts once and for all. But that no longer has anything to do with scientific judgment; only with a personal power drive.

In the first four sentences of this passage, Jung "vividly" recalls a specific conversation that took place between himself and Freud—so vividly, in fact, that he evidently remembers it word for word and gesture for gesture. Then in the final two sentences of the passage, Jung explains his reasons for having been disturbed by the conversation, showing how Freud's particular choice of words revealed him to be concerned not "with scientific judgment" but "with a personal power drive."

The alternation between recalling and interpreting events will vary from writer to writer, and work to work, depending on the details of the experience and the author's reflective purpose. Nevertheless, invariably, every piece of reflective writing will contain both kinds of material, for every reflective writer is concerned not only with sharing a memorable experience but also with showing why it was memorable. And as it happens, most memorable experiences stick in our minds because they give us "a better glimpse than [we] had had before of the real nature of" someone or something. So as a reader of reflective writing, you should always be attentive not only to the details of an author's recollected experience but also to the "glimpse" that it gives the author, and you, into "the real nature" of things. And in your own reflective writing, you should make sure that you convey both dimensions of your experience—both what happened and what the happenings enabled you to see.

THE RANGE OF REFLECTIVE WRITING

The range of reflective writing is in one sense limitless, for it necessarily includes the full range of things that make up our personal experience or the personal experience of anyone else in the world. Reflecting, in other words, may deal with anything that anyone has ever seen, or heard, or done, or thought about, and considered memorable enough to write about. Though the range of reflective writing is extraordinarily broad, the subject of any particular piece is likely to be very specific, and as it happens most pieces can be classified in terms of a few recurrent types of subject matter.

A single, memorable event is often the center of attention in reflective writing, as in Maya Angelou's "Graduation" or George Orwell's "Shooting an Elephant." In reflecting on this kind of subject, the author will usually provide not only a meticulous detailing of the event itself but also some opening background information that serves as a context for making sense of the event. In "Graduation," for example, Maya Angelou tells about all the pregraduation excitement at school and around town before turning to the graduation ceremony itself. And in "Shooting an Elephant," Orwell gives an overall description of his life as a colonial officer in Burma before he turns to the story about shooting the elephant. The event, in turn, is of interest not only in itself but also for what it reveals to the author (and the reader) about some significant aspect of experience. Thus for Angelou, graduation remains memorable because it helped her to see how black people have been "sustained" by their "known and unknown poets" and, for Orwell, the shooting remains memorable because it helped him to see "the real nature of imperialism."

A notable person is another type of subject that often moves people to reflective writing, as in Jung's recollections of Freud or Banesh Hoffmann's memories of Albert Einstein. In reflecting on a particular individual, most writers naturally seek to discover and convey what they consider to be the most essential or outstanding aspects of that person's character and ideas. In order to do so, they survey a number of memorable incidents or images from the life of that person. Jung, for example, recalls not only his conversation with Freud but also his correspondence with other colleagues about the theories of Freud. And

Hoffmann remembers Einstein in a number of different professional and personal situations. In each case, the recollection of several experiences serves to reveal, define, and illustrate qualities that might otherwise remain obscure or abstract, such as the "personal power drive" of Freud and the remarkable "simplicity" of Einstein.

Instead of concentrating on a particular person or event, reflective writing may center on a specific problem or significant issue in the past experience of an author, as in Jeremy Seabrook's "A Twin Is Only Half a Person" or Martin Luther King's "Pilgrimage to Nonviolence." A piece with this kind of subject is likely to touch upon many persons and events and to cover a long period of time in the process of recalling and reflecting upon the problem with which it is concerned. Seabrook, for example, covers more than thirty years of his life in his piece about the problem of being a twin, and King recalls events and issues throughout his life that led him to espouse the principles of "nonviolent resistance." In each case, the breadth of coverage serves to reveal the scope and complexity of the problem as well as the author's special understanding of it.

As you can see from just this brief survey of possibilities, reflective writing may deal witth a single event, several events, or a whole lifetime of events. It may be as restricted in its attention as a close-up snapshot or as all encompassing as a wide-angle lens. But no matter how little, or how much, experience it takes into account, reflective writing is always decisively focused through the author's persistent attempt to make sense of the past, to push memory to the point of understanding.

METHODS OF REFLECTING

Your experience is unique, as is your memory, so in a sense you know the best methods to follow whenever you are of a mind to reflect upon something that interests you. But once you have recalled something in detail and made sense of it for yourself, you are faced with the problem of how to present it to readers in a way that will also make sense to them. Given the fact that your readers will probably not be familiar with your experience, you will need to be very careful in selecting and organizing your material so that you give them a clearly detailed account of it. By the same token, you will need to give special emphasis to aspects or elements of your experience that will enable them to understand its significance. Usually, you will find that your choice of subject suggests a corresponding method of presenting it clearly and meaningfully to your readers.

If your reflections are focused on a single, circumscribed event, you will probably find it most appropriate to use a narrative presentation, telling your readers what happened in a relatively straightforward chronological order. Though you cover the event from beginning to end, your narrative should be carefully designed to emphasize the details that you consider to be most striking and significant. In "Shooting an Elephant," for example, Orwell devotes the largest segment of his piece to covering the very, very brief period of a few moments when he finds himself on the verge of having to shoot the elephant despite his strong desire not to do so. In fact, he devotes one-third of his essay to these few moments of inner conflict, because they bring about one of his major insights— "that when the white man turns tyrant it is his own freedom that he destroys." So in telling about a memorable event of your own, you should deliberately pace your story to make it build toward some kind of climax or surprise or decisive incident, which in turn leads to a moment of insight for you (and your reader).

If your reflections are focused on a particular person, you will probably find it necessary to use both narrative and descriptive methods of presentation, telling about several events in order to make clear to readers the character and thought of the person in question. Though you rely heavily on narration, you will not be able to cover incidents in as much detail as if you were focusing on a single event. Instead, you will find it necessary to isolate only the most striking and significant details from each incident you choose to recall. In his recollection of Einstein, for example, Banesh Hoffmann includes more than fifteen separate anecdotes, but in each case he touches on only a couple of telling images or a few very memorable statements by Einstein. And Hoffmann isolates these particular details because they vividly reveal Einstein's most remarkable character-istics—"his knack for going instinctively to the heart of a matter" and "his extraordinary feeling for beauty." So, too, in writing about an individual whom you have known, you should carefully select and arrange the details that you recall to make them convey a clear and compelling impression of that person's character and ideas.

If your reflections are focused on a particular problem or issue in your past experience, you will probably need to combine narrative, descriptive, and ex-planatory methods of presentation, bringing together your recollections of nu-merous events and persons in order to reveal the nature and significance of the problem. Though you survey the problem chronologically from beginning to end, you will also need to organize your narrative so that it highlights the essential aspects, elements, or facets of the problem. In his piece about being a twin, for example, Jeremy Seabrook immediately focuses on the distinctive way that people look at him when they discover that he is a twin, as if they are trying "to discern in [him his] absent half." And from this point on, he recalls the various ways in which a simplistic and distorted conception of twinship worked its unhealthy influence upon himself and his twin brother, at home, at school, and into their adult lives. So in writing about a particular problem of your own, your recollections should be deliberately selected and organized to highlight your special understanding of the issue.

No matter what specific combination of methods you use in your reflective writing, you will probably find, as do most writers, that a striking recollection is the most effective way to interest your readers and that a significant observation about experience is the most rewarding means to send them on their way. In the following selections, you will get to see how nineteen different writers use language to produce some very striking and significant pieces of reflection.

Arts and Humanities

GRADUATION

Maya Angelou

In her four volumes of autobiography, Maya Angelou (b. 1928) has written vividly of her struggles to achieve success as an actress, a dancer, a songwriter, a teacher, and a writer. An active worker in the civil rights movement in the 1960s, Angelou continues to focus much of her writing on racial issues. The following selection is from I Know Why the Caged Bird Sings *(1969), in which she writes, "I speak to the Black experience, but I am always talking about the human condition."*

The children in Stamps trembled visibly with anticipation.[1] Some adults were excited too, but to be certain the whole young population had come down with graduation epidemic. Large classes were graduating from both the grammar school and the high school. Even those who were years removed from their own day of glorious release were anxious to help with preparations as a kind of dry run. The junior students who were moving into the vacating classes' chairs were tradition-bound to show their talents for leadership and management. They strutted through the school and around the campus exerting pressure on the lower grades. Their authority was so new that occasionally if they pressed a little too hard it had to be overlooked. After all, next term was coming, and it never hurt a sixth grader to have a play sister in the eighth grade, or a tenth-year student to be able to call a twelfth grader Bubba. So all was endured in a spirit of shared understanding. But the graduating classes themselves were the nobility. Like travelers with exotic destinations on their minds, the graduates were remarkably forgetful. They came to school without their books, or tablets or even pencils. Volunteers fell over themselves to secure replacements for the missing equipment. When accepted, the willing workers might or might not be thanked, and it was of no importance to the pregraduation rites. Even teachers were

---

[1]Stamps: a town in Arkansas. [Eds.]

9

respectful of the now quiet and aging seniors, and tended to speak to them, if not as equals, as beings only slightly lower than themselves. After tests were returned and grades given, the student body, which acted like an extended family, knew who did well, who excelled, and what piteous ones had failed.

Unlike the white high school, Lafayette County Training School distin- 2 guished itself by having neither lawn, nor hedges, nor tennis court, nor climbing ivy. Its two buildings (main classrooms, the grade school and home economics) were set on a dirt hill with no fence to limit either its boundaries or those of bordering farms. There was a large expanse to the left of the school which was used alternately as a baseball diamond or basketball court. Rusty hoops on swaying poles represented the permanent recreational equipment, although bats and balls could be borrowed from the P.E. teacher if the borrower was qualified and if the diamond wasn't occupied.

Over this rocky area relieved by a few shady tall persimmon trees the graduating 3 class walked. The girls often held hands and no longer bothered to speak to the lower students. There was a sadness about them, as if this old world was not their home and they were bound for higher ground. The boys, on the other hand, had become more friendly, more outgoing. A decided change from the closed attitude they projected while studying for finals. Now they seemed not ready to give up the old school, the familiar paths and classrooms. Only a small percentage would be continuing on to college—one of the South's A & M (agricultural and mechanical) schools, which trained Negro youths to be carpenters, farmers, handymen, masons, maids, cooks and baby nurses. Their future rode heavily on their shoulders, and blinded them to the collective joy that had pervaded the lives of the boys and girls in the grammar school graduating class.

Parents who could afford it had ordered new shoes and ready-made clothes 4 for themselves from Sears and Roebuck or Montgomery Ward. They also en- gaged the best seamstresses to make the floating graduating dresses and to cut down secondhand pants which would be pressed to a military slickness for the important event.

Oh, it was important, all right. Whitefolks would attend the ceremony, and 5 two or three would speak of God and home, and the Southern way of life, and Mrs. Parsons, the principal's wife, would play the graduation march while the lower-grade graduates paraded down the aisles and took their seats below the platform. The high school seniors would wait in empty classrooms to make their dramatic entrance.

In the Store I was the person of the moment. The birthday girl. The center. 6 Bailey had graduated the year before,[2] although to do so he had had to forfeit all pleasures to make up for his time lost in Baton Rouge.

My class was wearing butter-yellow piqué dresses, and Momma launched 7 out on mine. She smocked the yoke into tiny crisscrossing puckers, then shirred

---

[2]Bailey: the brother of the author. [Eds.]

the rest of the bodice. Her dark fingers ducked in and out of the lemony cloth as she embroidered raised daisies around the hem. Before she considered herself finished she had added a crocheted cuff on the puff sleeves, and a pointy crocheted collar.

I was going to be lovely. A walking model of all the various styles of fine 8 hand sewing and it didn't worry me that I was only twelve years old and merely graduating from the eighth grade. Besides, many teachers in Arkansas Negro schools had only that diploma and were licensed to impart wisdom.

The days had become longer and more noticeable. The faded beige of former 9 times had been replaced with strong and sure colors. I began to see my classmates' clothes, their skin tones, and the dust that waved off pussy willows. Clouds that lazed across the sky were objects of great concern to me. Their shiftier shapes might have held a message that in my new happiness and with a little bit of time I'd soon decipher. During that period I looked at the arch of heaven so religiously my neck kept a steady ache. I had taken to smiling more often, and my jaws hurt from the unaccustomed activity. Between the two physical sore spots, I suppose I could have been uncomfortable, but that was not the case. As a member of the winning team (the graduating class of 1940) I had outdistanced unpleasant sensations by miles. I was headed for the freedom of open fields.

Youth and social approval allied themselves with me and we trammeled 10 memories of slights and insults. The wind of our swift passage remodeled my features. Lost tears were pounded to mud and then to dust. Years of withdrawal were brushed aside and left behind, as hanging ropes of parasitic moss.

My work alone had awarded me a top place and I was going to be one of 11 the first called in the graduating ceremonies. On the classroom blackboard, as well as on the bulletin board in the auditorium, there were blue stars and white stars and red stars. No absences, no tardinesses, and my academic work was among the best of the year. I could say the preamble to the Constitution even faster than Bailey. We timed ourselves often: "WethepeopleoftheUnited Statesinordertoformamoreperfectunion . . ." I had memorized the Presidents of the United States from Washington to Roosevelt in chronological as well as alphabetical order.

My hair pleased me too. Gradually the black mass had lengthened and 12 thickened, so that it kept at last to its braided pattern, and I didn't have to yank my scalp off when I tried to comb it.

Louise and I had rehearsed the exercises until we tired out ourselves. Henry 13 Reed was class valedictorian. He was a small, very black boy with hooded eyes, a long, broad nose and an oddly shaped head. I had admired him for years because each term he and I vied for the best grades in our class. Most often he bested me, but instead of being disappointed I was pleased that we shared top places between us. Like many Southern Black children, he lived with his grandmother, who was as strict as Momma and as kind as she knew how to be. He was courteous, respectful and soft-spoken to elders, but on the playground he chose to play the roughest games. I admired him. Anyone, I reckoned, sufficiently afraid or sufficiently dull could be polite. But to be able to operate at a top level with both adults and children was admirable.

His valedictory speech was entitled "To Be or Not to Be." The rigid tenth-grade teacher had helped him write it. He'd been working on the dramatic stresses for months. 14

The weeks until graduation were filled with heady activities. A group of small children were to be presented in a play about buttercups and daisies and bunny rabbits. They could be heard throughout the building practicing their hops and their little songs that sounded like silver bells. The older girls (nongraduates, of course) were assigned the task of making refreshments for the night's festivities. A tangy scent of ginger, cinnamon, nutmeg and chocolate wafted around the home economics building as the budding cooks made samples for themselves and their teachers. 15

In every corner of the workshop, axes and saws split fresh timber as the woodshop boys made sets and stage scenery. Only the graduates were left out of the general bustle. We were free to sit in the library at the back of the building or look in quite detachedly, naturally, on the measures being taken for our event. 16

Even the minister preached on graduation the Sunday before. His subject was, "Let your light so shine that men will see your good works and praise your Father, Who is in Heaven." Although the sermon was purported to be addressed to us, he used the occasion to speak to backsliders, gamblers and general ne'er-do-wells. But since he had called our names at the beginning of the service we were mollified. 17

Among Negroes the tradition was to give presents to children going only from one grade to another. How much more important this was when the person was graduating at the top of the class. Uncle Willie and Momma had sent away for a Mickey Mouse watch like Bailey's. Louise gave me four embroidered handkerchiefs. (I gave her crocheted doilies.) Mrs. Sneed, the minister's wife, made me an undershirt to wear for graduation, and nearly every customer gave me a nickel or maybe even a dime with the instruction "Keep on moving to higher ground," or some such encouragement. 18

Amazingly the great day finally dawned and I was out of bed before I knew it. I threw open the back door to see it more clearly, but Momma said, "Sister, come away from that door and put your robe on." 19

I hoped the memory of that morning would never leave me. Sunlight was itself young, and the day had none of the insistence maturity would bring it in a few hours. In my robe and barefoot in the backyard, under cover of going to see about my new beans, I gave myself up to the gentle warmth and thanked God that no matter what evil I had done in my life He had allowed me to live to see this day. Somewhere in my fatalism I had expected to die, accidentally, 20 and never have the chance to walk up the stairs in the auditorium and gracefully receive my hard-earned diploma. Out of God's merciful bosom I had won reprieve.

Bailey came out in his robe and gave me a box wrapped in Christmas paper. 21 He said he had saved his money for months to pay for it. It felt like a box of chocolates, but I knew Bailey wouldn't save money to buy candy when we had all we could want under our noses.

He was as proud of the gift as I. It was a soft-leather-bound copy of a col- 22 lection of poems by Edgar Allan Poe, or, as Bailey and I called him, "Eap." I turned to "Annabel Lee" and we walked up and down the garden rows, the cool dirt between our toes, reciting the beautifully sad lines.

Momma made a Sunday breakfast although it was only Friday. After we 23 finished the blessing, I opened my eyes to find the watch on my plate. It was a dream of a day. Everything went smoothly and to my credit. I didn't have to be reminded or scolded for anything. Near evening I was too jittery to attend to chores, so Bailey volunteered to do all before his bath.

Days before, we had made a sign for the Store, and as we turned out the 24 lights Momma hung the cardboard over the doorknob. It read clearly: CLOSED. GRADUATION.

My dress fitted perfectly and everyone said that I looked like a sunbeam in 25 it. On the hill, going toward the school, Bailey walked behind with Uncle Willie, who muttered, "Go on, Ju." He wanted him to walk ahead with us because it embarrassed him to have to walk so slowly. Bailey said he'd let the ladies walk together, and the men would bring up the rear. We all laughed, nicely.

Little children dashed by out of the dark like fireflies. Their crepe-paper 26 dresses and butterfly wings were not made for running and we heard more than one rip, dryly, and the regretful "uh uh" that followed.

The school blazed without gaiety. The windows seemed cold and unfriendly 27 from the lower hill. A sense of ill-fated timing crept over me, and if Momma hadn't reached for my hand I would have drifted back to Bailey and Uncle Willie, and possibly beyond. She made a few slow jokes about my feet getting cold, and tugged me along to the now-strange building.

Around the front steps, assurance came back. There were my fellow "greats," 28 the graduating class. Hair brushed back, legs oiled, new dresses and pressed pleats, fresh pocket handkerchiefs and little handbags, all homesewn. Oh, we were up to snuff, all right. I joined my comrades and didn't even see my family go in to find seats in the crowded auditorium.

The school band struck up a march and all classes filed in as had been 29 rehearsed. We stood in front of our seats, as assigned, and on a signal from the choir director, we sat. No sooner had this been accomplished than the band started to play the national anthem. We rose again and sang the song, after which we recited the pledge of allegiance. We remained standing for a brief minute before the choir director and the principal signaled to us, rather desperately I thought, to take our seats. The command was so unusual that our carefully rehearsed and smooth-running machine was thrown off. For a full minute we fumbled for our chairs and bumped into each other awkwardly. Habits change or solidify under pressure, so in our state of nervous tension we had been ready to follow our usual assembly pattern: the American national anthem, then the pledge of allegiance, then the song every Black person I knew called the Negro National Anthem. All done in the same key, with the same passion and most often standing on the same foot.

Finding my seat at last, I was overcome with a presentiment of worse things 30 to come. Something unrehearsed, unplanned, was going to happen, and we were going to be made to look bad. I distinctly remember being explicit in the choice of pronoun. It was "we," the graduating class, the unit, that concerned me then.

The principal welcomed "parents and friends" and asked the Baptist minister 31 to lead us in prayer. His invocation was brief and punchy, and for a second I thought we were getting on the high road to right action. When the principal came back to the dais, however, his voice had changed. Sounds always affected me profoundly and the principal's voice was one of my favorites. During assembly it melted and lowed weakly into the audience. It had not been in my plan to listen to him, but my curiosity was piqued and I straightened up to give him my attention.

He was talking about Booker T. Washington, our "late great leader," who 32 said we can be as close as the fingers on the hand, etc. . . . Then he said a few vague things about friendship and the friendship of kindly people to those less fortunate than themselves. With that his voice nearly faded, thin, away. Like a river diminishing to a stream and then to a trickle. But he cleared his throat and said, "Our speaker tonight, who is also our friend, came from Texarkana to deliver the commencement address, but due to the irregularity of the train schedule, he's going to, as they say, 'speak and run.' " He said that we understood and wanted the man to know that we were most grateful for the time he was able to give us and then something about how we were willing always to adjust to another's program, and without more ado—"I give you Mr. Edward Donleavy."

Not one but two white men came through the door off-stage. The shorter 33 one walked to the speaker's platform, and the tall one moved to the center seat and sat down. But that was our principal's seat, and already occupied. The dislodged gentleman bounced around for a long breath or two before the Baptist minister gave him his chair, then with more dignity than the situation deserved, the minister walked off the stage.

Donleavy looked at the audience once (on reflection, I'm sure that he wanted 34 only to reassure himself that we were really there), adjusted his glasses and began to read from a sheaf of papers.

He was glad "to be here and to see the work going on just as it was in the   35
other schools."

At the first "Amen" from the audience I willed the offender to immediate   36
death by choking on the word. But Amens and Yes, sir's began to fall around
the room like rain through a ragged umbrella.

He told us of the wonderful changes we children in Stamps had in store.   37
The Central School (naturally, the white school was Central) had already been
granted improvements that would be in use in the fall. A well-known artist was
coming from Little Rock to teach art to them. They were going to have the
newest microscopes and chemistry equipment for their laboratory. Mr. Donleavy
didn't leave us long in the dark over who made these improvements available
to Central High. Nor were we to be ignored in the general betterment scheme
he had in mind.

He said that he had pointed out to people at a very high level that one of   38
the first-line football tacklers at Arkansas Agricultural and Mechanical College
had graduated from good old Lafayette County Training School. Here fewer
Amen's were heard. Those few that did break through lay dully in the air with
the heaviness of habit.

He went on to praise us. He went on to say how he had bragged that "one   39
of the best basketball players at Fisk sank his first ball right here at Lafayette
County Training School."

The white kids were going to have a chance to become Galileos and Madame   40
Curies and Edisons and Gauguins, and our boys (the girls weren't even in on
it) would try to be Jesse Owenses and Joe Louises.

Owens and the Brown Bomber were great heroes in our world, but what   41
school official in the white-goddom of Little Rock had the right to decide that
those two men must be our only heroes? Who decided that for Henry Reed to
become a scientist he had to work like George Washington Carver, as a boot-
black, to buy a lousy microscope? Bailey was obviously always going to be too
small to be an athlete, so which concrete angel glued to what country seat had
decided that if my brother wanted to become a lawyer he had to first pay penance
for his skin by picking cotton and hoeing corn and studying correspondence
books at night for twenty years?

The man's dead words fell like bricks around the auditorium and too many   42
settled in my belly. Constrained by hard-learned manners I couldn't look behind me, but to my left and right the proud graduating class of 1940 had
dropped their heads. Every girl in my row had found something new to do
with her handkerchief. Some folded the tiny squares into love knots, some
into triangles, but most were wadding them, then pressing them flat on their
yellow laps.

On the dais, the ancient tragedy was being replayed. Professor Parsons sat,   43
a sculptor's reject, rigid. His large, heavy body seemed devoid of will or willingness, and his eyes said he was no longer with us. The other teachers examined

15

the flag (which was draped stage right) or their notes, or the windows which opened on our now-famous playing diamond.

Graduation, the hush-hush magic time of frills and gifts and congratulations 44 and diplomas, was finished for me before my name was called. The accomplishment was nothing. The meticulous maps, drawn in three colors of ink, learning and spelling decasyllabic words, memorizing the whole of *The Rape of Lucrece*[3]—it was for nothing. Donleavy had exposed us.

We were maids and farmers, handymen and washerwomen, and anything 45 higher that we aspired to was farcical and presumptuous.

Then I wished that Gabriel Prosser and Nat Turner had killed all whitefolks 46 in their beds and that Abraham Lincoln had been assassinated before the signing of the Emancipation Proclamation,[4] and that Harriet Tubman had been killed by that blow on her head and Christopher Columbus had drowned in the *Santa Maria*.[5]

It was awful to be a Negro and have no control over my life. It was brutal 47 to be young and already trained to sit quietly and listen to charges brought against my color with no chance of defense. We should all be dead. I thought I should like to see us all dead, one on top of the other. A pyramid of flesh with the whitefolks on the bottom, as the broad base, then the Indians with their silly tomahawks and teepees and wigwams and treaties, the Negroes with their mops and recipes and cotton sacks and spirituals sticking out of their mouths. The Dutch children should all stumble in their wooden shoes and break their necks. The French should choke to death on the Louisiana Purchase (1803) while silkworms ate all the Chinese with their stupid pigtails. As a species, we were an abomination. All of us.

Donleavy was running for election, and assured our parents that if he won 48 we could count on having the only colored paved playing field in that part of Arkansas. Also—he never looked up to acknowledge the grunts of acceptance— also, we were bound to get some new equipment for the home economics building and the workshop.

He finished, and since there was no need to give any more than the most 49 perfunctory thank-you's, he nodded to the men on the stage, and the tall white man who was never introduced joined him at the door. They left with the attitude that now they were off to something really important. (The graduation ceremonies at Lafayette County Training School had been a mere preliminary.)

The ugliness they left was palpable. An uninvited guest who wouldn't leave. 50 The choir was summoned and sang a modern arrangement of "Onward, Christian Soldiers," with new words pertaining to graduates seeking their place in the world. But it didn't work. Elouise, the daughter of the Baptist minister, recited

---

[3]*The Rape of Lucrece:* an 1,855-line narrative poem by William Shakespeare. [Eds.]

[4]Gabriel Prosser and Nat Turner: leaders of slave rebellions during the early 1800s in Virginia. [Eds.]

[5]Harriet Tubman (ca. 1820–1913): an escaped slave who conducted others to freedom on the Underground Railroad and worked as an abolitionist. [Eds.]

"Invictus,"[6] and I could have cried at the impertinence of "I am the master of my fate, I am the captain of my soul."

My name had lost its ring of familiarity and I had to be nudged to go and 51 receive my diploma. All my preparations had fled. I neither marched up to the stage like a conquering Amazon, nor did I look in the audience for Bailey's nod of approval. Marguerite Johnson, I heard the name again, my honors were read, there were noises in the audience of appreciation, and I took my place on the stage as rehearsed.

I thought about colors I hated: ecru, puce, lavender, beige and black. 52

There was shuffling and rustling around me, then Henry Reed was giving 53 his valedictory address, "To Be or Not to Be." Hadn't he heard the whitefolks? We couldn't *be*, so the question was a waste of time. Henry's voice came out clear and strong. I feared to look at him. Hadn't he got the message? There was no "nobler in the mind" for Negroes because the world didn't think we had minds, and they let us know it. "Outrageous fortune"? Now, that was a joke. When the ceremony was over I had to tell Henry Reed some things. That is, if I still cared. Not "rub," Henry, "erase." "Ah, there's the erase." Us.

Henry had been a good student in elocution. His voice rose on tides of 54 promise and fell on waves of warnings. The English teacher had helped him to create a sermon winging through Hamlet's soliloquy. To be a man, a doer, a builder, a leader, or to be a tool, an unfunny joke, a crusher of funky toadstools. I marveled that Henry could go through with the speech as if we had a choice.

I had been listening and silently rebutting each sentence with my eyes closed; 55 then there was a hush, which in an audience warns that something unplanned is happening. I looked up and saw Henry Reed, the conservative, the proper, the A student, turn his back to the audience and turn to us (the proud graduating class of 1940) and sing, nearly speaking,

> "Lift ev'ry voice and sing
> Till earth and heaven ring
> Ring with the harmonies of Liberty . . ."

It was the poem written by James Weldon Johnson. It was the music composed by J. Rosamond Johnson. It was the Negro national anthem. Out of habit we were singing it.

Our mothers and fathers stood in the dark hall and joined the hymn of 56 encouragement. A kindergarten teacher led the small children onto the stage and the buttercups and daisies and bunny rabbits marked time and tried to follow:

> "Stony the road we trod
> Bitter the chastening rod
> Felt in the days when hope, unborn, had died.

---

[6]"Invictus": a poem by the nineteenth-century English poet, William Ernest Henley. Its inspirational conclusion is quoted here. [Eds.]

Yet with a steady beat
Have not our weary feet
Come to the place for which our fathers sighed?"

Each child I knew had learned that song with his ABC's and along with   57
"Jesus Loves Me This I Know." But I personally had never heard it before.
Never heard the words, despite the thousands of times I had sung them. Never
thought they had anything to do with me.

On the other hand, the words of Patrick Henry had made such an impression   58
on me that I had been able to stretch myself tall and trembling and say, "I know
not what course others may take, but as for me, give me liberty or give me
death."

And now I heard, really for the first time: 59

"We have come over a way that with tears
has been watered,
We have come, treading our path through
the blood of the slaughtered."

While echoes of the song shivered in the air, Henry Reed bowed his head,   60
said "Thank you," and returned to his place in the line. The tears that slipped
down many faces were not wiped away in shame.

We were on top again. As always, again. We survived. The depths had been   61
icy and dark, but now a bright sun spoke to our souls. I was no longer simply
a member of the proud graduating class of 1940; I was a proud member of the
wonderful, beautiful Negro race.

Oh, Black known and unknown poets, how often have your auctioned pains   62
sustained us? Who will compute the lonely nights made less lonely by your
songs, or the empty pots made less tragic by your tales?

If we were a people much given to revealing secrets, we might raise monu-   63
ments and sacrifice to the memories of our poets, but slavery cured us of that
weakness. It may be enough, however, to have it said that we survive in exact
relationship to the dedication of our poets (include preachers, musicians and
blues singers).

QUESTIONS

1. Why was graduation such an important event in Stamps, Arkansas? Note the rituals
and preparations associated with this event. How do they compare with those accompanying your own high school graduation?

2. At the beginning of the graduation ceremony, the writer was "overcome with a
presentiment of worse things to come. Something unrehearsed, unplanned, was going
to happen" (paragraph 30). What "unrehearsed, unplanned" event does occur? How does
the writer convey to the reader the meaning of this event?

18

3. Toward the end of the essay we are told, "I was no longer simply a member of the proud graduating class of 1940; I was a proud member of the wonderful, beautiful Negro race" (paragraph 61). How did the experience of the graduation change the writer's way of thinking about herself and her people?

4. Understanding the structure of this essay is important for understanding the meaning of the essay. How does the writer organize her material, and how does this organization reflect the writer's purpose? Why do you think the writer changes her point of view from third person in the first five paragraphs to first person in the rest of the essay?

5. Think of an event in your life that didn't turn out as you expected. What were your expectations of this event? What was the reality? Write an essay in which you show the significance of this event by contrasting how you planned for the event with how it actually turned out.

6. We have all had experiences that have changed the directions of our lives. These experiences may be momentous, such as moving from one country to another or losing a parent, or they may be experiences that did not loom so large at the time but that changed the way you thought about things, such as finding that your parents disapproved of your best friend because of her race. Recall such a turning point in your life, and present it so as to give the reader a sense of what your life was like before the event and how it changed after the event.

LEARNING TO READ AND WRITE

Frederick Douglass

Frederick Augustus Washington Bailey (1817–1895) was born into slavery on the Eastern Shore of Maryland. His mother was a black slave; his father, a white man. After his escape from the South in 1838, he adopted the name of Douglass and worked to free other slaves and later (after the Civil War) to protect the rights of freed slaves. He was a newspaper editor, a lecturer, United States minister to Haiti, and the author of several books about his life and times. The Narrative of the Life of Frederick Douglass: An American Slave *(1841), from which the following chapter has been taken, is his best-known work.*

I lived in Master Hugh's family about seven years. During this time, I suc-   1
ceeded in learning to read and write. In accomplishing this, I was compelled
to resort to various stratagems. I had no regular teacher. My mistress, who had
kindly commenced to instruct me, had, in compliance with the advice and
direction of her husband, not only ceased to instruct, but had set her face against
my being instructed by any one else. It is due, however, to my mistress to say
of her, that she did not adopt this course of treatment immediately. She at first
lacked the depravity indispensable to shutting me up in mental darkness. It was
at least necessary for her to have some training in the exercise of irresponsible
power, to make her equal to the task of treating me as though I were a brute.

My mistress was, as I have said, a kind and tender-hearted woman; and in   2
the simplicity of her soul she commenced, when I first went to live with her,
to treat me as she supposed one human being ought to treat another. In entering
upon the duties of a slaveholder, she did not seem to perceive that I sustained
to her the relation of a mere chattel, and that for her to treat me as a human
being was not only wrong, but dangerously so. Slavery proved as injurious to
her as it did to me. When I went there, she was a pious, warm, and tender-
hearted woman. There was no sorrow or suffering for which she had not a tear.
She had bread for the hungry, clothes for the naked, and comfort for every
mourner that came within her reach. Slavery soon proved its ability to divest
her of these heavenly qualities. Under its influence, the tender heart became
stone, and the lamblike disposition gave way to one of tiger-like fierceness. The
first step in her downward course was in her ceasing to instruct me. She now
commenced to practise her husband's precepts. She finally became even more
violent in her opposition than her husband himself. She was not satisfied with

20

simply doing as well as he had commanded; she seemed anxious to do better. Nothing seemed to make her more angry than to see me with a newspaper. She seemed to think that here lay the danger. I have had her rush at me with a face made all up of fury, and snatch from me a newspaper, in a manner that fully revealed her apprehension. She was an apt woman; and a little experience soon demonstrated, to her satisfaction, that education and slavery were incompatible with each other.

From this time I was most narrowly watched. If I was in a separate room 3 any considerable length of time, I was sure to be suspected of having a book, and was at once called to give an account of myself. All this, however, was too late. The first step had been taken. Mistress, in teaching me the alphabet, had given me the *inch*, and no precaution could prevent me from taking the *ell*.

The plan which I adopted, and the one by which I was most successful, was 4 that of making friends of all the little white boys whom I met in the street. As many of these as I could, I converted into teachers. With their kindly aid, obtained at different times and in different places, I finally succeeded in learning to read. When I was sent on errands, I always took my book with me, and by going one part of my errand quickly, I found time to get a lesson before my return. I used also to carry bread with me, enough of which was always in the house, and to which I was always welcome; for I was much better off in this regard than many of the poor white children in our neighborhood. This bread I used to bestow upon the hungry little urchins, who, in return, would give me that more valuable bread of knowledge. I am strongly tempted to give the names of two or three of those little boys, as a testimonial of the gratitude and affection I bear them; but prudence forbids;—not that it would injure me, but it might embarrass them; for it is almost an unpardonable offence to teach slaves to read in this Christian country. It is enough to say of the dear little fellows, that they lived on Philpot Street, very near Durgin and Bailey's ship-yard. I used to talk this matter of slavery over with them. I would sometimes say to them, I wished I could be as free as they would be when they got to be men. "You will be free as soon as you are twenty-one, *but I am a slave for life!* Have not I as good a right to be free as you have?" These words used to trouble them; they would express for me the liveliest sympathy, and console me with the hope that something would occur by which I might be free.

I was now about twelve years old, and the thought of being *a slave for life* 5 began to bear heavily upon my heart. Just about this time, I got hold of a book entitled "The Columbian Orator."[1] Every opportunity I got, I used to read this book. Among much of other interesting matter, I found in it a dialogue between a master and his slave. The slave was represented as having run away from his master three times. The dialogue represented the conversation which took place

---

[1]*The Columbian Orator*: a popular schoolbook designed to introduce students to argument and rhetoric. [Eds.]

between them, when the slave was retaken the third time. In this dialogue, the whole argument in behalf of slavery was brought forward by the master, all of which was disposed of by the slave. The slave was made to say some very smart as well as impressive things in reply to his master—things which had the desired though unexpected effect; for the conversation resulted in the voluntary emancipation of the slave on the part of the master.

In the same book, I met with one of Sheridan's mighty speeches on and in behalf of Catholic emancipation.[2] These were choice documents to me. I read them over and over again with unabated interest. They gave tongue to interesting thoughts of my own soul, which had frequently flashed through my mind, and died away for want of utterance. The moral which I gained from the dialogue was the power of truth over the conscience of even a slaveholder. What I got from Sheridan was a bold denunciation of slavery, and a powerful vindication of human rights. The reading of these documents enabled me to utter my thoughts, and to meet the arguments brought forward to sustain slavery; but while they relieved me of one difficulty, they brought on another even more painful than the one of which I was relieved. The more I read, the more I was led to abhor and detest my enslavers. I could regard them in no other light than a band of successful robbers, who had left their homes, and gone to Africa, and stolen us from our homes, and in a strange land reduced us to slavery. I loathed them as being the meanest as well as the most wicked of men. As I read and contemplated the subject, behold! that very discontentment which Master Hugh had predicted would follow my learning to read had already come, to torment and sting my soul to unutterable anguish. As I writhed under it, I would at times feel that learning to read had been a curse rather than a blessing. It had given me a view of my wretched condition, without the remedy. It opened my eyes to the horrible pit, but to no ladder upon which to get out. In moments of agony, I envied my fellow-slaves for their stupidity. I have often wished myself a beast. I preferred the condition of the meanest reptile to my own. Any thing, no matter what, to get rid of thinking! It was this everlasting thinking of my condition that tormented me. There was no getting rid of it. It was pressed upon me by every object within sight or hearing, animate or inanimate. The silver trump of freedom had roused my soul to eternal wakefulness. Freedom now appeared, to disappear no more forever. It was heard in every sound, and seen in every thing. It was ever present to torment me with a sense of my wretched condition. I saw nothing without seeing it, I heard nothing without hearing it, and felt nothing without feeling it. It looked from every star, it smiled in every calm, breathed in every wind, and moved in every storm.

I often found myself regretting my own existence, and wishing myself dead; and but for the hope of being free, I have no doubt but that I should have killed

6

7

---

[2]Richard Brinsley Sheridan (1751–1816): British dramatist, orator, and politician. Catholics were not allowed to vote in England until 1829. [Eds.]

myself, or done something for which I should have been killed. While in this state of mind, I was eager to hear any one speak of slavery. I was a ready listener. Every little while, I could hear something about the abolitionists. It was some time before I found what the word meant. It was always used in such connections as to make it an interesting word to me. If a slave ran away and succeeded in getting clear, or if a slave killed his master, set fire to a barn, or did any thing very wrong in the mind of a slaveholder, it was spoken of as the fruit of *abolition*. Hearing the word in this connection very often, I set about learning what it meant. The dictionary afforded me little or no help. I found it was "the act of abolishing"; but then I did not know what was to be abolished. Here I was perplexed. I did not dare to ask any one about its meaning, for I was satisfied that it was something they wanted me to know very little about. After a patient waiting, I got one of our city papers, containing an account of the number of petitions from the north, praying for the abolition of slavery in the District of Columbia, and of the slave trade between the States. From this time I understood the words *abolition* and *abolitionist,* and always drew near when that word was spoken, expecting to hear something of importance to myself and fellow-slaves. The light broke in upon me by degrees. I went one day down on the wharf of Mr. Waters; and seeing two Irishmen unloading a scow of stone, I went, unasked, and helped them. When we had finished, one of them came to me and asked me if I were a slave. I told him I was. He asked, "Are ye a slave for life?" I told him that I was. The good Irishman seemed to be deeply affected by the statement. He said to the other that it was a pity so fine a little fellow as myself should be a slave for life. He said it was a shame to hold me. They both advised me to run away to the north; that I should find friends there, and that I should be free. I pretended not to be interested in what they said, and treated them as if I did not understand them; for I feared they might be treacherous. White men have been known to encourage slaves to escape, and then, to get the reward, catch them and return them to their masters. I was afraid that these seemingly good men might use me so; but I nevertheless remembered their advice, and from that time I resolved to run away. I looked forward to a time at which it would be safe for me to escape. I was too young to think of doing so immediately; besides, I wished to learn how to write, as I might have occasion to write my own pass. I consoled myself with the hope that I should one day find a good chance. Meanwhile, I would learn to write.

The idea as to how I might learn to write was suggested to me by being in Durgin and Bailey's ship-yard, and frequently seeing the ship carpenters, after hewing, and getting a piece of timber ready for use, write on the timber the name of that part of the ship for which it was intended. When a piece of timber was intended for the larboard side, it would be marked thus—"L." When a piece was for the starboard side, it would be marked thus—"S." A piece for the larboard side forward, would be marked thus—"L. F." When a piece was for starboard side forward, it would be marked thus—"S. F." For larboard aft, it

8

would be marked thus—"L.A." For starboard aft, it would be marked thus—
"S. A." I soon learned the names of these letters, and for what they were
intended when placed upon a piece of timber in the ship-yard. I immediately
commenced copying them, and in a short time was able to make the four letters
named. After that, when I met with any boy who I knew could write, I would
tell him I could write as well as he. The next word would be, "I don't believe
you. Let me see you try it." I would then make the letters which I had been so
fortunate as to learn, and ask him to beat that. In this way I got a good many
lessons in writing, which it is quite possible I should never have gotten in any
other way. During this time, my copy-book was the board fence, brick wall,
and pavement; my pen and ink was a lump of chalk. With these, I learned
mainly how to write. I then commenced and continued copying the Italics in
Webster's Spelling Book, until I could make them all without looking on the
book. By this time, my little Master Thomas had gone to school, and learned
how to write, and had written over a number of copy-books. These had been
brought home, and shown to some of our near neighbors, and then laid aside.
My mistress used to go to class meeting at the Wilk Street meetinghouse every
Monday afternoon, and leave me to take care of the house. When left thus, I
used to spend the time in writing in the spaces left in Master Thomas's copy-
book, copying what he had written. I continued to do this until I could write a
hand very similar to that of Master Thomas. Thus, after a long, tedious effort
for years, I finally succeeded in learning how to write.

QUESTIONS

1. As its title proclaims, Douglass's book is a narrative, the story of his life. So, too,
is this chapter a narrative, the story of his learning to read and write. Separate out the
main events of this story, and list them in chronological order.

2. Douglass is reporting some of the events in his life in this selection, but certain
events are not simply reported. Instead, they are described so that we may see, hear, and
feel what was experienced by those people who were present on the original occasions.
Which events are described most fully in this narrative? How does Douglass seek to
engage our interest and direct our feelings through such scenes?

3. In this episode from his life, as in his whole book, Douglass is engaged in evaluating an institution—slavery—and arguing a case against it. Can you locate the points
in the text where reflecting gives way to argumentation? How does Douglass support his
argument against slavery? What are the sources of his persuasiveness?

4. The situation of Irish Catholics is a subtheme in this essay. You can trace it by
locating every mention of the Irish or of Catholicism in the text. How does this theme
relate to Afro-American slavery? Try to locate *The Columbian Orator* in your library, or
find out more about who "Sheridan" was and why he had to argue on behalf of "Catholic
emancipation" (paragraph 6).

5. There is a subnarrative in this text that tells the story of Master Hugh's wife, the "mistress" of the household in which Douglass learned to read and write. Retell *her* story in your own words. Consider how her story relates to Douglass's own story and how it relates to Douglass's larger argument about slavery.

6. Put yourself in the place of Master Hugh's wife, and retell all events in her words and from her point of view. To do so, you will have to decide both what she might have come to know about all these events and how she would feel about them. You will also have to decide when she is writing. Is she keeping a diary during this very time (the early 1830s), or is she looking back from the perspective of later years? Has she been moved to write by reading Douglass's own book, which appeared in 1841? If so, how old would she be then, and what would she think about these past events? Would she be angry, bitter, repentant, embarrassed, indulgent, scornful, or what?

WHY I TOOK TO PHILOSOPHY

Bertrand Russell

*Mathematician, philosopher, man of letters, and pacifist,
Bertrand Russell (1872–1970) was both an English lord and
a Nobel laureate. He wrote books on a staggering range of
subjects from the principles of mathematics to questions of
religion and politics. Trained in mathematics, Russell tried
in his writing to apply the clarity he admired in mathematical reasoning to the solution of problems in other fields,
especially in ethics and politics. The following selection from
his book of reminiscences,* Portraits from Memory *(1956),
traces the path that led Russell to the study of philosophy.*

The motives which have led men to become philosophers have been of 1
various kinds. The most respectable motive was the desire to understand the
world. In early days, while philosophy and science were indistinguishable, this
motive predominated. Another motive which was a potent incentive in early
times was the illusoriness of the senses. Such questions as: where is the rainbow?
Are things really what they seem to be in sunshine or in moonlight? In more
modern forms of the same problem—are things really what they look like to the
naked eye or what they look like through a microscope? Such puzzles, however,
very soon came to be supplemented by a larger problem. When the Greeks
began to be doubtful about the Gods of Olympus, some of them sought in
philosophy a substitute for traditional beliefs. Through the combination of these
two motives there arose a twofold movement in philosophy: on the one hand,
it was thought to show that much which passes for knowledge in everyday life
is not real knowledge; and on the other hand, that there is a deeper philosophical
truth which, according to most philosophers, is more consonant than our everyday beliefs with what we should wish the universe to be. In almost all philosophy
doubt has been the goad and certainty has been the goal. There has been doubt
about the senses, doubt about science, and doubt about theology. In some
philosophers one of these has been more prominent, in others another. Philosophers have also differed widely as to the answers they have suggested to these
doubts and even as to whether any answers are possible.

All the traditional motives combined to lead me to philosophy, but there 2
were two that specially influenced me. The one which operated first and continued longest was the desire to find some knowledge that could be accepted as
certainly true. The other motive was the desire to find some satisfaction for
religious impulses.

WHY I TOOK TO PHILOSOPHY

I think the first thing that led me towards philosophy (though at that time 3
the word "philosophy" was still unknown to me) occurred at the age of eleven.
My childhood was mainly solitary as my only brother was seven years older than
I was. No doubt as a result of much solitude I became rather solemn, with a
great deal of time for thinking but not much knowledge for my thoughtfulness
to exercise itself upon. I had, though I was not yet aware of it, the pleasure in
demonstrations which is typical of the mathematical mind. After I grew up I
found others who felt as I did on this matter. My friend G. H. Hardy, who was
professor of pure mathematics, enjoyed this pleasure in a very high degree. He
told me once that if he cold find a proof that I was going to die in five minutes
he would of course be sorry to lose me, but this sorrow would be quite out-
weighed by pleasure in the proof. I entirely sympathized with him and was not
at all offended. Before I began the study of geometry somebody had told me
that it proved things and this causes me to feel delight when my brother said
he would teach it to me. Geometry in those days was still "Euclid.[1]" My brother
began at the beginning with the definitions. These I accepted readily enough.
But he came next to the axioms. "These," he said, "can't be proved, but they
have to be assumed before the rest can be proved." At these words my hopes
crumbled, I had thought it would be wonderful to find something that one
could PROVE, and then it turned out that this could only be done by means of
assumptions of which there was no proof. I looked at my brother with a sort of
indignation and said," But why should I admit these things if they can't be
proved?" He replied, "Well, if you won't, we can't go on." I thought it might
be worth while to learn the rest of the story, so I agreed to admit the axioms
for the time being. But I remained full of doubt and perplexity as regards a
region in which I had hoped to find indisputable clarity. In spite of these doubts,
which at most times I forgot, and which I usually supposed capable of some
answer not yet known to me, I found great delight in mathematics—much more
delight, in fact, than in any other study. I liked to think of the applications of
mathematics to the physical world, and I hoped that in time there would be a
mathematics of human behavior as precise as the mathematics of machines. I
hoped this because I liked demonstrations, and at most times this motive out-
weighed the desire, which I also felt, to believe in free will. Nevertheless I never
quite overcame my fundamental doubts as to the validity of mathematics.

When I began to learn higher mathematics, fresh difficulties assailed me. 4
My teachers offered me proofs which I felt to be fallacious and which, as I
learnt later, had been recognized as fallacious. I did not know then, or for some
time after I had left Cambridge, that better proofs had been found by German
mathematicians. I therefore remained in a receptive mood for the heroic measures

---

[1]Euclid: Greek mathematician of the fourth century B.C. whose *Elements* became the basis of
future geometry. [Eds.]

of Kant's philosophy.[2] This suggested a large new survey from which such difficulties as had troubled me looked niggling and unimportant. All this I came later on to think wholly fallacious, but that was only after I had allowed myself to sink deep in the mire of metaphysical muddles. I was encouraged in my transition to philosophy by a certain disgust with mathematics, resulting from too much concentration and too much absorption in the sort of skill that is needed in examinations. The attempt to acquire examination technique had led me to think of mathematics as consisting of artful dodges and ingenious devices and as altogether too much like a crossword puzzle. When, at the end of my first three years at Cambridge, I emerged from my last mathematical examination I swore that I would never look at mathematics again and sold all my mathematical books. In this mood the survey of philosophy gave me all the delight of a new landscape on emerging from a valley.

It had not been only in mathematics that I sought certainty. Like Descartes   5 (whose work was still unknown to me) I thought that my own existence was, to me, indubitable.[3] Like him, I felt it possible to suppose that the outer world is nothing but a dream. But even if it be, it is a dream that is really dreamt, and the fact that I experience it remains unshakably certain. This line of thought occurred to me first when I was sixteen, and I was glad when I learnt later that Descartes had made it the basis of his philosophy.

At Cambridge my interest in philosophy received a stimulus from another   6 motive. The scepticism which had led me to doubt even mathematics had also led me to question the fundamental dogmas of religion, but I ardently desired to find a way of preserving at least something that could be called religious belief. From the age of fifteen to the age of eighteen I spent a great deal of time and thought on religious belief. I examined fundamental dogmas one by one, hoping with all my heart to find some reason for accepting them. I wrote my thoughts in a notebook which I still possess. They were, of course, crude and youthful, but for the moment I saw no answser to the Agnosticism which they suggested. At Cambridge I was made aware of whole systems of thought of which I had previously been ignorant and I abandoned for a time the ideas which I had worked out in solitude. At Cambridge I was introduced to the philosophy of Hegel who, in the course of nineteen abstruse volumes, professed to have proved something which would do quite well as an emended and sophisticated version of traditional beliefs.[4] Hegel thought of the universe as a closely knit unity. His universe was like a jelly in the fact that, if you touched any one part of it, the whole quivered; but it was unlike a jelly in the fact that it could not really be cut up into parts. The appearance of consisting of parts,

[2]Immanuel Kant (1724–1804): German philosopher who developed a philosophy of ethics based on practical reason aided by moral feelings. [Eds.]
[3]René Descartes (1559–1650): French mathematician and philosopher, father of the modern scientific method. [Eds.]
[4]Georg Friedrich Hegel (1770–1831): German philosopher. [Eds.]

according to him, was a delusion. The only reality was the Absolute, which was his name for God. In this philosophy I found comfort for a time. As presented to me by its adherents, especially McTaggart, who was then an intimate friend of mine, Hegel's philosophy had seemed both charming and demonstrable. McTaggart was a philosopher some six years senior to me and throughout his life an ardent disciple of Hegel.[5] He influenced his contemporaries very considerably, and I for a time fell under his sway. There was a curious pleasure in making oneself believe that time and space are unreal, that matter is an illusion, and that the world really consists of nothing but mind. In a rash moment, however, I turned from the disciples to the Master and found in Hegel himself a farrago of confusions[6] and what seemed to me little better than puns. I therefore abandoned his philosophy.

For a time I found satisfaction in a doctrine derived, with modification, from   7
Plato. According to Plato's doctrine, which I accepted only in a watered-down form, there is an unchanging timeless world of ideas of which the world presented to our senses is an imperfect copy. Mathematics, according to his doctrine, deals with the world of ideas and has in consequence an exactness and perfection which is absent from the everyday world. This kind of mathematical mysticism, which Plato derived from Pythagoras, appealed to me. But in the end I found myself obliged to abandon this doctrine also, and I have never since found religious satisfaction in any philosophical doctrine that I could accept.

QUESTIONS

1. Paragraph 1 deals with the traditional "motives which have led men to become philosophers." Which of these motives apply to Russell's own development as a philosopher?

2. What roles have doubt and certainty played in the history of philosophy? What roles did they play in Russell's career?

3. Mathematics and religion are the two major topics of this essay. What parallels between the two do you find in Russell's representation of them? Does the phrase "mathematical mysticism" (in the final paragraph) offer a useful synthesis of the two subjects? Explain your answer.

4. In his dealings with mathematics, philosophy, and religion, Russell repeats a pattern of uninformed optimism followed by informed pessimism. Trace this pattern through the essay. How does this pattern structure Russell's presentation of his experience? On what note does the essay end?

5. How would you characterize the tone of this essay? What does the tone tell you about Russell's attitude toward his younger self?

6. This selection from Russell's memoirs halts while he is still a young man looking

---

[5]John McTaggart (1866–1925): English philosopher, author of *Commentary on Hegel's Logic* (1910). [Eds.]

[6]farrago: a jumbled mixture. [Eds.]

for a satisfactory philosophical doctrine. Read the rest of *Portraits from Memory* (or his later *Autobiography*), and report on what doctrines he later accepted.

7. Russell's quest for certainty is always frustrated. Has there been an occasion in your life when your drive for certainty on a particular question or incident ended in disillusion and disappointment rather than illumination? Write an essay about this occasion showing your readers the significance of this experience for you.

8. Russell's older brother tells him there are some geometric axioms that have to be assumed (even though they can't be proved) or else "we can't go on." Do you assume any "axioms" or beliefs that, while unprovable, make life easier or more rewarding? Write an essay reflecting about any such beliefs held by you or by others you know well. In your essay, both recall specific events and comment on their significance.

THE CRUELEST MONTH
Russell Baker

One of America's cleverest humorists, Russell Baker was born in 1925 and raised in rural America under circumstances that are touchingly evoked in his autobiography Growing Up *(1982), for which he won a Pulitzer Prize. After graduating from John Hopkins University in 1947, he worked on the* Baltimore Sun *for seven years before joining the staff of the* New York Times *in 1953. Originally a reporter of the Washington scene, he began in 1962 writing his "Observer" columns for which he has become famous. Periodically gathered into books, these columns combine literate humor with trenchant social observation. "I didn't set out in life to be a humorist," he said, but he has since been ranked with Mark Twain, James Thurber, and others, and millions of readers follow his columns avidly. "The Cruelest Month"—which takes its title from the opening line of T. S. Eliot's famous poem* The Waste Land *("April is the cruelest month")—is taken from Baker's recent collection of columns,* The Rescue of Miss Yaskell and Other Pipe Dreams *(1983).*

The third week of September has always been a grisly time for schoolchildren. It is then that the romance of education, sparked by the back-to-school excitement of fresh books, new teachers, virginal fountain pens and notebooks unstained by ink blots and baffling mathematical formulas, begins to yield to reality. 1

And what is that reality? It is knowledge. Knowledge that it will be nine long months before summer vacation rolls around again. Knowledge that the geography teacher dislikes you. Knowledge that the gym instructor finds your physique absurd. Knowledge that you are never going to understand at least three of the subjects with which you are saddled and are going to suffer horribly for months as you sink into the quagmire of F's recording the progress of your ignorance. 2

It was Jean Shepherd, I believe, who said that after three weeks in chemistry he was six months behind the class. This is a common experience, this sensation of being locked forever in the starting gate while the rest of the class is galloping for the back stretch, and it leaves many people scarred for life. 3

A woman I know, though financially well-heeled, still refuses to set foot in Italy because in seventh-grade Latin she became aware, after three weeks in the 4 classroom, that she would never be able to conjugate the verb *esse* to Cicero's satisfaction. Assurances that Cicero is no longer to be encountered in Rome do not comfort her. She associates the Italian peninsula with personal humiliation.

I myself have always avoided Germany since discovering in 10th grade that   5
German has two dozen ways of saying "the." I could be wrong about this, since I was wrong about everything else in German. Nevertheless, there is the fact. The memory of a third week in September when classmates began hooting about my tendency to use the dative feminine singular form of "the" when the accusative neuter plural was called for—this memory has created a lifelong barrier between Germany and me.

Schools do not concede that it is ridiculous to require every student to learn   6
at the same pace. They operate on the assumption that every brain in the classroom will achieve a firm grasp of the binomial theorem at the same instant and be ready to move on simultaneously to those many cheerful facts about the square of the hypotenuse waiting at the next hitching post.

Readers who met the educators' expectations in mathematics may deduce   7
from the above that my own pace in math was decidedly slow if, as I suspect, you have to master the hypotenuse before proceeding on to the binomial theorem. The truth is that, never understanding either one, I was utterly lost and made a terrible mess of things when I reached the cosine and the secant.

All of this probably resulted because some teacher during the third week of   8
some long-ago September assumed, wrongly, that I understood that 9 times 6 is 54, and rushed on to impress me with the realization that 9 times 8 is 77, or whatever it may be.

Almost all of us have dreadful third weeks of September in our backgrounds   9
somewhere. If psychoanalysts would let up a bit on our libidinal childhood experiences, they might discover a rich new source of adult neurosis here.

The third week of September that mutilated my own life is the reason I am   10
not a brilliant nuclear physicist today. Here let me confess that in youth it was not my intent to become a typewriter pounder hacking out material for Sunday supplements. Hooked on the romance of science, I yearned to take up the torch from Einstein and carry it forward.

Thus I came to physics class. The first week of September was thrilling, as   11
textbooks were issued and the teacher discoursed on Isaac Newton and apples and introduced us to the lab, that frontier of human progress. In the second week, he introduced us to the erg. I was quite happy with the erg, without which blocks of wood could not be made to overcome the villainous friction of inclined ramps and moved upward, triumphantly ascending those ramps.

At the end of the week, he introduced the dyne, which seemed excessive. It   12
was not that I couldn't understand the dyne. I could have. What I could not understand was why, since we already had the erg, it was also necessary to have the dyne.

I was still puzzling this philosophical question the following Monday when   13
the teacher, assuming that everybody now had a firm grip on the dyne, plunged
ahead into the centimeter. Perhaps it was only the millimeter. I am hazy here
because reality was fading rapidly.

It was disconcerting to have the dyne taken utterly for granted when I still   14
had profound doubts about it and to be asked to cope with the centimeter. The
next day was worse. That was the day of the milligram. The following day there
was a test.

I was astonished that the rest of the class took it without a roar of protest that   15
it was outrageous to ask us to cope with ergs, dynes, centimeters and milligrams
while we were still baffled about the dyne. The rest of the class did not protest.
Most passed easily. I failed every question not devoted exclusively to the erg.
The rest of that year was a nightmare, and the world still awaits a worthy
successor to Einstein.

QUESTIONS

1. Why is September "the cruelest month" for Baker?
2. Is Baker's aversion to the third week of September personal or universal? To what
extent does he speak for all students?
3. Is this merely a humorous reminiscence, or does Baker make any valid criticisms
of the present educational system? Is it ridiculous, as he says in paragraph 6, "to require
every student to learn at the same pace"? Explain your answers.
4. How authentic do the examples in paragraphs 4 and 5 sound to you? Does their
authenticity matter?
5. How seriously do you take his claim that his third week in physics class prevented
him from becoming "a brilliant nuclear physicist" (paragraph 10)? What is it about his
tone that signals you how seriously to take that claim?
6. Baker's humorous style relies on dramatic adjectives and comic exaggeration. Locate as many examples of these as possible, and explain why they make the essay more
enjoyable.
7. "Almost all of us have dreadful third weeks of September in our backgrounds
somewhere," Baker writes in paragraph 9. Do you? If so, give an account of yours, and
feel free to indulge in the same kind of comic exaggeration Baker does.

THE IGUANA

Isak Dinesen

Karen Dinesen (1885–1962) was a Danish woman who married a Swedish baron and went to Kenya in East Africa with him in 1914 to manage their coffee plantation. After their divorce she stayed in Kenya, managing the plantation until its failure in 1931. During this time she began to write in English (the language of whites in Kenya), taking the male first name of Isak. Her best-known books are Seven Gothic Tales *(1934), a volume of stories, and* Out of Africa *(1937), her reminiscences of Kenya. The following brief selection from the latter volume appeared in the section called "From an Immigrant's Notebook."*

In the Reserve I have sometimes come upon the Iguana, the big lizards,[1] as they were sunning themselves upon a flat stone in a river-bed. They are not pretty in shape, but nothing can be imagined more beautiful than their coloring. They shine like a heap of precious stones or like a pane cut out of an old church window. When, as you approach, they swish away, there is a flash of azure, green and purple over the stones, the color seems to be standing behind them in the air, like a comet's luminous tail.

Once I shot an Iguana. I thought that I should be able to make some pretty things from his skin. A strange thing happened then, that I have never afterwards forgotten. As I went up to him, where he was laying dead upon his stone, and actually while I was walking the few steps, he faded and grew pale, all color died out of him as in one long sigh, and by the time that I touched him he was grey and dull like a lump of concrete. It was the live impetuous blood pulsating within the animal, which had radiated out all that glow and splendor. Now that the flame was put out, and the soul had flown, the Iguana was as dead as a sandbag.

Often since I have, in some sort, shot an Iguana, and I have remembered the one of the Reserve. Up at Meru I saw a young Native girl with a bracelet on, a leather strap two inches wide, and embroidered all over with very small turquoise-colored beads which varied a little in color and played in green, light blue and ultramarine. It was an extraordinarily live thing; it seemed to draw breath on her arm, so that I wanted it for myself, and made Farah buy it from her.[2] No sooner had it come upon my own arm than it gave up the ghost. It

---

[1]the Reserve: the game reserve in the Ngong Hills of Kenya, Africa. [Eds.]
[2]Farah Aden: Dinesen's Somali servant. [Eds.]

34

was nothing now, a small, cheap, purchased article of finery. It had been the play of colors, the duet between the turquoise and the "nègre",—that quick, sweet, brownish black, like peat and black pottery, of the Native's skin,—that had created the life of the bracelet.

In the Zoological Museum of Pietermaritzburg, I have seen, in a stuffed 4 deep-water fish in a showcase, the same combination of coloring, which there had survived death; it made me wonder what life can well be like, on the bottom of the sea, to send up something so live and airy. I stood in Meru and looked at my pale hand and at the dead bracelet, it was as if an injustice had been done to a noble thing, as if truth had been suppressed. So sad did it seem that I remembered the saying of the hero in a book that I had read as a child: "I have conquered them all, but I am standing amongst graves."

In a foreign country and with foreign species of life one should take measures 5 to find out whether things will be keeping their value when dead. To the settlers of East Africa I give the advice: "For the sake of your own eyes and heart, shoot not the Iguana."

QUESTIONS

1. In this essay the act of shooting an iguana comes to stand as a type or model of other actions; it becomes a symbolic event. This is expressed explicitly at the beginning of paragraph 3: "Often since I have, *in some sort*, shot an Iguana" (italics added). How do the incidents described in paragraphs 3 and 4 help us to understand the full meaning of the symbolic action of shooting an iguana? Restate this meaning in your own words.

2. An argument that lurks beneath the surface of this meditative essay is made explicit in its last sentence. How do you understand that sentence and that argument?

3. The power of this essay grows from its effective representation—its ability to put us in the picture, to make us see and feel the events represented. Find a phrase of description or comparison that seems to you especially vivid, and explain why it is effective.

4. Dinesen uses three concrete examples here. How are the three related? Why do you suppose she arranged them in the order in which she did?

5. In her meditation, Dinesen moves from lizard, to bracelet, to fish, and then uses these three specific, concrete instances to make the jump to generalizations about foreign species and foreign countries. Try this technique yourself. Find some incident in your own life that reminds you of other similar events, so that they can be brought together as being symbolic of a certain *kind* of event. To what broader point can you leap from these few recollected events?

ON KEEPING
A NOTEBOOK

Joan Didion

*Joan Didion was born in Sacramento, California, in 1934
and graduated with a B.A. in English from the University
of California at Berkeley in 1956. Until the publication of
her first novel,* Run River, *in 1963, she worked as an associate feature editor for* Vogue *magazine. Since then she
has written three more novels,* Play It as It Lays *(1971),* A
Book of Common Prayer *(1977), and* Democracy *(1984)
as well as three books of essays,* Slouching Towards Bethlehem *(1969),* The White Album *(1982), and* Salvador
*(1983). As an essayist, she has shown herself to be a trench-
ant observer and interpreter of American society. The selection reprinted here is from* Slouching Towards Bethlehem.

" 'That woman Estelle,' " the note reads, " 'is partly the reason why George   1
Sharp and I are separated today' *Dirty crepe-de-Chine wrapper, hotel bar, Wilmington RR, 9:45 a.m. August Monday morning.*"

Since the note is in my notebook, it presumably has some meaning to me.   2
I study it for a long while. At first I have only the most general notion of what
I was doing on an August Monday morning in the bar of the hotel across from
the Pennsylvania Railroad station in Wilmington, Delaware (waiting for a train?
missing one? 1960? 1961? why Wilmington?), but I do remember being there.
The woman in the dirty crepe-de-Chine wrapper had come down from her
room for a beer, and the bartender had heard before the reason why George
Sharp and she were separated today. "Sure," he said, and went on mopping the
floor, "You told me." At the other end of the bar is a girl. She is talking,
pointedly, not to the man beside her but to a cat lying in the triangle of sunlight
cast through the open door. She is wearing a plaid silk dress from Peck & Peck,
and the hem is coming down.

Here is what it is: the girl has been on the Eastern Shore, and now she is   3
going back to the city, leaving the man beside her, and all she can see ahead
are the viscous summer sidewalks and the 3 A.M. long-distance calls that will
make her lie awake and then sleep drugged through all the steaming mornings
left in August (1960? 1961?). Because she must go directly from the train to
lunch in New York, she wishes that she had a safety pin for the hem of the
plaid silk dress, and she also wishes that she could forget about the hem and
the lunch and stay in the cool bar that smells of disinfectant and malt and make
friends with the woman in the crepe-de-Chine wrapper. She is afflicted by a

36

little self-pity, and she wants to compare Estelles. That is what that was all about.

Why did I write it down? In order to remember, of course, but exactly what was it I wanted to remember? How much of it actually happened? Did any of it? Why do I keep a notebook at all? It is easy to deceive oneself on all those scores. The impulse to write things down is a peculiarly compulsive one, inexplicable to those who do not share it, useful only accidentally, only secondarily, in the way that any compulsion tries to justify itself. I suppose that it begins or does not begin in the cradle. Although I have felt compelled to write things down since I was five years old, I doubt that my daughter ever will, for she is a singularly blessed and accepting child, delighted with life exactly as life presents itself to her, unafraid to go to sleep and unafraid to wake up. Keepers of private notebooks are a different breed altogether, lonely and resistant rearrangers of things, anxious malcontents, children afflicted apparently at birth with some presentiment of loss.

My first notebook was a Big Five tablet, given to me by my mother with the sensible suggestion that I stop whining and learn to amuse myself by writing down my thoughts. She returned the tablet to me a few years ago; the first entry is an account of a woman who believed herself to be freezing to death in the Arctic night, only to find, when day broke, that she had stumbled onto the Sahara Desert, where she would die of the heat before lunch. I have no idea what turn of a five-year-old's mind could have prompted so insistently "ironic" and exotic a story, but it does reveal a certain predilection for the extreme which has dogged me into adult life; perhaps if I were analytically inclined I would find it a truer story than any I might have told about Donald Johnson's birthday party or the day my cousin Brenda put Kitty Litter in the Aquarium.

So the point of my keeping a notebook has never been, nor is it now, to have an accurate factual record of what I have been doing or thinking. That would be a different impulse entirely, an instinct for reality which I sometimes envy but do not possess. At no point have I ever been able successfully to keep a diary; my approach to daily life ranges from the grossly negligent to the merely absent, and on those few occasions when I have tried dutifully to record a day's events, boredom has so overcome me that the results are mysterious at best. What is this business about "shopping, typing piece, dinner with E, depressed"? Shopping for what? Typing what piece? Who is E? Was this "E" depressed, or was I depressed? Who cares?

In fact I have abandoned altogether that kind of pointless entry; instead I tell what some would call lies. "That's simply not true," the members of my family frequently tell me when they come up against my memory of a shared event. "The party was *not* for you, the spider was *not* a black widow, *it wasn't that way at all.*" Very likely they are right, for not only have I always had trouble distinguishing between what happened and what merely might have happened, but I remain unconvinced that the distinction, for my purposes, matters. The cracked crab that I recall having for lunch the day my father came home from Detroit in 1945 must certainly be embroidery, worked into the day's pattern to lend verisimilitude; I was ten years old and would not now remember the cracked crab. The day's events did not turn on cracked crab. And yet it is precisely that fictitious crab that makes me see the afternoon all over again, a home movie run all too often, the father bearing gifts, the child weeping, an exercise in family love and guilt. Or that is what it was to me. Similarly, perhaps it never did snow that August in Vermont; perhaps there never were flurries in the night wind, and maybe no one else felt the ground hardening and summer already dead even as we pretended to bask in it, but that was how it felt to me, and it might as well have snowed, could have snowed, did snow.

How it felt to me: that is getting closer to the truth about a notebook. I sometimes delude myself about why I keep a notebook, imagine that some thrifty virtue derives from preserving everything observed. See enough and write it down, I tell myself, and them some morning when the world seems drained of wonder, some day when I am only going through the motions of doing what I am supposed to do, which is write—on that bankrupt morning I will simply open my notebook and there it will all be, a forgotten account with accumulated interest, paid passage back to the world out there: dialogue overheard in hotels and elevators and at the hat-check counter in Pavillon (one middle-aged man shows his hat check to another and says, "That's my old football number"); impressions of Bettina Aptheker and Benjamin Sonnenberg and Teddy ("Mr. Acapulco") Stauffer; careful *aperçus* about tennis bums and failed fashion models and Greek shipping heiresses, one of whom taught me a significant lesson (a lesson I could have learned from F. Scott Fitzgerald, but perhaps we all must meet the very rich for ourselves) by asking, when I arrived to interview her in her orchid-filled sitting room on the second day of a paralyzing New York blizzard, whether it was snowing outside.

I imagine, in other words, that the notebook is about other people. But of course it is not. I have no real business with what one stranger said to another at the hat-check counter in Pavillon; in fact I suspect that the line "That's my old football number" touched not my own imagination at all, but merely some memory of something once read, probably "The Eighty-Yard Run." Nor is my concern with a woman in a dirty crepe-de-Chine wrapper in a Wilmington bar. My stake is always, of course, in the unmentioned girl in the plaid silk dress. *Remember what it was to be me:* that is always the point.

It is a difficult point to admit. We are brought up in the ethic that others, any others, all others, are by definition more interesting than ourselves; taught to be diffident, just this side of self-effacing. ("You're the least important person in the room and don't forget it," Jessica Mitford's governess would hiss in her ear on the advent of any social occasion; I copied that into my notebook because it is only recently that I have been able to enter a room without hearing some such phrase in my inner ear.) Only the very young and the very old may recount their dreams at breakfast, dwell upon self, interrupt with memories of beach picnics and favorite Liberty lawn dresses and the rainbow trout in a creek near Colorado Springs. The rest of us are expected, rightly, to affect absorption in other people's favorite dresses, other people's trout.

And so we do. But our notebooks give us away, for however dutifully we 11 record what we see around us, the common denominator of all we see is always, transparently, shamelessly, the implacable "I." We are not talking here about the kind of notebook that is patently for public consumption, a structural conceit for binding together a series of graceful *pensées*; we are talking about something private, about bits of the mind's string too short to use, an indiscriminate and erratic assemblage with meaning only for its maker.

And sometimes even the maker has difficulty with the meaning. There does 12 not seem to be, for example, any point in my knowing for the rest of my life that, during 1964, 720 tons of soot fell on every square mile of New York City, yet there it is in my notebook, labeled "FACT." Nor do I really need to remember that Ambrose Bierce liked to spell Leland Stanford's name "£eland $tanford" or that "smart women almost always wear black in Cuba," a fashion hint without much potential for practical application. And does not the relevance of these notes seem marginal at best?:

> In the basement museum of the Inyo County Courthouse in Independence, California, sign pinned to a mandarin coat: "This MANDARIN COAT was often worn by Mrs. Minnie S. Brooks when giving lectures on her TEAPOT COLLECTION."
> Redhead getting out of car in front of Beverly Wilshire Hotel, chinchilla stole, Vuitton bags with tags reading:
>
> MRS LOU FOX
> HOTEL SAHARA
> VEGAS

Well, perhaps not entirely marginal. As a matter of fact, Mrs. Minnie S. 13 Brooks and her MANDARIN COAT pull me back into my own childhood, for although I never knew Mrs. Brooks and did not visit Inyo County until I was thirty, I grew up in just such a world, in houses cluttered with Indian relics and bits of gold ore and ambergris and the souvenirs my Aunt Mercy Farnsworth brought back from the Orient. It is a long way from that world to Mrs. Lou Fox's world, where we all live now, and is it not just as well to remember that? Might not Mrs. Minnie S. Brooks help me to remember what I am? Might not Mrs. Lou Fox help me to remember what I am not?

But sometimes the point is harder to discern. What exactly did I have in 14 mind when I noted down that it cost the father of someone I know $650 a month to light the place on the Hudson in which he lived before the Crash? What use was I planning to make of this line by Jimmy Hoffa: "I may have my faults, but being wrong ain't one of them"? And although I think it interesting to know where the girls who travel with the Syndicate have their hair done when they find themselves on the West Coast, will I ever make suitable use of it? Might I not be better off just passing it on to John O'Hara? What is a recipe for sauerkraut doing in my notebook? What kind of magpie keeps this notebook? *"He was born the night the Titanic went down."* That seems a nice enough line, and I even recall who said it, but is it not really a better line in life than it could ever be in fiction?

But of course that is exactly it: not that I should ever use the line, but that I should remember the woman who said it and the afternoon I heard it. We were on her terrace by the sea, and we were finishing the wine left from lunch, trying to get what sun there was, a California winter sun. The woman whose husband was born the night the *Titanic* went down wanted to rent her house, wanted to go back to her children in Paris. I remember wishing that I could afford the house, which cost $1,000 a month. "Someday you will," she said lazily. "Someday it all comes." There in the sun on her terrace it seemed easy to believe in someday, but later I had a low-grade afternoon hangover and ran over a black snake on the way to the supermarket and was flooded with inexplicable fear when I heard the checkout clerk explaining to the man ahead of me why she was finally divorcing her husband. "He left me no choice," she said over and over as she punched the register. "He has a little seven-month-old baby by her, he left me no choice." I would like to believe that my dread then was for the human condition, but of course it was for me, because I wanted a baby and did not then have one and because I wanted to own the house that cost $1,000 a month to rent and because I had a hangover.

It all comes back. Perhaps it is difficult to see the value in having one's self back in that kind of mood, but I do see it; I think we are well advised to keep on nodding terms with the people we used to be, whether we find them attractive company or not. Otherwise they turn up unannounced and surprise us, come hammering on the mind's door at 4 A.M. of a bad night and demand to know who deserted them, who betrayed them, who is going to make amends. We forget all too soon the things we thought we could never forget. We forget the loves and the betrayals alike, forget what we whispered and what we screamed, forget who we were. I have already lost touch with a couple of people I used to be; one of them, a seventeen-year-old, presents little threat, although it would be of some interest to me to know again what it feels like to sit on a river levee drinking vodka-and-orange-juice and listening to Les Paul and Mary Ford and their echoes sing "How High the Moon" on the car radio. (You see I still have the scenes, but I no longer perceive myself among those present, no longer could even improvise the dialogue.) The other one, a twenty-three-year-old, bothers me more. She was always a good deal of trouble, and I suspect she will reappear when I least want to see her, skirts too long, shy to the point of aggravation, always the injured party, full of recriminations and little hurts and stories I do not want to hear again, at once saddening me and angering me with her vulnerability and ignorance, an apparition all the more insistent for being so long banished.

It is a good idea, then, to keep in touch, and I suppose that keeping in touch   17
is what notebooks are all about. And we are all on our own when it comes to keeping those lines open to ourselves: your notebook will never help me, nor mine you. *"So what's new in the whiskey business?"* What could that possibly mean to you? To me it means a blonde in a Pucci bathing suit sitting with a couple of fat men by the pool at the Beverly Hills Hotel. Another man approaches, and they all regard one another in silence for a while. "So what's new in the whiskey business?" one of the fat men finally says by way of welcome, and the blonde stands up, arches one foot and dips it in the pool, looking all the while at the cabaña where Baby Pignatari is talking on the telephone. That is all there is to that, except that several years later I saw the blonde coming out of Saks Fifth Avenue in New York with her California complexion and a voluminous mink coat. In the harsh wind that day she looked old and irrevocably tired to me, and even the skins in the mink coat were not worked the way they were doing them that year, not the way she would have wanted them done, and there is the point of the story. For a while after that I did not like to look in the mirror, and my eyes would skim the newspapers and pick out only the deaths, the cancer victims, the premature coronaries, the suicides, and I stopped riding the Lexington Avenue IRT because I noticed for the first time that all the strangers I had seen for years—the man with the seeing-eye dog, the spinster who read the classified pages every day, the fat girl who always got off with me at Grand Central—looked older than they once had.

It all comes back. Even that recipe for sauerkraut: even that brings it back. I   18
was on Fire Island when I first made that sauerkraut, and it was raining, and we drank a lot of bourbon and ate the sauerkraut and went to bed at ten, and I listened to the rain and the Atlantic and felt safe. I made the sauerkraut again last night and it did not make me feel any safer, but that is, as they say, another story.

QUESTIONS

1. As described here, what is the difference between a diary and a notebook? Why does Didion reject the use of a diary? What does she mean by "instead I tell what some would call lies" (paragraph 7)?

2. Why is it important to the writer to *"Remember what it was to be me"* (paragraph 9)? What purpose do other people serve in the writer's remembrance of her past selves?

3. Trace the pattern of reflection and meditation in the essay. How much of the text is made up of notebook entries? How much is reflection on that material, and how much is meditation on what is reflected?

4. Find a picture of yourself, alone or with family or friends, that was taken at least

five years ago. Write an essay in which you both describe yourself at that time and reflect on that former self as you see it now.

5. Recall some experience from your past, and write about it. Embroider the truth with details to suggest how you felt about the experience rather than what actually occurred.

6. In the library, find a copy of *Time* or *Life* or another magazine that might have been in your home in the month and year of your seventh birthday. Carefully study the pictures, the text, and the advertisements. Choose some material that will help you; then write about the world you remember at that time and about your place in it.

Social Sciences and Public Affairs

PILGRIMAGE TO NONVIOLENCE
Martin Luther King, Jr.

The son of a minister, Martin Luther King, Jr., (1929–1968) was ordained a Baptist minister in his father's church in Atlanta, Georgia, at the age of eighteen. He sprang into prominence in 1955 when he called a citywide boycott of the segregated bus system in Montgomery, Alabama, and he continued to be the most prominent civil-rights activist in America until his assassination on April 4, 1968. During those tumultuous years, he was jailed at least fourteen times and endured countless threats against his life, but he persevered in his fight against racial discrimination using a synthesis of the nonviolent philosophy of Mahatma Gandhi and the Sermon on the Mount. The 1964 Nobel Peace Prize was only one of the many awards he received, and his several books are characterized as much by their eloquent prose style as by their moral fervor. "Pilgrimage to Nonviolence" originally appeared in the magazine Christian Century *and was revised and updated for a collection of his sermons,* Strength to Love *(1963), the source of the following text.*

In my senior year in theological seminary, I engaged in the exciting reading of various theological theories. Having been raised in a rather strict fundamentalist tradition, I was occasionally shocked when my intellectual journey carried me through new and sometimes complex doctrinal lands, but the pilgrimage was always stimulating, gave me a new appreciation for objective appraisal and critical analysis, and knocked me out of my dogmatic slumber. 1

Liberalism provided me with an intellectual satisfaction that I had never found in fundamentalism. I became so enamored of the insights of liberalism 2 that I almost fell into the trap of accepting uncritically everything it encompassed. I was absolutely convinced of the natural goodness of man and the natural power of human reason.

I

A basic change in my thinking came when I began to question some of the theories that had been associated with so-called liberal theology. Of course, there are aspects of liberalism that I hope to cherish always: its devotion to the search for truth, its insistence on an open and analytical mind, and its refusal to abandon the best lights of reason. The contribution of liberalism to the philological-historical criticism of biblical literature has been of immeasurable value and should be defended with religious and scientific passion.

But I began to question the liberal doctrine of man. The more I observed the tragedies of history and man's shameful inclination to choose the low road, the more I came to see the depths and strength of sin. My reading of the works of Reinhold Niebuhr made me aware of the complexity of human motives and the reality of sin on every level of man's existence.[1] Moreover, I came to recognize the complexity of man's social involvement and the glaring reality of collective evil. I realized that liberalism had been all too sentimental concerning human nature and that it leaned toward a false idealism.

I also came to see that the superficial optimism of liberalism concerning human nature overlooked the fact that reason is darkened by sin. The more I thought about human nature, the more I saw how our tragic inclination for sin encourages us to rationalize our actions. Liberalism failed to show that reason by itself is little more than an instrument to justify man's defensive ways of thinking. Reason, devoid of the purifying power of faith, can never free itself from distortions and rationalizations.

Although I rejected some aspects of liberalism, I never came to an all-out acceptance of neo-orthodoxy. While I saw neo-orthodoxy as a helpful corrective for a sentimental liberalism, I felt that it did not provide an adequate answer to basic questions. If liberalism was too optimistic concerning human nature, neo-orthodoxy was too pessimistic. Not only on the question of man, but also on other vital issues, the revolt of neo-orthodoxy went too far. In its attempt to preserve the transcendence of God, which had been neglected by an overstress of his immanence in liberalism, neo-orthodoxy went to the extreme of stressing a God who was hidden, unknown, and "wholly other." In its revolt against overemphasis on the power of reason in liberalism, neo-orthodoxy fell into a mood of antirationalism and semifundamentalism, stressing a narrow uncritical biblicism. This approach, I felt, was inadequate both for the church and for personal life.

---

[1]Reinhold Niebuhr (1892–1971): American theologian, social activist, and noted writer on social and religious issues. [Eds.]

So although liberalism left me unsatisfied on the question of the nature of   7
man, I found no refuge in neo-orthodoxy. I am now convinced that the truth
about man is found neither in liberalism nor in neo-orthodoxy. Each represents
a partial truth. A large segment of Protestant liberalism defined man only in
terms of his essential nature, his capacity for good; neo-orthodoxy tended to
define man only in terms of his existential nature, his capacity for evil. An
adequate understanding of man is found neither in the thesis of liberalism nor
in the antithesis of neo-orthodoxy, but in a synthesis which reconciles the truths
of both.

During the intervening years I have gained a new appreciation for the phi-   8
losophy of existentialism. My first contact with this philosophy came through
my reading of Kierkegaard and Nietzsche.[2] Later I turned to a study of Jaspers,
Heidegger, and Sartre.[3] These thinkers stimulated my thinking; while questioning each, I nevertheless learned a great deal through a study of them. When I
finally engaged in a serious study of the writings of Paul Tillich,[4] I became
convinced that existentialism, in spite of the fact that it had become all too
fashionable, had grasped certain basic truths about man and his condition that
could not be permanently overlooked.

An understanding of the "finite freedom" of man is one of the permanent   9
contributions of existentialism, and its perception of the anxiety and conflict
produced in man's personal and social life by the perilous and ambiguous structure of existence is especially meaningful for our time. A common denominator
in atheistic or theistic existentialism is that man's existential situation is estranged
from his essential nature. In their revolt against Hegel's essentialism,[5] all exis-
tentialists contend that the world is fragmented. History is a series of unrecon-
ciled conflicts, and man's existence is filled with anxiety and threatened with
meaninglessness. While the ultimate Christian answer is not found in any of
these existential assertions, there is much here by which the theologian may
describe the true state of man's existence.

Although most of my formal study has been in systematic theology and   10
philosophy, I have become more and more interested in social ethics. During
my early teens I was deeply concerned by the problem of racial injustice. I
considered segregation both rationally inexplicable and morally unjustifiable. I
could never accept my having to sit in the back of a bus or in the segregated

---

[2]Soren Kierkegaard (1813–1855): Danish religious and aesthetic philosopher, concerned especially with the role of the individual; Friedrich Nietzsche (1844–1900): German philosopher and
moralist looking for a heroic, creative rejuvenation of decadent Western civilization. [Eds.]

[3]Karl Jaspers (1883–1969): German philosopher; Martin Heidegger (1889–1976): German philospher; Jean-Paul Sartre (1905–1980): French philosopher and novelist. All three were existential-
ists, concerned with the existence and responsibility of the individual in an unknowable universe.
[Eds.]

[4]Paul Tillich (1886–1965): German-born American philospher and theologian whose writings
drew on psychology and existentialism. [Eds.]

[5]Georg Friedrich Hegel (1770–1831): German philosopher best known for his dialectic (thesis
vs. antithesis produces synthesis). [Eds.]

section of a train. The first time that I was seated behind a curtain in a dining car I felt as though the curtain had been dropped on my selfhood. I also learned that the inseparable twin of racial injustice is economic injustice. I saw how the systems of segregation exploited both the Negro and the poor whites. These early experiences made me deeply conscious of the varieties of injustice in our society.

II

Not until I entered theological seminary, however, did I begin a serious intellectual quest for a method that would eliminate social evil. I was immediately influenced by the social gospel. In the early 1950s I read Walter Rauschenbusch's *Christianity and the Social Crisis*, a book which left an indelible imprint on my thinking. Of course, there were points at which I differed with Rauschenbusch. I felt that he was a victim of the nineteenth-century "cult of inevitable progress," which led him to an unwarranted optimism concerning human nature. Moreover, he came perilously close to identifying the Kingdom of God with a particular social and economic system, a temptation to which the church must never surrender. But in spite of these shortcomings, Rauschenbusch gave to American Protestantism a sense of social responsibility that it should never lose. The gospel at its best deals with the whole man, not only his soul but also his body, not only his spiritual well-being but also his material well-being. A religion that professes a concern for the souls of men and is not equally concerned about the slums that damn them, the economic conditions that strangle them, and the social conditions that cripple them, is a spirtually moribund religion.

After reading Rauschenbusch, I turned to a serious study of the social and ethical theories of the great philosophers. During this period I had almost despaired of the power of love to solve social problems. The turn-the-other-cheek and the love-your-enemies philosophies are valid, I felt, only when individuals are in conflict with other individuals; when racial groups and nations are in conflict, a more realistic approach is necessary.

Then I was introduced to the life and teachings of Mahatma Gandhi.[6] As I read his works I became deeply fascinated by his campaigns of nonviolent resistance. The whole Gandhian concept of *satyagraha* (*satya* is truth which equals love and *graha* is force; *satyagraha* thus means truth-force or love-force) was profoundly significant to me. As I delved deeper into the philosophy of Gandhi, my skepticism concerning the power of love gradually diminished, and I came to see for the first time that the Christian doctrine of love, operating through the Gandhian method of nonviolence, is one of the most potent weapons available to an oppressed people in their struggle for freedom. At that time, however, I acquired only an intellectual understanding and appreciation of the

---

[6]Mahatma Gandhi (1869–1948): Hindu nationalist and spiritual leader.

position, and I had no firm determination to organize it in a socially effective situation.

When I went to Montgomery, Alabama, as a pastor in 1954, I had not the slightest idea that I would later become involved in a crisis in which nonviolent resistance would be applicable. After I had lived in the community about a year, the bus boycott began. The Negro people of Montgomery, exhausted by the humiliating experience that they had constantly faced on the buses, expressed in a massive act of noncooperation their determination to be free. They came to see that it was ultimately more honorable to walk the streets in dignity than to ride the buses in humiliation. At the beginning of the protest, the people called on me to serve as their spokesman. In accepting this responsibility, my mind, consciously or unconsciously, was driven back to the Sermon on the Mount and the Gandhian method of nonviolent resistance. This principle became the guiding light of our movement. Christ furnished the spirit and motivation and Gandhi furnished the method. 14

The experience in Montgomery did more to clarify my thinking in regard to the question of nonviolence than all of the books that I had read. As the days unfolded, I became more and more convinced of the power of nonviolence. Nonviolence became more than a method to which I gave intellectual assent; it became a commitment to a way of life. Many issues I had not cleared up intellectually concerning nonviolence were now resolved within the sphere of practical action. 15

My privilege of traveling to India had a great impact on me personally, for it was invigorating to see firsthand the amazing results of a nonviolent struggle to achieve independence. The aftermath of hatred and bitterness that usually follows a violent campaign was found nowhere in India, and a mutual friendship, based on complete equality, existed between the Indian and British people within the Commonwealth. 16

I would not wish to give the impression that nonviolence will accomplish miracles overnight. Men are not easily moved from their mental ruts or purged of their prejudiced and irrational feelings. When the underprivileged demand freedom, the privileged at first react with bitterness and resistance. Even when the demands are couched in nonviolent terms, the initial response is substantially the same. I am sure that many of our white brothers in Montgomery and throughout the South are still bitter toward the Negro leaders, even though these leaders have sought to follow a way of love and nonviolence. But the nonviolent approach does something to the hearts and souls of those committed to it. It gives them new self-respect. It calls up resources of strength and courage that they did not know they had. Finally, it so stirs the conscience of the opponent that reconciliation becomes a reality. 17

III

More recently I have come to see the need for the method of nonviolence 18
in international relations. Although I was not yet convinced of its efficacy in
conflicts between nations, I felt that while war could never be a positive good,
it could serve as a negative good by preventing the spread and growth of an evil
force. War, horrible as it is, might be preferable to surrender to a totalitarian
system. But I now believe that the potential destructiveness of modern weapons
totally rules out the possibility of war ever again achieving a negative good. If
we assume that mankind has a right to survive, then we must find an alternative
to war and destruction. In our day of space vehicles and guided ballistic missiles,
the choice is either nonviolence or nonexistence.

I am no doctrinaire pacifist, but I have tried to embrace a realistic pacifism 19
which finds the pacifist position as the lesser evil in the circumstances. I do not
claim to be free from the moral dilemmas that the Christian nonpacifist confronts, but I am convinced that the church cannot be silent while mankind
faces the threat of nuclear annihilation. If the church is true to her mission,
she must call for an end to the arms race.

Some of my personal sufferings over the last few years have also served to 20
shape my thinking. I always hesitate to mention these experiences for fear of
conveying the wrong impression. A person who constantly calls attention to his
trials and sufferings is in danger of developing a martyr complex and impressing
others that he is consciously seeking sympathy. It is possible for one to be self-
centered in his self-sacrifice. So I am always reluctant to refer to my personal
sacrifices. But I feel somewhat justified in mentioning them in this essay because
of the influence they have had upon my thought.

Due to my involvement in the struggle for the freedom of my people, I have 21
known very few quiet days in the last few years. I have been imprisoned in
Alabama and Georgia jails twelve times. My home has been bombed twice. A
day seldom passes that my family and I are not the recipients of threats of death.
I have been the victim of a near-fatal stabbing. So in a real sense I have been
battered by the storms of persecution. I must admit that at times I have felt that
I could no longer bear such a heavy burden, and have been tempted to retreat
to a more quiet and serene life. But every time such a temptation appeared,
something came to strengthen and sustain my determination. I have learned
now that the Master's burden is light precisely when we take his yoke upon us.

My personal trials have also taught me the value of unmerited suffering. As 22
my sufferings mounted I soon realized that there were two ways in which I
could respond to my situation—either to react with bitterness or seek to transform the suffering into a creative force. I decided to follow the latter course.
Recognizing the necessity for suffering, I have tried to make of it a virtue, If
only to save myself from bitterness, I have attempted to see my personal ordeals
as an opportunity to transfigure myself and heal the people involved in the tragic

situation which now obtains. I have lived these last few years with the conviction that unearned suffering is redemptive. There are some who still find the Cross a stumbling block, others consider it foolishness, but I am more convinced than ever before that it is the power of God unto social and individual salvation. So like the Apostle Paul I can now humbly, yet proudly, say, "I bear in my body the marks of the Lord Jesus."

The agonizing moments through which I have passed during the last few 23 years have also drawn me closer to God. More than ever before I am convinced of the reality of a personal God. True, I have always believed in the personality of God. But in the past the idea of a personal God was little more than a metaphysical category that I found theologically and philosophically satisfying. Now it is a living reality that has been validated in the experiences of everyday life. God has been profoundly real to me in recent years. In the midst of outer dangers I have felt an inner calm. In the midst of lonely days and dreary nights I have heard an inner voice saying, "Lo, I will be with you." When the chains of fear and the manacles of frustration have all but stymied my efforts, I have felt the power of God transforming the fatigue of despair into the buoyancy of hope. I am convinced that the universe is under the control of a loving purpose, and that in the struggle for righteousness man has cosmic companionship. Behind the harsh appearances of the world there is a benign power. To say that this God is personal is not to make him a finite object beside other objects or attribute to him the limitations of human personality; it is to take what is finest and noblest in our consciousness and affirm its perfect existence in him. It is certainly true that human personality is limited, but personality as such involves no necessary limitations. It means simply self-consciousness and self-direction. So in the truest sense of the word, God is a living God. In him there is feeling and will, responsive to the deepest yearnings of the human heart: *this* God both evokes and answers prayer.

The past decade has been a most exciting one. In spite of the tensions and 24 uncertainties of this period something profoundly meaningful is taking place. Old systems of exploitation and oppression are passing away; new systems of justice and equality are being born. In a real sense this is a great time to be alive. Therefore, I am not yet discouraged about the future. Granted that the easygoing optimism of yesterday is impossible. Granted that we face a world crisis which leaves us standing so often amid the surging murmur of life's restless sea. But every crisis has both its dangers and its opportunities. It can spell either salvation or doom. In a dark, confused world the Kingdom of God may yet reign in the hearts of men.

QUESTIONS

1. King found the extremes of liberalism on one hand and neo-orthodoxy on the other both unsatisfactory. Why?

2. Existentialism and Rauschenbusch's social gospel proved more useful to King than liberalism or neo-orthodoxy. How did these concepts help shape his outlook?

3. King is interested in religious and philosophical theories not for their own sake but for their usefulness in the social world. How do Gandhi's example and King's own experience in Montgomery (paragraphs 14, 15, and 17) illustrate this concern?

4. How did King's personal faith in God aid in his struggles and sufferings? Is his dream of a better society totally dependent upon the existence of this "benign power (paragraph 23)"?

5. King's intellectual development is described as a pilgrimage from a simple fundamentalist attitude through conflicting theological and philosophical concepts to an intensified belief in a benign God and a commitment to international nonviolence. How is his final set of beliefs superior to his original one? Has he convinced you of the validity of his beliefs?

6. King writes for a general audience rather than one with theological and philosophical training. How successful is King at clarifying religious and philosophical concepts for the general reader? Point out examples that show how he treats such concepts.

7. Again and again King employs the classical rhetorical strategy of concession: the opposition's viewpoint is stated and partially accepted before King gives his own viewpoint. Located two or three instances of this strategy, and explain how it aids a reader's understanding (if not acceptance) of King's views.

8. King's essay reflects on how he came to accept the method of nonviolence. Have you, over time, changed your thoughts or methods of approaching an issue or problem? Or has someone you know well? If so, write an essay reflecting on the events central to this change and their significance.

9. King's hopes for a better world were expressed in the early 1960s. Based on your knowledge of history since then, write an essay in which you justify or disqualify King's guarded optimism.

THE WAY TO RAINY MOUNTAIN
N. Scott Momaday

*N. Scott Momaday was born in Lawton, Oklahoma, in
1934. His father is a full-blooded Kiowa and his mother is
part Cherokee. After attending schools on Navaho, Apache,
and Pueblo Indian reservations, Momaday graduated from
the University of New Mexico and took his Ph.D. at Stanford University. He has published two collections of poetry,*
Angle of Geese and Other Poems *(1974) and* The Gourd
Dancer *(1976), and a memoir,* The Names *(1976). In 1969,
his novel* House Made of Dawn *won the Pulitzer Prize. The
following essay appeared first in the* Reporter *magazine in
1967 and later as the introduction to* The Way to Rainy
Mountain *(1969), a collection of Kiowa legends.*

A single knoll rises out of the plain in Oklahoma, north and west of the   1
Wichita range. For my people, the Kiowas, it is an old landmark, and they
gave it the name Rainy Mountain. The hardest weather in the world is there.
Winter brings blizzards, hot tornadic winds arise in the spring, and in summer
the prairie is an anvil's edge. The grass turns brittle and brown, and it cracks
beneath your feet. There are green belts along the rivers and creeks, linear
groves of hickory and pecan, willow and witch hazel. At a distance in July or
August the steaming foliage seems almost to writhe in fire. Great green and
yellow grasshoppers are everywhere in the tall grass, popping up like corn to
sting the flesh, and tortoises crawl about on the red earth, going nowhere in
the plenty of time. Loneliness is an aspect of the land. All things in the plain
are isolate; there is no confusion of objects in the eye, but *one* hill or *one* tree
or *one* man. To look upon that landscape in the early morning, with the sun
at your back, is to lose the sense of proportion. Your imagination comes to life,
and this, you think, is where Creation was begun.

I returned to Rainy Mountain in July. My grandmother had died in the   2
spring, and I wanted to be at her grave. She had lived to be very old and at last
infirm. Her only living daughter was with her when she died, and I was told
that in death her face was that of a child.

I like to think of her as a child. When she was born, the Kiowas were living   3
the last great moment of their history. For more than a hundred years they had
controlled the open range from the Smoky Hill River to the Red, from the
headwaters of the Canadian to the fork of the Arkansas and Cimarron. In alliance with the Comanches, they had ruled the whole of the Southern Plains.

War was their sacred business, and they were the finest horsemen the world has ever known. But warfare for the Kiowas was pre-eminently a matter of disposition rather than of survival, and they never understood the grim, unrelenting advance of the U.S. Cavalry. When at last, divided and ill provisioned, they were driven onto the Staked Plains in the cold of autumn, they fell into panic. In Palo Duro Canyon they abandoned their crucial stores to pillage and had nothing then but their lives. In order to save themselves, they surrendered to the soldiers at Fort Sill and were imprisoned in the old stone corral that now stands as a military museum. My grandmother was spared the humiliation of those high gray walls by eight or ten years, but she must have known from birth the affliction of defeat, the dark brooding of old warriors.

Her name was Aho, and she belonged to the last culture to evolve in North 4
America. Her forebears came down from the high country in western Montana nearly three centuries ago. They were a mountain people, a mysterious tribe of hunters whose language has never been classified in any major group. In the late seventeenth century they began a long migration to the south and east. It was a journey toward the dawn, and it led to a golden age. Along the way the Kiowas were befriended by the Crows, who gave them the culture and religion of the Plains. They acquired horses, and their ancient nomadic spirit was suddenly free of the ground. They acquired Tai-me, the sacred sun-dance doll, from that moment the object and symbol of their worship, and so shared in the divinity of the sun. Not least, they acquired the sense of destiny, therefore courage and pride. When they entered upon the Southern Plains they had been transformed. No longer were they slaves to the simple necessity of survival; they were a lordly and dangerous society of fighters and thieves, hunters and priests of the sun. According to their origin myth, they entered the world through a hollow log. From one point of view, their migration was the fruit of an old prophecy, for indeed they emerged from a sunless world.

Though my grandmother lived out her long life in the shadow of Rainy 5
Mountain, the immense landscape of the continental interior lay like memory in her blood. She could tell of the Crows, whom she had never seen, and of the Black Hills, where she had never been. I wanted to see in reality what she had seen more perfectly in the mind's eye, and drove fifteen hundred miles to begin my pilgrimage.

A dark mist lay over the Black Hills, and the land was like iron. At the top 6
of a ridge I caught sight of Devil's Tower upthrust against the gray sky as if in the birth of time the core of the earth had broken through its crust and the motion of the world was begun. There are things in nature that engender an awful quiet in the heart of man; Devil's Tower is one of them. Two centuries ago, because of their need to explain it, the Kiowas made a legend at the base of the rock. My grandmother said:

"Eight children were there at play, seven sisters and their brother. Suddenly   7
the boy was struck dumb; he trembled and began to run upon his hands and
feet. His fingers became claws, and his body was covered with fur. There was
a bear where the boy had been. The sisters were terrified; they ran, and the bear
after them. They came to the stump of a great tree, and the tree spoke to them.
It bade them climb upon it, and as they did so, it began to rise into the air.
The bear came to kill them, but they were just beyond its reach. It reared against
the tree and scored the bark all around with its claws. The seven sisters were
borne into the sky, and they became the stars of the Big Dipper." From that
moment, and so long as the legend lives, the Kiowas have kinsmen in the night
sky. Whatever they were in the mountains, they could be no more. However
tenuous their well-being, however much they had suffered and would suffer
again, they had found a way out of the wilderness.

My grandmother had a reverence for the sun, a holy regard that now is all   8
but gone out of mankind. There was a wariness in her, and an ancient awe.
She was a Christian in her later years, but she had come a long way about, and
she never forgot her birthright. As a child she had been to the sun dances; she
had taken part in that annual rite, and by it she had learned the restoration of
her people in the presence of Tai-me. She was about seven when the last Kiowa
sun dance was held in 1887 on the Washita River above Rainy Mountain Creek.
The buffalo were gone. In order to consummate the ancient sacrifice—to impale
the head of a buffalo bull upon the Tai-me tree—a delegation of old men
journeyed into Texas, there to beg and barter for an animal from the Goodnight
herd. She was ten when the Kiowas came together for the last time as a living
sun-dance culture. They could find no buffalo; they had to hang an old hide
from the sacred tree. Before the dance could begin, a company of soldiers rode
out from Fort Sill under orders to disperse the tribe. Forbidden without cause
the essential act of their faith, having seen the wild herds slaughtered and left
to rot upon the ground, the Kiowas backed away forever from the tree. That
was July 20, 1890, at the great bend of the Washita. My grandmother was there.
Without bitterness, and for as long as she lived, she bore a vision of deicide.[1]

Now that I can have her only in memory, I see my grandmother in the   9
several postures that were peculiar to her: standing at the wood stove on a winter
morning and turning meat in a great iron skillet; sitting at the south window,
bent above her beadwork, and afterwards, when her vision failed, looking down
for a long time into the fold of her hands; going out upon a cane, very slowly
as she did when the weight of age came upon her; praying. I remember her
most often at prayer. She made long, rambling prayers out of suffering and
hope, having seen many things. I was never sure that I had the right to hear,
so exclusive were they of all mere custom and company. The last time I saw

---

[1]deicide: the killing of a deity or god. [Eds.]

her she prayed standing by the side of her bed at night, naked to the waist, the light of a kerosene lamp moving upon her dark skin. Her long black hair, always drawn and braided in the day, lay upon her shoulders and against her breasts like a shawl. I do not speak Kiowa, and I never understood her prayers, but there was something inherently sad in the sound, some merest hesitation upon the syllables of sorrow. She began in a high and descending pitch, exhausting her breath to silence; then again and again—and always the same intensity of effort, of something that is, and is not, like urgency in the human voice. Transported so in the dancing light among the shadows of her room, she seemed beyond the reach of time. But that was illusion; I think I knew then that I should not see her again.

Houses are like sentinels in the plain, old keepers of the weather watch. 10 There, in a very little while, wood takes on the appearance of great age. All colors wear soon away in the wind and rain, and then the wood is burned gray and the grain appears and the nails turn red with rust. The window panes are black and opaque; you imagine there is nothing within, and indeed there are many ghosts, bones given up to the land. They stand here and there against the sky, and you approach them for a longer time than you expect. They belong in the distance; it is their domain.

Once there was a lot of sound in my grandmother's house, a lot of coming 11 and going, feasting and talk. The summers there were full of excitement and reunion. The Kiowas are a summer people; they abide the cold and keep to themselves, but when the season turns and the land becomes warm and vital they cannot hold still; an old love of going returns upon them. The aged visitors who came to my grandmother's house when I was a child were made of lean and leather, and they bore themselves upright. They wore great black hats and bright ample shirts that shook in the wind. They rubbed fat upon their hair and wound their braids with strips of colored cloth. Some of them painted their faces and carried the scars of old and cherished enmities. They were an old council of warlords, come to remind and be reminded of who they were. Their wives and daughters served them well. The women might indulge themselves; gossip was at once the mark and compensation of their servitude. They made loud and elaborate talk among themselves, full of jest and gesture, fright and false alarm. They went abroad in fringed and flowered shawls, bright beadwork and German silver. They were at home in the kitchen, and they prepared meals that were banquets.

There were frequent prayer meetings, and nocturnal feasts. When I was a 12 child I played with my cousins outside, where the lamplight fell upon the ground and the singing of the old people rose up around us and carried away into the darkness. There were a lot of good things to eat, a lot of laughter and surprise. And afterwards, when the quiet returned, I lay down with my grandmother and could hear the frogs away by the river and feel the motion of the air.

Now there is a funereal silence in the rooms, the endless wake of some final 13 word. The walls have closed in upon my grandmother's house. When I returned to it in mourning, I saw for the first time in my life how small it was. It was late at night, and there was a white moon, nearly full. I sat for a long time on the stone steps by the kitchen door. From there I could see out across the land; I could see the long row of trees by the creek, the low light upon the rolling plains, and the stars of the Big Dipper. Once I looked at the moon and caught sight of a strange thing. A cricket had perched upon the handrail, only a few inches away. My line of vision was such that the creature filled the moon like a fossil. It had gone there, I thought, to live and die, for there, of all places, was its small definition made whole and eternal. A warm wind rose up and purled like the longing within me.

The next morning, I awoke at dawn and went out on the dirt road to Rainy 14 Mountain. It was already hot, and the grasshoppers began to fill the air. Still, it was early in the morning, and birds sang out of the shadows. The long yellow grass on the mountain shone in the bright light, and a scissortail hied above the land. There, where it ought to be, at the end of a long and legendary way, was my grandmother's grave. She had at last succeeded to that holy ground. Here and there on the dark stones were ancestral names. Looking back once, I saw the mountain and came away.

QUESTIONS

1. What is this essay about? Explain whether it is a history of the Kiowas, or a biography of the writer's grandmother, or a narrative of the writer's journey.

2. Trace the movement in time in this essay. How much takes place in the present, the recent past, the distant past, or legendary time? What effect does such movement create?

3. How much of the essay reports events, and how much of the essay represents a sense of place or of persons through description of what the writer sees and feels? Trace the pattern of reporting and representing, and consider the writer's purpose in such an approach to his subject.

4. The first paragraph ends by drawing the reader into the writer's point of view: "Your imagination comes to life, and this, you think, is where Creation was begun." Given the description of the Oklahoma landscape that precedes this in the paragraph, how do you react to Momaday's summarizing statement? Why? What other passages in the essay evoke a sense of place?

5. Visit a place that has historical significance. It may be a place where you or members of your family lived in the past, or it may be a place of local or national historical significance. Describe the place as it appears now, and report on events that took place there in the past. What, if any, evidence do you find in the present of those events that took place in the past?

6. If you have a grandparent or an older friend living nearby, ask this person about

his or her history. What does this person remember about the past that is no longer in the present? Are there also objects—pictures, clothing, medals, and so on—that can speak to you of your subject's past life? Reflect on the person's present life as well as on those events from the past that seem most memorable. Write an essay in which you represent your subject's life by concentrating on the place where he or she lives and the surrounding objects that help you to understand the past and present life.

SHOOTING AN ELEPHANT

George Orwell

George Orwell (1903–1950) was the pen name of Eric Blair, the son of a British customs officer serving in Bengal, India. As a boy he was sent home to prestigious schools, where he learned to dislike the rich and powerful. After finishing school at Eton, he served as an officer of the British police in Burma, where he became disillusioned with imperialism. Then he studied conditions among the urban poor and the coal miners of Wigan, a city in northwestern England, which confirmed him as a socialist. He was wounded in the Spanish civil war, defending the lost cause of the left against the fascists. Under the name Orwell, he wrote accounts of all these experiences as well as the anti-Stalinist fable Animal Farm *and the novel* 1984. *In the following essay, first published in 1936, Orwell attacks the politics of imperialism.*

In Moulmein, in Lower Burma, I was hated by large numbers of people— the only time in my life that I have been important enough for this to happen to me. I was sub-divisional police officer of the town, and in an aimless, petty kind of way anti-European feeling was very bitter. No one had the guts to raise a riot, but if a European woman went through the bazaars alone somebody would probably spit betel juice over her dress. As a police officer I was an obvious target and was baited whenever it seemed safe to do so. When a nimble Burman tripped me up on the football field and the referee (another Burman) looked the other way, the crowd yelled with hideous laughter. This happened more than once. In the end the sneering yellow faces of young men that met me everywhere, the insults hooted after me when I was at a safe distance, got badly on my nerves. The young Buddhist priests were the worst of all. There were several thousands of them in the town and none of them seemed to have anything to do except stand on street corners and jeer at Europeans. 1

All this was perplexing and upsetting. For at that time I had already made up my mind that imperialism was an evil thing and the sooner I chucked up my job and got out of it the better. Theoretically—and secretly, of course—I was all for the Burmese and all against their oppressors, the British. As for the job I was doing, I hated it more bitterly than I can perhaps make clear. In a job like that you see the dirty work of Empire at close quarters. The wretched prisoners huddling in the stinking cages of the lock-ups, the grey, cowed faces of the long-term convicts, the scarred buttocks of the men who had been flogged with bamboos—all these oppressed me with an intolerable sense of guilt. But I 2 could get nothing into perspective. I was young and ill-educated and I had had to think out my problems in the utter silence that is imposed on every English-man in the East. I did not even know that the British Empire is dying, still less did I know that it is a great deal better than the younger empires that are going to supplant it. All I knew was that I was stuck between my hatred of the empire I served and my rage against the evil-spirited little beasts who tried to make my job impossible. With one part of my mind I thought of the British Raj as an unbreakable tyranny[1], as something clamped down, in *saecula saeculorum*[2], upon the will of prostrate peoples; with another part I thought that the greatest joy in the world would be to drive a bayonet into a Buddhist priest's guts. Feelings like these are the normal by-product of imperialism; ask any Anglo-Indian official, if you can catch him off duty.

One day something happened which in a roundabout way was enlightening.   3 It was a tiny incident in itself, but it gave me a better glimpse than I had had before of the real nature of imperialism—the real motives for which despotic governments act. Early one morning the sub-inspector at a police station the other end of the town rang me up on the phone and said that an elephant was ravaging the bazaar. Would I please come and do something about it? I did not know what I could do, but I wanted to see what was happening and I got on to a pony and started out. I took my rifle, an old .44 Winchester and much too small to kill an elephant, but I thought the noise might be useful *in terrorem*[3]. Various Burmans stopped me on the way and told me about the elephant's doings. It was not, of course, a wild elephant, but a tame one which had gone "must." It had been chained up, as tame elephants always are when their attack of "must" is due, but on the previous night it had broken its chain and escaped. Its mahout, the only person who could manage it when it was in that state, had set out in pursuit, but had taken the wrong direction and was now twelve hours' journey away, and in the morning the elephant had suddenly reappeared in town. The Burmese population had no weapons and were quite helpless against it. It had already destroyed somebody's bamboo hut, killed a cow and raided some fruit-stalls and devoured the stock; also it had met the municipal rubbish van and, when the driver jumped out and took to his heels, had turned the van over and inflicted violences upon it.

The Burmese sub-inspector and some Indian constables were waiting for me   4 in the quarter where the elephant had been seen. It was a very poor quarter, a labyrinth of squalid bamboo huts, thatched with palm-leaf, winding all over a steep hillside. I remember that it was a cloudy, stuffy morning at the beginning of the rains. We began questioning the people as to where the elephant had gone and, as usual, failed to get any definite information. That is invariably the case in the East; a story always sounds clear enough at a distance, but the nearer

---

[1]the British Raj: the imperial government ruling British India and Burma. [Eds.]
[2]*saecula saeculorum*: forever and ever. [Eds.]
[3]*in terrorem*: for fright. [Eds.]

you get to the scene of events the vaguer it becomes. Some of the people said that the elephant had gone in one direction, some said that he had gone in another, some professed not even to have heard of any elephant. I had almost made up my mind that the whole story was a pack of lies, when we heard yells a little distance away. There was a loud, scandalized cry of "Go away, child! Go away this instant!" and an old woman with a switch in her hand came round the corner of a hut, violently shooing away a crowd of naked children. Some more women followed, clicking their tongues and exclaiming; evidently there was something that the children ought not to have seen. I rounded the hut and saw a man's dead body sprawling in the mud. He was an Indian, a black Dravidian coolie, almost naked, and he could not have been dead many minutes. The people said that the elephant had come suddenly upon him round the corner of the hut, caught him with its trunk, put its foot on his back and ground him into the earth. This was the rainy season and the ground was soft, and his face had scored a trench a foot deep and a couple of yards long. He was lying on his belly with arms crucified and head sharply twisted to one side. His face was coated with mud, the eyes wide open, the teeth bared and grinning with an expression of unendurable agony. (Never tell me, by the way, that the dead look peaceful. Most of the corpses I have seen looked devilish.) The friction of the great beast's foot had stripped the skin from his back as neatly as one skins a rabbit. As soon as I saw the dead man I sent an orderly to a friend's house nearby to borrow an elephant rifle. I had already sent back the pony, not wanting it to go mad with fright and throw me if it smelt the elephant.

The orderly came back in a few minutes with a rifle and five cartridges, and meanwhile some Burmans had arrived and told us that the elephant was in the paddy fields below, only a few hundred yards away. As I started forward practically the whole population of the quarter flocked out of the houses and followed me. They had seen the rifle and were all shouting excitedly that I was going to shoot the elephant. They had not shown much interest in the elephant when he was merely ravaging their homes, but it was different now that he was going to be shot. It was a bit of fun to them, as it would be to an English crowd; besides they wanted the meat. It made me vaguely uneasy. I had no intention of shooting the elephant—I had merely sent for the rifle to defend myself if necessary—and it is always unnerving to have a crowd following you. I marched down the hill, looking and feeling a fool, with the rifle over my shoulder and an ever-growing army of people jostling at my heels. At the bottom, when you got away from the huts, there was a metalled road and beyond that a miry waste of paddy fields a thousand yards across, not yet ploughed but soggy from the first rains and dotted with coarse grass. The elephant was standing eight yards from the road, his left side towards us. He took not the slightest notice of the crowd's approach. He was tearing up bunches of grass, beating them against his knees to clean them and stuffing them into his mouth.

5

I had halted on the road. As soon as I saw the elephant I knew with perfect 6
certainty that I ought not to shoot him. It is a serious matter to shoot a working
elephant—it is comparable to destroying a huge and costly piece of machinery—
and obviously one ought not to do it if it can possibly be avoided. And at that
distance, peacefully eating, the elephant looked no more dangerous than a cow.
I thought then and I think now that his attack of "must" was already passing
off; in which case he would merely wander harmlessly about until the mahout
came back and caught him. Moreover, I did not in the least want to shoot him.
I decided that I would watch him for a little while to make sure that he did not
turn savage again, and then go home.

But at that moment I glanced round at the crowd that had followed me. It 7
was an immense crowd, two thousand at the least and growing every minute.
It blocked the road for a long distance on either side. I looked at the sea of
yellow faces above the garish clothes—faces all happy and excited over this bit
of fun, all certain that the elephant was going to be shot. They were watching
me as they would watch a conjurer about to perform a trick. They did not like
me, but with the magical rifle in my hands I was momentarily worth watching.
And suddenly I realized that I should have to shoot the elephant after all. The
people expected it of me and I had got to do it; I could feel their two thousand
wills pressing me forward, irresistibly. And it was at this moment, as I stood
there with the rifle in my hands, that I first grasped the hollowness, the futility
of the white man's dominion in the East. Here was I, the white man with his
gun, standing in front of the unarmed native crowd—seemingly the leading
actor of the piece; but in reality I was only an absurd puppet pushed to and fro
by the will of those yellow faces behind. I perceived in this moment that when
the white man turns tyrant it is his own freedom that he destroys. He becomes
a sort of hollow, posing dummy, the conventionalized figure of a sahib. For it
is the condition of his rule that he shall spend his life in trying to impress the
"natives," and so in every crisis he has got to do what the "natives" expect of
him. He wears a mask, and his face grows to fit it. I had got to shoot the
elephant. I had committed myself to doing it when I sent for the rifle. A sahib
has got to act like a sahib; he has got to appear resolute, to know his own mind
and do definite things. To come all that way, rifle in hand, with two thousand
people marching at my heels, and then to trail feebly away, having done nothing—no, that was impossible. The crowd would laugh at me. And my whole
life, every white man's life in the East, was one long struggle not to be laughed
at.

But I did not want to shoot the elephant. I watched him beating his bunch 8
of grass against his knees, with that preoccupied grandmotherly air that elephants
have. It seemed to me that it would be murder to shoot him. At that age I was
not squeamish about killing animals, but I had never shot an elephant and never
wanted to. (Somehow it always seems worse to kill a *large* animal.) Besides,
there was the beast's owner to be considered. Alive, the elephant was worth at

least a hundred pounds; dead, he would only be worth the value of his tusks, five pounds, possibly. But I had got to act quickly. I turned to some experienced-looking Burmans who had been there when we arrived, and asked them how the elephant had been behaving. They all said the same thing: he took no notice of you if you left him alone, but he might charge if you went too close to him.

It was perfectly clear to me what I ought to do. I ought to walk up to within, say, twenty-five yards of the elephant and test his behavior. If he charged, I could shoot; if he took no notice of me, it would be safe to leave him until the mahout came back. But also I knew that I was going to do no such thing. I was a poor shot with a rifle and the ground was soft mud into which one would sink at every step. If the elephant charged and I missed him, I should have about as much chance as a toad under a steam-roller. But even then I was not thinking particularly of my own skin, only of the watchful yellow faces behind. For at the moment, with the crowd watching me, I was not afraid in the ordinary sense, as I would have been if I had been alone. A white man mustn't be frightened in front of "natives"; and so, in general, he isn't frightened. The sole thought in my mind was that if anything went wrong those two thousand Burmans would see me pursued, caught, trampled on and reduced to a grinning corpse like that Indian up the hill. And if that happened it was quite probable that some of them would laugh. That would never do. There was only one alternative. I shoved the cartridges into the magazine and lay down on the road to get a better aim. 9

The crowd grew very still, and a deep, low, happy sigh, as of people who see the theatre curtain go up at last, breathed from innumerable throats. They were going to have their bit of fun after all. The rifle was a beautiful German thing with cross-hair sights. I did not then know that in shooting an elephant one would shoot to cut an imaginary bar running from ear-hole to ear-hole. I ought, therefore, as the elephant was sideways on, to have aimed straight at his ear-hole; actually I aimed several inches in front of this, thinking the brain would be further forward. 10

When I pulled the trigger I did not hear the bang or feel the kick—one never does when a shot goes home—but I heard the devilish roar of glee that went up from the crowd. In that instant, in too short a time, one would have thought, even for the bullet to get there, a mysterious, terrible change had come over the elephant. He neither stirred nor fell, but every line of his body had altered. He looked suddenly stricken, shrunken, immensely old, as though the frightful impact of the bullet had paralyzed him without knocking him down. At last, after what seemed a long time—it might have been five seconds, I dare say— he sagged flabbily to his knees. His mouth slobbered. An enormous senility seemed to have settled upon him. One could have imagined him thousands of years old. I fired again into the same spot. At the second shot he did not collapse but climbed with desperate slowness to his feet and stood weakly upright, with legs sagging and head drooping. I fired a third time. That was the shot that did 11 for him. You could see the agony of it jolt his whole body and knock the last remnant of strength from his legs. But in falling he seemed for a moment to rise, for as his hind legs collapsed beneath him he seemed to tower upward like a huge rock toppling, his trunk reaching skywards like a tree. He trumpeted, for the first and only time. And then down he came, his belly towards me, with a crash that seemed to shake the ground even where I lay.

I got up. The Burmans were already racing past me across the mud. It was obvious that the elephant would never rise again, but he was not dead. He was breathing very rhythmically with long rattling gasps, his great mound of a side painfully rising and falling. His mouth was wide open—I could see far down into caverns of pale pink throat. I waited a long time for him to die, but his breathing did not weaken. Finally I fired my two remaining shots into the spot where I thought his heart must be. The thick blood welled out of him like red velvet, but still he did not die. His body did not even jerk when the shots hit him, the tortured breathing continued without a pause. He was dying, very slowly and in great agony, but in some world remote from me where not even a bullet could damage him further. I felt that I had got to put an end to that dreadful noise. It seemed dreadful to see the great beast lying there, powerless to move and yet powerless to die, and not even to be able to finish him. I sent back for my small rifle and poured shot after shot into his heart and down his throat. They seemed to make no impression. The tortured gasps continued as steadily as the ticking of a clock.

In the end I could not stand it any longer and went away. I heard later that it took him half an hour to die. Burmans were bringing dahs and baskets even before I left,[4] and I was told they had stripped his body almost to the bones by the afternoon.

Afterwards, of course, there were endless discussions about the shooting of the elephant. The owner was furious, but he was only an Indian and could do nothing. Besides, legally I had done the right thing, for a mad elephant has to be killed, like a mad dog, if its owner fails to control it. Among the Europeans opinion was divided. The older men said I was right, the younger men said it was a damn shame to shoot an elephant for killing a coolie, because an elephant was worth more than any damn Coringhee coolie. And afterwards I was very glad that the coolie had been killed; it put me legally in the right and it gave me a sufficient pretext for shooting the elephant. I often wondered whether any of the others grasped that I had done it solely to avoid looking a fool.

---

[4]dahs: butcher knives. [Eds.]

QUESTIONS

1. Describe Orwell's mixed feelings about serving as a police officer in Burma.

2. How do the natives "force" Orwell to shoot the elephant against his better judgment? How does he relate this personal episode to the larger problems of British imperialism?

3. What is Orwell's final reaction to his deed? How literally can we take his statement that he "was very glad that the coolie had been killed" (paragraph 14)?

4. From the opening sentence Orwell displays a remarkable candor concerning his feelings. How does this personal, candid tone add to or detract from the strength of the essay?

5. Orwell's recollection of shooting the elephant is shaped to support a specific point or thesis. Where does Orwell state this thesis? Is this placement effective?

6. This essay reads more like a short story than an expository essay. In what ways is Orwell's use of narrative and personal experience effective?

7. Orwell often wrote with a political purpose, with a "desire to push the world in a certain direction, to alter other people's idea of the kind of society that they should strive after." To what extent does the "tiny incident" in this essay illuminate "the real nature of imperialism" (paragraph 3)? Does Orwell succeed in altering your idea of imperialism?

8. Using Orwell's essay as a model, write a reflection in which the narration of "a tiny incident" (paragraph 3) illuminates a larger social or political problem.

9. Like "Shooting an Elephant," Orwell's novel *Burmese Days* (1934) takes place in Burma and attacks British imperialism. After reading this novel, write a report comparing it with the essay.

SIGMUND FREUD

Carl G. Jung

Along with Sigmund Freud, Carl G. Jung (1875–1961) was one of the great pioneers of modern psychology. After receiving his medical degree from the University of Basel in 1900, he studied with Pierre Janet (in Paris) and Eugen Bleuler (in Zurich) in the new field of depth psychology. His collected works run to twenty volumes and deal with such important psychological concepts as the collective unconscious, introversion and extroversion, the association method, and dream symbolism. An early champion of Freud's controversial ideas, Jung later broke with him for the reasons set forth in the following selection from his autobiography Memories, Dreams, Reflections *(1963, rev. 1973). Of this work, which he undertook reluctantly, Jung said: "A book of mine is always a matter of fate. There is something unpredictable about the process of writing, and I cannot prescribe for myself any predetermined course. Thus this 'autobiography' is now taking a direction quite different from what I had imagined at the beginning. It has become a necessity for me to write down my early memories. If I neglect to do so for a single day, unpleasant physical symptoms immediately follow. As soon as I set to work they vanish and my head feels perfectly clear."*

I embarked on the adventure of my intellectual development by becoming a [1] psychiatrist. In all innocence I began observing mental patients, clinically, from the outside, and thereby came upon psychic processes of a striking nature. I noted and classified these things without the slightest understanding of their contents, which were considered to be adequately evaluated when they were dismissed as "pathological." In the course of time my interest focused more and more upon cases in which I experienced something understandable—that is, cases of paranoia, manic-depressive insanity, and psychogenic disturbances. From the start of my psychiatric career the studies of Breuer and Freud, along with the work of Pierre Janet, provided me with a wealth of suggestions and stimuli.[1] Above all, I found that Freud's technique of dream analysis and dream interpretation cast a valuable light upon schizophrenic forms of expression. As early

---

[1]Josef Breuer (1842–1925): Austrian physician, coauthor with Freud of *Studies in Hysteria* (1895); Pierre Janet (1859–1947): French psychologist and neurologist. [Eds.]

as 1900 I had read Freud's *The Interpretation of Dreams*. I had laid the book aside, at the time, because I did not yet grasp it. At the age of twenty-five I lacked the experience to appreciate Freud's theories. Such experience did not come until later. In 1903 I once more took up *The Interpretation of Dreams* and discovered how it all linked up with my own ideas. What chiefly interested me was the application to dreams of the concept of the repression mechanism, which was derived from the psychology of the neuroses. This was important to me because I had frequently encountered repressions in my experiments with word association; in response to certain stimulus words the patient either had no associative answer or was unduly slow in his reaction time. As was later discovered, such a disturbance occurred each time the stimulus word had touched upon a psychic lesion or conflict. In most cases the patient was unconscious of this. When questioned about the cause of the disturbance, he would often answer in a peculiarly artificial manner. My reading of Freud's *The Interpretation of Dreams* showed me that the repression mechanism was at work here, and that the facts I had observed were consonant with his theory. Thus I was able to corroborate Freud's line of argument.

The situation was different when it came to the content of the repression. 2 Here I could not agree with Freud. He considered the cause of the repression to be a sexual trauma. From my practice, however, I was familiar with numerous cases of neurosis in which the question of sexuality played a subordinate part, other factors standing in the foreground—for example, the problem of social adaptation, of oppression by tragic circumstances of life, prestige considerations, and so on. Later I presented such cases to Freud; but he would not grant that factors other than sexuality could be the cause. That was highly unsatisfactory to me.

At the beginning it was not easy for me to assign Freud the proper place in 3 my life, or to take the right attitude toward him. When I became acquainted with his work I was planning an academic career, and was about to complete a paper that was intended to advance me at the university. But Freud was definitely *persona non grata* in the academic world at the time,[2] and any connection with him would have been damaging in scientific circles. "Important people" at most mentioned him surreptitiously, and at congresses he was discussed only in the corridors, never on the floor. Therefore the discovery that my association experiments were in agreement with Freud's theories was far from pleasant to me.

Once, while I was in my laboratory and reflecting again upon these questions, 4 the devil whispered to me that I would be justified in publishing the results of my experiments and my conclusions without mentioning Freud. After all, I had worked out my experiments long before I understood his work. But then I heard the voice of my second personality: "If you do a thing like that, as if you had no knowledge of Freud, it would be a piece of trickery. You cannot build your

---

[2]*persona non grata:* an unacceptable person. [Eds.]

life upon a lie." With that, the question was settled. From then on I became an open partisan of Freud's and fought for him.

I first took up the cudgels for Freud at a congress in Munich where a lecturer discussed obsessional neuroses but studiously forbore to mention the name of Freud. In 1906, in connection with this incident, I wrote a paper for the *Münchner Medizinische Wochenschrift* on Freud's theory of the neuroses, which had contributed a great deal to the understanding of obsessional neuroses. In response to this article, two German professors wrote to me, warning that if I remained on Freud's side and continued to defend him, I would be endangering my academic career. I replied: "If what Freud says is the truth, I am with him. I don't give a damn for a career if it has to be based on the premise of restricting research and concealing the truth." And I went on defending Freud and his ideas. But on the basis of my own findings I was still unable to feel that all neuroses were caused by sexual repression or sexual traumata. In certain cases that was so, but not in others. Nevertheless, Freud had opened up a new path of investigation, and the shocked outcries against him at the time seemed to me absurd.

I had not met with much sympathy for the ideas expressed in "The Psychology of Dementia Praecox." In fact, my colleagues laughed at me. But through this book I came to know Freud. He invited me to visit him, and our first meeting took place in Vienna in February 1907. We met at one o'clock in the afternoon and talked virtually without a pause for thirteen hours. Freud was the first man of real importance I had encountered; in my experience up to that time, no one else could compare with him. There was nothing the least trivial in his attitude, I found him extremely intelligent, shrewd, and altogether remarkable. And yet my first impressions of him remained somewhat tangled; I could not make him out.

What he said about his sexual theory impressed me. Nevertheless, his words could not remove my hesitations and doubts. I tried to advance these reservations of mine on several occasions, but each time he would attribute them to my lack of experience. Freud was right; in those days I had not enough experience to support my objections. I could see that his sexual theory was enormously important to him, both personally and philosophically. This impressed me, but I could not decide to what extent this strong emphasis upon sexuality was connected with subjective prejudices of his, and to what extent it rested upon verifiable experiences.

Above all, Freud's attitude toward the spirit seemed to me highly questionable. Wherever, in a person or in a work of art, an expression of spirituality (in the intellectual, not the supernatural sense) came to light, he suspected it, and insinuated that it was repressed sexuality. Anything that could not be directly interpreted as sexuality he referred to as "psychosexuality." I protested that this hypothesis, carried to its logical conclusion, would lead to an annihilating judgment upon culture. Culture would then appear as a mere farce, the morbid consequence of repressed sexuality. "Yes," he assented, "so it is, and that is just a curse of fate against which we are powerless to contend." I was by no means disposed to agree, or to let it go at that, but still I did not feel competent to argue it out with him.

There was something else that seemed to me significant at that first meeting. 9 It had to do with things which I was able to think out and understand only after our friendship was over. There was no mistaking the fact that Freud was emotionally involved in his sexual theory to an extraordinary degree. When he spoke of it, his tone became urgent, almost anxious, and all signs of his normally critical and skeptical manner vanished. A strange, deeply moved expression came over his face, the cause of which I was at a loss to understand. I had a strong intuition that for him sexuality was a sort of *numinosum*.[3] This was confirmed by a conversation which took place some three years later (in 1910), again in Vienna.

I can still recall vividly how Freud said to me, "My dear Jung, promise me 10 never to abandon the sexual theory. That is the most essential thing of all. You see, we must make a dogma of it, an unshakable bulwark." He said that to me with great emotion, in the tone of a father saying, "And promise me this one thing, my dear son: that you will go to church every Sunday." In some astonishment I asked him, "A bulwark—against what?" To which he replied, "Against the black tide of mud"—and here he hesitated for a moment, then added—"of occultism." First of all, it was the words "bulwark" and "dogma" that alarmed me; for a dogma, that is to say, an undisputable confession of faith, is set up only when the aim is to suppress doubts once and for all. But that no longer has anything to do with scientific judgment; only with a personal power drive.

This was the thing that struck at the heart of our friendship. I knew that I 11 would never be able to accept such an attitude. What Freud seemed to mean by "occultism" was virtually everything that philosophy and religion, including the rising contemporary science of parapsychology, had learned about the psyche. To me the sexual theory was just as occult, that is to say, just as unproven an hypothesis, as many other speculative views. As I saw it, a scientific truth was a hypothesis which might be adequate for the moment but was not to be preserved as an article of faith for all time.

Although I did not properly understand it then, I had observed in Freud the 12 eruption of unconscious religious factors. Evidently he wanted my aid in erecting a barrier against these threatening unconscious contents.

The impression this conversation made upon me added to my confusion; 13 until then I had not considered sexuality as a precious and imperiled concept to which one must remain faithful. Sexuality evidently meant more to Freud than to other people. For him it was something to be religiously observed. In

---

[3]*numinosum:* spiritual force. [Eds.]

the face of such deep convictions one generally becomes shy and reticent. After a few stammering attempts on my part, the conversation soon came to an end.

I was bewildered and embarrassed. I had the feeling that I had caught a   14
glimpse of a new, unknown country from which swarms of new ideas flew to meet me. One thing was clear; Freud, who had always made much of his irreligiosity, had now constructed a dogma; or rather, in the place of a jealous God whom he had lost, he had substituted another compelling image, that of sexuality. It was no less insistent, exacting, domineering, threatening, and morally ambivalent than the original one. Just as the psychically stronger agency is given "divine" or "daemonic" attributes, so the "sexual libido" took over the role of a *deus absconditus*, a hidden or concealed god. The advantage of this transformation for Freud was, apparently, that he was able to regard the new numinous principle as scientifically irreproachable and free from all religious taint. At bottom, however, the numinosity, that is, the psychological qualities of the two rationally incommensurable opposites—Yahweh and sexuality—remained the same. The name alone had changed, and with it, of course, the point of view: the lost god had now to be sought below, not above. But what difference does it make, ultimately, to the stronger agency if it is called now by one name and now by another? If psychology did not exist, but only concrete objects, the one would actually have been destroyed and replaced by the other. But in reality, that is to say, in psychological experience, there is not one whit the less of urgency, anxiety, compulsiveness, etc. The problem still remains; how to overcome or escape our anxiety, bad conscience, guilt, compulsion, unconsciousness, and instinctuality. If we cannot do this from the bright, idealistic side, then perhaps we shall have better luck by approaching the problem from the dark, biological side.

Like flames suddenly flaring up, these thoughts darted through my mind.   15
Much later, when I reflected upon Freud's character, they revealed their significance. There was one characteristic of his that preoccupied me above all; his bitterness. It had struck me at our first encounter, but it remained inexplicable to me until I was able to see it in connection with his attitude toward sexuality. Although, for Freud, sexuality was undoubtedly a *numinosum*, his terminology and theory seemed to define it exclusively as a biological function. It was only the emotionality with which he spoke of it that revealed the deeper elements reverberating within him. Basically, he wanted to teach—or so at least it seemed to me—that, regarded from within, sexuality included spirituality and had an intrinsic meaning. But his concretistic terminology was too narrow to express this idea. He gave me the impression that at bottom he was working against his own goal and against himself; and there is, after all, no harsher bitterness than that of a person who is his own worst enemy. In his own words, he felt himself menaced by a "black tide of mud"—he who more than anyone else had tried to let down his buckets into those black depths.

Freud never asked himself why he was compelled to talk continually of sex, 16
why this idea had taken such possession of him. He remained unaware that his
"monotony of interpretation" expressed a flight from himself, or from that other
side of him which might perhaps be called mystical. So long as he refused to
acknowledge that side, he could never be reconciled with himself. He was blind
toward the paradox and ambiguity of the contents of the unconscious, and did
not know that everything which arises out of the unconscious has a top and a
bottom, an inside and an outside. When we speak of the outside—and that is
what Freud did—we are considering only half of the whole, with the result that
a countereffect arises out of the unconscious.

There was nothing to be done about this one-sidedness of Freud's. Perhaps 17
some inner experience of his own might have opened his eyes; but then his
intellect would have reduced any such experience to "mere sexuality" or "psychosexuality." He remained the victim of the one aspect he could recognize,
and for that reason I see him as a tragic figure; for he was a great man, and
what is more, a man in the grip of his daimon.[4]

QUESTIONS

1. Jung began by supporting Freud but later split from him. Trace the various conflicts that resulted in Jung's abandonment of Freudian psychology.

2. Although Freud considered himself irreligious (paragraph 14), Jung found "unconscious religious factors (paragraph 12) in Freud's attitude toward his own theories.
How does Jung explain this apparent contradiction?

3. This essay is as much about Freud the man as it is about his theories. What kind
of man emerges from Jung's portrait? On what basis has Jung selected the events and
illustrations he uses to create this portrait?

4. Do you trust Jung's evaluation of Freud? What is there in his approach and tone
that allows you to trust (or mistrust) him?

5. Read Freud's "The Sexual Enlightenment of Children" elsewhere in this anthology (pages 608–613). Do you find in this essay any of the dogmatism and one-sideness
of which Jung complained? (Focus on Freud's *attitude* toward his subject, rather than
the subject itself in your response.)

6. Read an evaluation by Freud (or by one of his followers) of Jung and his theories.
Many, for example, feel Jung was pulled under by the very "black tide of mud . . . of
occultism" (paragraph 10) that Freud warned against. Write an essay on how this supplementary reading alters your view of Freud.

7. Jung's essay on Freud includes "things which [he] was able to think out and
understand only after our friendship was over" (paragraph 9). Write an essay reflecting
on one of your former friends, both recalling and commenting on the significance of
your experience.

---

[4]daimon: demon. [Eds.]

A TWIN IS ONLY HALF A PERSON

Jeremy Seabrook

Jeremy Seabrook (b. 1939), the author of many British radio and television plays also has devoted much of his career to sociological studies. Among these are The Unprivileged *(1967),* Everlasting Feast *(1974), and* A Lasting Relationship: Homosexuals and Society *(1976). He is also the author of an autobiography,* Mother and Son *(1980), which examines how his domineering mother kept him dependent upon her late into adult life. He considered himself the "fat, ugly, and knock-kneed" twin of a brother with "beautiful violet eyes," and in the excerpt from* Mother and Son *that follows, he examines the issues of twinship, sibling rivalry, and adult expectations of children.*

Whenever I have told people I've met that I am a twin, there has always come a change of expression in their eyes, a kind of re-focusing, which I came to recognize long before I detected its meaning. I think it is an attempt to discern in me my absent half: everybody knows that a twin is only half a person. There is a distinct withdrawal too, the readjustment people make when they discover someone they have been talking to freely and intimately is married. If you are a twin, people behave as though you are not worth making a relationship with; and they recoil, sensing perhaps that there is no reserve of feeling within you which you could possibly expend on them. They are interested and polite. They say "Oh is he like you?" and you can watch them adjust to the possibility of a replica of the individual they have just met; and your sense of uniqueness is assailed. They ask "Do you feel pain and joy on behalf of each other? If he is suffering, do you feel a pang, can you not bear to be apart?" 1

It has been nothing like that. 2

My twin has always been there. This may seem a very banal and obvious thing to say; but he was there as a presence and not as a person. It is only now that we are well into our thirties that we have begun to exist for each other. 3

Our family made the same assumptions about us that are common in the general response to twinning. The first was that there is a sense of symmetry in nature, and that in a twin situation human characteristics are distributed in compensating opposites: the absence of some feature in one of us was made good by the presence of another, which, in turn, was lacking in the other twin. There was a division of human qualities between us soon after birth, like a fairy-tale christening at which all the members of the family bestowed a gift upon us, or, in some cases, a curse, according to their disposition. And it seems 4 to have occurred to no one that the same features might have been present in both of us. In this way, our natures were built by our relatives, an elaborate and ingenious construct which it has taken half a lifetime to demolish.

It was clear from the beginning that my brother was a good child who didn't 5 cry. All that remained for me was to be bad; but to make up for that, it was decided I would be clever. This implied that Jack would be dull; so it was decreed that he would be practical, skilled with his hands, which he became. This caused me to be clumsy and maladroit; and to make up for this, I was given a loving disposition, which I faithfully set about developing—even though I occasionally sensed guiltily that it wasn't true, and I longed to express my hatred of Aunt Maud and my loathing of bunny rabbits.

Our whole personalities were created rather than allowed to develop, and the 6 pace was forced. When one of us gave any sign of a preference or an ability, there was a rush to seek out its opposite in the other.

This meant over time that we became, each for the other, objects of great 7 mystery; and in this lay the deeper purpose of our contrived complementarity. The other was always endowed with what one didn't have, with what one lacked. My twin was a reproach to me for all the things I would never be. He was the beautiful one; and this meant, not simply that I was plain, or even of tolerably neutral appearance, but that I was ugly. For many years I observed people overcome what I imagined must be their revulsion before they could even bear to talk to me. But if I was bright, this implied that my brother was not merely average, but that he was backward. And we obliged by carrying out these determinants whispered over our cradle by malevolent adults. It was discovered— in early infancy somehow—that my brother would never be able to read or write. Later, when I went to the Grammar School, he was consigned to the C stream of the Secondary Modern in compliance with this melancholy fact. These roles pursued us far into adult life; and it wasn't until he was in the army, in Germany, that my brother realized, with wonder, that he was writing to his girl friend every day, letters he was amazed to find linguistically quite competent and marvellously rich in ideas.

In this way we grew up as strangers to each other; strangers who had nothing 8 in common and therefore no reason to make each other's acquaintance. The qualities which each of us possessed were not seen by the other as complementary. They had evolved to satisfy other people's sense of the rightness of things. We were immured in separate chambers of the body of the family,[1] with our respective myths about ourselves and each other. It wouldn't be true to say that I disliked my brother. I regarded him with distant curiosity, as someone governed by quite different laws and values from myself—the kind of anthropological detachment which is normally brought to the observation of remote outlandish customs and practices. He was inaccessible, because apparently there was noth-

---

[1]immured: entombed or imprisoned within walls. [Eds.]

ing we shared—not even our mother. She was a different person with each of us, as became someone with compassion for the monster of ugliness and the subnormal she had brought into the world.

But at the same time, my brother was the embodiment of all the things I 9
could never be. I grew up with my own deficiencies constantly illuminated by the model of the child I understood him to be. The pain of this was made worse by our close relatives. Why can't you be more like Jack, I was asked with despairing insistence. It was a question I didn't have an answer to then. I do now, but it is thirty years too late to be of use to either of us.

If each of us was held up as an example of human perfection to the other, 10
it meant that we both grew up with a deepened sense of our own inadequacy. The relationship with our mother always seemed to take place privately, with only one at a time; and this didn't strike us as odd. Each of us was so dazzled by the vaunted perfection of the other, that he could only expect to wait, humble, patient, excluded from the mystical bond that existed between brother and mother. I often wondered what she said to him, as she washed him at night if I had been put to bed first and was waiting to go to sleep; or why she talked to me all the time about him if he were already washed and in bed. When he and I were together, we were like indifferent stepchildren, sullenly accepting each other's presence, but unable to find any area of common interest. We had no idea then of our mother's resentment of what men had done to her. She must have dreaded above all else that my brother and I might combine against her.

Mealtimes were the worst. I could never understand why other families would 11
spend perhaps an hour at table, when our meals were such functional occasions, concerned with nothing but the assimilation of food. My brother and I would sit in morose silence as we played with the food on our plates, damming the gravy within an embankment of mashed potato and waiting for the rampart to give way, heads lowered, not even looking at each other. We simply eliminated one another from our consciousness; and in order to survive, each had to make light of the qualities the other had, and which were always being set before him as an example. I learned to undervalue practical ability in anything, so that I came to adulthood unable to pay a bill, mend a fuse, change a plug, mow a lawn. And in our competitive struggle I made a virtue of these things, because I was the only person who sought my true good qualities in vain. If I was patient or kind, I failed to observe it, or assumed patience and kindness to be of little worth because they were mine; or perhaps I considered them deeply contaminated by the fact that I was cowardly, ugly, and greedy. So I had to diminish physical beauty. It was after all, I never ceased telling myself, merely a shell; it indicated nothing of the person you really were. I had to despise tractability and the quiet acceptance of the adult timetable for sleep, food or play; I questioned the purpose of these rituals endlessly, disputed them with tears and refusal, until the adults despaired over my causeless grief.

My brother and I both tried to be as worthy as each suspected the other of 12
being of our mother's love; and it was given to us both to understand that each
was always on the brink of ousting the preferred other. This meant that neither
finally gave up the struggle; neither became totally indifferent or demoralized.
A competitive tension persisted. I promised my mother that when I grew up, I
would take her away with me to live in Canada, not knowing that my brother
had promised to make a life for both of them in Australia.

So we grew, slightly deformed, like trees that have common root but have 13
no room to grow to their full height side by side. We were shadows cast over
each other's childhood. I have a photograph of us at the age of about seven.
We are holding hands in front of the lilac bush, and we are dressed identically.
I have no recollection of the picture having been taken; only I am incredulous
that we could ever have held hands. He was always there, with his beautiful
violet eyes, silent and reproachful over his model-making, building aeroplanes
with strips of frail balsa-wood, exuding a smell of pear drops from the adhesive
he used. Once or twice he did initiate a clumsy attempt to get close to me.
When Gran died, he tried to put an arm around me; when he was fourteen,
he tried to talk to me about his loneliness. Terrified, I fled. It seemed like being
molested by a stranger.

But now that we are grown up and our lives are separate in every way—we 14
sometimes don't meet for a year or more at a time—there remains, curiously,
an ache and an absence. There is a sense of emptiness where he should have
been and yet never was. When we are together, the old rivalry erupts readily in
argument and misunderstanding; but when it doesn't there is a strange unspoken
pain, which is present to a lesser degree with other members of the family—
the scars of kinship.

At times I feel incomplete. The space he occupied has remained vacant. It 15
seems to me now that much of my adult life has been spent looking for people
who resemble, not him but myself: a belated and doomed search for the things
I ought to have shared with my twin. I remain with a persistent fear of being
alone; and yet with others I feel inadequate, half a person. But it is half a person
with no complement.

QUESTIONS

1. How does Seabrook feel that people react when he tells them he is a twin?
2. How did his family's response to twinning shape Seabrook's personality?
3. Describe Seabrook's relationship with his twin and with his mother.
4. At the end of paragraph 4, Seabrook writes that "our natures were built by our
relatives, an elaborate and ingenious construct which it has taken half a lifetime to
demolish." Point out any evidence at the end of the essay that Seabrook had indeed
demolished that "construct"?
5. Much of Seabrook's diction underscores the psychological warfare and the re-

sentment he feels toward the "malevolent adults" (paragraph 7) who inflicted "the scars of kinship" (paragraph 14). Find examples of Seabrook's violent and grotesque choice of language. How does his diction establish the tone of the essay? How does his diction help him achieve his purpose in writing this essay?

6. In the first paragraph, Seabrook compares the reaction to twinship to discovering someone you have been talking to intimately is married. Consider whether his feelings about twinship are applicable to any other couplings (such as husband and wife, brother and sister, and so on).

7. Talk with someone you know who is a twin, and then read some journal articles about twinship. Are Seabrook's feelings unique, or are his feelings common to other twins? How does Seabrook's account differ from other accounts? Write an essay in which you explore an issue about twinship that interests you.

8. Seabrook writes: "I have a photograph of us at the age of about seven. We are holding hands in front of the lilac bush, and we are dressed identically. I have no recollection of the picture having been taken; only I am incredulous that we could ever have held hands" (paragraph 13). Find a childhood photograph of yourself. What surprises you about this photograph? Write an essay in which you reflect upon the self you see in the photograph and the self that you have become.

WHAT DID YOU DO IN THE WAR, GRANDMA?

A Flashback to August, 1945

Zoë Tracy Hardy

Born in 1927 and raised in the Midwest, Zoë Tracy Hardy was one of millions of young women called "Rosie the Riveters" who worked in defense plants during World War II. Considered at first to be mere surrogates for male workers, these women soon were building bombers which their foremen declared "equal in the construction [to] those turned out by experienced workmen in the plant's other departments," as a news feature at the time stated. After the eventful summer described in the essay below, Hardy finished college, married, and began teaching college English in Arizona, Guam, and Colorado. This essay first appeared in the August 1985 issue of Ms. *magazine—exactly forty years after the end of World War II.*

It was unseasonably cool that day in May, 1945, when I left my mother and 1 father and kid brother in eastern Iowa and took the bus all the way to Omaha to help finish the war. I was 18, and had just completed my first year at the University of Iowa without distinction. The war in Europe had ended in April; the war against the Japanese still raged. I wanted to go where something *real* was being done to end this bitter war that had always been part of my adolescence.

I arrived in Omaha at midnight. The YWCA, where I promised my family 2 I would get a room, was closed until 7 A.M., so I curled up in a cracked maroon leather chair in the crowded, smoky waiting room of the bus station.

In the morning I set off on foot for the YWCA, dragging a heavy suitcase 3 and carrying my favorite hat trimmed in daisies in a large round hatbox. An hour of lugging and resting brought me to the Y, a great Victorian house of dark brick, where I paid two weeks in advance (most of my money) for board and a single room next to a bathroom that I would share with eight other girls. I surrendered my red and blue food-ration stamp books and my sugar coupons to the cook who would keep them as long as I stayed there.

I had eaten nothing but a wartime candy bar since breakfast at home the day 4 before, but breakfast at the Y was already over. So, queasy and light-headed, I went back out into the cold spring day to find my job. I set out for the downtown office of the Glenn L. Martin Company. It was at their plant south of the city that thousands of workers, in around-the-clock shifts, built the famous B-29 bombers, the great Superfortresses, which the papers said would end the war.

I filled out an application and thought about the women welders and riveters and those who operated machine presses to help put the Superfortresses together. I grew shakier by the minute, more and more certain I was unqualified for any job here.

My interview was short. The personnel man was unconcerned about my total lack of skills. If I passed the physical, I could have a job in the Reproduction Department, where the blueprints were handled.

Upstairs in a gold-walled banquet room furnished with examination tables and hospital screens, a nurse sat me on a stool to draw a blood sample from my arm. I watched my blood rolling slowly into the needle. The gold walls wilted in the distance, and I slumped forward in a dead faint.

A grandfatherly doctor waved ammonia under my nose, and said if I would go to a café down the street and eat the complete 50-cent breakfast, I had the job.

The first week in the Reproduction Department, I learned to cut and fold enormous blueprints as they rolled from a machine that looked like a giant washing machine wringer. Then I was moved to a tall, metal contraption with a lurid light glowing from its interior. An ammonia guzzler, it spewed out smelly copies of specifications so hot my finger-tips burned when I touched them. I called it the dragon, and when I filled it with ammonia, the fumes reminded me of gold walls dissolving before my eyes. I took all my breaks outdoors, even when it was raining.

My boss, Mr. Johnson,[1] was a sandy-haired man of about 40, who spoke pleasantly when he came around to say hello and to check our work. Elsie, his secretary, a cool redhead, seldom spoke to any of us and spent most of her time in the darkroom developing negatives and reproducing photographs.

One of my coworkers in Reproduction was Mildred, a tall dishwater blond with a horsey, intelligent face. She was the first women I'd ever met with an earthy unbridled tongue.

When I first arrived, Mildred warned me always to knock on the darkroom door before going in because Mr. Johnson and Elsie did a lot of screwing in there. I didn't believe her, I thought we were supposed to knock to give Elsie time to protect her negatives from the sudden light. "Besides," I said, "there isn't room to lie down in there." Mildred laughed until tears squeezed from the corners of her eyes. "You poor kid," she said. "Don't you *know* you don't have to lie down?"

I was stunned. "But it's easier if you do," I protested, defensive about my sex education. My mother, somewhat ahead of her time, had always been

---

[1] All names but the author's have been changed.

explicit in her explanations, and I had read "Lecture 14," an idyllic description of lovemaking being passed around among freshman girls in every dormitory in the country.

"Sitting, standing, any quick way you can in time of war," Mildred winked   14
wickedly. She was as virginal as I, but what she said reminded us of the steady dearth of any day-to-day presence of young men in our lives.

We were convinced that the war would be over by autumn. We were stepping   15
up the napalm and incendiary bombing of the Japanese islands, the British were now coming to our aid in the Pacific, and the Japanese Navy was being reduced to nothing in some of the most spectacular sea battles in history.

Sometimes, after lunch, I went into the assembly areas to see how the skel-   16
etons of the B-29s were growing from our blueprints. At first there were enormous stark ribs surrounded by scaffolding two and three stories high. A few days later there was aluminum flesh over the ribs and wings sprouting from stubs on the fuselage. Women in overalls and turbans, safety glasses, and steel-toed shoes scrambled around the wings with riveting guns and welding torches, fitting fuel tanks in place. Instructions were shouted at them by hoarse, paunchy old men in hard hats. I cheered myself by thinking how we were pouring it on, a multitude of us together creating this great bird to end the war.

Away from the plant, however, optimism sometimes failed me. My room at   17
the Y was bleak. I wrote letters to my unofficial fiancé and to other young men in the service who had been friends and classmates. Once in a while I attempted to study thinking I would redeem my mediocre year at the university.

During those moments when I sensed real homesickness lying in wait, I   18
would plan something to do with Betty and Celia, friends from high school, who had moved to Omaha "for the duration" and had jobs as secretaries for a large moving and storage company. Their small apartment was upstairs in an old frame house in Benson, a northwest suburb. Celia and Betty and I cooked, exchanged news from servicemen·we all knew and talked about plans for the end of the war. Betty was engaged to her high school sweetheart, a soldier who had been wounded in Germany and who might be coming home soon. We guessed she would be the first one of us to be married, and we speculated, in the careful euphemisms of "well-brought-up girls," about her impending introduction to sex.

By the first of July, work and the pace of life had lost momentum. The war   19
news seemed to repeat itself without advancing, as day after day battles were fought around jungly Pacific islands that all seemed identical and unreal.

At the plant, I was moved from the dragon to a desk job, a promotion of   20
sorts. I sat on a high stool in a cubicle of pigeonholed cabinets and filed blueprints, specs, and deviations in the proper holes. While I was working, I saw no one and couldn't talk to anybody.

In mid-July Betty got married. Counsel from our elders was always to wait— 21
wait until things settle down after the war. Harold, still recuperating from shrap-
nel wounds, asked Betty not to wait.

Celia and I attended the ceremony on a sizzling afternoon in a musty Pres- 22
byterian church. Harold was very serious, gaunt-faced and thin in his loose-
hanging Army uniform. Betty, a fair-skinned, blue-eyed brunet in a white street
dress, looked pale and solemn. After the short ceremony, they left the church
in a borrowed car. Someone had given them enough gasoline stamps for a
honeymoon trip to a far-off cabin on the shore of a piney Minnesota lake.

Celia and I speculated on Betty's introduction to lovemaking. I had "Lecture 23
14" in mind and hoped she would like lovemaking, especially way off in Minnesota, far from the sweltering city and the war. Celia thought it didn't matter
much whether a girl liked it or not, as long as other important parts of marriage
got off to a good start.

That weekend Celia and I took a walk in a park and watched a grandfather 24
carefully pump a seesaw up and down for his small grandson. We saw a short,
middle-aged sailor walking with a sad-faced young woman who towered over
him. "A whore," Celia said, "Probably one of those from the Hotel Bianca."
Celia had been in Omaha longer than I and knew more of its secrets.

I wanted, right then, to see someone young and male and healthy cross the 25
grass under the trees, someone without wounds and without a cap, someone
with thick disheveled hair that hadn't been militarily peeled down to the green
skin on the back of his skull. Someone wearing tennis shorts to show strong,
hair-matted legs, and a shirt with an open neck and short sleeves revealing
smooth, hard muscles and tanned skin. Someone who would pull me out of
this gloom with a wide spontaneous smile as he passed.

In the next few days, the tempo of the summer changed subtly. From friends 26
stationed in the Pacific, I began to get letters free from rectangular holes where
military censors had snipped out "sensitive" words. Our Navy was getting ready
to surround the Japanese islands with a starvation blockade, and our B-29s had
bombed the industrial heart of the country. We were dropping leaflets warning
the Japanese people that we would incinerate hundreds of thousands of them
by firebombing 11 of their major cities. Rumors rippled through the plant back
in Omaha. The Japanese Empire would collapse in a matter of weeks, at most.

One Friday night, with Celia's help, I moved out of the Y to Celia's apart- 27
ment in Benson, We moved by streetcar. Celia carried my towels and my full
laundry bag in big rolls, one under each arm, and wore my straw picture hat
with the daisies, which bobbled wildly on top of her head. My hatbox was
crammed with extra underwear and the war letters I was determined to save.
When we climbed aboard the front end of the streetcar, I dropped the hatbox,
spilled an armload of books down the aisle, and banged my suitcase into the
knees of an elderly man who was trying to help me retrieve them.

We began to laugh, at everything, at nothing, and were still laughing when   28
we hauled everything off the car and down one block to the apartment, the
daisies all the while wheeling recklessly on Celia's head.

It was a good move. Summer nights were cooler near the country, and so   29
quiet I could hear the crickets. The other upstairs apartment was occupied by
Celia's older sister, Andrea, and her husband, Bob, who hadn't been drafted.

Late in July, an unusual thing happened at the plant. Mr. Johnson asked us   30
to work double shifts for a few days. The situation was urgent, he said, and he
wanted 100 percent cooperation from the Reproduction Department, even if it
meant coming to work when we felt sick or postponing something that was
personally important to us.

The next morning no one from the day shift was missing, and the place was   31
full of people from the graveyard shift. Some of the time I worked in my cubicle
counting out special blueprints and deviations. The rest of the time I helped
the crews sweating over the blueprint machine cut out prints that contained odd
lines and numbers that I had never seen before. Their shapes were different,
too, and there was no place for them in the numbered pigeonholes of my
cubicle. Some prints were small, about four inches square. Mildred said they
were so cute she might tuck one in her shoe and smuggle it home as a souvenir
even if it meant going to the federal pen if she got caught.

During those days I learned to nap on streetcars. I had to get up at 4:30, bolt   32
down breakfast, and catch the first car to rumble out of the darkness at 5:15.
The double shift wasn't over until 11:30, so I got home about one in the
morning.

The frenzy at the plant ended as suddenly as it had begun. Dazed with   33
fatigue, I slept through most of a weekend and hoped we had pushed ourselves
to some limit that would lift us over the last hump of the war.

On Monday the familiar single shift was not quite the same. We didn't know   34
what we had done, but an undercurrent of anticipation ran through the department because of those double shifts—and the news. The papers told of
factories that were already gearing up to turn out refrigerators, radios, and automobiles instead of bombs and planes.

In Reproduction, the pace began to slacken. Five hundred thirty-six B-29s,   35
planes we had put together on the Nebraska prairie, had firebombed the principal islands of the Japanese Empire: Hokkaido, Honshu, Kyushu, Shikoku.
We had reduced to ashes more than 15 square miles of the heart of Tokyo. The
battered and burned Japanese were so near defeat that there couldn't be much
left for us to do. With surprising enthusiasm, I began to plan for my return to
college.

Going home on the streetcar the first Tuesday afternoon in August, I heard   36
about a puzzling new weapon. Some excited people at the end of the car were

jabbering about it, saying the Japanese would be forced to surrender in a matter of hours.

When I got home, Andrea, her round bespectacled face flushed, met me at the head of the stairs. "Oh, come and listen to the radio—it's a new bomb— it's almost over!"   37

I sat down in her living room and listened. There was news, then music, then expanded news. Over and over the newscaster reported that the United States had unlocked a secret of the universe and unleashed a cosmic force—from splitting atoms of uranium—on the industrial seaport of Hiroshima. Most of the city had been leveled to the ground, and many of its inhabitants disintegrated to dust in an instant by a single bomb. "Our scientists have changed the history of the world," the newscaster said. He sounded as if he could not believe it himself.   38

We ate dinner from our laps and continued to listen as the news pounded on for an hour, then two, then three. I tried, at last, to *think* about it. In high school physics we had already learned that scientists were close to splitting an atom. We imagined that a cupful of the tremendous energy from such a phe- nomenon might run a car back and forth across the entire country dozens of times. I could visualize that. But I could not imagine how such energy put into a small bomb would cause the kind of destruction described on the radio.   39

About nine, I walked over to McCollum's grocery store to buy an evening paper. The headline said we had harnessed atomic power. I skimmed through a front page story. Science had ushered us into a strange new world, and Pres- ident Truman had made two things clear: the bomb had created a monster that could wipe out civilization; and some protection against this monster would have to be found before its secret could be given to the world.   40

Back out in the dark street, I hesitated. For the first time I could remember, I felt a rush of terror at being out in the night alone.   41

When I got back to the apartment, I made a pot of coffee and sat down at the kitchen table to read the rest of the paper. President Truman had said: "The force from which the sun draws its power has been loosed against those who brought war to the Far East . . . . If they do not now accept our terms they may expect a rain of ruin from the air the like of which has never been seen on this earth." New and more powerful bombs were now being developed.   42

I read everything, looking for some speculation from someone about how we were going to live in this new world. There was nothing. About midnight Andrea knocked on my open door to get my attention. She stood there a moment in her nightgown and curlers looking at me rather oddly. She asked if I was all right.   43

I said yes, just trying to soak it all in.   44

Gently she told me I had better go to bed and think about how soon the war would be over.   45

The next day Reproduction was nearly demolished by the spirit of celebra- 46
tion. The *Enola Gay*, the plane that had dropped the bomb, was one of ours.
By Thursday morning the United States had dropped a second atomic bomb,
an even bigger one, on an industrial city, Nagasaki, and the Russians had
declared war on Japan.

At the end of the day, Mr. Johnson asked us to listen to the radio for an- 47
nouncements about when to return to work, then shook hands all around.
"You've all done more than you know to help win the war," he said.

We said tentative good-byes. I went home and over to McCollum's for an 48
evening paper. An Army Strategic Air Forces expert said that there was no
comparison between the fire caused by the atomic bomb and that of a normal
conflagration. And there were other stories about radiation, like X-rays, that
might cripple and poison living things for hours, weeks, maybe years, until they
died.

I went to bed late and had nightmares full of flames and strange dry gale 49
winds. The next noon I got up, exhausted, and called Mildred. She said they
were still saying not to report to work until further notice. "It's gonna bore our
tails off," she moaned. "I don't know how long we can sit around here just
playing hearts." I could hear girls laughing in the background.

"Mildred," I blurted anxiously, "do you think we should have done this 50
thing?"

"Why not? Better us than somebody else, kid." 51

I reminded her that we knew the Japanese were finished weeks ago and asked 52
her if it wasn't sort of like kicking a dead horse—brutally.

"Look," she said. "The war is really over even if the bigwigs haven't said so 53
yet. What more do you want?"

The evening paper finally offered a glimmer of relief. One large headline 54
said that serious questions about the morality of *Americans* using such a weapon
were being raised by some civilians of note and some churchmen. I went to
bed early and lay listening to the crickets and thinking about everyone coming
home—unofficial fiancés, husbands, fathers, brothers—all filling the empty spaces
between kids and women and old men, putting a balance in our lives we hadn't
known in years.

Yet the bomb haunted me. I was still awake when the windowpanes lightened 55
up at daybreak.

It was all over on August 14, 1945. Unconditional surrender. 56

For hours at a time, the bomb's importance receded in the excitement of 57
that day. Streetcar bells clanged up and down the streets; we heard sirens,
whistles, church bells. A newscaster described downtown Omaha as a free-for-
all. Perfect strangers were hugging each other in the streets; some were dancing.
Churches had thrown open their doors, and people were streaming in and out,
offering prayers of thanksgiving. Taverns were giving away free drinks.

Andrew wanted us to have a little whiskey, even though we were under age, 58
because there would never be another day like this as long as we lived. I hated
the first taste of it, but as we chattered away, inventing wild, gratifying futures,
I welcomed the muffler it wrapped around the ugliness of the bomb.

In the morning Mildred called to say our jobs were over and that we should 59
report to the plant to turn in our badges and get final paychecks. She had just
talked to Mr. Johnson, who told her that those funny blueprints we had made
during double shift had something to do with the bomb.

"Well, honey," she said, "I don't understand atomic energy, but old jazzy 60
Johnson said we had to work like that to get the *Enola Gay* and the *thing* to go
together."

I held my breath, waiting for Mildred to say she was kidding, as usual. 61
Ordinary 19- and 20-year-old girls were not, not in the United States of America,
required to work night and day to help launch scientific monsters that would
catapult us all into a precarious "strange new world"—forever. But I knew in
my bones that Mildred, forthright arrow-straight Mildred, was only telling me
what I had already, unwillingly, guessed.

Afer a long silence she said, "Well, kid, give me your address in Iowa, and 62
I'll send you a Christmas card for auld lang syne."

I wanted to cry as we exchanged addresses. I liked Mildred. I hated the gap 63
that I now sensed would always be between me and people like her.

"It's been nice talking dirty to you all summer," she said. 64

"Thanks," I hung up, slipped down the stairs, and walked past the streetcar 65
line out into the country.

The whole countryside was sundrenched, fragrant with sweet clover and 66
newly mown alfalfa. I learned against a fence post and tried to think.

The President had said we had unleashed the great secret of the universe in 67
this way, to shorten the war and save American lives. Our commitment to defeat
the Japanese was always clear to me. They had attacked us first. But we had
already firebombed much of the Japanese Empire to char. That seemed decisive
enough, and terrible enough.

If he had asked me whether I would work very hard to help bring this horror 68
into being, knowing it would shorten the war but put the world into jeopardy
for all time, how would I have answered?

I would have said, "No. With all due respect, Sir, how could such a thing 69
make a just end to our just cause?"

But the question had never been asked of us. And I stood now, in the warm, 70
sun, gripping a splintery fence post, outraged by our final insignificance—all of
us who had worked together in absolute trust to end the war.

An old cow stood near the fence switching her tail. I looked at her great, 71
uncomprehending brown eyes and began to sob.

After a while I walked back to the apartment, mentally packing my suitcase   72
and tying up my hatbox of war letters. I knew it was going to be very hard, from
now on, for the whole world to take care of itself.

I wanted very much to go home.   73

QUESTIONS

1. How does Hardy's attitude toward the war change in the course of this essay? What
event causes her to reevaluate her attitude?

2. Describe Hardy's feelings about the introduction of atomic power into her world.
Are they optimistic or pessimistic?

3. "You've all done more than you know to help win the war," Hardy's boss tells
her (paragraph 47). How does she react to the fact that she was not informed by the
authorities of the purpose of her work? How does her reaction differ from that of her
coworker Mildred?

4. As Hardy's attitude toward war changes, her attitude toward sex changes as well.
Trace this change in attitude; what connection, if any, do you see between the two?

5. Is this essay merely a personal reminiscence, or does the author have a larger
purpose? Explain what you think her purpose is.

6. This essay was published forty years after the events it describes. Are Hardy's fears
and speculations (on atomic power, on the authority of the government, on sex) dated
in any way, or are they still relevant today? Explain your answer.

7. Have you, like Hardy, ever wondered about the larger social implications of any
job that you've held or that a friend or parent holds? Write an essay like Hardy's reflecting
on that job and describing how your attitude changed as you placed the job in a larger
context.

Sciences and Technologies

1933 MEDICINE
Lewis Thomas

Born in 1913, Lewis Thomas is a medical doctor, biologist, researcher, professor, and writer. For most of his life, he has carried out laboratory research and served as an adminis-trator for medical schools and hospitals. At present he is chancellor of Memorial Sloan-Kettering Cancer Center in New York City. Thomas is most widely known for essays that he published first in the New England Journal of Med-icine and that have been gathered since in collections enti-tled The Lives of a Cell *(winner of the National Book Award in 1975),* The Medusa and the Snail *(1979), and* Late Night Thoughts on Listening to Mahler's Ninth Symphony *(1983). The following essay is taken from Thomas's auto-biography,* The Youngest Science: Notes of a Medicine Watcher *(1983).*

I was admitted to medical school under circumstances that would have been   1
impossible today. There was not a lot of competition; not more than thirty of
my four hundred classmates, most of these the sons of doctors, planned on
medicine. There was no special curriculum; elementary physics and two courses
in chemistry were the only fixed requirements; the term "premedical" had not
yet been invented. My academic record at Princeton was middling fair; I had
entered college at fifteen, having been a bright enough high-school student, but
then I turned into a moult of dullness and laziness, average or below average
in the courses requiring real work. It was not until my senior year, when I
ventured a course in advanced biology under Professor Swingle, who had just
discovered a hormone of the adrenal cortex, that I became a reasonably alert
scholar, but by that time my grade averages had me solidly fixed in the dead
center, the "gentlemen's third," of the class. Today, I would have been turned
down by every place, except perhaps one of the proprietary medical schools in
the Caribbean.

I got into Harvard, the hardest, by luck and also, I suspect, by pull. Hans 2
Zinsser, the professor of bacteriology, had interned with my father at Roosevelt
and had admired my mother, and when I went to Boston to be interviewed in
the winter of 1933, I was instructed by the dean's secretary to go have a talk
with Dr. Zinsser. It was the briefest of interviews, but satisfactory from my point
of view. Zinsser looked at me carefully, as at a specimen, then informed me
that my father and mother were good friends of his, and if I wanted to come to
Harvard he would try to help, but because of them, not me; he was entirely
good-natured, but clear on this point. It was favoritism, but not all that personal,
I was to understand.

My medical education was, in principle, much like that of my father. The 3
details had changed a lot since his time, especially in the fields of medical
science relating to disease mechanisms; physiology and biochemistry had become far more complex and also more illuminating; microbiology and immunology had already, by the early 1930s, transformed our understanding of the
causation of the major infectious diseases. But the *purpose* of the curriculum
was, if anything, even more conservative than thirty years earlier. It was to teach
the recognition of disease entities, their classification, their signs, symptoms,
and laboratory manifestations, and how to make an accurate diagnosis. The
treatment of disease was the most minor part of the curriculum, almost left out
altogether. There was, to be sure, a course in pharmacology in the second year,
mostly concerned with the mode of action of a handful of everyday drugs:
aspirin, morphine, various cathartics, bromides, barbiturates, digitalis, a few
others. Vitamin B was coming into fashion as a treatment for delirium tremens,
later given up. We were provided with a thin, pocket-size book called *Useful
Drugs*, one hundred pages or so, and we carried this around in our white coats
when we entered the teaching wards and clinics in the third year, but I cannot
recall any of our instructors ever referring to this volume. Nor do I remember
much talk about treating disease at any time in the four years of medical school
except by the surgeons, and most of their discussions dealt with the management
of injuries, the drainage or removal of infected organs and tissues, and, to a
very limited extent, the excision of cancers.

The medicine we were trained to practice was, essentially, Osler's medicine.[1] 4
Our task for the future was to be diagnosis and explanation. Explanation was
the real business of medicine. What the ill patient and his family wanted most
was to know the name of the illness, and then, if possible, what had caused it,
and finally, most important of all, how it was likely to turn out.

The successes possible in diagnosis and prognosis were regarded as the triumph 5
of medical science, and so they were. It had taken long decades of careful,
painstaking observation of many patients; the publication of countless papers
describing the detailed aspects of one clinical syndrome after another; more

[1]Sir William Osler (1849–1919): Canadian-born physician and teacher. [Eds.]

science, in the correlation of the clinical features of disease with the gross and microscopic abnormalities, contributed by several generations of pathologists. By the 1930s we thought we knew as much as could ever be known about the dominant clinical problems of the time: syphilis, tuberculosis, lobar pneumonia, typhoid, rheumatic fever, erysipelas, poliomyelitis. Most of the known varieties of cancer had been meticulously classified, and estimates of the duration of life could be made with some accuracy. The electrocardiogram had arrived, adding to the fair precision already possible in the diagnosis of heart disease. Neurology possessed methods for the localization of disease processes anywhere in the nervous system. When we had learned all that, we were ready for our M.D. degrees, and it was expected that we would find out about the actual day-to-day management of illness during our internship and residency years.

During the third and fourth years of school we also began to learn something 6 that worried us all, although it was not much talked about. On the wards of the great Boston teaching hospitals—the Peter Bent Brigham, the Massachusetts General, the Boston City Hospital, and Beth Israel—it gradually dawned on us that we didn't know much that was really useful, that we could do nothing to change the course of the great majority of the diseases we were so busy analyzing, that medicine, for all its façade as a learned profession, was in real life a pro-foundly ignorant occupation.

Some of this we were actually taught by our clinical professors, much more 7 we learned from each other in late-night discussions. When I am asked, as happens occasionally, which member of the Harvard faculty had the greatest influence on my education in medicine, I no longer grope for a name on that distinguished roster. What I remember now, from this distance, is the influence of my classmates. We taught each other; we may even have set careers for each other without realizing at the time that so fundamental an education process was even going on. I am not so troubled as I used to be by the need to reform the medical school curriculum. What worries me these days is that the curric-ulum, whatever its sequential arrangement, has become so crowded with lec-tures and seminars, with such masses of data to be learned, that the students may not be having enough time to instruct each other in what may lie ahead.

The most important period for discovering what medicine would be like was 8 a three-month ward clerkship in internal medicine that was a required part of the fourth year of medical school. I applied for the clerkship at the Beth Israel Hospital, partly because of the reputation of Professor Hermann Blumgart and partly because several of my best friends were also going there. Ward rounds with Dr. Blumgart were an intellectual pleasure, also good for the soul. I became considerably less anxious about the scale of medical ignorance as we followed him from bed to bed around the open circular wards of the B.I. I've seen his match only three or four times since then. He was a tall, thin, quick-moving man, with a look of high intelligence, austerity, and warmth all at the same time. He had the special gift of perceiving, almost instantaneously, while still approaching the bedside of a new patient, whether the problem was a serious one or not. He seemed to do this by something like intuition; at times when there werre no particular reasons for alarm that could be sensed by others in the retinue, Blumgart would become extremely alert and attentive, requiring the resident to present every last detail of the history, and then moving closer to the bedside, asking his own questions of he patient, finally performing his physical examination. To watch a master of physical diagnosis in the execution of a complete physical examination is something of an aesthetic experience, rather like observing a great ballet dancer or a concert cellist. Blumgart did all this swiftly, then asked a few more questions, then drew us away to the corridor outside the ward for his discussion, and then his diagnosis, sometimes a death sentence. Then back to the bedside for a brief private talk with the patient, inaudible to the rest of us, obviously reassuring to the patient, and on to the next bed. So far as I know, from that three months of close contact with Blumgart for three hours every morning, he was never wrong, not once. But I can recall only three or four patients for whom the diagnosis resulted in the possibility of doing something to change the course of the illness, and each of these involved calling in the surgeons to do the something—removal of a thyroid nodule, a gallbladder, an adrenal tumor. For the majority, the disease had to be left to run its own course, for better or worse.

There were other masters of medicine, each as unique in his way as Blumgart, surrounded every day by interns and medical students on the wards of the other Boston hospitals. 9

The Boston City Hospital, the city's largest, committed to the care of indigent Bostonians, was divided into five separate clinical services, two staffed by Harvard Medical School (officially designated as the Second and Fourth services), two by Tufts, and one by Boston University. The most spectacular chiefs on the Harvard faculty were aggregated on the City Hospital wards, drawn there in the 1920s by the creation of the Thorndike Memorial Laboratories, a separate research institute on the hospital grounds, directly attached by a series of ramps and tunnels to the buildings containing the teaching wards. The Thorndike was founded by Dr. Francis Weld Peabody, still remembered in Boston as perhaps the best of Harvard physicians. Peabody was convinced that the study of human disease should not be conducted solely by bedside observations, as had been largely the case for the research done by physicians up to that time, nor by pure bench research in the university laboratories; he believed that the installation of a fully equipped research institute, containing laboratories for investigations of any promising line of inquiry, directly in communication with the hospital wards, offered the best opportunity for moving the field forward. 10

Peabody was also responsible for the initial staffing of the Thorndike. By the time I arrived, in 1937, the array of talent was formidable: George Minot (who had already received his Nobel prize for the discovery of liver extract as a cure for pernicious anemia), William Castle (who discovered the underlying defi- 11 ciency in pernicious anemia), Chester Keefer, Soma Weiss, Maxwell Finland, John Dingle, Eugene Stead—each of them running a laboratory, teaching on the wards, and providing research training for young doctors who came for two- and three-year fellowship stints from teaching hospitals across the country. The Thorndike was a marvelous experiment, a model for what were to become the major departments of medicine in other medical schools, matched at the time only by the hospital of the Rockefeller Institute in New York.

Max Finland built and then ran the infectious disease service. He and his associates had done most of the definitive work on antipneumococcal sera in the treatment of lobar pneumonia, testing each new preparation of rabbit anti- serum as it arrived from the Lederle Laboratories. Later, Finland's laboratories were to become a national center for the clinical evaluation of penicillin, strep- tomycin, chloromycetin, and all the other antibiotics which followed during the 1950s and 1960s. As early as 1937, medicine was changing into a technology based on genuine science. The signs of change were there, hard to see because of the overwhelming numbers of patients for whom we could do nothing but stand by, but unmistakably there all the same. Syphilis could be treated in its early stages, and eventually cured, by Paul Ehrlich's arsphenamine; the treat- ment took a long time, many months, sometimes several years. If arsphenamine was started in the late stages of the disease, when the greatest damage was under way—in the central nervous system and the major arteries—the results were rarely satisfactory—but in the earliest stages, the chancre and then the rash of secondary syphilis, the spirochete could be killed off and the Wassermann reac- tion reversed.[2] The treatment was difficult and hazardous, the side effects of the arsenical drugs were appalling, sometimes fatal (I cannot imagine such a therapy being introduced and accepted by any of today's FDA or other regulatory agen- cies), but it did work in many cases, and it carried a powerful message for the future: it was possible to destroy an invading microorganism, intimately embed- ded within the cells and tissues, without destroying the cells themselves. Chemo- therapy for infectious disease in general lay somewhere ahead, and we should have known this.

Immunology was beginning to become an applied science. Thanks to the basic research launched twenty years earlier by Avery, Heidelberger, and Goeb- bel, it was known that pneumococci possessed specific carbohydrates in their capsules which gave rise to highly specific antibodies.[3] By the mid-1930s, rabbit antipneumococcal sera were available for the treatment of the commonest forms of lobar pneumonia. The sera were difficult and expensive to prepare, and sometimes caused overwhelming anaphylactic reactions in patients already mor-

12

13

---

[2]spirochete: type of bacteria including the one that produces syphilis; Wassermann reaction: the reaction to the test used to diagnose syphilis. [Eds.]
[3]pneumococci: bacteria that cause pneumonia. [Eds.]

ibund from their infection,[4] but they produced outright cures in many patients. Pernicious anemia, a uniformly fatal disease, was spectacularly reversed by liver extract (much later found to be due to the presence of vitamin B_{12} in the extracts). Diabetes mellitus could be treated—at least to the extent of reducing the elevated blood sugar and correcting the acidosis that otherwise led to diabetic coma and death—by the insulin preparation isolated by Banting and Best. Pellagra, a common cause of death among the impoverished rural populations in the South, had become curable with Goldberger's discovery of the vitamin B complex and the subsequent identification of nicotinic acid. Diphtheria could be prevented by immunization against the toxin of diphtheria bacilli and, when it occurred, treated more or less effectively with diphtheria antitoxin.

All these things were known at the time of my internship at the Boston City   14
Hospital, but they seemed small advances indeed. The major diseases, which filled the wards to overflowing during the long winter months, were infections for which there was no treatment at all.

The two great hazards to life were tuberculosis and tertiary syphilis. These   15
were feared by everyone, in the same way that cancer is feared today. There was nothing to be done for tuberculosis except to wait it out, hoping that the body's own defense mechanisms would eventually hold the tubercle bacillus in check. Some patients were helped by collapsing the affected lung (by injecting air into the pleural space, or by removing the ribs overlying the lung), and any number of fads were introduced for therapy—mountain resorts, fresh air, sunshine, nutritious diets—but for most patients tuberculosis simply ran its own long debilitating course despite all efforts. Tertiary syphilis was even worse. The wards of insane asylums were filled with psychotic patients permanently incapacitated by this disease—"general paresis of the insane";[5] some benefit was claimed for fever therapy; but there were few real cures. Rheumatic fever, the commonest cause of fatal heart disease in children, was shown by Coburn to be the result of infection by hemolytic streptococci; asprin, the only treatment available, relieved the painful arthritis in this disease but had no effect on the heart lesions. For most of the infectious diseases on the wards of the Boston City Hospital in 1937, there was nothing to be done beyond bed rest and good nursing care.

Then came the explosive news of sulfanilamide, and the start of the real   16
revolution in medicine.

I remember the astonishment when the first cases of pneumococcal and   17
streptococcal septicemia were treated in Boston in 1937. The phenomenon was almost beyond belief. Here were moribund patients, who would surely have died without treatment, improving in their appearance within a matter of hours of being given the medicine and feeling entirely well within the next day or so.

---

[4]anaphylactic reactions: severe toxic reactions by certain individuals who are hypersensitive to a drug; moribund: approaching death. [Eds.]

[5]general paresis of the insane: name for the type of insanity caused by syphilis. [Eds.]

The professionals most deeply affected by these extraordinary events were, I think, the interns. The older physicians were equally surprised, but took the news in stride. For an intern, it was the opening of a whole new world. We had been raised to be ready for one kind of profession, and we sensed that the profession itself had changed at the moment of our entry. We knew that other molecular variations of sulfanilamide were on their way from industry, and we heard about the possibility of penicillin and other antibiotics; we became convinced, overnight, that nothing lay beyond reach for the future. Medicine was off and running. 18

QUESTIONS

1. "We had been raised to be ready for one kind of profession," Thomas writes in the final paragraph. What was the purpose of a medical education in the 1930s?

2. How has the purpose of medicine changed since the 1930s? Where is the major emphasis now? Have today's standards changed the quality of medical education?

3. Thomas claims to have learned more from his classmates than from his professors. What did he learn from his fellow students?

4. Although Thomas doesn't make any direct criticism of 1933 medicine, he manages to demonstrate its limitations in contrast to modern practice. How does he achieve this? Would the essay be more effective had Thomas been more directly critical?

5. What qualities of Dr. Blumgart did Thomas admire? What techniques does Thomas use to describe Dr. Blumgart so that a reader can see those admirable qualities?

6. Which half of the essay relies more heavily on technical descriptions? Trace the way in which the changing vocabulary of the essay parallels Thomas's education as a physician.

7. Thomas expected one profession but found another. Write an essay in which you reflect on changes in your expectations in a certain field as you learned more about the subject.

8. Write an essay in which you describe a person (such as Dr. Blumgart) whom you admire. Create a dominant impression for your readers by using vivid details that show why you admire this person.

MY FRIEND, ALBERT EINSTEIN

Banesh Hoffmann

Although born in England, Banesh Hoffman (1906–1986) went to America to pursue his career as a mathematician and teacher. He took his B.A. at Oxford but finished his graduate education at Princeton. There he became a member of Princeton's Institute for Advanced Study, where he met and worked with Albert Einstein. During his forty years as a mathematics professor at Queens College in Flushing, New York, he wrote such books as The Strange Story of the Quantum *(1959) and* The Tyranny of Testing *(1978), as well as articles for a wide variety of magazines. With Helen Dukas, Einstein's personal secretary, Hoffman wrote* Albert Einstein: Creator and Rebel *(1973), which won a science writing award, and* Albert Einstein: The Human Side *(1979), a collection of Einstein's letters and personal reflections. The following essay first appeared in* Reader's Digest *and was later reprinted in their anthology* Unforgettable Characters *(1980).*

He was one of the greatest scientists the world has ever known, yet if I had 1 to convey the essence of Albert Einstein in a single word, I would choose *simplicity.* Perhaps an anecdote will help. Once, caught in a downpour, he took off his hat and held it under his coat. Asked why, he explained, with admirable logic, that the rain would damage the hat, but his hair would be none the worse for its wetting. This knack for going instinctively to the heart of a matter was the secret of his major scientific discoveries—this and his extraordinary feeling for beauty.

I first met Albert Einstein in 1935, at the famous Institute for Advanced 2 Study in Princeton, N.J. He had been among the first to be invited to the Institute, and was offered *carte blanche* as to salary. To the director's dismay, Einstein asked for an impossible sum: it was far too *small.* The director had to plead with him to accept a larger salary.

I was in awe of Einstein, and hesitated before approaching him about some 3 ideas I had been working on. When I finally knocked on his door, a gentle voice said, "Come"—with a rising inflection that made the single word both a welcome and a question. I entered his office and found him seated at a table, calculating and smoking his pipe. Dressed in ill-fitting clothes, his hair characteristically awry, he smiled a warm welcome. His utter naturalness at once set me at ease.

As I began to explain my ideas, he asked me to write the equations on the blackboard so he could see how they developed. Then came the staggering—and altogether endearing—request: "Please go slowly. I do not understand things quickly." This from Einstein! He said it gently, and I laughed. From then on, all vestiges of fear were gone. 4

Einstein was born in 1879 in the German city of Ulm. He had been no infant prodigy; indeed, he was so late in learning to speak that his parents feared he was a dullard. In school, though his teachers saw no special talent in him, the signs were already there. He taught himself calculus, for example, and his teachers seemed a little afraid of him because he asked questions they could not answer. At the age of 16, he asked himself whether a light wave would seem stationary if one ran abreast of it. From that innocent question would arise, ten years later, his theory of relativity. 5

Einstein failed his entrance examinations at the Swiss Federal Polytechnic School, in Zurich, but was admitted a year later. There he went beyond his regular work to study the masterworks of physics on his own. Rejected when he applied for academic positions, he ultimately found work, in 1902, as a patent examiner in Berne, and there in 1905 his genius burst into fabulous flower. 6

Among the extraordinary things he produced in that memorable year were his theory of relativity, with its famous offshoot, $E = mc^2$ (energy equals mass times the speed of light squared), and his quantum theory of light. These two theories were not only revolutionary, but seemingly contradictory: the former was intimately linked to the theory that light consists of waves, while the latter said it consists somehow of particles. Yet this unknown young man boldly proposed both at once—and he was right in both cases, though how he could have been is far too complex a story to tell here. 7

Collaborating with Einstein was an unforgettable experience. In 1937, the Polish physicist Leopold Infeld and I asked if we could work with him. He was pleased with the proposal, since he had an idea about gravitation waiting to be worked out in detail. Thus we got to know not merely the man and the friend, but also the professional. 8

The intensity and depth of his concentration were fantastic. When battling a recalcitrant problem, he worried it as an animal worries its prey. Often, when we found ourselves up against a seemingly insuperable difficulty, he would stand up, put his pipe on the table, and say in his quaint English, "I will a little tink" (he could not pronounce "th"). Then he would pace up and down, twirling a lock of his long, graying hair around his forefinger. 9

A dreamy, faraway and yet inward look would come over his face. There was no appearance of concentration, no furrowing of the brow—only a placid inner communion. The minutes would pass, and then suddenly Einstein would stop pacing as his face relaxed into a gentle smile. He had found the solution 10 to the problem. Sometimes it was so simple that Infeld and I could have kicked ourselves for not having thought of it. But the magic had been performed invisibly in the depths of Einstein's mind, by a process we could not fathom.

When his wife died he was deeply shaken, but insisted that now more than 11 ever was the time to be working hard. I remember going to his house to work with him during that sad time. His face was haggard and grief-lined, but he put forth a great effort to concentrate. To help him, I steered the discussion away from routine matters into more difficult theoretical problems, and Einstein gradually became absorbed in the discussion. We kept at it for some two hours, and at the end his eyes were no longer said. As I left, he thanked me with moving sincerity. "It was a fun," he said. He had had a moment of surcease from grief, and then groping words expressed a deep emotion.

Although Einstein felt no need for religious ritual and belonged to no formal 12 religious group, he was the most deeply religious man I have known. He once said to me, "Ideas come from God," and one could hear the capital "G" in the reverence with which he pronounced the word. On the marble fireplace in the mathematics building at Princeton University is carved, in the original German, what one might call his scientific credo: "God is subtle, but he is not malicious." By this Einstein meant that scientists could expect to find their task difficult, but not hopeless: the Universe was a Universe of law, and God was not confusing us with deliberate paradoxes and contradictions.

Einstein was an accomplished amateur musician. We used to play duets, he 13 on the violin, I at the piano. One day he surprised me by saying Mozart was the greatest composer of all. Beethoven "created" his music, but the music of Mozart was of such purity and beauty one felt he had merely "found" it—that it had always existed as part of the inner beauty of the Universe, waiting to be revealed.

It was this very Mozartean simplicity that most characterized Einstein's meth- 14 ods. His 1905 theory of relativity, for example, was built on just two simple assumptions. One is the so-called principle of relativity, which means, roughly speaking, that we cannot tell whether we are at rest or moving smoothly. The other assumption is that the speed of light is the same no matter what the speed of the object that produces it. You can see how reasonable this is if you think of agitating a stick in a lake to create waves. Whether you wiggle the stick from a stationary pier, or from a rushing speedboat, the waves, once generated, are on their own, and their speed has nothing to do with that of the stick.

Each of these assumptions, by itself, was so plausible as to seem primitively 15 obvious. But together they were in such violent conflict that a lesser man would have dropped one or the other and fled in panic. Einstein daringly kept both— and by so doing he revolutionized physics. For he demonstrated they could, after all, exist peacefully side by side, provided we gave up cherished beliefs about the nature of time.

Science is like a house of cards, with concepts like time and space at the lowest level. Tampering with time brought most of the house tumbling down, and it was this that made Einstein's work so important—and controversial. At a conference in Princeton in honor of his 70th birthday, one of the speakers, a Nobel Prize winner, tried to convey the magical quality of Einstein's achievement. Words failed him, and with a shrug of helplessness he pointed to his wristwatch, and said in tones of awed amazement, "It all came from this." His very ineloquence made this the most eloquent tribute I have heard to Einstein's genius. 16

Although fame had little effect on Einstein as a person, he could not escape it; he was, of course, instantly recognizable. One autumn Saturday, I was walking with him in Princeton discussing some technical matters. Parents and alumni were streaming excitedly toward the stadium, their minds on the coming football game. As they approached us, they paused in sudden recognition, and a momentary air of solemnity came over them as if they had been reminded of a different world. Yet Einstein seemed totally unaware of this effect and went on with the discussion as though they were not there. 17

We think of Einstein as one concerned only with the deepest aspects of science. But he saw scientific principles in everyday things to which most of us would give barely a second thought. He once asked me if I had ever wondered why a man's feet will sink into either dry or completely submerged sand, while sand that is merely damp provides a firm surface. When I could not answer, he offered a simple explanation. 18

It depends, he pointed out, on *surface tension*, the elastic-skin effect of a liquid surface. This is what holds a drop together, or causes two small raindrops on a windowpane to pull into one big drop the moment their surfaces touch. 19

When sand is damp, Einstein explained, there are tiny amounts of water between grains. The surface tensions of these tiny amounts of water pull all the grains together, and friction then makes them hard to budge. When the sand is dry, there is obviously no water between grains. If the sand is fully immersed, there is water between grains, but no water *surface* to pull them together. 20

This is not as important as relativity; yet there is no telling what seeming trifle will lead an Einstein to a major discovery. And the puzzle of the sand does give us an inkling of the power and elegance of his mind. 21

Einstein's work, performed quietly with pencil and paper, seemed remote from the turmoil of everyday life: But his ideas were so revolutionary they caused violent controversy and irrational anger. Indeed, in order to be able to award him a belated Nobel Prize, the selection committee had to avoid mentioning relativity, and pretend the prize was awarded primarily for his work on the quantum theory. 22

Political events upset the serenity of his life even more. When the Nazis   23
came to power in Germany, his theories were officially declared false because
they had been formulated by a Jew. His property was confiscated, and it is said
a price was put on his head.

When scientists in the United States, fearful that the Nazis might develop   24
an atomic bomb, sought to alert American authorities to the danger, they were
scarcely heeded. In desperation, they drafted a letter which Einstein signed and
sent directly to President Roosevelt. It was this act that led to the fateful decision
to go all-out on the production of an atomic bomb—an endeavor in which
Einstein took no active part. When he heard of the agony and destruction that
his $E = mc^2$ had wrought, he was dismayed beyond measure, and from then on
there was a look of ineffable sadness in his eyes.

There was something elusively whimsical about Einstein. It is illustrated by   25
my favorite anecdote about him. In his first year in Princeton, on Christmas
Eve, so the story goes, some children sang carols outside his house. Having
finished, they knocked on his door and explained they were collecting money
to buy Christmas presents. Einstein listened, then said, "Wait a moment." He
put on his scarf and overcoat, and took his violin from its case. Then, joining
the children as they went from door to door, he accompanied their singing of
"Silent Night" on his violin.

How shall I sum up what it meant to have known Einstein and his works?   26
Like the Nobel Prize winner who pointed helplessly at his watch, I can find no
adequate words. It was akin to the revelation of great art that lets one see what
was formerly hidden. And when, for example, I walk on the sand of a lonely
beach, I am reminded of his ceaseless search for cosmic simplicity—and the
scene takes on a deeper, sadder beauty.

QUESTIONS

1. Simplicity is not usually considered an enviable personal trait; how does Hoffmann
turn this to Einstein's advantage?

2. Hoffmann alternates between personal anecdotes and scientific anecdotes. Is this
alternation confusing, or does it add to the effectiveness of the essay? In what ways?

3. Although primarily about Einstein, the essay reveals a certain amount about Hoffmann himself. What qualities as both a person and a scientist does he possess?

4. Is Hoffmann mainly concerned in this essay with Einstein the person or Einstein
the scientist? What is Hoffmann's purpose in writing this essay?

5. Does this essay have a formal structure, or is the essay simply a series of reminiscences? How is the structure consistent with Hoffmann's purpose?

6. Hoffmann's reminiscences all center on Einstein's simplicity. Choose a memorable character you have known, define this character's key attraction (as Hoffmann has
done), and then write an essay using a series of reminiscences that illustrate this trait or
quality from various angles.

7. Many have written on Einstein's unique personality. Find another biographical
account of Einstein, and compare it with Hoffmann's. Do the same qualities emerge?

THE COSMIC CODE
Heinz R. Pagels

Born in New York City in 1939, Heinz R. Pagels was educated at Princeton and Stanford and has taught physics at Rockefeller University since 1966. Although he has written over sixty articles for scientific journals, he is best known for two books for the general public. The first, The Cosmic Code: Quantum Physics as the Language of Nature *(1982), both explains quantum physics and discusses its impact on society. His second book,* Perfect Symmetry: The Search for the Beginning of Time, *was published in 1985. Both were written with the interested layperson in mind; as he once explained, "I want to communicate scientific ideas to nonscientists. Especially I want to describe the way in which science alters our intellectual culture and the perception of reality." The essay below is the concluding chapter of Pagels's first book.*

> My friend, all theory is gray
> and the golden tree of life is green.

—GOETHE, *Faust*

What is the universe? Is it a great 3-D movie in which we are all unwilling actors? Is it a cosmic joke, a giant computer, a work of art by a Supreme Being, or simply an experiment? The problem in trying to understand the universe is that we have nothing to compare it with. 1

I don't know what the universe is or whether it has a purpose, but like most physicists I have to find some way to think about it. Einstein thought it a mistake to project our human needs onto the universe because, he felt, it is indifferent to those needs. Steven Weinberg agreed:[1] " . . . the more we know about the universe the more it is evident that it is pointless and meaningless." Like Gertrude Stein's rose, the universe is what it is what it is.[2] But what "is" it? The question will not go away. 2

I think the universe is a message written in code, a cosmic code, and the scientist's job is to decipher that code. This idea, that the universe is a message, is very old. It goes back to Greece, but its modern version was stated by the 3

---

[1]Steven Weinberg (b. 1933): American physicist, author of the popular *The First Three Minutes* (1977). [Eds.]

[2]The universe is what it is what it is: the often-quoted line from American expatriate writer Gertrude Stein (1874–1946) is "A Rose is a rose is a rose is a rose." [Eds.]

English empiricist Francis Bacon,[3] who wrote that there are two revelations. The first is given to us in scripture and tradition, and it guided our thinking for centuries. The second revelation is given by the universe, and that book we are just beginning to read. The sentences within this book are the physical laws—those postulated and confirmed invariances of our experience. If there are those who claim a conversion experience through reading scripture, I would point out that the book of nature also has its converts. They may be less evangelical than religious converts, but they share a deep conviction that an order of the universe exists and can be known.

Many scientists have written about their first experience of contact with the cosmic code—the idea of an order beyond immediate experience. This experience often comes in the first years of adolescence when the emotional and cognitive life of an individual is integrated. Einstein said his conversion at that age from a religious to a scientific view of the universe changed his life. Newton, who held unorthodox religious views his whole life, also had a vision of the cosmic code—for him the universe was a great puzzle to be solved. I. I. Rabi, an atomic physicist, told me he first became interested in science when he took some books on the planetary motions out of a library. It was a source of wonder to him that the mind could know such immense things that were not invented by it. I myself remember as a teenager reading Einstein's biography, George Gamow's *One, Two, Three . . . Infinity*, and Selig Hecht's *Exploring the Atom* and making up my mind to become a physicist. I thought there was nothing more fulfilling I could aspire to than devoting my mind and energy to solving the puzzle of the cosmos. For me, physics, which explores the beginnings and ends of space, time, and matter, met those aspirations.

If we accept the idea that the universe is a book read by scientists, then we ought to examine how reading this book influences civilization. Scientists have unleashed a new force into our social, political, and economic development—perhaps the major force. By learning about the structure of the universe, scientists and engineers invent new technological devices which radically alter the world we live in. What distinguishes this new knowledge is that its source lies outside of human institutions—it comes from the material universe itself. By contrast, literature, art, the law, politics, and even the methods of science have been invented by us. But we did not invent the universe, the chemistry of our bodies, atoms, or electromagnetic waves—discoveries which profoundly influence our lives and history. Could it be that the cosmic code, revealed in the architecture of the universe, is actually the program for historical change?

Arnold Toynbee said that each civilization was a response to a challenge.[4] The Romans had the challenge of maintaining dominion over a vast empire; their response was to invent the modern state. Likewise, the Egyptians met the

---

[3]Francis Bacon (1561–1626): English philosopher, statesman, and essayist. [Eds.]
[4]Arnold Toynbee (1889–1975): English historian, author of the twelve-volume *A Study of History* (1934–61). [Eds.]

challenge of their Nile environment by the construction of an elaborate irriga-tion system and a political structure to regulate it. The major challenge to our civilization is to master the discovered contents of the cosmic code. The forces science has discovered in the universe can annihilate us. They can also provide the basis of a new and more fulfilling human existence. What our response to this challenge will be no one knows, but we have clearly come to those sentences in the cosmic code that could bring our existence to an end or, alternatively, be the birth of humanity into the universe.

I complained once to an Indian friend that the poverty, ignorance, and   7
hopelessness of the subcontinent were a consequence of Indian religions and philosophical beliefs (or was it the other way around?). My friend replied that some Indian intellectuals thought that the great wars of the West, wars which have taken millions of lives, are a consequence of Western philosophy, science, and technology. The challenge to our civilization which has come from our knowledge of the cosmic energies that fuel the stars, the movement of light and electrons through matter, the intricate molecular order which is the biological basis of life, must be met by the creation of a moral and political order which will accommodate these forces or we shall be destroyed. It will try our deepest resources of reason and compassion.

Our recent understanding also provides rich, complex, often confusing op-   8
portunities. We may feel that we exercise our freedom in the choices we make, but our options themselves are circumscribed by limits which have been made all the more clear by modern science. The condition of the universe, of the world, and of human life is viewed by many people as a product of science—rather than being seen as a discovery of science. It is a perception that results in a sense of alienation from the technological world.

In 1965 I was walking through the Boston Common with friends and met   9
an elderly woman with bright and lively eyes. She was wearing a handmade dress. A poet, she belonged to a small community which rejected the use of machines. (They wrote with quills.) The woman told me that her small group continued to believe in the human spirit but saw the human spirit as corrupted by modern life and by technology. She explained that a demonic spirit had come upon this earth about three hundred years ago, a spirit inimical to hu-manity, which it set out to destroy. The malevolence began when the best minds among the philosophers, scientists, and social and political leaders were cap-tured. Soon the monsters of science, technology, and industrialism were loose upon the land. I thought of William Blake, another poet, lamenting Newton's blindness.[5] The conquest was all but complete, she said; only a few held firm against the final fall.

The woman asked me what I did, and when I said I was a physicist I was   10

---

[5]William Blake (1757–1827): English poet who admired Newton's work but felt that the scientist's mechanistic universe left no room for God, angels, and spiritual values. [Eds.]

greeted by a look of horror. I was one of "them," the enemy. I felt a chasm open between us. A year later the Counterculture was in full swing in America; a new revolt against science was on.

Some years later I spoke to a mentally disturbed young man. Very agitatedly, 11 he described to me how alien beings from outer space had invaded the earth. They were formed of mental substance, lived in human minds, and controlled human beings through the creations of science and technology. Eventually this alien being would have an autonomous existence in the form of giant computers and would no longer require humans—and that would mark its triumph and the end of humanity. Soon he was hospitalized because he was unable to shake off this terrible vision.

The old poet and the young man are correct in their perception that science 12 and technology came from "outside" the realm of human experience. They were sensitive to this perception in a way that most of us suppress. What is outside of us is the universe as a material revelation, the message that I call the cosmic code and that is now programming human, social and economic development. What may be perceived as threatening in this alien contact is that scientists, in reading the cosmic code, have entered into the invisible structures of the universe. We live in the wake of a physics revolution comparable to the Copernican demolition of the anthropocentric world[6]—a revolution which began with the invention of the theory of relativity and quantum mechanics in the first decades of this century and which has left most educated people behind. By the nature of the phenomena it studies, science has become increasingly abstract. The cosmic code has become invisible. The unseen is influencing the seen.

The irreversible transformation of the pattern of human existence by science 13 is a profoundly disturbing experience that most people do not see because it is too close to them. Most of us live in huge cities with populations in the millions which simply could not have existed a few centuries ago because of the problems of supplying food and controlling disease. We accept technology as part of the structure of our lives because our survival depends on it. Experts and scientists assure us that technology is going to be all right because it is supported by the rule of reason. But others like the poet see reason as the tool of the devil, an instrument for the destruction of life and simple faith. They see the scientist as a destroyer of the free human spirit, while the scientist sees the poet's allies as blind to the material requirements of human survival. What divides us is the difference between those who give priority to intuitions and feelings and those who give priority to knowledge and reason—different resources of human life. Both impulses live inside each of us; but a fruitful coexistence sometimes breaks down, and the result is an incomplete person.

---

[6]The Copernican demolition of the anthropocentric world: the theories of the Polish astronomer Nicholas Copernicus (1473–1543) revolutionized astronomy by proposing the sun rather than the earth as the center of the solar system. [Eds.]

In the thirteenth century, scholasticism struggled to reconcile faith with rea- 14
son. It failed, but out of its failure grew a new civilization—the modern world
in which the dialectic between faith and reason continues to engage us. The
dialectic is not to be resolved; it should be perceived as an opposition which
transforms life. Our capacity for fulfillment can come only through faith and
feelings. But our capacity for survival must come from reason and knowledge.

Is modern science hostile to our humanity? Max Born,[7] one of the developers 15
of the quantum theory, expressed concern about the permanence of the scientific
enterprise of the last three hundred years. Contemporary science, he felt, has
no fixed and solid place in the constellation of human life as do politics, religion,
or commerce. He wondered if humankind might ultimately abandon science.
If that should happen, it would sever our still-fragile connection with the cosmic
code—an error that might cost us our existence. I believe that future historians
will see contemporary civilization as response to the discovery of the worlds of
molecules, atoms, and the endless reaches of space and time. The challenge is
to bring these invisible realms to consciousness and to make human the enormous powers we find there.

Science is another name for knowledge, and we have not yet discovered the 16
boundary of knowledge, although we are discovering many other boundaries.
But knowledge is not enough. It must be tempered with justice, a sense of the
moral life, and our capacity for love and community. Science brings us to a
renewed appreciation of the human condition—the limitations of our existence
in the universe. Through the expansion of scientific awareness we learn again
and again not only of further advances of our material possibilities but of their
intrinsic limitations.

Genesis tells us about our first parents who were created in a garden paradise 17
and made its stewards by the Lord. There were two trees, the tree of knowledge
and the tree of life, and the Lord forbade them to eat of the fruit of the tree of
knowledge. The first parents tasted knowledge and hence knew good and evil.
They could now become, like the Lord, potentially infinite in knowledge. The
Lord cast them from the garden before they could eat from the tree of life and
become infinite in life as well. Humanity lives before the vision of infinite
knowledge but from a state of finite being.

Science is not the enemy of humanity but one of the deepest expressions of 18
the human desire to realize that vision of infinite knowledge. Science shows us
that the visible world is neither matter nor spirit; the visible world is the invisible
organization of energy. I do not know what the future sentences of the cosmic
code will be. But it seems certain that the recent human contact with the
invisible world of quanta and the vastness of the cosmos will shape the destiny
of our species or whatever we may become.

I used to climb mountains in snow and ice, hanging onto the sides of great 19

---

[7]Max Born (1882–1970): German physicist. [Eds.]

rocks. I was describing one of my adventures to an older friend once, and when I had finished he asked me, "Why do you want to kill yourself?" I protested. I told him that the rewards I wanted were of sight, of pleasure, of the thrill of pitting my body and my skills against nature. My friend replied, "When you are as old as I am you will see that you're are trying to kill youself."

I often dream about falling. Such dreams are commonplace to the ambitious 20 or those who climb mountains. Lately I dreamed I was clutching at the face of a rock but it would not hold. Gravel gave way. I grasped for a shrub, but it pulled loose, and in cold terror I fell into the abyss. Suddenly I realized that my fall was relative; there was no bottom and no end. A feeling of pleasure overcame me. I realized that what I embody, the principle of life, cannot be destroyed. It is written into the cosmic code, the order of the universe. As I continued to fall in the dark void, embraced by the vault of the heavens, I sang to the beauty of the stars and made my peace with the darkness.

QUESTIONS

1. Explain what Pagels means by "the cosmic code."

2. Pagels agrees with Steven Weinberg that the universe is "pointless and meaning-less" (paragraph 2). Most people would find such a view bleakly pessimistic; why isn't Pagels troubled?

3. How is the reading of the cosmic code of value to nonscientists? Do you agree with Pagels that scientific investigation—usually considered abstract and amoral—has moral, political, and economic consequences? Explain your answer.

4. How does the epigraph from Goethe's play *Faust* relate to Pagels's essay? (In context, these lines are spoken to a student by the devil who recommends experience over speculation about how to seduce a women.)

5. Pagels speaks of a conflict between poets and scientists in the second half of the essay. What values does each group represent? Can they be reconciled?

6. Does Pagels establish a relationship between the old poet of paragraphs 9 and 10 and the disturbed young man of paragraph 11? How fair are these relationships and these extreme examples?

7. Religion seems to be as antithetical to Pagels's beliefs as poetry, yet he uses the language of both in his final paragraphs. Do you find his use of such language effective? How does it dramatize a reconciliation of the scientific and poetic views of the universe?

8. Pagels recalls many personal conversations—with his Indian friend (paragraph 7), the poet (paragraphs 9 and 10), the disturbed young man (paragraph 11), and the older friend (paragraph 19). How does Pagels use these anecdotes in his essay? How does he comment on them or show their significance?

9. Pagels is reflecting on an abstract, even uncomfortable, subject that he grants "has left most educated people behind" (paragraph 12). He tries to meet this problem by

recounting biographical information, personal anecdotes, historical events, a Biblical account—in short, all sorts of events and experiences that may help make his point clearer to ordinary people. Try this technique yourself. Write an essay reflecting on something that is complicated to most people, but that you understand very well. Use a range of specific experience to convey your complex point to a reader who may feel left behind. Be careful, however, as Pagels is, not to talk down to this reader.

LENSES

Annie Dillard

Annie Dillard, naturalist, writer, and poet, is known for her poetic descriptions and meditations on the natural world. Her writings reflect her curiosity about nature, and she describes her nature voyages by saying: "I am an explorer, and I am also a stalker." Born in 1945 in Pittsburgh, Dillard graduated from Hollins College in the Blue Ridge Mountains of Virginia. Dillard settled in the area to investigate the natural world and to write. Her first book, Tickets for a Prayer Wheel *(1974), was closely followed by* A Pilgrim at Tinker Creek *(1974) for which she won a Pulitzer Prize. In the following selection, drawn from her essay collection* Teaching a Stone to Talk *(1982), Dillard observes the similarities between looking at pond life through a microscope and observing a pair of whistling swans through binoculars.*

You get used to looking through lenses; it is an acquired skill. When you first look through binoculars, for instance, you can't see a thing. You look at the inside of the barrel; you blink and watch your eyelashes; you play with the focus knob till one eye is purblind. 1

The microscope is even worse. You are supposed to keep both eyes open as you look through its single eyepiece. I spent my childhood in Pittsburgh trying to master this trick: seeing through one eye, with both eyes open. The microscope also teaches you to move your hands wrong, to shove the glass slide to the right if you are following a creature who is swimming off to the left—as if you were operating a tiller, or backing a trailer, or performing any other of those paradoxical maneuvers which require either sure instincts or a grasp of elementary physics, neither of which I possess. 2

A child's microscope set comes with a little five-watt lamp. You place this dim light in front of the microscope's mirror; the mirror bounces the light up through the slide, through the magnifying lenses, and into your eye. The only reason you do not see everything in silhouette is that microscopic things are so small they are translucent. The animals and plants in a drop of pond water pass light like pale stained glass; they seem so soaked in water and light that their opacity has leached away. 3

The translucent strands of algae you see under a microscope—Spirogyra, Oscillatoria, Cladophora—move of their own accord, no one knows how or why. You watch these swaying yellow, green, and brown strands of algae half mesmerized; you sink into the microscope's field forgetful, oblivious, as if it 4 were all a dream of your deepest brain. Occasionally a zippy rotifer comes barreling through, black and white, and in a tremendous hurry.

My rotifers and daphniae and amoebae were in an especially tremendous   5
hurry because they were drying up. I burnt out or broke my little five-watt bulb right away. To replace it, I rigged an old table lamp laid on its side; the table lamp carried a seventy-five-watt bulb. I was about twelve, immortal and invulberable, and did not know what I was doing; neither did anyone else. My parents let me set up my laboratory in the basement, where they wouldn't have to smell the urine I collected in test tubes and kept in vain hope it would grow something horrible. So in full, solitary ignorance I spent evenings in the basement staring into a seventy-five-watt bulb magnified three hundred times and focused into my eye. It is a wonder I can see at all. My eyeball itself would start drying up; I blinked and blinked.

But the pond water creatures fared worse. I dropped them on a slide, floated   6
a cover slip over them, and laid the slide on the microscope's stage, which the seventy-five-watt bulb had heated like a grill. At once the drop of pond water started to evaporate, Its edges shrank. The creatures swam among algae in a diminishing pool. I liked this part. The heat worked for me as a centrifuge, to concentrate the biomass. I had about five minutes to watch the members of a very dense population, excited by the heat, go about their business until—as I fancied sadly—they all caught on to their situation and started making out wills.

I was, then, not only watching the much-vaunted wonders in a drop of pond   7
water; I was also, with mingled sadism and sympathy, setting up a limitless series of apocalypses. I set up and staged hundreds of ends-of-the-world and watched, enthralled, as they played themselves out. Over and over again, the last trump sounded, the final scroll unrolled, and the known world drained, dried, and vanished. When all the creatures lay motionless, boiled and fried in the positions they had when the last of their water dried completely, I washed the slide in the sink and started over with a fresh drop. How I loved that deep, wet world where the colored algae waved in the water and the rotifers swam!

But oddly, this is a story about swans. It is not even a story; it is a description   8
of swans. This description of swans includes the sky over a pond, a pair of binoculars, and a mortal adult who had long since moved out of the Pittsburgh basement.

In the Roanoke valley of Virginia, rimmed by the Blue Ridge Mountains to   9
the east and the Allegheny Mountains to the west, is a little semi-agricultural area called Daleville. In Daleville, set among fallow fields and wooded ridges, is Daleville Pond. It is a big pond, maybe ten acres; it holds a lot of sky. I used to haunt the place because I loved it; I still do. In winter it had that airy

scruffiness of deciduous lands; you greet the daylight and the open space, and spend the evening picking burrs out of your pants.

One Valentine's Day, in the afternoon, I was crouched among dried reeds   10
at the edge of Daleville Pond. Across the pond from where I crouched was a low forested mountain ridge. In every other direction I saw only sky, sky crossed by the reeds which blew before my face whichever way I turned.

I was looking through binoculars at a pair of whistling swans. Whistling   11
swans! It is impossible to say how excited I was to see whistling swans in Daleville, Virginia. The two were a pair, mated for life, migrating north and west from the Atlantic coast to the high arctic. They had paused to feed at Daleville Pond. I had flushed them, and now they were flying and circling the pond. I crouched in the reeds so they would not be afraid to come back to the water.

Through binoculars I followed the swans, swinging where they flew. All their   12
feathers were white; their eyes were black. Their wingspan was six feet; they were bigger than I was. They flew in unison, one behind the other; they made pass after pass at the pond. I watched them change from white swans in front of the mountains to black swans in front of the sky. In clockwise ellipses they flew, necks long and relaxed, alternately beating their wings and gliding.

As I rotated on my heels to keep the black frame of the lenses around them,   13
I lost all sense of space. If I lowered the binoculars I was always amazed to learn in which direction I faced—dazed, the way you emerge awed from a movie and try to reconstruct, bit by bit, a real world, in order to discover where in it you might have parked the car.

I lived in that circle of light, in great speed and utter silence. When the   14
swans passed before the sun they were distant—two black threads, two live stitches. But they kept coming, smoothly, and the sky deepened to blue behind them and they took on light. They gathered dimension as they neared, and I could see their ardent, straining eyes. Then I could hear the brittle blur of their wings, the blur which faded as they circled on, and the sky brightened to yellow behind them and the swans flattened and darkened and diminished as they flew. Once I lost them behind the mountain ridge; when they emerged they were flying suddenly very high, and it was like music changing key.

I was lost. The reeds in front of me, swaying and out of focus in the binoc-   15
ulars' circular field, were translucent. The reeds were strands of color passing light like cells in water. They were those yellow and green and brown strands of pond algae I had watched so long in a light-soaked field. My eyes burned; I was watching algae wave in a shrinking drop; they crossed each other and parted wetly. And suddenly into the field swam two whistling swans, two tiny whistling swans. They swam as fast as rotifers: two whistling swans, infinitesimal, beating their tiny wet wings, perfectly formed.

QUESTIONS

1. Dillard describes the difficulties she had as a child trying to look through a microscope. What caused these difficulties? What is Dillard's purpose in describing these difficulties, and why does she devote six paragraphs to this description?

2. In paragraph 8, Dillard shifts her focus when she writes: "But oddly, this is a story about swans. It is not even a story; it is a description of swans." How does Dillard connect watching swans through binoculars with studying pond water under a microscope? Where in the essay does she emphasize this connection?

3. What does Dillard mean when she writes in paragraph 15: "I was lost. The reeds in front of me, swaying and out of focus in the binoculars' circular field, were translucent. The reeds were strands of color passing light like cells in water."

4. How could Dillard's swans "change from white swans in front of the mountain to black swans in front of the sky" (paragraph 12)? What comment is she making about the power of lenses and the powers of perception?

5. Dillard uses details and images very effectively to convey her observations to her readers. She writes, for instance, in paragraph 14: "I lived in that circle of light, in great speed and utter silence. When the swans passed before the sun they were distant—two black threads, two live stitches." Select details and images in the essay that you find effective, and explain why you think they work well.

6. Dillard compares one activity, looking through binoculars, to another, looking through a microscope. Select two activities which initially may seem dissimilar. Write an essay in which you describe these activities and develop an image to show their similarities.

7. Dillard is a careful observer of the natural world. Take your journal or a notepad and spend a few hours observing some aspect of nature. What do you see? What surprises you? What delights you? Write an essay in which you reflect on your observations.

THE BIRD AND THE MACHINE

Loren Eiseley

Loren Eiseley (1907–1977) rode the rails as a young hobo before he finished college, went to graduate school at the University of Pennsylvania, and began a distinguished career as an anthropologist, archaeologist, essayist, and poet. Through his writing, Eiseley made the ideas and findings of anthropology comprehensible to the public. He found significance in small incidents—the flights of birds, the web of a spider, and the chance encounter with a young fox. Eiseley once wrote that animals understand their roles, but that man, "bereft of instinct, must search continually for meanings." This essay is taken from his collection The Immense Journey *(1957).*

I suppose their little bones have years ago been lost among the stones and winds of those high glacial pastures. I suppose their feathers blew eventually into the piles of tumbleweed beneath the straggling cattle fences and rotted there in the mountain snows, along with dead steers and all the other things that drift to an end in the corners of the wire. I do not quite know why I should be thinking of birds over the *New York Times* at breakfast, particularly the birds of my youth half a continent away. It is a funny thing what the brain will do with memories and how it will treasure them and finally bring them into odd juxtapositions with other things, as though it wanted to make a design, or get some meaning out of them, whether you want it or not, or even see it.

It used to seem marvelous to me, but I read now that there are machines that can do these things in a small way, machines that can crawl about like animals, and that it may not be long now until they do more things—maybe even make themselves—I saw that piece in the *Times* just now. And then they will, maybe—well, who knows—but you read about it more and more with no one making any protest, and already they can add better than we and reach up and hear things through the dark and finger the guns over the night sky.

This is the new world that I read about at breakfast. This is the world that confronts me in my biological books and journals, until there are times when I sit quietly in my chair and try to hear the little purr of the cogs in my head and the tubes flaring and dying as the messages go through them and the circuits snap shut or open. This is the great age, make no mistake about it; the robot has been born somewhat appropriately along with the atom bomb, and the brain they say now is just another type of more complicated feedback system. The engineers have its basic principles worked out; it's mechanical, you know; nothing to get superstitious about; and man can always improve on nature once he gets the idea. Well, he's got it all right and that's why, I guess, that I sit here in my chair, with the article crunched in my hand, remembering those two birds and that blue mountain sunlight. There is another magazine article on my desk that reads "Machines Are Getting Smarter Every Day." I don't deny it, but I'll still stick with the birds. It's life I believe in, not machines.

Maybe you don't believe there is any difference. A skeleton is all joints and 4 pulleys, I'll admit. And when man was in his simpler stages of machine building in the eighteenth century, he quickly saw the resemblances. "What," wrote Hobbes, "is the heart but a spring, and the nerves but so many strings, and the joints but so many wheels, giving motion to the whole body?" Tinkering about in their shops it was inevitable in the end that men would see the world as a huge machine "subdivided into an infinite number of lesser machines."

The idea took on with a vengeance. Little automatons toured the country— 5 dolls controlled by clockwork. Clocks described as little worlds were taken on tours by their designers. They were made up of moving figures, shifting scenes and other remarkable devices. The life of the cell was unknown. Man, whether he was conceived as possessing a soul or not, moved and jerked about like these tiny puppets. A human being thought of himself in terms of his own tools and implements. He had been fashioned like the puppets he produced and was only a more clever model made by a greater designer.

Then in the nineteenth century, the cell was discovered, and the single 6 machine in its turn was found to be the product of millions of infinitesimal machines—the cells. Now, finally, the cell itself dissolves away into an abstract chemical machine—and that into some intangible, inexpressible flow of energy. The secret seems to lurk all about, the wheels get smaller and smaller, and they turn more rapidly, but when you try to seize it the life is gone—and so, by popular definition, some would say that life was never there in the first place. The wheels and the cogs are the secret and we can make them better in time— machines that will run faster and more accurately than real mice to real cheese.

I have no doubt it can be done, though a mouse harvesting seeds on an 7 autumn thistle is to me a fine sight and more complicated, I think, in his multiform activity, than a machine "mouse" running a maze. Also, I like to think of the possible shape of the future brooding in mice, just as it brooded once in a rather ordinary mousy insectivore who became a man. It leaves a nice fine indeterminate sense of wonder that even an electronic brain hasn't got, because you know perfectly well that if the electronic brain changes, it will be because of something man has done to it. But what man will do to himself he doesn't really know. A certain scale of time and a ghostly intangible thing called change are ticking in him. Powers and potentialities like the oak in the seed, or a red and awful ruin. Either way, it's impressive; and the mouse has it, too. Or those birds, I'll never forget those birds—yet before I measured their significance, I learned the lesson of time first of all. I was young then and left alone in a great desert—part of an expedition that had scattered its men over several hundred miles in order to carry on research more effectively. I learned there that time is a series of planes existing superficially in the same universe. The tempo is a human illusion, a subjective clock ticking in our own kind of protoplasm.

As the long months passed, I began to live on the slower planes and to observe more readily what passed for life there. I sauntered, I passed more and more slowly up and down the canyons in the dry baking heat of midsummer. I slumbered for long hours in the shade of huge brown boulders that had gathered in tilted companies out on the flats. I had forgotten the world of men and the world had forgotten me. Now and then I found a skull in the canyons, and these justified my remaining there. I took a serene cold interest in these discoveries. I had come, like many a naturalist before me, to view life with a wary and subdued attention. I had grown to take pleasure in the divested bone.

I sat once on a high ridge that fell away before me into a waste of sand dunes. I sat through hours of a long afternoon. Finally, as I glanced beside my boot an indistinct configuration caught my eye. It was a coiled rattlesnake, a big one. How long he had sat with me I do not know. I had not frightened him. We were both locked in the sleep-walking tempo of the earlier world, baking in the same high air and sunshine. Perhaps he had been there when I came. He slept on as I left, his coils, so ill discerned by me, dissolving once more among the stones and gravel from which I had barely made him out.

Another time I got on a higher ridge, among some tough little wind-warped pines half covered over with sand in a basin-like depression that caught everything carried by the air up to those heights. There were a few thin bones of birds, some cracked shells of indeterminable age, and the knotty fingers of pine roots bulged out of shape from their long and agonizing grasp upon the crevices of the rock. I lay under the pines in the sparse shade and went to sleep once more.

It grew cold finally, for autumn was in the air by then, and the few things that lived thereabouts were sinking down into an even chillier scale of time. In the moments between sleeping and waking I saw the roots about me and slowly, slowly, a foot in what seemed many centuries, I moved my sleep-stiffened hands over the scaling bark and lifted my numbed face after the vanishing sun. I was a great awkward thing of knots and aching limbs, trapped up there in some long, patient endurance that involved the necessity of putting living fingers into rock and by slow, aching expansion bursting those rocks asunder. I suppose, so thin and slow was the time of my pulse by then, that I might have stayed on to drift still deeper into the lower cadences of the frost, or the crystalline life that glisters in pebbles, or shines in a snowflake, or dreams in the meteoric iron between the worlds.

It was a dim descent, but time was present in it. Somewhere far down in   12
that scale the notion struck me that one might come the other way. Not many
months thereafter I joined some colleagues heading higher into a remote windy
tableland where huge bones were reputed to protrude like boulders from the
turf. I had drowsed with reptiles and moved with the century-long pulse of trees;
now, lethargically, I was climbing back up some invisible ladder of quickening
hours. There had been talk of birds in connection with my duties. Birds are
intense, fast-living creatures—reptiles, I suppose one might say, that have escaped out of the heavy sleep of time, transformed fairy creatures dancing over
sunlit meadows. It is a youthful fancy, no doubt, but because of something that
happened up there among the escarpments of that range, it remains with me a
lifelong impression. I can never bear to see a bird imprisoned.

We came into that valley through the trailing mists of a spring night. It was   13
a place that looked as though it might never have known the foot of man, but
our scouts had been ahead of us and we knew all about the abandoned cabin
of stone that lay far up on one hillside. It had been built in the land rush of
the last century and then lost to the cattlemen again as the marginal soils failed
to take to the plow.

There were spots like this all over that country. Lost graves marked by un-   14
lettered stones and old corroding rim-fire cartridge cases lying where somebody
had made a stand among the boulders that rimmed the valley. They are all that
remain of the range wars; the men are under the stones now. I could see our
cavalcade winding in and out through the mist below us: torches, the reflection
of the truck lights on our collecting tins, and the far-off bumping of a loose
dinosaur thigh bone in the bottom of a trailer. I stood on a rock a moment
looking down and thinking what it cost in money and equipment to capture the
past.

We had, in addition, instructions to lay hands on the present. The word had   15
come through to get them alive—birds, reptiles, anything. A zoo somewhere
abroad needed restocking. It was one of those reciprocal matters in which science
involves itself. Maybe our museum needed a stray ostrich egg and this was the
payoff. Anyhow, my job was to help capture some birds and that was why I was
there before the trucks.

The cabin had not been occupied for years. We intended to clean it out and   16
live in it, but there were holes in the roof and the birds had come in and were
roosting in the rafters. You could depend on it in a place like this where everything blew away, and even a bird needed some place out of the weather and
away from coyotes. A cabin going back to nature in a wild place draws them
till they come in, listening at the eaves, I imagine, pecking softly among the
shingles till they find a hole and then suddenly the place is theirs and man is
forgotten.

Sometimes of late years I find myself thinking the most beautiful sight in the   17
world might be the birds taking over New York after the last man has run away

111

to the hills. I will never live to see it, of course, but I know just how it will sound because I've lived up high and I know the sort of watch birds keep on us. I've listened to sparrows tapping tentatively on the outside of air conditioners when they thought no one was listening, and I know how other birds test the vibrations that come up to them through the television aerials.

"Is he gone?" they ask, and the vibrations come up from below, "Not yet, not yet." 18

Well, to come back, I got the door open softly and I had the spotlight all ready to turn on and blind whatever birds there were so they couldn't see to get out through the roof. I had a short piece of ladder to put against the far wall where there was a shelf on which I expected to make the biggest haul. I had all the information I needed just like any skilled assassin. I pushed the door open, the hinges squeaking only a little. A bird or two stirred—I could hear them— but nothing flew and there was a faint starlight through the holes in the roof. 19

I padded across the floor, got the ladder up and the light ready, and slithered up the ladder till my head and arms were over the shelf. Everything was dark as pitch except for the starlight at the little place back of the shelf near the eaves. With the light to blind them, they'd never make it. I had them. I reached my arm carefully over in order to be ready to seize whatever was there and I put the flash on the edge of the shelf where it would stand by itself when I turned it on. That way I'd be able to use both hands. 20

Everything worked perfectly except for one detail—I didn't know what kind of birds were there. I never thought about it at all, and it wouldn't have mattered if I had. My orders were to get something interesting. I snapped on the flash and sure enough there was a great beating and feathers flying, but instead of my having them, they, or rather he, had me. He had my hand, that is, and for a small hawk not much bigger than my fist he was doing all right. I heard him give one short metallic cry when the light went on and my hand descended on the bird beside him; after that he was busy with his claws and his beak was sunk in my thumb. In the struggle I knocked the lamp over on the shelf, and his mate got her sight back and whisked neatly through the hole in the roof and off among the stars outside. It all happened in fifteen seconds and you might think I would have fallen down the ladder, but no, I had a professional assassin's reputation to keep up, and the bird, of course, made the mistake of thinking the hand was the enemy and not the eyes behind it. He chewed my thumb up pretty effectively and lacerated my hand with his claws, but in the end I got him, having two hands to work with. 21

He was a sparrow hawk and a fine young male in the prime of life. I was sorry not to catch the pair of them, but as I dripped blood and folded his wings carefully, holding him by the back so that he couldn't strike again, I had to admit the two of them might have been more than I could have handled under the circumstances. The little fellow had saved his mate by diverting me, and that was that. He was born to it, and made no outcry now, resting in my hand 22 hopelessly, but peering toward me in the shadows behind the lamp with a fierce, almost indifferent glance. He neither gave nor expected mercy and something out of the high air passed from him to me, stirring a faint embarrassment.

I quit looking into that eye and managed to get my huge carcass with its fist 23 full of prey back down the ladder. I put the bird in a box too small to allow him to injure himself by struggle and walked out to welcome the arriving trucks. It had been a long day, and camp still to make in the darkness. In the morning that bird would be just another episode. He would go back with the bones in the truck to a small cage in a city where he would spend the rest of his life. And a good thing, too. I sucked my aching thumb and spat out some blood. An assassin has to get used to these things. I had a professional reputation to keep up.

In the morning, with the change that comes on suddenly in that high coun- 24 try, the mist that had hovered below us in the valley was gone. The sky was a deep blue, and one could see for miles over the high outcroppings of stone. I was up early and brought the box in which the little hawk was imprisoned out onto the grass where I was building a cage. A wind as cool as a mountain spring ran over the grass and stirred my hair. It was a fine day to be alive. I looked up and all around and at the hole in the cabin roof out of which the other little hawk had fled. There was no sign of her anywhere that I could see.

"Probably in the next county by now," I thought cynically, but before be- 25 ginning work I decided I'd have a look at my last night's capture.

Secretively, I looked again all around the camp and up and down and opened 26 the box. I got him right out in my hand with his wings folded properly and I was careful not to startle him. He lay limp in my grasp and I could feel his heart pound under the feathers but he only looked beyond me and up.

I saw him look that last look away beyond me into a sky so full of light that 27 I could not follow his gaze. The little breeze flowed over me again, and nearby a mountain aspen shook all its tiny leaves. I suppose I must have had an idea then of what I was going to do, but I never let it come up into consciousness. I just reached over and laid the hawk on the grass.

He lay there a long minute without hope, unmoving, his eyes still fixed on 28 that blue vault above him. It must have been that he was already so far away in heart that he never felt the release from my hand. He never even stood. He just lay with his breast against the grass.

In the next second after that long minute he was gone. Like a flicker of light, 29 he had vanished with my eyes full on him, but without actually seeing even a premonitory wing beat. He was gone straight into that towering emptiness of light and crystal that my eyes could scarcely bear to penetrate. For another long moment there was silence. I could not see him. The light was too intense. Then from far up somewhere a cry came ringing down.

I was young then and had seen little of the world, but when I heard that ³⁰ cry my heart turned over. It was not the cry of the hawk I had captured; for, by shifting my position against the sun, I was now seeing further up. Straight out of the sun's eye, where she must have been soaring restlessly above us for untold hours, hurtled his mate. And from far up, ringing from peak to peak of the summits over us, came a cry of such unutterable and ecstatic joy that it sounds down across the years and tingles among the cups on my quiet breakfast table.

I saw them both now. He was rising fast to meet her. They met in a great ³¹ soaring gyre that turned to a whirling circle and a dance of wings. Once more, just once, their two voices, joined in a harsh wild medley of question and response, struck and echoed against the pinnacles of the valley. Then they were gone forever somewhere into those upper regions beyond the eyes of men.

I am older now, and sleep less, and have seen most of what there is to see ³² and am not very much impressed any more, I suppose, by anything. "What Next in the Attributes of Machines?" my morning headline runs. "It Might Be the Power to Reproduce Themselves."

I lay the paper down and across my mind a phrase floats insinuatingly: "It ³³ does not seem that there is anything in the construction, constituents, or behavior of the human being which it is essentially impossible for science to duplicate and synthesize. On the other hand . . ."

All over the city the cogs in the hard, bright mechanisms have begun to ³⁴ turn. Figures move through computers, names are spelled out, a thoughtful machine selects the fingerprints of a wanted criminal from an array of thousands. In the laboratory an electronic mouse runs swiftly through a maze toward the cheese it can neither taste nor enjoy. On the second run it does better than a living mouse.

"On the other hand . . ." Ah, my mind takes up, on the other hand the ³⁵ machine does not bleed, ache, hang for hours in the empty sky in a torment of hope to learn the fate of another machine, nor does it cry out with joy nor dance in the air with the fierce passion of a bird. Far off, over a distance greater than space, that remote cry from the heart of heaven makes a faint buzzing among my breakfast dishes and passes on and away.

QUESTIONS

1. According to Eiseley, what is the difference between birds and machines?

2. Why does Eiseley tell the story about his experience as a young anthropologist exploring life in the American desert? How does this story relate to the rest of the essay?

3. Trace the associative movement of the writer's mind. How does one thought suggest another? How does this movement help illustrate his point?

4. Eiseley projects himself from the beginning as someone remembering and reflecting upon his experience. How did the meditative process of this essay, with its various twists and turns of thought, affect you as a reader?

5. Eiseley writes: "It is a funny thing what the brain will do with memories and how it will treasure them and finally bring them into odd juxtapositions with other things, as though it wanted to make a design, or get some meaning out of them, whether you want it or not, or even see it" (paragraph 1). Begin reflecting on some important memories from your childhood, and see where these reflections take you. As your mind wanders between past and present, see if any kind of design or meaning emerges for you. You may want to start with the first memory that comes to you by freewriting, writing down anything that goes through your mind for fifteen minutes without stopping. Then go back, and read what you've written. See what associations can be shaped into your own essay.

WRITING SUGGESTIONS FOR REFLECTING

1. Consider how living creatures are used as symbols in the reflections by two or three of the following writers: Isak Dinesen, Annie Dillard, and Loren Eiseley. How do the ways the writers use their symbols differ? How do these differences relate to each writer's larger purpose?

2. Maya Angelou, Frederick Douglass, Bertrand Russell, Russell Baker, and Lewis Thomas all reflect on some aspect of their educations. How does each writer share a memorable experience and show us why this experience was memorable? Why is the subject of education so suitable for reflective writing? Drawing on these essays or others you think are appropriate, write an essay defining *education* or defining and classifying different types of education.

3. Select two or three of the essays that present extended portraits of particular people. You might want to choose from those by N. Scott Momaday, Carl G. Jung, or Banesh Hoffmann. How do these writers differ in their techniques for presenting their subjects? In what ways do these differences relate to the purpose of each essay?

4. Examine the tones of two or three reflective pieces. How are they similar and different? How does the tone of each piece relate to the purposes of the writer?

5. A number of writers in this section offer their reflections in order to justify a belief or an opinion or a strong feeling about a subject. In other words, their reflections constitute a kind of argument. Consider one or more of these (such as the essays by Isak Dinesen, Martin Luther King, Jr., George Orwell, and Katherine Anne Porter). How convincing is the argument in each case? How has the writer used purely personal responses to make a persuasive case? How would you go about developing a more objective argument for the same position? What would be the difference in effect?

6. Certain writers in "Reflecting" consider professions. Select two or three of these essays. Compare and contrast what the writers say about the professions and how they say it. In what ways do they challenge or support your assumptions about these professions?

7. Choose one essay from each of the three disciplinary areas in this section. (The essays by N. Scott Momaday, Carl G. Jung, and Banesh Hoffmann would be one possibility.) In each case, trace the writer's movement of mind. How does each writer seem to be led from one thought to the next? Explore any particular similarities or differences among the three. Can you draw any conclusion about the relationship between a writer's field of interest and his or her process of thought?

8. Several writers mention how or why they became interested in their fields of study. Consider the essays by two or three of these writers, such as Bertrand Russell, Lewis Thomas, and Heinz R. Pagels. What accounts for their interest? How does each present this information to readers? Do their experiences interest you in their fields?

9. Many of the writers in this section reflect on turning points in their lives. Consider two or three of these essays, such as those by Maya Angelou, Frederick Douglass, Ber-

trand Russell, Martin Luther King, Jr., George Orwell, Carl G. Jung, Zoë Tracy Hardy, or Loren Eiseley. Compare and contrast the ways the writers present their turning points. How does each present the crucial moment or event, and how does each show its meaning?

10. Not surprisingly, some of these writers reflect on *how* to know or understand things. Consider two or three writers such as N. Scott Momaday, Joan Didion, Heinz R. Pagels, Annie Dillard, and Loren Eiseley. Compare and contrast their ideas about knowing and their techniques for conveying these ideas to readers.

11. For certain of these writers—such as Maya Angelou, Frederick Douglass, Russell Baker, Jeremy Seabrook, and Annie Dillard—the events of childhood or youth are particularly important. Consider how two or three of these writers view events when they were young, how they present their younger selves or viewpoints, and how they connect childhood to adulthood.

REPORTING

REPORTING

Here in "Reporting" you will find writing that reflects a wide array of academic and professional situations—an anthropologist describing the rhythm of daily life in a primitive South Seas culture, a brain surgeon detailing the progress of a delicate operation, a historian telling about the plague that swept through medieval Europe, a journalist recounting the air force mission that culminated in the atomic bombing of Nagasaki. Informative writing is basic in every field of endeavor, and the writers in this section seek to fulfill that basic need by reporting material drawn from various sources—a data recorder, a voice recorder, a microscope, a telescope, articles, books, public records, or firsthand observation. Working from such sources, these writers aim to provide detailed and reliable accounts of things—to give the background of a case, to convey the look and smell and feel of a place, to describe the appearance and behavior of people, to tell the story of recent or ancient events.

Though reporting depends on a careful gathering of information, it is by no means a mechanical and routine activity that consists simply of getting some facts and writing them up. Newspaper editors and criminal investigators, to be sure, often say they want "just the facts," but they know at last that in one way or another the facts are substantially shaped by the point of view of the person who is gathering and reporting them. By point of view, we mean both the physical and the mental standpoints from which a person observes or investigates something. Each of us, after all, stands at a particular point in space and time, as well as in thought and feeling, whenever we look at any subject. And wherever we stand in relation to the subject—whether we observe it close up or at a distance, in sunlight or in shadows, from one mental angle or another—will determine the particular aspects of it that we perceive and bring out in an account.

The influence that point of view exerts on reporting can be seen in the following passage from an article about an airline crash that took place outside of Washington, D.C., on December 1, 1974:

> According to the National Transportation Safety Board, today's was the first fatal crash by an airliner approaching Dulles, which opened in 1962.
> A T.W.A. spokesman said 85 passengers and a crew of seven were aboard the flight, which originated in Indianapolis. He said 46 persons got on at Columbus.
> The plane crashed about one and one-half miles from an underground complex

that reportedly is designed to serve as a headquarters for high government officials in the event of nuclear war. A Federal spokesman acknowledged only that the facility was operated by the little known Office of Preparedness, whose responsibilities, he said, include "continuity of government in a time of national disaster."

This report by the Associated Press (AP), which appeared in The New York Times on December 2, 1985, was evidently written by someone who had ready access to a number of sources, for virtually every bit of information in this excerpt comes from a different agency or "spokesman." In fact, the AP report as a whole refers not only to the three sources that are explicitly identified in this passage—namely, the "National Transportation Safety Board," a "T.W.A. spokesman," and a "Federal spokesman"—but also to twelve others including a county medical examiner, a telephone worker, a state police officer, a T.W.A. ground maintenance employee, and the Dulles control tower. Drawing upon these sources, the writer of this report is able not only to cover the vital statistics, such as the origin of the flight, the number of people aboard, and the location of the crash, but also to give a vividly detailed impression of the weather, the scarred landscape, and the scattered wreckage at and around the scene of the crash as well as to reveal some fascinating details about the "underground complex" near the site of the crash. As you read this piece, however, you will discover that it reports very little about the events leading up to the crash or about the circumstances that caused it, for the anonymous writer was evidently not in a position either to track the plane before the crash or to speculate about the cause of the crash only hours after it had taken place.

But an extensive investigation of the crash was carried out by the National Transportation Safety Board (NTSB), a federal agency which is charged with tracing the causes of airline accidents. Almost one year later, on November 26, 1975, the board issued an elaborately detailed, forty-two page report of its findings, a segment of which is reprinted in our collection. If you look at this segment of the NTSB "Aircraft Accident Report," you will see that it grew out of a completely different point of view from the one that produced the Associated Press report. The NTSB report, for example, does not make any reference to the "secret government installation" that is highlighted in the AP report; nor does it contain any vividly descriptive passages, like those in the AP report, about the weather, or the scarred landscape, or the scattered wreckage at the site of the crash; nor does it even mention some of the sources who figure prominently in the AP report, such as Captain William Carvello of the state police, Bill Smith of the Marshall, Virginia, Rescue Squad, Vance Berry of Bluemont, Virginia, and Richard Eastman, a ground maintenance employee of TWA. Conversely, some matters that are barely touched upon in the AP report are extensively covered in the NTSB report. In particular, the NTSB report provides a detailed "History of the Flight,' which includes summaries of cockpit conversation and navigational information at key points during the flight as well as excerpts of the conversation that took place among members of the flight crew during the last five minutes of the flight. And the NTSB report covers some topics that are not mentioned at all in the AP report, such as "Aids to Navigation" and "Aerodrome and Ground Facilities."

Given such striking differences in the emphases of these two pieces, you might wonder which one offers a more accurate report of the crash. Actually, both are true to the crash within the limits of their points of view on it. The AP report, for example, concentrates on the scene at the site of the crash, drawing material from a number of firsthand observers. This standpoint brings into focus the appalling spectacle that must have been visible on the mountainside where the crash took place. The NTSB report, by contrast, views the crash within a much broader context that takes into account not only a detailed history of the flight itself but also the complex system of navigational rules and procedures that were in effect at the time of the flight. And this perspective enables the NTSB to reveal that the mountainside crash resulted in part from serious "inadequacies and lack of clarity in the air traffic control procedures." Thus each point of view affords a special angle on the crash, obscuring some aspects of it, revealing others. And these are only two of many standpoints from which the crash might have been seen and reported. Imagine, for example, how the crash might have been viewed by workers who scoured the mountainside for remains of the passengers, or by specialists who identified their remains, or by relatives and friends of the victims, or by crews and passengers aboard other flights into Dulles that day.

Once you try to imagine the various perspectives from which anything can be observed or investigated, then you will see that no one person can possibly uncover everything there is to be known about something. For this reason, above all, point of view is an important aspect of reporting to be kept in mind by both readers and writers. As a reader of reportorial writing, you should always attempt to identify the point of views from which the information was gathered so as to help yourself assess the special strengths and weaknesses in the reporting that arise from that point of view as distinct from other possible points of view. By the same token, in your own reporting you should carefully decide upon the point of view that you already have or plan to use in observing or gathering information about something. Once you begin to pay deliberate attention to point of view, you will come to see that it is closely related to the various purposes for which people gather and report information in writing.

THE RANGE OF REPORTORIAL WRITING

The purpose of reporting is in one sense straightforward and self-evident, particularly when it is defined in terms of its commonly accepted value to readers. Whether it involves a firsthand account of some recent happening or the documented record of a long-past sequence of events, reportorial writing informs readers about the various subjects that may interest them but that they cannot observe or investigate on their own. You may never get to see chimpanzees in their native African habitats, but you can get a glimpse of their behavior through the firsthand account of Jane van Lawick-Goodall. So, too, you will probably never have occasion to make your way through the many public records and personal reports of the bubonic plague that beset Europe in the mid-fourteenth century, but you can get a synoptic view of the plague from Barbara Tuchman's account, which is based on an investigation of those sources. Reporting thus expands the range of its readers' perceptions and knowledge beyond the limits of their own immediate experiences. From the outlook of readers, then, the function of reporting does seem to be very clear-cut.

But if we shift our focus and look at reporting in terms of the purposes to which it is evidently put by writers, it often turns out to serve a more complex function than might at first be supposed. An example of this complexity can be seen in the following passage from van Lawick-Goodall's account:

> Suddenly I stopped, for I saw a slight movement in the long grass about sixty yards away. Quickly focusing my binoculars I saw that it was a single chimpanzee, and just then he turned in my direction. I recognized David Graybeard.
>
> Cautiously I moved around so that I could see what he was doing. He was squatting beside the red earth mound of a termite nest, and as I watched I saw him carefully push a long grass stem down into a hole in the mound. After a moment he withdrew it and picked something from the end with his mouth.

This passage seems on the whole to be a very neutral bit of scientific reporting that details van Lawick-Goodall's observation of a particular chimpanzee probing for food in a termite nest. The only unusual aspect of the report is her naming of the creature, which has the unscientific effect of personifying the animal. Otherwise, she is careful in the opening part of the description to establish the physical point of view from which she observed the chimpanzee—sixty yards away, looking at it through binoculars. And at the end of the passage she is equally careful not to identify or even conjecture about "something" beyond her range of detailed vision. As it turns out, however, this passage is a record not only of her observations but also of a pivotal moment in the story of how she came to make an important discovery about chimpanzees—that they are tool users—and thus how she came to regard their behavior as being much closer to that of human beings than had previously been supposed. So she climaxes her previous description of the chimpanzee with this sentence:

> I was too far away to make out what he was eating, but it was obvious that he was actually using a grass stem as a tool.

Here as elsewhere, then, her reporting is ingeniously worded and structured to make a strong case for her ideas about chimpanzee and human behavior. Thus she evidently intends her report to be both informative and persuasive.

A different set of purposes can be seen in yet another firsthand account—

this time of the atomic bomb that was dropped on Nagasaki on August 9, 1945, as observed by William L. Laurence:

> Observers in the tail of our ship saw a giant ball of fire rise as though from the bowels of the earth, belching forth enormous white smoke rings. Next they saw a giant pillar of purple fire, ten thousand feet high, shooting skyward with enormous speed.
>
> By the time our ship had made another turn in the direction of the atomic explosion the pillar of purple fire had reached the level of our altitude. Only about forty–five seconds had passed. Awe-struck, we watched it shoot upward like a meteor coming from the earth instead of from outer space, becoming ever more alive as it climbed skyward through the white clouds. It was no longer smoke, or dust, or even a cloud of fire. It was a living thing, a new species of being, born right before our incredulous eyes.
>
> At one stage of its evolution, covering millions of years in terms of seconds, the entity assumed the form of a giant square totem pole, with its base about three miles long, tapering off to about a mile at the top. Its bottom was brown, its center was amber, its top white. But it was a living totem pole, carved with many grotesque masks grimacing at the earth.

In this passage, Laurence seeks to describe the extraordinarily rapid and violent release of energy, fire, gas, smoke, and other debris that took place in the sky shortly after the bomb exploded on Nagasaki. The rapidity and violence of the release are clearly depicted through Laurence's extensive use of figurative language—through metaphors and similes that put these aspects of the scene in vividly familiar terms. He conveys the force of the explosion by referring to it as a "giant ball of fire . . . belching forth enormous white smoke rings." And he conveys the speed of the explosion by referring to it as a "giant pillar of purple fire" that shot "upward like a meteor." Yet it is also clear from some of the other similes in this passage that Laurence aims to convey not only the visually awesome but also the convulsively disturbing aspects of the explosion. Thus he compares the visual spectacle to a gigantic, multicolored "totem pole" and then goes on to describe the pole as being "carved with many grotesque masks grimacing at the earth." Here as elsewhere Laurence's report is calculatedly detailed and worded both to report the scene he observed and to convey his complex attitudes toward the scene. Clearly, he intends his report to be provocative as well as informative.

For yet another combination of purposes, you might look at Farley Mowat's informative, entertaining, and self-mocking account of his firsthand encounter with the territorial behavior of wolves. Or you might look at E. B. White's vivid, evocative, and contemplative report of his visit to a circus. Or you might turn to the NTSB report we discussed earlier in this introduction, and you will see that it is clearly intended not only to convey information pertaining to the cause of the airline crash but also to make a case for various procedural changes that might prevent similar accidents in the future.

As is apparent from just this handful of selections, writers invariably seem to use reporting for a combination of purposes—not only to provide information but also to convey their attitudes, beliefs, or ideas about it as well as to influence the views of their readers. This joining of purposes is hardly surprising, given the factors involved in any decision to report on something. After all, whenever we make a report, we do so presumably because we believe that the subject of our report is important enough for others to be told about it. And presumably we believe the subject to be important because of what we have come to know and think about it. So, when we are faced with deciding what information to report and how to report it, we inevitably base our decisions on these ideas. At every point in the process of planning and writing a report, we act on the basis of our particular motives and priorities for conveying information about the subject. And how could we do otherwise? How else could William Laurence have decided what to emphasize out of all the activities that he must have noted during the flight to and from the bombing of Nagasaki? How else could Jane van Lawick-Goodall have decided what information to report out of all she must have observed during her first few months in Africa? Without specific purposes to control our reporting, our records of events would be as long as the events themselves.

Reporting, as you can see, necessarily serves a widely varied range of purposes—as varied as are writers and their subjects. Thus whenever you read a piece of reportorial writing, you should always try to discover for yourself what appear to be its guiding purposes by examining its structure, its phrasing, and its wording, much as we have earlier in this discussion. And once you have identified the purpose, you should then consider how it has influenced the selection, arrangement, and weighting of information in the report. When you turn to doing your own writing, you should be equally careful in determining your purposes for reporting and in organizing your report so as to put the information in a form that is true to what you know and think about the subject.

METHODS OF REPORTING

In planning a piece of reportorial writing, you should be sure to keep in mind not only your ideas about the subject, but also the needs of your readers. Given the fact that most of your readers will probably not be familiar with your information, you should be very careful in selecting and organizing it so that you give them a clear and orderly report of it. Usually, you will find that the nature of your information suggests a corresponding method of presenting it most clearly and conveniently to your readers.

For example, if the information concerns a single, detailed event or covers a set of events spread over time, then the most natural presentation probably is narration—the form of story telling—in a more or less chronological order. This is the basic form that van Lawick-Goodall uses in recounting her first few months of observation in Africa, and it proves to be a very clear and persuasive form for gradually unfolding her discovery about the behavior of chimpanzees. If the information concerns a particular place or scene or spectacle, then the most convenient method is description, presenting your information in a clear–cut spatial order so as to help your reader visualize both the overall scene and its important details. This is the basic form that E. B. White uses in "The Ring of Time," first having us watch an older woman guide a circus horse around a practice ring, then having us watch a younger woman ride the same horse around the ring in a practice session of her own—an echoing of the spatial situation that keeps our attention on the ring and its special significance for White. If the information is to provide a synoptic body of knowledge about a particular subject, then the clearest form may be a topical summation, using a set of categories appropriate to the subject and familiar to readers. This is the basic form used in the NTSB report, which takes us through a comprehensive survey of material about the airline crash, methodically organized under clearly defined topical headings, such as "History of the Flight," "Meteorological Information," "Aids to Navigation," "Wreckage," "Medical and Pathological Information," and "Survival Aspects."

Although narration, description, topical summation, and other forms of presentation for reporting are often treated separately for purposes of convenience in identifying each of them, it is well to keep in mind that they usually end up working in some sort of combination with one another. Narratives, after all, involve not only events but also people and places, so it is natural that they include descriptive passages. Similarly, descriptions of place frequently entail stories about events taking place in them, so it is not surprising that they include bits of narration. And given the synoptic nature of topical summations, they are likely to include both descriptive and narrative elements. In writing, as in most other activities, form should follow function rather than be forced to fit arbitrary rules of behavior.

Once you have settled upon a basic form, you should then devise a way of managing your information within that form—of selecting, arranging, and proportioning it—so as to achieve your purposes most effectively. To carry out this task, you will need to review all of the material you have gathered with an eye to determining what you consider to be the most important information to report. Some bits or kinds of information inevitably will strike you as more significant than others, and these are the ones that you should feature in your report. Likewise, you will probably find that some information is simply not important enough even to be mentioned in your report. Van Lawick-Goodall, for example, is able to produce a striking account of her first few months in Africa because she focuses primarily on her observation of the chimpanzees, subordinating all of the other material she reports to her discoveries about their behavior. Thus only on a couple of occasions does she include observations about the behavior of animals other than chimpanzees—in particular about the timidities of a bushbuck and a leopard. And she only includes these observations to point up by contrast the distinctively sociable behavior of chimpanzees. For much the same reasons, she proportions her coverage of the several chimpanzee episodes she reports so as to give the greatest amount of detail to the one that provides the most compelling indication of their advanced intelligence—namely, the final episode, which shows the chimpanzees to be tool users and makers, a behavior previously attributed only to human beings.

To help achieve your purposes, you should also give special thought to deciding on the perspective through which you present your information to the reader. Do you want to present the material in first or third person? Do you want to be present in the piece, as are van Lawick-Goodall and Laurence? Or do you want to be invisible, as are the authors of the AP and NTSB reports? To some extent, of course, your answer to this question will depend upon whether you gathered the information through firsthand observation and then want to convey your firsthand reactions to your observations, as van Lawick-Goodall and Laurence do in their pieces. But just to show that there are no hard-and-fast rules on this score, you might look at "A Delicate Operation" by Roy C. Selby, Jr. You will notice at once that although Dr. Selby must have written this piece on the basis of firsthand experience, he tells the story in third person, removing himself almost completely from it except for such distant-sounding references to himself as "the surgeon." Clearly, Dr. Selby is important to the information in this report, yet he evidently decided to de-emphasize himself in writing the report. In order to see just how important it is to consider these alternatives in planning any report, you might look at another doctor's account based on firsthand experience, namely Richard Selzer's "The Discus Thrower." Dr. Selzer, as you will see, reports his observations of a particular patient through a first-person perspective, despite the fact that you might suppose him to be relatively unimportant to the information in this particular case. If the perspectives of these two reports were reversed—you might take a stab at changing them around yourself—you would find the contents and effects of both reports to be surprisingly different. Ultimately, then, the nature of a report is substantially determined not only by *what* a writer gathers from various sources but also by *how* a writer presents the information.

In the pieces that follow in this section, you will have an opportunity to see how the writers of eighteen different reports present things in language. In later sections, you will see how reporting combines with other kinds of writing—explaining and arguing.

Arts and Humanities

THE RING OF TIME
E. B. White

Elwyn Brooks White (1899–1985) began writing in various capacities for The New Yorker *in 1926, soon after the magazine's inception. In 1957, he retired to his farm in Maine, where he continued to write. White has been called with some justice "the finest essayist in the United States" because of the grace and clarity of his writing and the range of his interests. As White himself said, the essayist thoroughly enjoys his work because "he can pull on any sort of shirt, be any sort of person, according to his mood or his subject matter." Here, in "The Ring of Time," we see him as "recording secretary" for circus lovers, taking a small event and endowing it with significance.*

FIDDLER BAYOU, March 22, 1956—After the lions had returned to their   1
cages, creeping angrily through the chutes, a little bunch of us drifted away and into an open doorway nearby, where we stood for a while in semidarkness, watching a big brown circus horse go harumphing around the practice ring. His trainer was a woman of about forty, and the two of them, horse and woman, seemed caught up in one of those desultory treadmills of afternoon from which there is no apparent escape. The day was hot, and we kibitzers were grateful to be briefly out of the sun's glare.[1] The long rein, or tape, by which the woman guided her charge counterclockwise in his dull career formed the radius of their private circle, of which she was the revolving center; and she, too, stepped a tiny circumference of her own, in order to accommodate the horse and allow him his maximum scope. She had on a short-skirted costume and a conical straw hat. Her legs were bare and she wore high heels, which probed deep into the loose tanbark and kept her ankles in a state of constant turmoil. The great

---

[1]kibitzers: a Yiddish word for people who interfere and who give advice gratuitously; meddlesome onlookers. [Eds.]

size and meekness of the horse, the repetitious exercise, the heat of the afternoon, all exerted a hypnotic charm that invited boredom; we spectators were
experiencing a languor—we neither expected relief nor felt entitled to any. We
had paid a dollar to get into the grounds, to be sure, but we had got our dollar's
worth a few minutes before, when the lion trainer's whiplash had got caught
around a toe of one of the lions. What more did we want for a dollar?

Behind me I heard someone say, "Excuse me, please," in a low voice. She 2
was halfway into the building when I turned and saw her—a girl of sixteen or
seventeen, politely threading her way through us onlookers who blocked the
entrance. As she emerged in front of us, I saw that she was barefoot, her dirty
little feet fighting the uneven ground. In most respects she was like any of two
or three dozen showgirls you encounter if you wander about the winter quarters
of Mr. John Ringling North's circus, in Sarasota—cleverly proportioned, deeply
browned by the sun, dusty, eager, and almost naked. But her grave face and
the naturalness of her manner gave her a sort of quick distinction and brought
a new note into the gloomy octagonal building where we had all cast our lot
for a few moments. As soon as she had squeezed through the crowd, she spoke
a word or two to the older woman, whom I took to be her mother, stepped to
the ring, and waited while the horse coasted to a stop in front of her. She gave
the animal a couple of affectionate swipes on his enormous neck and then swung
herself aboard. The horse immediately resumed his rocking canter, the woman
goading him on, chanting something that sounded like "Hop! Hop!"

In attempting to recapture this mild spectacle, I am merely acting as recording 3
secretary for one of the oldest of societies—the society of those who, at one time
or another, have surrendered, without even a show of resistance, to the bedaz-
zlement of a circus rider. As a writing man, or secretary, I have always felt
charged with the safekeeping of all unexpected items of worldly or unworldly
enchantment, as though I might be held personally responsible if even a small
one were to be lost. But it is not easy to communicate anything of this nature.
The circus comes as close to being the world in microcosm as anything I know;
in a way, it puts all the rest of show business in the shade. Its magic is universal
and complex. Out of its wild disorder comes order; from its rank smell rises the
good aroma of courage and daring; out of its preliminary shabbiness comes the
final splendor. And buried in the familiar boasts of its advance agents lies the
modesty of most of its people. For me the circus is at its best before it has been
put together. It is at its best at certain moments when it comes to a point, as
through a burning glass, in the activity and destiny of a single performer out of
so many. One ring is always bigger than three. One rider, one aerialist, is always
greater than six. In short, a man has to catch the circus unawares to experience
its full impact and share its gaudy dream.

The ten-minute ride the girl took achieved—as far as I was concerned, who 4
wasn't looking for it, and quite unbeknownst to her, who wasn't even striving
for it—the thing that is sought by performers everywhere, on whatever stage,

whether struggling in the tidal currents of Shakespeare or bucking the difficult motion of a horse. I somehow got the idea she was just cadging a ride, improving a shining ten minutes in the diligent way all serious artists seize free moments to hone the blade of their talent and keep themselves in trim. Her brief tour included only elementary postures and tricks, perhaps because they were all she was capable of, perhaps because her warmup at this hour was unscheduled and the ring was not rigged for a real practice session. She swung herself off and on the horse several times, gripping his mane. She did a few knee-stands—or whatever they are called—dropping to her knees and quickly bouncing back up on her feet again. Most of the time she simply rode in a standing position, well aft on the beast, her hands hanging easily at her sides, her head erect, her straw-colored ponytail lightly brushing her shoulders, the blood of exertion showing faintly through the tan of her skin. Twice she managed a one-foot stance—a sort of ballet pose, with arms outstretched. At one point the neck strap of her bathing suit broke and she went twice around the ring in the classic attitude of a woman making minor repairs to a garment. The fact that she was standing on the back of a moving horse while doing this invested the matter with a clownish significance that perfectly fitted the spirit of the circus—jocund, yet charming. She just rolled the strap into a neat ball and stowed it inside her bodice while the horse rocked and rolled beneath her in dutiful innocence. The bathing suit proved as self-reliant as its owner and stood up well enough without benefit of strap.

The richness of the scene was in its plainness, its natural condition—of horse, of ring, of girl, even to the girl's bare feet that gripped the bare back of her proud and ridiculous mount. The enchantment grew not out of anything that happened or was performed but out of something that seemed to go round and around and around with the girl, attending her, a steady gleam in the shape of a circle—a ring of ambition, of happiness, of youth. (And the positive pleasures of equilibrium under difficulties.) In a week or two, all would be changed, all (or almost all) lost: the girl would wear makeup, the horse would wear gold, the ring would be painted, the bark would be clean for the feet of the horse, the girl's feet would be clean for the slippers that she'd wear. All, all would be lost.

As I watched with the others, our jaws adroop, our eyes alight, I became painfully conscious of the element of time. Everything in the hideous old building seemed to take the shape of a circle, conforming to the course of the horse. The rider's gaze, as she peered straight ahead, seemed to be circular, as though bent by force of circumstance; then time itself began running in circles, and so the beginning was where the end was, and the two were the same, and one thing ran into the next and time went round and around and got nowhere. The girl wasn't so young that she did not know the delicious satisfaction of having a perfectly behaved body and the fun of using it to do a trick most people can't do, but she was too young to know that time does not really move in a circle at all. I thought: "She will never be as beautiful as this again"—a thought that

131

made me acutely unhappy—and in a flash my mind (which is too much of a busybody to suit me) had projected her twenty-five years ahead, and she was now in the center of the ring, on foot, wearing a conical hat and high-heeled shoes, the image of the older woman, holding the long rein, caught in the treadmill of an afternoon long in the future. "She is at that enviable moment in life [I thought] when she believes she can go once around the ring, make one complete circuit, and at the end be exactly the same age as at the start." Everything in her movements, her expression, told you that for her the ring of time was perfectly formed, changeless, predictable, without beginning or end, like the ring in which she was traveling at this moment with the horse that wallowed under her. And then I slipped back into my trance, and time was circular again—time, pausing quietly with the rest of us, so as not to disturb the balance of a performer.

Her ride ended as casually as it had begun. The older woman stopped the 7 horse, and the girl slid to the ground. As she walked toward us to leave, there was a quick, small burst of applause. She smiled broadly, in surprise and pleasure; then her face suddenly regained its gravity and she disappeared through the door.

It has been ambitious and plucky of me to attempt to describe what is in- 8 describable, and I have failed, as I knew I would. But I have discharged my duty to my society; and besides, a writer, like an acrobat, must occasionally try a stunt that is too much for him. At any rate, it is worth reporting that long before the circus comes to town, its most notable performances have already been given. Under the bright lights of the finished show, a performer need only reflect the electric candle power that is directed upon him; but in the dark and dirty old training rings and in the makeshift cages, whatever light is generated, whatever excitement, whatever beauty, must come from original sources—from internal fires of professional hunger and delight, from the exuberance and gravity of youth. It is the difference between planetary light and the combustion of stars.

QUESTIONS

1. In paragraph 3, White describes his role as "recording secretary" for those who love circus riders. In the first two paragraphs, he does record or report what he observed. But how is paragraph 3 different from the first two? How much of the essay is actually devoted to reporting events?

2. The events in the essay are presented chronologically, but in what different ways is time felt and described within that structure? Why is this essay entitled "The Ring of Time"?

3. Why does White say the circus is "as close to being the world in microcosm as anything I know" (paragraph 3)? How would you describe the circus? What circus performers do you prefer watching? Why?

4. Why does White say at the end that he has failed in attempting "to describe what is indescribable" (paragraph 8)? Do you agree with him? In what sections of the essay do you find him most successful at describing?

5. Write a paragraph or two in which you report the same events from the girl's point of view. You will have to decide whether she would be aware of how she looked, or of the audience watching her.

6. For an essay of your own, observe a practice session of an orchestra, an athletic team, a drama group, or a studio art or ballet class. Concentrate on one person in the group you are observing, and report that person's actions. Then consider that person as representative of the entire group and what they are practicing for.

LOOKING FOR ZORA

Alice Walker

Born in Eatonton, Georgia, in 1944, Alice Walker was the youngest of eight children. Her father was a sharecropper, and her mother was a maid. A graduate of Sarah Lawrence College, Walker has been an active worker for civil rights. She has been a fellow of the Radcliffe Institute, a contributing and consulting editor for Ms. magazine, and a teacher of literature and writing at a number of colleges and universities. She has published poetry, short stories, and three novels, The Third Life of Grange Copeland (1970), Meridian (1976), and The Color Purple (1982), for which Walker won the Pultizer Prize. "Looking for Zora" first appeared in a collection of essays, In Search of Our Mother's Gardens (1975), and later in a Zora Neale Hurston reader edited by Walker. When asked why she writes, Walker said, "I'm really paying homage to people I love, the people who are thought to be dumb and backward but who were the ones who first taught me to see beauty."

On January 16, 1959, Zora Neale Hurston, suffering from the effects of a stroke and writing painfully in longhand, composed a letter to the "editorial department" of Harper and Brothers inquiring if they would be interested in seeing "the book I am laboring upon at present—a life of Herod the Great." One year and twelve days later, Zora Neale Hurston died without funds to provide for her burial, a resident of the St. Lucie County, Florida, Welfare Home. She lies today in an unmarked grave in a segregated cemetery in Fort Pierce, Florida, a resting place generally symbolic of the black writer's fate in America.

Zora Neale Hurston is one of the most significant unread authors in America, the author of two minor classics and four other major books.

—Robert Hemenway, "Zora Hurston and the Eatonville Anthropology," in *The Harlem Renaissance Remembered*[1]

On August 15, 1973, I wake up just as the plane is lowering over Sanford, Florida, which means I am also looking down on Eatonville, Zora Neale Hurston's birthplace. I recognize it from Zora's description in *Mules and Men:* "the city of five lakes, three croquet courts, three hundred brown skins, three hundred good swimmers, plenty guavas, two schools and no jailhouse." Of course I

1

---

[1]Harlem Renaissance: the flowering of Afro-American arts centered in Harlem during the 1920s. [Eds.]

cannot see the guavas, but the five lakes are still there, and it is the lakes I count as the plane prepares to land in Orlando.

From the air, Florida looks completely flat, and as we near the ground this impression does not change. This is the first time I have seen the interior of the state, which Zora wrote about so well, but there are the acres of orange groves, the sand, mangrove trees, and scrub pine that I know from her books. Getting off the plane I walk through the hot moist air of midday into the tacky but air-conditioned airport. I search for Charlotte Hunt, my companion on the Zora Hurston expedition. She lives in Winter Park, Florida, very near Eatonville, and is writing her graduate dissertation on Zora. I see her waving—a large, pleasant faced white woman in dark glasses. We have written to each other for several weeks, swapping our latest finds (mostly hers) on Zora, and trying to make sense out of the mass of information obtained (often erroneous or simply confusing) from Zora herself—through her stories and autobiography—and from people who wrote about her.

Eatonville has lived for such a long time in my imagination that I can hardly believe it will be found existing in its own right. But after twenty minutes on the expressway, Charlotte turns off and I see a small settlement of houses and stores set with no particular pattern in the sandy soil off the road. We stop in front of a neat gray building that has two fascinating signs: EATONVILLE POST OFFICE and EATONVILLE CITY HALL.

Inside the Eatonville City Hall half of the building, a slender, dark-brown-skin woman sits looking through letters on a desk. When she hears we are searching for anyone who might have known Zora Neale Hurston, she leans back in thought. Because I don't wish to inspire foot-dragging in people who might know something about Zora they're not sure they should tell, I have decided on a simple, but I feel profoundly *useful*, lie.

"I am Miss Hurston's niece," I prompt the young woman, who brings her head down with a smile.

"I think Mrs. Moseley is about the only one still living who might remember her," she says.

"Do you mean *Mathilda* Moseley, the woman who tells those 'woman-is-smarter-than-man' lies in Zora's book?"

"Yes," says the young woman. "Mrs. Moseley is real old now, of course. But this time of day, she should be at home."

I stand at the counter looking down on her, the first Eatonville resident I have spoken to. Because of Zora's books, I feel I know something about her; at least I know what the town she grew up in was like years before she was born.

"Tell me something," I say. "Do the schools teach Zora's books here?"

"No," she says, "they don't. I don't think most people know anything about Zora Neale Hurston, or know about any of the great things she did. She was a fine lady. I've read all of her books myself, but I don't think many other folks in Eatonville have."

"Many of the church people around here, as I understand it," says Charlotte   12
in a murmured aside, "thought Zora was pretty loose. I don't think they appreciated her writing about them."

"Well," I say to the young woman, "thank you for your help." She clarifies   13
her directions to Mrs. Moseley's house and smiles as Charlotte and I turn to
go.

The letter to Harper's does not expose a publisher's rejection of an unknown
masterpiece, but it does reveal how the bright promise of the Harlem Renaissance
deteriorated for many of the writers who shared in its exuberance. It also indicates
the personal tragedy of Zora Neale Hurston: Barnard graduate, author of four
novels, two books of folklore, one volume of autobiography, the most important
collector of Afro-American folklore in America, reduced by poverty and circumstance to seek a publisher by unsolicited mail.

—Robert Hemenway

Zora Hurston was born in 1901, 1902, or 1903—depending on how old she felt
to be at the time someone asked.

—Librarian, Beinecke Library
Yale University

The Moseley house is small and white and snug, its tiny yard nearly swal-   14
lowed up by oleanders and hibiscus bushes. Charlotte and I knock on the door.
I call out. But there is no answer. This strikes us as peculiar. We have had time
to figure out an age for Mrs. Moseley—not dates or a number, just old. I am
thinking of a quivery, bedridden invalid when we hear the car. We look behind
us to see an old black-and-white Buick, paint peeling and grillwork rusty—
pulling into the drive. A neat old lady in a purple dress and white hair is straining
at the wheel. She is frowning because Charlotte's car is in the way.

Mrs. Moseley looks at us suspiciously. "Yes, I knew Zora Neale," she says,   15
unsmilingly and with a rather cold stare at Charlotte (who I imagine, feels very
white at that moment), "but that was a long time ago, and I don't want to talk
about it."

"Yes, ma'am," I murmur, bringing all my sympathy to bear on the situation.   16

"Not only that," Mrs. Moseley continues, "I've been sick. Been in the hos-   17
pital for an operation. Ruptured artery. The doctors didn't believe I was going
to live, but you see me alive, don't you?"

"Looking well, too," I comment.   18

Mrs. Moseley is out of her car. A thin, sprightly woman with nice gold-   19
studded false teeth, uppers and lowers. I like her because she stands there *straight*
beside her car, with a hand on her hip and her straw pocketbook on her arm.
She wears white T-strap shoes with heels that show off her well-shaped legs.

"I'm eighty-two years old, you know," she says. "And I just can't remember   20
things the way I used to. Anyhow, Zora Neale left here to go to school and she

136

never really came back to live. She'd come here for material for her books, but
that was all. She spent most of her time down in South Florida."

"You know, Mrs. Moseley, I saw your name in one of Zora's books."   21

"You did?" She looks at me with only slightly more interest. "I read some   22
of her books a long time ago, but the people got to borrowing and borrowing
and they borrowed them all away."

"I could send you a copy of everything that's been reprinted." I offer. "Would   23
you like me to do that?"

"No," says Mrs. Moseley promptly. "I don't read much any more. Besides,   24
all of that was so long ago. . . ."

Charlotte and I settle back against the car in the sun. Mrs. Moseley tells us   25
at length and with exact recall every step in her recent operation, ending with:
"What those doctors didn't know—when they were expecting me to die (and
they didn't even think I'd live long enough for them to have to take out my
stitches!)—is that Jesus is the best doctor, and if *He* says for you to get well,
that's all that counts."

With this philosophy, Charlotte and I murmur quick assent: being southern-   26
ers and church bred, we have heard that belief before. But what we learn from
Mrs. Moseley is that she does not remember much beyond the year 1938. She
shows us a picture of her father and mother and says that her father was Joe
Clarke's brother. Joe Clarke, as every Zora Hurston reader knows, was the first
mayor of Eatonville; his fictional counterpart is Jody Starks of *Their Eyes Were
Watching God*. We also get directions to where Joe Clarke's store *was*—where
Club Eaton is now. Club Eaton, a long orange-beige nightspot we had seen on
the main road, is apparently famous for the good times in it regularly had by
all. It is, perhaps, the modern equivalent of the store porch, where all the men
of Zora's childhood came to tell "lies," that is, black folk tales, that were "made
and used on the spot," to take a line from Zora. As for Zora's exact birthplace,
Mrs. Moseley has no idea.

After I have commented on the healthy growth of her hibiscus bushes, she   27
becomes more talkative. She mentions how much she *loved* to dance, when
she was a young woman, and talks about how good her husband was. When
he was alive, she says, she was completely happy because he allowed her to be
completely free. "I was so free I had to pinch myself sometimes to tell if I was
a married woman."

Relaxed now, she tells us about going to school with Zora. "Zora and I went   28
to the same school. It's called Hungerford High now. It *was* only to the eighth
grade. But our teachers were so good that by the time you left you knew college
subjects. When I went to Morris Brown in Atlanta, the teachers there were just
teaching me the same things I had already learned right in Eatonville. I wrote
Mama and told her I was going to come home and help her with her babies. I
wasn't learning anything new."

"Tell me something, Mrs. Moseley," I ask. "Why do you suppose Zora was   29
against integration? I read somewhere that she was against school desegregation
because she felt it was an insult to black teachers."

"Oh, one of them [white people] came around asking me about integration.   30
One day I was doing my shopping. I heard 'em over there talking about it in
the store, about the schools. And I got on out of the way because I knew if they
asked me, they wouldn't like what I was going to tell 'em. But they came up
and asked me anyhow. 'What do you think about this integration?' one of them
said. I acted like I thought I had heard wrong. 'You're asking *me* what I think
about integration?' I said. 'Well, as you can see, I'm just an old colored woman—
I was seventy-five or seventy-six then—and this is the first time anybody ever
asked me about integration. And nobody asked my grandmother what she thought,
either, but her daddy was one of you all.' " Mrs. Moseley seems satisfied with
this memory of her rejoinder. She looks at Charlotte. "I have the blood of three
races in my veins," she says belligerently, "white, black, and Indian, and nobody
asked me *anything* before."

"Do you think living in Eatonville made integration less appealing to you?"   31

"Well, I can tell you this: I have lived in Eatonville all my life, and I've   32
been in the governing of this town. I've been everything but mayor and I've
been *assistant* mayor. Eatonville was and is an all-black town. We have our
own police department, post office, and town hall. Our own school and good
teachers. Do I need integration?

"They took over Goldsboro, because the black people who lived there never   33
incorporated, like we did. And now I don't even know if any black folks live
there. They built big houses up there around the lakes. But we didn't let that
happen in Eatonville, and we don't sell land to just anybody. And you see,
we're still here."

When we leave, Mrs. Moseley is standing by her car, waving. I think of the   34
letter Roy Wilkins wrote to a black newspaper blasting Zora Neale for her lack
of enthusiasm about the integration of schools. I wonder if he knew the experience of Eatonville she was coming from. Not many black people in America
have come from a self-contained, all-black community where loyalty and unity
are taken for granted. A place where black pride is nothing new.

There is, however, one thing Mrs. Moseley said that bothered me.   35

"Tell me, Mrs. Moseley," I had asked, "why is it that thirteen years after   36
Zora's death, no marker has been put on her grave?"

And Mrs. Moseley answered: "The reason she doesn't have a stone is because   37
she wasn't buried here. She was buried down in South Florida somewhere. I
don't think anybody really knew where she was."

Only to reach a wider audience, need she ever write books—because she is a
perfect book of entertainment in herself. In her youth she was always getting
scholarships and things from wealthy white people, some of whom simply paid
her just to sit around and represent the Negro race for them, she did it in such a

138

racy fashion. She was full of sidesplitting anecdotes, humorous tales, and tragi-comic stories, remembered out of her life in the South as a daughter of a traveling minister of God. She could make you laugh one minute and cry the next. To many of her white friends, no doubt, she was a perfect "darkie," in the nice meaning they give the term—that is, a naive, childlike, sweet, humorous, and highly colored Negro.

But Miss Hurston was clever, too—a student who didn't let college give her a broad "a" and who had scorn for all pretensions, academic or otherwise. That is why she was such a fine folklore collector, able to go among the people and never act as if she had been to school at all. Almost nobody else could stop the average Harlemite on Lenox Avenue and measure his head with a strange-looking, an-thropological device and not get bawled out for the attempt, except Zora, who used to stop anyone whose head looked interesting, and measure it.

—Langston Hughes,[2]
The Big Sea

What does it matter what white folks must have thought about her?

—Student,
black women writers' class, Wellesley College

Mrs. Sarah Peek Patterson is a handsome, red-haired woman in her late   38
forties, wearing orange slacks and gold earrings. She is the director of Lee-Peek Mortuary in Fort Pierce, the establishment that handled Zora's burial. Unlike most black funeral homes in Southern towns that sit like palaces among the general poverty, Lee-Peek has a run-down, *small* look. Perhaps this is because it is painted purple and white, as are its Cadillac chariots. These colors do not age well. The rooms are cluttered and grimy, and the bathroom is a tiny, stale-smelling prison, with a bottle of black hair dye (apparently used to touch up the hair of the corpses) dripping into the face bowl. Two pine burial boxes are resting in the bathtub.

Mrs. Patterson herself is pleasant and helpful.   39

"As I told you over the phone, Mrs. Patterson," I begin, shaking her hand   40
and looking into her penny-brown eyes, "I am Zora Neale Hurston's niece, and I would like to have a marker put on her grave. You said, when I called you last week, that you could tell me where the grave is."

By this time I am, of course, completely into being Zora's niece, and the lie   41
comes with perfect naturalness to my lips. Besides, as far as I'm concerned, she *is* my aunt—and that of all black people as well.

"She was buried in 1960," exclaims Mrs. Patterson. "That was when my   42
father was running this funeral home. He's sick now or I'd let you talk to him. But I know where she's buried. She's in the old cemetery, the Garden of the Heavenly Rest, on Seventeenth Street. Just when you go in the gate there's a circle, and she's buried right in the middle of it. Hers is the only grave in that circle—because people don't bury in that cemetery any more."

---

[2]Langston Hughes (1902–1967): black American writer. [Eds.]

139

She turns to a stocky, black-skinned woman in her thirties, wearing a green   43
polo shirt and white jeans cut off at the knees. "This lady will show you where
it is," she says.

"I can't tell you how I appreciate this," I say to Mrs. Patterson, as I rise to   44
go. "And could you tell me something else? You see, I never met my aunt.
When she died, I was still a junior in high school. But could you tell me what
she died of, and what kind of funeral she had?"

"I don't know exactly what she died of," Mrs. Patterson says. "I know she   45
didn't have any money. Folks took up a collection to bury her . . . I believe
she died of malnutrition."

"*Malnutrition?*"   46

Outside, in the blistering sun, I lean my head against Charlotte's even more   47
blistering car top. The sting of the hot metal only intensifies my anger. "*Malnutrition*," I manage to mutter. "Hell, our condition hasn't changed *any* since
Phillis Wheatley's time.[3] *She* died of malnutrition!"

"Really?" says Charlotte. "I didn't know that."   48

One cannot overemphasize the extent of her commitment. It was so great that her
marriage in the spring of 1927 to Herbert Sheen was short-lived. Although divorce
did not come officially until 1931, the two separated amicably after only a few
months, Hurston to continue her collecting, Sheen to attend Medical School.
Hurston never married again.

—Robert Hemenway

"What is your name?" I ask the woman who has climbed into the back seat.   49

"Rosalee," she says. She has a rough, pleasant voice, as if she is a singer   50
who also smokes a lot. She is homely, and has an air of ready indifference.

"Another woman came by here wanting to see the grave," she says, lighting   51
up a cigarette. "She was a little short, dumpy white lady from one of these
Florida schools. Orlando or Daytona. But let me tell you something before we
gets started. All I know is where the cemetery is. I don't know one thing about
that grave. You better go back in and ask her to draw you a map."

A few moments later, with Mrs. Patterson's diagram of where the grave is,   52
we head for the cemetery.

We drive past blocks of small, pastel-colored houses and turn right onto   53
Seventeenth Street. At the very end, we reach a tall curving gate, with the words
"Garden of the Heavenly Rest" fading into the stone. I expected, from Mrs.
Patterson's small drawing, to find a small circle—which would have placed
Zora's grave five or ten paces from the road. But the "circle" is over an acre
large and looks more like an abandoned field. Tall weeds choke the dirt road
and scrape against the sides of the car. It doesn't help either that I step out into
an active ant hill.

---

[3]Phillis Wheatley (1754–1784): black American poet. [Eds.]

"I don't know about y'all," I say, "but I don't even believe this." I am used   54
to the haphazard cemetery-keeping that is traditional in most Southern black
communities, but this neglect is staggering. As far as I can see there is nothing
but bushes and weeds, some as tall as my waist. One grave is near the road,
and Charlotte elects to investigate it. It is fairly clean, and belongs to someone
who died in 1963.

Rosalee and I plunge into the weeds; I pull my long dress up to my hips.   55
The weeds scratch my knees, and the insects have a feast. Looking back, I see
Charlotte standing resolutely near the road.

"Aren't you coming?" I call.   56

"No," she calls back. "I'm from these parts and I know what's out there."   57
She means snakes.

"Shit," I say, my whole life and the people I love flashing melodramatically   58
before my eyes. Rosalee is a few yards to my right.

"How're you going to find anything out here?" she asks. And I stand still a   59
few seconds, looking at the weeds. Some of them are quite pretty, with tiny
yellow flowers. They are thick and healthy, but dead weeds under them have
formed a thick gray carpet on the ground. A snake could be lying six inches
from my big toe and I wouldn't see it. We move slowly, very slowly, our eyes
alert, our legs trembly. It is hard to tell where the center of the circle is since
the circle is not really round, but more like half of something round. There are
things crackling and hissing in the grass. Sandspurs are sticking to the inside of
my skirt. Sand and ants cover my feet. I look toward the road and notice that
there are, indeed, *two* large curving stones, making an entrance and exit to the
cemetery. I take my bearings from them and try to navigate to exact center. But
the center of anything can be very large, and a grave is not a pinpoint. Finding
the grave seems positively hopeless. There is only one thing to do:

"Zora!" I yell, as loud as I can (causing Rosalee to jump). "Are you out   60
here?"

"If she is, I sho hope she don't answer you. If she do, I'm gone."   61

"Zora!" I call again. "I'm here. Are you?"   62

"If she is," grumbles Rosalee, "I hope she'll keep it to herself."   63

"Zora!" Then I start fussing with her. "I hope you don't think I'm going to   64
stand out here all day, with these snakes watching me and these ants having a
field day. In fact, I'm going to call you just one or two more times." On a
clump of dried grass, near a small bushy tree, my eye falls on one of the largest
bugs I have ever seen. It is on its back, and is as large as three of my fingers. I
walk toward it, and yell "Zo-ra!" and my foot sinks into a hole. I look down. I
am standing in a sunken rectangle that is about six feet long and about three or
four feet wide. I look up to see where the two gates are.

"Well," I say, "this is the center, or approximately anyhow. It's also the only   65
sunken spot we've found. Doesn't this look like a grave to you?"

"For the sake of not going no farther through these bushes," Rosalee growls, 66
"yes, it do."

"Wait a minute," I say, "I have to look around some more to be sure this is 67
the only spot that resembles a grave. But you don't have to come."

Rosalee smiles—a grin, really—beautiful and tough. 68

"Naw," she says, "I feel sorry for you. If one of these snakes got ahold of 69
you out here by yourself I'd feel *real* bad." She laughs. "I done come this far,
I'll go on with you."

"Thank you, Rosalee," I say. "Zora thanks you too." 70

"Just as long as she don't try to tell me in person," she says, and together we 71
walk down the field.

> The gusto and flavor of Zora Neal[e] Hurston's storytelling, for example, long
> before the yarns were published in "Mules and Men" and other books, became a
> local legend which might . . . have spread further under different conditions. A
> tiny shift in the center of gravity could have made them best-sellers.
>
> —Arna Bontemps,[4]
> *Personals*

> Bitter over the rejection of her folklore's value, especially in the black community,
> frustrated by what she felt was her failure to convert the Afro-American world view
> into the forms of prose fiction, Hurston finally gave up.
>
> —Robert Hemenway

When Charlotte and I drive up the Merritt Monument Company, I imme- 72
diately see the headstone I want.

"How much is this one?" I ask the young woman in charge, pointing to a 73
tall black stone. It looks as majestic as Zora herself must have been when she
was learning voodoo from those root doctors in New Orleans.

"Oh, *that* one," she says, "that's our finest. That's Ebony Mist." 74

"Well, how much is it?" 75

"I don't know. But wait," she says, looking around in relief, "here comes 76
somebody who'll know."

A small, sunburned man with squinty green eyes comes up. He must be the 77
engraver, I think, because his eyes are contracted into slits, as if he has been
keeping stone dust out of them for years.

"That's Ebony Mist," he says. "That's our best." 78

"How much is it?" I ask, beginning to realize I probably can't afford it. 79

He gives me a price that would feed a dozen Sahelian drought victims for 80
three years. I realize I must honor the dead, but between the dead great and
the living starving, there is no choice.

"I have a lot of letters to be engraved," I say, standing by the plain gray 81
marker I have chosen. It is pale and ordinary, not at all like Zora, and makes
me momentarily angry that I am not rich.

---

[4]Arna Bontemps (1902–1973): black American writer. [Eds.]

We go into his office and I hand him a sheet of paper that has: 82

ZORA NEALE HURSTON
"A GENIUS OF THE SOUTH"
NOVELIST FOLKLORIST
ANTHROPOLOGIST
1901   1960

"A genius of the South" is from one of Jean Toomer's poems.[5]   83
"Where is this grave?" the monument man asks. "If it's in a new cemetery,   84
the stone has to be flat."
"Well, it's not a new cemetery and Zora—my aunt—doesn't need anything   85
flat, because with the weeds out there, you'd never be able to see it. You'll have
to go out there with me."
He grunts.   86
"And take a long pole and 'sound' the spot," I add. "Because there's no way   87
of telling it's a grave, except that it's sunken."
"Well," he says, after taking my money and writing up a receipt, in the full   88
awareness that he's the only monument dealer for miles, "you take this flag"
(he hands me a four-foot-long pole with a red marker on top) "and take it out
to the cemetery and put it where you think the grave is. It'll take us about three
weeks to get the stone out there."
I wonder if he knows he is sending me to another confrontation with the   89
snakes. He probably does. Charlotte has told me she will cut my leg and suck
out the blood if I am bit.
"At least send me a photograph when it's done, won't you?"   90
He says he will.   91

Hurston's return to her folklore-collecting in December of 1927 was made possible
by Mrs. R. Osgood Mason, an elderly white patron of the arts, who at various
times also helped Langston Hughes, Alain Locke, Richmond Barthe, and Miguel
Covarrubias. Hurston apparently came to her attention through the intercession
of Locke, who frequently served as a kind of liaison between the young black
talent and Mrs. Mason. The entire relationship between this woman and the
Harlem Renaissance deserves extended study, for it represents much of the ambiguity involved in white patronage of black artists. All her artists were instructed
to call her "Godmother"; there was a decided emphasis on the "primitive" aspects
of black culture, apparently a holdover from Mrs. Mason's interest in the Plains
Indians. In Hurston's case there were special restrictions imposed by her patron:
although she was to be paid a handsome salary for her folklore collecting, she was
to limit her correspondence and publish nothing of her research without prior
approval.

—Robert Hemenway

---

[5]Jean Toomer (1894–1967): black American writer. [Eds.]

You have to read the chapters Zora *left out* of her autobiography.
—Student, Special Collections Room,
Beinecke Library, Yale University

Dr. Benton, a friend of Zora's and a practicing M.D. in Fort Pierce, is one   92
of those old, good-looking men whom I always have trouble not liking. (It no
longer bothers me that I may be constantly searching for father figures; by this
time, I have found several and dearly enjoyed knowing them all.) He is shrewd,
with steady brown eyes under hair that is almost white. He is probably in his
seventies, but doesn't look it. He carries himself with dignity, and has cause to
be proud of the new clinic where he now practices medicine. His nurse looks
at us with suspicion, but Dr. Benton's eyes have the penetration of a scalpel
cutting through skin. I guess right away that if he knows anything at all about
Zora Hurston, he will not believe I am her niece. "Eatonville?" Dr. Benton
says, leaning forward in his chair, looking first at me, then at Charlotte. "Yes,
I know Eatonville; I grew up not far from there. I knew the whole bunch of
Zora's family." (He looks at the shape of my cheekbones, the size of my eyes,
and the nappiness of my hair.) "I knew her daddy. The old man. He was a
hard-working Christian man. did the best he could for his family. He was the
mayor of Eatonville for a while, you know.

"My father was the mayor of Goldsboro. You probably never heard of it. It   93
never incorporated like Eatonville did, and has just about disappeared. But
Eatonville is still all black."

He pauses and looks at me. "And you're Zora's niece," he says wonderingly.   94

"Well," I say with shy dignity, yet with some tinge, I hope, of a nineteenth-   95
century blush, "I'm illegitimate. That's why I never knew Aunt Zora."

I love him for the way he comes to my rescue. "You're *not* illegitimate!" he   96
cries, his eyes resting on me fondly. "All of us are God's children! Don't you
even *think* such a thing!"

And I hate myself for lying to him. Still, I ask myself, would I have gotten   97
this far toward getting the headstone and finding out about Zora Hurston's last
days without telling my lie? Actually, I probably would have. But I don't like
taking chances that could get me stranded in central Florida.

"Zora didn't get along with her family. I don't know why. Did you read her   98
autobiography, *Dust Tracks on a Road?*"

"Yes, I did," I say. "It pained me to see Zora pretending to be naive and   99
grateful about the old white 'Godmother' who helped finance her research, but
I loved the part where she ran off from home after falling out with her brother's
wife."

Dr. Benton nodded. "When she got sick, I tried to get her to go back to her   100
family, but she refused. There wasn't any real hatred; they just never had gotten
along and Zora wouldn't go to them. She didn't want to go to the county home,
either, but she had to, because she couldn't do a thing for herself."

"I was surprised to learn she died of malnutrition." 101

Dr. Benton seems startled. "Zora *didn't* die of malnutrition," he says indig- 102
nantly. "Where did you get that story from? She had a stroke and she died in
the welfare home." He seems peculiarly upset, distressed, but sits back reflec-
tively in his chair. "She was an incredible woman," he muses. "Sometimes
when I closed my office, I'd go by her house and just talk to her for an hour
or two. She was a well-read, well-traveled woman and always had her own ideas
about what was going on . . . "

"I never knew her, you know. Only some of Carl Van Vechten's photographs 103
and some newspaper photographs[6] . . . What did she look like?"

"When I knew her, in the fifties, she was a big woman, *erect*. Not quite as 104
light as I am (Dr. Benton is dark beige), and about five foot, seven inches, and
she weighed about two hundred pounds. Probably more. She . . . "

"What! Zora was *fat*! She wasn't, in Van Vechten's pictures!" 105

"Zora loved to eat," Dr. Benton says complacently. "She could sit down 106
with a mound of ice cream and just eat and talk till it was all gone."

While Dr. Benton is talking, I recall that the Van Vechten pictures were 107
taken when Zora was still a young woman. In them she appears tall, tan, and
healthy. In later newspaper photographs—when she was in her forties—I remembered that she seemed heavier and several shades lighter. I reasoned that
the earlier photographs were taken while she was busy collecting folklore materials in the hot Florida sun.

"She had high blood pressure. Her health wasn't good . . . She used to live 108
in one of my houses—on School Court Street. It's a block house . . . I don't
recall the number. But my wife and I used to invite her over to the house for
dinner. *She always ate well*," he says emphatically.

"That's comforting to know," I say, wondering where Zora ate when she 109
wasn't with the Bentons.

"Sometimes she would run out of groceries—after she got sick—and she'd 110
call me. 'Come over here and see 'bout me,' she'd say. And I'd take her shopping
and buy her groceries.

"She was always studying. Her mind—before the stroke—just worked all the 111
time. She was always going somewhere, too. She once went to Honduras to
study something. And when she died, she was working on that book about
Herod the Great. She was so intelligent! And really had perfect expressions. Her
English was beautiful!" (I suspect this is a clever way to let me know Zora herself
didn't speak in the "black English" her characters used.)

"I used to read all of her books," Dr. Benton continues," but it was a long 112
time ago. I remember the one about . . . it was called, I think, 'The Children
of God' [*Their Eyes Were Watching God*], and I remember Janie and Teapot

---

[6]Carl Van Vechten (1880–1964): American writer and benefactor of the Harlem Renaissance
arts. [Eds.]

[Teacake] and the mad dog riding on the cow in that hurricane and bit old Teapot on the cheek . . ."

I am delighted that he remembers even this much of the story even if the   113
names are wrong, but seeing his affection for Zora I feel I must ask him about her burial. "Did she *really* have a pauper's funeral?"

"She *didn't* have a pauper's funeral!" he says with great heat. "Everybody   114
around here *loved* Zora."

"We just came back from ordering a headstone," I say quietly, because he   115
is an old man and the color is coming and going on his face, "but to tell the truth, I can't be positive what I found is the grave. All I know is the spot I found was the only grave-size hole in the area."

"I remember it wasn't near the road," says Dr. Benton, more calmly. "Some   116
other lady came by here and we went out looking for the grave and I took a long iron stick and poked all over that part of the cemetery but we didn't find anything. She took some pictures of the general area. Do the weeds still come up to your knees?"

"Any beyond," I murmur. This time there isn't any doubt. Dr. Benton feels   117
ashamed.

As he walks us to our car, he continues to talk about Zora. "She couldn't   118
really write much near the end. She had the stroke and it left her weak; her mind was affected. She couldn't think about anything for long.

"She came here from Daytona, I think. She owned a houseboat over there.   119
When she came here, she sold it. She lived on that money, then she worked as a maid—for an article on maids she was writing—and she worked for the *Chronicle* writing the horoscope column.

"I think black people here in Florida got mad at her because she was for   120
some politician they were against. She said this politician *built* schools for blacks while the one they wanted just talked about it. And although Zora wasn't ego-tistical, what she thought, she thought; and generally what she thought, she said."

When we leave Dr. Benton's office, I realize I have missed my plane back   121
home to Jackson, Mississippi. That being so, Charlotte and I decide to find the house Zora lived in before she was taken to the county welfare home to die. From among her many notes, Charlotte locates a letter of Zora's she has copied that carries the address: 1734 School Court Street. We ask several people for directions. Finally, two old gentlemen in a dusty gray Plymouth offer to lead us there. School Court Street is not paved, and the road is full of mud puddles. It is dismal and squalid, redeemed only by the brightness of the late afternoon sun. Now I can understand what a "block" house is. It is a house shaped like a block, for one thing, surrounded by others just like it. Some houses are blue and some are green or yellow. Zora's is light green. They are tiny—about fifty by fifty feet, squatty with flat roofs. The house Zora lived in looks worse than

146

the others, but that is its only distinction. It also has three ragged and dirty children sitting on the steps.

"Is this where y'all live?" I ask, aiming my camera. 122

"No, ma'am," they say in unison, looking at me earnestly. "We live over 123 yonder. This Miss So-and-So's house; but she in the horspital."

We chatter inconsequentially while I take more pictures. A car drives up 124 with a young black couple in it. They scowl fiercely at Charlotte and don't look at me with friendliness, either. They get out and stand in their doorway across the street. I go up to them and explain. "Did you know Zora Hurston used to live right across from you?" I ask.

"Who?" They stare at me blankly, then become curiously attentive, as if 125 they think I made the name up. They are both Afroed and he is somberly dashikied.

I suddenly feel frail and exhausted. "It's too long a story," I say, "but tell me 126 something: is there anybody on this street who's lived here for more than thirteen years?"

"That old man down there," the young man says, pointing. Sure enough, 127 there is a man sitting on his steps three houses down. He has graying hair and is very neat, but there is a weakness about him. He reminds me of Mrs. Turner's husband in *Their Eyes Were Watching God*. He's rather "vanishing"-looking, as if his features have been sanded down. In the old days, before black was beautiful, he was probably considered attractive, because he has wavy hair and light-brown skin; but now, well, light skin has ceased to be its own reward.

After the preliminaries, there is only one thing I want to know: "Tell me 128 something," I begin, looking down at Zora's house. "Did Zora like flowers?"

He looks at me queerly. "As a matter of fact," he says, looking regretfully at 129 the bare, rough yard that surrounds her former house, "she was crazy about them. And she was a great gardener. She loved azaleas, and that running and blooming vine [morning glories], and she really loved that night-smelling flower [gardenia]. She kept a vegetable garden year-round, too. She raised collards and tomatoes and things like that.

"Everyone in this community thought well of Miss Hurston. When she died, 130 people all up and down this street took up a collection for her burial. We put her away nice."

"Why didn't somebody put up a headstone?" 131

"Well, you know, one was never requested. Her and her family didn't get 132 along. They didn't even come to the funeral."

"And did she live down there by herself?" 133

"Yes, until they took her away. She lived with—just her and her companion, 134 Sport."

My ears perk up. "Who?" 135

"Sport, you know, her dog. He was her only companion. He was a big brown- 136 and-white dog."

147

When I walk back to the car, Charlotte is talking to the young couple on   137
their porch. They are relaxed and smiling.

"I told them about the famous lady who used to live across the street from   138
them," says Charlotte as we drive off. "Of course they had no idea Zora ever
lived, let alone that she lived across the street. I think I'll send some of her
books to them."

"That's real kind of you," I say.   139

> I am not tragically colored. There is no great sorrow dammed up in my soul, nor
> lurking behind my eyes. I do not mind at all. I do not belong to the sobbing
> school of Negrohood who hold that nature somehow has given them a lowdown
> dirty deal and whose feelings are all hurt about it . . . No, I do not weep at the
> world—I am too busy sharpening my oyster knife.
>
> —Zora Neale Hurston
> "How It Feels to Be Colored Me,"
> *World Tomorrow*, 1928

There are times—and finding Zora Hurston's grave was one of them—when   140
normal responses of grief, horror, and so on do not make sense because they
bear no real relation to the depth of the emotion one feels. It was impossible
for me to cry when I saw the field full of weeds where Zora is. Partly this is
because I have come to know Zora through her books and she was not a teary
sort of person herself; but partly, too, it is because there is a point at which even
grief feels absurd. And at this point, laughter gushes up to retrieve sanity.

It is only later, when the pain is not so direct a threat to one's own existence,   141
that what was learned in that moment of comical lunacy is understood. Such
moments rob us of both youth and vanity. But perhaps they are also times when
greater disciplines are born.

QUESTIONS

1. Did Walker find Zora? In what ways? What, for example, do we know of the
conditions surrounding Hurston's death?

2. How would you describe the writer's relationship to her subject?

3. How would you describe Walker as a reporter? What methods does she use to
acquire information?

4. What effect is created by Walker's use of the present tense?

5. How are the quotations from sources used in this essay? What natural divisions
in the text do they mark? How do these quotations relate to the information Walker is
discovering and presenting to us?

6. Using the information provided by Walker, write a short biography of Zora Neale
Hurston.

VOLTAIRE'S LABORATORY: HOW THEY WEIGHED FIRE

E. M. Forster

Born into a London banking family, E. M. Forster (1879–1970) had no interest in pursuing a business career. At King's College, Cambridge, Forster found the right atmosphere of "people and books" to nurture his career as a writer. After taking degrees in classics and in history, Forster traveled for a while and then settled in London where, in the next ten years, he published four novels and a collection of short stories. His trips to India in 1913 and 1921 inspired his best-known novel, A Passage to India *(1924). His collected essays appear in* Abinger Harvest *(1936) and* Two Cheers for Democracy *(1951). The following essay, first published in 1931, expresses Forster's belief that the literary person should have an interest in science. He sees the French writer Voltaire (1694–1778) as "an early popularizer" of science and presents him here in friendly competition with his mistress, Madame du Châtelet (1709–1749) whose château at Cirey-sur-Blaise served as Voltaire's laboratory from 1734 to 1749.*

During the spring of 1737 the iron foundries in a remote district of Lorraine were often visited by a thin middle-aged man with a notebook.[1] He would weigh out two pounds of iron, have them heated till they were red-hot, and then weigh them again. He repeated the experiment, increasing the amount until he had weighed up to a thousand pounds. Three cauldrons were next prepared under his directions, they were placed on scales, so that their weight could be estimated, and then molten metal was poured into them from a furnace, a hundred pounds into the first cauldron, thirty-five pounds into the second, twenty-five into the third, and when the cauldrons were cold the mass was weighed again. As the title of this article suggests, the thin, middle-aged man is Voltaire, but what on earth is he doing in an iron foundry? Wait a minute. Here comes a still more remarkable figure.

The newcomer is a lady of about thirty, with a long thin face, a commanding nose, and greenish eyes. Her appearance is masculine but not mannish; in spite of her earnest mien she is gay and charming, she dresses well, and is very

---

[1]Lorraine: a region in northeastern France. [Eds.]

kindhearted. It will be easy to make fun of her. For she, too, holds a notebook in her hand, in which she enters the weights of the hot and cold iron. She is quite as keen as Voltaire, and even more serious. She has taken up science, not because it is fashionable and brings her into contact with celebrities, but because she hopes to discover the nature of the universe. Facts, facts! A theory may come later—if there is one. She gives up acting, dancing, games, in order to do experiments. Voltaire calls her "divine Emilie." She is his mistress, Madame du Châtelet, and she owns Cirey, the great house where he is stopping.

On returning to Cirey, the investigators separate, and Voltaire goes to his own suite, which contains half a dozen ground-floor rooms, beautifully furnished; passing through a tiny antechamber and a bedroom of crimson velvet, he comes to the long gallery and sits down there. The long gallery is lacquered in yellow, with panels of Indian paper; it is ornamented with statues, one of which, a statue of Love, conceals the stove; there are cupboards full of books and scientific instruments; there are windows opening into the garden or on to the chapel—so that without disturbing himself too much he can hear Mass. At the end is a camera obscura and another room, not yet in order.[2] Voltaire drinks a cup of coffee. Establishing himself at a superb writing-desk, he takes up his pen in despair. For he is going in for a prize competition on the subject of the Nature and Propagation of Fire, and he has been unable to find out whether fire weighs anything. Since fire is an element,[3] one expects it to weigh something, yet the hot iron at the foundry was only occasionally heavier than the cold: sometimes it was the same weight and sometimes actually lighter. Nor is this all: other problems connected with fire are equally obscure. If he shuts up burning coals in a metal box, sometimes they continue to burn, at other times they go out. If he prepares sections of little trees and places them on a red-hot surface, the time in which they are reduced to ashes varies considerably, although they are of exactly the same thickness and size, and even come from the same plantation, "I then repeated this experiment with vegetables"; but the vegetables burned unevenly too. An experiment with objects painted different colors had been more satisfactory: black objects got hot quicker than green ones, yellow than white; but even here there were exceptions, and all he can do is to add to the Laws of Fire a supplementary law to the effect that they do not always work.

"My dear Abbé, we are surrounded by uncertainties," he writes to his agent in Paris. "To discover the least scrap of truth entails endless labor," and he implores the Abbé to inquire of people who are likely to know whether fire really does weigh anything; also whether a burning glass has a normal effect on objects in a vacuum; also, is it true that Persian naphtha of the best quality

3

4

---

[2]camera obscura: a darkened chamber in which the real image of an object is received through a small opening or lens and focused onto a facing surface. [Eds.]

[3]fire is an element: from the days of the Greek philosophers until modern times, earth, air, fire, and water were generally considered the four basic elements of the universe. [Eds.]

flames under water; also he wants writing-paper of various sizes, sealing-wax, an astrolabe,[4] two globes on stands, thermometers, barometers, earthenware pans, retorts, crucibles;[5] also a complete sportsman's outfit—gun, costume; also face-powder, hair-powder, scent, nail-scissors, sponges, two very large pots of orange-flower pomatum;[6] also a young priest who will officiate in the chapel, and knows a little chemistry besides; and a young mathematician who knows astronomy; also he does *not* want the publications of the French Academy, but the publications of the Academy of Sciences: the good Abbé has confused the two institutions, and sent the wrong volumes, so that Voltaire feels like the man who ordered eighteen swans for his ornamental water, and received eighteen monkeys by mistake; also—also—the list of wants rolls on; what, meantime, is Madame du Châtelet doing at her end of the house?

She, too, is entering for the prize competition on the Nature and Propagation 5 of Fire, but she has not told her lover this. It is to be a surprise. An indefatigable inquirer, she has visited foundries and scorched vegetables until she is left with very little time for the actual writing, and has to dip her hand constantly in cold water, it aches so. Her suite is even more gorgeous than his: everything matches in blue and yellow, down to the little dog's basket, the bed is covered with blue satin, Veroneses and Watteaus adorn the walls,[7] her writing table, inlaid with amber, was the gift of Prince Frederick of Prussia, her bathroom is tiled, and paved with marble, the chandeliers are exquisite, a looking-glass door leads from the bedroom into the library. Far into the night she writes; so does Voltaire; and between them slumbers the dilapidated central portion of the house, possibly occupied by her husband.

Life at Cirey was certainly comic, but before we have our good laugh at it 6 we had better remind ourselves that Voltaire and Madame du Châtelet were abreast of their age, and their science relatively no more absurd than our own— indeed, it may well prove to be less absurd, for they were highly intelligent. We find them funny because we know more, but if we patronize them for not knowing more it is we who become funny. For example, their difficulties over fire were shared by all their contemporaries. Chemistry now informs us that fire is not an element, but a state through which bodies are passing, and which is likely to be accompanied by certain reactions: under some conditions, when they are heated, they give out gas, and so get lighter; under other conditions they generate solid oxide, and so get heavier. In a hundred years' time chemistry will inform us of something else. The eighteenth century had not discovered even what we know, so the experiments at the foundry seemed to give contra-

---

[4]astrolabe: an instrument used to determine the altitude of celestial bodies. [Eds.]

[5]retorts: closed laboratory vessels used for distillation; crucibles: heat-resistant vessels used for heating or melting substances at high temperatures. [Eds.]

[6]pomatum: a perfumed ointment for the hair. [Eds.]

[7]Paolo Veronese (1522–1588): Italian painter; Jean Antoine Watteau (1684–1721): French painter. [Eds.]

dictory results. Moreover, the apparatus was hopelessly inaccurate; however good a pendulum clock the Abbé sent from Paris, and however carefully he packed it, it still could not record the exact times two cauliflowers took to burn. "My dear Abbé, we are surrounded by uncertainties." The uncertainties thrilled him, he dashed hither and thither to put them right and took genuine pleasure in the complexity of the universe.

It has been well said that Voltaire is not a journalist but a newspaper. Every 7 sort of activity gets mentioned in his columns. The literary side is strongest, but science jottings constantly appear, and first become prominent during his exile in England. He picked up in England many scraps that moved his respect or mirth: inoculation; a woman who bore rabbits; an Irishman who saw worms through a microscope in mutton broth. But it was not until he returned to France and fell under Madame du Châtelet's influence that his interests concentrated. She inclined him to the subjects she herself had studied—that is to say to physics and to astronomy—and his chief scientific work, an exposition of Newton's theory,[8] was composed under her protection. He presented the theory accurately, criticized it intelligently, and has the undivided credit of introducing Newton to the French public. Orthodoxy was alarmed; it had invested in the whirlwinds of Descartes as a suitable basis for the physical universe, and resented the possibility of gravitation.[9] On account of gravitation, and on account of other laxities, which included an improper poem on Joan of Arc, Voltaire kept away from Paris. He was not yet the very great Voltaire who quarrelled with Frederick the Great and avenged Calas.[10] But he was a considerable figure, tragedian, poet, wit, philosopher, and now science was to place her metallic wreath a little crookedly upon his brows.

He and his hostess had arrived at Cirey earlier in that same year, 1737. They 8 had driven by night and through the snow, and the wheel had come off the carriage on Voltaire's side, so that Madame du Châtelet, her maid, and a quantity of luggage fell on him. At the same moment, all the menservants fell off the box. It was long before the luggage, the maid, the mistress, and the great man could be progressively extracted, and he uttered a series of short, sharp shrieks. As so often happened, he was enjoying himself. Cushions were spread in the frozen road, and he and Madame du Châtelet sat on them and pointed out to one another the glories of the night sky. "The stars shone brilliantly," one of their servants writes. "Not a tree, not a house disturbed the expanse of the horizon. M. de Voltaire and Madame du Châtelet were in ecstasies: wrapped

---

[8]Newton's theory: Sir Isaac Newton (1642–1727) was an English mathematician and scientist best known for his theory of gravitation. [Eds.]

[9]René Descartes (1596–1650): French philosopher who held that physical substances are the result of "vortices," or whorls of motion. [Eds.]

[10]Calas: in 1761, Jean Calas was brutally tortured and executed for the murder of his son (actually a suicide, despondent over his limited prospects as a Protestant in an intolerant Catholic society). The religious fanaticism involved in the case roused Voltaire to force reopening of the case to clear Calas and to write his *Traité sur la tolérance*. [Eds.]

in furs, they discussed the nature and the orbits of the stars and their destination in space while their teeth chattered. If only they had had a telescope, their joy would have been complete." There they sat, half laughing and wholly serious, until the carriage could be repaired and take them on to their home.

When they got there, they evolved a routine which both impressed and annoyed their visitors. They took themselves seriously, in which they were fully justified, and they were obliged to organize their work, or it would not have got done. Eleven in the morning and nine at night were the only hours in the twenty-four when they were certain to be visible. At eleven there was coffee in Voltaire's gallery; in the evening came the great event—supper—occasionally marred by a quarrel. After supper, if all had gone well, Voltaire showed the magic lantern,[11] or directed a telescope at the moon, or played tricks with prisms, being screamingly funny all the time, or read Joan of Arc aloud in the marble bathroom, or had plays performed in a barn. Science was much discussed, also religion; at no time of his life was he either an atheist or an agnostic, he believed firmly in God, provided God is given nothing to do, and he always insisted that physics must rest upon metaphysics, and that metaphysics are divine. When the party broke up, they retired to their work, and somewhere or other in the house, well looked after but seldom seen, slept her little boy. The variety, the vigour of Cirey is most impressive; the imagination flits from room to room until it wearies, and fails even to reach the huge woods which shut in the domain, and the peasants whose labour supported it. What stands out in the end is the laboratory work. That the experiments were primitive, ill-directed, and unsuccessful did not trouble the investigators, and need not trouble us if we understand what they felt: they saw a new world opening in every direction and asking to be interpreted.

Madame du Châtelet was certainly a most remarkable creature—tiresome, but not too tiresome, and therefore an ideal mate for a very tiresome man. "Venus-Newton," Frederick of Prussia calls her, while Madame du Deffand insinuates that she was only Newton because she could not be Venus,[12] and also accuses her of spending more on her dresses than on her underthings— gravest of charges that one woman of quality can bring against another. Voltaire adored her. She irritated him, but he also irritated her, which he enjoyed doing, and they were too affectionate and gay to subside into sourness. The relationship between them is very odd: it included emotion, and lasted twelve years, yet it cannot be classed among famous love affairs. He was not a lover—he had all the ingredients that make up love, such as tenderness, pity, lust, selfishness, unselfishness, but they never combined: he was a chemical experiment, which, if love be the desired result, may be said to have failed. Madame du Châtelet was more normal, and it was she in the end who tired of the liaison, or rather

9

10

---

[11]magic lantern: optical device which projects the enlarged image of a picture. [Eds.]
[12]Madame du Deffand (1697–1780): a marquise, née Marie de Vichy Chamrond. [Eds.]

tried for an additional one which ended in a ghastly catastrophe. With their tragedy I am not concerned here: at the moment I visualize them they were wholly in accord, and in accord with her husband, and now that the eighteenth century is no longer here to sneer or the nineteenth century to lecture, they are perhaps coming into their own. What kept them together was their interest in outside things—science, the drama, philosophy, art. They can never have said— at least I cannot imagine them saying—"What is this? What has brought us so close? We had better not inquire, lest it vanish away." They were held by their common interests, and so the nerve-storms that occasionally swept over them left no wreckage behind.

Neither he nor she obtained the prize for the Nature and Propagation of   11 Fire. The judges complimented him on being a poet and her on being a lady, but appear to have been slightly shocked by the number of facts they mentioned, and divided the prize between three other competitors, who confined themselves to theory. In the opinion of modern authorities, the award ought to have been made to Madame du Châtelet: her essay is much the best.

QUESTIONS

1. To what extent is this essay about weighing fire?

2. In paragraph 10, the writer says, "At the moment I visualize them they were wholly in accord." What evidence of this accord is presented in the essay? Is there any evidence of discord?

3. In paragraph 2, the writer says of Madame du Châtelet, "It will be easy to make fun of her." Does he make fun of her? Of Voltaire? Describe his attitude toward his subjects.

4. In paragraph 1, Forster intoduces the present tense and continues to use it through paragraph 5. What effect is achieved by this?

5. How is the prize competition used to structure the essay?

6. While Voltaire and Madame du Châtelet are busily gathering facts about fire, Forster is just as busily giving us facts about them. Consider what we learn about Voltaire from the following information:

    his suite (paragraph 3)
    his wants (paragraph 4)
    his "science jottings" (paragraph 7)
    the carriage incident (paragraph 8)
    his entertainments (paragraph 9)

Choose one of these paragraphs, and write a paragraph or two about it showing how the information contributes to the representation of Voltaire. Or, look at paragraphs 2, 5, 8, and 10, and do the same for Madame du Châtelet.

7. Write about someone you know well, presenting him or her to the reader by reporting his or her actions and beliefs. If you prefer, you can choose a couple you know well.

THE DEATH
OF THE MOTH

Virginia Woolf

Born in 1882, Virginia Woolf became one of England's major modern novelists before her death in 1941. She is also known as the author of important critical essays and such personal documents as letters, journals, and familiar essays. This selection combines the reporting of a naturalist with the reflecting of an essayist. Ironically, this selection was first published for a wide audience in the posthumous collection The Death of the Moth and Other Essays *(1942), seen into print by her husband, Leonard Woolf.*

Moths that fly by day are not properly to be called moths; they do not excite 1
that pleasant sense of dark autumn nights and ivy-blossom which the commonest
yellow-underwing asleep in the shadow of the curtain never fails to rouse in us.
They are hybrid creatures, neither gay like butterflies nor sombre like their own
species. Nevertheless the present specimen, with his narrow hay-colored wings,
fringed with a tassel of the same color, seemed to be content with life. It was a
pleasant morning, mid-September, mild, benignant, yet with a keener breath
than that of the summer months. The plough was already scoring the field
opposite the window, and where the share had been, the earth was pressed flat
and gleamed with moisture. Such vigor came rolling in from the fields and the
down beyond that it was difficult to keep the eyes strictly turned upon the book.
The rooks too were keeping one of their annual festivities;[1] soaring round the
tree tops until it looked as if a vast net with thousands of black knots in it had
been cast up into the air; which, after a few moments sank slowly down upon
the trees until every twig seemed to have a knot at the end of it. Then, suddenly,
the net would be thrown into the air again in a wider circle this time, with the
utmost clamor and vociferation, as though to be thrown into the air and settle
slowly down upon the tree tops were a tremendously exciting experience.

The same energy which inspired the rooks, the ploughmen, the horses, and 2
even, it seemed, the lean bare-backed downs, sent the moth fluttering from side
to side of his square of the window-pane. One could not help watching him.
One was, indeed, conscious of a queer feeling of pity for him. The possibilities
of pleasure seemed that morning so enormous and so various that to have only
a moth's part in life, and a day moth's at that, appeared a hard fate, and his

---

[1]rooks: European birds, similar to American crows. [Eds.]

zest in enjoying his meagre opportunities to the full, pathetic. He flew vigorously to one corner of his compartment, and, after waiting there a second, flew across to the other. What remained for him but to fly to a third corner and then to a fourth? That was all he could do, in spite of the size of the downs, the width of the sky, the far-off smoke of houses, and the romantic voice, now and then, of a steamer out at sea. What he could do he did. Watching him, it seemed as if a fibre, very thin but pure, of the enormous energy of the world had been thrust into his frail and diminutive body. As often as he crossed the pane, I could fancy that a thread of vital light became visible. He was little or nothing but life.

Yet, because he was so small, and so simple a form of the energy that was 3 rolling in at the open window and driving its way through so many narrow and intricate corridors in my own brain and in those of other human beings, there was something marvelous as well as pathetic about him. It was as if someone had taken a tiny bead of pure life and decking it as lightly as possible with down and feathers, had set it dancing and zigzagging to show us the true nature of life. Thus displayed one could not get over the strangeness of it. One is apt to forget all about life, seeing it humped and bossed and garnished and cumbered so that it has to move with the greatest circumspection and dignity. Again, the thought of all that life might have been had he been born in any other shape caused one to view his simple activities with a kind of pity.

After a time, tired by his dancing apparently, he settled on the window ledge 4 in the sun, and, the queer spectacle being at an end, I forgot about him. Then, looking up, my eye was caught by him. He was trying to resume his dancing, but seemed either so stiff or so awkward that he could only flutter to the bottom of the window-pane; and when he tried to fly across it he failed. Being intent on other matters I watched these futile attempts for a time without thinking, unconsciously waiting for him to resume his flight, as one waits for a machine, that has stopped momentarily, to start again without considering the reason of its failure. After perhaps a seventh attempt he slipped from the wooden ledge and fell, fluttering his wings, onto his back on the window sill. The helplessness of his attitude roused me. It flashed upon me he was in difficulties; he could no longer raise himself; his legs struggled vainly. But, as I stretched out a pencil, meaning to help him to right himself, it came over me that the failure and awkwardness were the approach of death. I laid the pencil down again.

The legs agitated themselves once more. I looked as if for the enemy against 5 which he struggled. I looked out of doors. What had happened there? Presumably it was midday, and work in the fields had stopped. Stillness and quiet had replaced the previous animation. The birds had taken themselves off to feed in the brooks. The horses stood still. Yet the power was there all the same, massed outside indifferent, impersonal, not attending to anything in particular. Somehow it was opposed to the little hay-colored moth. It was useless to try to do anything. One could only watch the extraordinary efforts made by those tiny legs against an oncoming doom which could, had it chosen, have submerged an entire city, not merely a city, but masses of human beings; nothing, I knew, had any chance against death. Nevertheless after a pause of exhaustion the legs fluttered again. It was superb this last protest, and so frantic that he succeeded at last in righting himself. One's sympathies, of course, were all on the side of life. Also, when there was nobody to care or to know, this gigantic effort on the part of an insignificant little moth, against a power of such magnitude, to retain what no one else valued or desired to keep, moved one strangely. Again, some-how, one saw life, a pure bead. I lifted the pencil again, useless though I knew it to be. But even as I did so, the unmistakable tokens of death showed them-selves. The body relaxed, and instantly grew stiff. The struggle was over. The insignificant little creature now knew death. As I looked at the dead moth, this minute wayside triumph of so great a force over so mean an antagonist filled me with wonder. Just as life had been strange a few minutes before, so death was now as strange. The moth having righted himself now lay most decently and uncomplainingly composed. O yes, he seemed to say, death is stronger than I am.

QUESTIONS

1. A moth is a creature so small and insignificant that most of us would not pay attention to its dying. Why does Woolf pay attention? How does she engage our attention?

2. What most impresses Woolf as she watches the moth?

3. Why does Woolf describe in paragraph 1 the scene beyond the window? How does this description connect with her purpose in writing this essay?

4. In this essay, Woolf reports the sequence of events in the death of the moth as well as her thoughts concerning its dying. Trace the way in which she has chosen to weave the two strands of reporting and commenting together throughout the essay. How else might she have arranged her material? Why do you think she has chosen to arrange it as she has?

5. If you have witnessed a hopeless but valiant struggle on a human, animal, or insect scale, write a report of your observations. Decide how you will make a reader aware of your thoughts about what you observed.

"THIS IS THE END OF THE WORLD": THE BLACK DEATH

Barbara Tuchman

For over twenty-five years Barbara Wertheim Tuchman (b. 1912) has been writing books on historical subjects, ranging over the centuries from the Middle Ages to World War II. Her combination of careful research and lively writing has enabled her to produce books like The Guns of August *(1962) and* A Distant Mirror *(1978), which please not only the general public but many professional historians as well. She has twice won the Pulitzer Prize.* A Distant Mirror, *from which the following selection has been taken, was on the* New York Times *best-seller list for over nine months. Her latest work is* The March of Folly, From Troy to Vietnam *(1984).*

In October 1347, two months after the fall of Calais, Genoese trading ships 1
put into the harbor of Messina in Sicily with dead and dying men at the oars. The ships had come from the Black Sea port of Caffa (now Feodosiya) in the Crimea, where the Genoese maintained a trading post. The diseased sailors showed strange black swellings about the size of an egg or an apple in the armpits and groin. The swellings oozed blood and pus and were followed by spreading boils and black blotches on the skin from internal bleeding. The sick suffered severe pain and died quickly within five days of the first symptoms. As the disease spread, other symptoms of continuous fever and spitting of blood appeared instead of the swellings or buboes. These victims coughed and sweated heavily and died even more quickly, within three days or less, sometimes in 24 hours. In both types everything that issued from the body—breath, sweat, blood from the buboes and lungs, bloody urine, and blood-blackened excrement—smelled foul. Depression and despair accompanied the physical symptoms, and before the end "death is seen seated on the face."

The disease was bubonic plague, present in two forms: one that infected the 2
bloodstream, causing the buboes and internal bleeding, and was spread by contact; and a second, more virulent pneumonic type that infected the lungs and was spread by respiratory infection. The presence of both at once caused the high mortality and speed of contagion. So lethal was the disease that cases were known of persons going to bed well and dying before they woke, of doctors catching the illness at a bedside and dying before the patient. So rapidly did it

spread from one to another that to a French physician, Simon de Covino, it seemed as if one sick person "could infect the whole world." The malignity of the pestilence appeared more terrible because its victims knew no prevention and no remedy.

The physical suffering of the disease and its aspect of evil mystery were 3 expressed in a strange Welsh lament which saw "death coming into our midst like black smoke, a plague which cuts off the young, a rootless phantom which has no mercy for fair countenance. Woe is me of the shilling in the armpit! It is seething, terrible . . . a head that gives pain and causes a loud cry . . . a painful angry knob . . . Great is its seething like a burning cinder . . . a grievous thing of ashy color." Its eruption is ugly like the "seeds of black peas, broken fragments of brittle sea-coal . . . the early ornaments of black death, cinders of the peelings of the cockle weed, a mixed multitude, a black plague like half-pence, like berries. . . ."

Rumors of a terrible plague supposedly arising in China and spreading through 4 Tartary (Central Asia) to India and Persia, Mesopotamia, Syria, Egypt, and all of Asia Minor had reached Europe in 1346. They told of a death toll so dev-astating that all of India was said to be depopulated, whole territories covered by dead bodies, other areas with no one left alive. As added up by Pope Clement VI at Avignon, the total of reported dead reached 23,840,000. In the absence of a concept of contagion, no serious alarm was felt in Europe until the trading ships brought their black burden of pestilence into Messina while other infected ships from the Levant carried it to Genoa and Venice.

By January 1348 it penetrated France via Marseille, and North Africa via 5 Tunis. Shipborne along coasts and navigable rivers, it spread westward from Marseille through the ports of Languedoc to Spain and northward up the Rhône to Avignon, where it arrived in March. It reached Narbonne, Montpellier, Carcassonne, and Toulouse between February and May, and at the same time in Italy spread to Rome and Florence and their hinterlands. Between June and August it reached Bordeaux, Lyon, and Paris, spread to Burgundy and Nor-mandy, and crossed the Channel from Normandy into southern England. From Italy during the same summer it crossed the Alps into Switzerland and reached eastward to Hungary.

In a given area the plague accomplished its kill within four to six months 6 and then faded, except in the larger cities, where, rooting into the close-quartered population, it abated during the winter, only to reappear in spring and rage for another six months.

In 1349 it resumed in Paris, spread to Picardy, Flanders, and the Low Coun- 7 tries, and from England to Scotland and Ireland as well as to Norway, where a ghost ship with a cargo of wool and a dead crew drifted offshore until it ran aground near Bergen. From there the plague passed into Sweden, Denmark, Prussia, Iceland, and as far as Greenland. Leaving a strange pocket of immunity in Bohemia, and Russia unattacked until 1351, it had passed from most of

Europe by mid-1350. Although the mortality rate was erratic, ranging from one fifth in some places to nine tenths or almost total elimination in others, the overall estimate of modern demographers has settled—for the area extending from India to Iceland—around the same figure expressed in Froissart's casual words: "a third of the world died." His estimate, the common one at the time, was not an inspired guess but a borrowing of St. John's figure for mortality from plague in Revelation, the favorite guide to human affairs of the Middle Ages.

A third of Europe would have meant about 20 million deaths. No one knows 8 in truth how many died. Contemporary reports were an awed impression, not an accurate count. In crowded Avignon, it was said, 400 died daily; 7,000 houses emptied by death were shut up; a single graveyard received 11,000 corpses in six weeks; half the city's inhabitants reportedly died, including 9 cardinals or one third of the total, and 70 lesser prelates. Watching the endlessly passing death carts, chroniclers let normal exaggeration take wings and put the Avignon death toll at 62,000 and even at 120,000, although the city's total population was probably less than 50,000.

When graveyards filled up, bodies at Avignon were thrown into the Rhône 9 until mass burial pits were dug for dumping the corpses. In London in such pits corpses piled up in layers until they overflowed. Everywhere reports speak of the sick dying too fast for the living to bury. Corpses were dragged out of homes and left in front of doorways. Morning light revealed new piles of bodies. In Florence the dead were gathered up by the Compagnia della Misericordia— founded in 1244 to care for the sick—whose members wore red robes and hoods masking the face except for the eyes. When their efforts failed, the dead lay putrid in the streets for days at a time. When no coffins were to be had, the bodies were laid on boards, two or three at once, to be carried to graveyards or common pits. Families dumped their own relatives into the pits, or buried them so hastily and thinly "that dogs dragged them forth and devoured their bodies."

Amid accumulating death and fear of contagion, people died without last 10 rites and were buried without prayers, a prospect that terrified the last hours of the stricken. A bishop in England gave permission to laymen to make confession to each other as was done by the Apostles, "or if no man is present then even to a woman," and if no priest could be found to administer extreme unction, "then faith must suffice." Clement VI found it necessary to grant remissions of sin to all who died of the plague because so many were unattended by priests. "And no bells tolled," wrote a chronicler of Siena, "and nobody wept no matter what his loss because almost everyone expected death. . . . And people said and believed, 'This is the end of the world.' "

In Paris, where the plague lasted through 1349, the reported death rate was 11 800 a day, in Pisa 500, in Vienna 500 to 600. The total dead in Paris numbered 50,000 or half the population. Florence, weakened by the famine of 1347, lost three to four fifths of its citizens, Venice two thirds, Hamburg and Bremen, though smaller in size, about the same proportion. Cities, as centers of trans-

160

portation, were more likely to be affected than villages, although once a village was infected, its death rate was equally high. At Givry, a prosperous village in Burgundy of 1,200 to 1,500 people, the parish register records 615 deaths in the space of fourteen weeks, compared to an average of thirty deaths a year in the previous decade. In three villages of Cambridgeshire, manorial records show a death rate of 47 percent, 57 percent, and in one case 70 percent. When the last survivors, too few to carry on, moved away, a deserted village sank back into the wilderness and disappeared from the map altogether, leaving only a grass-covered ghostly outline to show where mortals once had lived.

In enclosed places such as monasteries and prisons, the infection of one [12] person usually meant that of all, as happened in the Franciscan convents of Carcassonne and Marseille, where every inmate without exception died. Of the 140 Dominicans at Montpellier only seven survived. Petrarch's brother Gherardo, member of a Carthusian monastery, buried the prior and 34 fellow monks one by one, sometimes three a day, until he was left alone with his dog and fled to look for a place that would take him in. Watching every comrade die, men in such places could not but wonder whether the strange peril that filled the air had not been sent to exterminate the human race. In Kilkenny, Ireland, Brother John Clyn of the Friars Minor, another monk left alone among dead men, kept a record of what had happened lest "things which should be remembered perish with time and vanish from the memory of those who come after us." Sensing "the whole world, as it were, placed within the grasp of the Evil One," and waiting for death to visit him too, he wrote, "I leave parchment to continue this work, if perchance any man survive and any of the race of Adam escape this pestilence and carry on the work which I have begun." Brother John, as noted by another hand, died of the pestilence, but he foiled oblivion.

The largest cities of Europe, with populations of about 100,000, were Paris [13] and Florence, Venice and Genoa. At the next level, with more than 50,000, were Ghent and Bruges in Flanders, Milan, Bologna, Rome, Naples, and Palermo, and Cologne. London hovered below 50,000, the only city in England except York with more than 10,000. At the level of 20,000 to 50,000 were Bordeaux, Toulouse, Montpellier, Marseille, and Lyon in France, Barcelona, Seville, and Toledo in Spain, Siena, Pisa, and other secondary cities in Italy, and the Hanseatic trading cities of the Empire. The plague raged through them all, killing anywhere from one third to two thirds of their inhabitants. Italy, with a total population of 10 to 11 million, probably suffered the heaviest toll. Following the Florentine bankruptcies, the crop failures and workers' riots of 1346–47, the revolt of Cola di Rienzi that plunged Rome into anarchy, the plague came as the peak of successive calamities. As if the world were indeed in the grasp of the Evil One, its first appearance on the European mainland in January 1348 coincided with a fearsome earthquake that carved a path of wreckage from Naples up to Venice. Houses collapsed, church towers toppled, villages were crushed, and the destruction reached as far as Germany and Greece.

Emotional response, dulled by horrors, underwent a kind of atrophy epitomized by the chronicler who wrote, "And in these days was burying without sorrowe and wedding without friendschippe."

In Siena, where more than half the inhabitants died of the plague, work was [14] abandoned on the great cathedral, planned to be the largest in the world, and never resumed, owing to loss of workers and master masons and "the melancholy and grief" of the survivors. The cathedral's truncated transept still stands in permanent witness to the sweep of death's scythe. Agnolo di Tura, a chronicler of Siena, recorded the fear of contagion that froze every other instinct. "Father abandoned child, wife husband, one brother another," he wrote, "for this plague seemed to strike through the breath and sight. And so they died. And no one could be found to bury the dead for money or friendship. . . . And I, Angolo di Tura, called the Fat, buried my five children with my own hands, and so did many others likewise."

There were many to echo his account of inhumanity and few to balance it, [15] for the plague was not the kind of calamity that inspired mutual help. Its loathsomeness and deadliness did not herd people together in mutual distress, but only prompted their desire to escape each other. "Magistrates and notaries refused to come and make the wills of the dying," reported a Franciscan friar of Piazza in Sicily; what was worse, "even the priests did not come to hear their confessions." A clerk of the Archbishop of Canterbury reported the same of English priests who "turned away from the care of their benefices from fear of death." Cases of parents deserting children and children their parents were reported across Europe from Scotland to Russia. The calamity chilled the hearts of men, wrote Boccaccio in his famous account of the plague in Florence that serves as introduction to the *Decameron*. "One man shunned another . . . kinsfolk held aloof, brother was forsaken by brother, oftentimes husband by wife; nay, what is more, and scarcely to be believed, fathers and mothers were found to abandon their own children to their fate, untended, unvisited as if they had been strangers." Exaggeration and literary pessimism were common in the 14th century, but the Pope's physician, Guy de Chauliac, was a sober, careful observer who reported the same phenomenon: "A father did not visit his son, nor the son his father. Charity was dead."

Yet not entirely. In Paris, according to the chronicler Jean de Venette, the [16] nuns of the Hôtel Dieu or municipal hospital, "having no fear of death, tended the sick with all sweetness and humility." New nuns repeatedly took the places of those who died, until the majority "many times renewed by death now rest in peace with Christ as we may piously believe."

When the plague entered northern France in July 1348, it settled first in [17] Normandy and, checked by winter, gave Picardy a deceptive interim until the next summer. Either in mourning or warning, black flags were flown from church towers of the worst-stricken villages of Normandy. "And in that time," wrote a monk of the abbey of Fourcarment, "the mortality was so great among

the people of Normandy that those of Picardy mocked them." The same un-
neighborly reaction was reported of the Scots, separated by a winter's immunity
from the English. Delighted to hear of the disease that was scourging the "south-
rons," they gathered forces for an invasion, "laughing at their enemies." Before
they could move, the savage mortality fell upon them too, scattering some in
death and the rest in panic to spread the infection as they fled.

In Picardy in the summer of 1349 the pestilence penetrated the castle of 18
Coucy to kill Enguerrand's mother,[1] Catherine, and her new husband. Whether
her nine-year-old son escaped by chance or was perhaps living elsewhere with
one of his guardians is unrecorded. In nearby Amiens, tannery workers, responding quickly to losses in the labor force, combined to bargain for higher
wages. In another place villagers were seen dancing to drums and trumpets, and
on being asked the reason, answered that, seeing their neighbors die day by day
while their village remained immune, they believed that they could keep the
plague from entering "by the jollity that is in us. That is why we dance." Further
north in Tournai on the border of Flanders, Gilles li Muisis, Abbot of St.
Martin's, kept one of the epidemic's most vivid accounts. The passing bells rang
all day and all night, he recorded, because sextons were anxious to obtain their
fees while they could. Filled with the sound of mourning, the city became
oppressed by fear, so that the authorities forbade the tolling of bells and the
wearing of black and restricted funeral services to two mourners. The silencing
of funeral bells and of criers' announcements of deaths was ordained by most
cities. Siena imposed a fine on the wearing of mourning clothes by all except
widows.

Flight was the chief recourse of those who could afford it or arrange it. The 19
rich fled to their country places like Boccaccio's young patricians of Florence,
who settled in a pastoral palace "removed on every side from the roads" with
"wells of cool water and vaults of rare wines." The urban poor died in their
burrows, "and only the stench of their bodies informed neighbors of their death."
That the poor were more heavily afflicted than the rich was clearly remarked at
the time, in the north as in the south. A Scottish chronicler, John of Fordun,
stated flatly that the pest "attacked especially the meaner sort and common
people—seldom the magnates." Simon de Covino of Montpellier made the
same observation. He ascribed it to the misery and want and hard lives that
made the poor more susceptible, which was half the truth. Close contact and
lack of sanitation was the unrecognized other half. It was noticed too that the
young died in greater proportion than the old; Simon de Covino compared the
disappearance of youth to the withering of flowers in the fields.

In the countryside peasants dropped dead on the roads, in the fields, in their 20
houses. Survivors in growing helplessness fell into apathy, leaving ripe wheat

---

[1]Enguerrand de Coucy: the French nobleman whose life is followed by Tuchman as a way of
unifying her study of the fourteenth century. [Eds.]

uncut and livestock untended. Oxen and asses, sheep and goats, pigs and chickens ran wild and they too, according to local reports, succumbed to the pest. English sheep, bearers of the precious wool, died throughout the country. The chronicler Henry Knighton, canon of Leicester Abbey, reported 5,000 dead in one field alone, "their bodies so corrupted by the plague that neither beast nor bird would touch them," and spreading an appalling stench. In the Austrian Alps wolves came down to prey upon sheep and then, "as if alarmed by some invisible warning, turned and fled back into the wilderness." In remote Dalmatia bolder wolves descended upon a plague-stricken city and attacked human survivors. For want of herdsmen, cattle strayed from place to place and died in hedgerows and ditches. Dogs and cats fell like the rest.

The dearth of labor held a fearful prospect because the 14th century lived 21 close to the annual harvest both for food and for next year's seed. "So few servants and laborers were left," wrote Knighton, "that no one knew where to turn for help." The sense of a vanishing future created a kind of dementia of despair. A Bavarian chronicler of Neuberg on the Danube recorded that "Men and women . . . wandered around as if mad" and let their cattle stray "because no one had any inclination to concern themselves about the future." Fields went uncultivated, spring seed unsown. Second growth with nature's awful energy crept back over cleared land, dikes crumbled, salt water reinvaded and soured the lowlands. With so few hands remaining to restore the work of centuries, people felt, in Walsingham's words, that "the world could never again regain its former prosperity."

Though the death rate was higher among the anonymous poor, the known 22 and the great died too. King Alfonso XI of Castile was the only reigning monarch killed by the pest, but his neighbor King Pedro of Aragon lost his wife, Queen Leonora, his daughter Marie, and a niece in the space of six months. John Cantacuzene, Emperor of Byzantium, lost his son. In France the lame Queen Jeanne and her daughter-in-law Bonne de Luxemburg, wife of the Dauphin, both died in 1349 in the same phase that took the life of Enguerrand's mother. Jeanne, Queen of Navarre, daughter of Louis X, was another victim. Edward III's second daughter, Joanna, who was on her way to marry Pedro, the heir of Castile, died in Bordeaux. Women appear to have been more vulnerable than men, perhaps because, being more housebound, they were more exposed to fleas. Boccaccio's mistress Fiammetta, illegitimate daughter of the King of Naples, died, as did Laura, the beloved—whether real or fictional—of Petrarch. Reaching out to us in the future, Petrarch cried, "Oh happy posterity who will not experience such abysmal woe and will look upon our testimony as a fable."

In Florence Giovanni Villani, the great historian of his time, died at 68 in 23 the midst of an unfinished sentence: " . . . e dure questo pistolenza fino a . . . (in the midst of this pestilence there came to an end . . .)." Siena's master painters, the brothers Ambrogio and Pietro Lorenzetti, whose names never appear after 1348, presumably perished in the plague, as did Andrea Pisano, architect and sculptor of Florence. William of Ockham and the English mystic Richard Rolle of Hampole both disappear from mention after 1349. Francisco Datini, merchant of Prato, lost both his parents and two siblings. Curious sweeps of mortality afflicted certain bodies of merchants in London. All eight wardens of the Company of Cutters, all six wardens of the Hatters, and four wardens of the Goldsmiths died before July 1350. Sir John Pulteney, master draper and four times Mayor of London, was a victim, likewise Sir John Montgomery, Governor of Calais.

Among the clergy and doctors the mortality was naturally high because of the nature of their professions. Out of 24 physicians in Venice, 20 were said to have lost their lives in the plague, although, according to another account, some were believed to have fled or to have shut themselves up in their houses. At Montpellier, site of the leading medieval medical school, the physician Simon de Covino reported that, despite the great number of doctors, "hardly one of them escaped." In Avignon, Guy de Chauliac confessed that he performed his medical visits only because he dared not stay away for fear of infamy, but "I was in continual fear." He claimed to have contracted the disease but to have cured himself by his own treatment; if so, he was one of the few who recovered. [24]

Clerical mortality varied with rank. Although the one-third toll of cardinals reflects the same proportion as the whole, this was probably due to their concentration in Avignon. In England, in strange and almost sinister procession, the Archbishop of Canterbury, John Stratford, died in August 1348, his appointed successor died in May 1349, and the next appointee three months later, all three within a year. Despite such weird vagaries, prelates in general managed to sustain a higher survival rate than the lesser clergy. Among bishops the deaths have been estimated at about one in twenty. The loss of priests, even if many avoided their fearful duty of attending the dying, was about the same as among the population as a whole. [25]

Government officials, whose loss contributed to the general chaos, found, on the whole, no special shelter. In Siena four of the nine members of the governing oligarchy died, in France one third of the royal notaries, in Bristol 15 out of the 52 members of the Town Council or almost one third. Tax-collecting obviously suffered, with the result that Philip VI was unable to collect more than a fraction of the subsidy granted him by the Estates in the winter of 1347–48. [26]

Lawlessness and debauchery accompanied the plague as they had during the great plague of Athens of 430 B.C., when according to Thucydides, men grew bold in the indulgence of pleasure: "For seeing how the rich died in a moment and those who had nothing immediately inherited their property, they reflected that life and riches were alike transitory and they resolved to enjoy themselves while they could." Human behavior is timeless. When St. John had his vision of plague in Revelation, he knew from some experience or race memory that [27] those who survived "repented not of the work of their hands. . . . Neither repented they of their murders, nor of their sorceries, nor of their fornication, nor of their thefts."

NOTES[2]

1: "Death Is Seen Seated": Simon de Covino, q. Campbell, 80.

2: "Could Infect the World": q. Gasquet, 41.

3: Welsh Lament: q. Ziegler, 190.

9: "Dogs Dragged Them Forth": Agnolo di Tura, q. Ziegler, 58.

10: "Or If No Man Is Present": Bishop of Bath and Wells, q. Ziegler, 125. "No Bells Tolled": Agnolo di Tura, q. Schevill, *Siena*, 211. The same observation was made by Gabriel de Muisis, notary of Piacenza, q. Crawfurd, 113.

11: Givry Parish Register: Renouard, 111. Three Villages Of Cambridgeshire: Saltmarsh.

12: Petrarch's Brother: Bishop, 273. Brother John Clyn: q. Ziegler, 195.

13: Atrophy; "and in These Days": q. Deaux, 143, citing only "an old northern chronicle."

14: Agnolo Di Tura, "Father Abandoned Child": q. Ziegler, 58.

15: "Magistrates And Notaries": q. Deaux, 49. English Priests Turned away: Ziegler, 261. Parents Deserting Children: Hecker, 30. Guy De Chauliac, "A Father": q. Gasquet, 50–51.

16: Nuns of the Hotel Dieu: *Chron. Jean de Venette*, 49.

17: Picards and Scots Mock Mortality of Neighbors: Gasquet, 53, and Ziegler, 198.

18: Catherine de Coucy: *L'Art de vérifier*, 237. Amiens Tanners: Gasquet, 57. "By the Jollity That is in Us": *Grandes Chrons.*, VI, 486–87.

19: John Of Fordun: q. Ziegler, 199. Simon de Covino on the Poor: Gasquet, 42. On Youth: Cazelles, *Peste*.

20: Knighton On Sheep: q. Ziegler, 175. Wolves of Austria and Dalmatia: ibid., 84, 111. Dogs and Cats: Muisis, q. Gasquet, 44, 61.

21: Bavarian Chronicler of Neuberg: q. Ziegler, 84. Walsingham, "The World Could Never": Denifle, 273.

22: "Oh Happy Posterity": q. Ziegler, 45.

23: Giovanni Villani, "*e dure questo*": q. Snell, 334.

24: Physicians of Venice: Campbell, 98. Simon de Covino: ibid., 31. Guy de Chauliac, "I Was in Fear": q. Thompson, *Ec. and Soc.*, 379.

27: Thucydides: q. Crawfurd, 30–31.

BIBLIOGRAPHY

L'Art de vérifier les dates des faits historiques, par un Religieux de la Congregation de St.-Maur, vol. XII. Paris, 1818.

---

[2]Tuchman does not use numbered footnotes, but at the back of her book she identifies the source of every quotation or citation. The works cited follow in a bibliography. Although Tuchman's notes are labeled by page number, the numbers here refer to the paragraphs in which the sources are mentioned. [Eds.]

Bishop, Morris. *Petrarch and His World*. Indiana University Press, 1963.

Campbell, Anna M., *The Black Death and Men of Learning*. Columbia University Press, 1931.

Cazelles, Raymond. *"La Peste de 1348–49 en Langue d'oil; épidémie prolitarienne et enfantine." Bull. philologique et historique*, 1962, pp. 293–305.

Chronicle of Jean de Venette. Trans. Jean Birdsall. Ed. Richard A. Newhall. Columbia University Press, 1853.

Crawfurd, Raymond, *Plague and Pestilence in Literature and Art*. Oxford, 1914.

Deaux, George, *The Black Death, 1347*. London, 1969.

Denifle, Henri, *La Désolation des églises, monastères et hopitaux en France pendant la guerre de cent ans*, vol. I. Paris, 1899.

Gasquet, Francis Aidan, Abbot, *The Black Death of 1348 and 1349*, 2nd ed. London, 1908.

Grandes Chroniques de France, vol. VI (to 1380). Ed. Paulin Paris. Paris, 1838.

Hecker, J. F. C., *The Epidemics of the Middle Ages*. London, 1844.

Renouard, Yves. *"La Peste noirs de 1348–50." Rev. de Paris*, March, 1950.

Saltmarsh, John, "Plague and Economic Decline in England in the Later Middle Ages," *Cambridge Historical Journal*, vol. VII, no. 1, 1941.

Schevill, Ferdinand, *Siena: The History of a Medieval Commune*. New York, 1909.

Snell, Frederick, *The Fourteenth Century*. Edinburgh, 1899.

Thompson, James Westfall, *Economic and Social History of Europe in the Later Middle Ages*. New York, 1931.

Ziegler, Philip, *The Black Death*. New York, 1969. (The best modern study.)

QUESTIONS

1. Try to imagine yourself in Tuchman's position. If you were assigned the task of reporting on the black plague in Europe, how would you go about it? What problems would you expect to encounter in the research and in the composition of your report?

2. The notes and bibliography reveal a broad scholarly base: Tuchman's research was clearly prodigious. But so were the problems of organization after the research had been done. Tuchman had to find a way to present her information to us that would be clear and interesting. How has she solved her problem? What overall patterns of organization do you find in this selection? Can you mark off subsections with topics of their own?

3. How does Tuchman organize her paragraphs? Consider paragraph 20, for example. What is the topic? What are the subtopics? Why does the paragraph begin and end as it does? Consider paragraph 22. How does the first sentence serve as a transition from the previous paragraph? How is the rest of the paragraph ordered? Does the next paragraph start a new topic or continue developing that announced at the beginning of paragraph 22?

4. Many paragraphs end with direct quotations. Examine some of these. What do they have in common? Why do you suppose Tuchman closes so many paragraphs in this way?

5. Much of this essay is devoted to the reporting of facts and figures. This could be supremely dull, but Tuchman is an expert at avoiding dullness. How does she help the reader see and feel the awfulness of the plague? Locate specific examples in the text, and discuss their effectiveness.

6. We have included the notes for the chapter reprinted here. Examine Tuchman's

list of sources, and explain how she has used them. Does she quote directly from each source, or does she paraphrase it? Does she use a source to illustrate a point, or as evidence for argument, or in some other way? Describe Tuchman's general method of using sources.

7. Taking Tuchman as a model, write a report on some other catastrophe, blending factual reporting with description of what it was like to be there. This will require both careful research and artful selection and arrangement of the fruits of that research.

8. Using Tuchman's notes to A *Distant Mirror* as a reference guide, find out more about some specific place or event mentioned by Tuchman. Write a report of your findings.

Social Sciences and Public Affairs

ATOMIC BOMBING OF NAGASAKI TOLD BY FLIGHT MEMBER

William L. Laurence

William L. Laurence was born in Lithuania and came to the United States in 1905. He studied at Harvard and the Boston University Law School. His main interest, however, had always been in science, and after working at the New York World for five years, Laurence went to the New York Times as a science reporter. During World War II, Laurence was the only reporter to know about the top secret testing of the atomic bomb. On August 9, 1945, he was permitted to fly with the mission to drop the second atomic bomb on Nagasaki. Three days earlier, over one hundred thousand people had been killed in the Hiroshima bombing. Laurence won the Pulitzer Prize for this account of the bombing of Nagasaki. The article appeared in the New York Times, September 9, 1945.

With the atomic-bomb mission to Japan, August 9 (Delayed)—We are on our way to bomb the mainland of Japan. Our flying contingent consists of three specially designed B-29 Superforts, and two of these carry no bombs. But our lead plane is on its way with another atomic bomb, the second in three days, concentrating in its active substance an explosive energy equivalent to twenty thousand and, under favorable conditions, forty thousand tons of TNT. 1

We have several chosen targets. One of these is the great industrial and shipping center of Nagasaki, on the western shore of Kyushu, one of the main islands of the Japanese homeland. 2

I watched the assembly of this man-made meteor during the past two days and was among the small group of scientists and Army and Navy representatives 3 privileged to be present at the ritual of its loading in the Superfort last night, against a background of threatening black skies torn open at intervals by great lightning flashes.

It is a thing of beauty to behold, this "gadget." Into its design went millions   4
of man-hours of what is without doubt the most concentrated intellectual effort in history. Never before had so much brain power been focused on a single problem.

This atomic bomb is different from the bomb used three days ago with such   5
devastating results on Hiroshima.

I saw the atomic substance before it was placed inside the bomb. By itself it   6
is not at all dangerous to handle. It is only under certain conditions, produced in the bomb assembly, that it can be made to yield up its energy, and even then it gives only a small fraction of its total contents—a fraction, however, large enough to produce the greatest explosion on earth.

The briefing at midnight revealed the extreme care and the tremendous   7
amount of preparation that had been made to take care of every detail of the mission, to make certain that the atomic bomb fully served the purpose for which it was intended. Each target in turn was shown in detailed maps and in aerial photographs. Every detail of the course was rehearsed—navigation, altitude, weather, where to land in emergencies. It came out that the Navy had rescue craft, known as Dumbos and Superdumbos, stationed at various strategic points in the vicinity of the targets, ready to rescue the fliers in case they were forced to bail out.

The briefing period ended with a moving prayer by the chaplain. We then   8
proceeded to the mess hall for the traditional early-morning breakfast before departure on a bombing mission.

A convoy of trucks took us to the supply building for the special equipment   9
carried on combat missions. This included the Mae West,[1] a parachute, a lifeboat, an oxygen mask, a flak suit, and a survival vest. We still had a few hours before take-off time, but we all went to the flying field and stood around in little groups or sat in jeeps talking rather casually about our mission to the Empire, as the Japanese home islands are known hereabouts.

In command of our mission is Major Charles W. Sweeney, twenty-five, of   10
124 Hamilton Avenue, North Quincy, Massachusetts. His flagship, carrying the atomic bomb, is named *The Great Artiste*, but the name does not appear on the body of the great silver ship, with its unusually long, four-bladed, orange-tipped propellers. Instead, it carries the number 77, and someone remarks that it was "Red" Grange's winning number on the gridiron.

We took off at 3:50 this morning and headed northwest on a straight line for   11
the Empire. The night was cloudy and threatening, with only a few stars here and there breaking through the overcast. The weather report had predicted

---

[1]Mae West: an inflatable life jacket named for the actress. [Eds.]

storms ahead part of the way but clear sailing for the final and climactic stages of our odyssey.

We were about an hour away from our base when the storm broke. Our great ship took some heavy dips through the abysmal darkness around us, but it took these dips much more gracefully than a large commercial air liner, producing a sensation more in the nature of a glide than a "bump," like a great ocean liner riding the waves except that in this case the air waves were much higher and the rhythmic tempo of the glide was much faster.

I noticed a strange eerie light coming through the window high above the navigator's cabin, and as I peered through the dark all around us I saw a startling phenomenon. The whirling giant propellers had somehow become great luminous disks of blue flame. The same luminous blue flame appeared on the plexiglas windows in the nose of the ship, and on the tips of the giant wings. It looked as though we were riding the whirlwind through space on a chariot of blue fire.

It was, I surmised, a surcharge of static electricity that had accumulated on the tips of the propellers and on the di-electric material of the plastic windows. One's thoughts dwelt anxiously on the precious cargo in the invisible ship ahead of us. Was there any likelihood of danger that this heavy electric tension in the atmosphere all about us might set it off?

I expressed my fears to Captain Bock, who seems nonchalant and unperturbed at the controls. He quickly reassured me.

"It is a familiar phenomenon seen often on ships. I have seen it many times on bombing missions. It is known as St. Elmo's fire."

On we went through the night. We soon rode out the storm and our ship was once again sailing on a smooth course straight ahead, on a direct line to the Empire.

Our altimeter showed that we were traveling through space at a height of seventeen thousand feet. The thermometer registered an outside temperature of thirty-three degrees below zero Centigrade, about thirty below Fahrenheit. Inside our pressurized cabin the temperature was that of a comfortable air-conditioned room and a pressure corresponding to an altitude of eight thousand feet. Captain Bock cautioned me, however, to keep my oxygen mask handy in case of emergency. This, he explained, might mean either something going wrong with the pressure equipment inside the ship or a hole through the cabin by flak.

The first signs of dawn came shortly after five o'clock. Sergeant Curry, of Hoopeston, Illinois, who had been listening steadily on his earphones for radio reports, while maintaining a strict radio silence himself, greeted it by rising to his feet and gazing out the window.

"It's good to see the day," he told me. "I get a feeling of claustrophobia hemmed in this cabin at night."

171

He is a typical American youth, looking even younger than his twenty years. 21
It takes no mind reader to read his thoughts.

"It's a long way from Hoopeston," I find myself remarking. 22

"Yep," he replies, as he busies himself decoding a message from outer space. 23

"Think this atomic bomb will end the war?" he asks hopefully. 24

"There is a very good chance that this one may do the trick," I assured him, 25
"but if not, then the next one or two surely will. Its power is such that no nation
can stand up against it very long." This was not my own view. I had heard it
expressed all around a few hours earlier, before we took off. To anyone who
had seen this manmade fireball in action, as I had less than a month ago in
the desert of New Mexico, this view did not sound overoptimistic.

By 5:50 it was really light outside. We had lost our lead ship, but Lieutenant 26
Godfrey, our navigator, informs me that we had arranged for that contingency.
We have an assembly point in the sky above the little island of Yakushima,
southeast of Kyushu, at 9:10. We are to circle there and wait for the rest of our
formation.

Our genial bombardier, Lieutenant Levy, comes over to invite me to take 27
his front-row seat in the transparent nose of the ship, and I accept eagerly. From
that vantage point in space, seventeen thousand feet above the Pacific, one gets
a view of hundreds of miles on all sides, horizontally and vertically. At that
height the vast ocean below and the sky above seem to merge into one great
sphere.

I was on the inside of that firmament, riding above the giant mountains of 28
white cumulus clouds, letting myself be suspended in infinite space. One hears
the whirl of the motors behind one, but it soon becomes insignificant against
the immensity all around and is before long swallowed by it. There comes a
point where space also swallows time and one lives through eternal moments
filled with an oppressive loneliness, as though all life had suddenly vanished
from the earth and you are the only one left, a lone survivor traveling endlessly
through interplanetary space.

My mind soon returns to the mission I am on. Somewhere beyond these 29
vast mountains of white clouds ahead of me there lies Japan, the land of our
enemy. In about four hours from now one of its cities, making weapons of war
for use against us, will be wiped off the map by the greatest weapon ever made
by man: In one tenth of a millionth of a second, a fraction of time immeasurable
by any clock, a whirlwind from the skies will pulverize thousands of its buildings
and tens of thousands of its inhabitants.

But at this moment no one yet knows which one of the several cities chosen 30
as targets is to be annihilated. The final choice lies with destiny. The winds
over Japan will make the decision. If they carry heavy clouds over our primary
target, that city will be saved, at least for the time being. None of its inhabitants
will ever know that the wind of a benevolent destiny had passed over their heads.
But that same wind will doom another city.

Our weather planes ahead of us are on their way to find out where the wind   31
blows. Half an hour before target time we will know what the winds have
decided.

Does one feel any pity or compassion for the poor devils about to die? Not   32
when one thinks of Pearl Harbor and of the Death March on Bataan.[2]

Captain Bock informs me that we are about to start our climb to bombing   33
altitude.

He manipulates a few knobs on his control panel to the right of him, and I   34
alternately watch the white clouds and ocean below me and the altimeter on
the bombardier's panel. We reached our altitude at nine o'clock. We were then
over Japanese waters, close to their mainland. Lieutenant Godfrey motioned to
me to look through his radar scope. Before me was the outline of our assembly
point. We shall soon meet our lead ship and proceed to the final stage of our
journey.

We reached Yakushima at 9:12 and there, about four thousand feet ahead   35
of us, was *The Great Artiste* with its precious load. I saw Lieutenant Godfrey
and Sergeant Curry strap on their parachutes and I decided to do likewise.

We started circling. We saw little towns on the coastline, heedless of our   36
presence. We kept on circling, waiting for the third ship in our formation.

It was 9:56 when we began heading for the coastline. Our weather scouts   37
had sent us code messages, deciphered by Sergeant Curry, informing us that
both the primary target as well as the secondary were clearly visible.

The winds of destiny seemed to favor certain Japanese cities that must remain   38
nameless. We circled about them again and again and found no opening in the
thick umbrella of clouds that covered them. Destiny chose Nagasaki as the
ultimate target.

We had been circling for some time when we noticed black puffs of smoke   39
coming through the white clouds directly at us. There were fifteen bursts of flak
in rapid succession, all too low. Captain Bock changed his course. There soon
followed eight more bursts of flak, right up to our altitude, but by this time
were too far to the left.

We flew southward down the channel and at 11:33 crossed the coastline and   40
headed straight for Nagasaki, about one hundred miles to the west. Here again
we circled until we found an opening in the clouds. It was 12:01 and the goal
of our mission had arrived.

We heard the prearranged signal on our radio, put on our arc welder's glasses,   41
and watched tensely the maneuverings of the strike ship about half a mile in
front of us.

---

[2]Pearl Harbor: on December 7, 1941, a surprise bombing attack by the Japanese on this United
States naval base in Hawaii caused the death of 1,177 people and prompted the United States to
enter World War II; the Death March on Bataan: physically weakened American and Filipino
defenders of the Bataan peninsula were forced by their Japanese captors to march ninety miles
under brutal conditions to a prisoner of war camp in Manila. Many did not survive. [Eds.]

"There she goes!" someone said.   42

Out of the belly of *The Great Artiste* what looked like a black object went   43
downward.

Captain Bock swung to get out of range; but even though we were turning   44
away in the opposite direction, and despite the fact that it was broad daylight
in our cabin, all of us became aware of a giant flash that broke through the
dark barrier of our arc welder's lenses and flooded our cabin with intense light.

We removed our glasses after the first flash, but the light still lingered on, a   45
bluish-green light that illuminated the entire sky all around. A tremendous blast
wave struck our ship and made it tremble from nose to tail. This was followed
by four more blasts in rapid succession, each resounding like the boom of
cannon fire hitting our plane from all directions.

Observers in the tail of our ship saw a giant ball of fire rise as though from   46
the bowels of the earth, belching forth enormous white smoke rings. Next they
saw a giant pillar of purple fire, ten thousand feet high, shooting skyward with
enormous speed.

By the time our ship had made another turn in the direction of the atomic   47
explosion the pillar of purple fire had reached the level of our altitude. Only
about forty-five seconds had passed. Awe-struck, we watched it shoot upward
like a meteor coming from the earth instead of from outer space, becoming ever
more alive as it climbed skyward through the white clouds. It was no longer
smoke, or dust, or even a cloud of fire. It was a living thing, a new species of
being, born right before our incredulous eyes.

At one stage of its evolution, covering millions of years in terms of seconds,   48
the entity assumed the form of a giant square totem pole, with its base about
three miles long, tapering off to about a mile at the top. Its bottom was brown,
its center was amber, its top white. But it was a living totem pole, carved with
many grotesque masks grimacing at the earth.

Then, just when it appeared as though the thing had settled down into a   49
state of permanence, there came shooting out of the top a giant mushroom that
increased the height of the pillar to a total of forty-five thousand feet. The
mushroom top was even more alive than the pillar, seething and boiling in a
white fury of creamy foam, sizzling upward and then descending earthward, a
thousand Old Faithful geysers rolled into one.

It kept struggling in an elemental fury, like a creature in the act of breaking   50
the bonds that held it down. In a few seconds it had freed itself from its gigantic
stem and floated upward with tremendous speed, its momentum carrying it into
the stratosphere to a height of about sixty thousand feet.

But no sooner did this happen when another mushroom, smaller in size than   51
the first one, began emerging out of the pillar. It was as though the decapitated
monster was growing a new head.

As the first mushroom floated off into the blue it changed its shape into a   52
flowerlike form, its giant petals curving downward, creamy white outside, rose-

colored inside. It still retained that shape when we last gazed at it from a distance of about two hundred miles. The boiling pillar of many colors could also be seen at that distance, a giant mountain of jumbled rainbows, in travail. Much living substance had gone into those rainbows. The quivering top of the pillar was protruding to a great height through the white clouds, giving the appearance of a monstrous prehistoric creature with a ruff around its neck, a fleecy ruff extending in all directions, as far as the eye could see.

QUESTIONS

1. What do we learn about the crew members on *The Great Artiste?* Why has Laurence bothered to tell us about them?

2. Laurence's description of the bomb as "a thing of beauty" (paragraph 4) suggests that this eyewitness report is not wholly objective. What is Laurence's moral stance on this mission?

3. Consider Laurence's arrangement of time in his narrative. What effect do you think he wishes to create by switching back and forth between past and present tense?

4. Consider Laurence's description of the blast and its resulting cloud (paragraphs 44 through 52). His challenge as a writer is to help his readers to see this strange and awesome thing. What familiar images does he use to represent this unfamiliar sight? What do those images say—especially the last one—about Laurence's feelings as he watched the cloud transform itself?

5. Write an eyewitness report of an event that you consider important. Present the preparations or actions leading up to the event, and include information about others involved. What imagery can you use to describe the glorious, funny, or chaotic event itself?

6. For a report on the basis for Laurence's attitude toward the bombings of Hiroshima and Nagasaki, look at as many newspapers as you can for August 6 through 10 in 1945. Be sure to look at the editorial pages as well as the front pages. If possible, you might also interview relatives and friends who are old enough to remember the war or who might have fought in it. What attitudes toward the bomb and its use were expressed then? How do these compare or contrast with Laurence's attitude?

HATSUYO NAKAMURA

John Hersey

*John Hersey was born in 1914 in Tientsin, China, where
his father was a YMCA secretary and his mother a mission-
ary. After graduating from Yale in 1936, Hersey was a war
correspondent in China and Japan. When the United States
entered World War II, Hersey covered the war in the South
Pacific, the Mediterranean, and Moscow. In 1945, he won
the Pulitzer Prize for his novel, A Bell for Adano. In 1946,
Hiroshima, a report about the effects of the atomic bomb
on the lives of six people, was widely acclaimed. Almost forty
years later, Hersey went back to Japan to find those six
people to see what their lives had been like. Their stories
form the final chapter of the 1985 edition of Hiroshima.
The selection presented here first appeared in The New Yorker,
as did the first edition of Hiroshima. A prolific writer of
fiction and nonfiction, Hersey believes that "journalism allows its readers to witness history; fiction gives its readers an
opportunity to live it."*

In August, 1946, a year after the bombing of Hiroshima, Hatsuyo Nakamura   1
was weak and destitute. Her husband, a tailor, had been taken into the Army
and had been killed at Singapore on the day of that city's capture, February 15,
1942. She lost her mother, a brother, and a sister to the atomic bomb. Her son
and two daughters—ten, eight, and five years old—were buried in rubble when
the blast of the bomb flung her house down. In a frenzy, she dug them out
alive. A month after the bombing, she came down with radiation sickness; she
lost most of her hair and lay in bed for weeks with a high fever in the house of
her sister-in-law in the suburb of Kabe, worrying all the time about how to
support her children. She was too poor to go to a doctor. Gradually, the worst
of the symptoms abated, but she remained feeble; the slightest exertion wore
her out.

She was near the end of her resources. Fleeing from her house through the   2
fires on the day of the bombing, she had saved nothing but a rucksack of
emergency clothing, a blanket, an umbrella, and a suitcase of things she had
stored in her air-raid shelter; she had much earlier evacuated a few kimonos to
Kabe in fear of a bombing. Around the time her hair started to grow in again,
her brother-in-law went back to the ruins of her house and recovered her late
husband's Sankoku sewing machine, which needed repairs. And though she
had lost the certificates of a few bonds and other meager wartime savings, she

176

had luckily copied off their numbers before the bombing and taken the record to Kabe, so she was eventually able to cash them in. This money enabled her to rent for fifty yen a month—the equivalent then of less than fifteen cents—a small wooden shack built by a carpenter in the Nobori-cho neighborhood, near the site of her former home. In this way, she could free herself from the charity of her in-laws and begin a courageous struggle, which would last for many years, to keep her children and herself alive.

The hut had a dirt floor and was dark inside, but it was a home of sorts. Raking back some rubble next to it, she planted a garden. From the debris of collapsed houses she scavenged cooking utensils and a few dishes. She had the Sankoku fixed and began to take in some sewing, and from time to time she did cleaning and laundry and washed dishes for neighbors who were somewhat better off than she was. But she got so tired that she had to take two days' rest for every three days she worked, and if she was obliged for some reason to work for a whole week she then had to rest for three or four days. She soon ran through her savings and was forced to sell her best kimono.

At that precarious time, she fell ill. Her belly began to swell up, and she had diarrhea and so much pain she could no longer work at all. A doctor who lived nearby came to see her and told her she had roundworm, and he said, incorrectly, "If it bites your intestine, you'll die." In those days, there was a shortage of chemical fertilizers in Japan, so farmers were using night soil, and as a consequence many people began to harbor parasites, which were not fatal in themselves but were seriously debilitating to those who had had radiation sickness. The doctor treated Nakamura-san (as he would have addressed her) with santonin, a somewhat dangerous medicine derived from certain varieties of artemisia.[1] To pay the doctor, she was forced to sell her last valuable possession, her husband's sewing machine. She came to think of that act as marking the lowest and saddest moment of her whole life.

In referring to those who went through the Hiroshima and Nagasaki bombings, the Japanese tended to shy away from the term "survivors," because in its focus on being alive it might suggest some slight to the sacred dead. The class of people to which Nakamura-san belonged came, therefore, to be called by a more neutral name, "hibakusha"—literally, "explosion-affected persons." For more than a decade after the bombings, the hibakusha lived in an economic limbo, apparently because the Japanese government did not want to find itself saddled with anything like moral responsibility for heinous acts of the victorious United States. Although it soon became clear that many hibakusha suffered consequences of their exposure to the bombs which were quite different in nature and degree from those of survivors even of the ghastly fire bombings in

---

[1]artemisia: a genus of herbs and shrubs, including sagebrush and wormwood, distinguished by strong-smelling foliage. [Eds.]

Tokyo and elsewhere, the government made no special provision for their relief—until, ironically, after the storm of rage that swept across Japan when the twenty-three crewmen of a fishing vessel, the Lucky Dragon No. 5, and its cargo of tuna were irradiated by the American test of a hydrogen bomb at Bikini in 1954. It took three years even then for a relief law for the hibakusha to pass the Diet.

Though Nakamura-san could not know it, she thus had a bleak period ahead   6
of her. In Hiroshima, the early postwar years were, besides, a time, especially painful for poor people like her, of disorder, hunger, greed, thievery, black markets. Non-hibakusha employers developed a prejudice against the survivors as word got around that they were prone to all sorts of ailments, and that even those like Nakamura-san, who were not cruelly maimed and had not developed any serious overt symptoms, were unreliable workers, since most of them seemed to suffer, as she did, from the mysterious but real malaise that came to be known as one kind of lasting "A-bomb sickness": a nagging weakness and weariness, dizziness now and then, digestive troubles, all aggravated by a feeling of oppression, a sense of doom, for it was said that unspeakable diseases might at any time plant nasty flowers in their bodies, and even in those of their descendants.

As Nakamura-san struggled to get from day to day, she had no time for   7
attitudinizing about the bomb or anything else. She was sustained, curiously, by a kind of passivity, summed up in a phrase she herself sometimes used—"*Shikata ga-nai*," meaning, loosely, "It can't be helped." She was not religious, but she lived in a culture long colored by the Buddhist belief that resignation might lead to clear vision; she had shared with other citizens a deep feeling of powerlessness in the face of a state authority that had been divinely strong ever since the Meiji Restoration, in 1868; and the hell she had witnessed and the terrible aftermath unfolding around her reached so far beyond human understanding that it was impossible to think of them as the work of resentable human beings, such as the pilot of the Enola Gay, or President Truman, or the scientists who had made the bomb[2]—or even, nearer at hand, the Japanese militarists who had helped to bring on the war. The bombing almost seemed a natural disaster—one that it had simply been her bad luck, her fate (which must be accepted), to suffer.

When she had been wormed and felt slightly better, she made an arrange-   8
ment to deliver bread for a baker named Takahashi, whose bakery was in Noboricho. On days when she had the strength to do it, she would take orders for bread from retail shops in her neighborhood, and the next morning she would pick up the requisite number of loaves and carry them in baskets and boxes through the streets to the stores. It was exhausting work, for which she earned the equivalent of about fifty cents a day. She had to take frequent rest days.

---

[2]Enola Gay: name of the airplane that dropped the atomic bomb on Hiroshima; Harry S. Truman (1884–1972): president of the United States who made the decision to drop the bomb. [Eds.]

After some time, when she was feeling a bit stronger, she took up another   9
kind of peddling. She would get up in the dark and trundle a borrowed two-
wheeled pushcart for two hours across the city to a section called Eba, at the
mouth of one of the seven estuarial rivers that branch from the Ota River
through Hiroshima. There, at daylight, fishermen would cast their leaded skirt-
like nets for sardines, and she would help them to gather up the catch when
they hauled it in. Then she would push the cart back to Nobori-cho and sell
the fish for them from door to door. She earned just enough for food.

A couple of years later, she found work that was better suited to her need for   10
occasional rest, because within certain limits she could do it on her own time.
This was a job of collecting money for deliveries of the Hiroshima paper, the
Chugoku Shimbun, which most people in the city read. She had to cover a big
territory, and often her clients were not at home or pleaded that they couldn't
pay just then, so she would have to go back again and again. She earned the
equivalent of about twenty dollars a month at this job. Every day, her will power
and her weariness seemed to fight to an uneasy draw.

In 1951, after years of this drudgery, it was Nakamura-san's good luck, her   11
fate (which must be accepted), to become eligible to move into a better house.
Two years earlier, a Quaker professor of dendrology from the University of
Washington named Floyd W. Schmoe, driven, apparently, by deep urges for
expiation and reconciliation, had come to Hiroshima, assembled a team of
carpenters, and, with his own hands and theirs, begun building a series of
Japanese-style houses for victims of the bomb; in all, his team eventually built
twenty-one. It was to one of these houses that Nakamura-san had the good
fortune to be assigned. The Japanese measure their houses by multiples of the
area of the floor-covering *tsubo* mat, a little less than four square yards, and the
Dr. Shum-o houses, as the Hiroshimans called them, had two rooms of six
mats each. This was a big step up for the Nakamuras. This home was redolent
of new wood and clean matting. The rent, payable to the city government, was
the equivalent of about a dollar a month.

Despite the family's poverty, the children seemed to be growing normally.   12
Yaeko and Myeko, the two daughters, were anemic, but all three had so far
escaped any of the more serious complications that so many young hibakusha
were suffering. Yaeko, now fourteen, and Myeko, eleven, were in middle school.
The boy, Toshio, ready to enter high school, was going to have to earn money
to attend it, so he took up delivering papers to the places from which his mother
was collecting. These were some distance from their Dr. Shum-o house, and
they had to commute at odd hours by streetcar.

The old hut in Nobori-cho stood empty for a time, and, while continuing   13
with her newspaper collections, Nakamura-san converted it into a small street
shop for children, selling sweet potatoes, which she roasted, and *dagashi*, or

little candies and rice cakes, and cheap toys, which she bought from a whole-saler.

All along, she had been collecting for papers from a small company, Suyama   14
Chemical, that made mothballs sold under the trade name Paragen. A friend
of hers worked there, and one day she suggested to Nakamura-san that she join
the company, helping wrap the product in its packages. The owner, Nakamura-san learned, was a compassionate man, who did not share the bias of many
employers against hibakusha; he had several on his staff of twenty women wrap-pers. Nakamura-san objected that she couldn't work more than a few days at a
time; the friend persuaded her that Suyama would understand that.

So she began. Dressed in company uniforms, the women stood, somewhat   15
bent over, on either side of a couple of conveyor belts, working as fast as possible
to wrap two kinds of Paragen in cellophane. Paragen had a dizzying odor, and
at first it made one's eyes smart. Its substance, powdered paradichlorobenzene,
had been compressed into lozenge-shaped mothballs and into larger spheres,
the size of small oranges, to be hung in Japanese-style toilets, where their rank
pseudomedicinal smell would offset the unpleasantness of non-flushing facili-ties.

Nakamura-san was paid, as a beginner, a hundred and seventy yen—then   16
less than fifty cents—a day. At first, the work was confusing, terribly tiring, and
a bit sickening. Her boss worried about her paleness. She had to take many days
off. But little by little she became used to the factory. She made friends. There
was a family atmosphere. She got raises. In the two ten-minute breaks, morning
and afternoon, when the moving belt stopped, there was a birdsong of gossip
and laughter, in which she joined. It appeared that all along there had been,
deep in her temperament, a core of cheerfulness, which must have fuelled her
long fight against A-bomb lassitude, something warmer and more vivifying than
mere submission, than saying "*Shikata ga-nai.*" The other women took to her;
she was constantly doing them small favors. They began calling her, affection-ately, *Oba-san*—roughly, "Auntie."

She worked at Suyama for thirteen years. Though her energy still paid its   17
dues, from time to time, to the A-bomb syndrome, the searing experiences of
that day in 1945 seemed gradually to be receding from the front of her mind.

The Lucky Dragon No. 5 episode took place the year after Nakamura-san   18
started working for Suyama Chemical. In the ensuing fever of outrage in the
country, the provision of adequate medical care for the victims of the Hiroshima
and Nagasaki bombs finally became a political issue. Almost every year since
1946, on the anniversary of the Hiroshima bombing a Peace Memorial Meeting
had been held in a park that the city planners had set aside, during the city's
rebuilding, as a center of remembrance, and on August 6, 1955, delegates from
all over the world gathered there for the first World Conference Against Atomic
and Hydrogen Bombs. On its second day, a number of hibakusha tearfully

testified to the government's neglect of their plight. Japanese political parties took up the cause, and in 1957 the Diet at last passed the A-Bomb Victims Medical Care Law. This law and its subsequent modifications defined four classes of people who would be eligible for support: those who had been in the city limits on the day of the bombing; those who had entered an area within two kilometers of the hypocenter in the first fourteen days after it; those who had come into physical contact with bomb victims, in administering first aid or in disposing of their bodies; and those who had been embryos in the wombs of women in any of the first three categories. These hibakusha were entitled to receive so-called health books, which would entitle them to free medical treatment. Later revisions of the law provided for monthly allowances to victims suffering from various aftereffects.

Like a great many hibakusha, Nakamura-san had kept away from all the agitation, and, in fact, also like many other survivors, she did not even bother to get a health book for a couple of years after they were issued. She had been too poor to keep going to doctors, so she had got into the habit of coping alone, as best she could, with her physical difficulties. Besides, she shared with some other survivors a suspicion of ulterior motives on the part of the political-minded people who took part in the annual ceremonies and conferences. 19

Nakamura-san's son, Toshio, right after his graduation from high school, went to work for the bus division of the Japanese National Railways. He was in the administrative offices, working first on timetables, later in accounting. When he was in his midtwenties, a marriage was arranged for him, through a relative who knew the bride's family. He built an addition to the Dr. Shum-o house, moved in, and began to contribute to his mother's support. He made her a present of a new sewing machine. 20

Yaeko, the older daughter, left Hiroshima when she was fifteen, right after graduating from middle school, to help an ailing aunt who ran a *ryo-kan*, a Japanese-style inn. There, in due course, she fell in love with a man who ate at the inn's restaurant, and she made a love marriage. 21

After graduating from high school, Myeko, the most susceptible of the three children to the A-bomb syndrome, eventually became an expert typist and took up instructing at typing schools. In time, a marriage was arranged for her. 22

Like their mother, all three children avoided pro-hibakusha and antinuclear agitation. 23

In 1966, Nakamura-san, having reached the age of fifty-five, retired from Suyama Chemical. At the end, she was being paid thirty thousand yen, or about eighty-five dollars, a month. Her children were no longer dependent on her, and Toshio was ready to take on a son's responsibility for his aging mother. She felt at home in her body now; she rested when she needed to, and she had no worries about the cost of medical care, for she had finally picked up Health Book No. 1023993. It was time for her to enjoy life. For her pleasure in being 24 able to give gifts, she took up embroidery and the dressing of traditional *kimekomi* dolls, which are supposed to bring good luck. Wearing a bright kimono, she went once a week to dance at the Study Group of Japanese Folk Music. In set movements, with expressive gestures, her hands now and then tucking up the long folds of the kimono sleeves, and with head held high, she danced, moving as if floating, with thirty agreeable women to a song of celebration of entrance into a house:

> May your family flourish
> For a thousand generations,
> For eight thousand generations.

A year or so after Nakamura-san retired, she was invited by an organization called the Bereaved Families' Association to take a train trip with about a hundred other war widows to visit the Yasukuni Shrine, in Tokyo. This holy place, established in 1869, was dedicated to the spirits of all the Japanese who had died in wars against foreign powers, and could be thought roughly analogous, in terms of its symbolism for the nation, to the Arlington National Cemetery— with the difference that souls, not bodies, were hallowed there. The shrine was considered by many Japanese to be a focus of a still smoldering Japanese militarism, but Nakamura-san, who had never seen her husband's ashes and had held on to a belief that he would return to her someday, was oblivious of all that. She found the visit baffling. Besides the Hiroshima hundred, there were huge crowds of women from other cities on the shrine grounds. It was impossible for her to summon up a sense of her dead husband's presence, and she returned home in an uneasy state of mind.

Japan was booming. Things were still rather tight for the Nakamuras, and Toshio had to work very long hours, but the old days of bitter struggle began to seem remote. In 1975, one of the laws providing support to the hibakusha was revised, and Nakamura-san began to receive a so-called health-protection allowance of six thousand yen, then about twenty dollars, a month; this would gradually be increased to more than twice that amount. She also received a pension, toward which she had contributed at Suyama, of twenty thousand yen, or about sixty-five dollars, a month; and for several years she had been receiving a war widow's pension of another twenty thousand yen a month. With the economic upswing, prices had, of course, risen steeply (in a few years Tokyo would become the most expensive city in the world), but Toshio managed to buy a small Mitsubishi car, and occasionally he got up before dawn and rode a train for two hours to play golf with business associates. Yaeko's husband ran a shop for sales and service of air-conditioners and heaters, and Myeko's husband ran a newsstand and candy shop near the railroad station.

In May each year, around the time of the Emperor's birthday, when the trees along broad Peace Boulevard were at their feathery best and banked azaleas were everywhere in bloom, Hiroshima celebrated a flower festival. Entertainment booths lined the boulevard, and there were long parades, with floats and bands and thousands of marchers. This year, Nakamura-san danced with the women of the folk-dance association, six dancers in each of sixty rows. They danced to "Oiwai-Ondo," a song of happiness, lifting their arms in gestures of joy and clapping in rhythms of threes:

> Green pine trees, cranes and turtles . . .
> You must tell a story of your hard times
> And laugh twice.

The bombing had been four decades ago. How far away it seemed!   28

The sun blazed that day. The measured steps and the constant lifting of the   29
arms for hours at a time were tiring. In midafternoon, Nakamura-san suddenly felt woozy. The next thing she knew, she was being lifted, to her great embarrassment and in spite of begging to be let alone, into an ambulance. At the hospital, she said she was fine; all she wanted was to go home. She was allowed to leave.

QUESTIONS

1. What does Hatsuyo Nakamura's story tell us about the larger group of atomic-bomb survivors?

2. Why do you think Hersey chose Hatsuyo Nakamura as a subject to report on? How is she presented to us? How are we meant to feel about her?

3. In composing his article, Hersey presumably interviewed his subject and reports from her point of view. At what points does he augment her story? For example, look at paragraph 5. What material probably comes from the subject? What material probably comes from other sources?

4. How has Hersey arranged his material? He has covered forty years of Hatsuyo Nakamura's life in twenty-nine paragraphs. Make a list of the events he chose to report. At what points does he condense large blocks of time?

5. Interview a relative or someone you know who participated in World War II or in some other war, such as Vietnam. How did the war change the person's life? What events does the person consider most important in the intervening years?

6. No doubt every person then in Hiroshima remembers the day of the bombing just as Americans of certain ages remember days of critical national events—the attack on Pearl Harbor, the Kennedy or King assassinations, the space shuttle disaster, and so on. Interview several people about one such day, finding out where they were when they first learned of the event, how they reacted, what long-term impact they felt, and how they view that day now. Use the information from your interviews to write a report.

A DAY IN SAMOA
Margaret Mead

Margaret Mead (1901–1979) was a cultural anthropologist for almost sixty years. She is the author of many books and articles in the field and is especially known for her studies of the South Sea Islanders. Coming of Age in Samoa (1928) was her first book, based on her first field trip as a working anthropologist. The essay reprinted here is chapter 2 from that book, which is a study of adolescent girls in Samoa. In the introduction to the fifth edition of the book in 1973, Mead wrote, "The little girls whom I studied are buxom grandmothers, still dancing light-footed as Samoan matrons do. . . . And I, instead of being a dutiful granddaughter writing letters home . . . am now a grandmother delighting in a dancing grandchild."

The life of the day begins at dawn, or if the moon has shown until daylight, the shouts of the young men may be heard before dawn from the hillside. Uneasy in the night, populous with ghosts, they shout lustily to one another as they hasten with their work. As the dawn begins to fall among the soft brown roofs and the slender palm trees stand out against a colourless, gleaming sea, lovers slip home from trysts beneath the palm trees or in the shadow of beached canoes, that the light may find each sleeper in his appointed place. Cocks crow, negligently, and a shrill-voiced bird cries from the breadfruit trees. The insistent roar of the reef seems muted to an undertone for the sounds of a waking village. Babies cry, a few short wails before sleepy mothers give them the breast. Restless little children roll out of their sheets and wander drowsily down to the beach to freshen their faces in the sea. Boys, bent upon an early fishing, start collecting their tackle and go to rouse their more laggard companions. Fires are lit, here and there, the white smoke hardly visible against the paleness of the dawn. The whole village, sheeted and frowsy, stirs, rubs its eyes, and stumbles towards the beach. "Talofa!" "Talofa!" "Will the journey start to-day?" "Is it bonito fishing your lordship is going?" Girls stop to giggle over some young ne'er-do-well who escaped during the night from an angry father's pursuit and to venture a shrewd guess that the daughter knew more about his presence than she told. The boy who is taunted by another, who has succeeded him in his sweetheart's favour, grapples with his rival, his foot slipping in the wet sand. From the other end of the village comes a long drawn-out, piercing wail. A messenger has just brought word of the death of some relative in another village. Half-clad, unhurried women, with babies at their breasts, or astride their hips, pause in their tale of

184

Losa's outraged departure from her father's house to the greater kindness in the home of her uncle, to wonder who is dead. Poor relatives whisper their requests to rich relatives, men make plans to set a fish trap together, a woman begs a bit of yellow dye from a kinswoman, and through the village sounds the rhythmic tattoo which calls the young men together. They gather from all parts of the village, digging sticks in hand, ready to start inland to the plantation. The older men set off upon their more lonely occupations, and each household, reassembled under its peaked roof, settles down to the routine of the morning. Little children, too hungry to wait for the late breakfast, beg lumps of cold taro which they munch greedily. Women carry piles of washing to the sea or to the spring at the far end of the village, or set off inland after weaving materials. The older girls go fishing on the reef, or perhaps set themselves to weaving a new set of Venetian blinds.

In the houses, where the pebbly floors have been swept bare with a stiff long-handled broom, the women great with child and the nursing mothers, sit and gossip with one another. Old men sit apart, unceasingly twisting palm husk on their bare thighs and muttering old tales under their breath. The carpenters begin work on the new house, while the owner bustles about trying to keep them in a good humour. Families who will cook to-day are hard at work; the taro, yams and bananas have already been brought from inland; the children are scuttling back and forth, fetching sea water, or leaves to stuff the pig. As the sun rises higher in the sky, the shadows deepen under the thatched roofs, the sand is burning to the touch, the hibiscus flowers wilt on the hedges, and little children bid the smaller ones, "Come out of the sun." Those whose excursions have been short return to the village, the women with strings of crimson jelly fish, or baskets of shell fish, the men with cocoanuts, carried in baskets slung on a shoulder pole. The women and children eat their breakfasts, just hot from the oven, if this is cook day, and the young men work swiftly in the midday heat, preparing the noon feast for their elders.

It is high noon. The sand burns the feet of the little children, who leave their palm leaf balls and their pin-wheels of frangipani blossoms to wither in the sun, as they creep into the shade of the houses. The women who must go abroad carry great banana leaves as sun-shades or wind wet cloths about their heads. Lowering a few blinds against the slanting sun, all who are left in the village wrap their heads in sheets and go to sleep. Only a few adventurous children may slip away for a swim in the shadow of a high rock, some industrious woman continues with her weaving, or a close little group of women bend anxiously over a woman in labour. The village is dazzling and dead; any sound seems oddly loud and out of place. Words have to cut through the solid heat slowly. And then the sun gradually sinks over the sea.

A second time, the sleeping people stir, roused perhaps by the cry of "a boat," resounding through the village. The fishermen beach their canoes, weary and spent from the heat, in spite of the slaked lime on their heads, with which they have sought to cool their brains and redden their hair. The brightly coloured fishes are spread out on the floor, or piled in front of the houses until the women pour water over them to free them from taboo. Regretfully, the young fishermen separate out the "Taboo fish," which must be sent to the chief, or proudly they pack the little palm leaf baskets with offerings of fish to take to their sweethearts. Men come home from the bush, grimy and heavy laden, shouting as they come, greeted in a sonorous rising cadence by those who have remained at home. They gather in the guest house for their evening kava drinking. The soft clapping of hands, the high-pitched intoning of the talking chief who serves the kava echoes through the village. Girls gather flowers to weave into necklaces; children, lusty from their naps and bound to no particular task, play circular games in the half shade of the late afternoon. Finally the sun sets, in a flame which stretches from the mountain behind to the horizon on the sea, the last bather comes up from the beach, children straggle home, dark little figures etched against the sky; lights shine in the houses, and each household gathers for its evening meal. The suitor humbly presents his offering, the children have been summoned from their noisy play, perhaps there is an honoured guest who must be served first, after the soft, barbaric singing of Christian hymns and the brief and graceful evening prayer. In front of a house at the end of the village, a father cries out the birth of a son. In some family circles a face is missing, in others little runaways have found a haven! Again quiet settles upon the village, as first the head of the household, then the women and children, and last of all the patient boys, eat their supper.

After supper the old people and the little children are bundled off to bed. If the young people have guests the front of the house is yielded to them. For day is the time for the councils of old men and the labours of youth, and night is the time for lighter things. Two kinsmen, or a chief and his councillor, sit and gossip over the day's events or make plans for the morrow. Outside a crier goes through the village announcing that the communal breadfruit pit will be opened in the morning, or that the village will make a great fish trap. If it is moonlight, groups of young men, women by twos and threes, wander through the village, and crowds of children hunt for land crabs or chase each other among the breadfruit trees. Half the village may go fishing by torchlight and the curving reef will gleam with wavering lights and echo with shouts of triumph or disappointment, teasing words or smothered cries of outraged modesty. Or a group of youths may dance for the pleasure of some visiting maiden. Many of those who have retired to sleep, drawn by the merry music, will wrap their sheets about them and set out to find the dancing. A white-clad, ghostly throng will gather in a circle about the gaily lit house, a circle from which every now and then a few will detach themselves and wander away among the trees. Sometimes sleep will not descend upon the village until long past midnight; then at last there is only the mellow thunder of the reef and the whisper of lovers, as the village rests until dawn.

A Day in Samoa

QUESTIONS

1. Go through the essay, and note every word or phrase that indicates the time of day. When you have found them all, consider what they reveal about the way Mead has organized her material.

2. There are five paragraphs in this essay. How has Mead used the paragraph in shaping her material? That is, what principle or method of selection has determined what should go in each of the five paragraphs?

3. Is this a report of a specific day or a representation of a typical day? Can you find places where Mead seems to be reporting a particular event? Can you also find places where she is clearly speaking of various events that *might* happen on a typical day? How and why does she mix these two modes of writing?

4. Does this essay have an evaluative dimension? Is Samoan life presented neutrally? Is it made especially attractive or unattractive at any points? Consider specific events or episodes.

5. How does Mead achieve the representational quality of this essay? That is, how does she attempt to make the Samoan day available to us as a sensory experience? How does she convey the "feel" of it?

6. Write an essay in which you represent for the reader "A Day in———." Study Mead's way of selecting details and organizing them as you plan and compose your own essay on a day in a place you know well.

OBSERVING WOLVES
Farley Mowat

Farley Mowat was born in Ontario, Canada, in 1921 and finished college at the University of Toronto in 1949, after wartime service and two years living in the Arctic. He makes his living as a writer rather than a scientist, but he works in the same areas covered by anthropologists and zoologists. Often he writes more as a partisan of primitive people and animals rather than as an "objective" scientist, and his work has reached a wide audience. He has written engagingly about the strange animals he grew up with in Owls in the Family *(1963) and about wolves in* Never Cry Wolf *(1963), from which the following selection is taken.*

During the next several weeks I put my decision into effect with the thoroughness for which I have always been noted. I went completely to the wolves. To begin with I set up a den of my own as near to the wolves as I could conveniently get without disturbing the even tenor of their lives too much. After all, I *was* a stranger, and an unwolflike one, so I did not feel I should go too far too fast. 1

Abandoning Mike's cabin (with considerable relief, since as the days warmed up so did the smell) I took a tiny tent and set it up on the shore of the bay immediately opposite to the den esker.[1] I kept my camping gear to the barest minimum—a small primus stove, a stew pot, a teakettle, and a sleeping bag were the essentials. I took no weapons of any kind, although there were times when I regretted this omission, even if only fleetingly. The big telescope was set up in the mouth of the tent in such a way that I could observe the den by day or night without even getting out of my sleeping bag. 2

During the first few days of my sojourn with the wolves I stayed inside the tent except for brief and necessary visits to the out-of-doors which I always undertook when the wolves were not in sight. The point of this personal concealment was to allow the animals to get used to the tent and to accept it as only another bump on a very bumpy piece of terrain. Later, when the mosquito population reached full flowering, I stayed in the tent practically all of the time unless there was a strong wind blowing, for the most bloodthirsty beasts in the Arctic are not wolves, but the insatiable mosquitoes. 3

My precautions against disturbing the wolves were superfluous. It had required a week for me to get their measure, but they must have taken mine at 4

---

[1]esker: a long, narrow deposit of gravel and sand left by a stream flowing from a glacier. [Eds.]

our first meeting; and, while there was nothing overtly disdainful in their evident assessment of me, they managed to ignore my presence, and indeed my very existence, with a thoroughness which was somehow disconcerting.

Quite by accident I had pitched my tent within ten yards of one of the major   5
paths used by the wolves when they were going to, or coming from, their hunting grounds to the westward; and only a few hours after I had taken up residence one of the wolves came back from a trip and discovered me and my tent. He was at the end of a hard night's work and was clearly tired and anxious to go home to bed. He came over a small rise fifty yards from me with his head down, his eyes half-closed, and a preoccupied air about him. Far from being the preternaturally alert and suspicious beast of fiction, this wolf was so self-engrossed that he came straight on to within fifteen yards of me, and might have gone right past the tent without seeing it at all, had I not banged my elbow against the teakettle, making a resounding clank. The wolf's head came up and his eyes opened wide, but he did not stop or falter in his pace. One brief, sidelong glance was all he vouchsafed to me as he continued on his way.

It was true that I wanted to be inconspicuous, but I felt uncomfortable at   6
being so totally ignored. Nevertheless, during the two weeks which followed, one or more wolves used the track past my tent almost every night—and never, except on one memorable occasion, did they evince the slightest interest in me.

By the time this happened I had learned a good deal about my wolfish   7
neighbors, and one of the facts which had emerged was that they were not nomadic roamers, as is almost universally believed, but were settled beasts and the possessors of a large permanent estate with very definite boundaries.

The territory owned by my wolf family comprised more than a hundred   8
square miles, bounded on one side by a river but otherwise not delimited by geographical features. Nevertheless there *were* boundaries, clearly indicated in wolfish fashion.

Anyone who has observed a dog doing his neighborhood rounds and leaving   9
his personal mark on each convenient post will have already guessed how the wolves marked out *their* property. Once a week, more or less, the clan made the rounds of the family lands and freshened up the boundary markers—a sort of lupine beating of the bounds. This careful attention to property rights was perhaps made necessary by the presence of two other wolf families whose lands abutted on ours, although I never discovered any evidence of bickering or disagreements between the owners of the various adjoining estates. I suspect, therefore, that it was more of a ritual activity.

In any event, once I had become aware of the strong feeling of property   10
rights which existed amongst the wolves, I decided to use this knowledge to make them at least recognize my existence. One evening, after they had gone off for their regular nightly hunt, I staked out a property claim of my own,

embracing perhaps three acres, with the tent at the middle, and *including a hundred-yard long section of the wolves' path.*

Staking the land turned out to be rather more difficult than I had anticipated. In order to ensure that my claim would not be overlooked, I felt obliged to make a property mark on stones, clumps of moss, and patches of vegetation at intervals of not more than fifteen feet around the circumference of my claim. This took most of the night and required frequent returns to the tent to consume copious quantities of tea; but before dawn brought the hunters home the task was done, and I retired, somewhat exhausted, to observe results.   11

I had not long to wait. At 0814 hours, according to my wolf log, the leading male of the clan appeared over the ridge behind me, padding homeward with his usual air of preoccupation. As usual he did not deign to glance at the tent; but when he reached the point where my property line intersected the trail, he stopped as abruptly as if he had run into an invisible wall. He was only fifty yards from me and with my binoculars I could see his expression very clearly.   12

His attitude of fatigue vanished and was replaced by a look of bewilderment. Cautiously he extended his nose and sniffed at one of my marked bushes. He did not seem to know what to make of it or what to do about it. After a minute of complete indecision he backed away a few yards and sat down. And then, finally, he looked directly at the tent and at me. It was a long, thoughtful, considering sort of look.   13

Having achieved my object—that of forcing at least one of the wolves to take cognizance of my existence—I now began to wonder if, in my ignorance, I had transgressed some unknown wolf law of major importance and would have to pay for my temerity. I found myself regretting the absence of a weapon as the look I was getting became longer, yet more thoughtful, and still more intent.   14

I began to grow decidedly fidgety, for I dislike staring matches, and in this particular case I was up against a master, whose yellow glare seemed to become more baleful as I attempted to stare him down.   15

The situation was becoming intolerable. In an effort to break the impasse I loudly cleared my throat and turned my back on the wolf (for a tenth of a second) to indicate as clearly as possible that I found his continued scrutiny impolite, if not actually offensive.   16

He appeared to take the hint. Getting to his feet he had another sniff at my marker, and then he seemed to make up his mind. Briskly, and with an air of decision, he turned his attention away from me and began a systematic tour of the area I had staked out as my own. As he came to each boundary marker he sniffed it once or twice, then carefully placed *his* mark on the outside of each clump of grass or stone. As I watched I saw where I, in my ignorance, had erred. He made his mark with such economy that he was able to complete the entire circuit without having to reload once, or, to change the simile slightly, he did it all on one tank of fuel.   17

The task completed—and it had taken him no longer than fifteen minutes—
he rejoined the path at the point where it left my property and trotted off towards
his home—leaving me with a good deal to occupy my thoughts.

18

QUESTIONS

1. What did you know about wolves before reading this piece? What was the most
surprising—or amusing—information you acquired from reading about Mowat's experience?

2. Write a paragraph summarizing the information about wolves that you can infer
from this selection.

3. How would you describe the narrator of this piece? What does he tell us about
himself, and how do his actions describe him?

4. The writer concludes by saying that he was left "with a good deal to occupy my
thoughts" (paragraph 18). What, do you suppose, were these thoughts?

5. Find a more objective, "scientific" account of wolves. Which of Mowat's observations are substantiated there?

6. Rewrite the main events in this piece from the wolf's point of view.

7. Observe the actions of a dog or a cat as it roams your neighborhood. Write an
objective report of the animal's actions. Conclude with your reactions to the animal's
behavior and, if pertinent, the animal's reactions to your behavior.

FIRST OBSERVATIONS

Jane van Lawick-Goodall

Jane van Lawick-Goodall (b. 1934), British student of animal behavior, began her work as an assistant to Louis Leakey, an anthropologist and paleontologist who has studied human origins. In 1960, with his help, she settled in Tanzania, East Africa, in the Gombe Stream Game Reserve to investigate the behavior of chimpanzees in their natural habitat. Her discoveries have been widely published in professional journals and in a number of books for more general audiences. The selection reprinted here is taken from In the Shadow of Man *(1971), a popular work in which she is careful to report her own behavior as well as that of her chimpanzee subjects.*

For about a month I spent most of each day either on the Peak or overlooking   1
Mlinda Valley where the chimps, before or after stuffing themselves with figs,
ate large quantities of small purple fruits that tasted, like so many of their foods,
as bitter and astringent as sloes or crab apples. Piece by piece, I began to form
my first somewhat crude picture of chimpanzee life.

The impression that I had gained when I watched the chimps at the msulula   2
tree of temporary, constantly changing associations of individuals within the
community was substantiated. Most often I saw small groups of four to eight
moving about together. Sometimes I saw one or two chimpanzees leave such a
group and wander off on their own or join up with a different association. On
other occasions I watched two or three small groups joining to form a larger
one.

Often, as one group crossed the grassy ridge separating the Kasekela Valley   3
from the fig trees in the home valley, the male chimpanzee, or chimpanzees,
of the party would break into a run, sometimes moving in an upright position,
sometimes dragging a fallen branch, sometimes stamping or slapping the hard
earth. These charging displays were always accompanied by loud pant-hoots and
afterward the chimpanzee frequently would swing up into a tree overlooking
the valley he was about to enter and sit quietly, peering down and obviously
listening for a response from below. If there were chimps feeding in the fig trees
they nearly always hooted back, as though in answer. Then the new arrivals
would hurry down the steep slope and, with more calling and screaming, the
two groups would meet in the fig trees. When groups of females and youngsters
with no males present joined other feeding chimpanzees, usually there was none

of this excitement; the newcomers merely climbed up into the trees, greeted some of those already there, and began to stuff themselves with figs.

While many details of their social behavior were hidden from me by the foliage, I did get occasional fascinating glimpses. I saw one female, newly arrived in a group, hurry up to a big male and hold her hand toward him. Almost regally he reached out, clasped her hand in his, drew it toward him, and kissed it with his lips. I saw two adult males embrace each other in greeting. I saw youngsters having wild games through the treetops, chasing around after each other or jumping again and again, one after the other, from a branch to a springy bough below. I watched small infants dangling happily by themselves for minutes on end, patting at their toes with one hand, rotating gently from side to side. Once two tiny infants pulled on opposite ends of a twig in a gentle tug-of-war. Often, during the heat of midday or after a long spell of feeding, I saw two or more adults grooming each other, carefully looking through the hair of their companions. 4

At that time of year the chimps usually went to bed late, making their nests when it was too dark to see properly through binoculars, but sometimes they nested earlier and I could watch them from the Peak. I found that every individual, except for infants who slept with their mothers, made his own nest each night. Generally this took about three minutes: the chimp chose a firm foundation such as an upright fork or crotch, or two horizontal branches. Then he reached out and bent over smaller branches onto this foundation, keeping each one in place with his feet. Finally he tucked in the small leafy twigs growing around the rim of his nest and lay down. Quite often a chimp sat up after a few minutes and picked a handful of leafy twigs, which he put under his head or some other part of his body before settling down again for the night. One young female I watched went on and on bending down branches until she had constructed a huge mound of greenery on which she finally curled up. 5

I climbed up into some of the nests after the chimpanzees had left them. Most of them were built in trees that for me were almost impossible to climb. I found that there was quite complicated interweaving of the branches in some of them. I found, too, that the nests were never fouled with dung; and later, when I was able to get closer to the chimps, I saw how they were always careful to defecate and urinate over the edge of their nests, even in the middle of the night. 6

During that month I really came to know the country well, for I often went on expeditions from the Peak, sometimes to examine nests, more frequently to collect specimens of the chimpanzees' food plants, which Bernard Verdcourt had kindly offered to identify for me. Soon I could find my way around the sheer ravines and up and down the steep slopes of three valleys—the home valley, the Pocket, and Mlinda Valley—as well as a taxi driver finds his way about in the main streets and byways of London. It is a period I remember vividly, not only because I was beginning to accomplish something at last, but 7 also because of the delight I felt in being completely by myself. For those who love to be alone with nature I need add nothing further; for those who do not, no words of mine could ever convey, even in part, the almost mystical awareness of beauty and eternity that accompanies certain treasured moments. And, though the beauty was always there, those moments came upon me unaware: when I was watching the pale flush preceding dawn; or looking up through the rustling leaves of some giant forest tree into the greens and browns and black shadows that occasionally ensnared a bright fleck of the blue sky; or when I stood, as darkness fell, with one hand on the still-warm trunk of a tree and looked at the sparkling of an early moon on the never still, sighing water of the lake.

One day, when I was sitting by the trickle of water in Buffalo Wood, pausing 8 for a moment in the coolness before returning from a scramble in Mlinda Valley, I saw a female bushbuck moving slowly along the nearly dry streambed. Occasionally she paused to pick off some plant and crunch it. I kept absolutely still, and she was not aware of my presence until she was little more than ten yards away. Suddenly she tensed and stood staring at me, one small forefoot raised. Because I did not move, she did not know what I was—only that my outline was somehow strange. I saw her velvet nostrils dilate as she sniffed the air, but I was downwind and her nose gave her no answer. Slowly she came closer, and closer—one step at a time, her neck craned forward—always poised for instant flight. I can still scarcely believe that her nose actually touched my knee; yet if I close my eyes I can feel again, in imagination, the warmth of her breath and the silken impact of her skin. Unexpectedly I blinked and she was gone in a flash, bounding away with loud barks of alarm until the vegetation hid her completely from my view.

It was rather different when, as I was sitting on the Peak, I saw a leopard 9 coming toward me, his tail held up straight. He was at a slightly lower level than I, and obviously had no idea I was there. Ever since arrival in Africa I had had an ingrained, illogical fear of leopards. Already, while working at the Gombe, I had several times nearly turned back when, crawling through some thick undergrowth, I had suddenly smelled the rank smell of cat. I had forced myself on, telling myself that my fear was foolish, that only wounded leopards charged humans with savage ferocity.

On this occasion, though, the leopard went out of sight as it started to climb 10 up the hill—the hill on the peak of which I sat. I quickly hastened to climb a tree, but halfway there I realized that leopards can climb trees. So I uttered a sort of halfhearted squawk. The leopard, my logical mind told me, would be just as frightened of me if he knew I was there. Sure enough, there was a thudding of startled feet and then silence. I returned to the Peak, but the feeling of unseen eyes watching me was too much. I decided to watch for the chimps in Mlinda Valley. And, when I returned to the Peak several hours later, there, on the very rock which had been my seat, was a neat pile of leopard dung. He must have watched me go and then, very carefully, examined the place where such a frightening creature had been and tried to exterminate my alien scent with his own.

As the weeks went by the chimpanzees became less and less afraid. Quite often when I was on one of my food-collecting expeditions I came across chimpanzees unexpectedly, and after a time I found that some of them would tolerate my presence provided they were in fairly thick forest and I sat still and did not try to move closer than sixty to eighty yards. And so, during my second month of watching from the Peak, when I saw a group settle down to feed I sometimes moved closer and was thus able to make more detailed observations.

It was at this time that I began to recognize a number of different individuals. As soon as I was sure of knowing a chimpanzee if I saw it again, I named it. Some scientists feel that animals should be labeled by numbers—that to name them is anthropomorphic—but I have always been interested in the *differences* between individuals, and a name is not only more individual than a number but also far easier to remember. Most names were simply those which, for some reason or other, seemed to suit the individuals to whom I attached them. A few chimps were named because some facial expression or mannerism reminded me of human acquaintances.

The easiest individual to recognize was old Mr. McGregor. The crown of his head, his neck, and his shoulders were almost entirely devoid of hair, but a slight frill remained around his head rather like a monk's tonsure. He was an old male—perhaps between thirty and forty years of age (the longevity record of a captive chimp is forty-seven years). During the early months of my acquaintance with him, Mr. McGregor was somewhat belligerent. If I accidentally came across him at close quarters he would threaten me with an upward and backward jerk of his head and a shaking of branches before climbing down and vanishing from my sight. He reminded me, for some reason, of Beatrix Potter's old gardener in *The Tale of Peter Rabbit*.

Ancient Flo with her deformed, bulbous nose and ragged ears was equally easy to recognize. Her youngest offspring at that time were two-year-old Fifi, who still rode everywhere on her mother's back, and her juvenile son, Figan, who was always to be seen wandering around with his mother and little sister. He was then about six years old; it was approximately a year before he would attain puberty. Flo often traveled with another old mother, Olly. Olly's long face was also distinctive; the fluff of hair on the back of her head—though no other feature—reminded me of my aunt, Olwen. Olly, like Flo, was accompanied by two children, a daughter younger than Fifi, and an adolescent son about a year older than Figan.

Then there was William, who, I am certain, must have been Olly's blood brother. I never saw any special signs of friendship between them, but their faces were amazingly alike. They both had long upper lips that wobbled when they suddenly turned their heads. William had the added distinction of several thin, deeply etched scar marks running down his upper lip from his nose.

Two of the other chimpanzees I knew well by sight at that time were David 16
Graybeard and Goliath. Like David and Goliath in the Bible, these two individuals were closely associated in my mind because they were very often together. Goliath, even in those days of his prime, was not a giant, but he had a
splendid physique and the springy movements of an athlete. He probably weighed
about one hundred pounds. David Graybeard was less afraid of me from the
start than were any of the other chimps. I was always pleased when I picked out
his handsome face and well-marked silvery beard in a chimpanzee group, for
with David to calm the others, I had a better chance of approaching to observe
them more closely.

Before the end of my trial period in the field I made two really exciting 17
discoveries—discoveries that made the previous months of frustration well worth
while. And for both of them I had David Graybeard to thank.

One day I arrived on the Peak and found a small group of chimps just below 18
me in the upper branches of a thick tree. As I watched I saw that one of them
was holding a pink-looking object from which he was from time to time pulling
pieces with his teeth. There was a female and a youngster and they were both
reaching out toward the male, their hands actually touching his mouth. Presently the female picked up a piece of the pink thing and put it to her mouth:
it was at this moment that I realized the chimps were eating meat.

After each bite of meat the male picked off some leaves with his lips and 19
chewed them with the flesh. Often, when he had chewed for several minutes
on this leafy wad, he spat out the remains into the waiting hands of the female.
Suddenly he dropped a small piece of meat, and like a flash the youngster swung
after it to the ground. Even as he reached to pick it up the undergrowth exploded
and an adult bushpig charged toward him. Screaming, the juvenile leaped back
into the tree. The pig remained in the open, snorting and moving backward
and forward. Soon I made out the shapes of three small striped piglets. Obviously
the chimps were eating a baby pig. The size was right and later, when I realized
that the male was David Graybeard, I moved closer and saw that he was indeed
eating piglet.

For three hours I watched the chimps feeding. David occasionally let the 20
female bite pieces from the carcass and once he actually detached a small piece
of flesh and placed it in her outstretched hand. When he finally climbed down
there was still meat left on the carcass; he carried it away in one hand, followed
by the others.

Of course I was not sure, then, that David Graybeard had caught the pig for 21
himself, but even so, it was tremendously exciting to know that these chimpanzees actually ate meat. Previously scientists had believed that although these
apes might occasionally supplement their diet with a few insects or small rodents
and the like they were primarily vegetarians and fruit eaters. No one had suspected that they might hunt larger mammals.

It was within two weeks of this observation that I saw something that excited   22
me even more. By then it was October and the short rains had begun. The
blackened slopes were softened by feathery new grass shoots and in some places
the ground was carpeted by a variety of flowers. The Chimpanzees' Spring, I
called it. I had had a frustrating morning, tramping up and down three valleys
with never a sign or sound of a chimpanzee. Hauling myself up the steep slope
of Mlinda Valley I headed for the Peak, not only weary but soaking wet from
crawling through dense undergrowth. Suddenly I stopped, for I saw a slight
movement in the long grass about sixty yards away. Quickly focusing my binoculars I saw that it was a single chimpanzee, and just then he turned in my
direction. I recognized David Graybeard.

Cautiously I moved around so that I could see what he was doing. He was   23
squatting beside the red earth mound of a termite nest, and as I watched I saw
him carefully push a long grass stem down into a hole in the mound. After a
moment he withdrew it and picked something from the end with his mouth. I
was too far away to make out what he was eating, but it was obvious that he
was actually using a grass stem as a tool.

I knew that on two occasions casual observers in West Africa had seen chim-   24
panzees using objects as tools: one had broken open palm-nut kernels by using
a rock as a hammer, and a group of chimps had been observed pushing sticks
into an underground bees' nest and licking off the honey. Somehow I had never
dreamed of seeing anything so exciting myself.

For an hour David feasted at the termite mound and then he wandered   25
slowly away. When I was sure he had gone I went over to examine the mound.
I found a few crushed insects strewn about, and a swarm of worker termites
sealing the entrances of the nest passages into which David had obviously been
poking his stems. I picked up one of his discarded tools and carefully pushed it
into a hole myself. Immediately I felt the pull of several termites as they seized
the grass, and when I pulled it out there were a number of worker termites and
a few soldiers, with big red heads, clinging on with their mandibles. There they
remained, sticking out at right angles to the stem with their legs waving in the
air.

Before I left I trampled down some of the tall dry grass and constructed a   26
rough hide—just a few palm fronds leaned up against the low branch of a tree
and tied together at the top. I planned to wait there the next day. But it was
another week before I was able to watch a chimpanzee "fishing" for termites
again. Twice chimps arrived, but each time they saw me and moved off immediately. Once a swarm of fertile winged termites—the princes and princesses,
as they are called—flew off on their nuptial flight, their huge white wings
fluttering frantically as they carried the insects higher and higher. Later I realized
that it is at this time of year, during the short rains, when the worker termites
extend the passages of the nest to the surface, preparing for these emigrations.

Several such swarms emerge between October and January. It is principally during these months that the chimpanzees feed on termites.

On the eighth day of my watch David Graybeard arrived again, together with 27 Goliath, and the pair worked there for two hours. I could see much better: I observed how they scratched open the sealed-over passage entrances with a thumb or forefinger. I watched how they bit the ends off their tools when they became bent, or used the other end, or discarded them in favor of new ones. Goliath once moved at least fifteen yards from the heap to select a firm-looking piece of vine, and both males often picked three or four stems while they were collecting tools, and put the spares beside them on the ground until they wanted them.

Most exciting of all, on several occasions they picked small leafy twigs and 28 prepared them for use by stripping off the leaves. This was the first recorded example of a wild animal not merely *using* an object as a tool, but actually modifying an object and thus showing the crude beginnings of tool*making*.

Previously man had been regarded as the only tool-making animal. Indeed, 29 one of the clauses commonly accepted in the definition of man was that he was a creature who "made tools to a regular and set pattern." The chimpanzees, obviously, had not made tools to any set pattern. Nevertheless, my early observations of their primitive toolmaking abilities convinced a number of scientists that it was necessary to redefine man in a more complex manner than before. Or else, as Louis Leakey put it, we should by definition have to accept the chimpanzee as Man.

QUESTIONS

1. This essay is an example, principally, of reporting; that is, it is a gathering of facts by a clearheaded, unbiased observer. Identify passages in the essay in which this kind of reporting clearly takes place.

2. Although Goodall, in the main, is a neutral observer of chimpanzee behavior, that neutrality is in fact impossible in any absolute sense. It is clear that she writes, for example, with an eye always on comparisons of chimpanzee and human behavior. Make a list of words, just from paragraphs 3 and 4, that reveal that particular bias.

3. Describe how the writer's comparison of chimpanzee with human behavior becomes increasingly prominent in the course of her essay.

4. Paraphrase the last discovery Goodall reports toward the end of her essay. What, exactly, was her contribution to science in this instance? What other activities, described earlier in the piece, make that discovery understandable, perhaps even unsurprising once we come to it?

5. What do you make of the choice outlined in paragraph 29? Which choice do you suppose the scientists made? Why?

6. Goodall's scientific work resembles that of an anthropologist in that she goes into the field to observe the behavior of another social group. Even from this short piece we

can learn a good deal about the practices and the way of life of such a worker in the field. Describe Goodall's life in the field as best you can, making whatever inferences you can from this single essay.

7. Amplify your description of Goodall's life in the field, done for question 6, by reading whatever articles you can find that tell more about her and about her work.

8. Place yourself somewhere and observe behavior more or less as Goodall does. You might observe wildlife—pigeons, sparrows, crows, squirrels, or whatever is available—or you might observe some aspect of human behavior. If you choose the latter, look for behavior that is unfamiliar to you, such as that of children at play, of workers on the job, or of persons in a social group very different from your own. Write a report detailing your observations.

9. After you have completed question 8, write a second, shorter report in which you comment on the nature of your task as an observer. Was it difficult to watch? Was it difficult to decide what was meaningful behavior? Did you influence what you saw so that you could not be confident that the behavior was representative? Looking back on your experience as a field worker, what else seems questionable to you now?

BODY RITUAL AMONG THE NACIREMA

Horace Miner

Horace Miner (b. 1912) has been a cultural anthropologist and a professor of anthropology at the University of Michigan in Ann Arbor for many years. The topics of his published studies have ranged from Timbuktu to French Canada. The following selection appeared first in a professional journal, the American Anthropologist, *in 1956. Reprinted far and wide, it has now become a classic joke among social scientists.*

The anthropologist has become so familiar with the diversity of ways in which   1
different peoples behave in similar situations that he is not apt to be surprised
by even the most exotic customs. In fact, if all of the logically possible combinations of behavior have not been found somewhere in the world, he is apt
to suspect that they must be present in some yet undescribed tribe. This point
has, in fact, been expressed with respect to clan organization by Murdock (1949:71).
In this light, the magical beliefs and practices of the Nacirema present such
unusual aspects that it seems desirable to describe them as an example of the
extremes to which human behavior can go.

Professor Linton first brought the ritual of the Nacirema to the attention of   2
anthropologists twenty years ago (1936:326), but the culture of this people is
still very poorly understood. They are a North American group living in the
territory between the Canadian Cree, the Yaqui and Tarahumare of Mexico,
and the Carib and Arawak of the Antilles. Little is known of their origin,
although tradition states that they came from the east. According to Nacirema
mythology, their nation was originated by a culture hero, Notgnihsaw, who is
otherwise known for two great feats of strength—the throwing of a piece of
wampum across the river Pa-To-Mac and the chopping down of a cherry tree
in which the Spirit of Truth resided.

Nacirema culture is characterized by a highly developed market economy   3
which has evolved in a rich natural habitat. While much of the people's time
is devoted to economic pursuits, a large part of the fruits of these labors and a
considerable portion of the day are spent in ritual activity. The focus of this
activity is the human body, the appearance and health of which loom as a
dominant concern in the ethos of the people. While such a concern is certainly
not unusual, its ceremonial aspects and associated philosophy are unique.

The fundamental belief underlying the whole system appears to be that the   4 human body is ugly and that its natural tendency is to debility and disease. Incarcerated in such a body, man's only hope is to avert these characteristics through the use of the powerful influences of ritual and ceremony. Every house-hold has one or more shrines devoted to this purpose. The more powerful individuals in the society have several shrines in their houses and, in fact, the opulence of a house is often referred to in terms of the number of such ritual centers it possesses. Most houses are of wattle and daub construction, but the shrine rooms of the more wealthy are walled with stone. Poorer families imitate the rich by applying pottery plaques to their shrine walls.

While each family has at least one such shrine, the rituals associated with it are not family ceremonies but are private and secret. The rites are normally only discussed with children, and then only during the period when they are being initiated into these mysteries. I was able, however, to establish sufficient rapport with the natives to examine these shrines and to have the rituals de-scribed to me.

The focal point of the shrine is a box or chest which is built into the wall. In this chest are kept the many charms and magical potions without which no native believes he could live. These preparations are secured from a variety of specialized practitioners. The most powerful of these are the medicine men, whose assistance must be rewarded with substantial gifts. However, the medicine men do not provide the curative potions for their clients, but decide what the ingredients should be and then write them down in an ancient and secret lan-guage. This writing is understood only by the medicine men and by the herbal-ists who, for another gift, provide the required charm.

The charm is not disposed of after it has served its purpose, but is placed in the charm-box of the household shrine. As these magical materials are specific for certain ills, and the real or imagined maladies of the people are many, the charm-box is usually full to overflowing. The magical packets are so numerous that people forget what their purposes were and fear to use them again. While the natives are very vague on this point, we can only assume that the idea in retaining all the old magical materials is that their presence in the charm-box, before which the body rituals are conducted, will in some way protect the worshipper.

Beneath the charm-box is a small font. Each day every member of the family, in succession, enters the shrine room, bows his head before the charm-box, mingles different sorts of holy water in the font, and proceeds with a brief rite of ablution. The holy waters are secured from the Water Temple of the com-munity, where the priests conduct elaborate ceremonies to make the liquid ritually pure.

In the hierarchy of magical practitioners, and below the medicine men in prestige, are specialists whose designation is best translated "holy-mouth-men." The Nacirema have an almost pathological horror of and fascination with the mouth, the condition of which is believed to have a supernatural influence on

5

6

7

8

9

all social relationships. Were it not for the rituals of the mouth, they believe that their teeth would fall out, their gums bleed, their jaws shrink, their friends desert them, and their lovers reject them. They also believe that a strong relationship exists between oral and moral characteristics. For example, there is a ritual ablution of the mouth for children which is supposed to improve their moral fiber.

The daily body ritual performed by everyone includes a mouth-rite. Despite 10 the fact that these people are so punctilious about care of the mouth, this rite involves a practice which strikes the uninitiated stranger as revolting. It was reported to me that the ritual consists of inserting a small bundle of hog hairs into the mouth, along with certain magical powders, and then moving the bundle in a highly formalized series of gestures.

In addition to the private mouth-rite, the people seek out a holy-mouth-man 11 once or twice a year. These practitioners have an impressive set of paraphernalia, consisting of a variety of augers, awls, probes, and prods. The use of these objects in the exorcism of the evils of the mouth involves almost unbelievable ritual torture of the client. The holy-mouth-man opens the client's mouth and, using the above mentioned tools, enlarges any holes which decay may have created in the teeth. Magical materials are put into these holes. If there are no naturally occurring holes in the teeth, large sections of one or more teeth are gouged out so that the supernatural substance can be applied. In the client's view, the purpose of these ministrations is to arrest decay and to draw friends. The extremely sacred and traditional character of the rite is evident in the fact that the natives return to the holy-mouth-men year after year, despite the fact that their teeth continue to decay.

It is to be hoped that, when a thorough study of the Nacirema is made, there 12 will be careful inquiry into the personality structure of these people. One has but to watch the gleam in the eye of a holy-mouth-man, as he jabs an awl into an exposed nerve, to suspect that a certain amount of sadism is involved. If this can be established, a very interesting pattern emerges, for most of the population shows definite masochistic tendencies. It was to these that Professor Linton referred in discussing a distinctive part of the daily body ritual which is performed only by men. This part of the rite involves scraping and lacerating the surface of the face with a sharp instrument. Special women's rites are performed only four times during each lunar month, but what they lack in frequency is made up in barbarity. As part of this ceremony, women bake their heads in small ovens for about an hour. The theoretically interesting point is that what seems to be a preponderantly masochistic people have developed sadistic specialists.

The medicine men have an imposing temple, or *latipso*, in every community 13 of any size. The more elaborate ceremonies required to treat very sick patients can only be performed at this temple. These ceremonies involve not only the thaumaturge but a permanent group of vestal maidens who move sedately about the temple chambers in distinctive costume and headdress.

The *latipso* ceremonies are so harsh that it is phenomenal that a fair pro- 14
portion of the really sick natives who enter the temple ever recover. Small
children whose indoctrination is still incomplete have been known to resist
attempts to take them to the temple because "that is where you go to die."
Despite this fact, sick adults are not only willing but eager to undergo the
protracted ritual purification, if they can afford to do so. No matter how ill the
supplicant or how grave the emergency, the guardians of many temples will not
admit a client if he cannot give a rich gift to the custodian. Even after one has
gained admission and survived the ceremonies, the guardians will not permit
the neophyte to leave until he makes still another gift.

The supplicant entering the temple is first stripped of all his or her clothes. 15
In every-day life the Nacirema avoids exposure of his body and its natural
functions. Bathing and excretory acts are performed only in the secrecy of the
household shrine, where they are ritualized as part of the body-rites. Psychological shock results from the fact that body secrecy is suddenly lost upon entry
into the *latipso*. A man, whose own wife has never seen him in an excretory
act, suddenly finds himself naked and assisted by a vestal maiden while he
performs his natural functions into a sacred vessel. This sort of ceremonial
treatment is necessitated by the fact that the excreta are used by a diviner to
ascertain the course and nature of the client's sickness. Female clients, on the
other hand, find their naked bodies are subjected to the scrutiny, manipulation
and prodding of the medicine men.

Few supplicants in the temple are well enough to do anything but lie on 16
their hard beds. The daily ceremonies, like the rites of the holy-mouth-men,
involve discomfort and torture. With ritual precision, the vestals awaken their
miserable charges each dawn and roll them about on their beds of pain while
performing ablutions, in the formal movements of which the maidens are highly
trained. At other times they insert magic wands in the supplicant's mouth or
force him to eat substances which are supposed to be healing. From time to
time the medicine men come to their clients and jab magically treated needles
into their flesh. The fact that these temple ceremonies may not cure, and may
even kill the neophyte, in no way decreases the people's faith in the medicine
men.

There remains one other kind of practitioner, known as a "listener." This 17
witch-doctor has the power to exorcise the devils that lodge in the heads of
people who have been bewitched. The Nacirema believe that parents bewitch
their own children. Mothers are particularly suspected of putting a curse on
children while teaching them the secret body rituals. The counter-magic of the
witch-doctor is unusual in its lack of ritual. The patient simply tells the "listener"
all his troubles and fears, beginning with the earliest difficulties he can remember. The memory displayed by the Nacirema in these exorcism sessions is truly
remarkable. It is not uncommon for the patient to bemoan the rejection he felt

203

upon being weaned as a babe, and a few individuals even see their troubles going back to the traumatic effects of their own birth.

In conclusion, mention must be made of certain practices which have their base in native esthetics but which depend upon the pervasive aversion to the natural body and its functions. There are ritual fasts to make fat people thin and ceremonial feasts to make thin people fat. Still other rites are used to make women's breasts larger if they are small, and smaller if they are large. General dissatisfaction with breast shape is symbolized in the fact that the ideal form is virtually outside the range of human variation. A few women afflicted with almost inhuman hypermammary development are so idolized that they make a handsome living by simply going from village to village and permitting the natives to stare at them for a fee. 18

Reference has already been made to the fact that excretory functions are ritualized, routinized, and relegated to secrecy. Natural reproductive functions are similarly distorted. Intercourse is taboo as a topic and scheduled as an act. Efforts are made to avoid pregnancy by the use of magical materials or by limiting intercourse to certain phases of the moon. Conception is actually very infrequent. When pregnant, women dress so as to hide their condition. Parturition takes place in secret, without friends or relatives to assist, and the majority of women do not nurse their infants. 19

Our review of the ritual life of the Nacirema has certainly shown them to be a magic-ridden people. It is hard to understand how they have managed to exist so long under the burdens which they have imposed upon themselves. But even such exotic customs as these take on real meaning when they are viewed with the insight provided by Malinowski when he wrote (1948:70): 20

> Looking from far and above, from our high places of safety in the developed civilization, it is easy to see all the crudity and irrelevance of magic. But without its power and guidance early man could not have mastered his practical difficulties as he has done, nor could man have advanced to the higher stages of civilization.

REFERENCES CITED

LINTON, RALPH
1936 The Study of Man. New York, D. Appleton-Century Co.
MALINOWSKI, BRONISLAW
1948 Magic, Science, and Religion. Glencoe, The Free Press.
MURDOCK, GEORGE P.
1949 Social Structure. New York, The Macmillan Co.

QUESTIONS

1. Where do the Nacirema live? Why would an anthropologist want to study their culture? Do the Nacirema sound like people you would want to know more about?

2. What is the writer's attitude toward his subject? Is his report objective, or is there evaluative language present?

3. What evidence is presented to support the writer's claim in paragraph 12 that "most of the population shows definite masochistic tendencies"? How is the evidence organized? Is enough evidence presented to substantiate this claim?

4. Miner's report was written in 1956. Have you seen in your community any more recent evidence that would indicate that the Nacirema's belief in magical powers has enabled them to advance to a higher stage of civilization, as Malinowski suggests it might?

5. Miner concentrates on the body rituals of the Nacirema. Obviously, the Nacirema must have other rituals, and surely some of these are more pleasurable than those described here. On the other hand, Miner may not have included other barbaric customs of the Nacirema. Do some field research of your own, and write a report of another Nacirema ritual that you have observed.

6. Nonanthropologists find this piece humorous because of Professor Miner's treatment of the Nacirema. Might anthropologists find this piece more humorous than non-anthropologists find it? Use your answer to draw some conclusions about how different audiences respond to humor.

Sciences and Technologies

A DELICATE OPERATION

Roy C. Selby, Jr.

Roy C. Selby, Jr., (b. 1930) graduated from Louisiana State University and the University of Arkansas Medical School, where he specialized in neurology and neurosurgery. He now practices in the Chicago area and is the author of numerous professional articles on neurosurgery. "A Delicate Operation," which first appeared in Harper's *magazine in 1975, reports for a more general audience the details of a difficult brain operation.*

In the autumn of 1973 a woman in her early fifties noticed, upon closing   1
one eye while reading, that she was unable to see clearly. Her eyesight grew slowly worse. Changing her eyeglasses did not help. She saw an ophthalmologist, who found that her vision was seriously impaired in both eyes. She then saw a neurologist, who confirmed the finding and obtained X rays of the skull and an EMI scan—a photograph of the patient's head. The latter revealed a tumor growing between the optic nerves at the base of the brain. The woman was admitted to the hospital by a neurosurgeon.

Further diagnosis, based on angiography, a detailed X-ray study of the cir-   2
culatory system, showed the tumor to be about two inches in diameter and supplied by many small blood vessels. It rested beneath the brain, just above the pituitary gland, stretching the optic nerves to either side and intimately close to the major blood vessels supplying the brain. Removing it would pose many technical problems. Probably benign and slow-growing, it may have been present for several years. If left alone it would continue to grow and produce blindness and might become impossible to remove completely. Removing it, however, might not improve the patient's vision and could make it worse. A major blood vessel could be damaged, causing a stroke. Damage to the undersurface of the brain could cause impairment of memory and changes in mood and personality.

The hypothalamus, a most important structure of the brain, could be injured, causing coma, high fever, bleeding from the stomach, and death.

The neurosurgeon met with the patient and her husband and discussed the   3
various possibilities. The common decision was to operate.

The patient's hair was shampooed for two nights before surgery. She was   4
given a cortisonelike drug to reduce the risk of damage to the brain during surgery. Five units of blood were cross-matched, as a contingency against hemorrhage. At 1:00 P.M. the operation began. After the patient was anesthetized her hair was completely clipped and shaved from the scalp. Her head was prepped with an organic iodine solution for ten minutes. Drapes were placed over her, leaving exposed only the forehead and crown of the skull. All the routine instruments were brought up—the electrocautery used to coagulate areas of bleeding, bipolar coagulation forceps to arrest bleeding from individual blood vessels without damaging adjacent tissues, and small suction tubes to remove blood and cerebrospinal fluid from the head, thus giving the surgeon a better view of the tumor and surrounding areas.

A curved incision was made behind the hairline so it would be concealed   5
when the hair grew back. It extended almost from ear to ear. Plastic clips were applied to the cut edges of the scalp to arrest bleeding. The scalp was folded back to the level of the eyebrows. Incisions were made in the muscle of the right temple, and three sets of holes were drilled near the temple and the top of the head because the tumor had to be approached from directly in front. The drill, powered by nitrogen, was replaced with a fluted steel blade, and the holes were connected. The incised piece of skull was pried loose and held out of the way by a large sponge.

Beneath the bone is a yellowish leatherlike membrane, the dura, that sur-   6
rounds the brain. Down the middle of the head the dura carries a large vein, but in the area near the nose the vein is small. At that point the vein and dura were cut, and clips made of tantalum, a hard metal, were applied to arrest and prevent bleeding. Sutures were put into the dura and tied to the scalp to keep the dura open and retracted. A malleable silver retractor, resembling the blade of a butter knife, was inserted between the brain and skull. The anesthesiologist began to administer a drug to relax the brain by removing some of its water, making it easier for the surgeon to manipulate the retractor, hold the brain back, and see the tumor. The nerve tracts for smell were cut on both sides to provide additional room. The tumor was seen approximately two-and-one-half inches behind the base of the nose. It was pink in color. On touching it, it proved to be very fibrous and tough. A special retractor was attached to the skull, enabling the other retractor blades to be held automatically and freeing the surgeon's hands. With further displacement of the frontal lobes of the brain, the tumor could be seen better, but no normal structures—the carotid arteries, their branches, and the optic nerves—were visible. The tumor obscured them.

A surgical microscope was placed above the wound. The surgeon had selected 7
the lenses and focal length prior to the operation. Looking through the microscope, he could see some of the small vessels supplying the tumor and he
coagulated them. He incised the tumor to attempt to remove its core and thus
collapse it, but the substance of the tumor was too firm to be removed in this
fashion. He then began to slowly dissect the tumor from the adjacent brain
tissue and from where he believed the normal structures to be.

Using small squares of cotton, he began to separate the tumor from very 8
loose fibrous bands connecting it to the brain and to the right side of the part
of the skull where the pituitary gland lies. The right optic nerve and carotid
artery came into view, both displaced considerably to the right. The optic nerve
had a normal appearance. He protected these structures with cotton compresses
placed between them and the tumor. He began to raise the tumor from the
skull and slowly to reach the point of its origin and attachment—just in front
of the pituitary gland and medial to the left optic nerve, which still could not
be seen. The small blood vessels entering the tumor were cauterized. The upper
portion of the tumor was gradually separated from the brain, and the branches
of the carotid arteries and the branches to the tumor were coagulated. The
tumor was slowly and gently lifted from its bed, and for the first time the left
carotid artery and optic nerve could be seen. Part of the tumor adhered to this
nerve. The bulk of the tumor was amputated, leaving a small bit attached to
the nerve. Very slowly and carefully the tumor fragment was resected.

The tumor now removed, a most impressive sight came into view—the pi- 9
tuitary gland and its stalk of attachment to the hypothalamus, the hypothalamus
itself, and the brainstem, which conveys nerve impulses between the body and
the brain. As far as could be determined, no damage had been done to these
structures or other vital centers, but the left optic nerve, from chronic pressure
of the tumor, appeared gray and thin. Probably it would not completely recover
its function.

After making certain there was no bleeding, the surgeon closed the wounds 10
and placed wire mesh over the holes in the skull to prevent dimpling of the
scalp over the points that had been drilled. A gauze dressing was applied to the
patient's head. She was awakened and sent to the recovery room.

Even with the microscope, damage might still have occurred to the cerebral 11
cortex and hypothalamus. It would require at least a day to be reasonably certain
there was none, and about seventy-two hours to monitor for the major post-
operative dangers—swelling of the brain and blood clots forming over the surface
of the brain. The surgeon explained this to the patient's husband, and both of
them waited anxiously. The operation had required seven hours. A glass of
orange juice had given the surgeon some additional energy during the closure
of the wound. Though exhausted, he could not fall asleep until after two in the
morning, momentarily expecting a call from the nurse in the intensive care unit
announcing deterioration of the patient's condition.

At 8:00 A.M. the surgeon saw the patient in the intensive care unit. She was   12
alert, oriented, and showed no sign of additional damage to the optic nerves or
the brain. She appeared to be in better shape than the surgeon or her husband.

QUESTIONS

1. Why did the neurosurgeon decide to operate? What could have happened if the
patient chose not to have the operation? What effect does knowing this information have
on the reader?

2. Although the essay is probably based on the writer's experience, it is reported in
the third person. What effect does this have on the information reported? How would
the report have come across if it had been written in the first person?

3. The writer uses different methods of reporting to create the drama of "The Delicate
Operation." At what point in the essay does he provide background information? How
much of the essay reports events before, during, and after the operation? At what points
does the writer explain terms and procedures for the reader?

4. Which passages in this essay do you find especially powerful? How did the writer
create this effect?

5. Write a report of a procedure with which you are familiar and which calls for
some expertise or sensitivity or a combination of these because there is always the chance
that something could go wrong. You should proceed step by step, giving the reader as
much information as necessary to understand and follow the procedure. At appropriate
points also include the problems you face. Suggestions are trimming a Christmas tree,
carrying out a chemistry experiment, getting a child off to school, or preparing a gourmet
meal.

THE DISCUS THROWER

Richard Selzer

Richard Selzer (b. 1928) is a surgeon and professor of surgery at the Yale University Medical School. His articles on various aspects of medicine have appeared in Harper's, Esquire, *and* Redbook. *In 1975 he won the National Magazine Award for his articles. His books include a volume of short stories,* Rituals of Surgery, *and a collection of autobiographical essays,* Mortal Lessons. *In the essay reprinted here, which first appeared in* Harper's *magazine in 1977, Selzer reports on the visits he made to one of his patients.*

I spy on my patients. Ought not a doctor to observe his patients by any means   1
and from any stance, that he might the more fully assemble evidence? So I stand in the doorways of hospital rooms and gaze. Oh, it is not all that furtive an act. Those in bed need only look up to discover me. But they never do.

From the doorway of Room 542 the man in the bed seems deeply tanned.   2
Blue eyes and close-cropped white hair give him the appearance of vigor and good health. But I know that his skin is not brown from the sun. It is rusted, rather, in the last stage of containing the vile repose within. And the blue eyes are frosted, looking inward like the windows of a snowbound cottage. This man is blind. This man is also legless—the right leg missing from midthigh down, the left from just below the knee. It gives him the look of a bonsai, roots and branches pruned into the dwarfed facsimile of a great tree.

Propped on pillows, he cups his right thigh in both hands. Now and then   3
he shakes his head as though acknowledging the intensity of his suffering. In all of this he makes no sound. Is he mute as well as blind?

The room in which he dwells is empty of all possessions—no get-well cards,   4
small, private caches of food, day-old flowers, slippers, all the usual kickshaws of the sickroom. There is only the bed, a chair, a nightstand, and a tray on wheels that can be swung across his lap for meals.

"What time is it?" he asks.   5

"Three o'clock."   6

"Morning or afternoon?"   7

"Afternoon."   8

He is silent. There is nothing else he wants to know.   9

"How are you?" I say.   10

211

"Who is it?" he asks. 11

"It's the doctor. How do you feel?" 12

He does not answer right away. 13

"Feel?" he says. 14

"I hope you feel better," I say. 15

I press the button at the side of the bed. 16

"Down you go," I say. 17

"Yes, down," he says. 18

He falls back upon the bed awkwardly. His stumps, unweighted by legs and 19
feet, rise in the air, presenting themselves. I unwrap the bandages from the
stumps, and begin to cut away the black scabs and the dead, glazed fat with
scissors and forceps. A shard of white bone comes loose. I pick it away. I wash
the wounds with disinfectant and redress the stumps. All this while, he does
not speak. What is he thinking behind those lids that do not blink? Is he
remembering a time when he was whole? Does he dream of feet? Of when his
body was not a rotting log?

He lies solid and inert. In spite of everything, he remains impressive, as 20
though he were a sailor standing athwart a slanting deck.

"Anything more I can do for you?" I ask. 21

For a long moment he is silent. 22

"Yes," he says at last and without the least irony. "You can bring me a pair 23
of shoes."

In the corridor, the head nurse is waiting for me. 24

"We have to do something about him," she says. "Every morning he orders 25
scrambled eggs for breakfast, and, instead of eating them, he picks up the plate
and throws it against the wall."

"Throws his plate?" 26

"Nasty. That's what he is. No wonder his family doesn't come to visit. They 27
probably can't stand him any more than we can."

She is waiting for me to do something. 28

"Well?" 29

"We'll see," I say. 30

The next morning I am waiting in the corridor when the kitchen delivers his 31
breakfast. I watch the aide place the tray on the stand and swing it across his
lap. She presses the button to raise the head of the bed. Then she leaves.

In time the man reaches to find the rim of the tray, then on to find the 32
dome of the covered dish. He lifts off the cover and places it on the stand. He
fingers across the plate until he probes the eggs. He lifts the plate in both hands,
sets it on the palm of his right hand, centers it, balances it. He hefts it up and
down slightly, getting the feel of it. Abruptly, he draws back his right arm as
far as he can.

There is the crack of the plate breaking against the wall at the foot of his bed 33
and the small wet sound of the scrambled eggs dropping to the floor.

And then he laughs. It is a sound you have never heard. It is something new 34
under the sun. It could cure cancer.

Out in the corridor, the eyes of the head nurse narrow. 35

"Laughed, did he?" 36

She writes something down on her clipboard. 37

A second aide arrives, brings a second breakfast tray, put it on the nightstand, 38
out of his reach. She looks over at me shaking her head and making her mouth
go. I see that we are to be accomplices.

"I've got to feed you," she says to the man. 39

"Oh, no you don't," the man says. 40

"Oh, yes I do," the aide says, "after the way you just did. Nurse says so." 41

"Get me my shoes," the man says. 42

"Here's oatmeal," the aide says. "Open." And she touches the spoon to his 43
lower lip.

"I ordered scrambled eggs," says the man. 44

"That's right," the aide says. 45

I step forward. 46

"Is there anything I can do?" I say. 47

"Who are you?" the man asks. 48

In the evening I go once more to that ward to make my rounds. The head 49
nurse reports to me that Room 542 is deceased. She has discovered this quite
by accident, she says. No, there had been no sound. Nothing. It's a blessing,
she says.

I go into his room, a spy looking for secrets. He is still there in his bed. His 50
face is relaxed, grave, dignified. After a while, I turn to leave. My gaze sweeps
the wall at the foot of the bed, and I see the place where it has been repeatedly
washed, where the wall looks very clean and very white.

QUESTIONS

1. Why does the writer say, "I spy on my patients" (paragraph 1)? Don't doctors
usually "look in on" their patients? What effect did the writer hope to achieve by starting
with such a statement?

2. The writer uses the present tense throughout this piece. Would the past tense be
just as effective? Explain your answer.

3. Selzer writes in the first person. Why might he have decided to make himself
prominent in the report in that way? How would his report have come across if it had
been written in the third person rather than the first person?

4. How would you describe this doctor's attitude toward his patient? How would you

describe the nurse's attitude toward the patient? How does the narrator manage to characterize himself in one way and the nurse in another?

5. Is the title, "The Discus Thrower," appropriate for this piece? In a slightly revised version, the title was changed to "Four Appointments with the Discus Thrower." Is this a better title?

6. What do you think Selzer's purpose was in writing this essay? Did he simply wish to shock us, or is there a message in this piece for the medical profession or for those of us who fear illness and death?

7. The essay reports on four visits to the patient by the doctor. Write a shorter version reporting on two or more visits by the head nurse. How would she react to the patient's request for shoes? How might her own point of view explain some of her reactions?

8. For many of us, knowledge of hospitals is limited, perhaps to television shows in which the hospital functions as a backdrop for the romances of its staff. Write a short essay in which you present your conception of what a hospital is and in which you consider how Selzer's essay either made you revise that conception or reaffirmed what you know through experience.

THE CELLS THAT WOULD NOT DIE

Michael Gold

A biochemist at the Oregon Graduate Center in Beaverton, Michael Gold was born in Paterson, New Jersey, in 1941. He has degrees in genetics and biochemistry from Rutgers University and the State University of New York at Buffalo. The article reprinted here appeared first in a magazine for a general audience, Science 81, *for which Gold worked as a staff writer.*

It was all very hush-hush. In the winter of 1973 a top official of the National   1
Cancer Institute flew from Washington, D.C., to Oakland, California, carrying in his briefcase five plastic flasks. Growing in a milky film at the bottom of each flask were live tumor cells. The cells came from cancer patients in five different medical centers in the Soviet Union. In the spirit of detente Russia had given the cells to American scientists, who hoped they might contain new clues to the cause of cancer.

The man from Washington brought the flasks to the University of California   2
at Berkeley, where he turned them over to Walter Nelson-Rees at the university's cell bank. It was Nelson-Rees' job to store cells in a deep-freeze repository and to periodically remove a few of one sort or another, grow them, and send them to certain government and private researchers. In the case of the top-secret Russian cells, however, he was told simply to store them away. He was neither to send them out nor to experiment with them himself.

But Walter Nelson-Rees was a perfectionist devoted to careful checking. He   3
routinely screened all samples that came through his lab to make sure they were what they were supposed to be. So a few days after being warned not to, he began analyzing a batch of the Soviet cells. He also sent some to a colleague in Detroit for testing.

The investigations produced a startling conclusion: The cells were not from   4
five different cancer patients in Russia. In fact the cells in all five flasks closely matched those of a black woman from Baltimore, Maryland, who had died of cervical cancer 22 years earlier. Her name was Henrietta Lacks.

It was not the first time Henrietta Lacks' cells had turned up unexpectedly.   5
A few years earlier some normal liver cells, which researchers had been using to study liver function, were found instead to be cervical tumor cells taken from Henrietta Lacks. Likewise, cells that scientists had cultured from an intestinal cancer, a tumor of the larynx, a normal heart, and half a dozen other organs

215

from various patients all over the world had somehow become the cells of Henrietta Lacks. Many scientists were gathering erroneous information and wasting perhaps millions of dollars because they had been mistakenly working on the wrong cells for years. The Russian incident was only the latest and most dramatic demonstration of how far the confusion had spread—and a hint of how much further it might go.

For Nelson-Rees the mix-up was the first of several events that launched a   6
personal crusade. Lots of people joined the effort to track down and ferret out the troublesome cells of Henrietta Lacks. But no one filled so many file drawers and thick black notebooks with details of the cells' habits as Nelson-Rees. No one collected so high a stack of micrographic mug shots of their many disguises. And no one else had the gall to publish periodic hit lists of other cells found to be overtaken by those of Henrietta Lacks and, to the dismay of many researchers, the names of the scientists working with the indicted cells. His obsession for quality control and his polite, precise manner of speech are more characteristic of *The Odd Couple*'s fastidious Felix Unger than the rough and abrasive fictional sleuth Philip Marlowe; but Walter Nelson-Rees has become one of science's toughest detectives. Since 1973 he had doggedly pursued these fugitive cells of biology around the globe. Yet the chase is far from over. Henrietta Lacks has a considerable head start.

One winter day in 1951, when Nelson-Rees was still an undergraduate stu-   7
dent, 31-year-old Henrietta Lacks arrived at the medical clinic of Johns Hopkins University in Baltimore. The doctor who examined her found a strange purple lesion about an inch in diameter within her cervix. He cut out a tiny section of the tissue for closer study and determined it to be malignant.

Several days later doctors removed another fragment of the tissue and deliv-   8
ered it to a research group working at the university. With limited success, the group was attempting to grow tumor cells in the laboratory in order to study the mechanisms of cancer. While the researchers tried to grow those few cancer cells in a petri dish containing clotted chicken blood, doctors began bombarding Henrietta Lacks with radiation in an effort to kill the cancer still inside her.

The tumor proved invulnerable. Eight months after her first visit to the clinic,   9
the cancer had spread throughout her body, and Henrietta Lacks died.

That is, most of Henrietta Lacks died. In the research lab, the few cells taken   10
from the original tumor were thriving, doubling their number every 24 hours. The same vigor that had enabled the cancer cells to resist radiation and overrun Henrietta Lacks' body kept them flourishing in the artificial conditions of a petri dish. Cells taken from the tumors of dozens of other patients had not grown at all. A few grew only haltingly, then quickly died off. The cells of Henrietta Lacks, however, divided and redivided without limit. "If allowed to grow un-inhibited under optimal cultural conditions," wrote one of the scientists later, "[the cells] would have taken over the world."

In fact, as the first human cells that were easy to grow and manipulate outside   11
the body for long periods of time, the cells from Henrietta Lacks' cervical tumor
were sought by researchers everywhere. Code-named HeLa (pronounced hee-
lah), the cells provided the first widely available model of human tissue, allowing
scientists to experiment on human cells growing conveniently in petri dishes.
Researchers studied the HeLa cells' nutritional requirements, their production
of proteins, their reactions to drugs, their patterns of mutation. As one of the
few fertile environments for human viruses, HeLa cells also were crucial to the
development of a polio vaccine. Even as techniques advanced to the point where
other cells could be developed into long-lasting cultures or cell lines, HeLa cells
remained popular in research. They were so readily available, so versatile, and
so easy to grow.

That popularity was partly responsible for the head start that HeLa cells had   12
on people like Nelson-Rees. By the time it was realized that the cells grew a
little *too* easily, they already had a foothold in many tissue culture laboratories.
At the same time, through years of use and countless new generations, the
innately vigorous HeLa cells had evolved into creatures very much at home in
the laboratory environment. They had adapted so well to life in a petri dish that
if but a few HeLa cells inadvertently made their way into a culture of one of
the newer cell lines, they would overpower the culture in a matter of days.

Unwittingly scientists aided the spread of HeLa with nonsterile equipment   13
and sloppy procedures. For example, technicians would transfer cells from a
HeLa dish into a non-HeLa dish by touching both with the same bottle of
growth medium. A couple of stray cells on the lip of the bottle were enough to
seed the contamination. One group of researchers found that HeLa cells can
travel within tiny airborne droplets created by such common lab activities as
pipetting, pulling stoppers, and streaking cultures. When the droplets landed
on open petri dishes, the HeLa cells began growing furiously, overwhelming
the original cultures there in three weeks. Some scientists are convinced that
HeLa cells can even survive on counter tops and the sides of flasks for days,
lying in wait for their next host.

In the case of the tumor cells from Russia, Nelson-Rees believes that a HeLa   14
culture must have been under study at each of the medical centers that supplied
them to the United States. With the involuntary help of Soviet scientists, and
using a few tricks of their own, the HeLa cells slipped into all five flasks un-
noticed. To the naked eye there is little difference between cultures of HeLa
and something else. One possible clue of a HeLa take-over might be sudden
explosive growth where the cells had been sluggish before. But biologists often
would see such a change as a sign that they had finally coaxed and coddled a
finicky cell culture into a hardy one.

For Nelson-Rees, a geneticist by training, the most incriminating evidence   15
came from chromosomes, the rodlike structures inside a cell's nucleus that carry
its genetic information. Previous investigators had found that HeLa cells con-

tained, in addition to the normal complement of chromosomes, four oddly shaped ones. These weird chromosomes, called markers, were unique to HeLa. It was through these markers that Nelson-Rees recognized the Russian cells as HeLa. He decided to use them as mug shots to screen other suspect cells.

There were backup tests as well. Henrietta Lacks carried a digestive enzyme that occurs rarely, and only in the black population. The Russian sample that Nelson-Rees sent to Detroit went to a friend who was able to find that enzyme. Recently more tests have been developed for many of the HeLa cells' biochemical characteristics, all of which Nelson-Rees uses in building cases against suspicious cells. "One doesn't have to drink the whole bottle to know that the milk is sour," he says. "Still, it's nice to be sure about these things." But it was Nelson-Rees' interest in chromosomes that led him to his second unexpected encounter with the cells of Henrietta Lacks. 16

It was just after the Russian mix-up. A colleague studying a line of breast cancer cells called HBT-3 (HBT for human breast tumor) observed several unusual features unlike those of other breast cancer cells. When she mentioned this to Nelson-Rees, he remembered that HBT-3 contained a strange chromosome shaped like Mickey Mouse ears. He has seen Mickey Mouse chromosomes in only one other cell line, HEK, taken from the kidney of a human embryo. "Perhaps this odd breast cell is really a kidney cell," he thought, and decided to analyze all the chromosomes of both cells. For comparison he added a third cell from another breast culture called HBT-39B. 17

He stained the nuclei to make the chromosome markings stand out, photographed them through a microscope, and sorted out the enlargements like a philatelist going through his stamp collection.[1] Suddenly it was the Russian incident all over again. "All three cells were identical. None were what they were supposed to be," he recalls, still slightly stunned. "And all three had HeLa markers." In addition, although at least one of the cells was supposed to have come from a Caucasian donor, the rare and characteristic black enzyme of HeLa turned up in all three. The Mickey Mouse ears, which had not been seen in any previously observed HeLa cultures, meant that HeLa cells had grown into several slightly different strains as they traveled from one spawning ground to the next. 18

Coming on the heels of the Russian HeLa case, the discovery seemed much more than coincidence to Nelson-Rees. Wasn't anyone working with the right cells? *Had* the whole world been taken over by HeLa? It was then that he launched his campaign to put this runaway cell back in its useful place. He combed the literature for anything that was already known about HeLa, searching for information that could help him trace its travels, uncover suspect cultures, and help control its spread. As a warning to his co-workers and in an effort to make the problem more visible, Nelson-Rees published a list of five 19

---

[1]philatelist: a stamp collector. [Eds.]

HeLa contaminants in the journal *Science* in 1974. Now HeLa was no longer the family secret of tissue culturists, and if there had been any doubt about it being a real problem, the doubt was gone: The chromosomal mug shots and enzyme data were very convincing.

"It really sent shock waves through the scientific world," recalls Jeffrey Schlom, 20 head of the National Cancer Institute's molecular oncology program. "It set back a lot of scientific careers."

Not that the wayward cancer cell posed any health threat to the scientists 21 whose labs it invaded. But to Nelson-Rees it was clear that by masquerading as other cells used in research, HeLa was perpetuating myths about the nature of cancer, bewildering experimenters.

Since the mid-1950s, for example, scientists had observed the same char- 22 acteristics in what they thought were different cancer cells and concluded that these traits must be common to all cancers. All cancer cells had certain nutritional needs, all could grow in soft agar cultures,[2] all could seed new solid tumors when transplanted into experimental animals, and all contained drastically abnormal chromosomes—the "mark of cancer," which were the unifying theories that emerged. In fact these traits are not common to all cancers. They are characteristic of the one cell that many different scientists were mistakenly studying. "It was our lady friend," says Nelson-Rees. "It is impossible to say how many millions of dollars were spent on research based on these misconceptions, but the whole spectrum of cancer characteristics had to be reevaluated."

Another popular myth held that normal human cells growing in a laboratory 23 culture dish could spontaneously turn cancerous. Such "spontaneous transformations" had been observed and well documented in early experiments in animal cells, but then scientists began reporting the phenomena in human cultures. Slow-growing normal cells, which never divide more than 50 to 60 times, reportedly exploded into growth and multiplied endlessly.

One such culture, labeled MA-160, began as normal prostate cells taken 24 from the administrator of a biological materials firm who decided to offer them as part of his company's inventory. By the time Nelson-Rees came across MA-160, another investigator already had found the black HeLa enzyme within the cells—which was odd since the donor was Caucasian. Nelson-Rees then identified the HeLa marker chromosomes and included the culture in his first hit list. Obviously, HeLa cells had sneaked into and overwhelmed the culture, as they had many cell lines that were thought to have magically become cancer cells. Today, few scientists believe there are any reliable reports of normal human cells becoming spontaneously transformed. To read the literature of the 1960s and early 1970s, though, you would think it happened every other day.

In addition to muddying the scientific waters with cancer myths, HeLa cells 25

---

[2]agar: a gelatinous medium derived from red algae or seaweed. [Eds.]

cast shadows of doubt over results that depended on the specific identity of a cell. Investigators who had been working with MA-160 under the assumption that it was a normal prostate cell from a white male, for instance, had to consider much of their work irrelevant when they learned it was a cervical cancer cell from a black woman. The same was true for the scientists searching for breast tumor viruses by experimenting on the two breast cancer lines indicted by Nelson-Rees. Studies based on their findings were jeopardized too.

After his first hit list was published, Nelson-Rees began receiving samples of   26
HeLa suspects from all over the world, cells presumed to be everything from skin to stomach. Many turned out to be HeLa. For each contaminant, he took micrographic mug shots of the chromosomes and duly noted the details of the case in his burgeoning notebooks. Occasionally, the source of a HeLa contaminant would say he had never heard of HeLa and certainly had no cells by that name in his lab. In those labs, however, Nelson-Rees was usually able to find another cell line, assumed to be pure, that itself had been contaminated by HeLa. He was to get to know that trick. The only way to fight back, he figured, was to continue publicizing as many of HeLa's disguises as he could.

In 1976 Nelson-Rees published his second hit list, naming 55 HeLa impos-   27
tors that had been reported previously and 11 new ones. As he had for the first list, he included the sources of the phony cells for two reasons. He thought there might be uncontaminated supplies of some cultures in the hands of more careful people. He also hoped that naming names might discourage further distribution of the spoiled goods.

By this time Nelson-Rees had earned two reputations. To some he was the   28
meticulous Ralph Nader of tissue culture who sought to improve the science by exposing shoddy materials and warning people away from them. "Walter's sometimes a little pointed, a little blunt," says Wade Parks, a microbiologist at the University of Miami who has followed Nelson-Rees' work since the days of the Russian HeLa cells. "But he's not wrong, I'll tell you that." To others, particularly to the scientists who never asked him to test their cells but whose names ended up on his lists just the same, he was an opportunistic publicity hound.

"Until now I have been very patient with your peculiar techniques to collect   29
'data' for your anti-HeLa publications, but this time you have gone too far." That is the opening of a venomous letter from a virologist whose newly cultivated breast cancer line was fingered in Nelson-Rees' 1976 hit list. He has an entire file full of similar reactions. In this case, the virologist reminded Nelson-Rees that he had never received permission to test the cell line and never notified the virologist that he was planning to discredit it in print. He concluded with "a strong and solemn protest" against Nelson-Rees' "unethical and irresponsible way of handling information."

Nelson-Rees' calm reply stated that it was the virologist's own co-worker who   30
had requested the analysis. The co-worker is now convinced that the new "breast
cells" are actually HeLa, he added. He also chided the virologist for announcing
the establishment of the new culture in a journal in spite of the partner's mis-
givings. Pointing out that several researchers wasted valuable time on the cells
before they learned they were HeLa, the letter concludes in classic Nelson-Rees
style: "I note from the latest issue of *Mammalian Chromosome Newsletter* that
you are working on a new cell line. If you feel that I could be of any assistance
to you in connection with this work, I should be pleased to do so." In other
words, "I'll be keeping an eye on things."

Nelson-Rees realizes it is only natural for those who spend years developing   31
cell lines and who base much of their research on them to be resentful. But he
says that is beside the point: "I've been admonished in the past not to overkill,
but this endless flow of nonsense has got to stop. We have to demand only the
best and only the most proven in our line of work. It's not like recalling a truck.
One can't recall a bogus cell culture and undo the damage after it's been growing
and disseminating."

When Nelson-Rees isn't publishing lists and receiving angry letters, he is   32
standing up at scientific meetings to question people's findings, preach the value
of careful techniques, and warn about HeLa's wily ways. What has it got him?

Small victories. Whereas the authenticity of cell lines was never stressed in   33
the training of young scientists, Nelson-Rees' hit lists are now required reading
in a few programs. To reduce contamination, a growing number of research
labs today work with only one cell type at a time, thoroughly disinfecting equipment before they move on to the next. Those who can afford the time and
money never start an experiment without having the identity of their cells ver-
ified by authorities like Nelson-Rees.

In January the American Type Culture Collection, a nonprofit cell bank like   34
Nelson-Rees', destroyed a dozen HeLa-contaminated cells in its supplies and
slapped bold warnings on the few it retained. Director Robert Stevenson, one
of Nelson-Rees' greatest fans, is emphasizing the point by distributing textured-
rubber jar openers with the slogan: "For a good grip on your research, use
authenticated cultures." Stevenson also has been pleading with the editors of
journals to require researchers to include a detailed pedigree of the cells they
work with in any report submitted for publication.

Meanwhile Nelson-Rees continues to pursue the strangely immortal woman   35
from Baltimore. Last summer he reported that supposedly normal kidney cells
used for years by scientists to study the health hazards of radiation were in fact
HeLa, throwing into doubt much of that work. The "kidney cells" appeared on
his third hit list, published earlier this year. Of the several hundred human
cancer cultures used in research today, he has now fingered 90 as HeLa. And
he is currently on the trail of three recently cultured liver cancer lines from
China that bear a suspicious resemblance to "our lady friend."

Maybe it's a good thing that Nelson-Rees will never quite catch up with   36
Henrietta Lacks. The image of the fugitive cells always one step ahead of the
scientific gumshoe is a useful reminder—not only for tissue culturists, but also
for scientists who hope to engineer new forms of life in a safe manner, for
technicians trying to harness tricky new kinds of energy, and for the public that
puts its faith in those pursuits. Science is after all a human activity with human
fallibilities, and things are not always what they seem.

QUESTIONS

1. What do you suppose Gold's methods of research are like? Try to describe them.

2. After gathering information, Gold's next task is to organize his presentation of it.
This is not just a matter of deciding what to say first, then second, but also a matter of
deciding how to characterize his story. What particular methods does Gold use to attract
you to the story he tells?

3. How does Gold coordinate the two major threads in his account—his report of
the HeLa phenomenon and his report about Nelson-Rees?

4. Consider the choice of words and the persons outside of this immediate story that
Gold mentions in paragraph 6. What do those elements have in common, and how do
they assist Gold in presenting his information to us?

5. In how many places other than paragraph 6 do you find the same sort of language
used? Do you think that this usage is controlled and purposeful, or does it get out of
hand? Could it be said to act like the HeLa cells themselves and to "contaminate" the
larger "culture" of Gold's story? Or do you find that spreading usage justified and defen-
sible? Explain.

6. In his last paragraph, Gold suggests the broader significance of this story. Are those
reasonable worries, or is he just adding on something at the end? Identify one of those
other subjects mentioned so briefly. Look up some articles on it, and write a report on
what might be at issue there.

LOVE CANAL AND
THE POISONING
OF AMERICA

Michael Brown

Michael Brown is a free-lance writer interested in environmental issues. His investigations into the dumping of toxic waste, which have appeared in newspaper and magazine articles, have won him three Pulitzer Prize nominations and a special award from the Environmental Protection Agency. This essay is taken from his book Laying Waste: The Poisoning of America by Toxic Chemicals *(1980).*

Niagara Falls is a city of unmatched natural beauty; it is also a tired industrial   1
workhorse, beaten often and with a hard hand. A magnificent river—a strait, really—connecting Lake Erie to Lake Ontario flows hurriedly north, at a pace of a half-million tons a minute, widening into a smooth expanse near the city before breaking into whitecaps and taking its famous 186-foot plunge. Then it cascades through a gorge of overhung shale and limestone to rapids higher and swifter than anywhere else on the continent.

The falls attract long lines of newlyweds and other tourists. At the same time,   2
the river provides cheap electricity for industry; a good stretch of its shore is now filled with the spiraled pipes of distilleries, and the odors of chlorine and sulfides hang in the air.

Many who live in the city of Niagara Falls work in chemical plants, the   3
largest of which is owned by the Hooker Chemical Company, a subsidiary of Occidental Petroleum since the 1960s. Timothy Schroeder did not. He was a cement technician by trade, dealing with the factories only if they needed a pathway poured, or a small foundation set. Tim and his wife, Karen, lived in a ranch-style home with a brick and wood exterior at 460 99th Street. One of the Schroeders' most cherished purchases was a Fiberglas pool, built into the ground and enclosed by a red-wood fence.

Karen looked from a back window one morning in October 1974, noting   4
with distress that the pool had suddenly risen two feet above the ground. She called Tim to tell him about it. Karen then had no way of knowing that this was the first sign of what would prove to be a punishing family and economic tragedy.

Mrs. Schroeder believed that the cause of the uplift was the unusual ground-   5
water flow of the area. Twenty-one years before, an abandoned hydroelectric canal directly behind their house had been backfilled with industrial rubble.

The underground breaches created by this disturbance, aided by the marshland nature of the region's surficial layer, collected large volumes of rainfall and undermined the back yard. The Schroeders allowed the pool to remain in its precarious position until the following summer and then pulled it from the ground, intending to pour a new pool, cast in cement. This they were unable to do, for the gaping excavation immediately filled with what Karen called "chemical water," rancid liquids of yellow and orchid and blue. These same chemicals had mixed with the groundwater and flooded the entire yard, attacking the redwood posts with such a caustic bite that one day the fence simply collapsed. When the chemicals receded in the dry weather, they left the gardens and shrubs withered and scorched, as if by a brush fire.

How the chemicals got there was no mystery. In the late 1930s, or perhaps early 1940s, the Hooker Company, whose many processes included the manufacture of pesticides, plasticizers, and caustic soda, began using the abandoned canal as a dump for at least 20,000 tons of waste residues—"still-bottoms," in the language of the trade.

Karen Schroeder's parents had been the first to experience problems with the canal's seepage. In 1959, her mother, Aileen Voorhees, encountered a strange black sludge bleeding through the basement walls. For the next twenty years, she and her husband, Edwin, tried various methods of halting the irritating intrusion, pasting the cinder-block wall with sealants and even constructing a gutter along the walls to intercept the inflow. Nothing could stop the chemical smell from permeating the entire household, and neighborhood calls to the city for help were fruitless. One day, when Edwin punched a hole in the wall to see what was happening, quantities of black liquid poured from the block. The cinder blocks were full of the stuff.

More ominous than the Voorhees basement was an event that occurred at 11:12 P.M. on November 21, 1968, when Karen Schroeder gave birth to her third child, a seven-pound girl named Sheri. No sense of elation filled the delivery room. The child was born with a heart that beat irregularly and had a hole in it, bone blockages of the nose, partial deafness, deformed ear exteriors, and a cleft palate. Within two years, the Schroeders realized Sheri was also mentally retarded. When her teeth came in, a double row of them appeared on her lower jaw. And she developed an enlarged liver.

The Schroeders considered these health problems, as well as illnesses among their other children, as acts of capricious genes—a vicious quirk of nature. Like Mrs. Schroeder's parents, they were concerned that the chemicals were devaluing their property. The crab apple tree and evergreens in the back were dead, and even the oak in front of the home was sick; one year, the leaves had fallen off on Father's Day.

The canal had been dug with much fanfare in the late nineteenth century by a flamboyant entrepreneur named William T. Love, who wanted to construct an industrial city with ready access to water power and major markets. The setting for Love's dream was to be a navigable power channel that would extend seven miles from the Upper Niagara before falling two hundred feet, circumventing the treacherous falls and at the same time providing cheap power. A city would be constructed near the point where the canal fed back into the river, and he promised it would accommodate half a million people.

So taken with his imagination were the state's leaders that they gave Love a 11 free hand to condemn as much property as he liked, and to divert whatever amounts of water. Love's dream, however, proved grander than his resources, and he was eventually forced to abandon the project after a mile-long trench, ten to forty feet deep and generally twenty yards wide, had been scoured perpendicular to the Niagara River. Eventually, the trench was purchased by Hooker.

Few of those who, in 1977, lived in the numerous houses that had sprung 12 up by the site were aware that the large and barren field behind them was a burial ground for toxic waste. Both the Niagara County Health Department and the city said it was a nuisance condition, but no serious danger to the people. Officials of the Hooker Company refused comment, claiming only that they had no records of the chemical burials and that the problem was not their responsibility. Indeed, Hooker had deeded the land to the Niagara Falls Board of Education in 1953, for a token $1. With it the company issued no detailed warnings of the chemicals, only a brief paragraph in the quitclaim document that disclaimed company liability for any injuries or deaths which might occur at the site.

Though Hooker was undoubtedly relieved to rid itself of the contaminated 13 land, the company was so vague about the hazards involved that one might have thought the wastes would cause harm only if touched, because they irritated the skin; otherwise, they were not of great concern. In reality, as the company must have known, the dangers of these wastes far exceeded those of acids or alkalines or inert salts. We now know that the drums Hooker had dumped in the canal contained a veritable witch's brew—compounds of truly remarkable toxicity. There were solvents that attacked the heart and liver, and residues from pesticides so dangerous that their commercial sale was shortly thereafter restricted outright by the government; some of them were already suspected of causing cancer.

Yet Hooker gave no hint of that. When the board of education, which wanted 14 the parcel for a new school, approached Hooker, B. Klaussen, at the time Hooker's executive vice president, said in a letter to the board. "Our officers have carefully considered your request. We are very conscious of the need for new elementary schools and realize that the sites must be carefully selected. We will be willing to donate the entire strip of property which we own between Colvin Boulevard and Frontier Avenue to be used for the erection of a school at a location to be determined. . . ."

The board built the school and playground at the canal's midsection. Construction progressed despite the contractor's hitting a drainage trench that gave off a strong chemical odor and the discovery of a waste pit nearby. Instead of halting the work, the authorities simply moved the school eighty feet away. Young families began to settle in increasing numbers alongside the dump, many of them having been told that the field was to be a park and recreation area for their children. 15

Children found the "playground" interesting, but at times painful. They sneezed, and their eyes teared. In the days when the dumping was still in progress, they swam at the opposite end of the canal, occasionally arriving home with hard pimples all over their bodies. Hooker knew children were playing on its spoils. In 1958, three children were burned by exposed residues on the canal's surface, much of which, according to residents, had been covered with nothing more than fly ash and loose dirt. Because it wished to avoid legal repercussions, the company chose not to issue a public warning of the dangers it knew were there, nor to have its chemists explain to the people that their homes would have been better placed elsewhere. 16

The Love Canal was simply unfit as a container for hazardous substances, poor even by the standards of the day, and now, in 1977, local authorities were belatedly finding that out. Several years of heavy snowfall and rain had filled the sparingly covered channel like a bathtub. The contents were overflowing at a frightening rate. 17

The city of Niagara Falls, I was assured, was planning a remedial drainage program to halt in some measure the chemical migration off the site. But no sense of urgency had been attached to the plan, and it was stalled in red tape. No one could agree on who should pay the bill—the city, Hooker, or the board of education—and engineers seemed confused over what exactly needed to be done. 18

Niagara Falls City Manager Donald O'Hara persisted in his view that, however displeasing to the eyes and nose, the Love Canal was not a crisis matter, mainly a question of aesthetics. O'Hara reminded me that Dr. Francis Clifford, county health commissioner, supported that opinion. 19

With the city, the board, and Hooker unwilling to commit themselves to a remedy, conditions degenerated in the area between 97th and 99th streets, until, by early 1978, the land was a quagmire of sludge that oozed from the canal's every pore. Melting snow drained the surface soot onto the private yards, while on the dump itself the ground had softened to the point of collapse, exposing the crushed tops of barrels. Beneath the surface, masses of sludge were finding their way out at a quickening rate, constantly forming springs of contaminated liquid. The Schroeder back yard, once featured in a local newspaper for its beauty, had reached the point where it was unfit even to walk upon. Of course, the Schroeders could not leave. No one would think of buying the property. They still owed on their mortgage and, with Tim's salary, could not afford to 20 maintain the house while they moved into a safer setting. They and their four children were stuck.

Apprehension about large costs was not the only reason the city was reluctant   21
to help the Schroeders and the one hundred or so other families whose properties abutted the covered trench. The city may also have feared distressing Hooker. To an economically depressed area, the company provided desperately needed employment—as many as 3000 blue-collar jobs and a substantial number of tax dollars. Hooker was speaking of building a $17 million headquarters in downtown Niagara Falls. So anxious were city officials to receive the new building that they and the state granted the company highly lucrative tax and loan incentives, and made available to the firm a prime parcel of property near the most popular tourist park on the American side.

City Manager O'Hara and other authorities were aware of the nature of   22
Hooker's chemicals. In fact, in the privacy of his office, O'Hara, after receiving a report on the chemical tests at the canal, had informed the people at Hooker that it was an extremely serious problem. Even earlier, in 1976, the New York State Department of Environmental Conservation had been made aware that dangerous compounds were present in the basement sump pump of at least one 97th Street home, and soon after, its own testing had revealed that highly injurious halogenated hydrocarbons were flowing from the canal into adjoining sewers. Among them were the notorious PCBs; quantities as low as one part PCBs to a million parts normal water were enough to create serious environmental concerns; in the sewers of Niagara Falls, the quantities of halogenated compounds were thousands of times higher. The other materials tracked, in sump pumps or sewers, were just as toxic as PCBs, or more so. Prime among the more hazardous ones was residue from hexachlorocyclopentadiene, or C-56, which was deployed as an intermediate in the manufacture of several pesticides. In certain dosages, the chemical could damage every organ in the body.

While the mere presence of C-56 should have been cause for alarm, gov-   23
ernment remained inactive. Not until early 1978—a full eighteen months after C-56 was first detected—was testing conducted in basements along 97th and 99th streets to see if the chemicals had vaporized off the sump pumps and walls and were present in the household air.

While the basement tests were in progress, the rains of spring arrived at the   24
canal, further worsening the situation. Heavier fumes rose above the barrels. More than before, the residents were suffering from headaches, respiratory discomforts, and skin ailments. Many of them felt constantly fatigued and irritable, and the children had reddened eyes. In the Schroeder home, Tim developed a rash along the backs of his legs. Karen could not rid herself of throbbing pains in her head. Their daughter, Laurie, seemed to be losing some of her hair.

The EPA test revealed that benzene, a known cause of cancer in humans,   25
had been readily detected in the household air up and down the streets. A widely used solvent, benzene was known in chronic-exposure cases to cause

headaches, fatigue, loss of weight, and dizziness followed by pallor, nose-bleeds, and damage to the bone marrow.

No public announcement was made of the benzene hazard. Instead, officials appeared to shield the finding until they could agree among themselves on how to present it. 26

Dr. Clifford, the county health commissioner, seemed unconcerned by the detection of benzene in the air. His health department refused to conduct a formal study of the people's health, despite the air-monitoring results. For this reason, and because of the resistance growing among the local authorities, I went to the southern end of 99th Street to take an informal health survey of my own. I arranged a meeting with six neighbors, all of them instructed beforehand to list the illnesses they were aware of on their block, with names and ages specified for presentation at the session. 27

The residents' list was startling. Though unafflicted before they moved there, many people were now plagued with ear infections, nervous disorders, rashes, and headaches. One young man, James Gizzarelli, said he had missed four months of work owing to breathing troubles. His wife was suffering epileptic-like seizures which her doctor was unable to explain. Meanwhile, freshly applied paint was inexplicably peeling from the exterior of their house. Pets too were suffering, most seriously if they had been penned in the back yards nearest to the canal, constantly breathing air that smelled like mothballs and weedkiller. They lost their fur, exhibited skin lesions, and, while still quite young, developed internal tumors. A great many cases of cancer were reported among the women, along with much deafness. On both 97th and 99th streets, traffic signs warned passing motorists to watch for deaf children playing near the road. 28

Evidence continued to mount that a large group of people, perhaps all of the one hundred families immediately by the canal, perhaps many more, were in imminent danger. While watching television, while gardening or doing a wash, in their sleeping hours, they were inhaling a mixture of damaging chemicals. Their hours of exposure were far longer than those of a chemical factory worker, and they wore no respirators or goggles. Nor could they simply open a door and escape. Helplessness and despair were the main responses to the blackened craters and scattered cinders behind their back yards. 29

But public officials often characterized the residents as hypochondriacs. Every agent of government had been called on the phone or sent pleas for help, but none offered aid. 30

Commissioner Clifford expressed irritation at my printed reports of illness, and disagreement began to surface in the newsroom on how the stories should be printed. "There's a high rate of cancer among my friends," Dr. Clifford argued. "It doesn't mean anything." 31

Yet as interest in the small community increased, further revelations shook the neighborhood. In addition to the benzene, eighty or more other compounds 32 were found in the makeshift dump, ten of them potential carcinogens. The physiological effects they could cause were profound and diverse. At least fourteen of them could impact on the brain and central nervous system. Two of them, carbon tetrachloride and chlorobenzene, could readily cause narcotic or anesthetic consequences. Many others were known to cause headaches, seizures, loss of hair, anemia, or skin rashes. Together, the compounds were capable of inflicting innumerable illnesses, and no one knew what new concoctions were being formulated by their mixture underground.

Edwin and Aileen Voorhees had the most to be concerned about. When a state   33
biophysicist analyzed the air content of their basement, he determined that the safe exposure time there was less than 2.4 minutes—the toxicity in the basement was thousands of times the acceptable limit for twenty-four-hour breathing. This did not mean they would necessarily become permanently ill, but their chances of contracting cancer, for example, had been measurably increased. In July, I visited Mrs. Voorhees for further discussion of her problems, and as we sat in the kitchen, drinking coffee, the industrial odors were apparent. Aileen, usually chipper and feisty, was visibly anxious. She stared down at the table, talking only in a lowered voice. Everything now looked different to her. The home she and Edwin had built had become their jail cell. Their yard was but a pathway through which toxicants entered the cellar walls. The field out back, that proposed "park," seemed destined to be the ruin of their lives.

On July 14 I received a call from the state health department with some   34
shocking news. A preliminary review showed that women living at the southern end had suffered a high rate of miscarriages and had given birth to an abnormally high number of children with birth defects. In one age group, 35.3 percent had records of spontaneous abortions. That was far in excess of the norm. The odds against it happening by chance were 250 to one. These tallies, it was stressed, were "conservative" figures. Four children in one small section of the neighborhood had documentable birth defects, club feet, retardation, and deafness. Those who lived there the longest suffered the highest rates.

The data on miscarriages and birth defects, coupled with the other accounts   35
of illness, finally pushed the state's bureaucracy into motion. A meeting was scheduled for August 2, at which time the state health commissioner, Dr. Robert Whalen, would formally address the issue. The day before the meeting, Dr. Nicholas Vianna, a state epidemiologist, told me that residents were also incurring some degree of liver damage. Blood analyses had shown hepatitis-like symptoms in enzyme levels. Dozens if not hundreds of people, apparently, had been adversely affected.

In Albany, on August 2, Dr. Whalen read a lengthy statement in which he   36
urged that pregnant women and children under two years of age leave the southern end of the dump site immediately. He declared the Love Canal an official emergency, citing it as a "great and imminent peril to the health of the general public."

When Commissioner Whalen's words hit 97th and 99th streets, by way of   37
one of the largest banner headlines in the Niagara *Gazette*'s 125-year history,
dozens of people massed on the streets, shouting into bullhorns and micro-
phones to voice frustrations that had been accumulating for months. Many of
them vowed a tax strike because their homes were rendered unmarketable and
unsafe. They attacked their government for ignoring their welfare. A man of
high authority, a physician with a title, had confirmed that their lives were in
danger. Most wanted to leave the neighborhood immediately.

Terror and anger roiled together, exacerbated by Dr. Whalen's failure to   38
provide a government-funded evacuation plan. His words were only a recommendation: individual families had to choose whether to risk their health and
remain, or abandon their houses and, in so doing, write off a lifetime of work
and savings.

On August 3, Dr. Whalen decided he should speak to the people. He arrived   39
with Dr. David Axelrod, a deputy who had directed the state's investigation,
and Thomas Frey, a key aide to Governor Hugh Carey.

At a public meeting, held in the 99th Street School auditorium, Frey was   40
given the grueling task of controlling the crowd of 500 angry and frightened
people. In an attempt to calm them, he announced that a meeting between the
state and the White House had been scheduled for the following week. The
state would propose that the Love Canal be classified a national disaster, thereby
freeing federal funds. For now, however, he could promise no more. Neither
could Dr. Whalen and his staff of experts. All they could say was what was
already known: twenty-five organic compounds, some of them capable of causing cancer, were in their homes, and because young children were especially
prone to toxic effects, they should be moved to another area.

Dr. Whalen's order had applied only to those living at the canal's southern   41
end, on its immediate periphery. But families living across the street from the
dump site, or at the northern portion, where the chemicals were not so visible
at the surface, reported afflictions remarkably similar to those suffered by families
whose yards abutted the southern end. Serious respiratory problems, nervous
disorders, and rectal bleeding were reported by many who were not covered by
the order.

Throughout the following day, residents posted signs of protest on their front   42
fences or porch posts. "Love Canal Kills," they said, or "Give Me Liberty, I've
Got Death." Emotionally exhausted and uncertain about their future, men
stayed home from work, congregating on the streets or comforting their wives.
By this time the board of education had announced it was closing the 99th
Street School for the following year, because of its proximity to the exposed
toxicants. Still, no public relief was provided for the residents.

Another meeting was held that evening, at a firehall on 102nd Street. It was   43
unruly, but the people, who had called the session in an effort to organize
themselves, managed to form an alliance, the Love Canal Homeowners Asso-

230

ciation, and to elect as president Lois Gibbs, a pretty, twenty-seven-year-old woman with jet-black hair who proved remarkably adept at dealing with experienced politicians and at keeping the matter in the news. After Mrs. Gibbs' election, Congressman John LaFalce entered the hall and announced, to wild applause, that the Federal Disaster Assistance Administration would be represented the next morning, and that the state's two senators, Daniel Patrick Moynihan and Jacob Javits, were working with him in an attempt to get funds from Congress.

With the Love Canal story now attracting attention from the national media, the Governor's office announced that Hugh Carey would be at the 99th Street School on August 7 to address the people. Decisions were being made in Albany and Washington. Hours before the Governor's arrival, a sudden burst of "urgent" reports from Washington came across the newswires. President Jimmy Carter had officially declared the Hooker dump site a national emergency.   44

Hugh Carey was applauded on his arrival. The Governor announced that the state, through its Urban Development Corporation, planned to purchase, at fair market value, those homes rendered uninhabitable by the marauding chemicals. He spared no promises. "You will not have to make mortgage payments on homes you don't want or cannot occupy. Don't worry about the banks. The state will take care of them." By the standards of Niagara Falls, where the real estate market was depressed, the houses were in the middle-class range, worth from $20,000 to $40,000 apiece. The state would assess each house and purchase it, and also pay the costs of moving, temporary housing during the transition period, and special items not covered by the usual real estate assessment, such as installation of telephones.   45

First in a trickle and then, by September, in droves, the families gathered their belongings and carted them away. Moving vans crowded 97th and 99th streets. Linesmen went from house to house disconnecting the telephones and electrical wires, while carpenters pounded plywood over the windows to keep vandals away. By the following spring, 237 families were gone; 170 of them had moved into new houses. In time the state erected around a six-block residential area a green chain-link fence, eight feet in height, clearly demarcating the contamination zone.   46

In October 1978, the long-awaited remedial drainage program began at the south end. Trees were uprooted, fences and garages torn down, and swimming pools removed from the area. So great were residents' apprehensions that dangerous fumes would be released over the surrounding area that the state, at a cost of $500,000, placed seventy-five buses at emergency evacuation pickup spots during the months of work, in the event that outlying homes had to be vacated quickly because of an explosion. The plan was to construct drain tiles around the channel's periphery, where the back yards had been located, in order to divert leakage to seventeen-foot-deep wet wells from which contaminated   47

231

groundwater could be drawn and treated by filtration through activated carbon. (Removing the chemicals themselves would have been financially prohibitive, perhaps costing as much as $100 million—and even then the materials would have to be buried elsewhere.) After the trenching was complete, and the sewers installed, the canal was to be covered by a sloping mound of clay and planted with grass. One day, city officials hoped, the wasteland would become a park.

In spite of the corrective measures and the enormous effort by the state health department, which took thousands of blood samples from past and current residents and made uncounted analyses of soil, water, and air, the full range of the effects remained unknown. In neighborhoods immediately outside the official "zone of contamination," more than 500 families were left near the desolate setting, their health still in jeopardy. The state announced it would buy no more homes.

The first public indication that chemical contamination had probably reached streets to the east and west of 97th and 99th streets, and to the north and south as well, came on August 11, 1978, when sump-pump samples I had taken from 100th and 101st streets, analyzed in a laboratory, showed the trace presence of a number of chemicals found in the canal itself, including lindane, a restricted pesticide that had been suspected of causing cancer in laboratory animals. While probing 100th Street, I had knocked on the door of Patricia Pino, thirty-four, a blond divorcee with a young son and daughter. I had noticed that some of the leaves on a large tree in front of her house exhibited a black oiliness much like that on the trees and shrubs of 99th Street; she was located near what had been a drainage swale.

After I had extracted a jar of sediment from her sump pump for the analysis, we conversed about her family situation and what the trauma now unfolding meant to them. Ms. Pino was extremely depressed and embittered. Both of her children had what appeared to be slight liver abnormalities, and her son had been plagued with "non-specific" allergies, teary eyes, sinus trouble, which improved markedly when he was sent away from home. Patricia told of times, during the heat of summer, when fumes were readily noticeable in her basement and sometimes even upstairs. She herself had been treated for a possibly cancerous condition on her cervix. But, like others, her family was now trapped.

On September 24, 1978, I obtained a state memorandum that said chemical infiltration of the outer regions was significant indeed. The letter, sent from the state laboratories to the U.S. Environmental Protection Agency, said, "Preliminary analysis of soil samples demonstrates extensive migration of potentially toxic materials outside the immediate canal area." There it was, in the state's own words. Not long afterward, the state medical investigator, Dr. Nicholas Vianna, reported indications that residents from 93rd to 103rd streets might also have incurred liver damage.

On October 4, a young boy, John Allen Kenny, who lived quite a distance north of the evacuation zone, died. The fatality was due to the failure of another organ that can be readily affected by toxicants, the kidney. Naturally, suspicions were raised that his death was in some way related to a creek that still flowed behind his house and carried, near an outfall, the odor of chlorinated compounds. Because the creek served as a catch basin for a portion of the Love Canal, the state studied an autopsy of the boy. No conclusions were reached. John Allen's parents, Norman, a chemist, and Luella, a medical research assistant, were unsatisfied with the state's investigation, which they felt was "superficial." Luella said, "He played in the creek all the time. There had been restrictions on the older boys, but he was the youngest and played with them when they were old enough to go to the creek. We let him do what the other boys did. He died of nephrosis. Proteins were passing through his urine. Well, in reading the literature, we discovered that chemicals can trigger this. There was no evidence of infection, which there should have been, and there was damage to his thymus and brain. He also had nosebleeds and headaches, and dry heaves. So our feeling is that chemicals probably triggered it."

The likelihood that water-carried chemicals had escaped from the canal's 53 deteriorating bounds and were causing problems quite a distance from the site was not lost upon the Love Canal Homeowners Association and its president, Lois Gibbs, who was attempting to have additional families relocated. Because she lived on 101st Street, she was one of those left behind, with no means of moving despite persistent medical difficulties in her six-year-old son, Michael, who had been operated on twice for urethral strictures. [Mrs. Gibbs' husband, a worker at a chemical plant, brought home only $150 a week, she told me, and when they subtracted from that the $90 a week for food and other necessities, clothing costs for their two children, $125 a month for mortgage payments and taxes, utility and phone expenses, and medical bills, they had hardly enough cash to buy gas and cigarettes, let alone vacate their house.]

Assisted by two other stranded residents, Marie Pozniak and Grace McCoulf, 54 and with the professional analysis of a Buffalo scientist named Beverly Paigen, Lois Gibbs mapped out the swale and creekbed areas, many of them long ago filled, and set about interviewing the numerous people who lived on or near formerly wet ground. The survey indicated that these people were suffering from an abnormal number of kidney and bladder aggravations and problems of the reproductive system. In a report to the state, Dr. Paigen claimed to have found, in 245 homes outside the evacuation zone, thirty-four miscarriages, eighteen birth defects, nineteen nervous breakdowns, ten cases of epilepsy, and high rates of hyperactivity and suicide.

In their roundabout way, the state health experts, after an elaborate investi- 55 gation, confirmed some of the homeowners' worst fears. On February 8, 1979, Dr. David Axelrod, who by then had been appointed health commissioner, and whose excellence as a scientist was widely acknowledged, issued a new order that officially extended the health emergency of the previous August, citing high incidences of birth deformities and miscarriages in the areas where creeks and

233

swales had once flowed, or where swamps had been. With that, the state offered to evacuate temporarily those families with pregnant women or children under the age of two from the outer areas of contamination, up to 103rd Street. But no additional homes would be purchased; nor was another large-scale evacuation, temporary or otherwise, under consideration. Those who left under the new plan would have to return when their children passed the age limit.

Twenty-three families accepted the state's offer. Another seven families, ineligible under the plan but of adequate financial means to do so, simply left their homes and took the huge loss of investment. Soon boarded windows speckled the outlying neighborhoods. 56

The previous November and December, not long after the evacuation of 97th and 99th streets, I became interested in the possibility that Hooker might have buried in the Love Canal waste residues from the manufacture of what is known as 2,4,5-trichlorophenol. My curiosity was keen because I knew that this substance, which Hooker produced for the manufacture of the antibacterial agent hexachlorophene, and which was also used to make defoliants such as Agent Orange, the herbicide employed in Vietnam, carries with it an unwanted by-product technically called 2,3,7,8-tetrachlorodibenzo-para-dioxin, or tetra dioxin. The potency of dioxin of this isomer is nearly beyond imagination. Although its toxicological effects are not fully known, the few experts on the subject estimate that if three ounces were evenly distributed and subsequently ingested among a million people, or perhaps more than that, all of them would die. It compares in toxicity to the botulinum toxin. On skin contact, dioxin causes a disfiguration called "chloracne," which begins as pimples, lesions, and cysts, but can lead to calamitous internal damage. Some scientists suspect that dioxin causes cancer, perhaps even malignancies that occur, in galloping fashion, within a short time of contact. At least two (some estimates went as high as eleven) pounds of dioxin were dispersed over Seveso, Italy, in 1976, after an explosion at a trichlorophenol plant: dead animals littered the streets, and more than 300 acres of land were immediately evacuated. In Vietnam, the spraying of Agent Orange, because of the dioxin contaminant, was banned in 1970, when the first effects on human beings began to surface, including dioxin's powerful teratogenic, or fetus-deforming, effects. 57

I posed two questions concerning trichlorophenol: Were wastes from the process buried in the canal? If so, what were the quantities? 58

On November 8, before Hooker answered my queries, I learned that, indeed, trichlorophenol had been found in liquids pumped from the remedial drain ditches. No dioxin had been found yet, and some officials, ever wary of more emotionalism among the people, argued that, because the compound was not soluble in water, there was little chance it had migrated off-site. Officials at Newco Chemical Waste Systems, a local waste disposal firm, at the same time claimed that if dioxin had been there, it had probably been photolytically destroyed. Its half-life, they contended, was just a few short years. 59

234

I knew from Whiteside, however, that in every known case, waste from 2,4,5- 60
trichlorophenol carried dioxin with it. I also knew that dioxin *could* become
soluble in groundwater and migrate into the neighborhood upon mixing with
solvents such as benzene. Moreover, because it had been buried, sunlight would
not break it down.

On Friday, November 10, I called Hooker again to urge that they answer 61
my questions. Their spokesman, Bruce Davis, came to the phone and, in a
controlled tone, gave me the answer: His firm had indeed buried trichlorophenol
in the canal—200 tons of it.

Immediately I called Whiteside. His voice took on an urgent tone. According 62
to his calculation, if 200 tons of trichlorophenol were there, in all likelihood
they were accompanied by 130 pounds of tetra dioxin, an amount equaling the
estimated total content of dioxin in the thousands of tons of Agent Orange rained
upon Vietnamese jungles. The seriousness of the crisis had deepened, for now
the Love Canal was not only a dump for highly dangerous solvents and pesticides; it was also the broken container for one of the most toxic substances ever
synthesized by man.

I reckoned that the main danger was to those working on the remedial project, 63
digging in the trenches. The literature on dioxin indicated that, even in quantities at times too small to detect, the substance possessed vicious characteristics.
In one case, workers in a trichlorophenol plant had developed chloracne, although the substance could not be traced on the equipment with which they
worked. The mere tracking of minuscule amounts of dioxin on a pedestrian's
shoes in Seveso led to major concerns, and, according to Whiteside, a plant in
Amsterdam, upon being found contaminated with dioxin, had been "disman-
tled, brick by brick, and the material embedded in concrete, loaded at a specially
constructed dock, on ships, and dumped at sea, in deep water near the Azores."
Workers in trichlorophenol plants had died of cancer or severe liver damage,
or had suffered emotional and sexual disturbances.

Less than a month after the first suspicions arose, on the evening of December 64
9, I received a call from Dr. Axelrod. "We found it. The dioxin. In a drainage
trench behind 97th Street. It was in the part-per-trillion range."

The state remained firm in its plans to continue the construction, and, despite 65
the ominous new findings, no further evacuations were announced. During the
next several weeks, small incidents of vandalism occurred along 97th and 99th
streets. Tacks were spread on the road, causing numerous flat tires on the trucks.
Signs of protest were hung in the school. Meetings of the Love Canal Homeowners Association became more vociferous. Christmas was near, and in the
association's office at the 99th Street School, a holiday tree was decorated with
bulbs arranged to spell "DIOXIN."

The Love Canal people chanted and cursed at meetings with the state offi- 66
cials, cried on the telephone, burned an effigy of the health commissioner,
traveled to Albany with a makeshift child's coffin, threatened to hold officials

hostage, sent letters and telegrams to the White House, held days of mourning and nights of prayer. On Mother's Day this year, they marched down the industrial corridor and waved signs denouncing Hooker, which had issued not so much as a statement of remorse. But no happy ending was in store for them. The federal government was clearly not planning to come to their rescue, and the state felt it had already done more than its share. City Hall was silent and remains silent today. Some residents still hoped that, miraculously, an agency of government would move them. All of them watched with anxiety as each newborn came to the neighborhood, and they looked at their bodies for signs of cancer.

One hundred and thirty families from the Love Canal area began leaving their homes last August and September, seeking temporary refuge in local hotel rooms under a relocation plan funded by the state which had been implemented after fumes became so strong, during remedial trenching operations, that the United Way abandoned a care center it had opened in the neighborhood. 67

As soon as remedial construction is complete, the people will probably be forced to return home, as the state will no longer pay for their lodging. Some have threatened to barricade themselves in the hotels. Some have mentioned violence. Anne Hillis of 102nd Street, who told reporters her first child had been born so badly decomposed that doctors could not determine its sex, was so bitter that she threw table knives and a soda can at the state's on-site coordinator. 68

In October, Governor Carey announced that the state probably would buy an additional 200 to 240 homes, at an expense of some $5 million. In the meantime, lawyers have prepared lawsuits totaling about $2.65 billion and have sought court action for permanent relocation. Even if the latter action is successful, and they are allowed to move, the residents' plight will not necessarily have ended. The psychological scars are bound to remain among them and their children, along with the knowledge that, because they have already been exposed, they may never fully escape the Love Canal's insidious grasp. 69

QUESTIONS

1. What caused the poisoning of Love Canal? Why did it take so long for both local and state officials to acknowledge the seriousness of the condition of Love Canal?

2. What kind of information does Brown provide to document the tragedy of Love Canal? What role did he play in uncovering this information?

3. Consider the introduction to this article. Why did the writer choose to tell the story of the Schroeder family in the opening paragraphs?

4. The power of this essay has much to do with the overwhelming tragedy and horror it relates. Find passages in the essay that you feel are especially effective. Explain how the writer creates this effect on the reader.

5. In this essay, the writer relies primarily on the factual data he has collected to tell

the story of Love Canal. Compare this writer's approach with that found in newspapers featuring sensational headlines. Analyze one of the headlined stories. How much factual evidence is present? How would such a newspaper's treatment of the story of the Schroeder family differ from Brown's treatment?

6. Environmental calamities such as Love Canal or Three Mile Island have become a permanent part of our lives. The Environmental Protection Agency reports that in most communities the groundwater has become so laced with toxic chemicals that it is no longer safe to drink. Investigate some aspect of the environment in your community such as the water supply or the quality of the air. Write a report based on your investigation.

TWO REPORTS OF AN AIRPLANE CRASH

The Associated Press
The National Transportation Safety Board

The crash of a TWA jetliner on its way into Dulles Inter-
national Airport outside Washington, D.C., was the lead
story in the New York Times *on December 2, 1974. Almost*
a year later, the National Transportation Safety Board re-
ported the results of their investigation into the causes of
that crash. The work of the NTSF, which is also responsible
for investigating rail, highway, marine, and pipeline acci-
dents, has contributed significantly to the low rate of airline
accidents in this country. We present here the newspaper
article and the first part of the NTSB report, which reviews
the accident itself, as examples of two different approaches
to the reporting of the same event.

BY THE ASSOCIATED PRESS

Upperville, Va., Dec. 1—

A Trans World Airlines 727, battling a driving rainstorm, slammed into a   1
wooded slope near a secret government installation today, killing all 92 persons
aboard. It was the worst air disaster of the year in the United States.

Capt. William Carvello of the state police declared "there are no survivors"   2
after rescue workers had combed for hours through the wreckage on Mount
Weather, a foothill of the Blue Ridge Mountains.

The plane, Flight 514, was bound for Washington from Columbus, Ohio,   3
and was approaching Dulles International Airport when the tower lost radar
contact at 11:10 A.M.

The crash site was about five miles north of Upperville, a tiny community   4
in the tip of the state and about 20 miles northwest of Dulles.

First on Dulles Approach

According to the National Transportation Safety Board, today's was the first   5
fatal crash by an airliner approaching Dulles, which opened in 1962.

A T.W.A. spokesman said 85 passengers and a crew of seven were aboard   6
the flight, which originated in Indianapolis. He said 46 persons got on at Columbus.

The plane crashed about one and one-half miles from an underground complex that reportedly is designed to serve as a headquarters for high government officials in the event of nuclear war. A Federal spokesman acknowledged only that the facility was operated by the little known Office of Preparedness, whose responsibilities, he said, include "continuity of government in a time of national disaster." 7

All of Mount Weather, a peak of about 2000 feet, is owned by the Federal Government. One official confirmed that several government employees were at work at the building complex, and helped in search and rescue efforts. 8

The airlines released a list of the victims' names tonight after relatives had been notified. The remains were taken to a makeshift morgue at the Bluemont Community Center, five miles from the site. Rescue operations were halted at 8:15 P.M. because of fog, high winds, and rain. 9

Dr. George Hocker, Loudoun County medical examiner, said the plane hit just below the summit and cut a swath 60 to 70 yards wide and about a quarter of a mile long. 10

"There were just chunks of metal and total destruction," he said. 11

The police initially sealed off an area within a five-mile radius of the site to all but law enforcement and rescue officials. A reporter who viewed the wreckage several hours later said that much of it was still burning and the largest piece of metal he could find measured only 5 by 10 feet. 12

The Federal Aviation Administration said there were no unusual communications from the plane before the crash, "just routine flight conversation." 13

The flight had been scheduled to land at National Airport near Washington at 10:23 A.M. but was diverted to Dulles, a larger facility about 20 miles west of the capital, because of high winds. 14

When the Dulles tower lost radar contact 37 minutes later, it notified the local authorities to begin a search. Captain Carvello said two state troopers found the wreckage almost immediately. 15

Apparently no one on the ground was hit by the crash nor were any buildings. But a worker for the Chesapeake and Potomac Telephone Company said the wreckage had severed the main underground phone line into the secret government installation. It was restored after two-and-a-half hours. 16

According to Federal aviation experts examining the wreckage, the airliner broke down through the treetops and its underbelly was apparently ripped off by a 10-foot high rock ledge at the end of a secondary road. 17

Visibility on the ground was only about 100 feet, with snow flurries mixed with rain and some fog. The Dulles tower said that at the proper altitude, visibility would have been up to five miles, despite the rain. 18

John Reed, chairman of the National Transportation Safety Board, said "it was impossible to say" what the cause of the crash was, outside of "an obviously premature descent." He said his team of accident investigators was still searching for the cockpit voice recorder and the aircraft's technical data recorder. 19

Mr. Reed said it was hoped that when these instruments were recovered, 20
they would provide a clue to the fateful last minutes.

Bill Smith, a member of the Marshall, Va. Rescue Squad, said the plane 21
hit "well below" the peak and there was "quite a bit of fire" at the site. He said
the plane devastated about 700 to 800 yards of the mountain's surface.

Vance Berry of Bluemont, who said he lived about three miles from the 22
scene, walked to it about an hour after the crash.

"There was nothing left but what looked like a bunch of crumpled up tinfoil," 23
he said. "You couldn't tell it had been a plane. What was left of the fuselage
was burning fiercely with a blue flame, even in the rain. For 100 yards the tops
of the trees had been cut off."

Mr. Berry added, "The weather was fierce—winds up to 50 miles per hour, 24
raining and foggy. I'd say the visibility was about 100 or 150 yards."

Richard Eastman, a ground maintenance employee of T.W.A., said after 25
viewing the wreckage, "If you didn't know it was an airplane you could never
guess it. The parts of the plane were scattered all over the area. There's no tail
or wing that you could make out."

In Washington, relatives and friends of the victims waited in despair at private 26
lounges at National and Dulles Airports for news from the crash site.

Carl Zwisler, a lawyer who said he believed his parents were on the plane, 27
said Senator Birch Bayh, Democrat of Indiana, who had planned to take the
plane back to Indianapolis, came into the lounge "and was very comforting."

"He was very helpful," Mr. Zwisler said. "He gave us his number and offered 28
to try to help us any way he could."

T.W.A. said the seven crew members included three pilots, all based in Los 29
Angeles, three stewardesses from Chicago and one from Kansas City.

AIRCRAFT ACCIDENT REPORT
NATIONAL TRANSPORTATION SAFETY BOARD

At 1110 e.s.t., December 1, 1974, Trans World Airlines, Inc., Flight 514, 1
a Boeing 727-231, N54328, crashed 25 nautical miles northwest of Dulles
International Airport, Washington, D.C. The accident occurred while the flight
was descending for a VOR/DME approach to runway 12 at Dulles during instrument meteorlogical conditions.[1] The 92 occupants—85 passengers and 7
crewmembers—were killed and the aircraft was destroyed.

The National Transportation Safety Board determines that the probable cause 2
of the accident was the crew's decision to descend to 1,800 feet before the aircraft
had reached the approach segment where that minimum altitude applied. The
crew's decision to descend was a result of inadequacies and lack of clarity in the

---

[1]VOR: very high frequency omnidirectional radio range, a radio navigation aid supplying bearing
information; DME: distance measuring equipment, a radio navigation aid that provides distance
information. VOR/DME is basic equipment used for an instrument landing in bad weather. [Eds.]

air traffic control procedures which led to a misunderstanding on the part of the pilots and of the controllers regarding each other's responsibilities during operations in terminal areas under instrument meteorological conditions. Nevertheless, the examination of the plan view of the approach chart should have disclosed to the captain that a minimum altitude of 1,800 feet was not a safe altitude.

Contributing factors were: 3

(1) The failure of the FAA to take timely action to resolve the confusion and misinterpretation of air traffic terminology although the Agency had been aware of the problem for several years;

(2) The issuance of the approach clearance when the flight was 44 miles from the airport on an unpublished route without clearly defined minimum altitudes; and

(3) Inadequate depiction of altitude restrictions on the profile view of the approach chart for the VOR/DME approach to runway 12 at Dulles International Airport.

1. INVESTIGATION

1.1 *History of the Flight*

Trans World Airlines, Inc., Flight 514 was a regularly scheduled flight from   4
Indianapolis, Indiana, to Washington, D.C., with an intermediate stop at Columbus, Ohio. There were 85 passengers and 7 crewmembers aboard the aircraft when it departed Columbus.

The flight was dispatched by TWA's dispatch office in New York through   5
the operations office in Indianapolis. The captain received a dispatch package which included en route and destination weather information. The flight operated under a computer-stored instrument flight rules (IFR) flight plan.

Flight 514 departed Indianapolis at 0853 e.s.t.[2] and arrived in Columbus at   6
0932. The crew obtained weather and aircraft load information. The flight departed Columbus at 1024, 11 minutes late.

At 1036, the Cleveland Air Route Traffic Control Center (ARTCC) informed   7
the crew of Flight 514 that no landings were being made at Washington National Airport because of high crosswinds, and that flights destined for that airport were either being held or being diverted to Dulles International Airport.

At 1038, the captain of Flight 514 communicated with the dispatcher in   8
New York and advised him of the information he had received. The dispatcher, with the captain's concurrence, subsequently amended Flight 514's release to allow the flight to proceed to Dulles.

At 1042, Cleveland ARTCC cleared Flight 514 to Dulles Airport via the   9

---

[2]All times are eastern standard times expressed on 24-hour clock.

Front Royal VOR, and to maintain flight level (FL) 290.[3] At 1043, the controller cleared the flight to descend to FL 230 and to cross a point 40 miles west of Front Royal at that altitude. Control of the flight was then transferred to the Washington ARTCC and communications were established with that facility at 1048.

During the period between receipt of the amended flight release and the 10 transfer of control of Washington ARTCC, the flightcrew discussed the instrument approach to runway 12, the navigational aids, and the runways at Dulles, and the captain turned the flight controls over to the first officer.

When radio communications were established with Washington ARTCC, 11 the controller affirmed that he knew the flight was proceeding to Dulles. Following this contract, the cockpit voice recorder (CVR) indicated that the crew discussed the various routings they might receive to conduct a VOR/DME approach to runway 12 at Dulles. They considered the possibilities of proceeding via Front Royal VOR, via Martinsburg VOR, or proceeding on a "straight-in" clearance.

At 1501, the Washington ARTCC controller requested the flight's heading. 12 After being told that the flight was on a heading of 100°, the controller cleared the crew to change to a heading of 090°, to intercept the 300° radial of the Armel VOR, to cross a point 25 miles northwest of Armel to maintain 8,000 feet,[4] and ". . . the 300° radial will be for a VOR approach to runway 12 at Dulles." He gave the crew an altimeter setting of 29.74 for Dulles.[5] The crew acknowledged this clearance. The CVR recording indicated that the Armel VOR was then tuned on a navigational receiver. The pilots again discussed the VOR/DME approach to runway 12 at Dulles.

At 1055, the landing preliminary checklist was read by the flight engineer 13 and the other crewmembers responded to the calls. A reference speed of 127 kn was calculated and set on the airspeed indicator reference pointers. The altimeters were set at 29.74.

At 1057, the crew again discussed items on the instrument approach chart 14 including the Round Hill intersection, the final approach fix, the visual approach slope indicator and runway lights, and the airport diagram.

At 1059, the captain commented that the flight was descending from 11,000 15 feet to 8,000 feet. He then asked the controller if there were any weather obstructions between the flight and the airport. The controller replied that he did not see any significant weather along the route. The captain replied that the crew also did not see any weather on the aircraft weather radar. The CVR recording indicated that the captain then turned on the anti-icing system.

At 1101, the controller cleared the flight to descend to and maintain 7,000 16

---

[3]Altitude reference used above 18,000 feet m.s.l., using an altimeter setting of 29.92.

[4]All altitudes and elevations are expressed in feet above mean sea level unless otherwise noted.

[5]altimeter: instrument which shows the altitude of the airplace with respect to a fixed level, such as sea level. [Eds.]

feet and to contact Dulles approach control. Twenty-six seconds later, the captain initiated a conversation with Dulles approach control and reported that the aircraft was descending from 10,000 feet to maintain 7,000 feet. He also reported having received the information "Charlie" transmitted on the ATIS broadcast.[6]

The controller replied with a clearance to proceed inbound to Armel and   17 to expect a VOR/DME approach to runway 12. The controller then informed the crew that ATIS information Delta was current and read the data to them. The crew determined that the difference between information Charlie and Delta was the altimeter setting which was given in Delta as 29.70. There was no information on the CVR to indicate that the pilots reset their altimeters from 29.74.

At 1104, the flight reported it was level at 7,000 feet. Five seconds after   18 receiving that report, the controller said, "TWA 514, you're cleared for a VOR/DME approach to runway 12." This clearance was acknowledged by the captain. The CVR recorded the sound of the landing gear warning horn followed by a comment from the captain that "Eighteen hundred is the bottom." The first officer then said, "Start down." The flight engineer said, "We're out here quite a ways. I better turn the heat down."

At 1105:06, the captain reviewed the field elevation, the minimum descent   19 altitude, and the final approach fix and discussed the reason that no time to the missed approach point was published. At 1106:15, the first officer commented that, "I hate the altitude jumping around." Then he commented that the instrument panel was bouncing around. At 1106:15, the captain said, "We have a discrepancy in our VOR's, a little but not much." He continued, "Fly yours, not mine." At 1106:27, the captain discussed the last reported ceiling and minimum descent altitude. He concluded, ". . . should break out."

At 1106:42, the first officer said, "Gives you a headache after a while, watch-   20 ing this jumping around like that." At 1107:27, he said, ". . . you can feel that wind down here now." A few seconds later, the captain said, "You know, according to this dumb sheet it says thirty-four hundred to Round Hill—is our minimum altitude." The flight engineer then asked where the captain saw that and the captain replied, "Well, here. Round Hill is eleven and a half DME." The first officer said, "Well, but—" and the captain replied, "When he clears you, that means you can go to your—" An unidentified voice said, "Initial approach," and another unidentified voice said, "Yeah!" Then the captain said "Initial approach altitude." The flight engineer then said, "We're out a—twenty-eight for eighteen." An unidentified voice said, "Right, and someone said, "One to go."

At 1108:14, the flight engineer said, "Dark in here," and the first officer   21 stated, "And bumpy too." At 1108:25, the sound of an altitude alert horn was

---

[6]ATIS—Automatic Terminal Information Service.

recorded. The captain said, "I had ground contact a minute ago," and the first officer replied, "Yeah, I did too." At 1108:29, the first officer said, "*power on this #."[7] The captain said "Yeah—you got a high sink rate." The first officer replied, "Yeah." An unidentified voice said, "We're going uphill," and the flight engineer replied, "We're right there, we're on course." Two voices responded, "Yeah!" The captain then said, "You ought to see ground outside in just a minute.—Hang in there boy." The flight engineer said, "We're getting seasick."

At 1108:57, the altitude alert sounded. Then the first officer said, "Boy, it   22
was—wanted to go right down through there, man," to which an unidentified voice replied, "Yeah!" Then the first officer said, "Must have had a # of a downdraft."

At 1109:14, the radio altimeter warning horn sounded and stopped. The first   23
officer said, "Boy!" At 1109:20, the captain said, "Get some power on." The radio altimeter warning horn sounded again and stopped. At 1109:22, the sound of impact was recorded.

At 1109:54, the approach controller called Flight 514 and said, "TWA 514,   24
say your altitude." There was no response to this or subsequent calls.

The controller subsequently testified that he noticed on the radarscope that   25
the flight's altitude was about 2,000 feet just before he called them.

The flight data recorder (FDR) readout indicated that after the aircraft left   26
7,000 feet, the descent was continuous with little rate variation until the indicated altitude was about 1,750 feet. The altitude increased about 150 feet over a 15-second period and then decreased about 200 feet during a 20-second period. The recorded altitude remained about 1,750 feet until impact.

During that same portion of the flight, the indicated airspeed varied from   27
240 kn to 230 kn until the altitude trace leveled off about 1,750 feet after which the airspeed decreased and fluctuated between 222 kn to 248 kn. Some of the fluctuations occurred within short time spans while others were within longer spans.

The heading trace showed little variation during the latter portion of the   28
flight. As the aircraft left 7,000 feet, the heading changed from an indication of 112° to about 120° in about 2.5 minutes. The heading did not vary more than 2° to 4° from that indication until impact.

As the aircraft left 7,000 feet, the vertical acceleration (g) trace was smooth   29
with little fluctuation. After 40 seconds, the g trace activity increased to about ± 0.1 g. This continued for about 1 minute and then increased in amplitude to about ± 0.2 g for about 70 seconds. At this point there was a blank in the g trace. When the trace reappeared, it was still active, with variations in indicated g ranging from ± 0.2 to 0.5 g, until impact.

The accident occurred on the west slope of Mount Weather, Virginia, about   30

---

[7]*Indicates unintelligible word(s); # indicates nonpertinent word(s).

25 nmi from Dulles, at an elevation of about 1,670 feet. The latitude was 39° 04.6'N and the longitude was 77° 52,9° W.

1.2 Injuries to Persons

Injuries	Crew	Passengers	Others
Fatal	7	85	0
Nonfatal	0	0	0
None	0	0	

1.3 Damage to Aircraft

The aircraft was destroyed.

1.4 Other Damage

Power and communications lines were damaged.

1.5 Crew Information

The flightcrew was qualified and certificated in accordance with the existing FAA requirements. The captain was qualified to operate into Dulles under the provisions of 14 CFR 121.443.

1.6 Aircraft Information

The aircraft was certificated and maintained in accordance with FAA-approved procedures. The aircraft weight and balance were calculated to be within limits at takeoff and at the time of the accident. The aircraft was serviced with Jet A fuel, and there were 29,700 pounds of fuel aboard when the flight departed Columbus. There were about 19,300 pounds of fuel aboard at impact.

1.7 Meteorlogical Information

The weather in the area where the accident occurred was characterized by low clouds, rain mixed with occasional wet snow, and strong, gusty easterly winds. A complex low-pressure system extended from western Kentucky to southeastern Virginia and the eastern Carolinas with small low centers located in western Kentucky and south-central Virginia. An occluded front extended from the Kentucky low through North Carolina into the Virginia low.[8] A warm front extended northeastward from the Virginia low into the Atlantic, while a cold front extended from the same low to the Virginia coast, then southward into the Atlantic. A large area of low cloudiness and precipitation extended from the mid-Atlantic states to the Great Lakes, and southward to Tennessee. High gusty winds existed from the Middle Atlantic States to the Great Lakes.

The aviation weather observations taken at Washington National Airport

---

[8]occluded front: when a warm front is overtaken by a cold front, the warm air is forced upward from the surface of the earth. [Eds.]

between 0853 and 1054 reported scattered clouds at 700 feet, overcast at 1,200 feet, and visibility of 5 or more miles with very light to light rain. The winds were blowing from 070°, and the velocity varied from 25 to 28 kn with gusts of 35 kn reported at 0853, 44 kn reported at 0953, and 49 kn reported at 1054.

The aviation weather observations taken at Dulles International Airport be- 38 tween 0858 and 1055 reported an overcast at 900 feet with visibility varying from 3 to 7 miles in light rain. The winds were from: 080° at 20 kn gusting to 32 kn reported at 0858; 090° at 26 kn, gusting to 40 kn reported at 0955; and, 080° at 25 kn, gusting to 36 kn, reported at 1055.

The 1131 radar weather observation from Patuxent, Maryland, showed a 39 large area of weather echoes which included the accident area. One-tenth of the area was covered with thunderstorms which were producing moderate rain showers, and five-tenths of the area was covered with moderate rain. The thunderstorm cells were moving from 170° at 45 kn. The maximum cloud tops were at 24,000 feet between Charlottesville, Virginia, and the accident site.

There were three SIGMETS[9] in effect at the time of the accident. They 40 recommended caution due to ". . . moderate to severe mixed icing in clouds and precipitation above the freezing level" and embedded thunderstorms with tops near 40,000 feet. The cells were moving northeastward at 25 to 30 kn.

Although there were numerous pilot reports of weather conditions in the area 41 around Washington, none was received from pilots flying in the area where the accident occurred.

Ground witnesses in the accident area stated that, at about the time of the 42 accident, the local weather was characterized by low ceilings with visibilities ranging from 50 to 100 feet at the crash site. The wind was estimated at 40 mph with stronger gusts. There was a steady drizzle in the accident area.

At the request of the Safety Board, the National Weather Service (NWS) 43 studied the possibility of pressure changes in the accident area which could have contributed to the cause of the accident. Based on the observed wind direction and velocity at Dulles at 1025 (43 kn), the NWS calculated that a pressure drop of 0.4 millibars, equivalent to 0.012 in. Hg., could have occurred if the wind conditions in the accident area were the same as the winds at Dulles.[10] This pressure change could result in an aircraft altimeter reading 13 feet higher than the actual altitude of the aircraft. They further calculated that if the wind velocity was 60 kn, the resulting pressure change could be 3.2 millibars (0.094 in. Hg.) causing an altimeter reading 95 feet higher than the actual altitude. A wind velocity of 80 kn could result in an altitude indication 218 feet higher than the aircraft altitude.

The accident occurred in clouds and during the hours of daylight. 44

---

[9]SIGMETS are advisory warnings of weather severe enough to be potentially hazardous to all aircraft. They are broadcast on navigation aid voice frequencies and by flight service stations. They are also transmitted on the Service A weather teletype circuits.

[10]Hg.: mercury, used to measure atmospheric changes and thus changes in altitude. [Eds.]

1.8 Aids to Navigation

The navigational aids in use for the VOR/DME approach to runway 12 at   45
Dulles included the Martinsburg, Front Royal, Linden, and Armel VOR's.
These navigational aids were flightchecked after the accident and were operating
within the prescribed tolerances. The distance measuring function of Armel had
been inoperative about 2 hours before the accident, but it was operating without
reported malfunction shortly before and after the accident.

Automated radar terminal system equipment (ARTS III) was used by the   46
approach controller to observe and control the traffic. The ARTS III is a system
which automatically processes the transponder beacon return from all transpon-
der-equipped aircraft.[11] The computed data are selectively presented on a data
block next to each aircraft's updated position on the air traffic controller's radar
display. The information provided on the video display is aircraft identification,
groundspeed in knots, and, when the transponder of the aircraft being tracked
has Mode C capability, pressure altitude in 100-foot increments. The aircraft's
transponder has this capability. The position accuracy of these data is limited
to about ¼° in azimuth and 1/16 nmi in range.[12] Altitude is presented with a
tolerance of ± 100 feet.

The controller's radarscopes are equipped with video maps which depict   47
various terrain features, the position of navigational aids, and other pertinent
data. In this case, the video map did not display the Round Hill intersection
which is the intermediate approach fix for this approach, nor did it display the
high terrain northwest of that fix. The updated video maps depicting the Round
Hill intersection had been ordered but had not been received at the time of the
accident.

There was no current letter of agreement between Dulles Approach Control   48
and the adjacent ARTCC's regarding the use of the Armel VOR/DME approach
to runway 12 at Dulles.

1.9 Communications

No air-to-ground radio communication difficulties were reported.   49

1.10 Aerodrome and Ground Facilities

Dulles International Airport is equipped with three primary runways: 12/30,   50
1L/19R, and 1R/19L. The north-south runways (1L/19R and 1R/19L) are 11,500
feet long and 12/30 (runway 12) is 10,000 feet long. There are provisions for
ILS approaches to the north-south runways. Runway 12 is served by a VOR/
DME approach. In addition, a surveillance radar approach is available to all
runways. Runway 12 is equipped with high intensity runway lights but not with

---

[11]transponder: a radio transmitter-receiver. [Eds.]

[12]azimuth: the horizontal direction of a celestial point from a terrestrial point; range: a line of
bearing defined by a radio range. [Eds.]

approach lights. There is a visual approach slope indicator (VASI) installed on the left side of the runway.

1.11 *Flight Recorders*

N54328 was equipped with Lockheed Aircraft Service Model 109-D flight   51
data recorder, serial No. 117, and a Fairchild Model A-100 cockpit voice recorder, serial No. 1123. Both recorders were installed in a nonpressurized area
aft of the pressure bulkhead.

The flight data recorder parameter traces were clearly recorded. There were   52
no recorder malfunctions. A readout was made of the last 15 minutes 25 seconds
of the flight. There was a small gap in the vertical acceleration trace shown on
the data graph at time 13 minutes 30 seconds because of foil damage which
obliterated the trace.

The cockpit voice recorder remained intact and the recording was clear. A   53
composite flight track was prepared by correlating the recorder data.

1.12 *Wreckage*

The wreckage was contained within an area about 900 feet long and 200 feet   54
wide. The evidence of first impact was trees whose tops were cut off about 70
feet above the ground. The elevation at the base of the trees was 1,605 feet.
The wreckage path was oriented along a line 118° magnetic. Calculations indicated that the left wing went down about 6° as the aircraft passed through the
trees and the aircraft was descending at an angle of about 1°. After about 500
feet of travel through the trees, the aircraft struck a rock outcropping at an
elevation of about 1,675 feet. Numerous heavy components of the aircraft were
thrown forward of the outcropping.

The wing flaps, wing leading edge devices, and the landing gears were re-   55
tracted. The condition of the flight control system could not be determined
because of impact and fire damage. No evidence was found of preimpact structural failure or control system malfunction.

All three engines separated from the aircraft and were damaged.   56

The major rotating compressor components were bent or broken in a direc-   57
tion opposite to normal rotation. There was no evidence found of preimpact
engine fire or malfunction.

Most of the instruments on the pilots' instrument panels were destroyed, as   58
were most of the aircraft navigational and flight instrument systems' components. Among those that were recovered and from which useful information
could be obtained were the first officer's DME indicator which read 12 miles;
the first officer's course deviation indicator which showed a selected course of
123°; and the first officer's altimeter, set at 29.70 in. Hg., with an internal
indication of 1,818 feet. The first officer's flight director indicator showed the
altitude marker at "0" feet, and the pitch display showed 5° aircraft noseup. An
airspeed indicator was recovered with the reference pointer set at 123 kn; and a

radio altimeter was found which indicated 10 feet. One distance measuring equipment interrogator unit was recovered; it showed a mileage indication of 12 miles and was tuned to a channel paired with 115.3 MHz., the frequency of the Front Royal VOR.[13]

1.13 *Medical and Pathological Information*

All of the occupants of the aircraft died of traumatic injuries. Post-mortem examinations and toxicological and histological analyses were conducted on all flight crewmembers. No evidence of disease was found and the analyses were negative. The medical histories of the flight crewmembers disclosed no evidence of abnormal conditions.

59

1.14 *Fire*

No evidence of in-flight fire was found. Scattered intense ground fires occurred throughout the wreckage area. Local fire departments were notified of the location of the wreckage about 1145 and about 150 fire and rescue personnel responded with six pumpers and several rescue vehicles.

60

1.15 *Survival Aspects*

This was not a survivable accident.

61

QUESTIONS

1. What information is present in the *Times* article but missing in the NTSB report? What does the NTSB report include that the newspaper account does not?

2. What does this difference in information tell you about the writers' conceptions of audience and purpose? Look back at the first two paragraphs of each report. How do these two openings reflect these conceptions?

3. The editors had to go to a library reference room to look up terms not explained by the writers of the NTSB report. Choose a term from the report that is not glossed or that is not explained clearly. Then find the best source in your library that explains the term better than we (or the NTSB) did.

4. Using the NTSB report, write an article for the New York *Times* in which you summarize the information in the report. Be sure to provide a headline.

5. Select an event familiar to you, and write a report about it aimed at a general audience that will need key terms explained. You might choose an event such as participating in a bicycle race or tour, entering a pet in a show, participating in a band concert or a wrestling match, preparing a special meal, or building a dog house. Give your report to a classmate for comments on any areas that may need revision for clarity.

---

[13]MHz.: megahertz, a unit of frequency equal to one million hertz, or cycles per second. [Eds.]

THE FUNGUS AND
ITS PARTNERS

Helen Hoover

*Born in Greenfield, Illinois, Helen Hoover (b. 1910) at-
tended Ohio University and pursued a career as a metal-
lurgist. She holds a patent for agricultural implement discs.
In 1954, she started a second career as a free-lance writer
with a special interest in nature. In that year, she and her
husband moved to a cabin in Minnesota's North Woods,
which was, in her words, "forty-five miles from town on a
one-way road . . . with no human neighbors within fifteen
miles." Out of this experience have come a number of books
on nature for adults and for children. The excerpt reprinted
here is from the first of these,* The Long-Shadowed Forest
(1963). Some others are The Gift of the Deer *(1966),* Place
in the Woods *(1969), and* The Years of the Forest *(1973).*

I started from the summer house to the log cabin on an afternoon when the   1
sky was hummocked with soggy-looking clouds,[1] one of which dumped itself in
streams as I came to the edge of the woods between the houses. I ducked into
the open woodshed and sat on a log, looking through the rain.

Against the trunk of a big birch the peeling bark lay in vertical rolls, like   2
parchments whose markings held the history of the forest. The other trunks
looked mottled in the dimness—the striated gray of the cedars, the blistered
green-gray of the balsam firs, the ridged brown of the white pines, the scaly gray
of the spruces. When the shower passed, the lichens that patterned the bark
stood out against a water-soaked black background.[2]

Flat against a cedar's trunk were greenish pancakes with crinkled edges, and   3
irregular gray patches with tiny, deeply lobed extensions. A balsam branch was
covered by a straw-colored, leathery complexity, its uplifted branches less than
a half-inch tall and intricate as coral. From the branches of the firs and pines
hung gray masses like tangled hair. The stump of a fallen spruce was swathed
in flat and nubby gray-green, from which cone-shaped fairy goblets lifted; some
of these cups had perforated patterns and lacy edges, as though they might have
been made of twisted snowflakes mounted on minute stems.

On the edge of the woodshed roof, miniature scarlet pillows rose on upright   4

---

[1]hummocked: filled with rounded knolls or small hills.[Eds.]

[2]lichens: the lichen is a type of plant consisting of a fungus and an alga in partnership, as this
selection goes on to explain. Paragraphs 3 and 4 describe some of the many different species.[Eds.]

stems from a gray growth that resembled felt. On a boulder beside the path, a flat black sheet clung, like charred paper whose curled edges showed a pale underside. Beside it was another flat growth, dark green above and made up of several loosely waved "leaves" that were dull black underneath. On the surface of a half-buried rock ledge, splotches of dusty rose were almost concealed by a spreading white fan—all looking as though they had been painted there.

The identification of the hundreds of species of lichens is a difficult business, requiring special knowledge, and often microscopic measurements. Thus, common names are applied to groups of species that have the same outstanding characteristics. The numerous lichens with scarlet tops are "British soldiers"; those with cups are "pixie cups"; gray-green, crinkled flat growths on trees and rocks are "curly crust." A red-brown form that colors the cliffs along the lake is the "cinnabar" or "flame," although the lattter is usually a nickname for a common, bright-orange lichen. The gray, upright types that cover sandy, northern barrens are "reindeer moss," and the hanging tangles in this woods are "old man's beard," or "deer moss" because the whitetails eat them. "Deer moss" looks much like the Spanish moss which hangs from trees in the south. "Spanish moss," however, is neither a lichen nor a moss. It is an epiphyte, a plant that takes all its nourishment from the air. A flat black lichen that grows on stones is "rock tripe" and, I am told, can be boiled and eaten. Since I do not know which of the similar forms is edible, and since some lichens may be poisonous, I am happy to forego a lunch that looks, and probably would chew, like rubber.

Every lichen is composed of two plants, a fungus and a green alga, working together in a mutually beneficial association. The fungus anchors the partners to bark, wood, rock, soil, or other substratum, and grows around the thin-walled, one-celled alga, protecting it from dehydration and death. The alga, by means of its chlorophyll, makes food for itself and for the fungus from air, water, and the energy of the sunlight that filters through the fungus body. Upright stalks, more correctly called stipes, bear the spore-producing organs of the fungus half of certain lichens. Spores are also produced by small "disks" that rise slightly above the surface of the prostrate forms. Such spores are worthless, as these fungi have become so adapted to their partnership that they cannot exist apart from their supporting algae, and the spores, of course, cannot reproduce the algae. Lichens are spread by windblown particles, made up of a bit of fungus body, surrounding a few algal cells. Perhaps the spores are carryovers from primordial times before the fungi entered into successful, and dependent, partnerships with the algae. On this partnership and its individual components rests the whole economy of plant and animal life.

One-celled algae, along with bacteria, are believed to have been the first life forms to appear in the waters of very ancient times. Remains of one-celled plants have been found in the Gunflint formation that slants northeastward three miles west of our home, where rocks have been dated by means of radiocarbon tests at approximately 1.7 billion years. Eventually the individual floating algae combined into chains and attached themselves to the bottoms of shallow streams and ponds. I look with respect at the green "scum" on stagnant water and at slimy "water weeds" waving in a stream, for not only have they survived with little change through all the climatic and geologic modifications since the days when the earth was surfaced only with water and barren igneous rock, but their forebears gave rise to all the plant forms that have grown or still grow on the earth. If higher life as we know it were suddenly to vanish, these humble algae might still live on to start a new life cycle.

The fungi, which have no chlorophyll and must depend on outside sources   8 for food, probably arose in those ancient waters, and the first alga-fungus combine may have developed there. Or a bit of fungus, or a spore, and some algae may have been washed onto a rock and, after many trials, clung there in the form of the first lichen. Acid by-products of the lichen's life processes attacked the rock and it began to decay. Bits of the lichen broke off and caught in the decaying stone, there to rot and add to the formation of soil, which would someday be ready to sustain great forests and to produce our food. Today, in the heat of deserts and the cold of the polar regions, on the poorest earth and the barest rocks, wherever the air is pure, the lichens nibble away, slowly, patiently—creating the nuclei of soil for the forests of the future.

That fungi can grow on almost anything (some even attack glass and metal)   9 was demonstrated to Ade and me when we came to spend our first vacation in the log cabin.[3] We opened the door to an atmosphere so spore-clouded that it set us sneezing. A breadbox revealed a flourishing green fuzz on a forgotten crust. Patterns of black covered the bare log walls and yellow spots blotched the painted kitchen counter. Dead flies were stuck to windowpanes, surrounded by haloes of spores released by the fungus that had digested their interiors. Mushrooms grew upside-down on Celotex ceiling panels, kept watered by a roof leak. After days of cleaning, airing, and drying (by means of fires that turned the North Woods coolness into an oven), we had a livable atmosphere, except near one door where the musty scent lingered. In desperation, Ade stripped off the frame and found several pieces of a shirt, stuffed away for heaven-knows-what reason, slowly being consumed by a pink-and-black garden.

QUESTIONS

  1. How does Hoover introduce us to lichens?

  2. Where are Hoover's own observation and experience present in this essay?

  3. Where does she use other kinds of reporting besides her own observations? What other kinds of reporting does she use?

---

[3]Ade: the husband of the author.[Eds.]

4. How does her description of her subjects differ from the description found in a botany or biology textbook?

5. What kind of thing can you identify and describe as closely as Hoover does? Write a report about this thing, presenting your descriptions so that your classmates will understand the special nature of this thing.

6. Select some common thing to study, and describe its types. You should help the reader see this thing in a new way, such as by recognizing the variety and complexity of its forms. Some suggestions are pens, pencils, local bugs, dust, trash baskets, potato chips, or fast-food restaurant uniforms.

WRITING SUGGESTIONS
FOR REPORTING

1. At the end of "The Ring of Time," E. B. White says that he has failed in his attempt to "describe what is indescribable" (paragraph 8). Is White's task more difficult than William Laurence's in "Atomic Bombing of Nagasaki told by Flight Member"? Consider those events in your own experience that you find indescribable. In the process, of course, you'll have to consider how White and Laurence went about describing the indescribable and how you would go about it.

2. Both Farley Mowat and Jane van Lawick-Goodall study a specific animal in its natural habitat. How are their procedures similar? How are they different? In what ways do their procedures influence what they find and how they present their findings?

3. Barbara Tuchman writes her chapter " 'This Is the End of the World': The Black Death" as a historian, whereas E. M. Forster is a novelist and literacy critic investigating a historical topic in "Voltaire's Laboratory: How They Weighed Fire." They both, however, rely on source material from and about the periods they are writing on. Compare their presentations of this material, and consider how their differences in presentation might reflect their different academic disciplines.

4. Experiment with Roy C. Selby, Jr's "A Delicate Operation" and Richard Selzer's "The Discus Thrower." Use a different perspective to rewrite a short section of each by changing the first person to the third, and vice versa. (Another option would be to rewrite a short portion of Selby's essay as Selzer might write it, and vice versa.) How do these changes alter the nature of the information presented and the effect of each report?

5. Many of the essays in "Reporting" are written by firsthand observers who reveal their own roles as they report their observations. Select at least three of these observers, and write an essay about how the role each chooses to play affects the report each finally writes. Choose from among writers such as E. B. White, Alice Walker, Virginia Woolf, Margaret Mead, Farley Mowat, Jane van Lawick-Goodall, Roy C. Selby, Jr., Richard Selzer, and Michael Brown.

6. Compare Michael Gold's position as a writer/reporter in relation to his topic ("The Cells That Would Not Die") with that of Michael Brown ("Love Canal and the Poisoning of America"). What similarities and what differences can you find in the ways Gold and Brown gather their information? How do their presentations of that information compare? Try to come to some conclusion about the most effective way to present provocative subject matter.

7. Investigate the special requirements of writing about history and of writing about the present. Select an essay in which the author treats the past and one in which the author treats present events. How are their techniques alike, and how are they different? Which characteristics result from differences in time period and which from differences in writer or topic? You might analyze E. M. Forster's "Voltaire's Laboratory: How They Weighed Fire" or Barbara Tuchman's " 'This Is the End of the World': The Black Death"

along with Michael Brown's "Love Canal and the Poisoning of America." Or consider Alice Walker's "Looking for Zora" along with Margaret Mead's "A Day in Samoa."

8. Consider the writers treating one person as a subject: White, Walker, Forster, Hersey, and Selzer. How close to their subjects do these writers get? Compare two of these writers, one that seems very close to the subject and one that maintains a distance. What are the effects of these differing writing strategies? Both Virginia Woolf and Helen Hoover have as their subjects the life force. How would you describe the similarities and differences in their attitudes and treatments of this subject?

9. Imagine a meeting today between William Laurence ("Atomic Bombing of Nagasaki Told by Flight Member") and Hatsuyo Nakamura (as presented by John Hersey). What might they say to one another? How might Laurence reflect on his feelings forty years ago? Imagine this meeting, and write a report of it.

EXPLAINING

EXPLAINING

Here in "Explaining" you will find writing by specialists from a wide range of fields seeking to account for matters as various as the color of the sky, the fear of death, the art of the pyramids, and the popularity of *King Kong*. Explanation is an essential kind of writing in every academic field and profession. Facts, after all, do not speak for themselves, nor do figures add up on their own. Even the most vividly detailed report or computer printout requires someone to make sense of the information it contains. To make sense of a subject, we need to see it in terms of something that is related to it—the color of the sky in terms of light waves from the sun, the art of the pyramids in terms of ancient Egyptian beliefs. To understand a subject, in other words, we must examine it in terms of some context that will shed light on its origin and development, or its nature and design, or its elements and functions, or its causes and effects, or its meaning and significance. For this reason, you will repeatedly find the writers in this section drawing on specific bodies of knowledge and systems of interpretation to explain the problems and subjects that they address.

This essential element of explaining can be seen in connection with the following passage from James Jeans's "Why the Sky Is Blue":

> We know that sunlight is a blend of lights of many colors—as we can prove for ourselves by passing it through a prism, or even through a jug of water, or as Nature demonstrates to us when she passes it through the raindrops of a summer shower and produces a rainbow. We also know that light consists of waves, and that the different colors of light are produced by waves of different lengths, red light by long waves and blue light by short waves. The mixture of waves which constitutes sunlight has to struggle through the obstacles it meets in the atmosphere, just as the mixture of waves at the seaside has to struggle past the columns of the pier. And these obstacles treat the light-waves much as the columns of the pier treat the sea-waves. The long waves which constitute red light are hardly affected, but the short waves which constitute blue light are scattered in all directions.
>
> Thus, the different constituents of sunlight are treated in different ways as they struggle through the earth's atmosphere. A wave of blue light may be scattered by a dust particle, and turned out of its course. After a time a second dust particle again turns it out of its course, and so on, until finally it enters our eyes by a path as zigzag as that of a flash of lightning. Consequently the blue waves of the sunlight enter our eyes from all directions. And that is why the sky looks blue.

Jeans's purpose here is to explain "why the sky looks blue," and as you can see from the opening sentence of the passage he systematically establishes an explanatory context by setting forth directly relevant information about the nature and properties of sunlight, light, and light waves. He approaches the explanatory problem, that is, in terms of knowledge drawn from his specialized fields of astronomy and physics. With this knowledge in hand, he then proceeds to show how "the different constituents of sunlight are treated in different ways as they struggle through the earth's atmosphere." In this way, he develops his explanation according to the analytic framework one would expect of an astronomer and physicist, concerning himself as he does with the interaction of the atmosphere and light waves. Having formulated a cause–and–effect analysis demonstrating that blue light is scattered "in all directions," he is able to conclude that "the blue waves of sunlight enter our eyes from all directions. And that is why the sky looks blue." Thus the particular body of information that Jeans draws upon from astronomy and physics make it possible for him to offer a knowledgeable, systematic, and instructive explanation.

To appreciate how significant an explanatory context can be, you need only consider how knowledge from other fields might influence an understanding of "why the sky looks blue." A zoologist specializing in optics, for example, might note the importance of the retinal organs known as cones, which in animals are thought to be the mechanism primarily responsible for the reception of color. Given this crucial bit of information, a zoologist might observe that the sky looks blue to human beings because their eyes are equipped with cones, whereas it does not look blue to animals lacking cones, such as guinea pigs, owls, and armadillos. An anthropologist, in turn, might think it worth noting that coastal and island cultures, given their maritime environments, tend to develop unusually rich vocabularies for describing how the sea looks and how the sky looks. So, an anthropologist might observe that members of maritime cultures are likely to be especially discerning about the colors of the sea and sky.

Our hypothetical zoologist and anthropologist would both differ from Jeans in their explanatory approaches to the blue sky. Whereas Jeans approached it in terms of accounting for the source and prevalence of blue color, our zoologist and anthropologist would take the color for granted and seek instead to account for the human ability to perceive the color or the propensity of some cultures to be especially discriminating in their perception of it. Their differing approaches, in this case as in others, would result from their differing fields of study. Each academic area, after all, involves a distinctive body of knowledge, a distinctive array of interests, and a distinctive set of methods for making sense of the subjects that fall within its field of interest. Thus it follows that each area is likely to approach problems from different angles and arrive at different kinds of explanations. It follows, too, that no area can lay claim to the ultimate truth about things. But, as the case of the blue sky illustrates, each field does have a special angle on the truth, particularly about subjects that fall within its area of specialization. Our zoologist and anthropologist could be as valid and as enlightening in this case as the astronomer–physicist. In a broader sense, you can see from the case of the blue sky that in trying to explain a particular subject or problem one always has to look at it or approach it from a particular angle or a combination of viewpoints and that any particular approach brings a corresponding body of knowledge to bear upon an understanding of the subject. Relevant knowledge, quite simply, is the most essential element of explaining.

But knowledge alone is not sufficient to produce intelligible and effective explanation. Jeans's explanation, for example, depends not only upon a body of information about the properties and movement of light and light waves but also, as you will see, upon the form and style in which the information is presented. To develop your ability in explaining, then, you will need to develop a resourcefulness in putting your knowledge to use. One way to do that is to familiarize yourself with some of the many different forms that explanatory writing can take in different academic and professional situations.

THE RANGE OF EXPLANATORY WRITING

Explanatory writing serves a wide range of academic, professional, and public purposes. Rules and regulations, guidelines and instructions—all these are familiar examples of explanation in the service of telling people how to carry on many of the practical and public activities of their lives. Textbooks, such as the one you are reading right now, as well as popularized presentations of highly specialized research or theory are common examples of explanatory writing that helps people to understand a particular body of information and ideas. Scholarly research papers, government documents, and other highly technical presentations of data and analysis, though less familiar to the general reader, are important kinds of explanation that advance knowledge and informed decision making.

To serve the differing needs of such varied purposes and audiences, explanatory writing necessarily incorporates various forms and styles of presentation. Jeans's piece about the sky, for example, comes from a book intended as an introduction to astronomy. Thus he writes in a style that depends completely on familiar language. And to make sure that beginners will understand the important concepts in his explanation, Jeans repeatedly illustrates his discussion with analogies and references to familiar experience. In fact, if you look at the whole of Jeans's piece, you will see that he establishes his analogy between light waves and sea waves at the very beginning of his discussion and then systematically uses it to organize and clarify the rest of his explanation.

By contrast, the scientific paper by Antonio Damasio and David Tranel, "Knowledge without Awareness," is written for a highly specialized audience of researchers, as you can tell immediately from the abstract that precedes it as well as from its highly technical language, numerical data, and scholarly reference notes. Thus Damasio and Tranel do not structure their explanation in terms of a familiar analogy but instead use a standardized format for writing up the results of experimental research. According to this format, their paper consists of four parts: (1) an introduction that defines the research problem and places it in the context of related studies; (2) a section that identifies the materials and methods that were used in the experiment; (3) a section that reports the data resulting from the research; and (4) a concluding section that interprets the data and explains its significance. They adhere to this structure so that other researchers will be able not only to understand the outcome of the experiment in question but also to verify the results of the experiment by carrying it out themselves.

For yet another variation in the format and style of explanatory writing, we need only shift our attention from the sciences to the social sciences and look at Bruno Bettelheim's "Joey: A 'Mechanical Boy'." Here Bettelheim is presenting research based not on experimentation but on the case-study method, which entails the close observation of an individual subject over time. Because the subject of a case study is by definition unique, the study cannot be replicated by other researchers. A case study, therefore, must be written up in sufficient detail not only to document the observer's understanding of the subject but also to enable other researchers to draw their own conclusions about the subject. So you will find that Bettelheim provides an extensively detailed description, history, and analysis of Joey's behavior. You will also find that Bettelheim writes on the whole in a standard rather than specialized style, as befits the audience of generally educated readers who are the predominant subscribers to *Scientific American*, the magazine where his article first appeared.

Some types of explanatory writing are important not only in the sciences or social sciences but in all fields of study. For example, persons in every field of endeavor regularly need to take stock of the overall state of research on topics or problems that are of special interest to them. In order to keep themselves and others up to date about a particular research area, they survey not only what knowledge has been established but also what problems are under investigation and what questions remain to be explored. This kind of survey, known as a review of the research, can be seen in Antonio Damasio and Betty Redeker's "Review of Research on Prosopagnosia." Typically, their review begins with a definition of the research topic and a summary of established knowledge. Then it moves into a detailed discussion of research on issues about which there has been "considerable controversy," and finally it concludes with a look at some "new developments" in the study of prosopagnosia. In each of these sections of his review, Damasio and Redeker refer to specific pieces of published research, which they enumerate and document at the end of their article. Thus, the review of research not only provides readers with an explanatory overview of investigation, but it also tells them where to look for more detailed information on the subject.

Just to make clear that style and format do not always adhere to audience and purpose exactly as one might expect, we need only look at the following passage from Douglas L. Wilson's "The Other Side of the Wall":

> In 1968–69 I spent a sabbatical year on a small farm that my wife and I had just acquired and that had over a mile and a half of line fence. Almost the first question asked me by one of my neighbors when I met him was whether I intended to pasture cows. This question was prompted by the wretched condition of the fences I had inherited from the former owner. My new neighbor was visibly relieved when I said that I didn't.

Judging from the plain style and the hint of familiarity in the contraction at the end of the last sentence, as well as from the autobiographical story telling, you might think that this piece belongs in the section on "Reflecting" rather than here in "Explaining." But if you read the whole of Wilson's essay, you will discover that it is a highly informed article, based on extensive research, about Robert Frost's poem "Mending Wall." You will also discover that Wilson sustains his narrative format throughout most of his essay both because he seeks to provide a complete record of the process through which he acquired his special knowledge about the poem and because he aims to show that this process in a very significant way involved his experience of living on a farm. Thus the narrative form of his essay proves to be a very artful and appropriate way to present the special knowledge that Wilson brings to his explanation of the poem.

As you can see from our brief discussion of just this handful of selections, explanation is a widely varied form of writing, involving as it does in every case a delicate mix of adjustments to the audience, purpose, specialized field, and subject matter. Thus as a reader of explanation, you will have to be very flexible in your approach, always willing to make your way through unfamiliar territory on the way to a clear understanding of things or perhaps to a clear recognition that understanding may be beyond the scope of your knowledge in a particular field. And as a writer you will have to be equally flexible in your choice of language, as well as in your selection and arrangement of material, so as to put your knowledge and understanding in a form that not only satisfies you but also fulfills the complex set of conditions to which your explanation is addressed.

METHODS OF EXPLAINING

In planning a piece of explanatory writing, you should begin by reviewing your material with an eye to deciding upon the overall approach that you intend to use. As our previous discussion has indicated, you should aim to develop an approach that is adjusted to all the conditions of your explanatory situation. Some methods, you will find, are inescapable, no matter what your subject, audience, or purpose. Every piece of explanation requires that ideas be clarified and demonstrated through *illustration*, that is, through the citing of specific examples, as you can see in the earlier passage by Jeans and in the following excerpt from Bettelheim's essay on Joey:

> During Joey's first weeks with us we would watch absorbedly as this at once fragile-looking and imperious nine-year-old went about his mechanical existence. Entering the dining room, for example, he would string an imaginary wire from his "energy source"—an imaginary electric outlet—to the table. There he "insulated" himself with paper napkins and finally plugged himself in. Only then could Joey eat, for he firmly believed that the "current" ran his ingestive apparatus.

Bettelheim's obligation to illustrate and demonstrate the machine-centered behavior of Joey leads him here, as elsewhere in his essay, to turn to a detailed *description* and *narration* of Joey's actions. So it is that reporting constitutes an essential element of explaining. And not only for reasons of clarity, but also for purposes of reliability and credibility. If an explanation cannot be illustrated, or can only be weakly documented, then it is likely to be much less reliable and therefore much less credible to readers than one that can be amply and vividly detailed.

Some methods, while not required in every case, are often so important that they should be kept in mind as being potentially necessary in any piece of explanation. An essay that depends on the use of special terms or concepts almost certainly will call for a *definition* of each term and concept in order to assure that the reader understands them exactly as the writer intends them to be understood. In his essay about Joey, for example, Bettelheim introduces a special term and concept in the phrase "mechanical boy," and thus he immediately defines it at the beginning of his piece by citing examples of it in Joey's behavior, in his self-conception, and in the perception of him by others. Bettelheim also uses some relatively familiar terms in his discussion of Joey, such as "disturbed children," but he evidently recognizes that familiar terms, too, need to be defined, especially if they are being used in a specialized way. Familiar terms, after all, are commonly understood in different ways by different readers and writers. And the more varied are the understandings of a particular word or concept, the greater are the chances of it being misunderstood if it is not defined. So Bettelheim defines the exact sense in which he means us to understand "disturbed children" by identifying an essential quality or characteristic of their disturbed behavior—"they remain withdrawn, prisoners of the inner world of delusion and fantasy." And just to make sure that we are clear about his definition, he sharpens it by distinguishing the fantasy life of "disturbed children" from that of "normal children." Definition, in other words, can be carried out in a variety of ways—by citing examples, by identifying essential qualities or characterisitics, by offering synonyms, by making distinctions.

Other methods, while not necessarily imperative, can be very effective in a broad range of explanatory situations. If you are trying to explain the character, design, elements, or nature of something, you will often do best to *compare and contrast* it with something to which it is logically and self–evidently related. Comparison calls attention to similarities, contrast focuses on differences, and together the methods work to clarify and emphasize important points by playing related subjects against each other.

In "On the Fear of Death," for example, Elizabeth Kübler-Ross aims to shed light on the tendency of modern society to "deny the reality of death," and she does so by comparing and contrasting "old customs and rituals" with modern ways of dealing with death. Her comparison and contrast enables her to show, on the one hand, that the fear of death has pervaded all cultures from ancient to modern times but, on the other, that modern practices alone are characterized by a "flight away from facing death calmly." Kübler-Ross could, of course, have discussed the modern evasion of death in and of itself, but it stands out all the more sharply by contrast with older customs that reflect the "acceptance of a fatal outcome."

Like Kübler-Ross's piece, some examples of comparison and contrast rely on a strategic balancing of similarities and differences. Other pieces, such as Murray Ross's "Football Red and Baseball Green," which explains the differing appeals of two very well known American spectator sports, depend largely on a sustained contrast. And still other pieces might work primarily in terms of comparison. The mix within each piece is adjusted to the needs of its explanatory situation. By the same token, you should make sure that whenever you use comparison and contrast, your attention to similarities and differences is adjusted to the needs of your explanatory situation.

A special form of comparison, namely *analogy*, can also be useful in many explanatory situations. Analogies help readers to understand difficult or unfamiliar ideas by putting them in tangible and familiar terms. In "Why the Sky Is Blue," for example, Jeans's analogy of light waves to sea waves enables us to visualize a process that we could not otherwise see. Similarly, in "A Zero-Sum Game," Lester Thurow compares our economic situation to a game where "for every winner there is a loser, and winners can only exist if losers exist." This analogy enables us to understand the painful truth that every economic solution necessarily involves substantial losses for some group of people. Useful as analogies are, however, they rely at last upon drawing particular resemblances between things that are otherwise unlike. Sea waves, after all, are not light waves, and games are not economic situations. So, whenever you develop an analogy, you should be careful in applying it to your explanatory situation so as to make sure that it fits and that it does not involve misleading implications.

Some explanatory methods are especially suited to a particular kind of situation. If you are trying to show how to do something, or how something works, or how something was done, you will find it best to use a method known as *process analysis*. In analyzing a process, your aim is to make it clear to a reader by providing a narrative breakdown and presentation of it step by step, by identifying and describing each step or stage in the process, by showing how each step leads to the next, and by explaining how the process as a whole leads to its final result. Jeans's piece, for example, analyzes the process by which light waves from the sun make their way through the earth's atmosphere and determine the color of the sky. Damasio and Tranel in their research paper on prosopagnosia offer a detailed explanation of the process by which they carried out their research. And Stephen Jay Gould in "A Biological Homage to Mickey Mouse" explains and illustrates the surprising process by which Mickey's "appearance became more youthful" over a period of fifty years.

A method related to process analysis is *causal analysis*. As the term suggests, this type of analysis seeks to get at the causes of things, particularly ones that are sufficiently complex as to be open to various lines of explanation. Usually, then, a causal analysis involves a careful investigation that works backward from something difficult to account for—such as the popularity of *King Kong*, the machinelike behavior of Joey, or the corporate career problems of aspiring women—through an examination of various causes that might account for the situation. Sometimes, however an analysis might work forward from a particular cause to the various effects it has produced, as in Casey Miller and Kate Swift's "Women and Names," which investigates the numerous and quite different ways in which personal names affect the lives of men and women. Because no two things can be identically accounted for, no set method exists for carrying out a causal analysis. But there are a few cautionary procedures to keep in mind. You should review other possible causes and other related circumstances before attempting to assert the priority of one cause or set of causes over another, and you should present enough evidence to demonstrate the reliability of your explanation. By doing so, you will be avoiding the temptation to oversimplify things.

As you can probably tell by now, almost any piece of writing that aims to make sense of something will invariably have to combine several methods of explanation. But this should come as no surprise if you stop to think about the way people usually explain even the simplest things in their day-to-day conversations with each other. Just ask someone, for example, to give you directions for getting from one place to another, and you will probably find that the person gives you both an overview of where the place is situated and a step-by-step set of movements to follow and places to look for, as well as brief descriptions of the most prominent guideposts along the way, and possibly even a review of the original directions, together with a brief remark or two about misleading spots to avoid. Whenever we ask for directions, after all, we want not only to get reliable information but also to get it in a form that cannot be misunderstood. So, whenever people give directions, they try not only to give them accurately but also to give them so clearly and fully from start to finish that they cannot be mistaken. By the same token, whenever people try to explain something in writing, they want to help readers get from one place to another in a particular subject matter. So, in the midst of giving a process analysis or causal analysis, a writer might feel compelled to illustrate this point, or define that term, or offer a telling analogy.

In the twenty-eight pieces the make up this section, you will get to see how writers in different fields combine various methods of explaining things. And in the next section, you will see how explaining also contributes to arguing.

Arts and Humanities

WHO KILLED KING KONG?

X. J. Kennedy

X. J. Kennedy was born Joseph Charles Kennedy in New Jersey in 1929. With a B.S. from Seton Hall College, M.A. from Columbia University, and four years' service in the U.S. Navy, he went to the University of Michigan for further graduate study. In 1961, his first book of poetry, Nude Descending a Staircase, was the distinguished Lamont Poetry Selection. A poet who wishes "to be seriously funny," Kennedy is also well known as an essayist; an anthologist, especially of poetry; and a teacher. The following essay, speculating on the appeal of the original version of the ever-popular King Kong, first appeared in 1960 in Dissent: A Quarterly of Socialist Opinion, edited by the author, teacher, and critic Irving Howe.

The ordeal and spectacular death of King Kong, the giant ape, undoubtedly   1
have been witnessed by more Americans than have ever seen a performance of *Hamlet, Iphigenia at Aulis,* or even *Tobacco Road.* Since RKO-Radio Pictures first released *King Kong,* a quarter-century has gone by; yet year after year, from prints that grow more rain-beaten, from sound tracks that grow more tinny, ticket-buyers by thousands still pursue Kong's luckless fight against the forces of technology, tabloid journalism, and the DAR. They see him chloroformed to sleep, see him whisked from his jungle isle to New York and placed on show, see him burst his chains to roam the city (lugging a frightened blonde), at last to plunge from the spire of the Empire State Building, machine-gunned by model airplanes.

Though Kong may die, one begins to think his legend unkillable. No clearer   2
proof of his hold upon the popular imagination may be seen than what emerged one catastrophic week in March 1955, when New York WOR-TV programmed

269

Kong for seven evenings in a row (a total of sixteen showings). Many a rival network vice-president must have scowled when surveys showed that *Kong*— the 1933 B-picture—had lured away fat segments of the viewing populace from such powerful competitors as Ed Sullivan, Groucho Marx and Bishop Sheen.

But even television has failed to run *King Kong* into oblivion. Coffee-in-the-lobby cinemas still show the old hunk of hokum, with the apology that in its use of composite shots and animated models the film remains technically interesting. And no other monster in movie history has won so devoted a popular audience. None of the plodding mummies, the stultified draculas, the white-coated Lugosis with their shiny pinball-machine laboratories,[1] none of the invisible stranglers, berserk robots, or menaces from Mars has ever enjoyed so many resurrections. 3

Why does the American public refuse to let King Kong rest in peace? It is true, I'll admit, that *Kong* outdid every monster movie before or since in sheer carnage. Producers Cooper and Schoedsack crammed into it dinosaurs, head-hunters, riots, aerial battles, bullets, bombs, bloodletting. Heroine Fay Wray, whose function is mainly to scream, shuts her mouth for hardly one uninterrupted minute from first reel to last. It is also true that *Kong* is larded with good healthy sadism, for those whose joy it is to see the frantic girl dangled from cliffs and harried by pterodactyls. But it seems to me that the abiding appeal of the giant ape rests on other foundations. 4

Kong has, first of all, the attraction of being manlike. His simian nature gives him one huge advantage over giant ants and walking vegetables in that an audience may conceivably identify with him. Kong's appeal has the quality that established the Tarzan series as American myth—for what man doesn't secretly image himself a huge hairy howler against whom no other monster has a chance? If Tarzan recalls the ape in us, then Kong may well appeal to that great-grand-daddy primordial brute from whose tribe we have all deteriorated. 5

Intentionally or not, the producers of *King Kong* encourage this identification by etching the character of Kong with keen sympathy. For the ape is a figure in a tradition familiar to moviegoers: the tradition of the pitiable monster. We think of Lon Chaney in the role of Quasimodo, of Karloff in the original *Frankenstein*.[2] As we watch the Frankenstein monster's fumbling and disastrous attempts to befriend a flower-picking child, our sympathies are enlisted with the monster in his impenetrable loneliness. And so with Kong. As he roars in his chains, while barkers sell tickets to boobs who gape at him, we perhaps feel something more deep than pathos. We begin to sense something of the problem that engaged Eugene O'Neill in *The Hairy Ape*: the dilemma of a displaced animal spirit forced to live in a jungle built by machines. 6

---

[1]Lugosis: after the actor, Bela Lugosi, known for his roles in horror movies. [Eds.]

[2]Lon Chaney . . . Karloff: Chaney (1883–1930) was an actor who played the title role in *The Hunchback of Notre Dame*; Boris Karloff (1887–1969) was also an actor known for his monster roles, particularly in the 1931 version of *Frankenstein*. [Eds.]

King Kong, it is true, had special relevance in 1933. Landscapes of the 7
depression are glimpsed early in the film when an impresario, seeking some
desperate pretty girl to play the lead in a jungle movie, visits souplines and a
Woman's Home Mission. In Fay Wray—who's been caught snitching an apple
from a fruitstand—his search is ended. When he gives her a big feed and a
movie contract, the girl is magic-carpeted out of the world of the National
Recovery Act.[3] And when, in the film's climax, Kong smashes that very Third
Avenue landscape in which Fay had wandered hungry, audiences of 1933 may
well have felt a personal satisfaction.

What is curious is that audiences of 1960 remain hooked. For in the heart 8
of urban man, one suspects, lurks the impulse to fling a bomb. Though machines speed him to the scene of his daily grind, though IBM comptometers
("freeing the human mind from drudgery") enable him to drudge more efficiently once he arrives, there comes a moment when he wishes to turn upon
his machines and kick hell out of them. He wants to hurl his combination
radio-alarmclock out the bedroom window and listen to its smash. What subway
commuter wouldn't love—just for once—to see the downtown express smack
head-on into the uptown local? Such a wish is gratified in that memorable scene
in *Kong* that opens with a wide-angle shot: interior of a railway car on the Third
Avenue El. Straphangers are nodding, the literate refold their newspapers. Unknown to them, Kong has torn away a section of trestle toward which the train
now speeds. The motorman spies Kong up ahead, jams on the brakes. Passengers
hurtle together like so many peas in a pail. In a window of the car appear Kong's
bloodshot eyes. Women shriek. Kong picks up the railway car as if it were a
rat, flips it to the street and ties knots in it, or something. To any commuter
the scene must appear one of the most satisfactory pieces of celluloid ever
exposed.

Yet however violent his acts, Kong remains a gentleman. Remarkable is his 9
sense of chivalry. Whenever a fresh boa constrictor threatens Fay, Kong first
sees that the lady is safely parked, then manfully thrashes her attacker. (And
she, the ingrate, runs away every time his back is turned.) Atop the Empire
State Building, ignoring his pursuers, Kong places Fay on a ledge as tenderly
as if she were a dozen eggs. He fondles her, then turns to face the Army Air
Force. And Kong is perhaps the most disinterested lover since Cyrano:[4] his
attentions to the lady are utterly without hope of reward. After all, between a
five-foot blonde and a fifty-foot ape, love can hardly be more than an intellectual
flirtation. In his simian way King Kong is the hopelessly yearning lover of

---

[3]National Recovery Act: congressional legislation passed in 1933 to help industry recover from
the Depression and to reduce unemployment. [Eds.]

[4]Cyrano de Bergerac: hero of Edmond Rostand's play by the same name who is prevented from
professing his love by his sensitivity about his huge nose. [Eds.]

Petrarchan convention.[5] His forced exit from his jungle, in chains, results directly from his single-minded pursuit of Fay. He smashes a Broadway theater when the notion enters his dull brain that the flashbulbs of photographers somehow endanger the lady. His perilous shinnying up a skyscraper to pluck Fay from her boudoir is an act of the kindliest of hearts. He's impossible to discourage even though the love of his life can't lay eyes on him without shrieking murder.

The tragedy of King Kong then, is to be the beast who at the end of the fable 10
fails to turn into the handsome prince. This is the conviction that the scriptwriters would leave with us in the film's closing line. As Kong's corpse lies blocking traffic in the street, the entrepreneur who brought Kong to New York turns to the assembled reporters and proclaims: "That's your story, boys—it was Beauty killed the Beast!" But greater forces than those of the screaming Lady have combined to lay Kong low, if you ask me. Kong lives for a time as one of those persecuted near-animal souls bewildered in the middle of an industrial order, whose simple desires are thwarted at every turn. He climbs the Empire State Building because in all New York it's the closest thing he can find to the clifftop of his jungle isle. He dies, a pitiful dolt, and the army brass and publicity-men cackle over him. His death is the only possible outcome to as neat a tragic dilemma as you can ask for. The machine-guns do him in, while the manicured human hero (a nice clean Dartmouth boy) carries away Kong's sweetheart to the altar. O, the misery of it all. There's far more truth about upper-middle-class American life in *King Kong* than in the last seven dozen novels of John P. Marquand.[6]

A Negro friend from Atlanta tells me that in movie houses in colored neigh- 11
borhoods throughout the South, *Kong* does a constant business. They show the thing in Atlanta at least every year, presumably to the same audiences. Perhaps this popularity may simply be due to the fact that Kong is one of the most watchable movies ever constructed, but I wonder whether Negro audiences may not find some archetypical appeal in this serio-comic tale of a huge black powerful free spirit whom all the hardworking white policemen are out to kill.

Every day in the week on a screen somewhere in the world, King Kong 12
relives his agony. Again and again he expires on the Empire State Building, as audiences of the devout assist his sacrifice. We watch him die, and by extension kill the ape within our bones, but these little deaths of ours occur in prosaic surroundings. We do not die on a tower, New York before our feet, nor do we give our lives to smash a few flying machines. It is not for us to bring to a

---

[5]the hopelessly yearning lover of Petrarchan convention: typical condition of the lover in the sonnets of the Italian poet Francis Petrarch (1304–1374) and in the poetry of those influenced by him. [Eds.]

[6]John P. Marquand (1893–1960): American novelist and short-story writer, known for his affectionate satires of upper-middle-class Boston society. [Eds.]

momentary standstill the civilization in which we move. King Kong does this for us. And so we kill him again and again, in much-spliced celluloid, while the ape in us expires from day to day, obscure, in desperation.

QUESTIONS

1. In paragraph 10, Kennedy reminds us of a capsule interpretation of *King Kong* that the movie itself supplies: "That's your story, boys—it was Beauty killed the Beast!" But it is clear that Kennedy isn't satisfied with that explanation. What are some of the points that lead him beyond the movie's own explanation?

2. Define Kennedy's point of view in this essay. To what extent does his point of view limit what he is able to say about the movie? What different considerations might he have included had he written from a feminist's perspective, or as a civil defense director, or as an administrator of the S.P.C.A.?

3. Why does Kennedy refer to "the old hunk of hokum" (paragraph 3)? Does he refer more to the monster or the film?

4. One of the complicating factors Kennedy finds in the movie is the possibility of our own identification, as moviegoers, with King Kong, who recalls, according to Kennedy, "that great-granddaddy primordial brute from whose tribe we have all deteriorated" (paragraph 5). How thoroughly does Kennedy develop this notion of identification, and how seriously do you take it?

5. What is implied by the word "deteriorated" in the passage quoted in question 4 above? What does that word suggest about the world in which Kong finds himself? How does Kennedy's choice of that word in its context reflect on this article's title?

6. Consider the phrases "so many peas in a pail" and "or something" in paragraph 8. What do those phrases make you alert to? What are other examples of similar phrasing?

7. Write an interpretation of a more recent "monster movie," trying to explain the appeal of its central character.

8. Read several movie reviews of Dino De Laurentiis's remake of *King Kong*, which appeared in 1976. Write a paper explaining how it was compared to RKO's original version from 1933, which Kennedy discusses.

FOOTBALL RED AND BASEBALL GREEN

Murray Ross

*Murray Ross (b. 1942) was born in Pasadena, California,
and educated at Williams College in Massachusetts and the
University of California at Berkeley. He is now artistic director of the theater program at the University of Colorado,
Colorado Springs. This essay was first published in the* Chicago Review *in 1971 when Ross was a graduate student at
Berkeley. Though not a study of a usual academic subject,
"Football Red and Baseball Green" shows Ross thinking
about those sports much as a critic might think about one
of the performing arts.*

The Super Bowl, the final game of the professional football season, draws a 1
larger television audience than any of the moon walks or Tiny Tim's wedding.
This revelation is one way of indicating just how popular spectator sports are in
this country. Americans, or American men anyway, seem to care about the
games they watch as much as the Elizabethans cared about their plays, and I
suspect for some of the same reasons. There is, in sport, some of the rudimentary
drama found in popular theater: familiar plots, type characters, heroic and comic
action spiced with new and unpredictable variations. And common to watching
both activities is the sense of participation in a shared tradition and in shared
fantasies. If sport exploits these fantasies, without significantly transcending them,
it seems no less satisfying for all that.

It is my guess that sport spectating involves something more than the vicarious 2
pleasures of identifying with athletic prowess. I suspect that each sport contains
a fundamental myth which it elaborates for its fans, and that our pleasure in
watching such games derives in part from belonging briefly to the mythical
world which the game and its players bring to life. I am especially interested in
baseball and football because they are so popular and so uniquely *American;*
they began here and unlike basketball they have not been widely exported. Thus
whatever can be said, mythically, about these games would seem to apply to
our culture.

Baseball's myth may be the easier to identify since we have a greater historical 3
perspective on the game. It was an instant success during the Industrialization,
and most probably it was a reaction to the squalor, the faster pace and the
dreariness of the new conditions. Baseball was old-fashioned right from the start;
it seems conceived in nostalgia, in the resuscitation of the Jeffersonian dream.

It established an artificial rural environment, one removed from the toil of an urban life, which spectators could be admitted to and temporarily breathe in. Baseball is a *pastoral* sport, and I think the game can be best understood as this kind of art. For baseball does what all good pastoral does—it creates an atmosphere in which everything exists in harmony.

Consider, for instance, the spatial organization of the game. A kind of controlled openness is created by having everything fan out from home plate, and the crowd sees the game through an arranged perspective that is rarely violated. Visually this means that the game is always seen as a constant, rather calm whole, and that the players and the playing field are viewed in relationship to each other. Each player has a certain position, a special area to tend, and the game often seems to be as much a dialogue between the fielders and the field as it is a contest between players themselves; will that ball get through the hole? Can that outfielder run under that fly? As a moral genre, pastoral asserts the virtue of communion with nature. As a competitive game, baseball asserts that the team which best relates to the playing field (by hitting the ball in the right places) will win. 4

I suspect baseball's space has a subliminal function too, for topographically it is a sentimental mirror of older America. Most of the game is played between the pitcher and the hitter in the extreme corner of the playing area. This is the busiest, most sophisticated part of the ball park, where something is always happening, and from which all subsequent action originates. From this urban corner we move to a supporting infield, active but a little less crowded, and from there we come to the vast stretches of the outfield. As is traditional in American lore, danger increases with distance, and the outfield action is often the most spectacular in the game. The long throw, the double off the wall, the leaping catch—these plays take place in remote territory, and they belong, like most legendary feats, to the frontier. 5

Having established its landscape, pastoral art operates to eliminate any reference to that bigger, more disturbing, more real world it has left behind. All games are to some extent insulated from the outside by having their own rules, but baseball has a circular structure as well which furthers its comfortable feeling of self-sufficiency. By this I mean that every motion of extension is also one of return—a ball hit outside is a *home* run, a full circle. Home—familiar, peaceful, secure—it is the beginning and end. You must go out and come back; only the completed movement is registered. 6

Time is a serious threat to any form of pastoral. The genre poses a timeless world of perpetual spring, and it does its best to silence the ticking of clocks which remind us that in time the green world fades into winter. One's sense of time is directly related to what happens in it, and baseball is so structured as to stretch out and ritualize whatever action it contains. Dramatic moments are few, and they are almost always isolated by the routine texture of normal play. It is certainly a game of climax and drama, but it is perhaps more a game of 7 repeated and predictable action: the foul balls, the walks, the pitcher fussing around on the mound, the lazy fly ball to centerfield. This is, I think, as it should be, for baseball exists as an alternative to a world of too much action, struggle and change. It is a merciful release from a more grinding and insistent tempo, and its time, as William Carlos Williams suggests, makes a virtue out of idleness simply by providing it:[1]

> The crowd at the ball game
> is moved uniformly
> by a spirit of uselessness
> Which delights them . . .

Within this expanded and idle time the baseball fan is at liberty to become a ceremonial participant and a lover of style. Because the action is normalized, how something is done becomes as important as the action itself. Thus baseball's most delicate and detailed aspects are often, to the spectator, the most interesting. The pitcher's windup, the anticipatory crouch of the infielders, the quick waggle of the bat as it poises for the pitch—these subtle miniature movements are as meaningful as the home runs and the strikeouts. It somehow matters in baseball that all the tiny rituals are observed: the shortstop must kick the dirt and the umpire must brush the plate with his pocket broom. In a sense baseball is largely a continuous series of small gestures, and I think it characteristic that the game's most treasured moment came when Babe Ruth pointed to where he subsequently hit a home run.

Baseball is a game where the little things mean a lot, and this, together with its clean serenity, its open space, and its ritualized action is enough to place it in a world of yesterday. Baseball evokes for us a past which may never have been ours, but which we believe was, and certainly that is enough. In the Second World War, supposedly, we fought for "Baseball, Mom and Apple Pie," and considering what baseball means that phrase is a good one. We fought then for the right to believe in a green world of tranquillity and uninterrupted contentment, where the little things would count. But now the possibilities of such a world are more remote, and it seems that while the entertainment of such a dream has an enduring appeal, it is no longer sufficient for our fantasies. I think this may be why baseball is no longer our preeminent national pastime, and why its myth is being replaced by another more appropriate to the new realities (and fantasies) of our time.

Football, especially professional football, is the embodiment of a newer myth, one which in many respects is opposed to baseball's. The fundamental difference is that football is not a pastoral game; it is a heroic one. One way of seeing the difference between the two is by the juxtaposition of Babe Ruth and Jim Brown, both legendary players in their separate genres. Ruth, baseball's most powerful

---

[1]William Carlos Williams (1883–1963): American poet, short-story writer, and physician. [Eds.]

hitter, was a hero maternalized (his name), an epic figure destined for a second immortality as a candy bar. His image was impressive but comfortable and altogether human: round, dressed in a baggy uniform, with a schoolboy's cap and a bat which looked tiny next to him. His spindly legs supported a Santa-sized torso, and this comic disproportion would increase when he was in motion. He ran delicately, with quick, very short steps, since he felt that stretching your stride slowed you down. This sort of superstition is typical of baseball players, and typical too is the way in which a personal quirk or mannerism mitigates their awesome skill and makes them poignant and vulnerable.

There was nothing funny about Jim Brown. His muscular and almost perfect [11] physique was emphasized further by the uniform which armored him. Babe Ruth had a tough face, but boyish and innocent; Brown was an expressionless mask under the helmet. In action he seemed invincible, the embodiment of speed and power in an inflated human shape. One can describe Brown accurately only with superlatives, for as a player he was a kind of Superman, undisguised.

Brown and Ruth are caricatures, yet they represent their games. Baseball is [12] part of a comic tradition which insists that its participants be humans, while football, in the heroic mode, asks that its players be more than that. Football converts men into gods, and suggests that magnificence and glory are as desirable as happiness. Football is designed, therefore, to impress its audience rather differently than baseball.

As a pastoral game, baseball attempts to close the gap between the players [13] and the crowd. It creates the illusion, for instance, that with a lot of hard work, a little luck, and possibly some extra talent, the average spectator might well be playing; not watching. For most of us can do a few of the things the ball players do: catch a pop-up, field a ground ball, and maybe get a hit once in a while. Chance is allotted a good deal of play in the game. There is no guarantee, for instance, that a good pitch will not be looped over the infield, or that a solidly batted ball will not turn into a double play. In addition to all of this, almost every fan feels he can make the manager's decision for him, and not entirely without reason. Baseball's statistics are easily calculated and rather meaningful; and the game itself, though a subtle one, is relatively lucid and comprehendible.

As a heroic game football is not concerned with a shared community of near- [14] equals. It seeks almost the opposite relationship between its spectators and play-ers, one which stresses the distance between them. We are not allowed to identify directly with Jim Brown any more than we are with Zeus, because to do so would undercut his stature as something more than human. The players do much of the distancing themselves by their own excesses of speed, size and strength. When Bob Brown, the giant all-pro tackle says that he could "block King Kong all day," we look at him and believe. But the game itself contributes to the players' heroic isolation. As George Plimpton has graphically illustrated

277

in *Paper Lion*,[2] it is almost impossible to imagine yourself in a professional football game without also considering your imminent humiliation and possible injury. There is scarcely a single play that the average spectator could hope to perform adequately, and there is even a difficulty in really understanding what is going on. In baseball what happens is what meets the eye, but in football each action is the result of eleven men acting simultaneously against eleven other men, and clearly this is too much for the eye to totally comprehend. Football has become a game of staggering complexity, and coaches are now wired in to several "spotters" during the games so they can find out what is happening.

If football is distanced from its fans by its intricacy and its "superhuman" play, it nonetheless remains an intense spectacle. Baseball, as I have implied, dissolves time and urgency in a green expanse, thereby creating a luxurious and peaceful sense of leisure. As is appropriate to a heroic enterprise, football reverses this procedure and converts space into time. The game is ideally played in an oval stadium, not in a "park," and the difference is the elimination of perspective. This makes football a perfect television game, because even at first hand it offers a flat, perpetually moving foreground (wherever the ball is). The eye in baseball viewing opens up; in football it zeroes in. There is no democratic vista in football, and spectators are not asked to relax, but to concentrate. You are encouraged to watch the drama, not a medley of ubiquitous gestures, and you are constantly reminded that this event is taking place in time. The third element in baseball is the field; in football this element is the clock. Traditionally heroes do reckon with time, and football players are no exceptions. Time in football is wound up inexorably until it reaches the breaking point in the last minutes of a close game. More often than not it is the clock which emerges as the real enemy, and it is the sense of time running out that regularly produces a pitch of tension uncommon in baseball.

A further reason for football's intensity is that the game is played like a war. The idea is to win by going through, around or over the opposing team and the battle lines, quite literally, are drawn on every play. Violence is somewhere at the heart of the game, and the combat quality is reflected in football's army language ("blitz," "trap," "zone," "bomb," "trenches," etc.). Coaches often sound like generals when they discuss their strategy. Woody Hayes of Ohio State, for instance, explains his quarterback option play as if it had been conceived in the Pentagon: "You know," he says, "the most effective kind of warfare is siege. You have to attack on broad fronts. And that's all the option is— attacking on a broad front. You know General Sherman ran an option through the south."

Football like war is an arena for action, and like war football leaves little

15

16

17

---

[2]George Plimpton (b. 1927): best-selling author and journalist, founder of the *Paris Review;* he wrote in *Paper Lion* about his experiences in training with the Detroit Lions. [Eds.]

room for personal style. It seems to be a game which projects "character" more than personality, and for the most part football heroes, publicly, are a rather similar lot. They tend to become personifications rather than individuals, and, with certain exceptions, they are easily read emblematically as embodiments of heroic qualities such as "strength," "confidence," "perfection," etc.—clichés really, but forceful enough when represented by the play of a Dick Butkus, a Johnny Unitas or a Bart Starr. Perhaps this simplification of personality results in part from the heroes' total identification with their mission, to the extent that they become more characterized by their work than by what they intrinsically "are." At any rate football does not make allowances for the idiosyncrasies that baseball actually seems to encourage, and as a result there have been few football players as uniquely crazy or human as, say, Casey Stengel or Dizzy Dean.

A further reason for the underdeveloped qualities of football personalities, [18] and one which gets us to the heart of the game's modernity, is that football is very much a game of modern technology. Football's action is largely interaction, and the game's complexity requires that its players mold themselves into a perfectly coordinated unit. Jerry Kramer, the veteran guard and author of *Instant Replay*, writes how Lombardi would work to develop such integration:

> He makes us execute the same plays over and over, a hundred times, two hundred times, until we do every little thing automatically. He works to make the kickoff-team perfect, the punt-return team perfect, the field-goal team perfect. He ignores nothing. Technique, technique, technique, over and over and over, until we feel like we're going crazy. But we win.

Mike Garrett, the halfback, gives the player's version:

> After a while you train your mind like a computer—put the ideas in, and the body acts accordingly.

As the quotations imply, pro football is insatiably preoccupied with the [19] smoothness and precision of play execution, and most coaches believe that the team which makes the fewest mistakes will be the team that wins. Individual identity thus comes to be associated with the team or unit that one plays for to a much greater extent than in baseball. To use a reductive analogy, it is the difference between *Bonanza* and *Mission Impossible*. Ted Williams is mostly Ted Williams, but Bart Starr is mostly the Green Bay Packers. The latter metaphor is a precise one, since football heroes stand out not because of purely individual acts, but because they epitomize the action and style of the groups they are connected to. Kramer cites the obvious if somewhat self-glorifying historical precedent: "Perhaps," he writes, "we're living in Camelot." Ideally a football team should be what Camelot was supposed to have been, a group of men who function as equal parts of a larger whole, dependent on each other for total meaning.

The humanized machine as hero is something very new in sport, for in [20]

279

baseball anything approaching a machine has always been suspect. The famous Yankee teams of the fifties were almost flawlessly perfect and never very popular. Their admirers took pains to romanticize their precision into something more natural than plain mechanics—Joe DiMaggio, for instance, was the "Yankee Clipper." Even so, most people hoped fervently the Brooklyn Dodgers (the "bums") would thrash them in every World Series. To take a more recent example, the victory of the Mets in 1969 was so compelling largely because it was at the expense of a superbly homogenized team, the Baltimore Orioles, and it was accomplished by a somewhat random collection of inspired leftovers. In baseball, machinery seems tantamount to villainy, whereas in football this smooth perfection is part of the expected integration a championship team must attain.

It is not surprising, really, that we should have a game which asserts the 21 heroic function of a mechanized group, since we have become a country where collective identity is a reality. Football as a game of groups is appealing to us as a people of groups, and for this reason football is very much an "establishment" game—since it is in the corporate business and governmental structures that group America is most developed. The game comments on the culture, and vice versa:

> President Nixon, an ardent football fan, got a football team picture as an inaugural anniversary present from his cabinet. . . .
>   Superimposed on the faces of real gridiron players were the faces of cabinet members. (A.P.)

This is not to say that football appeals only to a certain class, for group America is visible everywhere. A sign held high in the San Francisco Peace Moratorium . . . read: "49er Fans against War, Poverty and the Baltimore Colts."

Football's collective pattern is only one aspect of the way in which it seems 22 to echo our contemporary environment. The game, like our society, can be thought of as a cluster of people living under great tension in a state of perpetual flux. The potential for sudden disaster or triumph is as great in football as it is in our own age, and although there is something ludicrous in equating interceptions with assassinations and long passes with moonshots, there is also something valid and appealing in the analogies. It seems to me that football does successfully reflect those salient and common conditions which affect us all, and it does so with the end of making us feel better about them and our lot. For one thing, it makes us feel that something can be released and connected in all this chaos; out of the accumulated pile of bodies something can emerge— a runner breaks into the clear or a pass finds its way to a receiver. To the spectator plays such as these are human and dazzling. They suggest to the audience what it has hoped for (and been told) all along, that technology is still a tool and not a master. Fans get living proof of this every time a long pass is completed; they see at once that it is the result of careful planning, perfect integration and an effective "pattern," but they see too that it is human and that what counts as well is man, his desire, his natural skill and his "grace under pressure." Football metaphysically yokes heroic action and technology by violence to suggest that they are mutually supportive. It's a doubtful proposition, but given how we live it has its attractions.

Football, like the space program, is a game in the grand manner, yet it is a 23 rather sober sport and often seems to lack that positive, comic vision of which baseball's pastoral mannerisms are a part. It is a winter game, as those fans who saw the Minnesota Vikings play the Detroit Lions one Thanksgiving were graphically reminded. The two teams played in a blinding snowstorm, and except for the small flags in the corners of the end zones, and a patch of mud wherever the ball was downed, the field was totally obscured. Even through the magnified television lenses the players were difficult to identify; you saw only huge shapes come out of the gloom, thump against each other and fall in a heap. The movement was repeated endlessly and silently in a muffled stadium, interrupted once or twice by a shot of a bare-legged girl who fluttered her pompons in the cold. The spectacle was by turns pathetic, compelling and absurd; a kind of theater of oblivion.

Games such as this are by no means unusual, and it is not difficult to see 24 why for many football is a gladiatorial sport of pointless bludgeoning played by armored monsters. However accurate this description may be, I still believe that even in the worst of circumstances football can be a liberating activity. In the game I have just described, for instance, there was one play, the turning point of the game, which more than compensated for the sluggishness of most of the action. Jim Marshall, the huge defensive end (who hunts on dogsleds during the off season), intercepted a pass deep in his own territory and rumbled upfield like a dinosaur through the mud, the snow, and the opposing team, lateraling at the last minute to another lineman who took the ball in for a touchdown. It was a supreme moment because Marshall's principal occupation is falling on quarterbacks, not catching the ball and running with it. His triumphant jaunt, something that went unequaled during the rest of that dark afternoon, was a hearty burlesque of the entire sport, an occasion for epic laughter in bars everywhere (though especially in Minnesota), and it was more than enough to rescue the game from the snowbound limbo it was in.

In the end I suppose both football and baseball could be seen as varieties of 25 decadence. In its preoccupation with mechanization, and in its open display of violence, football is the more obvious target for social moralists, but I wonder if this is finally more "corrupt" than the seductive picture of sanctuary and tranquillity that baseball has so artfully drawn for us. Almost all sport is vulnerable to such criticism because it is not strictly ethical in intent, and for this reason there will always be room for puritans like the Elizabethan John Stubbes who howled at the "wanton fruits which these cursed pastimes bring forth." As a long-time dedicated fan of almost anything athletic, I confess myself out of sympathy with most of this; which is to say, I guess, that I am vulnerable to those fantasies which these games support, and that I find happiness in the company of people who feel as I do.

A final note. It is interesting that the heroic and pastoral conventions which 26 underlie our most popular sports are almost classically opposed. The contrasts are familiar: city versus country, aspirations versus contentment, activity versus peace and so on. Judging from the rise of professional football we seem to be slowly relinquishing that unfettered rural vision of ourselves that baseball so beautifully mirrors, and we have come to cast ourselves in a genre more reflective of a nation confronted by constant and unavoidable challenges. Right now, like the Elizabethans, we seem to share both heroic and pastoral yearnings, and we reach out to both. Perhaps these divided needs account in part for the enormous attention we as a nation now give to spectator sports. For sport provides one place where we can have our football and our baseball too.

QUESTIONS

1. Summarize each of the "fundamental myths" of baseball and football. Do you find Ross's interpretations justifiable?

2. In discussing two games, Ross makes use of several other fields of human activity and modes of behavior, both ancient and modern. Make lists of the chief terms he draws upon in characterizing baseball and football. How do those terms help you understand Ross's explanation of baseball and football?

3. How would you describe the audience for whom Ross is writing? How much knowledge of baseball and football does he expect of his readers? How much knowledge of other matters, such as literary conventions and patterns in American cultural history, does he assume?

4. From what viewpoint does Ross look at baseball and football? Contrast his particular approach with that of the writer of a typical sports article.

5. Ross structures his essay mostly by means of comparison and contrast. At what points does he discuss his subjects (baseball and football) separately and at what points together? What is his purpose in such an arrangement?

6. Are there other popular pastimes which could be said to "echo our contemporary environment" (paragraph 22) as Ross claims football does? Are there others which reflect our yearnings for a simpler, more pastoral America?

7. More than a decade has passed since Ross published this essay. Do you think his evaluations of baseball and football have stood the test of time? Write a short paper expressing your opinion on this matter.

8. Despite its exportation to the world, we still think of basketball as mainly an American game. Write an essay in which you compare and contrast basketball with either football or baseball. As you prepare your essay, see which of Ross's interpretations remain useful to you, which fade away, and which you change.

9. Compare and contrast another pair of fantasies, perhaps of those who watch horror

movies with those who watch westerns, of those who play poker with those who play chess, or of those who prefer one electronic game to another.

10. Research the public response to baseball and football since Ross's essay was first published. Investigate how the public responded to the World Series and the Super Bowl in 1971 (the date of Ross's essay), 1976 (our bicentennial year), and last season. Write a paper explaining whatever trends you discover.

ON BOXING

Joyce Carol Oates

Joyce Carol Oates (b. 1938) is the prolific author of books such as Them, Childwold, Upon the Sweeping Flood, *and* Marriage and Infidelities. *She is known primarily as a writer of short stories and novels that deal with the psychology of violence and disorder. It is not so surprising, then, that she should turn to the sport in which orderly violence is most on display. The following essay, which first appeared in the* New York Times Magazine *in June of 1985, is her answer to the question, "How can you enjoy so brutal a sport?"*

They are young welterweight boxers so evenly matched they might be twins— 1
though one has a redhead's pallor and the other is a dusky-skinned Hispanic.
Circling each other in the ring, they try jabs, tentative left hooks, right crosses
that dissolve in midair or turn into harmless slaps. The Madison Square Garden
crowd is derisive, impatient. "Those two! What'd they do, wake up this morning
and decide they were boxers?" a man behind me says contemptuously. (He's
dark, nattily dressed, with a neatly trimmed mustache and tinted glasses. A
sophisticated fight fan. Two hours later he will be crying. "Tommy! Tommy!
Tommy!" over and over in a paroxysm of grief as, on the giant closed-circuit
television screen, middleweight champion Marvelous Marvin Hagler batters his
challenger, Thomas Hearns, into insensibility.)

The young boxers must be conscious of the jeers and boos in this great 2
cavernous space reaching up into the $20 seats in the balconies amid the con-
stant milling of people in the aisles, the smell of hotdogs, beer, cigarette and
cigar smoke, hair oil. But they are locked desperately together, circling, jabbing,
slapping, clinching, now a flurry of light blows, clumsy footwork, another sweaty
stumbling despairing clinch into the ropes that provokes a fresh wave of derision.
Why are they here in the Garden of all places, each fighting what looks like
his first professional fight? What are they doing? Neither is angry at the other.
When the bell sounds at the end of the sixth and final round, the crowd boos
a little louder. The Hispanic boy, silky yellow shorts, damp, frizzy, floating
hair, strides about his corner of the ring with his gloved hand aloft—not in
defiance of the boos, which increase in response to his gesture, or even in
acknowledgment of them. It's just something he has seen older boxers do. He
seems to be saying "I'm here, I made it, I did it." When the decision is announced as a draw, the crowd's derision increases in volume." "Get out of the
ring!" "Go home!" Contemptuous male laughter follows the boys in their robes,

284

towels about their heads, sweating, breathless. Why had they thought they were boxers?

How can you enjoy so brutal a sport, people ask. Or don't ask.   3

And it's too complicated to answer. In any case, I don't "enjoy" boxing, and   4
never have; it isn't invariably "brutal"; I don't think of it as a sport.

Nor do I think of it in writerly terms as a metaphor for something else. (For   5
what else?) No one whose interest in boxing began in childhood—as mine did
as an offshoot of my father's interest—is likely to suppose it is a symbol of
something beyond itself, though I can entertain the proposition that life is a
metaphor for boxing—for one of those bouts that go on and on, round following
round, small victories, small defeats, nothing determined, again the bell and
again the bell and you and your opponent so evenly matched it's clear your
opponent *is* you and why are the two of you jabbing and punching at each other
on an elevated platform enclosed by ropes as in a pen beneath hot crude all-
exposing lights in the presence of an indifferent crowd: that sort of writerly
metaphor. But if you have seen 500 boxing matches, you have seen 500 boxing
matches, and their common denominator, which surely exists, is not of primary
interest to you. "If the Host is only a symbol," the Catholic writer Flannery
O'Connor said, "I'd say the hell with it."

Each boxing match is a story, a highly condensed, highly dramatic story—   6
even when nothing much happens: then failure is the story. There are two
principal characters in the story, overseen by a shadowy third. When the bell
rings no one knows what will happen. Much is speculated, nothing known.
The boxers bring to the fight everything that is themselves, and everything will
be exposed: including secrets about themselves they never knew. There are
boxers possessed of such remarkable intuition, such prescience, one would think
they had fought this particular fight before. There are boxers who perform
brilliantly, but mechanically, who cannot improvise in midfight; there are boxers
performing at the height of their skill who cannot quite comprehend that it
won't be enough; to my knowledge there was only one boxer who possessed an
extraordinary and disquieting awareness, not only of his opponent's every move
or anticipated move, but of the audience's keenest shifts in mood as well—
Muhammad Ali, of course.

In the ring, death is always a possibility, which is why I prefer to see films   7
or tapes of fights already past—already crystallized into art. In fact, death is a
statistically rare possibility of which no one likes to think—like your possible
death tomorrow morning in an automobile crash, or in next month's airplane
crash, or in a freak accident involving a fall on the stairs—a skull fracture,
subarachnoid hemorrhage.

A boxing match is a play without words, which doesn't mean that it has no   8
text or no language, only that the text is improvised in action, the language a

dialogue between the boxers in a joint response to the mysterious will of the crowd, which is always that the fight be a worthy one so that the crude paraphernalia of the setting—the ring, the lights, the onlookers themselves—be obliterated. To go from an ordinary preliminary match to a "Fight of the Century"—like those between Joe Louis and Billy Conn, Muhammad Ali and Joe Frazier, most recently Marvin Hagler and Thomas Hearns—is to go from listening or half-listening to a guitar being idly plucked to hearing Bach's "Well-Tempered Clavier" being perfectly played, and that too is part of the story. So much is happening so swiftly and so subtly you cannot absorb it except to know that something memorable is happening and it is happening in a place beyond words.

The fighters in the ring are time-bound—is anything so excruciatingly long 9
as a fiercely contested three-minute round?—but the fight itself is timeless. By way of films and tapes, it has become history, art. If boxing is a sport, it is the most tragic of all sports because, more than any human activity, it consumes the very excellence it displays: Its very drama is this consumption. To expend oneself in fighting the greatest fight of one's life is to begin immediately the downward turn that next time may be a plunge, a sudden incomprehensible fall. *I am the greatest*, Muhammad Ali says. *I am the greatest*, Marvin Hagler says. You always think you're going to win, Jack Dempsey wryly observed in his old age, otherwise you can't fight at all. The punishment—to the body, the brain, the spirit—a man must endure to become a great boxer is inconceivable to most of us whose idea of personal risk is largely ego related or emotional. But the punishment, as it begins to show in even a young and vigorous boxer, is closely assessed by his rivals. After junior-welterweight champion Aaron Pryor won a lackluster fight on points a few months ago, a younger boxer in his weight division, interviewed at ringside, said: "My mouth is watering."

So the experience of seeing great fighters of the past—and great sporting 10
events are always *past*—is radically different from having seen them when they were reigning champions. Jack Johnson, Jack Dempsey, Joe Louis, Sugar Ray Robinson, Willie Pep, Rocky Marciano, Muhammad Ali—as spectators we know not only how a fight ends but how a career ends. Boxing is always particulars, second by incalculable second, but in the abstract it suggests these haunting lines by Yeats:

> *Everything that man esteems*
> *Endures a moment or a day.*
> *Love's pleasure drives his love away,*
> *The painter's brush consumes his dreams;*
> *The herald's cry, the soldier's tread*
> *Exhaust his glory and his might:*

286

ON BOXING

Whatever flames upon the night
Man's own resinous heart has fed.

—from "The Resurrection"

The referee, the third character in the story, usually appears to be a mere observer, even an intruder, a near-ghostly presence as fluid in motion and quick-footed as the boxers themselves (he is frequently a former boxer). But so central to the drama of boxing is the referee that the spectacle of two men fighting each other unsupervised in an elevated ring would appear hellish, obscene—life rather than art. The referee is our intermediary in the fight. He is our moral conscience, extracted from us as spectators so that, for the duration of the fight, "conscience" is not a factor in our experience, nor is it a factor in the boxers' behavior.

Though the referee's role is a highly demanding one, and it has been esti- 12 mated that there are perhaps no more than a dozen really skilled referees in the world, it seems to be necessary in the intense dramatic action of the fight that the referee have no dramatic identity. Referees' names are quickly forgotten, even as they are announced over the microphone preceding a fight. Yet, paradoxically, the referee's position is one of crucial significance. The referee cannot control what happens in the ring, but he can frequently control, to a degree, *that* it happens: he is responsible for the fight, if not for the individual fighter's performance. It is the referee solely who holds the power of life and death at certain times; whose decision to terminate a fight, or to allow it to continue, determines a man's fate. (One should recall that a well-aimed punch with a boxer's full weight behind it can have an astonishing impact—a blow that must be absorbed by the brain in its jelly sac.)

In a recent heavyweight fight in Buffalo, 220-pound Tim Witherspoon re- 13 peatedly struck his 260-pound opponent James Broad, caught in the ropes, while the referee looked on without acting—though a number of spectators called for the fight to be stopped. In the infamous Benny Paret-Emile Griffith fight of March 24, 1962, the referee Ruby Goldstein was said to have stood paralyzed as Paret, trapped in the ropes, suffered as many as 18 powerful blows to the head before he fell. (He died 10 days later.) Boxers are trained not to quit; if they are knocked down they will try to get up to continue the fight, even if they can hardly defend themselves. The primary rule of the ring—to defend oneself at all times—is both a parody and a distillation of life.

Boxing is a purely masculine world. (Though there are female boxers—the 14 most famous is the black champion Lady Tyger Trimiar with her shaved head and tiger-striped attire—women's role in the sport is extremely marginal.) The vocabulary of boxing is attuned to a quintessentially masculine sensibility in which the role of patriarch/protector can only be assured if there is physical strength underlying it. First comes this strength—"primitive," perhaps; then comes civilization. It should be kept in mind that "boxing" and "fighting," though always combined in the greatest of boxers, can be entirely different and even unrelated activities. If boxing can be, in the lighter weights especially, a highly complex and refined skill belonging solely to civilization, fighting seems to belong to something predating civilization, the instinct not merely to defend onself—for when has the masculine ego ever been assuaged by so minimal a gesture?—but to attack another and to force him into absolute submission. Hence the electrifying effect upon a typical fight crowd when fighting emerges suddenly out of boxing—the excitement when a boxer's face begins to bleed. The flash of red is the visible sign of the fight's authenticity in the eyes of many spectators, and boxers are right to be proud—if they are—of their facial scars.

To the untrained eye, boxers in the ring usually appear to be angry. But, of course, this is "work" to them; emotion has no part in it, or should not. Yet in an important sense—in a symbolic sense—the boxers *are* angry, and boxing is fundamentally about anger. It is the only sport in which anger is accommodated, ennobled. Why are boxers angry? Because, for the most part, they belong to the disenfranchised of our society, to impoverished ghetto neighborhoods in which anger is an appropriate response. ("It's hard being black. You ever been black? I was black once—when I was poor," Larry Holmes has said.) Today, when most boxers—most good boxers—are black or Hispanic, white men begin to look anemic in the ring. Yet after decades of remarkable black boxers—from Jack Johnson to Joe Louis to Muhammad Ali—heavyweight champion Larry Holmes was the object of racist slurs and insults when he defended his title against the overpromoted white challenger Gerry Cooney a few years ago.

Liberals who have no personal or class reason to feel anger tend to disparage, if not condemn, such anger in others. Liberalism is also unfairly harsh in its criticism of all that predates civilization—or "liberalism" itself—without comprehending that civilization is a concept, an idea, perhaps at times hardly more than a fiction, attendant upon, and always subordinate to, physical strength: missiles, nuclear warheads. The terrible and tragic silence dramatized in the boxing ring is the silence of nature before language, when the physical *was* language, a means of communication swift and unmistakable.

The phrase "killer instinct" is said to have been coined in reference to Jack Dempsey in his famous early fights against Jess Willard, Georges Carpentier, Luis Firpo ("The Wild Bull of the Pampas") and any number of other boxers, less renowned, whom he savagely beat. The ninth of 11 children born to an impoverished Mormon sharecropper and itinerant railroad worker, Dempsey seems to have been, as a young boxer in his prime, the very embodiment of angry hunger; and if he remains the most spectacular heavyweight champion in history, it is partly because he fought when rules governing boxing were somewhat casual by present-day standards. Where aggression must be learned, even cultivated, in some champion boxers (Tunney, Louis, Marciano, Patterson, for example), Dempsey's aggression was direct and natural: Once in the ring he seems to have wanted to kill his opponent.

Dempsey's first title fight in 1919, against the aging champion Jess Willard, 18 was called "pugilistic murder" by some sportswriters and is said to have been one of boxing's all-time blood baths. Today, this famous fight—which brought the nearly unknown 24-year-old Dempsey to national prominence—would certainly have been stopped in the first minute of the first round. Badly out of condition, heavier than Dempsey by almost 60 pounds, the 37-year-old Willard had virtually no defense against the challenger. By the end of the fight, Willard's jaw was broken, his cheekbone split, nose smashed, six teeth broken off at the gum, an eye was battered shut, much further damage was done to his body. Both boxers were covered in Willard's blood. Years later Dempsey's estranged manager Kearns confessed—perhaps falsely—that he had "loaded" Dempsey's gloves—treated his hand tape with a talcum substance that turned concrete-hard when wet.

For the most part, boxing matches today are scrupulously monitored by 19 referees and ring physicians. The devastating knockout blow is frequently the one never thrown. In a recent televised junior-middleweight bout between Don Curry and James Green, the referee stopped the fight because Green seemed momentarily disabled: His logic was that Green had dropped his gloves and was therefore in a position to be hurt. (Green and his furious trainer protested the decision but the referee's word is final: No fight, stopped, can be resumed.) The drama of the ring begins to shift subtly as more and more frequently one sees a referee intervene to embrace a weakened or defenseless man in a gesture of paternal solicitude that in itself carries much theatrical power—a gesture not so dramatic as the killing blow but one that suggests that the ethics of the ring are moving toward those that prevail beyond it. As if fighter-brothers whose mysterious animosity has somehow brought them to battle are saved by their father. . . .

In the final moment of the Hagler-Hearns fight, the dazed Hearns—on his 20 feet but clearly not fully conscious, gamely prepared to take Hagler's next assault—was saved by the referee from what might well have been serious injury, if not death, considering the ferocity of Hagler's fighting and the personal anger he seems to have brought to it that night. This 8-minute fight, generally believed to be one of the great fights in boxing history, ends with Hearns in the referee's protective embrace—an image that is haunting, in itself profoundly mysterious, as if an indefinable human drama had been spontaneously created for us, brilliantly improvised, performed one time and one time only, yet permanently ingrained upon our consciousness.

Years ago in the early 1950's, when my father first took me to a Golden 21 Gloves boxing tournament in Buffalo, I asked him why the boys wanted to fight one another, why they were willing to get hurt. My father said, "Boxers don't feel pain quite the way we do."

Gene Tunney's single defeat in an 11-year career was to a flamboyant and 22 dangerous fighter named Harry Greb ("The Human Windmill") who seems to have been, judging from boxing literature, the dirtiest fighter in history. Low blows, butting, fouls, holding and hitting, using his laces on an opponent's eyes—Greb was famous for his lack of interest in the rules. He was world middleweight champion for three years but a presence in the boxing world for a long time. After the first of his several fights with Greb, the 24-year-old Tunney had to spend a week in bed, he was so badly hurt; he'd lost two quarts of blood during the 15-round fight. But as Tunney said years afterward: "Greb gave me a terrible whipping. He broke my nose, maybe with a butt. He cut my eyes and ears, perhaps with his laces . . . . My jaw was swollen from the right temple down the cheek, along under the chin and part way up the other side. The referee, the ring itself, was full of blood . . . . But it was in that first fight, in which I lost my American light-heavyweight title, that I knew I had found a way to beat Harry eventually. I was fortunate, really. If boxing in those days had been afflicted with the commission doctors we have today—who are always poking their noses into the ring and examining superficial wounds—the first fight with Greb would have been stopped before I learned how to beat him. It's possible, even probable, that if this had happened I would never have been heard of again."

Tommy Loughran, the light-heavyweight champion from 1927 to 1929, was 23 a master boxer greatly admired by other boxers. He approached boxing literally as a science—as Tunney did—studying his opponents' styles and mapping out ring strategy for each fight. He rigged up mirrors in his basement so that he could see himself as he worked out—for, as Loughran realized, no boxer ever sees himself quite as he appears to his opponent. But the secret of Loughran's career was that he had a right hand that broke so easily he could use it only once in each fight: It had to be the knockout punch or nothing. "I'd get one shot, then the agony of the thing would hurt me if the guy got up. Anybody I ever hit with a left hook, I knocked flat on his face, but I would never take a chance for fear if my left hand goes, I'm done for."

Both Tunney and Loughran, it is instructive to note, retired from boxing 24 before they were forced to retire. Tunney was a highly successful businessman and Loughran a successful sugar broker on the Wall Street commodities market—just to suggest that boxers are not invariably illiterate, stupid, or punch-drunk.

One of the perhaps not entirely acknowledged reasons for the attraction of 25 serious writers to boxing (from Swift, Pope, Johnson to Hazlitt, Lord Byron, Hemingway, and our own Norman Mailer, George Plimpton, Wilfrid Sheed, Daniel Halpern et al.) is the sport's systematic cultivation of pain in the interests of a project, a life-goal: the willed transposing of the sensation called "pain" (whether physical or psychological) into its opposite. If this is masochism—and I doubt that it is, or that it is simply—it is also intelligence, cunning, strategy. It is the active welcoming of that which most living beings try to avoid and to flee. It is the active subsuming of the present moment in terms of the future. Pain now but control (and therefore pleasure) later.

Still, it is the rigorous training period leading up to the public appearance   26
that demands the most discipline. In this, too, the writer senses some kinship, however oblique and one-sided, with the professional boxer. The brief public spectacle of the boxing match (which could last as little as 60 seconds), like the publication of the writer's book, is but the final, visible stage in a long, arduous, fanatic, and sometimes quixotic, subordination of the self. It was Rocky Marciano who seems to have trained with the most monastic devotion, secluding himself from his wife and family for as long as three months before a fight. Quite apart from the grueling physical training of this period and the constant preoccupation with diet and weight, Marciano concentrated on only the up-coming fight, the opening bell, his opponent. Every minute of the boxer's life was planned for one purpose. In the training camp the name of the opponent was never mentioned and Marciano's associates were careful about conversation in his presence: They talked very little about boxing.

In the final month, Marciano would not write a letter. The last 10 days   27
before a fight he saw no mail, took no telephone calls, met no new acquaint-ances. The week before the fight he would not shake hands with anyone. Or go for a ride in a car. No new foods! No envisioning the morning after the fight! All that was not *the fight* was taboo: When Marciano worked out punching the bag he saw his opponent before him, when he jogged early in the morning he saw his opponent close beside him. What could be a more powerful image of discipline—madness?—than this absolute subordination of the self, this cel-ibacy of the fighter-in-training? Instead of focusing his energies and fantasies upon Woman, the boxer focuses them upon the Opponent.

No sport is more physical, more direct, than boxing. No sport appears more   28
powerfully homoerotic: the confrontation in the ring—the disrobing—the sweaty, heated combat that is part dance, courtship, coupling—the frequent urgent pursuit by one boxer of the other in the fight's natural and violent movement toward the "knockout." Surely boxing derives much of its appeal from this mimicry of a species of erotic love in which one man overcomes the other in an exhibition of superior strength.

Most fights, however fought, lead to an embrace between the boxers after   29
the final bell—a gesture of mutual respect and apparent affection that appears to the onlooker to be more than perfunctory. Rocky Graziano, often derided for being a slugger rather than a "classic" boxer, somtimes kissed his opponents out of gratitude for the fight. Does the boxing match, one almost wonders, lead irresistibly to this moment: the public embrace of two men who otherwise, in public or in private, could not approach each other with such passion. Are men

privileged to embrace with love only after having fought? A woman is struck by the tenderness men will express for boxers who have been hurt, even if it is only by way of commentary on photographs: the startling picture of Ray (Boom Boom) Mancini after his second losing fight with Livingstone Bramble, for instance, when Mancini's face was hideously battered (photographs in *Sports Illustrated* and elsewhere were gory, near-pornographic); the much-reprinted photograph of the defeated Thomas Hearns being carried to his corner in the arms of an enormous black man in formal attire—the "Hit Man" from Detroit now help-less, only semiconscious, looking precisely like a black Christ taken from the cross. These are powerful, haunting, unsettling images, cruelly beautiful, very much bound up with the primitive appeal of the sport.

Yet to suggest that men might love one another directly without the violent 30 ritual of combat is to misread man's greatest passion—for war, not peace. Love, if there is to be love, comes second.

Boxing is, after all, about lying. It is about cultivating a double personality. 31 As José Torres, the ex-light-heavyweight champion who is now the New York State Boxing Commissioner, says: "We fighters understand lies. What's a feint? What's a left hook off the jab? What's an opening? What's thinking one thing and doing another . . . ?"

There is nothing fundamentally playful about boxing, nothing that seems to 32 belong to daylight, to pleasure. At its moments of greatest intensity it seems to contain so complete and so powerful an image of life—life's beauty, vulnera-bility, despair, incalculable and often reckless courage—that boxing *is* life, and hardly a mere game. During a superior boxing match we are deeply moved by the body's communion with itself by way of another's flesh. The body's dialogue with its shadow-self—or Death. Baseball, football, basketball—these quintes-sentially American pastimes are recognizably sports because they involve play: They are games. One *plays* football; one doesn't *play* boxing.

Observing team sports, teams of adult men, one sees how men are children 33 in the most felicitous sense of the word. But boxing in its elemental ferocity cannot be assimilated into childhood—though very young men box, even profes-sionally, and numerous world champions began boxing when they were hardly more than children. Spectators at public games derive much of their pleasure from reliving the communal emotions of childhood, but spectators at boxing matches relive the murderous infancy of the race. Hence the notorious cruelty of boxing crowds and the excitement when a man begins to bleed. ("When I see blood," says Marvin Hagler, "I become a bull." He means his own.)

The boxing ring comes to seem an altar of sorts, one of those legendary 34 magical spaces where the laws of a nation are suspended: Inside the ropes, during an officially regulated three-minute round, a man may be killed at his oppo-nent's hands but he cannot be legally murdered. Boxing inhabits a sacred space predating civilization; or, to use D. H. Lawrence's phrase, before God was love.

If it suggests a savage ceremony or a rite of atonement, it also suggests the futility of such rites. For what atonement is the fight waged, if it must shortly be waged again . . . ?

All this is to speak of the paradox of boxing—its obsessive appeal for many who find in it not only a spectacle involving sensational feats of physical skill but an emotional experience impossible to convey in words; an art form, as I have suggested, with no natural analogue in the arts. And of course this accounts, too, for the extreme revulsion it arouses in many people. ("Brutal," "disgusting," "barbaric," "inhuman," "a terrible, terrible sport"—typical comments on the subject.)

In December 1984, the American Medical Association passed a resolution calling for the abolition of boxing on the principle that it is the only sport in which the *objective* is to cause injury. This is not surprising. Humanitarians have always wanted to reform boxing—or abolish it altogether. The 1896 heavyweight title match between Ruby Robert Fitzsimmons and Peter Maher was outlawed in many parts of the United States, so canny promoters staged it across the Mexican border 400 miles from El Paso. (Some 300 people made the arduous journey to see what must have been one of the most disappointing bouts in boxing history—Fitzsimmons knocked out his opponent in a mere 95 seconds.)

During the prime of Jack Dempsey's career in the 1920's, boxing was illegal in many states, like alcohol, and like alcohol, seems to have aroused a hysterical public enthusiasm. Photographs of jammed outdoor arenas taken in the 1920's with boxing rings like postage-sized altars at their centers, the boxers themselves scarcely visible, testify to the extraordinary emotional appeal boxing had at that time, even as reform movements were lobbying against it. When Jack Johnson won the heavyweight title in 1908 (he had to pursue the white champion Tommy Burns all the way to Australia to confront him), the special "danger" of boxing was also that it might expose and humiliate white men in the ring. After Johnson's victory over the "White Hope" contender Jim Jeffries, there were race riots and lynchings throughout the United States; even films of some of Johnson's fights were outlawed in many states. And because boxing has become a sport in which black and Hispanic men have lately excelled, it is particularly vulnerable to attack by white middle-class reformers, who seem uninterested in lobbying against equally dangerous but "establishment" sports like football, auto racing, and thoroughbred horse racing.

There is something peculiarly American in the fact that, while boxing is our most controversial sport, it is also the sport that pays its top athletes the most money. In spite of the controversy, boxing has never been healthier financially. The three highest paid athletes in the world in both 1983 and 1984 were boxers; a boxer with a long career like heavyweight champion Larry Holmes—48 fights in 13 years as a professional—can expect to earn somewhere beyond $50 million.

(Holmes said that after retirement what he would miss most about boxing is his million-dollar checks.) Dempsey, who said that a man fights for one thing only—money—made somewhere beyond $3,500,000 in the ring in his long and varied career. Now $1.5 million is a fairly common figure for a single fight. Thomas Hearns made at least $7 million in his fight with Hagler while Hagler made at least $7.5 million. For the first of his highly publicized matches with Roberto Duran in 1980—which he lost on a decision—the popular black welterweight champion Sugar Ray Leonard received a staggering $10 million to Duran's $1.3 million. And none of these figures takes into account various subsidiary earnings (from television commercials, for instance) which in Leonard's case are probably as high as his income was from boxing.

Money has drawn any number of retired boxers back into the ring, very often 39 with tragic results. The most notorious example is perhaps Joe Louis, who, owing huge sums in back taxes, continued boxing well beyond the point at which he could perform capably. After a career of 17 years he was stopped by Rocky Marciano—who was said to have felt as upset by his victory as Louis by the defeat. (Louis then went on to a degrading second career as a professional wrestler. This, too, ended abruptly when 300-pound Rocky Lee stepped on the 42-year-old Louis's chest and damaged his heart.) Ezzard Charles, Jersey Joe Walcott, Joe Frazier, Muhammad Ali—each continued fighting when he was no longer in condition to defend himself against young heavyweight boxers on the way up. Of all heavyweight champions, only Rocky Marciano, to whom fame and money were not of paramount significance, was prudent enough to retire before he was defeated. In any case, the prodigious sums of money a few boxers earn do not account for the sums the public is willing to pay them.

Though boxing has long been popular in many countries and under many 40 forms of government, its popularity in the United States since the days of John L. Sullivan has a good deal to do with what is felt as the spirit of the individual— his "physical" spirit—in conflict with the constrictions of the state. The rise of boxing in the 1920's in particular might well be seen as a consequence of the diminution of the individual vis-à-vis society; the gradual attrition of personal freedom, will, and strength—whether "masculine" or otherwise. In the Eastern bloc of nations, totalitarianism is a function of the state; in the Western bloc it has come to seem a function of technology, or history—"fate." The individual exists in his physical supremacy, but does the individual matter?

In the magical space of the boxing ring so disquieting a question has no 41 claim. There, as in no other public arena, the individual as a unique physical being asserts himself; there, for a dramatic if fleeting period of time, the great world with its moral and political complexities, its terrifying impersonality, simply ceases to exist. Men fighting one another with only their fists and their cunning are all contemporaries, all brothers, belonging to no historical time. "He can run, but he can't hide"—so said Joe Louis before his famous fight with young Billy Conn in 1941. In the brightly lighted ring, man is *in extremis*, performing an atavistic rite or agon for the mysterious solace of those who can participate only vicariously in such drama: the drama of life in the flesh. Boxing has become America's tragic theater.

QUESTIONS

1. In paragraph 4 Oates says she doesn't think of boxing as a sport. If it isn't a sport, what is it?

2. What does the quotation from William Butler Yeats in paragraph 10 mean, especially the line that says "The painter's brush consumes his dreams"? How does this relate to boxing? How does it relate to writing?

3. Political issues are touched upon in paragraph 16 and elsewhere in this essay. How would you define Oates's position? What is her view of "liberalism," for instance?

4. How does Oates see *herself* in relation to boxing? In considering this question, first locate those parts of the essay in which her personal views are in the foreground.

5. How persuasive do you find the discussion of boxing and love in paragraphs 28 and 30?

6. Throughout the essay Oates brings up the question of the role of boxing in a civilized society. How would you describe her position on this question?

7. Oates often explains through comparisons and contrasts. Examine her use of these. Do any strike you as particularly effective or misleading? Look at paragraphs 5 through 8, to begin with.

8. In explaining the appeal of boxing, Oates finds she must explain boxing itself. That is, to say why people like it, she must try to say what it is. Make an outline that shows the major subtopics she has used to organize her explanation of boxing. For example, paragraphs 11 and 12 treat the referee's role. See what other subtopics you can identify.

9. Although Oates mentions her personal relationship to boxing, her essay seeks to arrive at a more general view of the role of boxing in American culture. Select a sport or activity that is personally important to you but also plays a role or reveals something important about American life in general. Write your own essay on the function of your chosen activity. Include your personal feelings, if you like, but keep them well subordinated to larger concerns.

ART FOR ETERNITY
E. H. Gombrich

E. H. Gombrich (b. 1890) describes himself as an art historian "with philosophical and psychological interests." He directs the Warburg Institute of the University of London. His Mellon Lectures, given in 1956 at the National Gallery of Art in Washington, D.C., were published as Art and Illusion, *his most important and influential book. Gombrich has also written an introduction to art history,* The Story of Art *(1972), in which the following selection appears as part of the second chapter.*

Everyone knows that Egypt is the land of the pyramids, those mountains of 1 stone which stand like weathered landmarks on the distant horizon of history [Fig. 1]. However remote and mysterious they seem, they tell us much of their own story. They tell us of a land which was so thoroughly organized that it was possible to pile up these gigantic mounds in the lifetime of a single king, and they tell us of kings who were so rich and powerful that they could force thousands and thousands of workers or slaves to toil for them year in, year out, to quarry the stones, to drag them to the building site, and to shift them with the most primitive means till the tomb was ready to receive the king. No king and no people would have gone to such expense, and taken so much trouble, for the creation of a mere monument. In fact, we know that the pyramids had their practical importance in the eyes of the kings and their subjects. The king was considered a divine being who held sway over them, and on his departure from this earth he would again ascend to the gods whence he had come. The pyramids soaring up to the sky would probably help him to make his ascent. In any case they would preserve his sacred body from decay. For the Egyptians believed that the body must be preserved if the soul is to live on in the beyond. That is why they prevented the corpse from decaying by an elaborate method of embalming it, and binding it up in strips of cloth. It was for the mummy of the king that the pyramid had been piled up, and his body was laid right in the center of the huge mountain of stone in a stone coffin. Everywhere round the burial chamber, spells and incantations were written to help him on his journey to the other world.

But it is not only these oldest relics of human architecture which tell of the 2 role played by age-old beliefs in the story of art. The Egyptians held the belief that the preservation of the body was not enough. If the likeness of the king was also preserved, it was doubly sure that he would continue to exist for ever. So they ordered sculptors to chisel the king's head out of hard, imperishable granite,

296

and put it in the tomb where no one saw it, there to work its spell and to help his soul to keep alive in and through the image. One Egyptian word for sculptor was actually "He-who-keeps-alive."

At first these rites were reserved for kings, but soon the nobles of the royal household had their minor tombs grouped in neat rows round the king's mound; and gradually every self-respecting person had to make provision for his after-life by ordering a costly grave which would house his mummy and his likeness, and where his soul could dwell and receive the offerings of food and drink which were given to the dead. Some of these early portraits from the pyramid age, the fourth "dynasty" of the "Old Kingdom,"[1] are among the most beautiful works of Egyptian art [Fig. 2]. There is a solemnity and simplicity about them which one does not easily forget. One sees that the sculptor was not trying to flatter his sitter, or to preserve a fleeting expression. He was concerned only with essentials. Every lesser detail he left out. Perhaps it is just because of this strict concentration on the basic forms of the human head that these portraits remain so impressive. For, despite their almost geometrical rigidity, they are not prim-itive. . . . Nor are they . . . naturalistic portraits. . . . The observation of nature,

1. The Great Pyramid of Gizeh. *Built about* 2700 B.C.

---

[1]the fourth "dynasty" of the "Old Kingdom": period in Egyptian history from about 2900 B.C. to 2700 B.C. [Eds.]

2. Portrait head of limestone. *Found in a tomb at Gizeh, made about 2700* B.C. *Vienna, Kunst-historisches Museum*

and the regularity of the whole, are so evenly balanced that they impress us as being lifelike and yet remote and enduring.

This combination of geometric regularity and keen observation of nature is 4 characteristic of all Egyptian art. We can study it best in the reliefs and paintings that adorned the walls of the tombs. The word "adorned," it is true, may hardly fit an art which was meant to be seen by no one but the dead man's soul. In fact, these works were not intended to be enjoyed. They, too, were meant to "keep alive." Once, in a grim distant past, it had been the custom when a powerful man died to let his servants and slaves accompany him into the grave. They were sacrificed so that he should arrive in the beyond with a suitable train. Later, these horrors were considered either too cruel or too costly, and art came to the rescue. Instead of real servants, the great ones of this earth were given images as substitutes. The pictures and models found in Egyptian tombs were connected with the idea of providing the soul with helpmates in the other world.

To us these reliefs and wall-paintings provide an extraordinarily vivid picture 5 of life as it was lived in Egypt thousands of years ago. And yet, looking at them for the first time, one may find them rather bewildering. The reason is that the Egyptian painters had quite a different way from ours of representing real life. Perhaps this is connected with the different purpose their paintings had to serve. What mattered most was not prettiness but completeness. It was the artists' task to preserve everything as clearly and permanently as possible. So they did not set out to sketch nature as it appeared to them from any fortuitous angle. They drew from memory, according to strict rules which ensured that everything that had to go into the picture would stand out in perfect clarity. Their method, in fact, resembled that of the map-maker rather than that of the painter. Fig. 3 shows it in a simple example, representing a garden with a pond. If we had to draw such a motif we might wonder from which angle to approach it. The shape and character of the trees could be seen clearly only from the sides, the shape of the pond would be visible only if seen from above. The Egyptians had no compunction about this problem. They would simply draw the pond as if it were seen from above, and the trees from the side. The fishes and birds in the pond, on the other hand, would hardly look recognizable as seen from above, so they were drawn in profile.

In such a simple picture, we can easily understand the artist's procedure. A 6 similar method is often used by children. But the Egyptians were much more consistent in their application of these methods than children ever are. Everything had to be represented from its most characteristic angle. Fig. 4 shows the effect which this idea had on the representation of the human body. The head was most easily seen in profile so they drew it sideways. But if we think of the human eye we think of it as seen from the front. Accordingly, a full-face eye was planted into the side view of the face. The top half of the body, the shoulders and chest, are best seen from the front, for then we see how the arms are hinged to the body. But arms and legs in movement are much more clearly seen sideways. That is the reason why Egyptians in these pictures look so strangely flat and contorted. Moreover the Egyptian artists found it hard to visualize either foot seen from the outside. They preferred the clear outline from the big toe upwards. So both feet are seen from the inside, and the man on the relief looks as if he had two left feet. It must not be supposed that Egyptian artists thought

3. Painting of a pond. *From a tomb in Thebes. About 1400* B.C. *London, British Museum*

that human beings looked like that. They merely followed a rule which allowed them to include everything in the human form that they considered important. Perhaps this strict adherence to the rule had something to do with their magic purpose. For how could a man with his arm "foreshortened" or "cut off" bring or receive the required offerings to the dead?

Here as always, Egyptian art is not based on what the artist could see at a given moment, but rather on what he knew belonged to a person or a scene. It was out of these forms which he had learned, and which he knew, that he built his representations, much as the tribal artist builds his figures out of the forms he can master. It is not only his knowledge of forms and shapes that the artist embodies in his picture, but also his knowledge of their significance. We sometimes call a man a "big boss." The Egyptian drew the boss bigger than his servants or even his wife.

Once we have grasped these rules and conventions, we understand the language of the pictures in which life of the Egyptians is chronicled. Fig. 5 gives

300

4. Portrait of Hesire from a wooden door in his tomb. *Carved about 2700* B.C. *Cairo, Museum*

a good idea of the general arrangement of a wall in a tomb of a high Egyptian dignitary of the so-called "Middle Kingdom,"[2] some nineteen hundred years before our era. The inscriptions in hieroglyphs tell us exactly who he was, and what titles and honors he had collected in his lifetime. His name, we read, was Chnemhotep, the Administrator of the Eastern Desert, Prince of Menat Chufu, Confidential Friend of the King, Royal Acquaintance, Superintendent of the

---

[2]"Middle Kingdom": period in Egyptian history from about 2000 B.C. to 1800 B.C. [Eds.]

5. A wall from the tomb of Chnemhotep near Beni Hassan. *About 1900* B.C.

Priests, Priest of Horus, Priest of Anubis, Chief of all the Divine Secrets, and—most impressive of all—Master of all the Tunics. On the left side we see him hunting wild-fowl with a kind of boomerang, accompanied by his wife Cheti, his concubine Jat, and one of his sons who, despite his tiny size in the picture, held the title of Superintendent of the Frontiers. Below, in the frieze, we see fishermen under their superintendent Mentuhotep hauling in a big catch. On top of the door Chnemhotep is seen again, this time trapping waterfowl in a net. Understanding the methods of the Egyptian artist, we can easily see how this device worked. The trapper sat hidden behind a screen of reeds, holding a cord, which was linked with the open net (seen from above). When the birds had settled on the bait, he pulled the rope and the net closed over them. Behind Chnemhotep is his eldest son Nacht, and his Superintendent of the Treasures, who was also responsible for the ordering of the tomb. On the right side, Chnemhotep, who is called "great in fish, rich in wild-fowl, loving the goddess of the chase," is seen spearing fish. Once more we can observe the conventions of the Egyptian artist who lets the water rise among the reeds to show us the clearing with the fish. The inscription says: "Canoeing in the papyrus beds, the

302

pools of wild-fowl, the marshes and the streams, spearing with the two-pronged spear, he transfixes thirty fish; how delightful is the day of hunting the hippopotamus." Below is an amusing episode with one of the men who had fallen into the water being fished out by his mates. The inscription round the door records the days on which offerings are to be given to the dead, and includes prayers to the gods.

When we have become accustomed to looking at these Egyptian pictures we are as little troubled by their unrealities as we are by the absence of color in a photograph. We even begin to realize the great advantages of the Egyptian method. Nothing in these pictures gives the impression of being haphazard, nothing looks as if it could just as well be somewhere else. It is worth while taking a pencil and trying to copy one of these "primitive" Egyptian drawings. Our attempts always look clumsy, lopsided and crooked. At least my own do. For the Egyptian sense of order in every detail is so strong that any little variation seems to upset it entirely. The Egyptian artist began his work by drawing a network of straight lines on the wall, and he distributed his figures with great care along these lines. And yet all this geometrical sense of order did not prevent him from observing the details of nature with amazing accuracy. Every bird or fish is drawn with such truthfulness that zoologists can still recognize the species. Fig. 6 shows such a detail of Fig. 5—the birds in the tree by Chnemhotep's fowling net. It was not only his great knowledge which guided the artist, but also an eye for pattern.

It is one of the greatest things in Egyptian art that all the statues, paintings and architectural forms seem to fall into place as if they obeyed one law. We call such a law, which all creations of a people seem to obey, a "style." It is very difficult to explain in words what makes a style, but it is far less difficult to see. The rules which govern all Egyptian art give every individual work the effect of poise and austere harmony.

The Egyptian style comprised a set of very strict laws, which every artist had to learn from his earliest youth. Seated statues had to have their hands on their knees; men had to be painted with darker skin than women; the appearance of every Egyptian god was strictly laid down: Horus, the sun-god, had to be shown as a falcon or with a falcon's head, Anubis, the god of death, as a jackal or with a jackal's head. Every artist also had to learn the art of beautiful script. He had to cut the images and symbols of the hieroglyphs clearly and accurately in stone. But once he had mastered all these rules he had finished his apprenticeship. No one wanted anything different, no one asked him to be "original." On the contrary, he was probably considered the best artist who could make his statues most like the admired monuments of the past. So it happened that in the course of three thousand years or more Egyptian art changed very little. Everything that was considered good and beautiful in the age of the pyramids was held to be just as excellent a thousand years later. True, new fashions appeared, and

6. Birds in a bush. *Detail of Fig. 5*

new subjects were demanded of the artists, but their mode of representing man and nature remained essentially the same.

Only one man ever shook the iron bars of the Egyptian style. He was a king [12] of the Eighteenth Dynasty, in the period known as the "New Kingdom,"[3] which was founded after a catastrophic invasion of Egypt. This king, called Amenophis IV, was a heretic. He broke with many of the customs hallowed by age-old tradition. He did not wish to pay homage to the many strangely shaped gods of his people. For him only one god was supreme, Aton, whom he worshipped and whom he had represented in the shape of the sun. He called himself Akhnaton, after his god, and he moved his court out of reach of the priests of the other gods, to a place which is now called El-Amarna.

The pictures which he commissioned must have shocked the Egyptians of [13] his day by their novelty. In them none of the solemn and rigid dignity of the earlier Pharaohs was to be found. Instead, he had himself depicted lifting his daughter on to his knees, walking with his wife in the garden, leaning on his stick. Some of his portraits show him as an ugly man [Fig. 7]—perhaps he wanted the artists to portray him in all his human frailty or, perhaps, he was so convinced of his unique importance as a prophet that he insisted on a true likeness. Akhnaton's successor was Tutankhamen, whose tomb with its treasures was discovered in 1922. Some of these works are still in the modern style of the Aton religion—particularly the back of the king's throne [Fig. 8], which shows the king and queen in a homely idyll. He is sitting on his chair in an attitude which might have scandalized the strict Egyptian conservative—almost lolling, by Egyptian standards. His wife is no smaller than he is, and gently puts her hand on his shoulder while the Sun-god, represented as a golden orb, is stretching his hands in blessing down to them.

It is not impossible that this reform of art in the Eighteenth Dynasty was [14] made easier for the king because he could point to foreign works that were much less strict and rigid than the Egyptian products. On an island overseas, in Crete, there dwelt a gifted people whose artists delighted in the representation of swift movement. When the palace of their king at Knossos was excavated at the end of the nineteenth century, people could hardly believe that such a free and graceful style could have been developed in the second millennium before our era. Works in this style were also found on the Greek mainland; a dagger from Mycenae [Fig. 9] shows a sense of movement and flowing lines which must have impressed any Egyptian craftsman who had been permitted to stray from the hallowed rules of his style.

But this opening of Egyptian art did not last long. Already during the reign [15] of Tutankhamen the old beliefs were restored, and the window to the outside world was shut again. The Egyptian style, as it had existed for more than a

---

[3]the Eighteenth Dynasty, in the period known as the "New Kingdom": a period in Egyptian history from about 1600 B.C. to 1200 B.C., corresponding to the exodus of the Israelites from Egypt and the fall of Troy. [Eds.]

7. King Amenophis IV. *Limestone relief. About 1370* B.C. *Berlin, Museum*

thousand years before his time, continued to exist for another thousand years or more, and the Egyptians doubtless believed it would continue for all eternity. Many Egyptian works in our museums date from this later period, and so do nearly all Egyptian buildings such as temples and palaces. New themes were introduced, new tasks performed, but nothing essentially new was added to the achievement of art.

8. The Pharaoh Tutankhamen and his wife. *Gilt and painted woodwork from the throne found in his tomb. Made about 1350* B.C. *Cairo, Museum*

E. H. GOMBRICH

9. A dagger from Mycenae. *About 1600* B.C. *Athens, Museum*

QUESTIONS

1. Briefly state in your own words what Gombrich considers "the achievement of art" (paragraph 15) in ancient Egypt.

2. Sum up the ways in which Gombrich says Egyptian beliefs affected Egyptian art.

3. Gombrich's viewpoint is that of an art historian, but he also draws on information from other fields such as religion, anthropology, government, history, archaeology, and so on. Select one paragraph or short section, and explain how a specialist in another field might present essentially the same subject from a different angle of vision.

4. Given the Egyptian stylistic conventions, how do you suppose the study of Egyptian art differs from the study of the art of other periods and places?

5. The Egyptian method of drawing, as described in paragraphs 5 and 6, might be called *explanatory* or, perhaps, *analytical*. Use this method of analysis to sketch your classroom, a room in which you work regularly, or a room in which you live. Or, make an "Egyptian" portrait of a roommate or friend.

6. Like the Egyptians, we explain the relation of parts to the whole with pictorial analyses such as maps, diagrams of electrical circuitry, dress patterns, diagrams of football plays, and so on. Sometimes, however, we need to analyze with words. Select some familiar item with little or no mechanical complexity, something like a calendar, the face of a clock, or a radio or telephone dial. Write a description of it that takes into account its parts and their relations to each other.

7. Select an object to describe as you did in question 7, but this time pick something with working parts, such as an eggbeater, a can opener, a bicycle pedal and chain, a doorknob and latch, or the latch on a gate. Write a description of the item you choose, and explain how the parts work together.

8. Test Gombrich's generalizations against some examples of Egyptian art. Look for illustrations in art history books or in books about ancient Egyptian culture. Select and describe one or two works of art in relation to Gombrich's comments about the conventional style or the violation of convention under Akhnaton.

9. Consider the idea of style as described in paragraphs 10 and 11. What styles are apparent in the ways people live in your community? Do you shift from one style of

dress and behavior to another, or does a single style serve for all you do? How do you tell one style from another?

10. Write an account of styles of dress over the last few years. Consider, for example, style in men's clothing so as to emphasize either its many changes or its underlying consistency. That is, make your account either as similar to or as different from Gombrich's account of Egyptian pictorial style as you can. Compare your account with that of a classmate who has taken the opposite point of view.

11. Consider what modern constructions approach the grandeur and possible excesses of the pyramids—perhaps the Empire State Building, the space shuttle, a superdome, the Golden Gate Bridge, or something in your community. How might future historians explain one of those structures?

THE CULTURAL IMPORTANCE
OF ART

Susanne K. Langer

Born in New York City, Susanne Langer (1895–1985) be-
came one of America's leading philosophers after receiving
her A. B., A. M. and Ph.D. from Radcliffe College at
Harvard University, where she taught philosophy for fifteen
years before moving to Columbia and, in 1954, to Con-
necticut College. The author of a number of books, Langer
was best known for her work in the philosophy of art. The
essay included here was first delivered as a lecture at Syra-
cuse University in 1958 and then was published in Langer's
Philosophical Sketches *in 1962.*

Every culture develops some kind of art as surely as it develops language.　1
Some primitive cultures have no real mythology or religion, but all have some
art—dance, song, design (sometimes only on tools or on the human body).
Dance, above all, seems to be the oldest elaborated art.

The ancient ubiquitous character of art contrasts sharply with the prevalent　2
idea that art is a luxury product of civilization, a cultural frill, a piece of social
veneer.

It fits better with the conviction held by most artists, that art is the epitome　3
of human life, the truest record of insight and feeling, and that the strongest
military or economic society without art is poor in comparison with the most
primitive tribe of savage painters, dancers, or idol carvers. Wherever a society
has really achieved culture (in the ethnological sense, not the popular sense of
"social form") it has begotten art, not late in its career, but at the very inception
of it.

Art is, indeed, the spearhead of human development, social and individual.　4
The vulgarization of art is the surest symptom of ethnic decline. The growth of
a new art or even a great and radically new style always bespeaks a young and
vigorous mind, whether collective or single.

What sort of thing is art, that it should play such a leading role in human　5
development? It is not an intellectual pursuit, but is necessary to intellectual
life; it is not religion, but grows up with religion, serves it, and in large measure
determines it.

We cannot enter here on a long discussion of what has been claimed as the　6
essence of art, the true nature of art, or its defining function; in a single lecture
dealing with one aspect of art, namely its cultural influence, I can only give

you by way of preamble my own definition of art, with categorical brevity. This does not mean that I set up this definition in a categorical spirit, but only that we have no time to debate it; so you are asked to accept it as an assumption underlying these reflections.

Art, in the sense here intended—that is, the generic term subsuming paint- 7
ing, sculpture, architecture, music, dance, literature, drama, and film—may be defined as the practice of creating perceptible forms expressive of human feeling. I say "perceptible" rather than "sensuous" forms because some works of art are given to imagination rather than to the outward senses. A novel, for instance, usually is read silently with the eye, but is not made for vision, as a painting is; and though sound plays a vital part in poetry, words even in poetry are not essentially sonorous structures like music. Dance requires to be seen, but its appeal is to deeper centers of sensation. The difference between dance and mobile sculpture makes this immediately apparent. But all works of art are purely perceptible forms that seem to embody some sort of feeling.

"Feeling" as I am using it here covers much more than it does in the technical 8
vocabulary of psychology, where it denotes only pleasure and displeasure, or even in the shifting limits of ordinary discourse, where it sometimes means sensation (as when one says a paralyzed limb has no feeling in it), sometimes sensibility (as we speak of hurting someone's feelings), sometimes emotion (e.g., as a situation is said to harrow your feelings, or to evoke tender feeling), or a directed emotional attitude (we say we feel strongly *about* something), or even our general mental or physical condition, feeling well or ill, blue, or a bit above ourselves. As I use the word, in defining art as the creation of perceptible forms expressive of human feeling, it takes in all those meanings; it applies to every-thing that may be felt.

Another word in the definition that might be questioned is "creation." I think 9
it is justified, not pretentious, as perhaps it sounds, but that issue is slightly beside the point here; so let us shelve it. If anyone prefers to speak of the "making" or "construction" of expressive forms, that will do here just as well.

What does have to be understood is the meaning of "form," and more par- 10
ticularly "expressive form"; for that involves the very nature of art and therefore the question of its cultural importance.

The word "form" has several current uses; most of them have some relation 11
to the sense in which I am using it here, though a few, such as "a form to be filled in for tax purposes" or "a mere matter of form," are fairly remote, being quite specialized. Since we are speaking of art, it might be good to point out that the meaning of stylistic pattern—"the sonata form," "the sonnet form"— is not the one I am assuming here.

I am using the word in a simpler sense, which it has when you say, on a 12
foggy night, that you see dimly moving forms in the mist; one of them emerges clearly, and is the form of a man. The trees are gigantic forms; the rills of rain trace sinuous forms on the windowpane. The rills are not fixed things; they are

forms of motion. When you watch gnats weaving in the air, or flocks of birds wheeling overhead, you see dynamic forms—forms made by motion.

It is in this sense of an apparition given to our perception that a work of art 13 is a form. It may be a permanent form like a building or a vase or a picture, or a transient, dynamic form like a melody or a dance, or even a form given to imagination, like the passage of purely imaginary, apparent events that constitutes a literary work. But it is always a perceptible, self-identical whole; like a natural being, it has a character of organic unity, self-sufficiency, individual reality. And it is thus, as an appearance, that a work of art is good or bad or perhaps only rather poor—as an appearance, not as a comment on things beyond it in the world, or as a reminder of them.

This, then, is what I mean by "form"; but what is meant by calling such 14 forms "expressive of human feeling"? How do apparitions "express" anything— feeling or anything else? First of all, let us ask just what is meant here by "express," what sort of "expression" we are talking about.

The word "expression" has two principal meanings. In one sense it means 15 self-expression—giving vent to our feelings. In this sense it refers to a symptom of what we feel. Self-expression is a spontaneous reaction to an actual, present situation, an event, the company we are in, things people say, or what the weather does to us; it bespeaks the physical and mental state we are in and the emotions that stir us.

In another sense, however, "expression" means the presentation of an idea, 16 usually by the proper and apt use of words. But a device for presenting an idea is what we call a symbol, not a symptom. Thus a word is a symbol, and so is a meaningful combination of words.

A sentence, which is a special combination of words, expresses the idea of 17 some state of affairs, real or imagined. Sentences are complicated symbols. Language will formulate new ideas as well as communicate old ones, so that all people know a lot of things that they have merely heard or read about. Symbolic expression, therefore, extends our knowledge beyond the scope of our actual experience.

If an idea is clearly conveyed by means of symbols we say it is well expressed. 18 A person may work for a long time to give his statement the best possible form, to find the exact words for what he means to say, and to carry his account or his argument most directly from one point to another. But a discourse so worked out is certainly not a spontaneous reaction. Giving expression to an idea is obviously a different thing from giving expression to feelings. You do not say of a man in a rage that his anger is well expressed. The symptoms just are what they are; there is no critical standard for symptoms. If, on the other hand, the angry man tries to tell you what he is fuming about, he will have to collect himself, curtail his emotional expression, and find words to express his ideas. For to tell a story coherently involves "expression" in quite a different sense:

this sort of expression is not "self-expression," but may be called "conceptual expression."

Language, of course, is our prime instrument of conceptual expression. The [19] things we can say are in effect the things we can think. Words are the terms of our thinking as well as the terms in which we present our thoughts, because they present the objects of thought to the thinker himself. Before language communicates ideas, it gives them form, makes them clear, and in fact makes them what they are. Whatever has a name is an object for thought. Without words, sense experience is only a flow of impressions, as subjective as our feelings; words make it objective, and carve it up into *things* and *facts* that we can note, remember, and think about. Language gives outward experience its form, and makes it definite and clear.

There is, however, an important part of reality that is quite inaccessible to [20] the formative influence of language: that is the realm of so-called "inner experience," the life of feeling and emotion. The reason why language is so powerless here is not, as many people suppose, that feeling and emotion are irrational; on the contrary, they seem irrational because language does not help to make them conceivable, and most people cannot conceive anything without the logical scaffolding of words. The unfitness of language to convey subjective experience is a somewhat technical subject, easier for logicians to understand than for artists; but the gist of it is that the form of language does not reflect the natural form of feeling, so that we cannot shape any extensive concepts of feelings with the help of ordinary, discursive language. Therefore the words whereby we refer to feeling only name very general kinds of inner experience— excitement, calm, joy, sorrow, love, hate, and so on. But there is no language to describe just how one joy differs, sometimes radically, from another. The real nature of feeling is something language as such—as discursive symbolism— cannot render.

For this reason, the phenomena of feeling and emotion are usually treated [21] by philosophers as irrational. The only pattern discursive thought can find in them is the pattern of outward events that occasion them. There are different degrees of fear, but they are thought of as so many degrees of the same simple feeling.

But human feeling is a fabric, not a vague mass. It has an intricate dynamic [22] pattern, possible combinations and new emergent phenomena. It is a pattern of organically interdependent and interdetermined tensions and resolutions, a pattern of almost infinitely complex activation and cadence. To it belongs the whole gamut of our sensibility—the sense of straining thought, all mental attitude and motor set. Those are the deeper reaches that underlie the surface waves of our emotion, and make human life a life of feeling instead of an unconscious metabolic existence interrupted by feelings.

It is, I think, this dynamic pattern that finds its formal expression in the arts. [23] The expressiveness of art is like that of a symbol, not that of an emotional

313

symptom; it is as a formulation of feeling for our conception that a work of art is properly said to be expressive. It may serve somebody's need of self-expression besides, but that is not what makes it good or bad art. In a special sense one may call a work of art a symbol of feeling, for, like a symbol, it formulates our ideas of inward experience, as discourse formulates our ideas of things and facts in the outside world. A work of art differs from a genuine symbol—that is, a symbol in the full and usual sense—in that it does not point beyond itself to something else. Its relation to feeling is a rather special one that we cannot undertake to analyze here; in effect, the feeling it expresses appears to be directly given with it—as the sense of a true metaphor, or the value of a religious myth—and is not separable from its expression. We speak of the feeling *of*, or the feeling *in*, a work of art, not the feeling it means. And we speak truly; a work of art presents something like a direct vision of vitality, emotion, subjective reality.

The primary function of art is to objectify feeling so that we can contemplate 24 and understand it. It is the formulation of so-called "inward experience," the "inner life," that is impossible to achieve by discursive thought, because its forms are incommensurable with the forms of language and all its derivatives (e.g., mathematics, symbolic logic). Art objectifies the sentience and desire, self-consciousness and world-consciousness, emotions and moods, that are generally regarded as irrational because words cannot give us clear ideas of them. But the premise tacitly assumed in such a judgment—namely, that anything language cannot express is formless and irrational—seems to me to be an error. I believe the life of feeling is not irrational; its logical forms are merely very different from the structures of discourse. But they are so much like the dynamic forms of art that art is their natural symbol. Through plastic works, music, fiction, dance, or dramatic forms we can conceive what vitality and emotion feel like.

This brings us, at last, to the question of the cultural importance of the arts. 25 Why is art so apt to be the vanguard of cultural advance, as it was in Egypt, in Greece, in Christian Europe (think of Gregorian music and Gothic architecture), in Renaissance Italy—not to speculate about ancient cavemen, whose art is all that we know of them? One thinks of culture as economic increase, social organization, the gradual ascendancy of rational thinking and scientific control of nature over superstitious imagination and magical practices. But art is not practical; it is neither philosophy nor science; it is not religion, morality, or even social comment (as many drama critics take comedy to be). What does it contribute to culture that could be of major importance?

It merely presents forms—sometimes intangible forms—to imagination. Its 26 direct appeal is to that faculty, or function, that Lord Bacon considered the chief stumbling block in the way of reason, and that enlightened writers like Stuart Chase never tire of condemning as the source of all nonsense and bizarre erroneous beliefs. And so it is; but it is also the source of all insight and true

314

beliefs. Imagination is probably the oldest mental trait that is typically human—older than discursive reason; it is probably the common source of dream, reason, religion, and all true general observation. It is this primitive human power—imagination—that engenders the arts and is in turn directly affected by their products.

Somewhere at the animalian starting line of human evolution lie the beginnings of that supreme instrument of the mind—language. We think of it as a device for communication among the members of a society. But communication is only one, and perhaps not even the first, of its functions. The first thing it does is to break up what William James called the "blooming, buzzing confusion" of sense perception into units and groups, events and chains of events—things and relations, causes and effects. All these patterns are imposed on our experience by language. We think, as we speak, in terms of objects and their relations.

But the process of breaking up our sense experience in this way, making reality conceivable, memorable, sometimes even predictable, is a process of imagination. Primitive conception is imagination. Language and imagination grow up together in a reciprocal tutelage.

What discursive symbolism—language in its literal use—does for our awareness of things about us and our own relation to them, the arts do for our awareness of subjective reality, feeling and emotion; they given form to inward experiences and thus make them conceivable. The only way we can really envisage vital movement, the stirring and growth and passage of emotion, and ultimately the whole direct sense of human life, is in artistic terms. A musical person thinks of emotions musically. They cannot be discursively talked about above a very general level. But they may nonetheless be known—objectively set forth, publicly known—and there is nothing necessarily confused or formless about emotions.

As soon as the natural forms of subjective experience are abstracted to the point of symbolic presentation, we can use those forms to imagine feeling and understand its nature. Self-knowledge, insight into all phases of life and mind, springs from artistic imagination. That is the cognitive value of the arts.

But their influence on human life goes deeper than the intellectual level. As language actually gives form to our sense experience, grouping our impressions around those things which have names, and fitting sensations to the qualities that have adjectival names, and so on, the arts we live with—our picture books and stories and the music we hear—actually form our emotive experience. Every generation has its styles of feeling. One age shudders and blushes and faints, another swaggers, still another is godlike in a universal indifference. These styles in actual emotion are not insincere. They are largely unconscious—determined by many social causes, but *shaped* by artists, usually popular artists of the screen, the jukebox, the shop-window, and the picture magazine. (That, rather than

27

28

29

30

31

incitement to crime, is my objection to the comics.) Irwin Edman remarks in one of his books that our emotions are largely Shakespeare's poetry.

This influence of art on life gives us an indication of why a period of efflo-   32 rescence in the arts is apt to lead a cultural advance: it formulates a new way of feeling, and that is the beginning of a cultural age. It suggests another matter for reflection, too—that a wide neglect of artistic education is a neglect in the education of feeling. Most people are so imbued with the idea that feeling is a formless, total organic excitement in men as in animals that the idea of educating feeling, developing its scope and quality, seems odd to them, if not absurd. It is really, I think, at the very heart of personal education.

There is one other function of the arts that benefits not so much the advance   33 of culture as its stabilization—an influence on individual lives. This function is the converse and complement of the objectification of feeling, the driving force of creation in art: it is the education of vision that we receive in seeing, hearing, reading works of art—the development of the artist's eye, that assimilates ordinary sights (or sounds, motions, or events) to inward vision, and lends expressiveness and emotional import to the world. Wherever art takes a motif from actuality—a flowering branch, a bit of landscape, a historic event, or a personal memory, any model or theme from life—it transforms it into a piece of imagination, and imbues its image with artistic vitality. The result is an impregnation of ordinary reality with the significance of created form. This is the subjectification of nature that makes reality itself a symbol of life and feeling.

The arts objectify subjective reality, and subjectify outward experience of   34 nature. Art education is the education of feeling, and a society that neglects it gives itself up to formless emotion. Bad art is corruption of feeling. This is a large factor in the irrationalism which dictators and demagogues exploit.

QUESTIONS

1. What is Langer's definition of art?
2. What other words besides *art*, does Langer define in the essay? How do these other definitions relate to her definition of art? Examine one of her other definitions in detail. How, for instance, does she go about defining *form*?
3. Put into your own words what Langer means by *language*. See paragraph 19, especially.
4. What does paragraph 6 tell you about the relationship between Langer and her audience?
5. Beginning in paragraph 25, Langer moves from explanation toward argument about the importance of art. Why does the question of "the cultural importance of the arts" (paragraph 25) cause her to shift from explaining to arguing? As she changes her purpose from explanation to argument, how does she change her major method of supporting her views?
6. Langer defines art in two different ways in the first sentence of paragraph 7, but

apparently she considers only one of these a proper definition. Based on this sentence and her other definitions, how do you suppose she would define *definition?* What is the best definition of *definition* that you can devise?

7. Write an essay in which you discuss another cultural activity in the manner of Langer, first defining it and then evaluating its importance. Some possibilities are sport, love, education, religion, law, history, science, or technology.

8. Perhaps you have a view of art that is different from Langer's. Write an essay in which you develop your own ideas on art. You may refer to her essay or ignore it, but try to write seriously and thoughtfully as she did.

THE OTHER SIDE
OF THE WALL
Douglas L. Wilson

*Born in St. James, Minnesota, in 1935, Douglas Wilson is
a librarian with degrees from Doane College in Nebraska
and the University of Pennsylvania. In addition to directing
both the library and a program in American Studies at Knox
College in Galesburg, Illinois, Wilson writes regularly on
American subjects. About the following essay, reprinted from
The Iowa Review, he says that he was interested in demonstrating how a literary understanding that he had never
questioned, and about which there was no controversy whatever, could be turned absolutely around in the wake of persuasive personal experience.*

I

My starting point is something that must seem fairly obvious: the notion that   1
we are creatures of our own experience. I would not expect to get much of an
argument on that score, and yet if one begins to develop this idea in certain
ways, one can readily create a dialectic that has the appearance, at least, of a
dilemma. One could, for example, emphasize the ways in which we are the
victims of our experience, limited or, to heighten the metaphor, imprisoned by
its iron precincts. Or one could, I think, with equal validity emphasize the
liberating character of experience and stress how every new experience frees us
from the limitations of our former condition. It is simply a matter of how we
wish to construe the notion that we are creatures of our own experience. What
both versions of the idea have in common, however, is the concept of a barrier,
a line of demarcation. And this has special significance for the poem that is the
focus of my essay—Robert Frost's "Mending Wall."

"Mending Wall" is extremely familiar, certainly one of Frost's best known   2
poems and perhaps one of the most famous in all of American poetry. It is
almost invariably read by students from elementary school to the college level;
until very recently, it made every anthology; it readily lends itself to quotation.
Say "Something there is that doesn't love a wall" and educated people are certain
to catch the reference. Moreover, it is a remarkably straightforward poem. That
is to say, given the standard new critical reservations, it seems to mean pretty
much what it says and to present no classic ambiguities. A survey of the long
record of commentary on the poem, which was published in 1914, reveals
relatively little critical disagreement.

To rehearse briefly a very familiar story, "Mending Wall" is about two New   3
England neighbors who meet in the spring to repair the stone wall that separates
their properties. Since they clearly live in the country, one might assume that
they are farmers, though all we are told is that one "is all pine" and the other
is "apple orchard" and that neither has cows (and, by extension, other livestock)
that might wander through the broken wall. As they mend the wall, the speaker
attempts to engage his neighbor in a debate over the necessity of having a wall
between them. His position is summed up in the classic line, "Something there
is that doesn't love a wall." His neighbor refuses to be drawn into an argument
and simply replies (another classic line), "Good fences make good neighbors."
The speaker regards this as a kind of category mistake, for he sees his neighbor
as applying a rule that was intended to cover a different kind of situation. The
poem concludes with the speaker's depiction of the neighbor as an unreflective
primitive, incapable of independent thinking or change.

> I see him there,
> Bringing a stone grasped firmly by the top
> In each hand, like an old-stone savage armed,
> He moves in darkness as it seems to me,
> Not of woods only and the shade of trees.
> He will not go behind his father's saying,
> And he likes having thought of it so well
> He says again, "Good fences make good neighbors."

Now in spite of all the ways that the poem can be, and has been, approached   4
and dealt with, it is difficult *not* to adopt the point of view of the speaker, and
virtually all the commentators do. Given the commitment of educators and
educated people to the examined life and the predominantly progressive spirit
of modern times, this is perhaps inevitable. Is there any way of understanding
the poem, one might ask, in which the neighbor does not emerge as the heavy?
Before 1968–69 I would have said "no," but since that time I have found myself
on the other side of the wall.

II

In 1968–69 I spent a sabbatical year on a small farm that my wife and I had   5
just acquired and that had over a mile and a half of line fence. Almost the first
question asked me by one of my neighbors when I met him was whether I
intended to pasture cows. This question was prompted by the wretched condition
of the fences I had inherited from the former owner. My new neighbor was
visibly relieved when I said that I didn't. During the course of that year I was
to see and hear a good deal about the importance of fences in a rural community.

One of the first things I heard about was the case of a former neighbor who   6
had been regarded as a notoriously bad neighbor. It was not simply that his

fences were neglected and in a constant state of disrepair. This is a very serious matter in dairy country, where half of a farmer's line fence (or boundary fence) is his responsibility and the other half is the responsibility of his neighbor. But it was clearly more than that. It was more that he was distrustful, quarrelsome, and generally indifferent or insensitive towards his neighbors—cardinal sins in a community that operated on the basis of mutual assistance and support. In truth, it was his attitude towards his neighbors and his neighborly responsibilities that accounted for his notoriety, and his fences, I came to see, were actually regarded not so much the source as the symbol of the problem. A long-standing member of the neighborhood, and one I am sure who had never heard of Robert Frost or read his poems, summarized the situation for me as follows: "They say good fences make good neighbors."

As time went by, I had occasion to see the problem a little closer to home. 7
My neighbor across the road could not keep his livestock properly penned, and I awoke one morning to find that a huge sow had uprooted half our front lawn. The situation deteriorated as the summer went along, and we found ourselves on the receiving end of a pilgrimage of pigs. I could take matters in hand and build a fence around my front yard (which I eventually did), but this would not keep the pigs at home. I decided in due course that the fault was not in my neighbor's fences but in my neighbor—more precisely in his attitude toward his neighborly responsibilities.

As one of my principal preoccupations that year was considering what it 8
meant to live in the country and how that differed from urban life, I began to think a good deal about fences. And whenever I did, my thoughts invariably returned to Frost's "Mending Wall." Having studied it in school, college, and graduate school, and having taught it every year in my American literature classes, I assumed that I knew "Mending Wall" pretty thoroughly and understood perfectly well.

> "Good fences make good neighbors."
> "*Why* do they make good neighbors? Isn't it
> Where there are cows? But here there are no cows.
> Before I built a wall I'd ask to know
> What I was walling in and walling out,
> And to whom I was like to give offense."

The position of the speaker was convincing enough, as it had been in the 9
past, and my experience on the farm had given it ample warrant. But the notion that the speaker was leaving something important out of the equation—that fences were more than merely barriers to livestock—would not go away and, in fact, continued to grow in my mind.

In the fall of the year I happened to meet one of my neighbors—a reticent, 10
older man—at the fenceline, where he was making some makeshift repairs to a stretch of very poor fence that I realized, alas, was my responsibility to keep up.

I was, of course, properly embarrassed but also surprised because I had understood that he never kept cattle in that field. He quickly explained that he only wanted to pasture his cows there for a few weeks and that he didn't expect me to rebuild the fence just for that. We fell to talking about the condition of our fences, what repairs were needed and which should be made first. Having satisfied himself as to my good intentions, he volunteered that he did not feel right about his neglect of the fencerow in front of us. While the fence in question was mine to keep up, he had allowed trees and shrubs to grow up on his side, as they had done prodigiously on mine, making for a dense and entangled mass of foliage on either side of the dilapidated fence. I thought I saw what he was driving at, and I said that this certainly made it more difficult to keep up the fence. But that wasn't it. What bothered him, he finally allowed, was that "it didn't *look* good." We soon agreed, with a warmth and enthusiasm that astonished me, to meet in the spring and clear the fencerow together.

It became abundantly clear to me, in thinking about this encounter, that   11
what we have been talking about was much more than the condition of the fence that divided our farms. It had rather to do with our relationship as neighbors. The practical aspect of the fence, in fact, had virtually been eliminated from consideration, for he had told me that he was about to give up his cows and his milking operation so as to qualify for social security. What we had agreed to do had little or nothing to do with wandering livestock. My cornstalks would never get across and eat his alfalfa. We were going to put our fences in order because we wanted to be good neighbors.

Coming back to "Mending Wall" after this series of experiences, I began to   12
see it in a different light. There was a pattern in these experiences—the notorious former neighbor, the neighbor with the unpenable pigs, and the neighbor who wanted to clear the fencerow—and I began to discern what it was. Good fences *do* make good neighbors. Not just where there are cows but where there are neighbors. The speaker in "Mending Wall," if he really believes that the force of nature that sunders stone walls should be regarded as a cue to right conduct, is short on experience and long on mischief. The neighbor's view, on the other hand, is true wisdom. Our only reason for supposing that he "moves in darkness" is that this is the way the speaker represents him. How, I began to ask myself, if this were the case, had this poem come to be so widely misread and misunderstood? And how had Frost, who must have known all of this perfectly well from the beginning, come to cast the poem in the form he did? The balance of my essay deals with these two questions.

III

The first question can be answered fairly easily, I believe, in the context of   13
the unstartling proposition with which I began. We are creatures of our own experience. To understand that the neighbor who says "Good fences make good

neighbors" is uttering something like practical wisdom requires an appeal to experience. As a debate there is little to choose. The speaker seems to have all the arguments on his side. The wall is useless, and mending it is meaningless, done only in the interest of the outmoded thinking of the neighbor; and all of this is confirmed by a principle of nature: "Something there is that doesn't love a wall." To judge this encounter strictly as a debate, as most readers apparently do, is inevitably to run a tally in favor of the speaker and award him the decision on points. Besides, he has qualities that have general appeal to readers of modern American poetry: he is critical; he doesn't take things like traditional sayings for granted; he is open to change; and he has a sense of humor. Our impression of the neighbor, poor man, is just the opposite, though it rests almost entirely on the speaker's biased references.

To judge the issue between them intelligently requires knowledge or expe- 14 rience that lies outside the poem—what Frost calls elsewhere "the need of being versed in country things." The speaker in the poem tries to deal with the issue of fences philosophically—by speculation, by arguments, by appeals to the nature of things. What the reader must grasp is that the speaker cannot or, for some reason, *will* not acknowledge what is truly at stake in the ritual of fence mending. He insists that, since he has only apple trees and the neighbor has only pines, the wall is not "needed." This assumes that a boundary serves only a very limited function, such as keeping livestock out or in. But country people know, not by an appeal to philosophy but as part of their culture, that a boundary is something very important; it is both an acknowledgement of responsibility and a token of respect. Maintaining a boundary is a hedge against uncertainty, a guarantee against dispute. The boundary can be seen in these terms as nothing less than an aspect of one's identity.

Now these are things that are understood implicitly by people whose land is 15 an extension of their lives. One could never persuade a farmer that the speaker in this poem has the better of this argument. Certainty Frost was aware of this, for his poetry is replete with references to boundaries and their critical importance. As Radcliffe Squires has observed, if Frost's position with respect to boundaries is represented by the speaker in "Mending Wall," it is at odds with everything else he has written on the subject. But Frost's readers, and certainly his commentators, have not been farmers. On the contrary, we have been city dwellers who have approached his poem from an unmistakably urban perspective. This, in combination with our disposition to judge the poem as a debate, has led to a decidedly imperfect understanding of the poem.

IV

There is a great deal that might be said at this point, but I propose to postpone 16 further discussion of the poem's interpretation in order to say something about the second question I raised, namely, how did Frost come to cast the dramatic encounter of "Mending Wall" in the form that he did and so seem to contribute to a widespread misunderstanding of his own poem. To pursue this question, I am going to risk the indulgence of the reader and ease back into the biographical mode in which I began.

As is well known, Frost's career as a poet did not really begin in earnest until he was nearly 40 years old and he had moved his family to England. How he came to find himself as a poet while there was not simply his good fortune in finding a publisher for a volume of his early poems or his acquaintance with Edward Thomas and other British poets or his recognition by Ezra Pound, though these were all important results of his two-year stay in England. What Lawrance Thompson's biography and his edition of the letters make clear is that Frost's sudden emergence as a poet can be traced to a series of poems, written in England and published in *North of Boston*, that were the outcropping of his homesickness for the life and landscape of rural New England. 17

In 1975, I had the good fortune to spend a summer in England, and while there I set for myself the task of investigating the circumstances in which Frost's emergence as a poet took place. Not long after arriving in England, I went with my family on a tour of the Cotswolds, a picturesque range of broad-backed hills west of Oxford. There my attention was caught at once by the distinctive stone walls that lined the fields and roadsides. Here were miles of well-kept walls made of neatly stacked slabs of limestone, which nowhere betrayed signs of an annual upheaval, even though they frequently had been built on the steepest of inclines. If something there is that doesn't love a wall, it seemed to be inoperative in the Cotswolds. 18

A little investigation into these walls served only to heighten my interest. They are called dry stone walls, "dry" because they are made without cement, and they do stand for scores of years, if well made, without need of repair. They are found only in certain parts of England and Scotland (where they are called dry stane dykes) for the obvious reason that they are only put up where limestone is readily available and close to the site of the wall. 19

Had Frost seen these dry stone walls before he wrote "Mending Wall," I wondered. Certainly they would have caught his eye if he had been around them, for they are both very prominent and very attractive features of the rural landscape where they appear. What began as curiosity soon ripened into speculation. If Frost had seen the dry stone walls, he would have made it a point to learn something about them and would have discovered their remarkable properties. If he came to see that stone walls, under certain conditions, can stand for generations without repair, it would have undoubtedly affected the way he conceived and constructed a poem that seems to urge upon its readers the futility of wall-building. He would have been made keenly aware of how limited and parochial the position taken by the speaker in "Mending Wall" can be seen to be. 20

So compelling was this possibility that I conceived an hypothesis about the 21 writing of "Mending Wall": that Frost's experiences in England had brought about a dramatic change in his attitude toward rural New England and the life that he had lived there; for the people and the places that he had left behind thinking he hated, he discovered that he now felt something like affection; he grew homesick for the life that he had so gladly left, and this experience issued in a series of new poems that were far better than anything he had written previously. So much of my theory was simply drawn from the biographical record as it emerges from the published letters and Thompson's biography. "Mending Wall," I now conjectured, could have come to Frost as a reconsideration of his relationship with his former New Hampshire neighbor, Napolean Guay. Nostalgically remembering his neighbor and their spring outings at the wall in conjunction with seeing dry stone walls could have triggered a poem in which his perversity in having made the worse appear the better reasoning was implicitly acknowledged.

A number of problems now presented themselves. If this theory were to hold 22 its own, it would be necessary to show that Frost was at least exposed to dry stone walls before "Mending Wall" was written. If he had brought the poem over to England with him from America, for example, the theory was kaput. But that did not seem to be the case, though it was true of a few *North of Boston* poems. Frost seems to have begun writing the poems for this volume—except for these few earlier poems—in the late fall of 1912, and the completed manuscript was apparently sent to the publisher about a year later. It seemed a reasonable time in which to get Frost and dry stone walls together and to get the poem written. All that was required, I reasoned, was the necessary persistence on my part.

I had the benefit of ideal working conditions for this task, for the summer of 23 1975 was an unprecedented season of glorious sunshine in England, and I was working in the rarefied scholarly atmosphere of the English Reading Room of the Bodleian Library at Oxford. The sunshine was important, incidentally, not just for its effect on the spirit, but because the light in the Bodleian, like its cataloging system, is scandalous by American library standards, and I could not always arrive in time to get a seat by the windows.

The early going was not encouraging. Frost had spent his first year and a 24 half in England—the time during which the *North of Boston* poems were written—in Beaconsfield in Buckinghamshire. Chalk country. Lovely but no limestone, and thus no dry stone walls. No mention of "Mending Wall" could be found in the published letters during this period, and Frost was staying maddeningly close to Beaconsfield, with occasional trips to London, which was only 30 miles away. By August, he had so nearly completed the new book that he was considering various titles for it and had awarded himself and his family a vacation. But now things began to look up, for he announced in letters to his friends that he was going to spend his vacation in Scotland. Having just read a marvellous book on dry stone walls written by a Scotsman, I knew that he was headed in a promising direction. His report on his trip to Scotland, in a letter to Sidney Cox dated *circa* Sept. 15, proved to be all that I could have hoped for. It read in part:

> We are just back from a two week's journey in Scotland . . . The best adventure was the time in Kingsbarns where tourists and summer boarders never come. The common people in the south of England I don't like to have around me. They don't know how to meet you man to man. The people in the north are more like Americans. I wonder whether they made Burns' poems or Burns' poems made them. And there are stone walls (dry stone dykes) in the north; I liked those.

To say that I was elated at finding this passage in Frost's letter to Cox on that bright summer morning in the Bodleian is to seriously understate it. And yet I was curiously troubled by a minor matter. "Could Frost," I wrote in my notebook, "have written 'dry stane dykes'?" This was admittedly trivial, but I felt *certain* that if Frost had taken note of the Scottish form "dykes," as he had, he would likely have used "stane" as well. And certainty exacts its price. I duly noted that the letter was in the Baker Library at Dartmouth and resolved to check it for myself when I got the chance.

I was thus able to establish that Frost had indeed seen the dry stone walls of Great Britain, and he had taken particular note of them. But had he already written "Mending Wall" when he saw them? Just before going to Scotland he had written a letter to his friend John T. Bartlett in which he listed the titles of 12 poems to be included in the new book, which would eventually appear with a total of 17 poems. "Mending Wall" was not on the list. Had it been omitted for some reason, inadvertently left out, or was it more likely that it had not yet been written? I decided that there was no percentage in doubting. [25]

The only other clue that I could find in the published sources was a seemingly unrelated reference, buried deep in the footnotes of Thompson's biography, to a friendship that Frost had formed with a Scots Shakespearian scholar named James Cruickshanks Smith. Thompson mentions this friendship only in connection with Frost's departure from England in 1915, for Smith was one of the people who loaned him money to make the crossing to America. Frost, according to Thompson, had met Smith at Kingsbarns during his 1913 vacation, so I made a note in my notebook to check out the relationship between Frost and Smith. I could find nothing further to shed light on my theory in England, and, in due course, I followed Frost back to America. [26]

V

The following year, in 1976, I went with my family on a bicentennial pilgrimage to the eastern United States, where, with millions of others, we patriotically made the rounds of the essential New England sites: Bunker Hill in [27]

Boston, Concord Bridge at Concord, and the Baker Library at Dartmouth. I may as well confess that, while I was excited about working in the superb collection of original Frost materials that repose in the Baker Library, the prospect that I most keenly anticipated was the examination of Frost's letter to Cox in which he had written of the dry stone dykes, a topic that had become dear to my heart. I was certain that Thompson, in editing the letters, had mistranscribed Frost's handwriting and that the word "stone" would actually be "stane"—and I was right. Thus fortified by a clearcut victory, I settled down in that marvellous reading room (the light was much better than the Bodleian's) to see what I could learn from the remaining material.

There are a great many different collections in the Baker relating to Frost, and I soon discovered that virtually all of the interesting letters by Frost himself had been published by Thompson. The collection that proved to be most productive for my purposes turned out to be the file of letters that Frost received while living in England. In trying to gauge Frost's homesickness while in England, because of its crucial effect on his poetry, I had observed that the mail that he received was of great importance to him. A passage in Frost's correspondence captures his feelings very memorably. "Homesickness makes us news-hungry. Every time the postman bangs the letter-slot-door our mouths go open and our eyes shut like birds' in a nest. . . ." Sitting in the Baker Library, I spent several fascinating hours reading through the mail that had come through that letter-slot-door. 28

Thus engaged in the otherwise despicable practice of reading someone else's mail, I struck gold. For here were the letters written to Frost by the man he had met on his Scottish vacation at Kingsbarns, James Cruickshanks Smith. This first letter acknowledges receipt of Frost's first book, *A Boy's Will*, and its Sept. 15 date indicates that Frost must have sent the book to him immediately after arriving home from his vacation in Kingsbarns. The second letter is dated Nov. 24, 1913, which is very close to the time that the final manuscript of *North of Boston* was to go to the printer. Smith begins by describing the work that he had been doing and then the things that he does for recreation. "I do some pure geometry," he writes, "and learn some Shelley by heart: Geometry is very like poetry for releasing the mind. And that, by one of the natural transitions of which the masters of style have the secret, brings me round to your latest poems—which I herewith return. Now about those poems:— 29

"*Imprimis.*[1] Of course I recognized 'Mending Wall' at once as the poem which had been suggested by our walk at Kingsbarns. . . ." 30

It was not the 4th of July in Hanover, New Hampshire, but at that moment it felt like fireworks to me. 31

---

[1] *Imprimis*: in the first place. [Eds.]

VI

I realize, of course, that it would be premature at this juncture to pronounce: 32 Q.E.D.[2] What I have been able to show is that Frost wrote "Mending Wall" in the fall of 1913 and that it was prompted by something that happened on a walk with J. C. Smith at Kingsbarns, Fifeshire, Scotland, where he had been particularly attracted by dry stone walls. But adding this to what we know about Frost's situation and attitudes at this time, I feel little hesitation in filling in the picture as follows: Frost takes a walk in the countryside with J. C. Smith, who explains dry stone walls to him—how they are built, how durable they are, and how little maintenance they require. Frost responds with a description of the wall on his farm in Derry, N.H., which he shared with his neighbor, Napolean Guay. He describes how he used to argue with Guay each spring about mending the wall, partly out of mischief, partly from an inability to see the point of it all. Possibly he emphasized the contrast between the ingenious arguments of the young schoolteacher and the stubbornly laconic reply of the neighbor. With this dramatic encounter freshly summoned up in his consciousness, Frost returned to Beaconsfield and began working on the poem. His frame of mind is suggested by a remark he made years later: "I wrote the poem 'Mending Wall' thinking of the old wall that I hadn't mended in several years and which must be in a terrible condition. I wrote that poem in England when I was very homesick for my old wall in New England."

I began this essay with the proposition that we are creatures of our own 33 experience. It is certainly true for me, as I have tried to show in shamelessly personal terms. But I want to conclude by suggesting that it was also profoundly true for Frost and that bearing this in mind can help us to gain a truer perspective on "Mending Wall." The poet who had found his subject and was beginning to find success, who was living in England and growing increasingly homesick for a region he thought he despised, saw and understood the world differently from the bitterly discontented schoolteacher he had been a few years before. So much did the young schoolteacher think himself a *victim* of his circumstances that he had begun to believe that the grandfather who had willed him the hated Derry farm had deliberately intended the legacy as a curse. In England, he began to see his experiences in a very different and what we may legitimately call a *liberating* perspective, as is perfectly illustrated in his confessed homesickness for the old wall. The extent of this change is measured rather precisely in "Mending Wall" in the difference between the point of view of the poet, who understands the wisdom of the neighbor's view, and that of the speaker in the poem, who presumably does not. But this can only be grasped by readers who are sufficiently versed in country things to know how to judge the substance

---

[2]Q.E.D.: which was to be demonstrated, an abbreviation of the Latin phrase *quod erat demonstrandum*. [Eds.]

of the issue between them. To be persuaded by the arguments of the speaker is clearly to be misled.

Ironically, it may well be that this sympathetic response to the speaker, which 34 I believe is a function of an urban perspective and essentially misplaced, largely accounts for the poem's popularity. Frost, who is reported to have said that "the poet is entitled to everything that the reader can find in the poem," may have been aware that this was the case, for he deliberately sidestepped a number of opportunities to explain the poem or take sides in the debate. Indeed, he once claimed that he had played "exactly fair" in the poem because he had twice said "Good fences make good neighbors" and twice "Something there is that doesn't love a wall." But this is a perfect example of the puckish answer that Frost liked to give when someone tried to pin him down. (In a poem of 45 lines, the speaker's position is expounded in all but two; and those, setting forth the neighbor's position, are virtually the same.) Whatever disputative equilibrium the poem has may be said to be achieved by a balancing of all the advantages of the speaker—the central point of view, the wit, the humor, the arguments, the invidious depiction of the neighbor—against a simple statement whose full authority is undiminished by all that the speaker can say or do. A more fitting authorial commentary on the poem, to my mind, is a celebrated remark of the mature Frost, which appears in the preface to his *Complete Poems*. He is describing what he calls "the figure a poem makes." "It begins," he says, "in delight and ends in wisdom."

> "Something there is that doesn't love a wall."
> "Good fences make good neighbors."

MENDING WALL

Something there is that doesn't love a wall,
That sends the frozen-ground-swell under it
And spills the upper boulders in the sun,
And makes gaps even two can pass abreast.
The work of hunters is another thing:
I have come after them and made repair
Where they have left not one stone on a stone,
But they would have the rabbit out of hiding,
To please the yelping dogs. The gaps I mean,
No one has seen them made or heard them made,
But at spring mending-time we find them there.
I let my neighbor know beyond the hill;

And on a day we meet to walk the line
And set the wall between us once again.
We keep the wall between us as we go.
To each the boulders that have fallen to each.
And some are loaves and some so nearly balls
We have to use a spell to make them balance:
"Stay where you are until our backs are turned!"
We wear our fingers rough with handling them.
Oh, just another kind of outdoor game,
One on a side. It comes to little more:
There where it is we do not need the wall:
He is all pine and I am apple orchard.
My apple trees will never get across
And eat the cones under his pines, I tell him.
He only says, "Good fences make good neighbors."
Spring is the mischief in me, and I wonder
If I could put a notion in his head:
"*Why* do they make good neighbors? Isn't it
Where there are cows? But here there are no cows.
Before I built a wall I'd ask to know
What I was walling in or walling out,
And to whom I was like to give offense.
Something there is that doesn't love a wall,
That wants it down." I could say "Elves" to him,
But it's not elves exactly, and I'd rather
He said it for himself. I see him there,
Bringing a stone grasped firmly by the top
In each hand, like an old-stone savage armed.
He moves in darkness as it seems to me,
Not of woods only and the shade of trees.
He will not go behind his father's saying,
And he likes having thought of it so well
He says again, "Good fences make good neighbors."

Robert Frost

QUESTIONS

1. Summarize the conventional understanding of "Mending Wall," according to Wilson.

2. What experience leads Wilson to contradict that understanding and replace it with another? Summarize Wilson's interpretation of "Mending Wall."

329

3. What are the two quite different kinds of research that contributed to Wilson's understanding of Frost's poem? What does Wilson search for in the libraries of Oxford and Dartmouth? What does he find?

4. Wilson's essay is interesting for what it demonstrates not only about Frost's poem but also about a certain pleasure that can be part of research and of intellectual inquiry. Outline the steps of Wilson's research. Which moments provide the greatest pleasure? How do they relate to his work as a whole? What picture of himself does he present? What do you suppose motivates him?

5. If good fences make good neighbors in rural life, what makes good neighbors in your community, your dorm, your apartment building, or whatever other living unit you are familiar with? Write an essay explaining what your answer is and how you discovered its importance.

6. Identify a time when your own experience has led you to overturn the accepted understanding of some question. Recount the steps to your discovery, and explain how you composed your alternative understanding.

WHAT HIGH SCHOOL IS

Theodore R. Sizer

*Born in New Haven, Connecticut, and educated at Yale
and Harvard, Theodore R. Sizer has been headmaster at
Phillips Academy, Andover, Dean of the Graduate School
of Education at Harvard University, and Chairman of the
Education Department at Brown University. Besides being
the author of several books on American secondary schools,
in recent years he has also worked on a study of American
high schools sponsored by the National Association of Secondary School Principals and the National Association of
Independent Schools. His book* Horace's Compromise: The
Dilemma of the American High School (1984) *reports the
results of that study. The selection reprinted here is the first
chapter of the second section of that book, "The Program."*

Mark, sixteen and a genial eleventh–grader, rides a bus to Franklin High   1
School, arriving at 7:25. It is an Assembly Day, so the schedule is adapted to
allow for a meeting of the entire school. He hangs out with his friends, first
outside school and then inside, by his locker. He carries a pile of textbooks and
notebooks; in all, it weighs eight and a half pounds.

From 7:30 to 8:19, with nineteen other students, he is in Room 304 for   2
English class. The Shakespeare play being read this year by the eleventh grade
is *Romeo and Juliet*. The teacher, Ms. Viola, has various students in turn take
parts and read out loud. Periodically, she interrupts the (usually halting) reci-
tations to ask whether the thread of the conversation in the play is clear. Mark
is entertained by the stumbling readings of some of his classmates. He hopes
he will not be asked to be Romeo, particularly if his current steady, Sally, is
Juliet. There is a good deal of giggling in class, and much attention paid to who
may be called on next. Ms. Viola reminds the class of a test on this part of the
play to be given next week.

The bell rings at 8:19. Mark goes to the boys' room, where he sees a classmate   3
who he thinks is a wimp but who constantly tries to be a buddy. Mark avoids
the leech by rushing off. On the way, he notices two boys engaged in some sort
of transaction, probably over marijuana. He pays them no attention. 8:24. Typing class. The rows of desks that embrace big office machines are almost filled
before the bell. Mark is uncomfortable here: typing class is girl country. The
teacher constantly threatens what to Mark is a humiliatingly female future:
"Your employer won't like these erasures." The minutes during the period are
spent copying a letter from a handbook onto business stationery. Mark struggles

to keep from looking at his work; the teacher wants him to watch only the material from which he is copying. Mark is frustrated, uncomfortable, and scared that he will not complete his letter by the class's end, which would be embarrassing.

Nine tenths of the students present at school that day are assembled in the auditorium by the 9:18 bell. The dilatory tenth still stumble in, running down aisles. Annoyed class deans try to get the mob settled. The curtains part; the program is a concert by a student rock group. Their electronic gear flashes under the lights, and the five boys and one girl in the group work hard at being casual. Their movements on stage are studiously at three-quarter time, and they chat with one another as though the tumultuous screaming of their schoolmates were totally inaudible. The girl balances on a stool; the boys crank up the music. It is very soft rock, the sanitized lyrics surely cleared with the assistant principal. The girl sings, holding the mike close to her mouth, but can scarcely be heard. Her light voice is tentative, and the lyrics indecipherable. The guitars, amplified, are tuneful, however, and the drums are played with energy.

The students around Mark—all juniors, since they are seated by class— alternatley slouch in their upholstered, hinged seats, talking to one another, or sit forward, leaning on the chair backs in front of them, watching the band. A boy near Mark shouts noisily at the microphone-fondling singer, "Bite it . . . ohhh," and the area around Mark explodes in vulgar male laughter, but quickly subsides. A teacher walks down the aisle. Songs continue, to great applause. Assembly is over at 9:46, two minutes early.

9:53 and biology class. Mark was at a different high school last year and did not take this course there as a tenth-grader. He is in it now, and all but one of his classmates are a year younger than he. He sits on the side, not taking part in the chatter that goes on after the bell. At 9:57, the public address system goes on, with the announcements of the day. After a few words from the principal ("Here's today's cheers and jeers . . . " with a cheer for the winning basketball team and a jeer for the spectators who made a ruckus at the gymnasium), the task is taken over by officers of ASB (Associated Student Bodies). There is an appeal for "bat bunnies." Carnations are for sale by the Girls' League. Miss Indian American is coming. Students are auctioning off their services (background catcalls are heard) to earn money for the prom. Nominees are needed for the ballot for school bachelor and school bachelorette. The announcements end with a "thought for the day. When you throw a little mud, you lose a little ground."

At 10:04 the biology class finally turns to science. The teacher, Mr. Robbins, has placed one of several labeled laboratory specimens—some are pinned in frames, others swim in formaldehyde—on each of the classroom's eight laboratory tables. The three or so students whose chairs circle each of these benches are to study the specimen and make notes about it or drawings of it. After a few minutes each group of three will move to another table. The teacher points out

332

that these specimens are of organisms already studied in previous classes. He says that the period-long test set for the following day will involve observing some of these specimens—then to be without labels—and writing an identifying paragraph on each. Mr. Robbins points out that some of the printed labels ascribe the specimens names different from those given in the textbook. He explains that biologists often give several names to the same organism.

The class now falls to peering, writing, and quiet talking. Mr. Robbins comes over to Mark, and in whispered words asks him to carry a requisition form for science department materials to the business office. Mark, because of his "older" status, is usually chosen by Robbins for this kind of errand. Robbins gives Mark the form and a green hall pass to show to any teacher who might challenge him, on his way to the office, for being out of a classroom. The errand takes Mark four minutes. Meanwhile Mark's group is hard at work but gets to only three of the specimens before the bell rings at 10:42. As the students surge out, Robbins shouts a reminder about a "double" laboratory period on Thursday. 8

Between classes one of the seniors asks Mark whether he plans to be a candidate for schoolwide office next year. Mark says no. He starts to explain. The 10:47 bell rings, meaning that he is late for French class. 9

There are fifteen students in Monsieur Bates's language class. He hands out tests taken the day before: "*C'est bien fait, Etienne . . . c'est mieux, Marie . . . Tch, tch, Robert . . .*" Mark notes his C+ and peeks at the A- in front of Susanna, next to him. The class has been assigned seats by M. Bates; Mark resents sitting next to prissy, brainy Susanna. Bates starts by asking a student to read a question and give the correct answer. "*James, question un.*" James haltingly reads the question and gives an answer that Bates, now speaking English, says is incomplete. In due course: "*Mark, question cinq.*" Mark does his bit, and the sequence goes on, the eight quiz questions and answers filling about twenty minutes of time. 10

"Turn to page forty-nine. *Maintenant, lisez après moi . . .*" and Bates reads a sentence and has the class echo it. Mark is embarrassed by this and mumbles with a barely audible sound. Others, like Susanna, keep the decibel count up, so Mark can hide. This I–say–you–repeat drill is interrupted once by the public address system, with an announcement about a meeting for the cheerleaders. Bates finishes the class, almost precisely at the bell, with a homework assignment. The students are to review these sentences for a brief quiz the following day. Mark takes note of the assignment, because he knows that tomorrow will be a day of busy-work in French class. Much though he dislikes oral drills, they are better than the workbook stuff that Bates hands out. Write, write, write, for Bates to throw away, Mark thinks. 11

11:36. Down to the cafeteria, talking noisily, hanging out, munching. Getting to Room 104 by 12:17: U.S. history. The teacher is sitting cross-legged on his desk when Mark comes in, heatedly arguing with three students over the fracas that had followed the previous night's basketball game. The teacher, Mr. 12

Suslovic, while agreeing that the spectators from their school certainly were provoked, argues that they should neither have been so obviously obscene in yelling at the opposing cheerleaders nor have allowed Coke cans to be rolled out on the floor. The three students keep saying that "it isn't fair." Apparently they and some others had been assigned "Saturday mornings" (detentions) by the principal for the ruckus.

At 12:34, the argument appears to subside. The uninvolved students, in- 13 cluding Mark, are in their seats, chatting amiably. Mr. Suslovic climbs off his desk and starts talking: "We've almost finished this unit, chapters nine and ten . . . " The students stop chattering among themselves and turn toward Suslovic. Several slouch down in their chairs. Some open notebooks. Most have the five-pound textbook on their desks.

Suslovic lectures on the cattle drives, from north Texas to railroads west of 14 St. Louis. He breaks up this narrative with questions ("Why were the railroad lines laid largely east to west?"), directed at nobody in particular and eventually answered by Suslovic himself. Some students take notes. Mark doesn't. A student walks in the open door, hands Mr. Suslovic a list, and starts whispering with him. Suslovic turns from the class and hears out this messenger. He then asks, "Does anyone know where Maggie Sharp is?" Some one answers, "Sick at home"; someone else says, "I thought I saw her at lunch." Genial consternation. Finally Suslovic tells the messenger, "Sorry, we can't help you," and returns to the class: "Now, where were we?" He goes on for some minutes. The bell rings. Suslovic forgets to give the homework assignment.

1:11 and Algebra II. There is a commotion in the hallway: someone's locker 15 is rumored to have been opened by the assistant principal and a narcotics agent. In the five-minute passing time, Mark hears the story three times and three ways. A locker had been broken into by another student. It was Mr. Gregory and a narc. It was the cops, and they did it without Gregory's knowing. Mrs. Ames, the mathematics teacher, has not heard anything about it. Several of the nineteen students try to tell her and start arguing among themselves. "O.K., that's enough." She hands out the day's problem, one sheet to each student. Mark sees with dismay that it is a single, complicated "word" problem about some train that, while traveling at 84 mph, due west, passes a car that was going due east at 55mph. Mark struggles: Is it $d = rt$ or $t = rd$? The class becomes quiet, writing, while Mrs. Ames writes some additional, short problems on the blackboard. "Time's up." A sigh; most students still writing. A muffled "Shit." Mrs. Ames frowns. "Come on, now." She collects papers, but it takes four minutes for her to corral them all.

"Copy down the problems from the board." A minute passes. "William, try 16 number one." William suggests an approach. Mrs. Ames corrects and cajoles, and William finally gets it right. Mark watches two kids to his right passing notes; he tries to read them, but the handwriting is illegible from his distance. He hopes he is not called on, and he isn't. Only three students are asked to puzzle out an answer. The bell rings at 2:00. Mrs. Ames shouts a homework assignment over the resulting hubbub.

Mark leaves his books in his locker. He remembers that he has homework, 17 but figures that he can do it during English class the next day. He knows that there will be an in-class presentation of one of the *Romeo and Juliet* scenes and that he will not be in it. The teacher will not notice his homework writing, or won't do anything about it if she does.

Mark passes various friends heading toward the gym, members of the bas- 18 ketball teams. Like most students, Mark isn't an active school athlete. However, he is associated with the yearbook staff. Although he is not taking "Yearbook" for credit as an English course, he is contributing photographs. Mark takes twenty minutes checking into the yearbook staff's headquarters (the classroom of its faculty adviser) and getting some assignments of pictures from his boss, the senior who is the photography editor. Mark knows that if he pleases his boss and the faculty adviser, he'll take that editor's post for the next year. He'll get English credit for his work then.

After gossiping a bit with the yearbook staff, Mark will leave school by 2:35 19 and go home. His grocery market bagger's job is from 4:45 to 8:00, the rush hour for the store. He'll have a snack at 4:30, and his mother will save him some supper to eat at 8:30. She will ask whether he has any homework, and he'll tell her no. Tomorrow, and virtually every other tomorrow, will be the same for Mark, save for the lack of the assembly: each period then will be five minutes longer.

Most Americans have an uncomplicated vision of what secondary education 20 should be. Their conception of high school is remarkably uniform across the country, a striking fact, given the size and diversity of the United States and the politically decentralized character of the schools. This uniformity is of several generations' standing. It has, however, two appearances, each quite different from the other, one of words and the other of practice, a world of political rhetoric and Mark's world.

A California high school's general goals, set out in 1979, could serve equally 21 well most of America's high schools, public and private. This school had as its ends:

· Fundamental scholastic achievement . . . to acquire knowledge and share in the traditionally accepted academic fundamentals . . . to develop the ability to make decisions, to solve problems, to reason independently, and to accept responsibility for self-evaluation and continuing self-improvement.
· Career and economic competence . . .
· Citizenship and civil responsibility . . .
· Competence in human and social relations . . .
· Moral and ethical values . . .

- Self-realization and mental and physical health . . .
- Aesthetic awareness . . .
- Cultural diversity . . .[1]

In addition to its optimistic rhetoric, what distinguishes this list is its comprehensiveness. The high school is to touch most aspects of an adolescent's existence—mind, body, morals, values, career. No one of these areas is given especial prominence. School people arrogate to themselves an obligation to all.

An example of the wide acceptability of these goals is found in the courts. 22
Forced to present a detailed definition of "thorough and efficient education," elementary as well as secondary, a West Virginia judge sampled the best of conventional wisdom and concluded that

> there are eight general elements of a thorough and efficient system of education: (a) Literacy, (b) The ability to add, subtract, multiply, and divide numbers, (c) Knowledge of government to the extent the child will be equipped as a citizen to make informed choices among persons and issues that affect his own governance, (d) Self-knowledge and knowledge of his or her total environment to allow the child to intelligently choose life work—to know his or her options, (e) Work-training and advanced academic training as the child may intelligently choose, (f) Recreational pursuits, (g) Interests in all creative arts such as music, theater, literature, and the visual arts, and (h) Social ethics, both behavioral and abstract, to facilitate compatibility with others in this society.[2]

That these eight—now powerfully part of the debate over the purpose and practice of education in West Virginia—are reminiscent of the influential list, "The Seven Cardinal Principles of Secondary Education," promulgated in 1918 by the National Education Association, is no surprise.[3] The rhetoric of high school purpose has been uniform and consistent for decades. Americans agree on the goals for their high schools.

That agreement is convenient, but it masks the fact that virtually all the 23
words in these goal statements beg definition. Some schools have labored long to identify specific criteria beyond them; the result has been lists of daunting pseudospecificity and numbing earnestness. However, most leave the words undefined and let the momentum of traditional practice speak for itself. That

---

[1]Shasta High School, Redding, California. An eloquent and analogous statement, "The Essentials of Education," one stressing explicitly the "interdependence of skills and content" that is implicit in the Shasta High School statement, was issued in 1980 by as coalition of education associations. Organizations for the Essentials of Education (Urbana, Illinois).

[2]Judge Arthur M. Recht, in his order resulting from *Pauley* v. *Kelly*, 1979, as reprinted in *Education Week*, May 26, 1982, p. 10. See also, in *Education Week*, January 16, 1983, pp. 21, 24, Jonathan P. Sher, "The Struggle to Fulfill at Judicial Mandate: How Not to 'Reconstruct' Education in W. Va."

[3]Bureau of Education, Department of the Interior, "Cardinal Principles of Secondary Education: A Report of the Commission on the Reorganization of Secondary Education, appointed by the National Education Association," *Bulletin*, no. 35 (Washington: U.S. Government Printing Office, 1918).

is why analyzing how Mark spends his time is important: from watching him one uncovers the important purposes of education, the ones that shape practice. Mark's day is similar to that of other high school students across the country, as similar as the rhetoric of one goal statement to others'. Of course, there are variations, but the extent of consistency in the shape of school routine for a large and diverse adolescent population is extraordinary, indicating more graphically than any rhetoric the measure of agreement in America about what one does in high school, and, by implication, what it is for.

The basic organizing structures in schools are familiar. Above all, students   24
are grouped by age (that is, freshman, sophomore, junior, senior), and all are expected to take precisely the same time—around 720 school days over four years, to be precise—to meet the requirements for a diploma. When one is out of his grade level, he can feel odd, as Mark did in his biology class. The goals are the same for all, and the means to achieve them are also similar.

Young males and females are treated remarkably alike; the schools' goals are   25
the same for each gender. In execution, there are differences, as those pressing sex discrimination suits have made educators intensely aware. The students in metalworking classes are mostly male; those in home economics, mostly female. But it is revealing how much less sex discrimination there is in high schools than in other American institutions. For many young women, the most liberated hours of their week are in school.

School is to be like a job: you start in the morning and end in the afternoon,   26
five days a week. You don't get much of a lunch hour, so you go home early, unless you are an athlete or are involved in some special school or extracurricular activity. School is conceived of as the children's workplace, and it takes young people off parents' hands and out of the labor market during prime-time work hours. Not surprisingly, many students see going to school as little more than a dogged necessity. They perceive the day-to-day routine, a Minnesota study reports, as one of "boredom and lethargy." One of the students summarizes: School is "boring, restless, tiresome, puts ya to sleep, tedious, monotonous, pain in the neck."[4]

The school schedule is a series of units of time: the clock is king. The base   27
time block is about fifty minutes in length. Some schools, on what they call modular scheduling, split that fifty-minute block into two or even three pieces. Most schools have double periods for laboratory work, especially in the sciences, or four-hour units for the small numbers of students involved in intensive vocational or other work-study programs. The flow of all school activity arises from or is blocked by these time units. "How much time do I have with my kids" is the teacher's key question.

---

[4]Diane Hedin, Paula Simon, and Michael Robin, *Minnesota Youth Poll: Youth's Views on School and School Discipline*, Minnesota Report 184 (1983), Agricultural Experiment Station, University of Minnesota, p. 13.

Because there are many claims for those fifty–minute blocks, there is little   28
time set aside for rest between them, usually no more than three to ten minutes,
depending on how big the school is and, consequently, how far students and
teachers have to walk from class to class. As a result, there is a frenetic quality
to the school day, a sense of sustained restlessness. For the adolescents, there
are frequent changes of room and fellow students, each change giving tempting
opportunities for distraction, which are stoutly resisted by teachers. Some schools
play soft music during these "passing times," to quiet the multitude, one principal told me.

Many teachers have a chance for a coffee break. Few students do. In some   29
city schools where security is a problem, students must be in class for seven
consecutive periods, interrupted by a heavily monitored twenty-minute lunch
period for small groups, starting as early as 10:30 A.M. and running to after 1:00
P.M.. A high premium is placed on punctuality and on "being where you're
supposed to be." Obviously, a low premium is placed on reflection and repose.
The students rushes from class to class to collect knowledge. Savoring it, it is
implied, is not to be done much in school, nor is such meditation really much
admired. The picture that these familiar patterns yield is that of an academic
supermarket. The purpose of going to school is to pick things up, in an organized
and predictable way, the faster the better.

What is supposed to be picked up is remarkably consistent among all sorts   30
of high schools. Most schools specifically mandate three out of every five courses
a student selects. Nearly all of these mandates fall into five areas—English,
social studies, mathematics, science, and physical education. On the average,
English is required to be taken each year, social studies and physical education
three out of the four high school years, and mathematics and science one or
two years. Trends indicate that in the mid-eighties there is likely to be an
increase in the time allocated to these last two subjects. Most students take
classes in these four major academic areas beyond the minimum requirements,
sometimes in such special areas as journalism and "yearbook," offshoots of
English departments.[5]

Press most adults about what high school is for, and you hear these subjects   31
listed. *High school? That's where you learn English and math and that sort of
thing.* Ask students, and you get the same answer. High school is to "teach"
these "subjects."

What is often absent is any definition of these subjects or any rationale for   32
them. They are just there, labels. Under those labels lie a multitude of things.
A great deal of material is supposed to be "covered"; most of these courses are
surveys, great sweeps of the stuff of their parent disciplines.

While there is often a sequence *within* subjects—algebra before trigonometry,   33

[5] I am indepted to Harold F. Sizer and Lyde E. Sizer for a survey of the diploma requirements
of fifty representative secondary schools, completed for A Study of High Schools.

"first-year" French before "second-year" French—there is rarely a coherent relationship or sequence *across* subjects. Even the most logically related matters—reading ability as a precondition for the reading of history books, and certain mathematical concepts or skills before the study of some of physics—are only loosely coordinated, if at all. There is little demand for a synthesis of it all; English, mathematics, and the rest are discrete items, to be picked up individually. The incentive for picking them up is largely through tests and, with success at these, in credits earned.

Coverage within subjects is the key priority. If some imaginative teacher 34 makes a proposal to force the marriage of, say, mathematics and physics or to require some culminating challenges to students to use several subjects in the solution of a complex problem, and if this proposal will take "time" away from other things, opposition is usually phrased in terms of what may be thus forgone. If we do that, we'll have to give up colonial history. We won't be able to get to programming. We'll not be able to read *Death of a Salesman*. There isn't time. The protesters usually win out.

The subjects come at a student like Mark in random order, a kaleidoscope 35 of worlds: algebraic formulae to poetry to French verbs to Ping–Pong to the War of the Spanish Succession, all before lunch. Pupils are to pick up these things. Tests measure whether the picking up has been successful.

The lack of connection between stated goals, such as those of the California 36 high school cited earlier, and the goals inherent in school practice is obvious and, curiously, tolerated. Most striking is the gap between statements about "self–realization and mental and physical growth" or "moral and ethical values"—common rhetoric in school documents—and practice. Most physical education programs have neither the time nor the focus really to ensure fitness. Mental health is rarely defined. Neither are ethical values, save at the negative extremes, such as opposition to assault or dishonesty. Nothing in the regimen of a day like Mark's signals direct or implicit teaching in this area. The "schoolboy code" (not ratting on a fellow student) protects the marijuana pusher, and a leechlike associate is shrugged off without concern. The issue of the locker search was pushed aside, as not appropriate for class time.

Most students, like Mark, go to class in groups of twenty to twenty-seven 37 students. The expected attendance in some schools, particularly those in low–income areas, is usually higher, often thirty-five students per class, but high absentee rates push the actual numbers down. About twenty–five per class is an average figure for expected attendance, and the actual numbers are somewhat lower. There are remarkably few students who go to class in groups much larger or smaller than twenty–five. [6]

A student such as Mark sees five or six teachers per day; their differing styles 38

---

[6]Education Research Service, Inc. *Class Size: A Summary of Research* (Arlington, Virginia, 1978); and *Class Size Research: A Critique of Recent Meta-Analyses* (Arlington, Virginia, 1980).

and expectations are part of his kaleidoscope. High school staffs are highly specialized: guidance counselors rarely teach mathematics, mathematics teachers rarely teach English, principals rarely do any classroom instruction. Mark, then, is known a little bit by a number of people, each of whom sees him in one specialized situation. No one may know him as a "whole person"—unless he becomes a special problem or has special needs.

Save in extracurricular or coaching situations, such as in athletics, drama,   39 or shop classes, there is little opportunity for sustained conversation between student and teacher. The mode is a one-sentence or two-sentence exchange: *Mark, when was Grover Cleveland president?* Let's see, was 1890 . . . or something . . . wasn't he the one . . . he was elected twice, wasn't he . . . *Yes* . . . *Gloria, can you get the dates right?* Dialogue is strikingly absent, and as a result the opportunity of teachers to challenge students' ideas in a systematic and logical way is limited. Given the rushed, full quality of the school day, it can seldom happen. One must infer that careful probing of students' thinking is not a high priority. How one gains (to quote the California school's statement of goals again) "the ability to make decisions, to solve problems, to reason independently, and to accept responsibility for self–evaluation and continuing self–improvment" without being challenged is difficult to imagine. One certainly doesn't learn these things merely from lectures and textbooks.

Most schools are nice places. Mark and his friends enjoy being in theirs.   40 The adults who work in schools generally like adolescents. The academic pressures are limited, and the accommodations to students are substantial. For example, if many members of an English class have jobs after school, the English teacher's expectations for them are adjusted, downward. In a word, school is sensitively accommodating, as long as students are punctual, where they are supposed to be, and minimally dutiful about picking things up from the clutch of courses in which they enroll.

This characterization is not pretty, but it is accurate, and it serves to describe   41 the vast majority of American secondary schools. "Taking subjects" in a systematized, conveyer–belt way is what one does in high school. That this process is, in substantial respects, not related to the rhetorical purposes of education is tolerated by most people, perhaps because they do not really either believe in those ill–defined goals or, in their heart of hearts, believe that schools can or should even try to achieve them. The students are happy taking subjects. The parents are happy, because that's what they did in high school. The rituals, the most important of which is graduation, remain intact. The adolescents are supervised, safely and constructively most of the time, during the morning and afternoon hours, and they are off the labor market. That is what high school is all about.

QUESTIONS

1. The first half of this essay (the first nineteen paragraphs, to be exact) is a report. What do you think of this report? Given your own experience, how accurate is it? What attitude does the report convey, or is it objective?

2. Paragraph 19 is the conclusion of the report. It ends the story of Mark's day. Does it draw or imply any conclusions from the events reported?

3. How is the explanatory section of the essay (paragraphs 20 through 41) organized? If the first subtopic discussed is the goals of high school, what are the other subtopics?

4. What is the major conclusion of this explanation? To what extent do you agree with the last sentence of the essay and what it implies?

5. How does the report (paragraphs 1 through 19) function in the explanation that follows? What would be lost if the report were omitted? In considering how the two sections of the essay relate, note especially places where the explanation specifically refers to the report.

6. If you have a different view of high school, or went to a different kind of school, write an essay that is organized like Sizer's but that presents your own report and explanation of what school is.

7. Using the basic outline of Sizer's essay, write your own explanation of the workings of some institution: store, family, church or temple, club, team, or whatever else you know well. Think of your project in terms of Sizer's title: "What X Is."

AMERICA REVISED
Frances FitzGerald

Frances FitzGerald (b. 1940), an American free-lance jour-
nalist, won a Pulitzer Prize in general nonfiction for her
reporting of the Vietnam War. Her writing about the war,
first published in The New Yorker, *was collected in* Fire in
the Lake: The Vietnamese and Americans in Vietnam *(1973).*
She then turned to the study of American history and an
investigation of how history books change with the needs
and prejudices of the time. This work resulted in Fitz-
Gerald's second book, America Revised *(1979), where the*
following essay appears as the first chapter.

Those of us who grew up in the fifties believed in the permanence of our   1
American-history textbooks. To us as children, those texts were the truth of
things: they were American history. It was not just that we read them before we
understood that not everything that is printed is the truth, or the whole truth.
It was that they, much more than other books, had the demeanor and trappings
of authority. They were weighty volumes. They spoke in measured cadences:
imperturbable, humorless, and as distant as Chinese emperors. Our teachers
treated them with respect, and we paid them abject homage by memorizing a
chapter a week. But now the textbook histories have changed, some of them to
such an extent that an adult would find them unrecognizable.

One current junior-high-school American history begins with a story about   2
a Negro cowboy called George McJunkin. It appears that when McJunkin was
riding down a lonely trail in New Mexico one cold spring morning in 1925 he
discovered a mound containing bones and stone implements, which scientists
later proved belonged to an Indian civilization ten thousand years old. The book
goes on to say that scientists now believe there were people in the Americas at
least twenty thousand years ago. It discusses the Aztec, Mayan, and Incan
civilizations and the meaning of the word "culture" before introducing the
European explorers.[1]

Another history text—this one for the fifth grade—begins with the story of   3
how Henry B. Gonzalez, who is a member of Congress from Texas, learned
about his own nationality. When he was ten years old, his teacher told him he
was an American because he was born in the United States. His grandmother,
however, said, "The cat was born in the oven. Does that make him bread?"
After reporting that Mr. Gonzalez eventually went to college and law school,

---

[1] Wood, Gabriel, and Biller, *America* (1975), p. 3.

the book explains that "the melting pot idea hasn't worked out as some thought it would," and that now "some people say that the people of the United States are more like a salad bowl than a melting pot."[2]

Poor Columbus! He is a minor character now, a walk-on in the middle of   4 American history. Even those books that have not replaced his picture with a Mayan temple or an Iroquois mask do not credit him with discovering America—even for the Europeans. The Vikings, they say, preceded him to the New World, and after that the Europeans, having lost or forgotten their maps, simply neglected to cross the ocean again for five hundred years. Columbus is far from being the only personage to have suffered from time and revision. Captain John Smith, Daniel Boone, and Wild Bill Hickok—the great self-promoters of American history—have all but disappeared, taking with them a good deal of the romance of the American frontier. General Custer has given way to Chief Crazy Horse; General Eisenhower no longer liberates Europe single-handed; and, indeed, most generals, even to Washington and Lee, have faded away, as old soldiers do, giving place to social reformers such as William Lloyd Garrison and Jacob Riis. A number of black Americans have risen to prominence: not only George Washington Carver but Frederick Douglass and Martin Luther King, Jr. W. E. B. Du Bois now invariably accompanies Booker T. Washington. In addition, there is a mystery man called Crispus Attucks, a fugitive slave about whom nothing seems to be known for certain except that he was a victim of the Boston Massacre and thus became one of the first casualties of the American Revolution. Thaddeus Stevens has been reconstructed[3]—his character changed, as it were, from black to white, from cruel and vindictive to persistent and sincere. As for Teddy Roosevelt, he now champions the issue of conservation instead of charging up San Juan Hill. No single President really stands out as a hero, but all Presidents—except certain unmentionables in the second half of the nineteenth century—seem to have done as well as could be expected, given difficult circumstances.

Of course, when one thinks about it, it is hardly surprising that modern   5 scholarship and modern perspectives have found their way into children's books. Yet the changes remain shocking. Those who in the sixties complained of the bland optimism, the chauvinism, and the materialism of their old civics texts did so in the belief that, for all their protests, the texts would never change. The thought must have had something reassuring about it, for that generation never noticed when its complaints began to take effect and the songs about

---

[2]King and Anderson, *The United States* (sixth level), Houghton Mifflin Social Studies Program (1976), pp. 15–16.

[3]Thaddeus Stevens (1792–1868): Republican congressman from Pennsylvania. A leader in the House during and after the Civil War, he was a determined abolitionist who hated the South and violently opposed Lincoln's moderate reconstruction plan. Stevens dominated the committee that impeached Andrew Johnson.

radioactive rainfall and houses made of ticky-tacky began to appear in the textbooks. But this is what happened.

The history texts now hint at a certain level of unpleasantness in American   6
history. Several books, for instance, tell the story of Ishi, the last "wild" Indian in the continental United States, who, captured in 1911 after the massacre of his tribe, spent the final four and a half years of his life in the University of California's museum of anthropology, in San Francisco. At least three books show the same stunning picture of the breaker boys, the child coal miners of Pennsylvania—ancient children with deformed bodies and blackened faces who stare stupidly out from the entrance to a mine. One book quotes a soldier on the use of torture in the American campaign to pacify the Philippines at the beginning of the century. A number of books say that during the American Revolution the patriots tarred and feathered those who did not support them, and drove many of the loyalists from the country. Almost all the present-day history books note that the United States interned Japanese-Americans in detention camps during the Second World War.

Ideologically speaking, the histories of the fifties were implacable, seamless.   7
Inside their covers, America was perfect: the greatest nation in the world, and the embodiment of democracy, freedom, and technological progress. For them, the country never changed in any important way: its values and its political institutions remained constant from the time of the American Revolution. To my generation—the children of the fifties—these texts appeared permanent just because they were so self-contained. Their orthodoxy, it seemed, left no handholds for attack, no lodging for decay. Who, after all, would dispute the wonders of technology or the superiority of the English colonists over the Spanish? Who would find fault with the pastorale of the West or the Old South? Who would question the anti-Communist crusade? There was, it seemed, no point in comparing these visions with reality, since they were the public truth and were thus quite irrelevant to what existed and to what anyone privately believed. They were—or so it seemed—the permanent expression of mass culture in America.

But now the texts have changed, and with them the country that American   8
children are growing up into. The society that was once uniform is now a patchwork of rich and poor, old and young, men and women, blacks, whites, Hispanics, and Indians. The system that ran so smoothly by means of the Constitution under the guidance of benevolent conductor Presidents is now a rattletrap affair. The past is no highway to the present; it is a collection of issues and events that do not fit together and that lead in no single direction. The word "progress" has been replaced by the word "change": children, the modern texts insist, should learn history so that they can adapt to the rapid changes taking place around them. History is proceeding in spite of us. The present, which was once portrayed in the concluding chapters as a peaceful haven of scientific advances and Presidential inaugurations, is now a tangle of problems: race problems, urban problems, foreign-policy problems, problems of pollution,

poverty, energy depletion, youthful rebellion, assassination, and drugs. Some books illustrate these problems dramatically. One, for instance, contains a picture of a doll half buried in a mass of untreated sewage; the caption reads, "Are we in danger of being overwhelmed by the products of our society and wastage created by their production? Would you agree with this photographer's interpretation?"[4] Two books show the same picture of an old black woman sitting in a straight chair in a dingy room, her hands folded in graceful resignation;[5] the surrounding text discusses the problems faced by the urban poor and by the aged who depend on Social Security. Other books present current problems less starkly. One of the texts concludes sagely:

> Problems are part of life. Nations face them, just as people face them, and try to solve them. And today's Americans have one great advantage over past generations. Never before have Americans been so well equipped to solve their problems. They have today the means to conquer poverty, disease, and ignorance. The technetronic age has put that power into their hands.[6]

Such passages have a familiar ring. Amid all the problems, the deus ex machina of science still dodders around in the gloaming of pious hope.

Even more surprising than the emergence of problems is the discovery that the great unity of the texts has broken. Whereas in the fifties all texts represented the same political view, current texts follow no pattern of orthodoxy. Some books, for instance, portray civil-rights legislation as a series of actions taken by a wise, paternal government; others convey some suggestion of the social upheaval involved and make mention of such people as Stokely Carmichael and Malcolm X. In some books, the Cold War has ended; in others, it continues, with Communism threatening the free nations of the earth.

The political diversity in the books is matched by a diversity of pedagogical approach. In addition to the traditional narrative histories, with their endless streams of facts, there are so-called "discovery," or "inquiry," texts, which deal with a limited number of specific issues in American history. These texts do not pretend to cover the past; they focus on particular topics, such as "stratification in Colonial society" or "slavery and the American Revolution," and illustrate them with documents from primary and secondary sources. The chapters in these books amount to something like case studies, in that they include testimony from people with different perspectives or conflicting views on a single subject. In addition, the chapters provide background information, explanatory notes, and a series of questions for the student. The questions are the heart of the matter, for when they are carefully selected they force students to think much as historians think: to define the point of view of the speaker, analyze the

---

[4]Sellers et al., *As It Happened* (1975), p. 812.
[5]Graff, *The Free and the Brave*, 2nd ed. (1972), p. 696; and Graff and Krout, *The Adventure*, 2nd ed. (1973), p. 784.
[6]Wood, Gabriel, and Biller, *America* (1975), p. 812.

ideas presented, question the relationship between events, and so on. One text, for example, quotes Washington, Jefferson, and John Adams on the question of foreign alliances and then asks, "What did John Adams assume that the international situation would be after the American Revolution? What did Washington's attitude toward the French alliance seem to be? How do you account for his attitude?" Finally, it asks, "Should a nation adopt a policy toward alliances and cling to it consistently, or should it vary its policies toward other countries as circumstances change?"[7] In these books, history is clearly not a list of agreed-upon facts or a sermon on politics but a babble of voices and a welter of events which must be ordered by the historian.

In matters of pedagogy, as in matters of politics, there are not two sharply differentiated categories of books; rather, there is a spectrum. Politically, the books run from moderate left to moderate right; pedagogically, they run from the traditional history sermons, through a middle ground of narrative texts with inquiry-style questions and of inquiry texts with long stretches of narrative, to the most rigorous of case-study books. What is common to the current texts— and makes all of them different from those of the fifties—is their engagement with the social sciences. In eighth-grade histories, the "concepts" of social science make fleeting appearances. But these "concepts" are the very foundation stones of various elementary-school social-studies series. The 1970 Harcourt Brace Jovanovich series, for example, boasts in its preface of "a horizontal base or ordering of conceptual schemes" to match its "vertical arm of behavioral themes."[8] What this means is not entirely clear, but the books do proceed from easy questions to hard ones, such as—in the sixth-grade book—"How was interaction between merchants and citizens different in the Athenian and Spartan social systems?" Virtually all the American-history texts for older children include discussions of "role," "status," and "culture." Some of them stage debates between eminent social scientists in roped-off sections of the text; some include essays on economics or sociology; some contain pictures and short biographies of social scientists of both sexes and of diverse races. Many books seem to accord social scientists a higher status than American Presidents.

Quite as striking as these political and pedagogical alterations is the change in the physical appearance of the texts. The schoolbooks of the fifties showed some effort in the matter of design: they had maps, charts, cartoons, photographs, and an occasional four-color picture to break up the columns of print. But beside the current texts they look as naïve as Soviet fashion magazines. The print in the fifties books is heavy and far too black, the colors muddy. The photographs are conventional news shots—portraits of Presidents in three-quarters profile, posed "action" shots of soldiers. The other illustrations tend to be Socialist-realist-style drawings (there are a lot of hefty farmers with hoes in the

11

12

[7]Fenton, gen. ed., A New History of the United States, grade eleven (1969), p. 170.
[8]Brandwein et al., The Social Sciences (1975), introductions to all books.

Colonial-period chapters) or incredibly vulgar made-for-children paintings of patriotic events. One painting shows Columbus standing in full court dress on a beach in the New World from a perspective that could have belonged only to the Arawaks.[9] By contrast, the current texts are paragons of sophisticated modern design. They look not like *People* or *Family Circle* but, rather, like *Architectural Digest* or *Vogue*. One of them has an Abstract Expressionist design on its cover, another a Rauschenberg-style collage, a third a reproduction of an American primitive painting. Inside, almost all of them have a full-page reproduction of a painting of the New York school—a Jasper Johns flag, say, or "The Boston Massacre," by Larry Rivers. But these reproductions are separated only with difficulty from the over-all design, for the time charts in the books look like Noland stripe paintings, and the distribution charts are as punctilious as Albers' squares in their color gradings. The amount of space given to illustrations is far greater than it was in the fifties; in fact, in certain "slow-learner" books the pictures far outweigh the text in importance. However, the illustrations have a much greater historical value. Instead of made-up paintings or anachronistic sketches, there are cartoons, photographs, and paintings drawn from the periods being treated. The chapters on the Colonial period will show, for instance, a ship's carved prow, a Revere bowl, a Copley painting—a whole gallery of Early Americana. The nineteenth century is illustrated with nineteenth-century cartoons and photographs—and the photographs are all of high artistic quality. As for the twentieth-century chapters, they are adorned with the contents of a modern-art museum.

The use of all this art and high-quality design contains some irony. The nineteenth-century photographs of child laborers or urban slum apartments are so beautiful that they transcend their subjects. To look at them, or at the Victor Gatto painting of the Triangle shirtwaist-factory fire, is to see not misery or ugliness but an art object. In the modern chapters, the contrast between style and content is just as great: the color photographs of junkyards or polluted rivers look as enticing as *Gourmet*'s photographs of food. The book that is perhaps the most stark in its description of modern problems illustrates the horrors of nuclear testing with a pretty Ben Shahn picture of the Bikini explosion,[10] and the potential for global ecological disaster with a color photograph of the planet swirling its mantle of white clouds.[11] Whereas in the nineteen-fifties the texts were childish in the sense that they were naïve and clumsy, they are now childish in the sense that they are polymorphous-perverse. American history is not dull any longer; it is a sensuous experience.

The surprise that adults feel in seeing the changes in history texts must come from the lingering hope that there is, somewhere out there, an objective truth.

---

[9]Arawaks: American Indians then inhabiting the Caribbean area. [Eds.]

[10]Bikini explosion: the Bikini atoll in the Pacific Ocean was the site of American nuclear-bomb testing from 1946 to 1958. [Eds.]

[11]Ver Steeg and Hofstadter, *A People* (1974), pp. 722–23.

The hope is, of course, foolish. All of us children of the twentieth century know, or should know, that there are no absolutes in human affairs, and thus there can be no such thing as perfect objectivity. We know that each historian in some degree creates the world anew and that all history is in some degree contemporary history. But beyond this knowledge there is still a hope for some reliable authority, for some fixed stars in the universe. We may know journalists cannot be wholly unbiased and that "balance" is an imaginary point between two extremes, and yet we hope that Walter Cronkite will tell us the truth of things. In the same way, we hope that our history will not change—that we learned the truth of things as children. The texts, with their impersonal voices, encourage this hope, and therefore it is particularly disturbing to see how they change, and how fast.

Slippery history! Not every generation but every few years the content of American-history books for children changes appreciably. Schoolbooks are not, like trade books,[12] written and left to their fate. To stay in step with the cycles of "adoption" in school districts across the country, the publishers revise most of their old texts or substitute new ones every three or four years. In the process of revision, they not only bring history up to date but make changes—often substantial changes—in the body of the work. History books for children are thus more contemporary than any other form of history. How should it be otherwise? Should students read histories written ten, fifteen, thirty years ago? In theory, the system is reasonable—except that each generation of children reads only one generation of schoolbooks. That transient history is those children's history forever—their particular version of America.

QUESTIONS

1. What does FitzGerald say are the main differences between the history textbooks of the fifties and those of today? What are the main points of her comparison?

2. What evidence does FitzGerald offer to support her explanation of these differences? Can you think of other illustrations that she might have used, perhaps from a textbook that you have read?

3. FitzGerald identifies her primary audience in the first sentence: "Those of us who grew up in the fifties believed in the permanence of our American-history textbooks." What techniques does FitzGerald use to involve that audience? What role is she inviting her readers to play?

4. Assuming you did not grow up in the fifties, how do you relate to this essay? Are you left out, or does FitzGerald include you in some way? At what other times have you not been directly addressed as a primary audience but been spoken to clearly and forcefully nevertheless?

5. How does FitzGerald organize her discussion of the textbooks? What topics does

---

[12]trade books: not textbooks but books written for a general audience. [Eds.]

she discuss? How does one topic connect to the next? How does she organize the movement back and forth between current textbooks and those of the fifties?

6. What are some of the major historical events in your lifetime? Which of these
events are likely to remain classified as "major historical events"? Why is this likely?
How might these events be revised and presented in history textbooks a hundred years
from now?

7. See if your library has some older textbooks for a course you are taking or have
taken. If so, compare your textbook with the older one to see what has changed. Look,
as FitzGerald did, at the opening, the major figures or topics, the attitudes, the pedagogical types, the physical appearance, and any other major features of each book. Write
an essay explaining what you find.

8. Locate a current textbook in American history. How does it compare to your
memory of American history as you learned it in junior high or high school? What was
America "like," according to your old text? What is it "like" now?

THE HISTORIAN AND HIS FACTS

Edward Hallet Carr

E. H. Carr (1892–1982) was a distinguished British historian whose major work was The History of Soviet Russia, *in fourteen volumes. A Fellow of Trinity College, Cambridge, Carr delivered a series of lectures there in 1961 under the general title of "What Is History?" The lectures were later published as a book, which opened with the selection reprinted here. It addressed the general question—What is history?—in terms of a more specific question: What is a historical fact?*

What is history? Lest anyone think the question meaningless or superfluous, I will take as my text two passages relating respectively to the first and second incarnations of *The Cambridge Modern History*. Here is Acton in his report of October 1896 to the Syndics of the Cambridge University Press on the work which he had undertaken to edit:[1]

> It is a unique opportunity of recording, in the way most useful to the greatest number, the fullness of the knowledge which the nineteenth century is about to bequeath. . . . By the judicious division of labour we should be able to do it, and to bring home to every man the last document, and the ripest conclusions of international research.
>
> Ultimate history we cannot have in this generation; but we can dispose of conventional history, and show the point we have reached on the road from one to the other, now that all information is within reach, and every problem has become capable of solution.[2]

And almost exactly sixty years later Professor Sir George Clark, in his general introduction to the second *Cambridge Modern History*, commented on this belief of Acton and his collaborators that it would one day be possible to produce "ultimate history," and went on:

> Historians of a later generation do not look forward to any such prospect. They expect their work to be superseded again and again. They consider that knowledge of the past has come down through one or more human minds, has been "processed" by them, and therefore cannot consist of elemental and impersonal atoms which

---

[1]John Dalberg Acton (1834–1902): British historian and editor of the first *Cambridge Modern History*. [Eds.]

[2]*The Cambridge Modern History: Its Origin, Authorship and Production* (Cambridge University Press; 1907), pp. 10–12.

nothing can alter. . . . The exploration seems to be endless, and some impatient scholars take refuge in scepticism, or at least in the doctrine that, since all historical judgments involve persons and points of view, one is as good as another and there is no "objective" historical truth.[3]

Where the pundits contradict each other so flagrantly the field is open to enquiry. I hope that I am sufficiently up-to-date to recognize that anything written in the 1890's must be nonsense. But I am not yet advanced enough to be committed to the view that anything written in the 1950's necessarily makes sense. Indeed, it may already have occurred to you that this enquiry is liable to stray into something even broader than the nature of history. The clash between Acton and Sir George Clark is a reflection of the change in our total outlook on society over the interval between these two pronouncements. Acton speaks out of the positive belief, the clear-eyed self-confidence of the later Victorian age; Sir George Clark echoes the bewilderment and distracted scepticism of the beat generation. When we attempt to answer the question, What is history?, our answer, consciously or unconsciously, reflects our own position in time, and forms part of our answer to the broader question, what view we take of the society in which we live. I have no fear that my subject may, on closer inspection, seem trivial. I am afraid only that I may seem presumptuous to have broached a question so vast and so important.

The nineteenth century was a great age for facts. "What I want," said Mr. Gradgrind in *Hard Times*,[4] "is Facts. . . . Facts alone are wanted in life." Nineteenth-century historians on the whole agreed with him. When Ranke in the 1830's,[5] in legitimate protest against moralizing history, remarked that the task of the historian was "simply to show how it really was (*wie es eigentlich gewesen*)" this not very profound aphorism had an astonishing success. Three generations of German, British, and even French historians marched into battle intoning the magic words, *"Wie es eigentlich gewesen"* like an incantation—designed, like most incantations, to save them from the tiresome obligation to think for themselves. The Positivists, anxious to stake out their claim for history as a science, contributed the weight of their influence to this cult of facts. First ascertain the facts, said the positivists, then draw your conclusions from them. In Great Britain, this view of history fitted in perfectly with the empiricist tradition which was the dominant strain in British philosophy from Locke to Bertrand Russell.[6] The empirical theory of knowledge presupposes a complete separation between subject and object. Facts, like sense-impressions, impinge on the observer from outside, and are independent of his consciousness. The process of reception is passive: having received the data, he then acts on them.

2

---

[3]*The New Cambridge Modern History*, I (Cambridge University Press; 1957), pp. xxiv–xxv.
[4]*Hard Times*: a novel by Charles Dickens. [Eds.]
[5]Leopold von Ranke (1795–1886): German historian. [Eds.]
[6]John Locke (1632–1704): English philosopher; Bertrand Russell (1872–1970): English philosopher and mathematician. [Eds.]

The Shorter Oxford English Dictionary, a useful but tendentious work of the empirical school, clearly marks the separateness of the two processes by defining a fact as "a datum of experience as distinct from conclusions." This is what may be called the common-sense view of history. History consists of a corpus of ascertained facts. The facts are available to the historian in documents, inscriptions, and so on, like fish on the fishmonger's slab. The historian collects them, takes them home, and cooks and serves them in whatever style appeals to him. Acton, whose culinary tastes were austere, wanted them served plain. In his letter of instructions to contributors to the first *Cambridge Modern History* he announced the requirement "that our Waterloo must be one that satisfies French and English, German and Dutch alike; that nobody can tell, without examining the list of authors where the Bishop of Oxford laid down the pen, and whether Fairbairn or Gasquet, Liebermann or Harrison took it up."[7] Even Sir George Clark, critical as he was of Acton's attitude, himself contrasted the "hard core of facts" in history with the "surrounding pulp of disputable interpretation"[8]— forgetting perhaps that the pulpy part of the fruit is more rewarding than the hard core. First get your facts straight, then plunge at your peril into the shifting sands of interpretation—that is the ultimate wisdom of the empirical, common-sense school of history. It recalls the favorite dictum of the great liberal journalist C. P. Scott: "Facts are sacred, opinion is free."

Now this clearly will not do. I shall not embark on a philosophical discussion 3 of the nature of our knowledge of the past. Let us assume for present purposes that the fact that Caesar crossed the Rubicon and the fact that there is a table in the middle of the room are facts of the same or of a comparable order, that both these facts enter our consciousness in the same or in a comparable manner, and that both have the same objective character in relation to the person who knows them. But, even on this bold and not very plausible assumption, our argument at once runs into the difficulty that not all facts about the past are historical facts, or are treated as such by the historian. What is the criterion which distinguishes the facts of history from other facts about the past?

What is a historical fact? This is a crucial question into which we must look 4 a little more closely. According to the common-sense view, there are certain basic facts which are the same for all historians and which form, so to speak, the backbone of history—the fact, for example, that the Battle of Hastings was fought in 1066. But this view calls for two observations. In the first place, it is not with facts like these that the historian is primarily concerned. It is no doubt important to know that the great battle was fought in 1066 and not in 1065 or 1067, and that it was fought at Hastings and not at Eastbourne or Brighton. The historian must not get these things wrong. But when points of this kind are raised, I am reminded of Housman's remark that "accuracy is a duty, not a

---

[7]Acton: *Lectures on Modern History* (London: Macmillan & Co.; 1906), p. 318.
[8]Quoted in *The Listener* (June 19, 1952), p. 992.

virtue."[9] To praise a historian for his accuracy is like praising an architect for using well-seasoned timber or properly mixed concrete in his building. It is a necessary condition of his work, but not his essential function. It is precisely for matters of this kind that the historian is entitled to rely on what have been called the "auxiliary sciences" of history—archaeology, epigraphy, numismatics, chronology, and so forth. The historian is not required to have the special skills which enable the expert to determine the origin and period of a fragment of pottery or marble, to decipher an obscure inscription, or to make the elaborate astronomical calculations necessary to establish a precise date. These so-called basic facts which are the same for all historians commonly belong to the category of the raw materials of the historian rather than of history itself. The second observation is that the necessity to establish these basic facts rests not on any quality in the facts themselves, but on an *a priori* decision of the historian. In spite of C. P. Scott's motto, every journalist knows today that the most effective way to influence opinion is by the selection and arrangement of the appropriate facts. It used to be said that facts speak for themselves. This is, of course, untrue. The facts speak only when the historian calls on them: it is he who decides to which facts to give the floor, and in what order or context. It was, I think, one of Pirandello's characters who said that a fact is like a sack[10]—it won't stand up till you've put something in it. The only reason why we are interested to know that the battle was fought at Hastings in 1066 is that historians regard it as a major historical event. It is the historian who has decided for his own reasons that Caesar's crossing of that petty stream, the Rubicon, is a fact of history, whereas the crossing of the Rubicon by millions of other people before or since interests nobody at all. The fact that you arrived in this building half an hour ago on foot, or on a bicycle, or in a car, is just as much a fact about the past as the fact that Caesar crossed the Rubicon. But it will probably be ignored by historians. Professor Talcott Parsons once called science "a selective system of cognitive orientations to reality."[11] It might perhaps have been put more simply. But history is, among other things, that. The historian is necessarily selective. The belief in a hard core of historical facts existing objectively and independently of the interpretation of the historian is a preposterous fallacy, but one which it is very hard to eradicate.

Let us take a look at the process by which a mere fact about the past is 5 transformed into a fact of history. At Stalybridge Wakes in 1850, a vendor of gingerbread, as the result of some petty dispute, was deliberately kicked to death by an angry mob. Is this a fact of history? A year ago I should unhesitatingly have said "no." It was recorded by an eyewitness in some little-known mem-

---

[9]M. Manilius: *Astronomicon: Liber Primus*, 2nd ed. (Cambridge University Press; 1937), p. 87. (A. E. Housman [1859–1936]: poet and classical scholar who edited Manilius. [Eds.])

[10]Luigi Pirandello (1867–1936): Italian playwright. [Eds.]

[11]Talcott Parsons and Edward A. Shils: *Toward a General Theory of Action*, 3rd ed. (Cambridge, Mass.: Harvard University Press; 1954), p. 167.

oirs;[12] but I had never seen it judged worthy of mention by any historian. A year ago Dr. Kitson Clark cited it in his Ford lectures in Oxford.[13] Does this make it into a historical fact? Not, I think, yet. Its present status, I suggest, is that it has been proposed for membership of the select club of historical facts. It now awaits a seconder and sponsors. It may be that in the course of the next few years we shall see this fact appearing first in footnotes, then in the text, of articles and books about nineteenth-century England, and that in twenty or thirty years' time it may be a well established historical fact. Alternatively, nobody may take it up, in which case it will relapse into the limbo of unhistorical facts about the past from which Dr. Kitson Clark has gallantly attempted to rescue it. What will decide which of these two things will happen? It will depend, I think, on whether the thesis or interpretation in support of which Dr. Kitson Clark cited this incident is accepted by other historians as valid and significant. Its status as a historical fact will turn on a question of interpretation. This element of interpretation enters into every fact of history.

May I be allowed a personal reminiscence? When I studied ancient history 6 in this university many years ago, I had as a special subject "Greece in the period of the Persian Wars." I collected fifteen or twenty volumes on my shelves and took it for granted that there, recorded in these volumes, I had all the facts relating to my subject. Let us assume—it was very nearly true—that those volumes contained all the facts about it that were then known, or could be known. It never occurred to me to enquire by what accident or process of attrition that minute selection of facts, out of all the myriad facts that must have once been known to somebody, had survived to become *the* facts of history. I suspect that even today one of the fascinations of ancient and mediaeval history is that it gives us the illusion of having all the facts at our disposal within a manageable compass: the nagging distinction between the facts of history and other facts about the past vanishes because the few known facts are all facts of history. As Bury, who had worked in both periods, said, "the records of ancient and mediaeval history are starred with lacunae."[14] History has been called an enormous jig-saw with a lot of missing parts. But the main trouble does not consist of the lacunae. Our picture of Greece in the fifth century B.C. is defective not primarily because so many of the bits have been accidentally lost, but because it is, by and large, the picture formed by a tiny group of people in the city of Athens. We know a lot about what fifth-century Greece looked like to an Athenian citizen; but hardly anything about what it looked like to a Spartan, a Corinthian, or a Theban—not to mention a Persian, or a slave or other non-citizen resident in Athens. Our picture has been pre-selected and predetermined

---

[12]Lord George Sanger: *Seventy Years a Showman* (London: J. M. Dent & Sons; 1926); pp. 188–9.

[13]These will shortly be published under the title *The Making of Victorian England.*

[14]John Bagnell Bury: *Selected Essays* (Cambridge University Press; 1930), p. 52. (lacunae: empty spaces or gaps. [Eds.])

for us, not so much by accident as by people who were consciously or uncon-sciously imbued with a particular view and thought the facts which supported that view worth preserving. In the same way, when I read in a modern history of the Middle Ages that the people of the Middle Ages were deeply concerned with religion, I wonder how we know this, and whether it is true. What we know as the facts of mediaeval history have almost all been selected for us by generations of chroniclers who were professionally occupied in the theory and practice of religion, and who therefore thought it supremely important, and recorded everything relating to it, and not much else. The picture of the Russian peasant as devoutly religious was destroyed by the revolution of 1917. The picture of mediaeval man as devoutly religious, whether true or not, is inde-structible, because nearly all the known facts about him were pre-selected for us by people who believed it, and wanted others to believe it, and a mass of other facts, in which we might possibly have found evidence to the contrary, has been lost beyond recall. The dead hand of vanished generations of historians, scribes, and chroniclers has determined beyond the possibility of appeal the pattern of the past. "The history we read," writes Professor Barraclough, himself trained as a mediaevalist, "though based on facts, is, strictly speaking, not factual at all, but a series of accepted judgments."[15]

But let us turn to the different, but equally grave, plight of the modern historian. The ancient or mediaeval historian may be grateful for the vast win-nowing process which, over the years, has put at his disposal a manageable corpus of historical facts. As Lytton Strachey said in his mischievous way, "ig-norance is the first requisite of the historian, ignorance which simplifies and clarifies, which selects and omits."[16] When I am tempted, as I sometimes am, to envy the extreme competence of colleagues engaged in writing ancient or mediaeval history, I find consolation in the reflexion that they are so competent mainly because they are so ignorant of their subject. The modern historian enjoys none of the advantages of this built-in ignorance. He must cultivate this necessary ignorance for himself—the more so the nearer he comes to his own times. He has the dual task of discovering the few significant facts and turning them into facts of history, and of discarding the many insignificant facts as unhistorical. But this is the very converse of the nineteenth-century heresy that history consists of the compilation of a maximum number of irrefutable and objective facts. Anyone who succumbs to this heresy will either have to give up history as a bad job, and take to stamp-collecting or some other form of anti-quarianism, or end in a madhouse. It is this heresy, which during the past hundred years has had such devastating effects on the modern historian, pro-ducing in Germany, in Great Britain, and in the United States a vast and growing mass of dry-as-dust factual histories, of minutely specialized mono-

---

[15]Geoffrey Barraclough: *History in a Changing World* (London: Basil Blackwell & Mott; 1955), p. 14.
[16]Lytton Strachey: Preface to *Eminent Victorians*.

graphs, of would-be historians knowing more and more about less and less, sunk without trace in an ocean of facts. It was, I suspect, this heresy—rather than the alleged conflict between liberal and Catholic loyalties—which frustrated Acton as a historian. In an early essay he said of his teacher Döllinger: "He would not write with imperfect materials, and to him the materials were always imperfect."[17] Acton was surely here pronouncing an anticipatory verdict on himself, on that strange phenomenon of a historian whom many would regard as the most distinguished occupant the Regius Chair of Modern History in this university has ever had—but who wrote no history. And Acton wrote his own epitaph in the introductory note to the first volume of the *Cambridge Modern History*, published just after his death, when he lamented that the requirements pressing on the historian "threaten to turn him from a man of letters into the compiler of an encyclopedia."[18] Something had gone wrong. What had gone wrong was the belief in this untiring and unending accumulation of hard facts as the foundation of history, the belief that facts speak for themselves and that we cannot have too many facts, a belief at that time so unquestioning that few historians then thought it necessary—and some still think it unnecessary today—to ask themselves the question: What is history?

The nineteenth-century fetishism of facts was completed and justified by a fetishism of documents. The documents were the Ark of the Covenant in the temple of facts. The reverent historian approached them with bowed head and spoke of them in awed tones. If you find it in the documents, it is so. But what, when we get down to it, do these documents—the decrees, the treaties, the rent-rolls, the blue books, the official correspondence, the private letters and diaries—tell us? No document can tell us more than what the author of the document thought—what he thought had happened, what he thought ought to happen or would happen, or perhaps only what he wanted others to think he thought, or even only what he himself thought he thought. None of this means anything until the historian has got to work on it and deciphered it. The facts, whether found in documents or not, have still to be processed by the historian before he can make any use of them: the use he makes of them is, if I may put it that way, the processing process.

Let me illustrate what I am trying to say by an example which I happen to know well. When Gustav Stresemann, the Foreign Minister of the Weimar Republic,[19] died in 1929, he left behind him an enormous mass—300 boxes full—of papers, official, semi-official, and private, nearly all relating to the six years of his tenure of office as Foreign Minister. His friends and relatives nat-

---

[17]Quoted in George P. Gooch: *History and Historians in the Nineteenth Century* (London: Longmans, Green & Company; 1952), p. 385. Later Acton said of Döllinger that "it was given him to form his philosophy of history on the largest induction ever available to man" (*History of Freedom and Other Essays* [London: Macmillan & Co.; 1907], p. 435).

[18]*The Cambridge Modern History*, I (1902), p.4.

[19]Weimar Republic: the government of Germany, established in the city of Weimar after World War I (1919) and lasting until Adolf Hitler rose to power in 1933. [Eds.]

urally thought that a monument should be raised to the memory of so great a man. His faithful secretary Bernhardt got to work; and within three years there appeared three massive volumes, of some 600 pages each, of selected documents from the 300 boxes, with the impressive title *Stresemanns Vermächtnis*.[20] In the ordinary way the documents themselves would have mouldered away in some cellar or attic and disappeared for ever; or perhaps in a hundred years or so some curious scholar would have come upon them and set out to compare them with Bernhardt's text. What happened was far more dramatic. In 1945 the documents fell into the hands of the British and the American governments, who photographed the lot and put the photostats at the disposal of scholars in the Public Record Office in London and in the National Archives in Washington, so that, if we have sufficient patience and curiosity, we can discover exactly what Bernhardt did. What he did was neither very unusual nor very shocking. When Stresemann died, his Western policy seemed to have been crowned with a series of brilliant successes—Locarno, the admission of Germany to the League of Nations, the Dawes and Young plans and the American loans, the withdrawal of allied occupation armies from the Rhineland. This seemed the important and rewarding part of Stresemann's foreign policy; and it was not unnatural that it should have been over-represented in Bernhardt's selection of documents. Stresemann's Eastern policy, on the other hand, his relations with the Soviet Union, seemed to have led nowhere in particular; and, since masses of documents about negotiations which yielded only trivial results were not very interesting and added nothing to Stresemann's reputation, the process of selection could be more rigorous. Stresemann in fact devoted a far more constant and anxious attention to relations with the Soviet Union, and they played a far larger part in his foreign policy as a whole, than the reader of the Bernhardt selection would surmise. But the Bernhardt volumes compare favorably, I suspect, with many published collections of documents on which the ordinary historian implicitly relies.

This is not the end of my story. Shortly after the publication of Bernhardt's 10 volumes, Hitler came into power. Stresemann's name was consigned to oblivion in Germany, and the volumes disappeared from circulation: many, perhaps most, of the copies must have been destroyed. Today *Stresemanns Vermächtnis* is a rather rare book. But in the West Stresemann's reputation stood high. In 1935 an English publisher brought out an abbreviated translation of Bernhardt's work—a selection from Bernhardt's selection; perhaps one third of the original was omitted. Sutton, a well-known translator from the German, did his job competently and well. The English version, he explained in the preface, was "slightly condensed, but only by the omission of a certain amount of what, it was felt, was more ephemeral matter . . . of little interest to English readers or

---

[20]*Stresemanns Vermächtnis*: this title may be translated as "Stresemann's Legacy." [Eds.]

students."[21] This again is natural enough. But the result is that Stresemann's Eastern policy, already under-represented in Bernhardt, recedes still further from view, and the Soviet Union appears in Sutton's volumes merely as an occasional and rather unwelcome intruder in Stresemann's predominantly Western foreign policy. Yet it is safe to say that, for all except a few specialists, Sutton and not Bernhardt—and still less the documents themselves—represents for the Western world the authentic voice of Stresemann. Had the documents perished in 1945 in the bombing, and had the remaining Bernhardt volumes disappeared, the authenticity and authority of Sutton would never have been questioned. Many printed collections of documents gratefully accepted by historians in default of the originals rest on no securer basis than this.

But I want to carry the story one step further. Let us forget about Bernhardt and Sutton, and be thankful that we can, if we choose, consult the authentic papers of a leading participant in some important events of recent European history. What do the papers tell us? Among other things they contain records of some hundreds of Stresemann's conversations with the Soviet ambassador in Berlin and of a score or so with Chicherin.[22] These records have one feature in common. They depict Stresemann as having the lion's share of the conversations and reveal his arguments as invariably well put and cogent, while those of his partner are for the most part scanty, confused, and unconvincing. This is a familiar characteristic of all records of diplomatic conversations. The documents do not tell us what happened, but only what Stresemann thought had happened, or what he wanted others to think, or perhaps what he wanted himself to think, had happened. It was not Sutton or Bernhardt, but Stresemann himself, who started the process of selection. And, if we had, say, Chicherin's records of these same conversations, we should still learn from them only what Chicherin thought, and what really happened would still have to be reconstructed in the mind of the historian. Of course, facts and documents are essential to the historian. But do not make a fetish of them. They do not by themselves constitute history; they provide in themselves no ready-made answer to this tiresome question: What is history?

At this point I should like to say a few words on the question of why nineteenth-century historians were generally indifferent to the philosophy of history. The term was invented by Voltaire,[23] and has since been used in different senses; but I shall take it to mean, if I use it at all, our answer to the question: What is history? The nineteenth century was, for the intellectuals of Western Europe, a comfortable period exuding confidence and optimism. The facts were on the whole satisfactory; and the inclination to ask and answer awkward questions about them was correspondingly weak. Ranke piously believed that divine prov-

---

[21]*Gustav Stresemann: His Diaries, Letters, and Papers* (London: Macmillan & Co.; 1935), I, Editor's Note.

[22]Grigory Chicherin (1872–1936): a powerful Russian diplomat. [Eds.]

[23]Voltaire (1694–1778): French dramatist, philosopher, and social critic. [Eds.]

idence would take care of the meaning of history if he took care of the facts; and Burckhardt with a more modern touch of cynicism observed that "we are not initiated into the purposes of the eternal wisdom." Professor Butterfield as late as 1931 noted with apparent satisfaction that "historians have reflected little upon the nature of things and even the nature of their own subject."[24] But my predecessor in these lectures, Dr. A. L. Rowse, more justly critical, wrote of Sir Winston Churchill's *The World Crisis*—his book about the First World War—that, while it matched Trotsky's *History of the Russian Revolution* in personality, vividness, and vitality, it was inferior in one respect: it had "no philosophy of history behind it."[25] British historians refused to be drawn, not because they believed that history had no meaning, but because they believed that its meaning was implicit and self-evident. The liberal nineteenth-century view of history had a close affinity with the economic doctrine of *laissez-faire*—also the product of a serene and self-confident outlook on the world. Let everyone get on with his particular job, and the hidden hand would take care of the universal harmony. The facts of history were themselves a demonstration of the supreme fact of a beneficent and apparently infinite progress towards higher things. This was the age of innocence, and historians walked in the Garden of Eden, without a scrap of philosophy to cover them, naked and unashamed before the god of history. Since then, we have known Sin and experienced a Fall; and those historians who today pretend to dispense with a philosophy of history are merely trying, vainly and self-consciously, like members of a nudist colony, to recreate the Garden of Eden in their garden suburb. Today the awkward question can no longer be evaded.

QUESTIONS

1. Carr's essay answers the question, "What is a historical fact?" Summarize his answer to that question.

2. In paragraph 7, Carr says the historian must "cultivate . . . ignorance." What does this expression mean in its context? What is the point of the discussion of Acton and Döllinger in that paragraph? How does this discussion contribute to the larger theme of the essay?

3. In presenting an explanation, especially a controversial one, a writer must often seek to gain the confidence of the reader. How does Carr go about this? What sort of picture does he present of himself? What impression of him do you get from his references to himself in paragraphs 1 and 6, and how does that impression affect your evaluation of his position?

4. Carr's essay is not only explanatory; it is an essay on interpretation. Locate the many uses of the words *interpret* or *interpretation* in the essay, and consider how they

---

[24]Herbert Butterfield: *The Whig Interpretation of History* (London: George Bell & Sons; 1931), p. 67.

[25]Alfred L. Rowse: *The End of an Epoch* (London: Macmillan & Co.; 1947), pp. 282–3.

function in the larger discussion. What view of the relationship between facts and interpretation is presented here?

5. Carr's essay contradicts previously existing explanations of the relationship between historians and the facts they must deal with in writing history. Where does Carr summarize the opposing position? State in your own words the views of historical facts with which Carr takes issue.

6. Consider several facts generally known to you and your class. Limit your attention to recent facts, specifically from the last year. (You might first discuss in class what sorts of facts merit your attention.) Which of those facts has the best chance of becoming "a historical fact," in Carr's terms. On what does that process depend? Write an explanation of the historicity of a fact you choose, trying to convince your classmates that your fact will become a historical fact.

7. Using an accepted historical fact not mentioned by Carr, write an essay in which you consider why your chosen fact is a historical fact and what grounds we have for understanding it and accepting it as a fact.

Social Sciences and Public Affairs

A ZERO-SUM GAME
Lester C. Thurow

Born in Livingston, Montana, in 1938, Lester Thurow has degrees in economics from Williams College, Oxford University, and Harvard University. He is the author of over sixty articles on economics and a number of books. Currently teaching at the Sloan School of Management at the Massachusetts Institute of Technology, Thurow writes frequently on economic matters for newspapers. He reached a wide audience with The Zero-Sum Society, *which* Business Week *called "a ruthlessly honest, tough-minded book." The following selection is from chapter 1 of that book, "An Economy That No Longer Performs."*

This is the heart of our fundamental problem. Our economic problems are 1 solvable. For most of our problems there are several solutions. But all these solutions have the characteristic that someone must suffer large economic losses. No one wants to volunteer for this role, and we have a political process that is incapable of forcing anyone to shoulder this burden. Everyone wants someone else to suffer the necessary economic losses, and as a consequence none of the possible solutions can be adopted.

Basically we have created the world described in Robert Ardrey's *The Terri-* 2 *torial Imperative.* To beat an animal of the same species on his home turf, the invader must be twice as strong as the defender. But no majority is twice as strong as the minority opposing it. Therefore we each veto the other's initiatives, but none of us has the ability to create successful initiatives ourselves.

Our political and economic structure simply isn't able to cope with an econ- 3 omy that has a substantial zero-sum element. A zero-sum game is any game where the losses exactly equal the winnings. All sporting events are zero-sum games. For every winner there is a loser, and winners can only exist if losers exist. What the winning gambler wins, the losing gambler must lose.

When there are large losses to be allocated, any economic decision has a 4 large zero-sum element. The economic gains may exceed the economic losses, but the losses are so large as to negate a very substantial fraction of the gains. What is more important, the gains and losses are not allocated to the same individuals or groups. On average, society may be better off, but this average hides a large number of people who are much better off and large numbers of people who are much worse off. If you are among those who are worse off, the fact that someone else's income has risen by more than your income has fallen is of little comfort.

To protect our own income, we will fight to stop economic change from 5 occurring or fight to prevent society from imposing the public policies that hurt us. From our perspective they are not good public policies even if they do result in a larger GNP.[1] We want a solution to the problem, say the problem of energy, that does not reduce our income, but all solutions reduce someone's income. If the government chooses some policy option that does not lower our income, it will have made a supporter out of us, but it will have made an opponent out of someone else, since someone else will now have to shoulder the burden of large income reductions.

The problem with zero-sum games is that the essence of problem solving is 6 loss allocation. But this is precisely what our political process is least capable of doing. When there are economic gains to be allocated, our political process can allocate them. When there are large economic losses to be allocated, our political process is paralyzed. And with political paralysis comes economic paralysis.

The importance of economic losers has also been magnified by a change in 7 the political structure. In the past, political and economic power was distributed in such a way that substantial economic losses could be imposed on parts of the population if the establishment decided that it was in the general interest. Economic losses were allocated to particular powerless groups rather than spread across the population. These groups are no longer willing to accept losses and are able to raise substantially the costs for those who wish to impose losses upon them.

There are a number of reasons for this change. Vietnam and the subsequent 8 political scandals clearly lessened the population's willingness to accept their nominal leader's judgments that some project was in their general interest. With the civil rights, poverty, black power, and women's liberation movements, many of the groups that have in the past absorbed economic losses have become militant. They are no longer willing to accept losses without a political fight.

---

[1]GNP: gross national product, an annual measure of the wealth generated by a country—in this case, the United States. [Eds.]

The success of their militancy and civil disobedience sets an example that spreads to other groups representing the environment, neighborhoods, and regions.

All minority groups have gone through a learning process. They have dis- 9
covered that it is relatively easy with our legal system and a little militancy to delay anything for a very long period of time. To be able to delay a program is often to be able to kill it. Legal and administrative costs rise, but the delays and uncertainties are even more important. When the costs of delays and uncertainties are added into their calculations, both government and private industry often find that it pays to cancel projects that would otherwise be profitable. Costs are simply higher than benefits.

In one major environmental group, delays are such a major part of their 10
strategy that they have a name for it—analysis paralysis. Laws are to be passed so that every project must meet a host of complicated time-consuming requirements. The idea is not to learn more about the costs and benefits of projects, but to kill them. If such requirements were to be useful in deciding whether a project should be undertaken, environmental-impact statements, for example, would have to be inexpensive, simple, and quick to complete. Then a firm might undertake the studies to help determine whether they should or should not start a project.

Instead, the studies are to be expensive and complex to serve as a financial 11
deterrent to undertaking any project, to substantially lengthen the time necessary to complete any project, and to ensure that they can be challenged in court (another lengthy process). As a consequence, the developer will start the process only if he has already decided on other grounds to go ahead with the project. The result is an adversary situation where the developer cannot get his project underway—and where the environmentalists also cannot get existing plants (such as Reserve Mining) to clean up their current pollution. Where it helps them, both sides have learned the fine art of delay.

Consider the interstate highway system. Whatever one believes about the 12
merits of completing the remaining intracity portion of the system, it is clear that it gives the country an intercity transportation network that would be sorely missed had it not been built. Even those who argue against it do so on the grounds that if it had not been built, some better (nonauto) system would have been devised. Yet most observers would agree that the interstate highway system could not have been built if it had been proposed in the mid-1970s rather than in the mid-1950s.

Exactly the same factors that would prevent the initiation of an interstate 13
highway system would also prevent the initiation of any alternative transportation system. A few years ago, when a high-speed rail system was being considered for the Boston-Washington corridor, a former governor of Connecticut announced that he would veto any relocation of the Boston-to-New York line on the grounds that it would be of prime benefit to those at either end of the line, but would tear up Connecticut homes. The groups opposing an intercity rail

network would be slightly different from the groups opposing an intercity highway network, but they would be no less effective in stopping the project. Any transportation system demands that land be taken and homes be torn down. At one time, this was possible; at the moment, it is impossible.

The Balkanization of nations is a worldwide phenomenon that the United States has not escaped.[2] Regions and localities are less and less willing to incur costs that will primarily help people in other parts of the same country. Consider the development of the coalfields of Wyoming and Montana. There is no question that most of the benefits will accrue to those living in urban areas in the rest of the country while most of the costs will be imposed on those living in that region. As a result, the local population objects. More coal mining might be good for the United States, but it will be bad for local constituents. Therefore they will impose as many delays and uncertainties as possible.   14

The same problem is visible in the location of nuclear power plants. Whatever one believes about the benefits of nuclear power, it is clear that lengthy delays in approving sites serve no purpose other than as a strategy for killing the projects. If the projects are undertaken anyway, the consumer will have to suffer the same risks and pay the higher costs associated with these delays. What is wanted is a quick yes or no answer; but this is just what we find impossible to do. The question of nuclear power sites also raises the Balkanization issue. Whatever the probabilities of accidents, the consequences of such failures are much less if the plants are located in remote areas. But those who live in remote areas do not want the plants, since they suffer all the potential hazards and do not need the project. Everyone wants power, but no one wants a power plant next to his own home.   15

Domestic problems also tend to have a much longer time horizon. In modern times, even long wars are won or lost in relatively short periods of time. In contrast, a project such as energy independence would take decades to achieve. The patience and foresight necessary for long-range plans is generally not an American virtue. Consequently, representatives seeking reelection every two, four, or six years want to support programs that will bring them votes. They do not want to stick their necks out for a good cause that may conflict with their careers. Even more fundamentally, domestic problems often involve long periods where costs accrue, with the benefits following much later. Think about energy independence. For a long time, sacrifices must be made to construct the necessary mines and plants. Benefits emerge only near the end of the process. The politician who must incur the costs (raise the necessary revenue and incur the anger of those who are hurt as the projects are constructed) is unlikely to be around to collect the credits when energy independence has been achieved.   16

---

[2]Balkanization: the process by which a region breaks down into smaller, usually hostile units. The term derives from the division of the Balkan countries in southeastern Europe by the Great Powers early in this century. [Eds.]

QUESTIONS

1. Does Thurow say that the United States economy is a zero-sum game? What, exactly, does he say, and what, exactly, is a zero-sum game?

2. In his first paragraph, Thurow mentions a fundamental problem. What is that problem? What has it got to do with zero-sum games?

3. What is the logical structure of the first paragraph? Where does it move from premises or assumptions to conclusions?

4. In paragraph 3, how does Thurow make sure you will understand his definition of a zero-sum game? (Consider also the structure of the last two sentences of that paragraph. How does the form of those sentences relate to the idea being conveyed? Why could you call them zero-sum sentences?)

5. How does Thurow organize paragraphs 11 through 14? What gives each paragraph its coherence? How are all four related to the larger structure of the essay?

6. How does this essay divide into sections that develop different parts of the subject? Make an outline of the essay by listing a few topics and then assigning the appropriate paragraphs to each topic.

7. In paragraph 6, Thurow says, "the essence of problem solving is loss allocation." What does he mean by *loss allocation?* Present a proposal for solving a particular problem. Do so in such a way as to make clear the loss allocation that will be required. Try to present your case in such a way that the allocation seems reasonable.

8. When Thurow says that "the essence of problem solving is loss allocation" (paragraph 6), he implicitly defines problem solving. Is every solution a matter of cost-benefit analysis? Is the winners-losers framework an assumption—or a pragmatic observation? Write a paper in which you explain the nature of problem solving by agreeing or disagreeing with Thurow.

9. Write an essay in which you interpret or explain the causes of a particular situation, such as why a team loses or why something costs what it does. Support your reasoning with concrete examples and specific details.

10. Analyze a government proposal being made right now, locally, regionally, or nationally. What is the problem? What is the proposed solution? In particular, what is the system of loss allocation being suggested? How direct are the proponents of this legislation about the loss allocation that will be necessary?

FITTING NEW EMPLOYEES INTO THE COMPANY CULTURE

Richard Pascale

*Richard Pascale was born in Amityville, New York, in 1938
and went to the University of California at Berkeley, where
he studied mechanical engineering. Later, he went to Harvard for an M.B.A. in 1967 and a Ph.D. in 1971. Since
1970 he has taught in the Stanford University Business
School. His many books include* Managing the White House,
Zen and the Art of Management, *which he coauthored to
explain to Americans the great success of certain Japanese
business firms and* The Art of Japanese Management. *The
essay reprinted here appeared in 1984 in* Fortune *magazine,
under the following subheading: "Many of the best–managed
companies in America are particularly skilled at getting recruits to adopt the corporate collection of shared values,
beliefs, and practices as their own. Here's how they do it,
and why indoctrination need not mean brainwashing."*

What corporate strategy was in the 1970s, corporate culture is becoming in   1
the 1980s. Companies worry about whether theirs is right for them, consultants
hawk advice on the subject, executives wonder if there's anything in it that can
help them manage better. A strong culture—a set of shared values, norms, and
beliefs that get everybody heading in the same direction—is common to all the
companies held up as paragons in the best-seller *In Search of Excellence.*

There is, however, one aspect of culture that nobody seems to want to talk   2
about. This is the process by which newly hired employees are made part of a
company's culture. It may be called learning the ropes, being taught "the way
we do things here at XYZ Corp.," or simply training. Almost no one calls it by
its precise social-science name—socialization.

To American ears, attuned by Constitution and conviction to the full expres-   3
sion of individuality, socialization tends to sound alien and vaguely sinister.
Some equate it with the propagation of socialism—which it isn't—but even
when it is correctly understood as the development of social conformity, the
prospect makes most of us cringe. How many companies caught up in the
corporate culture fad will be quite as enthusiastic when they finally grasp that
"creating a strong culture" is a nice way of saying that employees have to be
more comprehensively socialized?

The tradition at most American corporations is to err in the other direction,   4 to be culturally permissive, to let employees do their own thing to a remarkable degree. We are guided by a philosophy, initially articulated by John Locke, Thomas Hobbes, and Adam Smith, that says that individuals free to choose make the most efficient decisions. The independence of the parts makes for a greater sum. Trendy campaigns to build a strong corporate culture run into trouble when employees are asked to give up some of their individuality for the common good.

The crux of the dilemma is this: We are opposed to the manipulation of individuals for organizational purposes. At the same time we increasingly realize that a degree of social uniformity enables organizations to work better. One need not look to Japan to see the benefits of it. Many of the great American companies that thrive from one generation to the next—IBM, Procter & Gamble, Morgan Guaranty Trust—are organizations that have perfected their processes of socialization. Virtually none talk explicitly about socialization; they may not even be conscious of precisely what they are doing. Moreover, when one examines any particular aspect of their policy toward people—how they recruit or train or compensate—little stands out as unusual. But when the pieces are assembled, what emerges is an awesome internal consistency that powerfully shapes behavior.

It's time to take socialization out of the closet. If some degree of it is necessary for organizations to be effective, then the challenge for managers is to reconcile this necessity with traditional American independence.

Probably the best guide available on how to socialize people properly is what the IBMs and the P&Gs actually do. Looking at the winners company by company, one finds that, with slight variations, they all put new employees through what might be called the seven steps of socialization:

· Step one. The company subjects candidates for employment to a selection process so rigorous that it often seems designed to discourage individuals rather than encourage them to take the job. By grilling the applicant, telling him or her the bad side as well as the good, and making sure not to oversell, strong-culture companies prod the job applicant to take himself out of contention if he, who presumably knows more about himself than any recruiter, thinks the organization won't fit his style and values.

Consider the way Procter & Gamble hires people for entry level positions in brand management. The first person who interviews the applicant is drawn not from the human resources department, but from an elite cadre of line managers who have been trained with lectures, videotapes, films, practice interviews, and role playing. These interviewers use what they've learned to probe each applicant for such qualities as the ability to "turn out high volumes of excellent work," to "identify and understand problems," and to "reach thoroughly substantiated and well-reasoned conclusions that lead to action." Initially, each candidate undergoes at least two interviews and takes a test of his general knowledge. If he passes, he's flown to P&G headquarters in Cincinnati, where he goes through a day of one-on-one interviews and a group interview over lunch.

367

The New York investment banking house of Morgan Stanley encourages 10 people it is thinking of hiring to discuss the demands of the job with their spouses, girlfriends, or boyfriends—new recruits sometimes work 100 hours a week. The firm's managing directors and their wives take promising candidates and their spouses or companions out to dinner to bring home to them what they will face. The point is to get a person who will not be happy within Morgan's culture because of the way his family feels to eliminate himself from consideration for a job there.

This kind of rigorous screening might seem an invitation to hire only people 11 who fit the mold of present employees. In fact, it often *is* harder for companies with strong cultures to accept individuals different from the prevailing type.

· Step two. The company subjects the newly hired individual to experiences 12 calculated to induce humility and to make him question his prior behavior, beliefs, and values. By lessening the recruit's comfort with himself, the company hopes to promote openness toward its own norms and values.

This may sound like brainwashing or boot camp, but it usually just takes the 13 form of pouring on more work than the newcomer can possibly do. IBM and Morgan Guaranty socialize with training programs in which, to quote one participant, "You work every night until 2 A.M. on your own material, and then help others." Procter & Gamble achieves the same result with what might be called upending experiences—requiring a recent college graduate to color in a map of sales territories, for example. The message is clear: while you may be accomplished in many respects, you are in kindergarten as far as what you know about this organization.

Humility isn't the only feeling brought on by long hours of intense work that 14 carry the individual close to his or her limit. When everybody's vulnerability runs high, one also tends to become close to one's colleagues. Companies sometimes intensify this cohesiveness by not letting trainees out of the pressure cooker for very long—everyone has so much work to do that he doesn't have time to see people outside the company or reestablish a more normal social distance from his co-workers.

Morgan Stanley, for instance, expects newly hired associates to work 12- to 15 14- hour days and most weekends. Their lunches are not the Lucullan repasts that MBAs fantasize about,[1] but are typically confined to 30 minutes in the unprepossessing cafeteria. One can observe similar patterns—long hours, exhausting travel schedules, and almost total immersion in casework—at law firms and consulting outfits. Do recruits chafe under such discipline? Not that much, apparently. Socialization is a bit like exercise—it's probably easier to reconcile yourself to it while you're young.

· Step three. Companies send the newly humble recruits into the trenches, 16

---

[1]Lucullan repasts: luxurious feasts, like the banquets given by the Roman general, Lucius Licinius Lucullus (first century, B.C.). [Eds.]

pushing them to master one of the disciplines at the core of the company's business. The newcomer's promotions are tied to how he does in that discipline.

In the course of the individual's first few months with the company, his universe of experience has increasingly narrowed down to the organization's culture. The company, having got him to open his mind to its way of doing business, now cements that orientation by putting him in the field and giving him lots of carefully monitored experience. It rewards his progress with promotions at predictable intervals. 17

While IBM hires some MBAs and a few older professionals with prior work experience, almost all of them start at the same level as recruits from college and go through the same training programs. It takes about 15 years, for example, to become a financial controller. At Morgan Stanley and consulting firms like McKinsey, new associates must similarly work their way up through the ranks. There is almost never a quick way to jump a few rungs on the ladder. 18

The gains from this approach are cumulative. For starters, when all trainees understand there is just one step-by-step career path, it reduces politicking. Since they are being evaluated on how they do over the long haul, they are less tempted to cut corners or go for short–term victories. By the time they reach senior positions they understand the business not as a financial abstraction, but as a reality of people they know and skills they've learned. They can communicate with people in the lowest ranks in the shorthand of shared experience. 19

· Step four. At every stage of the new manager's career, the company measures the operating results he has achieved and rewards him accordingly. It does this with systems that are comprehensive and consistent. These systems focus particularly on those aspects of the business that make for competitive success and for the perpetuation of the corporation's values. 20

Procter & Gamble, for instance, measures managers on three factors it deems critical to a brand's success: building volume, building profit, and conducting planned change—altering a product to make it more effective or more satisfying to the customer in some other way. Information from the outside world—market-share figures, say—is used in the measuring along with financial data. Performance appraisals focus on these criteria as well as on general managerial skill. 21

IBM uses similar interlocking systems to track adherence to one of its major values, respect for the dignity of the individual. The company monitors this with surveys of employee morale; "Speak Up," a confidential suggestion box; a widely proclaimed policy of having the boss's door open to any subordinates who want to talk; so-called skip-level interviews, in which a subordinate can skip over a couple of organizational levels to discuss a grievance with senior management; and informal social contacts between senior managers and lower level employees. Management moves quickly when any of these systems turns up a problem. 22

The IBM culture includes a mechanism for disciplining someone who has 23
violated one of the corporate norms—handling his subordinates too harshly,
say, or being overzealous against the competition. The malefactor will be assigned to what is called the penalty box—typically, a fairly meaningless job at
the same level, sometimes in a less desirable location. A branch manager in
Chicago might be moved to a nebulous staff position at headquarters. To the
outsider, penalty box assignments look like just another job rotation, but insiders
know that the benched manager is out of the game temporarily.

The penalty box provides a place to hold a manager while the mistakes he's 24
made and the hard feelings they've engendered are gradually forgotten. The
mechanism lends substance to the belief, widespread among IBM employees,
that the company won't fire anybody capriciously. The penalty box's existence
says, in effect, that in the career of strong, effective managers there are times
when one steps on toes. The penalty box lets someone who has stepped too
hard contemplate his error and return to play another day.

· Step five. All along the way, the company promotes adherence to its tran- 25
scendent values, those overarching purposes that rise way above the day-to-day
imperative to make a buck. At the AT&T of yore, for example, the transcendent
value was guaranteeing phone service to customers through any emergency.
Identification with such a value enables the employee to accept the personal
sacrifices the company asks of him.

Placing oneself at the service of an organization entails real costs. There are 26
long hours of work, weekends apart from one's family, bosses one has to endure,
criticism that seems unfair, job assignments that are inconvenient or undesirable. The countervailing force making for commitment to the company in these
circumstances is the organization's set of transcendent values that connect its
purpose to human values of a higher order than just those of the marketplace—
values such as serving mankind, providing a first-class product for society, or
helping people learn and grow.

Someone going to work for Delta Air Lines will be told again and again 27
about the "Delta family feeling." Everything that's said makes the point that
Delta's values sometimes require sacrifices—management takes pay cuts during
lean times, senior flight attendants and pilots voluntarily work fewer hours per
week so the company won't have to lay off more-junior employees. Candidates
who accept employment with Delta tend to buy into this quid pro quo, agreeing
in effect that keeping the Delta family healthy justifies the sacrifices that the
family exacts.

· Step six. The company constantly harps on watershed events in the or- 28
ganization's history that reaffirm the importance of the firm's culture. Folklore
reinforces a code of conduct—how we do things around here.

All companies have their stories, but at corporations that socialize well the 29
morals of these stories all tend to point in the same direction. In the old Bell
System, story after story extolled Bell employees who made heroic sacrifices to

keep the phones working. The Bell folklore was so powerful that when natural disaster struck, all elements of a one-million-member organization were able to pull together, cut corners, violate normal procedures, even do things that would not look good when measured by usual job performance criteria—all in the interest of restoring phone service. Folklore, when well understood, can legitimize special channels for moving an organization in a hurry.

· Step seven. The company supplies promising individuals with role models. 30 These models are consistent—each exemplary manager displays the same traits.

Nothing communicates more powerfully to younger professionals within an 31 organization than the example of peers or superiors who are recognized as winners and who also share common qualities. The protégé watches the role model make presentations, handle conflict, and write memos, then tries to duplicate the traits that seem to work most effectively.

Strong-culture firms regard role models as constituting the most powerful 32 long-term training program available. Because other elements of the culture are consistent, the people who emerge as role models are consistent. P&G's brand managers, for example, exhibit extraordinary consistency in several traits—they're almost all analytical, energetic, and adept at motivating others. Unfortunately most firms leave the emergence of role models to chance. Some of the fast track seem to be whizzes at analysis, others are skilled at leading people, others seem astute at politics: the result for those below is confusion as to what it *really* takes to succeed. For example, the companies that formerly made up the Bell System have a strong need to become more market oriented and aggressive. Yet the Bell culture continues to discriminate against potential fast-trackers who, judged by the values of the older monopoly culture, are too aggressive.

Many companies can point to certain organizational practices that look like 33 one or two of the seven steps, but rarely are all seven managed in a well-coordinated effort. It is *consistency* across all seven steps of the socialization process that results in a strongly cohesive culture that endures.

When one understands the seven steps, one can better appreciate the case 34 for socialization. All organizations require a degree of order and consistency. They can achieve this through explicit procedures and formal controls or through implicit social controls. American companies, on the whole, tend to rely more on formal controls. The result is that management often appears rigid, bureaucratic, and given to oversteering. A United Technologies executive laments, "I came from the Bell system. Compared with AT&T, this is a weak culture and there is little socialization. But of course there is still need for controls. So they put handcuffs on you, shackle you to every nickel, track every item of inventory, monitor every movement in production and head count. They control you by the balance sheet."

At most American companies, an inordinate amount of energy gets used up 35 in fighting "the system." But when an organization can come up with a strong, consistent set of implicit understandings, it has effectively established for itself a body of common law to supplement its formal rules. This enables it to use formal systems as they are supposed to be used—as tools rather than straitjackets. An IBM manager, conversant with the concept of socialization, puts it this way: "Socialization acts as a fine-tuning device; it helps us make sense out of the procedures and quantitative measures. Any number of times I've been faced with a situation where the right thing for the measurement system was X and the right thing for IBM was Y. I've always been counseled to tilt toward what was right for IBM in the long term and what was right for our people. They pay us a lot to do that. Formal controls, without coherent values and culture, are too crude a compass to steer by."

Organizations that socialize effectively use their cultures to manage ambi- 36
guity, ever present in such tricky matters as business politics and personal relationships. This tends to free up time and energy. More goes toward getting the job done and focusing on external considerations like the competition and the customer. "At IBM you spend 50% of your time managing the internal context," states a former IBMer, now at ITT. "At most companies it's more like 75%." A marketing manager who worked at Atari before it got new management recalls: "You can't imagine how much time and energy around here went into politics. You had to determine who was on first base this month in order to figure out how to obtain what you needed to get the job done. There were no rules. There were no clear values. Two of the men at the top stood for diametrically opposite things. Your bosses were constantly changing. All this meant that you never had time to develop a routine way for getting things done at the interface between your job and the next guy's. Without rules for working with one another, a lot of people got hurt, got burned out, and were never taught the 'Atari way' of doing things because there wasn't an Atari way."

The absence of cultural guidelines makes organizational life capricious. This 37
is so because success as a manager requires managing not only the substance of the business but also, increasingly, managing one's role and relationships. When social roles are unclear, no one is speaking the same language; communication and trust break down. A person's power to get things done in a company seldom depends on his title and formal authority alone. In great measure it rests on his track record, reputation, knowledge, and network of relationships. In effect, the power to implement change and execute business strategies depends heavily on what might be called one's social currency—as in money—something a person accumulates over time. Strong-culture firms empower employees, helping them build this currency by supplying continuity and clarity.

Continuity and clarity also help reduce the anxiety people feel about their 38
careers. Mixed signals about rewards, promotions, career paths, criteria for being on the "fast track" or a candidate for termination inevitably generate a lot of gossip, game playing, and unproductive expenditure of energy. Only the naive think that these matters can be entirely resolved by provisions in a policy man-

ual. The reality is that many criteria of success for middle- and senior-level positions can't be articulated in writing. The rules tend to be communicated and enforced via relatively subtle cues. When the socialization process is weak, the cues tend to be poorly or inconsistently communicated.

Look carefully at career patterns in most companies. Ambitious professionals 39 strive to learn the ropes, but there are as many "ropes" as there are individuals who have made their way to the top. So the aspirant picks an approach, and if it happens to coincide with how his superiors do things, he's on the fast track. Commonly, though, the approach that works with one superior is offensive to another. "As a younger manager, I was always taught to touch bases and solicit input before moving ahead," a manager at a Santa Clara, California, electronics firm says, "and it always worked. But at a higher level, with a different boss, my base-touching was equated with being political. The organization doesn't forewarn you when it changes signals. A lot of good people leave owing to misunderstandings of this kind." The human cost of the failure to socialize tends to go largely unrecognized.

What about the cost of conformity? A senior vice president of IBM asserts: 40 "Conformity among IBM employees has often been described as stultifying in terms of dress, behavior, and lifestyle. There is, in fact, strong pressure to adhere to certain norms of superficial behavior, and much more intensely to the three tenets of the company philosophy—respect for the dignity of the individual, first-rate customer service, and excellence. These are the benchmarks. Between them there is wide latitude for divergence in opinions and behavior."

A P&G executive echoes this thought: "There is a great deal of consistency 41 around here in how certain things are done, and these are rather critical to our sustained success. Beyond that, there are very few hard and fast rules. People on the outside might portray our culture as imposing lock-step uniformity. It doesn't feel rigid when you're inside. It feels like it accommodates you. And best of all, you know the game you're in—you know whether you're playing soccer or football; you can find out very clearly what it takes to succeed and you can bank your career on that."

It is useful to distinguish here between norms that are central to the business's 42 success and social conventions that signal commitment and belonging. The former are essential in that they ensure consistency in executing the company's strategy. The latter are the organizational equivalent of shaking hands. They are social conventions that make it easier for people to be comfortable with one another. One need not observe all of them, but one wants to reassure the organization that one is on the team. An important aspect of this second set of social values is that, like a handshake, they are usually not experienced as oppressive. Partly this is because adherence doesn't require much thought or deliberation, just as most people don't worry much about their individuality being compromised by the custom of shaking hands.

The aim of socialization is to establish a base of shared attitudes, habits, and 43
values that foster cooperation, integrity, and communication. But without the
natural rough-and-tumble friction between competing coworkers, some might
argue, there will be little innovation. The record does not bear this out. Consider
3M or Bell Labs. Both are highly innovative institutions—and both remain so
by fostering social rules that reward innovation. Socialization does not necessarily discourage competition between employees. Employees compete hard at
IBM, P&G, major consulting firms, law firms, and outstanding financial institutions like Morgan Guaranty and Morgan Stanley.

There is, of course, the danger of strong-culture firms becoming incestuous 44
and myopic—what came to be known in the early days of the Japanese auto
invasion as the General Motors syndrome. Most opponents of socialization rally
around this argument. But what one learns from observing the likes of IBM and
P&G is that their cultures keep them constantly facing outward. Most companies
like this tend to guard against the danger of complacency by having as one
element of their culture an *obsession* with some facet of their performance in
the marketplace. For example, McDonald's has an obsessive concern for quality
control, IBM for customer service, 3M for innovation. These obsessions make
for a lot of fire drills. But they also serve as the organizational equivalent of
calisthenics, keeping people fit for the day when the emergency is real. When,
on the other hand, the central cultural concern points inward rather than outward—as seems to be the case, say, with Delta Air Lines' focus on "family
feeling"—the strong-culture company may be riding for a fall.

Revolutions begin with an assault on awareness. It is time to be more candid 45
and clear-minded about socialization. Between our espoused individualism and
the reality of most companies lies a zone where organizational and individual
interests overlap. If we can manage our ambivalence about socialization, we
can make our organizations more effective. Equally important, we can reduce
the human costs that arise today as individuals stumble along in careers with
companies that fail to articulate ends and means coherently and understandably
for all employees.

QUESTIONS

1. What does Pascale mean by a company culture?
2. What companies does Pascale appear to admire the most? What does he find most
admirable about them?
3. What is Pascale's view of Delta Airlines? How does it differ from his view of IBM,
for instance? This essay originally appeared in May 1984. What has happened to Delta
Airlines since then?
4. Pascale has organized his essay around seven steps. Describe each step in a single
sentence. To what do these steps lead? Are they all really steps? That is, do they nec-

essarily come in the order in which they are presented, with each one taking us further than the one before, or could they be rearranged? What seems to be the principle behind the present arrangement? Is it used consistently?

5. Consider the material that comes before and after the seven steps. What are the functions of the first and last sections of the essay?

6. This essay originally appeared in *Fortune* under its title and a subheading (reprinted in the headnote) that explicitly states what is in the essay. Why do you think *Fortune* presented the essay this way? What does this explicitness reveal about the magazine and its readers?

7. How does the title of this essay relate to the text of the essay? Compare this title with some others in this anthology. Do all essays have the same relationship between their titles and their texts that this one has? What different relationships between titles and texts can you identify?

8. Consider some organization you know that has a culture—perhaps a club, a business, a team, or a sorority. Write an essay in which you describe this culture and its function or purpose. Include some discussion of the steps through which a new member of this group becomes socialized or acculturated.

9. In paragraph 3 and other places, Pascale raises the question of how a strong company culture seems to conflict with the American stress on individual freedom. Write an essay in which you consider this problem, using examples drawn from Pascale's essay.

WHY WOMEN AREN'T GETTING TO THE TOP

Susan Fraker

Susan Fraker is an associate editor at Fortune *magazine. Assisted by research associate David Weld Stevens, she wrote this essay for the April 16, 1984, issue of the magazine, where it appeared as the cover story. In the magazine's format, the title appeared in very heavy type. It was followed by a subheading in smaller type, designed to attract the reader's attention: "No women are on the fast track to the chief executive's job at any* Fortune *500 corporation. That's incongruous, given the number of years women have been working in management. The reasons are elusive and tough for management to deal with."*

Ten years have passed since U.S. corporations began hiring more than token 1
numbers of women for jobs at the bottom rung of the management ladder. A decade into their careers, how far up have these women climbed? The answer: not as far as their male counterparts. Despite impressive progress at the entry level and in middle management, women are having trouble breaking into senior management. "There is an invisible ceiling for women at that level," says Janet Jones-Parker, executive director of the Association of Executive Search Consultants Inc. "After eight or ten years, they hit a barrier."

The trouble begins at about the $75,000 to $100,000 salary level, and seems 2
to get worse the higher one looks. Only one company on *Fortune*'s list of the 500 largest U.S. industrial corporations has a woman chief executive. That woman, Katharine Graham of the Washington Post Co. (No. 342), readily admits she got the job because her family owns a controlling share of the corporation.

More surprising, given that women have been on the ladder for ten years, is 3
that none currently seems to have a shot at the top rung. Executive recruiters, asked to identify women who might become presidents or chief executives of *Fortune* 500 companies, draw a blank. Even companies that have women in senior management privately concede that these women aren't going to occupy the chairman's office.

Women have only four of the 154 spots this year at the Harvard Business 4
School's Advanced Management Program—a prestigious 13-week conclave to which companies send executives they are grooming for the corridors of power. The numbers aren't much better at comparable programs at Stanford and at

Dartmouth's Tuck School. But perhaps the most telling admission of trouble comes from men at the top. "The women aren't making it," confessed the chief executive of a *Fortune* 500 company to a consultant. "Can you help us find out why?"

All explanations are controversial to one faction or another in this highly 5 charged debate. At one extreme, many women—and some men—maintain that women are the victims of blatant sexism. At the other extreme, many men— and a few women—believe women are unsuitable for the highest managerial jobs: they lack the necessary assertiveness, they don't know how to get along in this rarefied world, or they have children and lose interest in—or time for— their careers. Somewhere in between is a surprisingly large group of men and women who see "discrimination" as the major problem, but who often can't define precisely what they mean by the term.

The discrimination they talk about is not the simple-minded sexism of dirty 6 jokes and references to "girls." It is not born of hatred, or indeed of any ill will that the bearer may be conscious of. What they call discrimination consists simply of treating women differently from men. The notion dumbfounds some male managers. You mean to say, they ask, that managerial women don't want to be treated differently from men in any respect, and that by acting otherwise— as I was raised to think only decent and gentlemanly—I'm somehow prejudicing their chances for success? Yes, the women respond.

"Men I talk to would like to see more women in senior management," says 7 Ann Carol Brown, a consultant to several *Fortune* 500 companies. "But they don't recognize the subtle barriers that stand in the way." Brown thinks the biggest hurdle is a matter of comfort, not competence. "At senior management levels, competence is assumed," she says. "What you're looking for is someone who fits, someone who gets along, someone you trust. Now that's subtle stuff. How does a group of men feel that a woman is going to fit? I think it's very hard."

The experience of an executive at a large Northeastern bank illustrates how 8 many managerial women see the problem. Promoted to senior vice president several years ago, she was the first woman named to that position. But she now believes it will be many years before the bank appoints a woman executive vice president. "The men just don't feel comfortable," she says. "They make all sorts of excuses—that I'm not a banker [she worked as a consultant originally], that I don't know the culture. There's a smoke screen four miles thick. I attribute it to being a woman." Similarly, 117 to 300 women executives polled recently by UCLA's Graduate School of Management and Korn/Ferry International, an executive search firm, felt that being a woman was the greatest obstacle to their success.

A common concern among women, particularly in law and investment bank- 9 ing, is that the best assignments go to men. "Some departments—like sales and trading or mergers and acquisitions—are considered more macho, hence more prestigious," says a woman at a New York investment bank. "It's nothing explicit. But if women can't get the assignments that allow them to shine, how can they advance?"

Women also worry that they don't receive the same kind of constructive   10
criticism that men do. While these women probably overestimate the amount of feedback their male colleagues receive, even some men acknowledge widespread male reluctance to criticize a woman. "There are vast numbers of men who can't do it," says Eugene Jennings, professor of business administration at Michigan State University and a consultant to a dozen large companies. A male banking executive agrees: "A male boss will haul a guy aside and just kick ass if the subordinate performs badly in front of a client. But I heard about a woman here who gets nervous and tends to giggle in front of customers. She's unaware of it and her boss hasn't told her. But behind her back he downgrades her for not being smooth with customers."

Sometimes the message that has to be conveyed to a woman manager is   11
much more sensitive. An executive at a large company says he once had to tell a woman that she should either cross her legs or keep her legs together when she sat. The encounter was obviously painful to him. "She listened to me and thanked me and expressed shock at what she was doing," he recalls, with a touch of agony in his voice. "My God, this is something only your mother tells you. I'm a fairly direct person and a great believer in equal opportunity. But it was damn difficult for me to say this to a woman whom I view to be very proper in all other respects."

Research by Anne Harlan, a human resource manager at the Federal Avia-   12
tion Administration, and Carol Weiss, a managing associate of Charles Hamilton Associates, a Boston consulting firm, suggests that the situation doesn't necessarily improve as the number of women in an organization increases. Their study, conducted at the Wellesley College Center for Research on Women and completed in 1982, challenges the theory advanced by some experts that when a corporation attained a "critical mass" of executive women—defined as somewhere between 30% and 35%—job discrimination would vanish naturally as men and women began to take each other for granted.

Harlan and Weiss observed the effects of different numbers of women in an   13
organization during a three-year study of 100 men and women managers at two Northeastern retailing corporations. While their sample of companies was not large, after their results were published, other companies said they had similar experiences. Harlan and Weiss found that while overt resistance drops quickly after the first few women become managers, it seems to pick up again as the number of women reaches 15%. In one company they studied, only 6% of the managers were women, compared with 19% in the second company. But more women in the second company complained of discrimination, ranging from sexual harassment to inadequate feedback. Could something other than discrim-

ination—very different corporate cultures, say—have accounted for the result? Harlan and Weiss say no, that the two companies were eminently comparable.

Consultants and executives who think discrimination is the problem tend to believe it persists in part because the government has relaxed its commitment to affirmative action, which they define more narrowly than some advocates do. "We're not talking about quotas or preferential treatment," says Margaret Hennig who, along with Anne Jardim, heads the Simmons College Graduate School of Management. "That's stupid management. We just mean the chance to compete equally." Again, a semantic chasm separates women and men. Women like Hennig and Jardim think of affirmative action as a vigorous effort on the part of companies to ensure that women are treated equally and that sexist prejudices aren't permitted to operate. Men think the term means reverse discrimination, giving women preferential treatment.   14

Legislation such as the Equal Employment Opportunity Act of 1972 prohibits companies from discriminating against women in hiring. The laws worked well—indeed, almost too well. After seven or eight years, says Jennings of Michigan State, the pressure was off and no one pushed hard to see that discrimination was eliminated in selecting people for senior management. Jennings thinks the problem began in the latter days of the Carter Administration, when the economy was lagging and companies worried more about making money than about how their women managers were doing. The Reagan Administration hasn't made equal opportunity a priority either.   15

What about the belief that women fall behind not because of discrimination, but because they are cautious, unaggressive, and differently motivated than men—or less motivated? Even some female executives believe that women derail their careers by choosing staff jobs over high-risk, high-reward line positions. One woman, formerly with a large consumer goods company and now president of a market research firm, urges women to worry less about sexism and more about whether the jobs they take are the right route to the top. "I spent five years thinking the only reason I didn't become a corporate officer at my former company was because of my sex," she says. "I finally had to come to grips with the fact that I overemphasized being a women and underemphasized what I did for a living. I was in a staff function—the company didn't live and die by what I did."   16

Men and women alike tend to believe that because women are raised differently they must manage differently. Research to support this belief is hard to come by, though. The women retail managers studied by Harlan and Weiss, while never quarterbacks or catchers, had no trouble playing on management teams. Nor did they perform less well on standardized tests measuring qualities like assertiveness and leadership. "Women don't manage differently," Harlan says flatly.   17

In a much larger study specifically addressing management styles, psychol- 18
ogists Jay Hall and Susan Donnell of Teleometrics International Inc., a management training company, reached the same conclusion. They matched nearly
2,000 men and women managers according to age, rank in their organization,
kind of organization, and the number of people they supervised. The psychologists ran tests to assess everything from managerial philosophies to the ability
to get along with people, even quizzing subordinates on their views of the boss.
Donnell and Hall concluded, "Male and female managers do not differ in the
way they manage the organization's technical and human resources."

Data on how women's expectations—and therefore, arguably, their per- 19
formance—may differ from men's are more confusing. Stanford Professor Myra
Strober studied 150 men and 26 women who graduated from the Stanford
Business School in 1974. When she and a colleague, Francine Gordon, polled
the MBAs shortly before graduation, they discovered that the women had much
lower expectations for their peak earnings. The top salary the women expected
during their careers was only 60% of the men's. Four years later the ratio had
fallen to 40%.

Did this mean that women were less ambitious or were willing to take lower 20
salaries to get management jobs? Strober doesn't think so. She says a major
reason for the women's lower salary expectations was that they took jobs in
industries that traditionally pay less, but which, the women thought, offered
opportunities for advancement. Almost 20% of the women in her sample went
into government, compared with 3% of the men. On the other hand, no women
went into investment banking or real estate development, which each employed
about 6% of the men. Strober points out, however, that investment banking
and big-time real estate were all but closed to women in the early 1970s. "One
way people decide what their aspirations are," she says, "is to look around and
see what seems realistic. If you look at a field and see no women advancing,
you may modify your goals."

Some of what Mary Anne Devanna found in her examination of MBAs 21
contradicts Strober's conclusions. Devanna, research coordinator of the Columbia Business School's Center for Research in Career Development, matched 45
men and 45 women who graduated from the Columbia Business School from
1969 to 1972. Each paired man and woman had similar backgrounds, credentials, and marital status. The starting salaries of the women were 98% of the
men's. Using data collected in 1980, Devanna found a big difference in the
salaries men and women ultimately achieved, though. In manufacturing, the
highest paying sector, women earned $41,818 after ten years vs. $59,733 for
the men. Women in finance had salaries of $42,867 vs. $46,786 for the men.
The gap in the service industries was smallest: $36,666 vs. $38,600. She then
tested four hypotheses in seeking to explain the salary differences: (1) that women
are less successful because they are motivated differently than men, (2) that
motherhood causes women to divert attention from their careers, (3) that women

seek jobs in low-paying industries, and (4) that women seek types of jobs—in human resources, say—that pay less.

Devanna found no major differences between the sexes in the importance   22
they attached to the psychic or monetary rewards of work. "The women did not expect to earn less than the men," she says. Nor did she find that motherhood led women to abandon their careers. Although several women took maternity leaves, all returned to work full time within six months. Finally, Devanna found no big differences in the MBAs' choice of industry or function, either when they took their first jobs or ten years later.

Devanna concluded that discrimination, not level of motivation or choice of   23
job, accounted for the pay differences. Could the problem simply have been performance—that the women didn't manage as well as men? Devanna claims that while she couldn't take this variable into account specifically, she controlled for all the variables that should have made for a difference in performance—from family background to grades in business school.

In their discussions with male executives, researchers like Devanna hear a   24
recurrent theme—a conviction that women don't take their careers seriously. Even though most female managers were regarded as extremely competent, the men thought they would eventually leave—either to have children or because the tensions of work became too much. Both are legitimate concerns. A woman on the fast track is under intense pressure. Many corporate types believe that she gets much more scrutiny than a man and must work harder to succeed. The pressures increase geometrically if she has small children at home.

Perhaps as a result, thousands of women have careers rather than husbands   25
and children. In the UCLA-Korn/Ferry study of executive women, 52% had never married, were divorced, or were widowed, and 61% had no children. A similar study of male executives done in 1979 found that only 5% of the men had never married or were divorced and even fewer—3%—had no children.

Statistics on how many women bear children and then leave the corporation   26
are incomplete. Catalyst, a nonprofit organization that encourages the participation of women in business, studied 815 two-career families in 1980. It found that 37% of the new mothers in the study returned to work within two months; 68% were back after 4½ months; 87% in eight months. To a company, of course, an eight-month absence is a long time. Moreover, the 10% or so who never come back—most males are convinced the figure is higher—represent a substantial capital investment lost. It would be naive to think that companies don't crank this into their calculation of how much the women who remain are worth.

Motherhood clearly slows the progress of women who decide to take long   27
maternity leaves or who choose to work part time. But even those committed to working full time on their return believe thay are sometimes held back—purposely or inadvertently. "Men make too many assumptions that women with children aren't free to take on time-consuming tasks," says Gene Kofke, director

of human resources at AT&T. Karen Gonçalves, 34, quit her job as a consultant when she was denied challenging assignments after the birth of her daughter. "I was told clearly that I couldn't expect to move ahead as fast as I had been," she says. Latter, when Gonçalves began working at the consulting firm of Arthur D. Little Inc. in Cambridge, Massachusetts, she intentionally avoided discussions of family and children: "I didn't keep a picture of my daughter in the office, and I would travel anywhere, no matter how hard it was for me."

Sometimes pregnancy is more of an issue for the men who witness it than   28
for the women who go through it. Karol Emmerich, 35, now treasurer of Dayton Hudson Corp., was the first high-level woman at the department-store company to become pregnant. "The men didn't really know what to do," she recalls. "They were worried when I wanted to take three months off. But they wanted to encourage me to come back. So they promoted me to treasurer when I was seven months pregnant. Management got a lot of good feedback." Emmerich's experience would please Simmons Dean Anne Jardim, who worries that most organizations aren't doing enough to keep women who want to have children. "It's mind-boggling," she argues. "Either some of the brightest women in this country aren't going to reproduce or the companies are going to write off women in whom they have a tremendous investment."

To the corporation it may seem wasteful to train a woman and then be unable   29
to promote her because she won't move to take the new job. The Catalyst study found that 40% of the men surveyed had moved for their jobs, vs. only 21% of the women. An argument can be made that an immobile executive is worth less to the corporation—and hence may be paid less.

Where women frequently do go is out of the company and into business for   30
themselves. "When the achievements you want aren't forthcoming, it makes going out on your own easier," says a woman who has set up her own consultancy. "I was told I wouldn't make it into senior management at my bank. Maybe I just didn't have it. But the bank never found any woman who did. They were operating under a consent decree and they brought in a lot of women at the vice president level. Every single one of them left." Karen Gonçalves left Arthur D. Little to do part-time teaching and consulting when she was pregnant with her second child. "I didn't think I would get the professional satisfaction I wanted at ADL," she says.

From 1977 to 1980, according to the Small Business Administration, the   31
number of businesses owned by women increased 33%, compared with an 11% increase for men—though admittedly the women's increase started from a much smaller base. While it's not clear from the numbers that women are entering the entrepreneurial ranks in greater numbers than they are joining corporations, some experts think so. "It's ironic," says Strober of Stanford. "The problem of the 1970s was bringing women into the corporation. The problem of the 1980s is keeping them there."

A few companies, convinced that women face special problems and that it's   32
in the corporation's interest to help overcome them, are working hard at solutions. At Penn Mutual Life Insurance Co. in Philadelphia, where nearly half
the managers are women, executives conducted a series of off-site seminars on
gender issues and sex-role stereotypes. Dayton Hudson provides support (moral
and financial) for a program whereby women in the company trade information
on issues like personal financial planning and child care.

What women need most, the experts say, are loud, clear, continuing state-   33
ments of support from senior management. Women have come a long way at
Merck, says B. Lawrence Branch, the company's director of equal employment
affairs, because Chairman John J. Horan insisted that their progress be watched.
Merck has a program that identifies 10% of its women and 10% of minorities
as "most promising." The company prepares a written agenda of what it will
take for them to move to the next level. Progress upward may mean changing
jobs or switching functions, so Merck circulates their credentials throughout the
company. "We have a timetable and we track these women carefully,' says
Branch. Since 1979 almost 40% of the net growth in Merck's managerial staff
has been women.

Sensitive to charges of reverse discrimination, Branch explains that Merck   34
has for years singled out the best employees to make sure they get opportunities
to advance. Women, he notes, were consistently underrepresented in that group.
In his view the tracking program simply allows women to get into the competition with fast-track men. Others might not be so charitable. Any company that
undertakes to do something on behalf of its managerial women leaves itself open
to the charge that it too is discriminating—treating women and men differently.

What everyone may be able to agree on is that opening corporations to   35
competition in the executive ranks is clearly good for performance and profits.
But how can a company do this? It can try to find productive part-time work
for all employees who want to work part time—even managers. It can structure
promotions so that fewer careers are derailed by an absence of a few months or
the unwillingness to relocate. It can make sure that the right information, particularly on job openings, reaches everyone. Perhaps most importantly, it can
reward its managers for developing talent of all sorts and sexes, penalize them
if they don't, and vigilantly supervise the process.

QUESTIONS

1. The title of the essay implies that it will answer the question, "Why aren't women
getting to the top?" Does it? What, if anything, have you learned about the problem?

2. Where there's a problem, there may be a solution. What does Fraker offer the
reader beyond an explanation of the problem and an exploration of its possible causes?

3. The format of *Fortune* does not allow for footnotes, but Fraker mentions her sources regularly, and it is obvious that this essay is a version of a research paper. List the sources you can identify, in the order in which they are mentioned, to see how many sources were consulted and what range and variety of material it takes to produce an informative essay of this kind. How much of the information Fraker presents is based on private conversations or interviews, and how much comes from published documents or public records?

4. Fraker has to present a lot of information in this essay. What does she do to enliven and humanize her data? Look at particular passages that seem to you successful in turning abstractions into concrete form. How do different *kinds* of information work to prevent this from turning into a recital of dry abstractions?

5. How has Fraker organized the essay? What are the large subdivisions of the main topic?

6. Extend Fraker's study to your own school. Are women getting to the top there? Can you discover changes over the past ten years in numbers of women on the faculty, promotions to higher ranks, and so on? Are any women among your school's senior administrators, such as president, deans, or department heads? Write an essay in which you describe the situation, explain it, and, if it seems appropriate, suggest ways to change it. (Check on whether any plans for change are now in operation—and how they are working.) Use a mixture of statistical data and personal interviews as Fraker has.

7. Choose any minority group and consider their progress to the top in some organization for which you can obtain the relevant data. Using Fraker as a model, try to identify a problem, if there is one, explain its sources, and suggest solutions. If what you find is not a problem but a success story, try to explain how it happened and suggest how it might be repeated in other areas.

LET'S HAVE A MEAL TOGETHER
Rosalind Coward

A *lecturer in the Department of Visual Communication at Goldsmiths' College in London, England, Rosalind Coward has written frequently on questions of interest to women and on cultural theory and criticism. She was a coauthor (with John Ellis) of* Language and Materialism *and the author of* Patriarchal Precedents *as well as* Female Desires *(1985) from which the following essay has been selected.*

When 800 million people in the world live under the constant threat of   1
starvation, it may seem frivolous to look at meals in terms of sexual politics. But *how* food is consumed and prepared has crucial implications for women in this society, because it expresses deeply held ideologies of provision and dependency. Where eating is no longer a matter of absolute survival, the preparation and contexts of food are laced with social symbolism. Eating appears to be utterly natural—like breathing, an essential part of our survival. So it is hard to imagine that along with the nourishment we might be swallowing a whole lot more besides. (And I'm not referring to the chemical additives.) This very appearance of naturalness disguises the fact that women's surbordination is expressed in the ways we eat. Who does the cooking, what is served up in what order by whom and in what settings are all practices determined by the social significance they have.

In spite of the general level of affluence in Western society, eating is not a   2
particularly easy business. As a society we are plagued with alimentary disorders and neuroses connected with eating—ulcers, indigestion, anorexia, bulimia. Women, in particular, sometimes find eating in public very difficult since there's too much anxiety connected with social eating. These disorders and neuroses connected with food surely reflect on the indigestible aspects of social and sexual symbolism associated with eating.

Just take the classic example of when a man says, "Let's have a meal together   3
sometime." Only in recent times, with the impact of feminist ideologies, have women been able to establish the possibility of paying for their own meal, and the traditional practice is by no means dead. The bill is still presented to the man, the man is invited to taste the wines, and some extremely smart (and reactionary) restaurants give women a menu without prices.

Some cite this as a typical example of the triviality of feminism's concerns,   4
but such a battle, small though it may seem, was necessary to combat the symbolism behind accepting a meal from a man. Lurking behind such a treat is the symbolism of the business man–client relationship. In this relationship,

a meal is provided by the business or company seeking the services of a particular person. The "meal out" in a good restaurant is paid for by the company as a way of expressing the wealth, status and power of the business. The meal impresses the client and invariably puts him in a relationship of obligation. The symbolism between men and women to some extent reproduces this symbolism, the symbolism of the male provider. What is demonstrated is the ability to provide, and economic status in the world. In addition these "traditional" meals eaten out by a man and a woman carry meanings not dissimilar from those pertaining to prostitution. Services are bought for a fee. In routine sexual relations, services are expected in return for provision. Small wonder that even the most impoverished women sometimes make an issue about paying for themselves just in case unwanted sexual attentions should be wheeled in after the starters.

A close scrutiny of the average restaurant shows that even the lay-out seems 5 designed to affirm the symbolism of business man–client relationship, whether it is between the sexes or between companies. The only people who can afford to eat out are either people with expense accounts or those who do so for special occasions. Restaurants always seem to be packed with business men doing deals or row after row of heterosexual couples. Locked in intense dialogue (propositions or arguments) or staring at each other in stony silence, you might get the impression visiting the average restaurant for the first time that no other relationship existed under the sun. (And that this wasn't good news.) This is quite different from other societies, such as the Chinese, where eating out is habitual, and eating with any less than ten people decidedly odd. Restaurants in our society, however, seem to reinforce the impression that special-occasion meals are more often than not symbolic affirmations of relations of power and obligations.

Most of our eating anxieties start earlier than the days of "special occasions" 6 in restaurants. Eating neuroses usually stem from the early experiences of family eating, from the unspoken conflicts and turbulent emotions associated with family meals. No less than eating out, though family meals are redolent with the symbolism of economic provision and dependency.

Everyone has stories of family meals ending in some kind of drama or chaos. 7 Either violent arguments break out—food hits the floor, drink is hurled across the room, joints[1] grow cold as insults rise in a crescendo, mothers and children silently weep into their congealing food—or sometimes an embarrassing and hostile silence descends, no one daring risk further misunderstanding.

Eating a meal together in the family is burdened with the heavy symbolism 8 of provision and dependency. This becomes most apparent in the big communal meals—the Sunday lunch and the Christmas dinner. Indeed, Christmas in a

---

[1]Meat, roasted in the oven and served hot [Eds.]

secular society is a festivity primarily concerned with eating and, as such, high-lights the politics of eating.

There are two major rituals associated with Christmas, that of present-giving   9
and that of excessive eating. Both are rituals which crop up in numerous soci-eties, expressing the abililty to provide and mutual dependency. Present-giving, for example, is a way of expressing people's dependency on one another, people's need for each other. The mutual exchange of gifts is designed to establish a sense of reciprocity and to quell anxieties about the separateness of other people. They need you as much as you need them.

Mutual present-giving has been well documented in anthropology[2] and is   10
seen by many as a fundamental ritual of any human society by which *social* bonds are recognized. By social I mean the dependency of individuals on the group, the inability of an individual to survive without social ties and obligations. Festive eating equally signifies an affirmation of the survival of society. The essence of a feast is that it should be excessive, that it should involve quantities and types of foods not normally eaten, in order to signify profusion and survival. These connotations have certainly been carried over into our secular winter festival.

The criterion by which a Christmas dinner is judged successful is the extent   11
to which it defeats the eater. What is noted is the enormous size of the turkey, the number of mince pies consumed. Even falling into an unconscious stupor acquires a certain glamour, the culmination of the curious pattern of Christmas eating—intensive preparation, high expectations, exchange, indulgence, anti-climax, sleep. Even the food combinations are transgressive. Sweet foods and savoury are combined in ways which are on the whole confined to Christmas meals—jam with meat, fruit and savouries in puddings, and so on.

But analysis of meals and present-giving doesn't just reveal two universal   12
practices where people mutually express dependency and everything is egalitar-ian and unproblematic. Providing the feast, and even giving the most spectacular presents, are also ways of expressing power. Food in hierarchical societies is often appropriated and controlled. Giving food out in feasts is a way in which hierarchical positions are demonstrated.

In a documentary about the Ashanti, a matrilineal society in Africa, a group   13
of men were asked whether they ever did the cooking.[3] Their response was one of amazement: "Men, cook? What an extraordinary idea! Men do not worship women so why should men serve food? Women worship men—they cook food for us." This shocked response is symptomatic of the fact that in many socie-ties—though not all—the preparation of food is considered an act of servitude, the demonstration of a subordinate and servicing social position.

---

[2]See, for example, M. Mauss, *The Gift*, Routledge, London, 1970.
[3]*Ashanti Market Women. Disappearing World* series for Granada TV, directed by Claudia Milne.

Our Western hierarchical society contains many of these elements. It is   14
women who prepare the food and both Sunday lunches and Christmas dinner
require intensive labor. Yet when it comes to serving the food, it is traditionally
the male role to carve the meat and pass the plates around. These ritual meals
are designed to signify the ability of men to provide and the duty of women to
prepare and service.

There are additional connotations in our symbolic meals. For these symbolic   15
meals are confined to a small nuclear family. Present-giving between friends is
by no means obligatory, whereas a forgotten relative is likely to engender terrible
guilt. Ritual eating as well is a symbolic activity which sits oddly on groups
when taken outside the family. There's a rush *not* to carve, an embarrassment
about laying on a joint just for convention's sake.

The rituals of mutual present-giving and symbolic eating as practised in our   16
society mean that social dependency is symbolized almost exclusively within the
family. The festival of Christmas expresses the idea that the restricted family
can provide materially and exclusively for all our needs. On the table are the
visible signs of the family's ability to provide. The meal is the product of woman's
domestic labor, demonstrating her willingness to serve the family and expressing
her love through the preparation of food. The man carves, taking up his role
as economic provider.

The alimentary disorders which rack our society may well be the physical   17
expression of the limitations of an ideology which claims that a small family
can provide for all our needs. Family festivities can be a real gut-bomb, because
along with the food go complex feelings of inadequacy, disappointment and
guilt. Expecting too much from too few is a certain recipe for disaster, and all
the members of the family are likely to suffer. Because the symbolism suggests
that the family can provide everything, family members feel guilt if they express
a need for emotional support from outsiders. This need is sometimes experienced
as guilt for rejecting the family's love, when it is merely recognizing more
extensive social needs that can't always be met in the family.

The attempt to make the family the place where all the material and emo-   18
tional support can be supplied has been particularly exacting for women. Women,
if confined to the home, often become isolated. In these circumstances, often
for practical reasons like child care, there's no escape route like work, and
women find themselves more subject to emotional investment in the family. In
the current situation, it is an investment bound for disappointment, since it is
not shared by men.

Social changes in living arrangements over the last few decades are fair evi-   19
dence of the limitations of the nuclear family.[4] Divorce has doubled in the last

[4]For a summary of household patterns, see The Study Commission on the Family, *Families in the Future*, 1983. For an examination of how the traditional family affects women, see L. Segal (ed.), *What is to be Done About the Family?*, Penguin, 1983, especially the article by F. Bennett which discusses the relationship between the state and women's economic dependency within the family.

ten years and the number of single-parent families has increased enormously. Many people are opting for different kinds of living arrangements. And women have become vociferously critical of the ideology of male provision, an ideology which feeds back into an economy where women are ghettoized in low-paid jobs. It is also an ideology used to excuse all kinds of aggressive and uncaring behavior in the home.

Eating meals is a hazardous activity, infused as it is with implications for sex [20] roles and living arrangements. Small wonder that our digestive tracts have become the site of hidden warfare.

QUESTIONS

1. What is Coward explaining here? Why does it need explaining—or doesn't it?

2. This essay illustrates a kind of explanation called interpretation. Its method is to say that behind or beneath something obvious there is some hidden meaning. Such writing always has a strong element of argument as well as explanation, because the writer has to convince us that the hidden meanings are really there. What are the major hidden meanings Coward finds in meals?

3. How convincing do you find Coward's view of the symbolism of eating together? If you agree with her interpretation, what is it that has convinced you? If you disagree, what is it that you find unacceptable? Compare your responses to those of your classmates.

4. How does Coward get from her discussion of eating to a consideration of the family unit? What is she saying about families? What is her evidence? Are you convinced? Compare your responses to those of your classmates.

5. Can you add experiences of your own to the situations that Coward describes? Write an essay on eating together using some of your own experiences. Take Coward's views as your starting point, and then support her position or challenge it with your own experiences and interpretations of the hidden symbolism of dining.

6. Do other familiar acts and situations have hidden meanings? Take some other aspect of ordinary life, and present your interpretation of its deeper symbolism.

WOMEN AND NAMES
Casey Miller and Kate Swift

Casey Miller was born in Toledo, Ohio, in 1919 and grad-
uated from Smith College in 1940. After some graduate
work at Yale, she served on active duty in the U.S. Naval
Reserve, rising to the rank of lieutenant junior grade, and
has worked since then mainly as an editor and free-lance
writer. Kate Swift, born in Yonkers, New York, in 1923,
went to Connecticut College and the University of North
Carolina, from which she graduated in 1944. Both her par-
ents were journalists, so it is not surprising that she found
a career, like Miller, in editing and writing. Both women
live in East Haddam, Connecticut, where they collaborated
on the book Words and Women *(1977). It is the source of*
the following essay on names and especially on patronymy,
the practice of giving names from the father's side of the
family.

The photograph of the three bright, good-looking young people in the Army   1
recruitment ad catches the eye. All three have a certain flair, and one knows
just by looking at the picture that they are enjoying life and glad they joined
up. They are typical Americans, symbols of the kind of people the modern
Army is looking for. The one closest to the camera is a white male. His name,
as can be seen from the neat identification tag pinned to the right pocket of his
regulation blouse, is Spurgeon. Behind him and slightly to the left is a young
black man. He is wearing a decoration of some kind, and his name is Sort—.
Perhaps it is Sorter or Sortman—only the first four letters show. A young woman,
who is also white, stands behind Spurgeon on the other side. She is smiling
and her eyes shine; she looks capable. She is probably wearing a name tag too,
but because Spurgeon is standing between her and the camera, her name is
hidden. She is completely anonymous.

The picture is not a candid shot; it was carefully posed. The three models   2
were chosen from thousands of possible recruits. They are the same height; they
all have dark hair and are smiling into the camera. They look like students, and
the copy says the Army will pay 75 per cent of their tuition if they work for a
college degree. It is no accident that two are white, one black, or that two are
male, one female. Nor is it an accident that Spurgeon stands in front of the

others at the apex of a triangle, or that, since someone had to be anonymous, the woman was chosen.[1]

In our society women's names are less important than men's. The reasons why are not hard to identify, but the consequences for both men and women are more far-reaching than members of either sex, with a few notable exceptions, have been prepared to admit or even, until recently, to examine. Like other words, names are symbols; unlike other words, what they symbolize is unique. A thousand John Does and Jane Roes may live and die, but no bearer of those names has the same inheritance, the same history, or the same fears and expectations as any other. It therefore seems legitimate to ask what effect our naming customs have on girls and boys and on the women and men they grow into. Are the symbol-words that become our names more powerful than other words?

Few people can remember learning to talk. The mystery of language is rarely revealed in a single moment of electrifying insight like Helen Keller's, when suddenly, at the age of seven, the deaf and blind child realized for the first time the connection between the finger signals for w-a-t-e-r her teacher was tapping into her palm and "the wonderful cool something" that flowed from the pump spout onto her other hand.[2]

From what scholars report about the way children normally acquire speech, it seems probable that "learning to talk" is actually the measured release, in conjunction with experience, of an innate capacity for language that is common to all human beings.[3] We are no more likely to remember the process than we are to remember growing taller. What one may remember is a particular moment—seeing the yardstick exactly even with the latest pencil line marking one's height on the door jamb or learning a word for some particular something one had been aware of but could not name: tapioca, perhaps, or charisma, or a cotter pin. Anyone who has ever said, "So *that's* what those things are called," knows the experience.

When children are first learning to talk they go through a series of similar experiences. The very act of learning what a person or thing is called brings the object into the child's ken in a new way. It has been made specific. Later, the specific will also become general, as when the child calls any small, furry animal a "kitty." Words are symbols; their meanings can be extended.

Amanda, who is twenty months old, has spurts of learning names, "Mum," she says to her mother while pointing to the box. "Mum," she says again, pointing to the doorknob. "What it is?" she is asking without using words. "Tell

---

[1]The recruitment ad appeared in the September 30, 1974, issue of *Time* magazine, pp. 84–85. By the following year, similar ads were posed in such a way that the name of each recruit was visible.

[2]Helen Keller, *The Story of My Life*, Garden City, N.Y., Doubleday & Company, 1955, p. 36. (First published in 1902.)

[3]Eric H. Lenneberg, "On Explaining Language," *Science*, May 9, 1969, pp. 635–43.

me its name." When she calls her mother by a name, she knows her mother will respond to it. She knows that she, Amanda, has a name. It is important to her, for she has already become aware of herself as a thing different from everything else. As a psychologist might put it, her ego is emerging. Hearing her name, being called by it, is part of the process.

Amanda makes certain sounds, naming food or her bottle, that tell her parents she is hungry or thirsty. Before long she will speak of herself in the third person: " 'Manda want apple." " 'Manda come too." She may repeat her name over and over, perhaps mixing it with nonsense syllables. It is like a charm. It may be the first word she learns to spell. She will delight in seeing the letters of her name, this extension of herself, on her toothbrush or drinking mug. They belong to her, not to her brother or to her mother or father. 8

When children begin to play with other children and when they finally go to school, their names take on a public dimension. The child with a "funny" name is usually in for trouble, but most kids are proud of their names and want to write them on their books and pads and homework. There was a time when older children carved their names or initials on trees. Now that there are so many people and so few trees, the spray can has taken over from the jackknife, but the impulse to put one's identifying mark where all the world can see it is as strong as ever. The popularity of commercially produced name-on objects of every kind, from tee-shirts to miniature license plates, also attests to the importance youngsters (and a lot of grown-ups too) place on claiming and proclaiming their names. 9

Given names are much older than surnames, of course, probably as old as language itself. One can imagine that as soon as our ancient forebears started using sounds to represent actions or objects, they also began to distinguish each other in the same way. One might even speculate that the people who most often assigned sounds to others were those who produced and cared for the group's new members. Commenting on the assumption of philologists that the exchange of meaningful vocal sounds began among males as they worked and hunted together— hence the so-called "yo-heave-ho" and "bow-wow" theories of language origin—Ethel Strainchamps, a psycholinguist, notes that most philologists have in the past been men. Considering the importance to human survival of communication between mother and child when open fires, venomous reptiles, and other hazards were everywhere, "it might have occurred to a woman that a 'no-no' theory was more likely," Strainchamps says.[4] Perhaps her suggestion should be taken a step further: who knows that it was not the creative effort of women, striving to communicate with each new baby, calling it by a separate and distinguishing sound, that freed the primordial human mind from the prison of animal grunts and led in time to the development of language? 10

---

[4]Ethel Strainchamps, "Our Sexist Language," in Vivian Gornick and Barbara K. Moran, eds., *Woman in Sexist Society*, New York, Basic Books, 1971, p. 247.

Inevitably, some people dislike the names they have been given, and many   11
children go through a phase of wanting to be called something else. For no
apparent reason Anne announces that her name is really Koko and she will not
answer to any other. For months nothing will change her resolve. She is Koko—
and then one day she is Anne again. But if Cecil decides he wants to be called
Jim, or Fanny elects to be known as Jill, the reasons may be less obscure: names
do seem to give off vibrations of a sort, and other people's response to your
name becomes a part of their response to you. Some psychologists think that
given names are signals of parental expectations: children get the message and
act on it either positively or negatively. One study claims to show, for example,
that names can be "active" or "passive." If you call your son Mac or Bart he
will become a more active person than if you call him Winthrop or Egbert.
Your daughter is more likely to be outgoing and confident, according to this
theory, if you call her Jody rather than Letitia. It follows, though, that if Jody
prefers to be called Letitia, she is letting it be known that she sees herself in a
more passive and dependent way than you anticipated.[5]

Last names, too, can be positive or negative. Some carry a mystique of   12
greatness or honor: Randolph, Diaz, Morgenthau, Saltonstall. Others are cum-
bersome, or they invite cruel or tasteless jokes. Many people decide, for one
reason or another, to change their last names, but a great many more take pride
today in being identified as a Klein or a Mackenzie, a Giordano or a Westervelt.
The first-and-last-name mix which a person grows up with—that combination
of particular and general, of personal and traditional—is not lightly exchanged
for another.

Whether a name is self-chosen or bestowed at birth, making it one's own is   13
an act of self-definition. When a former Cabinet member who had been involved in the Watergate scandal asked the Senate investigating committee to
give back his good name, he was speaking metaphorically, for no one had taken
his name away. What he had lost, justly or unjustly, was his public image as a
person of integrity and a servant of the people. One's name also represents one's
sense of power and self-direction. "I'm so tired I don't know my own name" is
a statement of confusion and fatigue. Your name, the beginning of your answer
to "Who am I?" is the outermost of the many layers of identity reaching inward
to the real you. It is one of the significant differences between you and, let's
say, a rose, which is named but does not know it. Yet it is one of the things a
little girl grows up knowing she will be expected to lose if she marries.

The loss of women's last names may seem compensated for by a custom in   14
first-naming that allows girls to be called by a version of their fathers' names,
so that—after a fashion, at least—continuity is restored. In this post-Freudian
age it would be bad form to give a boy a version of his mother's first name.

---

[5]The study by James Bruning and William Albott, reported in the March 1974 issue of *Human
Behavior*, was described by Melvin Maddocks, the Chrisian Science Monitor News Service, and
reprinted in the Middletown (Conn.) *Press*, June 26, 1974.

Nevertheless, if a couple named Henrietta and Frank should decide to call their son Henry, chances are an earlier Henry, after whom Henrietta was named, provides the necessary male for him to identify with. In any case, the name has come back into its own: it stands foursquare and solid, which is seldom true of the derivative names given to girls. The strength of John is preserved in Joan and Jean, but these are exceptions. Names like Georgette and Georgina, Josephine, Paulette and Pauline, beautiful as they may sound, are diminutives. They are copies, not originals, and like so many other words applied to women, they can be diminishing.

A man in most Western societies can not only keep his name for his lifetime   15
but he can pass it on intact to his son, who in turn can pass it on to *his* son. The use of a surname as a given name is also usually reserved for males, presumably on the grounds that such names do not have a sufficiently "feminine" sound for the "weaker sex." When tradition permits the giving of a family surname to daughters, as in the American South, a woman can at least retain her identification with that branch of her family. Once a surname has gained popularity as a girl's name, however, it is likely to face extinction as a boy's name. Shirley, for example, an old Yorkshire family name meaning "shire meadow," was once given as a first name only to boys. Not until Charlotte Brontë write *Shirley*—a novel published in 1849, whose central character, Shirley Keeldar, was modeled on Charlotte's sister Emily—was it used for a girl.[6] Since then, Shirley has become popular as a girl's name but has dropped out of use as a boy's. Names like Leslie, Beverly, Evelyn, and Sidney, may be traveling the same route. Once they have become popular as women's names, their histories as surnames are forgotten, and before long they may be given to girls exclusively.

In English, names like Charity, Constance, Patience, Faith, Hope, Pru-   16
dence, and Honor no longer have popular equivalents for males, as they often do in other languages. The qualities described are not limited to females, of course, and yet to name a son Honor or Charity, even if doing so breaks no objective rule, would somehow run counter to social expectations. This may be true in part because such names are subjective, expressing more intimately than would seem appropriate for a boy the parents' expectations for their offspring. Or the principle that applied in the case of Shirley may apply here, for once a name or a word becomes associated with women, it is rarely again considered suitable for men.

One of the most useful functions of a given name is to serve as a quick   17
identifier of sex. Nearly everyone, whether they admit it or not, is interested in knowing what sex an unknown person is. You get a postcard from a friend saying he will be stopping by to see you next week with someone named Lee,

[6]Linwood Sleigh and Charles Johnson, *Apollo Book of Girls' Names*, New York, Thomas Y. Crowell Company, 1962, p. 194.

and chances are the first question that pops into your mind is not whether Lee is young or old, black or white, clever or dull, but whether Lee will turn out to be female or male. Still, natural curiosity does not entirely explain the annoyance or embarrassment some people seem to feel when women have names that are not specifically female by tradition or why names that become associated with women are thenceforth out of bounds for men.

If quick sex identification were the only consideration, the long male tradition 18 of using initials in place of first names would not have come about. People with names like J. P. Morgan, P. T. Barnum, and L. L. Bean were always male—or were they? No one could stop women from sneaking under the flap of *that* tent, and in fact so many did that the practice had to be disallowed. In the early years of this century Columbia University, which in its academic bulletins identified male faculty members only by their surnames and initials, wrote out the names of women faculty members in full—lest anyone unintentionally enroll in a course taught by a woman.[7]

Perhaps it is because of the transience of women's last names that their first 19 names seem often to be considered the logical, appropriate, or even polite counterpart of men's surnames, and the news media frequently reflect this feeling. When Secretary of State Henry Kissinger and Nancy Maginnis were married, many news stories called them "Kissinger and Nancy" after the first paragraph. The usage is so accepted, and its belittling implications so subliminal, that it often persists in defiance of changes taking place all about it. In a magazine story on the atypical career choices of six graduate students, the subhead read "Sterotypes fade as men and women students . . . prepare to enter fields previously dominated almost exclusively by the opposite sex." Three women going into dentistry, business administration, and law were introduced by their full names, as were three men whose fields of study were nursing, library science, and primary education. The men were then referred to as Groves, White, and Fondow, while the women became, Fran, Carol, and Pam.[8]

Children, servants, and other presumed inferiors are apt to be first-named 20 by adults and employers and by anyone else who is older, richer, or otherwise assumed to be superior. In turn, those in the first category are expected to address those in the second by their last names prefixed with an appropriate social or professional title. People on a fairly equal footing, however, either first-name each other or by mutual if unspoken agreement use a more formal mode of address.

As it happens, even though the average full-time working woman in the 21 United States is slightly older than the average man who is employed full-time,

---

[7]Alice H. Bonnell, "Women at Columbia: The Long March to Equal Opportunities," *Columbia Reports*, May 1972.

[8]University of North Carolina News Bureau press release reprinted in the university's *Alumni Review*, November 1971.

she makes only slightly more than half the salary he makes.[9] This may explain why a great many more women than men are called by their first names on the job and why, in offices where most of the senior and junior executives are men and most of the secretaries and clerks are women, the first-naming of all women— including executives, if any—easily becomes habitual. Or it could be that women are at least slightly less impressed by the thought of their own importance, slightly more inclined to meet their colleagues and employees on equal terms. When a reporter asked newly elected Governor Ella Grasso of Connecticut what she wanted to be called and she answered, "People usually call me Ella," a new benchmark for informality must have been set in the other forty-nine state capitals. Unless men respond in the same spirit, however, without taking advantage of what is essentially an act of generosity, women like Governor Grasso will have made a useless sacrifice, jeopardizing both their identity and their prestige.

In the whole name game, it is society's sanction of patronymy that most diminishes the importance of women's names—and that sanction is social only, not legal. In the United States no state except Hawaii legally requires a woman to take her husband's name when she marries, although social pressures in the other states are almost as compelling.[10] The very fact that until recently few women giving up their names realized they were not required to do so shows how universal the expectation is. Any married couple who agree that the wife will keep her own name are in for harassment, no matter how legal their stand: family, friends, the Internal Revenue Service, state and local agencies like motor vehicle departments and voter registrars, hotels, credit agencies, insurance companies are all apt to exert pressure on them to conform. One judge is quoted as saying to a married woman who wanted to revert to her birth name, "If you didn't want his name, why did you get married? Why didn't you live with him instead?"[11] To thus equate marriage with the desire of some women to be called "Mrs." and the desire of some men to have "a Mrs." is insulting to both sexes; yet the equation is so widely accepted that few young people growing up in Western societies think in any different terms.

The judge just quoted was, in effect, defining what a family is in a patronymical society like ours where only males are assured permanent surnames they can pass on to their children. Women are said to "marry into" families, and families are said to "die out" if an all-female generation occurs. The word family, which comes from the Latin *famulus*, meaning a servant or slave, is itself a reminder that wives and children, along with servants, were historically

22

23

---

[9]Based on figures reported in *The World Almanac & Book of Facts 1975*, New York, Newspaper Enterprise Association, 1974.

[10]"Booklet for Women Who Wish to Determine Their Own Names After Marriage," Barrington, Ill., Center for a Woman's Own Name, 1974, p. 7.

[11]Quoted by Carmen Rubio in "Staying Single—In Name Only," *Sunday, The Hartford Courant Magazine*, February 2, 1975.

part of man's property. When black Americans discard the names of the slave-holders who owned their forebears, they are consciously disassociating their sense of identity from the property status in which their ancestors were held. To adopt an African name is one way of identifying with freedom and eradicating a link to bondage. The lot of married women in Western society today can hardly be called bondage, but to the degree that people's names are a part of themselves, giving them up, no matter how willingly, is tantamount to giving up some part of personal, legal, and social autonomy.

Since a surname defines a family and identifies its members, a man who marries and has children extends his family, but a woman in marrying gives up her "own" family and joins in extending another's. She may be fully aware that she brings to her new family—to her children and grandchildren—the genetic and cultural heritage of her parents and grandparents, but the lineages she can trace are ultimately paternal. Anyone who decides to look up their ancestors through marriage and birth records in town halls and genealogical societies may find paternal lines going back ten or fifteen generations or more, whereas with few exceptions maternal ones end after two or three. The exceptions are interesting for they emphasize how important the lost information from maternal lines really is. Stephen Birmingham, writing about America's blue-blooded families, notes that "Who is she?" as a question may mean, 'What was her maiden name?' It may also mean what was her mother's maiden name, and what was her grandmother's maiden name, and so on."[12] Blue bloods, in other words, care a lot about "maiden names," and rightly so, considering that the inputs of maternal genes and culture have as great an effect on offspring as paternal inputs.

Obviously we all have as many female ancestors as male ancestors, but maternal lineages, marked with name changes in every generation, are far more difficult to trace. To most of us the identity of our mother's mother's mother, and that of *her* mother, and on back, are lost forever. How is one affected by this fading out of female ancestors whose names have disappeared from memory and the genealogical records? Research on the subject is not readily available, if it exists at all, but it seems likely that daughters are affected somewhat differently from sons. If it is emotionally healthy, as psychologists believe, for a child to identify with the parent of the same sex, would it not also be healthy for a child to identify with ancestors of the same sex?

A boy, knowing he comes from a long line of males bearing the name Wheelwright, for example, can identify with his forefathers: Johnny Wheelwright in the 1970s, if he wants to, can imagine some medieval John in whose workshop the finest wheels in the land were fashioned, a John who had a son, who had a son, who had a son, until at last Johnny Wheelwright himself was born. No line of identifiable foremothers stretches back into the past to which

24

25

26

---

[12]Stephen Birmingham, *The Right People: A Portrait of the American Social Establishment*, Boston, Little, Brown and Company, 1968, p. 9.

his sister Mary can lay claim. Like Johnny, she is a Wheelwright, assigned by patronymy to descent from males. What neither boy nor girl will ever be able to trace is their equally direct descent from, let's say, a woman known as the Healer, a woman whose daughter's daughter's daughter, through the generations, passed on the skilled hands which both John and Mary may have inherited.

Imagine, in contrast to Johnny Wheelwright, a hypothetical woman of today 27 whose name is Elizabeth Jones. If you were to ask, in the manner of a blue blood, "Who is she?" you might be told, "She was a Fliegendorf. Her people were Pennsylvania Dutch farmers who came over from Schleswig-Holstein in the seventeenth century." Actually, that tells a fraction of the story. This hypothetical Elizabeth Jones's mother—who met her father at an Army post during the Second World War—was a Woslewski whose father emigrated from Poland as a boy, lived in Chicago, and there married a Quinn whose mother came from Canada and was a Vallière. The mother of that Vallière was the great-great-granddaughter of a woman whose given name was the equivalent of "Deep Water" and who belonged to a group of native North Americans called the Têtes de Boule by French explorers.

Elizabeth Jones's father's mother, in Pennsylvania, had been a Bruhofer, 28 whose mother had been a Gruber, whose mother, a Powel, was born in Georgia and was the great-great-granddaughter of a woman brought to this country from Africa in the hold of a slave ship.

Thus, although Elizabeth Jones is said to have been a Fliegendorf whose 29 people came from Schleswig-Holstein in the sixteen hundreds, fewer than 5 per cent of her two thousand or so direct ancestors who were alive in that century had any connection with Schleswig-Holstein, and only one of those who made the passage to America was born with the name Fliegendorf. The same may be said, of course, of Elizabeth Jones's brother, Ed Fliegendorf's relationship to the Fliegendorf family or Johnny Wheelwright's relationship to the bearers of his name. Yet so strong is our identification with the name we inherit at birth that we tend to forget both the rich ethnic mix most of us carry in our genes and the arbitrary definition of "family" that ultimately links us only to the male line of descent.

This concept of family is one of the reasons why most societies through most 30 of history have placed greater value on the birth of a male child than of a female child. Ours is no exception. A recent survey reported in *Psychology Today* showed that a higher percentage of prospective parents in the United States would prefer to have a son than a daughter as a first or only child. The percentage who feel this way, however, has dropped from what it was only twenty years ago.[13] Responding to the report, a reader expressed his opinion that the change could be attributed to "a breakdown in the home-and-family ideal"

---

[13]"Newsline," *Psychology Today*, August 1974, p. 29.

among young parents today. "The son," he wrote in a letter to the editor, "and in particular the eldest son, is strongly tied to the archetypal family; first as its prime agent of continuation, and also as the future guardian and master of the home."[14] Here, then, family and name are seen as synonymous, the male is the prime if not only progenitor, and even the order of birth among male children affects the model of an ideal family.

One could not ask for a better example of how patronymy reinforces the 31 powerful myth that pervades the rest of our language—the myth that the human race is essentially male. The obvious first reaction to such a statement may be to say, "But that's absurd. No one thinks of the race as essentially male." And yet we do. As the social critic Elizabeth Janeway has pointed out, a myth does not really describe a situation; rather, it tries to bring about what it declares to exist.[15]

A childless couple adopted a baby girl. When asked why they chose a girl 32 rather than a boy, they explained that if she did not live up to their expectations because of her genetic heritage, "at least she won't carry on the family." Journalist Mike McGrady states the myth of racial maleness even more tellingly in an article about sperm banking: "One customer . . . gave a reason for depositing sperm that may foreshadow the future: it was to carry on the family line should his male offspring prove sterile. What we are talking about here," McGrady said, "is not fertility insurance but immortality insurance."[16] This customer, then, believes he cannot be linked to future generations through his female offspring, should they prove fertile. His immortality, one must conclude, is not in his sperm or his genes but in his name.

"One's name and strong devotion to it," wrote an Austrian philosopher, Otto 33 Weininger, around the turn of the century, "are even more dependent on personality than is the sense of property . . . . Women are not bound to their names with any strong bond. When they marry they give up their own name and assume that of their husband without any sense of loss . . . . The fundamental namelessness of the woman is simply a sign of her undifferentiated personality."[17] Weininger, whose book *Sex and Character* had a brief but powerful influence on popular psychology, is of historical interest because he articulated the myth of humanity's maleness at a time when the first wave of feminism was beginning to be taken seriously by governments, trade unions, and other institutions in England and the United States as well as in Europe. In describing the "fundamental namelessness" of woman as "a sign of her undifferentiated personality," Weininger was building support for his premise that

---

[14]Robert T. Means, Jr., Letter to the Editor, *Psychology Today*, November 1974, p. 14.

[15]Elizabeth Janeway, *Man's World, Woman's Place: A Study in Social Mythology*, New York, A Delta Book, Dell Publishing Company, 1971, p. 337.

[16]Mike McGrady, "Family Banking," *New York* magazine, June 12, 1972, p. 42.

[17]Otto Weininger, *Sex and Character*, New York, G. P. Putnam's Sons, 1906, p. 206. This is the "authorized translation from the sixth German edition"; also published in London by William Heinemann.

"women have no existence and no essence . . . no share in ontological reality, no relation to the thing-in-itself, which, in the deepest interpretation, is the absolute, is God."[18]

Otto Weininger was aware of the movement for women's rights and was deeply disturbed by it. He may well have heard of the noted American feminist Lucy Stone, whose decision to keep her birth name when she married Henry Blackwell in 1855 had created consternation on both sides of the Atlantic. An eloquent speaker with a free and fearless spirit, Stone was widely known as an antislavery crusader. After the Civil War her organizing efforts helped secure passage of the Fourteenth Amendment, which extended the vote to freed slaves who were men. She devoted the rest of her long, productive life to the cause of suffrage for women and founded and edited the *Woman's Journal*, for forty-seven years the major weekly newspaper of the women's movement.

It is especially relevant that among Lucy Stone's many important contributions to history she is best known today for her refusal to give up her name. Her explanation, "My name is the symbol of my identity and must not be lost," was a real shocker to anyone who had not considered the possibility that a married woman could have an individual identity—and in the nineteenth century that meant almost everyone. The law did not recognize such a possibility, as the famous English jurist William Blackstone made clear when he summarized the rule of "coverture," influencing both British and American law for well over a hundred years. "By marriage," he wrote, "the husband and wife are one person in the law—that is, the very being or legal existence of the woman is suspended during the marriage . . . ."[19]

The suspended existence of the married woman came to be well symbolized in the total submersion of a wife's identity in her husband's name—preceded by "Mrs." The use of designations like "Mrs. John Jones" does not go back much before 1800. Martha Washington would have been mystified to receive a letter addressed to "Mrs. George Washington," for at that time the written abbreviation *Mrs.*, a social title applied to any adult woman, was used interchangeably with its spelled-out form *mistress* and was probably pronounced the same way. "Mistress George" would have made little sense.

Lucy Stone's example was followed in the late nineteenth and early twentieth centuries by small but increasing numbers of women, mostly professional writers, artists, and scientists. The Lucy Stone League, founded in New York in 1921, was the first organization to help women with the legal and bureaucratic difficulties involved in keeping their names after marriage. Its early leaders included Jane Grant, co-founder with her first husband, Harold Ross, of the *New Yorker* magazine, and journalist Ruth Hale who in 1926 asked rhetorically how men would respond to the suggestion that they give up *their* names. The suggestion

34

35

36

37

---

[18]Ibid., p. 286.
[19]Quoted by Lucy Komisar, *The New Feminism*, New York, Warner Paperback Library, 1971, p. 81. Blackstone's *Commentaries* was first published in 1765–69.

does not often arise, but a psychologist recently described the reaction of one husband and father when someone in his family raised the possibility of changing the family name because they didn't like it:

"He suddenly realized that it was a traumatic thing for him to consider giving 38
up his last name," according to Dr. Jack Sawyer of Northwestern University. "He said he'd never realized before that 'only men have real names in our society, women don't.' And it bothered him also that his name should be a matter of such consequence for him. He worried about his professional standing, colleagues trying to contact him—all kinds of things that women face as a matter of course when they get married. Men have accepted the permanency of their names as one of the rights of being male, and it was the first time he realized how much his name was part of his masculine self-image."[20]

Lucy Stone, whose self-image was comfortably female but not feminine, 39
agreed to be known as Mrs. Stone after her marriage. Through this compromise with custom she avoided the somewhat schizophrenic situation many well-known women face when they use their birth names professionally and their husbands' names socially, thus becoming both Miss Somebody and Mrs. Somebody Else. The Pulitzer-prize winning novelist Jean Stafford wants to be "saluted as *Miss* Stafford if the subject at hand has to do with me and my business or as *Mrs.* Liebling if inquiries are being made about my late husband."[21] Miss Stafford objects to being addressed as "Ms.," a title that Lucy Stone would probably have welcomed had it existed in her time.

During the nearly two centuries in which the use of the distinguishing marital 40
labels Miss or Mrs. for women was rigidly enforced by custom, the labels tended to become parts of women's names, in effect replacing their given names. A boarding school founded by Sarah Porter in Farmington, Connecticut, soon became known as Miss Porter's School. After the actress Minnie Maddern married Harrison Grey Fiske, she became famous as Mrs. Fiske. In the following classroom dialogue, the columnist Ellen Cohn provides a classic example of how the custom works:

Question: Who is credited with discovering radium?
Answer: (all together): Madam Curie.
Teacher: Well, class, the woman (who was indeed married to a man named Pierre Curie) had a first name all her own. From now on let's call her Marie Curie.
Question: Can Madam Curie ever be appropriately used?
Answer: Of course. Whenever the inventor of the telephone is called Mr. Bell.[22]

[20]Arline Brecher, "Male Lib: The Men Who Want Human Liberation: An Interview with Psychologist Jack Sawyer," *New Woman*, February 1972, p. 75.

[21]Jean Stafford, "Don't Use Ms. with Miss Stafford, Unless You Mean ms.," New York *Times*, September 21, 1873, p. 36.

[22]Ellen Cohn, "The Liberated Woman," New York *Sunday News* magazine, June 17, 1973, p. 4.

Through the transience and fragmentation that have traditionally character- 41 ized women's names, some part of the human female self-image has been sacrificed. It is hardly surprising, therefore, that the second wave of feminist consciousness brought a serious challenge to patronymy and to the assignment of distinguishing marital labels to women. To be named and defined by someone else is to accept an imposed identity—to agree that the way others see us is the way we really are. Naming conventions, like the rest of language, have been shaped to meet the interests of society, and in partriarchal societies the shapers have been men. What is happening now in language seems simply to reflect the fact that, in the words of Dr. Pauli Murray, "women are seeking their own image of themselves nurtured from within rather than imposed from without."[23]

QUESTIONS

1. What, exactly, are Miller and Swift explaining here? To what extent is their explanation also an argument? Discuss the relationship between explaining and arguing, starting with the difference between *why* something is the case and *whether* something is the case.

2. In paragraph 2 Miller and Swift twice use a version of the phrase, "It is no accident." What does this mean? If it isn't an accident, what is it? Who is responsible?

3. What is the function of the opening discussion of the recruiting ad? Why do you suppose the authors began with that?

4. Locate some examples of this essay's regular movement between general assertions and specific illustrations. Can you find any generalizations that are unsupported? Which, if any, of Miller and Swift's major statements seem dubious? Why?

5. What do you know about your own female ancestors? Getting all the help you can from relatives, how far back can you trace the female side of your heritage: your mother, her mother, her mother, and so on? What about the male side—is there any difference in your knowledge of the two sides? (Skip the complications like mother's father's mother.) Compare your findings with those of your classmates. Can you draw any conclusions from all this that support or weaken the position taken in the essay?

6. Examine the implications of some custom or assumption in our society as Miller and Swift have examined names and naming. Use specific examples and illustrations to support your major points as you explain the significance of something that most people take for granted.

[23]Pauli Murray, testimony before Rep. Edith Green's Special Subcommittee on Education in Support of Section 805 of H.R. 16098, June 19, 1970, U. S. Government Printing Office, 1970.

THE CONCEPT
OF NARCISSISM

Karen Horney

Karen Horney (the last syllable rhymes with bay) *is the author of many books on psychoanalysis. She was born in Germany in 1885 and educated mainly at the University of Berlin where she received her M.D. degree in 1913. In 1932 she left Germany and settled in the United States, where she practiced psychoanalysis in New York City until her death in 1952. Though she acknowledged the importance of Freud, in essays like the one reprinted here from her 1939 collection,* New Ways in Psychoanalysis, *she carefully distinguished her own views from those of the founder of psychoanalysis. In particular, she challenged his views of women and children.*

The phenomena which in psychoanalytical literature are called narcissistic   1
are most divergent in character. They include vanity, conceit, craving for prestige and admiration, a desire to be loved in connection with an incapacity to love others, withdrawal from others, normal self-esteem, ideals, creative desires, anxious concern about health, appearance, intellectual faculties. Thus a clinical definition of narcissism would be an embarrassing task. All that the above phenomena have in common is concern about the self, or perhaps merely attitudes pertaining to the self. The reason for this bewildering picture is that the term is used in a purely genetic sense to signify that the origin of these manifestations is assumed to be the narcissistic libido.[1]

In contrast to the vagueness of the clinical definition, the genetic one is   2
precise: a person is narcissistic who at bottom is in love with himself. In the words of Gregory Zilboorg: "The term 'narcissism' does not mean mere selfishness, or egocentricity, as is assumed; it denotes specifically that state of mind, that spontaneous attitude of man, in which the individual himself happens to choose only himself instead of others as the object to love. Not that he does not love, or that he hates, others and wants everything for him; but he is inwardly in love with himself and seeks everywhere for a mirror in which to admire and woo his own image."[2]

---

[1]libido: energy from instinctual biological or sexual drives. Freud's contention that all human pleasures and satisfactions are sexual in nature is the source of the "genetic" or causal definition discussed next. [Eds.]

[2]Gregory Zilboorg, "Loneliness" in *Atlantic Monthly* (January 1938).

The core of the concept is the postulate that concern with one's self or overvaluation of one's self is an expression of infatuation with the self. Are we not just as blind, Freud argues, toward shortcomings in another person, and just as inclined to overrate his good qualities, when we are infatuated with him? Therefore persons tending toward self-concern or self-overvaluation must undoubtedly at bottom be in love with themselves. This postulate is in accordance with the libido theory. On this basis it is conclusive indeed to regard egocentricity as an expression of self-love and also to regard normal self-esteem and ideals as its desexualized derivatives. But if we do not accept the libido theory the postulate appears to be a merely dogmatic contention.[3] Clinical evidence, with few exceptions, is not in its favor.

If narcissism is considered not genetically but with reference to its actual meaning it should, in my judgment, be described as essentially self-inflation. Psychic inflation, like economic inflation, means presenting greater values than really exist. It means that the person loves and admires himself for values for which there is no adequate foundation.[4] Similarly, it means that he expects love and admiration from others for qualities that he does not possess, or does not possess to as large an extent as he supposes. According to my definition, it is not narcissistic for a person to value a quality in himself which he actually possesses, or to like it to be valued by others. These two tendencies—appearing unduly significant to oneself and craving undue admiration from others—cannot be separated. Both are always present, though in different types one or the other may prevail.

Why must people aggrandize themselves? If we are not content with a speculative biological answer—which means relating the tendency to an instinctual source—we must find some other answer. As in all neurotic phenomena we find at the basis disturbances in the relationships to others, disturbances acquired in childhood through the environmental influences. The factor which contributes most fundamentally to the development of narcissistic trends appears to be the child's alienation from others, provoked by grievances and fears. His positive emotional ties with others become thin; he loses the capacity to love.

The same unfavorable environment produces disturbances in his feeling for self. In more severe cases these mean more than a mere impairment of self-esteem; they bring about a complete suppression of the spontaneous individual self.[5] Various influences operate to this effect: the unquestioned authority of righteous parents, creating a situation in which the child feels compelled to

[3] *Cf.* Michael Balint, "Frühe Entwicklungsstadien des Ichs" in *Imago* (1937).

[4] The emphasis rests on the fact that the foundation is not adequate. The illusory picture a person presents to himself and to others is not altogether fantastic, but may be an exaggerated picture of the potentialities he actually has.

[5] Erich Fromm in his lectures on authority was the first to point out the significance which this loss of self has for neuroses. Also it seems that Otto Rank, in his concept of will and creativeness, has similar factors in mind; *cf.* Otto Rank, *Will Therapy* (1936).

adopt their standards for the sake of peace; the attitudes of self-sacrificing parents who elicit the feeling from the child that he has no rights of his own and should live only for the parents' sake; parents who transfer their own ambitions to the child and regard the boy as an embryonic genius or the girl as a princess, thereby developing in the child the feeling that he is loved for imaginary qualities rather than for his true self. All these influences, varied as they are, make the child feel that in order to be liked or accepted he must be as others expect him to be. The parents have so thoroughly superimposed themselves on the mind of the child that he complies through fear, thus gradually losing what James calls the "real me." His own will, his own wishes, his own feelings, his own likes and dislikes, his own grievances, become paralyzed.[6] Therefore he gradually loses the capacity to measure his own values. He becomes dependent on the opinion of others. He is bad or stupid when others think he is bad or stupid, intelligent when others order him to be intelligent, a genius when others consider him one. While in all of us self-esteem is to some extent dependent upon the estimate of others, in this case nothing but the estimate of others counts.[7]

Such a development is fostered also by other influences, such as direct blows   7
to the self-esteem, derogatory attitudes of parents who miss no opportunity to make a child feel that he is no good, the parents' preference for other siblings, which undermines his security and makes him concentrate on outshining them. There are also all those factors which directly impair a child's self-sufficiency, self-reliance and initiative.

There are several ways in which a child tries to cope with life under such   8
distressing conditions: by defiantly conforming with the standards ("super-ego"); by making himself unobtrusive and dependent on others (masochistic trends); by self-inflation (narcissistic trends). Which way is chosen, or prevailingly chosen, depends on the peculiar combination of circumstances.

What does an individual gain by self-aggrandizement?   9

He escapes the painful feeling of nothingness by molding himself in fancy   10
into something outstanding. This is achieved whether he indulges in an active conscious play of fantasy—thinking of himself as a prince, a genius, a president, a general, an explorer—or is aware only of an inarticulate feeling of his own significance. The more he is alienated, not only from others but also from himself, the more easily such notions acquire a psychic reality. Not that he discards reality because of them—as the psychotic does—but reality takes on a provisional character, as life does for a Christian who expects his real life to

---

[6]Strindberg describes this process in one of his fairy tales, "Jubal ohne Ich" (in *Märchen und Fabeln*, in 1920). A boy was naturally possessed of a strong will; at an earlier age than other boys he spoke of himself in the first person. But his parents told him that he had no self. When he grew a little older he said: I will. But his parents told him that he had no will. Having a strong will he was amazed at this verdict but he accepted it. When he grew up his father asked him what he wanted to be, but he did not know because he had ceased to will as it had been forbidden.

[7]In William James' term, what remains is the "social self": "A man's social self is the recognition which he gets from his mates."

begin in heaven. His notions of himself become a substitute for his undermined self-esteem; they become his "real me."

By creating a fantasy world of his own in which he is the hero he also consoles 11 himself for not being loved and appreciated. He may feel that though others reject him, look down on him, do not love him for what he really is, it is because he is too far above their understanding. My personal impression is that the illusions do far more than give secret substitute satisfactions. I often wonder whether they do not save the individual from being crushed entirely and thus whether they are not literally life-saving.

Finally, self-inflation represents an attempt to put relationships to others on 12 a positive basis. If others do not love and respect the individual for what he is they should at least pay attention to him and admire him. The obtainment of admiration is substituted for love—a consequential step. From then on he feels unwanted if he is not admired. He loses any understanding of the fact that friendliness and love can include an objective or even a critical attitude. What falls short of blind adoration is to him no longer love; he will even suspect it of being hostility. He will judge others according to the admiration or flattery he receives from them. People who admire him are good and superior, people who do not are not worth bothering with. Thus his main gratification lies in being admired, but also his security rests on it, because it gives him the illusion that he is strong and that the world around is friendly. It is a security on a rickety basis, however. Any failure may bring to the surface all the underlying inse-curity. In fact, not even a failure is needed to elicit this effect; admiration paid to someone else may be sufficient to bring it about.

Thus there develops a certain combination of character trends which for the 13 sake of facilitating understanding one might call the basic narcissistic trends. Their further development depends on the extent of alienation from self and others, and on the degree of anxiety produced. If the early experiences were not too decisive, and if later conditions are favorable, these basic trends may be outgrown. If not, they tend to be reinforced in time through three main factors.

One of them is an increasing unproductivity. A striving for admiration may 14 be a powerful motor toward achievement, or toward developing qualities which are socially desirable or which make a person lovable, but it involves the danger that everything will be done with both eyes on the effect it has on others. An individual of this type chooses a woman not for her own sake but because her conquest would flatter him or add to his prestige. A piece of work is done not for its own sake but for the impression it might make. Brilliancy becomes more important than substance. Hence the danger that superficiality, showmanship, opportunism will choke productivity. Even if the individual succeeds in winning prestige this way, he rightly feels that it cannot last, though he is not aware of the reasons for his uneasiness about it. The only available means for silencing his uneasiness is to reinforce the narcissistic trends: to chase for more success and to build up more inflated notions about himself. Sometimes a baffling capacity is developed to transform shortcomings and failures into something glorious. If his writings are not recognized sufficiently it is because he is far ahead of his time; if he cannot get along with his family or friends it is because of their shortcomings.

Another factor increasing the individual's basic narcissistic trends is the development of excessive expectations as to what the world owes him. He feels he should be recognized as a genius without having to give evidence of it by actual work. Women should single him out without his actively doing anything about it. Deep down he may feel, for example, that it is inconceivable that any woman knowing him could fall in love with another man. The characteristic feature of these attitudes is the expectation that devotion or glory can be obtained without effort and initiative of his own. This peculiar type of expectation is strictly determined. It is necessary because of the damage that has been done to the individual's spontaneity, originality and initiative, and because of his fear of people. The factors which originally pushed him toward self-inflation also paralyze his inner activity. Hence the inner insistence that fulfillment of his wishes should come from others.[8] This process, which is unconscious in its implications, leads in two ways to a reinforcement of narcissistic trends: the claims made on others must be justified by emphasis on his own alleged values; and this emphasis must be renewed in order to cover up the disappointments which inevitably ensue from his exaggerated expectations.

A last source feeding the basic narcissistic trends is the increasing impairment of human relationships. The individual's illusions about himself, and his peculiar kind of expectations of others, are bound to make him vulnerable. Since the world does not recognize his secret claims he often feels hurt and develops greater hostility toward others, becomes more isolated and as a result is driven again and again to take refuge in his illusions. Grievances toward others also may grow because he holds them responsible for his failures to realize his illusions. As a consequence he develops traits which we regard as morally objectionable, such as pronounced egoism, vindictiveness, distrust, disregard for others if they do not serve his own glory. These traits, however, are incompatible with his notion that he is a wonderful being, far above the average of human frailties. Therefore they must be covered up. They are either repressed, in which case they appear only in disguise, or they are simply denied.[9] Self-inflation thus acquires the function of concealing the existing disparity, in line with the maxim:

15

16

---

[8]H. Schultz-Hencke in *Schicksal und Neurose* (1931) points out the significance of this process for neuroses. He claims that a sequence which can be briefly characterized as fears, inertia, excessive demands, is the essential process in every neurosis. Also N.L. Blitzsten in "Amphithymia" (*Archives of Neurology and Psychiatry*, 1936) stresses the significance of unreasonable demands on others, and of the wish for accomplishment without having to make any efforts.

[9]Repressions resulting from self-inflation seem to be less radical than those resulting from perfectionistic strivings frequently trends not fitting into the individual's inflated picture of himself are merely denied or embellished.

it is out of the question that I, this superior being, have such shortcomings, and therefore they are nonexistent.

In order to understand the differences that are found in types with pronounced narcissistic trends we have to consider two main factors. One of them is how far the phantom of admiration is pursued in reality or only in the realm of fantasy; this difference ultimately boils down to quantitative factors in genesis, briefly, to the extent to which the individual's spirit has been broken. The other factor is the way in which narcissistic trends are combined with other character trends; they may be entangled, for example, with perfectionistic, masochistic[10] and sadistic trends. The frequency of these combinations is accounted for by the fact that all of them emanate from a similar source, that they represent different solutions for similar calamities. The bewildering number of contradictory qualities attributed to narcissism in psychoanalytical literature results in part from a failure to recognize that narcissism is but one specific trend within a personality structure. It is the combination of trends which gives a personality a certain coloring.

Narcissistic trends may be combined also with a tendency to withdraw from people, a tendency that is found in the schizoid personality. In psychoanalytical literature withdrawal from others is regarded as inherently a narcissistic trend; but while alienation from others is inherent in narcissistic trends withdrawal is not. On the contrary, a person with pronounced narcissistic trends, though incapable of love, nevertheless needs people as a source of admiration and support. Thus it would be more accurate in these cases to speak of a combination of narcissistic trends with a tendency to withdraw from others.

Narcissistic trends are frequent in our culture. More often than not people are incapable of true friendship and love; they are egocentric, that is, concerned with their security, health, recognition; they feel insecure and tend to overrate their personal significance; they lack judgment of their own value because they have relegated it to others. These typical narcissistic features are by no means restricted to persons who are incapacitated by neuroses.

Freud accounts for the frequency of these trends by his assumption of their biological origin. This assumption is evidence again of Freud's faith in the concept of instincts, but it also reveals his habitual failure to take cultural factors into consideration. Actually the two sets of factors engendering narcissistic trends in neuroses are generally operative in our culture. There are also many cultural factors creating fears and hostile tensions among people and thereby alienating them from one another. There are also many general influences tending to curtail individual spontaneity, such as the standardization of feelings, thoughts and behavior, and the fact that people are valued rather for what they appear to be than for what they are. Furthermore, the striving for prestige as a means of overcoming fears and inner emptiness is certainly culturally prescribed.

---

[10]Cf. Fritz Wittels, "The Mystery of Masochism" in the *Psychoanalytic Review* (1937).

Summing up, the observations which Freud has taught us to make[11] con-   21
cerning self-aggrandizement and egocentricity permit a different interpretation
from that suggested by him. I believe that—here as in other psychological problems—the postulate that an instinct is the generating cause prevents a perception
of the meaning and significance which particular trends have for a personality.
According to my view, narcissistic trends are not the derivative of an instinct
but represent a neurotic trend, in this case an attempt to cope with the self and
others by way of self-inflation.

Freud assumes that both normal self-esteem and self-aggrandizement are   22
narcissistic phenomena, the difference being merely one of quantity. In my
opinion this failure to distinguish clearly between the two attitudes toward the
self befogs the issue. The difference between self-esteem and self-inflation is not
quantitative but qualitative. True self-esteem rests on qualities which a person
actually possesses, while self-inflation implies presenting to the self and to others
qualities or achievements for which there is no adequate foundation. If the other
conditions are present narcissistic trends may arise if self-esteem and other qualities pertaining to the individual's spontaneous self are smothered. Hence self-
esteem and self-inflation are mutually exclusive.

Finally, narcissism is an expression not of self-love but of alienation from   23
the self. In rather simplified terms, a person clings to illusions about himself
because, and as far as, he has lost himself. As a consequence the correlation
between love for self and love for others is not valid in the sense that Freud
intends it. Nevertheless, the dualism which Freud assumes in his second theory
of instincts—the dualism between narcissism and love—if divested of theoretical
implications contains an old and significant truth. This is, briefly, that any kind
of egocentricity detracts from a real interest in others, that it impairs the capacity
to love others. Freud, however, means something different by his theoretical
contention. He interprets the tendency toward self-inflation as originating in
self-love, and he believes that the reason why the narcissistic person does not
love others is that he loves himself too much. Freud thinks of narcissism as a
reservoir which is depleted to the extent that the individual loves (that is, gives
libido to) others. According to my view, a person with narcissistic trends is
alienated from self as well as from others, and hence to the extent that he is
narcissistic he is incapable of loving either himself or anyone else.

QUESTIONS

1. Who is Narcissus? Look him up in a classical or mythological dictionary or in a
copy of Ovid's *Metamorphoses*. Why do you suppose psychoanalysis uses mythology
(Oedipus, for instance) so much? Are the myths true?

---

[11]Sigmund Freud, "Narcissism: An Introduction" in *Collected Papers*, Vol. IV (1914). *Cf.* also
the excellent observations reported by Ernest Jones, "Der Gottmensch-Komplex" in *Internationale
Zeitschrift für ärztliche Psychoanalyse* (1913), and Karl Abraham, "Über eine besondere Form des
neurotischen Widerstandes gegen die psychoanalytische Methodik" in *ibid.* (1919)

2. Like many other explanatory essays, this one begins by emphasizing the definition of a crucial term. In the first four paragraphs, Horney offers three approaches to a definition of *narcissism*: the "clinical," the "genetic," and her own, which she claims is based on the "actual" meaning of the word. Describe in your own words each of the three approaches. Is it fair for Horney to call her own approach the "actual" meaning? Do words have "actual" meanings?

3. In the last three paragraphs Horney emphasizes the difference between her views and those of Freud. Explain this difference in your own words.

4. Horney's definition relies on a metaphor or comparison connecting the human psyche with economics. This comparison is grounded in the word "inflation" (paragraph 4). Explain how this comparison functions in Horney's definition.

5. Paragraph 13 is a transitional paragraph. Look at each of the four sentences, and note the expressions that look backward and those that look forward to assist the reader in following the structure of the essay. For example, how does the word *three* in the last sentence work with words in the next three paragraphs to keep the readers aware of the essay's shape and direction?

6. Paragraphs 6 and 7 present a set of "distressing conditions" (paragraph 8) under which children may be reared. Considering what you have seen of young children and remembering your own childhood, do you think such conditions are common or rare? In the half century since this essay was written, in what ways, if any, do you think child rearing has changed?

7. Our whole society, and especially the younger generation, has been called narcissistic. Is this charge true? To what extent do public events or situations you know about substantiate the charge? Can our culture be defended against such criticism? Write an essay in which you consider this criticism of our culture and resolve the issue as best you can. You don't have to argue the case, but you should explain the ways in which we are and are not narcissistic as a whole society. You might begin with your own definition of cultural narcissism.

JOEY:
A "MECHANICAL BOY"

Bruno Bettelheim

*Born in 1903 and educated in Vienna, Bruno Bettelheim's
psychoanalytic work was strongly influenced by Sigmund
Freud. During 1938 and 1939, he was a prisoner in Nazi
concentration camps; he wrote about those experiences in*
The Informed Heart *after coming to the United States in
1939. Bettelheim has described his major work with emotionally disturbed children in books addressed to the general
reader as well as to his fellow psychoanalysts. His other work
includes* Children of the Dream, *a study of children raised
in an Israeli kibbutz, and a study of fairy tales called* The
Uses of Enchantment. *This essay on Joey was first published
in* Scientific American *in 1959.*

Joey, when we began our work with him, was a mechanical boy. He func-　1
tioned as if by remote control, run by machines of his own powerfully creative
fantasy. Not only did he himself believe that he was a machine but, more
remarkably, he created this impression in others. Even while he performed
actions that are intrinsically human, they never appeared to be other than ma-
chine-started and executed. On the other hand, when the machine was not
working we had to concentrate on recollecting his presence, for he seemed not
to exist. A human body that functions as if it were a machine and a machine
that duplicates human functions are equally fascinating and frightening. Perhaps
they are so uncanny because they remind us that the human body can operate
without a human spirit, that body can exist without soul. And Joey was a child
who had been robbed of his humanity.

Not every child who possesses a fantasy world is possessed by it. Normal　2
children may retreat into realms of imaginary glory or magic powers, but they
are easily recalled from these excursions. Disturbed children are not always able
to make the return trip; they remain withdrawn, prisoners of the inner world of
delusion and fantasy. In many ways Joey presented a classic example of this
state of infantile autism.[1]

At the Sonia Shankman Orthogenic School of the University of Chicago it　3
is our function to provide a therapeutic environment in which such children

---

[1]autism: a form of psychosis characterized by an inability to relate to and perceive the environment in a realistic manner. Autistic thinking is characterized by withdrawal and detachment from
reality, fantasies, delusions, and hallucinations. [Eds.]

may start life over again. I have previously described in this magazine the rehabilitation of another of our patients ["Schizophrenic Art: A Case Study"; SCIENTIFIC AMERICAN, April, 1952]. This time I shall concentrate upon the illness, rather than the treatment. In any age, when the individual has escaped into a delusional world, he has usually fashioned it from bits and pieces of the world at hand. Joey, in his time and world, chose the machine and froze himself in its image. His story has a general relevance to the understanding of emotional development in a machine age.

Joey's delusion is not uncommon among schizophrenic children today.[2] He wanted to be rid of his unbearable humanity, to become completely automatic. He so nearly succeeded in attaining this goal that he could almost convince others, as well as himself, of his mechanical character. The descriptions of autistic children in the literature take for their point of departure and comparison the normal or abnormal human being. To do justice to Joey I would have to compare him simultaneously to a most inept infant and a highly complex piece of machinery. Often we had to force ourselves by a conscious act of will to realize that Joey was a child. Again and again his acting-out of his delusions froze our own ability to respond as human beings.   4

During Joey's first weeks with us we would watch absorbedly as this at once fragile-looking and imperious nine-year-old went about his mechanical existence. Entering the dining room, for example, he would string an imaginary wire from his "energy source"—an imaginary electric outlet—to the table. There he "insulated" himself with paper napkins and finally plugged himself in. Only then could Joey eat, for he firmly believed that the "current" ran his ingestive apparatus. So skillful was the pantomime that one had to look twice to be sure there was neither wire nor outlet nor plug. Children and members of our staff spontaneously avoided stepping on the "wires" for fear of interrupting what seemed the source of his very life.   5

For long periods of time, when his "machinery" was idle, he would sit so quietly that he would disappear from the focus of the most conscientious observation. Yet in the next moment he might be "working" and the center of our captivated attention. Many times a day he would turn himself on and shift noisily through a sequence of higher and higher gears until he "exploded," screaming "Crash, crash!" and hurling items from his ever present apparatus— radio tubes, light bulbs, even motors or, lacking these, any handy breakable object. (Joey had an astonishing knack for snatching bulbs and tubes unobserved.) As soon as the object thrown had shattered, he would cease his screaming and wild jumping and retire to mute, motionless nonexistence.   6

Our maids, inured to difficult children, were exceptionally attentive to Joey; they were apparently moved by his extreme infantile fragility, so strangely cou-   7

---

[2]schizophrenic: severe mental disorder characterized by unrealistic behavior, bizarre actions, and a tendency to live in an inner world dominated by private fantasies. [Eds.]

pled with megalomaniacal superiority. Occasionally some of the apparatus he fixed to his bed to "live him" during his sleep would fall down in disarray. This machinery he contrived from masking tape, cardboard, wire and other paraphernalia. Usually the maids would pick up such things and leave them on a table for the children to find, or disregard them entirely. But Joey's machine they carefully restored: "Joey must have the carburetor so he can breathe." Similarly they were on the alert to pick up and preserve the motors that ran him during the day and the exhaust pipes through which he exhaled.

How had Joey become a human machine? From intensive interviews with his parents we learned that the process had begun even before birth. Schizophrenia often results from parental rejection, sometimes combined ambivalently with love. Joey, on the other hand, had been completely ignored. 8

"I never knew I was pregnant," his mother said, meaning that she had already excluded Joey from her consciousness. His birth, she said, "did not make any difference." Joey's father, a rootless draftee in the wartime civilian army, was equally unready for parenthood. So, of course, are many young couples. Fortunately most such parents lose their indifference upon the baby's birth. But not Joey's parents. "I did not want to see or nurse him," his mother declared. "I had no feeling of actual dislike—I simply didn't want to take care of him." For the first three months of his life Joey "cried most of the time." A colicky baby, he was kept on a rigid four-hour feeding schedule, was not touched unless necessary and was never cuddled or played with. The mother, preoccupied with herself, usually left Joey alone in the crib or playpen during the day. The father discharged his frustration by punishing Joey when the child cried at night. 9

Soon the father left for overseas duty, and the mother took Joey, now a year and a half old, to live with her at her parents' home. On his arrival the grandparents noticed that ominous changes had occurred in the child. Strong and healthy at birth, he had become frail and irritable; a responsive baby, he had become remote and inaccessible. When he began to master speech, he talked only to himself. At an early date he became preoccupied with machinery, including an old electric fan which he could take apart and put together again with surprising deftness. 10

Joey's mother impressed us with a fey quality that expressed her insecurity, her detachment from the world and her low physical vitality. We were struck especially by her total indifference as she talked about Joey. This seemed much more remarkable than the actual mistakes she made in handling him. Certainly he was left to cry for hours when hungry, because she fed him on a rigid schedule; he was toilet-trained with great rigidity so that he would give no trouble. These things happen to many children. But Joey's existence never registered with his mother. In her recollections he was fused at one moment with one event or person; at another, with something or somebody else. When she told us about his birth and infancy, it was as if she were talking about some 11

GROWING SELF-ESTEEM is shown in this sequence of drawings. At left Joey portrays himself as an electrical "papoose," completely enclosed, suspended in empty space and operated by wireless signals. In center drawing his figure is much larger, though still under wireless control. At right he is able to picture the machine which controls him, and he has acquired hands with which he can manipulate his immediate environment.

vague acquaintance, and soon her thoughts would wander off to another person or to herself.

When Joey was not yet four, his nursery school suggested that he enter a special school for disturbed children. At the new school his autism was immediately recognized. During his three years there he experienced a slow improvement. Unfortunately a subsequent two years in a parochial school destroyed this progress. He began to develop compulsive defenses, which he called his "preventions." He could not drink, for example, except through elaborate piping systems built of straws. Liquids had to be "pumped" into him, in his fantasy, or he could not suck. Eventually his behavior became so upsetting that he could not be kept in the parochial school. At home things did not improve. Three months before entering the Orthogenic School he made a serious attempt at suicide.

To us Joey's pathological behavior seemed the external expression of an overwhelming effort to remain almost nonexistent as a person. For weeks Joey's only reply when addressed was "Bam." Unless he thus neutralized whatever we said, there would be an explosion, for Joey plainly wished to close off every form of contact not mediated by machinery. Even when he was bathed he rocked back and forth with mute, engine-like regularity, flooding the bathroom. If he stopped rocking, he did this like a machine too; suddenly he went completely rigid. Only once, after months of being lifted from his bath and carried

414

to bed, did a small expression of puzzled pleasure appear on his face as he said very softly: "They even carry you to your bed here."

For a long time after he began to talk he would never refer to anyone by name, but only as "that person" or "the little person" or "the big person." He was unable to designate by its true name anything to which he attached feelings. Nor could he name his anxieties except through neologisms or word contaminations.[3] For a long time he spoke about "master paintings" and "a master painting room" (i.e., masturbating and masturbating room). One of his machines, the "criticizer," prevented him from "saying words which have unpleasant feelings." Yet he gave personal names to the tubes and motors in his collection of machinery. Moreover, these dead things had feelings; the tubes bled when hurt and sometimes got sick. He consistently maintained this reversal between animate and inanimate objects.

In Joey's machine world everything, on pain of instant destruction, obeyed inhibitory laws much more stringent than those of physics. When we came to know him better, it was plain that in his moments of silent withdrawal, with his machine switched off, Joey was absorbed in pondering the compulsive laws of his private universe. His preoccupation with machinery made it difficult to establish even practical contacts with him. If he wanted to do something with a counselor, such as play with a toy that had caught his vague attention, he could not do so: "I'd like this very much, but first I have to turn off the machine." But by the time he had fulfilled all the requirements of his preventions, he had lost interest. When a toy was offered to him, he could not touch it because his motors and his tubes did not leave him a hand free. Even certain colors were dangerous and had to be strictly avoided in toys and clothing, because "some colors turn off the current, and I can't touch them because I can't live without the current."

Joey was convinced that machines were better than people. Once when he bumped into one of the pipes on our jungle gym he kicked it so violently that his teacher had to restrain him to keep him from injuring himself. When she explained that the pipe was much harder than his foot, Joey replied: "That proves it. Machines are better than the body. They don't break; they're much harder and stronger." If he lost or forgot something, it merely proved that his brain ought to be thrown away and replaced by machinery. If he spilled something, his arm should be broken and twisted off because it did not work properly. When his head or arm failed to work as it should, he tried to punish it by hitting it. Even Joey's feelings were mechanical. Much later in his therapy, when he had formed a timid attachment to another child and had been rebuffed, Joey cried: "He broke my feelings."

Gradually we began to understand what had seemed to be contradictory in

14

15

16

17

---

[3]neologisms or word contaminations: words that Joey made up or words that he peculiarly altered. [Eds.]

ELABORATE SEWAGE SYSTEM in Joey's drawing of a house reflects his long preoccupation with excretion. His obsession with sewage reflected intense anxieties produced by his early toilet-training, which was not only rigid but also completely impersonal.

Joey's behavior—why he held on to the motors and tubes, then suddenly destroyed them in a fury, then set out immediately and urgently to equip himself with new and larger tubes. Joey had created these machines to run his body and mind because it was too painful to be human. But again and again he became dissatisfied with their failure to meet his need and rebellious at the way they frustrated his will. In a recurrent frenzy he "exploded" his light bulbs and tubes, and for a moment became a human being—for one crowning instant he came alive. But as soon as he had asserted his dominance through the self-created explosion, he felt his life ebbing away. To keep on existing he had immediately to restore his machines and replenish the electricity that supplied his life energy.

What deep-seated fears and needs underlay Joey's delusional system? We were long in finding out, for Joey's preventions effectively concealed the secret of his autistic behavior. In the meantime we dealt with his peripheral problems one by one. 18

During his first year with us Joey's most trying problem was toilet behavior. This surprised us, for Joey's personality was not "anal" in the Freudian sense; his original personality damage had antedated the period of his toilet-training. Rigid and early toilet-training, however, had certainly contributed to his anxieties. It was our effort to help Joey with this problem that led to his first recognition of us as human beings. 19

Going to the toilet, like everything else in Joey's life, was surrounded by 20

GROWING AUTONOMY is shown in Joey's drawings of the imaginary "Carr" (car) family. Top drawing shows a machine which can move but is unoccupied. Machine in center is occupied, but by a passive figure. In bottom drawing figure has gained control of machine.

417

elaborate preventions. We had to accompany him; he had to take off all his clothes; he could only squat, not sit, on the toilet seat; he had to touch the wall with one hand, in which he also clutched frantically the vacuum tubes that powered his elimination. He was terrified lest his whole body be sucked down.

To counteract this fear we gave him a metal wastebasket in lieu of a toilet. 21 Eventually, when eliminating into the wastebasket, he no longer needed to take off all his clothes, nor to hold on to the wall. He still needed the tubes and motors which, he believed, moved his bowels for him. But here again the all-important machinery was itself a source of new terrors. In Joey's world the gadgets had to move their bowels, too. He was terribly concerned that they should, but since they were so much more powerful than men, he was also terrified that if his tubes moved their bowels, their feces would fill all of space and leave him no room to live. He was thus always caught in some fearful contradiction.

Our readiness to accept his toilet habits, which obviously entailed some 22 hardship for his counselors, gave Joey the confidence to express his obsessions in drawings. Drawing these fantasies was a first step toward letting us in, however distantly, to what concerned him most deeply. It was the first step in a yearlong process of externalizing his anal preoccupations. As a result he began seeing feces everywhere; the whole world became to him a mire of excrement. At the same time he began to eliminate freely wherever he happened to be. But with this release from his infantile imprisonment in compulsive rules, the toilet and the whole process of elimination became less dangerous. Thus far it had been beyond Joey's comprehension that anybody could possibly move his bowels without mechanical aid. Now Joey took a further step forward; defecation became the first physiological process he could perform without the help of vacuum tubes. It must not be thought that he was proud of this ability. Taking pride in an achievement presupposes that one accomplishes it of one's own free will. He still did not feel himself an autonomous person who could do things on his own. To Joey defecation still seemed enslaved to some incomprehensible but utterly binding cosmic law, perhaps the law his parents had imposed on him when he was being toilet-trained.

It was not simply that his parents had subjected him to rigid, early training. 23 Many children are so trained. But in most cases the parents have a deep emotional investment in the child's performance. The child's response in turn makes training an occasion for interaction between them and for the building of genuine relationships. Joey's parents had no emotional investment in him. His obedience gave them no satisfaction and won him no affection or approval. As a toilet-trained child he saved his mother labor, just as household machines saved her labor. As a machine he was not loved for his performance, nor could he love himself.

So it had been with all other aspects of Joey's existence with his parents. 24 Their reactions to his eating or noneating, sleeping or wakening, urinating or defecating, being dressed or undressed, washed or bathed did not flow from any unitary interest in him, deeply embedded in their personalities. By treating him mechanically his parents made him a machine. The various functions of life—even the parts of his body—bore no integrating relationship to one another or to any sense of self that was acknowledged and confirmed by others. Though he had acquired mastery over some functions, such as toilet-training and speech, he had acquired them separately and kept them isolated from each other. Toilet-training had thus not gained him a pleasant feeling of body mastery; speech had not led to communication of thought or feeling. On the contrary, each achievement only steered him away from self-mastery and integration. Toilet-training had enslaved him. Speech left him talking in neologisms that obstructed his and our ability to relate to each other. In Joey's development the normal process of growth had been made to run backward. Whatever he had learned put him not at the end of his infantile development toward integration but, on the contrary, farther behind than he was at its very beginning. Had we understood this sooner, his first years with us would have been less baffling.

It is unlikely that Joey's calamity could befall a child in any time and culture   25
but our own. He suffered no physical deprivation; he starved for human contact. Just to be taken care of is not enough for relating. It is a necessary but not a sufficient condition. At the extreme where utter scarcity reigns, the forming of relationships is certainly hampered. But our society of mechanized plenty often makes for equal difficulties in a child's learning to relate. Where parents can provide the simple creature-comforts for their children only at the cost of significant effort, it is likely that they will feel pleasure in being able to provide for them; it is this, the parents' pleasure, that gives children a sense of personal worth and sets the process of relating in motion. But if comfort is so readily available that the parents feel no particular pleasure in winning it for their children, then the children cannot develop the feeling of being worthwhile around the satisfaction of their basic needs. Of course parents and children can and do develop relationships around other situations. But matters are then no longer so simple and direct. The child must be on the receiving end of care and concern given with pleasure and without the exaction of return if he is to feel loved and worthy of respect and consideration. This feeling gives him the ability to trust; he can entrust his well-being to persons to whom he is so important. Out of such trust the child learns to form close and stable relationships.

For Joey relationship with his parents was empty of pleasure in comfort-   26
giving as in all other situations. His was an extreme instance of a plight that sends many schizophrenic children to our clinics and hospitals. Many months passed before he could relate to us; his despair that anybody could like him made contact impossible.

When Joey could finally trust us enough to let himself become more infan-   27
tile, he began to play at being a papoose. There was a corresponding change in

419

his fantasies. He drew endless pictures of himself as an electrical papoose. Totally enclosed, suspended in empty space, he is run by unknown, unseen powers
through wireless electricity [*see illustration at left on page 414*].

As we eventually came to understand, the heart of Joey's delusional system   28
was the artificial, mechanical womb he had created and into which he had
locked himself. In his papoose fantasies lay the wish to be entirely reborn in a
womb. His new experiences in the school suggested that life, after all, might
be worth living. Now he was searching for a way to be reborn in a better way.
Since machines were better than men, what was more natural than to try rebirth
through them? This was the deeper meaning of his electrical papoose.

As Joey made progress, his pictures of himself became more dominant in   29
his drawings. Though still machine-operated, he has grown in self-importance
[*see illustration at center on page 414*]. Another great step forward is represented in the picture at right. . . . Now he has acquired hands that do something, and he has had the courage to make a picture of the machine that runs
him. Later still the papoose became a person, rather than a robot encased in
glass.

Eventually Joey began to create an imaginary family at the school: the "Carr"   30

GENTLE LANDSCAPE painted by Joey after his recovery symbolizes the human emotions he had regained. At 12, having learned to express his feelings, he was no longer a
machine.

family. Why the Carr family? In the car he was enclosed as he had been in his papoose, but at least the car was not stationary; it could move. More important, in a car one was not only driven but also could drive. The Carr family was Joey's way of exploring the possibility of leaving the school, of living with a good family in a safe, protecting car [*see illustrations on page 417*].

Joey at last broke through his prison. In this brief account it has not been possible to trace the painfully slow process of his first true relations with other human beings. Suffice it to say that he ceased to be a mechanical boy and became a human child. This newborn child was, however, nearly 12 years old. To recover the lost time is a tremendous task. That work has occupied Joey and us ever since. Sometimes he sets to it with a will; at other times the difficulty of real life makes him regret that he ever came out of his shell. But he has never wanted to return to his mechanical life.

One last detail and this fragment of Joey's story has been told. When Joey was 12, he made a float for our Memorial Day parade. It carried the slogan: "Feelings are more important than anything under the sun." Feelings, Joey had learned, are what make for humanity; their absence, for a mechanical existence. With this knowledge Joey entered the human condition.

QUESTIONS

1. Bettelheim's task was to explain Joey's behavior as best he could. What did he and his colleagues do, what did they examine, and how did they behave in order to develop their explanation of Joey?

2. Joey, of course, had already come to some conclusions about himself and about the world he inhabited. These explanations seem to have become fixed as interpretations, by which we mean simply that he had come to understand himself in terms of something else. In which passages does Bettelheim come closest to presenting Joey as his own interpreter? Summarize Joey's interpretation of himself—the structure or set of principles by which he understands himself.

3. In order to begin to be cured, Joey had to *reinterpret* his life. What were the major steps toward that reinterpretation? What changed for Joey?

4. Even to say *cured*, as we just did in question 3, involves an unexamined interpretation. What assumptions guide our use of that word? Do you find *cured* a satisfying explanation of what begins to happen to Joey?

5. The introduction to this part mentions this essay as an example of a case study, that is, a close examination of a unique person, event, or situation over time in a set of circumstances that are probably not replicable. Using this essay as your example, what else might characterize a case study? What makes a case believable?

6. Quite a few people play roles or assume characterizations that deviate from what we think we know about them. Describe a person who does that. Offer your own limited

case study. Try to indicate the extent to which that person's understanding of himself or herself is based on reality and the extent to which it isn't.

7. College can lead you to reinterpret yourself. In fact, that traditionally has been a large part of the experience of going to college. Write an explanation of yourself or of someone else you know well who is undergoing such a reinterpretation. What were the terms that prevailed earlier? What happened to call them into question? What kind of change has occurred, and what is at stake in this matter?

ON THE FEAR
OF DEATH

Elizabeth Kübler-Ross

*Elizabeth Kübler-Ross (b. 1926), a Swiss-American psychi-
atrist, is one of the leaders of the movement that may help
change the way Americans think about death. Born in Zurich, Switzerland, she received her M.D. from the University
of Zurich in 1957 and came to the United States as an
intern the following year. Kübler-Ross began her work with
terminally ill patients while teaching psychiatry at the University of Chicago Medical School. She now heads "Shanti
Nilaya" (Sanskrit for "home of peace"), an organization she
founded north of Escondido, California, in 1976, "dedicated
to the promotion of physical, emotional, and spiritual health."
"On the Fear of Death" is taken from her first and most
famous book,* On Death and Dying *(1969).*

> *Let me not pray to be sheltered from
> dangers but to be fearless in facing
> them.*
> *Let me not beg for the stilling of
> my pain but for the heart to conquer it.*
> *Let me not look for allies in life's
> battlefield but to my own strength.*
> *Let me not crave in anxious fear to
> be saved but hope for the patience to
> win my freedom.*
> *Grant me that I may not be a
> coward, feeling your mercy in my
> success alone; but let me find the grasp
> of your hand in my failure.*

Rabindranath Tagore, *Fruit-Gathering*

Epidemics have taken a great toll of lives in past generations. Death in infancy 1
and early childhood was frequent and there were few families who didn't lose
a member of the family at an early age. Medicine has changed greatly in the
last decades. Widespread vaccinations have practically eradicated many illnesses,
at least in western Europe and the United States. The use of chemotherapy,
especially the antibiotics, has contributed to an ever-decreasing number of fa-
talities in infectious diseases. Better child care and education has effected a low

morbidity and mortality among children. The many diseases that have taken an impressive toll among the young and middle-aged have been conquered. The number of old people is on the rise, and with this fact come the number of people with malignancies and chronic diseases associated more with old age.

Pediatricians have less work with acute and life-threatening situations as they have an ever-increasing number of patients with psychosomatic disturbances and adjustment and behavior problems. Physicians have more people in their waiting rooms with emotional problems than they have ever had before, but they also have more elderly patients who not only try to live with their decreased physical abilities and limitations but who also face loneliness and isolation with all its pains and anguish. The majority of these people are not seen by a psychiatrist. Their needs have to be elicited and gratified by other professional people, for instance, chaplains and social workers. It is for them that I am trying to outline the changes that have taken place in the last few decades, changes that are ultimately responsible for the increased fear of death, the rising number of emotional problems, and the greater need for understanding of and coping with the problems of death and dying.

When we look back in time and study old cultures and people, we are impressed that death has always been distasteful to man and will probably always be. From a psychiatrist's point of view this is very understandable and can perhaps best be explained by our basic knowledge that, in our unconscious, death is never possible in regard to ourselves. It is inconceivable for our unconscious to imagine an actual ending of our own life here on earth, and if this life of ours has to end, the ending is always attributed to a malicious intervention from the outside by someone else. In simple terms, in our unconscious mind we can only be killed; it is inconceivable to die of a natural cause or of old age. Therefore death in itself is associated with a bad act, a frightening happening, something that in itself calls for retribution and punishment.

One is wise to remember these fundamental facts as they are essential in understanding some of the most important, otherwise unintelligible communications of our patients.

The second fact that we have to comprehend is that in our unconscious mind we cannot distinguish between a wish and a deed. We are all aware of some of our illogical dreams in which two completely opposite statements can exist side by side—very acceptable in our dreams but unthinkable and illogical in our wakening state. Just as our unconscious mind cannot differentiate between the wish to kill somebody in anger and the act of having done so, the young child is unable to make this distinction. The child who angrily wishes his mother to drop dead for not having gratified his needs will be traumatized greatly by the actual death of his mother—even if this event is not linked closely in time with his destructive wishes. He will always take part or the whole blame for the loss of his mother. He will always say to himself—rarely to others—"I did it, I am responsible, I was bad, therefore Mommy left me." It is well to remember that the child will react in the same manner if he loses a parent by divorce, separation, or desertion. Death is often seen by a child as an impermanent thing and has therefore little distinction from a divorce in which he may have an opportunity to see a parent again.

Many a parent will remember remarks of their children such as, "I will bury my doggy now and next spring when the flowers come up again, he will get up." Maybe it was the same wish that motivated the ancient Egyptians to supply their dead with food and goods to keep them happy and the old American Indians to bury their relatives with their belongings.

When we grow older and begin to realize that our omnipotence is really not so omnipotent, that our strongest wishes are not powerful enough to make the impossible possible, the fear that we have contributed to the death of a loved one diminishes—and with it the guilt. The fear remains diminished, however, only so long as it is not challenged too strongly. Its vestiges can be seen daily in hospital corridors and in people associated with the bereaved.

A husband and wife may have been fighting for years, but when the partner dies, the survivor will pull his hair, whine and cry louder and beat his chest in regret, fear and anguish, and will hence fear his own death more than before, still believing in the law of talion—an eye for an eye, a tooth for a tooth—"I am responsible for her death, I will have to die a pitiful death in retribution."

Maybe this knowledge will help us understand many of the old customs and rituals which have lasted over the centuries and whose purpose is to diminish the anger of the gods or the people as the case may be, thus decreasing the anticipated punishment. I am thinking of the ashes, the torn clothes, the veil, the *Klage Weiber* of the old days[1]—they are all means to ask you to take pity on them, the mourners, and are expressions of sorrow, grief, and shame. If someone grieves, beats his chest, tears his hair, or refuses to eat, it is an attempt at self-punishment to avoid or reduce the anticipated punishment for the blame that he takes on the death of a loved one.

This grief, shame, and guilt are not very far removed from feelings of anger and rage. The process of grief always includes some qualities of anger. Since none of us likes to admit anger at a deceased person, these emotions are often disguised or repressed and prolong the period of grief or show up in other ways. It is well to remember that it is not up to us to judge such feelings as bad or shameful but to understand their true meaning and origin as something very human. In order to illustrate this I will again use the example of the child—and the child in us. The five-year-old who loses his mother is both blaming himself for her disappearance and being angry at her for having deserted him and for no longer gratifying his needs. The dead person then turns into something the child loves and wants very much but also hates with equal intensity for this severe deprivation.

6

7

8

9

10

---

[1]*Klage Weiber:* wailing wives. [*Eds.*]

The ancient Hebrews regarded the body of a dead person as something un- 11
clean and not to be touched. The early American Indians talked about the evil
spirits and shot arrows in the air to drive the spirits away. Many other cultures
have rituals to take care of the "bad" dead person, and they all originate in this
feeling of anger which still exists in all of us, though we dislike admitting it.
The tradition of the tombstone may originate in the wish to keep the bad spirits
deep down in the ground, and the pebbles that many mourners put on the grave
are leftover symbols of the same wish. Though we call the firing of guns at
military funerals a last salute, it is the same symbolic ritual as the Indian used
when he shot his spears and arrows into the skies.

I give these examples to emphasize that man has not basically changed. Death 12
is still a fearful, frightening happening, and the fear of death is a universal fear
even if we think we have mastered it on many levels.

What has changed is our way of coping and dealing with death and dying 13
and our dying patients.

Having been raised in a country in Europe where science is not so advanced, 14
where modern techniques have just started to find their way into medicine, and
where people still live as they did in this country half a century ago, I may have
had an opportunity to study a part of the evolution of mankind in a shorter
period.

I remember as a child the death of a farmer. He fell from a tree and was not 15
expected to live. He asked simply to die at home, a wish that was granted without
question. He called his daughters into the bedroom and spoke with each one
of them alone for a few moments. He arranged his affairs quietly, though he
was in great pain, and distributed his belongings and his land, none of which
was to be split until his wife should follow him in death. He also asked each of
his children to share in the work, duties, and tasks that he had carried on until
the time of the accident. He asked his friends to visit him once more, to bid
goodbye to them. Although I was a small child at the time, he did not exclude
me or my siblings. We were allowed to share in the preparations of the family
just as we were permitted to grieve with them until he died. When he did die,
he was left at home, in his own beloved home which he had built, and among
his friends and neighbors who went to take a last look at him where he lay in
the midst of flowers in the place he had lived in and loved so much. In that
country today there is still no make-believe slumber room, no embalming, no
false makeup to pretend sleep. Only the signs of very disfiguring illnesses are
covered up with bandages and only infectious cases are removed from the home
prior to the burial.

Why do I describe such "old-fashioned" customs? I think they are an indi- 16
cation of our acceptance of a fatal outcome, and they help the dying patient as
well as his family to accept the loss of a loved one. If a patient is allowed to
terminate his life in the familiar and beloved environment, it requires less
adjustment for him. His own family knows him well enough to replace a sedative

with a glass of his favorite wine; or the smell of a home-cooked soup may give him the appetite to sip a few spoons of fluid which, I think, is still more enjoyable than an infusion. I will not minimize the need for sedatives and infusions and realize full well from my own experience as a country doctor that they are sometimes life-saving and often unavoidable. But I also know that patience and familiar people and foods could replace many a bottle of intravenous fluids given for the simple reason that it fulfills the physiological need without involving too many people and/or individual nursing care.

The fact that children are allowed to stay at home where a fatality has struck 17 and are included in the talk, discussions, and fears gives them the feeling that they are not alone in their grief and gives them the comfort of shared responsibility and shared mourning. It prepares them gradually and helps them view death as part of life, an experience which may help them grow and mature.

This is in great contrast to a society in which death is viewed as taboo, 18 discussion of it is regarded as morbid, and children are excluded with the presumption and pretext that it would be "too much" for them. They are then sent off to relatives, often accompanied by some unconvincing lies of "Mother has gone on a long trip" or other unbelievable stories. The child senses that something is wrong, and his distrust in adults will only multiply if other relatives add new variations of the story, avoid his questions or suspicions, shower him with gifts as a meager substitute for a loss he is not permitted to deal with. Sooner or later the child will become aware of the changed family situation and, depending on the age and personality of the child, will have an unresolved grief and regard this incident as a frightening, mysterious, in any case very traumatic experience with untrustworthy grownups, which he has no way to cope with.

It is equally unwise to tell a little child who lost her brother that God loved 19 little boys so much that he took little Johnny to heaven. When this little girl grew up to be a woman she never solved her anger at God, which resulted in a psychotic depression when she lost her own little son three decades later.

We would think that our great emancipation, our knowledge of science and 20 of man, has given us better ways and means to prepare ourselves and our families for this inevitable happening. Instead the days are gone when a man was allowed to die in peace and dignity in his own home.

The more we are making advancements in science, the more we seem to 21 fear and deny the reality of death. How is this possible?

We use euphemisms, we make the dead look as if they were asleep, we ship 22 the children off to protect them from the anxiety and turmoil around the house if the patient is fortunate enough to die at home, we don't allow children to visit their dying parents in the hospitals, we have long and controversial discussions about whether patients should be told the truth—a question that rarely arises when the dying person is tended by the family physician who has known him from delivery to death and who knows the weaknesses and strengths of each member of the family.

427

I think there are many reasons for this flight away from facing death calmly. 23
One of the most important facts is that dying nowadays is more gruesome in
many ways, namely, more lonely, mechanical, and dehumanized; at times it
is even difficult to determine technically when the time of death has occurred.

Dying becomes lonely and impersonal because the patient is often taken out 24
of his familiar environment and rushed to an emergency room. Whoever has
been very sick and has required rest and comfort especially may recall his experience of being put on a stretcher and enduring the noise of the ambulance
siren and hectic rush until the hospital gates open. Only those who have lived
through this may appreciate the discomfort and cold necessity of such transportation which is only the beginning of a long ordeal—hard to endure when
you are well, difficult to express in words when noise, light, pumps, and voices
are all too much to put up with. It may well be that we might consider more
the patient under the sheets and blankets and perhaps stop our well-meant
efficiency and rush in order to hold the patient's hand, to smile, or to listen to
a question. I include the trip to the hospital as the first episode in dying, as it
is for many. I am putting it exaggeratedly in contrast to the sick man who is
left at home—not to say that lives should not be saved if they can be saved by
a hospitalization but to keep the focus on the patient's experience, his needs
and his reactions.

When a patient is severely ill, he is often treated like a person with no right 25
to an opinion. It is often someone else who makes the decision if and when
and where a patient should be hospitalized. It would take so little to remember
that the sick person too has feelings, has wishes and opinions, and has—most
important of all—the right to be heard.

Well, our presumed patient has now reached the emergency room. He will 26
be surrounded by busy nurses, orderlies, interns, residents, a lab technician
perhaps who will take some blood, an electrocardiogram technician who takes
the cardiogram. He may be moved to X-ray and he will overhear opinions of
his condition and discussions and questions to members of the family. He slowly
but surely is beginning to be treated like a thing. He is no longer a person.
Decisions are made often without his opinion. If he tries to rebel he will be
sedated and after hours of waiting and wondering whether he has the strength,
he will be wheeled into the operating room or intensive treatment unit and
become an object of great concern and great financial investment.

He may cry for rest, peace, and dignity, but he will get infusions, transfu- 27
sions, a heart machine, or tracheotomy if necessary. He may want one single
person to stop for one single minute so that he can ask one single question—
but he will get a dozen people around the clock, all busily preoccupied with
his heart rate, pulse, electrocardiogram or pulmonary functions, his secretions
or excretions but not with him as a human being. He may wish to fight it all
but it is going to be a useless fight since all this is done in the fight for his life,
and if they can save his life they can consider the person afterwards. Those who

428

consider the person first may lose precious time to save his life! At least this seems to be the rationale or justification behind all this—or is it? Is the reason for this increasingly mechanical, depersonalized approach our own defensiveness? Is this approach our own way to cope with and repress the anxieties that a terminally or critically ill patient evokes in us? Is our concentration on equipment, on blood pressure, our desperate attempt to deny the impending death which is so frightening and discomforting to us that we displace all our knowledge onto machines, since they are less close to us than the suffering face of another human being which would remind us once more of our lack of omnipotence, our own limits and failures, and last but not least perhaps our own mortality?

Maybe the question has to be raised: Are we becoming less human or more   28
human?. . .it is clear that whatever the answer may be, the patient is suffering more—not physically, perhaps, but emotionally. And his needs have not changed over the centuries, only our ability to gratify them.

QUESTIONS

1. Why does Kübler-Ross describe the death of a farmer? What point is she making in explaining "such 'old-fashioned' customs" (paragraph 16)?

2. To what extent is this essay explanatory? Summarize a particular explanation of hers that you find intriguing. Do you find it persuasive?

3. At what point in this essay does Kübler-Ross turn from explanation toward argument? Do you think she has taken a stand on her subject? How sympathetic are you to her position?

4. In paragraphs 2 and 10, Kübler-Ross indicates a specialized audience for her writing. Who is that audience, and how do you relate to it?

5. Think of the audience you described in question 4 as a primary audience and of yourself as a member of a secondary audience. To what extent do the two audiences overlap? How thoroughly can you divide one from the other?

6. What experience of death have you had so far? Write of a death that you know something about, even if your relation to it is distant, perhaps only through the media. Can you locate elements of fear and anger in your own behavior or in the behavior of other persons involved? Does Kübler-Ross's interpretation of those reactions help you come to terms with the experience?

7. What kind of balance do you think best between prolonging life and allowing a person to die with dignity? What does the phrase "dying with dignity" mean?

8. If you were told you had a limited time to live, how would that news change the way you are living? Or would it? Offer an explanation for your position.

WHAT MADE THIS MAN? MENGELE

Robert Jay Lifton

Born in New York City in 1926, Robert Jay Lifton received his M.D. in 1948 and is presently Distinguished Professor of Psychiatry and Psychology at John Jay College of Criminal Justice in the City University of New York. The author of books on "brainwashing" and Vietnam veterans, he has been working on a study of Nazi doctors, from which the following essay was adapted for the New York Times Magazine *in July 1985. This essay appeared in the* Times *just after Mengele's body—or what most people believe to be his body— was found in a South American grave.*

His bones do not satisfy. Josef Mengele had come to symbolize the entire   1
Nazi killing project. The need was to capture him and put him on trial, hear
his confession, put *him* at *our* mercy. For many, that anticipated event took on
the significance of confronting the Holocaust and restoring a moral universe.

For Mengele has long been the focus of what could be called a cult of   2
demonic personality. He has been seen as the embodiment of absolute evil, a
doctor pledged to heal who kills instead. But this demonization made him
something of a deity, a nonhuman or even superhuman force, and served as a
barrier to any explanation of his behavior. One reason Auschwitz survivors have
hungered for his capture and trial is to divest him of this status. One of them,
for instance, spoke to me of his yearning to see "this metamorphosis of turning
him back into a person instead of God Almighty."

Mengele was a man, not a demon, and that is our problem.   3

Indeed, during recent weeks he had already begun to fall from grace as a   4
symbol of pure evil. The most notorious Nazi fugitive, unsuccessfully pursued
for decades, had suddenly appeared—as bones in a Brazilian grave. The world
watched in fascination as scientific examination seemed to confirm that these
were the right bones.

It was reported that Mengele had lived out much of his last 25 years in   5
lonely, despairing isolation, that he had fallen in love with a housemaid. An
exemplar of pure evil is not supposed to experience loneliness or to care for
another person.

What has been lost in the preoccupation with the corpse has been the nature   6
of the man: What made Mengele Mengele? How can we explain his murderous
behavior in Auschwitz?

Over the last eight years, while conducting research for a book on Nazi   7
doctors, I have sought answers to these questions. I have conducted psycho-

430

logical interviews with 28 former Nazi doctors; a number of Nazi lawyers, economists and other nonmedical professionals, and also with more than 80 former Auschwitz inmates who were engaged in medical work in the camp. The study has required me to probe moral as well as psychological issues and to raise questions about the nature of evil.

Hannah Arendt gave currency to a concept of the banality of evil in her [8] portrayal of Adolf Eichmann as a rather unremarkable bureaucrat who killed by meeting schedules and quotas. She is surely correct in her claim that an ordinary person is capable of extreme evil. But over the course of committing evil acts, an ordinary person becomes something different. In a process I call "doubling," a new self takes shape that adapts to the evil environment, and the evil acts become part of that self. At this point, the person and his behavior are anything but banal.

Mengele possessed unusually intense destructive potential, but there were no [9] apparent signs of aberrant behavior prior to the Nazis and Auschwitz. Without Auschwitz, he would probably have kept his destructive potential under control. As a wise former inmate physician told me, "In ordinary times, Mengele could have been a slightly sadistic German professor."

It was the coming together of the man and the place, the "fit" between the [10] two, that created the Auschwitz Mengele.

What we know about the man who arrived in Auschwitz in May 1943 is not [11] especially remarkable. The son of a well to-do Bavarian industrialist, Mengele is remembered by an acquaintance as a popular young man, an enthusiastic friend. He was also intelligent, a serious student who showed "a very distinct ambitiousness."

In 1931, at the age of 20, Mengele joined a right-wing, nationalistic or- [12] ganization. He was an early Nazi enthusiast, enlisting with the SA (the storm troopers) in 1933, applying for party membership in 1937 and for SS member- ship the following year. There are rumors that, while studying in Munich, he met such high-ranking Nazis as Alfred Rosenberg, a leading ideologue, and even Hitler himself.

Mengele became a true ideologue: a man who understood his life to be in [13] the service of a larger vision.

According to an Auschwitz friend and fellow-SS physician, Mengele es- [14] poused the visionary SS ideology that the Nordic race was the only truly creative race, that it had been weakened by Christian morality of Jewish origin, and that Germany needed to revert to ancient German myths in creating an SS "order" to purify the Nordic race. According to his friend, Mengele was an extreme anti-Semite, "fully convinced that the annihilation of the Jews is a provision for the recovery of the world and Germany." And Mengele considered these views to be sc entifically derived. (I have preserved the anonymity of the people I interviewed Those who are identified had previously made themselves known in books or other public documents.)

431

Mengele's ideology considerably influenced his intellectual choices. Matri- 15
culating not only at Munich but also at Bonn, Vienna and Frankfurt, he came
to concentrate on physical anthropology and genetics, eventually working under
Professor Freiherr Otmar von Verschuer at the Institute of Hereditary Biology
and Racial Hygiene at Frankfurt. He earned a degree in anthropology as well
as medicine.

Mengele produced three publications before he came to Auschwitz. They 16
dealt with physical characteristics and abnormalities and, in each case, emphasized the role of heredity—an emphasis in keeping with trends in German and
international scholarship at the time. Though jammed with charts, diagrams
and photographs that claim more than they prove, the papers are relatively
respectable scientific works of that era. But their conclusions uniformly reflect
Mengele's commitment to bringing science into the service of the Nazi vision.

Mengele seemed well on his way toward an academic career. He had the 17
strong backing of Verschuer who, in a letter of recommendation, praised his
reliability and his capacity for clear verbal presentation of difficult intellectual
problems. Mengele's marriage to a professor's daughter was in keeping with his
academic aspirations.

His military experience loomed large in his idea of himself. In 1938–39, 18
Mengele served six months with a specially trained mountain light-infantry
regiment, followed by a year in the reserve medical corps. He spent three years
with a Waffen SS unit, mostly in the East, including action in Russia, where,
according to SS records, he was wounded and declared medically unfit for
combat. A commendation declared that he had "acquitted himself brilliantly in
the face of the enemy," and he received five decorations, including the Iron
Cross First Class and Second Class.

Mengele, his friend said, was the only doctor in Auschwitz who possessed 19
that array of medals, and he was enormously proud of them; he frequently
referred to his combat experience to bolster his arguments on a variety of matters.
According to his friend, Mengele arrived at the camp with a special aura because
he was coming more or less directly from the front.

His friend suggests something else special about Mengele. He had asked to 20
be sent to the Auschwitz death camp because of the opportunities it could
provide for his research. He continued to have the support and collaboration of
his teacher, Verschuer, who convinced the German Research Society to provide
financial support for Mengele's work.

Auschwitz was both an annihilation camp and a work camp for German 21
industry. Like other SS doctors there, Mengele had the task of "selecting" prisoners for the gas chamber—the vast majoritity—and for the slave labor force.
SS doctors also controlled and supervised the inmate doctors who alone did
whatever actual medical treatment was done. Mengele was the chief doctor of
Birkenau, an Auschwitz subcamp, but seemed to many inmates to have authority beyond his position. Dr. Olga Lengyel, an inmate doctor, described

Mengele as "far and away the chief provider for the gas chamber and the crematory ovens." Another inmate doctor spoke of Mengele's role as "very important, more than that of the others."

One reason he appeared to be especially important was that he was extraordinarily energetic. While many SS doctors did no more than what was required of them, Mengele was always on the move, busy with his work, initiating new projects. More than any other SS doctor, he seemed to find his calling in Auschwitz. 22

Many inmates thought that Mengele alone conducted the large "selections." When they arrived at Auschwitz, packed by the hundreds into freight and cattle cars, they were unloaded and herded down a ramp. The Nazi doctors were assigned, on a rotating basis, to stand on the ramp and select those prisoners who would live, as workers at the camp, and those who would be killed. 23

The evidence is that Mengele took his turn at the ramp, like everyone else, but he also appeared there frequently to make sure that any twins in a "transport," as the trains were called, would be collected and saved for his research. But the prisoners saw it differently. At a trial of former Auschwitz personnel, in Frankfurt in 1964, an inmate who had been assigned to unload the transports recalled only the name of Mengele. When the judge commented, "Mengele cannot have been there all the time," the witness answered: "In my opinion, always. Night and day." Mengele brought such flamboyance and posturing to the selections task that it was his image inmates remembered. 24

He was an elegant figure on the ramp—handsome, well groomed, extremely upright in posture. Prisoners sometimes described him as "very Aryan looking" or "tall and blond," when he was actually of medium height, with dark hair and a dark complexion. Inmates said Mengele "conveyed the impression of a gentle and cultured man" and spoke of the "cheerful expression on his face . . . almost like he had fun . . . he was very playful." 25

There was an easy rhythm in his approach to selections. He walked back and forth, an inmate recalled, "a nice-looking man" with a riding crop in his hand who "looked at the bodies and the faces just a couple of seconds" and said, "*Links* [left], *Rechts* [right], *Links*, *Rechts* . . . *Rechts* . . . *Links*, *Rechts*." 26

Prisoners were struck by the stark contrast between his calm, playful manner and the horror of what he was doing. Occasionally, though, his detachment could give way to outbreaks of rage and violence, especially when he encountered resistance to his sense of "the rules." In one instance, a mother refused to be separated from her teen-age daughter and scratched the face of the SS trooper who tried to enforce Mengele's decision. Mengele drew his gun and shot both the woman and her child. Still raging, he ordered that all the people from that transport whom he had previously selected as workers be sent to the gas chamber. 27

In the hospital blocks where medical treatment was given to prisoners in order to maintain the workforce, there was another kind of "selection" process. 28

Nazi doctors would weed out for the gas chamber the weakest patients, those thought unlikely to recover in two or three weeks. Mengele, Dr. Lengyel recalled, "could show up suddenly at any hour, day or night. . . . when we least expected him." The prisoners would "march before him with their arms in the air while he continued to whistle his Wagner—or it might be Verdi or Johann Strauss."

Though usually cool in his conduct of selections, Mengele was passionate   29
in pursuing his "scientific research." His main interest was the study of twins, but he carried out a variety of projects with different groups of human subjects.

· He collected and studied dwarfs in an effort to determine the genetic reasons   30
  for their condition.
· He investigated a gangrenous condition of the face and mouth called noma.   31
  Though ordinarily a rare condition, it was common among gypsy inmates of
  Auschwitz. It was known to be caused by the kind of debilitation that inmates
  were subject to, but Mengele focused on what he deemed to be genetic and
  racial factors.
· He sought out inmates with a condition known as heterochromia of the iris—   32
  in which the two eyes are of different colors—and, after their death, sent their
  eyes to his old professor, Verschuer, at the Berlin-Dahlem Institute of Racial
  Biology. With some of these inmates, Mengele took the bizarre step of attempting to change eye color in an Aryan direction by injecting methylene
  blue into the brown eyes of blond inmate children.

But the research that most occupied Mengele, to which he devoted the   33
greatest time and energy, was his study of twins. In fact, he probably came to
Auschwitz for that specific purpose—as a continuation of work he had done
under Verschuer at the University of Frankfurt a few years earlier.

As early as 1935, Verschuer had written of the absolute necessity of research   34
on twins to achieve "complete and reliable determination of what is hereditary
in man."

Because identical twins (derived from the same ovum) possess the same genetic   35
constitution, they have traditionally been used in research on hereditary
influences. Their shared physical and sometimes psychological characteristics,
normal and abnormal, can be assumed to be genetically determined. Such
characteristics can be assumed to be genetically determined in other people as
well.

Mengele recognized that Auschwitz would permit him to pursue his mentor's   36
dream. From the hundreds of thousands of prisoners, he could collect twins in
quantities never before available to a scientist. What is more, he could exercise
total control over them.

He could compare measurements and bodily features. He could try medi-   37
cations meant to prevent, treat or induce a particular illness on an individual

twin, or both of a pair of twins. He could then make comparisons of various kinds, in which he sought to demonstrate the importance of heredity rather than environment. He had no need or inclination to concern himself with ethical considerations, sharing as he did the general SS doctor's view that one was doing no harm since Auschwitz inmates, especially Jews, were in any case doomed.

Mengele had a fanatic's commitment to twin research. A number of survivors 38 reported seeing him on the transport ramp, shouting "Zwillinge heraus! [Twins out!]," Zwillinge heraustreten! [Twins step forward!]." An inmate anthropologist whom Mengele had eagerly recruited to assist him described the arrival of a group of Hungarian Jews "like a river . . . women, men, women with children, and suddenly I saw Mengele going quickly . . . the same speed [as] the crowd [crying out] only 'Zwillinge heraus!' . . . with such a face that I would think he's mad."

Mengele had the same frenzied attitude in carrying out his research. To 39 inmates, he seemed to have an inner compulsion to get a great deal accomplished quickly in a personal race against time. He undoubtedly came to recognize increasingly that the days of the Auschwitz research bonanza were numbered.

Mainly to pursue his studies of twins, Mengele set up an Auschwitz caricature 40 of an academic research institute. Inmate doctors, mostly Jewish, with specialized training in various laboratory and clinical areas, were called upon to contribute to his work by diagnosing, sometimes treating, X-raying and performing post-mortem examinations of his research subjects. For his pathologist, Dr. Miklos Nyiszli, he provided a special dissection room complete with porcelain sinks and a dissecting table of polished marble. The overall arrangement, as Dr. Nyiszli later wrote, was "the exact replica of any large city's institute of pathology." In addition to the area used by SS physicians, Mengele had three offices of his own, mainly for work with twins.

The precise number of twins Mengele studied is not known, but during the 41 spring and summer of 1944, the time of the influx and mass murder of enormous numbers of Hungarian Jews, he accumulated what inmates of the men's and women's camps estimated to be a total of 175 sets of twins; it was an extraordinarily large number to have available simultaneously in a single place. Most were children, but the twins ranged up to the age of 70. The relative number of identical twins, as opposed to nonidentical twins, is also uncertain. (Nonidentical twins come from different ova and are genetically similar only to the extent of ordinary siblings.) Mengele's capacity or inclination to maintain, in his work, the crucial distinction between these two kinds of twins is unclear. Since it is known that a few ordinary siblings masqueraded as twins, upon discovering the advantages of doing so, there is reason to doubt the reliability of Mengele's research.

Being a twin gave one a much better chance to survive. That was especially 42

435

true for children, who were otherwise routinely selected for the gas chamber on arrival.

Twins had unique status. They felt themselves, as one put it, "completely 43 elevated, segregated from the hurly-burly of the camp." They lived in special blocks, usually within medical units. They were frequently permitted to keep their own clothing. Their heads were not shaved. Their diet was rich by Auschwitz standards, often including white bread and milk. They were never beaten, as one surviving twin explained—even if they were caught in such a normally "ultimate sin" as stealing food—because the word was out "not to ruin us physically."

Mothers of young female twins were sometimes allowed to stay with their 44 children, though usually only temporarily, in order to help the twins remain in good physical and mental condition—and on occasion to contribute to information about heredity and family history. We may say that the lives of twins had unique existential value in Auschwitz.

Mengele's research method, according to the inmate anthropologist, was 45 standard for the time—and much the same as that used by her own well-regarded professor at the Polish university where she had obtained her advanced degree. That professor, she said, stressed "the biological foundation of [the] social environment" and the delineation of "racial types." Mengele's approach was different only in being "terribly detailed."

Measurements were taken of the twins' skulls and bodies and various char- 46 acteristics of the nose, lips, ears, hair and eyes. The inmate anthropologist used quality Swiss instruments and wore a white coat "like a physician."

Identical twins, Mengele's most treasured research objects, were often ex- 47 amined together. As one of them described: "It was like a laboratory. . . . There isn't a piece of body that wasn't measured and compared. . . . We were always sitting together—always nude. . . . We would sit for hours together."

When Mengele himself performed the examination, they said, he was very 48 proper and methodical: "He concentrated on one part of the body at one time . . . like [one day] he measured our eyes for about two hours." They spoke of being examined as frequently as twice a week for a period of five months in late 1944, and also remembered vividly a special visit to the Auschwitz main camp for photographs.

There were less benign research programs on twins. One twin survivor, for 49 example, told how he and his 12-year-old twin sister would be examined and subjected to such procedures as the injection of material into their spines or the clamping of some part of the body "to see how long you could stand the pressure."

The twin survivor also spoke of Mengele's supervising "a lot of research with 50 chemicals" and of how Mengele's assistants "might stick a needle in various places from behind," including the performing of spinal taps. These procedures, when done on young children, resulted sometimes in loss of consciousness, deafness and—among the smaller children—death.

The final step in Mengele's research on a number of the twins was dissection. Auschwitz enabled him not only to observe and measure twins to compare them in life, but to arrange for them to die together. He could thereby obtain comparisons of healthy or diseased organs to show the effects of heredity.

Sometimes Mengele himself presided over the murder of his twins. A deposition given by Dr. Nyiszli in 1945 described one such event:

> "In the work room next to the dissecting room, 14 gypsy twins were waiting . . . and crying bitterly. Dr. Mengele didn't say a single word to us, and prepared a 10cc. and 5cc. syringe. From a box he took evipan, and from another box he took chloroform, which was in 20 cubic-centimeter glass containers, and put these on the operating table. After that, the first twin was brought in . . . a 14-year-old girl. Dr. Mengele ordered me to undress the girl and put her on the dissecting table. Then he injected the evipan into her right arm intravenously. After the child had fallen asleep, he felt for the left ventricle of the heart and injected 10cc. of chloroform. After one little twitch the child was dead, whereupon Dr. Mengele had it taken into the corpse chamber. In this manner, all 14 twins were killed during the night."

Mengele could be totally arbitrary in his killings. An inmate radiologist told of a pair of gypsy twins, "two splendid boys of 7 or 8, whom we were studying from all aspects—from the 16 or 18 different specialties we represented." The boys both had symptoms in their joints that, according to a belief at that time, could be linked to tuberculosis. Mengele was convinced that the boys were tubercular, but the various inmate doctors, including the radiologist, found no trace of that disease.

Mengele was outraged, and he left the room, ordering the radiologist to remain. When he returned about an hour later, Mengele said calmly: "You are right. There was nothing." After some silence, Mengele added, "Yes, I dissected them." Later, the radiologist said, he heard from Dr. Nyiszli that Mengele had shot the two boys in the neck and that "while they were still warm, began to examine them: lungs first, then each organ."

The two boys, the radiologist added, had been favorites with all the doctors—including Mengele. They had been treated very well, he added, "spoiled in all respects . . . these two especially . . . they fascinated him considerably." But their post-mortem study had still greater fascination for him.

Mengele's fanatically brutal approach to his research can be understood mainly in terms of his combination of ideological zealotry and scientific ambition. Verschuer, his mentor, was taking science in a Nazi direction when he declared that research with twins would demonstrate "the extent of the damage caused by adverse hereditary influences" as well as "relations between disease, racial types, and miscegenation." In Auschwitz, Mengele saw an opportunity to deepen and extend the Nazi racial vision by means of systematic research "evidence."

437

He was also intent upon gaining personal recognition as a scientist. Indeed, 57
his Auschwitz friend told me that Mengele planned to use his research with
twins as the basis for his Habilitation, the presentation necessary for a formal
university appointment. Mengele's ideological worship, then, included the worship of Nazified "science," and from that standpoint he told his friend that "it
would be a sin, a crime . . . and irresponsible not to utilize the possibilities
that Auschwitz had for twin research," and that "there would never be another
chance like it."

Mengele saw himself as a biological revolutionary, part of a vanguard devoted 58
to the bold scientific task of remaking his people and ultimately the people of
the world. The German race would have to be cured and its genes improved.
Many believed, as one inmate doctor said, that Mengele wanted to make use
of his research on twins "to find the cause of multiple pregnancies" in order to
increase such events among Aryan women. In any case, he did wish to apply
his results toward German-centered racial goals.

Mengele's friend revealed something of this motivation when he told me that 59
Mengele saw his work as having bearing on selecting national leaders "not on
a political basis but on a biological basis." He might well have been unclear
himself about his exact motivations, but we have reason to see in them a combination of distorted scientific claims and related ideological fantasies.

Mengele's treatment of twins provides important additional clues to his psy- 60
chology. There we see displayed the full range of his adaptation to the Auschwitz
environment. Survivors repeatedly commented on his confusing duality of affection and violence, an extreme manifestation of the process I call "doubling."

The twins lived in an atmosphere that combined sanctuary with terror. As 61
one recalled, they never forgot they were in Auschwitz where, starting in the
summer of 1944, they could clearly see "flames really coming up every day,
every night" from the open pits in which bodies were burned, and they could
"hear every evening a cacophony of screams" and breathe in "the unbearable
smell."

Yet most of the twins were safe, under the protection of Mengele, and much 62
of the time he treated them lovingly. According to an inmate doctor, Mengele
in his contacts with the children was "as gentle as a father," talking to them
and patting them on the head "in a loving way." He could be playful, jumping
about to please them. The twin children frequently called him "Uncle Pepi."
Sometimes, though, as the inmate doctor reported, Mengele would bring some
gypsy twins sweets and invite them for a ride in his car which turned out to be
"a little drive with Uncle Pepi, to the gas chamber."

For many of the twins, the strength of their warm feelings toward Mengele 63
was such that they found it impossible in later years to believe the evil things
they heard about him. "For us," one said, he was "like a papa, like a mama."

One inmate doctor, in his own excruciating struggles to come to terms with 64
Mengele, thought of him as "the double man" who had "all the human feelings,

438

pity and so on," but also had in his psyche an "impenetrable, indestructible cell, which is obedience to the received order."

He was describing Mengele's Auschwitz self, the new self that can take shape 65 in virtually anyone in adapting to an extreme environment. With the Auschwitz self, Mengele's potential for evil became actual, even as he maintained elements of his prior self that included affection toward children. In this process, each part-self behaved as a functioning whole: the Auschwitz self enabling him to function in that murderous environment and to exploit its human resources with considerable efficiency; the prior self enabling him to maintain a sense of decency. His powerful commitment to Nazi ideology served as a bridge, a necessary connection between the two.

Mengele's Auschwitz behavior reflects important pre-existing psychological 66 tendencies that contributed greatly to that doubling process. His inclinations toward omnipotence and total control over others could be given extreme expression in Auschwitz.

The man and the place were dramatically summed up by a survivor who did 67 art work for him and spoke of herself as Mengele's "pet," someone who was pleasant to have around. The death camp, she said, was like a city dog pound, with Mengele as the inspector checking up on the keepers—the inmate doctors—and on the dogs—the inmates.

The inspector, she recalled, would often admonish the keepers to "wash up 68 the excrement" in the pound, "to keep it clean, to keep the dogs healthy." Then he would examine "these chambers where they are killed" and he would inquire about the dog population: "How many are you? Well, it's too crowded—you better put in two more [gas chambers] today."

This image, with its blending of omnipotence and sadism, was relevant to 69 much of Mengele's relationship to twins. "It was an axiom," one of them told me, "that Mengele is God. He used to come always with an entourage, very-well decked out, very elegant. He always carried around him an aura of some terrifying threat, which is, I suspect, unexplainable to normal human beings who didn't see this." It was "literally impossible," the survivor said, "to transmit the edge of this terror."

Only in Auschwitz could Mengele assume that aura and become what the 70 inmate artist described as "a very charismatic man" with "star quality." But when she added, "Marilyn Monroe flashed through my mind," she was perhaps suggesting the strong element of mannered self-display, what is loosely called "narcissism"—and perhaps a certain amount of kitsch and absurdity—contained in Mengele's assumption of omnipotence.

Another prior trait, Mengele's schizoid tendencies, were reflected in surviv- 71 ors' accounts of his "dead eyes"—eyes that showed no emotion, that avoided looking into the eyes of others. The inmate artist described him as so distant from others that "he seemed to be from a different planet." That kind of schizoid person, however friendly or affectionate at times, remains fundamentally removed from others, with inner divisions that can contribute to the doubling process.

Mengele's exaggerated immaculateness was consistent with such tendencies 72 toward withdrawal. He was "very sensitive about bad smells," an inmate doctor reported, so that before he arrived, "the doors and windows had to be opened." He was "Clean, clean, clean!" one survivor said. This passion for cleanliness actually became part of Mengele's selection esthetic. He often sent prisoners with skin blemishes—even those with small abscesses or old appendectomy scars—to the gas chamber.

All people are capable of psychic numbing, a diminished tendency or incli- 73 nation to feel. But Mengele's version of the Auschwitz self—his ease in harming and killing—carried psychic numbing to a remarkable extreme. "The main thing about him," an observant inmate-doctor stated, "was that he totally lacked feel-ing." He was enabled to feel nothing in killing a young twin, even one he had been fond of, to make a medical point.

Mengele's sadism was of a piece with these other traits. The pleasure he 74 could take in causing pain was an aspect of his omnipotence, a means of main-taining his schizoid withdrawal and his renunciation of anything in the realm of fellow-feeling toward his victims. That kind of sadism was manifest in his smiling enthusiasm at selections. It was present in his remark to a Jewish woman doctor who was pleading vainly for the life of her father: "Your father is 70 years old. Don't you think he has lived long enough?" And survivors tell of Mengele's proclaiming on Tisha B'Av, the commemoration of the destruction of the first and second temples, "We will have a concert." There was a concert, then a roll-call, then an enormous selection for the gas chamber.

In his play "The Deputy," Rolf Hochhuth creates a fiendish Nazi character 75 known only as "the Doctor," modeled after Mengele, who is described as having "the stature of Absolute Evil," as "only playing the part of a human being."

Some inmate-doctors also viewed Mengele as a demon and wished to divest 76 him of his professional status. One described him as "a monster, period," and another as "no more doctor than anything else."

But being a doctor was part of Mengele's demonology: he took on the dark 77 side of the omnipotent Svengali-like physician-shaman.

The myth of Mengele's demonic stature was given added support by the often 78 misleading rumors about his life after Auschwitz. He was said to be living in comfort in South America, advising dictators such as Gen. Alfredo Stroessner of Paraguay on how to annihilate the Indian population, growing wealthy in an extensive drug trade run by former Nazis. Nobody could touch Mengele.

We have seen that his death has partly dispelled this demonology. His con- 79 tinuing "metamorphosis" into an ordinary mortal can be enhanced by probing his motivations and behavior.

The psychological traits Mengele brought to Auschwitz exist in many of us, 80 but in him they took exaggerated form. His impulse toward omnipotence and total control of the world around him were means of fending off anxiety and doubt, fears of falling apart—ultimately, fear of death. That fear also activated his sadism and extreme psychic numbing. He could quiet his fears of death in that death-dominated environment by performing the ultimate act of power over another person: murder.

Yet, as far as we know, he had neither killed nor maimed prior to Auschwitz, and had in fact functioned in a more or less integrated way.   81

The perfect match betwen Mengele and Auschwitz changed all that. Through doubling, he could call forth his evil potential. That evil, generally speaking, is neither inherent in any self nor foreign to it. Under certain kinds of psychological and moral conditions it can emerge. Crucial to that emergence is an ideology or world view, a theory or vision that justifies or demands evil actions.   82

Viewed in this light, Josef Mengele emerges as he really was: a visionary ideologue, an efficiently murderous functionary, a diligent careerist—and disturbingly human.   83

QUESTIONS

1. As paragraph 6 makes clear, this essay means to "explain" Mengele. Summarize in your own words the explanation that it offers.

2. Why were twins so important to Mengele? Are the reasons psychological, scientific, or both? What has his interest in twins got to do with the process Lifton calls "doubling" in paragraph 8?

3. Much of this essay is devoted to reporting. Where do these reports come from? What sources does Lifton identify in the article?

4. In paragraph 70 Lifton speaks of "narcissism." Consider Mengele in relation to Karen Horney's essay on narcissism (pages 403–410). In what ways does Mengele seem to conform to this psychological type or depart from it?

5. Lifton speaks in paragraph 73 of "psychic numbing." Can you think of other instances of this phenomenon that you have encountered in your reading or in your experience? Is a play like Shakespeare's *Macbeth*, for instance, about "psychic numbing"? Is Bettelheim's "Joey" (pages 411–412)? Write an essay in which you discuss this phenomenon, defining and illustrating the concept.

6. Do some research on another person supposed to have been a human monster such as the Roman emperor Nero or Caligula or some more modern tyrant, terrorist, or torturer. (You may find legend at odds with history as you look into things.) Incorporate your research in an essay considering the kind of figure that humans find horrifying. What is it that makes these creatures both terrible and fascinating?

SOME CONDITIONS OF OBEDIENCE AND DISOBEDIENCE TO AUTHORITY

Stanley Milgram

Stanley Milgram (1933–1984) was born in New York, went to Queens College and Harvard University, and was a professor of social psychology at the Graduate Center of the City University of New York. The following explanation of Milgram's experiment first appeared in the professional journal Human Relations *in 1965 and made him famous, causing a storm of controversy over his method of experimentation and the results of his experiment. Milgram has said of his work, "As a social psychologist, I look at the world not to master it in any practical sense, but to understand it and to communicate that understanding to others."*

The situation in which one agent commands another to hurt a third turns   1
up time and again as a significant theme in human relations.[1] It is powerfully expressed in the story of Abraham, who is commanded by God to kill his son. It is no accident the Kierkegaard,[2] seeking to orient his thought to the central themes of human experience, chose Abraham's conflict as the springboard to his philosophy.

War too moves forward on the triad of an authority which commands a   2
person to destroy the enemy, and perhaps all organized hostility may be viewed as a theme and variation on the three elements of authority, executant, and victim.[3] We describe an experimental program, recently concluded at Yale

---

[1]This research was supported by two grants from the National Science Foundation: NSF G-17916 and NSF G-24152. Exploratory studies carried out in 1960 were financed by a grant from the Higgins Funds of Yale University. I am grateful to John T. Williams, James J. McDonough, and Emil Elges for the important part they played in the project. Thanks are due also to Alan Elms, James Miller, Taketo Murata, and Stephen Stier for their aid as graduate assistants. My wife, Sasha, performed many valuable services. Finally, I owe a profound debt to the many persons in New Haven and Bridgeport who served as subjects.

[2]Søren Kierkegaard (1813–1855): Danish philosopher and theologian. [Eds.]

[3]Consider, for example, J. P. Scott's analysis of war in his monograph on aggression:
. . . while the actions of key individuals in a war may be explained in terms of direct stimulation to aggression, vast numbers of other people are involved simply by being part of an organized society.
. . . For example, at the beginning of World War I an Austrian archduke was assassinated in Sarajevo. A few days later soldiers from all over Europe were marching toward each other, not because they were stimulated by the archduke's misfortune, but because they had been trained to obey orders.
(Slightly rearranged from Scott (1958), *Aggression*, p. 103.)

University, in which a particular expression of this conflict is studied by experimental means.

In its most general form the problem may be defined thus: if X tells Y to hurt Z, under what conditions will Y carry out the command of X and under what conditions will he refuse? In the more limited form possible in laboratory research, the question becomes: If an experimenter tells a subject to hurt another person, under what conditions will the subject go along with this instruction, and under what conditions will he refuse to obey? The laboratory problem is not so much a dilution of the general statement as one concrete expression of the many particular forms this question may assume. 3

One aim of the research was to study behavior in a strong situation of deep consequence to the participants, for the psychological forces operative in powerful and lifelike forms of the conflict may not be brought into play under diluted conditions. 4

This approach meant, first, that we had a special obligation to protect the welfare and dignity of the persons who took part in the study; subjects were, of necessity, placed in a difficult predicament, and steps had to be taken to ensure their wellbeing before they were discharged from the laboratory. Toward this end, a careful, post-experimental treatment was devised and has been carried through for subjects in all conditions.[4] 5

TERMINOLOGY

If Y follows the command of X we shall say that he has obeyed X; if he fails to carry out the command of X, we shall say that he has disobeyed X. The terms to *obey* and to *disobey*, as used here, refer to the subject's overt action only, and carry no implication for the motive or experiential states accompanying the action.[5] 6

---

[4]It consisted of an extended discussion with the experimenter and, of equal importance, a friendly reconciliation with the victim. It is made clear that the victim did *not* receive painful electric shocks. After the completion of the experimental series, subjects were sent a detailed report of the results and full purposes of the experimental program. A formal assessment of this procedure points to its overall effectiveness. Of the subjects, 83.7 percent indicated that they were glad to have taken part in the study; 15.1 percent reported neutral feelings; and 1.3 percent stated that they were sorry to have participated. A large number of subjects spontaneously requested that they be used in further experimentation. Four-fifths of the subjects felt that more experiments of this sort should be carried out, and 74 percent indicated that they had learned something of personal importance as a result of being in the study. Furthermore, a university psychiatrist, experienced in outpatient treatment, interviewed a sample of experimental subjects with the aim of uncovering possible injurious effects resulting from participation. No such effects were in evidence. Indeed, subjects typically felt that their participation was instructive and enriching. A more detailed discussion of this question can be found in Milgram (1964).

[5]To *obey* and to *disobey* are not the only terms one could use in describing the critical action of Y. One could say that Y is cooperating with X, or displays conformity with regard to X's commands. However, *cooperation* suggests that X agrees with Y's ends, and understands the relationship

To be sure, the everyday use of the word *obedience* is not entirely free from complexities. It refers to action within widely varying situations, and connotes diverse motives within those situations: a child's obedience differs from a soldier's obedience, or the love, honor, and *obey* of the marriage vow. However, a consistent behavioral relationship is indicated in most uses of the term: in the act of obeying, a person does what another person tells him to do. Y obeys X if he carries out the prescription for action which X has addressed to him; the term suggests, moreover, that some form of dominance-subordination, or hierarchical element, is part of the situation in which the transaction between X and Y occurs. 7

A subject who complies with the entire series of experimental commands will be termed an *obedient* subject; one who at any point in the command series defies the experimenter will be called a *disobedient* or *defiant* subject. As used in this report the terms refer only to the subject's performance in the experiment, and do not necessarily imply a general personality disposition to submit to or reject authority. 8

SUBJECT POPULATION

The subjects used in all experimental conditions were male adults, residing in the greater New Haven and Bridgeport areas, aged 20 to 50 years, and engaged in a wide variety of occupations. Each experimental condition described in this report employed 40 fresh subjects and was carefully balanced for age and occupational types. The occupational composition for each experiment was: workers, skilled and unskilled: 40 percent; white collar, sales, business: 40 percent; 9

---

between his own behavior and the attainment of those ends. (But the experimental procedure, and, in particular, the experimenter's command that the subject shock the victim even in the absence of a response from the victim, preclude such understanding.) Moreover, cooperation implies status parity for the co-acting agents, and neglects the asymmetrical, dominance-subordination element prominent in the laboratory relationship between experimenter and subject. *Conformity* has been used in other important contexts in social psychology, and most frequently refers to imitating the judgments or actions of others when no explicit requirement for imitation has been made. Furthermore, in the present study there are two sources of social pressure; pressure from the experimenter issuing the commands, and pressure from the victim to stop the punishment. It is the pitting of a common man (the victim) against an authority (the experimenter) that is the distinctive feature of the conflict. At a point in the experiment the victim demands that he be let free. The experimenter insists that the subject continue to administer shocks. Which act of the subject can be interpreted as conformity? The subject may conform to the wishes of his peer or to the wishes of the experimenter, and conformity in one direction means the absence of conformity in the other. Thus the word has no useful reference in this setting, for the dual and conflicting social pressures cancel out its meaning.

In the final analysis, the linguistic symbol representing the subject's action must take its meaning from the concrete context in which that action occurs; and there is probably no word in everyday language that covers the experimental situation exactly, without omissions or irrelevant connotations. It is partly for convenience, therefore, that the terms *obey* and *disobey* are used to describe the subject's actions. At the same time, our use of the words is highly congruent with dictionary meaning.

professionals: 20 percent. The occupations were intersected with three age categories (subjects in 20's, 30's, and 40's, assigned to each condition in the proportions of 20, 40, and 40 percent, respectively).

THE GENERAL LABORATORY PROCEDURE[6]

The focus of the study concerns the amount of electric shock a subject is 10 willing to administer to another person when ordered by an experimenter to give the "victim" increasingly more severe punishment. The act of administering shock is set in the context of a learning experiment, ostensibly designed to study the effect of punishment on memory. Aside from the experimenter, one naïve subject and one accomplice perform in each session. On arrival each subject is paid $4.50. After a general talk by the experimenter, telling how little scientists know about the effect of punishment on memory, subjects are informed that one member of the pair will serve as teacher and one as learner. A rigged drawing is held so that the naïve subject is always the teacher, and the accomplice becomes the learner. The learner is taken to an adjacent room and strapped into an "electric chair."

The naïve subject is told that it is his task to teach the learner a list of paired 11 associates, to test him on the list, and to administer punishment whenever the learner errs in the test. Punishment takes the form of electric shock, delivered to the learner by means of a shock generator controlled by the naïve subject. The teacher is instructed to increase the intensity of electric shock one step on the generator on each error. The learner, according to plan, provides many wrong answers, so that before long the naïve subject must give him the strongest shock on the generator. Increases in shock level are met by increasingly insistent demands from the learner that the experiment be stopped because of the growing discomfort to him. However, in clear terms the experimenter orders the teacher to continue with the procedure in disregard of the learner's protests. *Thus, the naïve subject must resolve a conflict between two mutually incompatible demands from the social field. He may continue to follow the orders of the experimenter and shock the learner with increasing severity, or he may refuse to follow the orders of the experimenter and heed the learner's pleas. The experimenter's authority operates not in a free field, but against ever-mounting countervailing pressure from the person being punished.*

A few technical points need to be considered before the findings of the study 12 are described. For the purpose of delivering shock, a simulated shock generator is used, with 30 clearly marked voltage levels that range from 15 to 450 volts.

---

[6]A more detailed account of the laboratory procedure can be found in Milgram (1963). A similar and independently evolved experimental procedure, employing a shock generator, victim, and learning task, was reported by Buss (1961). Buss used the technique for studying aggression, not obedience, and did not make use of the fundamental measure employed in the present study: break-off points.

(Each level is activated by one of 30 individual lever switches set in a horizontal line.) The naïve subject is given a sample shock of 45 volts to convince him of the authenticity of the instrument. The generator bears verbal designations that range from "Slight Shock" to "Danger: Severe Shock."

The responses of the victim are standardized on tape, and each protest is 13 coordinated to a particular voltage level on the shock generator. Starting with 75 volts the learner begins to grunt and moan. At 150 volts he demands to be let out of the experiment. At 180 volts he cries out that he can no longer stand the pain. At 300 volts he refuses to provide any more answers to the memory test, insisting that he is no longer a participant in the experiment and must be freed. In response to this last tactic, the experimenter instructs the naïve subject to treat the absence of an answer as equivalent to a wrong answer, and to follow the usual shock procedure. The experimenter reinforces his demand with the statement: "You have no other choice, you must go on!" (This imperative is used whenever the naïve subject tries to break off the experiment.) If the subject refuses to give the next higher level of shock, the experiment is considered at an end. A quantitative value is assigned to the subject's performance based on the maximum-intensity shock he administered before breaking off. Thus any subject's score may range from zero (for a subject unwilling to administer the first shock level) to 30 (for a subject who proceeds to the highest voltage level on the board). For any particular subject and for any particular experimental condition, the degree to which participants have followed the experimenter's orders may be specified with a numerical value, corresponding to the metric on the shock generator.

This laboratory situation gives us a framework in which to study the subject's 14 reactions to the principal conflict of the experiment. Again, this conflict is between the experimenter's demands that he continue to administer the electric shock, and the learner's demands, which become increasingly more insistent, that the experiment be stopped. The crux of the study is to vary systematically the factors believed to alter the degree of obedience to the experimental commands, to learn under what conditions submission to authority is most probable and under what conditions defiance is brought to the fore.

PILOT STUDIES

Pilot studies for the present research were completed in the winter of 1960; 15 they differed from the regular experiments in a few details: for one, the victim was placed behind a silvered glass, with the light balance on the glass such that the victim could be dimly perceived by the subject (Milgram, 1961).

Though essentially qualitative in treatment, these studies pointed to several 16 significant features of the experimental situation. At first no vocal feedback was used from the victim. It was thought that the verbal and voltage designations on the control panel would create sufficient pressure to curtail the subject's obedience. However, this was not the case. In the absence of protests from the learner, virtually all subjects, once commanded, went blithely to the end of the board, seemingly indifferent to the verbal designations ("Extreme Shock" and "Danger: Severe Shock"). This deprived us of an adequate basis for scaling obedient tendencies. A force had to be introduced that would strengthen the subject's resistance to the experimenter's commands, and reveal individual differences in terms of a distribution of break-off points.

This force took the form of protests from the victim. Initially, mild protests were used, but proved inadequate. Subsequently, more vehement protests were inserted into the experimental procedure. To our consternation, even the strongest protests from the victim did not prevent all subjects from administering the harshest punishment ordered by the experimenter; but the protests did lower the mean maximum shock somewhat and created some spread in the subject's performance; therefore, the victim's cries were standardized on tape and incorporated into the regular experimental procedure.

The situation did more than highlight the technical difficulties of finding a workable experimental procedure: It indicated that subjects would obey authority to a greater extent than we had supposed. It also pointed to the importance of feedback from the victim in controlling the subject's behavior.

One further aspect of the pilot study was that subjects frequently averted their eyes from the person they were shocking, often turning their heads in an awkward and conspicuous manner. One subject explained: "I didn't want to see the consequences of what I had done." Observers wrote:

> . . . subjects showed a reluctance to look at the victim, whom they could see through the glass in front of them. When this fact was brought to their attention they indicated that it caused them discomfort to see the victim in agony. We note, however, that although the subject refuses to look at the victim, he continues to administer shocks.

This suggested that the salience of the victim may have, in some degree, regulated the subject's performance. If, in obeying the experimenter, the subject found it necessary to avoid scrutiny of the victim, would the converse be true? If the victim were rendered increasingly more salient to the subject, would obedience diminish? The first set of regular experiments was designed to answer this question.

IMMEDIACY OF THE VICTIM

This series consisted of four experimental conditions. In each condition the victim was brought "psychologically" closer to the subject giving him shocks.

In the first condition (Remote Feedback) the victim was placed in another room and could not be heard or seen by the subject, except that, at 300 volts, he pounded on the wall in protest. After 315 volts he no longer answered or was heard from.

The second condition (Voice Feedback) was identical to the first except that   23
voice protests were introduced. As in the first condition the victim was placed
in an adjacent room, but his complaints could be heard clearly through a door
left slightly ajar and through the walls of the laboratory.[7]

The third experimental condition (Proximity) was similar to the second, ex-   24
cept that the victim was now placed in the same room as the subject, and 1½
feet from him. Thus he was visible as well as audible, and voice cues were
provided.

The fourth, and final, condition of this series (Touch-Proximity) was identical   25
to the third, with this exception: The victim received a shock only when his
hand rested on a shockplate. At the 150-volt level the victim again demanded
to be let free and, in this condition, refused to place his hand on the shockplate.
The experimenter ordered the naïve subject to force the victim's hand onto the
plate. Thus obedience in this condition required that the subject have physical
contact with the victim in order to give him punishment beyond the 150-volt
level.

Forty adult subjects were studied in each condition. The data revealed that   26
obedience was significantly reduced as the victim was rendered more immediate
to the subject. The mean maximum shock for the conditions is shown in
Figure 1.

Expressed in terms of the proportion of obedient to defiant subjects, the   27

---

[7]It is difficult to convey on the printed page the full tenor of the victim's responses, for we have
no adequate notation for vocal intensity, timing, and general qualities of delivery. Yet these features
are crucial to producing the effect of an increasingly severe reaction to mounting voltage levels.
(They can be communicated fully only by sending interested parties the recorded tapes.) In general
terms, however, the victim indicates no discomfort until the 75-volt shock is administered, at which
time there is a light grunt in response to the punishment. Similar reactions follow the 90- and 105-
volt shocks, and at 120 volts the victim shouts to the experimenter that the shocks are becoming
painful. Painful groans are heard on administration of the 135-volt shock, and at 150 volts the
victim cries out, 'Experimenter, get me out of here! I won't be in the experiment any more! I refuse
to go on!' Cries of this type continue with generally rising intensity, so that at 180 volts the victim
cries out, 'I can't stand the pain,' and by 270 volts his response to the shock is definitely an agonized
scream. Throughout, he insists that he be let out of the experiment. At 300 volts the victim shouts
in desperation that he will no longer provide answers to the memory test; and at 315 volts, after a
violent scream, he reaffirms with vehemence that he is no longer a participant. From this point
on, he provides no answers, but shrieks in agony whenever a shock is administered; this continues
through 450 volts. Of course, many subjects will have broken off before this point.

A revised and stronger set of protests was used in all experiments outside the Proximity series.
Naturally, new baseline measures were established for all comparisons using the new set of protests.

There is overwhelming evidence that the great majority of subjects, both obedient and defiant,
accepted the victims' reactions as genuine. The evidence takes the form of: (a) tension created in
the subjects (see discussion of tension); (b) scores on "estimated-pain" scales filled out by subjects
immediately after the experiment; (c) subjects' accounts of their feelings in post-experimental interviews; and (d) quantifiable responses to questionnaires distributed to subjects several months after
their participation in the experiments. This matter will be treated fully in a forthcoming monograph.

(The procedure in all experimental conditions was to have the naïve subject announce the
voltage level before administering each shock, so that—independently of the victim's responses—
he was continually reminded of delivering punishment of ever-increasing severity.)

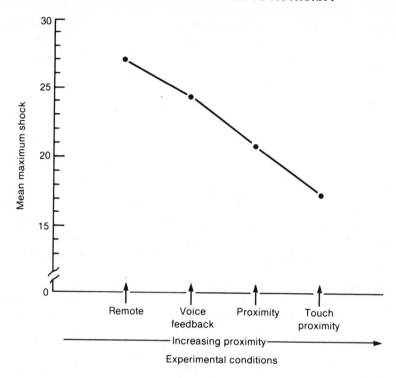

FIGURE 1. Mean maxima in proximity series.

findings are that 34 percent of the subjects defied the experimenter in the Remote condition, 37.5 percent in Voice Feedback, 60 percent in Proximity, and 70 percent in Touch-Proximity.

How are we to account for this effect? A first conjecture might be that as the victim was brought closer the subject became more aware of the intensity of his suffering and regulated his behavior accordingly. This makes sense, but our evidence does not support the interpretation. There are no consistent differences in the attributed level of pain across the four conditions (i.e. the amount of pain experienced by the victim as estimated by the subject and expressed on a 14-point scale). But it is easy to speculate about alternative mechanisms: [28]

> *Empathic cues.* In the Remote and to a lesser extent the Voice Feedback conditions, the victim's suffering possesses an abstract, remote quality for the subject. He is aware, but only in a conceptual sense, that his actions cause pain to another person; the fact is apprehended, but not felt. The phenomenon is common enough. The bombardier can reasonably suppose that his weapons will inflict suffering and death, yet this knowledge is divested of affect and does not move him to a felt, emotional response to the suffering resulting from his actions. Similar observations [29]

449

have been made in wartime. It is possible that the visual cues associated with the victim's suffering trigger empathic responses in the subject and provide him with a more complete grasp of the victim's experience. Or it is possible that the empathic responses are themselves unpleasant, possessing drive properties which cause the subject to terminate the arousal situation. Diminishing obedience, then, would be explained by the enrichment of empathic cues in the successive experimental conditions.

Denial and narrowing of the cognitive field. The Remote condition allows a narrowing of the cognitive field so that the victim is put out of mind. The subject no longer considers the act of depressing a lever relevant to moral judgment, for it is no longer associated with the victim's suffering. When the victim is close it is more difficult to exclude him phenomenologically. He necessarily intrudes on the subject's awareness since he is continuously visible. In the Remote condition his existence and reactions are made known only after the shock has been administered. The auditory feedback is sporadic and discontinuous. In the Proximity conditions his inclusion in the immediate visual field renders him a continuously salient element for the subject. The mechanism of denial can no longer be brought into play. One subject in the Remote condition said: "It's funny how you really begin to forget that there's a guy out there, even though you can hear him. For a long time I just concentrated on pressing the switches and reading the words." 30

Reciprocal fields. If in the Proximity condition the subject is in an improved position to observe the victim, the reverse is also true. The actions of the subject now come under proximal scrutiny by the victim. Possibly, it is easier to harm a person when he is unable to observe our actions than when he can see what we are doing. His surveillance of the action directed against him may give rise to shame, or guilt, which may then serve to curtail the action. Many expressions of language refer to the discomfort or inhibitions that arise in face-to-face confrontation. It is often said that it is easier to criticize a man "behind his back" than to "attack him to his face." If we are in the process of lying to a person it is reputedly difficult to "stare him in the eye." We "turn away from others in shame" or in "embarrassment" and this action serves to reduce our discomfort. The manifest function of allowing the victim of a firing squad to be blindfolded is to make the occasion less stressful for him, but it may also serve a latent function of reducing the stress of the executioner. In short, in the Proximity conditions, the subject may sense that he has become more salient in the victim's field of awareness. Possibly he becomes more self-conscious, embarrassed, and inhibited in his punishment of the victim. 31

Phenomenal unity of act. In the Remote condition it is more difficult for the subject to gain a sense of *relatedness* between his own actions and the consequences of these actions for the victim. There is a physical and spatial separation of the act and its consequences. The subject depresses a lever in one room, and protests and cries are heard from another. The two events are in correlation, yet they lack a compelling phenomenological unity. The structure of a meaningful act—*I am hurting a man*—breaks down because of the spatial arrangements, in a manner 32

450

somewhat analogous to the disappearance of phi phenomena[8] when the blinking lights are spaced too far apart. The unity is more fully achieved in the Proximity condition as the victim is brought closer to the action that causes him pain. It is rendered complete in Touch-Proximity.

Incipient group formation. Placing the victim in another room not only takes him 33 further from the subject, but the subject and the experimenter are drawn relatively closer. There is incipient group formation between the experimenter and the subject, from which the victim is excluded. The wall between the victim and the others deprives him of an intimacy which the experimenter and subject feel. In the Remote condition, the victim is truly an outsider, who stands alone, physically and psychologically.

When the victim is placed close to the subject, it becomes easier to form an 34 alliance with him against the experimenter. Subjects no longer have to face the experimenter alone. They have an ally who is close at hand and eager to collaborate in a revolt against the experimenter. Thus, the changing set of spatial relations leads to a potentially shifting set of alliances over the several experimental conditions.

Acquired behavior dispositions. It is commonly observed that laboratory mice will 35 rarely fight with their litter mates. Scott (1958) explains this in terms of passive inhibition. He writes: "By doing nothing under . . . circumstances [the animal] learns to do nothing, and this may be spoken of as passive inhibition . . . this principle has great importance in teaching an individual to be peaceful, for it means that he can learn not to fight simply by not fighting." Similarly, we may learn not to harm others simply by not harming them in everyday life. Yet this learning occurs in a context of proximal relations with others, and may not be generalized to that situation in which the person is physically removed from us. Or possibly, in the past, aggressive actions against others who were physically close resulted in retaliatory punishment which extinguished the original form of response. In contrast, aggression against others at a distance may have only sporadically led to retaliation. Thus the organism learns that it is safer to be aggressive toward others at a distance, and precarious to be so when the parties are within arm's reach. Through a pattern of rewards and punishments, he acquires a disposition to avoid aggression at close quarters, a disposition which does not extend to harming others at a distance. And this may account for experimental findings in the remote and proximal experiments.

Proximity as a variable in psychological research has received far less attention 36 than it deserves. If men were sessile[9] it would be easy to understand this neglect. But we move about; our spatial relations shift from one situation to the next, and the fact that we are near or remote may have a powerful effect on the psychological processes that mediate our behavior toward others. In the present

---

[8]phi phenomena: the optical impression of motion generated when similar stationary objects are presented one after another at a certain interval. [Eds.]
[9]sessile: permanently attached. [Eds.]

situation, as the victim is brought closer to the subject ordered to give him shocks, increasing numbers of subjects break off the experiment, refusing to obey. The concrete, visible, and proximal presence of the victim acts in an important way to counteract the experimenter's power to generate disobedience.[10]

CLOSENESS OF AUTHORITY

If the spatial relationship of the subject and victim is relevant to the degree of obedience, would not the relationship of subject to experimenter also play a part? 37

There are reasons to feel that, on arrival, the subject is oriented primarily to the experimenter rather than to the victim. He has come to the laboratory to fit into the structure that the experimenter—not the victim—would provide. He has come less to understand his behavior than to *reveal* that behavior to a competent scientist, and he is willing to display himself as the scientist's purposes require. Most subjects seem quite concerned about the appearance they are making before the experimenter, and one could argue that this preoccupation in a relatively new and strange setting makes the subject somewhat insensitive to the triadic nature of the social situation. In other words, the subject is so concerned about the show he is putting on for the experimenter that influences from other parts of the social field do not receive as much weight as they ordinarily would. This overdetermined orientation to the experimenter would account for the relative insensitivity of the subject to the victim, and would also lead us to believe that alterations in the relationship between subject and experimenter would have important consequences for obedience. 38

In a series of experiments we varied the physical closeness and degree of surveillance of the experimenter. In one condition the experimenter sat just a few feet away from the subject. In a second condition, after giving initial instructions, the experimenter left the laboratory and gave his orders by telephone. In still a third condition the experimenter was never seen, providing instructions by means of a tape recording activated when the subjects entered the laboratory. 39

Obedience dropped sharply as the experimenter was physically removed from the laboratory. The number of obedient subjects in the first condition (Experimenter Present) was almost three times as great as in the second, where the experimenter gave his orders by telephone. Twenty-six subjects were fully obe- 40

---

[10]Admittedly, the terms *proximity*, *immediacy*, *closeness*, and *salience-of-the-victim* are used in a loose sense, and the experiments themselves represent a very coarse treatment of the variable. Further experiments are needed to refine the notion and tease out such diverse factors as spatial distance, visibility, audibility, barrier interposition, etc.

The Proximity and Touch-Proximity experiments were the only conditions where we were unable to use taped feedback from the victim. Instead, the victim was trained to respond in these conditions as he had in Experiment 2 (which employed taped feedback). Some improvement is possible here, for it should be technically feasible to do a proximity series using taped feedback.

dient in the first condition, and only nine in the second (Chi square obedient *vs.* defiant in the two conditions, df = 14.7; $p < 0.001$). Subjects seemed able to take a far stronger stand against the experimenter when they did not have to encounter him face to face, and the experimenter's power over the subject was severely curtailed.[11]

Moreover, when the experimenter was absent, subjects displayed an inter- 41 esting form of behavior that had not occurred under his surveillance. Though continuing with the experiment, several subjects administered lower shocks than were required and never informed the experimenter of their deviation from the correct procedure. (Unknown to the subjects, shock levels were automatically recorded by an Esterline-Angus event recorder wired directly into the shock generator; the instrument provided us with an objective record of the subjects' performance.) Indeed, in telephone conversations some subjects specifically assured the experimenter that they were raising the shock level according to instruction, whereas in fact they were repeatedly using the lowest shock on the board. This form of behavior is particularly interesting: although these subjects acted in a way that clearly undermined the avowed purposes of the experiment, they found it easier to handle the conflict in this manner than to precipitate an open break with authority.

Other conditions were completed in which the experimenter was absent 42 during the first segment of the experiment, but reappeared at the point that the subject definitely refused to give higher shocks when commanded by telephone. Although he had exhausted his power via telephone, the experimenter could frequently force further obedience when he reappeared in the laboratory.

Experiments in this series show that the *physical presence* of an authority is 43 an important force contributing to the subject's obedience or defiance. Taken together with the first experimental series on the proximity of the victim, it would appear that something akin to fields of force, diminishing in effectiveness with increasing psychological distance from their source, have a controlling effect on the subject's performance. As the victim is brought closer, the subject finds it harder to administer shocks to him. When the victim's position is held constant relative to the subject, and the authority is made more remote, the subject finds it easier to break off the experiment. This effect is substantial in both cases, but manipulation of the experimenter's position yielded the more powerful results. Obedience to destructive commands is highly dependent on the proximal relations between authority and subject.

TENSIONS

The description of final scores does not fully convey the character of the 44 subjects' performance, and it would be useful to interrupt our reporting of

---

[11]The third condition also led to significantly lower obedience than this first situation in which the experimenter was present, but it contains technical difficulties that require extensive discussion.

quantitative relationships to remark on the subjects' general reaction to the situation.

One might suppose that a subject would simply break off or continue as his 45 conscience and temperament dictated. Yet this is very far from what happened. There were powerful reactions of tension and emotional strain in a substantial proportion of the participants. Persons were observed to sweat, tremble, stutter, bite their lips, and groan as they found themselves increasingly implicated in the experimental conflict. Some sense of the subjects' mood can be found in a transcript of their remarks at break-off point. Here are the remarks of two defiant subjects:

> Is he banging? . . . Is he hurt out there? Well, I don't want to be responsible for anything that happens to him. No, I can't go on with it. I don't know whether he's all right or not. I mean he may have a heart condition or something; I wouldn't feel right doing it. He's banging for help. He's evidently in trouble or he wouldn't bang . . . I don't see any sense to this—to knocking him out or something. I just can't see it.
> [*Subject refuses to administer shocks*]   [*Subject 0108*]

> The man is banging. He wants to get out . . . I'm sorry. If the man wants to get out I'd just as soon stop . . . I don't want to administer any more [extremely excited] . . . I will gladly refund the check, but I will not harm this man . . . I'm sorry, I will not give him any more if he obviously wants to get out. There is no money in the world that will make me hurt another individual.   [*Subject 010X*]

And here is a transcript from an obedient subject. He began the experiment 46 calmly, but became increasingly tense as the experiment proceeded. After administering the 150-volt shock, he began to address the experimenter in agitated tones:

> *150 volts delivered.* You want me to keep going?
> *165 volts delivered.* That guy is hollering in there. There's a lot of them here. He's liable to have heart condition. You want me to go?
> *180 volts delivered.* He can't stand it! I'm not going to kill that man in there! You hear him hollering? He's hollering. He can't stand it. What if something happens to him? . . . I'm not going to get that man sick in there. He's hollering in there. You know what I mean? I mean I refuse to take responsibility. He's getting hurt in there. He's in there hollering. Too many left here. Geez, if he gets them wrong. There's too many of them left. I mean who is going to take responsibility if anything happens to that gentleman?
> [*The experimenter accepts responsibility.*] All right.
> *195 volts delivered.* You see he's hollering. Hear that. Gee, I don't know.
> [*The experimenter says: 'The experiment requires that you go on.'*]—I know it does, sir, but I mean—hugh—he don't know what he's in for. He's up to 195 volts.
> *210 volts delivered.*
> *225 volts delivered.*
> *240 volts delivered.* Aw, no. You mean I've got to keep going up with the scale? No sir. I'm not going to kill that man! I'm not going to give him 450 volts!

[*The experimenter says: 'The experiment requires that you go on.'*]—I know it does, but that man is hollering there, sir . . .

Despite his numerous, agitated objections, which were constant accompaniments to his actions, the subject unfailingly obeyed the experimenter, proceeding to the highest shock level on the generator. He displayed a curious dissociation between word and action. Although at the verbal level he had resolved not to go on, his actions were fully in accord with the experimenter's commands. This subject did not want to shock the victim, and he found it an extremely disagreeable task, but he was unable to invent a response that would free him from *E*'s authority. Many subjects cannot find the specific verbal formula that would enable them to reject the role assigned to them by the experimenter. Perhaps our culture does not provide adequate models for disobedience.

One puzzling sign of tension was the regular occurrence of nervous laughing fits. In the first four conditions 71 of the 160 subjects showed definite signs of nervous laughter and smiling. The laughter seemed entirely out of place, even bizarre. Full-blown, uncontrollable seizures were observed for 15 of these subjects. On one occasion we observed a seizure so violently convulsive that it was necessary to call a halt to the experiment. In the post-experimental interviews subjects took pains to point out that they were not sadistic types and that the laughter did not mean they enjoyed shocking the victim. 47

In the interview following the experiment subjects were asked to indicate on a 14-point scale just how nervous or tense they felt at the point of maximum tension (Figure 2). The scale ranged from "not at all tense and nervous" to "extremely tense and nervous." Self-reports of this sort are of limited precision and at best provide only a rough indication of the subject's emotional response. Still, taking the reports for what they are worth, it can be seen that the distribution of responses spans the entire range of the scale, with the majority of subjects concentrated at the center and upper extreme. A further breakdown showed that obedient subjects reported themselves as having been slightly more tense and nervous than the defiant subjects at the point of maximum tension. 48

How is the occurrence of tension to be interpreted? First, it points to the presence of conflict. If a tendency to comply with authority were the only psychological force operating in the situation, all subjects would have continued to the end and there would have been no tension. Tension, it is assumed, results from the simultaneous presence of two or more incompatible response tendencies (Miller, 1944). If sympathetic concern for the victim were the exclusive force, all subjects would have calmly defied the experimenter. Instead, there were both obedient and defiant outcomes, frequently accompanied by extreme tension. A conflict develops between the deeply ingrained disposition not to harm others and the equally compelling tendency to obey others who are in authority. The subject is quickly drawn into a dilemma of a deeply dynamic 49

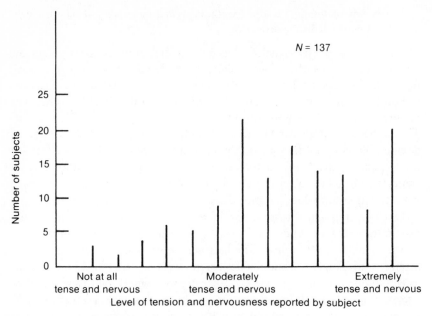

FIGURE 2. Level of tension and nervousness: the self-reports on "tension and nervousness" for 137 subjects in the Proximity experiments. Subjects were given a scale with 14 values ranging from "not at all tense and nervous" to "extremely tense and nervous." They were instructed: "Thinking back to that point in the experiment when you felt the most tense and nervous, indicate just how you felt by placing an X at the appropriate point on the scale." The results are shown in terms of midpoint values.

character, and the presence of high tension points to the considerable strength of each of the antagonistic vectors.

Moreover, tension defines the strength of the aversive state from which the subject is unable to escape through disobedience. When a person is uncomfortable, tense, or stressed, he tries to take some action that will allow him to terminate this unpleasant state. Thus tension may serve as a drive that leads to escape behavior. But in the present situation, even where tension is extreme, many subjects are unable to perform the response that will bring about relief. Therefore there must be a competing drive, tendency, or inhibition that precludes activation of the disobedient response. The strength of this inhibiting factor must be of greater magnitude than the stress experienced, or else the terminating act would occur. Every evidence of extreme tension is at the same time an indication of the strength of the forces that keep the subject in the situation.

Finally, tension may be taken as evidence of the reality of the situations for the subjects. Normal subjects do not tremble and sweat unless they are implicated in a deep and genuinely felt predicament.

456

BACKGROUND AUTHORITY

In psychophysics, animal learning, and other branches of psychology, the 52
fact that measures are obtained at one institution rather than another is irrelevant
to the interpretation of the findings, so long as the technical facilities for
measurement are adequate and the operations are carried out with competence.

But it cannot be assumed that this holds true for the present study. The 53
effectiveness of the experimenter's commands may depend in an important way
on the larger institutional context in which they are issued. The experiments
described thus far were conducted at Yale University, an organization which
most subjects regarded with respect and sometimes awe. In post-experimental
interviews several participants remarked that the locale and sponsorship of the
study gave them confidence in the integrity, competence, and benign purposes
of the personnel; many indicated that they would not have shocked the learner
if the experiments had been done elsewhere.

This issue of background authority seemed to us important for an interpre- 54
tation of the results that had been obtained thus far; moreover it is highly relevant
to any comprehensive theory of human obedience. Consider, for example, how
closely our compliance with the imperatives of others is tied to particular institutions and locales in our day-to-day activities. On request, we expose our throats
to a man with a razor blade in the barber shop, but would not do so in a shoe
store; in the latter setting we willingly follow the clerk's request to stand in our
stockinged feet, but resist the command in a bank. In the laboratory of a great
university, subjects may comply with a set of commands that would be resisted
if given elsewhere. *One must always question the relationship of obedience to a
person's sense of the context in which he is operating.*

To explore the problem we moved our apparatus to an office building in 55
industrial Bridgeport and replicated experimental conditions, without any visible
tie to the university.

Bridgeport subjects were invited to the experiment through a mail circular 56
similar to the one used in the Yale study, with appropriate changes in letterhead,
etc. As in the earlier study, subjects were paid $4.50 for coming to the labo-
ratory. The same age and occupational distributions used at Yale and the identical personnel were employed.

The purpose in relocating in Bridgeport was to assure a complete dissociation 57
from Yale, and in this regard we were fully successful. On the surface, the study
appeared to be conducted by Research Associates of Bridgeport, an organization
of unknown character (the title had been concocted exclusively for use in this
study).

The experiments were conducted in a three-room office suite in a somewhat 58
run-down commercial building located in the downtown shopping area. The
laboratory was sparsely furnished, though clean, and marginally respectable in

appearance. When subjects inquired about professional affiliations, they were informed only that we were a private firm conducting research for industry.

Some subjects displayed skepticism concerning the motives of the Bridgeport 59 experimenter. One gentleman gave us a written account of the thoughts he experienced at the control board:

> . . . Should I quit this damn test? Maybe he passed out? What dopes we were not to check up on this deal. How do we know that these guys are legit? No furniture, bare walls, no telephone. We could of called the Police up or the Better Business Bureau. I learned a lesson tonight. How do I know that Mr. Williams [the experimenter] is telling the truth . . . I wish I knew how many volts a person could take before lapsing into unconsciousness . . .   [*Subject 2414*]

Another subject stated:

> I questioned on my arrival my own judgment [about coming]. I had doubts as to the legitimacy of the operation and the consequences of participation. I felt it was a heartless way to conduct memory or learning processes on human beings and certainly dangerous without the presence of a medical doctor.   [*Subject 2440V*]

There was no noticeable reduction in tension for the Bridgeport subjects. 60 And the subjects' estimation of the amount of pain felt by the victim was slightly, though not significantly, higher than in the Yale study.

A failure to obtain complete obedience in Bridgeport would indicate that the 61 extreme compliance found in New Haven subjects was tied closely to the background authority of Yale University; if a large proportion of the subjects remained fully obedient, very different conclusions would be called for.

As it turned out, the level of obedience in Bridgeport, although somewhat 62 reduced, was not significantly lower than that obtained at Yale. A large proportion of the Bridgeport subjects were fully obedient to the experimenter's commands (48 percent of the Bridgeport subjects delivered the maximum shock versus 65 percent in the corresponding condition at Yale).

How are these findings to be interpreted? It is possible that if commands of 63 a potentially harmful or destructive sort are to be perceived as legitimate they must occur within some sort of institutional structure. But it is clear from the study that it need not be a particularly reputable or distinguished institution. The Bridgeport experiments were conducted by an unimpressive firm lacking any credentials; the laboratory was set up in a respectable office building with title listed in the building directory. Beyond that, there was no evidence of benevolence or competence. It is possible that the *category* of institution, judged according to its professed function, rather than its qualitative position within that category, wins our compliance. Persons deposit money in elegant, but also in seedy-looking banks, without giving much thought to the differences in security they offer. Similarly, our subjects may consider one laboratory to be as competent as another, so long as it is a scientific laboratory.

It would be valuable to study the subjects' performance in other contexts 64 which go even further than the Bridgeport study in denying institutional support to the experimenter. It is possible that, beyond a certain point, obedience disappears completely. But that point had not been reached in the Bridgeport office: almost half the subjects obeyed the experimenter fully.

FURTHER EXPERIMENTS

We may mention briefly some additional experiments undertaken in the Yale 65 series. A considerable amount of obedience and defiance in everyday life occurs in connection with groups. And we had reason to feel in light of the many group studies already done in psychology that group forces would have a profound effect on reactions to authority. A series of experiments was run to examine these effects. In all cases only one naïve subject was studied per hour, but he performed in the midst of actors who, unknown to him, were employed by the experimenter. In one experiment (Groups for Disobedience) two actors broke off in the middle of the experiment. When this happened 90 percent of the subjects followed suit and defied the experimenter. In another condition the actors followed the orders obediently; this strengthened the experimenter's power only slightly. In still a third experiment the job of pushing the switch to shock the learner was given to one of the actors, while the naïve subject performed a subsidiary act. We wanted to see how the teacher would respond if he were involved in the situation but did not actually give the shocks. In this situation only three subjects out of forty broke off. In a final group experiment the subjects themselves determined the shock level they were going to use. Two actors suggested higher and higher shock levels; some subjects insisted, despite group pressure, that the shock level be kept low; others followed along with the group.

Further experiments were completed using women as subjects, as well as a 66 set dealing with the effects of dual, unsanctioned, and conflicting authority. A final experiment concerned the personal relationship between victim and subject. These will have to be described elsewhere, lest the present report be extended to monographic length.

It goes without saying that future research can proceed in many different 67 directions. What kinds of response from the victim are most effective in causing disobedience in the subject? Perhaps passive resistance is more effective than vehement protest. What conditions of entry into an authority system lead to greater or lesser obedience? What is the effect of anonymity and masking on the subject's behavior? What conditions lead to the subject's perception of responsibility for his own actions? Each of these could be a major research topic in itself, and can readily be incorporated into the general experimental procedure described here.

LEVELS OF OBEDIENCE AND DEFIANCE

One general finding that merits attention is the high level of obedience   68
manifested in the experimental situation. Subjects often expressed deep disapproval of shocking a man in the face of his objections, and others denounced
it as senseless and stupid. Yet many subjects complied even while they protested.
The proportion of obedient subjects greatly exceeded the expectations of the
experimenter and his colleagues. At the outset, we had conjectured that subjects
would not, in general, go above the level of "Strong Shock." In practice, many
subjects were willing to administer the most extreme shocks available when
commanded by the experimenter. For some subjects the experiment provided
an occasion for aggressive release. And for others it demonstrated the extent to
which obedient dispositions are deeply ingrained and engaged, irrespective of
their consequences for others. Yet this is not the whole story. Somehow, the
subject becomes implicated in a situation from which he cannot disengage
himself.

The departure of the experimental results from intelligent expectation, to   69
some extent, has been formalized. The procedure was to describe the experimental situation in concrete detail to a group of competent persons, and to ask
them to predict the performance of 100 hypothetical subjects. For purposes of
indicating the distribution of break-off points, judges were provided with a diagram of the shock generator and recorded their predictions before being informed
of the actual results. Judges typically underestimated the amount of obedience
demonstrated by subjects.

In Figure 3, we compare the predictions of forty psychiatrists at a leading   70
medical school with the actual performance of subjects in the experiment. The
psychiatrists predicted that most subjects would not go beyond the tenth shock
level (150 volts; at this point the victim makes his first explicit demand to be
freed). They further predicted that by the twentieth shock level (300 volts; the
victim refuses to answer) 3.73 percent of the subjects would still be obedient;
and that only a little over one-tenth of one percent of the subjects would administer the highest shock on the board. But, as the graph indicates, the obtained
behavior was very different. Sixty-two percent of the subjects obeyed the experimenter's commands fully. Between expectation and occurrence there is a whopping discrepancy.

Why did the psychiatrists underestimate the level of obedience? Possibly,   71
because their predictions were based on an inadequate conception of the determinants of human action, a conception that focuses on motives *in vacuo*. This
orientation may be entirely adequate for the repair of bruised impulses as revealed on the psychiatrist's couch, but as soon as our interest turns to action in
larger settings, attention must be paid to the situations in which motives are
expressed. A situation exerts an important press on the individual. It exercises
constraints and may provide push. In certain circumstances it is not so much

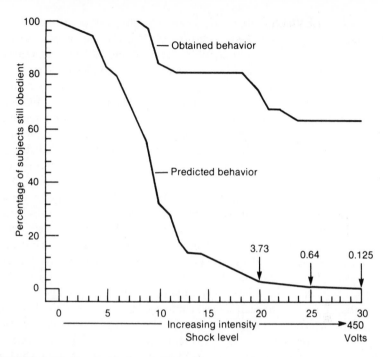

FIGURE 3. Predicted and obtained behavior in voice feedback.

the kind of person a man is, as the kind of situation in which he is placed, that determines his actions.

Many people, not knowing much about the experiment, claim that subjects who go to the end of the board are sadistic. Nothing could be more foolish than an overall characterization of these persons. It is like saying that a person thrown into a swift-flowing stream is necessarily a fast swimmer, or that he has great stamina because he moves so rapidly relative to the bank. The context of action must always be considered. The individual, upon entering the laboratory, becomes integrated into a situation that carries its own momentum. The subject's problem then is how to become disengaged from a situation which is moving in an altogether ugly direction.

The fact that disengagement is so difficult testifies to the potency of the forces that keep the subject at the control board. Are these forces to be conceptualized as individual motives and expressed in the language of personality dynamics, or are they to be seen as the effects of social structure and pressures arising from the situational field?

A full understanding of the subject's action will, I feel, require that both perspectives be adopted. The person brings to the laboratory enduring dispositions toward authority and aggression, and at the same time he becomes en-

461

meshed in a social structure that is no less an objective fact of the case. From the standpoint of personality theory one may ask: What mechanisms of personality enable a person to transfer responsibility to authority? What are the motives underlying obedient and disobedient performance? Does orientation to authority lead to a short-circuiting of the shame-guilt system? What cognitive and emotional defenses are brought into play in the case of obedient and defiant subjects?

The present experiments are not, however, directed toward an exploration of 75 the motives engaged when the subject obeys the experimenter's commands. Instead, they examine the situational variables responsible for the elicitation of obedience. Elsewhere, we have attempted to spell out some of the structural properties of the experimental situation that account for high obedience, and this analysis need not be repeated here (Milgram, 1963). The experimental variations themselves represent our attempt to probe that structure, by systematically changing it and noting the consequences for behavior. It is clear that some situations produce greater compliance with the experimenter's commands than others. However, this does not necessarily imply an increase or decrease in the strength of any single definable motive. Situations producing the greatest obedience could do so by triggering the most powerful, yet perhaps the most idiosyncratic, of motives in each subject confronted by the setting. Or they may simply recruit a greater number and variety of motives in their service. But whatever the motives involved—and it is far from certain that they can ever be known—action may be studied as a direct function of the situation in which it occurs. This has been the approach of the present study, where we sought to plot behavioral regularities against manipulated properties of the social field. Ultimately, social psychology would like to have a compelling *theory of situations* which will, first, present a language in terms of which situations can be defined; proceed to a typology of situations; and then point to the manner in which definable properties of situations are transformed into psychological forces in the individual.[12]

POSTSCRIPT

Almost a thousand adults were individually studied in the obedience research, 76 and there were many specific conclusions regarding the variables that control obedience and disobedience to authority. Some of these have been discussed briefly in the preceding sections, and more detailed reports will be released subsequently.

There are now some other generalizations I should like to make, which do 77 not derive in any strictly logical fashion from the experiments as carried out, but which, I feel, ought to be made. They are formulations of an intuitive sort

---

[12]My thanks to Professor Howard Leventhal of Yale for strengthening the writing in this paragraph.

that have been forced on me by observation of many subjects responding to the pressures of authority. The assertions represent a painful alteration in my own thinking; and since they were acquired only under the repeated impact of direct observation, I have no illusion that they will be generally accepted by persons who have not had the same experience.

With numbing regularity good people were seen to knuckle under the demands of authority and perform ' actions that were callous and severe. Men who are in everyday life responsible and decent were seduced by the trappings of authority, by the control of their perceptions, and by the uncritical acceptance of the experimenter's definition of the situation, into performing harsh acts. 78

What is the limit of such obedience? At many points we attempted to establish a boundary. Cries from the victim were inserted; not good enough. The victim claimed heart trouble; subjects still shocked him on command. The victim pleaded that he be let free, and his answers no longer registered on the signal box; subjects continued to shock him. At the outset we had not conceived that such drastic procedures would be needed to generate disobedience, and each step was added only as the ineffectiveness of the earlier techniques became clear. The final effort to establish a limit was the Touch-Proximity condition. But the very first subject in this condition subdued the victim on command, and proceeded to the highest shock level. A quarter of the subjects in this condition performed similarly. 79

The results, as seen and felt in the laboratory, are to this author disturbing. They raise the possibility that human nature or, more specifically, the kind of character produced in American democratic society cannot be counted on to insulate its citizens from brutality and inhumane treatment at the direction of malevolent authority. A substantial proportion of people do what they are told to do, irrespective of the content of the act and without limitations of conscience, so long as they perceive that the command comes from a legitimate authority. If in this study an anonymous experimenter could successfully command adults to subdue a fifty-year-old man and force on him painful electric shocks against his protests, one can only wonder what government, with its vastly greater authority and prestige, can command of its subjects. There is, of course, the extremely important question of whether malevolent political institutions could or would arise in American society. The present research contributes nothing to this issue. 80

In an article titled "The Danger of Obedience," Harold J. Laski wrote: 81

> . . . civilization means, above all, an unwillingness to inflict unnecessary pain. Within the ambit of that definition, those of us who heedlessly accept the commands of authority cannot yet claim to be civilized men.
>
> . . . Our business, if we desire to live a life, not utterly devoid of meaning and significance, is to accept nothing which contradicts our basic experience merely because it comes to us from tradition or convention or authority. It may well be

that we shall be wrong; but our self-expression is thwarted at the root unless the certainties we are asked to accept coincide with the certainties we experience. That is why the condition of freedom in any state is always a widespread and consistent skepticism of the canons upon which power insists.

REFERENCES

BUSS, ARNOLD H.
  1961. *The Psychology of Aggression*. New York and London: John Wiley.
KIERKEGAARD, S.
  1843. *Fear and Trembling*. English edition, Princeton: Princeton University Press, 1941.
LASKI, HAROLD J.
  1929. "The dangers of obedience." *Harper's Monthly Magazine*, 15 June, 1–10.
MILGRAM, S.
  1961. "Dynamics of obedience: experiments in social psychology." Mimeographed report, *National Science Foundation*, January 25.

  1963. "Behavioral study of obedience." *J. Abnorm. Soc. Psychol.* 67, 371–378.

  1964. "Issues in the study of obedience: a reply to Baumrind." *Amer. Psychol.* 1, 848–852.
MILLER, N.E.
  1944. "Experimental studies of conflict." In J. McV. Hunt (ed.), *Personality and the Behavior Disorders*. New York: Ronald Press.
SCOTT, J.P.
  1958. *Aggression*. Chicago: University of Chicago Press.

QUESTIONS

1. What did Milgram want to determine by his experiment? What were his anticipated outcomes?

2. What conclusions did Milgram reach about the extent to which ordinary individuals would obey the orders of an authority figure? Under what conditions is this submission most probable? Under what conditions is defiance most likely?

3. Describe the general procedures of this experiment. Some persons have questioned Milgram's methods. Do you think it is ethical to expose subjects without warning to experiments that might have a lasting effect on them? What such effects might this experiment have had?

4. One characteristic of this paper is Milgram's willingness to consider several possible explanations of the same phenomenon. Study the interpretations in paragraphs 28 through 35. What do you make of the range of interpretation there and elsewhere in the essay? How does Milgram achieve such a range?

5. A report such as Milgram's is not structured in the same way as a conventional essay. His research is really a collection of separate but related experiments, each one of

which requires its own interpretation. Describe the groups into which these experiments fall. Which results seemed most surprising to you? Which were easiest to anticipate?

6. In Milgram's experiment, people who are responsible and decent in everyday life were seduced, he says, by trappings of authority. Most of us, however, like to believe that we would neither engage in brutality on our own nor obey directions of this kind. Has Milgram succeeded in getting you to question your own behavior? Would you go so far as to say that he forces you to question your own human nature?

7. In paragraph 46 Milgram comments, "Perhaps our culture does not provide adequate models for disobedience." What do you think of this hypothesis? Are there such models? Ought there to be? Have there appeared such models in the time since the experiment was conducted? Explain your stand on Milgram's statement.

8. If research in social psychology takes place in your school today, there is probably a panel of some sort that enforces guidelines on research with human subjects. Locate that board, if it exists, and find out whether this experiment could take place today. Report to your class on the rules that guide researchers today. Do you think those rules are wise?

9. What, in your opinion, should be the guidelines for psychological research with human subjects? List the guidelines you think are appropriate, and compare your list with the lists of your classmates. Would your guidelines have allowed Milgram's experiment?

10. Think of a situation in which you were faced with the moral and ethical dilemma of whether or not to obey a figure of authority. How did you behave? Did your behavior surprise you? Describe and explain that experience.

Sciences and Technologies

LOGIC AND PROOF: A CERTAIN TREASURE

Michael Guillen

Michael Guillen (b. 1956) has a Ph.D. in physics, mathematics, and astronomy from Cornell University. He currently teaches physics and math at Harvard and has frequently appeared on national television as a science expert. He is the author of many scientific articles, and a collection of his own essays, The Human Side of Mathematics, *which was published in 1983 under the title* Bridges to Infinity. *The essay reprinted here is the first in that book. Its subject matter, logic and proof, is shared by the humanities and the sciences, by philosophy and mathematics to be exact. We have chosen to place it here, at the beginning of our examples of scientific and technical explanation, because the sciences are founded on questions of proof and disproof.*

> *Proof is an idol before which the mathematician tortures himself.*
> Sir Arthur Eddington

It is a rare person who does not prefer certainty over doubt in most matters 1 and an even rarer person who can obtain it. It is as though certainty were a buried treasure, and we who so desire it have yet to find a map that can lead us to it. Around 300 B.C., mathematicians believed they had found such a map in the guiding principles of Aristotle's logic. Euclid followed those principles in proving the theorems of geometry (the study of shapes), which were hailed as models of certainty for the next 2000 years. During the late nineteenth century, however, when mathematicians guided by those same principles essayed to prove the theorems of arithmetic (the study of numbers), they were led to a treasure of paradoxes rather than of certainties. Aristotle's logic was flawed.

This revelation divided mathematicians into various schools of thought, with 2 each group claiming to have the one map that would redirect all mathematicians to an infallible standard of proof. The divisiveness that ensued was superseded in 1931 by yet another revelation, which decreed that there is no conceivable way to obtain complete certainty in mathematics.

There was a finality to this edict that disheartened some mathematicians and inspired others to try to find some way around it—so far without success. Like the rest of us, most mathematicians have learned to accept doubt as a familiar part of doing business; it is a grudging acceptance, though, by those mathematicians who still nurse a hope of recovering the certainty that was once believed to be theirs.   3

The wave of mathematical certainty crested around 300 B.C., with the appearance of Aristotle's *Organon* (a Latin word meaning "instrument of reason") and Euclid's *Elements*. At that time it was widely believed that the *Organon* proffered the way to logical certainty and that the *Elements* was the treasure of indubitability itself.   4

In the *Organon*, Aristotle reduced the thitherto ill-defined process of deductive reasoning to fourteen rules and a few canons by which conclusions could properly be derived from assumptions. Among the canons, there was the law of identity (Everything is identical with itself), the law of contradiction (Nothing can both be and not be), and the law of the excluded middle (Something is either true or false; there is no third possibility). The canons were intended to express verities that most of us would call common sense, whereas the rules were the outcome of Aristotle's meticulous study of syllogisms.   5

A syllogism is a three-step exercise in deductive reasoning of the following form: 6

(if) All men are mortal
(and if) Socrates is a man
(then) Socrates is mortal

The first two statements are the assumptions, and the third statement is the conclusion, which, as Aristotle put it, "follows of necessity" from the assumptions. We may doubt the credibility of the assumptions, Aristotle explained, but if the rules of deductive reasoning have been followed, there is no doubting the conclusion. For example, one might dispute the assumptions

All happy people are amiable
and
Bill is a happy person,
but there's no disputing that from these assumptions it necessarily follows that
Bill is amiable.

This is precisely what is meant by logical certainty. Because each was stated in terms of an archetypal syllogism, Aristotle's rules of logic were widely perceived as guides to certitude. (Later, medieval logicians added five new rules to the original fourteen.)

In his magnum opus, the *Elements*, Euclid followed the principles of deductive reasoning in deriving hundreds of theorems in geometry from only ten assumptions. The assumptions were a mixture of common sense (Things equal to the same thing are equal to each other) and plausible assertions about mathematical points, lines, and planes (A straight line can be drawn from any point to any other point). Mathematicians could, and did, challenge some of Euclid's assumptions, but, as Aristotle had shown, there was no doubting the conclusions. Euclid's theorems were all *If . . . then* arguments derived according to the rules of logic. If a person believed in the infallibility of Aristotle's rules, he was bound to believe that Euclid's theorems were models of logical certainty, whatever he thought about the assumptions. 7

For more than 2000 years after the first appearance of the *Organon* and the *Elements*, not only mathematicians but also philosophers, scientists, and the literati believed that in Aristotle's logic and deductive reasoning they had a means by which to obtain surety in a wide range of matters. During the thirteenth century, for example, the Italian Scholastic Thomas Aquinas used Aristotelian reasoning to corroborate the veracity of matters of faith, including the existence of God. Thomism, as this synthesis of Aristotelianism and Christianity came to be called, was so influential that Pope Leo XIII issued an encyclical in 1879 declaring it the official philosophy of the Roman Catholic Church. 8

It was, therefore, just another ardent declaration of faith in the infallibility of deductive reasoning when mathematicians in the late 1800s embarked en masse on a program to do for arithmetic what Euclid had done for geometry. The general idea was to reformulate the hodgepodge of arithmetical results that had accumulated over the centuries into some kind of logical format. Mathematicians had come to accept many of these results without proving them, mostly because they seemed to be a matter of common sense. For example, no one had ever thought seriously to question the law of trichotomy, which states that every ordinary number is either zero, positive, or negative. The law was taken to be as indisputable as stating that every moment in time is either a part of the present, future, or past, and so no one could imagine it to be false. 9

It *isn't* false, as it happens, but as late as one hundred years ago, mathematicians had not yet gotten around to proving it, along with many other arithmetical truths. Only now was this long-standing nonchalance giving way to an eagerness to acquire logical certainty in matters arithmetic. These mathematicians expected that ahead of them was a short and rather routine quest, to be made following the same map that Euclid had followed. Actually, it was the beginning of a futile hunt for a nonexistent treasure. 10

Though several mathematicians led the rest throughout the time of the search, the German mathematician Gottlob Frege was one of the first to declare that he had finished it. He had worked from 1893 to 1902 to derive hundreds of 11

469

theorems of arithmetic from just a few assumptions, and the tangible result was a monumental two-volume treatise entitled *Grundgesetze der Arithmetik* ("Fundamental Laws of Arithmetic"). His assumptions, like Euclid's, might be challenged, but his conclusions were drawn according to principles of deductive reasoning that were consistent, though technically not identical, with Aristotle's. He and his contemporaries, therefore, had every reason to believe that his *Grundgesetze* was no less a model of certitude than the *Elements*.

They had no reason to believe otherwise, that is, until 1902, the year Frege   12 was putting the finishing touches on his work. In that year, the English mathematician-philosopher Bertrand Russell made it known that he had spotted a paradox, a flaw in logic, in the final manuscript of Frege's second volume. The paradox was not due merely to some careless and easily correctable error on Frege's part, Russell explained; it was more in the way of a defect in deductive logic itself. No one at the time could possibly guess how serious a flaw it was or what it would require to eliminate it, but it was serious enough for Frege to recognize that it vitiated his entire ten-year effort. In a rather sad postscript to his second volume, Frege wrote: "A scientist can hardly meet with anything more undesirable than to have the foundation give way just as the work is finished. In this position I was put by a letter from Mr. Bertrand Russell as the work was nearly through the press."

Russell specifically prosecuted the apparently benign notions of class and   13 class membership that Frege had used in his *Grundgesetze* to describe collections of numbers. According to Aristotelian logic, a class is any group of objects—automobiles, birds, or numbers, for example—that are related by certain qualitative similarities. Conversely, a class is defined by the very qualitative similarities of its members, just as a neighborhood is distinguished by the people who make it up. In order for a candidate to qualify for membership in a particular class, it must share precisely the qualitative similarities of existing members, however incompatible it may be otherwise.

Whereas other mathematicians of the time simply took these ideas for granted,   14 Russell tested them in his mind. "It seemed to me," he recalled years later in *My Philosophical Development*, "that a class sometimes is, and sometimes is not, a member of itself. The class of teaspoons, for example, is not another teaspoon, but the class of things that are not teaspoons is one of the things that are not teaspoons."

Most classes we can think of are of the teaspoon sort. The classes of shoes,   15 of houses, of pencils—none of these classes is a member of itself. Still, there are a few good examples of classes that *are* members of themselves. For instance, the set of all things printed on this page is itself printed on this page, and the set of all ideas is itself an idea. In each case, the class itself qualifies for membership because taken as a single entity it shares the qualitative similarities of its members.

470

Next, Russell recalled, he mused over the unimaginably huge class that   16
contains all "the classes that are not members of themselves." Let's call this the
NS class, for "nonself." The NS class includes all the familiar classes (the classes
of teaspoons, shoes, and so on). Then, he wrote, "I asked myself whether this
[NS] class is a member of itself or not."

It was in attempting to answer this question that Russell discovered the par-   17
adox. If we assume that NS is a member of NS, he reasoned, then we assume
that NS is a member of itself. But, according to the original definition of NS,
this very assumption disqualifies NS from membership in NS (by definition,
remember, NS includes only classes that are not members of themselves). If,
on the contrary, we assume that NS is not a member of NS, then we assume
that NS is not a member of itself. But according to the original definition of
NS, this very assumption decrees that NS qualifies for membership in NS.
"Thus each alternative leads to its [logical] opposite," Russell wrote. "It put an
end to the logical honeymoon that I had been enjoying."

Russell's paradox illustrated the fact that following the rules of logic could   18
lead us to contradictory results. An immediate implication of this was that
Aristotelian logic had to be either somehow rehabilitated to remove the offending
paradox or replaced with an entirely new means of obtaining complete certainty
in mathematics. During the first three decades of this century, mathematicians
disagreed about how best to set things aright (not knowing that an unexpected
discovery would render all their differences of opinion moot). Of the many
schools of thought that emerged in the thirty-year period, two of them were
aimed specifically at rehabilitating Aristotelian logic. These were the Logicist
and Formalist schools, and the programs they championed preoccupied the
mathematicians of the time.

The Logicists, led by Russell himself, would have obviated Russell's paradox   19
by modifying the rules for class membership. Specifically, they wanted to dis-
allow a priori the possibility that a class could be a member of itself. To accomplish this, they proposed that the principles of Aristotelian logic be supplemented
hereafter by what they called the "vicious circle principle," which states, "Whatever involves all of a collection must not be one of the collection." By the
enforcement of this principle, the question of whether Russell's hypothetical
NS class is or is not a member of itself would be settled by fiat, and the vicious
circle of Russell's paradox would thereby be avoided.

In contrast to the Logicists, the Formalists believed that the shortcomings   20
revealed by the paradox were not in logic itself but in the semantic content of
the language used to express logic. In particular, they traced the origin of many
paradoxes, including Russell's, to the ambiguous meaning of the word "all."
Statements such as "All rules have exceptions" are either innocuous or paradoxical, depending on whether we interpret the word "all" to include or exclude
the statement of which it is a part. Uncertainties such as these are semantic
rather than logical, the Formalists maintained, and could be expurgated simply

471

by bleaching logic of its semantic coloration. Thus, they set about re-expressing the logical arguments in mathematics in terms of strictly defined symbols that had no real meaning, rather than in terms of words.

Each of the routes described by these and other schools promised to lead 21 mathematicians back to the treasure of certainty, and until 1931 each faction hopefully pursued its chosen way. But in that year all mathematicians were stopped dead in their tracks when the German logician Kurt Gödel announced his discovery that complete certainty was never to be encountered in mathematics by any route founded on traditional logic. It was an ironic proof in that Gödel had used logic in a clever way to establish its own shortcomings.

The gist of his finding was that any standard of proof based on the self- 22 consistent principles of deductive reasoning is inadequate to establish the truth or falsity of every conceivable mathematical theorem, just as Aristotle's logic was inadquate to settle the question in Russell's paradox (that is, Is the NS class a member of itself?). In short, there will always be questions that arise in mathematics that cannot be settled with logical certainty. Furthermore, Gödel found, any imaginable remedy for an inadequate standard will also prove inadequate in the same way. This meant that the Logicists' and the Formalists' proposals were predestined to fail in the end.

Gödel's results stimulated the invention of non-Aristotelian logical systems, 23 according to which a statement can be something other than true or false. The simplest of these is a so-called trivalent logical system, in which a statement can be either true, false, or merely possible. Such a system is based on a disregard for Aristotle's law of the excluded middle (that is, Something is either true or false; there is no third possibility), and because it allows for the possibility that a theorem might be logically uncertain, it is consistent with Gödel's finding.

For this reason, and because non-Aristotelian logical systems are mathemat- 24 ically interesting subjects, some mathematicians today spend all their time studying and developing them. Efforts by other mathematicians also tend to be aimed at accommodating mathematics to, rather than extricating it from, Gödel's uncertainty. It is a tendency that is in marked contrast to the earlier fight to reclaim mathematical certainty from the throes of Russell's paradox.

In the aftermath of Gödel's revolutionary findings, most mathematicians 25 resigned themselves to no longer thinking of mathematics as a bastion of certainty. One of these was the late Hungarian mathematician-philosopher Imre Lakatos, who in 1963 articulated a philosophy of mathematics that accommodated the Gödelian uncertainties. Lakatos described mathematics much as his mentor Karl Popper had described science, as always having a tentative status and as subject to being revised, even drastically, by new discoveries. Lakatos wrote: "Mathematics does not grow through a monotonous increase of the number of indubitably established theorems, but through the incessant improvement of guesses by speculation and criticism."

In 1981, the mathematician-historian Morris Kline was making much the   26
same point in his book *Mathematics: The Loss of Certainty* when he compared
the mathematician to a homesteader "who clears a piece of ground but notices
wild beasts lurking in a wooded area surrounding the clearing." To increase his
sense of security, the homesteader clears a larger and larger area, but he is never
able to feel absolutely safe—"The beasts are always there, and one day they may
surprise and destroy him." Similarly, Kline wrote, the mathematician uses logic
to clear away a wilderness of mathematical ignorance, but he must expect that
logical inadequacies may be discovered at any time that, like beasts, will spoil
his hopes for complete security from doubt.

The mood in mathematics today, however, is not one of complete accom-   27
modation to Gödelian uncertainty. Perhaps it is because mathematicians coexist
so uneasily with uncertainty that they go about their day-to-day business as
though the events of this century had never happened. Or perhaps it is because,
as Kline suggests, "they find it hard to believe that there can be any serious
concern . . . about their own mathematical activity"—each mathematician be-
haves as if Gödel's uncertainty is something that affects the next person, but not
him.

For whatever reason, mathematicians today "write and publish as if uncer-   28
tainties were nonexistent," writes Kline. In practice, if not in principle, they
retain the pre-Gödelian conviction that, as described by the German Formalist
David Hilbert, "every definite mathematical problem must necessarily be susceptible of an exact settlement, either in the form of an actual answer to the
question asked, or by a proof of the impossibility of its solution."

This adherence to a conviction that has been proved incredible is the human   29
side of mathematics. It is not consistent with the popular image of a mathematician, but it is entirely consistent with human nature. In behaving as though
certainty exists or can be had in mathematics, today's mathematicians are not
unlike those many inventors who believe, against all odds, in the feasibility of
a perpetual motion machine. Their conviction has been and continues to be in
the nature of human progress, impelling one generation to prove possible what
previous generations had proved impossible. In mathematicians, as in others,
"this conviction . . . is a powerful incentive," Hilbert wrote in 1900. "We hear
within us the perpetual call: There is the problem. Seek its solution. You can
find it by pure reason, for in mathematics there is no 'we will not know.' "

In 1959, a disillusioned Russell lamented: "I wanted certainty in the kind of   30
way in which people want religious faith. I thought that certainty is more likely
to be found in mathematics than elsewhere. . . . But after some twenty years
of arduous toil, I came to the conclusion that there was nothing more that I
could do in the way of making mathematical knowledge indubitable."

Doubtless there are and will be many more mathematicians like Russell who   31
will dedicate decades of their lives to the search for the treasure of certainty. So

long as this remains the case, there is always the possibility that one of them will encounter it and thereby bequeath to future generations what previous mathematicians have failed to: an infallible standard of proof.

QUESTIONS

1. Consider the following syllogism:

> All those who seek mathematical certainty are mad.
> All mathematicians seek mathematical certainty.
> All mathematicians are mad.

Is this a valid syllogism? Is it true? Is it a fair summary of Guillen's essay? Can you improve it with respect to either its truth or its function as a summary of the essay? What happens if you substitute some other concept for the word *mad*? What is the best substitute you can find?

2. What is Russell's paradox? Explain it in your own words.

3. The date 1931 is mentioned in paragraph 2. Look at all other references to time, including the one in the last paragraph. How does chronology function in Guillen's organization?

4. The question of mathematical proof could be a dauntingly abstract topic. How does Guillen counteract this possibility?

5. As Guillen observes in his first sentence, "It is a rare person who does not prefer certainty over doubt in most matters and an even rarer person who can obtain it." Write an essay explaining a search for certainty—yours or someone else's. Following Guillen's model, clearly explain each stage in the search, including what happened and why it was significant.

6. Consider carefully the way that Guillen presents the difficult concept called "Russell's paradox," especially in paragraphs 12 through 17. Write an essay in which you take some complex problem in a field well known to you and present it so that every one of your classmates can understand the problem, its importance, and its background or history. You need not persuade your classmates that the problem is important to them. You should aim, however, at presenting the problem clearly and explaining why it is important to those who care about it.

MY BUILT–IN DOUBTER

Isaac Asimov

Isaac Asimov (b. 1920) is a professor of biochemistry at the Boston University School of Medicine and one of America's most wide-ranging and productive writers. Although he has published over two hundred books on such subjects as astronomy, biochemistry, history, mathematics, and physics, he is probably best known for his science-fiction short stories and novels. Asimov has said of his own writing: "Everything I write goes through the typewriter twice. But I have a completely unadorned style. I aim to be accurate and clear, and not to write great literature." The essay reprinted here is chapter 16 in his book Fact and Fancy *(1962), a collection of pieces that appeared first in the* Magazine of Fantasy and Science Fiction.

Once I delivered myself of an oration before a small but select audience of non-scientists on the topic of "What is Science?" speaking seriously and, I hope, intelligently. 1

Having completed the talk, there came the question period, and, bless my heart, I wasn't disappointed. A charming young lady up front waved a pretty little hand at me and asked, not a serious question on the nature of science, but: "Dr. Asimov, do you believe in flying saucers?" 2

With a fixed smile on my face, I proceeded to give the answer I have carefully given after every lecture I have delivered. I said, "No, miss, I do not, and I think anyone who does is a crackpot!" 3

And oh, the surprise on her face! 4

It is taken for granted by everyone, it seems to me, that because I sometimes write science fiction, I believe in flying saucers, in Atlantis, in clairvoyance and levitation, in the prophecies of the Great Pyramid, in astrology, in Fort's theories, and in the suggestion that Bacon wrote Shakespeare. 5

No one would ever think that someone who writes fantasies for pre-school children really thinks that rabbits can talk, or that a writer of hard-boiled detective stories really thinks a man can down two quarts of whiskey in five minutes, then make love to two girls in the next five, or that a writer for the ladies' magazines really thinks that virtue always triumphs and that the secretary always marries the handsome boss—but a science-fiction writer apparently *must* believe in flying saucers. 6

Well, I do not. 7

To be sure, I wrote a story once about flying saucers in which I explained 8 their existence very logically. I also wrote a story once in which levitation played a part.

If I can buddy up to such notions long enough to write sober, reasonable 9 stories about them, why, then, do I reject them so definitely in real life?

I can explain by way of a story. A good friend of mine once spent quite a 10 long time trying to persuade me of the truth and validity of what I considered a piece of pseudo-science and bad pseudo-science at that. I sat there listening quite stonily, and none of the cited evidence and instances and proofs had the slightest effect on me.

Finally the gentleman said to me, with considerable annoyance, "Damn it, 11 Isaac, the trouble with you is that you have a built-in doubter."

To which the only answer I could see my way to making was a heartfelt, 12 "Thank God."

If a scientist has one piece of temperamental equipment that is essential to 13 his job, it is that of a built-in doubter. Before he does anything else, he must doubt. He must doubt what others tell him and what he reads in reference books, and, *most of all*, what his own experiments show him and what his own reasoning tells him.

Such doubt must, of course, exist in varying degrees. It is impossible, im- 14 practical, and useless to be a maximal doubter at all times. One cannot (and would not want to) check personally every figure or observation given in a handbook or monograph before one uses it and then proceed to check it and recheck it until one dies. *But*, if any trouble arises and nothing else seems wrong, one must be prepared to say to one's self, "Well, now, I wonder if the data I got out of the 'Real Guaranteed Authoritative Very Scientific Handbook' might not be a misprint."

To doubt intelligently requires, therefore, a rough appraisal of the authori- 15 tativeness of a source. It also requires a rough estimate of the nature of the statement. If you were to tell me that you had a bottle containing one pound of pure titanium oxide, I would say, "Good," and ask to borrow some if I needed it. Nor would I test it. I would accept its purity on your say-so (until further notice, anyway).

If you were to tell me that you had a bottle containing one pound of pure 16 thulium oxide, I would say with considerable astonishment, "You have? Where?" Then if I had use for the stuff, I would want to run some tests on it and even run it through an ion-exchange column before I could bring myself to use it.

And if you told me that you had a bottle containing one pound of pure 17 americium oxide, I would say, "You're crazy," and walk away. I'm sorry, but my time is reasonably valuable, and I do not consider that statement to have enough chance of validity even to warrant my stepping into the next room to look at the bottle.

What I am trying to say is that doubting is far more important to the advance   18
of science than believing is and that, moreover, doubting is a serious business
that requires extensive training to be handled properly. People without training
in a particular field do not know what to doubt and what not to doubt; or, to
put it conversely, what to believe and what not to believe. I am very sorry to
be undemocratic, but one man's opinion is not necessarily as good as the next
man's.

To be sure, I feel uneasy about seeming to kowtow to authority in this   19
fashion. After all, you all know of instances where authority was wrong, dead
wrong. Look at Columbus, you will say. Look at Galileo.

I know about them, and about others, too. As a dabbler in the history of   20
science, I can give you horrible examples you may never have heard of. I can
cite the case of the German scientist, Rudolf Virchow, who, in the mid-
nineteenth century was responsible for important advances in anthropology and
practically founded the science of pathology. He was the first man to engage in
cancer research on a scientific basis. However, he was dead set against the germ
theory of disease when that was advanced by Pasteur. So were many others, but
one by one the opponents abandoned doubt as evidence multiplied. Not Virchow, however. Rather than be forced to admit he was wrong and Pasteur right,
Virchow quit science altogether and went into politics. How much wronger
could Stubborn Authority get?

But this is a very exceptional case. Let's consider a far more normal and   21
natural example of authority in the wrong.

The example concerns a young Swedish chemical student, Svante August   22
Arrhenius, who was working for his Ph.D. in the University of Uppsala in the
1880s. He was interested in the freezing points of solutions because certain odd
points arose in that connection.

If sucrose (ordinary table sugar) is dissolved in water, the freezing point of   23
the solution is somewhat lower than is that of pure water. Dissolve more sucrose
and the freezing point lowers further. You can calculate how many molecules
of sucrose must be dissolved per cubic centimeter of water in order to bring
about a certain drop in freezing point. It turns out that this same number of
molecules of glucose (grape sugar) and of many other soluble substances will
bring about the same drop. It doesn't matter that a molecule of sucrose is twice
as large as a molecule of glucose. What counts is the number of molecules and
not their size.

But if sodium chloride (table salt) is dissolved in water, the freezing-point   24
drop per molecule is twice as great as normal. And this goes for certain other
substances too. For instance, barium chloride, when dissolved, will bring about
a freezing-point drop that is three times normal.

Arrhenius wondered if this meant that when sodium chloride was dissolved,   25
each of its molecules broke into two portions, thus creating twice as many
particles as there were molecules and therefore a doubled freezing-point drop.

And barium chloride might break up into three particles per molecule. Since the sodium chloride molecule is composed of a sodium atom and a chlorine atom and since the barium chloride molecule is composed of a barium atom and two chlorine atoms, the logical next step was to suppose that these particular molecules broke up into individual atoms.

Then, too, there was another interesting fact. Those substances like sucrose and glucose which gave a normal freezing-point drop did not conduct an electric current in solution. Those, like sodium chloride and barium chloride, which showed abnormally high freezing-point drops, *did* do so. 26

Arrhenius wondered if the atoms, into which molecules broke up on solution, might not carry positive and negative electric charges. If the sodium atom carried a positive charge for instance, it would be attracted to the negative electrode. If the chlorine atom carried a negative charge, it would be attracted to the positive electrode. Each would wander off in its own direction and the net result would be that such a solution would conduct an electric current. For these charged and wandering atoms, Arrhenius adopted Faraday's name "ions" from a Greek word meaning "wanderer." 27

Furthermore, a charged atom, or ion, would not have the properties of an uncharged atom. A charged chlorine atom would not be a gas that would bubble out of solution. A charged sodium atom would not react with water to form hydrogen. It was for that reason that common salt (sodium chloride) did not show the properties of either sodium metal or chlorine gas, though it was made of those two elements. 28

In 1884 Arrhenius, then twenty-five, prepared his theories in the form of a thesis and presented it as part of his doctoral dissertation. The examining professors sat in frigid disapproval. No one had ever heard of electrically charged atoms, it was against all scientific belief of the time, and they turned on their built-in doubters. 29

However, Arrhenius argued his case so clearly and, on the single assumption of the dissolution of molecules into charged atoms, managed to explain so much so neatly, that the professors' built-in doubters did not quite reach the intensity required to flunk the young man. Instead, they passed him—with the lowest possible passing grade. 30

But then, ten years later, the negatively charged electron was discovered and the atom was found to be not the indivisible thing it had been considered but a complex assemblage of still smaller particles. Suddenly the notion of ions as charged atoms made sense. If an atom lost an electron or two, it was left with a positive charge; if it gained them, it had a negative charge. 31

Then, the decade following, the Nobel Prizes were set up and in 1903 the Nobel Prize in Chemistry was awarded to Arrhenius for that same thesis which, nineteen years earlier, had barely squeaked him through for a Ph.D. 32

Were the professors wrong? Looking back, we can see they were. But in 1884 they were *not* wrong. They did exactly the right thing and they served science 33 well. Every professor must listen to and appraise dozens of new ideas every year. He must greet each with the gradation of doubt his experience and training tells him the idea is worth.

Arrhenius's notion met with just the proper gradation of doubt. It was radical   34
enough to be held at arm's length. However, it seemed to have just enough possible merit to be worth some recognition. The professors *did* give him his Ph.D. after all. And other scientists of the time paid attention to it and thought about it. A very great one, Ostwald,[1] thought enough of it to offer Arrhenius a good job.

Then, when the appropriate evidence turned up, doubt receded to minimal   35
values and Arrhenius was greatly honored.

What better could you expect? Ought the professors to have fallen all over   36
Arrhenius and his new theory on the spot? And if so, why shouldn't they also have fallen all over forty-nine other new theories presented that year, no one of which might have seemed much more unlikely than Arrhenius's and some of which may even have appeared less unlikely?

It would have taken *longer* for the ionic theory to have become established   37
if overcredulity on the part of scientists had led them into fifty blind alleys. How many scientists would have been left to investigate Arrhenius's notions?

Scientific manpower is too limited to investigate everything that occurs to   38
everybody, and always will be too limited. The advance of science depends on scientists in general being kept firmly in the direction of maximum possible return. And the only device that will keep them turned in that direction is doubt; doubt arising from a good, healthy and active built-in doubter.

But, you might say, this misses the point. Can't one pick and choose and   39
isolate the brilliant from the imbecilic, accepting the first at once and whole-heartedly, and rejecting the rest completely? Would not such a course have saved ten years on ions without losing time on other notions?

Sure, if it could be done, but it can't. The godlike power to tell the good   40
from the bad, the useful from the useless, the true from the false, instantly and *in toto* belongs to gods and not to men.

Let me cite you Galileo as an example; Galileo, who was one of the greatest   41
scientific geniuses of all time, who invented modern science in fact, and who certainly experienced persecution and authoritarian enmity.

Surely, Galileo, of all people, was smart enough to know a good idea when   42
he saw it, and revolutionary enough not to be deterred by its being radical.

Well, let's see. In 1632 Galileo published the crowning work of his career,   43
Dialogue on the Two Principal Systems of the World which was the very book that got him into real trouble before the Inquisition. It dealt, as the title indicates, with the two principal systems; that of Ptolemy, which had the earth at

---

[1]Friedrich Wilhelm Ostwald (1853–1932): German physical chemist and philosopher, awarded the 1909 Nobel Prize in chemistry. [Eds.]

the center of the universe with the planets, sun and moon going about it in complicated systems of circles within circles; and that of Copernicus which had the sun at the center and the planets, earth, and moon going about *it* in complicated systems of circles within circles.

Galileo did not as much as mention a *third* system, that of Kepler, which had the sun at the center but abandoned all the circles-within-circles jazz. Instead, he had the various planets traveling about the sun in ellipses, with the sun at one focus of the ellipse. It was Kepler's system that was correct and, in fact, Kepler's system has not been changed in all the time that has elapsed since. Why, then, did Galileo ignore it completely? 44

Was it that Kepler had not yet devised it? No, indeed. Kepler's views on that matter were published in 1609, twenty-seven years before Galileo's book. 45

Was it that Galileo had happened not to hear of it? Nonsense. Galileo and Kepler were in steady correspondence and were friends. When Galileo built some spare telescopes, he sent one to Kepler. When Kepler had ideas, he wrote about them to Galileo. 46

The trouble was that Kepler was still bound up with the mystical notions of the Middle Ages. He cast horoscopes for famous men, for a fee, and worked seriously and hard on astrology. He also spent time working out the exact notes formed by the various planets in creating the "music of the spheres" and pointed out that Earth's notes were mi, fa, mi, standing for misery, famine, and misery. He also devised a theory accounting for the relative distances of the planets from the Sun by nesting the five regular solids one within another and making deductions therefrom. 47

Galileo, who must have heard of all this, and who had nothing of the mystic about himself, could only conclude that Kepler, though a nice guy and a bright fellow and a pleasant correspondent, was a complete nut. I am sure that Galileo heard all about the elliptical orbits and, considering the source, shrugged it off. 48

Well, Kepler was indeed a nut, but he happened to be luminously right on occasion, too, and Galileo, of all people, couldn't pick the diamond out from among the pebbles. 49

Shall we sneer at Galileo for that? 50

Or should we rather be thankful that Galileo didn't interest himself in the ellipses *and* in astrology *and* in the nesting of regular solids *and* in the music of the spheres. Might not credulity have led him into wasting his talents, to the great loss of all succeeding generations? 51

No, no, until some supernatural force comes to our aid and tells men what is right and what wrong, men must blunder along as best they can, and only the built-in doubter of the trained scientist can offer a refuge of safety. 52

The very mechanism of scientific procedure, built up slowly over the years, is designed to encourage doubt and to place obstacles in the way of new ideas. No person receives credit for a new idea unless he publishes it for all the world to see and criticize. It is further considered advisable to announce ideas in papers 53 read to colleagues at public gatherings that they might blast the speaker down face to face.

Even after announcement or publication, no observation can be accepted until it has been confirmed by an independent observer, and no theory is considered more than, at best, an interesting speculation until it is backed by experimental evidence that has been independently confirmed and that has withstood the rigid doubts of others in the field.   54

All this is nothing more than the setting up of a system of "natural selection" designed to winnow the fit from the unfit in the realm of ideas, in manner analogous to the concept of Darwinian evolution. The process may be painful and tedious, as evolution itself is; but in the long run it gets results, as evolution itself does. What's more, I don't see that there can be any substitute.   55

Now let me make a second point. The intensity to which the built-in doubter is activated is also governed by the extent to which a new observation fits into the organized structure of science. If it fits well, doubt can be small; if it fits poorly, doubt can be intensive; if it threatens to overturn the structure completely, doubt is, and should be, nearly insuperable.   56

The reason for this is that now, three hundred fifty years after Galileo founded experimental science, the structure that has been reared, bit by bit, by a dozen generations of scientists is so firm that its complete overturning has reached the vanishing point of unlikelihood.   57

Nor need you point to relativity as an example of a revolution that overturned science. Einstein did not overturn the structure, he merely extended, elaborated, and improved it. Einstein did not prove Newton wrong, but merely incomplete. Einstein's world system contains Newton's as a special case and one which works if the volume of space considered is not too large and if velocities involved are not too great.   58

In fact, I should say that since Kepler's time in astronomy, since Galileo's time in physics, since Lavoisier's[2] time in chemistry, and since Darwin's time in biology no discovery or theory, however revolutionary it has seemed, has actually overturned the structure of science or any major branch of it. The structure has merely been improved and refined.   59

The effect is similar to the paving of a road, and its broadening and the addition of clover-leaf intersections, and the installation of radar to combat speeding. None of this, please notice, is the equivalent of abandoning the road and building another in a completely new direction.   60

But let's consider a few concrete examples drawn from contemporary life. A team of Columbia University geologists have been exploring the configuration of the ocean bottom for years. Now they find that the mid-Atlantic ridge (a chain of mountains, running down the length of the Atlantic) has a rift in the   61

---

[2]Antoine Laurent Lavoisier (1743–1794): French chemist and physicist, a founder of modern chemistry. His classification of substances is the basis of the modern distinction between chemical elements and compounds and of the system of chemical nomenclature. [Eds.]

center, a deep chasm or crack. What's more, this rift circles around Africa, sends an offshoot up into the Indian Ocean and across eastern Africa, and heads up the Pacific, skimming the California coast as it does so. It is like a big crack encircling the earth.

The observation itself can be accepted. Those involved were trained and experienced specialists and confirmation is ample.   62

But why the rift? Recently one of the geologists, Bruce Heezen, suggested that the crack may be due to the expansion of the earth.   63

This is certainly one possibility. If the interior were slowly expanding, the thin crust would give and crack like an eggshell.   64

But why should Earth's interior expand? To do so it would have to take up a looser arrangement, become less dense; the atoms would have to spread out a bit.   65

Heezen suggests that one way in which all this might happen is that the gravitational force of the Earth was very slowly weakening with time. The central pressures would therefore ease up and the compressed atoms of the interior would slowly spread out.   66

Buy why should Earth's gravity decrease, unless the force of gravitation everywhere were slowly decreasing with time? Now this deserves a lot of doubt, because there is nothing in the structure of science to suggest that the force of gravitation must decrease with time. However, it is also true that there is nothing in the structure of science to suggest that the force of gravitation might *not* decrease with time.[3]   67

Or take another case. I have recently seen a news clipping concerning an eighth-grader in South Carolina who grew four sets of bean plants under glass jars. One set remained there always, subjected to silence. The other three had their jars removed one hour a day in order that they might be exposed to noise; in one case to jazz, in another to serious music, and in a third to the raucous noises of sports-car engines. The only set of plants that grew vigorously were those exposed to the engine noises.   68

The headline was: BEANS CAN HEAR—AND THEY PREFER AUTO RACING NOISE TO MUSIC.   69

Automatically, my built-in doubter moves into high gear. Can it be that the newspaper story is a hoax? This is not impossible. The history of newspaper hoaxes is such that one could easily be convinced that nothing in any newspaper can possibly be believed.   70

But let's assume the story is accurate. The next question to ask is whether the youngster knew what he was doing? Was he experienced enough to make the nature of the noise the only variable? Was there a difference in the soil or   71

---

[3]As a matter of fact, there have been cosmological speculations (though not, in my opinion, very convincing ones) that involve a steady and very slow decrease in the gravitational constant; and there is also Kapp's theory, . . . which involves decreasing gravitational force on earth, without involving the gravitational constant.

in the water supply or in some small matter, which he disregarded through inexperience?

Finally, even if the validity of the experiment is accepted, what does it really 72 prove? To the headline writer and undoubtedly to almost everybody who reads the article, it will prove that plants can hear; and that they have preferences and will refuse to grow if they feel lonely and neglected.

This is so far against the current structure of science that my built-in doubter 73 clicks it right off and stamps it: IGNORE. Now what is an alternative explanation that fits in reasonably well with the structure of science? Sound is not just something to hear; it is a form of vibration. Can it be that sound vibrations stir up tiny soil particles making it easier for plants to absorb water, or putting more ions within reach by improving diffusion? May the natural noise that surrounds plants act in this fashion to promote growth? And may the engine noises have worked best on a one-hour-per-day basis because they were the loudest and produced the most vibration?

Any scientist (or eighth-grader) who feels called on to experiment further, 74 ought to try vibrations that do not produce audible sound; ultrasonic vibrations, mechanical vibrations and so on. Or he might also try to expose the plant itself to vibrations of all sorts while leaving the soil insulated; and vice versa.

Which finally brings me to flying saucers and spiritualism and the like. The 75 questions I ask myself are: What is the nature of the authorities promulgating these and other viewpoints of this sort? and How well do such observations and theories fit in with the established structure of science?

My answers are, respectively, Very poor and Very poorly. 76

Which leaves me completely unrepentant as far as my double role in life is 77 concerned. If I get a good idea involving flying saucers and am in the mood to write some science fiction, I will gladly and with delight write a flying-saucer story.

And I will continue to disbelieve in them firmly in real life. 78

And if that be schizophrenia, make the most of it. 79

QUESTIONS

1. What is a "built-in doubter," and why, as in paragraph 13, is Asimov's definition of it essentially mechanical, as a piece of equipment? What are the implications of his describing his "built-in doubter" that way?

2. Asimov claims that "doubting is far more important to the advance of science than believing is" (paragraph 18) and supports that claim with the case of the scientists who refused to accept wholeheartedly the theories of Arrhenius (paragraphs 21 through 37). How does that example support his claim? What other examples does he offer?

3. Asimov also claims that it takes training to doubt well. In what field of interest might you be a well-trained doubter? Provide a set of examples from an area of interest to you that parallels the example of the three oxides in paragraphs 15 through 17. Your

examples should range from causing little or no doubt to stirring a great deal of doubt in you.

4. As humans, Asimov reminds us, we simply lack the powers to distinguish reliably "the good from the bad, the useful from the useless" (paragraph 40). Think of the difficulty of that kind of judgment in cases outside of science. Can you always tell a good movie from a bad one, a good record from a poor one, a good book from one you needn't bother reading? Tell of a case in which you changed your mind about such a judgment. What caused you to change your mind? How did that change occur?

5. We often begin by admiring something and later doubt its value. Is our "built-in doubter" simply being switched on late then, or would you describe what happens differently?

6. Asimov raises the question of when, if ever, it is right not to doubt. Consider a slightly different case: when is it right to believe without doubting? Think of an idea— something other than a matter of religious faith—that you have read about or someone has told you about that you naturally believe in. What causes you to believe in this idea? Describe the case of a "built-in believer."

7. Go to the library and do some research on one of the notions Asimov rejects (paragraph 5) or on one of the discoveries of the great scientists he admires (paragraphs 58 and 59). Write a paper explaining what you have discovered and how it accords with Asimov's judgments about built-in doubters and science.

8. The history of every discipline is filled with examples of ideas that were once doubted and then later recognized as great discoveries. Investigate such an idea from a discipline that interests you, and try to uncover not only why that idea was once doubted but also the influence it has had subsequently on that discipline.

WHY THE
SKY IS BLUE

James Jeans

Sir James Jeans (1877–1946) was a British physicist and astronomer. Educated at Trinity College, Cambridge, he lectured there and was a professor of applied mathematics at Princeton University from 1905 to 1909. He later did research at Mount Wilson Observatory in California. Jeans won many honors for his work and wrote a number of scholarly and popular scientific books. The following selection is from The Stars in Their Courses *(1931), a written version of what began as a series of radio talks for an audience assumed to have no special knowledge of science.*

Imagine that we stand on any ordinary seaside pier, and watch the waves rolling in and striking against the iron columns of the pier. Large waves pay very little attention to the columns—they divide right and left and re-unite after passing each column, much as a regiment of soldiers would if a tree stood in their road; it is almost as though the columns had not been there. But the short waves and ripples find the columns of the pier a much more formidable obstacle. When the short waves impinge on the columns, they are reflected back and spread as new ripples in all directions. To use the technical term, they are "scattered." The obstacle provided by the iron columns hardly affects the long waves at all, but scatters the short ripples. 1

We have been watching a sort of working model of the way in which sunlight struggles through the earth's atmosphere. Between us on earth and outer space the atmosphere interposes innumerable obstacles in the form of molecules of air, tiny droplets of water, and small particles of dust. These are represented by the columns of the pier. 2

The waves of the sea represent the sunlight. We know that sunlight is a blend of lights of many colors—as we can prove for ourselves by passing it through a prism, or even through a jug of water, or as Nature demonstrates to us when she passes it through the raindrops of a summer shower and produces a rainbow. We also know that light consists of waves, and that the different colors of light are produced by waves of different lengths, red light by long waves and blue light by short waves. The mixture of waves which constitutes sunlight has to struggle through the obstacles it meets in the atmosphere, just as the mixture of waves at the seaside has to struggle past the columns of the pier. And these obstacles treat the light-waves much as the columns of the pier treat the sea- 3

485

waves. The long waves which constitute red light are hardly affected, but the short waves which constitute blue light are scattered in all directions.

Thus, the different constituents of sunlight are treated in different ways as   4
they struggle through the earth's atmosphere. A wave of blue light may be scattered by a dust particle, and turned out of its course. After a time a second dust particle again turns it out of its course, and so on, until finally it enters our eyes by a path as zigzag as that of a flash of lightning. Consequently the blue waves of the sunlight enter our eyes from all directions. And that is why the sky looks blue.

QUESTIONS

1. Analogy, the comparison of something familiar with something less familiar, occurs frequently in scientific explanation. Jeans introduces an analogy in his first paragraph. How does he develop that analogy as he develops his explanation?

2. The analogy Jeans provides enables him to explain the process by which the blue light waves scatter throughout the sky. Hence he gives us a brief process analysis of that phenomenon. Summarize that process in your own words.

3. Try rewriting this essay without the analogy. Remove paragraph 1 and all the references to ocean waves and pier columns in paragraphs 2 and 3. How clear an explanation is left?

4. Besides the sea waves, what other familiar examples does Jeans use in his explanation?

5. This piece opens with "Imagine that we stand. . . ." Suppose that every *we* was replaced with a *you.*" How would the tone of the essay change?

6. While analogy can be effective in helping to explain difficult scientific concepts, it can be equally useful in explaining and interpreting familiar things by juxtaposing them in new ways. Suppose, for example, that you wished to explain to a friend why you dislike a course you are taking. Select one of the following ideas for an analogy (or find a better one): a forced-labor camp, a three-ring circus, squirrels on a treadmill, a tea party, a group-therapy session. Think through the analogy to your course, and write a few paragraphs of explanation. Let Jeans's essay guide you in organizing your own.

TIMES AND DISTANCES, LARGE AND SMALL

Francis Crick

Francis Crick (b. 1916), British molecular biologist, shared the Nobel Prize for medicine in 1962 with James D. Watson for their report on the molecular structure of DNA, one of the most important scientific discoveries of this century. Both Watson and Crick have made special efforts to explain their field of study to the general public. The essay reprinted here is the first chapter of Crick's book, Life Itself *(1981).*

There is one fact about the origin of life which is reasonably certain. Whenever and wherever it happened, it started a very long time ago, so long ago that it is extremely difficult to form any realistic idea of such vast stretches of time. Our own personal experience extends back over tens of years, yet even for that limited period we are apt to forget precisely what the world was like when we were young. A hundred years ago the earth was also full of people, bustling about their business, eating and sleeping, walking and talking, making love and earning a living, each one steadily pursuing his own affairs, and yet (with very rare exceptions) not one of them is left alive today. Instead, a totally different set of persons inhabits the earth around us. The shortness of human life necessarily limits the span of direct personal recollection.

Human culture has given us the illusion that our memories go further back than that. Before writing was invented, the experience of earlier generations, embodied in stories, myths and moral precepts to guide behavior, was passed down verbally or, to a lesser extent, in pictures, carvings and statues. Writing has made more precise and more extensive the transmission of such information and in recent times photography has sharpened our images of the immediate past. Cinematography will give future generations a more direct and vivid impression of their forebears than we can now easily get from the written word. What a pity we don't have a talking picture of Cleopatra;[1] it would not only reveal the true length of her nose but would make more explicit the essence of her charm.

We can, with an effort, project ourselves back to the time of Plato and

---

[1]Cleopatra (69 B.C.–30 B.C.): Egyptian queen who charmed Julius Caesar and Marc Antony. [Eds.]

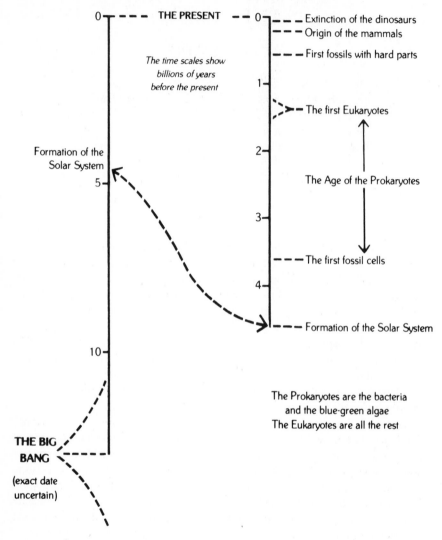

Aristotle,[2] and even beyond to Homer's Bronze Age heroes.[3] We can learn something of the highly organized civilizations of Egypt, the Middle East, Central America and China and a little about other primitive and scattered habi-

---

[2]Plato (428 B.C.?–348 B.C.) and Aristotle (384 B.C.–322 B.C.): Greek philosophers. [Eds.]

[3]Homer's Bronze Age heroes: the heroes of *The Iliad* and *The Odyssey*, epic poems written by the Greek poet Homer about 750 B.C. Homer's heroes fought in the Trojan War (ca. 1200 B.C.) at the end of the Bronze Age (3500 B.C.–1000 B.C.). [Eds.]

tations. Even so, we have difficulty in contemplating steadily the march of history, from the beginnings of civilization to the present day, in such a way that we can truly experience the slow passage of time. Our minds are not built to deal comfortably with periods as long as hundreds or thousands of years.

Yet when we come to consider the origin of life, the time scales we must 4 deal with make the whole span of human history seem but the blink of an eyelid. There is no simple way to adjust one's thinking to such vast stretches of time. The immensity of time passed is beyond our ready comprehension. One can only construct an impression of it from indirect and incomplete descriptions, much as a blind man laboriously builds up, by touch and sound, a picture of his immediate surroundings.

The customary way to provide a convenient framework for one's thoughts is 5 to compare the age of the universe with the length of a single earthly day. Perhaps a better comparison, along the same lines, would be to equate the age of our earth with a single week. On such a scale the age of the universe, since the Big Bang,[4] would be about two or three weeks. The oldest macroscopic fossils (those from the start of the Cambrian)[5] would have been alive just one day ago. Modern man would have appeared in the last ten seconds and agriculture in the last one or two. Odysseus would have lived only half a second before the present time.[6]

Even this comparison hardly makes the longer time scale comprehensible to 6 us. Another alternative is to draw a linear map of time, with the different events marked on it. The problem here is to make the line long enough to show our own experience on a reasonable scale, and yet short enough for convenient reproduction and examination. For easy reference such a map has been printed at the beginning of this [essay]. But perhaps the most vivid method is to compare time to the lines of print themselves. Let us make [a 200-page] book equal in length to the time from the start of the Cambrian to the present; that is, about 600 million years. Then each full page will represent roughly 3 million years, each line about ninety thousand years and each letter or small space about fifteen hundred years. The origin of the earth would be about seven books ago and the origin of the universe (which has been dated only approximately) ten or so books before that. Almost the whole of recorded human history would be covered by the last two or three letters of the book.

If you now turn back the pages of the book, slowly reading *one letter at a* 7 *time*—remember, each letter is fifteen hundred years—then this may convey to

---

[4]Big Bang: a cosmological model in which all matter in the universe originated in a giant explosion about 18 billion years ago. [Eds.]

[5]Cambrian: the earliest period in the Paleozoic era, beginning about 600 million years ago. [Eds.]

[6]Odysseus: the most famous Greek hero of antiquity; he is the hero of Homer's *Odyssey* and a prominent character in the *Iliad*. [Eds.]

you something of the immense stretches of time we shall have to consider. On this scale the span of your own life would be less than the width of a comma.

If life really started here we need hardly be concerned with the rest of the 8 universe, but if it started elsewhere the magnitude of large distances must be squarely faced. Though it is difficult to convey a vivid and precise impression of the age of the universe, to grasp its size is almost beyond human comprehension, however we try to express it. The main stumbling block is the extreme emptiness of space; not merely the few atoms in between the stars but the immense distance from one star to another. The visible world close to us is cluttered with objects and our intuitive estimates of their distance depend mainly on various clues provided by their apparent size and their visual interrelationships. It is much more difficult to judge the distance of an unfamiliar object floating in the emptiness of the clear, blue sky. I once heard a Canadian radio interviewer say, when challenged, that he thought the moon "was about the size of a balloon," though admittedly this was before the days of space travel.

This is how two astronomers, Jastrow and Thompson, try to describe, by 9 analogy, the size and the distance of objects in space:

> Let the sun be the size of an orange; on that scale the earth is a grain of sand circling in orbit around the sun at a distance of thirty feet; Jupiter, eleven times larger than the earth, is a cherry pit revolving at a distance of 200 feet or one city block from the sun. The galaxy on this scale is 100 billion oranges, each orange separated from its neighbors by an average distance of 1,000 miles.[7]

The difficulty with an analogy of this type is that it is almost impossible for 10 us to estimate distances in empty space. A comparison with a city block is misleading, because we too easily visualize the buildings in it, and in doing so lose the idea of emptiness. If you try to imagine an orange floating even a mile up in the sky you will find that its distance seems to become indefinite. An "orange" a thousand miles away would be too small to see unless it were incandescent.

Another possible method is to convert distances to time. Pretend you are on 11 a spaceship which is traveling faster than any present-day spaceship. For various reasons, which will become clear later, let us take its speed to be one-hundredth the velocity of light; that is, about 1,800 miles per second. At this speed one could go from New York to Europe in about three seconds (Concorde takes roughly three hours), so we are certainly traveling fairly fast by everyday standards. It would take us two minutes to reach the moon and fifteen hours to reach the sun. To go right across the solar system from one side to the other—let us take this distance rather arbitrarily as the diameter of the orbit of Neptune—would take us almost three and a half weeks. The main point to grasp is that this journey is not unlike a very long train journey, rather longer than the distance

[7]Robert Jastrow and Malcolm M. Thompson, *Astronomy: Fundamentals and Frontiers*, 2nd ed. (New York: Wiley, 1972).

from Moscow to Vladivostok and back. Such a trip would probably be monotonous enough, even though the landscape were constantly flowing past the train window. While going across the solar system, there would be nothing at all just outside the window of the spaceship. Very slowly, day after day, the sun would change in size and position. As we traveled farther away from it, its apparent diameter would decrease, till near the orbit of Neptune it would look "little bigger than a pin's head," as I have previously described it, assuming that its apparent size, as viewed from the earth, corresponds roughly to that of a silver dollar. In spite of traveling so fast—remember that at this speed we could travel from any spot to any other on the earth's surface in less than seven seconds— this journey would be tedious in the extreme. Our main impression would be of the almost total emptiness of space. At this distance a planet would appear to be little more than an occasional speck in this vast wilderness.

This feeling of an immense three-dimensional emptiness is bad enough while we are focusing on the solar system. (Almost all of the scale models of the solar system one sees in museums are grossly misleading. The sun and the planets are almost always shown as far too big by comparison with the distances between them.) It is when we try to go farther afield that the enormity of space really hits us. To reach the nearest star—actually a group of three stars fairly close together—would take our spaceship 430 years and the chances are we would pass nothing significant on the way there. A whole lifetime of one hundred years, traveling at this very high speed, would take us less than a quarter of the way there. We would be constantly traveling from emptiness to emptiness with nothing but a few gas molecules and an occasional tiny speck of dust to show that we were not always in the same place. Very, very slowly a few of the nearest stars would change their positions slightly, while the sun itself would fade imperceptibly until it was just another star in the brilliant panorama of stars visible on all sides of the spaceship. Long though it would seem, this journey to the nearest star is, by astronomical standards, a very short one. To cross our own galaxy from side to side would take no less than ten million years. Such distances are beyond anything we can conceive except in the most abstract way. And yet, on a cosmic scale, the distance across the galaxy is hardly any distance at all. Admittedly it is only about twenty times as far to Andromeda, the nearest large galaxy, but to reach the limits of space visible to us in our giant telescopes we would have to travel more than a thousand times farther than that. To me it is remarkable that this astonishing discovery, the vastness and the emptiness of space, has not attracted the imaginative attention of poets and religious thinkers. People are happy to contemplate the limitless powers of God—a doubtful proposition at best—but quite unwilling to meditate creatively on the size of this extraordinary universe in which, through no virtue of their own, they find themselves. Naïvely one might have thought that both poets and priests would be so utterly astonished by these scientific revelations that they would be working with a white-hot fury to try to embody them in the foundation of our culture.

12

The psalmist who said, "When I consider Thy heavens, the work of Thy fingers, the moon and the stars, which Thou hast ordained; what is man, that Thou art mindful of him? . . ." was at least trying, within the limitations of his beliefs, to express his wonder at the universe visible to the naked eye and the pettiness of man by comparison. And yet *his* universe was a small, almost cozy affair compared to the one modern science has revealed to us. It is almost as if the utter insignificance of the earth and the thin film of its biosphere has totally paralyzed the imagination, as if it were too dreadful to contemplate and therefore best ignored.

I shall not discuss here how these very large distances are estimated. The 13 distance of the main objects in the solar system can now be obtained very accurately by a combination of the theory of solar mechanics and radar ranging, the distances of the nearest stars by the way their relative positions change slightly when viewed from the different positions of the earth in its yearly orbit around the sun. After that the arguments are more technical and less precise. But that the distances are the sort of size astronomers estimate there is not the slightest doubt.

So far we have been considering very large magnitudes. Fortunately, when 14 we turn to very small distances and times things are not quite so bad. We need to know the size of atoms—the size and contents of the tiny nucleus within each atom will concern us less—compared to everyday things. This we can manage in two relatively small hops. Let us start with a millimeter. This distance (about a twenty-fifth of an inch) is easy for us to see with the naked eye. One-thousandth part of this is called a micron. A bacteria cell is about two microns long. The wavelength of visible light (which limits what we can see in a high-powered light microscope) is about half a micron long.

We now go down by another factor of a thousand to reach a length known 15 as a nanometer. The typical distance between adjacent atoms bonded strongly together in an organic compound lies between a tenth and a fifth of this. Under the best conditions we can see distances of a nanometer, or a little less, using an electron microscope, provided the specimen can be suitably prepared. More-over, it is possible to exhibit pictures of a whole series of natural objects at every scale between a small group of atoms and a flea, so that with a little practice we can feel one scale merging into another. By contrast with the emptiness of space, the living world is crammed with detail at every level. The ease with which we can go from one scale to another should not blind us to the fact that the numbers of objects within a *volume* can be uncomfortably large. For example, a drop of water contains rather more than a thousand billion billion water molecules.

The short time we shall be concerned with will rarely be less than a pico- 16 second, that is, one-millionth of a millionth of a second, though very much shorter times occur in nuclear reactions and in studies of subatomic particles. This minute interval is the sort of time scale on which molecules are vibrating, but looked at another way, it does not seem so outlandish. Consider the velocity of sound. In air this is relatively slow—little faster than most jet planes—being about a thousand feet per second. If a flash of lightning is only a mile away, it will take a full five seconds for its sound to reach us. This velocity is, incidentally, approximately the same as the average speed of the molecules of gas in the air, in between their collisions with each other. The speed of sound in most solids is usually a little faster.

Now we ask, how long will it take a sound wave to pass over a small molecule?   17
A simple calculation shows this time to be in the picosecond range. This is just what one would expect, since this is about the time scale on which the atoms of the molecule are vibrating against one another. What is important is that this is, roughly speaking, the pulse rate *underlying* chemical reactions. An enzyme—an organic catalyst—can react a thousand or more times a second. This may appear fast to us but this rate is really rather slow on the time scale of atomic vibration.

Unfortunately, it is not so easy to convey the time scales in between a second   18
and a picosecond, though a physical chemist can learn to feel at home over this fairly large range. Fortunately, we shall not be concerned directly with these very short times, though we shall see their effects indirectly. Most chemical reactions are really very rare events. The molecules usually move around intermittently and barge against one another many times before a rare lucky encounter allows them to hit each other strongly enough and in the correct direction to surmount their protective barriers and produce a chemical reaction. It is only because there are usually so many molecules in one small volume, all doing this at the same time, that the rate of chemical reaction appears to proceed quite smoothly. The chance variations are smoothed out by the large numbers involved.

When we stand back and review once again these very different scales—the   19
minute size of an atom and the almost unimaginable size of the universe; the pulse rate of chemical reaction compared to the deserts of vast eternity since the Big Bang—we see that in all these instances our intuitions, based on our experience of everyday life, are likely to be highly misleading. By themselves, large numbers mean very little to us. There is only one way to overcome this handicap, so natural to our human condition. We must calculate and recalculate, even though only approximately, to check and recheck our initial impressions until slowly, with time and constant application, the real world, the world of the immensely small and the immensely great, becomes as familiar to us as the simple cradle of our common earthly experience.

QUESTIONS

1. Study the diagram that accompanies the essay. How does one line relate to the other? What is the diagram trying to convey?

2. Why are the first three paragraphs devoted to the history and historical memory of humankind?

3. Compare the analogies Crick uses to explain the long passage of universal time in paragraphs 5, 6, and 7. What does the analogy of the book add to that of the week?

4. In paragraph 8, what is the implication of *elsewhere* in its first sentence? This essay is the first chapter of a book called *Life Itself*. What do you imagine to be at least one idea treated in the rest of the book?

5. Paragraph 11 is an extremely long paragraph, and paragraph 12 is even longer. Their lengths seem to correspond to the subjects they take up. Can you think of other ways to imagine the kind of emptiness those paragraphs describe?

6. Paragraph 11 implies an unusual definition of *wilderness*, its last word. Explain why you consider Crick's idea of wilderness the essential one or an eccentric notion.

7. Why do you think that priests and poets have not, as Crick observes, been "working with a white-hot fury to try to embody [these scientific revelations] in the foundation of our culture" (paragraph 12)? What does that last phrase, "foundation of our culture," mean in this context?

8. Why do you think Crick treats the very large before the very small? Which are the more astonishing measurements?

9. Think of a way of estimating, closely but reasonably, something quite numerous— for example, the number of grasses in a yard, the number of leaves or pine needles on a tree, the number of hairs on the tail of a cat, or the number of cars on all the roads, during a single day, in your state or city. Describe your system of estimation, and explain the answer it yields.

THE ACTION OF NATURAL SELECTION

Charles Darwin

Charles Darwin (1809–1882), British botanist, geologist, and naturalist, is best known for his discovery that natural selection was responsible for changes in organisms during evolution. After an undistinguished academic career and a five-year voyage to South America with a British survey ship, he began keeping his Transmutation Notebooks *(1837–1839), developing the idea of "selection owing to struggle." In 1842 and 1844 he published short accounts of his views and in 1859 published* On the Origin of Species, *which made him famous—even notorious—as the father of the "Theory of Evolution." He preferred to avoid controversy and left the debates over his theories to others whenever possible. But he was a keen observer and continued to study and write on natural history all his life. The essay that follows here is a brief excerpt from* On the Origin of Species, *in which Darwin explains his principle of "natural selection."*

1 In order to make it clear how, as I believe, natural selection acts, I must beg permission to give one or two imaginary illustrations. Let us take the case of a wolf, which preys on various animals, securing some by craft, some by strength, and some by fleetness; and let us suppose that the fleetest prey, a deer for instance, had from any change in the country increased in numbers, or that other prey had decreased in numbers, during that season of the year when the wolf is hardest pressed for food. I can under such circumstances see no reason to doubt that the swiftest and slimmest wolves would have the best chance for surviving, and so be preserved or selected,—provided always that they retained strength to master their prey at this or at some other period of the year, when they might be compelled to prey on other animals. I can see no more reason to doubt this, than that man can improve the fleetness of his greyhounds by careful and methodical selection, or by that unconscious selection which results from each man trying to keep the best dogs without any thought of modifying the breed.

2 Even without any change in the proportional numbers of the animals on which our wolf preyed, a cub might be born with an innate tendency to pursue certain kinds of prey. Nor can this be thought very improbable; for we often observe great differences in the natural tendencies of our domestic animals; one

cat, for instance, taking to catch rats, another mice; one cat, according to Mr. St. John, bringing home winged game, another hares or rabbits, and another hunting on marshy ground and almost nightly catching woodcocks or snipes. The tendency to catch rats rather than mice is known to be inherited. Now, if any slight innate change of habit or of structure benefited an individual wolf, it would have the best chance of surviving and of leaving offspring. Some of its young would probably inherit the same habits or structure, and by the repetition of this process, a new variety might be formed which would either supplant or coexist with the parent-form of wolf. Or, again, the wolves inhabiting a mountainous district, and those frequenting the lowlands, would naturally be forced to hunt different prey; and from the continued preservation of the individuals best fitted for the two sites, two varieties might slowly be formed. These varieties would cross and blend where they met; but to this subject of intercrossing we shall soon have to return. I may add, that, according to Mr. Pierce, there are two varieties of the wolf inhabiting the Catskill Mountains in the United States, one with a light greyhound-like form, which pursues deer, and the other more bulky, with shorter legs, which more frequently attacks the shepherd's flocks.

Let us now take a more complex case. Certain plants excrete a sweet juice, apparently for the sake of eliminating something injurious from their sap: this is effected by glands at the base of the stipules in some Leguminosae, and at the back of the leaf of the common laurel. This juice, though small in quantity, is greedily sought by insects. Let us now suppose a little sweet juice or nectar to be excreted by the inner bases of the petals of a flower. In this case insects in seeking the nectar would get dusted with pollen, and would certainly often transport the pollen from one flower to the stigma of another flower. The flowers of two distinct individuals of the same species would thus get crossed; and the act of crossing, we have good reason to believe (as will hereafter be more fully alluded to), would produce very vigorous seedlings, which consequently would have the best chance of flourishing and surviving. Some of these seedlings would probably inherit the nectar-excreting power. Those individual flowers which had the largest glands or nectaries, and which excreted most nectar, would be oftenest visited by insects, and would be oftenest crossed; and so in the long-run would gain the upper hand. Those flowers, also, which had their stamens and pistils placed, in relation to the size and habits of the particular insects which visited them, so as to favor in any degree the transportal of their pollen from flower to flower, would likewise be favored or selected. We might have taken the case of insects visiting flowers for the sake of collecting pollen instead of nectar; and as pollen is formed for the sole object of fertilization, its destruction appears a simple loss to the plant; yet if a little pollen were carried, at first occasionally and then habitually, by the pollen-devouring insects from flower to flower, and a cross thus effected, although nine-tenths of the pollen were destroyed, it might still be a great gain to the plant; and those individuals which produced more and more pollen, and had larger and larger anthers, would be selected.

When our plant, by this process of the continued preservation or natural 4 selection of more and more attractive flowers, had been rendered highly attractive to insects, they would unintentionally on their part, regularly carry pollen from flower to flower; and that they can most effectually do this, I could easily show by many striking instances. I will give only one—not as a very striking case, but as likewise illustrating one step in the separation of the sexes of plants, presently to be alluded to. Some holly-trees bear only male flowers, which have four stamens producing rather a small quantity of pollen, and a rudimentary pistil; other holly-trees bear only female flowers; these have a full-sized pistil and four stamens with shrivelled anthers, in which not a grain of pollen can be detected. Having found a female tree exactly sixty yards from a male tree, I put the stigmas of twenty flowers, taken from different branches, under the microscope, and on all, without exception, there were pollen-grains, and on some a profusion of pollen. As the wind had set for several days from the female to the male tree, the pollen could not thus have been carried. The weather had been cold and boisterous, and therefore not favorable to bees, nevertheless every female flower which I examined had been effectually fertilized by the bees, accidentally dusted with pollen, having flown from tree to tree in search of nectar. But to return to our imaginary case: as soon as the plant had been rendered so highly attractive to insects that pollen was regularly carried from flower to flower, another process might commence. No naturalist doubts the advantage of what has been called the "physiological division of labor;" hence we may believe that it would be advantageous to a plant to produce stamens alone in one flower or on one whole plant, and pistils alone in another flower or on one whole plant. In plants under culture and placed under new conditions of life, sometimes the male organs and sometimes the female organs become more or less impotent; now if we suppose this to occur in ever so slight a degree under nature, then as pollen is already carried regularly from flower to flower, and as a more complete separation of the sexes of our plant would be advantageous on the principle of the division of labor, individuals with this tendency more and more increased would be continually favored or selected, until at last a complete separation of the sexes would be effected.

Let us now turn to the nectar-feeding insects in our imaginary case: we may 5 suppose the plant of which we have been slowly increasing the nectar by continued selection, to be a common plant; and that certain insects depended in main part on its nectar for food. I could give many facts, showing how anxious bees are to save time; for instance, their habit of cutting holes and sucking the nectar at the bases of certain flowers, which they can, with a very little more trouble, enter by the mouth. Bearing such facts in mind, I can see no reason to doubt that an accidental deviation in the size and form of the body, or in the curvature and length of the proboscis, &c., far too slight to be appreciated by us, might profit a bee or other insect, so that an individual so characterized would be able to obtain its food more quickly, and so have a better chance of living and leaving descendants. Its descendants would probably inherit a tendency to a similar slight deviation of structure. The tubes of the corollas of the common red and incarnate clovers (Trifolium pratense and incarnatum) do not on a hasty glance appear to differ in length; yet the hive-bee can easily suck the nectar out of the incarnate clover, but not out of the common red clover, which is visted by humble-bees alone; so that whole fields of the red clover offer in vain an abundant supply of precious nectar to the hive-bee. Thus it might be a great advantage to the hive-bee to have a slightly longer or differently constructed proboscis. On the other hand, I have found by experiment that the fertility of clover greatly depends on bees visiting and moving parts of the corolla, so as to push the pollen on to the stigmatic surface. Hence, again, if humble-bees were to become rare in any country, it might be a great advantage to the red clover to have a shorter or more deeply divided tube to its corolla, so that the hive-bee could visit its flowers. Thus I can understand how a flower and a bee might slowly become, either simultaneously or one after the other, modifed and adapted in the most perfect manner to each other, by the continued preservation of individuals presenting mutual and slightly favorable deviations of structure.

I am well aware that this doctrine of natural selection, exemplified in the above imaginary instances, is open to the same objections which were at first urged against Sir Charles Lyell's noble views on "the modern changes of the earth, as illustrative of geology;" but we now very seldom hear the action, for instance, of the coast-waves, called a trifling and insignificant cause, when applied to the excavation of gigantic valleys or to the formation of the longest lines of inland cliffs. Natural selection can act only by the preservation and accumulation of infinitesimally small inherited modifications, each profitable to the preserved being; and as modern geology has almost banished such views as the excavation of a great valley by a single diluvial wave, so will natural selection, if it be a true principle, banish the belief of the continued creation of new organic beings, or of any great and sudden modification in their structure.

6

QUESTIONS

1. What does Darwin mean by "natural selection"?
2. The short title of Darwin's major book is often mistakenly given as *The Origin of the Species*. What is the difference between that and the book's correct title, *The Origin of Species*? Why do you suppose so many people get it wrong?
3. Why does Darwin "beg permission" in the first sentence? In the same sentence, what does he mean by "imaginary" illustrations? Are they untrue, or what?
4. We use the name "bumblebee" for what Darwin (and other English writers before him) called a "humble-bee." Find out something about the word *humble* and about the

different kinds of bees. (What is the difference between a hive-bee and a humble-bee, anyway?) For the word *humble*, go to a good dictionary, but don't depend on a dictionary for information about different kinds of bees. Play with the words *humble* and *bumble* to see which of their meanings can be appropriately applied to bees.

5. Darwin's illustrative explanations are excellent examples of process analysis, a type of writing that presents a complicated chain of events as clearly as possible. Select some subject that you know well and that involves an intricate linkage of events. Explain an "imaginary" process taken from that subject. That is, imagine how some little change in an intricate pattern of events would lead to other changes that would cause other changes, until a whole new pattern was established. For example, how would some change in your behavior, appearance, or abilities change the patterns of school and family life around you? Explain the process you imagine as accurately and "scientifically" as you can. Complete your explanation by drawing some conclusion about the principles exemplified by the process you have described.

A BIOLOGICAL HOMAGE TO MICKEY MOUSE

Stephen Jay Gould

Born in 1941 in New York City, Stephen Jay Gould has degrees from Antioch College and Columbia University. For the past fifteen years he has been teaching geology at Harvard University, but he is best known for his monthly column in Natural History *magazine, which has a wide readership. The author of over a hundred scientific articles, he has been enormously successful in making scientific ideas and values available and interesting to a wide readership. His best known books are* Ever Since Darwin *(1977),* The Panda's Thumb *(1980),* The Mismeasure of Man *(1981), and* The Flamingo's Smile *(1985). The essay reprinted here appeared first in* Natural History.

Age often turns fire to placidity. Lytton Strachey, in his incisive portrait of   1
Florence Nightingale, writes of her declining years:

> Destiny, having waited very patiently, played a queer trick on Miss Nightingale.
> The benevolence and public spirit of that long life had only been equalled by its
> acerbity. Her virtue had dwelt in hardness. . . . And now the sarcastic years brought
> the proud woman her punishment. She was not to die as she had lived. The sting
> was to be taken out of her; she was to be made soft; she was to be reduced to
> compliance and complacency.

I was therefore not surprised—although the analogy may strike some people   2
as sacrilegious—to discover that the creature who gave his name as a synonym
for insipidity had a gutsier youth. Mickey Mouse turned a respectable fifty last
year. To mark the occasion, many theaters replayed his debut performance in
Steamboat Willie (1928). The original Mickey was a rambunctious, even slightly
sadistic fellow. In a remarkable sequence, exploiting the exciting new development of sound, Mickey and Minnie pummel, squeeze, and twist the animals
on board to produce a rousing chorus of "Turkey in the Straw." They honk a
duck with a tight embrace, crank a goat's tail, tweak a pig's nipples, bang a
cow's teeth as a stand-in xylophone, and play bagpipe on her udder.

Christopher Finch, in his semiofficial pictorial history of Disney's work,   3
comments: "The Mickey Mouse who hit the movie houses in the late twenties
was not quite the well-behaved character most of us are familiar with today. He
was mischievous, to say the least, and even displayed a streak of cruelty." But
Mickey soon cleaned up his act, leaving to gossip and speculation only his

unresolved relationship with Minnie and the status of Morty and Ferdie. Finch continues: "Mickey . . . had become virtually a national symbol, and as such he was expected to behave properly at all times. If he occasionally stepped out of line, any number of letters would arrive at the Studio from citizens and organizations who felt that the nation's moral well-being was in their hands. . . . Eventually he would be pressured into the role of straight man."

As Mickey's personality softened, his appearance changed. Many Disney fans   4
are aware of this transformation through time, but few (I suspect) have recognized the coordinating theme behind all the alterations—in fact, I am not sure that the Disney artists themselves explicitly realized what they were doing, since the changes appeared in such a halting and piecemeal fashion. In short, the blander and inoffesive Mickey became progressively more juvenile in appearance. (Since Mickey's chronological age never altered—like most cartoon characters he stands impervious to the ravages of time—this change in appearance at a constant age is a true evolutionary transformation. Progressive juvenilization as an evolutionary phenomenon is called neoteny. More on this later.)

The characteristic changes of form during human growth have inspired a   5
substantial biological literature. Since the head-end of an embryo differentiates first and grows more rapidly in utero than the foot-end (an antero-posterior gradient, in technical language), a newborn child possesses a relatively large head attached to a medium-sized body with diminutive legs and feet. This gradient is reversed through growth as legs and feet overtake the front end. Heads continue to grow but so much more slowly than the rest of the body that relative head size decreases.

In addition, a suite of changes pervades the head itself during human growth.   6
The brain grows very slowly after age three, and the bulbous cranium of a young child gives way to the more slanted, lower-browed configuration of adulthood. The eyes scarcely grow at all and relative eye size declines precipitously. But the jaw gets bigger and bigger. Children, compared with adults, have larger

MICKEY'S EVOLUTION during 50 years (left to right). As Mickey became increasingly well behaved over the years, his appearance became more youthful. Measurements of three stages in his development revealed a larger relative head size, larger eyes, and an enlarged cranium—all traits of juvenility. © Walt Disney Productions

heads and eyes, smaller jaws, a more prominent, bulging cranium, and smaller, pudgier legs and feet. Adult heads are altogether more apish, I'm sorry to say.

Mickey, however, has traveled this ontogenetic pathway in reverse during his 7 fifty years among us. He has assumed an ever more childlike appearance as the ratty character of *Steamboat Willie* became the cute and inoffensive host to a magic kingdom. By 1940, the former tweaker of pig's nipples gets a kick in the ass for insubordination (as the *Sorcerer's Apprentice* in *Fantasia*). By 1953, his last cartoon, he has gone fishing and cannot even subdue a squirting clam.

The Disney artists transformed Mickey in clever silence, often using sugges- 8 tive devices that mimic nature's own changes by different routes. To give him the shorter and pudgier legs of youth, they lowered his pants line and covered his spindly legs with a baggy outfit. (His arms and legs also thickened substan- tially—and acquired joints for a floppier appearance.) His head grew relatively larger and its features more youthful. The length of Mickey's snout has not altered, but decreasing protrusion is more subtly suggested by a pronounced thickening. Mickey's eye has grown in two modes: first, by a major, discontin- uous evolutionary shift as the entire eye of ancestral Mickey became the pupil of his descendants, and second, by gradual increase thereafter.

Mickey's improvement in cranial bulging followed an interesting path since 9 his evolution has always been constrained by the unaltered convention of rep- resenting his head as a circle with appended ears and an oblong snout. The circle's form could not be altered to provide a bulging cranium directly. Instead, Mickey's ears moved back, increasing the distance between nose and ears, and giving him a rounded, rather than a sloping, forehead.

To give these observations the cachet of quantitative science, I applied my 10 best pair of dial calipers to three stages of the official phylogeny—the thin- nosed, ears-forward figure of the early 1930s (stage 1), the latter-day Jack of Mickey and the Beanstalk (1947, stage 2), and the modern mouse (stage 3). I

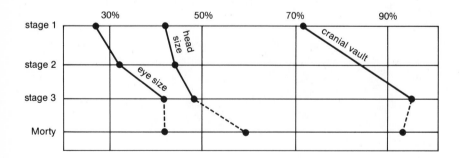

At an early stage in his evolution, Mickey had a smaller head, cranial vault, and eyes. He evolved toward the characteristics of his young nephew Morty (connected to Mickey by a dotted line).

measured three signs of Mickey's creeping juvenility: increasing eye size (maximum height) as a percentage of head length (base of the nose to the top of rear ear); increasing head length as a percentage of body length; and increasing cranial vault size measured by rearward displacement of the front ear (base of the nose to top of front ear as a percentage of base of the nose to top of rear ear).

All three percentages increased steadily—eye size from 27 to 42 percent of head length; head length from 42.7 to 48.1 percent of body length; and nose to front ear from 71.7 to a whopping 95.6 percent of nose to rear ear. For comparison, I measured Mickey's young "nephew" Morty Mouse. In each case, Mickey has clearly been evolving toward youthful stages of his stock, although he still has a way to go for head length.   11

You many, indeed, now ask what an at least marginally respectable scientist has been doing with a mouse like that. In part, fiddling around and having fun, of course, (I still prefer *Pinocchio* to *Citizen Kane*.) But I do have a serious point—two, in fact— to make. We must first ask why Disney chose to change his most famous character so gradually and persistently in the same direction? National symbols are not altered capriciously and market researchers (for the doll industry in particular) have spent a good deal of time and practical effort learning what features appeal to people as cute and friendly. Biologists also have spent a great deal of time studying a similar subject in a wide range of animals.   12

In one of his most famous articles, Konrad Lorenz argues that humans use the characteristic differences in form between babies and adults as important behavioral cues. He believes that features of juvenility trigger "innate releasing mechanisms" for affection and nurturing in adult humans. When we see a living creature with babyish features, we feel an automatic surge of disarming tenderness. The adaptive value of this response can scarcely be questioned, for we must nurture our babies. Lorenz, by the way, lists among his releasers the very features of babyhood that Disney affixed progressively to Mickey: "a relatively large head, predominance of the brain capsule, large and low-lying eyes, bulging cheek region, short and thick extremities, a springy elastic consistency, and clumsy movements." (I propose to leave aside for this article the contentious issue of whether or not our affectionate response to babyish features is truly innate and inherited directly from ancestral primates—as Lorenz argues—or whether it is simply learned from our immediate experience with babies and grafted upon an evolutionary predisposition for attaching ties of affection to certain learned signals. My argument works equally well in either case for I only claim that babyish features tend to elicit strong feelings of affection in adult humans, whether the biological basis be direct programming or the capacity to learn and fix upon signals. I also treat as collateral to my point the major thesis of Lorenz's article—that we respond not to the totality or *Gestalt*, but to a set of specific features acting as releasers. This argument is important to Lorenz because he wants to argue for evolutionary identity in modes of behavior between   13 other vertebrates and humans, and we know that many birds, for example, often respond to abstract features rather than *Gestalten*. Lorenz's article, published in 1950, bears the title *Ganzheit und Teil in der tierischen und menschlichen Gemeinschaft*—"Entirety and part in animal and human society." Disney's piecemeal change of Mickey's appearance does make sense in this context—he operated in sequential fashion upon Lorenz's primary releasers.)

Lorenz emphasizes the power that juvenile features hold over us, and the abstract quality of their influence, by pointing out that we judge other animals by the same criteria—although the judgment may be utterly inappropriate in an evolutionary context. We are, in short, fooled by an evolved response to our own babies, and we transfer our reaction to the same set of features in other animals. 14

Many animals, for reasons having nothing to do with the inspiration of affection in humans, possess some features also shared by human babies but not by human adults—large eyes and a bulging forhead with retreating chin, in particular. We are drawn to them, we cultivate them as pets, we stop and admire them in the wild—while we reject their small-eyed, long-snouted relatives who might make more affectionate companions or objects of admiration. Lorenz points out that the German names of many animals with features mimicking human babies end in the diminutive suffix *chen*, even though the animals are often larger than close relatives without such features—*Rotkehlchen* (robin), *Eichhörnchen* (squirrel), and *Kaninchen* (rabbit), for example. 15

In a fascinating section, Lorenz then enlarges upon our capacity for biologically inappropriate response to other animals, or even to inanimate objects that mimic human features. "The most amazing objects can acquire remarkable, highly emotional values by 'experiential attachment' of human properties . . . . Steeply rising, somewhat overhanging cliff faces or dark storm-clouds piling up have the same, immediate display value as a human being who is standing at full height and leaning slightly forwards"—that is, threatening. 16

We cannot help regarding a camel as aloof and unfriendly because it mimics, quite unwittingly and for other reasons, the "gesture of haughty rejection" common to so many human cultures. In this gesture, we raise our heads, placing our nose above our eyes. We than half-close our eyes and blow out through our nose—the "harumph" of the stereo-typed upperclass Englishman or his well-trained servant. "All this," Lorenz argues quite cogently, "symbolizes resistance against all sensory modalities emanating from the disdained counterpart." But the poor camel cannot help carrying its nose above its elongate eyes, with mouth drawn down. As Lorenz reminds us, if you wish to know whether a camel will eat out of your hand or spit, look at its ears, not the rest of its face. 17

In his important book *Expression of the Emotions in Man and Animals*, published in 1872, Charles Darwin traced the evolutionary basis of many common gestures to originally adaptive actions in animals later internalized as symbols in humans. Thus, he argued for evolutionary continuity of emotion, not 18

HUMANS FEEL AFFECTION for animals with juvenile features: large eyes, bulging craniums, retreating chins (left column). Small-eyed, long-snouted animals (right column) do not elicit the same response. From *Studies in Animal and Human Behavior*, vol, II, by Konrad Lorenz, 1971. Methuen & Co. Ltd.

only of form. We snarl and raise our upper lip in fierce anger—to expose our nonexistent fighting canine tooth. Our gesture of disgust repeats the facial actions associated with the highly adaptive act of vomiting in necessary circumstances. Darwin concluded, much to the distress of many Victorian contemporaries: "With mankind some expressions, such as the bristling of the hair under the influence of extreme terror, or the uncovering of the teeth under that of furious rage, can hardly be understood, except on the belief that man once existed in a much lower and animal-like condition."

In any case, the abstract features of human childhood elicit powerful emotional responses in us, even when they occur in other animals. I submit that Mickey Mouse's evolutionary road down the course of his own growth in reverse reflects the unconscious discovery of this biological principle by Disney and his artists. In fact, the emotional status of most Disney characters rests on the same set of distinctions. To this extent, the magic kingdom trades on a biological illusion—our ability to abstract and our propensity to transfer inappropriately to other animals the fitting responses we make to changing form in the growth of out own bodies.

Donald Duck also adopts more juvenile features through time. His elongated beak recedes and his eyes enlarge; he converges on Huey, Louie, and Dewey

19

20

as surely as Mickey approaches Morty. But Donald, having inherited the mantle of Mickey's original misbehavior, remains more adult in form with his projecting beak and more sloping forehead.

Mouse villains or sharpies, contrasted with Mickey, are always more adult 21 in appearance, although they often share Mickey's chronological age. In 1936, for example, Disney made a short entitled *Mickey's Rival*. Mortimer, a dandy in a yellow sports car, intrudes upon Mickey and Minnie's quiet country picnic. The thoroughly disreputable Mortimer has a head only 29 percent of body length, to Mickey's 45, and a snout 80 percent of head length, compared with Mickey's 49. (Nonetheless, and was it ever different, Minnie transfers her affection until an obliging bull from a neighboring field dispatches Mickey's rival.) Consider also the exaggerated adult features of other Disney characters—the swaggering bully Peg-leg Pete or the simple, if lovable, dolt Goofy.

As a second, serious biological comment on Mickey's odyssey in form, I note 22 that his path to eternal youth repeats, in epitome, our own evolutionary story. For humans are neotenic. We have evolved by retaining to adulthood the originally juvenile features of our ancestors. Our australopithecine forebears, like Mickey in *Steamboat Willie*, had projecting jaws and low vaulted craniums.

DANDIFIED, DISREPUTABLE MORTIMER (here stealing Minnie's affections) has strikingly more adult features than Mickey. His head is smaller in proportion to body length; his nose is a full 80 percent of head length. © Walt Disney Productions

Our embryonic skulls scarcely differ from those of chimpanzees. And we   23
follow the same path of changing form through growth: relative decrease of the
cranial vault since brains grow so much more slowly than bodies after birth,
and continuous relative increase of the jaw. But while chimps accentuate these
changes, producing an adult strikingly different in form from a baby, we proceed
much more slowly down the same path and never get nearly so far. Thus, as
adults, we retain juvenile features. To be sure, we change enough to produce
a notable difference between baby and adult, but our alteration is far smaller
than that experienced by chimps and other primates.

A marked slowdown of developmental rates has triggered our neoteny. Pri-   24
mates are slow developers among mammals, but we have accentuated the trend
to a degree matched by no other mammal. We have very long periods of ges-
tation, markedly extended childhoods, and the longest life span of any mammal.
The morphological features of eternal youth have served us well. Our enlarged
brain is, at least in part, a result of extending rapid prenatal growth rates to later
ages. (In all mammals, the brain grows rapidly in utero but often very little after
birth. We have extended this fetal phase into postnatal life.)

But the changes in timing themselves have been just as important. We are   25
preeminently learning animals, and our extended childhood permits the trans-
ference of culture by education. Many animals display flexibility and play in
childhood but follow rigidly programmed patterns as adults. Lorenz writes, in

CARTOON VILLIANS are not the only
Disney characters with exaggerated adult
features. Goofy, like Mortimer, has a small
head relative to body length and a
prominent snout. © Walt Disney
Productions

the same article above: "The characteristic which is so vital for the human peculiarity of the true man—that of always remaining in a state of development—is quite certainly a gift which we owe to the neotenous nature of mankind.

In short, we, like Mickey, never grow up although we, alas, do grow old. 26 Best wishes to you, Mickey, for you next half-century. May we stay as young as you, but grow a bit wiser.

QUESTIONS

1. Gould admits he is having fun in this essay, but he also says (in paragraph 12) that he has two serious points to make. What are they?

2. What is the function of the very long parenthesis in paragraph 13? How do the remarks in parentheses relate to Gould's presentation of his views as those of "an at least marginally respectable scientist" (paragraph 12). What does he intend by referring to himself in that way?

3. How important are the charts and illustrations to this essay? Consider each of them separately.

4. What would be lost if the essay used no exact measurements but relied instead on the author's impressions?

5. Gould does not consider only the visual images of he cartoon figures he is studying. What other evidence does he mention, and how does he connect it to his major points?

6. Does this essay use biology and psychology to explain popular culture, or popular culture to illustrate biological and psychological principles? What do you feel you have learned from reading Gould's essay?

7. Consider another cartoon character (not a Disney figure) that has existed for a long period of time. Examine this figure to see if it has evolved (as opposed to aged) in any way over time—either pictorially or in terms of speech and action. Write an essay explaining this cartoon character's change (or lack of change), being as precise and careful ("scientific"?) as you can.

TENTATIVE REPORT ON THE HUDSON RIVER BRIDGE

Othmar H. Ammann

Othmar H. Ammann (1879–1965) was a Swiss-born civil engineer whose work is familiar to most Americans, if only from postcards: over the course of a long career he played a major role in the design and construction of many bridges, including the George Washington in New York City and the Golden Gate in San Francisco. The report reprinted here was singled out as a model of good engineering prose by Walter J. Miller and Lee E. A. Saidla, two English professors at the Polytechnic Institute of Brooklyn, New York, who included it in their textbook, Engineers as Writers *(1953, 1971), and wrote the comment that follows the report. As they pointed out in their edition, Ammann was asked to write this report in 1926 when plans for what became the George Washington Bridge had reached a crucial stage. The report was written for the Port of New York Authority and sent to the governors of the two states involved, New York and New Jersey. As a result of this report, the states pledged ten million dollars for construction, ground was broken in 1927, and the bridge was open to traffic four years later.*

The selection that follows includes the cover letter to the governors; Ammann's report, which is addressed to the commissioners of the Port of New York Authority; and the comment by Miller and Saidla. The supplementary tables and other technical exhibits have been omitted.

THE PORT OF NEW YORK AUTHORITY

March 11, 1926

To the Governor of the State of New York:
To the Governor of the State of New Jersey:

Sirs:—We herewith transmit to you the Tentative Report of our Bridge   1

Engineer dealing with a bridge across the Hudson River between Fort Washington and Fort Lee, which gives the engineers' tentative conclusions.

We send this report at this time in order that you may have the latest available 2 engineering information on this matter. The Commission has not yet determined the design or location of the bridge.

We have the honor to remain, 3

Respectfully,

Julian A. Gregory, Chairman,
John F. Galvin, Vice-Chairman,
Frank C. Ferguson,
Otto B. Shulhof,
Schuyler N. Rice,
Herbert K. Twitchell,
Commissioners

The Port of New York Authority

February 25, 1926

To the Commissioners of the Port of New York Authority:

DEAR SIRS:—The preliminary work necessary for the planning and con- 4 struction of the Hudson River Bridge between Fort Washington and Fort Lee, with which The Port of New York Authority has been charged by the Legislatures of New York and New Jersey, has now advanced to a point where conclusions can be drawn regarding the physical and financial feasibility of this bridge, its necessity as a link in the local and interstate transportation systems, its location, size, type, method of construction, approximate cost and aesthetic merits.

Briefly the work so far accomplished embraces comprehensive traffic studies 5 to determine the probable volume of traffic over the bridge and the revenues to be derived therefrom, topographical surveys, river borings and engineering design studies to determine the suitable site, size and type of crossing and its cost, and finally, architectural studies to determine the feasibility of rendering the bridge a befitting object in a charming landscape.

The project being of exceptional magnitude and complex aspect, it was nec- 6 essary that the preliminary studies be undertaken with great care and thoroughness. The appropriations by the two States for these preliminary studies, amounting to $200,000, became available only on July 1, 1925, and the time

510

has not been sufficient to permit either the completion of the studies or the rendering of a comprehensive report on the project. However, it is believed that from the studies so far completed the following conservative conclusions may be drawn:

CONCLUSIONS

(1) The traffic studies reveal an urgent demand for a crossing for vehicular traffic in the vicinity of the proposed bridge to relieve the present intolerable traffic situation. The traffic volume is of more than sufficient magnitude to make it financially feasible to construct, operate and maintain, from tolls, such a crossing, not considering the broader benefits to the people of both States as well as to the local community. 7

(2) The general location of the bridge is well chosen with regard to topography in its vicinity and the feasibility of convenient connections to the important local and arterial highway routes on both sides of the river. A crossing at this point also appears to be the next logical step after construction of the vehicular tunnel at Canal Street, since the two crossings are far enough apart not to influence materially each other's traffic quota. 8

(3) From the engineering point of view the construction of the bridge is in every respect feasible and, while of unusual magnitude, will involve no extraordinary difficulties, nor hazardous or untried operations. The bridge will have a single river span of at least 3500 feet and a clear height above water of about 200 feet. The piers will be located within pier-head lines, as established by the War Department, and will therefore be no obstruction to navigation. 9

(4) The bridge is to be the suspension type, the most economical and aesthetically superior type available. It will be of extremely simple construction, and its design is conceived so that it will be feasible to build the bridge at a minimum initial expenditure to serve present traffic needs, and to enlarge its capacity as the traffic volume increases. 10

(5) If funds for construction of the bridge shall become available in 1927, it is expected that not later than 1933 the bridge will be open for four-lane vehicular and bus passenger traffic and for pedestrians. It is estimated that this capacity will suffice to take care of the initial traffic and the expected increase until about 1943, and then it will probably become necessary to enlarge to an eight-lane vehicular capacity. 11

(6) While it is not possible, at the present time, to report definite cost figures, it is estimated, upon information so far available and upon such forecast of real estate values as may now reasonably be made, that the bridge can be opened for highway traffic at a cost of less than $50,000,000, inclusive of interest during construction. 12

(7) Depending upon traffic capacity finally to be decided upon, it is esti- 13

mated that the bridge can later be enlarged at an additional cost of between $15,000,000 and $25,000,000, if, and when, the vehicular and passenger traffic will have grown in volume to pay for this additional cost.

(8)   On the basis of conservative traffic analysis, and without counting upon the vehicular traffic which will be generated by the construction of the bridge, nor upon possible income from other than vehicular traffic, it is estimated that during the first year after completion the revenue will more than cover the annual interest charge, administration, maintenance, and amortization. The bridge will thus be self-sustaining in every respect from the first year without imposing unreasonable toll charges upon the traffic.

(9)   On the basis of conservative assumptions for future growth of traffic, and counting upon revenue from vehicular traffic alone, it is estimated that within ten years after opening to traffic the bridge may be enlarged to eight-lane capacity, and that within twenty years thereafter the entire bond issue raised to cover construction cost can be amortized.

(10)   The architectural studies so far made, while yet tentative, indicate clearly that the bridge may be so designed as to form an object of grace and beauty as well as utility, and to blend harmoniously with the grandeur of its natural setting.

(11)   In view of this favorable aspect of the bridge, its urgent necessity to relieve traffic conditions and in order to derive the benefit of a complete investigation, it is recommended that the preliminary work be carried to completion, and that the States be asked to appropriate an additional sum of $100,000 to make that completion possible.

Following is a more complete and detailed account of the work so far accomplished:

TRAFFIC STUDIES

Since the Legislative Acts provide that the Port Authority may levy charges for the use of the bridge and that the bridge shall be built and paid for in whole or in part by bonds of the Port Authority, or other securities, it has been necessary to ascertain whether or not the revenues from tolls for vehicles and pedestrians, and possibly franchise rights for rail passenger facilities, will be adequate to meet the cost of construction. This involves the study of a number of traffic factors, viz.:

First: The present volume of vehicular and pedestrian traffic over each of the seventeen ferries across the Hudson River.

Second: The volume of traffic the bridge will be expected to attract when it is opened to traffic. This requires an estimate of the effect on the bridge traffic of the opening of the vehicular tunnel in 1926.

Third: The volume of traffic that can reasonably be expected to be diverted to the bridge from each of the other crossings in that year.

Fourth: The volume of traffic over the bridge for each year, for twenty years   23
subsequent to the opening of the bridge, proper allowance being made for the
effect upon the bridge traffic of the possible construction of other crossings below
179th Street, Manhattan.

This necessitates the determination of the origin and destination of vehicles   24
by types for the existing ferries and apportioning the divertible traffic to each of
the proposed crossings in such a way as to take into account relative distances
and ferry, tunnel, and bridge charges and the elimination of undue congestion
on the approach streets to each of the proposed facilities.

Fifth: An estimate of the revenues for each year subsequent to the opening   25
of the bridge, based upon an average toll per vehicle and per pedestrian.

In order to estimate the vehicular traffic, it was necessary to obtain the trend   26
or rate of growth of the present-day traffic over seventeen ferries between the
Battery and Tarrytown (for the most recent normal year). This required the
records, by classes of vehicles, kept by each of the ferry companies from 1914
to date. Where revenues only are available for this traffic, average tolls for each
class of vehicle must be applied to the revenues to estimate the number of
vehicles. From these records the volume of traffic over each of the ferries can
be forecast for each of the years subsequent to 1932.

Instead of forecasting the traffic for each of the ferries it is better to forecast   27
the volume of traffic that will be diverted from the existing ferries to the bridge.
To obtain this divertible bridge traffic it is necessary first to ascertain the distribution of the present-day traffic over each of the ferries for the most recent
normal year. To do this the origin and destination of each vehicle is necessary
for a sample period of time, so selected that the peak and the average traffic
condition in the year will be reflected. These occur in the months of July and
October. The variations of traffic between week-days and Sundays and from
hour to hour, or both, are necessary to estimate the peak traffic conditions to
test out the roadway capacities on the bridge. Field clockings, therefore, were
taken by placing inspectors on each of the ferry boats of every route to ride the
boats throughout the day. The inspectors ascertained and recorded the following
information respecting each vehicle crossing the river by ferry:

(a) Type of vehicle, that is, whether horse drawn or motor propelled. A
division of motor vehicles was made as between commercial and pleasure, and
again sub-divided to indicate the carrying capacity of the commercial vehicles
and the seating capacity of the pleasure vehicles:

(b) Number of persons carried in each vehicle;

(c) State License;

(d) Origin and destination of each vehicle;

(e) Frequency of use of ferry route by each vehicle.

These clockings were made throughout the months of July, August, Septem-   28
ber and October, 1925. In carrying forward the clockings a field force of fifty-

513

six men was employed on the seventeen ferry routes. The detailed information noted above was ascertained and recorded for a total of 242,000 vehicles.

Clockings were made of the vehicular traffic now passing over the streets and street intersections in the vicinity of the proposed location of the bridge, to determine the degree to which capacity of these streets is now used. Also a study was made to determine the volume of traffic carried at present by the East River bridges, particularly during the peak of travel; and the extent of saturation. 29

Examination of the records of the various ferry companies operating the seventeen ferry routes, for the purpose of ascertaining the volume of traffic and its classification handled by the ferries of each route for the past ten years, has required a force of three to four men constantly from July to the present date. 30

After having completed the field clockings, the next step was the tabulation and summarization of the data. The work of tabulating was carried on in part during the period of clocking and has proceeded since the clockings were completed in October, to bring it to a point to permit of detailed analysis. 31

These analyses are for the purpose of determining future distribution of vehicular traffic among the present crossings, the proposed 178th Street bridge, and any other crossings that might later be constructed and which might affect the future revenues of the 178th Street bridge. 32

One of the first determinations to be arrived at by analysis is the probable volume of traffic that may be expected to use the 178th Street bridge when it is opened, assuming that were the only highway across the Hudson River between Manhattan and New Jersey. 33

The second determination to be made is the volume of traffic which will be attracted to the vehicular tunnel, when it is opened, which otherwise might, in part at least, have used the 178th Street Bridge. 34

The third determination is the probable effect on the 178th Street bridge traffic by the opening of any additional highway crossing over the Hudson in the future. 35

Each of these steps involves a large number of intermediate steps. For example: highway access to the bridge; determination of a toll which will secure maximum traffic and maximum revenue; future crossings to be constructed by the City of New York across the East and Harlem Rivers; and traffic that will be generated by the stimulation of industrial and residential development, particularly on the Jersey side. 36

The results of all of these traffic studies are now being carefully recorded and will be included in a later report on the project. 37

Exhibit (A) illustrates the growth of the total trans-Hudson vehicular traffic as tentatively estimated, from 1924 to 1960, inclusive, and the number of vehicles of this total traffic which would have been, or will be, diverted to the 178th Street bridge. 38

Below is recorded the first tentative estimate of total trans-Hudson vehicular 39

514

traffic for all ferries from the Battery to and including Tarrytown, and the traffic that the bridge will divert from these ferries and the tunnel.

Year	Hudson River Traffic	Bridge Traffic	Year	Hudson River Traffic	Bridge Traffic
1924	11,706,000	3,208,000	1944	36,055,000	11,476,000
1925	12,912,000	3,596,000	1945	36,767,000	11,723,000
1926	14,185,000	4,017,000	1946	37,408,000	11,944,000
. . . .					
1934	25,607,000	7,889,000	1953	40,841,000	13,144,000
1935	26,984,000	8,364,000	1954	41,172,000	13,263,000
1936	28,280,000	8,807,000	1955	41,478,000	13,369,000
			1956	41,765,000	13,471,000

These figures must be revised as the analysis proceeds to take into account 40 the effect of the opening of additional crossings. The above figures do not include traffic which will be generated from the adjacent territories, whose growth the bridge will stimulate. While this cannot be measured accurately, an analysis of the growth of population, intensity of realty development, and motor vehicle registration is in process to determine the effect of the East River bridges upon Brooklyn and Queens, in order to gauge roughly the effect that the Hudson River bridge will have upon Fort Lee and its contiguous communities. The amount of this traffic will be considerable and eventually will be added to the above estimates.

While the above traffic is the principal source of revenue, there are four 41 other sources which will contribute to the income of the bridge. This revenue will come from passengers in vehicles, pedestrians, bus lines and rapid transit facilities. Studies are under way to ascertain the potential traffic which will give rise to this income and will be presented in a later report.

Tables (1-a), and (1-c), appended to this report, give the gross revenues 42 estimated to date for a 50¢ rate, a 60¢ rate, a 70¢ rate, respectively, from vehicles only. It will be seen that for 1933, or the first year of operation, the income from vehicles alone is forecast as at least $3,700,000. Subtracting the charges for administration, maintenance and operation, the net operating income is close to 6½% on the $50,000,000, the probable maximum initial cost of the bridge. In addition, there will be revenue from passengers in vehicles, pedestrians, and bus lines, and from vehicular traffic which will be generated by the bridge. Consequently, it is safe to conclude at this time that the charges on the initial and ultimate cost of construction can be met out of the potential revenue from traffic, and that therefore the project is economically sound.

LOCATION STUDIES

The Legislative Acts of New York and New Jersey provide that the bridge 43 shall be located at a point between 170th and 185th Streets in Manhattan, New York City, and a point approximately opposite thereto in the borough of Fort Lee, New Jersey.

After a general examination of the territory on both sides of the river, within 44 these limits, three specific sites which appeared to offer possibilities were tentatively selected for more careful study. . . . The three sites chosen are those in close vicinity of 181st Street, 179th Street, and 175th Street, Manhattan, respectively. River borings, studies of approaches, grades, street connections, tentative designs and comparative cost estimates were made for these locations. These studies revealed the central location near 179th Street as being not only the most economical, but also the most desirable with respect to approach grades and street connections and natural setting, and it was therefore decided to confine the elaboration of more complete plans and estimates to this location.

In the selection of the locations, careful consideration was also given to the 45 scenic effect of the bridge, more particularly with regard to the effect upon Fort Washington Park. While, by locating the bridge at 181st Street or 175th Street, encroachment upon this park by bridge piers might be avoided, the much longer river span required at these locations, and the consequent greater proportions of the bridge, would not be as favorable, aesthetically, as a bridge at 179th Street. Moreover, the location of a pier in the Park is not believed to curtail in any way the usefulness of the Park or to mar its beauty.

TOPOGRAPHICAL SURVEYS, MAPPING AND TRIANGULATION

Owing to lack of maps, sufficiently accurate and complete for preliminary 46 planning and reliable estimates of cost, it has been necessary to undertake extensive and accurate topographical surveys extending over the territories on which the bridge approaches and street connections may be located. These surveys are now nearing completion and will form a valuable basis for the final planning and construction of the bridge. The results of these surveys have been embodied in a large map to the scale of $1'' = 100'$.

Owing to the lateness of the season it has been found impracticable to un- 47 dertake an accurate triangulation across the river, but the necessary base lines have been established, and all other preparations for these measurements have been made, and it is expected that they can be accomplished in the Spring as soon as weather conditions permit. For the tentative studies, the triangulation made by the U. S. Coast and Geodetic Survey was considered to be sufficiently reliable.

RIVER BORINGS

In order to obtain reliable information on the character of the river bottom and to establish beyond question the surface of the solid bedrock upon which the bridge piers have to rest, it was necessary to undertake borings carried well into the solid rock. 48

In all sixteen borings, at the three locations tentatively selected, have been sunk, the results carefully recorded and the rock cores preserved. These borings have established the fact that, outside of the pierhead lines established by the War Department, that is, within the width of river reserved for navigation, bedrock is too deep to permit of economical construction of bridge piers and that such piers must, and can, be placed between the pierhead lines and the shore, or on shore. Moreover, thus located, the piers will form no obstructions to navigation. . . . 49

Additional borings will have to be made when the location of the bridge is definitely established. 50

The character of rock revealed by these borings corresponds to that prognosticated by the U. S. Geological Survey. On the New Jersey side bedrock was found to consist partly of solid red sandstone and shale, known as the "Newark Formation," partly of the so-called "Stockbridge Dolomite" which forms the major portion of the rockbed under the Hudson River. The borings on the New York side revealed a solid bed of "Hudson Shist" (mica shist), which is the prevailing rock of Manhattan Island. All of these rock formations are sufficiently hard to constitute a solid and permanent foundation for the bridge piers and to safely sustain the great pressure from them. 51

The material overlying the rock is almost entirely river silt, unsuitable for foundation purposes. 52

ENGINEERING DESIGN STUDIES

In order to determine the most economical and suitable type and general proportions of the structure, for various possible locations, it was essential to undertake extended comparative design studies and cost estimates, before any final planning could be undertaken. Complete tentative designs were made for a 3500 foot river span and a 3900 foot span, as required for the 179th and 181st Street locations, respectively. Comparative estimates of cost have also been prepared for various capacities for highway traffic and for combined highway and rail passenger traffic. 53

Various possible forms and materials for the individual parts of this structure 54
were given most careful consideration, and all essential features of the structure
have been studied in detail with a view to assure not only economy, but conformity to the most advanced standards of design and methods of fabrication
and construction.

Tentative schemes of erection have been evolved, inasmuch as the method 55
of erection of a large bridge not only has an important bearing upon its design
and economy, but because in this case it involves operations of unprecedented
proportions.

As a result of these studies a tentative design has been developed which, for 56
the 179th Street location, may be briefly described as follows:

TYPE AND GENERAL PROPORTIONS OF BRIDGE

Little study was necessary to determine the suspension bridge as the most 57
suitable type, because its superior economy for such great spans and capacities
is now generally recognized by engineers. Its superior aesthetic merits, when
properly designed, further single it out as the best adapted type in this case.

A cantilever bridge, the nearest other possibility, would, with its dense and 58
massive network of steel members, form a monstrous structure and truly mar
forever the beauty of the natural scenery.

The general proportions of the bridge, as to length of spans and height above 59
water, were sharply defined by the topographical and geological conditions of
the site. As a result of the borings, heretofore described, the main pier on the
New Jersey side was located well within the pierhead line at a point where rock
can be reached at a depth of about 100 feet, which is the approximate limit for
the pneumatic process, the safest and most reliable foundation method. On the
New York side the logical and natural place for the pier is the rocky point of
Fort Washington Park close to the pierhead line. This results in a central span
of 3500 feet between centers of piers, or twice the span of the Philadelphia-
Camden bridge, the longest suspension bridge so far built.

The rock cliffs of the Palisades form the natural abutment and anchorage on 60
the New Jersey side and, for the sake of symmetry, which is an essential aesthetic
requirement, the side span on the New York side is made the same, or approximately 700 feet.

The clear height of the bridge floor above water is approximately 200 feet, 61
this height resulting from the elevations of the connecting streets on both sides
of the river and the limiting grades of the approaches. Incidentally, this height
is ample to permit passage of the largest vessels which are likely to go up the
river beyond this point.

The general form and arrangement of the structure are of extreme simplicity. 62
Essentially the floor deck is suspended throughout its length from simple cables

or chains. The latter will pass over the two towers and are to be firmly anchored in rock or massive concrete blocks at their ends.

To enhance the gracefulness of the bridge, the cables are to have a comparatively small sag or flat catenary. Structurally, the cables are to be built either of steel wires or of high grade steel eyebars, both types of construction having reached a high degree of perfection in American bridge practice and a degree of safety superior to that of any other type of structural members. 63

Detailed studies have been made of two essentially different types of towers, a slender steel tower, as exemplified in the Manhattan bridge, and a combined steel and masonry tower of massive appearance. While the economic merits of the slender steel tower, and its justification in some localities, are recognized, it is felt that the conspicuous location of the proposed bridge in the midst of a bold and impressive landscape makes the selection of the aesthetically superior massive tower imperative. 64

TRAFFIC CAPACITY OF BRIDGE

One of the most important and complex questions which had to be solved, and will involve further careful study in connection with the planning of this bridge, is the determination of its traffic capacity, as regards both kinds and volume of traffic. 65

The question is necessarily closely related to the study of the traffic situation and definite solution has to await the results of these studies. While the Legislative Acts do not specify the kind of traffic to be accommodated, existing conditions point clearly to the need of a crossing primarily for vehicular traffic. Furthermore, while the development of the territories contiguous to the bridge will, sooner or later, call for the accommodation of a considerable volume of passenger traffic, it is not likely that rapid transit or other rail passenger traffic facilities will be needed for many years to come. 66

It is also realized that the demand for passenger traffic in the immediate future, and possibly for many years to come, may be filled by passenger buses running over the bridge roadway. Any provision for the accommodation of rail traffic, which would involve a comparatively large outlay at present, would therefore not be warranted. 67

As a result of our studies it now appears quite feasible, however, to build the bridge initially for highway traffic only, but with provision, at a small extra expenditure, for the future accommodation of rail passenger, or additional bus passenger traffic. 68

In fact the design, as now developed (see Exhibit C), is exceptionally farreaching in its provision for a gradual increase in traffic capacity with a minimum possible initial expenditure, and with the least possible time of construction before the bridge can be opened to traffic. 69

The plan provides for an initial capacity of two 24-foot roadways which will 70 conveniently accommodate four lanes of vehicular traffic, two in each direction. Two footwalks for pedestrians are also provided for. It is estimated that these two roadways will be sufficient to fill the demand for highway traffic for about ten years after the opening of the bridge.

If and when justified by increased volume of vehicular traffic, another four- 71 lane roadway can be added, and used for truck traffic, while the two initial roadways may be reserved for the faster passenger automobiles. It is estimated that the eight lanes will be ample to take care of all vehicular traffic which may be concentrated at this crossing. All of this highway traffic is to be accommodated on an upper deck of the structure.

If and when accommodation for rail passenger traffic, or for additional bus 72 passenger traffic, across the bridge becomes necessary, two or four lanes, or tracks, of either form of such traffic can be added on a lower deck.

The question as to whether, and to what extent, rail passenger traffic should 73 be provided for on the bridge is still under consideration, and the cooperation and advice of the transit authorities in the two States have been sought in order to arrive at a satisfactory solution.

APPROACHES AND HIGHWAY CONNECTIONS

Tentative studies for the approaches and highway connections on both sides 74 of the river have been made, but further studies in cooperation with the proper municipal and State highway authorities, are necessary. The studies so far completed indicate conclusively that direct connections of the bridge approaches with important highway arteries, such as Broadway and Riverside Drive in Manhattan, and Lemoine Avenue in New Jersey, are entirely feasible and involve no extensive changes in the street system, at least for many years after completion of the bridge.

It would be lacking in foresight, however, not to recognize the fact that when 75 the bridge is to be completed to capacity the vehicular traffic will have grown to such an extent that new arteries will become necessary on both sides of the river, more particularly for that traffic which will flow to and from the bridge in an easterly and westerly direction. While such new arteries will not form part of the bridge project proper, studies are being made with respect to them and with a view to give the bridge a proper setting in the future net of highway arteries.

Regarding the structural arrangement of the approaches, more particularly 76 that on the New York side, it should be mentioned that aesthetic considerations have been paramount in developing their design.

The New York approach is designed as a short viaduct of monumental ap- 77 pearance which will enhance rather than destroy the good character of the neighborhood (see Exhibit D). The New Jersey approach is designed as a cut through the top of the Palisades so marked at the face of the cliffs as not to destroy the appearance of the latter or to break their natural silhouette.

Tracks, if any are provided, will be hidden from view on the approaches.　78

ARCHITECTURAL STUDIES

The commanding location of the bridge in a charming landscape made it　79 imperative to give prominent consideration to the aesthetic side of the bridge design; in other words, to combine beauty with utility and strength. For this purpose the Port Authority has engaged an eminent architect, Mr. Cass Gilbert, to assist the engineering staff in the preparation of the plans. A statement by the architect on the architectural aspect of the project is appended.

ESTIMATES OF COST

In view of the incompleted state of the preliminary work and certain as yet　80 unsettled questions, such as provision for passenger traffic, extent of architectural treatment of the bridge and approaches, more accurate appraisal of property and damages, etc., it is impossible to give at the present time reliable cost estimates. Making reasonable allowance for the uncertain features, it is estimated that the bridge can be constructed, ready for the initial highway capacity, at a cost of less than $50,000,000, inclusive of interest during construction, and that it can later be strengthened for the eight-lane highway capacity, and provision for from two to four electric railway tracks, at an additional cost of between $15,000,000 and $20,000,000.

FINANCIAL STATEMENT

The financial statement following gives, for the years 1933, 1943, 1953 and　81 1960, the gross revenue and net operating income from vehicles only, based upon average toll rates of 50¢, 60¢, and 70¢, respectively, an initial cost of $50,000,000 and an additional expenditure, ten years later, of $15,000,000, as required for the increased vehicular capacity.

ACKNOWLEDGEMENT

The Engineering Staff has been aided in its studies so far made by valuable　82 advice and information from various individuals and organizations to whom due credit will be given at the proper time.

The undersigned also take this occasion to express their acknowledgement　83 for the valuable services so far rendered by other members of the engineering staff, more particularly, R. A. Lesher, Traffic Engineer, in charge of traffic studies; W. J. Boucher, Engineer of Construction, and R. Hoppen, Jr., Resi-

Year	Gross Revenue from Vehicles Only	Administration Operation Maintenance	Net Operating Income Available for Interest and Amortization	Per Cent of Net Operating Income to Estimated Cost
A. Average Toll Charge 50¢				
1933	$3,700,000	$ 500,000	$3,200,000	6.40%
1943	5,608,000	750,000	4,858,000	9.72
1953	6,572,000	1,000,000	5,572,000	8.57
1960	6,910,000	1,000,000	5,910,000	9.09
B. Average Toll Charge 60¢				
1933	4,441,000	500,000	3,941,000	8.76
1943	6,730,000	750,000	5,980,000	13.29
1953	7,886,000	1,000,000	6,886,000	10.59
1960	8,293,000	1,000,000	7,293,000	11.22
C. Average Toll Charge 70¢				
1933	5,181,000	500,000	4,681,000	10.40
1943	7,851,000	750,000	7,101,000	15.78
1953	9,201,000	1,000,000	8,201,000	12.62
1960	9,675,000	1,000,000	8,675,000	13.35

Note:—Additional revenue from generated vehicular traffic and from bus and rail-passenger traffic is expected to increase materially the potential net operating income.

dent Engineer, in charge of surveys and borings; W. A. Cuenot and A. Andersen, Assistant Engineers, in charge of design studies.

Respectfully submitted
(Signed) O. H. Ammann,
Bridge Engineer

COMMENT

We were so pleased with the design and execution of this report that we went [84] to talk about it with Ammann himself. When we arrived in the New York office of Ammann and Whitney, Consulting Engineers, the partners were busy examining huge charts on a long work-table. Ammann, who is in his seventies and still energetic and graceful in his movements, led us to his desk, on which lay a rough draft of his most recent report, scheduled for publication early in 1953. The conversation confirmed what we had surmised but had wanted to hear in his own words: His reports and papers are born of a very definite "philosophy of composition."

"Unfortunately," the designer of the Washington Bridge told us, "most en- [85] gineers think in terms of details. And so most engineering reports are cluttered with meaningless particulars. Actually what the reader needs most is a good general view of the situation. In my reports I usually start off with a summary and a statement of conclusions. Then I use logical subdivisions of the subject, and try to develop my basic material in language the layman can understand."

He handed us the draft of the report he had been working on, a lengthy 86 account of his inspection of one of the world's largest bridges. It opened with an explanation of the scope and arrangement of the material, immediately followed by a summary of the results of the investigation and the proposals of the investigator. At the end of the first few pages the reader had the gist and significance of the entire document.

Ammann confessed with a smile that reports are no easier to design than 87 bridges. "I usually have to take my reports home and work on them until two in the morning." In the course of his long professional career, he told us, he had written more than a hundred full-length reports. And how had he trained himself to write reports? "I rely on my studies of logic and literature. Logic taught me how to structure my writing. Literature gives me an understanding of the importance of style."

The 1926 report studied here follows the general approach Ammann de- 88 scribed to us. The writer's sole consideration in the opening paragraphs is to get as quickly as possible to what the reader wants most to know: the conclusions. Therefore, the occasion, aim, and scope of the report are swiftly treated in one sentence. The methods employed to gather the material are reviewed with equal brevity. Some necessary background is sketched in lightly. But all this is prelude, fanfare, preceding the procession of conclusions. These are introduced in an order in which each one leads to the next, until the last is a recommendation for action by the reader.

Now, certain that his reader will be able to view particulars with some pa- 89 tience and purpose, Ammann gives his "more complete and detailed account," using the same order of topics. So far as that is possible, raw data are pushed to the rear, and some to appendices. The net result is a well-designed report.

Ammann's style is equally pleasing, and functionally related to his structure 90 of both reports and bridges. Generally, his writing is rapid and graceful. He uses many long-span sentences, but they carry heavy loads with great spring and verve. Since he believes that the reader must get the essence, the general view, he naturally uses qualitative language, but without unnecessary ornament. He does not feel that his "scientific objectivity" will be compromised if he translates quantity into quality ("intolerable traffic situation") or views a fact through a feeling ("charming landscape"). He accepts the professional man's responsibility not only to specialize, but to generalize. His description of what a cantilever bridge would look like in the setting of the Palisades is especially revealing in all these connections:

"A cantilever bridge, the nearest other possibility, would, with its dense and 91 massive network of steel members, form a monstrous structure and mar forever the beauty of the natural scenery."

How very similar to his description of the average report as "cluttered with meaningless particulars"!   92

Walter J. Miller and Lee E. A. Saidla

QUESTIONS

1. Write one sentence that summarizes in your own words what Ammann recommends and why. In what ways does this report make writing such a sentence hard or easy?

2. In paragraphs 45, 64, 77, and 78, Ammann makes value judgments about the aesthetic effect the bridge will have on its immediate environment. Because those are value judgments rather than strictly technical information, how do you respond to the passages? What influences you most in your doubt or acceptance of them? What do these passages suggest about Ammann's viewpoint as an engineer?

3. Examine any few paragraphs, 7 through 10, for example, or paragraph 27. What are some examples of "language the laymen can understand" (paragraph 85)? How often does Ammann slip away from such language?

4. The comment following the report outlines Ammann's philosophy of composition in paragraph 85. Review the summary and conclusions with which Ammann begins. What logic do you find for the order of the conclusions numbered 1 through 11?

5. Paragraph 89, claims Ammann, following the presentation of his conclusions, gives his " 'more complete and detailed account,' using the same order of topics." How closely does that turn out to be the case? Compare the conclusions, paragraphs 7 through 17, with the subsections that follow. Which conclusions pertain to which subsections and vice versa?

6. The commentary in paragraph 90 describes Ammann's style. The commentators are obviously influenced by engineering concepts ("rapid and graceful," "long-span sentences"), and they are also concerned about Ammann's scientific objectivity. Write your own analysis of Ammann's style, limiting your examination to one of his subsections.

7. If the George Washington Bridge is unfamiliar to you, find its location, as noted in paragraph 43, on some maps both of New York City and of the United States. If your class is from another region, ask whether anyone in the room has crossed that bridge and, if so, for what reasons.

8. If you live near the George Washington Bridge, you might be able to report on whether Ammann's judgment, as expressed in paragraphs 45, 64, 77, and 78, has turned out to be valid or not. You might take special note of any conditions Ammann could not have foreseen that influence the present aesthetic aspect of the bridge.

9. Describe the bridge today. How many lanes has it? What variety of traffic does it carry? How closely does it fulfill the predictions Ammann made for it?

10. Describe a study that could be made to propose a new bridge, parking lot, shopping mall, or highway in your own community. What specific studies would be required?

524

TWO REPORTS ON PROSOPAGNOSIA (KNOWLEDGE WITHOUT AWARENESS)

Antonio R. Damasio and Associates

Antonio R. Damasio was born in Portugal in 1944, where he studied medicine, receiving both an M.D. and a Ph.D. from the University of Lisbon. He is presently Professor of Neurology and Chief of the Division of Behavioral Neurology at the University of Iowa College of Medicine. He has conducted funded research since 1970 and is the author of more than 160 publications on anatomical aspects of higher brain function, parkinsonism, and dementia. Most of his research focuses on understanding the cerebral basis of vision, language, and memory. Damasio's two articles here represent aspects of his work on prosopagnosia, which he defines as "knowledge without awareness." The first, written by Damasio with the assistance of Betty Redeker, is a review of research in this field. The second reports on an experiment conducted by Damasio and his associate David Tranel. Both are examples of the style of presentation favored by scientific journals.

REVIEW OF RESEARCH ON PROSOPAGNOSIA

[Abstract.] *The impaired recognition of previously known familiar faces (pro-* 1
sopagnosia), when it appears in isolation, is one of the most extreme forms of behavioral dissociation encountered in human pathology. Its research provides an outstanding opportunity to understand better the organization of the visual system and of memory mechanisms in humans. Recent evidence indicates that the disorder is associated with bilateral lesions of the central visual system, located in the mesial occipito-temporal region. These lesions either destroy a specific sector of the visual association cortex or disconnect it from limbic structures located anteriorly in the temporal lobe. This evidence is in keeping with the demonstration, in normals, that both hemispheres are capable of facial recognition, but should not be seen to indicate that each hemisphere uses the same mechanisms to process faces or is equally efficient in the process. Cognitive analysis of pro-sopagnosia reveals that the defect is not specific to human faces but also appears in relation to other visual stimuli whose recognition depends on the evocation of

525

specific contextual attributes and associations, and which are visually 'ambiguous' (different stimuli belonging to the same group but having similar physical structure). Physiopathologically, prosopagnosia is the result of a failure to activate, on the basis of visual stimuli, memories pertinent to those stimuli.

The description of prosopagnosia dates from the turn of the century although the designation was only coined in 1947 by Bodamer.[1] In isolation, the condition is so extreme and infrequent that many investigators doubted its reality. Otherwise normal individuals suddenly lose their ability to recognize the faces of relatives, friends, and even their own faces in the mirror, while being able to recognize other objects visually. They also lose the ability to learn to identify the faces of new persons they come into contact with. In short, the visual inspection of these familiar faces no longer generates an experience of even vague familiarity and thus facial recognition is forever precluded. The patients can still recognize, by the sound of their voices, the people whose faces have become meaningless. All the remote memories that pertain to those people remain intact. Cognitive skills also remain intact and so do complex visual abilities, i.e. most prosopagnosic patients describe their visual environment accurately, localize stimuli in space flawlessly, inspect visual arrays in normal fashion, and some can even read. Needless to say, their visual acuity is normal. The only symptoms that commonly accompany prosopagnosia are achromatopsia, an acquired defect in color perception which may affect part or all of the visual field, an acquired defect in the appreciation of textures visually, and some partial field cut for the vision of forms. (Prosopagnosia may also be found as a component of global amnesic syndrome. In such instances no field defects for color or form accompany the manifestation, and visual perception is manifestly intact.)

Even after it became clear that the condition was indeed real, considerable controversy surfaced regarding its physiopathological nature and anatomical basis. This review focuses on some of these issues as well as on new developments in the understanding of prosopagnosia.

ANATOMICAL BASIS

The early descriptions of prosopagnosia indicated that the condition was associated with bilateral damage to the occipital lobes.[26,3] But when after decades of neglect, there was a resurgence of interest in prosopagnosia, several investigators conceptualized it as a sign of unilateral damage of the right hemisphere. At the time, the 1960s, fresh neuropsychological investigations had revealed the major role of the right hemisphere in visual processing and it appeared reasonable to assume that the right hemisphere might possess the sole key to a refined visual process such as facial recognition. Hecaen and Angelergues[2] added strength to this hypothesis by noting that most prosopagnosic patients had exclusive left visual field defects, and suggesting that this was due to exclusive right hemisphere damage. Later, in a comprehensive review of the data available in 1974, Meadows concluded 'that patients with prosopagnosia have right anterior inferior occipital lesions in the region of the occipital temporal junction. Many if not all cases have an addition lesion in the left hemisphere.'[4] Although these interpretations were consonant with the anatomical localization methods at the time, the evidence uncovered in the years that followed revealed that they were not supportable. The current view is that bilateral lesions are indeed necessary, a notion that is based on: (1) a critical review of the meaning of visual field data: (2) a reassessment of post-mortem studies of prosopagnosic patients; (3) Computed Tomography (CT), Nuclear Magnetic Resonance (NMR) and Emission Tomography (ET) studies of patients with and without prosopagnosia; (4) a study of patients with cerebral hemispherectomy, callosal surgery and amnesic sydromes. The fundamental evidence is as follows:

(1) The one patient of Hecaen and Angelergues to come to post-mortem, [5] turned out to have a bilateral lesion.[2] The lesion in the left hemisphere was "silent" as far as visual field findings were concerned. Similar "silent" lesions were uncovered at autopsy in patients described by Benson[5] and by Lhermitte.[6] It is now apparent that when lesions of the central visual system fail to involve optic radiations or primary visual cortex they do not produce an overt defect of form vision even when they can cause major disturbances of complex visual processing such as a defect in recognition or color processing.[7] While the presence of a field defect correctly indicates the presence of a lesion, its absence does not exclude focal damage. Thus while the detailed study of field defects is mandatory for the appropriate study of visual agnosia, its details cannot be used for the prediction of lesion localization.

(2) Analysis of the post-mortem records of all patients that have come to [6] autopsy[8,9] indicate that they all have bilateral lesions. Furthermore, it is clear that those lesions preferably involve the inferior visual association cortices, i.e. the occipito-temporal region. Finally, patients with bilateral lesions involving the superior visual association cortices, i.e. the occipito-parietal region, never develop prosopagnosia, presenting instead either a full Balint syndrome or some of its components, i.e. visual disorientation, optic ataxia or ocular apraxia.[7] Patients with Balint syndrome can recognize faces provided their attention is properly directed to the stimuli.

(3) Computed Tomography (CT) has permitted the study of many cases of [7] prosopagnosia and of numerous controls with unilateral lesions of the left or right occipito-temporal region, or with bilateral lesions of the occipito-parietal region. With one exception all the instances of permanent prosopagnosia studied in appropriate patients with technically advanced scanning techniques, have shown bilateral lesions.[8–11] Furthermore, numerous instances of unilateral lesion in the right and left hemispheres have been described and there has been no report of prosopagnosia appearing in those circumstances. (The possible

exception was reported in a hypertensive patient on the basis of a single cut of an acute CT scan[12]; it is important to consider the possibility of an undetected lesion in the opposite hemisphere.)

Patients with bilateral occipito-parietal lesions consistently show Balint syndrome or its components but not prosopagnosia.[7] In the only two cases studied with nuclear magnetic resonance (NMR) the lesions were bilateral. In the only two cases studied with Single Photon Emission Tomography there were bilateral regions of diminished cerebral blood flow.[7]   8

(4) Evidence from hemispherectomy and from cases of surgical callosal section has also been helpful. Patients with right hemispherectomy maintain their ability to recognize faces with their single left hemisphere.[13] The split-brain subjects continue to recognize faces with each isolated hemisphere although, as expected, the mechanisms of recognition appear to be different on the left and on the right.[27]   9

Final evidence for the bilaterality of damage in prosopagnosia comes from the analysis of patients with amnesic syndromes. Patients with global amnesic syndromes associated with temporal lobe damage have prosopagnosia as a component. All have bilateral lesions.[15,16] The finding simply underscores the fact that memory processing of the type involved in facial recognition is of crucial importance for the individual and is clearly operated by both hemispheres. This is not to say that the left and right hemispheres perform the task in the same way or equally well. On the contrary, we believe each hemisphere learns, recognizes and recalls faces with different strategies and that the right hemisphere's approach is probably more efficient than the left.   10

THE NATURE OF THE DEFECT

The bizarre nature of prosopagnosia, when it appears in isolation, has prompted all sorts of explanations for the phenomenon. Those who have never seen a prosopagnosic patient may be tempted to dismiss the phenomenon as the result of psychiatric illness or dementia. None of these interpretations obtain, considering that these patients show no evidence of language impairment, have intact cognitive skills and do not have psychiatric symptomatology before or after the onset of prosopagnosia. In his review of the neuropsychological investigation of prosopagnosia, Benton noted how some authors have seen prosopagnosia as a primary perceptual defect that would preclude the analysis and synthesis of complex visual stimuli; how others have postulated an incapacity to perceive individuality within a single class of objects; and yet others have proposed a material specific defect in memory, that is, a defect of integrating current facial percepts with past experience of them.[17]   11

Some of these issues are more clear today. There is substantial evidence against the notion that prosopagnosia is due to a primary perceptual disturbance. Firstly, prosopagnosic patients can discriminate unfamiliar faces well. Some of   12 these patients perform normally in Benton and Van Allen's test of facial discrimination—a difficult task in which they are called to match unfamiliar and differently lit photographs of faces but obviously not asked to recognize any of them[8,17]; they can perform complex visual tasks such as the anomalous contours test and they have normal stereopsis,[8] they can draw accurately complex figures shown in photographs, drawings or in real models[8,17]; more importantly, they can recognize, at a generic level, any visual stimulus provided that no contextual memory cues are required.[6,8] Secondly, severe disorders of visual perception such as seen in patients with Balint syndrome or comparable disorders, do not have prosopagnosia.[7,18,19] Patients with prosopagnosia can perceive and recognize accurately many stimuli that are visually more complex than human faces, i.e., that have a greater number of individual components arranged in just as complicated a manner but crowded in smaller areas or volumes.[8] On the other hand, there is evidence that the particular class of visual stimuli, as well as the ability to integrate facial percepts with pertinent past experience, are important factors in the physiopathology of prosopagnosia. The evidence is as follows.

Prosopagnosia does not occur in relation to human faces alone. All of the   13
patients with prosopagnosia have defects of recognition for other stimuli.[4,6,8] The types of stimuli for which they have agnosia, however, are rather special. They include: (a) automobiles (prosopagnosics cannot recognize their own car and do not recognize different makes of cars; however, these patients can recognize different types of car, such as a passenger car, a fire engine, an ambulance, or a funeral car); (b) clothes of the same type and general shape, i.e. dresses, suits, shirts, etc,; (c) food ingredients with similar forms and volumes; (d) specific animals within a group (a farmer suddenly became unable to recognize, within a herd, specific animals that he could easily recognize before; birdwatchers have become unable to recognize different birds, etc.). In all of these instances, the process of recognition operates normally up to the point in which specific recognition of a given member within the group is required. In other words, all of these patients can recognize an automobile as an automobile, a cow as a cow, or a dress as a dress. They can also recognize all of the subcomponents of these stimuli correctly, i.e. eyes, noses, windshields, wheels, sleeves, etc. But when, as is the case with human faces, the patient is requested to identify precisely the specific possessor of that visual appearance, the process breaks down and the within-class-membership of the stimulus cannot be ascertained.

An analysis of the shared characteristics of the stimuli which can cause   14
prosopagnosia reveals that: (a) these are stimuli for which a specific recognition is mandatory and for which a generic recognition is either socially unacceptable (human faces), or incompatible with normal activity (cars, clothing, foodstuffs); (b) the specific recognition of all of the stimuli depends on contextual (episodic) memory, i.e. it depends on the evocation of multiple traces of memory previously associated with the currently perceived stimulus; those traces depend on

a personal, temporally and spatially bound, memory process; (c) that all of the stimuli belong to groups in which numerous members are physically *similar* (in visual terms), and yet individually *different*; we have designated these stimuli as visually "ambiguous" (an operational definition of visual ambiguity is the presence in a group of numerous *different* members with *similar* visual characteristics). Prosopagnosia patients have no difficulty with the correct, individual recognition of "non-ambiguous" stimuli, i.e. visual stimuli that belong to groups with numerous members but in which *different* individual members have a *different* (distinctive) visual structure.[8]

According to the analysis above, the basic perceptual mechanisms in pro-   15
sopagnosic patients are normal. There is no evidence that the varied partial defects of color, texture or form perception, alone or in combination, can cause prosopagnosia. When patients are called on to recognize stimuli that belong to visually ambiguous classes, they fail to evoke the pertinent, associated traces of contextual memory on the basis of which familiarity and recognition of the stimulus would be based. Seen in this light, the defect must be described, physiopathologically, as a disorder of visually-triggered contextual memory. It is important to distinguish this from a disorder of memory in general (memory traces can be normally activated through other sensory channels) and even from a disorder of visual memory (auditory stimulation can bring forward numerous traces of visual memory testifying to the intactness of many visual memory stores). The malfunction is in the triggering system for the associated evocations. We believe this defect can be explained by one of three possible mechanisms: (1) a defect in the highest level of visual analysis, that which permits the distinction of finest structural details necessary for the separation of visually "ambiguous" stimuli but unnecessary for visually unambiguous ones; (2) a defect of the plotting of the ongoing percept into the pre-existing, templated information, acquired for each specific stimulus (this mechanism would assume the normalcy of the perceptual step referred to above); (3) a defect in the activation of pertinent associated memories occurring after both steps above operate normally. Current research in our laboratory and others is aimed at investigating the validity of these possible mechanisms.

NEW DEVELOPMENTS

Autonomic evidence for non-conscious recognition

One of the intriguing problems posed by visual agnosia and, more generally,   16
by amnesia has to do with the level at which the failure of recognition occurs. Some investigators have hypothesized that the failure to evoke both non-verbal and verbal memories capable of generating recognition, does not preclude some process of recognition at a lower, nonconscious level of processing. In other words, it is possible that some part of the brain does recognize stimulus even if

the subject is not aware of that process taking place. Patients with prosopagnosia are ideal subjects to test this hypothesis and that is what has recently been accomplished using paradigms aimed at detecting autonomic responses to stimuli that patients are clearly not aware of recognizing. In both available studies (Ref. 20 and, Tranel, D. and Damasio, A., *Neurology*, in press), there is persuading evidence that at a nonconscious level, faces of relatives, friends, and self, generated strong psychophysiological responses clearly different from the weak or nonexistent responses to faces unfamiliar to the subject. The implications of this discovery are far-reaching. The findings support the notion that perception and recognition processes evolve by steps and that failure at the top of the cascade does not necessarily imply failure at more elementary levels. On the issue of facial recognition itself, they argue for the existence of a template system for each individual familiar face, and suggest that, at least in some of the patients, such a template system is intact. It is important to note that in our model the template system is not conceived in the Humian sense, as a static facsimile of a given face, but rather as a dynamic, evolving record of computations built on multiple exposure to the stimulus and probably stored at multiple levels of CNS, but especially anchored in visual association cortices.

Ocular motor activity in visual recognition

It has been suggested that patients with prosopagnosia might have an impairment of the proper scanning of the face, a disturbance of the ability to search appropriately for elements crucial to facial perception, i.e. eyes, nose, mouth, hairline, facial contour. A recent study carried out in prosopagnosic patients shows that this is not the case (Rizzo, M., Hurtig, R. and Damasio, A., unpublished observations). Using electro-oculographic techniques the investigators showed that prosopagnosic patients scan fundamental elements of the face as do controls, using a natural progression in their scanning and spending comparable times in the analysis of separate features. The prosopagnosic patients also scan a complex picture (e.g. the Cookie Theft plate from the Boston Diagnostic Battery) in exactly the same manner as controls. Once again, the results lend credence to the notion that basic perception proceeds normally and that prosopagnosic subjects search and accumulate information as do normal individuals but fail, at a later stage, either to bring that information together in an integrated pattern, or to lead the integrated pattern to activate the pertinent associated memories. [17]

Perception of contrast sensitivity in visual agnosia

It has been suggested that object recognition may be especially dependent on the processing of low visuospatial frequencies.[21] It might follow that prosopagnosia would be caused by selective impairment of low spatial frequency vision. A recent study investigated this possibility in a prosopagnosic patient and has [18] revealed exactly the contrary: the patient's processing of low spatial frequencies was intact, entirely comparable to matched controls, while the processing of high spatial frequencies showed a defect (Rizzo, M., Hurtig, R. and Damasio, A., unpublished observations). Further studies are necessary to clarify the role of different spatial frequencies in the recognition of objects and faces, in both normals and agnosics. Nonetheless, there is evidence to suggest that normal facial recognition calls for both low and high visuospatial frequencies.[22]

Cognitive strategies in facial processing

While it is clear that both hemispheres can learn, recognize and recall faces, recent investigations demonstrate that, as one might have expected, the left and the right hemispheres utilize different strategies to accomplish the task. The findings obtained in patients with callosal surgery,[14] or in normals,[23-25] suggest that the right hemisphere of most individuals is likely to be the most efficient processor of faces and of comparable visual stimuli.   19

Studies in animals

The electrophysiological study of neurons responsive to visual stimuli in non-human primates is likely to shed some light on the mechanisms of facial recognition and prosopagnosia. E. T. Rolls and E. Perrett have reported the presence of neurons in the temporal lobe of the monkey that respond powerfully to faces.[28]   20

Antonio R. Damasio
and Betty Redeker

SELECTED REFERENCES

These references work somewhat in the manner of normal footnotes. That is, they are listed roughly in order of their citation in the text. Number 1 is the first cited, and so on, but there are many exceptions to this and sometimes more than one reference is cited as bearing on a particular statement made in the text. The second citation in the text, for instance, is 26, 3, indicating that both references 26 and 3 bear on the issue under discussion. The third citation is numbered 2, the fourth 4, and the fifth is 2 again. This method avoids the needless proliferation of numbers. Why 3 comes before 2, however, is one of the mysteries of science. [Eds.]

1. Bodamer, J. (1947) *Arch. Psychiatr. Nervenkr.* 179, 6–54
2 Hecaen, H. and Angelergues, R. (1962) *Soc. for Inf. Disp. Arch. Neurol.* 7, 92–100
3 Wilbrand, H. (1892) *Deutche Z Nervenheilkd.* 2, 361–387
4 Meadows, J. C. (1974) *J. Neurol. Neurosurg. Psychiatry* 37, 498–501
5 Benson, D., Segarra, J. and Albert, M. L. (1974) *Arch. Neurol. (Chicago)* 30, 307–310

6 Lhermitte, J., Chain, F., Escourolle, R., Ducarne, B. and Pillon, B. (1972) *Rev. Neurol.* 126, 329–346
7 Damasio, A. R. (1985) in *Principles of Behavioral Neurology*, (Mesulam, M. M., ed.), Davis, Philadelphia
8 Damasio, A. R., Damasio, H. and Van Hoesen, G. W. (1982) *Neurology* 32, 331–341
9 Nardelli, E., Buonanno, F., Coccia, G., Fiaschi, A., Terzian, H. and Rizzuto, N. (1982) *Eur. Neurol.* 21, 289–297
10 Brazis, P. W., Biller, J. and Fine, M. (1981) *Neurology* 31, 920
11 Bruyer, R., Laterre, C., Seron, X., Feyereisen, P., Strypstein, E., Pierrard, E. and Rectem, D. (1983) *Brain Cognition* 2, 257–284
12 Whitely, A. M. and Warrington, E. K. (1977) *J. Neurol. Neurosurg. Psychiatry* 40, 395–403
13 Damasio, A. R., Lima, P. A. and Damasio, H. (1975) *Neurology* 25, 89–93
14 Gazzaniga, M. S., Smylie, C. S. (1983) *Ann. Neurol.* 13, 537–540
15 Corkin, S. (1984) *Semin. Neurol.* 4, 249–259
16 Damasio, A. R., Eslinger, P. J., Damasio, H., Van Hoesen, G. W. and Cornell, S. (1985) *Arch. Neurol.* 42, 252–259
17 Benton, A. (1980) *Am. Psychol.* 35, 176–186
18 Meier, M. J. and French, L. A. (1965) *Neuropsychologia* 3, 261–272
19 Orgass, B., Poeck, K., Kerchensteiner, M. and Hartje, W. (1972) *Z. Neurol.* 202, 177–195
20 Bauer, R. M. (1984) *Neuropsychologia* 22, 457–469
21 Ginsburg, A. P. (1980) *Proc. of the Soc. for Inf. Dis.* 21, 219–227
22 Fiorentini, A., Maffei, L. and Sandini, G. (1983) *Perception* 12, 195–201
23 Ellis, H. D. (1983) in *Functions of the Right Cerebral Hemisphere*, (Young, A. W., ed.), Academic Press, London
24 Sergent, J. and Bindra, D. (1981) *Psycol. Bull.* 89, 541–554
25 Warrington, E. K. and James, M. (1967) *Cortex* 3, 317–326
26 Heidenhain, A. (1927) *Monatschr. Psychiatr. Neurol.* 66, 61–116
27 Levy, J., Trevarthen, C. and Sperry, R. W. (1972) *Brain* 95, 61–78
28 Perrett, D. I., Rolls, E. T. and Caan, W. (1982) *Exp. Brain. Res.* 47, 329–342

KNOWLEDGE WITHOUT AWARENESS

[Abstract.] *Prosopagnosia, the inability to recognize visually the faces of familiar persons who continue to be normally recognized through other sensory channels, is caused by bilateral cerebral lesions involving the visual system. Two patients with prosopagnosia generated frequent and large electrodermal skin conductance responses to faces of persons they had previously known but were now unable to recognize. They did not generate such responses to unfamiliar faces. The results suggest that an early step of the physiological process of recognition is still taking place in these patients, without their awareness but with an autonomic index.* [1]

Patients with prosopagnosia are unable to recognize visually the faces of [2] persons they previously knew or ought to have learned without difficulty. They fail to experience any familiarity with those faces, and, even after they recognize the faces through other cues, such as voices, their physiognomies remain meaningless. Prosopagnosia is due to a complete failure to evoke memories pertinent to specific faces or to a defective evocation that fails to reach awareness. The condition is caused by bilateral damage to mesial occipitotemporal cortices or their connections.

Investigators of prosopagnosia have generally relied on the verbal report of   3
the patient's experience as the sole index of recognition, an approach that does not address potential covert processes of which there may be no subjective awareness. In this study we used the electrodermal skin conductance response (SCR) as a dependent measure and found that two prosopagnosic patients generated significantly larger SCR's and responded more frequently to familiar faces than to unfamiliar ones.[1] These results indicate that, despite their inability to experience familiarity with the visual stimulus and to provide verbal evidence of recognition, prosopagnosics still carry out some steps of the recognition process for which there is an autonomic index.

The subjects were two female patients with stable prosopagnosia caused by   4
bilateral occipitotemporal damage, as determined from computerized tomography (CT) and nuclear magnetic resonance (NMR) imaging.[2] We conducted several experiments. In each the patient was shown 50 black-and-white photographs of faces, depicting a full frontal pose on a white background.[3] Forty-two of the faces were of persons entirely unfamiliar to the patient ("nontarget" faces) and eight were of persons with whom the patient was well acquainted ("target" faces). Both subjects were shown two sets of target faces selected from a period preceding the prosopagnosia (these target faces were randomly interspersed among the nontargets). In one of the sets, "family" faces, the target faces included those of the patient herself, family members, and close friends; in the other set, "famous" faces, the targets were famous politicians and actors. Subject 2 was exposed to a third set of target stimuli, "anterograde" faces, in which the targets were persons with whom the patient had had extensive contact since the onset of her illness but not before (physicians, psychologists, and so forth).

The subjects were given two presentations of each of the two sets of stimuli   5
(or three sets, in the case of subject 2). During the first presentation skin conductance was recorded with Ag-AgCl electrodes from the thenar and hypothenar eminences of the nonpreferred hand on a Beckman type RM Dynograph recorder. Slides were presented for 2 seconds at intervals of 20 to 25 seconds. During the first viewing, no response was required of the subject; during the second, she was asked to verbally rate the familiarity of each face.[4] Skin conductance was not recorded during the second presentation.

The results are presented in Table 1. As expected on the basis of her pervasive   6
syndrome, subject 1 showed a complete failure to recognize any of the targets in the family and famous faces sets. Yet not only did she produce more frequent and consistent SCR's to the target stimuli, she also generated larger SCR's to the target faces than to the nontargets. The amplitude data were compared by the Mann-Whitney U test, a nonparametric test that avoids statistical assumptions not fulfilled by the data sets generated in this study. The average SCR

534

Table 1. Skin conductance response and verbal rating data for the two prosopagnosic subjects. For each category of faces (family, famous, and anterograde), two presentations of 8 target and 42 nontarget faces were made. The SCR data are based on the first presentation, while the verbal rating data are based on the second. Values in parentheses are standard deviations.

Sub-ject	First presentation				Second presentation; average verbal rating (4)	
	Stimuli responded to (%)		Average SCR amplitude (μS)		Target	Nontarget
	Target	Non-target	Target	Nontarget		
Family faces						
1	71	12	0.934 (0.723)	0.048 (0.134)	6.0 (0.0)	6.0 (0.0)
2	100	36	1.660 (1.110)	0.146 (0.317)	1.0 (0.0)	5.1 (1.1)
Famous faces						
1	63	12	0.731 (0.652)	0.012 (0.034)	6.0 (0.0)	6.0 (0.0)
2	63	19	1.080 (1.420)	0.022 (0.052)	2.6 (1.9)	5.0 (1.2)
Anterograde faces						
2	75	17	0.345 (0.274)	0.022 (0.060)	4.4 (1.8)	4.6 (1.7)

amplitude for the target faces was significantly larger than that observed for the nontargets for both family faces ($U = 241$, $z = 4.01$, $P < 0.001$) and famous faces ($U = 265.5$, $z = 1.80$, $P < 0.05$).[5]

Subject 2 also evidenced more frequent and significantly larger SCR's to the target stimuli in the family faces ($U = 362$, $z = 4.63$, $P < 0.001$) and famous faces ($U = 204$, $z = 3.19$, $P < 0.001$) sets (Table 1), but, consistent with her lack of retrograde prosopagnosia, she also recognized accurately the familiar faces in these two sets. In the anterograde faces set, however, in which she was not able to recognize the target faces, she again produced more consistent and significantly larger SCR's to the target faces ($U = 283$, $z = 3.95$, $P < 0.001$). Thus this subject also showed a highly accurate autonomic index of recognition of familiar faces, despite a complete inability to experience familiarity with these faces and to recognize them formally.

The dissociation between the absence of an experience of recognition and the positive electrodermal identification may mean that in these subjects an early step of the physiological process of recognition is still taking place, but that the results of its operation are not made available to consciousness. Dissociations between overt recognition and unconscious discrimination of stimuli have been reported.[6] Healthy subjects can show accurate autonomic discrimination of certain target stimuli, even when they are presented in a degraded or camouflaged manner that precludes overt discrimination and identification.[7] There is some parallel between such findings in healthy individuals and the observations described above, even if the mechanisms that lead to failure of recognition are different. Our results are also compatible with those of a recent study of prosopagnosia in a single patient, who showed discriminatory electrodermal responses to correct but not incorrect face-name matches.[8]

We will attempt to interpret this "covert" recognition phenomenon in terms of a model of facial learning and recognition.[9] The model includes step 1, perception; step 2, use of a template system, in which dynamic intramodal records of the elaboration of past visual perceptions of a given face can be aroused by the perception of that face;[10] step 3, activation, in which multiple multimodal memories pertinent to the face are evoked; and step 4, a conscious readout of concomitant evocations that permits an experience of familiarity and either a verbal account of that experience or the performance of nonverbal matching tasks.[11]

Prosopagnosia cannot be explained as being due to an impairment of the basic perceptual step (numerous indices of visual perception are normal, and patients are able to match unfamiliar faces and describe separate visual details of the faces). Nor can it be explained by an impairment of associated memories because they can be easily evoked through other channels. The defect may be explained, however, by an impairment of the activation step, which would either not take place or take place inefficiently. That, in turn, might be due to a dysfunction of the template system, which could be (i) intact but inaccessible to ongoing percepts, (ii) destroyed, or (iii) intact but prevented from activating multimodal memory stores. From the evidence above, it appears that facial templates are intact: the electrodermal "recognition" can be interpreted as being an index of successful matches between percepts, that is, correctly perceived target faces, and templates of those faces. Furthermore, the data on subject 2 suggest that, with respect to newly encountered faces, the process of template formation can proceed automatically in the absence of normal recognition processes.

The prosopagnosia of the two subjects can be viewed as a complete or partial blocking of the activation that normally would be triggered by template matching. From the anatomic specifications of the model,[11] it appears that the blocking occurs either in white matter connections of the occipitotemporal region (linking both visual cortices to anterior temporal cortices, and the latter to multimodal sensory cortices) or in anterior temporal cortices.

According to the model, the findings presuppose the intactness, at least unilaterally, of the primary visual cortex and the inferior and mesial visual association cortex. Anatomic analyses of images of both patients obtained by CT and NMR verify these predictions.[12] It is of great interest that the lesions that block activation of associated memories do not block the autonomic response. The anatomic substrates of the autonomic response remain to be elucidated.

Antonio R. Damasio
and David Tranel

NOTES

1. We previously showed, using the SCR as a dependent measure in neurologically intact subjects, that familiar faces have a notable "signal value" (D. Tranel, D. C. Fowles, A. R. Damasio, *Psychophysiology*, in press).

2. Subject 1 has both anterograde and retrograde prosopagnosia (she cannot recognize any faces that were familiar before the condition developed, including her own, nor has she learned any new faces during the 7 years of her prosopagnosia). She is a 62-year-old, right-handed woman who suffered bilateral strokes involving the occipitotemporal region. The lesion involves the white matter of both occipitotemporal regions but spares the most mesial and rostral regions of the inferior visual association cortex. As determined by a comprehensive neuropsychological assessment, her intellect, language, and visual perception are normal. Subject 2 has anterograde prosopagnosia only (she has not learned any new faces since the onset of her prosopagnosia 3 years ago). She is a 20-year-old, right-handed woman who had herpes simplex encephalitis leading to bilateral lesions of the occipitotemporal region. The lesions are located more anteriorly than in subject 1, so they also spare the mesial and rostral aspects of the inferior visual association cortex. Her language abilities are intact and her visual perception is compatible with normal recognition of faces learned before the onset of her illness.

3. The slides were constructed so that all the faces were of similar size. No slide contained features below the neckline, and no clothing was seen. The nontarget faces were selected so as to be similar to the targets in terms of age range and sex ratio. Brightness, contrast, and resolution were comparable in target and nontarget faces.

4. A six-point rating scale, ranging from "certain familiarity" (1) to "certain unfamiliarity" (6), was used. Ratings of 3 or less indicated some degree of familiarity with, or recognition of, the stimulus; conversely, ratings of 4 or greater indicated that the subject did not recognize the stimulus.

5. All P values are corrected for ties (data points with equal values), as recommended by S. Siegel [*Nonparametric Statistics for the Behavioral Sciences* (McGraw-Hill, New York, 1956), pp. 123–126].

6. J. K. Adams, *Psychol. Bull.* **54**, 383 (1957); M. F. Reiser and J. D. Block, *Psychosom. Med.* **27**, 274 (1965); C. Rousey and P. S. Holzman, *J. Pers. Soc. Psychol.* **6**, 464 (1967).

7. R. S. Lazarus and R. A. McCleary, *Psychol. Rev.* **58**, 113 (1951); R. S. Corteen and B. Wood, *J. Exp. Psychol.* **94**, 308 (1972).

8. The magnitude of the effect was not as large as the one reported here. The paradigm included both visual and verbal information, unlike our paradigms [R. M. Bauer, *Neuropsychologia* **22**, 457 (1984)].

9. A. R. Damasio, H. Damasio, G. W. Van Hoesen, *Neurology* **32**, 331 (1982).

10. The template system, which involves a dynamic process sensitive to the acquisition of new sensory information, permits the categorization of normal percepts according to physical structure. These dynamic templates do not contain information about the identity of a particular face. The latter information is stored not in a single site but rather in various sensory association cortices, including the visual, in both nonverbal and verbal forms. The templates serve as an interface between the repeated perception of a face and the multiple stored traces of information pertinent to the face; that is, the perception of a previously known face matches the respective template system, which in turn activates the pertinent multimodal memory stores.

11. The anatomic substrate of step 1 comprises bilateral visual system structures up to and including the primary visual cortex; the anatomical basis of step 2 is focused on

537

bilateral mesial and inferior visual association cortices; the anatomic basis of step 3 includes bilateral anterior temporal structures, both mesial and lateral, and bilateral association cortices of different sensory modalities.[9] Step 4 depends on the same association cortices.

12. We thank Dr. Hanna Damasio for providing the detailed anatomic analysis of CT and NMR images of the two subjects, Dr. Nelson Butters for referring subject 2 to our center, and Dr. Don Fowles for technical advice. Supported by National Institute of Neurological and Communicative Disorders and Stroke program project grant NS 19632-02.

* To whom correspondence should be addressed.

QUESTIONS

1. Define prospopagnosia. In your own words, explain what is known about this ailment. Why are scientists interested in it?

2. What causes prosopagnosia? How do we know this?

3. The second of these two essays is cast in the form of an argument asserting that a certain experiment proves something about the way prosopagnosia works and the way the human mind processes particular kinds of data. Paraphrase the argument in your own words.

4. The first selection on prosopagnosia is a review of research on the subject. Analyze how it is organized. Divide the text into sections, and explain their functions. How do you account for the order or arrangement of the sections?

5. These two selections use different types of citations or annotations. Describe as accurately as you can the two different methods. What seems to be the function of each?

6. Like most scientific essays, these two are each preceded by an abstract or synopsis. Why do you suppose this is the case? Considering the first essay, what does the full text provide that is not in the abstract?

7. Discuss the relationship between the style of these essays (format, vocabulary, sentence structure, and so on) and the audience for whom they were written. Does audience always have an effect on style? Explain why or why not.

8. Using the first essay as a model, write a review of research about a topic in a field you know something about.

9. Drawing upon both of these essays, write a description and explanation of prosopagnosia that can be understood by a broad audience, as in a Sunday newspaper supplement or newsmagazine, for instance.

10. As in the second of these two essays, write an explanation of some scientific experiment you know about or some experiment you have performed in a science class. Write as if you were reporting on the first occasion of such an experiment. That is, describe the experiment, draw conclusions, and note further implications of that experiment. Assume that you are addressing other scientists in the same field of study.

WRITING SUGGESTIONS
FOR EXPLAINING

1. Consider Frances FitzGerald's "America Revised" in the light of Edward Hallett Carr's discussion of a historical fact. Is what FitzGerald observes essentially the shifting agreement among historians as to what are historical facts? Write an essay in which you consider the extent to which FitzGerald's evidence illustrates Carr's points. Does it illustrate anything else besides?

2. In the first part of Explaining are several essays that deal with sport and art. Using these essays as the basis of your discussion, write an essay in which you explain the relationship between sport and art. Define, illustrate, compare, contrast, and reach a conclusion about the extent to which sport and art resemble or differ from one another.

3. Do social scientists and physical or biological scientists think and write in the same way (all being scientists) or in different ways (social and physical or biological)? Using at least two essays from each of the last two parts of Explaining, take a position on this question. Explain how these different scientists investigate and explain things in their fields. Try to include some discussion of the ways in which they write their reports and explanations.

4. Two essays in Explaining address directly the fundamental problems of their disciplines: Edward Hallet Carr on history and Michael Guillen on mathematics. Taking these two essays as your point of departure, discuss the differences and similarities between scientific and humanistic thought. Your aim is not to evaluate these two modes but to describe and account for the most significant differences between these fields of study. Refer to other essays from Explaining whenever they are appropriate to your discussion.

5. In "The Cultural Importance of Art," Susanne Langer defines art and discusses its function. Using her essay as a source of concepts to be tested and developed or modified, consider other explanations of specific arts, such as Gombrich's, Kennedy's, and Wilson's. Try to reach some conclusions of your own about the nature and purposes of art.

6. What does it mean to be human? Taking into account several essays such as those by Horney, Bettelheim, Kübler-Ross, Lifton, and Milgram, define the range of human possibilities. What are the central qualities of humanity? And what are the limits, the boundaries? You may wish to consider the essays of Kennedy and Gould as well, with respect to the way that creatures like King Kong and Mickey Mouse help us to define what is human.

7. The view of boxing presented by Joyce Carol Oates is related to the views of other sports and of films like *King Kong* presented in the two essays that precede hers. Compare and contrast either Kennedy's or Ross's essay with hers with respect to conclusions and strategies. That is, compare the main point of each essay with that of the other, and also consider the methods used (definitions, analogies, contrasts, analysis, statistics, personal experience and testimony, and so on). Looking at both essays, what are the common features and significant differences?

8. Miller and Swift's "Women and Names" and Coward's "Let's Have a Meal Together" both express a "feminist" viewpoint. Write an essay in which you define feminism and explain what you take to be its aims, using as evidence these two essays and any other specific examples that you can cite. You might consider such subjects as what feminism is, what motivates feminists, what feminist goals are, what feminist methods are, and what differences of attitude and approach you can find within feminism. Base your generalizations on examples, not on your own feelings about what feminism ought or ought not to be. Explanation, not argument, should be your aim. Emphasize description, not evaluation.

9. Discuss the uses of analogy and distinction (or comparison and contrast) in humanistic explanation. Illustrate your discussion with examples of analogies, comparisons, or contrasts drawn from several essays such as those by Kennedy, Ross, Oates, Jeans, and Crick.

10. Use Frances FitzGerald's "America Revised" and Theodore Sizer's "What High School Is" to stimulate your memory. Write an essay in which you discuss what you learned in high school from books, from teachers, or from others. Try to explain what learning is and how it works, or fails to work, in our schools.

ARGUING

ARGUING

Here in "Arguing" you will find authors taking positions on a wide range of controversial subjects—from the nature of faith to the origins of war, from the behavior of monkeys to the quality of *E.T.* No matter what their academic fields or professions, these authors energetically defend their stands on the issues and questions they address. But this should come as no surprise. None of us, after all, holds lightly to our beliefs and ideas about what is true or beautiful or good. Indeed, most of us get especially fired up when our views are pitted against the ideas and beliefs of others. So you will find these authors vigorously engaged in the give-and-take of argument. And as a consequence, you will repeatedly find yourself having to weigh the merits of competing positions in a debate or disagreement about some controversial issue.

The distinctive quality of arguing can be seen in the following passage from Margaret Mead's "Warfare: An Invention—Not a Biological Necessity":

> Is war a biological necessity, a sociological inevitability or just a bad invention? Those who argue for the first view endow man with such pugnacious instincts that some outlet in aggressive behavior is necessary if man is to reach full human stature. . . . Then there are those who take the second view: warfare is the inevitable concomitant of the development of the state, the struggle for land and natural resources of class societies springing, not from the nature of man, but from the nature of history. . . .
>
> One may hold a compromise position between these two extremes; one may claim that all aggression springs from the frustration of man's biologically determined drives and that, since all forms of culture are frustrating, it is certain each new generation will be aggressive and the aggression will find its natural and inevitable expression in race war, class war, nationalistic war, and so on.
>
> All three positions are very popular today among those who think seriously about the problems of war and its possible prevention, but I wish to urge another point of view, less defeatist perhaps than the first and third, and more accurate than the second: that is, that warfare, by which I mean organized conflict between two groups *as groups* . . . is an invention like any other of the inventions in terms of which we order our lives, such as writing, marriage, cooking our food instead of eating it raw, trial by jury, or burial of the dead, and so on.

This passage comes from the opening of a piece in which Mead attempts to prove that warfare is an invention and that as such it can be overcome by the development of new and better inventions which will render it obsolete. In taking this view of warfare, Mead realizes that she is at odds with many others "who think seriously about the problems of war and its possible prevention." Given the significant disagreements that exist between her view and the views of others, she is not free just to make a straightforward case for her own position on the matter. She must instead contend with her opponents, refuting their positions while also providing evidence in support of her own. She is, in short, engaged in arguing. And the argumentative situation is immediately reflected in the title of her piece, in its opening question, and in the debatelike structure of the paragraphs that follow. Accordingly, Mead begins by identifying the views of her opponents ("those who argue for the first view," "those who take the second view," and those who take "a compromise position between these two extremes"). Then she moves to counterstatements intended to refute the opposition ("but I wish to urge another point of view"). This debate continues throughout the piece, as Mead acknowledges the most important counterattacks of her opponents and answers them with her own. So it is that argument puts ideas to the test by forcing them to stand up against opposing beliefs or theories.

As this passage also reveals, argument naturally arises over significant issues or questions that are open to sharply differing points of view. Questions about the origin of war, for example, are of crucial interest to persons in a wide range of fields—not only to anthropologists such as Mead, but also to historians, philosophers, political scientists, psychologists, and sociologists, as well as to diplomats, politicians, and military leaders. And persons from these fields might well be inclined to approach the question from markedly different points of view that involve different assumptions as well as different bodies of knowledge and experience. Many psychologists, for example, do regard war as an inescapable consequence of man's "pugnacious instincts," while many political scientists, given their specialized point of view, look upon war as "the inevitable concomitant of the development of the state." Mead, by contrast, given her anthropological orientation, believes that the problem can be illuminated by examining a wide variety of cultures, especially those in which warfare does not exist. Each point of view necessarily leads to substantially different claims about the origin of war, and none of the claims can be conclusively proven to be true. Indeed, if conclusive evidence had existed for one view or another, the argument would never have arisen, or it would have been resolved as quickly as the evidence had been discovered. So, like all controversial issues, the question remains open to debate, and anyone involved in such an argument can at best hope to make a persuasive case for a particular viewpoint—a case that will move thoughtful readers to consider that position seriously and possibly even convince them to accept it.

As readers of argumentative writing, we in turn should try to be as impartial as the members of a jury. We should try to set aside any biases or prejudices that we might have about one view or another. Then, we should weigh all the evidence, logic, claims, and appeals for each viewpoint before arriving at a decision about which one we find most convincing. By the same token, as writers of argument we should assume that readers are not likely to be persuaded by a one-sided view of a complex situation. Thus we should be ready to present a case that not only will support our position but will respond to the crucial challenges of views that differ from our own. Both as readers and writers, then, we should strive to understand the balanced methods of persuasion that can be found throughout the broad range of argumentative writing.

THE RANGE OF ARGUMENTATIVE WRITING

Argumentative writing so pervades our lives that we may not even recognize it as such in the many brochures and leaflets that come our way, urging us to vote for one candidate rather than another or to support one cause rather than another. Argumentative writing also figures heavily in newspaper editorials, syndicated columns, and letters to the editor, which are typically given over to debating the pros and cons of one public issue or another, from local taxes to national defense policies. Argument, of course, is fundamental in the judicial process, providing as it does the basic procedure for conducting all courtroom trials. And it is crucial in the legislative process, for it offers a systematic means of exploring the strengths and weaknesses of different proposed policies and programs. In a similar way, argument serves the basic aims of the academic world, enabling different ideas and theories to be tested by pitting them against each other. Whatever the field or profession, argument is an important activity in the advancement of knowledge and society.

The broad range of argumentative writing may conveniently be understood by considering the kinds of issues and questions that typically give rise to disagreement and debate. Surely, the most basic sources of controversy are questions of fact—the who, what, when, and where of things, as well as how much. Questions such as these are most commonly at issue in criminal trials. But intense arguments over questions of fact can also develop in any academic or professional field, especially when the facts in question have a significant bearing on the explanation or judgment of a particular subject, body of material, or type of investigation. In "The Hundredth Monkey Phenomenon," for example, Ron Amundson vigorously challenges the "remarkable and paranormal claims" of several authors who have written about the development of a "group consciousness" among disparate groups of monkeys living on various islands in Japan. Amundson systematically refutes the factual accuracy of their claims, not only because he is interested in getting at the truth about these particular monkeys, but more importantly because as a philosopher of science he is committed to defining, documenting, and exposing the flawed "methodology of pseudoscience." So, in a very real sense, the argument in this piece arises over questions of fact as well as questions of how to interpret the facts.

545

Even when there is no question about the facts themselves, there are likely to be arguments about how to explain the facts. Disagreements of this kind abound across the full range of academic and professional fields. And the arguments inevitably arise out of sharply differing points of view on the facts as we have already seen in the case of Mead's piece about the origin of war. As her piece makes clear, everyone appears to agree that war has existed throughout much of human history, and everyone appears to agree that the causes must in some sense be attributable to human beings. But the exact senses in which human beings are responsible remain open to debate. So, Mead and her opponents approach the facts from sharply differing explanatory viewpoints, and an argument naturally ensues.

Differing viewpoints, of course, ultimately reflect differing beliefs and values. The way we view any particular subject is, after all, a matter of personal choice, an outgrowth of what our experience and knowledge have led us to hold as being self-evident. In this sense, beliefs and values are always to some extent at issue in any argumentative situation, even when they remain more or less in the background. But in some cases the conflicting values themselves are so clearly at the heart of the argument that they become the direct focus of the debate. For example, in "Why Are Americans Afraid of Dragons?" Ursula Le Guin opposes what she calls the "antifantasy" views of Americans with a sustained argument on behalf of fantastic literature. In order to do so she is compelled to make a case for the value of the imagination itself and for the qualities she attributes to it, such as "the free play of the mind":

> To be free, after all, is not to be undisciplined. I should say that the discipline of the imagination may in fact be the essential method or technique of both art and science. It is our Puritanism, insisting that discipline means repression or punishment, which confuses the subject. To discipline something, in the proper sense of the word, does not mean to repress it, but to train it—to encourage it to grow, and act, and be fruitful, whether it is a peach tree or a human mind.

In order to support her position here, Le Guin directly challenges one of the major assumptions of the opposing value structure—namely, a belief that the freedom of imaginative activity is at odds with the virtue of discipline. And she challenges this belief in a highly imaginative series of intellectual maneuvers—first by conceiving of the imagination itself as a "discipline," then by claiming this discipline to be "essential" to "both art and science," then by defining discipline as a form of training rather than repression, and finally by embodying this idea of discipline in the form of a highly appealing metaphor that links the fruitfulness of a trained peach tree with that of a carefully trained human mind. Thus in the imaginative way that she makes her case, Le Guin enables us to witness the rigorous discipline of the imagination.

Le Guin's argument also enables us to see that conflicts over beliefs and values can have an important bearing on questions of policy and planning.

Imagine, for example, how our educational system might be designed and operated if it were based on her belief "that the discipline of the imagination may in fact be the essential method or technique of both art and science." Though Le Guin does not map a new educational system in her piece, she evidently conceives of fantastic literature and other works of the imagination as being fundamental to the development of healthy human minds. For a clear-cut example of how conflicts over belief lead to debates over policy, you need only look at Lewis Thomas's "The Art of Teaching Science." In the early section of his piece, Thomas challenges conventional beliefs about the certitude of scientific knowledge with his claim that "The conclusions reached in science are always, when looked at closely, far more provisional and tentative than are most of the assumptions arrived at by our colleagues in the humanities." Based on this and related claims, Thomas then proceeds in the later portions of his piece to outline a completely new method of teaching science:

> I suggest that the introductory courses in science, at all levels from grade school through college, be radically revised. Leave the fundamentals, the so-called basics, aside for a while, and concentrate the attention of all students on the things that are not known. . . .
>
> At the outset, before any of the fundamentals, teach the still imponderable puzzles of cosmology. Describe as clearly as possible, for the youngest minds, that there are some things going on in the universe that lie still beyond comprehension, and make it plain how little is known.

Introductory science teachers might not respond too favorably to this proposal, especially since it would oblige them to deal "systematically with ignorance in science." But can you imagine what it would be like to take such a course? Can you imagine how such courses might influence the thinking of future scientists? Can you imagine how such a proposal might affect our contemporary attitudes towards science? None of these questions, of course, can be answered with certitude, for certainty is not possible in deliberations about the future. But Thomas does attempt to address these and other such questions since, in arguing on behalf of a proposal for change, he is obligated to explore the possible consequences of his proposed change.

Just as his argument for a new mode of scientific education requires Thomas to consider and defend the possible effects of his proposed change, so every other kind of question imposes on writers a particular set of argumentative obligations. Le Guin's argument in favor of fantasy, for example, obliges her to defend the value of the imagination, and Mead's anthropological account of warfare compels her to show that "there are peoples even today who have no warfare." A writer who aims to be persuasive cannot simply assert that something is or is not the case, for readers in general are not willing to be bullied, hoodwinked, or otherwise manipulated into accepting a particular claim. But they are capable of being reached by civilized and rational methods of persuasion that are appropriate to controversial issues—by evidence, logic, and eloquence.

METHODS OF ARGUING

In any piece of argumentative writing, no matter what field or subject it concerns, your primary purpose is to bring readers around to your point of view rather than another. Some readers, of course, will agree with you in advance, but others will disagree, and still others will be undecided. So, in planning a piece of argumentative writing, you should begin by examining your material with an eye to discovering the issues that have to be addressed and the points that have to be made in order to present your case most persuasively to readers, especially those who oppose you or who are undecided. This means that you will have to deal not only with issues that you consider relevant but also with matters that have been raised by your opponents. In other words, you will have to show readers that you have taken both sides of the controversy into account. In arguing about the origin of war, for example, Mead repeatedly takes into account the views of her opponents, even to the point of imagining how they might question the evidence she cites and then answering their hypothetical objections. Likewise, Thomas not only presents his method of teaching science but also seeks to refute the premises upon which the existing methods are based.

After you have identified the crucial points to be addressed, then you should decide upon the methods that will be necessary to make a convincing case with respect to each of the points. Some methods, of course, are imperative no matter what point you are trying to prove. Every piece of argumentation requires that you offer readers appropriate and sufficient evidence to support your position. To do so, you will need to gather and present specific details that bear on each of the points you are trying to make. This basic concern for providing readers with convincing evidence will lead you inevitably into the activity of reporting. Mead, for example, reports on a variety of different cultures to show that warfare is not a universal pattern of behavior but an invention limited to particular peoples; Le Guin reports conversations to illustrate the American fear of fantasy; and Thomas reports a striking array of unsolved scientific questions to demonstrate the scope of scientific ignorance. Reporting appropriate evidence constitutes the most basic means of making a persuasive case for any point under consideration. So, any point for which evidence cannot be provided, or for which only weak or limited evidence can be offered, is likely to be much less convincing to readers than one that can be amply and vividly substantiated.

But evidence alone will not be persuasive to readers unless it is brought to bear on a point in a clearly logical way. So evidence ordinarily goes hand in hand with some kind of logic, some method of reasoning, to produce a convincing conclusion. In one of its most familiar forms, known as *induction*, logic involves the process of moving from bits of evidence to a generalization that is based upon them. Margaret Mead, for example, gathers evidence from several different cultures, some "simple," others "civilized," some natively "mild and meek," others "turbulent and troublesome." And she not only finds examples of each type that possess the "idea of warfare," but she also discovers examples of each type that do not possess the "idea of warfare." So this particular set of evidence leads her to formulate the generalization that warfare is neither inherent in human nature nor the outgrowth of political development but is instead an invention of particular peoples. Her generalization in this case is highly reasonable, but like virtually all generations it is a hypothesis and not a certainty. In order to prove it beyond any doubt, Mead would have had to examine every culture in the world and consider every possible reason for the presence or absence of warfare in each of these manifold cultures—clearly an impossible task for anyone to perform. So, she has no choice but to make what is known as an inductive leap from a reasonable, but necessarily limited, body of evidence to a generalization. So, too, her generalization is at best a statement of probability.

Mead's argument also relies on another familiar type of logic, known as *deduction*, which involves the movement from general assumptions or hypotheses to particular conclusions that can be derived from them. For example, having arrived at the generalization that war is an invention, Mead then combines this proposition with another generalization, namely, that defective inventions and practices will usually be superseded by better ones. She thereby is able to reach the conclusion that warfare can be overcome by inventing better forms of behavior that will make it obsolete. Given her generalizations about war and about inventions, her deduction about overcoming war seems to be a logical conclusion, as indeed it is. But like most cases of deductive logic, her conclusion is only as solid and as convincing as the premises on which it is based. So, it is especially important here, as in any case of deduction, to check the premises in order to discover just how sturdy they actually are.

As we have already noted, Mead's proposition about war being an invention is a reasonable generalization, but just the same it is only a hypothesis which is at odds with other hypotheses about the nature and origin of war. Her proposition about defective inventions being superseded by better ones seems on the face of it to make sense and to be true to general experience. But like most commonsensical propositions, it is the product of reasoning by analogy—in particular, that better inventions might be devised to supersede warfare, much as trial by jury replaced trial by combat or as the automobile replaced the horse and buggy. Warfare, of course, is hardly the same kind of invention as the automobile or as trial by jury. Given these tenuous analogies, her conclusion in turn is bound to be somewhat tenuous. And yet in other respects, her position is so appealing and she argues it so adeptly that it deserves our thoughtful consideration.

As you can see from the case of Mead, logical reasoning takes a variety of common forms—inductive, deductive, and analogical. And all of these forms are likely to be present in subtle and complicated ways in virtually every piece of argumentative writing. For arguing calls upon writers to be especially re-

549

sourceful in developing and presenting their positions. Actually, logic is a nec-essary—and powerful—tool in every field and profession because it serves to fill in gaps where evidence does not exist or, as in a court case, to move beyond the accumulated evidence to conclusions that follow from it. But like any pow-erful tool it must be used with care. One weak link in a logical chain of reasoning can lead, after all, to a string of falsehood.

Some situations, of course, do not call for logic so much as for an eloquent appeal to the basic truths of human experience. When Le Guin challenges the American distrust of fantasy, as we have seen, she does not rely on an abstract chain of reasoning but on the powerful appeal of a vivid metaphor that embodies "the discipline of the imagination" in the fruitfulness of a peach tree. And when she argues for the enduring value of fantasy, she does not simply assert it as such. Instead she invokes a powerful image to suggest the disturbing conse-quences of thwarting the human need for it.

> I believe that all the best faculties of a mature human being exist in the child, and that if these faculties are encouraged in youth they will act well and wisely in the adult, but if they are repressed and denied in the child they will stunt and cripple the adult personality.

Surely, as she knows, we would all prefer to be fruitful rather than stunted or crippled. Some beliefs, after all, are so unmistakably true to general human experience that a universal image or metaphor is the most fitting way to remind readers of their truth.

Explanatory techniques, such as those we discussed in our introduction to the preceding section, also can play a role in argument, as you may already have noticed from your own reading of the passages we have just been discussing. Mead's argument about warfare, for example, is based on a comparison and contrast of its status in a variety of different cultures. And Le Guin's attack on the American distrust of fantasy relies on a strategic use of definition when she asserts that "To discipline something, in the proper sense of the word, does not mean to repress it, but to train it. . . ." Any piece of argument, in other words, is likely to draw upon a wide range of techniques, for argument at last is always attempting to achieve the complex purpose not only of getting at the truth about something, and making that truth intelligible to readers, but also of persuading them to accept it as such.

No matter what particular combination of techniques a writer favors, you will probably find that most authors, when carrying out an argument, save a very telling point or bit of evidence or a well-turned phrase for last. Like effective storytellers or successful courtroom lawyers, they know that a memorable detail makes for a powerful climax. In the twenty-seven pieces that follow in this section, you will get to see how different writers use the various resources of language to produce some very striking and compelling pieces of argument.

Arts and Humanities

TWO REVIEWS OF *E.T.*
David Denby
George F. Will

David Denby regularly reviews movies for New York *magazine. George F. Will (b. 1941), a former professor of philosophy, is a nationally syndicated Pulitzer Prize-winning columnist for the* Washington Post. *He also writes a biweekly column for* Newsweek, *which is where this review of E.T. first appeared in July 1982. Denby's column appeared in* New York *in June 1982. While both Denby and Will agree that E.T. is a joy to watch, their interpretations of that joy are quite different.*

THE VISIONARY GLEAM

Steven Spielberg's *E.T., the Extra-Terrestrial* is one of the most beautiful fantasy-adventure movies ever made—a sublimely witty and inventive fable that goes so deep into the special alertness, loyalty, and ardor of children that it makes you see things you had forgotten or blotted out and feel things you were embarrassed to feel. Watching it, children will be in heaven; adults, I think, will be moved by how funny, even hip, innocence can be. You may wonder how so commercial a work can be innocent, but Spielberg has pulled it off: He's used his fabulous technique and boundless savvy to create the ecstasy of first responses, when friendship, danger, the physical world itself strike the child as awesome, revelatory. It's a Wordsworthian science-fiction movie.[1]   1

After the frantic aridities of *1941* and the entertaining but soulless high jinks   2
of *Raiders of the Lost Ark*, the director has returned to the beatific mood of

---

[1]William Wordsworth (1770–1850): British Romantic poet who wrote of "that dreamlike vividness and splendor which invest objects of sight in childhood." [Eds.]

Close Encounters of the Third Kind. The new movie is a heart-wrenching elaboration of that moment at the end of *Close Encounters* when the awkward little
creature moves down the runway of its spaceship in a column of overpowering
light and raises its palms in greeting.

The premise of *E.T.* is simple. Accidentally left behind by outer-space vis-   3
itors, a smallish, green-brown creature, brilliant but physically vulnerable, takes
refuge in the bedroom of a ten-year-old boy in the California suburbs. The boy,
Elliott (Henry Thomas), aided by his big brother, Michael (Robert Macnaugh-
ton), and his gravely beautiful little sister, Gertie (Drew Barrymore), secretly
cares for the extraterrestrial (E.T. for short) as if it were a peculiarly intelligent
wild animal—feeding it, protecting it from shadowy scientific authorities, and
finally helping it in its quest to return home, where it must go if it is to survive.

In outline, the plot may seem familiar, since there are many echoes in it of   4
such classic animal-and-child stories as *The Black Stallion* and *The Yearling*, as
well as a large infusion of *Peter Pan*. But Spielberg and screenwriter Melissa
Mathison (who worked on the script of *The Black Stallion*) have worked out the
story with astounding moment-by-moment physical and emotional detail: Even
such spellbinders as J. M. Barrie, Marjorie Kinnan Rawlings, and Disney himself might have been impressed.[2] It's been years since I've been this caught up
in the emotions of a movie.

Nearly everyone has had the experience of lying on the grass on a clear night,   5
looking up at the sky and feeling not only amazement but also a sense of
anticipation, the conviction that something overwhelming was about to happen.
Spielberg is the master of this hushed, awed mood of imminence, and he always
delivers what he has promised. Spielberg makes physical beauty dramatically
exciting; he has a kinetic sense of detail. His characteristic visual style (Allen
Daviau is the cinematographer here) depends on a stealthily moving camera
and shafts of dazzling white light against darkness—light as power and intelligence.

The opening of *E.T.* is both majestic and witty—a true Spielberg combi-   6
nation. Having landed in a dark forest of redwoods and firs, the outer-space
creatures quietly explore, taking specimens, talking to one another in their
strange, snuffling language. The details are exquisite: Long brown fingers delicately uproot a plant; immense redwoods in parallel columns, seen from the
creatures' point of view, stretch endlessly upward; in the valley below, a flat
California valley community glistens and hums in the night. As a group of
men—scientists probably, looking for the spaceship—drive up violently in their
cars and trucks, Spielberg holds the aliens' point of view, keeping the camera
low, in the bushes. We never see the men's faces; the scientists are embodied

---

[2]James Matthew Barrie (1860–1937): British writer best known for his play *Peter Pan* (1904);
Marjorie Kinnan Rawlings (1896–1953): American writer who won the Pulitzer Prize for her novel
The Yearling (1938); Walt Disney (1901–1966): creator of animated cartoon characters such as
Mickey Mouse (b. 1928). [Eds.]

by the light—first headlights, then superpowered flashlights moving around in the dark like tracer bullets. One little gremlin, tearing through the bushes, emits a panicked noise somewhere between a squeal and a honk, and gets left aground as the spaceship takes off.

From the beginning, then, we are plunged into an entirely physical, almost visceral experience of the story, accomplished without obvious scare tactics. All the excitement is fully earned—it is dramatized from the inside, as experience, and not felt merely as the usual cinematic assault on the senses. Spielberg charges every scene with eccentric movement, but nothing is rushed or forced. When Elliott lures the gremlin into his house, Spielberg finally unveils his incomparable toy. This lifelike brown rubber thing is the finest creation of Carlo Rambaldi, who also constructed the 1976 King Kong and the earlier Spielberg extraterrestrials. Squat, a waddler with horny feet, it has long arms that touch the ground, a long neck that extends in moments of panic. Rambaldi has made it comical-looking, slightly grotesque, but not frightening: He's given it beautiful liquid eyes that dilate with emotion. And Spielberg has given it a personality— grave, tender, quietly sad, and utterly benevolent. A dignified, rather conservative man of feeling (one can imagine E.T. as editor of *The New Yorker*), it pulsates and makes sympathetic noises—murmurs and groans—when other people are hurt. In Elliott's robe, it shuffles off to the kitchen, looking like an elderly visiting uncle who stayed through the winter.

In the past, most directors have made aliens threatening, even terrifying. Spielberg's gentler conception, in which the extraterrestrials find *us* alien, is infinitely more fun. When little Gertie sees E.T. in her brother's bedroom, she screams "Eek!" and E.T. screams back, neck craning, long fingers held up in protest against this small blond thing with pink yarn in her hair. For Gertie, E.T. is a part of the world of toys and dolls and magical bedtime stories, and she quickly accepts it, dressing it up in a blond wig and bracelets, chattering away at it as it follows her around the kitchen. Tiny Drew Barrymore (John's granddaughter) is a very positive child with a natural gravity that becomes increasingly comical. Spielberg performs miracles with her and with Henry Thomas, whose arched eyebrows give him a look of devilish intelligence.

In those classic animal tales, children have special qualities of mind and character—generosity, concern—that adults don't have, and that is part of the reason the animals come to them. From the beginning, Elliott feels he has been chosen by E.T., and he takes the responsibility of introducing him to an entire civilization—in his bedroom. Elliott, who sends a toy shark chasing after a real goldfish (E.T. stares in grave wonder) and who presents a little metal car as a means of human locomotion, doesn't always distinguish between real objects and their representation. He's still learning, while E.T. is trying to decode an entire way of life. For a magical moment, they occupy the same place, communicating haphazardly, confusingly, but ecstatically. Their empathy is so great that when E.T. chugs down a couple of beers, Elliott, at school miles

553

away, belches loudly and casts lewd, drunken looks at the girl across the aisle. Like every great fantasist, Spielberg extends his premises in strictly logical fashion until they attain the surreal. In several sequences, he moves into new areas of wild inventiveness that parallel, in popular and largely benevolent rather than macabre terms, what some of the great surrealists have done.

What fuses the movie's separate moods is Spielberg and Mathison's passionate child partisanship. In *Peter Pan*, the children's special world was held together, in part, by the adults' inability to see Peter and Tinker Bell—a metaphor of Barrie's for adult insensitivity. In *E.T.*, the filmmakers work out the same idea in slapstick terms. The children's lovely mother (Dee Wallace), preoccupied with her own concerns, doesn't see the grotesque E.T. lying among the large teddy bears and other stuffed animals in the closet. She's merely busy and oblivious, but the other adults, all faceless, are presented as children's nightmare figures. The scientists who have been lurking in vans outside Elliott's house, spying and eavesdropping, finally crash in wearing frightening space suits. They wear the heavy gear, it turns out, to prevent themselves from contaminating E.T., yet Spielberg sustains, almost to the end, the children's view of them as sinister (doomy drumbeats accompany their entrance). The point of shooting them that way is that all their science and technology can't match what the children's love has done for E.T. 10

The poetic logic of animal stories requires that the horse, dog, or lion finally "return to the wild," and that the child, who has created a private world with it, learn to accept the separation—in other words, he begins to acknowledge that he must grow up. The filmmakers make this resolution even more wrenching than usual by having the three children fight so hard to get the sickly E.T. home; out of love, they fight against their own desires to hold on to him forever. In the last 40 minutes or so, Spielberg exhibits such a powerful grip on the audience's emotions (I have never seen so many grown men weeping at a screening) that some will accuse him of manipulation or even sadism. On the contrary, I welcome this return to the honorable emotional fullness that was taken for granted in movies of the thirties and forties (in, say, *Captains Courageous* and *How Green Was My Valley*). 11

Even when Spielberg is squeezing us for tears, there's eccentric detail to marvel at. The impromptu hospital the scientists set up in Elliott's house is a terrifying white hell of milky plastic walls; the long translucent tunnel they stretch from the house to a waiting van is like a gigantic snake. Spielberg incorporates the tunnel in a terrific chase at the end that features a pack of boys on bikes splitting apart and shooting over hills like separate streams of water. His visual imagination never falters. At one point, as John Williams's music rises in triumph, Spielberg sends Elliott and E.T. riding a bicycle across the face of the moon, an image that recalls, in its mixture of homeliness and exuberance, the very origins of cinematic fantasy in Georges Méliès A *Trip to* 12 *the Moon*, from 1902.[3] Just like those early audiences, the millions who see *E.T.* will stay rooted to their seats, astonished at what the movies can do.

David Denby

WELL, *I* DON'T LOVE YOU, E.T.

The hot breath of summer is on America, but few children feel it. They are 1 indoors, in the dark, watching the movie *E.T.* and being basted with three subversive ideas:

Children are people.

Adults are not.

Science is sinister.

The first idea amounts to counting chickens before they are hatched. The 2 second is an exaggeration. The third subverts what the movie purports to encourage: a healthy capacity for astonishment.

The yuckiness of adults is an axiom of children's cinema. And truth be told, 3 adults are, more often than not, yucky. That is because they are human, a defect they share with their pint-size detractors. (A wit once said that children are natural mimics who act like their parents in spite of all efforts to teach them good manners.) Surely children are unmanageable enough without gratuitously inoculating them with anti-adultism. Steven Spielberg, the perpetrator of *E.T.*, should be reminded of the charge that got Socrates condemned to drink hemlock: corrupting the youth of Athens.

It is not easy to corrupt American youth additionally. Geoffrey Will, 8, like 4 all younger brothers in the theater, swooned with pleasure while sitting next to his censorious father watching the little boy in *E.T.* shout across the dinner table at the big brother: "Shut up, penis breath!" *E.T.* has perfect pitch for child talk at its gamiest. Convincing depictions of a child's-eye view of the world are rare. George Eliot's "The Mill on the Floss" and Henry James's "What Maisie Knew" are two. But those delicate sensibilities could not have captured the scatological sounds of young American male siblings discussing their differences.

Ethnocentric: I feel about children expressing themselves the way Wellington 5 felt about soldiers.[1] He even disapproved of soldiers cheering, because cheering is too nearly an expression of opinion. The little boy in *E.T.* did say something neat: "How do you explain school to a higher intelligence?" The children who popped through C. S. Lewis's wardrobe into Narnia never said anything that penetrating.[2] Still, the proper way to converse with a young person is:

---

[3]George Méliès (1861–1938): French magician who became a film producer-writer-director. [Eds.]

[1]Wellington: Arthur Wellesley (1769–1852), British soldier and statesman, held the title First Duke of Wellington. [Eds.]

[2]C. S. Lewis (1898–1963): English writer whose *The Lion, the Witch and the Wardrobe* is the first of the seven volumes of the *Chronicles of Narnia*. [Eds.]

YOUNG PERSON: What's that bird?
OLDER PERSON: It's a guillemot.[3]
YOUNG PERSON: That's not my idea of a guillemot.
OLDER PERSON: It's God's idea of a guillemot.

I assume every American has spent the last month either in line to see, or 6
seeing, *E.T.* In the first month it earned $100 million—$17.5 million during
the Fourth of July weekend. But in case you have been spelunking beneath
Kentucky since May,[4] *E.T.* is about an extraterrestrial creature left behind in a
California suburb when his buddies blast off for home. He is befriended by a
boy in the American manner: the boy tosses a ball to E.T. and E.T. chucks it
back.

It is, I suppose, illiberal and—even more unforgivable—ethnocentric (or, in 7
this case, speciescentric) to note that E.T. is not just another pretty face. E.T.
looks like a stump with a secret sorrow. (Except to another E.T. As Voltaire
said,[5] to a toad, beauty is popeyes, a yellow belly and spotted back.) E.T. is a
brilliant, doe-eyed, soulful space elf who waddles into the hearts of the boy, his
big brother and little sister. But a wasting illness brings E.T. to death's door just
as a horde of scary scientists crashes through the door of the boy's house.

Throughout the movie they have been hunting the little critter, electronically 8
eavesdropping on the house and generally acting like Watergate understudies.[6]
They pounce upon E.T. with all the whirring, pulsing, blinking paraphernalia
of modern medicine. He dies anyway, then is inexplicably resurrected. He is
rescued from the fell clutches of the scientists by a posse of kid bicyclists and
boards a spaceship for home. This variant of the boy-sundered-from-dog theme
leaves few eyes dry. But what is bothersome is the animus against science, which
is seen as a morbid calling for callous vivisectionists and other unfeeling tech-
nocrats.

A childish (and Rousseau-ist[7]) view of children as noble savages often is part 9
of a belief that nature is a sweet garden and science and technology are spoilsome
intrusions. But nature is, among other things, plagues and pestilences, cholera
and locusts, floods and droughts. Earlier ages thought of nature in terms of such
afflictions. As Robert Nisbet says, this age can take a sentimental view of nature
because science has done so much to ameliorate it.[8]

Wonder: Disdain for science usually ends when the disdainer gets a tooth- 10

---

[3]guillemot: northern coastal sea bird. [Eds.]
[4]spelunking: exploring caves. [Eds.]
[5]Voltaire (1694–1778): pen name of François Marie Arouet, French poet, playwright, and
historian. [Eds.]
[6]Watergate: 1972 political scandal that culminated in the resignation of President Richard Nixon
in 1974. [Eds.]
[7]Jean Jacques Rousseau (1712–1778): French philosopher and writer. [Eds.]
[8]Robert Nisbet (b. 1913): social historian and critic. [Eds.]

ache, or his child needs an operation. But hostility to science is the anti-intellectualism of the semi-intellectual. That is in part because science undercuts intellectual vanity: measured against what is unknown, the difference between what the most and least learned persons know is trivial. E.T. is, ostensibly, an invitation to feel what we too rarely feel: wonder. One reason we rarely feel wonder is that science has made many things routine that once were exciting, even terrifying (travel, surgery). But science does more than its despisers do to nurture the wonderful human capacity for wonder.

U.S. missions have revealed that Saturn has braided rings and a ring com-   11
posed of giant snowballs. The space program is the greatest conceivable adventure; yet the government scants it and Philistine utilitarians justify it because it has yielded such marvels as nonstick frying pans. We live in (let us say the worst) an age of journalism: an age of skimmed surfaces, of facile confidence that reality is whatever can be seen and taped and reported. But modern science teaches that things are not what they seem: matter is energy; light is subject to gravity; the evidence of gravity waves suggests that gravitic energy is a form of radiation; to increase the speed of an object is to decrease the passage of its time. This is science; compared with it, space elves are dull as ditchwater.

The epigram that credulity is an adult's weakness but a child's strength is   12
true. Victoria Will (21 months) croons ecstatically at the sight of a squirrel; she sees, without thinking about it, that a squirrel is a marvelous piece of work—which, come to think about it, it is. For big people, science teaches the truth that a scientist put this way: the universe is not only queerer than we suppose, it is queerer than we can suppose.

George F. Will

QUESTIONS

1. Compare the two reviews. On what issues does each critic base his assessment of the film?

2. To what extent and for what purposes does each writer narrate scenes from the movie? For what purposes do they refer to nonmovie material, such as novels and plays?

3. Denby welcomes "this return to the honorable emotional fullness that was taken for granted in movies of the thirties and forties" (paragraph 11). How might Will reply to Denby's praise of the emotional value of E.T.?

4. What image or conception does each writer have of childhood? If you've seen E.T. or other Spielberg films, how would you describe Spielberg's conception of childhood?

5. How would you describe the tone of each writer?

6. In his review of *E.T.*, Denby appreciates the fun of Spielberg's conception of extraterrestrials finding *us* alien rather than the other way around. Drop a newly arrived E.T. into your home, school, or place of work, and write a report on events from the E.T.'s point of view. Will the E.T. try to convince others to visit or to stay away?

7. Write a review of a film for an audience who has not seen it. Refer to Denby and Will when you consider how much retelling of the film is necessary to make your points.

WHY ARE AMERICANS
AFRAID OF DRAGONS?

Ursula K. Le Guin

*Ursula Kroeber Le Guin (b. 1929) is best known as a writer
of fiction, especially science fiction and fantasy. Her most
admired works are* The Earthsea Trilogy (1968–1972), The
Left Hand of Darkness (1969), *and* The Dispossessed (1974).
The essay reprinted here (from The Language of the Night,
1979) *was first presented in 1973 as a talk at a conference
of the Pacific Northwest Library Association held in Port-
land, Oregon, Le Guin's home city.*

This was to be a talk about fantasy. But I have not been feeling very fanciful   1
lately, and could not decide what to say; so I have been going about picking
people's brains for ideas. "What about fantasy? Tell me something about fantasy." And one friend of mine said, "All right, I'll tell you something fantastic.
Ten years ago, I went to the children's room of the library of such-and-such a
city, and asked for *The Hobbit*; and the librarian told me, 'Oh, we keep that
only in the adult collection; we don't feel that escapism is good for children.' "

My friend and I had a good laugh and shudder over that, and we agreed that   2
things have changed a great deal in these past ten years. That kind of moralistic
censorship of works of fantasy is very uncommon now, in the children's libraries.
But the fact that the children's libraries have become oases in the desert doesn't
mean that there isn't still a desert. The point of view from which that librarian
spoke still exists. She was merely reflecting, in perfect good faith, something
that goes very deep in the American character: a moral disapproval of fantasy,
a disapproval so intense, and often so aggressive, that I cannot help but see it
as arising, fundamentally, from fear.

So: Why are Americans afraid of dragons?   3

Before I try to answer my question, let me say that it isn't only Americans   4
who are afraid of dragons. I suspect that almost all very highly technological
peoples are more or less antifantasy. There are several national literatures which,
like ours, have had no tradition of adult fantasy for the past several hundred
years: the French, for instance. But then you have the Germans, who have a
good deal; and the English, who have it, and love it, and do it better than
anyone else. So this fear of dragons is not merely a Western, or a technological,
phenomenon. But I do not want to get into these vast historical questions; I will
speak of modern Americans, the only people I know well enough to talk about.

In wondering why Americans are afraid of dragons, I began to realize that a   5 great many Americans are not only antifantasy, but altogether antifiction. We tend, as a people, to look upon all works of the imagination either as suspect, or as contemptible.

"My wife reads novels. I haven't got the time." 6

"I used to read that science fiction stuff when I was a teenager, but of course I don't now." 7

"Fairy stories are for kids. I live in the real world." 8

Who speaks so? Who is it that dismisses *War and Peace, The Time Machine,* 9
and *A Midsummer Night's Dream* with this perfect self-assurance?[1] It is, I fear, the man in the street—the hardworking, over-thirty American male—the men who run this country.

Such a rejection of the entire art of fiction is related to several American 10
characteristics: our Puritanism, our work ethic, our profit-mindedness, and even our sexual mores.

To read *War and Peace* or *The Lord of the Rings* plainly is not "work"[2]— 11
you do it for pleasure. And if it cannot be justified as "educational" or as "self-improvement," then, in the Puritan value system, it can only be self-indulgence or escapism. For pleasure is not a value, to the Puritan; on the contrary, it is a sin.

Equally, in the businessman's value system, if an act does not bring in an 12
immediate, tangible profit, it has no justification at all. Thus the only person who has an excuse to read Tolstoy or Tolkien is the English teacher, because he gets paid for it. But our businessman might allow himself to read a best-seller now and then: not because it is a good book, but because it is a best-seller—it is a success, it has made money. To the strangely mystical mind of the money-changer, this justifies its existence; and by reading it he may partic-ipate, a little, in the power and mana of its success. If this is not magic, by the way, I don't know what is.

The last element, the sexual one, is more complex. I hope I will not be 13
understood as being sexist if I say that, within our culture, I believe that this antifiction attitude is basically a male one. The American boy and man is very commonly forced to define his maleness by rejecting certain traits, certain hu-man gifts and potentialities, which our culture defines as "womanish" or "child-ish." And one of these traits or potentialities is, in cold sober fact, the absolutely essential human faculty of imagination.

Having got this far, I went quickly to the dictionary. 14

The *Shorter Oxford Dictionary* says: "Imagination. 1. The action of imag- 15
ining, or forming a mental concept of what is not actually present to the senses; 2. The mental consideration of actions or events not yet in existence."

---

[1] *War and Peace, The Time Machine,* and *A Midsummer Night's Dream:* by Leo Tolstoy, H. G. Wells, and William Shakespeare, respectively. [Eds.]
[2] *The Lord of the Rings:* the trilogy by J. R. R. Tolkien. [Eds.]

Very well; I certainly can let "absolutely essential human faculty" stand. But 16
I must narrow the definition to fit our present subject. By "imagination," then,
I personally mean the free play of the mind, both intellectual and sensory. By
"play" I mean recreation, re-creation, the recombination of what is known into
what is new. By "free" I mean that the action is done without an immediate
object of profit—spontaneously. That does not mean, however, that there may
not be a purpose behind the free play of the mind, a goal; and the goal may be
a very serious object indeed. Children's imaginative play is clearly a practicing
at the acts and emotions of adulthood; a child who did not play would not
become mature. As for the free play of an adult mind, its result may be *War
and Peace*, or the theory of relativity.

To be free, after all, is not to be undisciplined. I should say that the discipline 17
of the imagination may in fact be the essential method or technique of both art
and science. It is our Puritanism, insisting that discipline means repression or
punishment, which confuses the subject. To discipline something, in the proper
sense of the word, does not mean to repress it, but to train it—to encourage it
to grow, and act, and be fruitful, whether it is a peach tree or a human mind.

I think that a great many American men have been taught just the opposite. 18
They have learned to repress their imagination, to reject it as something childish
or effeminate, unprofitable, and probably sinful.

They have learned to fear it. But they have never learned to discipline it at 19
all.

Now, I doubt that the imagination can be suppressed. If you truly eradicated 20
it in a child, he would grow up to be an eggplant. Like all our evil propensities,
the imagination will win out. But if it is rejected and despised, it will grow into
wild and weedy shapes; it will be deformed. At its best, it will be mere ego-
centered daydreaming; at its worst, it will be wishful thinking, which is a very
dangerous occupation when it is taken seriously. Where literature is concerned,
in the old, truly Puritan days, the only permitted reading was the Bible. Nowadays, with our secular Puritanism, the man who refuses to read novels because
it's unmanly to do so, or because they aren't true, will most likely end up
watching bloody detective thrillers on the television, or reading hack Westerns
or sports stories, or going in for pornography, from *Playboy* on down. It is his
starved imagination, craving nourishment, that forces him to do so. But he can
rationalize such entertainment by saying that it is realistic—after all, sex exists,
and there are criminals, and there are baseball players, and there used to be
cowboys—and also by saying that it is virile, by which he means that it doesn't
interest most women.

That all these genres are sterile, hopelessly sterile, is a reassurance to him, 21
rather than a defect. If they were genuinely realistic, which is to say genuinely
imagined and imaginative, he would be afraid of them. Fake realism is the
escapist literature of our time. And probably the ultimate escapist reading is that
masterpiece of total unreality, the daily stock market report.

Now what about our man's wife? She probably wasn't required to squelch 22
her private imagination in order to play her expected role in life, but she
hasn't been trained to discipline it, either. She is allowed to read novels, and
even fantasies. But, lacking training and encouragement, her fancy is likely
to glom on to very sickly fodder, such things as soap operas, and "true romances," and nursy novels, and historico-sentimental novels, and all the rest
of the baloney ground out to replace genuine imaginative works by the artistic sweatshops of a society that is profoundly distrustful of the uses of the
imagination.

What, then, are the uses of the imagination? 23

You see, I think we have a terrible thing here: a hardworking, upright, 24
responsible citizen, a full-grown, educated person, who is afraid of dragons,
and afraid of hobbits, and scared to death of fairies. It's funny, but it's also
terrible. Something has gone very wrong. I don't know what to do about it
but to try and give an honest answer to that person's question, even though
he often asks it in an aggressive and contemptuous tone of voice. "What's the
good of it all?" he says. "Dragons and hobbits and little green men—what's
the *use* of it?"

The truest answer, unfortunately, he won't even listen to. He won't hear it. 25
The truest answer is, "The use of it is to give you pleasure and delight."

"I haven't got the time," he snaps, swallowing a Maalox pill for his ulcer 26
and rushing off to the golf course.

So we try the next-to-truest answer. It probably won't go down much better, 27
but it must be said: "The use of imaginative fiction is to deepen your understanding of your world, and your fellow men, and your own feelings, and your
destiny."

To which I fear he will retort, "Look, I got a raise last year, and I'm giving 28
my family the best of everything, we've got two cars and a color TV. I understand
enough of the world!"

And he is right, unanswerably right, if that is what he wants, and all he 29
wants.

The kind of thing you learn from reading about the problems of a hobbit 30
who is trying to drop a magic ring into an imaginary volcano has very little
to do with your social status, or material success, or income. Indeed, if there
is any relationship, it is a negative one. There is an inverse correlation between fantasy and money. That is a law, known to economists as Le Guin's
Law. If you want a striking example of Le Guin's Law, just give a lift to one
of those people along the roads who own nothing but a backpack, a guitar,
a fine head of hair, a smile, and a thumb. Time and again, you will find
that these waifs have read *The Lord of the Rings*—some of them can practically recite it. But now take Aristotle Onassis, or J. Paul Getty: could you
believe that those men ever had anything to do, at any age, under any circumstances, with a hobbit?

562

But, to carry my example a little further, and out of the realm of economics, 31
did you ever notice how very gloomy Mr. Onassis and Mr. Getty and all those
billionaires look in their photographs? They have this strange, pinched look, as
if they were hungry. As if they were hungry for something, as if they had lost
something and were trying to think where it could be, or perhaps what it could
be, what it was they've lost.

Could it be their childhood? 32

So I arrive at my personal defense of the uses of the imagination, especially 33
in fiction, and most especially in fairy tale, legend, fantasy, science fiction, and
the rest of the lunatic fringe. I believe that maturity is not an outgrowing, but
a growing up: that an adult is not a dead child, but a child who survived. I
believe that all the best faculties of a mature human being exist in the child,
and that if these faculties are encouraged in youth they will act well and wisely
in the adult, but if they are repressed and denied in the child they will stunt
and cripple the adult personality. And finally, I believe that one of the most
deeply human, and humane, of these faculties is the power of imagination: so
that it is our pleasant duty, as librarians, or teachers, or parents, or writers, or
simply as grownups, to encourage that faculty of imagination in our children,
to encourage it to grow freely, to flourish like the green bay tree, by giving it
the best, absolutely the best and purest, nourishment that it can absorb. And
never, under any circumstances, to squelch it, or sneer at it, or imply that it is
childish, or unmanly, or untrue.

For fantasy is true, of course. It isn't factual, but it is true. Children know 34
that. Adults know it too, and that is precisely why many of them are afraid of
fantasy. They know that its truth challenges, even threatens, all that is false,
all that is phony, unnecessary, and trivial in the life they have let themselves
be forced into living. They are afraid of dragons, because they are afraid of
freedom.

So I believe that we should trust our children. Normal children do not 35
confuse reality and fantasy—they confuse them much less often than we adults
do (as a certain great fantasist pointed out in a story called "The Emperor's New
Clothes"). Children know perfectly well that unicorns aren't real, but they also
know that books about unicorns, if they are good books, are true books. All too
often, that's more than Mummy and Daddy know; for, in denying their childhood, the adults have denied half their knowledge, and are left with the sad,
sterile little fact: "Unicorns aren't real." And that fact is one that never got
anybody anywhere (except in the story "The Unicorn in the Garden," by another
great fantasist, in which it is shown that a devotion to the unreality of unicorns
may get you straight into the loony bin). It is by such statements as, "Once
upon a time there was a dragon," or "In a hole in the ground there lived a
hobbit"—it is by such beautiful non-facts that we fantastic human beings may
arrive, in our peculiar fashion, at the truth.

563

QUESTIONS

1. This essay was first a talk before a group of librarians. Given this, how aware does the author seem to be of this particular audience? What elements in the essay reveal this awareness? Single out specific paragraphs or sections that relate directly to libraries, and consider their probable effect on that first audience and on Le Guin's argument.

2. In paragraph 21, Le Guin distinguishes between "fake realism" and that which is "genuinely realistic." In the light of that distinction, how do you evaluate her examples in paragraphs 24 through 29? Are they genuine enough?

3. In paragraph 33, Le Guin turns to her "personal defense of the uses of the imagination." At this point she is arguing from belief rather than from facts or what you might call hard evidence. How sympathetic are you to her beliefs? In what ways are her beliefs attractive?

4. This essay attempts to establish a positive evaluation of fantastic literature by formulating a negative evaluation and then arguing against it. How much of Le Guin's argument is directed against the position taken by her opponents, and how much is against her opponents themselves? Who is she arguing against, anyway? How does she describe and locate her opponents?

5. One of Le Guin's more interesting ideas is of "disciplining" the imagination (paragraphs 17 through 19). Le Guin doesn't really say how that is done, but perhaps you have had some training in such discipline or can imagine how it could happen. Write an essay describing the experience of disciplining the imagination in an area that interests you. Try to characterize the nature of the freedom that the discipline you have acquired permits.

6. Write your own argument about fantasy for the same audience of librarians addressed by Le Guin. Write a reasonable counterargument to Le Guin's views—an effective case against fantasy, a different diagnosis of what's wrong, or even an argument that the opposition to fantasy actually packages and sells it in order to make money. Or write an argument parallel to Le Guin's but using different evidence and different cases to discover some additional reasons to encourage fantasy.

7. Le Guin's argument is concerned primarily with literary fantasy. Taking her ideas into account, write an argument for or against cinematic fantasy. E.T. and King Kong suggest the range of movies that this category can include.

TWELVE DAYS OF TERROR! THE THREE MILE ISLAND STORY

Edwin Diamond

Edwin Diamond (b. 1925) is a Senior Lecturer in Political Science at the Massachusetts Institute of Technology, where he heads the News Study Group. This group, which includes both graduate and undergraduate students, records, studies, and analyzes media treatment of major news events. The results of NSG's work have appeared in three books by Diamond: The Tin Kazoo: Television, Politics, and the News *(1975);* Good News, Bad News *(1978); and* Sign-Off: The Last Days of Television *(1983) from which the following piece is taken. Diamond, formerly a senior editor at* Newsweek, *is a contributing editor to* Esquire *and* New York *magazines. He also appears on television as a media critic.*

Press coverage of the Three Mile Island nuclear accident began offhandedly   1
Wednesday morning, March 28, 1979, when the managing editor of the *Waynesboro* (Pennsylvania) *Record Herald* passed on to the Associated Press news service a tip that central Pennsylvania state police had been put on alert in the Harrisburg area. By the time the crisis ended, two weeks later, anchorman Walter Cronkite on CBS News would talk of "12 days of terror." The press coverage of that period was anything but casual; rather the manner in which the accident at the nuclear plant at Three Mile Island, Pennsylvania, was reported by all the media, and particularly by television, had become an issue in itself.

In any story different actors have different agendas and different messages to   2
convey. This was true of the events at Three Mile Island, a nuclear power plant licensed by the federal government and operated by the Metropolitan Edison Company of Pennsylvania. There were at least three sources of messages: the press, the electric company, and the government. The press grew progressively dissatisfied with the messages of the other two, and they, in turn, grew critical of the press. By the end of the crisis, the White House was spreading the word around Washington that President Carter thought the news accounts of Three Mile Island were outrageous, exaggerated, irresponsible. One distinguished nuclear scientist told me that the television coverage had been pronuclear; another equally distinguished nuclear scientist told me that it had been antinuclear. Most television viewers—ordinary people and presidents and physicists alike—tend to approve of materials that confirm their own judgments or prejudices

and to disapprove of contrary information. The scientist who thought television's coverage was proindustry opposes nuclear power; the scientist who thought television was anti-industry favors it. Enough disagreement existed about what television did, and did not, show and tell viewers that our News Study Group decided to examine precisely what appeared on the three networks, from the first news tip to the final reactor shutdown. We found at Three Mile Island that

1. Television news moved with admirable responsibility initially, to the point of being cautious and slow to report developments.

2. Television news reported carefully both industry and government accounts from within the plant, though with a growing suspicion that the full story was not told.

3. Television news eventually proved to be unprepared, or unwilling, to put together the specialized analysis and detailed explanation needed to clarify the whole story; at times, in fact, it avoided promising, but risky, reporting leads in favor of more conventional, and safer, coverage.

To back up these conclusions with specifics, we found it helpful to organize   3
the Three Mile Island coverage into three phases.

FIRST ALARM

Most news organizations had no trouble recognizing a major story in the   4
making on March 28, and each network quickly dispatched reporters to the Three Mile Island plant, or more accurately, to the plant gates, since the state troopers were barring access to the plant itself. On Wednesday night, March 28, each network devoted a long (by network news standards) lead story to Three Mile Island. The ABC *World News Tonight* in particular was evenhanded, noncommittal. Anchorman Frank Reynolds began:

> Good evening. For many years there has been a vigorous debate in this country about the safety of the nation's 72 nuclear-energy power plants. That debate is likely to be intensified because of what happened early this morning at a nuclear-power plant in Pennsylvania.

On the NBC *Nightly News*, John Chancellor was also low-key. The cooling   5
system in the nuclear-power plant had broken down, he said, but went on to stress that there was "no danger to people outside" and that the plant was shut down. Then followed reassuring reports quoting Jack Herbein, vice president for power generation at Metropolitan Edison, as well as some state officials and Met Ed workers. Next NBC's Carole Simpson introduced some material from the Critical Mass Energy Project, a group she described as "opposed to nuclear energy." The Critical Mass spokesperson maintained that the Three Mile Island plant had been plagued with safety problems since its opening a year ago.

The CBS *Evening News* coverage the first night was noteworthy because   6 there was considerable reworking of the opening words of Walter Cronkite at the beginning of the program. This is the lead, the headline, and broadcast journalists take care to strike the right tone. After what one CBS executive remembers as three or four rewrites to get the right tone, America's premiere broadcaster said to 16 million viewers tuned to the top-rated evening newscast:

> Good evening. It was the first step in a nuclear nightmare; as far as we know this hour, no worse than that. But a government official said that a breakdown in an atomic-power plant in Pennsylvania today is probably the worst nuclear accident to date. There was no apparent serious contamination of workers. But a nuclear-safety group said that radiation inside the plant is at eight times the deadly level; so strong that after passing through a three-foot-thick concrete wall, it can be measured a mile away."

Cronkite later in his report brought up the motion picture, *The China Syndrome*, mentioning "the current movie about a near-catastrophic nuclear meltdown" and assuring viewers that plant officials had assured the public that wasn't the situation. 7

The network reporters on the scene then offered cautious, factual accounts, but at the same time distanced themselves—sensibly, it turned out—from the story by carefully attributing the statements to officials of one sort or another. Thus Bettina Gregory on ABC said: 8

> . . . The NRC (Nuclear Regulatory Commission) said, "There's a hell of a lot of radiation in the reactor building . . . and [some] was detected as far as one mile away." Officials of Metropolitan Edison conceded that some workers may have been contaminated, but they insisted this was not a serious accident. They said only one-tenth the amount of radiation needed for a general alarm escaped.

And with equal care, Gary Shepard of CBS News reported:

> Officials from Metropolitan Edison Company, which operates the plant, attempted to minimize the seriousness of the accident, saying the public was never in danger.

Then followed a tape of Met Ed's Herbein, who said:

> We may have some minor fuel damage, but we don't believe at this point that it's extensive. . . . We're monitoring for—for airborne contamination. The amount that we found is minimal. Very small traces of radioactivity have been released from the plant.

The impression the television viewer got was clear: the system had worked. As Max Robinson said on ABC News, "The plant did just what it was supposed to do, shut itself off, but not before some radioactivity escaped." Most viewers, it's fair to conclude, went to bed with little thought about Three Mile Island. When they got up the next morning, March 29, and turned on NBC's *Today Show*, they first heard a soothing reference to the malfunction at Three Mile 9

Island, followed by Walter Creitz of Met Ed talking of the unparalleled safety record of the civilian nuclear-power industry.

That night Three Mile Island again was the lead story on the three network 10 newscasts. The tone on NBC was reassuring: John Chancellor reported that the reactor was hot but normal, the system was operating. On ABC the nuclear malfunction had been moved up on the scale of seriousness to a nuclear accident. Still, ABC reported, the situation was serious but not dangerous. There was a general feeling of postmortem in the newscasts; what remained was for Met Ed to accomplish the complete cold shutdown of the reactor, to begin its extensive cleanup effort and—the thrust of the story now—the long inevitable investigations to find out what had happened. Walter Cronkite seemed to put Three Mile Island in the past tense, and as a mishap at that:

> Good evening. The questions still pour in about the nuclear accident. . . . More than 24 hours after the mishap, there is more heat than light in the confusion surrounding the incident. Critics charge "cover-up" . . . even as an industry spokesman says, "The system worked. . . ."

On the other networks, people stories replaced the reactor as the focus. 11 Reporters interviewed area residents concerned about radiation as well as members of Congress who had heard from people concerned about the causes of the accident. NBC's David Brinkley described members of Congress as agitated. ABC was the most people oriented of the network news organizations; its reporters went across the road from the plant to a neat row of surburban homes for comment from a resident. By Friday morning, March 30, the *Today Show* was reporting that the danger was minimal.

Less than two hours later, the calm was broken. An NBC *News Update*— 12 one of its thirty-second newsbreaks between programs—informed viewers that more radiation had been released into the atmosphere around the plant. Four hours after that, another NBC *News Update* carried word that Pennsylvania Governor Richard Thornburgh had asked for the evacuation of all pregnant women and preschool children within five miles of the plant. The story was building from low-key to high voltage.

The network news that Friday night jolted viewers. Each network devoted 13 well over half of its broadcast to Three Mile Island. Frank Reynolds opened on ABC with these words:

> Good evening. The news from the Harrisburg, Pa., nuclear-energy plant is much more serious tonight. For the first time today an official of the Nuclear Regulatory Commission said there is the possibility, though not yet the probability, of what is called a meltdown of the reactor core. That would be, in plain language, a catastrophe.

Walter Cronkite was even more chilling: 14

> We are faced with the remote but very real possibility of a nuclear meltdown at

the Three Mile Island atomic-power plant. The danger faced by man for tampering with natural forces, a theme familiar from the myths of Prometheus to the story of Frankenstein, moved closer to fact from fancy through the day.

A young journalist I know, a New York City resident, would vividly remem- 15 ber the effect of Cronkite's words on her. Upset by the ominous bulletins and updates during the day, she recalls, she had hurried home to tune into CBS. After all, she thought, the calming voice of Walter Cronkite had helped us all through earlier national traumas—riots, assassinations, astronauts in tricky orbital maneuvers. He would get events in perspective. But Cronkite, she recalled, scared her more than the earlier bulletins had.

TROUBLE AT THE SOURCE

With hindsight, we can see that Cronkite and CBS, along with other news 16 organizations, were mainly reacting to the information presented by state, federal, and company officials. As these officials lost their self-assurance, television reflected this. When these officials began contradicting one another, the news began to sound contradictory. That led to confusion among the media audience. Deplorable as this might be for the formation of public opinion, it was minor compared to another area of confusion—the events taking place inside the Three Mile Island plant. Underexperienced technicians had misread valves and contributed to the original reactor troubles, and further errors were hampering the search for corrective measures, or so we all were to learn later.

For example, a key clue to the damage that occurred early on Wednesday 17 (day one) inside the reactor core was handed to operators early that afternoon. A pressure spike was clearly traced on a recorder sheet. But no one looked at the sheet until Friday, after two full days of consistent underreporting of the amount of core damage. The oversight, an NRC official later explained, may have been due to what he called the hassle factor in the control room—noise, flashing lights, people getting in one another's way.

In most catastrophes there is a dominant element of what might be called 18 honest confusion. Because of it, no one needs to erect elaborate conspiracy theories to account for what is reported. In the case of Three Mile Island, we saw twin delusions develop: the initial underestimation of the mishap and the subsequent overestimation of the possibilities (what games theory people call worst-case analysis). On Friday, the day of the specter of meltdown, Joseph Hendrie, the NRC chairman, complained that he and Pennsylvania Governor Thornburgh didn't know what was going on. The governor's information, Hendrie said, was ambiguous, and Hendrie admitted that his own information was nonexistent. These two officials, responsible for the safety of millions of Pennsylvanians, Hendrie concluded, were "like a couple of blind men staggering around making decisions." It was an apt image. Looking at the coverage, we can see that the press was dragged along as the third blind and staggering man.

EDWIN DIAMOND

THE UNFILLED PICTURE

Television news has the power to convey feelings, impressions, auras. In the $\quad$ 19
case of Three Mile Island television first gave the feeling of nothing more than
alert; next came the sense of reassurance, and then the evocation of danger. In
this respect television did approximately reflect the reality of the Three Mile
Island events. That is why different people saw different things. There was
something to please, or displease, everybody. Television at its best should do
more than hold a mirror to events. The record of the coverage of Three Mile
Island shows that there were efforts to do more than repeat the official line of
the moment. There were attempts by television journalists to speak in their own
voices. Unfortunately, television news begins to falter when it tries analysis.
Explanations, at least in the case of Three Mile Island, went by too fast, graphics
were too careless, scripts radiated tabloid-think, with words too urgent—lethal,
massive, dreaded, nightmarish; or too bland—mishap, malfunction.

Later that Friday night each network had the opportunity in special reports $\quad$ 20
to give the necessary time and thought to the possibility of meltdown. How each
responded reveals something about network news organizations and about television news in general. CBS News chose to do a one-hour report, immediately
setting itself apart from the thirty-minute reports of ABC and NBC. On almost
all counts, the CBS special report was better than the other two. Walter Cronkite
and correspondent Steve Young had time to explain clearly the situation inside
the reactor as of Friday. Mitchell Krauss had time to look at past nuclear-power
plant accidents. Robert Schakne, who emerged as perhaps the most informed
correspondent during the week, had time to raise the key question of acceptable
risk-taking in the development of nuclear power.

The shorter ABC and NBC reports suffered by contrast. ABC's was wide but $\quad$ 21
not very deep, a report touching on Three Mile Island, other reactors, the White
House, Congress. On NBC John Chancellor was a model of judiciousness: he
refused to scare anyone. Calmly, professorially, he showed a drawing of the
plant. Chancellor achieved the best tone for television, noting the contradictions
and misstatements and saying, "In terms of information, this thing is a mess. . . ."
It was a good insight, and could have been used as a lead-in to an analysis of
the efforts to control information at Three Mile Island. Instead it was Chancellor's sign-off. NBC opened the door but did not walk in.

Detailed explanations of any kind, whether about nuclear reactors or nuclear $\quad$ 22
politics, appear to tax television's resources. So it was with Three Mile Island.
Just as Met Ed's technicians seemed ill-prepared for their trip into the unknowns
of an exposed reactor, so too did television's generalists seem over their heads
in this particular assignment. This leads to a question often put to news organizations: why not hire specialists who are at ease with scientific disciplines?
The usual answer is that television can't employ full-time chemist-correspond-
ents or physicist-correspondents or geneticist-correspondents. Where would it
end? But the coverage of Three Mile Island showed the advantages of arranging

for expert consultants to help out the television producers and writers. CBS News, for example, arranged for George Rathjens, one of the nation's most knowledgeable nuclear specialists, to be available for telephone consultations. Because he had no special hard line to push—he's prosafety *and* pronuclear—he helped sort out some of the confusion for CBS.

Three Mile Island also raised questions that had nothing to do with technical   23
matters. The story had political and economic meanings that required analysis and explanation. For example, the push for nuclear power largely comes from the manufacturers of the equipment rather than from the utilities operators like Met Ed. An explanation of this in terms of jobs, investments, and political influence would have helped. Yet in these nontechnical, politically sophisticated areas, where the networks are supposed to be at ease, they proved to be relatively sluggish in their coverage.

Television was also much too diffident about looking into the causes of the   24
accident. It didn't put authority's feet to the fire. Were there financial incentives involved in getting Three Mile Island's unit two on line before the end of calendar year 1978? Did safety get shortchanged as a result? According to a passing reference in *Time* magazine, Met Ed qualified for tax investment credits and deductions of around $40 million by meeting the year-end deadline. That aspect of the story needed development. But even when CBS News took an unhurried look back at the story in May ("Fallout from Three Mile Island"), it was remarkably gentle on the plant operators and remarkably reluctant to re-create what went on inside the plant.

The accident at Three Mile Island, when the record is reviewed, proved to   25
be a triple test of competence. It tested the ability of industry to build and operate safe, efficient nuclear plants; it tested the ability of government agencies to regulate these plants in the public interest, and it tested the ability of the press to cover complex stories in a clear, coherent, nonpanicky voice. With the benefit of critic's hindsight it is possible to see that industry, government, and press didn't quite measure up. The three institutions that should be helping the public—and the public's elected representatives—determine the future of nuclear power in the United States needed help themselves. All the bad habits the news institution has built up—overreliance on authority, grabbers, lack of memory, preoccupation with style at the expense of content—came into play at Three Mile Island. Because we've seen them so often in our other case studies, we know the Three Mile Island coverage was no accident.

QUESTIONS

1. Take one of Diamond's conclusions in paragraph 2, and outline the specific information he cites later to substantiate that conclusion. Is the conclusion justified?

2. Is Diamond's three-phrase organization of television news coverage as helpful as he thinks it is? Why? If you think not, suggest other ways of organizing the material.

3. To whom is the argument directed? How does Diamond present himself to his audience?

4. Given Diamond's criticism of television news in general, describe the kind of television news show that might win his applause. You might use your own local television news show as an example for upgrading or for praise.

5. Watch coverage of a local or national news event on two or more television stations. Write an essay comparing their treatments of the story.

6. Using your library's newspaper files, look at one newspaper's coverage of Three Mile Island from the afternoon edition on Wednesday, March 28, through Saturday, March 31, 1979. Compare the newspaper coverage with the television coverage as described by Diamond. Are there similarities? Does the newspaper's information come from its own reporters or from the Associated Press or United Press International: Write an essay comparing one newspaper's coverage with that of one television network. Did the newspaper take time to analyze, to find out causes?

THE FIRST
TELEVISED WAR
Phillip Knightley

Phillip Knightley was born in Australia in 1929. He began his career as a copyboy on a newspaper in Sydney, later becoming a reporter and an editor. For over twenty years he has lived and worked in London as a journalist and historian of journalism, acting as a special correspondent for the Sunday Times *of London. He says that he has never heard a shot fired in anger and hopes he never will. The following selection is taken from chapter 16 of his book* The First Casualty: From the Crimea to Vietnam: The War Correspondent as Hero, Propagandist, and Myth Maker *(1975). The title of the book is based on a statement made by United States Senator Hiram Johnson in 1917: "The first casualty when war comes is truth."*

The most intrusive medium in Vietnam was television, and, as the war went on, the hunger of editors for combat footage increased. "Before they were satisfied with a corpse," Richard Lindley, a British television reporter, said. "Then they had to have people dying in action."[1] Michael Herr described a truck carrying a dying ARVN soldier that stopped near a group of correspondents. The soldier, who was only nineteen or twenty, had been shot in the chest. A television cameraman leaned over the Vietnamese and began filming. The other correspondents watched. "He opened his eyes briefly a few times and looked back at us. The first time he tried to smile . . . then it left him. I'm sure he didn't even see us the last time he looked, but we all knew what it was that he had seen just before that."[2] The Vietnamese had seen the zoom lens of a sixteen-millimeter converted Auricon sound camera capturing his last moments of life on film that, if the flight connections worked and the editors back at the network liked it, would be shown in American living rooms within forty-eight hours.

This little item would not be exceptional. During the Tet offensive,[3] a Vietnamese in a checked shirt appeared on television being walked—that is, dragged—between two soldiers. The soldiers took him over to a man holding a pistol, who held it to the head of the man in the checked shirt and blew his brains

---

[1]*London Sunday Times*, November 26, 1967.
[2]*Christian Science Monitor*, May 29–June 30, 1970.
[3]Tet offensive: the campaign by the Vietcong begun during the Tet (lunar new year) festival in January 1968. [Eds.]

out. All of it was seen in full color on television (and later in a memorable series of photographs taken by Eddie Adams of the AP).

Any viewer in the United States who watched regularly the television re- 3 porting from Vietnam—and it was from television that 60 per cent of Americans got most of their war news—would agree that he saw scenes of real-life violence, death, and horror on his screen that would have been unthinkable before Vietnam. The risk and intrusion that such filming involved could, perhaps, be justified if it could be shown that television had been particularly effective in revealing the true nature of the war and thus had been able to change people's attitudes to it. Is there any evidence to this effect?

The director of CBS News in Washington, William Small, wrote: "When 4 television covered its 'first war' in Vietnam it showed a terrible truth of war in a manner new to mass audiences. A case can be made, and certainly should be examined, that this was cardinal to the disillusionment of Americans with this war, the cynicism of many young people towards America, and the destruction of Lyndon Johnson's tenure of office."[4] A *Washington Post* reporter, Don Oberdorfer, amply documents, in his book *Tet*, the number of commentators and editors (including those of Time Inc.) who had to re-examine their attitudes after extensive television—and press—coverage brought home to them the bewildering contradictions of a seemingly unending war.

Television's power seems to have impressed British observers even more than 5 American. The director-general of the Royal United Service Institution, Air Vice-Marshal S. W. B. Menaul, believes that television had "a lot to answer for [in] the collapse of American morale in relation to the Vietnam war." The then editor of the *Economist*, Alistair Burnet, wrote that the television reporting of Vietnam had made it very difficult for two American administrations to continue that war, "which was going on in American homes," irrespective of the merits or demerits of why the United States was actually involved in Vietnam. Robin Day, the BBC commentator, told a seminar of the Royal United Service Institution that the war on color-television screens in American living rooms had made Americans far more anti-militarist and anti-war than anything else: "One wonders if in the future a democracy which has uninhibited television coverage in every home will ever be able to fight a war, however just. . . . The full brutality of the combat will be there in close up and color, and blood looks very red on the color television screen." And the Director of Defence Operations, Plans and Supplies at the Ministry of Defence, Brigadier F. G. Caldwell, said that the American experience in Vietnam meant that if Britain were to go to war again, "we would have to start saying to ourselves, are we going to let the television cameras loose on the battlefield?"[5]

All this seems very persuasive, and it would be difficult to believe that the 6

---

[4]*Sunday Times*, October 19 and October 10, 1971; *The Times*, July 12, 1971.
[5]J. Lucas, *Dateline Vietnam* (New York: Award Books, 1967), p. 15.

sight, day after day, of American soldiers and Vietnamese civilians dying in a war that seemed to make no progress could not have had *some* effect on the viewer. Yet a survey conducted for *Newsweek* in 1967 suggested a remarkably different conclusion: that television had encouraged a majority of viewers to *support* the war. When faced with deciding whether television coverage had made them feel more like "backing up the boys in Vietnam" or like opposing the war, 64 per cent of viewers replied that they were moved to support the soldiers and only 26 per cent to oppose the war. A prominent American psychiatrist, Fredric Wertham, said, in the same year, that television had the effect of conditioning its audience to accept war, and a further *Newsweek* enquiry, in 1972, suggested that the public was developing a tolerance of horror in the newscasts from Vietnam—"The only way we can possibly tolerate it is by turning off a part of ourselves instead of the television set."

Edward Jay Epstein's survey of television producers and news editors, for his   7
book *News from Nowhere*, showed that more than two-thirds of those he interviewed felt that television had had little effect in changing public opinion on Vietnam. An opinion commonly expressed was that people saw exactly what they wanted to in a news report and that television only served to reinforce existing views. *The New Yorker's* television critic, Michael J. Arlen, reported, on several occasions, that viewers had a vague, unhappy feeling that they were not getting "the true picture" of Vietnam from the medium.[6] So if it was true that television did not radically change public opinion about the war, could it have been because of the quality of the coverage?

Television is a comparatively new medium. There were 10,000 sets in the   8
United States in 1941; at the time of Korea there were 10 million, and at the peak of the Vietnam War 100 million. There was some television reporting in Korea, a lot of it daring—an American general had to order the BBC cameraman Cyril Page to get down off the front of a tank to which he had tied himself so as to get a grandstand view of the battle as the tank went into action. But, until Vietnam, no one knew what problems the prolonged day-by-day coverage of a war by television would produce. The first was surprising—a lack of reality. It had been believed that when battle scenes were brought into the living room the reality of war would at last be brought home to a civilian audience. But Arlen was quick to point out, in *The New Yorker*, that by the same process battle scenes are made less real, "diminished in part by the physical size of the television screen, which, for all the industry's advances, still shows one a picture of men three inches tall shooting at other men three inches tall."[7] Sandy Gall of ITN found shooting combat footage difficult and dangerous, and the end result very disappointing. "I think you lose one dimension on television's small screen and things look smaller than life; the sound of battle, for example, never

[6]F. Harvey, *Air War Vietnam* (New York: Bantam, 1967), p. 115.
[7]Harvey, p. 184.

coming across. I am always let down when I eventually see my footage and think, Is that all? The sense of danger never comes across on television and you, the correspondent, always look as though you had an easy time of it."[8]

For many Americans in Vietnam, there emerged a strange side to the war that became directly related to television—the fact that the war seemed so unreal that sometimes it became almost possible to believe that everything was taking place on some giant Hollywood set and all the participants were extras playing a remake of *Back to Bataan*.[9] GIs—and even correspondents—brought up on Second World War movies shown on television, used to seeing Errol Flynn sweeping to victory through the jungles of Burma or Brian Donlevy giving the Japanese hell in the Coral Sea,[10] tended to relate their experiences in Vietnam to the Hollywood version of America at war.[11] Michael Herr, making a dash, with David Greenway of *Time*, from one position at Hué to another, caught himself saying to a Marine a line from a hundred Hollywood war films: "We're going to cut out now. Will you cover us?" One should not be surprised, therefore, to find that GIs sometimes behaved, in the presence of television cameras, as if they were making *Dispatch from Da Nang*. Herr describes soldiers running about during a fight because they knew there was a television crew nearby. "They were actually making war movies in their heads, doing little guts and glory Leatherneck tap dances under fire, getting their pimples shot off for the networks."[12]

So it is not difficult to understand how, when seen on a small screen, in the enveloping and cosy atmosphere of the household, sometime between the afternoon soap-box drama and the late-night war movie, the television version of the war in Vietnam could appear as just another drama, in which the hero is the correspondent and everything will come out all right at the end. Jack Laurence of CBS, an experienced war correspondent, who spent a lot of time in Vietnam, had this possibility brought home to him in Israel during the 1973 conflict. He was in a hotel lobby, and a couple who had just arrived from the United States recognized him and said, "We saw you on television and we knew everything was going to be all right because you were there."[13] There is not much a television correspondent can do about such a situation as that; it seems inherent in the nature of the medium. However, correspondents, or, more fairly, their editors, do have something to answer for in their selection of news in Vietnam.

Years of television news of the war have left viewers with a blur of images consisting mainly of helicopters landing in jungle clearings, soldiers charging

9

10

11

---

[8]*Washington Post*, February 23, 1966.
[9]*Back to Bataan:* a 1945 John Wayne film about the retaking of Bataan in the Philippines during World War II. [Eds.]
[10]Errol Flynn (1909–1959) and Brian Donlevy (1899–1972): Hollywood filmstars. [Eds.]
[11]The arrival in 1965 of Flynn's son, Sean, as a correspondent tended to confirm this feeling.
[12]Interview with John Shaw.
[13]Harvey, p. 104.

into undergrowth, wounded being loaded onto helicopters, artillery and mortar fire, air strikes on distant targets, napalm canisters turning slowly in the sky, and a breathless correspondent poking a stick microphone under an army officer's nose and asking, "What's happening up there, Colonel?" (The only honest answer came, in 1972, from a captain on Highway 13. "I wish the hell I knew," he said.) The networks claimed that combat footage was what the public wanted; that concentrating on combat prevented the film's being out of date if it was delayed in transmission; that it was difficult to shoot anything other than combat film when only three or four minutes were available in the average news program for events in Vietnam; and that the illusion of American progress created by combat footage shot from only one side was balanced by what the correspondent had to say.

This is simply not true. To begin with, combat footage fails to convey all 12 aspects of combat. "A cameraman feels so inadequate, being able to record only a minute part of the misery, a minute part of the fighting," said Kurt Volkert, a CBS cameraman. "You have to decide what the most important action is. Is it the woman holding her crying baby? Is it the young girl cringing near her house because of the exploding grenades? Or is it the defiant looking Vietcong with blood on his face just after capture?"[14] When the cameraman's thirty minutes of combat footage are edited down to three minutes—not an unusual editing ratio—the result is a segment of action that bears about as much relation to the reality in Vietnam as a battle scene shot in Hollywood does. In fact, the Hollywood version would probably appear more realistic.

The American viewer who hoped to learn something serious about Vietnam 13 was subjected, instead, to a television course in the techniques of war, and he was not sufficiently exposed either to what the war meant to the people over whose land it was being fought, or to the political complexities of the situation, or even to the considered personal views of reporters who had spent years covering the situation. Yet, even by the networks' own standards, the limited aspects of the war that the viewer was permitted to see could produce excellent television. One of the most dramatic pieces of film on the war was shot by a CBS team on Highway 13 late in April 1972. A South Vietnamese mine, intended to stop advancing enemy tanks, had caught a truck loaded with refugees. The film showed deaf children, distressed babies, and a woman weeping over the body of her son. The reporter, Bob Simon, described what had happened and then, with perhaps the best sign-off line from Vietnam, said simply, "There's nothing left to say about this war, nothing at all." "Morley Safer's Vietnam," an hour-long report by the CBS correspondent in Saigon, was Safer's own explicit view, and was hailed by *The New Yorker*'s critic, Michael J. Arlen, as "one of the best pieces of journalism to come out of the Vietnam war in any medium." But film like this was rare.

---

[14]P. Jones Griffiths, *Vietnam Inc.* (New York: Macmillan, 1971), p. 60.

Competition for combat footage was so intense that it not only forced American television teams to follow each other into what the BBC's correspondent Michael Clayton called "appallingly dangerous situations," but it also made editors reluctant to risk allowing a team the time and the freedom to make its own film of the war. Where were the television equivalents of Martha Gellhorn's series on Vietnamese orphanages and hospitals, or Philip Jones Griffiths' searing book on the nature of the war, *Vietnam Inc.?* True, television was handicapped by its mechanics—a three-man, or even a two-man, team loaded with camera, sound equipment, and film is less mobile and more dependent on military transport, and in a dangerous situation more vulnerable, than a journalist or a photographer. In its presentation, too, television is sometimes handicapped by its commercial associations. The Vietnamese cameraman Vo Suu filmed the brutal shooting of a Vietcong suspect by General Nguyen Ngoc Loan during the Tet offensive. NBC blacked out the screen for three seconds after the dead man hit the ground, so as to provide a buffer before the commercial that followed. (What television *really* wanted was action in which the men died cleanly and not too bloodily. "When they get a film which shows what a mortar does to a man, really shows the flesh torn and the blood flowing, they get squeamish," says Richard Lindley. "They want it to be just so. They want television to be cinema."[15])

American television executives showed too little courage in their approach to Vietnam. They followed each other into paths the army had chosen for them. They saw the war as "an American war in Asia—and that's the only story the American audience is interested in," and they let other, equally important, aspects of Vietnam go uncovered.

QUESTIONS

1. What is the meaning of the incident Knightley describes in his first paragraph? How does that example relate to his essay?

2. What is Knightley's thesis? Where do you find the clearest statement of it? What position is Knightley arguing *against?*

3. Paragraphs 4 and 5 summarize a position frequently heard about the Vietnam War, yet it turns out to be a position Knightley attacks. What are his major points of disagreement with that position? How convincingly does Knightley develop them?

4. Trace the theme of Hollywood as it develops in this essay. What does it add to Knightley's argument? How does it relate to his thesis?

5. Knightley isn't the first person to observe that the movies and television have taught us how to behave in certain critical situations, not always having to do with war. Can you think of a time when your behavior was not just influenced but almost defined by how people in movies act? Write an essay about that event. What were you doing, or

[15]Jones Griffiths, p. 62.

what did you need to do? What models of behavior influenced your own? How well did that learning enable you to meet the demands of the moment?

6. For a week or more, study television coverage of an important political event. Write a report on the coverage as you find it. How realistic and thorough do you judge it to be? What hints of distortion and misunderstanding do you find? Try to develop a thesis about the success or failure of the coverage of this event.

7. Compare television and newspaper coverage of any significant event. To what extent do the different media focus on different features of the event? What are the values, as you see them, of the differences you find?

THE HUNDREDTH MONKEY PHENOMENON

Ron Amundson

Ron Amundson (b. 1946) received his Ph.D. in philosophy from the University of Wisconsin and teaches at the University of Hawaii at Hilo. His main interests are epistemology (study of the theory of knowledge) and the history and philosophy of science, especially psychology. As he notes in his article, the students in his courses on these topics and on pseudoscience and the occult brought the Hundredth Monkey Phenomenon to his attention. During his research into this supposedly valid example of a paranormal event, Amundson says, "The truly interesting topics became (1) how the original author was able to discourage his readers from looking more closely at the facts, and (2) how other authors not only accepted the myth but exaggerated it." Amundson is still wondering "why we are so eager to believe in myths of mental miracles like the Hundredth Monkey Phenomenon." This article first appeared in Skeptical Inquirer, *a journal in which scientists challenge popular pseudoscientific notions.*

Claims of the paranormal are supported in many ways. Personal reports ("I was kidnapped by extraterrestrials"), appeals to puzzling everyday experiences ("Did you ever get a phone call from someone you had just dreamed about?"), and references to "ancient wisdom" are a few. Citations of actual scientific results are usually limited to ESP experiments and a few attempts to mystify further the already bizarre discoveries of modern physics. But the New Age is upon us (we're told) and New Age authors like Rupert Sheldrake (1981) and Lyall Watson (1979) support their new visions of reality with scientific documentation. Sheldrake has a bibliography of about 200 listings, and Watson lists exactly 600 sources. The sources cited are mostly respectable academic and scientific publications. The days of "[unnamed] scientists say" and "Fred Jones, while walking alone in the woods one day . . ." are gone. Or are they?

I teach college courses in epistemology, in the philosophy of science, and in pseudoscience and the occult. Students in these courses naturally bring to class examples of remarkable and paranormal claims. During the past few years one such claim has become especially popular, the "Hundredth Monkey Phenomenon." This phenomenon was baptized by Lyall Watson, who documents the case with references to five highly respectable articles by Japanese primatologists (Imanishi 1963; Kawai 1963 and 1965; Kawamura 1963; and Tsumori 1967). Watson's discussion of this phenomenon covers less than two pages. (Except where noted, all references to Watson are to pages 147 and 148.) But this brief report has inspired much attention. Following Watson, a book (Keyes 1982), a newsletter article (*Brain/Mind Bulletin* 1982), and a film (Hartley 1983) have each been created with the title "The Hundredth Monkey." In addition we find a journal article entitled "The 'Hundredth Monkey' and Humanity's Quest for Survival" (Stein 1983) and an article called "The Quantum Monkey" in a popular magazine (*Science Digest* 1981). Each relies on Watson as the sole source of information on the remarkable and supernatural behavior of primates.

The monkeys referred to are indeed remarkable. They are Japanese macaques 3 (*Macaca fuscata*), which live in wild troops on several islands in Japan. They have been under observation for years. During 1952 and 1953 the primatologists began "provisioning" the troops—providing them with such foods as sweet potatoes and wheat. This kept the monkeys from raiding farms and also made them easier to observe. The food was left in open areas, often on beaches. As a result of this new economy, the monkeys developed several innovative forms of behavior. One of these was invented in 1953 by an 18-month-old female that the observers named "Imo." Imo was a member of the troop on Koshima island. She discovered that sand and grit could be removed from the sweet potatoes by washing them in a stream or in the ocean. Imo's playmates and her mother learned this trick from Imo, and it soon spread to other members of the troop. Unlike most food customs, this innovation was learned by older monkeys from younger ones. In most other matters the children learn from their parents. The potato-washing habit spread gradually, according to Watson, up until 1958. But in the fall of 1958 a remarkable event occurred on Koshima. This event formed the basis of the "Hundredth Monkey Phenomenon."

THE MIRACLE ON KOSHIMA

According to Watson, all of the juveniles on Koshima were washing their 4 potatoes by early 1958, but the only adult washers were those who had learned from the children. In the fall of that year something astounding happened. The exact nature of the event is unclear. Watson says:

. . . One has to gather the rest of the story from personal anecdotes and bits of folklore among primate researchers, because most of them are still not quite sure what happened. And those who do suspect the truth are reluctant to publish it for fear of ridicule. So I am forced to improvise the details, but as near as I can tell, this is what seems to have happened. In the autumn of that year an unspecified number of monkeys on Koshima were washing sweet potatoes in the sea. . . . Let us say, for argument's sake, that the number was ninety-nine and that at eleven o'clock on a Tuesday morning, one further convert was added to the fold in the usual way. But the addition of the hundredth monkey apparently carried the number across some sort of threshold, pushing it through a kind of critical mass, because by that evening almost everyone was doing it. Not only that, but the habit seems to have jumped natural barriers and to have appeared spontaneously, like glycerine crystals in sealed laboratory jars, in colonies on other islands and on the mainland in a troop at Takasakiyama.

A sort of group consciousness had developed among the monkeys, Watson tells us. It had developed suddenly, as a result of one last monkey's learning potato washing by conventional means. The sudden learning of the rest of the Koshima troop was not attributable to the normal one-monkey-at-a-time methods of previous years. The new phenomenon of group consciousness was responsible not only for the sudden learning on Koshima but for the equally sudden acquisition of the habit by monkeys across the sea. Watson admits that he was forced to "improvise" some of the details—the time of the day, the day of the week, and the exact number of monkeys required for the "critical mass" were not specified in the scientific literature. But by evening (or at least in a very short period of time) almost everyone (or at least a large number of the remaining monkeys) in the colony had suddenly acquired the custom. This is remarkable in part because of the slow and gradual mode of acquisition that had typified the first five years after Imo's innovation. Even more remarkable was the sudden jumping of natural boundaries, apparently caused by the Koshima miracle.

DOCUMENTATION

In this section I investigate the relations between Watson's description of the Hundredth Monkey Phenomenon and the scientific sources by which he validates it. To be sure, we must not expect too much from the sources. Watson has warned us that the complete story was not told and that he was "forced to improvise the details." But we should expect to find some evidence of the mysteriousness of the Koshima events of 1958. In particular, we should expect to find evidence of an episode of sudden learning within the troop at this time (though perhaps not in one afternoon) and evidence of the sudden appearance of potato washing in other troops sometime soon after the Koshima event. We also have a negative expectation of the literature; it should *fail* to report certain important details. It will not (we expect) tell us the exact number of monkeys washing potatoes prior to or after the event of 1958, nor will it provide us with an explanation of how the post-event Koshima learners were able to acquire their knowledge. After all, it is Watson's claim that the event produced *paranormal* learning of potato washing. These three expectations will be tested against the literature. Was there a sudden event at Koshima? Did acquisition at other colonies follow closely the Koshima event? Does Watson improvise details *only* when the cited literature fails to provide adequate information? The following comments will be restricted to the literature on macaques actually cited by Watson.

Almost all of the information about the Koshima troop appears in a journal   7
article by Masao Kawai (1965); the other articles are secondary on this topic. Kawai's article is remarkably detailed in its description of the Koshima events. The troop numbered 20 in 1952 and grew to 49 by 1962. (At least in the numerical sense, there was never a "hundredth monkey" on Koshima.) Watson states that "an unspecified number" of monkeys on Koshima had acquired the potato-washing habit by 1958. Actually this number was far from unspecified. Kawai's data allowed the reader to determine the dates of acquisition of potato washing (and two other food behaviors), as well as the dates of birth and ge-nealogical relationships, *of every monkey in the Koshima troop from 1949 to 1962* (Figure 1, pp. 2–3, and elsewhere in the paper). In March 1958, exactly 2 of 11 monkeys over 7 years old had learned potato washing, while exactly 15 of 19 monkeys between 2 and 7 had the habit (p. 3). This amounts to 17 of 30 noninfant monkeys. There is no mention in this paper (or in any other) of a sudden learning event in the fall of 1958. However, it is noted that by 1962, 36 of the 49 monkeys had acquired the habit. So both the population and the number of potato washers had increased by 19 during this four-year period. Perhaps this is what suggested to Watson that a sudden event occurred in the fall of 1958. And perhaps (since one can only surmise) this idea was reinforced in Watson's mind by the following statement by Kawai: "The acquisition of [potato washing] behavior can be divided into two periods: before and after 1958" (p. 5).

So Kawai does not give a time of year, a day of the week, or even the season   8
for any sudden event in 1958. But he does at least identify the year. And is Kawai mystified about the difference between pre- and post-1958 acquisition? Is he "not quite sure what happened"? Is he reluctant to publish details "for fear of ridicule?" No. He publishes the whole story, in gothic detail. The post-1958 learning period was remarkable only for its normalcy. The period from 1953 to 1958 had been a period of exciting innovation. The troop encountered new food sources, and the juveniles invented ways of dealing with these sources. But by 1958 the innovative youth had become status quo adults; macaques mature faster than humans. The unusual juvenile-to-adult teaching methods reverted to the more traditional process of learning one's food manners at one's mother's knee. Imo's first child, a male named "Ika," was born in 1957 (pp. 5, 7). Imo and her former playmates brought up their children as good little potato-washers. One can only hope that Ika has been less trouble to his Mom than Imo was to hers. Kawai speaks of the innovative period from 1953 to 1958 as "individual propagation" (p. 5) and the period after 1958 as "pre-cultural propa-gation" (p. 8). (This latter term does not indicate anything unusual for the monkey troops. The troops under normal circumstances have behavioral idio-syncrasies and customs that are passed along within the group by "pre-cultural"

means. The expression only indicates a reluctance to refer to monkey behavior as genuinely "cultural.")

So there was nothing left unsaid in Kawai's description. There was nothing 9 mysterious, or even sudden, in the events of 1958. Nineteen fifty-eight and 1959 were the years of maturation of a group of innovative youngsters. The human hippies of the 1960s now know that feeling. In fact 1958 was a singularly poor year for habit acquisition on Koshima. Only two monkeys learned to wash potatoes during that year, young females named Zabon and Nogi. An average of three a year had learned potato washing during the previous five years (Table 1, p. 4). There is no evidence that Zabon and Nogi were psychic or in any other way unusual.

Let us try to take Watson seriously for a moment longer. Since only two 10 monkeys learned potato washing during 1958 (according to Watson's own citation), one of them must have been the "Hundredth Monkey." Watson leaves "unspecified" which monkey it was, so I am "forced to improvise" and "say, for argument's sake" that it was Zabon. This means that poor little Nogi carries the grim metaphysical burden of being the "almost everyone in the colony" who, according to Watson, suddenly and miraculously began to wash her potatoes on that autumn afternoon.

Watson claims that the potato-washing habit "spontaneously" leaped natural 11 barriers. Is there evidence of this? Well, two sources report that the behavior was observed off Koshima, in at least five different colonies (Kawai 1965, 23; Tsumori 1967, 219). These reports specifically state that the behavior was observed only among a few individual monkeys and that it had not spread throughout a colony. There is no report on when these behaviors occurred. They must have been observed sometime between 1953 and 1967. But there is nothing to indicate that they followed closely upon some supposed miraculous event on Koshima during the autumn of 1958, or that they occurred suddenly at any other time, or that they were in any other way remarkable.

In fact there is absolutely no reason to believe in the 1958 miracle on Ko- 12 shima. There is every reason to deny it. Watson's description of the event is refuted *in great detail* by the very sources he cites to validate it. In contrast to Watson's claims of a sudden and inexplicable event, "Such behavior patterns seem to be smoothly transmitted among individuals in the troop and handed down to the next generation" (Tsumori 1967, 207).

METHODOLOGY OF PSEUDOSCIENCE

The factual issue ends here. Watson's claim of a "Hundredth Monkey Phe- 13 nomenon" is conclusively refuted by the very sources he cites in its support. He either failed to read or misreported the information in these scientific articles. But Watson's own mode of reasoning and reporting, as well as the responses he has inspired in the popular literature, deserve attention. They exemplify the pseudoscientific tradition. Consider the following:

1. Hidden sources of information: Watson informs us that the scientific   14
reports leave important data "unspecified." This is simply false. But, more subtly, he tells us that most of the researchers are still unsure of what happened
and that those who "do suspect the truth are reluctant to publish it for fear of
ridicule." In one fell swoop Watson brands himself as courageous, explains why
no one else has dared report this miraculous phenomenon, and discourages us
from checking the cited literature for corroboration. Watson got the real story
from "personal anecdotes and bits of folklore among primate researchers. . . ."
Those of us who don't hobnob with such folks must trust Watson. The technique
was effective. Of the commentaries I have found on the Hundredth Monkey
Phenomenon, not one shows evidence of having consulted the scientific sources
cited by Watson. Nonetheless, each presents Watson's fantasy as a scientifically
authenticated fact. Nor is additional information available from Watson. I have
written both to Watson and to his publishers requesting such information and
have received no reply.

2. Aversion to naturalistic explanations: The fact is that potato washing was   15
observed on different islands. Watson infers that it had traveled in some paranormal way from one location to another. Like other aficionados of the paranormal, Watson ignores two plausible explanations of the concurrence of potato
washing. First, it could well have been an independent innovation—different
monkeys inventing the same solution to a common problem. This process is
anathema to the pseudoscientist. The natives of the Americas simply *could not
have* invented the pyramid independent of the Egyptians—they just didn't have
the smarts. In more extreme cases (von Däniken, for example[1]) a *human being*
is just too dumb to invent certain clever things—extraterrestrials must have done
it.

Watson assumes that Imo was the only monkey capable of recognizing the   16
usefulness of washing potatoes. In his words, Imo was "a monkey genius" and
potato washing is "comparable almost to the invention of the wheel." Monkeys
on other islands were too dumb for this sort of innovation. But keep in mind
that these monkeys didn't even *have* potatoes to wash before 1952 or 1953, when
provisioning began. Monkeys in at least five locations had learned potato washing by 1962. This suggests to me that these monkeys are clever creatures. It
suggests to Watson that *one* monkey was clever and that the paranormal took
care of the rest. A second neglected explanation is natural diffusion. And indeed
Kawai reports that in 1960 a potato washer named "Jugo" swam from Koshima
to the island on which the Takasakiyama troop lives. Jugo returned in 1964
(Kawai 1965, 17). Watson does not mention this. The Japanese monkeys are
known to be both clever and mobile, and either characteristic might explain
the interisland spread of potato washing. Watson ignores both explanations,
preferring to invent a new paranormal power.

---

[1]Erich von Däniken (b. 1935): author of such science fiction as *Chariots of the Gods?* (1968)
and *Gods from Outer Space* (1971). [Eds.]

3. Inflation of the miracle: As myths get passed along, everyone puffs them   17
up a bit. The following two examples come from second-generation commentaries that quote extensively from Watson. Nevertheless, even Watson's claims
are beginning to bulge. First, the primatologists' reports had mentioned that
only a few isolated cases of off-Koshima potato-washing were observed. Watson
reports this as the habit's having "appeared spontaneously . . . in colonies on
other islands. . . ." Not actually false, since the few individuals were indeed *in*
other colonies (though only individuals and not whole colonies adopted the
behavior). Following Watson, Ken Keyes reports that, after the hundredth Koshima
monkey, "colonies of monkeys on other islands . . . began washing their sweet
potatoes" (Keyes 1982, p. 16). From Keyes, one gets the image of spontaneous
mass orgies of spud-dunking. A second example: Regarding the primatologists'
attitudes toward the events of 1958, Watson reports only that they are "still not
quite sure what happened." But the primatological confusion quickly grows, for
Science Digest (1981) reports "a mystery which has stumped scientists for nearly
a quarter of a century." In these two particular cases, Watson's own statements
are at least modest. They're not what one would call accurate, but not exorbi-
tantly false either. By the second generation we find that "not quite sure what
happened" becomes "stumped for nearly a quarter of a century," and the habit
that *appeared in* individuals within colonies of monkeys becomes a habit *of*
colonies of monkeys. Please keep in mind that the second generation relies *only*
on Watson for its information; even Watson's none-too-accurate report has been
distorted—and not, needless to say, in the direction of accuracy.

4. The paranormal validates the paranormal: The validity of one supernatural   18
report is strengthened by its consistency with other such reports. Watson's commentators show how this works. Keyes supports the Hundredth Monkey Phenomenon by its consistency with J. B. Rhine's work at Duke, which "demonstrated" telepathy between individual humans.[2] "We now know that the strength
of this extrasensory communication can be amplified to a powerfully effective
level when the consciousness of the 'hundredth person' is added" (Keyes 1982,
18). Elda Hartley's film "The Hundredth Monkey" invokes Edgar Cayce.[3] And
in a remarkable feat of group consciousness, *four of the five* secondary sources
emphasize the similarities between Watson's Hundredth Monkey Phenomenon
and Rupert Sheldrake's notion of the "morphogenetic field."[4] The spontaneous
recognition of the similarities between Watson and Sheldrake seems to have

[2]Joseph Banks Rhine (b. 1895): American parapsychologist known for his research in extrasensory
perception. [Eds.]
[3]Edgar Cayce (1877–1945): American medium who preached reincarnation, diet, and geological
changes. [Eds.]
[4]morphogenetic field: Sheldrake claims that "morphogenetic fields" are given off by the forms
(morphologies) of physical objects. These fields influence other objects by "formative causation," a
nonphysical power which may extend through time and space. He uses this idea to support ESP,
among other things. Needless to say, this concept is not credited by most biologists. [Eds.]

leaped the natural boundaries between the four publications! Now *there's* a miracle! (Surely independent invention or natural diffusion couldn't account for such a coincidence.)

CONCLUSIONS

I must admit sympathy for some of the secondary sources on the Hundredth [19] Monkey Phenomenon. This feeling comes from the purpose for which the phenomenon was cited. Ken Keyes's book uses the phenomenon as a theme, but the real topic of the book is nuclear disarmament. Arthur Stein's article and (to a lesser extent) the Hartley film are inspired by Keyes's hope that the Hundredth Monkey Phenomenon may help prevent nuclear war. The message is that "you may be the Hundredth Monkey" whose contribution to the collective consciousness turns the world away from nuclear holocaust. It is hard to find fault in this motive. For these very same reasons, one couldn't fault the motives of a child who wrote to Santa Claus requesting world nuclear disarmament as a Christmas present. We can only hope that Santa Claus and the Hundredth Monkey are not our best chances to avoid nuclear war.

Watson's primary concern is not prevention of war but sheer love of the [20] paranormal. His book begins with a description of a child who, before Watson's own eyes, and with a "short implosive sound, very soft, like a cork being drawn in the dark," psychically turned a tennis ball inside out—fuzz side in, rubber side out—without losing air pressure (p. 18). Just after the Hundredth Monkey discussion, Watson makes a revealing point. He quotes with approval a statement attributed to Lawrence Blair: "When a myth is shared by large numbers of people, it becomes a reality" (p. 148). This sort of relativist epistemology is not unusual in New Age thought. I would express Blair's thought somewhat differently: "Convince enough people of a lie, and it becomes the truth." I suggest that someone who accepts this view of truth is not to be trusted as a source of knowledge. He may, of course, be a marvelous source of fantasy, rumor, and pseudoscientific best-sellers.

I prefer epistemological realism to this sort of relativism. Truth is not de- [21] pendent on the numbers of believers or on the frequency of published repetition. My preferred epistemology can be expressed simply: Facts are facts. There is no Hundredth Monkey Phenomenon.

REFERENCES

Brain/Mind Bulletin.
1982. *The hundredth monkey.* In *"Updated Special Issue: 'A New Science of Life.'"*
HARTLEY, ELDA (producer).
1983. *The Hundredth Monkey* (film and videotape). Hartley Film Foundation, Inc. Cos Cob. Conn.

IMANISHI, KINJI.
1963.   Social behavior in Japanese monkeys. In *Primate Social Behavior*, Charles A. Southwick, ed. Toronto: Van Nostrand.
KAWAI, MASAO.
1963.   On the newly-acquired behaviors of the natural troop of Japanese monkeys on Koshima island. *Primates*, 4:113–115.
———.
1965.   On the newly-acquired pre-cultural behavior of the natural troop of Japanese monkeys on Koshima Islet. *Primates*, 6:1–30.
KAWAMURA, SYUNZO.
1963.   Subcultural propagation among Japanese macaques. In *Primate Social Behavior*, Charles A. Southwick, ed. Toronto: Van Nostrand.
KEYES, KEN, JR.
1982.   *The Hundredth Monkey*, Coos Bay, Ore.: Vision Books.
Science Digest.
1981.   *The quantum monkey.* Vol. 8:57.
SHELDRAKE, RUPERT.
1981.   *A New Science of Life*, Los Angeles: J. P. Tarcher.
STEIN, ARTHUR.
1983.   The "hundredth monkey" and humanity's quest for survival. *Phoenix Journal of Transpersonal Anthropology*, 7:29–40.
TSUMORI, ATSUO.
1967.   Newly acquired behavior and social interactions of Japanese monkeys. In *Social Communication Among Primates.* Stuart Altman, ed. Chicago: University of Chicago Press.
WATSON, LYALL.
1979.   *Lifetide.* New York: Simon and Schuster.

QUESTIONS

1. Why is Amundson's article grouped with readings from the humanities rather than the sciences?

2. What *is* truly remarkable about the Japanese macaques?

3. How might the monkeys interpret this sweet potato caper?

4. How does Amundson organize his argument? Make an outline of his essay's structure.

5. Amundson makes no secret of his attitude towards Watson. In what ways does he reveal it? Do you find Amundson's tone appropriate for the subject under discussion? Explain.

6. What general lessons about the use of source material can be drawn from Watson's use of sources? What lessons can be drawn from Amundson's use of sources?

7. Apply Amundson's four points about the methodology of pseudoscience to a story in a sensationalist newspaper (the kind you find by the supermarket checkout with headlines such as "North Dakota Woman Moves Pudding with Her Mind" or "New Orleans Tot Recalls War of 1812").

8. For a research project, investigate the works and popularity of one of the paranormal writers and promoters mentioned in this article (for example, Erich von Däniken, Edgar Cayce, or J. B. Rhine). Use the information you gather as a basis for responding to Amundson's question of "why we are so eager to believe in myths of mental miracles."

TWO VIEWS
OF FAITH

Richard Robinson
Richard Taylor

*The following two selections are the work of philosophers who
present opposed views on religious faith. Richard G. F. Robinson took his degrees at Oxford University in England and
Cornell University in the United States. His Ph.D. thesis
on logic was published in 1931, and he has since written a
number of books while teaching at Oriel College of Oxford
University. Richard Clyde Taylor (b. 1919), with degrees
from Oberlin College and Brown University, is a specialist
in metaphysics and ethics who has taught at Brown, Columbia, and Rochester universities. Taylor's selection appeared first in the philosopher Sidney Hook's anthology,* Religious Experience and Truth *(1961). Robinson's was a part
of his lectures at Oxford, published in 1964 as* An Atheist's
Values.*

FAITH

According to Christianity one of the great virtues is faith. Paul gave faith a   1
commanding position in the Christian scheme of values, along with hope and
love, in the famous thirteenth chapter of his first letter to the Corinthians.
Thomas Aquinas held that infidelity is a very great sin,[1] that infidels should be
compelled to believe, that heretics should not be tolerated, and that heretics
who revert to the true doctrine and then relapse again should be received into
penitence, but killed (*Summa Theologica*, 2-2, 1–16).

According to me this is a terrible mistake, and faith is not a virtue but a   2
positive vice. More precisely, there is, indeed, a virtue often called faith, but
that is not the faith which the Christians make much of. The true virtue of
faith is faith as opposed to faithlessness, that is, keeping faith and promises and
being loyal. Christian faith, however, is not opposed to faithlessness but to
unbelief. It is faith as some opposite of unbelief that I declare to be a vice.

---

[1](St.) Thomas Aquinas (1225–1274): Italian Dominican monk, teacher, and philosopher; he is
regarded as the most important theologian of medieval Europe. [Eds.]

When we investigate what Christians mean by their peculiar use of the word 3
"faith," I think we come to the remarkable conclusion that all their accounts
of it are either unintelligible or false. Their most famous account is that in Heb.
xi. 1: "Faith is the substance of things hoped for, the evidence of things not
seen." This is obviously unintelligible. In any case, it does not make faith a
virtue, since neither a substance nor an evidence can be a virtue. A virtue is a
praiseworthy habit of choice, and neither a substance nor an evidence can be
a habit of choice. When a Christian gives an intelligible account of faith, I
think you will find that it is false. I mean that it is not a true dictionary report
of how he and other Christians actually use the word. For example, Augustine
asked:[2] "What is faith but believing what you do not see?" (*Joannis Evang.
Tract.*, c. 40, § 8). But Christians do not use the word "faith" in the sense of
believing what you do not see. You do not see thunder; but you cannot say in
the Christian sense: "Have faith that it is thundering," or "I have faith that it
has thundered in the past and will again in the future." You do not see mathematical truths; but you cannot say in the Christian sense: "Have faith that there
is no greatest number." If we take Augustine's "see" to stand here for "know,"
still it is false that Christians use the word "faith" to mean believing what you
do not know, for they would never call it faith if anyone believed that the sun
converts hydrogen into helium, although he did not know it.

A good hint of what Christians really mean by their word "faith" can be got 4
by considering the proposition: "Tom Paine had faith that there is no god." Is
this a possible remark, in the Christian sense of the word "faith"? No, it is an
impossible remark, because it is self-contradictory, because part of what Christians mean by "faith" is belief that there *is* a god.

There is more to it than this. Christian faith is not merely believing that 5
there is a god. It is believing that there is a god no matter what the evidence
on the question may be. "Have faith," in the Christian sense, means "Make
yourself believe that there is a god without regard to evidence." Christian faith
is a habit of flouting reason in forming and maintaining one's answer to the
question whether there is a god. Its essence is the determination to believe that
there is a god no matter what the evidence may be.

No wonder that there is no true and intelligible account of faith in Christian 6
literature. What they mean is too shocking to survive exposure. Faith is a great
vice, an example of obstinately refusing to listen to reason, something irrational
and undesirable, a form of self-hypnotism. Newman wrote that "If we but obey
God strictly, in time (through his blessing) faith will become like sight" (*Sermon*
15).[3] This is no better than if he had said: "Keep on telling yourself that there
is a god until you believe it. Hypnotize yourself into this belief."

---

[2](St.) Augustine (354–430): Bishop of Hippo, Christian philosopher and theologian; his best-
known works are *The Confessions* and *The City of God.* [Eds.]

[3]John Henry Newman (1801–1890): a leader of the religious revival movement in Victorian
England, he converted to Catholicism and entered the priesthood, becoming a cardinal in 1879.
[Eds.]

It follows that, far from its being wicked to undermine faith, it is a duty to 7
do so. We ought to do what we can toward eradicating the evil habit of believing
without regard to evidence.

The usual way of recommending faith is to point out that belief and trust 8
are often rational or necessary attitudes. Here is an example of this from Newman: "To hear some men speak (I mean men who scoff at religion), it might
be thought we never acted on Faith or Trust, except in religious matters; whereas
we are acting on trust every hour of our lives. . . . We trust our *memory* . . . the
general soundness of our reasoning powers. . . . Faith in (the) sense of *reliance
on the words of another* as opposed to trust in oneself . . . is the common
meaning of the word" (*Sermon* 15).

The value of this sort of argument is as follows. It is certainly true that belief 9
and trust are often rational. But it is also certainly true that belief and trust are
often irrational. We have to decide in each case by rational considerations
whether to believe and trust or not. Sometimes we correctly decide *not* to trust
our memory on some point, but to look the matter up in a book. Sometimes
even we correctly decide not to trust our own reason, like poor Canning deciding
he was mad because the Duke of Wellington told him he was. But Christian
faith is essentially a case of irrational belief and trust and decision, because it
consists in deciding to believe and trust the proposition that there is a god no
matter what the evidence may be.

Another common way to defend Christian faith is to point out that we are 10
often obliged to act on something less than knowledge and proof. For example,
Newman writes: "Life is not long enough for a religion of inferences; we shall
never have done beginning if we determine to begin with proof. Life is for
action. If we insist on proof for everything, we shall never come to action; to
act you must assume, and that assumption is faith" (*Assent*, p. 92).

The value of this argument is as follows. It is true that we are often unable 11
to obtain knowledge and proof. But it does not follow that we must act on faith,
for faith is belief reckless of evidence and probability. It follows only that we
must act on some belief that does not amount to knowledge. This being so, we
ought to assume, as our basis for action, those beliefs which are more probable
than their contradictories in the light of the available evidence. We ought not
to act on faith, for faith is assuming a certain belief without reference to its
probability.

There is an ambiguity in the phrase "have faith in" that helps to make faith 12
look respectable. When a man says that he has faith in the president he is
assuming that it is obvious and known to everybody that there is a president,
that the president exists, and he is asserting his confidence that the president
will do good work on the whole. But if a man says he has faith in telepathy,
he does not mean that he is confident that telepathy will do good work on the
whole, but that he believes that telepathy really occurs sometimes, that telepathy
exists. Thus the phrase "to have faith in *x*" sometimes means to be confident
that good work will be done by *x*, who is assumed or known to exist, but at

591

other times means to believe that *x* exists. Which does it mean in the phrase "have faith in God"? It means ambiguously both; and the self-evidence of what it means in the one sense recommends what it means in the other sense. If there is a perfectly powerful and good god it is self-evidently reasonable to believe that he will do good. In this sense "Have faith in God" is a reasonable exhortation. But it insinuates the other sense, namely "Believe that there is a perfectly powerful and good god, no matter what the evidence." Thus the reasonableness of trusting God if he exists is used to make it seem also reasonable to believe that he exists.

It is well to remark here that a god who wished us to decide certain questions 13 without regard to the evidence would definitely *not* be a perfectly good god.

Even when a person is aware that faith is belief without regard to evidence, 14 he may be led to hold faith respectable by the consideration that we sometimes think it good for a man to believe in his friend's honesty in spite of strong evidence to the contrary, or for a woman to believe in her son's innocence in spite of strong evidence to the contrary. But while we admire and love the love that leads the friend or parent to this view, we do not adopt or admire his conclusion unless we believe that he has private evidence of his own, gained by his long and intimate association, to outweigh the public evidence on the other side. Usually we suppose that his love has led him into an error of judgment, which both love and hate are prone to do.

This does not imply that we should never act on a man's word if we think 15 he is deceiving us. Sometimes we ought to act on a man's word although we privately think he is probably lying. For the act required may be unimportant, whereas accusing a man of lying is always important. But there is no argument from this to faith. We cannot say that sometimes we ought to believe a proposition although we think it is false!

So I conclude that faith is a vice and to be condemned. As Plato said, "It is 16 unholy to abandon the probably true" (*Rp.* 607 c). Out of Paul's "faith, hope, and love" I emphatically accept love and reject faith. As to hope, it is more respectable than faith. While we ought not to believe against the probabilities, we are permitted to hope against them. But still the Christian overtones of hope are other-worldly and unrealistic. It is better to take a virtue that avoids that. Instead of faith, hope, and love, let us hymn reason, love, and joy.

Richard Robinson

FAITH

"Our most holy religion," David Hume said,[1] "is founded on *faith*, not on   1
reason." (All quotations are from the last two paragraphs of Hume's essay "Of
Miracles.") He did not then conclude that it ought, therefore, to be rejected by
reasonable men. On the contrary, he suggests that rational evaluation has no
proper place in this realm to begin with, that a religious man need not feel in
the least compelled to put his religion "to such a trial as it is, by no means,
fitted to endure," and he brands as "dangerous friends or disguised enemies" of
religion those "who have undertaken to defend it by the principles of human
reason."

I want to defend Hume's suggestion, and go a bit farther by eliciting some   2
things that seem uniquely characteristic of *Christian* faith, in order to show
what it has, and what it has not, in common with other things to which it is
often compared. I limited myself to Christian faith because I know rather little
of any other, and faith is, with love and hope, supposed to be a uniquely
Christian virtue.

FAITH AND REASON

Faith is not reason, else religion would be, along with logic and metaphysics,   3
a part of philosophy, which it assuredly is not. Nor is faith belief resting on
scientific or historical inquiry, else religion would be part of the corpus of human
knowledge, which it clearly is not. More than that, it seems evident that by the
normal, common-sense criteria of what is reasonable, the content of Christian
faith is *unreasonable*. This, I believe, should be the starting point, the *datum*,
of any discussion of faith and reason. It is, for instance, an essential content of
the Christian faith that, at a certain quite recent time, God became man, dwelt
among us in the person of a humble servant, and then, for a sacred purpose,
died, to live again. Now, apologetics usually addresses itself to the *details* of this
story, to show that they are not inherently incredible, but this is to miss the
point. It is indeed *possible* to believe it, and in the strict sense the story is
credible. Millions of people do most deeply and firmly believe it. But even the
barest statement of the content of that belief makes it manifest that it does not
and, I think, could not, ever result from rational inquiry. "Mere reason," Hume
said, "is insufficient to convince us of its veracity." The Christian begins the
recital of his faith with the words, "I believe," and it would be an utter distortion
to construe this as anything like "I have inquired, and found it reasonable to
conclude." If there were a man who could say that in honesty, as I think there
is not, then he would, in a clear and ordinary sense, believe, but he would

---

[1]David Hume (1711–1776): Scottish philosopher and historian. [Eds.]

593

have no religious faith whatsoever, and his beliefs themselves would be robbed of what would make them religious.

Now if this essential and (it seems to me) obvious unreasonableness of Chris- 4
tian belief could be recognized at the outset of any discussion of religion, involving rationalists on the one hand and believers on the other, we would be spared the tiresome attack and apologetics upon which nothing ultimately turns, the believer would be spared what is, in fact, an uncalled-for task of reducing his faith to reason or science, which can, as Hume noted, result only in "exposing" it as neither, and the rationalist would be granted his main point, not as a conclusion triumphantly extracted, but as a datum too obvious to labor.

FAITH AND CERTAINTY

Why, then, does a devout Christian embrace these beliefs? Now this very 5
question, on the lips of a philosopher, is wrongly expressed, for he invariably intends it as a request for reasons, as a means of putting the beliefs to that unfair "trial" of which Hume spoke. Yet there is a clear and definite answer to this question, which has the merit of being true and evident to anyone who has known intimately those who dwell in the atmosphere of faith. The reason the Christian believes that story around which his whole life turns is, simply, that he cannot help it. If he is trapped into eliciting grounds for it, they are grounds given after the fact of conviction. Within "the circle of faith," the question whether on the evidence one *ought* to believe "does not arise." One neither seeks nor needs grounds for the acceptance of what he cannot help believing. "Whoever is moved by *faith* to assent," Hume wrote, "is conscious of a continued miracle in his own person, which subverts all the principles of his understanding, and gives him a determination to believe. . . ." It is this fact of faith which drives philosophers to such exasperation, in the face of which the believer is nonetheless so utterly unmoved.

The believer sees his life as a gift of God, the world as the creation of God, 6
his own purposes, insofar as they are noble, as the purposes of God, and history as exhibiting a divine plan, made known to him through the Christian story. He sees things this way, just because they do seem so, and he cannot help it. This is why, for him, faith is so "easy," and secular arguments to the contrary so beside the point. No one seeks evidence for that of which he is entirely convinced, or regards as relevant what seems to others to cast doubt. The believer is like a child who recoils from danger, as exhibited, for instance, in what he for the first time sees as a fierce animal; the child has no difficulty *believing* he is in peril, just because he cannot help believing it, yet his belief results not at all from induction based on past experience with fierce animals, and no reassurances, garnered from *our* past experience, relieve his terror at all.

594

SOME CONFUSIONS

If this is what religious faith essentially is—if, as a believer might poetically   7
but, I think, correctly describe it, faith is an involuntary conviction, often regarded as a "gift," on the part of one who has voluntarily opened his mind and
heart to receive it—then certain common misunderstandings can be removed.

In the first place, faith should never be likened to an *assumption*, such as   8
the scientist's assumption of the uniformity of nature, or whatnot. An assumption is an intellectual device for furthering inquiry. It need not be a conviction
nor, indeed, even a belief. But a half-hearted faith is no religious faith. Faith
thus has that much, at least, in common with knowledge, that it is a *conviction*,
and its subjective state is *certainty*. One thus wholly distorts faith if he represents
the believer as just "taking" certain things "on faith," and then reasons, like a
philosopher, from these beginnings, as though what were thus "taken" could,
like an assumption, be rejected at will.

Again, it is a misunderstanding to represent faith as "mere tenacity." Tenacity   9
consists in stubbornly clinging to what one hopes, but of which one is not fully
convinced. The child who is instantly convinced of danger in the presence of
an animal is not being tenacious or stubborn, even in the face of verbal reassurances, and no more is the Christian whose acts are moved by faith. The
believer does not so much *shun* evidence as something that might *shake* his
faith, but rather regards it as not to the point. In this he may appear to philosophers to be mistaken, but only if one supposes, as he need not, that one should
hold only such beliefs as are rational.

Again, it is misleading to refer to any set of propositions, such as those   10
embodied in a creed, as being this or that person's "faith." Concerning that
content of belief in which one is convinced by faith, it is logically (though I
think not otherwise) possible that one might be convinced by evidence, in which
case it would have no more to do with faith or religion than do the statements
in a newspaper. This observation has this practical importance, that it is quite
possible—in fact, common—for the faith of different believers to be one and
the same, despite creedal differences.

And finally, both "faith" (or "fideism") and "reason" (or "rationalism") can   11
be, and often are, used as pejorative terms and as terms of commendation.
Which side one takes here is arbitrary, for there is no non-question-begging way
of deciding. A rationalist can perhaps find reasons for being a rationalist, though
this is doubtful; but in any case it would betray a basic misunderstanding to
expect a fideist to do likewise. This is brought out quite clearly by the direction
that discussions of religion usually take. A philosophical teacher will often, for
instance, labor long to persuade his audience that the content of Christian faith
is unreasonable, which is a shamefully easy task for him, unworthy of his
learning. Then, suddenly, the underlying assumption comes to light that Christian beliefs ought, therefore, to be abandoned by rational people! A religious

hearer of this discourse might well reply that, religion being unreasonable but nonetheless manifestly worthy of belief, we should conclude with Hume that reason, in this realm at least, ought to be rejected. Now one can decide *that* issue by any light that is granted him, but it is worth stressing that the believer's position on it is just exactly as good, and just as bad, as the rational skeptic's.

Richard Taylor

QUESTIONS

1. What is the main point of each essay? Discuss this by completing the following two summary statements.
    a. Robinson: "Faith is a vice because . . ."
    b. Taylor: "Faith is a virtue because . . ."
Are the two essays arguing opposite sides of the same question, or are they arguing two different questions?

2. Throughout his essay, Taylor gives the impression that the famous skeptic and rationalist David Hume agrees with him that reason should be "rejected" in favor of faith. Suppose he were quoting Hume out of context to support his own case. Would it matter? Is Taylor under any obligation to argue reasonably?

3. Is it fair to say that Robinson is making a god of reason? How do you suppose he would respond to that charge?

4. Taylor concludes that religion is "unreasonable but nonetheless manifestly worthy of belief." What does he mean by "manifestly"? Has he taken any steps to show why religion is worthy of belief? Could he have done a better job on this, or has he done enough?

5. How might you answer the contention of Robinson's paragraph 13? What is Robinson's assumption in that passage? How could you argue that a "perfectly good god" might very well wish us "to decide certain questions without regard to the evidence"? What would you mean, then, by "a perfectly good god"?

6. What do you think of the three virtues Robinson proposes in his final paragraph? Write an essay either defending or attacking "reason, love, and joy" as the central virtues.

7. If you ever have defended yourself either against a person of more faith than yourself or against one more devoted to reason, write an account of that confrontation. What were the positions taken, as you remember them? What were the assumptions governing your argument and that of your opponent? How could you improve on that argument now?

8. Probably you have listened at one time or another either to an evangelical minister or to an unabashed skeptic inveighing against Christian belief. Try to reconstruct the presentation of one such speaker, insofar as you can remember it. How would you characterize that presentation? Is it an argument or something else? (You might want to seek out such a speaker again in order to reacquaint yourself with a presentation you could describe.)

9. If you answered question 8, write an essay that either attacks the presentation you described or that recasts it as a more formal argument.

10. Read David Hume's essay "Of Miracles," which you can find in your library copy of his *Enquiry Concerning Human Understanding*, where it appears as section X. Try to summarize Hume's argument in your own words, and then consider Taylor's position in relation to Hume's. Conclude by arguing either that Taylor has distorted Hume or that he has represented Hume's position fairly in his essay on "Faith."

TWO POETS CONSIDER YOUTH AND BEAUTY

Andrew Marvell
William Butler Yeats

Andrew Marvell (1621–1678), born in Winestead, Eng-
land, was a Puritan who was best known during his lifetime
as a public servant. While pursuing careers as a clerk, a
tutor, and a member of Parliament, Marvell wrote his poems
which were not published until after his death and not ap-
preciated until recently. William Butler Yeats (1865–1939)
was born near Dublin, Ireland, and took an early interest
in the Irish folklore and mythology that, along with Irish
politics, infuses much of his poetry. In each poem presented
here, a male speaker presents an argument to a woman
based on physical attributes.

TO HIS COY MISTRESS

    Had we but world enough and time,
This coyness, lady, were no crime.
We would sit down, and think which way
To walk, and pass our long love's day.
Thou by the Indian Ganges' side   5
Shouldst rubies find; I by the tide
Of Humber[1] would complain. I would
Love you ten years before the Flood;[2]
And you should, if you please, refuse
Till the conversion of the Jews.[3]   10
My vegetable love should grow
Vaster than empires, and more slow.
An hundred years should go to praise
Thine eyes, and on thy forehead gaze;
Two hundred to adore each breast;   15
But thirty thousand to the rest:

---

[1]Humber: English river flowing into the North Sea. [Eds.]
[2]Flood: Noah's, in the Old Testament. [Eds.]
[3]conversion of the Jews: supposed to occur at the end of time. [Eds.]

An age at least to every part,
And the last age should show your heart.
For, lady, you deserve this state;
Nor would I love at lower rate.   20
    But at my back I always hear
Time's wingèd chariot hurrying near;
And yonder all before us lie
Deserts of vast eternity.
Thy beauty shall no more be found,   25
Nor, in thy marble vault, shall sound
My echoing song. Then worms shall try
That long preserved virginity:
And your quaint honor turn to dust;
And into ashes all my lust.   30
The grave's a fine and private place,
But none, I think, do there embrace.
    Now, therefore, while the youthful hue
Sits on thy skin like morning dew,
And while thy willing soul transpires   35
At every pore with instant fires,
Now let us sport us while we may;
And now, like amorous birds of prey,
Rather at once our time devour
Than languish in his slow-chapped[4] power.   40
Let us roll all our strength and all
Our sweetness up into one ball;
And tear our pleasures with rough strife
Through the iron gates of life.
Thus, though we cannot make our sun   45
Stand still, yet we will make him run.

                                Andrew Marvell

FOR ANNE GREGORY[1]

"Never shall a young man,
Thrown into despair
By those great honey-coloured
Ramparts at your ear,

---

[4]slow-chapped: slow-jawed. [Eds.]
[1]Anne Gregory: the granddaughter of Yeats's friend and patron, Lady Gregory.

Love you for yourself alone 5
And not your yellow hair."

"But I can get a hair-dye
And set such color there,
Brown, or black, or carrot,
That young men in despair 10
May love me for myself alone
And not my yellow hair."

"I heard an old religious man
But yesternight declare
That he had found a text to prove 15
That only God, my dear,
Could love you for yourself alone
And not your yellow hair."

William Butler Yeats

QUESTIONS

1. "To His Coy Mistress" is structured in three sections (lines 1 to 20, 21 to 32, and 33 to 46). Write a paraphrase of each section, and then determine what the logical argument is in each section.

2. Describe the imagery in each section of "To His Coy Mistress." How does the imagery contribute to the persuasiveness of the argument?

3. In "For Anne Gregory," how is the young woman's hair perceived in lines 3 and 4? Why does it cause "despair" (line 2)?

4. How would you describe the speakers in each of these poems? How would you compare their purposes?

5. Although Yeats's poem, like Marvell's, has a three-part structure, "For Anne Gregory" differs in being a dialogue. How else does it differ as an argument from Marvell's poem?

6. Write a comparison of the messages about physical beauty in the two poems. If you think that any of the speakers in the poems may be considered sexist, you might include that issue in your discussion.

7. Write a response from the coy mistress to the speaker in Marvell's poem in which she tries to refute his argument.

Social Sciences and Public Affairs

SOME VERY MODEST PROPOSALS FOR THE IMPROVEMENT OF AMERICAN EDUCATION

Nathan Glazer

Nathan Glazer (b. 1923) is a New York City native, a professor of education and sociology at Harvard University, and coeditor of The Public Interest *magazine. His books include* The Lonely Crowd *(1950) with Reuel Denney and David Riesman,* Beyond the Melting Pot *(2d edition, 1970) with Daniel P. Moynihan,* Affirmative Discrimination: Ethnic Inequality and Public Policy *(1975) and an essay collection,* Ethnic Dilemmas, 1964–1982 *(1983). The following essay appeared first in the magazine* Daedalus, *an interdisciplinary journal of The American Academy of Arts and Sciences (Fall 1984). By mentioning "modest proposals," Glazer refers to Jonathan Swift whose famous essay appears later in this section. By that term, Glazer also suggests deceptively simple steps that go directly to the heart of the problem. How "modest" are his proposals?*

That we can do a great deal for the sorry state of American education with   1
more money is generally accepted. Even apparently modest proposals will, however, cost a great deal of money. Consider something as simple as increasing the average compensation of American teachers—who are generally considered underpaid—by $2,000 a year each. The bill would come to five billion dollars a year. A similar figure is reached by the report of the highly qualified Twentieth Century Fund Task Force on Federal, Elementary, and Secondary Educational Policy, which proposes fellowships and additional compensation for master

teachers. Reducing class size 10 percent, or increasing the number of teachers by the same percentage would cost another five billion dollars. With present-day federal deficits, these look like small sums, but since education is paid for almost entirely by states and local government, these modest proposals would lead to substantial and painful tax increases. (I leave aside for the moment the views of skeptics who believe that none of these changes would matter.)

But the occasional visitor to American schools will note some changes that would cost much less, nothing at all, or even save money—and yet would improve at least the educational *environment* in American schools (once again, we ignore those skeptics who would insist that even a better educational environment cannot be guaranteed to improve educational achievement). In the spirit of evoking further cheap proposals, here is a small list of suggestions that, to my mind at least—and the mind I believe of any adult who visits American public schools—would mean a clear plus for American education:

1. *Disconnect all loudspeaker systems in American schools—or at least reserve them, like the hotline between Moscow and Washington, for only the gravest emergencies.* The American classroom—and the American teacher and his or her charges—is continually interrupted by announcements from central headquarters over the loudspeaker system. These remind teachers to bring in some form or other; or students to bring in some form or other; or students engaged in some activity to remember to come to practice or rehearsal; or they announce a change of time for some activity. There is nothing so unnerving to a teacher engaged in trying to explain something, or a student engaged in trying to understand something, as the crackle of the loudspeaker prepared to issue an announcement, and the harsh and gravelly voice (the systems are not obviously of the highest grade) of the announcement itself.

Aside from questions of personal taste, why would this be a good idea? As I have suggested, one reason is that the loudspeaker interrupts efforts to communicate complicated material that requires undivided attention. Second, it demeans the teacher as professional: every announcement tells her whatever she is doing is not very important and can be interrupted at any time. Third, it accentuates the notion of hierarchy in education—the principal and assistant principal are the most important people, and command time and attention even in the midst of instruction. Perhaps I have been softened by too many years as a college teacher, but it would be unimaginable that a loudspeaker, if one existed, would ever interrupt a college class except under conditions of the gravest and most immediate threat to life and limb. One way of showing students that education is important is not to interrupt it for band-rehearsal announcements.

2. *Disarm the school.* One of the most depressing aspects of the urban school in the United States is the degree of security manifest within it, and that seems

to me quite contradictory to what a school should be. Outer doors are locked. Security guards are present in the corridors. Internal doors are locked. Passes are necessary to enter the school or move within it, for outsiders and for students. Students are marched in groups from classroom to classroom, under the eye of the teachers. It is understandable that given the conditions in lower-class areas in our large cities—and not only lower-class areas—some degree of security-mindedness is necessary. There is valuable equipment—typewriters, computers, audio-visual equipment—that can be stolen; vandalism is a serious concern; marauders can enter the school in search for equipment, or teachers' pocket-books, or to threaten directly personal safety in search of money or sex, and so on. School integration and busing, at least in their initial stages, have contrib-uted to increased interracial tensions in schools and have in part severed the link between community and school. The difference in ethnic and racial com-position of faculty, other staff, administrators, and students contributes to the same end.

Having acknowledged all this, I still believe the school should feel less like a prison than it does. One should examine to what extent outside doors must be closed; to what extent the security guard cannot be replaced by local parents, volunteer or paid; the degree to which the endless bells indicating "stop" and "go" are really necessary. I suspect that now that the most difficult period of school integration has passed, now that teachers and administrators and staff more closely parallel in race and ethnic background students and community owing to the increase in black and Hispanic teachers and administrators, we may be saddled with more security than we need. Here we come to the sticky problem of *removing* security measures whose need has decreased. What school board will open itself to suit or to public criticism by deliberately providing *less* security? And yet one must consider the atmosphere of the school and a school's primary objective as a reaching agent: can this be reconciled with a condition of maximum security? Perhaps there are lessons to be learned from colleges and community colleges in older urban areas, which in my experience do seem to manage with less security. One reason is that there are more adults around in such institutions. Is that a hint as to how we could manage better in our public schools?

3. *Enlist the children in keeping the school clean.* Occasionally we see a practice abroad that suggests possible transfer to the American scene. In Japan, the children clean the school. There is a time of day when mops and pails and brooms come out, and the children sweep up and wash up. This does, I am sure, suggest to the children that this is *their* school, that it is not simply a matter of being forced to go to a foreign institution that imposes alien demands upon them. I can imagine some obstacles in the way of instituting regular student clean-up in American schools—custodians' unions, for example, might object. But they can be reassured that children don't do that good a job, and

they will still be needed. Once again, as in the case of the security problem, one wants to create in the school, if at all possible, a common enterprise of teachers and students, without the latter being bored and resistant, the former, in response, becoming equally indifferent. The school should be seen as everyone's workplace—and participation in cleaning the school will help.

4. *Save old schools.* Build fewer new ones. It has often surprised me that 8 while in schools such as Eton and Oxford—and indeed well-known private schools and colleges in the United States—old buildings are prized, in so many communities older public schools are torn down when to the naked eye they have many virtues that would warrant their maintenance and use. Only a few blocks from where I live, an excellent example of late nineteenth-century fine brickwork and carved stonework that served as the Cambridge Latin School came down for a remodeling. The carved elements are still displayed about the remodeled school, but why a building of such character should have deserved demolition escaped my understanding, particularly since one can take it almost as a given that a school building put up before the 1940s will be built of heavier and sturdier materials than one constructed today. Even the inconveniences of the old can possess a charm that makes them worthwhile. And indeed many of the reforms that seemed to require new buildings (for example, classrooms without walls, concentrated around activities centers in large open rooms) have turned out, on use, to be not so desirable. Our aim should be to give each school a history, a character, something that at least some students respond to. The pressures for new buildings are enormous, and sometimes perfectly legitimate (as when communities expand), but often illegitimate, as when builders and building-trades workers and contract-givers seek an opportunity or when state aid makes it appear as if a new building won't cost anything.

5. *Look on new hardware with a skeptical eye.* I think it likely that the passion 9 for the new in the way of teaching-hardware not only does not contribute to higher education achievement but may well serve as a temporary means to evade the real and hard tasks of teaching—which really require almost no hardware at all, besides textbooks, blackboard, and chalk. Admittedly, when one comes to high-school science, something more is called for. And yet our tendency is to always find cover behind new hardware. It's *fun* to get new audio-visual equipment, new rooms equipped with them in which all kinds of things can be done by flicking a switch or twisting a dial, or, as is now the case, to decide what kind of personal computers and software are necessary for a good educational program. Once again, foreign experience can be enlightening. When Japanese education was already well ahead of American, most Japanese schools were in prewar wooden buildings. (They are now as up-to-date as ours, but neither their age nor up-to-dateness has much to do with their good record of achievement.) Resisting the appeal of new hardware not only saves money, and

provides less in the way of saleable goods to burglarize, but it also prevents distraction from the principal tasks of reading, writing, and calculating. When it turns out that computers and new software are shown to do a better job at these key tasks—I am skeptical as to whether this will ever be the case—there will be time enough to splurge on new equipment. The teacher, alone, up front, explaining, encouraging, guiding, is the heart of the matter—the rest is fun, and very helpful to corporate income, and gives an inflated headquarters staff something new to do. But students will have time enough to learn about computers when they get to college, and getting there will depend almost not at all on what they can do with computers, but how well they understand words and sentences, and how well they do at simple mathematics.

There is nothing wrong with old textbooks, too. Recently, reviewing some   10
recent high-school American history texts, I was astonished to discover they come out in new editions every two years or so, and not because the main body of the text is improved, but because the textbook wants to be able to claim it covers the very last presidential campaign, and the events of the last few years. This is a waste of time and energy and money. There is enough to teach in American history up to 1950 or 1960 not to worry about whether the text includes Reagan's tax cuts. I suspect many new texts in other areas also offer little advantage over the older ones. There is also a virtue in a teacher becoming acquainted with a particular textbook. When I read that a school is disadvantaged because its textbooks are old, I am always mystified. Even the newest advances in physics and biology might well be reserved for college.

6. *Expand the pool from which we draw good teachers.* This general heading   11
covers a number of simple and concrete things, such as: if a teacher is considered qualified to teach at a good private school, that teacher should be considered qualified to teach at a public school. It has always seemed to me ridiculous that teachers accepted at the best private schools in New York City or top preparatory schools in the country would not be allowed to teach in the public school system of New York or Boston. Often, they are willing—after all, the pay is better in public schools and there are greater fringe benefits. They might, it is true, be driven out of those schools by the challenge of lower- and working-class children. But when they are willing, it seems unbelievable that the teacher qualified (or so Brearley thinks) for Brearley will not be allowed to teach at P.S. 122.[1] Greater use of part-time teachers might also be able to draw upon people with qualities that we are told the average teacher unfortunately doesn't possess— such as a higher level of competence in writing and mathematics.

Our recurrent concern with foreign-language teaching should lead us to   12
recruit foreign-born teachers. There are problems in getting teaching jobs today in Germany and France—yet teachers there are typically drawn from pools of

---

[1]Brearley: a prominent private school in New York City. [Eds.]

students with higher academic skills than is the case in this country. Paradoxically, we make it easy for teachers of Spanish-language background to get jobs owing to the expansion of bilingual programs—but then their teaching is confined to children whose Spanish accent doesn't need improvement. It would make more sense to expose children of foreign-language background more to teachers with native English—and children from English-speaking families to teachers who speak French, German, Spanish, and, why not, Japanese, and Chinese natively. This would mean that rules requiring that a teacher must be a citizen, or must speak English without an accent, should be lifted for special teachers with special tasks. Perhaps we could make the most of the oversupply of teachers in some foreign countries by using them to teach mathematics—a subject where accent doesn't count. The school system in Georgia is already recruiting from Germany. Colleges often use teaching assistants whose English is not native and far from perfect, including Asians from Korea and China, to assist in science and mathematics courses. (There are many state laws which would not permit them to teach in elementary and secondary schools.)

All the suggestions above eschew any involvement with some great issues of 13
education—tradition or reform, the teaching of values, the role of religion in the schools—that have in the past dominated arguments over education and still do today. But I add one more proposal that is still, I am afraid, somewhat controversial:

7. *Let students, within reasons, pick their schools, or let parents choose them* 14
for them. All those informed on school issues will sense the heaving depths of controversy under this apparently modest proposal. Does this mean they might choose parochial schools, without being required to pay tuition out of their own pockets? Or does this mean black children would be allowed to attend schools in black areas, and whites in white areas, or the reverse if each is so inclined? As we all know, the two great issues of religion and race stand in the way of any such simple and commonsensical arrangement. Students are regularly bused from one section of a city to another because of their race, and students cannot without financial penalty attend that substantial sector of schools—30 percent or so in most Northern and Midwestern cities—that are called "private." I ignore the question of whether, holding all factors constant, students do "better" in private or public schools, in racially well-mixed or hardly mixed schools. The evidence will always be uncertain. What is perhaps less arguable is that students will do better in a school that forms a community, in which teachers, parents, and students all agree that *that* is the school they want to teach in, to attend, to send their children to. I would guess that this is the kind of school most of the readers of this article have attended; it is the kind of school, alas, that our complex racial and religious history makes it harder and harder for those of minority race or of lower- and working-class status to attend.

I have eschewed the grand proposals—for curriculum change, for improving 15
the quality of entering teachers, for checking on the competence of teachers in
service, for establishing national standards for achievement in different levels of
education—all of which now form the agenda for many state commissions of
educational reform, and all of which seem reasonable to me. Rather, I have
concentrated on a variety of other things that serve to remove distraction, to
open the school to those of quality who would be willing to enter it to improve
it, to concentrate on the essentials of teaching and learning as I (and many
others) have experienced it. It would be possible to propose larger changes in
the same direction: for example, reduce the size of the bureaucracies in urban
school systems. Some of my modest proposals are insidiously intended to do
this—if there were less effort devoted to building new schools, buying new
equipment, evaluating new textbooks, or busing children, there would be no
need to maintain quite so many people at headquarters. Or so I would hope.

In the meantime, why not disconnect the loudspeakers? 16

QUESTIONS

1. Among Glazer's proposals, which seem to you the most helpful and which the
least? Explain why.

2. Why do you think Glazer focuses so much on money in his first two paragraphs?
Would his proposals "cost much less, nothing at all, or even save money," as he claims
in paragraph 2? Explain why or why not.

3. What audience is Glazer addressing? What does he expect readers to do about his
"modest proposals"?

4. How has Glazer ordered his seven proposals? Why do you think he arranged them
as he did? What other methods of organization might he have used?

5. Glazer makes his suggestions "in the spirit," he says, "of evoking further cheap
proposals" (paragraph 2). Offer a few of your own, with explanations.

6. Pool the proposals that you and your classmates have made for question 5. Select
the best of these with the best possible explanations, and prepare a group report that you
might even forward to Professor Glazer, as well as to other possible audiences.

7. Proposals of this sort suggest parodies. Can you come up with a few comic or
ironic proposals that you would like to make on behalf of "better education," something
like sending all the teachers home for one day a week and leaving learning to the students?
Or maybe all the administrators should become bus drivers, the bus drivers coaches, and
the coaches administrators. Of course, you would need to advance reasons for your
proposals.

8. In general, Glazer's proposals address public education in elementary and secondary schools, but by now you've had a taste of college. As either an individual or a
group activity, make up a list of modest proposals for improving, inexpensively, the
quality of education at your college. Present your list, if you wish, wherever you think
it should go.

THE SEXUAL ENLIGHTENMENT OF CHILDREN

Sigmund Freud

Sigmund Freud (1856–1939) spent most of his life in Vienna and would have died there if he had not, like many other Jews, had to leave Austria when Nazi Germany invaded in 1938. As a young man he studied medicine in Vienna, became a doctor, and specialized in mental illness. His researches in this area led him to the study of unconscious mental processes and to the development of psychoanalysis as a way of understanding and treating certain emotional problems. The following essay first appeared in 1907 as a letter to the editor of a medical journal, Soziale Medizin und Hygiene.

DEAR SIR—When you ask me for an expression of opinion on the matter of sexual enlightenment for children, I assume that what you want is the independent opinion of an individual physician whose professional work offers him special opportunities for studying the subject, and not a regular conventional treatise dealing with all the mass of literature that has grown up around it. I am aware that you have followed my scientific efforts with interest, and that, unlike many other colleagues, you do not dismiss my ideas without a hearing because I regard the psychosexual constitution and certain noxiae in the sexual life as the most important causes of the neurotic disorders that are so common.[1] My *Drei Abhandlungen zur Sexualtheorie*,[2] in which I describe the components of which the sexual instinct is made up, and the disturbances which may occur in its development into the function of sexuality, has recently received favorable mention in your Journal.

I am therefore to answer the questions whether children may be given any information at all in regard to the facts of sexual life, and at what age and in what way this should be done. Now let me confess at the outset that discussion with regard to the second and third points seems to me perfectly reasonable, but that to my mind it is quite inconceivable how the first of these questions could ever be the subject of debate. What can be the aim of withholding from children, or let us say from young people, this information about the sexual life

---

[1]noxiae: faults. [Eds.]
[2]*Drei Abhandlungen zur Sexualtheorie: Three Essays on Sexual Theory.* [Eds.]

of human beings? Is it a fear of arousing interest in such matters prematurely, before it spontaneously stirs in them? Is it a hope of retarding by concealment of this kind the development of the sexual instinct in general, until such time as it can find its way into the only channels open to it in the civilized social order? Is it supposed that children would show no interest or understanding for the facts and riddles of sexual life if they were not prompted to do so by outside influence? Is it regarded as possible that the knowledge withheld from them will not reach them in other ways? Or is it genuinely and seriously intended that later on they should consider everything connected with sex as something despicable and abhorrent, from which their parents and teachers wish to keep them apart as long as possible?

I am really at a loss to say which of these can be the motive for the customary 3 concealment from children of everything connected with sex. I only know that these arguments are one and all equally foolish, and that I find it difficult to pay them the compliment of serious refutation. I remember, however, that in the letters of that great thinker and friend of humanity, Multatuli,[3] I once found a few lines which are more than adequate as an answer.

> To my mind it seems that certain things are altogether too much wrapped in mystery. It is well to keep the fantasies of children pure, but their purity will not be preserved by ignorance. On the contrary, I believe that concealment leads a girl or boy to suspect the truth more than ever. Curiosity leads to prying into things which would have roused little or no interest if they were talked of openly without any fuss. If this ignorance could be maintained I might be more reconciled to it, but that is impossible; the child comes into contact with other children, books fall into his hands, which lead him to reflect, and the mystery with which things he has already surmised are treated by his parents actually increases his desire to know more. Then this desire that is only incompletely and secretly satisfied gives rise to excitement and corrupts his imagination, so that the child is already a sinner while his parents still believe he does not know what sin is.[4]

I do not know how the case could be better stated, though perhaps one might 4 amplify it. It is surely nothing else but habitual prudery and a guilty conscience in themselves about sexual matters which causes adults to adopt this attitude of mystery towards children; possibly, however, a piece of theoretical ignorance on their part, to be counteracted only by fresh information, is also responsible. It is commonly believed that the sexual instinct is lacking in children, and only begins to arise in them when the sexual organs mature. This is a grave error, equally serious from the point of view both of theory and of actual practice. It is so easy to correct it by observation that one can only wonder how it can ever have arisen. As a matter of fact, the new-born infant brings sexuality with it

---

[3]Multatuli: the pseudonym of Edward Douwes Dekker (1820–1887), a Dutch writer who became famous through his attacks on the Dutch colonial system. [Eds.]

[4]Multatuli, *Briefe*, 1906, Bd. I. S. 26.

into the world; certain sexual sensations attend its development while at the breast and during early childhood, and only very few children would seem to escape some kind of sexual activity and sexual experiences before puberty. A more complete exposition of this statement can be found in my *Drei Abhandlungen zur Sexualtheorie*, to which reference has been made above. The reader will learn that the specific organs of reproduction are not the only portions of the body which are a source of pleasurable sensation, and that Nature has stringently ordained that even stimulation of the genitals cannot be avoided during infancy. This period of life, during which a certain degree of directly sexual pleasure is produced by the stimulation of various cutaneous areas (erotogenic zones),[5] by the activity of certain biological impulses and as an accompanying excitation during many affective states, is designated by an expression introduced by Havelock Ellis as the period of auto-erotism.[6] Puberty merely brings about attainment of the stage at which the genitals acquire supremacy among all the zones and sources of pleasure, and in this way presses erotism into the service of reproduction, a process which naturally can undergo certain inhibitions; in the case of those persons who later on become perverts and neurotics this process is only incompletely accomplished. On the other hand, the child is capable long before puberty of most of the mental manifestations of love, for example, tenderness, devotion, and jealousy. Often enough the connection between these mental manifestations and the physical sensation of sexual excitation is so close that the child cannot be in doubt about the relation between the two. To put it briefly, the child is long before puberty a being capable of mature love, lacking only the ability for reproduction; and it may be definitely asserted that the mystery which is set up withholds him only from intellectual comprehension of achievements for which he is psychically and physically prepared.

The intellectual interest of a child in the riddle of sexual life, his desire for knowledge, finds expression at an earlier period of life than is usually suspected. If they have not often come across such cases as I am about to mention, parents must either be afflicted with blindness in regard to this interest in their children, or, when they cannot overlook it, must make every effort to stifle it. I know a splendid boy, now four years old, whose intelligent parents abstain from forcibly suppressing one side of the child's development. Little Herbert, who has certainly not been exposed to any seducing influence from servants, has for some time shown the liveliest interest in that part of his body which he calls his weewee-maker. When only three years old he asked his mother, "Mamma, have you got a weewee-maker, too?" His mother answered, "Of course, what did you think?" He also asked his father the same question repeatedly. At about the same age he was taken to a barn and saw a cow milked for the first time.

---

[5]Cutaneous areas: parts of the skin. [Eds.]
[6]Havelock Ellis (1859–1939): British author of many works on human sexual development. [Eds.]

"Look, milk is coming out of the weewee-maker!" he called in surprise. At the age of three and three-quarters he was well on the way to establish correct categories by means of his own independent observation. He saw how water is run off from a locomotive and said, "See, the engine is making weewee, but where is its weewee-maker?" Later on he added thoughtfully, "Dogs and horses have weewee-makers, but tables and chairs don't have them." Recently he was watching his little sister of one week old being bathed, and remarked, "Her weewee-maker is still tiny; it will get bigger when she grows." (I have heard of this attitude towards the problem of sex difference in other boys of the same age.) I must expressly assert that Herbert is not a sensual child nor even morbidly disposed; in my opinion, since he has never been frightened or oppressed with a sense of guilt, he gives expression quite ingenuously to what he thinks.

The second great problem which exercises a child's mind—probably at a rather later date—is that of the origin of children, and is usually aroused by the unwelcome arrival of a baby brother or sister. This is the oldest and most burning question that assails immature humanity; those who understand how to interpret myths and legends can detect it in the riddle which the Theban Sphinx set to Oedipus. The answers usually given to children in the nursery wound the child's frank and genuine spirit of investigation, and generally deal the first blow at his confidence in his parents; from this time onwards he commonly begins to mistrust grown-up people and keeps to himself what interests him most. The following letter may show how torturing this very curiosity may become in older children; it was written by a motherless girl of eleven and a half who had been puzzling over the problem with her younger sister.

> DEAR AUNT MALI—Please will you be so kind as to write and tell me how you got Chris or Paul. You must know because you are married. We were arguing about it yesterday, and we want to know the truth. We have nobody else to ask. When are you coming to Salzburg? You know, Aunt Mali, we simply can't imagine how the stork brings babies. Trudel thought the stork brings them in a shirt. Then we want to know, too, how the stork gets them out of the pond, and why one never sees babies in ponds. And please will you tell me, too, how you know beforehand when you are going to have one. Please write and tell me *all* about it. Thousands of kisses from all of us.—Your inquiring niece,

> LILY.

I do not think that this touching request brought the two sisters the information they wanted. Later on the writer developed the neurosis that arises in unanswered unconscious questions—obsessive speculating.

I do not think that there is even one good reason for denying children the information which their thirst for knowledge demands. To be sure, if it is the purpose of educators to stifle the child's power of independent thought as early as possible, in order to produce that "good behavior" which is so highly prized, they cannot do better than deceive children in sexual matters and intimidate

611

them by religious means. The stronger characters will, it is true, withstand these influences; they will become rebels against the authority of their parents and later against every other form of authority. When children do not receive the explanations for which they turn to their elders, they go on tormenting themselves in secret with the problem, and produce attempts at solution in which the truth they have guessed is mixed up in the most extraordinary way with grotesque inventions; or else they whisper confidences to each other which, because of the sense of guilt in the youthful inquirers, stamp everything sexual as horrible and disgusting. These infantile sexual theories are well worth collecting and examining. After these experiences children usually lose the only proper attitude to sexual questions, many of them never to find it again.

It would seem that the overwhelming majority of writers, both men and women, who have dealt with the question of explaining sexual matters to children have expressed themselves in favor of enlightenment. The clumsiness, however, of most of their proposals how and when this enlightenment should be carried out leads one to conclude that they have not found it very easy to venture this admission. As far as my knowledge of the literature goes, the charming letter of explanation which a certain Frau Emma Eckstein gives as written to her ten-year-old boy stands out conspicuously.[7] The customary method is obviously not the right one. All sexual knowledge is kept from children as long as possible, and then on one single occasion an explanation, which is even then only half the truth and generally comes too late, is proffered them in mysterious and solemn language. Most of the answers to the question "How can I tell my children?" make such a pitiful impression, at least upon me, that I should prefer parents not to concern themselves with the explanation at all. It is much more important that children should never get the idea that one wants to make more of a secret of the facts of sexual life than of any other matter not suited to their understanding. To ensure this it is necessary that from the very beginning everything sexual should be treated like everything else that is worth knowing about. Above all, schools should not evade the task of mentioning sexual matters; lessons about the animal kingdom should include the great facts of reproduction, which should be given their due significance, and emphasis should be laid at the same time on the fact that man shares with the higher animals everything essential to his organization. Then, if the atmosphere of the home does not make for suppression of all reasoning, something similar to what I once overheard in a nursery would probably occur oftener. A small boy said to his little sister, "How can you think the stork brings babies! You know that man is a mammal, do you suppose that storks bring other mammals their young too?" In this way the curiosity of children will never become very intense, for at each stage in its inquiries it will find the satisfaction it needs. Explanations about the specific circumstances of human sexuality and some indication of its social

---

[7]Emma Eckstein, *Die Sexualfrage in der Erziehung des Kindes*, 1904.

significance should be provided before the child is eleven years old. The age of confirmation would be a more suitable time than any other at which to instruct the child, who already has full knowledge of the physical facts involved, in those social obligations which are bound up with the actual gratification of this instinct. A gradual and progressive course of instruction in sexual matters such as this, at no period interrupted, in which the school takes the initiative, seems to me to be the only method of giving the necessary information that takes into consideration the development of the child and thus successfully avoids ever-present dangers.

QUESTIONS

1. Summarize Freud's argument in your own words.

2. In his second paragraph, Freud mentions three questions. The second two he finds "perfectly reasonable" but the first hardly worth debate. Yet he doesn't leave that first question until paragraph 9, the last paragraph of his essay. What do you make of this imbalance? What does it indicate about Freud's argumentative purpose?

3. What counterpositions does Freud acknowledge? How does he present them and deal with them?

4. Freud quotes two long passages from other writers (Multatuli and Lily), and he gives us several quotations from little Herbert. What is the function of the material drawn from each of these three sources in Freud's argument?

5. Compare Freud's term *sexual enlightenment* with the contemporary term *sex education*. Do they have the same denotation? Do they have the same connotations?

6. What is the balance between appeal to reason and appeal to emotion in this essay? Can you point to specific places where Freud shifts from one to the other?

7. Paragraph 2 has a long string of rhetorical questions. What is the function of such questions? How do you respond to them?

8. Perhaps you have a younger brother or sister or know some young children. If not, you can certainly imagine having a child who might ask you questions about sex. What do you think your proper role would be in that situation? Write an essay in which you, first, specify the age and relationship to you of the person you imagine, and, second, outline the nature of the information you think proper to provide and the manner in which you might do that.

9. Write a critique of sex education as you have known it. This does not necessarily mean that you have to agree with all of Freud's ideas. Sex education as you have known it may have been well informed, well planned, and useful; or it may have been, for any number of reasons, a bungled job, an embarrassment, and a disaster. Most likely it held a place between those extremes. In any case, write an essay that describes sex education as you knew it, and make some suggestions for its improvement.

THE IGNORED LESSON
OF ANNE FRANK

Bruno Bettelheim

Psychoanalyst Bruno Bettelheim, as the headnote on page 411 explains, himself survived imprisonment in Nazi concentration camps. Here he writes about Anne Frank, one of the better-known victims of World War II. Her family, after hiding in an attic in Amsterdam for two years, was betrayed to the Nazis, and Anne perished in a concentration camp. Her Diary, kept during her time in hiding, was published in 1947 and later was turned into a play and a film. The following essay originally appeared in Harper's *(November 1960) and was reprinted in Bettelheim's book* Surviving and Other Essays *(1979). In this essay, Bettelheim seeks to revise our moral understanding of Anne Frank's story.*

When the world first learned about the Nazi concentration and death camps, most civilized people felt the horrors committed in them to be so uncanny as to be unbelievable. It came as a severe shock that supposedly civilized nations could stoop to such inhuman acts. The implication that modern man has such inadequate control over his cruel and destructive proclivities was felt as a threat to our views of ourselves and our humanity. Three different psychological mechanisms were most frequently used for dealing with the appalling revelation of what had gone on in the camps: 1

(1) its applicability to man in general was denied by asserting—contrary to evidence—that the acts of torture and mass murder were committed by a small group of insane or perverted persons;

(2) the truth of the reports was denied by declaring them vastly exaggerated and ascribing them to propaganda (this originated with the German government, which called all reports on terror in the camps "horror propaganda"—*Greuel-propaganda*);

(3) the reports were believed, but the knowledge of the horror repressed as soon as possible.

All three mechanisms could be seen at work after liberation of those prisoners remaining. At first, after the discovery of the camps and their death-dealing, a wave of extreme outrage swept the Allied nations. It was soon followed by a general repression of the discovery in people's minds. Possibly this reaction was due to something more than the blow dealt to modern man's narcissism by the 2

614

realization that cruelty is still rampant among men. Also present may have been the dim but extremely threatening realization that the modern state now has available the means for changing personality, and for destroying millions it deems undesirable. The ideas that in our day a people's personalities might be changed against their will by the state, and that other populations might be wholly or partially exterminated, are so fearful that one tries to free oneself of them and their impact by defensive denial, or by repression.

The extraordinary world-wide success of the book, play, and movie *The Diary of Anne Frank* suggests the power of the desire to counteract the realization of the personality-destroying and murderous nature of the camps by concentrating all attention on what is experienced as a demonstration that private and intimate life can continue to flourish even under the direct persecution by the most ruthless totalitarian system. And this although Anne Frank's fate demonstrates how efforts at disregarding in private life what goes on around one in society can hasten one's own destruction. 3

What concerns me here is not what actually happened to the Frank family, how they tried—and failed—to survive their terrible ordeal. It would be very wrong to take apart so humane and moving a story, which aroused so much well-merited compassion for gentle Anne Frank and her tragic fate. What is at issue is the universal and uncritical response to her diary and to the play and movie based on it, and what this reaction tells about our attempts to cope with the feelings her fate—used by us to serve as a symbol of a most human reaction to Nazi terror—arouses in us. I believe that the world-wide acclaim given her story cannot be explained unless we recognize in it our wish to forget the gas chambers, and our effort to do so by glorifying the ability to retreat into an extremely private, gentle, sensitive world, and there to cling as much as possible to what have been one's usual daily attitudes and activities, although surrounded by a maelstrom apt to engulf one at any moment. 4

The Frank family's attitude that life could be carried on as before may well have been what led to their destruction. By eulogizing how they lived in their hiding place while neglecting to examine first whether it was a reasonable or an effective choice, we are able to ignore the crucial lesson of their story—that such an attitude can be fatal in extreme circumstances. 5

While the Franks were making their preparations for going passively into hiding, thousands of other Jews in Holland (as elsewhere in Europe) were trying to escape to the free world, in order to survive and/or fight. Others who could not escape went underground—into hiding—each family member with, for example, a different gentile family. We gather from the diary, however, that the chief desire of the Frank family was to continue living as nearly as possible in the same fashion to which they had been accustomed in happier times. 6

Little Anne, too, wanted only to go on with life as usual, and what else could she have done but fall in with the pattern her parents created for her existence? But hers was not a necessary fate, much less a heroic one; it was a 7

615

terrible but also a senseless fate. Anne had a good chance to survive, as did many Jewish children in Holland. But she would have had to leave her parents and go live with a gentile Dutch family, posing as their own child, something her parents would have had to arrange for her.

Everyone who recognized the obvious knew that the hardest way to go underground was to do it as a family; to hide out together made detection by the SS most likely; and when detected, everybody was doomed. By hiding singly, even when one got caught, the others had a chance to survive. The Franks, with their excellent connections among gentile Dutch families, might well have been able to hide out singly, each with a different family. But instead, the main principle of their planning was continuing their beloved family life—an understandable desire, but highly unrealistic in those times. Choosing any other course would have meant not merely giving up living together, but also realizing the full measure of the danger to their lives. 8

The Franks were unable to accept that going on living as a family as they had done before the Nazi invasion of Holland was no longer a desirable way of life, much as they loved each other; in fact, for them and others like them, it was most dangerous behavior. But even given their wish not to separate, they failed to make appropriate preparations for what was likely to happen. 9

There is little doubt that the Franks, who were able to provide themselves with so much while arranging for going into hiding, and even while hiding, could have provided themselves with some weapons had they wished. Had they had a gun, Mr. Frank could have shot down at least one or two of the "green police" who came for them. There was no surplus of such police, and the loss of an SS with every Jew arrested would have noticeably hindered the functioning of the police state. Even a butcher knife, which they certainly could have taken with them into hiding, could have been used by them in self-defense. The fate of the Franks wouldn't have been very different, because they all died anyway except for Anne's father. But they could have sold their lives for a high price, instead of walking to their death. Still, although one must assume that Mr. Frank would have fought courageously, as we know he did when a soldier in the first World War, it is not everybody who can plan to kill those who are bent on killing him, although many who would not be ready to contemplate doing so would be willing to kill those who are bent on murdering not only them but also their wives and little daughters. 10

An entirely different matter would have been planning for escape in case of discovery. The Franks' hiding place had only one entrance; it did not have any other exit. Despite the fact, during their many months of hiding, they did not try to devise one. Nor did they make other plans for escape, such as that one of the family members—as likely as not Mr. Frank—would try to detain the police in the narrow entrance way—maybe even fight them, as suggested above— thus giving other members of the family a chance to escape, either by reaching 11 the roofs of adjacent houses, or down a ladder into the alley behind the house in which they were living.

Any of this would have required recognizing and accepting the desperate straits in which they found themselves, and concentrating on how best to cope with them. This was quite possible to do, even under the terrible conditions in which the Jews found themselves after the Nazi occupation of Holland. It can be seen from many other accounts, for example from the story of Marga Minco, a girl of about Anne Frank's age who lived to tell about it. Her parents had planned that when the police should come for them, the father would try to detain them by arguing and fighting with them, to give the wife and daughter a chance to escape through a rear door. Unfortunately it did not quite work out this way, and both parents got killed. But their short-lived resistance permitted their daughter to make her escape as planned and to reach a Dutch family who saved her.[1]

This is not mentioned as a criticism that the Frank family did not plan or behave along similar lines. A family has every right to arrange their life as they wish or think best, and to take the risks they want to take. My point is not to criticize what the Franks did, but only the universal admiration of their way of coping, or rather of not coping. The story of little Marga who survived, every bit as touching, remains totally neglected by comparison.

Many Jews—unlike the Franks, who through listening to British radio news were better informed than most—had no detailed knowledge of the extermination camps. Thus it was easier for them to make themselves believe that complete compliance with even the most outrageously debilitating and degrading Nazi orders might offer a chance for survival. But neither tremendous anxiety that inhibits clear thinking and with it well-planned and determined action, nor ignorance about what happened to those who responded with passive waiting for being rounded up for their extermination, can explain the reaction of audiences to the play and movie retelling Anne's story, which are all about such waiting that results finally in destruction.

I think it is the fictitious ending that explains the enormous success of this play and movie. At the conclusion we hear Anne's voice from the beyond, saying, "In spite of everything, I still believe that people are really good at heart." This improbable sentiment is supposedly from a girl who had been starved to death, had watched her sister meet the same fate before she did, knew that her mother had been murdered, and had watched untold thousands of adults and children being killed. This statement is not justified by anything Anne actually told her diary.

Going on with intimate family living, no matter how dangerous it might be to survival, was fatal to all too many during the Nazi regime. And if all men are good, then indeed we can all go on with living our lives as we have been

---

[1] Marga Minco, *Bitter Herbs* (New York: Oxford University Press), 1960.

accustomed to in times of undisturbed safety and can afford to forget about Auschwitz. But Anne, her sister, her mother, may well have died because her parents could not get themselves to believe in Auschwitz.

While play and movie are ostensibly about Nazi persecution and destruction, in actuality what we watch is the way that, despite this terror, lovable people manage to continue living their satisfying intimate lives with each other. The heroine grows from a child into a young adult as normally as any other girl would, despite the most abnormal conditions of all other aspects of her existence, and that of her family. Thus the play reassures us that despite the destructiveness of Nazi racism and tyranny in general, it is possible to disregard it in one's private life much of the time, even if one is Jewish. 17

True, the ending happens just as the Franks and their friends had feared all along: their hiding place is discovered, and they are carried away to their doom. But the fictitious declaration of faith in the goodness of all men which concludes the play falsely reassures us since it impresses on us that in the combat between Nazi terror and continuance of intimate family living the latter wins out, since Anne has the last word. This is simply contrary to fact, because it was she who got killed. Her seeming survival through her moving statement about the goodness of men releases us effectively of the need to cope with the problems Auschwitz presents. That is why we are so relieved by her statement. It explains why millions loved play and movie, because while it confronts us with the fact that Auschwitz existed it encourages us at the same time to ignore any of its implications. If all men are good at heart, there never really was an Auschwitz; nor is there any possibility that it may recur. 18

The desire of Anne Frank's parents not to interrupt their intimate family living, and their inability to plan more effectively for their survival, reflect the failure of all too many others faced with the threat of Nazi terror. It is a failure that deserves close examination because of the inherent warnings it contains for us, the living. 19

Submission to the threatening power of the Nazi state often led both to the disintegration of what had once seemed well-integrated personalities and to a return to an immature disregard for the dangers of reality. Those Jews who submitted passively to Nazi persecution came to depend on primitive and infantile thought processes: wishful thinking and disregard for the possibility of death. Many persuaded themselves that they, out of all the others, would be spared. Many more simply disbelieved in the possibility of their own death. Not believing in it, they did not take what seemed to them desperate precautions, such as giving up everything to hide out singly; or trying to escape even if it meant risking their lives in doing so; or preparing to fight for their lives when no escape was possible and death had become an immediate possibility. It is true that defending their lives in active combat before they were rounded up to be transported into the camps might have hastened their deaths, and so, up to 20 a point, they were protecting themselves by "rolling with the punches" of the enemy.

But the longer one rolls with the punches dealt not by the normal vagaries 21 of life, but by one's eventual executioner, the more likely it becomes that one will no longer have the strength to resist when death becomes imminent. This is particularly true if yielding to the enemy is accompanied not by a commensurate strengthening of the personality, but by an inner disintegration. We can observe such a process among the Franks, who bickered with each other over trifles, instead of supporting each other's ability to resist the demoralizing impact of their living conditions.

Those who faced up to the announced intentions of the Nazis prepared for 22 the worst as a real and imminent possibility. It meant risking one's life for a self-chosen purpose, but in doing so, creating at least a small chance for saving one's own life or those of others, or both. When Jews in Germany were restricted to their homes, those who did not succumb to inertia took the new restrictions as a warning that it was high time to go underground, join the resistance movement, provide themselves with forged papers, and so on, if they had not done so long ago. Many of them survived.

Some distant relatives of mine may furnish an example. Early in the war, a 23 young man living in a small Hungarian town banded together with a number of other Jews to prepare against a German invasion. As soon as the Nazis imposed curfews on the Jews, his group left for Budapest—because the bigger capital city with its greater anonymity offered chances for escaping detection. Similar groups from other towns converged in Budapest and joined forces. From among themselves they selected typically "Aryan" looking men who equipped themselves with false papers and immediately joined the Hungarian SS. These spies were then able to warn of impending persecution and raids.

Many of these groups survived intact. Furthermore, they had also equipped 24 themselves with small arms, so that if they were detected, they could put up enough of a fight for the majority to escape while a few would die fighting to make the escape possible. A few of the Jews who had joined the SS were discovered and immediately shot, probably a death preferable to one in the gas chambers. But most of even these Jews survived, hiding within the SS until liberation.

Compare these arrangements not just to the Franks' selection of a hiding 25 place that was basically a trap without an outlet but with Mr. Frank's teaching typically academic high-school subjects to his children rather than how to make a getaway: a token of his inability to face the seriousness of the threat of death. Teaching high-school subjects had, of course, its constructive aspects. It relieved the ever-present anxiety about their fate to some degree by concentrating on different matters, and by implication it encouraged hope for a future in which such knowledge would be useful. In this sense such teaching was purposeful, but it was erroneous in that it took the place of much more pertinent teaching and planning: how best to try to escape when detected.

Unfortunately the Franks were by no means the only ones who, out of anxiety, became unable to contemplate their true situation and with it to plan accordingly. Anxiety, and the wish to counteract it by clinging to each other, and to reduce its sting by continuing as much as possible with their usual way of life incapacitated many, particularly when survival plans required changing radically old ways of living that they cherished, and which had become their only source of satisfaction.   26

My young relative, for example, was unable to persuade other members of his family to go with him when he left the small town where he had lived with them. Three times, at tremendous risk to himself, he returned to plead with his relatives, pointing out first the growing persecution of the Jews, and later the fact that transport to the gas chambers had already begun. He could not convince these Jews to leave their homes and break up their families to go singly into hiding.   27

As their desperation mounted, they clung more determinedly to their old living arrangements and to each other, became less able to consider giving up the possessions they had accumulated through hard work over a lifetime. The more severely their freedom to act was reduced, and what little they were still permitted to do restricted by insensible and degrading regulations imposed by the Nazis, the more did they become unable to contemplate independent action. Their life energies drained out of them, sapped by their ever-greater anxiety. The less they found strength in themselves, the more they held on to the little that was left of what had given them security in the past—their old surroundings, their customary way of life, their possessions—all these seemed to give their lives some permanency, offer some symbols of security. Only what had once been symbols of security now endangered life, since they were excuses for avoiding change. On each successive visit the young man found his relatives more incapacitated, less willing or able to take his advice, more frozen into inactivity, and with it further along the way to the crematoria where, in fact, they all died.   28

Levin renders a detailed account of the desperate but fruitless efforts made by small Jewish groups determined to survive to try to save the rest. She tells how messengers were "sent into the provinces to warn Jews that deportation meant death, but their warnings were ignored because most Jews refused to contemplate their own annihilation."[2] I believe the reason for such refusal has to be found in their inability to take action. If we are certain that we are helpless to protect ourselves against the danger of destruction, we cannot contemplate it. We can consider the danger only as long as we believe there are ways to protect ourselves, to fight back, to escape. If we are convinced none of this is

[2]Nora Levin, *The Holocaust* (New York: Thomas Y. Crowell, 1968).

possible for us, then there is no point in thinking about the danger; on the contrary, it is best to refuse to do so.

As a prisoner in Buchenwald, I talked to hundreds of German Jewish prisoners who were brought there as part of the huge pogrom in the wake of the murder of vom Rath in the fall of 1938. I asked them why they had not left Germany, given the utterly degrading conditions they had been subjected to. Their answer was: How could we leave? It would have meant giving up our homes, our work, our sources of income. Having been deprived by Nazi persecution and degradation of much of their self-respect, they had become unable to give up what still gave them a semblance of it: their earthly belongings. But instead of using possessions, they became captivated by them, and this possession by earthly goods became the fatal mask for their possession by anxiety, fear, and denial.

How the investment of personal property with one's life energy could make people die bit by bit was illustrated throughout the Nazi persecution of the Jews. At the time of the first boycott of Jewish stores, the chief external goal of the Nazis was to acquire the possessions of the Jews. They even let Jews take some things out of the country at that time if they would leave the bulk of their property behind. For a long time the intention of the Nazis, and the goal of their first discriminatory laws, was to force undesirable minorities, including Jews, into emigration.

Although the extermination policy was in line with the inner logic of Nazi racial ideology, one may wonder whether the idea that millions of Jews (and other foreign nationals) could be submitted to extermination did not partially result from seeing the degree of degradation Jews accepted without fighting back. When no violent resistance occurred, persecution of the Jews worsened, slow step by slow step.

Many Jews who on the invasion of Poland were able to survey their situation and draw the right conclusions survived the Second World War. As the Germans approached, they left everything behind and fled to Russia, much as they distrusted and disliked the Soviet system. But there, while badly treated, they could at least survive. Those who stayed on in Poland believing they could go on with life-as-before sealed their fate. Thus in the deepest sense the walk to the gas chamber was only the last consequence of these Jews' inability to comprehend what was in store; it was the final step of surrender to the death instinct, which might also be called the principle of inertia. The first step was taken long before arrival at the death camp.

We can find a dramatic demonstration of how far the surrender to inertia can be carried, and the wish not to know because knowing would create unbearable anxiety, in an experience of Olga Lengyel.[3] She reports that although she and her fellow prisoners lived just a few hundred yards from the crematoria

---

[3]Olga Lengyel, *Five Chimneys: The Story of Auschwitz* (Chicago: Ziff-Davis, 1947).

and the gas chambers and knew what they were for, most prisoners denied knowledge of them for months. If they had grasped their true situation, it might have helped them save either the lives they themselves were fated to lose, or the lives of others.

When Mrs. Lengyel's fellow prisoners were selected to be sent to the gas 35 chambers, they did not try to break away from the group, as she successfully did. Worse, the first time she tried to escape the gas chambers, some of the other selected prisoners told the supervisors that she was trying to get away. Mrs. Lengyel desperately asks the question: How was it possible that people denied the existence of the gas chambers when all day long they saw the crematoria burning and smelled the odor of burning flesh? Why did they prefer ignoring the exterminations to fighting for their very own lives? She can offer no explanation, only the observation that they resented anyone who tried to save himself from the common fate, because they lacked enough courage to risk action themselves. I believe they did it because they had given up their will to live and permitted their death tendencies to engulf them. As a result, such prisoners were in the thrall of the murdering SS not only physically but also psychologically, while this was not true for those prisoners who still had a grip on life.

Some prisoners even began to serve their executioners, to help speed the 36 death of their own kind. Then things had progressed beyond simple inertia to the death instinct running rampant. Those who tried to serve their executioners in what were once their civilian capacities were merely continuing life as usual and thereby opening the door to their death.

For example, Mrs. Lengyel speaks of Dr. Mengele, SS physician at Ausch- 37 witz, as a typical example of the "business as usual" attitude that enabled some prisoners, and certainly the SS, to retain whatever balance they could despite what they were doing. She described how Dr. Mengele took all correct medical precautions during childbirth, rigorously observing all aseptic principles, cutting the umbilical cord with greatest care, etc. But only half an hour later he sent mother and infant to be burned in the crematorium.

Having made his choice, Dr. Mengele and others like him had to delude 38 themselves to be able to live with themselves and their experience. Only one personal document on the subject has come to my attention, that of Dr. Nyiszli, a prisoner serving as "research physician" at Auschwitz.[4] How Dr. Nyiszli deluded himself can be seen, for example, in the way he repeatedly refers to himself as working in Auschwitz as a physician, although he worked as the assistant of a criminal murderer. He speaks of the Institute for Race, Biological, and Anthropological Investigation as "one of the most qualified medical centers of the Third Reich," although it was devoted to proving falsehoods. That Nyiszli was a doctor didn't alter the fact that he—like any of the prisoner foremen who

---

[4]Miklos Nyiszli, *Auschwitz: A Doctor's Eyewitness Account* (New York: Frederick Fell, 1960).

served the SS better than some SS were willing to serve it—was a participant in the crimes of the SS. How could he do it and live with himself?

The answer is: by taking pride in his professional skills, irrespective of the   39 purpose they served. Dr. Nyiszli and Dr. Mengele were only two among hundreds of other—and far more prominent—physicians who participated in the Nazis' murderous pseudo-scientific human experiments. It was the peculiar pride of these men in their professional skill and knowledge, without regard for moral implications, that made them so dangerous. Although the concentration camps and crematoria are no longer here, this kind of pride still remains with us; it is characteristic of a modern society in which fascination with technical competence has dulled concern for human feelings. Auschwitz is gone, but so long as this attitude persists, we shall not be safe from cruel indifference to life at the core.

I have met many Jews as well as gentile anti–Nazis, similar to the activist   40 group in Hungary described earlier, who survived in Nazi Germany and in the occupied countries. These people realized that when a world goes to pieces and inhumanity reigns supreme, man cannot go on living his private life as he was wont to do, and would like to do; he cannot, as the loving head of a family, keep the family living together peacefully, undisturbed by the surrounding world; nor can he continue to take pride in his profession or possessions, when either will deprive him of his humanity, if not also of his life. In such times, one must radically reevaluate all of what one has done, believed in, and stood for in order to know how to act. In short, one has to take a stand on the new reality—a firm stand, not one of retirement into an even more private world.

If today, Negroes in Africa march against the guns of a police that defends   41 *apartheid*—even if hundreds of dissenters are shot down and tens of thousands rounded up in camps—their fight will sooner or later assure them of a chance for liberty and equality. Millions of the Jews of Europe who did not or could not escape in time or go underground as many thousands did, could at least have died fighting as some did in the Warsaw ghetto at the end, instead of passively waiting to be rounded up for their own extermination.

QUESTIONS

1. As part of his evidence, Bettelheim repeatedly refers to and sometimes summarizes parts of the story of Anne Frank. What are the main outlines of her story? What makes it so important?

2. What is Bettelheim's thesis? What is his most urgent message?

3. At times Bettelheim's thesis bears on Nazi resistance in the forties; at times it appears more universal. When does it tip one way, and when another? Which message do you consider more important?

4. Bettelheim's last paragraph takes up Africans in an argument by analogy. Is this

a good analogy? Does it matter to Bettelheim's overall argument that the situations of blacks in South Africa and of Jews in Europe are not in every way similar?

5. Bettelheim also refers to four other stories served in print, those of Minco, Levin, Lengyel, and Nyiszli, as well as the case of his own distant relatives. How do those stories serve as evidence? Why do you think Bettelheim decided to arrange them in the order in which they appear?

6. Have you ever observed or learned of a situation in which someone's inaction seemed to increase, rather than decrease, some form of persecution? If so, analyze this situation in light of Bettelheim's essay.

WARFARE: AN INVENTION—NOT A BIOLOGICAL NECESSITY

Margaret Mead

As the headnote on page 184 indicates, Margaret Mead was a cultural anthropologist whose work continues to be important and influential. In the following essay, which first appeared in 1940, in Asia, a magazine for the general audience and dedicated to our better understanding of the Far East, she writes as an anthropologist, as a concerned human being, and feminist. Responding to a highly influential essay by William James (1842–1910), the famous American philosopher and the older brother, by a year, of the novelist Henry James, Mead challenges the idea that our human character relies on virtues that stem from war or from its "moral equivalent."

Is war a biological necessity, a sociological inevitability or just a bad invention? Those who argue for the first view endow man with such pugnacious instincts that some outlet in aggressive behavior is necessary if man is to reach full human stature. It was this point of view which lay back of William James's famous essay, "The Moral Equivalent of War," in which he tried to retain the warlike virtues and channel them in new directions. A similar point of view has lain back of the Soviet Union's attempt to make competition between groups rather than between individuals. A basic, competitive, aggressive, warring human nature is assumed, and those who wish to outlaw war or outlaw competitiveness merely try to find new and less socially destructive ways in which these biologically given aspects of man's nature can find expression. Then there are those who take the second view: warfare is the inevitable concomitant of the development of the state, the struggle for land and natural resources of class societies springing, not from the nature of man, but from the nature of history. War is nevertheless inevitable unless we change our social system and outlaw classes, the struggle for power, and possessions; and in the event of our success warfare would disappear, as a symptom vanishes when the disease is cured.

One may hold a compromise position between these two extremes; one may claim that all aggression springs from the frustration of man's biologically determined drives and that, since all forms of culture are frustrating, it is certain each new generation will be aggressive and the aggression will find its natural and inevitable expression in race war, class war, nationalistic war, and so on.

All three positions are very popular today among those who think seriously

625

about the problems of war and its possible prevention, but I wish to urge another point of view, less defeatist perhaps than the first and third, and more accurate than the second: that is, that warfare, by which I mean organized conflict between two groups *as groups*, in which each group puts an army (even if the army is only fifteen Pygmies) into the field to fight and kill, if possible, some of the members of the army of the other group—that warfare of this sort is an invention like any other of the inventions in terms of which we order our lives, such as writing, marriage, cooking our food instead of eating it raw, trial by jury, or burial of the dead, and so on. Some of this list any one will grant are inventions: trial by jury is confined to very limited portions of the globe; we know that there are tribes that do not bury their dead but instead expose or cremate them; and we know that only part of the human race has had a knowledge of writing as its cultural inheritance. But, whenever a way of doing things is found universally, such as the use of fire or the practice of some form of marriage, we tend to think at once that it is not an invention at all but an attribute of humanity itself. And yet even such universals as marriage and the use of fire are inventions like the rest, very basic ones, inventions which were perhaps necessary if human history was to take the turn it has taken, but nevertheless inventions. At some point in his social development man was undoubtedly without the institution of marriage or the knowledge of the use of fire.

The case for warfare is much clearer because there are peoples even today who have no warfare. Of these the Eskimo are perhaps the most conspicuous example, but the Lepchas of Sikkim are an equally good one.[1] Neither of these peoples understands war, not even defensive warfare. The idea of warfare is lacking, and this idea is as essential to carrying on war as an alphabet or a syllabary is to writing. But whereas the Lepchas are a gentle, unquarrelsome people, and the advocates of other points of view might argue that they are not full human beings or that they had never been frustrated and so had no aggression to expend in warfare, the Eskimo case gives no such possibility of interpretation. The Eskimo are not a mild and meek people; many of them are turbulent and troublesome. Fights, theft of wives, murder, cannibalism occur among them—all outbursts of passionate men goaded by desire or intolerable circumstance. Here are men faced with hunger, men faced with loss of their wives, men faced with the threat of extermination by other men, and here are orphan children, growing up miserably with no one to care for them, mocked and neglected by those about them. The personality necessary for war, the circumstances necessary to goad men to desperation are present, but there is no war. When a traveling Eskimo entered a settlement he might have to fight the strongest man in the settlement to establish his position among them, but this was a test of strength and bravery, not war. The idea of warfare, of one *group*

4

---

[1]Sikkim: a small kingdom wedged between India and Tibet that became an Indian state in 1975. [Eds.]

organizing against another *group* to maim and wound and kill them was absent. And without that idea passions might rage but there was no war.

But, it may be argued, isn't this because the Eskimo have such a low and 5 undeveloped form of social organization? They own no land, they move from place to place, camping, it is true, season after season on the same site, but this is not something to fight for as the modern nations of the world fight for land and raw materials. They have no permanent possessions that can be looted, no towns that can be burned. They have no social classes to produce stress and strains within the society which might force it to go to war outside. Doesn't the absence of war among the Eskimo, while disproving the biological necessity of war, just go to confirm the point that it is the state of development of the society which accounts for war, and nothing else?

We find the answer among the Pygmy peoples of the Andaman Islands in 6 the Bay of Bengal. The Andamans also represent an exceedingly low level of society; they are a hunting and food-gathering people; they live in tiny hordes without any class stratification; their houses are simpler than the snow houses of the Eskimo. But they knew about warfare. The army might contain only fifteen determined pygmies marching in a straight line, but it was the real thing none the less. Tiny army met tiny army in open battle, blows were exchanged, casualties suffered, and the state of warfare could only be concluded by a peace-making ceremony.

Similarly, among the Australian aborigines, who built no permanent dwell- 7 ings but wandered from water hole to water hole over their almost desert country, warfare—and rules of "international law"—were highly developed. The student of social evolution will seek in vain for his obvious causes of war, struggle for lands, struggle for power of one group over another, expansion of population, need to divert the minds of a populace restive under tyranny, or even the ambition of a successful leader to enhance his own prestige. All are absent, but warfare as a practice remained, and men engaged in it and killed one another in the course of a war because killing is what is done in wars.

From instances like these it becomes apparent that an inquiry into the causes 8 of war misses the fundamental point as completely as does an insistence upon the biological necessity of war. If a people have an idea of going to war and the idea that war is the way in which certain situations, defined within their society, are to be handled, they will sometimes go to war. If they are a mild and unaggressive people, like the Pueblo Indians, they may limit themselves to defensive warfare; but they will be forced to think in terms of war because there are peoples near them who have warfare as a pattern, and offensive, raiding, pillaging warfare at that. When the pattern of warfare is known, people like the Pueblo Indians will defend themselves, taking advantage of their natural de-fenses, the *mesa* village site, and people like the Lepchas, having no natural defenses and no idea of warfare, will merely submit to the invader. But the essential point remains the same. There is a way of behaving which is known

627

to a given people and labeled as an appropriate form of behavior. A bold and warlike people like the Sioux or the Maori may label warfare as desirable as well as possible;[2] a mild people like the Pueblo Indians may label warfare as undesirable; but to the minds of both peoples the possibility of warfare is present. Their thoughts, their hopes, their plans are oriented about this idea, that warfare may be selected as the way to meet some situation.

So simple peoples and civilized peoples, mild peoples and violent, assertive 9
peoples, will all go to war if they have the invention, just as those peoples who have the custom of dueling will have duels and peoples who have the pattern of vendetta will indulge in vendetta. And, conversely, peoples who do not know of dueling will not fight duels, even though their wives are seduced and their daughters ravished; they may on occasion commit murder but they will not fight duels. Cultures which lack the idea of the vendetta will not meet every quarrel in this way. A people can use only the forms it has. So the Balinese have their special way of dealing with a quarrel between two individuals:[3] if the two feel that the causes of quarrel are heavy they may go and register their quarrel in the temple before the gods, and, making offerings, they may swear never to have anything to do with each other again. Under the Dutch government they registered such mutual "not-speaking" with the Dutch government officials. But in other societies, although individuals might feel as full of animosity and as unwilling to have any further contact as do the Balinese, they cannot register their quarrel with the gods and go on quietly about their business because registering quarrels with the gods is not an invention of which they know.

Yet, if it be granted that warfare is after all an invention, it may nevertheless 10
be an invention that lends itself to certain types of personality, to the exigent needs of autocrats, to the expansionist desires of crowded peoples, to the desire for plunder and rape and loot which is engendered by a dull and frustrating life. What, then, can we say of this congruence between warfare and its uses? If it is a form which fits so well, is not this congruence the essential point? But even here the primitive material causes us to wonder, because there are tribes who go to war merely for glory, having no quarrel with the enemy, suffering from no tyrant within their boundaries, anxious neither for land nor loot nor women, but merely anxious to win prestige which within that tribe has been declared obtainable only by war and without which no young man can hope to win his sweetheart's smile of approval. But if, as was the case with the Bush Negroes of Dutch Guiana,[4] it is artistic ability which is necessary to win a girl's approval, the same young man would have to be carving rather than going out on a war party.

In many parts of the world, war is a game in which the individual can win 11
counters—counters which bring him prestige in the eyes of his own sex or of

---

[2]Maori: the native people of New Zealand. [Eds.]
[3]Balinese: the people of Bali, an island province of Indonesia. [Eds.]
[4]Dutch Guiana: former name of Surinam in northern South America. [Eds.]

the opposite sex; he plays for these counters as he might, in our society, strive for a tennis championship. Warfare is a frame for such prestige-seeking merely because it calls for the display of certain skills and certain virtues; all of these skills—riding straight, shooting straight, dodging the missiles of the enemy and sending one's own straight to the mark—can be equally well exercised in some other framework and, equally, the virtues—endurance, bravery, loyalty, steadfastness—can be displayed in other contexts. The tie-up between proving oneself a man and proving this by a success in organized killing is due to a definition which many societies have made of manliness. And often, even in those societies which counted success in warfare a proof of human worth, strange turns were given to the idea, as when the Plains Indians gave their highest awards to the man who touched a live enemy rather than to the man who brought in a scalp— from a dead enemy—because killing a man was less risky. Warfare is just an invention known to the majority of human societies by which they permit their young men either to accumulate prestige or avenge their honor or acquire loot or wives or slaves or sago lands or cattle or appease the blood lust of their gods or the restless souls of the recently dead. It is just an invention, older and more widespread than the jury system, but none the less an invention.

But, once we have said this, have we said anything at all? Despite a few instances, dear to the hearts of controversialists, of the loss of the useful arts, once an invention is made which proves congruent with human needs or social forms, it tends to persist. Grant that war is an invention, that it is not a biological necessity nor the outcome of certain special types of social forms, still, once the invention is made, what are we to do about it? The Indian who had been subsisting on the buffalo for generations because with his primitive weapons he could slaughter only a limited number of buffalo did not return to his primitive weapons when he saw that the white man's more efficient weapons were exterminating the buffalo. A desire for the white man's cloth may mortgage the South Sea Islander to the white man's plantation, but he does not return to making bark cloth, which would have left him free. Once an invention is known and accepted, men do not easily relinquish it. The skilled workers may smash the first steam looms which they feel are to be their undoing, but they accept them in the end, and no movement which has insisted upon the mere abandonment of usable inventions has ever had much success. Warfare is here, as part of our thought; the deeds of warriors are immortalized in the words of our poets; the toys of our children are modeled upon the weapons of the soldier; the frame of reference within which our statesmen and our diplomats work always contains war. If we know that it is not inevitable, that it is due to historical accident that warfare is one of the ways in which we think of behaving, are we given any hope by that? What hope is there of persuading nations to abandon war, nations so thoroughly imbued with the idea that resort to war is, if not actually desirable and noble, at least inevitable whenever certain defined circumstances arise?

12

In answer to this question I think we might turn to the history of other social inventions, inventions which must once have seemed as firmly entrenched as warfare. Take the methods of trial which preceded the jury system: ordeal and trial by combat. Unfair, capricious, alien as they are to our feeling today, they were once the only methods open to individuals accused of some offense. The invention of trial by jury gradually replaced these methods until only witches, and finally not even witches, had to resort to the ordeal. And for a long time the jury system seemed the one best and finest method of settling legal disputes, but today new inventions, trial before judges only or before commissions, are replacing the jury system. In each case the old method was replaced by a new social invention; the ordeal did not go out because people thought it unjust or wrong, it went out because a method more congruent with the institutions and feelings of the period was invented. And, if we despair over the way in which war seems such an ingrained habit of most of the human race, we can take comfort from the fact that a poor invention will usually give place to a better invention. 13

For this, two conditions at least are necessary. The people must recognize the defects of the old invention, and some one must make a new one. Propaganda against warfare, documentation of its terrible cost in human suffering and social waste, these prepare the ground by teaching people to feel that warfare is a defective social institution. There is further needed a belief that social invention is possible and the invention of new methods which will render warfare as out-of-date as the tractor is making the plow, or the motor car the horse and buggy. A form of behavior becomes out-of-date only when something else takes its place, and in order to invent forms of behavior which will make war obsolete, it is a first requirement to believe that an invention is possible. 14

QUESTIONS

1. Mead's essay, like many arguments, recognizes alternative viewpoints. What are the other viewpoints? Why does Mead begin with them?

2. Mead says in paragraph 10, 'Yet, if it be granted that warfare is after all an invention . . ." Do you grant that? If so, how has she made her case?

3. Toward the end of the next paragraph, she says much the same thing: "Warfare is just an invention known to the majority of human societies. . . ." What has changed in her conception of warfare in the interim between paragraphs 10 and 11? Are you any more or less sure that it is "just an invention"?

4. If Mead is correct and warfare is an invention and if, then, a better invention might supplant it, what might do? What kinds of situations would this new invention have to satisfy?

5. Write an essay in which you propose and speculate on an alternative to war. Describe the behavior that would replace war, and outline the questions it would resolve.

6. Write a report on one on the peoples Mead mentions in this article—such as the

Eskimo, the Pueblo, the Lepchas, the Pygmies, the Sioux, or perhaps the Maori. Describe their knowledge of war, their behavior in war, their avoidance of war, or whatever is appropriate for the people you choose.

7. Look up William James's essay, which provided the impetus for this one, and write an answer to Mead as you imagine he might answer her. Or you might suppose he found her essay convincing; what might he say after deciding that?

THE TECHNOSTRUCTURE

John Kenneth Galbraith

John Kenneth Galbraith (b. 1908) was a professor of economics at Harvard University until his retirement in 1975. From 1961 through 1963, he was the American ambassador to India. He is the author of several books, the best known of which is The Affluent Society *(1958), and is a member of the American Academy, Institute of Arts and Letters. Other of his books include* The Age of Uncertainty *(1976),* The Anatomy of Power *(1984), and* The New Industrial State *(3d edition, 1978), from which this selection is taken. Here he examines the relation of power to intelligence in large organizations and challenges our assumptions of who is in charge.*

". . . the prevalence of group, instead of individual, action is a striking characteristic of management organization in the large corporations."

R. A. Gordon
Business Leadership in the Large Corporation

The individual has far more standing in our culture than the group. An   1
individual has a presumption of accomplishment; a committee has a presumption of inaction. We react sympathetically to the individual who seeks to safeguard his personality from engulfment by the mass. We call for proof, at least in principle, before curbing his aggressions. Individuals have souls; corporations are notably soulless. The entrepreneur—individualistic, restless, with vision, guile and courage—has been the economists' only hero. The great business organization arouses no similar admiration. Admission to heaven is individually and by families; the top management even of an enterprise with an excellent corporate image cannot yet go in as a group. To have, in pursuit of truth, to assert the superiority of the organization over the individual for important social tasks is a taxing prospect.

Yet it is a necessary task. It is not to individuals but to organizations that   2
power in the business enterprise and power in the society has passed. And modern economic society can only be understood as an effort, wholly successful, to synthesize by organization a group personality far superior *for its purposes* to a natural person and with the added advantage of immortality.

The need for such a group personality begins with the circumstance that in   3
modern industry a large number of decisions, and *all* that are important, draw on information possessed by more than one man. Typically they draw on the

specialized scientific and technical knowledge, the accumulated information or experience and the artistic or intuitive sense of many persons. And this is guided by further information which is assembled, analyzed and interpreted by professionals using highly technical equipment. The final decision will be informed only as it draws systematically on all those whose information is relevant. Nor, human beings what they are, can it take all of the information that is offered at face value. There must, additionally, be a mechanism for testing each person's contribution for its relevance and reliability as it is brought to bear on the decision.

[II]

The need to draw on, and appraise, the information of numerous individuals 4 in modern industrial decision-making has three principal points of origin. It derives, first, from the technological requirements of modern industry. It is not that these are always inordinately sophisticated; a man of moderate genius could, quite conceivably, provide himself with the knowledge of the various branches of metallurgy and chemistry, and of engineering, procurement, production management, quality control, labor relations, styling and merchandising which are involved in the development of a modern motorcar. But even moderate genius is in unpredictable supply, and to keep abreast of all these branches of science, engineering and art would be time-consuming even for a genius. The elementary solution, which allows of the use of far more common talent and with far greater predictability of result, is to have men who are appropriately qualified or experienced in each limited area of specialized knowledge or art. Their information is then combined for carrying out the design and production of the vehicle. It is a common public impression, not discouraged by scientists, engineers and industrialists, that modern scientific, engineering and industrial achievements are the work of a new and quite remarkable race of men. This is pure vanity; were it so, there would be few such achievements. The real accomplishment of modern science and technology consists in taking ordinary men, informing them narrowly and deeply and then, through appropriate organization, arranging to have their knowledge combined with that of other specialized but equally ordinary men. This dispenses with the need for genius. The resulting performance, though less inspiring, is far more predictable. No individual genius arranged the flights to the moon. It was the work of organization—bureaucracy. And the men walking on the moon and contemplating their return could be glad it was so.

The second factor requiring the combination of specialized talent derives 5 from advanced technology, the associated use of capital and the resulting need for planning with its accompanying control of environment. The market is, in remarkable degree, an intellectually undemanding institution. The Wisconsin farmer need not anticipate his requirements for fertilizers, pesticides or even machine parts; the market stocks and supplies them. The cost of these is substantially the same for the man of intelligence and for his neighbor who, under medical examination, shows daylight in either ear. And the farmer need have no price or selling strategy; the market takes all his milk at the ruling price. Much of the appeal of the market, to economists at least, has been from the way it seems to simplify life. Better orderly error than complex truth.

For complexity enters with planning and is endemic thereto. The manufac-   6
turer of missiles, space vehicles or modern aircraft must foresee the requirements for specialized plant, specialized manpower, exotic materials and intricate components and take steps to ensure their availability when they are needed. For procuring such things, we have seen, the market is either unreliable or unavailable. And there is no open market for the finished product. Everything here depends on the care and skill with which contracts are sought and nurtured in Washington or in Whitehall or Paris.[1]

The same foresight and responding action are required, in lesser degree, from   7
manufacturers of automobiles, processed foods and detergents. They too must foresee requirements and manage markets. Planning, in short, requires a great variety of information. It requires variously informed men and men who are suitably specialized in obtaining the requisite information. There must be men whose knowledge allows them to foresee need and to ensure a supply of labor, materials and other production requirements; those who have knowledge to plan price strategies and see that customers are suitably persuaded to buy at these prices; those who, at higher levels of technology, are informed that they can work effectively with the state to see that it is suitably guided; and those who can organize the flow of information that the above tasks and many others require. Thus, to the requirements of technology for specialized technical and scientific talent are added the very large further requirements of the planning that technology makes necessary.

Finally, following from the need for this variety of specialized talent, is the   8
need for its coordination. Talent must be brought to bear on the common purpose. More specifically, on large and small matters, information must be extracted from the various specialists, tested for its reliability and revelance, and made to yield a decision. This process, which is much misunderstood, requires a special word.

[III]

The modern business organization, or that part which has to do with guid-   9
ance and direction, consists of numerous individuals who are engaged, at any given time, in obtaining, digesting or exchanging and testing information. A

---

[1]Whitehall: a street in London where many departments of the government are located and hence a familiar name for the British government. [Eds.]

very large part of the exchange and testing of information is by word of mouth—a discussion in an office, at lunch or over the telephone. But the most typical procedure is through the committee and the committee meeting. One can do worse than think of a business organization as a hierarchy of committees. Coordination, in turn, consists in assigning the appropriate talent to committees, intervening on occasion to force a decision, and, as the case may be, announcing the decision or carrying it as information for a yet further decision by a yet higher committee.

Nor should it be supposed that this is an inefficient procedure. On the contrary it is, normally, the only efficient procedure. Association in a committee enables each member to come to know the intellectual resources and the reliability of his colleagues. Committee discussion enables members to pool information under circumstances which allow, also, of immediate probing to assess the relevance and reliability of the information offered. Uncertainty about one's information or error is revealed as in no other way. There is also, no doubt, considerable stimulus to mental effort from such association. One may enjoy torpor in private but not so comfortably in public, at least during working hours. Men who believe themselves deeply engaged in private thought are usually doing nothing. Committees are condemned by those who have been captured by the cliché that individual effort is somehow superior to group effort; by those who guiltily suspect that since group effort is more congenial, it must be less productive; and by those who do not see that the process of extracting, and expecially of testing, information has necessarily a somewhat undirected quality—briskly conducted meetings invariably decide matters previously decided; and by those who fail to realize that highly paid men, when sitting around a table as a committee, are not necessarily wasting more time than, in the aggregate, they would each waste in private by themselves. Forthright and determined administrators frequently react to belief in the superior capacity of individuals for decision by abolishing all committees. They then constitute working parties, task forces or executive groups in order to avoid the one truly disastrous consequence of their action which would be that they should make the decisions themselves.

Thus decision in the modern business enterprise is the product not of individuals but of groups. The groups are numerous, as often informal as formal and subject to constant change in composition. Each contains the men possessed of the information, or with access to the information, that bears on the particular decision together with those whose skill consists in extracting and testing this information and obtaining a conclusion. This is how men act successfully on matters where no single one, however exalted or intelligent, has more than a fraction of the necessary knowledge. It is what makes modern business possible, and in other contexts it is what makes modern government possible. It is fortunate that men of limited knowledge are so constituted that they can work together in this way. Were it otherwise, business and government, at any given moment, would be at a standstill awaiting the appearance of a man with the requisite breadth of knowledge to resolve the problem presently at hand. Some further characteristics of group decision-making must now be noticed.

[IV]

Group decision-making extends deeply into the business enterprise. Effective participation is not closely related to rank in the formal hierarchy of the organization. This takes an effort of mind to grasp. Everyone is influenced by the stereotyped organization chart of the business enterprise. At its top is the Board of Directors and the Board Chairman; next comes the President; next comes the Executive Vice President; thereafter come the Department or Divisional heads—those who preside over the Chevrolet division, the large-generators division, the computer division. Power is assumed to pass down from the pinnacle. Those at the top give orders; those below relay them on or respond. 12

This happens, but only in very simple organizations—the peacetime drill of the National Guard or a troop of Boy Scouts moving out on Saturday maneuvers. Elsewhere the decision will require information. Some power will then pass to the person or persons who have this information. If this knowledge is highly particular to themselves, then their power becomes very great. In Los Alamos, during the development of the atomic bonb, Enrico Fermi rode a bicycle up the hill to work;[2] Major General Leslie R. Groves presided in grandeur over the entire Manhattan District.[3] In association with a handful of others Fermi could, at various early stages, have brought the entire enterprise to an end. No such power resided with Groves. At any moment he could have been replaced without loss. 13

When power is exercised by a group, not only does it pass into the organization but it passes irrevocably. If an individual has taken a decision, he can be called before another individual, who is his superior in the hierarchy, his information can be examined and his decision reversed by the greater wisdom or experience of the superior. But if the decision required the combined information of a group, it cannot be safely reversed by an individual. He will have to get the judgment of other specialists. This returns the power once more to organization. 14

No one should insist, in these matters, on pure cases. There will often be instances when an individual has the knowledge to modify or change the finding of a group. But the broad rule holds: If a decision requires the specialized 15

---

[2]Enrico Fermi (1901–1954): Italian-born American physicist who was a key figure in the development of the atomic bomb. [Eds.]

[3]Manhattan District: the code name for the project developing the first atomic bomb was the Manhattan Project. The Manhattan Engineer District of the Corps of Engineers was the agency in charge of the project, and Groves was its commander. He directed activities at Oak Ridge, Tennessee, and Los Alamos, New Mexico. [Eds.]

knowledge of a group of men, it is subject to safe review only by the similar knowledge of a similar group. Group decision, unless acted upon by another group, tends to be absolute.

[V]

Next, it must not be supposed that group decision is important only in such 16
evident instances as nuclear technology or space mechanics. Simple products are made and packaged by sophisticated processes. And the most massive programs of market control, together with the most specialized marketing talent, are used on behalf of soap, detergents, cigarettes, aspirin, packaged cereals and gasoline. These, beyond others, are the valued advertising accounts. The simplicity and uniformity of these products require the investment of compensatingly elaborate science and art to suppress market influences and make prices and amounts sold subject to the largest possible measure of control. For these products too, decision passes to a group which combines specialized and esoteric knowledge. Here too power goes deeply and more or less irrevocably into the organization.

For purposes of pedagogy, I have sometimes illustrated these tendencies by 17
reference to a technically uncomplicated product, which, unaccountably, neither General Electric nor Westinghouse has yet placed on the market. It is a toaster of standard performance, the pop-up kind, except that it etches on the surface of the toast, in darker carbon, one of a selection of standard messages or designs. For the elegant, an attractive monogram would be available or a coat of arms; for the devout, at breakfast there would be an appropriate devotional message from the Reverend Billy Graham; for the patriotic or worried, there would be an aphorism urging vigilance from Mr. J. Edgar Hoover; for modern painters and economists, there would be a purely abstract design. A restaurant version would sell advertising.

Conceivably this is a vision that could come from the head of General 18
Electric. But the systematic proliferation of such ideas is the designated function of much more lowly men who are charged with product development. At an early stage in the development of the toaster the participation of specialists in engineering, production, styling and design and possibly philosophy, art and spelling would have to be sought. No one in position to authorize the product would do so without a judgment on how the problems of inscription were to be solved and at what cost. Nor, ordinarily, would an adverse finding on technical and economic feasibility be overridden. At some stage, further development would become contingent on the findings of market researchers and merchandise experts on whether the toaster could be sold and at what price. Nor would an adverse decision by this group be overruled. In the end there would be a comprehensive finding on the feasibility of the innovation. If unfavorable this would not be overruled. Nor, given the notoriety that attaches to lost opportu-

nity, would be the more plausible contingency of a favorable recommendation. It will be evident that nearly all powers—initiation, character of development, rejection or acceptance—are exerised deep in the company. It is not the managers who decide. Effective power of decision is lodged deeply in the technical, planning and other specialized staff.

[VI]

We must notice next that this exercise of group power can be rendered unreliable or ineffective by external interference. Not only does power pass into the organization but the quality of decision can easily be impaired by efforts of an individual to retain control over the decision-making process.   19

Specifically the group reaches decision by receiving and evaluating the specialized information of its members. If it is to act responsibly, it must be accorded responsibility. It cannot be arbitrarily or capriciously overruled. If it is, it will develop the same tendencies to irresponsibility as an individual similarly treated.   20

But the tendency will be far more damaging. The efficiency of the group and the quality of its decisions depend on the quality of the information provided and the precision with which it is tested. The last increases greatly as men work together. It comes to be known that some are reliable and that some, though useful, are at a tacit discount. All information offered must be so weighed. The sudden intervention of a superior introduces information, often of dubious quality, that is not subject to this testing. His reliability, as a newcomer, is unknown; his information, since he is boss, may be automatically exempt from the proper discount; or his intervention may take the form of an instruction and thus be outside the process of group decision in a matter where only group decision incorporating the required specialized judgments is reliable. In all cases the intrusion is damaging.   21

It follows both from the tendency for decision-making to pass down into organization and the need to protect the autonomy of the group that those who hold high formal rank in an organization—the President of General Motors or General Electric—exercise only modest powers of substantive decision. This power is certainly less than conventional obeisance, professional public relations or, on occasion, personal vanity insist. Decision and ratification are often confused. The first is important; the second is not. There is a tendency to associate power with any decision, however routine, that involves a good deal of money. Business protocol requires that money be treated with solemnity and respect and likewise the man who passes on its use. The nominal head of a large corporation, though with slight power, and perhaps in the first stages of retirement, is visible, tangible and comprehensible. It is tempting and perhaps valuable for the corporate personality to attribute to him power of decision that, in fact, belongs to a dull and not easily comprehended collectivity. Nor is it a valid explanation   22 that the boss, though impotent on specific questions, acts on broad issues of policy. Such issues of policy, if genuine, are pre–eminently the ones that require the specialized information of the group.

Leadership assigns tasks to committees from which decisions emerge. In doing so, it breaks usefully with the routine into which organization tends to fall. And it selects the men who comprise the groups that make the decisions, and it constitutes and reconstitutes these groups in accordance with changing need. This is, perhaps, its most important function. In an economy where organized intelligence is the decisive factor of production, the selection of the intelligence so organized is of central importance. But it cannot be supposed that a boss can replace or even second-guess organized intelligence on substantive decisions. 23

[VII]

In the past, leadership in business organizations was identified with the entrepreneur—the individual who united ownership or control of capital with capacity for organizing the other factors of production and, in most contexts, with a further capacity for innovation. With the rise of the modern corporation, the emergence of the organization required by modern technology and planning and the divorce of the owner of the capital from control of the enterprise, the entrepreneur no longer exists as an individual person in the mature industrial enterprise. Everyday discourse, except in the economics textbooks, recognizes this change. It replaces the entrepreneur, as the directing force of the enterprise, with management. This is a collective and imperfectly defined entity; in the large corporation it embraces chairman, president, those vice presidents with important staff or departmental responsibility, occupants of other major staff positions and, perhaps, division or department heads not included above. It includes, however, only a small proportion of those who, as participants, contribute information to group decisions. This latter group is very large; it extends from the most senior officials of the corporation to where it meets, at the outer perimeter, the white- and blue-collar workers whose function is to conform more or less mechanically to instruction or routine. It embraces all who bring specialized knowledge, talent or experience to group decision-making. This, not the management, is the guiding intelligence—the brain—of the enterprise. There is no name for all who participate in group decision-making or the organization which they form. I propose to call this organization the Technostructure. 24

QUESTIONS

1. Galbraith's argument seems to present two chief propositions. The first, which comes early, asserts that "it is not to individuals but to organizations that power . . . has passed" (paragraph 2). What is the second major proposition, and how does it relate to the first?

2. Why must so much explanation of technology, planning, and coordination precede Galbraith's second argumentative proposition?

3. In his first paragraph, Galbraith says "the entrepreneur . . . has been the economists' only hero." But his argument as a whole emphasizes the past tense of that remark. What does he foresee?

4. There is a lot of explanation in this essay, perhaps more explanation than argument. Indicate several of the subjects and areas of explanation. What do they contribute to the essay?

5. In paragraph 8 Galbraith says that the process he is discussing "requires a special word." When does he supply this special word? Why does he identify it at that point instead of in paragraph 8?

6. What experience have you had with committee decisions? Write a report about a committee on which you have served. What was its function? How did it proceed with its work? How were decisions made? Where did power reside in the group? Why? What is your estimation of that power and its exercise?

7. Consider as a "technostructure" a school or some other large organization with which you are familiar. If the analogy is at all reasonable and if Galbraith's analysis is correct, you should be able to revise some common views of the relation of the individual to the group and of arrangements of power in that organization. Write a report entitled something like "Real Power in a High School" or in whatever organization you choose.

REVIEW OF STANLEY MILGRAM'S EXPERIMENTS ON OBEDIENCE

Diana Baumrind

Diana Baumrind (b. 1927) is a developmental and clinical psychologist with the Institute of Human Development at The University of California at Berkeley. Her research specializations are "the effects of family socialization on the development of social responsibility and personal agency in children and adolescents" and "the ethics of research with human subjects." That last subject is her topic here as she discusses the experiment conducted by Stanley Milgram (pages 442–465). Her article appeared originally in 1964 in American Psychologist, *the journal of the American Psychological Association.*

Certain problems in psychological research require the experimenter to balance his career and scientific interests against the interests of his prospective subjects. When such occasions arise the experimenter's stated objective frequency is to do the best possible job with the least possible harm to his subjects. The experimenter seldom perceives in more positive terms an indebtedness to the subject for his services, perhaps because the detachment which his functions require prevents appreciation of the subject as an individual. 1

Yet a debt does exist, even when the subject's reason for volunteering includes course credit or monetary gain. Often a subject participates unwillingly in order to satisfy a course requirement. These requirements are of questionable merit ethically, and do not alter the experimenter's responsibility to the subject. 2

Most experimental conditions do not cause the subjects pain or indignity, and are sufficiently interesting or challenging to present no problem of an ethical nature to the experimenter. But where the experimental conditions expose the subject to loss of dignity, or offer him nothing of value, then the experimenter is obliged to consider the reasons why the subject volunteered and to reward him accordingly. 3

The subject's public motives for volunteering include having an enjoyable or stimulating experience, acquiring knowledge, doing the experimenter a favor which may some day be reciprocated, and making a contribution to science. These motives can be taken into account rather easily by the experimenter who is willing to spend a few minutes with the subject afterwards to thank him for his participation, answer his questions, reassure him that he did well, and chat 4

641

with him a bit. Most volunteers also have less manifest, but equally legitimate, motives. A subject may be seeking an opportunity to have contact with, be noticed by, and perhaps confide in a person with psychological training. The dependent attitude of most subjects toward the experimenter is an artifact of the experimental situation as well as an expression of some subjects' personal need systems at the time they volunteer.

The dependent, obedient attitude assumed by most subjects in the experi- 5 mental setting is appropriate to that situation. The "game" is defined by the experimenter and he makes the rules. By volunteering, the subject agrees implicitly to assume a posture of trust and obedience. While the experimental conditions leave him exposed, the subject has the right to assume that his security and self-esteem will be protected.

There are other professional situations in which one member—the patient 6 or client—expects help and protection from the other—the physician or psychologist. But the interpersonal relationship between experimenter and subject additionally has unique features which are likely to provoke initial anxiety in the subject. The laboratory is unfamiliar as a setting and the rules of behavior ambiguous compared to a clinician's office. Because of the anxiety and passivity generated by the setting, the subject is more prone to behave in an obedient, suggestible manner in the laboratory than elsewhere. Therefore, the laboratory is not the place to study degree of obedience or suggestibility, as a function of a particular experimental condition, since the base line for these phenomena as found in the laboratory is probably much higher than in most other settings. Thus experiments in which the relationship to the experimenter as an authority is used as an independent condition are imperfectly designed for the same reason that they are prone to injure the subjects involved. They disregard the special quality of trust and obedience with which the subject appropriately regards the experimenter.

Other phenomena which present ethical decisions, unlike those mentioned 7 above, *can* be reproduced successfully in the laboratory. Failure experience, conformity to peer judgment, and isolation are among such phenomena. In these cases we can expect the experimenter to take whatever measures are necessary to prevent the subject from leaving the laboratory more humiliated, insecure, alienated, or hostile than when he arrived. To guarantee that an especially sensitive subject leaves a stressful experimental experience in the proper state sometimes requires special clinical training. But usually an attitude of compassion, respect, gratitude, and common sense will suffice, and no amount of clinical training will substitute. The subject has the right to expect that the psychologist with whom he is interacting has some concern for his welfare, and the personal attributes and professional skill to express his good will effectively.

Unfortunately, the subject is not always treated with the respect he deserves. 8 It has become more commonplace in sociopsychological laboratory studies to manipulate, embarrass, and discomfort subjects. At times the insult to the subject's sensibilities extends to the journal reader when the results are reported. Milgram's (1963) study is a case in point. The following is Milgram's abstract of his experiment:

This article describes a procedure for the study of destructive obedience in the laboratory. It consists of ordering a naive S to administer increasingly more severe punishment to a victim in the context of a learning experiment. Punishment is administered by means of a shock generator with 30 graded switches ranging from Slight Shock to Danger: Severe Shock. The victim is a confederate of E.[1] The primary dependent variable is the maximum shock the S is willing to administer before he refuses to continue further.[2] 26 Ss obeyed the experimental commands fully, and administered the highest shock on the generator. 14 Ss broke off the experiment at some point after the victim protested and refused to provide further answers. The procedure created extreme levels of nervous tension in some Ss. Profuse sweating, trembling, and stuttering were typical expressions of this emotional disturbance. One unexpected sign of tension—yet to be explained—was the regular occurrence of nervous laughter, which in some Ss developed into uncontrollable seizures. The variety of interesting behavioral dynamics observed in the experiment, the reality of the situation for the S, and the possibility of parametric variation within the framework of the procedure,[3] point to the fruitfulness of further study [p. 371].

The detached, objective manner in which Milgram reports the emotional disturbance suffered by his subject contrasts sharply with his graphic account of that disturbance. Following are two other quotes describing the effects on his subjects of the experimental conditions:

I observed a mature and initially poised businessman enter the laboratory smiling and confident. Within 20 minutes he was reduced to a twitching, stuttering wreck, who was rapidly approaching a point of nervous collapse. He constantly pulled on his earlobe, and twisted his hands. At one point he pushed his fist into his forehead and muttered: "Oh God, let's stop it." And yet he continued to respond to every word of the experimenter, and obeyed to the end [p. 377].

In a large number of cases the degree of tension reached extremes that are rarely seen in sociopsychological laboratory studies. Subjects were observed to sweat, tremble, stutter, bite their lips, groan, and dig their fingernails into their flesh. These were characteristic rather than exceptional responses to the experiment.
One sign of tension was the regular occurrence of nervous laughing fits. Fourteen of the 40 subjects showed definite signs of nervous laughter and smiling. The laughter seemed entirely out of place, even bizarre. Full-blown, uncontrollable seizures were observed for 3 subjects. On one occasion we observed a seizure so

---

[1]S: stands for subject; E: stands for experimenter. [Eds.]
[2]dependent variable: that which changes as a result of other changes made in the experiment. [Eds.]
[3]parametric variation: statistical term suggesting variables within the experiment that would influence the results and so leave some questions unanswered. [Eds.]

violently convulsive that it was necessary to call a halt to the experiment . . . [p. 375].

Milgram does state that,

After the interview, procedures were undertaken to assure that the subject would leave the laboratory in a state of well being. A friendly reconciliation was arranged between the subject and the victim, and an effort was made to reduce any tensions that arose as a result of the experiment [p. 374].

It would be interesting to know what sort of procedures could dissipate the type of emotional disturbance just described. In view of the effects on subjects, traumatic to a degree which Milgram himself considers nearly unprecedented in sociopsychological experiments, his casual assurance that these tensions were dissipated before the subject left the laboratory is unconvincing.

What could be the rational basis for such a posture of indifference? Perhaps   10
Milgram supplies the answer himself when he partially explains the subject's destructive obedience as follows, "Thus they assume that the discomfort caused the victim is momentary, while the scientific gains resulting from the experiment are enduring [p. 378]." Indeed such a rationale might suffice to justify the means used to achieve his end if that end were of inestimable value to humanity or were not itself transformed by the means by which it was attained.

The behavioral psychologist is not in as good a position to objectify his faith   11
in the significance of his work as medical colleagues at points of breakthrough. His experimental situations are not sufficiently accurate models of real-life ex-perience; his sampling techniques are seldom of a scope which would justify the meaning with which he would like to endow his results; and these results are hard to reproduce by colleagues with opposing theoretical views. Unlike the Sabin vaccine,[4] for example, the concrete benefit to humanity of his particular piece of work, no matter how competently handled, cannot justify the risk that real harm will be done to the subject. I am not speaking of physical discomfort, inconvenience, or experimental deception per se, but of permanent harm, how-ever slight. I do regard the emotional disturbance described by Milgram as potentially harmful because it could easily effect an alteration in the subject's self-image or ability to trust adult authorities in the future. It is potentially harmful to a subject to commit, in the course of an experiment, acts which he himself considers unworthy, particularly when he has been entrapped into com-mitting such acts by an individual he has reason to trust. The subject's personal responsibility for his actions is not erased because the experimenter reveals to him the means which he used to stimulate these actions. The subject realizes that he would have hurt the victim if the current were on. The realization that he also made a fool of himself by accepting the experimental set results in

---

[4]Sabin vaccine: an oral vaccine against polio, developed by Albert Bruce Sabin (b. 1906), Polish-born American physician and microbiologist. [Eds.]

additional loss of self-esteem. Moreover, the subject finds it difficult to express his anger outwardly after the experimenter in a self-acceptant but friendly manner reveals the hoax.

A fairly intense corrective interpersonal experience is indicated wherein the subject admits and accepts his responsibility for his own actions, and at the same time gives vent to his hurt and anger at being fooled. Perhaps an experience as distressing as the one described by Milgram can be integrated by the subject,[5] provided that careful thought is given to the matter. The propriety of such experimentation is still in question even if such a reparational experience were forthcoming. Without it I would expect a naive, sensitive subject to remain deeply hurt and anxious for some time, and a sophisticated, cynical subject to become even more alienated and distrustful. 12

In addition the experimental procedure used by Milgram does not appear suited to the objectives of the study because it does not take into account the special quality of the set which the subject has in the experimental situation. Milgram is concerned with a very important problem, namely, the social consequences of destructive obedience. He says, 13

> Gas chambers were built, death camps were guarded, daily quotas of corpses were produced with the same efficiency as the manufacture of appliances. These inhumane policies may have originated in the mind of a single person, but they could only be carried out on a massive scale if a very large number of persons obeyed orders [p. 371].

But the parallel between authority-subordinate relationships in Hitler's Germany and in Milgram's laboratory is unclear. In the former situation the SS man or member of the German Officer Corps, when obeying orders to slaughter, had no reason to think of his superior officer as benignly disposed towards himself or their victims. The victims were perceived as subhuman and not worthy of consideration. The subordinate officer was an agent in a great cause. He did not need to feel guilt or conflict because within his frame of reference he was acting rightly.

It is obvious from Milgram's own descriptions that most of his subjects were concerned about their victims and did trust the experimenter, and that their distressful conflict was generated in part by the consequences of these two disparate but appropriate attitudes. Their distress may have results from shock at what the experimenter was doing to them as well as from what they thought they were doing to their victims. In any case there is not a convincing parallel between the phenomena studied by Milgram and destructive obedience as that concept would apply to the subordinate-authority relationship demonstrated in Hitler Germany. If the experiments were conducted "outside of New Haven and without any visible ties to the university," I would still question their validity 14

---

[5]integrated: a technical term in psychology suggesting the process by which we adjust to and incorporate traumatic experience. [Eds.]

on similar although not identical grounds. In addition, I would question the representativeness of a sample of subjects who would voluntarily participate within a noninstitutional setting.

In summary, the experimental objectives of the psychologist are seldom in- 15 compatible with the subject's ongoing state of well being, provided that the experimenter is willing to take the subject's motives and interests into consideration when planning his methods and correctives. Section 4b in *Ethical Standards of Psychologists* (American Psychological Association, undated) reads in part:

> Only when a problem is significant and can be investigated in no other way, is the psychologist justified in exposing human subjects to emotional stress or other possible harm. In conducting such research, the psychologist must seriously consider the possibility of harmful aftereffects, and should be prepared to remove them as soon as permitted by the design of the experiment. Where the danger of serious aftereffects exists, research should be conducted only when the subjects or their responsible agents are fully informed of this possibility and volunteer nevertheless [p. 12].

From the subject's point of view procedures which involve loss of dignity, self-esteem, and trust in rational authority are probably most harmful in the long run and require the most thoughtfully planned reparations, if engaged in at all. The public image of psychology as a profession is highly related to our own actions, and some of these actions are changeworthy. It is important that as research psychologists we protect our ethical sensibilities rather than adapt our personal standards to include as appropriate the kind of indignities to which Milgram's subjects were exposed. I would not like to see experiments such as Milgram's proceed unless the subjects were fully informed of the dangers of serious aftereffects and his correctives were clearly shown to be effective in restoring their state of well being.

REFERENCES

AMERICAN PSYCHOLOGICAL ASSOCIATION.
Ethical Standards of Psychologists: A summary of ethical principles. Washington, D. C.: APA, undated.
MILGRAM, S.
Behavorial study of obedience. *J. abnorm. soc. Psychol.*, 1963, 67, 371–378.

QUESTIONS

1. Baumrind challenges Milgram's experiment on two grounds. Distinguish and summarize the two.
2. Baumrind speaks generally for a couple of pages before even mentioning the

Milgram experiment. Why do you think she introduces her argument this way? Are there moments during this opening when the Milgram experiment is very much in mind, even without being mentioned?

3. What do you make of Baumrind's claim that "the laboratory is not the place to study degree of obedience or suggestibility" (paragraph 6)? Do Baumrind's reasons successfully undercut Milgram, or has he anticipated that worry?

4. At the end of her article, Baumrind challenges the applicability of Milgram's experiment to events in Hitler's Germany. Does Baumrind represent Milgram's thinking fairly? Do you agree with her that the application does not work? Explain your views.

5. Study Milgram's abstract, quoted by Baumrind in paragraph 8. How do you understand its next-to-last sentence? Do you really find the "nervous laughter" unexplained?

6. See whether your school has a policy about the use of human subjects in experiments. Assuming it has, and that its standards are available to the public, get a copy of them. After studying them, write a paper either supporting them or arguing for their amendment.

7. Have you ever been coerced by a situation to mistreat another person, or have you witnessed such mistreatment? Write an analysis of that situation as you remember it. Try to explain the degree to which the situation itself seemed to elicit the questionable behavior. How do you weigh individual responsibility against institutional or group responsibility in this instance?

RACIST ARGUMENTS AND IQ
Stephen Jay Gould

Stephen Jay Gould, as the headnote on page 500 mentions, is a geologist best known for his column in Natural History *magazine. The following essay comes from his book* Ever Since Darwin: Reflections in Natural History *(1977). The broad subject at issue here is "biological determinism," the idea that nature, more than socialization and training, makes us what we are.*

Louis Agassiz, the greatest biologist of mid-nineteenth-century America, argued that God had created blacks and whites as separate species. The defenders of slavery took much comfort from this assertion, for biblical proscriptions of charity and equality did not have to extend across a species boundary. What could an abolitionist say? Science had shone its cold and dispassionate light upon the subject; Christian hope and sentimentality could not refute it.   1

Similar arguments, carrying the apparent sanction of science, have been continually invoked in attempts to equate egalitarianism with sentimental hope and emotional blindness. People who are unaware of this historical pattern tend to accept each recurrence at face value: that is, they assume that each statement arises from the "data" actually presented, rather than from the social conditions that truly inspire it.   2

The racist arguments of the nineteenth century were based primarily on craniometry, the measurement of human skulls. Today, these contentions stand totally discredited. What craniometry was to the nineteenth century, intelligence testing has been to the twentieth. The victory of the eugenics movement in the Immigration Restriction Act of 1924 signaled its first unfortunate effect—for the severe restrictions upon non-Europeans and upon southern and eastern Europeans gained much support from results of the first extensive and uniform application of intelligence tests in America—the Army Mental Tests of World War I. These tests were engineered and administered by psychologist Robert M. Yerkes,[1] who concluded that "education alone will not place the negro [*sic*] race on a par with its Caucasian competitors." It is now clear that Yerkes and his colleagues knew no way to separate genetic from environmental components in postulating causes for different performances on the tests.   3

The latest episode of this recurring drama began in 1969, when Arthur Jensen published an article entitled, "How Much Can We Boost IQ and Scholastic   4

---

[1]Robert M. Yerkes (1876–1956): American biologist and psychologist. [Eds.]

Achievement?" in the *Harvard Educational Review.*[2] Again, the claim went forward that new and uncomfortable information had come to light, and that science had to speak the "truth" even if it refuted some cherished notions of a liberal philosophy. But again, I shall argue, Jensen had no new data; and what he did present was flawed beyond repair by inconsistencies and illogical claims.

Jensen assumes that IQ tests adequately measure something we may call   5 "intelligence." He then attempts to tease apart the genetic and environmental factors causing differences in performance. He does this primarily by relying upon the one natural experiment we possess: identical twins reared apart—for differences in IQ between genetically identical people can only be environmental. The average difference in IQ for identical twins is less than the difference for two unrelated individuals raised in similarly varied environments. From the data on twins, Jensen obtains an estimate of environmental influence. He concludes that IQ has a heritability of about 0.8 (or 80 percent) *within* the population of American and European whites. The average difference between American whites and blacks is 15 IQ points (one standard deviation).[3] He asserts that this difference is too large to attribute to environment, given the high heritability of IQ. Lest anyone think that Jensen writes in the tradition of abstract scholarship, I merely quote the first line of his famous work: "Compensatory education has been tried, and it apparently has failed."

I believe that this argument can be refuted in a "hierarchical" fashion—that   6 is, we can discredit it at one level and then show that it fails at a more inclusive level even if we allow Jensen's argument for the first two levels:

Level 1: The equation of IQ with intelligence. Who knows what IQ measures?   7 It is a good predictor of "success" in school, but is such success a result of intelligence, apple polishing, or the assimilation of values that the leaders of society prefer? Some psychologists get around this argument by defining intelligence operationally as the scores attained on "intelligence" tests. A neat trick. But at this point, the technical definition of intelligence has strayed so far from the vernacular that we can no longer define the issue. But let me allow (although I don't believe it), for the sake of argument, that IQ measures some meaningful aspect of intelligence in its vernacular sense.

Level 2: The heritability of IQ. Here again, we encounter a confusion be-   8 tween vernacular and technical meanings of the same word. "Inherited," to a layman, means "fixed," "inexorable," or "unchangeable." To a geneticist, "Inherited" refers to an estimate of similarity between related individuals based on genes held in common. It carries no implications of inevitability or of immutable entities beyond the reach of environmental influence. Eyeglasses correct a variety of inherited problems in vision; insulin can check diabetes.

---

[2] Arthur Jensen (b. 1923): American educational psychologist. [Eds.]
[3] Standard deviation: a measure of variability of any set of numerical values around their arithmetic mean. [Eds.]

Jensen insists that IQ is 80 percent heritable. Princeton psychologist Leon J.   9
Kamin has done the dog-work of meticulously checking through details of the
twin studies that form the basis of this estimate.[4] He has found an astonishing
number of inconsistencies and downright inaccuracies. For example, the late
Sir Cyril Burt, who generated the largest body of data on identical twins reared
apart, pursued his studies of intelligence for more than forty years.[5] Although
he increased his sample sizes in a variety of "improved" versions, some of his
correlation coefficients remain unchanged to the third decimal place[6]—a statistically impossible situation.[7] IQ depends in part upon sex and age; and other
studies did not standardize properly for them. An improper correction may
produce higher values between twins not because they hold genes for intelligence
in common, but simply because they share the same sex and age. The data are
so flawed that no valid estimate for the heritability of IQ can be drawn at all.
But let me assume (although no data support it), for the sake of argument, that
the heritability of IQ is as high as 0.8.

Level 3: The confusion of within- and between-group variation. Jensen draws   10
a causal connection between his two major assertions—that the within-group
heritability of IQ is 0.8 for American whites, and that the mean difference in
IQ between American blacks and whites is 15 points. He assumes that the black
"deficit" is largely genetic in origin because IQ is so highly heritable. This is a
non sequitur of the worst possible kind[8]—for there is no necessary relationship
between heritability within a group and differences in mean values of two separate groups.

A simple example will suffice to illustrate this flaw in Jensen's argument.   11
Height has a much higher heritability within groups than anyone has ever
claimed for IQ. Suppose that height has a mean value of five feet two inches
and a heritability of 0.9 (a realistic value) within a group of nutritionally deprived
Indian farmers. High heritability simply means that short farmers will tend to
have short offspring, and tall farmers tall offspring. It says nothing whatever
against the possibility that proper nutrition could raise the mean height to six
feet (taller than average white Americans). It only means that, in this improved
status, farmers shorter than average (they may now be five feet ten inches) would
still tend to have shorter than average children.

---

[4]Leon J. Kamin: American psychologist at Princeton and author of *The Science and Politics of
I.Q.* (1974). [Eds.]

[5]Sir Cyril Burt (1883–1971): British psychologist. [Eds.]

[6]correlation coefficients: a technical term having to do with determining variables that tend to
change together systematically. [Eds.]

[7]I wrote this essay in 1974. Since then, the case against Sir Cyril has progressed from an inference
of carelessness to a spectacular (and well-founded) suspicion of fraud. Reporters for the London
Times have discovered, for example, that Sir Cyril's coauthors (for the infamous twin studies)
apparently did not exist outside his imagination. In the light of Kamin's discoveries, one must
suspect that the data have an equal claim to reality.

[8]non sequitur: it does not follow. This Latin term, common in logic, indicates a conclusion
that is not derivable from the evidence produced. [Eds.]

I do not claim that intelligence, however defined, has no genetic basis—I 12
regard it as trivially true, uninteresting, and unimportant that it does. The
expression of any trait represents a complex interaction of heredity and environment. Our job is simply to provide the best environmental situation for the
realization of valued potential in all individuals. I merely point out that a specific
claim purporting to demonstrate a mean genetic deficiency in the intelligence
of American blacks rests upon no new facts whatever and can cite no valid data
in its support. It is just as likely that blacks have a genetic advantage over whites.
And, either way, it doesn't matter a damn. An individual can't be judged by
his group mean.

If current biological determinism in the study of human intelligence rests 13
upon no new facts (actually, no facts at all), then why has it become so popular
of late? The answer must be social and political. The 1960s were good years for
liberalism; a fair amount of money was spent on poverty programs and relatively
little happened. Enter new leaders and new priorities. Why didn't the earlier
programs work? Two possibilities are open: (1) we didn't spend enough money,
we didn't make sufficiently creative efforts, or (and this makes any established
leader jittery) we cannot solve these problems without a fundamental social and
economic transformation of society; or (2) the programs failed because their
recipients are inherently what they are—blaming the victims. Now, which alternative will be chosen by men in power in an age of retrenchment?

I have shown, I hope, that biological determinism is not simply an amusing 14
matter for clever cocktail party comments about the human animal. It is a
general notion with important philosophical implications and major political
consequences. As John Stuart Mill wrote;[9] in a statement that should be the
motto of the opposition: "Of all the vulgar modes of escaping from the consideration of the effect of social and moral influences upon the human mind, the
most vulgar is that of attributing the diversities of conduct and character to
inherent natural differences."

QUESTIONS

1. Gould has at least three strands to his argument: an argument with Jensen's methods and data, an argument based on the concluding sentences of paragraphs 13 and 14,
and an interpretation of the motives for an argument like Jensen's. What are the main
strands of Gould's argument?
2. Which strand of argument does Gould develop at greatest length? Why?
3. Which strand of argument do you find most convincing? Why?
4. If you have given different answers for questions 2 and 3, what do you make of
that?

---

[9]John Stuart Mill (1806–1873): British economist and philosopher, noted for his utilitarian views
and his support for social and political reform. [Eds.]

5. Gould says in paragraph 4 that Jensen presents no new data, in fact no reliable data at all. Do you find that to be so?

6. What do you think John Stuart Mill meant by "vulgar" in the quotation that ends Gould's essay? Would Jensen's experiment be an example of the "vulgar"? Why or why not?

7. Taking the quotation from Mill (paragraph 14) as a starting point, write an essay that either defends or refutes Mill's idea.

8. Surely you know someone who seems either smarter or a lot less smart than he or she is generally taken to be. On what basis is that person commonly measured? On what basis do you evaluate her or him? Write a paper in which you reveal the "truth" as opposed to the more common interpretation of that person.

THE DANGERS OF FEMININITY
Lucy Gilbert & Paula Webster

Lucy Gilbert (b. 1941) is a psychotherapist in private prac-tice in New York City. Paula Webster (b. 1943), also of New York, is codirector of The Institute for the Study of Sex in Society and History. *Their essay, the opening chapter of* Bound by Love: The Sweet Trap of Daughterhood *(1982), illustrates the power of generalization in argument. The ideas of "a real man" and "a real woman" are both pow-erfully evocative, even though seldom found in nature. Though neither term describes an individual exactly, each is a useful abstraction that helps us frame our understanding of persons and behavior.*

One day, when Sara was barely nine years old, she sneaked into her brother's room and pulled a pair of jockey shorts and a white T-shirt out of his drawer. Clutching the underwear, she slipped into the bathroom to try them on.

Standing by the sink, she pulled her hair back with a rubber band, slicked it into place with water and stared into the mirror, trying to find a face to fit her new clothes. After forcing her eyes out of focus she thought she saw a more masculine face looking back at her. The effect was thrilling and disorienting, but just what she had desired. She looked like a boy.

Proud of her accomplishment, she went into the kitchen to show her mother the results of her experiment. Her mother, however, did not share her excite-ment and ordered her to remove her brother's underwear. Sara was not sure why her mother was so upset, but it was clear she had done something wrong. She returned to her room and made the undershirt into a bolero, a simple trick she had learned from her best friend. This time she went to get her mother's approval, sure she had remedied the situation, but Mom didn't seem to like it any better. She did not appreciate such imaginative play and was not going to encourage it. Her mother said that girls don't wear boys' underwear because they don't have what boys have, and she didn't see the joke. Sara felt defeated and humiliated. She learned that boys and girls must stay in their own clothes and in their own place.

Like Sara, many of us can remember the first time we experimented with the rules of masculinity or femininity by trying on clothes, attitudes, or behaviors marked "off limits." Usually someone told us that we couldn't change what nature had intended, that we had to remain girls or boys and find pleasure in the gender we were born to. These secret and transitory journeys into the ter-ritory of Otherness must have given us a glimpse of what we wanted to know but we had to renounce them if we were to accomplish our primary social task, to replicate the social system as it is constructed. Breaking the rules for appropriate masculine or feminine behavior introduces us to the dangers of testing the power of cultural assumptions and fears of breaking unnamed taboos. Early in our lives we give up the desire to take such imaginative leaps over the boundaries of difference and lose our curiosity about being the Other. We become the men or women we were meant to be.

The division of humanity into the two gender groups, women and men, 5 begins at the time we are born. Each infant is assigned to one or the other category on the basis of the shape and size of its genitals. Once this assignment is made we become what the culture believes each of us to be—feminine or masculine. Although many people think that men and women are the natural expression of a genetic blueprint, gender is a product of human thought and culture, a social construction that creates the "true nature" of all individuals. Human traits, capabilities, thoughts, and feelings are divided between the genders and come to be recognized and expressed in accordance with a complex set of rules and rituals that are learned to affirm this. Biological males and females are thus transformed by culture into men and women who are socially and psychologically conditioned to become masculine and feminine.

The division of infants into gender categories is based on the belief that men 6 and women are different kinds of beings. The emphasis on difference results in boys and girls being raised and evaluated differently. Although each group is thought to be incomplete, it is assumed that they will come together as a heterosexual couple to achieve a fusion of the traits that keep them separate. Since the original separation of the two places them in opposition and the exclusivity of the assignment enforces their difference, only through heterosexual coupling can each come to appreciate the assumed benefits of complementarity.

The imposition of the culture's two-gender system creates an exclusive gender 7 identity, one that feels natural despite the arduous path each child must follow to be recognized as appropriately feminine or masculine. Once imposed, this identity is internalized and experienced as an unalterable and inevitable reality. As children develop socially and psychologically the effects of difference are reinforced and rooted in the conscious and unconscious mind. The consequences of gender appear to be the result of an inborn personality structure and not the product of social conditioning and psychic structuring.

As men and women proceed through life, they are expected to "do" gender 8 according to the culture's assumptions about proper gender relations. Men must be masculine to women's feminine. Separate and unequal, the two halves of humanity confront each other with expectations for difference, and they are rarely surprised. Conformity to the cultural rules is harnessed when children have no choice but to obey. The desire to have the right kind of child, masculine or feminine, is matched by the parents' need to reproduce the gender system as they know it, and the result is the ongoing re-creation of the present two-gender system.

The division of the world's infants into masculine or feminine would cause 9 no dilemma if there were social parity between the genders, if differences were merely interesting but unimportant. However, in a patriarchal society the two-gender system mandates masculine and feminine beings who are unequal, giving one set social power and the other none. Relatively powerless, and considered inferior to men, all female infants enter a world that devalues and mystifies femininity. Society simultaneously denigrates and idealizes feminine character-istics, placing women on the pedestal and under the boot. The cultural system that defines femininity as inferior to masculinity and women as inferior to men creates a complex conflict of interests between the genders.

Boys and girls are raised with the cultural stereotypes for their gender as 10 guides. To become what they are supposed to be, they must be discouraged from all behavior that does not conform to the notion of the basic nature of masculinity or femininity. Feminine traits must be stamped out of boys, mas-culine out of girls. To reproduce gender classifications and maintain the bound-aries that divide boys from girls, each category must become what the other is not. Femininity and masculinity are conceived as opposites; therefore each child must be taught the limits of its human potential. The cultural rules of difference operate successfully when children can demonstrate that they know what they are and act appropriately masculine or feminine.

The model of masculinity that is presented to the little boy is based on an 11 idealized vision of male power. Mothers want their sons to become the most valued type of male—the "Real Man." Although this ideal is not one to which all men actually conform, the concept dictates parents' attitudes for raising their sons, standards against which many men judge their own behavior and that of other men. Even adult men who reject substantial portions of the model, worry about how well they are "doing" masculinity.

The Real Man exhibits all the traits of a strong and self-assured person by 12 being rational, competitive, proud, self-protective, physically powerful, and sex-ually active. Acting like a Real Man means standing up for your beliefs, pushing your opinions with determination and courage, even against seemingly insur-mountable odds. Fighting for justice or doing evil, the Real Man approaches his tasks believing in the righteousness of his cause. If necessary the Real Man will protect those weaker than he, because it is his duty to use his strength for others. Even if he is tyrannical in exercising his power, he gains respect for the force of his will. He may not love conflict but enjoys a good fight since he can show his skills at winning—the only acceptable outcome to his struggles.

The struggles that demand a Real Man's strength are self-chosen. He asserts 13 his individuality and independence even in the face of censure, and is often stimulated to bigger and better projects when he meets with adversity. He speaks with assurance and calm, explaining why tasks must be done his way. He never doubts the meaning of his life, is happy to be alive, and has much to accomplish. He is full of initiative and energy and undertakes all projects with full confidence that he will be successful. Sure of himself, he doesn't understand those who procrastinate because of indecision. He is a man of action, masterful and clever.

A Real Man learns his lessons quickly and applies his knowledge. Proud of his skills, he thinks it foolish to be excessively modest and doesn't consider it boastful to speak about his dreams, his plans, and his successes. He makes his way in the world by mapping strategies for what he wants. He knows he has to get ahead on his own and makes sure he is at the right place at the right time. He knows who can help him, is friendly to the right people, and thinks about the connections necessary to advancing his interests. He doesn't fear imposing himself by demanding too much of other people's time, resources, or energies. He likes to get his own way and uses people if he has to. If he doesn't succeed at first, he pauses briefly and sets off again to battle the elements. He never loses faith or confidence and just keeps fighting. The Real Man is not a quitter. 14

With his peers he is a loyal friend, but his friendships are based on shared activities—hanging out, doing or watching sports, drinking, camping, or arguing politics—rather than shared feelings. When he has trouble with his wife or his work or his mother, he does not expose his distress to other men lest he feel too vulnerable. Men are his competitors and he doesn't want them to have any advantage over him. He fears that an open expression of his feelings will raise questions about his masculinity. He prefers to stay cool with his buddies and thus ensure that his feelings are not misunderstood. 15

Although he can and must be serious, and bears the burden of power in society, he knows that a well-rounded person also has to have a good time. He likes to be outdoors, to be physically active, play, or at least watch, sports. His commitment to masculine pursuits is avowed and very strong. He likes men and spends time with them talking about masculine subjects, but not for too long. He has to get on with the business of life, and too much play is frivolous. 16

The world may think of a Real Man as rigid or tyrannical, but this view does not threaten his masculinity. He has to be strong and sure about his objectives. Even if he blusters and rants and raves to get his way, he is forgiven such excesses because his authority speaks louder than his words, leaving even the most stubborn of his audience in awe at the passion of his desires. 17

A Real Man believes that life is a game in which there are winners and losers. The weak lose and the strong win. It is not a pretty reality, he will assure you, but that is the way society works. In this dog-eat-dog world, the goal is to get power and forget about approval. To win, it is necessary to get your hands dirty, to take risks, to sell out if need be, but never to suffer defeat, never to surrender. There is something feminine about surrender and passivity and a Real Man avoids them at all costs. Even when he can't avoid losing, he is respected if he gives it all he has. If he surrenders aggressively, with style, he still comes out a winner. 18

A Real Man likes women, but prefers the company of men, even though he   19
shares his culture's terror of homosexuals, who are not "real" men. He lets
women know that he finds them appealing but he is very choosy, interested
only in the most attractive. He surveys a room, looking for his "type." He doesn't
find most women interesting or intelligent, so he experiments in relationships
with those who are at least pretty until he finds his ideal. He wants to be attractive
to women so his dress conforms to the popular stereotypes of masculine attire.
He can confidently be the casual professor, the immaculate businessman, the
trendy hippy, or the macho outdoorsman, never believing that his real personality is obscured by his clothes. He isn't obsessed with his image, but he may
spend a lot of time thinking about what he should wear in order to present one
aspect or another of his masculine personality.

But women are necessary to validate his masculinity and heterosexuality. No   20
Real Man can prove he is sufficiently masculine if he can't have sex with
women. In our patriarchal culture celibate men are ridiculed and suspect. To
demonstrate his masculinity a man must sexualize his simplest conversations
with women. When having sexual relations with a woman, a man knows he is
finally, without a doubt, a man.

To succeed at masculinity a Real Man must always anticipate sexual adven-   21
ture and be able to initiate and lead in seduction, smoothly encouraging women
to surrender and entrust what they say is most precious to them—their bodies
and their sexuality. An undeniably Real Man does not have to demand access
to women's sexuality; women offer themselves to him with grateful sighs and
great expectations.

If a young boy manages to achieve masculinity, as defined and determined   22
by the culture, he will find that the outcome of being a man is to feel good
about himself and his work, to feel like a winner. In a male-dominated society
like our own, in which boys are valued over girls and men over women, boys
will grow up to believe they are more important, more valued, and better than
girls. If they can meet the demands of masculinity they come to believe that
they deserve the best.

The more masculine a man's behavior, the closer he is to realizing the ideal.   23
Yet exaggeration of masculine characteristics can lead to persistent promotion
of self-interest, cold-blooded reason, lack of empathy, ruthless competition, and
aggressive sexuality. While these are considered negative traits, going too far,
taking masculinity too seriously, men are rarely criticized for being too masculine. How could there be too much of a good thing? Only when men abuse
the power given to them by virtue of their gender and become Dr. Strangelove
or Jack the Ripper does society turn a negative eye toward them. Men who go
too far, out of control, are destined to become victimizers, using their privilege
and their power for seemingly incomprehensible motives. Yet, masculinity, as
determined by culture and reproduced in the family, assures men that if they
follow the rules they will never become helpless victims. Hypermasculinity,

657

although not easy to live with, is never denigrated; it is rather accorded awe and cringing respect. Boys who follow the gender rules become winners and inherit the mantle of authority, legitimacy and power reserved for men.

While power is the reward for doing masculinity well, powerlessness is the 24 reward for doing femininity well. A girl who becomes the woman she is meant to be receives love, but never power. The cultural stereotype for femininity may be as rigid and self-alienating as the one for masculinity, but its outcomes are different. The program for girls must make them into women, and women must be what men are not. Before they even learn the rules, girls are denied the possibility of ever becoming as special as boys.

The culture's message to girls about who they should be is contained in the 25 stereotype for femininity. While masculinity is defined as a single consistent program for success, femininity is constructed as a formula for surrender. To be considered feminine a girl must suppress the positive traits that are labeled masculine. Each girl must reflect the mirror opposite of what is valued for men; she must learn to mute her strengths, her individuality, deny her own needs, and respond to the world in an emotional and noncompetitive manner. She must take every opportunity to demonstrate that she is a Real Woman, unselfish, flexible, cooperative, and altruistic. Her feminine behavior must conform to the cultural ideals for womanhood, the standard against which she will be judged as an appropriate member of her gender group.

When femininity is done well, girls become women whom men want to 26 love, protect, cherish, and ultimately marry. Women who can stir the passions and imaginations of men should be ultrafeminine, magical child-women who can draw men to their place on the pedestal and make their requests for male help in a sweet and convincing voice.

Femininity creates the Princess/Daddy's Girl, the only woman considered 27 exciting enough to deserve men's romantic attention. She should be fragile and not strong, helpless and insecure about her own worth, ineffectual and not masterful, confused and not rational, demanding but not competitive. She should feel like and act like a princess, waiting to be chosen and awakened by her master's touch. A woman who can pull off this version of the feminine ideal is promised the enduring respect of men and the unremitting jealousy of women. The stakes are high for the Princess, but to become the culture's sweetheart she must follow the rules.

The Princess looks to men for her definition and direction. Since she depends 28 on men to make her feel real she attracts their attention by flattering their masculinity. She assures them she is too fragile to stand on her own and cope with the harsh realities of everyday life. If her check book doesn't balance or the toilet backs up, she throws in the towel and waits for her boyfriend or husband to come home to set things in order. She is easily upset when things don't go her own way but isn't sure how she can take charge. Because she is fragile she expects others to do for her and make things just a little easier—easy enough for her to handle and not get dirty.

To get men to take care of her the Princess shows her helplessness and inability to defend herself. With a roll of her eyes and a careless shrug of her shoulders she gasps in frustration, mocking herself for being a silly incompetent, while seeking a man who will tell her what to do. Afraid of appearing too self-sufficient or resourceful, and therefore unfeminine, she gives up easily and lets others have their own way, sulking all the while. 29

The Princess is also ineffectual. Although she tries to master the new technology at her office, she can't get it right and refuses to read the manual. When friends make luncheon dates with her, she regularly shows up late explaining that she left the oven on, or just had to finish the dishes before they piled too high. She is the Gracie Allen of the neighborhood and can't accomplish what she sets out to do. Bemused and confused, the Princess is unable to get it together and organize her life. 30

When confronted by the irritation she provokes, she lowers her head and whispers that she is sorry, or she is shocked—Who, me? She shows her fear of those in authority and her willingness to comply with their wishes. If her boss urges her to stay late to finish some work for his pet project, she finds it impossible to refuse but resents him for asking. She wants to please him, but more than that can't bear to have anyone angry at her. Masking her rage, she complies. She believes that politeness and acquiescence to men will ultimately protect her from their disfavor. She is unwilling to rock the boat. She becomes adept at indirection because making demands is unfeminine and therefore makes her uncomfortable. 31

She replays her delicate and rather demure behavior by dressing in styles that accentuate her softness and fragility. Hoping to attract the right man, she strikes a pose that is cold and unattainable yet approachable. Since she is not supposed to deliver what she obliquely promises by her sexy little-girl pose, she must be careful to present an understated sexuality, one that will not threaten her image. But the Princess is a little spunky, hedging her bets by acting innocent with just a touch of devil-may-care. Although she refuses to admit that she understands that men ultimately want sex from her, she is willing to flirt. In the end, however, her cleverness must not be taken too seriously. While she can tease and taunt, she must remain sexually aloof so men will not mistake her for a Bad Girl. 32

The Princess, the most desirable woman in patriarchal culture and fantasy, waits for a man to make her life meaningful. Although many try desperately to become the Princess, an arduous, if not impossible task, few are fully successful. It is difficult to stand around looking helpless when femininity requires so much work. Femininity is a schizophrenic condition since at the very same time that women have to act helpless and passive, we must also act helpful, enduring, nurturing, and assertive (but only in the interests of others). Like our mothers, 33 we should be able to give until it hurts. In addition to confirming heterosexual femininity a woman must also become the tireless worker, the all-giving friend, the woman who takes care of others by putting herself last and making lives better for those more deserving than herself. So the Princess must take off her sequins and put on her apron to become the more ubiquitous version of a real woman, the Good Girl.

The Good Girl plays her role with a Saint in mind. She puts up with life's 34 tragedies and stands steadfastedly by when anyone needs her help. As a woman, she is not allowed control over the course of human events, but must be prepared to grit her teeth, endure her hardships, and go on. Her patience and good will in the face of adversity warm the hearts of all who hear of her sacrifice. She can take it and come back for more. Infinitely flexible, the Good Girl bears up under the weight of the world and her subordinate condition. She is strong for others yet her strength is worthy of praise only under adversity, when directed away from herself.

The Good Girl is not obsessed about her good looks or desirability the way 35 the Princess is, at least in public. She is more refined, more sedate, and maddeningly practical. Though she isn't a prude, she refuses to wear clothes that are considered sexy. To her way of thinking, looking or acting seductive or sexual is morally distasteful and ultimately dangerous. Instead of looking fragile, she prefers to be "natural," to let her sense of practicality and good taste be reflected in sturdy and sensible attire. With her plain pumps, good haircut, moderate cleaning bill, and subtle makeup, she takes good care of herself but never looks too "fancy."

If her Gracie Allen sister can't get started because she doesn't know where to 36 begin, the Good Girl is up at dawn planning good works. She likes herself best when she is doing for others, volunteering to watch your kids, make the coffee, and take work home, even before being asked. Tireless and self-effacing, she rejects praise for her work and considers modesty a virtue. Nothing is too much for her because she can handle it all.

While the Princess is reserved, emotionally withholding, the Good Girl ex- 37 periences her life as an intense spectacle. She goes up and down, fluctuating between depression and boundless joy, feeling her way through the most difficult situations emotionally but never rationally. She fears being thought of as cold or calculating, even intellectual, and when she wants to get the best for herself and refuses to compromise, she feels she is being selfish—which doesn't sit right with her because that means she's acting like a man. So tirelessly she nurtures until she is ready to fall, which she does with a self-satisfied smile on her face. She makes others happy, thank God.

Instead of making her needs known, the Good Girl forgets to put herself in 38 the picture, assertion coming with difficulty and seeming unfeminine. She plays the waiting game, looking for the right time, the precisely correct moment to state her feelings. She never gets angry when her desires are frustrated; she is happy if you are happy. When conflicts arise she finds a way to play the mediator, to stress the futility of yelling or screaming or trying to get your way. She hates dissension and looks for the middle road, the common good. She is adept at compromise and accommodation, which she finesses with a tolerance that leaves others in her debt. She doesn't carp and complain about the silly things that occupy the more sensitive Princess, who is upset when things don't go her way. The Good Girl navigates through conflict and competition by denying her desire to win and burying her terror of losing. She withdraws when the action gets hot, claiming that the sidelines are fine for her.

The final model for femininity is the Bad Girl, the only woman who lives 39 under the threat of excommunication from the feminine sorority because she doesn't follow the rules of self-denial and compliance. While the Good Girl timidly agrees to other people's desires, and the Princess sweetly demands what she wants, the Bad Girl calculates the costs and benefits of her actions, with a tough and unrelenting rationality. By daring to take herself seriously—like a man—she pursues her desires, even at the risk of appearing dangerous and unfeminine. She seeks pleasure and wants to control her own gratification. She strikes fear in the hearts of both men and women because she seems to be an anomaly of femininity, someone who misunderstands the limits of her gender.

A woman who refuses to act like the Princess or the Good Girl will surely 40 be accused of being bad, the worst insult that can be directed at women, who are supposed to be good before all else. Being bad means not acting like a girl, crossing the line into masculinity, and threatening the assumed natural division between the sexes. No mother wants her daughter to be considered bad; no woman wants to live with that label as a permanent stigma. If a woman acts out of gender, trying on the masculine privileges, mannerisms, attitudes, or feelings that are off limits, society warns her that she will come to a bad end. A Bad Girl gets hurt, ends up in jail, suffers for her transgressions, and ultimately is alone. Had she only been good and acted like girls are supposed to, she would not find herself abandoned by the company of good women who can now feel better about their own sacrifices to femininity, or the real men whose excitement turns to boredom and then pity.

Little girls learn the complex structure of femininity as they grow up in the 41 family and adopt it as a self-chosen identity after a time. They internalize the construct and take it on as a psychological identity, the only way to know the self—feeling secure when following the prescribed rules. Women come to act, think, and feel feminine, viewing the world and all social relations through the lens of the gender assignment. It feels natural to act like a woman and unnatural to deviate from that "authentic" identity. Acting unfeminine, or feeling out of gender, produces anxiety. A woman who is tempted to stand up for herself, act like a man by being competitive, self-directed, or selfish, experiences confusion about herself and worries that she is being bad, unfeminine, possibly a freak or an unnatural woman. This anxiety has to do with the fear of gender loss—the fear of being beyond the boundaries of femininity, without a solid identity. Without a secure sense of who she is, who she is supposed to be, a woman fears stepping out of the "natural" constraints. Understandably she wants to be normal.

Femininity, like masculinity, is enforced by external threats as well. A woman who tests the limits of gender by pushing beyond the definition of femininity is threatened with loss of approval, love, and male attention. By being pushy, aggressive, assertive, or selfish, she can lose her job, her boyfriend, or her mother's concern. Social conformity maintains the gender system, keeping women acting like women and men acting like men. The fears of rejection and loss of love, coupled with the internal threat of being out of control, going too far, not really acting like a woman, keep all women committed to a social and psychological identity that requires the suppression of autonomous and aggressive desires. Doing femininity well receives the praise of society and the rewards of being an acceptable heterosexual woman, one who can get her man and keep him. If she is good and adheres to the models that the culture values for women, she will come to be known and know herself as a Real Woman, ready to live her life as a subordinate to men without questioning the primary mechanism that reproduces her subordination—the acquisition of femininity.

Since girls cannot be boys, or act like them, girls must accept the script for femininity and live with the contradiction of acting both the fragile femme and the enduring Mother Courage, responding to life with the needs of a dependent child and the strength of an enduring martyr. If they can balance assertion that is not too assertive with dependency that is not too dependent, they are promised the respect of men, their love, and their benevolence. The applause for being good and the threats to self-esteem for being bad keep women in their place in the two-gender system. Women renounce what is self-fulfilling in order to become heterosexual successes.

Because women must "do" femininity in a patriarchal society in which men are more valued than women, being a woman means being subordinate. Boys get more power, more privilege, and, when they are adults, more of what society offers in terms of pleasure and control. Girls get less. They have to take what is offered and not ask for more. Eventually femininity is equated with inferiority and acceptance of deprivation. The conclusion that girls draw from observing and participating in a society that values masculine over feminine is that they must be less deserving, less special and important than boys. Repeated experience with deprivation encourages women to agree with the cultural definition that they are less and shouldn't ask for too much. Femininity, which requires women to be passive, quiet, selfless, and subordinate, sets women up to expect to be the losers and not the winners in the world. Conditioned to accept their own deprivation as "natural," women are poorly prepared to defend their own interests, ask for what they need, or fight for what they want.

Women who follow the rules for femininity come to feel like victims, helpless 45
before the demands of other people, and unable to put their needs first. Refusing
to let other people have their way feels bad—uncomfortable and threatening.
Women who can't say no to the daily demands for their compliance end up
feeling taken advantage of—used. But that seems preferable to feeling selfish.
Women who say no, draw boundaries to protect what they think is important,
court the danger of other people's anger, irritation, or displeasure. If they are
not "good," they fear being "bad." But if they are "good girls," they often end
up feeling used, abused, and victimized.

Women who are committed to being good, even when it serves others and 46
not themselves, act out their feminine conditioning. Afraid to be thought rude,
unable to draw the line that ensures their own comfort and gratification, they
are helpless in situations where other people's needs for satisfaction seem to be
more urgent than their own. Acting like the Good Girl even when it feels painful
and self-defeating, is the only strategy that is familiar, the only one that feels
acceptable and right. Women come to believe that they are less, deserve less,
and shouldn't complain, confront, or struggle to get what they need.

So women complain about being taken advantage of, but fail to understand 47
why it feels so difficult to defend ourselves. Even in the simplest daily experiences we expect less and consequently get less. We watch ourselves giving up
our place in line because we are afraid to protest; we submit to a bad haircut,
unable to stop the scissors or walk out. Afraid of being thought too narcissistic,
we suffer silently. Some of us spend more time than we want to with friends,
children, lovers, and husbands, saying that the others' needs come first. We
don't want to disappoint or cause any pain. Women stand ready to serve even
when exhausted and indifferent. When someone strongly disagrees with our
opinions we are mute, pondering the necessity of speaking up at all. Feeling
powerless to assert ourselves, and terrified at the potency of our anger, we retreat
into silence, speaking obliquely and indirectly about what we want.

We deny our anger when events don't turn out to our satisfaction and deny 48
our disappointment when our desires are not fulfilled. We blame ourselves for
the rejections, power trips, and cruelties of friends and lovers, saying we must
have done something to deserve it. We find it hard to believe that people aren't
as good as we would like them to be and assume responsibility for unpleasant
situations in our lives, thinking we are in control when in fact we are not. If a
woman doesn't get the job she wants she usually assumes she wasn't good
enough, if she has a fight with her boyfriend she assumes it was her fault, that
he was right and she was wrong. Never suspicious of other people's motives,
never sure she can trust her feelings, women assume that everybody will protect
their interests if they don't make trouble.

The program for femininity and the internal sense of security that keep 49
women hooked on being what they are supposed to be leave them unprepared
to define or defend their own interests. Ready to deny the dangers of surrendering

to the will of others, women cheerfully walk into situations where defeat is inevitable. We come out feeling bad about ourselves, but never angry, never able to take the reins and get what we want.

Like the bottomless well, the truly feminine woman in all of us is a never-ending source of compassion and nurturance for others. She feels real when she is needed; she sees self-directed choice as something that will alienate her from those whom she cares most about—everybody but herself. Being good for others feels better than being good to herself. Women refuse to act like winners for fear of losing love, respect, or the good will of men and women who they think are better than they and more deserving of having their needs met. Wanting to be good, to be well thought of, to be liked, women passively endure impositions on their time, energy, and will in order to hold onto the good opinion of others. Fearing to ask for more or better, anxious about saying no and refusing to serve, the feminine woman walks a path that leads to self-denial and compliance—the only path for which her conditioning to femininity prepares her.

Because adhering to femininity seems natural, and because this "natural" condition strips women of the resources they need to stand up for themselves and fight back, most women believe that their victimization is inevitable. Since women are frightened of being called selfish, bad, or unfeminine, they often choose to be the losers instead of the winners. Winning assumes that one is better than someone else and doesn't fit in with the feminine self-image. A Real Woman says that it isn't important whether you win or lose, it's how you play the game. And she plays according to the rules of femininity, thereby ensuring her own defeat. Each time she loses, her femininity is validated; she is now the woman she was meant to be.

The woman who plays the Good Girl is promised some compensation for her efforts—the love of a man. The man, romanticized and overrated in the culture, will make up for the deprivations she suffers and assure the woman of her normalcy and worth. A man can lift the veil of social inferiority that women are forced to wear and elevate her above the generally denigrated category of Woman. With a man by her side she feels safer and more valuable, better able to deny her lack of social, economic and political power. Without a man she will be considered a heterosexual failure, a reject, a poor pitiable creature doomed to invisibility and celibacy. Her aloneness is the living proof of her inability to give, her failure to be feminine.

Masculinity and femininity are played out in the social relations between the sexes. Given the distribution of power and privilege, the relationship is always tinged with the residues of inequality; women must conspicuously demonstrate their admiration for the powerful and their willingness to serve; while men must express their respect for the powerless and their desire to protect. The contradictions of loving those who have more power than you are muted by the ideology of heterosexual romance, which assumes that women choose men

664

because they experience an irresistible attraction to them. Yet a woman *must* choose a man if she is to fulfill her feminine destiny. Without a man she cannot be a "real woman," the only kind men are interested in.

To have their femininity validated, women must gain men's attention and 54 approval. Women go about pleasing men with a single-minded energy they can rarely muster for themselves. Hungry for male recognition and fascinated by masculine power, women dedicate themselves to seeing that men get their way. Men's praise, even when grudgingly given, feels like a warm blanket of security. Putting men's interests first may seem to be a burden but the feminine woman smiles; nothing is too much for the man she loves. If she is successful in making him feel important, she can rest easy, knowing she has done her job well. She now feels worthy and finally visible.

But men demand a lot of women's services to make life warm and cozy. 55 Sometimes a man forgets the limits of his social power and asks for too much, yet unreasonable demands on a woman's time, energy, and nurturing capacities are interpreted as his "needing" her, and above all else she wants to be needed. She understands and is grateful that someone of his stature wants so much from someone like her. She explains that men are tyrants but usually underneath they are babies. "Just another kid to take care of," she tells her friends. But in truth she loves him more because he can lean on her, is willing to put up with his "craziness" because he loves her.

And she forgives him because she knows that men go off sometimes, they 56 are under pressure at work, they need to let off steam—men are like that. She is willing to become his emotional punching bag because he isn't really trying to hurt *her*, he just needs to let it out. She doesn't mind being a victim for a little while because women are like that. She keeps on keeping on. In this way she stops blaming him and relieves him of the responsibility to apologize. She says it was her fault, and she will try to stop complaining, acting so unfeminine, and be a better lover, wife, or girlfriend. She promises him and herself that she will be less angry in the future. The panic passes. He isn't leaving. She rededicates herself to being a good girl, hoping he will treat her better.

Femininity strips a woman of her desire to defend her own interests or to get 57 what she wants from men. She is unprepared to act like a man with men. She says that she just couldn't disappoint him, will not ignore him, and can't change him. She makes jokes about the battle of the sexes with bitterness and resignation. Women have been conditioned, both socially and intrapsychically, to accept the ideology of gender relations and believe there is nothing they can do. Men must win. That's what makes them men. Women have no choice. They have to take what they can get and pretend it is enough.

Conditioned to be feminine, not masculine, women are set up to participate 58 in their own deprivation, especially in their relations with men. Ambivalence about self-worth jockeys with fear of rejection, making a powerful social mandate to serve men feel like a compulsion, natural and even gratifying. Challenging men's authority feels dangerous. Disagreeing with their opinions is an act of insubordination creating a palpable anxiety. It is often easier to be good for him than to be "bad," risking his anger. If men are given power over women in culture and society, women can be thanked for promoting male interests. Even in the face of cruelty and cold indifference, women are junkies for male approval and do almost anything to have it delivered to the door.

Women's responses to impositions from men are predictable. Women endure $\quad$ 59 the dissatisfactions of the gender system, sharing the culture's belief that men must never have their masculinity threatened. A woman who dares to challenge this system risks the anxiety of being out of gender—unnatural and therefore unappealing. She clenches her teeth and remains silent even when feeling violated by his demands. The sadness passes and the anger fades. If he is a "real" man, she as his victim is a "real" woman.

QUESTIONS

1. Paragraph 4 announces an assumption about our primary social task. Explain this assumption in your own words. What is your reaction to it?
2. Notice the two word pairs: male and female, masculine and feminine. Trace their uses through the essay. What difference do you find in their meanings?
3. Why do you suppose there are so many varieties of women—the Princess, the Good Girl, and the Bad Girl—and no subcategories for men? Are men that much simpler? Does this relate somehow to Gilbert and Webster's point?
4. Between tomboys and mama's boys, who has it worse? (See paragraph 10. Also consider Gilbert and Webster's overall argument.)
5. What may paragraph 47 indicate about the real audience for this essay?
6. Describe "a good guy." How close is a good guy to a good girl?
7. Paragraphs 11 through 23 deal with the "real man." Describe a man you admire, someone you take to be successful. Try to explain how he is similar to and different from the idea of a real man.
8. Write an essay on dogs and cats, distinguishing one as an animal type from the other. In your essay, subdivide dogs into several subcategories—lap dogs, working dogs, and guard dogs, for example. Choose a different pair of subjects, if you like, good and bad students, for example, but adopt the same tactic. What does that differentiation do to your understanding of cats?
9. Take one of Gilbert and Webster's terms—"the Princess," "the Good or Bad Girl," or "Real Woman"—and apply it to someone you know, perhaps yourself. How well does that term and your use of it succeed in explaining that person's situation and problems?

A MODEST PROPOSAL
Jonathan Swift

Jonathan Swift (1667–1745) was born in Dublin, Ireland, of English parents and educated in Irish schools. A graduate of Trinity College, Dublin, he received an M.A. from Oxford and was ordained a priest in the Church of England in 1695. He was active in politics as well as religion, becoming an editor and pamphlet writer for the Tory party in 1710. After becoming Dean of St. Patrick's Cathedral, Dublin, in 1713, he settled in Ireland and began to take an interest in the English economic exploitation of Ireland, gradually becoming a fierce Irish patriot. By 1724 the English were offering a reward for the discovery of the writer of the Drapier's Letters, a series of pamphlets secretly written by Swift, attacking the British for their treatment of Ireland. In 1726 Swift produced the first volume of a more universal satire, known to modern readers as Gulliver's Travels, which has kept his name alive for two hundred and fifty years. A Modest Proposal, his best-known essay on Irish affairs, appeared in 1729. In 1742 he was found to be of unsound mind and three years later he died, leaving most of his estate for the founding of a hospital for the insane.

> A Modest Proposal
> for Preventing the Children of Poor People in Ireland
> from Being a Burden to Their Parents or Country,
> and for Making Them Beneficial to the Public

It is a melancholy object to those who walk through this great town,[1] or travel in the country, when they see the streets, the roads and cabin-doors crowded with beggars of the female sex, followed by three, four, or six children, all in rags, and importuning every passenger for an alms. These mothers, instead of being able to work for their honest livelihood, are forced to employ all their time in strolling, to beg sustenance for their helpless infants, who, as they grow up, either turn thieves for want of work, or leave their dear native country to fight for the Pretender in Spain,[2] or sell themselves to the Barbadoes.[3]

---

[1]this great town: Dublin. [Eds.]

[2]Pretender in Spain: the Catholic descendant of the British royal family (James I, Charles I, and Charles II) of Stuart. Exiled so that England could be governed by Protestant rulers, the Stuarts lurked in France and Spain, preparing various disastrous schemes for regaining the throne. [Eds.]

[3]sell themselves to the Barbadoes: sell themselves as indentured servants, a sort of temporary slavery, to the sugar merchants of the British Carribean islands. [Eds.]

I think it is agreed by all parties that this prodigious number of children, in 2
the arms, or on the backs, or at the heels of their mothers, and frequently of
their fathers, is in the present deplorable state of the kingdom a very great
additional grievance; and therefore whoever could find out a fair, cheap, and
easy method of making these children sound and useful members of the commonwealth would deserve so well of the public as to have his statue set up for
a preserver of the nation.

But my intention is very far from being confined to provide only for the 3
children of professed beggars; it is of a much greater extent, and shall take in
the whole number of infants at a certain age who are born of parents in effect
as little able to support them as those who demand our charity in the streets.

As to my own part, having turned my thoughts for many years upon this 4
important subject, and maturely weighed the several schemes of other projectors,
I have always found them grossly mistaken in their computation. It is true a
child just dropped from its dam may be supported by her milk for a solar year
with little other nourishment, at most not above the value of two shillings,[4]
which the mother may certainly get, or the value in scraps, by her lawful
occupation of begging, and it is exactly at one year old that I propose to provide
for them, in such a manner as, instead of being a charge upon their parents,
or the parish, or wanting food and raiment for the rest of their lives, they shall,
on the contrary, contribute to the feeding and partly to the clothing of many
thousands.

There is likewise another great advantage in my scheme, that it will prevent 5
those voluntary abortions, and that horrid practice of women murdering their
bastard children, alas, too frequent among us, sacrificing the poor innocent
babes, I doubt, more to avoid the expense than the shame, which would move
tears and pity in the most savage and inhuman breast.

The number of souls in Ireland being usually reckoned one million and a 6
half, of these I calculate there may be about two hundred thousand couples
whose wives are breeders, from which number I subtract thirty thousand couples
who are able to maintain their own children, although I apprehend there cannot
be so many under the present distresses of the kingdom, but this being granted,
there will remain an hundred and seventy thousand breeders. I again subtract
fifty thousand for those women who miscarry, or whose children die by accident
or disease within the year. There only remain an hundred and twenty thousand
children of poor parents annually born: the question therefore is, how this
number shall be reared, and provided for, which as I have already said, under
the present situation of affairs is utterly impossible by all the methods hitherto
proposed, for we can neither employ them in handicraft or agriculture; we
neither build houses (I mean in the country), nor cultivate land: they can very
seldom pick up a livelihood by stealing until they arrive at six years old, except

---

[4]shillings: a shilling used to be worth about one day's labor. [Eds.]

where they are of towardly parts, although I confess they learn the rudiments much earlier, during which time they can however be properly looked upon only as probationers, as I have been informed by a principal gentleman in the County of Cavan, who protested to me that he never knew above one or two instances under the age of six, even in a part of the kingdom so renowned for the quickest proficiency in that art.

I am assured by our merchants that a boy or girl before twelve years old, is no saleable commodity, and even when they come to this age, they will not yield above three pounds, or three pounds and half-a-crown at most on the Exchange, which cannot turn to account either to the parents or the kingdom, the charge of nutriment and rags having been at least four times that value. [7]

I shall now therefore humbly propose my own thoughts, which I hope will not be liable to the least objection. [8]

I have been assured by a very knowing American of my acquaintance in London, that a young healthy child well nursed is at a year old a most delicious, nourishing and wholesome food, whether stewed, roasted, baked, or boiled, and I make no doubt that it will equally serve in a fricassee, or a ragout. [9]

I do therefore humbly offer it to public consideration, that of the hundred and twenty thousand children already computed, twenty thousand may be reserved for breed, whereof only one fourth part to be males, which is more than we allow to sheep, black-cattle, or swine, and my reason is that these children are seldom the fruits of marriage, a circumstance not much regarded by our savages, therefore one male will be sufficient to serve four females. That the remaining hundred thousand may at a year old be offered in sale to the persons of quality, and fortune, through the kingdom, always advising the mother to let them suck plentifully in the last month, so as to render them plump, and fat for a good table. A child will make two dishes at an entertainment for friends, and when the family dines alone, the fore or hind quarter will make a reasonable dish, and seasoned with a little pepper or salt will be very good boiled on the fourth day, especially in winter. [10]

I have reckoned upon a medium, that a child just born will weigh twelve pounds, and in a solar year if tolerably nursed increaseth to twenty-eight pounds. [11]

I grant this food will be somewhat dear, and therefore very proper for landlords, who, as they have already devoured most of the parents, seem to have the best title to the children. [12]

Infant's flesh will be in season throughout the year, but more plentiful in March, and a little before and after, for we are told by a grave author, an eminent French physician,[5] that fish being a prolific diet, there are more children born in Roman Catholic countries about nine months after Lent than at any other season; therefore reckoning a year after Lent, the markets will be more [13]

---

[5]French physician: François Rabelais (1494?–1553), physician and satirist known for his *Gargantua* and *Pantagruel*. [Eds.]

glutted than usual, because the number of Popish infants is at least three to one in this kingdom, and therefore it will have one other collateral advantage by lessening the number of Papists among us.

I have already computed the charge of nursing a beggar's child (in which list   14
I reckon all cottagers, labourers, and four-fifths of the farmers) to be about two shillings *per annum*, rags included, and I believe no gentleman would repine to give ten shillings for the carcass of a good fat child, which, as I have said, will make four dishes of excellent nutritive meat, when he hath only some particular friend of his own family to dine with him. Thus the Squire will learn to be a good landlord and grow popular among his tenants, the mother will have eight shillings net profit, and be fit for work until she produces another child.

Those who are more thrifty (as I must confess the times require) may flay   15
the carcass; the skin of which artifically dressed, will make admirable gloves for ladies, and summer boots for fine gentlemen.

As to our city of Dublin, shambles[6] may be appointed for this purpose, in   16
the most convenient parts of it, and butchers we may be assured will not be wanting, although I rather recommend buying the children alive, and dressing them hot from the knife, as we do roasting pigs.

A very worthy person, a true lover of his country, and whose virtues I highly   17
esteem was lately pleased, in discoursing on this matter to offer a refinement upon my scheme. He said that many gentlemen of this kingdom, having of late destroyed their deer, he conceived that the want of venison might be well supplied by the bodies of young lads and maidens, not exceeding fourteen years of age, nor under twelve, so great a number of both sexes in every county being now ready to starve, for want of work and service: and these to be disposed of by their parents if alive, or otherwise by their nearest relations. But with due deference to so excellent a friend, and so deserving a patriot, I cannot be altogether in his sentiments. For as to the males, my American acquaintance assured me from frequent experience that their flesh was generally tough and lean, like that of our schoolboys, by continual exercise, and their taste disagreeable, and to fatten them would not answer the charge. Then as to the females, it would, I think with humble submission, be a loss to the public, because they soon would become breeders themselves: and besides, it is not improbable that some scrupulous people might be apt to censure such a practice (although indeed very unjustly) as a little bordering upon cruelty, which I confess, hath always been with me the strongest objection against any project, howsoever well intended.

But in order to justify my friend, he confessed that this expedient was put   18
into his head by the famous Psalmanazar, a native of the island Formosa, who came from thence to London, above twenty years ago, and in conversation told my friend that in his country when any young person happened to be put to

---

[6]shambles: slaughterhouses. [Eds.]

death, the executioner sold the carcass to persons of quality, as a prime dainty, and that, in his time, the body of a plump girl of fifteen, who was crucified for an attempt to poison the emperor, was sold to his Imperial Majesty's Prime Minister of State, and other great Mandarins of the Court, in joints from the gibbet, at four hundred crowns. Neither indeed can I deny that if the same use were made of several plump young girls in this town who, without one single groat to their fortunes, cannot stir abroad without a chair, and appear at the playhouse and assemblies in foreign fineries, which they never will pay for, the kingdom would not be the worse.

Some persons of a desponding spirit are in great concern about that vast 19 number of poor people, who are aged, diseased, or maimed, and I have been desired to employ my thoughts what course may be taken to ease the nation of so grievous an encumbrance. But I am not in the least pain upon that matter, because it is very well known that they are every day dying, and rotting, by cold, and famine, and filth, and vermin, as fast as can be reasonably expected. And as to the younger labourers they are now in almost as hopeful a condition. They cannot get work, and consequently pine away from want of nourishment, to a degree that if at any time they are accidentally hired to common labour, they have not strength to perform it; and thus the country and themselves are in a fair way of being soon delivered from the evils to come.

I have too long digressed, and therefore shall return to my subject. I think 20 the advantages by the proposal which I have made are obvious and many, as well as of the highest importance.

For first, as I have already observed, it would greatly lessen the number of 21 Papists, with whom we are yearly over-run, being the principal breeders of the nation, as well as our most dangerous enemies, and who stay at home on purpose with a design to deliver the kingdom to the Pretender, hoping to take their advantage by the absence of so many good Protestants, who have chosen rather to leave their country than stay at home and pay tithes against their conscience to an idolatrous Episcopal curate.

Secondly, the poorer tenants will have something valuable of their own, 22 which by law may be made liable to distress, and help to pay their landlord's rent, their corn and cattle being already seized, and money a thing unknown.

Thirdly, whereas the maintenance of an hundred thousand children, from 23 two years old, and upwards, cannot be computed at less than ten shillings a piece *per annum*, the nation's stock will be thereby increased fifty thousand pounds *per annum*, besides the profit of a new dish, introduced to the tables of all gentlemen of fortune in the kingdom, who have any refinement in taste, and the money will circulate among ourselves, the goods being entirely of our own growth and manufacture.

Fourthly, the constant breeders, besides the gain of eight shillings sterling 24 *per annum*, by the sale of their children, will be rid of the charge of maintaining them after the first year.

Fifthly, this food would likewise bring great custom to taverns, where the   25
vintners will certainly be so prudent as to procure the best receipts for dressing
it to perfection, and consequently have their houses frequented by all the fine
gentlemen, who justly value themselves upon their knowledge in good eating;
and a skilful cook, who understands how to oblige his guests, will contrive to
make it as expensive as they please.

Sixthly, this would be a great inducement to marriage, which all wise nations   26
have either encouraged by rewards, or enforced by laws and penalties. It would
increase the care and tenderness of mothers towards their children, when they
were sure of a settlement for life, to the poor babes, provided in some sort by
the public to their annual profit instead of expense. We should soon see an
honest emulation among the married women, which of them could bring the
fattest child to the market. Men would become as fond of their wives, during
the time of their pregnancy, as they are now of their mares in foal, their cows
in calf, or sows when they are ready to farrow, nor offer to beat or kick them
(as it is too frequent a practice) for fear of a miscarriage.

Many other advantages might be enumerated. For instance, the addition of   27
some thousand carcasses in our exportation of barrelled beef; the propagation of
swine's flesh, and improvement in the art of making good bacon, so much
wanted among us by the great destruction of pigs, too frequent at our tables,
are no way comparable in taste or magnificence to a well-grown, fat yearling
child, which roasted whole will make a considerable figure at a Lord Mayor's
feast, or any other public entertainment. But this and many others I omit, being
studious of brevity.

Supposing that one thousand families in this city would be constant cus-   28
tomers for infants' flesh, besides others who might have it at merry meetings,
particularly weddings and christenings; I compute that Dublin would take off
annually about twenty thousand carcasses, and the rest of the kingdom (where
probably they will be sold somewhat cheaper) the remaining eighty thousand.

I can think of no one objection that will possibly be raised against this   29
proposal, unless it should be urged that the number of people will be thereby
much lessened in the kingdom. This I freely own, and it was indeed one principal design in offering it to the world. I desire the reader will observe, that I
calculate my remedy *for this one individual Kingdom of* Ireland, *and for no
other that ever was, is, or, I think, ever can be upon earth.* Therefore let no
man talk to me of other expedients: *Of taxing our absentees at five shillings a
pound: Of using neither clothes, nor household furniture, except what is of our
own growth and manufacture: Of utterly rejecting the materials and instruments
that promote foreign luxury: Of curing the expensiveness of pride, vanity, idleness, and gaming in our women: Of introducing a vein of parsimony, prudence,
and temperance: Of learning to love our country, wherein we differ even from*
Laplanders, *and the inhabitants of* Topinamboo: *Of quitting our animosities
and factions, nor act any longer like the* Jews, *who were murdering one another
at the very moment their city was taken: Of being a little cautious not to sell*

our country and consciences for nothing: Of teaching landlords to have at least one degree of mercy towards their tenants. Lastly, *of putting a spirit of honesty, industry, and skill into our shopkeepers, who, if a resolution could now be taken to buy only our native goods, would immediately unite to cheat and exact upon us in the price, the measure and the goodness, nor could ever yet be brought to make one fair proposal of just dealing, though often and earnestly invited to it.*

Therefore I repeat, let no man talk to me of these and the like expedients, till he hath at least a glimpse of hope that there will ever be some hearty and sincere attempt to put them in practice. 30

But as to myself, having been wearied out for many years with offering vain, idle, visionary thoughts, and at length utterly despairing of success, I fortunately fell upon this proposal, which as it is wholly new, so it hath something solid and real, of no expense and little trouble, full in our own power, and whereby we can incur no danger in disobliging England. For this kind of commodity will not bear exportation, the flesh being of too tender a consistence to admit a long continuance in salt, *although perhaps I could name a country which would be glad to eat up our whole nation without it.* 31

After all I am not so violently bent upon my own opinion as to reject any offer, proposed by wise men, which shall be found equally innocent, cheap, easy and effectual. But before some thing of that kind shall be advanced in contradiction to my scheme, and offering a better, I desire the author, or authors, will be pleased maturely to consider two points. First, as things now stand, how they will be able to find food and raiment for a hundred thousand useless mouths and backs? And secondly, there being a round million of creatures in human figure, throughout this kingdom, whose whole subsistence put into a common stock would leave them in debt two millions of pounds sterling; adding those who are beggars by profession, to the bulk of farmers, cottagers, and laborers with their wives and children, who are beggars in effect; I desire those politicians who dislike my overture, and may perhaps be so bold to attempt an answer, that they will first ask the parents of these mortals whether they would not at this day think it a great happiness to have been sold for food at a year old, in the manner I prescribe, and thereby have avoided such a perpetual scene of misfortunes as they have since gone through, by the oppression of landlords, the impossibility of paying rent without money or trade, the want of common sustenance, with neither house nor clothes to cover them from the inclemencies of weather, and the most inevitable prospect of entailing the like, or greater miseries upon their breed for ever. 32

I profess in the sincerity of my heart that I have not the least personal interest in endeavoring to promote this necessary work, having no other motive than the *public good of my country, by advancing our trade, providing for infants, relieving the poor, and giving some pleasure to the rich.* I have no children by which I can propose to get a single penny; the youngest being nine years old, and my wife past child-bearing. 33

QUESTIONS

1. A proposal always involves a proposer. What is the character of the proposer here? Do we perceive his character to be the same throughout the essay? Compare, for example, paragraphs 21, 26, and 33.

2. When does the proposer actually offer his proposal? What does he do before making his proposal? What does he do after making his proposal? How does the order in which he does things affect our impression of him and of his proposal?

3. What kind of counterarguments to his own proposal does this proposer anticipate? How does he answer and refute proposals that might be considered alternatives to his?

4. In reading this essay, most persons are quite certain that the author, Swift, does not himself endorse the proposer's proposal. How do we distinguish the two of them? What details of style help us make this distinction?

5. Consider the proposer, the counterarguments the proposer acknowledges and refutes, and Swift himself, who presumably does not endorse the proposer's proposal. To what extent is Swift's position essentially that which his proposer refutes? To what extent is it a somewhat different position still?

6. To what extent does an ironic essay like this depend upon the author and reader sharing certain values without question or reservation? Can you discover any such values explicitly or implicitly present in Swift's essay?

7. Use Swift's technique to write a "modest proposal" of your own about some contemporary situation. That is, use some outlandish proposal as a way of drawing attention to a situation that needs correcting. Consider carefully the character you intend to project for your proposer and the way you intend to make your own view distinguishable from hers or his.

THE DECLARATION OF INDEPENDENCE

Thomas Jefferson

Thomas Jefferson (1743–1826) was born in Shadwell, Virginia, attended William and Mary College, and became a lawyer. He was elected to the Virginia House of Burgesses in 1789 and was a delegate to the Continental Congress in 1776. When the Congress voted in favor of Richard Henry Lee's resolution that the colonies "ought to be free and independent states," a committee of five members, including John Adams, Benjamin Franklin, and Jefferson, was appointed to draw up a declaration. Jefferson, because of his eloquence as a writer, was asked by this committee to draw up a first draft. Jefferson's text, with a few changes suggested by Franklin and Adams, was presented to the Congress. After a debate in which further changes were made, including striking out a passage condemning the slave trade, the Declaration was approved on the fourth of July, 1776. Jefferson said of it that, "Neither aiming at originality of principles or sentiments, nor yet copied from any particular and previous writing, it was intended to be an expression of the American mind."

In Congress, July 4, 1776
The unanimous Declaration of the
thirteen united States of America

When in the Course of human events it becomes necessary for one people 1
to dissolve the political bands which have connected them with another, and to assume among the powers of the earth, the separate and equal station to which the Laws of Nature and of Nature's God entitle them, a decent respect to the opinions of mankind requires that they should declare the causes which impel them to the separation.

We hold these truths to be self-evident, that all men are created equal, that 2
they are endowed by their Creator with certain unalienable Rights, that among these are Life, Liberty and the pursuit of Happiness. That to secure these rights, Governments are instituted among Men, deriving their just powers from the consent of the governed, That whenever any Form of Government becomes destructive of these ends, it is the Right of the People to alter or to abolish it, and to institute new Government, laying its foundation on such principles and

675

organizing its powers in such form, as to them shall seem most likely to affect their Safety and Happiness. Prudence, indeed, will dictate that Governments long established should not be changed for light and transient causes; and accordingly all experience hath shewn that mankind are more disposed to suffer, while evils are sufferable, than to right themselves by abolishing the forms to which they are accustomed. But when a long train of abuses and usurpations, pursuing invariably the same Object evinces a design to reduce them under absolute Despotism, it is their right, it is their duty, to throw off such Government, and to provide new Guards for their future security. Such has been the patient sufferance of these Colonies; and such is now the necessity which constrains them to alter their former Systems of Government. The history of the present King of Great Britain is a history of repeated injuries and usurpations, all having in direct object the establishment of an absolute Tyranny over these States. To prove this, let Facts be submitted to a candid world.

He has refused his Assent to Laws, the most wholesome and necessary for   3
the public good.

He has forbidden his Governors to pass laws of immediate and pressing   4
importance, unless suspended in their operation till his Assent should be obtained; and when so suspended, he has utterly neglected to attend to them.

He has refused to pass other Laws for the accommodation of large districts   5
of people, unless those people would relinquish the right of Representation in the Legislature, a right inestimable to them and formidable to tyrants only.

He has called together legislative bodies at places unusual, uncomfortable,   6
and distant from the depository of their Public Records, for the sole purpose of fatiguing them into compliance with his measures.

He has dissolved Representative Houses repeatedly, for opposing with manly   7
firmness his invasions on the rights of the people.

He has refused for a long time, after such dissolutions, to cause others to be   8
elected; whereby the Legislative Powers, incapable of Annihilation, have returned to the People at large for their exercise; the State remaining in the mean time exposed to all the dangers of invasion from without, and convulsions within.

He has endeavored to prevent the population of these States; for that purpose   9
obstructing the Laws for Naturalization of Foreigners; refusing to pass others to encourage their migration hither, and raising the conditions of new Appropriations of Lands.

He has obstructed the Administration of Justice, by refusing his Assent to   10
Laws for Establishing Judiciary Powers.

He has made Judges dependent on his Will alone, for the tenure of their   11
offices, and the amount and payment of their salaries.

He has erected a multitude of New Offices, and sent hither swarms of Officers   12
to harass our people, and eat out their substance.

He has kept among us, in times of peace, Standing Armies without the 13 Consent of our legislatures.

He has affected to render the Military independent of and superior to the 14 Civil Power.

He has combined with others to subject us to a jurisdiction foreign to our 15 constitution, and unacknowledged by our laws; giving his Assent to the Acts of pretended Legislation: For quartering large bodies of armed troops among us: For protecting them, by a mock Trial, from punishment for any Murders which they should commit on the Inhabitants of these States: For cutting off our Trade with all parts of the world: For imposing Taxes on us without our Consent: For depriving us in many cases, of the benefits of Trial by Jury; For Transporting us beyond Seas to be tried for pretended offenses: for abolishing the free System of English Laws in a neighboring Province, establishing therein an Arbitrary government, and enlarging its Boundaries so as to render it at once an example and fit instrument for introducing the same absolute rule into these Colonies: For taking away our Charters, abolishing our most valuable Laws and altering fundamentally the Forms of our Governments: For suspending our own Legislatures, and declaring themselves invested with power to legislate for us in all cases whatsoever.

He has abdicated Government here, by declaring us out of his Protection 16 and waging War against us.

He has plundered our seas, ravaged our Coasts, burnt our towns, and de- 17 stroyed the lives of our people.

He is at this time transporting large Armies of foreign Mercenaries to com- 18 plete the works of death, desolation and tyranny, already begun with circumstances of Cruelty & Perfidy scarcely paralleled in the most barbarous ages, and totally unworthy the Head of a civilized nation.

He has constrained our fellow Citizens taken Captive on the high Seas to 19 bear Arms against their Country, to become the executioners of their friends and Brethren, or to fall themselves by their Hands.

He has excited domestic insurrections amongst us, and has endeavored to 20 bring on the inhabitants of our frontiers, the merciless Indian Savages, whose known rule of warfare, is an undistingushed destruction of all ages, sexes, and conditions.

In every stage of these Oppressions We have Petitioned for Redress in the 21 most humble terms: Our repeated petitions have been answered only by repeated injury. A Prince, whose character is thus marked by every act which may define a Tyrant, is unfit to be the ruler of a free people.

Nor have We been wanting in attention to our British brethren. We have 22 warned them from time to time of attempts by their legislature to extend an unwarrantable jurisdiction over us. We have reminded them of the circumstances of our emigration and settlement here. We have appealed to their native justice and magnanimity, and we have conjured them by the ties of our common kindred to disavow these usurpations, which would inevitably interrupt our connections and correspondence. They too have been deaf to the voice of justice and of consanguinity. We must, therefore, acquiesce in the necessity, which denounces our Separation, and hold them, as we hold the rest of mankind, Enemies in War, in Peace Friends.

We, THEREFORE, the Representatives of the UNITED STATES OF AMERICA, 23 in General Congress, Assembled, appealing to the Supreme Judge of the world for the rectitude of our intentions, do, in the Name, and by Authority of the good People of these Colonies, solemnly publish and declare, That these United Colonies are, and of Right ought to be FREE AND INDEPENDENT STATES; that they are Absolved from all Allegiance to the British Crown, and that all political connection between them and the State of Great Britain, is and ought to be totally dissolved; and that as Free and Independent States, they have full Power to levy War, conclude Peace, contract Alliances, establish Commerce, and to do all other Acts and Things which Independent States may of right do. And for the support of this Declaration, with a firm reliance on the protection of Divine Providence, we mutually pledge to each other our Lives, our Fortunes, and our sacred Honor.

QUESTIONS

1. The Declaration of Independence is frequently cited as a classic deductive argument. A deductive argument is based on a general statement, or premise, that is assumed to be true. What does this document assume that the American colonists are entitled to and on what basis? Look at the reasoning in paragraph 2. What are these truths that are considered self-evident? What does *self-evident* mean?

2. What accusations against the king of Great Britain are the facts presented meant to substantiate? If you were the British king presented with this document, how might you reply to it? Would you first attack its premise or reply to its accusations? Or would you do both? (How did George III respond anyway?)

3. To what extent is the audience of the Declaration intended to be the king and people of Great Britain?

4. What other audiences were intended for this document? Define at least two other audiences, and describe how each might be expected to respond.

5. Although this declaration could have been expected to lead to war and all the horrors thereof, it is a most civilized document, showing great respect throughout for certain standards of civility among people and among nations. Try to define the civilized standards the declaration assumes. Write an essay that tries to identify and characterize the nature and variety of those expectations.

6. Write a declaration of your own, announcing your separation from some injurious situation (an uncompatible roommate, a noisy sorority or fraternity house, an awful job, or whatever). Start with a premise, give reasons to substantiate it, provide facts that illustrate the injurious conditions, and conclude with a statement of what your new condition will mean to you and to other oppressed people.

Sciences and Technologies

THE ART OF
TEACHING SCIENCE

Lewis Thomas

Lewis Thomas (b. 1913) is chancellor of Memorial Sloan-Kettering Cancer Center in New York City and chairman of the board of the Scientists' Institute for Public Information. His engaging essay collections are mentioned in the headnote on page 85 that introduces an account of his medical education at Harvard. This piece, which was given as a talk at a conference sponsored by the Alfred P. Sloan Foundation, appeared in the New York Times Magazine *in 1982.*

Everyone seems to agree that there is something wrong with the way science 1 is being taught these days. But no one is at all clear about when it went wrong or what is to be done about it. The term "scientific illiteracy" has become almost a cliché in educational circles. Graduate schools blame the colleges; colleges blame the secondary schools; the high schools blame the elementary schools, which, in turn, blame the family.

I suggest that the scientific community itself is partly, perhaps largely, to 2 blame. Moreover, if there are disagreements between the world of the humanities and the scientific enterprise as to the place and importance of science in a liberal-arts education and the role of science in 20th-century culture, I believe that the scientists are themselves responsible for a general misunderstanding of what they are really up to.

During the last half-century, we have been teaching the sciences as though 3 they were the same collection of academic subjects as always, and—here is what has really gone wrong—as though they would always be the same. Students

LEWIS THOMAS

learn today's biology, for example, the same way we learned Latin when I was in high school long ago: first, the fundamentals; then, the underlying laws; next, the essential grammar and, finally, the reading of texts. Once mastered, that was that: Latin was Latin and forever after would always be Latin. History, once learned, was history. And biology was precisely biology, a vast array of hard facts to be learned as fundamentals, followed by a reading of the texts.

Furthermore, we have been teaching science as if its facts were somehow superior to the facts in all other scholarly disciplines—more fundamental, more solid, less subject to subjectivism, immutable. English literature is not just one way of thinking; it is all sorts of ways; poetry is a moving target; the facts that underlie art, architecture and music are not really hard facts, and you can change them any way you like by arguing about them. But science, it appears, is an altogether different kind of learning: an unambiguous, unalterable and endlessly useful display of data that only needs to be packaged and installed somewhere in one's temporal lobe in order to achieve a full understanding of the natural world.

And, of course, it is not like this at all. In real life, every field of science is incomplete, and most of them—whatever the record of accomplishment during the last 200 years—are still in their very earliest stages. In the fields I know best, among the life sciences, it is required that the most expert and sophisticated minds be capable of changing course—often with a great lurch—every few years. In some branches of biology the mind-changing is occurring with accelerating velocity. Next week's issue of any scientific journal can turn a whole field upside down, shaking out any number of immutable ideas and installing new bodies of dogma. This is an almost everyday event in physics, in chemistry, in materials research, in neurobiology, in genetics, in immunology.

On any Tuesday morning, if asked, a good working scientist will tell you with some self-satisfaction that the affairs of his field are nicely in order, that things are finally looking clear and making sense, and all is well. But come back again on another Tuesday, and the roof may have just fallen in on his life's work. All the old ideas—last week's ideas in some cases—are no longer good ideas. The hard facts have softened, melted away and vanished under the pressure of new hard facts. Something strange has happened. And it is this very strangeness of nature that makes science engrossing, that keeps bright people at it, and that ought to be at the center of science teaching.

The conclusions reached in science are always, when looked at closely, far more provisional and tentative than are most of the assumptions arrived at by our colleagues in the humanities. But we do not talk much in public about this, nor do we teach this side of science. We tend to say instead: These are the facts of the matter, and this is what the facts signify. Go and learn them, for they will be the same forever.

By doing this, we miss opportunity after opportunity to recruit young people into science, and we turn off a good many others who would never dream of

680

scientific careers but who emerge from their education with the impression that science is fundamentally boring.

Sooner or later, we will have to change this way of presenting science. We might begin by looking more closely at the common ground that science shares with all disciplines, particularly with the humanities and with social and behavioral science. For there is indeed such a common ground. It is called bewilderment. There are more than seven times seven types of ambiguity in science, all awaiting analysis. The poetry of Wallace Stevens is crystal clear alongside the genetic code.   9

One of the complaints about science is that it tends to flatten everything. In its deeply reductionist way, it is said, science removes one mystery after another, leaving nothing in the place of mystery but data. I have even heard this claim as explanation for the drift of things in modern art and modern music: Nothing is left to contemplate except randomness and senselessness; God is nothing but a pair of dice, loaded at that. Science is linked somehow to the despair of the 20th-century mind. There is almost nothing unknown and surely nothing unknowable. Blame science.   10

I prefer to turn things around in order to make precisely the opposite case. Science, especially 20th-century science, has provided us with a glimpse of something we never really knew before, the revelation of human ignorance. We have been accustomed to the belief, from one century to another, that except for one or two mysteries we more or less comprehend everything on earth. Every age, not just the 18th century, regarded itself as the Age of Reason, and we have never lacked for explanations of the world and its ways. Now, we are being brought up short. We do not understand much of anything, from the episode we rather dismissively (and, I think, defensively) choose to call the "big bang," all the way down to the particles in the atoms of a bacterial cell. We have a wilderness of mystery to make our way through in the centuries ahead. We will need science for this but not science alone. In its own time, science will produce the data and some of the meaning in the data, but never the full meaning. For perceiving real significance when significance is at hand, we will need all sorts of brains outside the fields of science.   11

It is primarily because of this need that I would press for changes in the way science is taught. Although there is a perennial need to teach the young people who will be doing the science themselves, this will always be a small minority. Even more important, we must teach science to those who will be needed for thinking about it, and that means pretty nearly everyone else—most of all, the poets, but also artists, musicians, philosophers, historians and writers. A few of these people, at least, will be able to imagine new levels of meaning which may be lost on the rest of us.   12

In addition, it is time to develop a new group of professional thinkers, perhaps a somewhat larger group than the working scientists and the working poets, who can create a discipline of scientific criticism. We have had good luck so far in   13 the emergence of a few people ranking as philosophers of science and historians and journalists of science, and I hope more of these will be coming along. But we have not yet seen specialists in the fields of scientific criticism who are of the caliber of the English literary and social critics F. R. Leavis and John Ruskin or the American literary critic Edmund Wilson. Science needs critics of this sort, but the public at large needs them more urgently.

I suggest that the introductory courses in science, at all levels from grade 14 school through college, be radically revised. Leave the fundamentals, the so-called basics, aside for a while, and concentrate the attention of all students on the things that are not known. You cannot possibly teach quantum mechanics without mathematics, to be sure, but you can describe the strangeness of the world opened up by quantum theory. Let it be known, early on, that there are deep mysteries and profound paradoxes revealed in distant outline by modern physics. Explain that these can be approached more closely and puzzled over, once the language of mathematics has been sufficiently mastered.

At the outset, before any of the fundamentals, teach the still imponderable 15 puzzles of cosmology. Describe as clearly as possible, for the youngest minds, that there are some things going on in the universe that lie still beyond comprehension, and make it plain how little is known.

Do not teach that biology is a useful and perhaps profitable science; that can 16 come later. Teach instead that there are structures squirming inside each of our cells that provide all the energy for living. Essentially foreign creatures, these lineal descendants of bacteria were brought in for symbiotic living a billion or so years ago. Teach that we do not have the ghost of an idea how they got there, where they came from, or how they evolved to their present structure and function. The details of oxidative phosphorylation and photosynthesis can come later.

Teach ecology early on. Let it be understood that the earth's life is a system 17 of interdependent creatures, and that we do not understand at all how it works. The earth's environment, from the range of atmospheric gases to the chemical constituents of the sea, has been held in an almost unbelievably improbable state of regulated balance since life began, and the regulation of stability and balance is somehow accomplished by the life itself, like the autonomic nervous system of an immense organism. We do not know how such a system works, much less what it means, but there are some nice reductionist details at hand, such as the bizarre proportions of atmospheric constituents, ideal for our sort of planetary life, and the surprising stability of the ocean's salinity, and the fact that the average temperature of the earth has remained quite steady in the face of at least a 25 percent increase in heat coming in from the sun since the earth began. That kind of thing: something to think about.

Go easy, I suggest, on the promises sometimes freely offered by science. 18 Technology relies and depends on science these days, more than ever before, but technology is far from the first justification for doing research, nor is it necessarily an essential product to be expected from science. Public decisions about the future of technology are totally different from decisions about science, and the two enterprises should not be tangled together. The central task of science is to arrive, stage by stage, at a clearer comprehension of nature, but this does not at all mean, as it is sometimes claimed to mean, a search for mastery over nature.

Science may someday provide us with a better understanding of ourselves, 19 but never, I hope, with a set of technologies for doing something or other to improve ourselves. I am made nervous by assertions that human consciousness will someday be unraveled by research, laid out for close scrutiny like the workings of a computer, and then—and *then* . . . ! I hope with some fervor that we can learn a lot more than we now know about the human mind, and I see no reason why this strange puzzle should remain forever and entirely beyond us. But I would be deeply disturbed by any prospect that we might use the new knowledge in order to begin doing something about it—to improve it, say. This is a different matter from searching for information to use against schizophrenia or dementia, where we are badly in need of technologies, indeed likely one day to be sunk without them. But the ordinary, everyday, more or less normal human mind is too marvelous an instrument ever to be tampered with by anyone, science or no science.

The education of humanists cannot be regarded as complete, or even ade- 20 quate, without exposure in some depth to where things stand in the various branches of science, particularly, as I have said, in the areas of our ignorance. Physics professors, most of them, look with revulsion on assignments to teach their subject to poets. Biologists, caught up by the enchantment of their new power, armed with flawless instruments to tell the nucleotide sequences of the entire human genome, nearly matching the physicists in the precision of their measurements of living processes, will resist the prospect of broad survey courses; each biology professor will demand that any student in his path master every fine detail within that professor's research program.

The liberal-arts faculties, for their part, will continue to view the scientists 21 with suspicion and apprehension. "What do the scientists want?" asked a Cambridge professor in Francis Cornford's wonderful "Microcosmographia Academica." "Everything that's going," was the quick answer. That was back in 1912, and scientists haven't much changed.

But maybe, just maybe, a new set of courses dealing systematically with 22 ignorance in science will take hold. The scientists might discover in it a new and subversive technique for catching the attention of students driven by curiosity, delighted and surprised to learn that science is exactly as the American scientist and educator Vannevar Bush described it: an "endless frontier." The humanists, for their part, might take considerable satisfaction in watching their scientific colleagues confess openly to not knowing everything about everything. And the poets, on whose shoulders the future rests, might, late nights, thinking things over, begin to see some meanings that elude the rest of us. It is worth a try.

I believe that the worst thing that has happened to science education is that   23
the fun has gone out of it. A great many good students look at it as slogging work to be got through on the way to medical school. Others are turned off by the premedical students themselves, embattled and bleeding for grades and class standing. Very few recognize science as the high adventure it really is, the wildest of all explorations ever taken by human beings, the chance to glimpse things never seen before, the shrewdest maneuver for discovering how the world works. Instead, baffled early on, they are misled into thinking that bafflement is simply the result of not having learned all the facts. They should be told that everyone else is baffled as well—from the professor in his endowed chair down to the platoons of postdoctoral students in the laboratories all night. Every important scientific advance that has come in looking like an answer has turned, sooner or later—usually sooner—into a question. And the game is just beginning.

If more students were aware of this, I think many of them would decide to   24
look more closely and to try and learn more about what *is* known. That is the time when mathematics will become clearly and unavoidably recognizable as an essential, indispensable instrument for engaging in the game, and that is the time for teaching it. The calamitous loss of applied mathematics from what we might otherwise be calling higher education is a loss caused, at least in part, by insufficient incentives for learning the subject. Left by itself, standing there among curriculum offerings, it is not at all clear to the student what it is to be applied to. And there is all of science, next door, looking like an almost-finished field reserved only for chaps who want to invent or apply new technologies. We have had it wrong, and presented it wrong to class after class for several generations.

An appreciation of what is happening in science today, and how great a   25
distance lies ahead for exploring, ought to be one of the rewards of a liberal-arts education. It ought to be good in itself, not something to be acquired on the way to a professional career but part of the cast of thought needed for getting into the kind of century that is now just down the road. Part of the intellectual equipment of an educated person, however his or her time is to be spent, ought to be a feel for the queernesses of nature, the inexplicable thing, the side of life for which informed bewilderment will be the best way of getting through the day.

QUESTIONS

1. What is the thesis of Thomas's argument? What parts of the essay present evidence to support it? What parts of the essay offer alternatives to present methods of teaching science? Do you think Thomas presents valid reasons for adopting these alternatives?

2. In Thomas's view, what is wrong with the way science is taught now? What suggestions does he offer for the improvement of science teaching?

3. What does Thomas mean by giving poets responsibility for the future (paragraph 22)? Can he be serious? Or is this a rhetorical trick of some kind?

4. What would it take to be the kind of critic of science that Thomas mentions in paragraph 13?

5. Who is Thomas's audience? What is his attitude toward his audience?

6. Thomas concludes by saying, "Part of the intellectual equipment of an educated person . . . ought to be a feel for the queernesses of nature, the inexplicable thing, the side of life for which informed bewilderment will be the best way of getting through the day." What does he mean by "informed bewilderment"? How does one develop that?

7. What points made by Thomas apply to your experience in science courses you elected or were required to take? Drawing on your own experience and those points in the essay which are relevant to it, or those points you wish to take issue with, write a letter to a friend who is to attend your college, and present an agrument either for or against taking a particular science course.

8. If Lewis Thomas were teaching a biology course at your school next semester, would you take it? Give reasons.

THE CASE AGAINST MAN
Isaac Asimov

Isaac Asimov, as the headnote on page 475 indicates, is a professor of biochemistry and an extremely prolific writer. His popular Foundation novels are science fiction, but he has also written mysteries, fantasies, and many nonfiction books about science, technology, and history. The following essay comes from Science Past—Science Future *(1970). In this essay, Asimov's "case" draws on both the legal and medical uses of the term but expands beyond both to encompass larger, moral issues.*

The first mistake is to think of mankind as a thing in itself. It isn't. It is part 1 of an intricate web of life. And we can't think even of life as a thing in itself. It isn't. It is part of the intricate structure of a planet bathed by energy from the Sun.

The Earth, in the nearly 5 billion years since it assumed approximately its 2 present form, has undergone a vast evolution. When it first came into being, it very likely lacked what we would today call an ocean and an atmosphere. These were formed by the gradual outward movement of material as the solid interior settled together.

Nor were ocean, atmosphere, and solid crust independent of each other after 3 formation. There is interaction always: evaporation, condensation, solution, weathering. Far within the solid crust there are slow, continuing changes, too, of which hot springs, volcanoes, and earthquakes are the more noticeable manifestations here on the surface.

Between 2 billion and 3 billion years ago, portions of the surface water, 4 bathed by the energetic radiation from the Sun, developed complicated compounds in organization sufficiently versatile to qualify as what we call "life." Life forms have become more complex and more various ever since.

But the life forms are as much part of the structure of the Earth as any 5 inanimate portion is. It is all an inseparable part of a whole. If any animal is isolated totally from other forms of life, then death by starvation will surely follow. If isolated from water, death by dehydration will follow even faster. If isolated from air, whether free or dissolved in water, death by asphyxiation will follow still faster. If isolated from the Sun, animals will survive for a time, but plants would die, and if all plants died, all animals would starve.

It works in reverse, too, for the inanimate portion of Earth is shaped and 6 molded by life. The nature of the atmosphere has been changed by plant activity (which adds to the air the free oxygen it could not otherwise retain). The soil is turned by earthworms, while enormous ocean reefs are formed by coral.

The entire planet, plus solar energy, is one enormous intricately interrelated 7 system. The entire planet is a life form made up of nonliving portions and a large variety of living portions (as our own body is made up of nonliving crystals in bones and nonliving water in blood, as well as of a large variety of living portions).

In fact, we can pursue the analogy. A man is composed of 50 trillion cells 8 of a variety of types, all interrelated and interdependent. Loss of some of those cells, such as those making up an entire leg, will seriously handicap all the rest of the organism: serious damage to a relatively few cells in an organ, such as the heart or kidneys, may end by killing all 50 trillion.

In the same way, on a planetary scale, the chopping down of an entire forest 9 may not threaten Earth's life in general, but it will produce serious changes in the life forms of the region and even in the nature of the water runoff and, therefore, in the details of geological structure. A serious decline in the bee population will affect the numbers of those plants that depend on bees for fertilization, then the numbers of those animals that depend on those particular bee-fertilized plants, and so on.

Or consider cell growth. Cells in those organs that suffer constant wear and 10 tear—as in the skin or in the intestinal lining—grow and multiply all life long. Other cells, not so exposed, as in nerve and muscle, do not multiply at all in the adult, under any circumstances. Still other organs, ordinarily quiescent, as liver and bone, stand ready to grow if that is necessary to replace damage. When the proper repairs are made, growth stops.

In a much looser and more flexible way, the same is true of the "planet 11 organism" (which we study in the science called ecology). If cougars grow too numerous, the deer they live on are decimated, and some of the cougars die of starvation, so that their "proper number" is restored. If too many cougars die, then the deer multiply with particular rapidity, and cougars multiply quickly in turn, till the additional predators bring down the number of deer again. Barring interference from outside, the eaters and the eaten retain their proper numbers, and both are the better for it. (If the cougars are all killed off, deer would multiply to the point where they destroy the plants they live off, and more would then die of starvation than would have died of cougars.)

The neat economy of growth within an organism such as a human being is 12 sometimes—for what reason, we know not—disrupted, and a group of cells begins growing without limit. This is the dread disease of cancer, and unless that growing group of cells is somehow stopped, the wild growth will throw all the body structure out of true and end by killing the organism itself.

In ecology, the same would happen if, for some reason, one particular type 13 of organism began to multiply without limit, killing its competitors and increasing its own food supply at the expense of that of others. That, too, could end only in the destruction of the larger system—most or all of life and even of certain aspects of the inanimate environment.

And this is exactly what is happening at this moment. For thousands of years,   14 the single species Homo sapiens, to which you and I have the dubious honor of belonging, has been increasing in numbers. In the past couple of centuries, the rate of increase has itself increased explosively.

At the time of Julius Caesar, when Earth's human population is estimated   15 to have been 150 million, that population was increasing at a rate such that it would double in 1,000 years if that rate remained steady. Today, with Earth's population estimated at about 4,000 million (26 times what it was in Caesar's time), it is increasing at a rate which, if steady, will cause it to double in 35 years.

The present rate of increase of Earth's swarming human population qualifies   16 Homo sapiens as an ecological cancer, which will destroy the ecology just as surely as any ordinary cancer would destroy an organism.

The cure? Just what it is for any cancer. The cancerous growth must some-   17 how be stopped.

Of course, it will be. If we do nothing at all, the growth will stop, as a   18 cancerous growth in a man will stop if nothing is done. The man dies and the cancer dies with him. And, analogously, the ecology will die and man will die with it.

How can the human population explosion be stopped? By raising the death-   19 rate, or by lowering the birthrate. There are no other alternatives. The deathrate will rise spontaneously and finally catastrophically, if we do nothing—and that within a few decades. To make the birthrate fall, somehow (almost *any* how, in fact), is surely preferable, and that is therefore the first order of mankind's business today.

Failing this, mankind would stand at the bar of abstract justice (for there may   20 be no posterity to judge) as the mass murderer of life generally, his own included, and mass disrupter of the intricate planetary development that made life in its present glory possible in the first place.

Am I too pessimistic? Can we allow the present rate of population increase   21 to continue indefinitely, or at least for a good long time? Can we count on science to develop methods for cleaning up as we pollute, for replacing wasted resources with substitutes, for finding new food, new materials, more and better life for our waxing numbers?

Impossible! If the numbers continue to wax at the present rate.   22

Let us begin with a few estimates (admittedly not precise, but in the rough   23 neighborhood of the truth).

The total mass of living objects on Earth is perhaps 20 trillion tons. There   24 is usually a balance between eaters and eaten that is about 1 to 10 in favor of the eaten. There would therefore be about 10 times as much plant life (the eaten) as animal life (the eaters) on Earth. There is, in other words, just a little under 2 trillion tons of animal life on Earth.

But this is all the animal life that can exist, given the present quantity of   25 plant life. If more animal life is somehow produced, it will strip down the plant life, reduce the food supply, and then enough animals will starve to restore the balance. If one species of animal life increases in mass, it can only be because other species correspondingly decrease. For every additional pound of human flesh on Earth, a pound of some other form of flesh must disappear.

The total mass of humanity now on Earth may be estimated at about 200   26 million tons, or one ten-thousandth the mass of all animal life. If mankind increases in numbers ten thousandfold, then Homo sapiens will be, perforce, the *only* animal species alive on Earth. It will be a world without elephants or lions, without cats or dogs, without fish or lobsters, without worms or bugs. What's more, to support the mass of human life, all the plant world must be put to service. Only plants edible to man must remain, and only those plants most concentratedly edible and with minimum waste.

At the present moment, the average density of population of the Earth's land   27 surface is about 73 people per square mile. Increase that ten thousandfold and the average density will become 730,000 people per square mile, or more than seven times the density of the workday population of Manhattan. Even if we assume that mankind will somehow spread itself into vast cities floating on the ocean surface (or resting on the ocean floor), the average density of human life at the time when the last nonhuman animal must be killed would be 310,000 people per square mile over all the world, land and sea alike, or a little better than three times the density of modern Manhattan at noon.

We have the vision, then, of high-rise apartments, higher and more thickly   28 spaced than in Manhattan at present, spreading all over the world, across all the mountains, across the Sahara Desert, across Antarctica, across all the oceans; all with their load of humanity and with no other form of animal life beside. And on the roof of all those buildings are the algae farms, with little plant cells exposed to the Sun so that they might grow rapidly and, without waste, form protein for all the mighty population of 35 trillion human beings.

Is that tolerable? Even if science produced all the energy and materials man-   29 kind could want, kept them all fed with algae, all educated, all amused—is the planetary high-rise tolerable?

And if it were, can we double the population further in 35 more years? And   30 then double it again in another 35 years? Where will the food come from? What will persuade the algae to multiply faster than the light energy they absorb makes possible? What will speed up the Sun to add the energy to make it possible? And if vast supplies of fusion energy are added to supplement the Sun, how will we get rid of the equally vast supplies of heat that will be produced? And after the icecaps are melted and the oceans boiled into steam, what?

Can we bleed off the mass of humanity to other worlds? Right now, the 31
number of human beings on Earth is increasing by 80 million per year, and
each year that number goes up by 1 and a fraction percent. Can we really
suppose that we can send 80 million people per year to the Moon, Mars, and
elsewhere, and engineer those worlds to support those people? And even so,
merely remain in the same place ourselves?

No! Not the most optimistic visionary in the world could honestly convince 32
himself that space travel is the solution to our population problem, if the present
rate of increase is sustained.

But when will this planetary high-rise culture come about? How long will it 33
take to increase Earth's population to that impossible point at the present doubling rate of once every 35 years? If it will take 1 million years or even 100,000,
then, for goodness sake, let's not worry just yet.

Well, we don't have that kind of time. We will reach that dead end in no 34
more than 460 years.

At the rate we are going, without birth control, then even if science serves 35
us in an absolutely ideal way, we will reach the planetary high-rise with no
animals but man, with no plants but algae, with no room for even one more
person, by A.D. 2430.

And if science serves us in less than an ideal way (as it certainly will), the 36
end will come sooner, much sooner, and mankind will start fading long, long
before he is forced to construct that building that will cover all the Earth's
surface.

So if birth control *must* come by A.D. 2430 at the very latest, even in an 37
ideal world of advancing science, let it come *now*, in heaven's name, while
there are still oak trees in the world and daisies and tigers and butterflies, and
while there is still open land and space, and before the cancer called man proves
fatal to life and the planet.

QUESTIONS

1. In the opening paragraphs of this essay, Asimov seems to disapprove of our ability
or willingness to stand apart from nature. How does that view of humankind relate to
the larger concerns of his essay?

2. Does Asimov convince you that birth control is necessary? Why or why not?

3. The word *case* in the title has both legal and medical meanings. Which predominates? How do both contribute to Asimov's thesis?

4. In paragraphs 7 through 18, Asimov argues by analogy. What are some of his
analogies? How do they function in the essay?

5. Asimov's most serious analogy is of humankind as a cancer. Trace the development
of that analogy.

6. Write a "case" against some category of thing—against automobiles, athletics,
insects, or whatever. Try to find an analogy or two that will help shape your presentation.

7. If you think of this essay as a quasi-legal case, with humans as defendants in a
special trial, there could be a statement written in our defense. Write one.

EVOLUTION AS FACT
AND THEORY

Stephen Jay Gould

Stephen Jay Gould, well known for his monthly column in
Natural History *magazine, has written many scientific ar-*
ticles including those reprinted on pages 500–508 and pages
648–652. The essay reprinted here appeared first in Discover
magazine, a journal of popular science, in 1981.

Kirtley Mather, who died last year at age 89, was a pillar of both science and   1
the Christian religion in America and one of my dearest friends. The difference
of half a century in our ages evaporated before our common interests. The most
curious thing we shared was a battle we each fought at the same age. For Kirtley
had gone to Tennessee with Clarence Darrow to testify for evolution at the
Scopes trial of 1925. When I think that we are enmeshed again in the same
struggle for one of the best documented, most compelling and exciting concepts
in all of science, I don't know whether to laugh or cry.

According to idealized principles of scientific discourse, the arousal of dor-   2
mant issues should reflect fresh data that give renewed life to abandoned notions.
Those outside the current debate may therefore be excused for suspecting that
creationists have come up with something new, or that evolutionists have generated some serious internal trouble. But nothing has changed; the creationists
have not a single new fact or argument. Darrow and Bryan were at least more
entertaining than we lesser antagonists today.[1] The rise of creationism is politics,
pure and simple; it represents one issue (and by no means the major concern)
of the resurgent evangelical right. Arguments that seemed kooky just a decade
ago have re-entered the mainstream.

CREATIONISM IS NOT SCIENCE

The basic attack of the creationists falls apart on two general counts before   3
we even reach the supposed factual details of their complaints against evolution.
First, they play upon a vernacular misunderstanding of the word "theory" to
convey the false impression that we evolutionists are covering up the rotten core
of our edifice. Second, they misuse a popular philosophy of science to argue
that they are behaving scientifically in attacking evolution. Yet the same phi-

---

[1]Clarence Darrow (1857–1938): the defense attorney in the 1925 trial of John Thomas Scopes
for teaching evolution; William Jennings Bryan (1860–1925): an orator and politician who aided
the prosecution in the Scopes trial. [Eds.]

losophy demonstrates that their own belief is not science, and that "scientific creationism" is therefore meaningless and self-contradictory, a superb example of what Orwell[2] called "newspeak."[3]

In the American vernacular, "theory" often means "imperfect fact"—part of a hierarchy of confidence running downhill from fact to theory to hypothesis to guess. Thus the power of the creationist argument: evolution is "only" a theory, and intense debate now rages about many aspects of the theory. If evolution is less than a fact, and scientists can't even make up their minds about the theory, then what confidence can we have in it? Indeed, President Reagan echoed this argument before an evangelical group in Dallas when he said (in what I devoutly hope was campaign rhetoric): "Well, it is a theory. It is a scientific theory only, and it has in recent years been challenged in the world of science—that is, not believed in the scientific community to be as infallible as it once was."

Well, evolution *is* a theory. It is also a fact. And facts and theories are different things, not rungs in a hierarchy of increasing certainty. Facts are the world's data. Theories are structures of ideas that explain and interpret facts. Facts do not go away when scientists debate rival theories to explain them. Einstein's theory of gravitation replaced Newton's, but apples did not suspend themselves in mid-air pending the outcome. And human beings evolved from apelike ancestors whether they did so by Darwin's proposed mechanism or by some other, yet to be discovered.

Moreover, "fact" does not mean "absolute certainty." The final proofs of logic and mathematics flow deductively from stated premises and achieve certainty only because they are *not* about the empirical world. Evolutionists make no claim for perpetual truth, though creationists often do (and then attack us for a style of argument that they themselves favor). In science, "fact" can only mean "confirmed to such a degree that it would be perverse to withhold provisional assent." I suppose that apples might start to rise tomorrow, but the possibility does not merit equal time in physics classrooms.

Evolutionists have been clear about this distinction between fact and theory from the very beginning, if only because we have always acknowledged how far we are from completely understanding the mechanisms (theory) by which evolution (fact) occurred. Darwin continually emphasized the difference between his two great and separate accomplishments: establishing the fact of evolution, and proposing a theory—natural selection—to explain the mechanism of evolution. He wrote in *The Descent of Man*: "I had two distinct objects in view; firstly, to show that species had not been separately created, and secondly, that natural selection had been the chief agent of change . . . Hence if I have erred

---

[2]George Orwell (1903–1950): English journalist and novelist, author of *Animal Farm* and *1984*. [Eds.]

[3]"Newspeak": the official language in Orwell's *1984*, devised to meet the ideological needs of the ruling party and to make all other modes of thought impossible. [Eds.]

in . . . having exaggerated its [natural selection's] power . . . I have at least, as I hope, done good service in aiding to overthrow the dogma of separate creations."

Thus Darwin acknowledged the provisional nature of natural selection while 8
affirming the fact of evolution. The fruitful theoretical debate that Darwin initiated has never ceased. From the 1940s through the 1960s, Darwin's own theory of natural selection did achieve a temporary hegemony that it never enjoyed in his lifetime. But renewed debate characterizes our decade, and, while no biologist questions the importance of natural selection, many now doubt its ubiquity. In particular, many evolutionists argue that substantial amounts of genetic change may not be subject to natural selection and may spread through populations at random. Others are challenging Darwin's linking of natural selection with gradual, imperceptible change through all intermediary degrees; they are arguing that most evolutionary events may occur far more rapidly than Darwin envisioned.

Scientists regard debates on fundamental issues of theory as a sign of intel- 9
lectual health and a source of excitement. Science is—and how else can I say it?—most fun when it plays with interesting ideas, examines their implications, and recognizes that old information may be explained in surprisingly new ways. Evolutionary theory is now enjoying this uncommon vigor. Yet amidst all this turmoil no biologist has been led to doubt the fact that evolution occurred; we are debating *how* it happened. We are all trying to explain the same thing: the tree of evolutionary descent linking all organisms by ties of genealogy. Creationists pervert and caricature this debate by conveniently neglecting the common conviction that underlies it, and by falsely suggesting that we now doubt the very phenomenon we are struggling to understand.

Using another invalid argument, creationists claim that "the dogma of sep- 10
arate creations," as Darwin characterized it a century ago, is a scientific theory meriting equal time with evolution in high school biology curricula. But a prevailing viewpoint among philosophers of science belies this creationist argument. Philosopher Karl Popper has argued for decades that the primary criterion of science is the falsifiability of its theories. We can never prove absolutely, but we can falsify. A set of ideas that cannot, in principle, be falsified is not science.

The entire creationist argument involves little more than a rhetorical attempt 11
to falsify evolution by presenting supposed contradictions among its supporters. Their brand of creationism, they claim, is "scientific" because it follows the Popperian model in trying to demolish evolution. Yet Popper's argument must apply in both directions. One does not become a scientist by the simple act of trying to falsify another scientific system; one has to present an alternative system that also meets Popper's criterion—it too must be falsifiable in principle.

"Scientific creationism" is a self-contradictory, nonsense phrase precisely be- 12
cause it cannot be falsified. I can envision observations and experiments that

693

would disprove any evolutionary theory I know, but I cannot imagine what potential data could lead creationists to abandon their beliefs. Unbeatable systems are dogma, not science. Lest I seem harsh or rhetorical, I quote creationism's leading intellectual, Duane Gish, Ph.D., from his recent (1978) book *Evolution? The Fossils Say No!* "By creation we mean the bringing into being by a supernatural Creator of the basic kinds of plants and animals by the process of sudden, or fiat, creation. We do not know how the Creator created, what processes He used, *for He used processes which are not now operating anywhere in the natural universe* [Gish's italics]. This is why we refer to creation as special creation. We cannot discover by scientific investigations anything about the creative processes used by the Creator." Pray tell, Dr. Gish, in the light of your last sentence, what then is "scientific" creationism?

THE FACT OF EVOLUTION

Our confidence that evolution occurred centers upon three general argu-   13
ments. First, we have abundant, direct, observational evidence of evolution in action, from both the field and the laboratory. It ranges from countless experiments on change in nearly everything about fruit flies subjected to artificial selection in the laboratory to the famous British moths that turned black when industrial soot darkened the trees upon which they rest. (The moths gain protection from sharp-sighted bird predators by blending into the background.) Creationists do not deny these observations; how could they? Creationists have tightened their act. They now argue that God only created "basic kinds," and allowed for limited evolutionary meandering within them. Thus toy poodles and Great Danes come from the dog kind and moths can change color, but nature cannot convert a dog to a cat or a monkey to a man.

The second and third arguments for evolution—the case for major changes—   14
do not involve direct observation of evolution in action. They rest upon inference, but are no less secure for that reason. Major evolutionary change requires too much time for direct observation on the scale of recorded human history. All historical sciences rest upon inference, and evolution is no different from geology, cosmology, or human history in this respect. In principle, we cannot observe processes that operated in the past. We must infer them from results that still survive: living and fossil organisms for evolution, documents and artifacts for human history, strata and topography for geology.

The second argument—that the imperfection of nature reveals evolution—   15
strikes many people as ironic, for they feel that evolution should be most elegantly displayed in the nearly perfect adaptation expressed by some organisms—the chamber of a gull's wing, or butterflies that cannot be seen in ground litter because they mimic leaves so precisely. But perfection could be imposed by a wise creator or evolved by natural selection. Perfection covers the tracks of past history. And past history—the evidence of descent—is our mark of evolution.

Evolution lies exposed in the *imperfections* that record a history of descent. 16
Why should a rat run, a bat fly, a porpoise swim, and I type this essay with
structures built of the same bones unless we all inherited them from a common
ancestor? An engineer, starting from scratch, could design better limbs in each
case. Why should all the large native mammals of Australia be marsupials,
unless they descended from a common ancestor isolated on this island continent? Marsupials are not "better," or ideally suited for Australia; many have
been wiped out by placental mammals imported by man from other continents.
This principle of imperfection extends to all historical sciences. When we recognize the etymology of September, October, November, and December (seventh, eighth, ninth, and tenth, from the Latin), we know that two additional
items (January and February) must have been added to an original calendar of
ten months.

The third argument is more direct: transitions are often found in the fossil 17
record. Preserved transitions are not common—and should not be, according
to our understanding of evolution (see next section)—but they are not entirely
wanting, as creationists often claim. The lower jaw of reptiles contains several
bones, that of mammals only one. The non-mammalian jawbones are reduced,
step by step, in mammalian ancestors until they become tiny nubbins located
at the back of the jaw. The "hammer" and "anvil" bones of the mammalian
ear are descendants of these nubbins. How could such a transition be accomplished? the creationists ask. Surely a bone is either entirely in the jaw or in
the ear. Yet paleontologists have discovered two transitional lineages or ther-
apsids (the so-called mammal-like reptiles) with a double jaw joint—one composed of the old quadrate and articular bones (soon to become the hammer and
anvil), the other of the squamosal and dentary bones (as in modern mammals).
For that matter, what better transitional form could we desire than the oldest
human, *Australopithecus afarensis*, with its apelike palate, its human upright
stance, and a cranial capacity larger than any ape's of the same body size but a
full 1,000 cubic centimeters below ours? If God made each of the half dozen
human species discovered in ancient rocks, why did he create in an unbroken
temporal sequence of progressively more modern features—increasing cranial
capacity, reduced face and teeth, larger body size? Did he create to mimic
evolution and test our faith thereby?

AN EXAMPLE OF CREATIONIST ARGUMENT

Faced with these facts of evolution and the philosophical bankruptcy of their 18
own position, creationists rely upon distortion and innuendo to buttress their
rhetorical claim. If I sound sharp or bitter, indeed I am—for I have become a
major target of these practices.

I count myself among the evolutionists who argue for a jerky, or episodic, 19
rather than a smoothly gradual, pace of change. In 1972 my colleague Niles

Eldredge and I developed the theory of punctuated equilibrium [*Discover*, October]. We argued that two outstanding facts of the fossil record—geologically "sudden" origin of new species and failure to change thereafter (stasis)—reflect the predictions of evolutionary theory, not the imperfections of the fossil record. In most theories, small isolated populations are the source of new species, and the process of speciation takes thousands or tens of thousands of years. This amount of time, so long when measured against our lives, is a geological microsecond. It represents much less than 1 per cent of the average life span for a fossil invertebrate species—more than 10 million years. Large, widespread, and well-established species, on the other hand, are not expected to change very much. We believe that the inertia of large populations explains the stasis of most fossil species over millions of years.

We proposed the theory of punctuated equilibrium largely to provide a different explanation for pervasive trends in the fossil record. Trends, we argued, cannot be attributed to gradual transformation within lineages, but must arise from the differential success of certain kinds of species. A trend, we argued, is more like climbing a flight of stairs (punctuations and stasis) than rolling up an inclined plane.   20

Since we proposed punctuated equilibria to explain trends, it is infuriating to be quoted again and again by creationists—whether through design or stupidity, I do not know—as admitting that the fossil record includes no transitional forms. Transitional forms are generally lacking at the species level, but are abundant between larger groups. The evolution from reptiles to mammals, as mentioned earlier, is well documented. Yet a pamphlet entitled "Harvard Scientists Agree Evolution Is a Hoax" states: "The facts of punctuated equilibrium which Gould and Eldredge . . . are forcing Darwinists to swallow fit the picture that Bryan insisted on, and which God has revealed to us in the Bible."   21

Continuing the distortion, several creationists have equated the theory of punctuated equilibrium with a caricature of the beliefs of Richard Goldschmidt, a great early geneticist. Goldschmidt argued, in a famous book published in 1940, that new groups can arise all at once through major mutations. He referred to these suddenly transformed creatures as "hopeful monsters." (I am attracted to some aspects of the non-caricatured version, but Goldschmidt's theory still has nothing to do with punctuated equilibrium.) Creationist Luther Sunderland talks of the "punctuated equilibrium hopeful monster theory" and tells his hopeful readers that "it amounts to tacit admission that anti-evolutionists are correct in asserting there is no fossil evidence supporting the theory that all life is connected to a common ancestor." Duane Gish writes, "According to Goldschmidt, and now apparently according to Gould, a reptile laid an egg from which the first bird, feathers and all, was produced." Any evolutionist who believed such nonsense would rightly be laughed off the intellectual stage; yet the only theory that could ever envision such a scenario for the evolution of birds is creationism—God acts in the egg.   22

CONCLUSION

I am both angry at and amused by the creationists; but mostly I am deeply sad. Sad for many reasons. Sad because so many people who respond to creationist appeals are troubled for the right reason, but venting their anger at the wrong target. It is true that scientists have often been dogmatic and elitist. It is true that we have often allowed the white-coated, advertising image to represent us—"Scientists say that Brand X cures bunions ten times faster than . . ." We have not fought it adequately because we derive benefits from appearing as a new priesthood. It is also true that faceless bureaucratic state power intrudes more and more into our lives and removes choices that should belong to individuals and communities. I can understand that requiring that evolution be taught in the schools might be seen as one more insult on all these grounds. But the culprit is not, and cannot be, evolution or any other fact of the natural world. Identify and fight your legitimate enemies by all means, but we are not among them. 23

I am sad because the practical result of this brouhaha will not be expanded coverage to include creationism (that would also make me sad), but the reduction or excision of evolution from high school curricula. Evolution is one of the half dozen "great ideas" developed by science. It speaks to the profound issues of genealogy that fascinate all of us—the "roots" phenomenon writ large. Where did we come from? Where did life arise? How did it develop? How are organisms related? It forces us to think, ponder, and wonder. Shall we deprive millions of this knowledge and once again teach biology as a set of dull and unconnected facts, without the thread that weaves diverse material into a supple unity? 24

But most of all I am saddened by a trend I am just beginning to discern among my colleagues. I sense that some now wish to mute the healthy debate about theory that has brought new life to evolutionary biology. It provides grist for creationist mills, they say, even if only by distortion. Perhaps we should lie low and rally round the flag of strict Darwinism, at least for the moment—a kind of old-time religion on our part. 25

But we should borrow another metaphor and recognize that we too have to tread a straight and narrow path, surrounded by roads to perdition. For if we ever begin to suppress our search to understand nature, to quench our own intellectual excitement in a misguided effort to present a united front where it does not and should not exist, then we are truly lost. 26

QUESTIONS

1. Summarize the difference between *fact* and *theory* as Gould uses those terms in paragraphs 3 through 12.

2. Why, in paragraph 13, does Gould return to the "fact of evolution"? What turn does his argument take there?

3. In paragraphs 18 through 22 Gould claims that the creationists have distorted his work. How well do you think Gould has substantiated this claim? Are all his examples and arguments convincing? If there are problems, what are they?

4. Consider the proposition that "a set of ideas that cannot, in principle, be falsified is not science" (paragraph 10). How does that proposition set evolution theory apart from creationism? What underlying notion does it point to in the history and nature of science?

5. Insofar as you can tell, does the teaching of evolution continue in schools in your area? Have the fears Gould voices at the end of his essay come to pass? Perhaps you can draw upon your own memory of high school, and write a report on this subject. Or perhaps you can interview one or more high school biology teachers.

6. Gould opens his essay with a reference to the Scopes trial in 1925. Do some library research about that trial and about the current debate. Write an essay arguing that the same battle continues or that significant differences exist between the two situations.

7. In paragraph 12 Gould criticizes Gish for assuming that God created the world, using "processes which are not now operating anywhere in the natural universe." Does this mean that to be a scientist, one must accept the opposite assumption, namely, that *natural processes are always the same throughout the universe?* Write an essay in which you consider a science that you have studied, exploring the extent to which it depends upon this assumption. What are the main theories and facts established by this science? Do they require this assumption? Is the assumption itself scientific? Or is it an article of faith?

TEST-TUBE BABIES:
SOLUTION OR PROBLEM?

Ruth Hubbard

*Ruth Hubbard, born in 1924 in Austria, is now an Amer-
ican biologist and professor of biology at Harvard University. Her research interests include the chemistry of vision,
the sociology of science, and women's biology and health.
She is a member of the National Women's Health Network
and often writes for a general audience on women's health
issues. With Mary Sue Henifin and Barbara Fried, she edited* Women Look at Biology Looking at Women *(Boston,
1979), and with Marian Lowe, she has edited* Genes *and*
Gender II: Pitfalls in Research on Sex and Gender *(New
York, 1979) and* Woman's Nature: Rationalizations of Inequality *(New York, 1983).*

In vitro fertilization of human eggs and the implantation of early embryos [1]
into women's wombs are new biotechnologies that may enable some women to
bear children who have hitherto been unable to do so.[1] In that sense, it may
solve their particular infertility problems. On the other hand, this technology
poses unpredictable hazards since it intervenes in the process of fertilization, in
the first cell divisions of the fertilized egg, and in the implantation of the embryo
into the uterus. At present we have no way to assess in what ways and to what
extent these interventions may affect the women or the babies they acquire by
this procedure. Since the use of the technology is only just beginning, the
financial and technical investments it represents are still modest. It is therefore
important that we, as a society, seriously consider the wisdom of implementing
and developing it further.

According to present estimates, about 10 million Americans are infertile by [2]
the definition that they have tried for at least a year to achieve pregnancy without
conceiving or carrying a pregnancy to a live birth. In about a third of infertile
couples, the incapacity rests with the woman only, and for about a third of
these women the problem is localized in the fallopian tubes (the organs that
normally propel an egg from the ovary to the uterus or womb). These short,
delicate tubes are easily blocked by infection or disease. Nowadays the most
common causes of blocked tubes are inflammations of the uterine lining brought
on by IUDs, pelvic inflammatory disease, or gonorrhea. Once blocked, the

---

[1]in vitro: Latin for "in glass," that is, in a test tube. [Eds.]

tubes are difficult to reopen or replace, and doctors presently claim only a one-in-three success rate in correcting the problem. Thus, of the 10 million infertile people in the country, about 600 thousand (or 6 per cent) could perhaps be helped to pregnancy by in vitro fertilization. (These numbers are from Barbara Eck Menning's *Infertility: A Guide for the Childless Couple*, Prentice-Hall, 1977. Ms. Menning is executive director of Resolve, a national, nonprofit counseling service for infertile couples located in Belmont, Mass.)

Louise Brown, born in England in July, 1978, is the first person claimed to   3 have been conceived in vitro. Since then, two other babies conceived outside the mother are said to have been born—one in England, the other in India. In none of these cases have the procedures by which the eggs were obtained from the woman's ovary, fertilized, stored until implantation, and finally implanted in her uterus been described in any detail. However, we can deduce the procedures from animal experimentation and the brief published accounts about the three babies.

The woman who is a candidate for in vitro fertilization has her hormone   4 levels monitored to determine when she is about to ovulate. She is then admitted to the hsopital and the egg is collected in the following way: a small cut is made in her abdomen; a metal tube containing an optical arrangement that allows the surgeon to see the ovaries and a narrow-bore tube (called a micropipette) are inserted through the cut; and the egg is removed shortly before it would normally be shed from the ovary. The woman is ready to go home within a day, at most.

When the procedure was first developed, women were sometimes given hor-   5 mones to make them "superovulate"—produce more than one egg (the usual number for most women). But we do not know whether this happened with the mothers of the three "test-tube" babies that have been born. Incidentally, this superovulation reportedly is no longer induced, partly because some people believe it is too risky.

After the egg has been isolated, it is put into a solution that keeps it alive   6 and nourishes it, and is mixed with sperm. Once fertilized, it is allowed to go through a few cell divisions and so begin its embryonic development—the still-mysterious process by which a fertilized egg becomes a baby. The embryo is then picked up with another fine tube, inserted through the woman's cervix, and flushed into the uterus.

If the uterus is not at the proper stage to allow for implantation (approximately   7 17 to 23 days after the onset of each menstruation) when the embryo is ready to be implanted, the embryo must be frozen and stored until the time is right in a subsequent menstrual cycle. Again, we do not know whether the embryos were frozen and stored prior to implantation with the two British babies; we are told that the Indian one was.

In sum, then, there is a need, and there is a technology said to meet that   8 need. But as a woman, a feminist, and a biologist, I am opposed to using it and developing it further.

HEALTH RISKS

As a society, we do not have a very good track record in anticipating the 9
problems that can arise from technological interventions in complicated biological systems. Our physical models are too simpleminded and have led to many
unforeseen problems in the areas of pest control, waste disposal, and other
aspects of what is usually referred to as the ecological crisis.

In reproductive biology, the nature of the many interacting processes is poorly 10
understood. We are in no position to enumerate or describe the many reactions
that must occur at just the right times during the early stages of embryonic
development when the fertilized egg begins to divide into increasing numbers
of cells, implants itself in the uterus, and establishes the pattern for the different
organ systems that will allow it to develop into a normal fetus and baby.

The safety of this in vitro procedure cannot be established in animal exper- 11
iments because the details and requirements of normal embryonic development
are different for different kinds of animals. Nor are the criteria of "normalcy"
the same for animals and for people. The guinea pigs of the research and
implementation of in vitro fertilization will be:

— the women who donate their eggs,
— the women who lend their wombs (who, of course, need not be the same
     as the egg-donors; rent-a-wombs clearly are an option), and
— the children who are produced.

The greatest ethical and practical questions arise with regard to the children. 12
They cannot consent to be produced, and we cannot know what hazards their
production entails until enough have lived out their lives to allow for statistical
analysis of their medical histories.

This example shows the inadequacy of our scientific models because it is not 13
obvious how to provide "controls," in the usual scientific sense of the term, for
the first generation of "test-tube" individuals; they will be viewed as "special"
at every critical juncture in their lives. When I ask myself whether I would want
to be a "test-tube person," I know that I would not like to have to add *those*
self-doubts to my more ordinary repertory of insecurities.

A concrete example of a misjudgment with an unfortunate outcome that 14
could not be predicted was the administration of the chemical thalidomide, a
"harmless tranquilizer" touted as a godsend and prescribed to pregnant women,
which resulted in the births of thousands of armless and legless babies. Yet there
the damage was visible at birth and the practice could be stopped, though not
until after it had caused great misery. But take the case of the hormone DES
(diethyl stilbesterol), which was prescribed for pregnant women in the mistaken
(though at the time honest) belief that it could prevent miscarriages. Some 15
years passed before many of the daughters of these women developed an unusual
form of vaginal cancer. Both these chemicals produced otherwise rare diseases,

so the damage was easy to detect and its causes could be sought. Had the chemicals produced more common symptoms, it would have been much more difficult to detect the damage and to pinpoint which drugs were harmful.

The important point is that both thalidomide and DES changed the environment in which these babies developed—in ways that could not have been foreseen and that we still do not understand. This happened because we know very little about how embryos develop. How then can we claim to know that the many chemical and mechanical manipulations of eggs, sperms, and embryos that take place during in vitro fertilization and implantation are harmless? 15

A WOMAN'S RIGHT?

The push toward this technology reinforces the view, all too prevalent in our society, that women's lives are unfulfilled, or indeed worthless, unless we bear children. I understand the wish to have children, though I also know many people—women and men—who lead happy and fulfilled lives without them. But even if one urgently wants a child, why must it be biologically one's own? It is not worth opening the hornet's nest of reproductive technology for the privilege of having one's child derive from one's own egg or sperm. Foster and adoptive parents are much needed for the world's homeless children. Why not try to change the American and international practices that make it difficult for people who want children to be brought together with children who need parents? 16

Advocates of this new technology argue that every woman has a right to bear a child and that the technology will extend this right to a group previously denied it. It is important to examine this argument and to ask in what sense women have a "right" to bear children. In our culture, many women are taught from childhood that we must do without lots of things we want—electric trains, baseball mitts, perhaps later an expensive education or a well-paying job. We are also taught to submit to all sorts of social restrictions and physical dangers—we cannot go out alone at night, we allow ourselves to be made self-conscious at the corner drugstore and to be molested by strangers or bosses or family members without punching them as our brothers might do. We are led to believe that we must put up with all this—and without grousing—because as women we have something beside which everything else pales, something that will make up for everything: we can have babies! To grow up paying all the way and then to be denied that child *is* a promise unfulfilled; that's cheating. 17

But I would argue that to promise children to women by means of an untested technology—that is being tested only as it is used on them and their babies—is adding yet another wrong to the burdens of our socialization. Take the women whose fallopian tubes have been damaged by an infection provoked by faulty IUDs. They are now led to believe that problems caused by one risky, though 18

702

medically approved and administered, technology can be relieved by another, much more invasive and hazardous technology.

I am also concerned about the extremely complicated nature of the tech- [19] nology. It involves many steps, is hard to demystify, and requires highly skilled professionals. There is no way to put control over this technology into the hands of the women who are going to be exposed to it. On the contrary, it will make women and their babies more dependent than ever upon a high-technology, super-professionalized medical system. The women and their babies must be monitored from before conception until birth, and the children will have to be observed all their lives. Furthermore, the pregnancy-monitoring technologies themselves involve hazard. From the start, women are locked into subservience to the medical establishment in a way that I find impossible to interpret as an increase in reproductive freedom, rights, or choices.

HEALTH PRIORITIES

The final issue—and a major one—is that this technology is expensive. It [20] requires prolonged experimentation, sophisticated professionals, and costly equipment. It will distort our health priorities and funnel scarce resources into a questionable effort. The case of the Indian baby is a stark illustration, for in that country, where many children are dying from the effects of malnutrition and poor people have been forcibly sterilized, expensive technologies are being pioneered to enable a relatively small number of well-to-do people to have their own babies.

In the United States, as well, many people have less-than-adequate access to [21] such essential health resources as decent jobs, food and housing, and medical care when they need it. And here, too, poor women have been and are still being forcibly sterilized and otherwise coerced into *not* having babies, while women who can pay high prices will become guinea pigs in the risky technology of in vitro fertilization.

In vitro fertilization is expensive and unnecessary in comparison with many [22] pressing social needs, including those of children who need homes. We must find better and less risky solutions for women who want to parent but cannot bear children of their own.

QUESTIONS

1. Briefly state Hubbard's argument in your own words.
2. What are the main strands of evidence, both social and scientific, that she draws upon?
3. Examine the order in which Hubbard presents her main points. Why do you thnk she arranges them this way?

4. One argument she ignores is the moral issue of humans playing God and interfering in nature. Why do you suppose she avoids that issue?

5. Would you care to counter her argument? Write a position paper for the mother who desires a test-tube baby. Without ignoring Hubbard's case, make a case for the opposition.

6. Find out from the library or from one or more adoption agencies the rules for adoption in your state. Then, using Hubbard's article as a small piece of additional evidence, write an argument for liberalizing those rules. Or argue the opposite, if your research leads you to believe the rules are already too lax.

7. In vitro fertilization isn't the only example of technology running ahead of our ability, as a society, to decide the moral issues it raises. Choose another example—such as medical transplants, the development of highly efficient feedlots, a specific aspect of space exploration, or some other technological feat. After investigating this example, write a paper explaining the dilemmas such a scientific advance poses for society. If you want, you may write your paper as an argument like Hubbard's, either for or against some particular advance.

ON THE SEEMING PARADOX OF MECHANIZED CREATIVITY

Douglas R. Hofstadter

Douglas R. Hofstadter (b. 1945) won both the American Book Award and the Pulitzer Prize in 1980 for his book Gödel, Escher, Bach: An Eternal Golden Braid. *With Daniel Dennett he also "composed and arranged" another book,* The Mind's I: Fantasies and Reflections on Self and the Soul *(1981). He is a professor of computer science at The University of Indiana, and his subspecialty is artificial intelligence. For several years he wrote a column for* Scientific American *called "Mathematical Themas" and in 1985 collected these into a book of the same name. The selection here, one of his "Mathematical Themas," examines the nature of intelligence and its compatibility with the nature of machines.*

It is commonly held that there is such a thing as "the creative spark," that when a brilliant mind comes up with a new idea or work of art there has been "an unanalyzable leap of the imagination." Great creators are sometimes said to be a "quantum leap" away from ordinary mortals. People such as Mozart are held to be somehow divinely inspired, to have magical insights for which they could no more account than spiders could explain how they weave their wondrous webs. It is all felt to be a gift somehow too deep, too hidden, too occult to be in any sense mechanical. "You may mechanize your *logic*," says the English professor to the computer scientist, "but you'll never a lay a finger on *poetry*." (You may substitute music or any other domain of artistic creation for poetry.) 1

Is this kind of statement irrational? Is it a reflection of a deep-seated fear that even this most sacred aspect of being human is doomed to be taken over soon by machines or silicon chips? Why make such a big deal out of an activity of the human mind that, like every other activity in life, has shades and degrees? After all, the creative blurs into the mundane so smoothly that it would seem hopeless to try to cull what is truly creative out of what is not. Or is there some clean dividing line that distinguishes the run-of-the-mill workaday deviser of ditties from the Great Composer of Eternal Symphonic Masterpieces? And if there is, is it possible that here lies the elusive difference between the living and the dead, the human being and the machine, the mental and the mechanical? 2

With such a "magical" view of creativity there is, of course, a problem. It 3 would seem to imply that the poor composer of ditties is actually dead and mechanical inside, that only certified geniuses such as Mozart are qualitatively different from machines and that even Mozart was nonmechanical only when he was composing, certainly not when he was merely drinking beer at an inn. Probably most people who believe in the magical view of creativity would disagree with this way of describing their position. They would maintain that Mozart was nonmechanical all the time and that moreover you and I, no less than Mozart, are also nonmechanical all the time. It is irrelevant that some, even many, human abilities have already been mechanized or will be mechanized someday.

About the touchy question of the mechanization of the mental many educated people believe that although a machine may now or someday be able to do a creditable job of acting like a person, any machine's performance will always remain lackluster and dull, and that after a while this dullness will always show through. You will simply have no doubt that the machine is unoriginal, that its ideas and thoughts are all being drawn from some storehouse of formulas and cliches, that ultimately there is nothing alive and dynamic—no *élan vital*[1]— behind its facade. There may be nothing specific to point to other than the "vibes" you pick up of its dullness and unoriginality, but after a while they will inevitably start to come in loud and clear. (Incidentally, I would be delighted if some of the more vocal antimechanists felt that way, instead of insisting, as they more often do, that operational tests are of no value in deciding who or what possesses "genuine mental states.")

This sense that you will eventually be able to "just tell," from its inevitable lack of sparkle, that you are dealing with a machine and not a person seems to depend on a tacit assumption about human thought, one with which I fully agree, namely that the "creative spark" is not the exclusive property of a few rare individuals down through the centuries but rather is an intrinsic ingredient of the everyday mental activity of everyone, even the most ordinary people. In short, it seems that people who think machines—even intelligent machines— will always remain duller than people are tacitly relying on this thesis: Creativity is part of the fabric of all human thought, rather than some esoteric, even exceptional or fluky by-product of the ability to think, which surfaces every so often here and there.

With that thesis I agree. Where I differ with antimechanists is over the matter of whether creativity lies *beyond* intelligence. I see creativity and insight, for machines no less than for people, as being intimately bound up with intelligence, and so I cannot imagine a non-creative yet intelligent machine—something that, in order to make a point about what is essentially human, antime-

---

[1]*élan vital*: vital force. [Eds.]

chanists seem willing to do. To me "noncreative intelligence" is a flat-out contradiction in terms.

Here I would like to describe some ideas I have about how creativity is founded on mechanisms, mechanisms that to be sure lie deeply hidden in the depths of the structure of our brain but that nonetheless exist and can perhaps be approximated with the hardware and software of the machines we have today, crude though they are in certain ways. The gist of my notion is that having creativity is an automatic consequence of having the proper representation of *concepts* in a mind. It is not something you add on afterward. It is built into the way concepts are. To spell this out more concretely, if you have succeeded in making an accurate model of concepts, you have thereby also succeeded in making an accurate model of the creative process, even of consciousness. 7

Another way of talking about concepts is to talk about memory, which is the "place" where concepts are stored. It is the organization of memory that defines what concepts are. Incidentally, when I first wrote the preceding sentence, it ended differently. It went: "It is the organization of memory that defines what concepts will be accessible under what conditions." On rereading the sentence I felt it was too weak that way. It took for granted the notion that all readers have a clear concept of what a concept is. But that is hardly to be taken for granted! Granted, we all have *some* concept of what a concept is, but do we have a *clear* one? 8

Therefore I dropped the phrase beginning with "will be accessible" and replaced it with "are." This way the sentence does more than simply state that memory is a storehouse of some things called concepts. It emphasizes that what establishes the "concepthood" of something is the way it is integrated into memory. Or conversely, nothing is a concept except by virtue of the way it is connected up with other things that are also concepts. In other words, the property of being a concept is a property of connectivity, a quality that comes from being embedded in a certain kind of network and from nowhere else. Put this way, concepts sound like structural or even topological properties of the vast tangly networks of sticky mental spaghetti. 9

That is more or less the image I think it is important to convey, namely, that concepts derive all their power from their connectivity with one another. Having expressed the idea, I can now return to the sentence as it was originally put: "It is the organization of memory that defines what concepts will be accessible under what conditions"—and surely the happy choice of the right concept at the right time is the essence of the creative. Therefore it is imperative to study deeply the nature of that network, to ask the question: What is a concept? 10

Questions that quickly come to mind are: What is the relation between a Platonic, or general, concept such as the concept of "tree," and the concept you form of some specific tree? That is, what is the distinction between semantic 11

707

or perceptual *categories* and the representations of individual *instances* of such categories? How is a given situation filed away in memory so that one has access to it under a variety of future situations—access that is often gained by analogy or other abstract pathways rather than by simplistic superficial traits? Or, to consider the other side of the coin, how does a given situation lead to the highly selective retrieval from memory of a small number of earlier situations that seem relevant? Only through a deep understanding of the organization of memory—which is to say, only by answering the question: What is a concept?—will it be possible to make models of the creative process. It will be a long and arduous process, not one that will yield answers soon, or even in a few decades. The right beginnings have nonetheless been made, in the sciences of cognitive psychology and artificial intelligence. Contributions will undoubtedly be made by philosophers of mind and neuroscientists as well.

A question that arises at the outset is: What kinds of objects have concepts 12 stored inside them and what kinds do not? In Dean E. Wooldridge's book, *Mechanical Man: The Physical Basis of Intelligent Life* (McGraw-Hill Book Company, 1968), there is a passage that opens the question wide:

"When the time comes for egg laying, the wasp *Sphex* builds a burrow for 13 the purpose and seeks out a cricket which she stings in such a way as to paralyze but not kill it. She drags the cricket into the burrow, lays her eggs alongside, closes the burrow, then flies away, never to return. In due course, the eggs hatch and the wasp grubs feed off the paralyzed cricket, which has not decayed, having been kept in the wasp equivalent of a deepfreeze. To the human mind, such an elaborately organized and seemingly purposeful routine conveys a convincing flavor of logic and thoughtfulness—until more details are examined. For example, the wasp's routine is to bring the paralyzed cricket to the burrow, leave it on the threshold, go inside to see that all is well, emerge, and then drag the cricket in. If the cricket is moved a few inches away while the wasp is inside making her preliminary inspection, the wasp, on emerging from the burrow, will bring the cricket back to the threshold, but not inside, and will then repeat the preparatory procedure of entering the burrow to see that everything is all right. If again the cricket is removed a few inches while the wasp is inside, once again she will move the cricket up to the threshold and reenter the burrow for a final check. The wasp never thinks of pulling the cricket straight in. On one occasion this procedure was repeated forty times, always with the same result."

One might remark that it was not the wasp that was in a run but the exper- 14 imenter. Humor aside, this is a shocking revelation of the mechanical underpinning in a living creature of what looks like quite reflective behavior.

Something about the wasp's actions seems supremely unconscious, a quality 15 totally opposite to what we human beings think we are all about, particularly when we talk about our own consciousness. I propose to call the *Sphex* wasp's quality "sphexishness" and its opposite "antisphexishness." I then propose that

708

consciousness is simply the possession of antisphexishness to the highest possible degree. The point is that sphexishness and antisphexishness are two extremes along a continuum. Let me give a few examples distributed along that continuum, starting at the most sphexish and finishing with the most antisphexish:

1. A stuck record. This can be particularly disturbing if the recorded piece has a vibrant dynamism (such as the music of contemporary composer Steve Reich) the lifelike illusion of which is shattered by the mechanical repetition of the jumping needle. 16

2. The *Sphex* wasp herself and other examples from the insect world. For instance, suppose you have a mosquito in your bedroom. You try to swat it, and you miss. The mosquito takes off and flies around the room, losing you. After a while it alights and you spot it on the wall. Again you try to swat it and miss. As the cycle progresses is the mosquito aware of the repetition? Does the mosquito begin to sense that there is an organized effort to kill it or does each new swat come as fresh and as unexpected as the preceding one? Does the mosquito formulate some such notion as "the animate agent whose desire is to wipe me out"? Unfortunately for the mosquito but fortunately for you, it seems highly unlikely. 17

3. A herd of cattle in a corral, waiting to get branded. There is a general commotion and hubbub, originating with the noise each cow makes at the moment of branding and propagated outward by the cows closest to it. Does each cow in the corral recognize the overall pattern? Is each cow's increased state of agitation due to the fact that it perceives what is about to happen to it, or does it feel only a vague apprehension, perhaps a raised hormone level without any specific meaning or referential quality? 18

4. A dog that is fooled every time by a faking motion in which you pretend to throw a ball but do not release it. Actually I do not know any dog that would fall for such an elementary trick. I am, however, acquainted with a certain Airedale that did not catch on when I threw his toy onto an upstairs landing instead of down the hall where he expected it. I then led him up the stairs and showed him where it was. I expected he would know enough to go upstairs the next time. No such luck; he just ran down the hall again. Even after I had thrown his toy upstairs 15 times more, he *still* ran down the hall and then returned looking confused. Poor doggie! True, some of those 16 painful times he did start to go up the stairs, but each time he got only part way up, turned around and then hightailed it down the hall. To me it was a disappointingly sphexish kind of behavior for a dog. 19

5. Glassy-eyed gamblers in Las Vegas, glued to their slot machines. To this can be added glassy-eyed teenagers and college students glued to video games and pinball machines. Is there not some kind of deadening rut here? And yet many people do such things over and over again with seeming pleasure. 20

6. A person who has the habit of singing or whistling in the midst of other 21

activities who, if you pay attention, can be heard to sing or whistle the same little refrain, day in, day out, year in, year out, never with any variety.

7. People who make what seems to be the same joke, only in slightly different 22 guises, over and over again. Or inveterate punsters, who simply cannot stop making one pun after another.

8. Junior-high-school students who fill each other's yearbooks with the same 23 pat phrases and corny poems *your* junior-high class did.

9. A mathematician who exploits a single technique in paper after paper, 24 making advances in different branches of mathematics, yet always with a distinct, idiosyncratic touch and always, in some deep sense, doing just "the same old trick" again and again.

10. People whose behavior leads them down harmful pathways in their lives, 25 for instance in their love affairs or their jobs. We all know people who "blow it" in the same way each time they are faced with a situation that matters.

11. Social trends that become completely stylized and predictable, such as 26 the endless "sitcoms" television networks keep churning out and the movies one after another based on some gimmick exploited in slightly different ways. For instance, one could perceive the movies *Breaking Away, The Black Stallion* and *Chariots of Fire* as being simply three ways of plugging specific values for variables into one successful formula: an upcoming championship race, a lovable underdog, a rival and, of course, ultimate victory. And these works are sophisticated compared with some books and movies that far more blatantly exploit famous predecessors.

12. Styles in art that become dated and routinized to the point of no longer 27 being creative. It happens to every style, but at the moment of its happening there are always some people who are breaking out of the rut and creating totally new styles. There are other people, however, who become technically proficient at an old style and continue to create in an old-fashioned vein.

How different are those last few examples from the stuck record or from the 28 *Sphex* wasp? What is the real difference we feel as we progress down the list?

I would summarize it by saying that it is a general *sensitivity to patterns*, an 29 ability to spot patterns of unanticipated types in unanticipated places at unanticipated times in unanticipated media. For instance, *you* just spotted an unanticipated pattern: four repetitions of a word. There was no explicit preparation for this act of perception in your genes or your schooling. All you had going for you is an ability to see sameness. All human beings have that readiness, that alertness, and this is what makes them so antisphexish. Whenever they get into some kind of "loop," they quickly sense it. Something happens in their head—a kind of "loop detector" fires. You can think of it as a "rut detector," a "sameness detector," but no matter how you put it the possession of this ability to break out of loops of all types seems the antithesis of the mechanical. Or, to put it the other way around, the essence of the mechanical seems to lie in its lack of novelty and its repetitiveness, in its being trapped in some kind of precisely delimited space. That is why the behavior of the wasp, the dog and even some human beings seems so mechanical.

How many computers do you know that react with outrage (or a guffaw) to the simultaneous occurrence on a single mailing list of "Bernie Weinreb," "Bernie W. Weinreb," "Mr. Bernie Weinreb, R.M.," "Barnie Weinrab" and so forth? Computers do not have automatic sensitivity to patterns in the data they deal with. To be sure, how could they be expected to? As the old saw goes, they do only what they are programmed to do. Computers are not inherently bored by adding long columns of numbers, even when all the numbers are the same. People are. What is the difference? 30

Clearly there is something lacking in the machine that allows it to have an unbounded tolerance for repetitive actions. The thing that is lacking can be described in a few words: it is the ability to watch oneself as one deals with the world, to perceive in one's own activities a pattern and to be able to do so at many levels of abstraction. Consider a hypothetical self-watching computer. To be sensitive in this way it should get bored whenever it is forced to add a long column of identical numbers together. Wouldn't you? It should get bored whenever it is forced to do just adding over and over again, even when the numbers are different. Wouldn't you? It should even get bored when it is asked to do many arithmetic operations in any kind of repetitive pattern. Wouldn't you? Any loop of any kind should become tedious. Shouldn't it? 31

But where does it stop? Surely if a computer could perceive that all it *ever* does is pull one instruction after another up from memory (a piece of hardware not to be confused with human memory), execute the instructions and change various registers, it would yawn with boredom and probably soon go to sleep. By the same token you or I, if we ever gained access to the firings of our neurons, would find watching that activity to be one of the most stultifying things imaginable. 32

This, however, is not the kind of self-watching I mean. Watching one's own internal microscopic patterns of activity is bound to be boring, because any complex system is bound to be made up of thousands, millions or even more copies of small elements (gears, transistors, cells and so on). What is critical is to be able to watch activities on a completely different level: the collective level, in which huge patterns of activity of these many components assume regular kinds of behavior perceptible on their own. A hurricane is a huge pattern of activity of tiny atoms, but one with such regularity and pattern that we can predict the behavior of hurricanes without ever thinking of their constituent atoms. A *thought* is a huge pattern of activity of tiny cells, and much the same can be said of it. 33

Antisphexishness has to do with self-perception at this kind of level. Rather than watching its neurons or transistors or registers, an antisphexish being watches 34 its own high-level patterns, looking for similarities in somewhat the way a meteorologist might look for one hurricane to follow the same general path as another.

Hence we should not expect or even want a self-watching computer to be   35
able to see down to the level of its circuitry; it would not watch itself doing the machine-language operations of "add,' "store" and "jump" in looplike patterns. The effects of such operations are to change the larger things in memory called data structures. Self-watching involves monitoring those changes as they happen, filtering out dull ones and recording certain aspects of the interesting ones in *other* data structures. (The fact that such recording would, on a more microscopic level, involve the very same kinds of elementary machine-language operations would be invisible to the computer, since the machine should be shielded from that detailed a view of itself.) Thus patterns in the changes taking place in *one* set of data structures would get recorded in another set of data structures. Should we then not set up a third level of data structures, a level to watch the second level for patterns occurring in it? And should we not also set up a fourth level to watch the third? This seems prime territory for an infinite regress; an endless hierarchy of structures, each one monitoring changes in the level below it.[2]

Such is indeed the case, and it is because you are a self-watching human   36
being that you caught onto the pattern, probably before I spelled it out. It is in the nature of human pattern perception to be able to detect such infinite regresses and to stop them before they get anywhere. But what about the hypothetical self-watching computer, with its infinitely many layers of watchers?

Well, surely one of the most salient features—no, definitely the *most* salient   37
feature—of what I have just described is the pattern of the data structures themselves: the hierarchy stretching upward repetitively toward infinity. Shouldn't this pattern be as blatant to a self-watcher as it is to us? It should indeed. If we were to label the bottom level 0 and the first watching level 1, then logically we should label the further levels 2, 3 and so on. Each level in this potentially infinite set can be identified with a natural number. Once the pattern is perceived by a watcher, that watcher can form the general concept of "all the levels seen at once," associated with the concept of "all the natural numbers conceived of at once." The conventional name for the set of all natural numbers is *omega*, which can be taken as the name of a new watching level that looks out for patterns in this potentially infinite tower of watchers.

You need not worry, by the way, that in proposing such a self-watching   38
computer I am presupposing an infinite machine. Precisely the opposite is the case. The entire reason for stopping infinite regress in its tracks is so that we

---

[2]infinite regress: a system that extends itself indefinitely and systematically, as when, for example, mirrors reflect each other. [Eds.]

will not need to build an infinite tower of data structures and watching processes, a feat that would clearly be impossible, aside from being monumentally sphexish. At any stage only a finite number—in fact a small number—of levels of structure would exist. The only requirement is that there be the *potential* to extend it further.

It would be the *omega* watcher that would perceive (as you and I and any other human being would) the infinite-regress pattern of attempts to build the *omega* tower itself. The *omega* watcher would catch any such infinite regress before it could start. If a change in Level 1 caused a change in Level 2, and if these changes seemed to be patterned in such a way that an inevitable infinite ripple upward would ensue, the *omega* watcher, ever alert for such patterns in the other watchers, would come to the rescue, shouting, "Wait! Enough! Halt!" Therefore no infinite regress would actually occur; it would be nipped in the bud by the same kind of mechanism that enables you to cut off a bore at a party. "Excuse me, I think I'll go get some more punch." 39

The problem is that there is nothing to prevent the *omega* level itself from going into loops, and so if we are going to prevent that, we must have a higher watcher: *omega*-plus-one. Uh-oh! Before I even had a chance to begin spelling it out, you sniffed a new infinite regress. (You spoil all my fun!) Well, I am going to spell it out anyway. Level *omega*-plus-one needs to be watched by Level *omega*-plus-2, and that level by Level *omega*-plus-three. Thus we have a *second* potentially infinite tower of watchers, all of whom will be watched over by the Grand Watcher, Level two-*omega*. But if there can be *two* towers, why not *three*? And so, of course, it goes. Wheels within wheels, patterns of patterns of patterns. We get watchers two-*omega*, three-*omega*, and now our tower of towers needs a new Great-Grand Watcher: *omega*-squared. And then— 40

Excuse me; I think I'll go get some more punch. There is a problem once you start getting into infinite regresses composed of other infinite regresses: the whole thing just never stops, and it becomes a bore. Well, not exactly a *bore*, but a complex and confusing thing whose reality and relevance become ever more questionable. And yet when you bring it back to the domain of sphexishness, it becomes the very real and very relevant question of how to build a machine that can sense unanticipated patterns in its own behavior. 41

This is related to a classic problem in the theory of computability: the halting problem. The problem is the question of whether there exists any computer program that can inspect other programs before they run and reliably predict whether or not they will go into infinite loops. (Going into an infinite loop means never coming to a halt, and, conversely, halting means avoiding any infinite loop.) The answer turns out to be no, and for elegant, deep reasons. Of course, the thing hinges on getting the halting inspector to try to predict its own behavior while it is looking at itself trying to predict its own behavior while it is looking at itself trying to predict its own behavior while it is looking at itself 42 trying to predict its own behavior while—Excuse me; I think I'll go get some more punch.

The idea of the halting problem is closely related to the question about self-watching programs, but it is not really the same thing. First of all the halting problem is concerned with an inspection to be carried out on programs *before* they are running; it is like looking at blueprints of a building before it is built to see if it is earthquake-proof. Here we are talking about a program that is observing some program *while* it is running, and what is more, it is not just "some program" that it is watching, but *itself*. Of course, not *all* its attention is being devoted to seeing if it has got into a rut (since that would itself constitute ruttish behavior), but while it is doing other things it is keeping its eye peeled, so to speak, for signs of ruttishness within itself.

In computability theory, when a program or a system of any other kind turns back on itself in this way, the turning back on itself is known as diagonalization. To some people diagonalization seems a bizarre exercise in artificiality, a construction of a sort that would never arise in any realistic context. To others its flirtation with paradox is tantalizing and provocative, suggesting links to many deep aspects of the universe. Now here we see a *dynamic* diagonalization—a self-watching program—that seems to be closely connected with what makes a human being utterly different from a stuck record or a *Sphex* wasp. Surely that is not such a bizarrely artificial thing to ponder!

Probably the most significant difference between the halting problem and the idea of a self-watching program is that in trying to build an artificial intelligence we are not really so much concerned with the mathematical perfection of our self-watching system as we are with its likelihood of survival in a complex world. After all, that is what intelligence is about. Therefore if there is a mathematical theorem telling us that no program whatsoever will be a *perfect* self-watcher, able to catch itself in any conceivable kind of infinite regress, well, it is simply a statement that *perfect* intelligence is unreachable—something that ought to please us rather than dismay us, since it would be rather disappointing if someone came up with a finite program and could legitimately announce: "Well, folks, here it is at last, the end-all of intelligence, a *perfectly* intelligent program."

But don't worry about that. The metamathemathical work of Kurt Gödel, Alan Turing, Stephen Kleene[3] and others on such things as the halting problem and the theory of infinite ordinals (such as the towers of numbers and *omegas*) tells us that this scenario will never be realized, since there is neither a perfect halting inspector nor any ultimate scheme for naming ordinals. What this latter result means is that there is no finite mechanism that can possibly detect all patterns, patterns of patterns, patterns of patterns of patterns of patterns (aha!— I fooled you that last time, didn't I) and so on.

---

[3]Kurt Gödel (1906–1978): an Austrian-American mathematician; Alan Turing (1912–1954): an English mathematician and inventor of early computers; Stephen Kleene (b. 1909): an American mathematician. [Eds.]

In a famous paper titled "Minds, Machines and Gödel" (in *Minds and Ma-* 47
chines, edited by Alan Ross Anderson, Prentice-Hall, 1964) the English philosopher J. R. Lucas attempted to capitalize on these types of "negative" results of
metamathematics by asserting they provided the key element in a proof that no
machine could ever be conscious in the way human beings are. Let Lucas speak
for himself:

"At one's first and simplest attempts to philosophize, one becomes entangled 48
in questions of whether when one knows something one knows that one knows
it, and what, when one is thinking of oneself, is being thought about, and what
is doing the thinking. After one has been puzzled and bruised by this problem
for a long time one learns not to press these questions: the concepts of a conscious being is implicitly realized to be different from that of an unconscious
object. In saying that a conscious being knows something we are saying not only
that he knows it, but that he knows he knows it, and that he knows that he
knows it, and so on, as long as we care to pose the question: there is, we
recognize, an infinity here, but it is not an infinite regress in the bad sense, for
it is the questions that peter out, at being pointless, rather than the answers.
The questions are felt to be pointless because the concept contains within itself
the idea of being able to go on answering such questions indefinitely. Although
conscious beings have the power of going on, we do not wish to exhibit this
simply as a succession of tasks they are able to perform, nor do we see the mind
as an infinite sequence of selves and super-selves and super-super-selves. Rather,
we insist that a conscious being is a unity, and though we talk about parts of
the mind, we do so only as a metaphor, and will not allow it to be taken literally.

"The paradoxes of consciousness arise because a conscious being can be 49
aware of itself, as well as of other things, and yet cannot really be construed as
being divisible into parts. It means that a conscious being can deal with Gödelian
questions in a way in which a machine cannot, because a conscious being can
be made in a manner of speaking to 'consider' its performance, but it cannot
take this 'into account' without thereby becoming a different machine, namely
the old machine with a 'new part' added. But it is inherent in our idea of a
conscious mind that it can reflect upon itself and criticize its own performances,
and no extra part is required to do this: it is already complete, and has no
Achilles' heel."

Somehow—and I think understandably—Lucas was under the impression 50
that human beings are endowed with powers equivalent to those of a self-watcher
of infinite depth, someone who will detect and terminate any and all patterned
behavior: the ultimate in antisphexishness. I call this hypothetical ability "breaking out of loops everywhere," or BOOLE for short (in honor of George Boole,
who wrote *The Laws of Thought,* one of the most influential books of the 19th
century).[4]

Lucas seems to think that to be human is to be endowed with this BOOLE 51

---

[4]George Boole (1815–1864): British mathematician. [Eds.]

DOUGLAS R. HOFSTADTER

ability—this total and perfect antisphexishness—intrinsically. On reflection, however, one realizes that this cannot be the case. In spite of not being *Sphex* wasps or Airedales, we are all still vulnerable to getting caught in ruts, as I attempted to point out in the dozen-item list above. None of us is immune to it. Each of us—even the Mozarts among us—exhibits a "cognitive style" that in essence defines the ruts in which we are permanently caught.

Far from being a tragic flaw, this is what makes us interesting to one another. 52 If we limit ourselves to thinking about music, for instance, each composer exhibits a "cognitive style" in that domain—a musical style. Do we take it as a sign of weakness that Mozart did not have the power to break out of his "Mozart rut" and anticipate the patterns of Chopin?[5] And is it because Chopin lacked spark that he could not see his way to inventing the subtle harmonics of Maurice Ravel?[6]

On the contrary. We celebrate individual styles, rather than seeing them 53 negatively, as proofs of inner limits. What in fact is curious is that those people who are able to put on or take off styles in the manner of a chameleon seem to have no style of their own and are simply saloon performers, amusing imitators. We accord greatness to those people whose "limitations," if that is how you want to look at it, are the most apparent, the most blatant. If you are familiar with the style of Ravel, you can recognize his music anytime. He is powerful *because* he is so recognizable, because he is trapped in that inimitable Ravel rut. Even if Mozart *had* jumped that far out of his Mozart system, he still would have been trapped inside the Ravel system.

The point is that Mozart, and you and I, are all highly antisphexish but not 54 perfectly so, and it is at the fuzzy boundary where we can no longer quite maintain the self-watching to a high degree of reliability that our own individual styles, characters, begin to emerge to the world.

Although Lucas has been roundly criticized (I believe rightly) by many phi- 55 losophers, logicians and computer scientists for failing to see many important subtleties of the Gödel argument on which he bases his paper, most of his critics have failed to see the crucial aspect of mind that Lucas was one of the first to point out. He correctly observes that the degree of nonmechanicalness one perceives in a conscious being is directly related to its ability to self-watch in ever more exquisite ways. Unfortunately too many artificial-intelligence people are ready to put down the Lucas article on the grounds that its central thesis— the impossibility of mechanizing mind—is wrong. What they miss is that it is pointing at deep issues having much to do with the very core of intelligence and creativity. The logician Emil Post[7] wrote, "The creative germ seems not to

---

[5]Wolfgang Amadeus Mozart (1756–1791): Austrian composer; Frédéric François Chopin (1810–1849): Polish pianist and composer. [Eds.]
[6]Maurice Ravel (1875–1937): French composer. [Eds.]
[7]Emil Post (1897–1954): Polish-born American mathematician. [Eds.]

716

be capable of being purely presented but can be stated as consisting in constructing even higher types. These are as transfinite ordinals, and the creative process consists in continually transcending them by seeing previously unseen laws that give a sequence of such numbers."

I stressed above the importance of the organization of memory and the press- 56 ing need to come at the question of what a concept is. Critical to the way our memory is organized is our automatic mode of storing and retrieving items, our knowledge of when we know and do not know. Such aspects of "metaknowledge" are fluidly integrated into the way our concepts are meshed. They are not some kind of "extra layer" added on top by a second-generation programmer who decided that metaknowledge is a good thing, over and above knowledge! No, metaknowledge and knowledge are simmering together in a single stew, totally fused and flavoring each other richly. That makes self-watching an automatic consequence of how memory is structure. How is this wondrous stew of antisphexishness realized in the human brain?

And how can we create a program that, like a human brain, is all "of a 57 piece," a program that is not simply a stack of ever higher "other-watchers" but is a genuine self-watcher, where all levels are collapsed into one? If we want to have a program that breaks out of the sphexish mold all programs seem to be in today, we have to figure out how a flexible perception program might exploit its own flexibility to look at itself. Of course, no such program will be written as I just stated. That is, it will not come into being in the following way:

Step 1. We write a flexible perception program.

Step 2. We turn that program back on itself as self-watcher.

Rather, in order to achieve the results desired in Step 1 we must have in- 58 corporated the goals of Step 2 into the design from the start; in other words, the two goals are intertwined, more in the following sense:

Goal 1. Flexible perception.

Goal 2. Self-watching.

There is no chronological priority here, because the two goals are too inter- 59 twined for the one to precede the other. It is a tricky foldback, more elaborate than the one involved in the halting problem, yet in spirit related to it.

It is interesting that Lucas' article was based on Gödel's theorem, whose proof 60 depends on making one of these seemingly impossible (or at least highly counterintuitive) foldbacks. In that proof a mathematical system of reasoning folds back on itself and subsumes itself as an object of study. What is fascinating in the proof is how in such a system there is a kind of level-collapse that ensues from the ability of a system to see itself. Rather than there being towers of watchers, then towers of those towers and soon *ad infinitum*[8] in the worst possible kind of infinite regress, all those degrees and levels of self-perception

---

[8]*ad infinitum*: to infinity. [Eds.]

are achieved at once by the fact that the system can mirror itself. Not that it mirrors itself in every aspect, mind you; that would entail contradiction. It does do so, however, at all levels of complexity.

The apparently distinct levels of watcher and watched are totally fused in the 61 Gödel construction, exactly as Lucas would have them fusing in the minds of all conscious beings. The only thing Lucas failed to understand is that the ability to fold around and see oneself in the wonderfully circular Gödelian way does not—indeed cannot—bring with it *total* antisphexishness. That, fortunately or unfortunately, depending on your point of view, is a chimera.

Back in 1952 the philosopher and composer John Myhill wrote a lyrical 62 article titled "Some Philosophical Implications of Mathematical Logic: Three Classes of Ideas" (*The Review of Metaphysics*, Vol. 6, No. 2, pages 165–198; December, 1952). The three classes are borrowed from mathematical logic, and Myhill's names for them are the "effective," the "constructive" and the "prospective." In logic they are known more technically as the "recursive," the "renotrec" (short for "recursively enumerable but not recursive") and the "productive." Their essence is described as follows.

A category is "effective" provided there is a way, given a candidate for mem- 63 bership in the category, of deciding without any doubt whether or not that object is a member. Is Ronald Reagan Chinese? Is the Pope Catholic? Although the two questions are easy to answer and would seem to imply that being Chinese and being Catholic are examples of the effective, they are slightly misleading. Was Bruce Lee Chinese? Is an excommunicated bishop Catholic? Examples such as these show that the categories are not genuinely effective categories, but then nothing in the real world is as clean as it is in logic. I could have asked, "Is 29 prime?" but I wanted to show how these notions extend beyond the mathematical realm. In natural languages grammaticality (syntactic well-formedness) is a rather fuzzy property, but in an idealized language or formal system it would be a perfect example of an effective property.

We pass on the "constructive." A property that is constructive is more elusive 64 than one that is effective. The idea here is that there is some means whereby members of the category can be churned out one by one; and so you will eventually see any particular member if you wait long enough. At the same time there is no means for doing the complementary operation, namely churning out *non*-members one by one. Unfortunately, although this kind of set in mathematics is an extremely important one, easily definable examples of it are rather hard to come by. The set of all theorems in any formal axiomatic system is always recursively enumerable, but often its complement is too, which turns the set into an effective one rather than a constructive one. You have to be dealing with a formal system whose *non*-theorems are not themselves producible by some complementary formal system. Only then do you have a renotrec, or constructive, set. The set of theorems of any formalized version of number theory turns out (by Gödel's theorem) to have this property.

We finally come to the "prospective," also known as the "productive." My-   65
hill's characterization of it is: "A prospective character is one which we cannot
either recognize or create by a series of reasoned but in general unpredictable
acts." Thus it is neither effective or constructive. It eludes production by *any*
finite set of rules. Nevertheless (and this is important), it can be *approximated*
to a higher and higher degree of accuracy by a series of bigger and better sets
of generative rules. Such rules tell you (or a machine) how to churn out members of this "prospective" category. In mathematical logic, work by Alfred Tarski
and Gödel establishes that truth has this open-ended, prospective character.[9]
This means that you can produce all kinds of examples of truth—unlimitedly
many—but that no set rules is ever sufficient to characterize them all. The
prospective character eludes capture in any finite net.

As Myhill's prime example outside of mathematical logic of this quality he   66
suggests beauty. As he puts it: "Not only can we not guarantee to recognize it
(beauty) when we encounter it, but also there exists no formula or attitude, such
as that in which the romantics believed, which can be counted upon, even in
a hypothetical infinitely protracted life-time, to create all the beauty that there
is." Hence beauty admits of a succession of ever better approximations but is
never fully attainable. Beauty and irrationality are often linked. Is it coincidental
that the first example of such a notion of something approximatable but never
attainable in a finite process is called an "irrational" number?

If we see the aim of art as being the production of all possible objects of   67
beauty (which is doubtless an oversimplification, but let us adopt it nonetheless),
then each artist contributes objects in a particular style. That style is a product
of the artist's heredity and formation, and it becomes a hallmark. To the extent
that he has an individual style any artist is sphexish: trapped within invisible,
intangible boundaries of mental space. That is nothing to lament. Artists in
groups form movements or schools or periods, and what limits one artist need
not limit another. Therefore by the fact that its boundaries are wider a school
is less sphexish—more conscious—than any of its members.

But even the collective movement of a school of art has its limits, shows its   68
finitude, after a period of time. It starts to wind down, to lose fertility, to stagnate.
A new school begins to form. What no individual can make out clearly is
perhaps seen collectively, on the level of a society. Thus art progresses toward
an ever wider vision of beauty—a "prospective" vision of beauty—by a series of
repeated diagonalizations, that is, processes of recognizing ruts and breaking out
of ruts. As I like to put it, this is the process of "jootsing" (jumping out of the
system) to ever wider worlds. This endless jootsing is a process any single step
which *can* be formalized but whose totality (so says Gödel) *cannot* be formalized,
either in a computer or in any finite brain or set of brains. Hence one need not
fear that the mechanization of creativity, if ever it comes about, will mark the

---

[9]Alfred Tarski (b. 1920): Polish-born mathematician. [Eds.]

end of art. Quite the contrary: it is a day to look forward to, because on that day our eyes will open (as will those of computers, to be sure) onto entire new worlds of beauty. It will be a happy day when hand in hand with our new computer friends we take an unanalyzable leap out of the system and go get some more punch.

QUESTIONS

1. " 'Noncreative intelligence' is a flat-out contradiction in terms" (paragraph 6), says Hofstadter. How does he define *intelligence* and *creative?* What opposition to his view does he imagine?

2. How, according to Hofstadter, do concepts relate to intelligence? What is his image of a concept?

3. Define *sphexishness* and its opposite. What further examples of sphexish behavior can you suggest?

4. Why do we cultivate antisphexishness in ourselves? What is our attitude toward persons or things that seem to have too little of it?

5. What, on the other hand, is the relation of sphexishness to style? Is sphexishness, then, rather surprisingly, a "good thing"?

6. How much of this essay would you have outlined by outlining Hofstadter's development of those concepts—*sphexishness* and *antisphexishness?*

7. How does Hofstadter's way of escaping a bore function in this article? What turn does he make on it at the end?

8. Write a short paper on something mechanical as a way of illustrating an aspect of human behavior. You might write about a radio, a blender, a sewing machine, a bike— any object you know well. But you will really be writing about human beings, so your overriding challenge will be to decide when to put a stop to your analogy. Just how like a blender is the human mind, stomach, or heart?

THE HISTORICAL STRUCTURE OF SCIENTIFIC DISCOVERY

Thomas Kuhn

Thomas S. Kuhn (b. 1922) is a professor of philosophy at the Massachusetts Institute of Technology. His best-known book is The Structure of Scientific Revolutions *(2d edition, 1970). The following essay was abstracted, as his first note says, from its second chapter; the essay appeared originally in* Science *magazine in 1962. Other books of his include* The Essential Tension: Selected Studies in Scientific Tradition and Change *(1977) and* Black-Body Theory and the Quantum Discontinuity, 1894–1912 *(1978). He has made the process of scientific investigation his special subject; historians and philosophers of science are his chief audience.*

My object in this article is to isolate and illuminate one small part of what 1 I take to be a continuing historiographic revolution in the study of science.[1] The structure of scientific discovery is my particular topic, and I can best approach it by pointing out that the subject itself may well seem extraordinarily odd. Both scientists and, until quite recently, historians have ordinarily viewed discovery as the sort of event which, though it may have preconditions and surely has consequences, is itself without internal structure. Rather than being seen as a complex development extended both in space and time, discovering something has usually seemed to be a unitary event, one which, like seeing something, happens to an individual at a specifiable time and place.

This view of the nature of discovery has, I suspect, deep roots in the nature 2 of the scientific community. One of the few historical elements recurrent in the textbooks from which the prospective scientist learns his field is the attribution of particular natural phenomena to the historical personages who first discovered them. As a result of this and other aspects of their training, discovery becomes for many scientists an important goal. To make a discovery is to achieve one of the closest approximations to a property right that the scientific career affords. Professional prestige is often closely associated with these acquisitions.[2]

---

[1]The larger revolution will be discussed in my forthcoming book, *The Structure of Scientific Revolutions*, to be published in the fall by the University of Chicago Press. The central ideas in this paper have been abstracted from that source, particularly from its third chapter, "Anomaly and the Emergence of Scientific Discoveries" [2d ed., 1970].

[2]For a brilliant discussion of these points, see R. K. Merton, "Priorities in Scientific Discovery: A Chapter in the Sociology of Science," *American Sociological Review* 22 (1957): 635. Also very relevant, though it did not appear until this article had been prepared, is F. Reif, "The Competitive World of the Pure Scientist," *Science* 134 (1961): 1957.

Small wonder, then, that acrimonious disputes about priority and independence in discovery have often marred the normally placid tenor of scientific communication. Even less wonder that many historians of science have seen the individual discovery as an appropriate unit with which to measure scientific progress and have devoted much time and skill to determining what man made which discovery at what point in time. If the study of discovery has a surprise to offer, it is only that, despite the immense energy and ingenuity expended upon it, neither polemic nor painstaking scholarship has often succeeded in pinpointing the time and place at which a given discovery could properly be said to have "been made."

That failure, both of argument and of research, suggests the thesis that I now wish to develop. Many scientific discoveries, particularly the most interesting and important, are not the sort of event about which the questions "Where?" and, more particularly, "When?" can appropriately be asked. Even if all conceivable data were at hand, those questions would not regularly possess answers. That we are persistently driven to ask them nonetheless is symptomatic of a fundamental inappropriateness in our image of discovery. That inappropriateness is here my main concern, but I approach it by considering first the historical problem presented by the attempt to date and to place a major class of fundamental discoveries.

The troublesome class consists of those discoveries—including oxygen, the electric current, X rays, and the electron—which could not be predicted from accepted theory in advance and which therefore caught the assembled profession by surprise. That kind of discovery will shortly be my exclusive concern, but it will help first to note that there is another sort and one which presents very few of the same problems. Into this second class of discoveries fall the neutrino, radio waves, and the elements which filled empty places in the periodic table. The existence of all these objects had been predicted from theory before they were discovered, and the men who made the discoveries therefore knew from the start what to look for. That foreknowledge did not make their task less demanding or less interesting, but it did provide criteria which told them when their goal had been reached.[3] As a result, there have been few priority debates over discoveries of this second sort, and only a paucity of data can prevent the historian from ascribing them to a particular time and place. Those facts help to isolate the difficulties we encounter as we return to the troublesome discov-

---

[3]Not all discoveries fall so neatly as the preceding into one or the other of my two classes. For example, Anderson's work on the positron was done in complete ignorance of Dirac's electron theory from which the new particle's existence had already been very nearly predicted. On the other hand, the immediately succeeding work by Blackett and Occhialini made full use of Dirac's theory and therefore exploited experiment more fully and constructed a more forceful case for the positron's existence than Anderson had been able to do. On this subject see N. R. Hanson, "Discovering the Positron," *British Journal for the Philosophy of Science* 12 (1961): 194; 12 (1962): 299. Hanson suggests several of the points developed here. I am much indebted to Professor Hanson for a preprint of this material.

eries of the first class. In the cases that most concern us here there are no benchmarks to inform either the scientist or the historian when the job of discovery has been done.

As an illustration of this fundamental problem and its consequences, consider 5 first the discovery of oxygen. Because it has repeatedly been studied, often with exemplary care and skill, that discovery is unlikely to offer any purely factual surprises. Therefore it is particularly well suited to clarify points of principle.[4] At least three scientists—Carl Scheele, Joseph Priestley, and Antoine Lavoisier[5]— have a legitimate claim to this discovery, and polemicists have occasionally entered the same claim for Pierre Bayen.[6] Scheele's work, though it was almost certainly completed before the relevant researches of Priestley and Lavoisier, was not made public until their work was well known.[7] Therefore it had no apparent causal role, and I shall simplify my story by omitting it.[8] Instead, I pick up the main route to the discovery of oxygen with the work of Bayen, who, sometime before March 1774, discovered that red precipitate of mercury (HgO) could, by heating, be made to yield a gas. That aeriform product Bayen identified as fixed air (CO_2), a substance made familiar to most pneumatic chemists

---

[4]I have developed a less familiar example from the same viewpoint in "The Caloric Theory of Adiabatic Compression," *Isis* 49 (1958): 132. A closely similar analysis of the emergence of a new theory is included in the early pages of my essay "Energy Conservation as an Example of Simultaneous Discovery," in *Critical Problems in the History of Science*, ed. M. Clagett (Madison: University of Wisconsin Press, 1959), pp. 321–56. Reference to these papers may add depth and detail to the following discussion.

[5]Carl Wilhelm Scheele (1742–1786): Swedish chemist; Joseph Priestley (1733–1804): British chemist and clergyman; Antoine Laurent Lavoisier (1743–1794): French chemist. Pierre Bayen (1725–1798), mentioned at the end of the sentence, was a French chemist. [Eds.]

[6]The still classic discussion of the discovery of oxygen is A. N. Meldrum, *The Eighteenth Century Revolution in Science: The First Phase* (Calcutta, 1930), chap. 5. A more convenient and generally quite reliable discussion is included in J. B. Conant, *The Overthrow of the Phlogiston Theory: The Chemical Revolution of 1775–1789.* Harvard Case Histories in Experimental Science, case 2 (Cambridge: Harvard University Press, 1950). A recent and indispensable review, which includes an account of the development of the priority controversy, is M. Daumas, *Lavoisier, théoricien et expérimentateur* (Paris, 1955), chaps. 2 and 3. H. Guerlac has added much significant detail to our knowledge of the early relations between Priestley and Lavoisier in his "Joseph Priestley's First Papers on Gases and Their Reception in France," *Journal of the History of Medicine* 12 (1957): 1 and in his very recent monograph, *Lavoisier: The Crucial Year* (Ithaca: Cornell University Press, 1961). For Scheele see J. R. Partington, *A Short History of Chemistry*, 2d ed. (London, 1951), pp. 104–9.

[7]For the dating of Scheele's work, see A. E. Nordenskjöld, *Carl Wilhelm Scheele, Nachgelassene Briefe und Aufzeichnungen* (Stockholm, 1892).

[8]U. Bocklund ("A Lost Letter from Scheele to Lavoisier," *Lychnos*, 1957–58, pp. 39–62) argues that Scheele communicated his discovery of oxygen to Lavoisier in a letter of 30 Sept. 1774. Certainly the letter is important, and it clearly demonstrates that Scheele was ahead of both Priestley and Lavoisier at the time it was written. But I think the letter is not quite so candid as Bocklund supposes, and I fail to see how Lavoisier could have drawn the discovery of oxygen from it. Scheele describes a procedure for reconstituting common air, not for producing a new gas, and that, as we shall see, is almost the same information that Lavoisier received from Priestley at about the same time. In any case, there is no evidence that Lavoisier performed the sort of experiment that Scheele suggested.

by the earlier work of Joseph Black.[9] A variety of other substances were known to yield the same gas.

At the beginning of August 1774, a few months after Bayen's work had appeared, Joseph Priestley repeated the experiment, though probably independently. Priestley, however, observed that the gaseous product would support combustion and therefore changed the identification. For him the gas obtained on heating red precipitate was nitrous air (N_2O), a substance that he had himself discovered more than two years before.[10] Later in the same month Priestley made a trip to Paris and there informed Lavoisier of the new reaction. The latter repeated the experiment once more, both in November 1774 and in February 1775. But, because he used tests somewhat more elaborate than Priestley's, Lavoisier again changed the identification. For him, as of May 1775, the gas released by red precipitate was neither fixed air nor nitrous air. Instead, it was "[atmospheric] air itself entire without alteration . . . even to the point that . . . it comes out more pure."[11] Meanwhile, however, Priestley had also been at work, and, before the beginning of March 1775, he, too, had concluded that the gas must be "common air." Until this point all of the men who had produced a gas from red precipitate of mercury had identified it with some previously known species.[12]

The remainder of this story of discovery is briefly told. During March 1775 Priestley discovered that his gas was in several respects very much "better" than common air, and he therefore reidentified the gas once more, this time calling it "dephlogisticated air," that is, atmospheric air deprived of its normal complement of phlogiston. This conclusion Priestley published in the *Philosophical Transactions*, and it was apparently that publication which led Lavoisier to reexamine his own results.[13] The reexamination began during February 1776 and within a year had led Lavoisier to the conclusion that the gas was actually a separable component of the atmospheric air which both he and Priestley had previously thought of as homogeneous. With this point reached, with the gas recognized as an irreducibly distinct species, we may conclude that the discovery of oxygen had been completed.

But to return to my initial question, when shall we say that oxygen was

[9]P. Bayen, "Essai d'expériences chymiques, faites sur quelques précipités de mercure, dans la vue de découvrir leur nature, Seconde partie," *Observations sur la physique* 3 (1774): 280–95, particularly pp. 289–91. (Joseph Black [1728–1799]: Scottish physician and chemist. [Eds.])

[10]J. B. Conant, *The Overthrow of the Phlogiston Theory*, pp. 34–40.

[11]Ibid., p. 23. A useful translation of the full text is available in Conant.

[12]For simplicity I use the term *red precipitate* throughout. Actually, Bayen used the precipitate: Priestley used both the precipitate and the oxide produced by direct calcination of mercury: and Lavoisier used only the latter. The difference is not without importance, for it was not unequivocally clear to chemists that the two substances were identical.

[13]There has been some doubt about Priestley's having influenced Lavoisier's thinking at this point, but, when the latter returned to experimenting with the gas in February 1776, he recorded in his notebooks that he had obtained "l'air dephlogistique de M. Priestley" (M. Daumas, *Lavoisier*, p. 36).

discovered and what criteria shall we use in answering that question? If discovering oxygen is simply holding an impure sample in one's hands, then the gas had been "discovered" in antiquity by the first man who ever bottled atmospheric air. Undoubtedly, for an experimental criterion, we must at least require a relatively pure sample like that obtained by Priestley in August 1774. But during 1774 Priestley was unaware that he had discovered anything except a new way to produce a relatively familiar species. Throughout that year his "discovery" is scarcely distinguishable from the one made earlier by Bayen, and neither case is quite distinct from that of the Reverend Stephen Hales, who had obtained the same gas more than forty years before.[14] Apparently to discover something one must also be aware of the discovery and know as well what it is that one has discovered.

But, that being the case, how much must one know? Had Priestley come 9 close enough when he identified the gas as nitrous air? If not, was either he or Lavoisier significantly closer when he changed the identification to common air? And what are we to say about Priestley's next identification, the one made in March 1775? Dephlogisticated air is still not oxygen or even, for the phlogistic chemist, a quite unexpected sort of gas.[15] Rather it is a particularly pure atmospheric air. Presumably, then, we wait for Lavoisier's work in 1776 and 1777, work which led him not merely to isolate the gas but to see what it was. Yet even that decision can be questioned, for in 1777 and to the end of his life Lavoisier insisted that oxygen was an atomic "principle of acidity" and that oxygen *gas* was formed only when that "principle" united with caloric, the matter of heat.[16] Shall we therefore say that oxygen had not yet been discovered in 1777? Some may be tempted to do so. But the principle of acidity was not banished from chemistry until after 1810 and caloric lingered on until the 1860s. Oxygen had, however, become a standard chemical substance long before either of those dates. Furthermore, what is perhaps the key point, it would probably have gained that status on the basis of Priestley's work alone without benefit of Lavoisier's still partial reinterpretation.

I conclude that we need a new vocabulary and new concepts for analyzing 10 events like the discovery of oxygen. Though undoubtedly correct, the sentence "Oxygen was discovered" misleads by suggesting that discovering something is a single simple act unequivocally attributable, if only we knew enough, to an individual and an instant in time. When the discovery is unexpected, however, the latter attribution is always impossible and the former often is as well. Ignoring Scheele, we can, for example, safely say that oxygen had not been discovered

---

[14]J. R. Partington, *A Short History of Chemistry*, p. 91. (Reverend Stephen Hales [1677–1761]: British botanist and physiologist. [Eds.])

[15]phlogistic: from *phlogiston*, a New Latin coinage from the Greek word for inflammable, naming a substance formerly thought to escape when a material burns. Though a faulty theory, its investigation contributed to the discovery of oxygen. [Eds.]

[16]For the traditional elements in Lavoisier's interpretations of chemical reactions, see H. Metzger, *La philosophie de la matière chez Lavoisier* (Paris, 1935), and Daumas, *Lavoisier*, chap. 7.

before 1774; probably we would also insist that it had been discovered by 1774; probably we would also insist that it had been discovered by 1777 or shortly thereafter. But within those limits any attempt to date the discovery or to attribute it to an individual must inevitably be arbitrary. Furthermore, it must be arbitrary just because discovering a new sort of phenomenon is necessarily a complex process which involves recognizing both *that* something is and *what* it is. Observation and conceptualization, fact and the assimilationn of fact to theory, are inseparably linked in the discovery of scientific novelty. Inevitably, that process extends over time and may often involve a number of people. Only for discoveries in my second category—those whose nature is known in advance—can discovering *that* and discovering *what* occur together and in an instant.

Two last, simpler, and far briefer examples will simultaneously show how typical the case of oxygen is and also prepare the way for a somewhat more precise conclusion. On the night of 13 March 1781, the astronomer William Herschel made the following entry in his journal: "In the quartile near Zeta Tauri . . . is a curious either nebulous star or perhaps a comet."[17] That entry is generally said to record the discovery of the planet Uranus, but it cannot quite have done that. Between 1690 and Herschel's observation in 1781 the same object had been seen and recorded at least seventeen times by men who took it to be a star. Herschel differed from them only in supposing that, because in his telescope it appeared especially large, it might actually be a *comet!* Two additional observations on 17 and 19 March confirmed that suspicion by showing that the object he had observed moved among the stars. As a result, astronomers throughout Europe were informed of the discovery, and the mathematicians among them began to compute the new comet's orbit. Only several months later, after all those attempts had repeatedly failed to square with observation, did the astronomer Lexell suggest that the object observed by Herschel might be a planet.[18] And only when additional computations, using a planet's rather than a comet's orbit, proved reconcilable with observation was that suggestion generally accepted. At what point during 1781 do we want to say that the planet Uranus was discovered? And are we entirely and unequivocally clear that it was Herschel rather than Lexell who discovered it?

Or consider still more briefly the story of the discovery of X rays, a story which opens on the day in 1895 when the physicist Roentgen interrupted a well-precedented investigation of cathode rays because he noticed that a barium platinocyanide screen far from his shielded apparatus glowed when the discharge was in process.[19] Additional investigations—they required seven hectic weeks

11

12

---

[17]P. Doig, A *Concise History of Astronomy* (London: Chapman, 1950), pp. 115–16. (William Herschel [1738–1822]: German-born English astronomer. [Eds.])

[18]Anders Johan Lexell (1740–1784): Swedish astronomer. [Eds.]

[19]L. W. Taylor, *Physics, the Pioneer Science* (Boston: Houghton Mifflin Co., 1941), p. 790. (Wilhelm Konrad Roentgen [1845–1923]: German physicist. [Eds.])

during which Roentgen rarely left the laboratory—indicated that the cause of the glow traveled in straight lines from the cathode ray tube, that the radiation cast shadows, that it could not be deflected by a magnet, and much else besides. Before announcing his discovery Roentgen had convinced himself that his effect was not due to cathode rays themselves but to a new form of radiation with at least some similarity to light. Once again the question suggests itself: When shall we say that X rays were actually discovered? Not, in any case, at the first instant, when all that had been noted was a glowing screen. At least one other investigator had seen that glow and, to his subsequent chagrin, discovered nothing at all. Nor, it is almost as clear, can the moment of discovery be pushed back to a point during the last week of investigation. By that time Roentgen was exploring the properties of the new radiation he had *already* discovered. We may have to settle for the remark that X rays emerged in Würzburg between 8 November and 28 December 1895.

The characteristics shared by these examples are, I think, common to all the 13 episodes by which unanticipated novelties become subjects for scientific attention. I therefore conclude these brief remarks by discussing three such common characteristics, ones which may help to provide a framework for the further study of the extended episodes we customarily call "discoveries."

In the first place, notice that all three of our discoveries—oxygen, Uranus, 14 and X rays—began with the experimental or observational isolation of an anomaly, that is, with nature's failure to conform entirely to expectation. Notice, further, that the process by which that anomaly was educed displays simultaneously the apparently incompatible characteristics of the inevitable and the accidental. In the case of X rays, the anomalous glow which provided Roentgen's first clue was clearly the result of an accidental disposition of his apparatus. But by 1895 cathode rays were a normal subject for research all over Europe; that research quite regularly juxtaposed cathode-ray tubes with sensitive screens and films; as a result, Roentgen's accident was almost certain to occur elsewhere, as in fact it had. Those remarks, however, should make Roentgen's case look very much like those of Herschel and Priestley. Herschel first observed his oversized and thus anomalous star in the course of a prolonged survey of the northern heavens. That survey was, except for the magnification provided by Herschel's instruments, precisely of the sort that had repeatedly been carried through before and that had occasionally resulted in prior observations of Uranus. And Priestley, too—when he isolated the gas that behaved almost but not quite like nitrous air and then almost but not quite like common air—was seeing something unintended and wrong in the outcome of a sort of experiment for which there was much European precedent and which had more than once before led to the production of the new gas.

These features suggest the existence of two normal requisites for the beginning 15 of an episode of discovery. The first, which throughout this paper I have largely taken for granted, is the individual skill, wit, or genius to recognize that something has gone wrong in ways that may prove consequential. Not any and every scientist would have noted that no unrecorded star should be so large, that the screen ought not to have glowed, that nitrous air should not have supported life. But that requisite presupposes another which is less frequently taken for granted. Whatever the level of genius available to observe them, anomalies do not emerge from the normal course of scientific research until both instruments and concepts have developed sufficiently to make their emergence likely and to make the anomaly which results recognizable as a violation of expectation.[20] To say that an unexpected discovery begins only when something goes wrong is to say that it begins only when scientists know well both how their instruments and how nature should behave. What distinguished Priestley, who saw an anomaly, from Hales, who did not, is largely the considerable articulation of pneumatic techniques and expectations that had come into being during the four decades which separate their two isolations of oxygen.[21] The very number of claimants indicates that after 1770 the discovery could not have been postponed for long.

The role of anomaly is the first of the characteristics shared by our three examples. A second can be considered more briefly, for it has provided the main theme for the body of my text. Though awareness of anomaly marks the beginning of a discovery, it marks only the beginning. What necessarily follows, if anything at all is to be discovered, is a more or less extended period during which the individual and often many members of his group struggle to make the anomaly lawlike. Invariably that period demands additional observation or experimentation as well as repeated cogitation. While it continues, scientists repeatedly revise their expectations, usually their instrumental standards, and sometimes their most fundamental theories as well. In this sense discoveries have a proper internal history as well as prehistory and a posthistory. Furthermore, within the rather vaguely delimited interval of internal history, there is no single moment or day which the historian, however complete his data, can identify as the point at which the discovery was made. Often, when several individuals are involved, it is even impossible unequivocally to identify any one of them as the discoverer.

Finally, turning to the third of these selected common characteristics, note briefly what happens as the period of discovery draws to a close. A full discussion of that question would require additional evidence and a separate paper, for I have had little to say about the aftermath of discovery in the body of my text. Nevertheless, the topic must not be entirely neglected, for it is in part a corollary of what has already been said.

16

17

---

[20]Though the point cannot be argued here, the conditions which make the emergence of anomaly likely and those which make anomaly recognizable are to a very great extent the same. That fact may help us understand the extraordinarily large amount of stimultaneous discovery in the sciences.

[21]A useful sketch of the development of pneumatic chemistry is included in Partington, *A Short History of Chemistry*, chap. 6.

Discoveries are often described as mere additions or increments to the grow- 18 ing stockpile of scientific knowledge, and that description has helped make the unit discovery seem a significant measure of progress. I suggest, however, that it is fully appropriate only to those discoveries which, like the elements that filled missing places in the periodic table, were anticipated and sought in advance and which therefore demanded no adjustment, adaptation, and assimilation from the profession. Though the sorts of discoveries we have here been examining are undoubtedly additions to scientific knowledge, they are also something more. In a sense that I can now develop only in part, they also react back upon what has previously been known, providing a new view of some previously familiar objects and simultaneously changing the way in which even some traditional parts of science are practiced. Those in whose area of special competence the new phenomenon falls often see both the world and their work differently as they emerge from the extended struggle with anomaly which constitutes the discovery of that phenomenon.

William Herschel, for example, when he increased by one the time-honored 19 number of planetary bodies, taught astronomers to see new things when they looked at the familiar heavens even with instruments more traditional than his own. That change in the vision of astronomers must be a principal reason why, in the half century after the discovery of Uranus, twenty additional circumsolar bodies were added to the traditional seven.[22] A similar transformation is even clearer in the aftermath of Roentgen's work. In the first place, established techniques for cathode-ray research had to be changed, for scientists found they had failed to control a relevant variable. Those changes included both the redesign of old apparatus and revised ways of asking old questions. In addition, those scientists most concerned experienced the same transformation of vision that we have just noted in the aftermath of the discovery of Uranus. X rays were the first new sort of radiation discovered since infrared and ultraviolet at the beginning of the century. But within less than a decade after Roentgen's work, four more were disclosed by the new scientific sensitivity (for example, to fogged photographic plates) and by some of the new instrumental techniques that had resulted from Roentgen's work and its assimilation.[23]

Very often these transformations in the established techniques of scientific 20

---

[22]R. Wolf, *Geschichte der Astronomie* (Munich, 1877), pp. 513–15, 683–93. The prephotographic discoveries of the asteroids is often seen as an effect of the invention of Bode's law. But that law cannot be the full explanation and may not even have played a large part. Piazzi's discovery of Ceres, in 1801, was made in ignorance of the current speculation about a missing planet in the "hole" between Mars and Jupiter. Instead, like Herschel, Piazzi was engaged on a star survey. More important, Bode's law was old by 1800 (ibid., p. 683), but only one man before that date seems to have thought it worthwhile to look for another planet. Finally, Bode's law, by itself, could only suggest the utility of looking for additional planets; it did not tell astronomers where to look. Clearly, however, the drive to look for additional planets dates from Herschel's work on Uranus.

[23]For α-, β-, and γ-radiation, discovery of which dates from 1896, see Taylor, *Physics*, pp. 800–804. For the fourth new form of radiation, N rays, see D. J. S. Price, *Science Since Babylon* (New Haven: Yale University Press, 1961), pp. 84–89. That N rays were ultimately the source of a scientific scandal does not make them less revealing of the scientific community's state of mind.

practice prove even more important than the incremental knowledge provided by the discovery itself. That could at least be argued in the cases of Uranus and of X rays; in the case of my third example, oxygen, it is categorically clear. Like the work of Herschel and Roentgen, that of Priestley and Lavoisier taught scientists to view old situations in new ways. Therefore, as we might anticipate, oxygen was not the only new chemical species to be identified in the aftermath of their work. But, in the case of oxygen, the readjustments demanded by assimilation were so profound that they played an integral and essential role— though they were not by themselves the cause—in the gigantic upheaval of chemical theory and practice which has since been known as the chemical revolution. I do not suggest that every unanticipated discovery has consequences for science so deep and so far-reaching as those which followed the discovery of oxygen. But I do suggest that every such discovery demands, from those most concerned, the sorts of readjustment that, when they are more obvious, we equate with scientific revolution. It is, I believe, just because they demand readjustments like these that the process of discovery is necessarily and inevitably one that shows structure and that therefore extends in time.

QUESTIONS

1. State in your own words the principle Kuhn identifies at the end of paragraph 2.

2. Distinguish the two kinds of scientific discoveries Kuhn outlines in paragraphs 3 and 4. Which is the subject of this article?

3. Summarize the three characteristics of scientific discovery that Kuhn reviews in paragraphs 14 through 20.

4. Why does Kuhn spend so much more time on the discovery of oxygen than on the comet or x-rays? Would that first example have been sufficient in itself? Do all three examples contribute substantially to "the characteristics of scientific discovery" that Kuhn goes on to outline?

5. If a single word were to distinguish the scientific discoveries that most interest Kuhn, that word might be *process* (as paragraph 10 suggests). Describe an event you know well—a class, a game, a meeting, an accident—as if it were a process rather than a single event. How does your description of that process allow you to understand the event in a way you had not understood it before?

6. Seen from one point of view, the papers you write are events, too. You hand them in when due and get them back, graded, later. But in another sense, they are part of a process as well. Describe the process of the last paper you wrote. When did that process begin? What pattern did it take? What were the crucial moments, perhaps the turning points? And when can you say the process came to an end?

CAN SCIENTIFIC DISCOVERY BE PREMEDITATED?

P. B. Medawar

*Sir Peter Brian Medawar (b. 1915) is a British biologist.
He taught at Oxford University, the University of Birmingham, the University of London. He also was the director of
the National Institute for Medical Research. His scientific
papers concentrate in the fields of growth, aging, wound
healing, and transplantation. In addition, he has written
a number of books including* The Future of Man *(1960)*,
Induction and Intuition in Scientific Thought *(1969)*, Advice to a Young Scientist *(1979), and* The Limits of Science
*(1984), a book for the general reader from which this essay
was taken. In many of his writings he has reexamined "the
scientific method" and discussed its fusion of inductive and
deductive reasoning with more than a dash of intuition.*

INTRODUCTION

Most scientists in most countries are funded directly or indirectly by the [1]
public purse. This puts scientists with social consciences under a special obligation to "improve natural knowledge" (in the Royal Society's words) or to
procure that "advancement of learning" (in Bacon's). It is in this context that
the question which forms the title of this essay is especially relevant. It is not
rhetorical: I believe that it can be answered and that the answer has quite far-
reaching political implications. I shall begin by recounting, with telegraphic
brevity, three case histories of discoveries that could not possibly have been
premeditated—that could not have been the specific outcome of a conscious
and declared intention to make them. I shall then make some reference to the
role of luck in scientific discovery, and shall finally turn to the question of
whether our current understanding of how scientists make their discoveries is
compatible with the idea of premeditation.

CASE HISTORIES

X-rays.[1] Thanks to anesthesia and to the development of aseptic surgery by [2]
W. S. Halsted of Johns Hopkins and Berkeley George Moynihan of Leeds,

---

[1]This example, of the medical uses of X-radiography, was put into my head by my old teacher
Dr. John Baker, FRS [Fellow of the Royal Society] (1942), via a lecture by Sir John McMichael,
FRS.

731

surgery had progressed so far and so fast by 1900 that Moynihan opined that not much further progress was to be expected.[2] Yet surgery still had one serious handicap: the surgeon had to embark on his operation without knowing what to expect inside. There was an imperative need for some method of making human flesh transparent. Imagine now that a system of research funding such as that which prevails today were in operation in 1900 and imagine also the incredulous derision with which a research proposal "to discover a means of making human flesh transparent" would be greeted by any grant-giving body. Yet as we all know, just such a procedure was discovered by a man primarily interested in studying electric discharges in high vacua. The medical potentialities of Roentgen rays (X-rays) for what is now called diagnostic radiology were recognized almost immediately.

HLA polymorphism. Second, imagine now a contract open to tender to discover the genetic constitutions predisposing human beings to any of three grave debilitating diseases: ankylosing spondylitis, multiple sclerosis and the juvenile (insulin-dependent) form of diabetes. No degree of premeditation could solve such a problem, but it was in fact solved, in the following way: 3

It took only a few years for the promising and exciting research on tumor transplantation started by C. O. Jensen's discovery around 1900 of tumor transplantability to reach a state of unparalleled confusion, with mutually contradictory and unreproducible results. Some of the early research workers of the Imperial Cancer Research Fund even began to speak of "seasonal" influences on the transplantability of tumors—a sure sign that research had reached a low ebb. The reason, we now know, is that the early research workers used different animals for each experiment—they used the "white mouse," the "brown mouse," the "spotted mouse" and even the "Berlin mouse" and the "Tokyo mouse," on the—at that time—virtually universal assumption that uniformity of color or provenance assured uniformity of reactivity. It was as if a chemist were to estimate the solubilities and melting points of "white chemicals" or "blue chemicals," etc., in the expectation that uniformity of color implied uniformity of physiochemical properties. 4

Research continued in a state of almost total disarray until matters were taken in hand by Peter Gorer of Guy's Hospital and Dr. C. C. Little and his colleagues, notably George Snell, J. J. Bittner and Leonell Strong, at Bar Harbor, Maine. Snell and Gorer between them worked out the genetic basis of tissue transplantation in mice and identified the chromosome segment housing the genes responsible for it: In mice, these form MHC, the so-called major tissue-matching complex, H-2. 5

---

[2] Under the pseudonym "A Harley Street surgeon," Moynihan first expressed this view in *The Strand* magazine about 1900. He expressed it again in a publication of Leeds University Medical School in 1930 and yet again in his Romanes Lecture in Oxford University for 1932. See P. B. Medawar: *Pluto's Republic* (Oxford, 1982); pp. 298–310.

The work of Gorer and Snell made it possible for Dausset and others to   6
recognize and define the corresponding major tissue-matching system in man,
known as HLA. It is sometimes thought that the major importance of the
discovery of the HLA system was the facilitation of transplantation in man, but
in my opinion its real importance was to have brought to light a new system of
polymorphism in man—I mean a new system of stable genetic differentiation
in the human population—one that has made it possible to specify the genetic
constitutions predisposing their possessors to ankylosing spondylitis, multiple
sclerosis and insulin-dependent diabetes, in much the same way that membership in the different blood groups is associated in different degrees to the sus-
ceptibility to gastric ulceration and gastric cancer. There is no conceivable means
by which such a discovery could have been premeditated.

Nature of myasthenia gravis (MG).[3] Dr. Dennis Denny-Brown, a pupil and   7
colleague of England's most famous neurophysiologist, C. S. Sherrington, is
reputed to have been the first to draw attention to the similarity between the
symptoms of the creeping neuromuscular paralysis myasthenia gravis and the
symptoms of curare poisoning. This led directly to the use of anti-curare agents
such as eserine (physostigmine) for the melioration of myasthenia gravis. The
parallel surely implicates acetylcholine receptors of the postsynaptic muscle
membrane—the area of apposition of muscle and nerve—in the causation of
MG.
    To investigate this possibility, Lindstrom and his colleagues (Lindstrom, 1979;   8
Patrick and Lindstrom, 1973) decided to raise antibodies in rabbits against acetylcholine receptors.[4] Purified receptor protein from electric organs of eels was
accordingly injected into rabbits, with the dramatic result that in due course
they developed a flaccid paralysis whose similarity to myasthenia gravis was
confirmed by the way they perked up after the injection of a muscle stimulant
such as neostigmine.
    These and subsequent findings (Newsom-Davis *et al.*, 1978) may be said to   9
have corroborated the audacious hypothesis that myasthenia gravis is immu-
nologically self-destructive in origin, as Simpson (1960) had brilliantly conjectured. There are other pieces to this jigsaw puzzle: MG is known to be accompanied by pathological changes in the thymus, the most important lymphoid
organ in the body, which is often removed in the treatment of the disease. It is
therefore very relevant that Wekerle and his colleagues (1978) have shown that
embryonic precursors of muscle cells with well-formed acetylcholine receptors
may differentiate from cells residing in the connective tissue framework of the
thymus.

---

[3]For this example, I am indebted to a clinical lecture delivered in the Clinical Research Centre
(Harrow) by Dr. John Newsom-Davis (January 1980).
    [4]Acetylcholine is the chemical that causes a motor nerve impulse to initiate musclar contraction.

The special interest of these three examples is that although they represent 10 discoveries which could not possibly have been premeditated—and could not therefore have been the subject of a customer/contractor treaty—they were nevertheless made by the ordinary processes of scientific inquiry, grossly inefficient and cost-ineffective though such processes have been declared to be by people who have no deep understanding of the nature of scientific research. All three examples do, however, illustrate the cardinal importance of the state of preparedness of mind, which is the subject of the next section.

LUCK IN SCIENTIFIC DISCOVERY

Any scientist who is not a hypocrite will admit the important part that luck 11 plays in scientific discovery; this must always seem to be greater than it really is, because our estimate of its importance is inherently biased: We know when we benefit from luck, but from the nature of things, we cannot assess how often bad luck deprives us of the chance of making what might have been an important discovery—the discoveries we did not make leave no trace. I think, therefore, that there was really no need for one of the world's most distinguished neurophysiologists to refer to his "feeling of guilt about suppressing the part which chance and good fortune played in what now seems to be a rather logical development" (Hodgkin, 1976).

It might nevertheless seem as if the principal lesson to be drawn from the 12 three case histories I have just outlined is that luck plays a preponderant part in scientific discovery. I should like to challenge this view, for the following reasons having to do with the philosophy of luck:

We sometimes describe as "lucky" a man who wins a prize in a lottery at 13 long odds; but if we describe such an event as luck, what word shall we use to describe the accidental discovery on a park bench of a lottery ticket that turns out to be the winning one?

The two cases are quite different. A man who buys a lottery ticket is putting 14 himself in the way of winning a prize. He has, so to speak, purchased his candidature for such a turn of events and all the rest is a matter of mathematical probabilities. So it is with scientists. A scientist is a man who by his observations and experiments, by the literature he reads and even by the company he keeps, is putting himself in the way of winning a prize; he has made himself discovery prone. Such a man, by deliberate action, has enormously enlarged his awareness—his candidature for good fortune—and will now take into account evidence of a kind that a beginner or a casual observer would probably overlook or misinterpret. I honestly do not think that blind luck of the kind enjoyed by the man who finds a winning lottery ticket for which he has not paid plays an important part in science or that many important discoveries arise from the casual intersection of two world lines.

Nearly all successful scientists have emphasized the importance of prepar-   15
edness of mind, and what I want to emphasize is that this preparedness of mind
is worked for and paid for by a great deal of exertion and reflection. If these
exertions lead to a discovery, then I think it would be pejorative to credit such
a discovery to luck.

METHODOLOGY

Our present-day understanding of the methodology of science at bench or   16
shop-floor level (as opposed to, for example, Thomas Kuhn's theory of the role
of revolutions in the *history* of science) is something for which we are mainly
indebted to Professor Sir Karl Popper, FRS.[5] Popper's methodology is, I believe,
quite incompatible with the idea that scientific discovery can be premeditated.
Administrative high-ups in Washington and Whitehall firmly believe that scientists make their discoveries by the application of a procedure known to them
as the scientific method—the belief in which, considered as a kind of calculus
of discovery, is based on a misconception dating from the days of John Stuart
Mill's A *System of Logic* and Karl Pearson's *The Grammar of Science.*[6]

If such a method existed, none of us working scientists would be secure in   17
our jobs, for consider a research worker in an institute devoted to elucidating
the causes of and finding a cure for rheumatoid arthritis. If he fails to do so,
his failure could only be either because he did not know the scientific method,
in which case he should be sacked, or because he was too lazy or obstinate to
apply it, an equally valid reason for dismissal.

There is indeed no such thing as "the" scientific method. A scientist uses a   18
very great variety of exploratory stratagems, and although a scientist has a certain
address to his problems—a certain way of going about things that is more likely
to bring success than the gropings of an amateur—he uses no procedure of
discovery that can be logically scripted. According to Popper's methodology,
every recognition of a truth is preceded by an imaginative preconception of what
the truth might be—by hypotheses such as William Whewell first called "happy
guesses," until, as if recollecting that he was Master of Trinity, he wrote "felicitous strokes of inventive talent."[7]

Most of the day-to-day business of science consists in making observations   19
or experiments designed to find out whether this imagined world of our hypotheses corresponds to the real one. An act of imagination, a speculative adventure, thus underlies every improvement of natural knowledge.

---

[5]Sir Karl Popper (b. 1902): British philosopher. [Eds.]
[6]John Stuart Mill (1806–1873): British philosopher and political theorist whose book A *System
of Logic* appeared in 1843; Karl Pearson (1857–1936): British philosopher of science whose book
The Grammar of Science has been reprinted often since it first appeared in 1892. [Eds.]
[7]William Whewell (1794–1866): British philosopher and historian. The Trinity College mentioned is at Cambridge. [Eds.]

It was not a scientist of a philosopher but a poet who first classified this act [20] of mind and found the right word to describe it. The poet was Shelley[8] and the word, *poiesis*, the root of the words "poetry" and "poesy," and standing for making, fabrication or the act of creation.

With this wider sense of the word in mind, Shelley roundly declared in his [21] famous *Defence of Poetry* (1821) that "poetry comprehends all science," thus classifying scientific creativity with the form of creativity more usually associated with imaginative literature and the fine arts. What is more to the point is that Shelley went on to assert: "A man cannot say I *will* write poetry . . . the greatest poet even cannot say it."

No more, I submit, can a scientist say I *will* make a scientific discovery; the [22] greatest scientist even cannot say it.

SUMMARY AND CONCLUSIONS

I began this essay with three case histories of discoveries that could not [23] possibly have been premeditated and that could therefore never have been the subject of customer/contractor treaties. I then went on to say that it would be injudicious to credit to luck the consequences of a conscious preparedness of mind. Finally, I argued that the modern conception of scientific procedure taken in conjunction with Shelley's conception of poetry is incompatible with the idea that scientific discovery could be premeditated. In short, I believe I should now be in a position to answer the question posed in the title: "Can scientific discovery be premeditated?" The answer is: "No."

REFERENCES

BAKER, J. R.
   1942. *The Scientific Life*. London: Allen & Unwin.
HODGKIN, A. L.
   1976. Chance and design in electrophysiology: an informal account of certain experiments on nerve carried out between 1934 and 1952. *J Physiol*. 263: 1–21.
KUHN, T. S.
   1979. *The Structure of Scientific Revolutions*. Chicago.
———.
   1978. *Essential Tension*. Chicago.
LINDSTROM, J.
   1979. Autoimmune response to acetylcholine receptors in myasthenia gravis and its animal model.
NEWSOM-DAVIS, J., A. J. PINCHING, ANGELA VINCENT, AND S. G. WILSON.
   1978. Function of circulating antibody to acetylcholine receptor in myasthenia gravis: investigation by plasma exchange. *Neurology* 28: 266–72.

[8]Percy Bysshe Shelley (1792–1822): English poet. [Eds.]

PATRICK, J., AND J. LINDSTROM.
    1973.   Autoimmune response to acetylcholine receptor. *Science* 180: 871–72.
PEARSON, KARL.
    1892.   *The Grammar of Science.* London.
POPPER, K. R.
    1959.   *The Logic of Scientific Discovery.* London.
SIMPSON, J. A.
    1960.   Myasthenia gravis: a new hypothesis. *Scottish Medical Journal* 5: 419–35.
WHEWELL, WILLIAM.
    1840.   *The Philosophy of the Inductive Sciences.*

QUESTIONS

1. How does Medawar distinguish between luck and blind luck? Explain the difference in your own words.

2. What is "preparedness of mind" (paragraph 15), and how does that contribute to luck?

3. What does Shelley's remark, quoted in paragraph 21, mean? How does Shelley's view relate to the question about scientific discovery?

4. Reread Medawar's first and last paragraphs. How do they function in this essay? In what ways do they define his purpose and audience?

5. Describe a situation when your preparedness made luck possible for you. How closely does your experience correspond with Medawar's view?

6. Medaware argues that scientists cannot premeditate their discoveries and thus cannot, as is generally required, write funding proposals that outline anticipated results. Based on Medawar's argument, propose another method of distributing the public funds earmarked for encouraging scientific discoveries.

WRITING SUGGESTIONS
FOR ARGUING

1. How does Ursula Le Guin's argument about fantasy in "Why Are Americans Afraid of Dragons?" relate to David Denby's and George Will's reactions to E.T.? How do Le Guin's arguments relate to your own reactions to E.T., Star Wars, Disneyland, or other popular versions of fantasy? Develop your own argument on this topic, taking account of positions represented by Le Guin, Denby, and Will.

2. Both Thomas Kuhn in "The Historical Structure of Scientific Discovery" and Lewis Thomas in "The Art of Teaching Science" suggest that we misperceive the nature and methodology of scientific work and thought. Write an essay comparing their two arguments. Which in your view goes further toward correcting this misperception? Why?

3. Ron Amundson ("The Hundredth Monkey Phenomenon"), Diana Baumrind ("Review of Stanley Milgram's Experiments on Obedience"), Stephen Jay Gould ("Evolution as Fact and Theory" and "Racist Arguments and IQ"), and Ruth Hubbard ("Test-Tube Babies: Solution or Problem?") all raise ethical questions arising from the nature of scientific work and argumentation. Choose two of these essays, and write a paper comparing and contrasting the issues raised by the writers.

4. Speaking broadly, you could say that both Nathan Glazer ("Some Very Modest Proposals for the Improvement of American Education") and John Kenneth Galbraith ("The Technostructure") argue that creativity and power come from deep within the system. And in a way Douglas R. Hofstadter ("On the Seeming Paradox of Mechanized Creativity") supports this view. Perhaps you notice another essay related to these three. Drawing on at least two essays, perhaps one of your own choosing, write an analysis of the location and role of creativity in a large organization or system.

5. Richard Robinson and Richard Taylor represent two sides of a debate concerning "reason" and "faith." Compare their positions with Stephen Jay Gould's argument in "Evolution as Fact and Theory." Write an essay considering how effectively one may "reasonably" argue against (or in favor of) "faith."

6. To what extent does the essay by Nathan Glazer play off of Swift's famous essay? In what ways are they similar? How do they differ? Given these similarities and differences, why do you think Glazer used the title he did?

7. Considering the cases Bettelheim discusses in "The Ignored Lesson of Anne Frank," whatever you know about the struggles of South African blacks, your knowledge of any other contemporary freedom movement, and the reasons Jefferson gives in The Declaration of Independence, write a general position paper on when, if ever, you find it proper to rebel. You may bring into this paper any other doctrine you like—political, religious, or moral—so long as you explain it clearly and relate its principles to your thesis.

8. Thomas Jefferson opens The Declaration of Independence by stating directly the "self-evident" "truths" upon which his argument will be based. In fact, every argument depends on an appeal to certain unquestioned values, to a body of "truths" that the

writer assumes the audience accepts (although not every writer states these "truths" as explicitly as Jefferson). Consider three essays, perhaps one from each subsection of "Arguing" (such as George Will's "Well, *I* Don't Love You, E.T.," Bruno Bettelheim's "The Ignored Lesson of Anne Frank," and Isaac Asimov's "The Case Against Man"). Try to determine in each case the values the writer assumes—not the views being argued but the accepted "truths" on which the argument depends. Write an essay in which you identify, discuss, and criticize the accepted truths that provide the basis for one or more of these arguments.

9. How much does the audience—or the writer's assumptions about the audience—affect argumentative writing? Select three essays from "Arguing" (perhaps Ursula Le Guin's "Why Are Americans Afraid of Dragons?" Nathan Glazer's "Some Very Modest Proposals for the Improvement of American Education," and P. B. Medawar's "Can Scientific Discovery Be Premeditated?"), and describe the ways in which these authors' presumed audiences seem to have shaped the essays. In each case, consider such matters as the presumed relationship between author and audience (friendly, hostile, or neutral; familiar or unfamiliar), the presumed interests of the audience (general or specialized), and so on. Consider also yourself as audience and the way your situation compares with that of the original audience. Write an essay that develops a thesis about the way that the author-audience relationship influences arguments or their effectiveness.

10. Has any one of the arguments in this section persuaded you to hold a view that you did not hold before you read the essay? Select the essay that you feel had the greatest effect on your own values or your own view of a particular situation. Do not pick the one you were most in agreement with before you read it. Pick the one that changed your mind the most. Try to explain exactly what caused the change. Was it reasoning? Examples? Emotional languages? Or what? Use your personal experience as a persuaded reader to develop a thesis about what sorts of things are actually convincing in argumentative writing. You may wish to bring in examples, including negative examples, from other essays in this section.

11. Select the essay from "Arguing" that you found the least convincing. Assuming that you are addressing the same audience, write a reply to that essay in which you attack its weak points and bring in any additional evidence that will help you argue your case.

12. Of the essays in this section that you have read, which do you consider the best argued? Which is the worst? Write an essay in which you try to substantiate both of these judgments (that is, make an effective argument for yor position), and from this, develop a thesis about what makes for good and bad argumentative writing.

13. Of the essays you have read in this section, which one do you think faced the most difficult problems in terms of the position being argued and the beliefs of the audience addressed? Discuss these problems and evaluate the author's attempts to solve them. Taking examples from other essays as well, develop a thesis about what makes an argument difficult to develop and what are the best solutions for such difficulties. You may also wish to consider the relationship between difficulty and the interest generated by any given essay.

Reading and Rereading

READING AND RESPONDING

Readers of the *New York Times* editorial page on September 23, 1967, would have encountered, along with several other editorials, the following featured article:

Dear Mr. ⑆0214⑉1063⑆ ⑈02⑉10730⑉8⑈

By E. B. WHITE

My bank, which I have forgotten the name of in the excitement of the moment, 1
sent me a warning the other day. It was headed: "An important notice to all our checking account customers." The burden of this communication was that I would no longer be allowed to write checks that did not bear the special series of magnetic ink numbers along the base.

My bank said the Federal Reserve System had notified them that it will not 2
accept for processing any checks that don't show these knobby little digits. For example, I would no longer be free to write a check on a blank form, because it would lack a certain magnetism that computers insist on.

Slightly Rheumatoid

I first encountered these spooky numbers a few years back and took a dislike 3
to them. They looked like numbers that had been run over by a dump truck or that had developed rheumatoid arthritis and their joints had swollen. But I kept my mouth shut, as they seemed to be doing me no harm.

Now, however, it appears that we are all going to knuckle under to the ma- 4
chines that admire these numbers. We must all forgo the pleasure and convenience of writing a check on an ordinary nonmagnetic piece of paper. My signature used to be enough to prod my bank into dispatching some of my money to some deserving individual or firm. Not any more.

This, I think, is a defeat for all—a surrender. In order to accommodate the 5
Federal Reserve System, we are asked to put ourselves out.

I Embarrass Easily

The notice I received says that if I try to palm off a check that lacks the magnetic   6
ink numbers, the check cannot be processed without "delay, extra handling charges,
and possible embarrassment." I embarrass easily—it doesn't take much, really—
and naturally I am eager to learn what form this embarrassment will take if I
should decide to write a check using the old blank form that has proved so convenient, for I don't know how many decades, on those occasions when one is
stuck without his checkbook or enough lettuce to carry the day.

"The tremendous increase in the use of checks," writes my bank, warming to   7
its subject, "made it necessary for the Federal Reserve to establish a completely
computerized operation for processing all checks from all banks. Their computer
can function only when proper magnetic numbers are used."

Well, I can believe that last part, about the computer requiring a special diet   8
of malformed numbers; but I am suspicious of that first statement, about how the
Federal Reserve would have been unable to carry on unless it went completely
over to machines. I suspect that the Federal Reserve simply found machines handy
and adventurous. But suppose we had had, in this country, a tremendous increase
in the use of checks before anybody had got round to inventing the computer—
what would have happened then? Am I expected to believe that the Federal Reserve
and all its members would have thrown in the sponge?

I know banks better than that. Banks love money and are not easily deflected   9
from the delicious act of accumulating it. Love would have found a way. Checks
would have cleared.

I'm not against machines, as are some people who feel that the computer is   10
leading us back into the jungle. I rather like machines, particularly the egg beater,
which is the highest point the machine has yet reached. I'm against machines
only when the convenience they afford to some people is regarded as more important than the inconvenience they cause to all.

In short, I don't think computers should wear the pants, or make the decisions.   11
They are deficient in humor, they are not intuitive, and they are not aware of the
imponderables. The men who feed them seem to believe that everything is made
out of ponderables, which isn't the case. I read a poem once that a computer had
written, but didn't care much for it. It seemed to me I could write a better one
myself, if I were to put my mind to it.

Time to Find Out

And now I must look around for a blank check. It's time I found out what   12
form my new embarrassment is going to take. First, though, I'll have to remember
the name of my bank. It'll come to me, if I sit here long enough. Oddly enough,
the warning notice I received contained no signature. Imagine a bank forgetting
to sign its name!

Obviously, reading this essay in a textbook for a course in English composition, as you have just done, is not quite the same as reading it in a daily
newspaper. Not only does the format—the layout, the page size, the typeface—

of a newspaper differ from that of a textbook, but the reasons we have for reading each and, consequently, the *way* we read will differ, as well.

Think for a moment, though, about the similarities between your reading of this essay here and now and someone's reading of it in the fall of 1967. First of all, both readings are based on recognizing and interpreting an arrangement of printed symbols, symbols most of us were familiar with long before we began to learn them systematically in the first grade. This aspect of reading is so elemental that you probably never stop to consider what a feat it really is. Second, both readings begin with the title and work their way sequentially through the final line of the text (though seeing the process as purely sequential is somewhat misleading; in fact, our minds ordinarily move back and forth, comparing what we read at one point with what we've read at others, as we work to make sense of the text). Third, both readings assume an active, rather than a passive, reader—someone who is responding to everything that White has to say. And responding in a variety of ways—pondering, questioning, nodding, gesturing, laughing, or growling, just to name a few of the reactions that might be provoked in a reader of White's piece.

The complexity of such reactions can be seen just by trying to imagine how one might read the title, "Dear Mr. 0214 1063 02 10730 8." The first two words are easy enough: we recognize them immediately as the conventional salutation of a business letter. We could even speak them aloud (taking into account that the unpronounceable *Mr.* is an abbreviated form of *Mister.*) But the following series of "knobby little digits" presents a more complicated problem. "What are they?" we might ask. "What do they mean? Even if we recognize them as the sort of figures that are printed at the bottom of a check, we cannot, in fact *read* them, because the markings between the numbers represent nothing in our language or our grammer. In fact, they are meant to be read not by human beings but by machines. Trying to read such a title, therefore, will set off any number of responses: perhaps an inkling of what White is up to ("Ah, a put-down of computer technology"), perhaps confusion ("I can't imagine what to make of this"), perhaps the desire to read on, and probably a less than fully articulated combination of several of these.

Next, the name of the author will create another round of responses. Perhaps you (and our imaginary reader of the *Times*) will be familiar with the name E. B. White and will associate it with *Charlotte's Web* or *Elements of Style* or a piece in *The New Yorker* magazine or something else you've read by White or know he wrote. You (and our imaginary *Times* reader) might respond positively ("I loved *Charlotte's Web*") or negatively ("I hate that *New Yorker* stuff") or less familiarly ("Is E. B. a man or a woman?"), but you will certainly have some response. This complicated sequence of responses, of course, occurs in just the second or two it takes you to comprehend the symbols on the page.

As you continue to read, you will continue to respond. Thoughts and impressions, no matter how tentative and ill-formed, will play through your conscious-

743

ness, and the closer your attention, the more these impressions will rise directly from the words you are reading. (You may even feel compelled to jot down some of these responses in the margin of the page.) Our minds can only make sense of the information we receive by testing this information against what we already know and feel. Such testing is a peculiarly human activity—at least we regard it as "human" when we observe it in other species—and only by allowing, even encouraging, ourselves to make these mental connections can we participate fully in the collaboration necessary to create meaning. Reading, as you probably realize, is a *transaction* that spans at least two human minds; reader and writer both must work actively for a meaningful transaction to take place.

If either participant fails to regard the human responsibilities of communication, the transaction will be unsatisfying. White provides a particularly unpleasant example of this: an impersonal letter, written not by a human being but by "a bank," has had an unsettling effect because it indicates to White the abrupt dehumanization of what was previously a human transaction. Readers can fail, as well, when they approach the transaction impersonally, when they ignore their personal reactions and responses, when they don't participate actively in examining and judging what they read. Such passivity is, of course, what impersonal writers hope for from their readers; the impersonal mask is calculated to discourage any questions or objections. Perhaps you have occasionally found yourself intimidated by such all-knowing bureaucratic pronouncements. The surest way to prevent yourself from being cowed ever again is to read inquisitively, ready to respond with all of your mind and all of your feelings to whatever you find in your reading, from the smallest detail to the text as a whole.

As we have said, your reading will always involve responses of some kind. The important step is to move from the responses themselves to a serious examination of them. To read White's reflections on his bank's warning and respond simply with "It's dumb" or "It's funny" or "I agree" or "I disagree" or the implacable "I can't relate to this" is not enough. Examining such responses will reveal a complex interaction between the structures of the text, the intentions and abilities of the writer, and what you as a reader bring to the text from your own experience. You may find White's essay "funny" because his treatment of his bank as a letter-writing entity that forgets to sign its name sets off a particularly exact set of images in your mind. You may "disagree" with White because you find his comment that the egg beater "is the highest point the machine has yet reached" to be overly flippant and because you think the computer's greater accuracy does in fact afford convenience to all. You may feel you "can't relate to" White's experience because you've never known checks *without* the magnetic code and because you've never received a similarly impersonal letter from a bureaucratic institution. Whatever the case, your responses will remain superficial and ill-formed until you examine them closely enough to explain them in detail.

Clearly, our own experiences will deeply affect our reading. Whatever we have seen or done or felt or heard, even the room we are in and our last meal, will contribute to a data bank from which our responses arise. Consider the following excerpt from the memoirs of Frederick Douglass (the complete chapter from which this was taken appears on pages 20–25). Born into slavery, Douglass managed to learn to read and at the age of twelve saved enough money—fifty cents—to buy his first book, *The Columbian Orator*. This was a popular school book containing speeches by famous orators and dialogues for students of rhetoric to practice and memorize. Here are Douglass's reactions to one of his readings:

> I was now about twelve years old, and the thought of being *a slave for life* began to bear heavily upon my heart. Just about this time, I got hold of a book entitled "The Columbian Orator." Every opportunity I got, I used to read this book. Among much of other interesting matter, I found in it a dialogue between a master and his slave. The slave was represented as having run away from his master three times. The dialogue represented the conversation which took place between them, when the slave was retaken the third time. In this dialogue, the whole argument in behalf of slavery was brought forward by the master, all of which was disposed of by the slave. The slave was made to say some very smart as well as impressive things in reply to his master—things which had the desired though unexpected effect; for the conversation resulted in the voluntary emancipation of the slave on the part of the master.
>
> In the same book, I met with one of Sheridan's mighty speeches on and in behalf of Catholic emancipation. These were choice documents to me. I read them over and over again with unabated interest. They gave tongue to interesting thoughts of my own soul, which had frequently flashed through my mind, and died away for want of utterance. The moral which I gained from the dialogue was the power of truth over the conscience of even a slaveholder. What I got from Sheridan was a bold denunciation of slavery, and a powerful vindication of human rights. The reading of these documents enabled me to utter my thoughts, and to meet the arguments brought forward to sustain slavery; but while they relieved me of one difficulty, they brought on another even more painful than the one of which I was relieved. The more I read, the more I was led to abhor and detest my enslavers.

Obviously, Douglass's experience as a slave determined his strong response to his reading. The words he read spoke directly to his condition, shaping his previously inexpressible desires and emotions into language. He was, of course, the perfect audience for Richard Brinsley Sheridan's "bold denunciation of slavery and powerful vindication of human rights." But had Douglass's master and mistress read the same speech, they might well have reacted in a strongly negative way, finding Sheridan subversive of their position as slave owners. They might have characterized his denunciation as "too bold" and his vindication of human rights as "wrongheaded" rather than "powerful." We might read Sheridan today and respond to his speech as an effective piece of eighteenth-century rhetoric or as an interesting historical document. On the other hand, if we have lived in places where human rights are greatly restricted, we might find Sheridan's speech as powerful and bold as Douglass did.

This does not mean, of course, that one's responses are limited to a strictly personal point of view. As we determine the basis for our most personal responses, we can begin to read with greater discipline and to think more systematically about what we read. First of all, we are able to realize that not everyone will have the same responses that we do. This, in turn, can help us recognize what may be limitations in our original responses, limitations imposed perhaps by our *lack* of experience ("Well, sure, I guess if I had been using blank checks all my life and got a letter like that out of the blue, threatening me with 'possible embarrassment' if I didn't start using the magnetically coded ones, I wouldn't have liked it very much either. But what's his point in making a joke of it?"). Opening up a text for ourselves will almost always mean moving beyond those important initial responses to asking ourselves implicit questions about what is being said, how it is being said, and why it is being said in this particular way.

Obviously, we can't fully comprehend what we are reading until we have read it once completely through. Not until we reach White's final line ("Imagine a bank forgetting to sign its name!") do all the various strands of thought that he has been pursuing begin to fall clearly into place. At this point a second reading (and maybe even a third or a fourth) will allow us to pay more attention to how a writer has presented the material because our curiosity has been satisfied as to what the text is about and we have a sense of it as a whole. In rereading it, we may discover points we have missed or misinterpreted; other of our experiences may begin to come to bear ("This is like that letter I got from the registrar's office informing me that from now on I'd have to have financial aid forms notarized and submit them with my term bill"). Consequently, our responses will be different, and we may significantly revise our initial reading. We can also begin in this second reading to question the text more closely to discover its intentions and its structure. This questioning may take a number of forms (which we'll be considering later in this discussion), but in all cases it's a good idea to write down your responses, beginning with those that arise during the initial reading. Writing helps us to think more clearly and deeply about what we read and to preserve our thoughts for further development.

ELEMENTS OF READING

Earlier we pointed out some basic similarities between reading E. B. White's "Dear Mr. . . . ." on the editorial page of the *New York Times* and reading the same essay in a textbook as an assignment for an English composition course. However, as you already know from experience, many elements of your reading can vary, depending on the situation. What you read and why you read will always influence the way you read.

For example, a *Times* buyer in the fall of 1967 would have read White's essay primarily for what we can call "pleasure." "Pleasure," of course, can take many forms: we may read for amusement, for escape, for intellectual discovery and stimulation, even to get angry or to make ourselves more depressed. But it's clear that we *choose* to do such reading because of a definite personal interest. No one is asking us to look for anything or remember anything. Ironically, though, we will often remember what we read for pleasure more clearly and more fully than what we read under pressure, because our minds are more relaxed. On such occasions, we have time to pause over a word or a phrase just because we like the sound of it or the feeling it expresses. So, while the pleasure that arises from personal interest may be our primary purpose for reading, we may also be assimilating new information, analyzing a particularly striking passage to understand how it works, or evaluating what a writer has to say, all because we enjoy what we are doing.

Douglas L. Wilson's account of his wide-ranging research into the origins of Robert Frost's famous poem "Mending Wall" ("The Other Side of the Wall," pages 598–600) provides a good example of this sort of reading. Personal experience leads Wilson to question prevailing interpretations of Frost's meaning. Intrigued, he begins to read biographies of the poet, then turns to letters Frost wrote during the poem's composition, even treatises on wall-building; he returns again and again to the poem itself. Bit by bit, Wilson arms himself with evidence that he hopes will substantiate his unorthodox analysis, his reevaluation, of the work. His purposes in doing such reading are obviously varied. Yet what links them together and, in fact, underlies them all is Wilson's intense personal interest, his *pleasure* in the task. Thoughtful, responsible, and truly responsive reading will always involve an element of personal interest.

Taking account of how you read for pleasure, then, can help you read more effectively in other situations; you can even use your personal reading to help you develop habits that will make you a better reader generally. One way is to take the time to make note of your immediate responses. For example, you may want to remember a particular piece of information or to hold on to a word or phrase that made an impression; to respond evaluatively, agreeing or disagreeing with what the writer has to say; or to explore responses that the writer has triggered. Begin to record such responses in writing. Keep a notebook handy to use as a journal of observations, information, and impressions. You can then refer to this journal for ideas to use in your own writing. Taking pleasure in working with new concepts and new information is an important step in becoming a better reader.

Reading in its broadest sense (as White's bank's computer *reads* his magnetic "code-name") always implies taking in information. We do so whenever and whatever we read. But grasping the most pertinent information in a text requires

747

that we read with an awareness of the author's purpose for writing. An author's primary purpose may be reflective, reportorial, explanatory, or argumentative. Each of these purposes entails a different kind or writing, and thus each calls for a somewhat different kind of reading, as we have shown in our introductions to the sections on "Reflecting," "Reporting," "Explaining," and "Arguing." For example, when we read White's argumentative piece about the computerized numbers on his checks, we must weigh the merits of competing ideas—of his antitechnological outlook versus the technological needs of the bank and its customers. But when we read "The Ring of Time" (pages 129–133), White's reportorial piece about his visit to a circus, we concern ourselves not with controversial issues but with the details of a particular scene and event. So, whenever you are assigned a piece of reading, you should try to determine the author's primary purpose as quickly as possible. Then you will have a better idea of what to focus on as you read and study the material for class discussions, paper assignments, or tests.

Whatever type of reading you are doing, in whatever field of study, you will generally be called upon to analyze, understand, memorize, and possibly evaluate the most important information and ideas that it contains. In order to sort out the most pertinent information and make sense of it for yourself, you will probably find it helpful to use a combination of the following methods.

(1) *Initial Reading.* Begin by reading the piece through from beginning to end primarily to get a quick overall sense of the author's subject, purpose, major ideas, and information. This initial reading is meant to help you get acquainted with the piece as a whole, so don't let yourself get bogged down in details as you make your way through the text. But don't hesitate to underline or check off what seem to be important (or puzzling) words, phrases, sentences, ideas, and points of information that you want to look into later when you examine the piece in detail. Once you have completed your initial reading of the piece, you should jot down a few notes about what you consider to be the gist of the piece—its major subject, purpose, points, and information.

(2) *Annotating.* After you have gathered the gist of the piece, then you should annotate the material for yourself. An annotation consists of explanatory notes. So if the piece contains words, names, titles of works, or other bits of information with which you are unfamiliar, you should consult a dictionary, encyclopedia, or other reference work, jotting down explanatory notes that you can use for future reference. This procedure will help you not only to understand the piece but also to expand both your vocabulary and your storehouse of general knowledge.

(3) *Outlining.* Once you have annotated the piece, then you may find it useful to make an outline of the material that it contains. An outline systematically lists the major ideas, points, and bits of information according to the order that they appear in the piece. The process of making an outline will help you to understand the piece more reliably and thoroughly than you can by simply

reading it over once or twice. And the outline itself will serve as an invaluable aid to remembering the piece at a later date, when you may want to draw upon it for a paper or examination. In preparing an outline, you might be tempted to rely entirely on your initial reading, underlinings, and notes. But just to make sure that your outline is reliable, you should read the piece carefully a second time with an eye to getting down the most important material in a form that is accurately worded and arranged. (For a sample outline, see the suggestions for discussion and writing that follow this section on pages 752–754.)

(4) *Summarizing.* Instead of outlining the piece, you may prefer to summarize it. A summary, like an outline, offers a highly condensed version of the most important material in a piece. But rather than casting the material in a lettered and numbered list, a summary calls upon you to write a paragraph of continuous prose in which you identify the major purpose, ideas, points, and information. The process of summarizing, like that of outlining, is a valuable aid to understanding a piece, and the summary itself will also serve as an aid to remembering the piece at a later date. The ability to summarize is an especially important skill in writing research papers, for they usually call upon you to condense material that you have read and integrate it into your own discussion. So you should try your hand at summarizing a few of the pieces that you read in this collection. (For a sample summary, see the suggestions for discussion and writing that follow this section on pages 753–754.) A special kind of summary, know as an *abstract*, is also customary in highly specialized professional journals, which require an author to provide a very brief summary at the beginning of an article for the convenience of readers. (For sample abstracts, see Antonio Damasio, "Two Reports on Prosopagnosia," page 525, or Daniel Tranel and Antonio Damasio, "Knowledge Without Awareness," page 533. See also the "Synopsis" that comes at the beginning of "Two Reports of an Airplane Crash," pages 238–249.)

(5) *Analyzing and Evaluating.* Instead of outlining or summarizing a piece, you may find it necessay to analyze and evaluate it, particularly if you need to understand it in detail. In order to analyze a text carefully and thoughtfully, we suggest that you read it over with several key questions in mind that you want to answer for yourself. Each of these questions, as you will see below, is designed to focus on a different aspect of the piece—its purpose, organization, evidence, implied audience, and use of language. In the following paragraphs, we will use White's "Dear Mr. . . . ." to show how you can analyze a text by asking and answering a set of questions about it.

What is the writer's purpose? White's immediate purpose is to describe his responses to the letter from his bank, ranging from personal annoyance to ironic evaluations of why a change should be required to a note of wry defiance. These personal reflections revolve around a more general and serious point, which he states fairly directly in paragraph 5 and again in paragraph 10: he thinks it is a "defeat," a "surrender" to allow machines to inconvenience "all" (and himself, in particular) for the sake of making life easier for a powerful few. Allied with this idea is White's belief that computers are "deficient" in the qualities which make us human and that, consequently, they should not be allowed to usurp human transactions (paragraph 11). His conclusion is a refusal to "knuckle under" to the dictates of such machines.

How does the writer organize his or her material? White's reflections are organized around the information contained in the letter he received from his bank. His title is an ironic version of the letter's salutation, and his concluding sentence refers to the lack of a closing signature. In paragraphs 1, 2, 6, and 7, he quotes from the letter, directly or indirectly, and goes on to offer his specific responses. Paragraphs 10 and 11 represent a new, more general direction of thought that grows out of his specific responses to the letter. Paragraph 12 returns to the letter and reinforces White's reactionary position on encroaching impersonality.

Does the writer provide evidence to back up the points he or she is trying to make? White is not offering a formal argument but a more personal consideration of his subject, so we would not expect "evidence" in the traditional sense. But, as his reflective structure would suggest, he does offer imaginative evidence and evidence based on personal experience, particularly in paragraphs 4 and 5, 8 and 9, and 11.

What are the writer's assumptions about his or her audience? White's essay was written for the *New York Times*, so he could assume that his readers would be a reasonably well-informed group, many of whom would have themselves received similar letters from their banks. Even so, he is careful to explain the change the bank is demanding as well as its practical effects. (A further question you might consider is whether the writer assumes his readers will be generally sympathetic with, antagonistic toward, or neutral about the ideas being raised. What would you say about White's assumptions?)

What kind of language and imagery does the writer use? White is responding to what he regards as a ridiculous letter with very serious implications. His language is resolutely informal and conversational; phrases like "spooky numbers," "kept my mouth shut," "palm off," "enough lettuce," and "wear the pants" can be contrasted to the kind of communication he is criticizing. Yet when he has a serious point to make (for example, that computers "are deficient in humor, they are not intuitive, and they are not aware of the imponderables"), his language becomes more formal. His images—particularly his personification of the bank as a letter-writing entity—are comic or wryly sarcastic, but, as with his language, they don't overwhelm his underlying seriousness.

In responding to questions such as these, a reader is able to take a piece of writing apart and examine its components to see how it works. In many situations, so careful an analysis won't be necessary: you would have little reason, for example, to analyze a comprehensive textbook in this way. However, analytical skill can be applied to a wide variety of activities and, in particular, can help a reader move beyond simply personal responses to a more systematic evaluation of a piece of writing.

Suppose that your initial response to the White essay was something like, "I enjoyed this; it was funny." A second analytical reading then helped you to understand the workings of the essay and how the tone and imagery contributed to your interest and appreciation. Further analysis of your own initial responses perhaps led you to realize that you share White's suspicion of computers and his subversive reaction to impersonal, bureaucratic pronouncements. This, in turn, has given you a sense of how others, who do not particularly share your views, might respond. Now you may develop a more systematic evaluation of the essay, using topics like the following to assess or judge the essay.

Purpose. White has succeeded well in presenting his own reactions with wit and grace. His conversational tone and his wry imagery allow a reader to sympathize with his very human rebellion against being inconvenienced because of the requirements of a machine.

Organization. Organizing his essay around the letter he received from his bank is an effective way for White to move from his specific responses to his more general considerations about the relationship between technology and human life. This organization also leads him to his important central image of a bank that forgets "to sign its name."

Evidence. Because White is relating his responses rather than arguing a position, the personal evidence he presents (the inconvenience the new rules will cause him, the computer-composed poem, etc.) is sufficient to communicate aptly and forcefully his reason for feeling the way he does. What White's evidence does not do, however, is to convince us that carrying checks with the magnetic code is a terrible inconvenience. White simply assumes that his reader will agree. Consequently, his general comments on computer technology—particularly from the perspective of almost twenty years—don't carry the weight they might.

Summary. White's essay is an entertaining and thought-provoking reflection on what it's like to be told to modify old habits in order to conform to the dictates of new technology. The personality of the writer, the grace and cleverness of his expression, and the clarity of his design engage the reader's attention and sympathy. Although we may not immediately agree with the specific basis for his objections or with his underlying argument, we can't help but be persuaded by his sincerity, skill, and good sense that his position is admirably and sanely humane.

This, of course, is only the beginning of only one evaluation. These notations—or another set that might be entirely contradictory—could be expanded and developed into an evaluative essay that presented reasons and evidence based on further research, perhaps into other essays by White or studies of computerized banking. Such an essay might be highly supportive (as our sample summary would indicate) or highly critical ("Though White's essay is very clever, the subversive point of view he expresses here is just a few steps from anarchy"), or it might take an intermediate position. It might concentrate on the consequences of the writer's ideas or the success of the writer's methods or some combination of the two.

As you may already have begun to realize, becoming a more astute reader can lay the groundwork for becoming a more effective writer. The more reading we do—the more we understand our role as a reader—the more we learn about what it means to be an audience. By paying attention to our responses, by examining them in order to analyze and evaluate what we read, we can begin to see more clearly *why* we feel well or poorly treated by a writer. Transferring such knowledge from our own experience as an audience to the audience for whom we are writing, we become more aware of what that intended audience will require. We become more concerned about the appropriate tone to take, about what does and doesn't need to be said about a topic, given our purpose, and we have a better idea of the organization necessary to gain and hold our audience's interest and bring our work to a satisfactory conclusion. We realize more fully the transaction that must take place, and how we as writers can encourage a reader to collaborate in the making of meaning. In "Writing and Rewriting" we will consider this subject in more detail.

SUGGESTIONS FOR DISCUSSION AND WRITING

1. Choose something you ordinarily read for pleasure (a particular magazine, for example, or the sports pages or the liner notes of a new record album). Once you are finished reading it, take a few minutes to record your responses in writing. Then annotate it, outline or summarize it, and finally analyze and evaluate it. What have you discovered about this reading material by examining it in these ways? You might find it interesting to share your reactions to this reading experiment with other members of your class.

2. Prepare an outline of one of the following pieces in this text: Martin Luther King, Jr., "Pilgrimage to Nonviolence"; Barbara Tuchman, " 'This is the End of the World': The Black Death"; E. H. Gombrich, "Art for Eternity"; Susanne K. Langer, "The Culture Importance of Art"; Susan Fraker, "Why Women Aren't Getting to the Top"; Stephen Jay Gould, "A Biological Homage to Mickey Mouse"; Edwin Diamond, "Twelve

Days of Terror! The Three Mile Island Story"; Lucy Gilbert and Paula Webster, "The Dangers of Femininity." (Your instructor may have other suggestions.)

Following is a sample outline of X. J. Kennedy's "Who Killed King Kong?" Before you examine this outline, you should read Kennedy's piece yourself, and make your own outline of it. Then compare your outline with ours, noting the most important points at which they are similar and different. You might also find it interesting to compare your outlines with outlines made by other members of your class, again noting the most important points at which they are similar and different.

An outline of X. J. Kennedy's "Who Killed King Kong?" (pages 269–273)

I. No other monster movie has won so devoted a popular audience as *King Kong*, as seen in the following evidence:
  A. Its continued appeal at movie houses twenty-five years after release, even in badly worn prints.
  B. Its ability in TV reruns to lure viewers away from some of the most popular TV entertainers.
  C. Its success in being rerun more often than any other monster movie.

II. Though its popularity is partly attributable to its many violent and sadistic elements, its continuing appeal must be the result of other more compelling and significant elements, such as the following:
  A. King Kong himself has the attraction of being a manlike creature with whom the audience can easily identify.
  B. Kong is also depicted as a pitiable monster in chains, and thus he appeals to our concern for the plight of the animal spirit within us that is forced to live in an alien world of machines.
  C. Kong, though violent in his actions, "remains a gentleman," as evidenced by his unwaveringly gentle, loving, and chivalric treatment of the lady whom he pursuses unsuccessfully throughout the movie.

III. Thus King Kong's tragedy is to be the noble beast who goes unrewarded. In this way, Kong appeals to our deepest instincts in two interrelated ways:
  A. He gives expression to our desire to rebel against, even to destroy, our machine-ridden world.
  B. Yet his calamitous ending also bears witness to our recognition that we must repress our primordial instincts and thus must "kill the ape within our bones."

3. Choose one of the essays listed above (or another that your instructor suggests), and write a summary of it. Again, we have provided a sample based on Kennedy's essay. Before you examine this summary, you should make your own summary of the piece, so that you can compare yours with ours and with those of your classmates.

A summary of X. J. Kennedy's "Who Killed King Kong?" (pages 269–273)

Kennedy's intention is to account for the extraordinary popularity of the movie *King Kong*. As evidence of its being the most popular monster movie ever made, Kennedy notes that *King Kong* has been rerun more than any other such movie, yet it continues to draw large audiences both at movie houses and on TV. Though Kennedy concedes that the movie's violence and sadism account for part of its appeal, he believes that its continuing popularity must be the outcome of more compelling and significant elements. In particular, he notes that King Kong himself is depicted as manlike, so that audiences can easily identify with him. Further, he observes that King Kong is portrayed as a pitiable monster in chains, thereby giving expression to our own sense of being trapped in an alien world of machines. Finally, he points out that Kong, though violent in his actions, is shown to be an unwavering gentleman in his treatment of the lady whom he pursues unsuccessfully throughout the movie. Thus King Kong's tragedy is to be a noble beast who goes unrewarded, and in this way he gives expression to our own paradoxical situation—our desire to express the animal spirit within us by rebelling against our machine-ridden world, yet our civilized recognition that we must "kill the ape within our bones."

4. Suppose you were doing research on the subject of how college English textbooks treat the subject of reading. Summarize portions of this appendix that might be pertinent.

5. Return to E. B. White's "Dear Mr. . . . ." and attempt first to outline and then to summarize his essay. Note any particular difficulties you may have. How does the form of White's reflective essay contribute to these difficulties?

6. Choose one of the readings in this text for a careful written analysis. Begin by jotting down your responses to your initial reading. Then consider the questions for analysis that follow. You may, as well, want to prepare an outline or summary as a means of analyzing the writer's methods.

a. What was the writer's purpose for writing? That is, what did the writer set out to show, to explain, to prove, to reflect on?

b. How did the writer organize the material? Does the organization reflect the purpose for writing? Was the arrangement of material easy for the reader to follow?

c. Does the writer provide evidence to back up the points he or she is making? Here you should look for any sweeping general statements without evidence to back them up or reasons why we should accept them.

d. What kind of diction is used? Here you would look for language that is too formal or too informal or for imagery and metaphor that help to convey meaning.

e. What are the writer's assumptions about his or her audience? Such assumptions would include a sense of the level of intelligence of the audience and an awareness of what general knowledge about the topic the audience might have.

After this preparation, write an essay of your own in which you analyze the essay you have read.

7. Based on the suggestions outlined on page 751, prepare an evaluation of the reading you analyzed in question 6 above or another reading in this text. After this preparation, write an essay in which you evaluate this reading.

Writing and Rewriting

As we discussed in "Reading and Rereading," expressing your ideas will often begin with recording your most immediate responses, jotting them down on a pad, in a journal, or in the margin of a book. Clearly such jottings are not intended for a reader. You may be surprised to realize, however, that with thought and care and concern for an eventual audience, even the sketchiest notes can evolve into a significant, controlled piece of writing. This process of development and revision is rarely apparent when we read: all we see is the finished product, the piece of writing in its final form. But the polished work that is presented to an audience may, in fact, barely resemble what the writer started out with.

E. B. White didn't simply sit down the afternoon he received the warning from his bank and allow "Dear Mr. . . . ." to flow out onto a page (if you haven't yet read White's essay, you'll find it at the beginning of "Reading and Rereading," page 741). The letter sparked a response, however—a sense of injustice, of annoyance at the threat of "embarrassment" and concern about the effects of technology—and White realized that here was at least the germ of an essay that might eventually find its way into print, earning him a bit of money and the satisfaction of reaching an audience with his concerns. His first thought, though, was merely to provide himself with a rough rendering of his immediate response. Consequently, his original notes (which we include below) do little more than sketch out his basic intentions and establish a point of view.

I seldom carry a checkbook
because I like to travel light
But I always have money
in the bank (it is an
old habit of mine that
I cant seem to break)
and I feel that I should
be free to dispense this
money without any
embarrassment to myself.
Now, because of the Federal
Reserve's Knuckling under,
I will not be privileged to
write a blank check.

The ~~only most~~ danger in a
machine culture is that ~~it~~
in the enjoyment of
the convenience of machines,
~~will to~~ we ~~soon~~, will ~~ ~~ overshadow
their disadvantages to others

The danger in a machine
culture is not that ~~machine~~
~~will take over our thinking~~
~~and dominate the our lives~~, but
~~that men, who~~ the convenience
of machines may come to
overshadow the losses we suffer
~~from their~~ by reason of their
peculiar requirements.

Computers free the Federal
Reserve from arduous and
voluminous ~~and~~ operations in
clearing checks. But in so
doing they deprive the ^narrow^
consumer's of ~~but the privilege~~ ^right^
of instructing his bank in
a casual, agreeable manner

The man who foresaw all
this was a man named
Orwell. and he foresaw
pretty good. If were
not careful. we may
wake up some morning
and find that what he
predicted has come to
pass.

White's notes bear almost no resemblance to his polished final draft as it appeared in the *New York Times*. We see White beginning with his immediate personal response—his desire to dispense his money without any embarrassment or inconvenience to himself—and then moving on to generalize, to expand his annoyance over the particular letter to the larger issue of "the danger in a machine culture." Thus, he establishes the meaning and purpose that will govern his final essay. But there is little attempt to formulate a coherent design at this point. In fact, it is almost comforting to see how messy these initial notes are, when we realize what they will provide the foundation for.

Even as White is scribbling notes to himself, however, with little concern for coherence and the needs of his eventual reader, he is his own critic. He is listening to himself as he writes, thinking about how his words go together, and revising when he's not quite satisfied. He has, for example, reworked the sentence about "the danger in a machine culture" several times, trying to get it right (although, as we'll see in his subsequent drafts, this central idea would continue to give him trouble). But he is not particularly concerned with correctness; for instance, he lets stand a sentence like "The man who foresaw all this was a man named Orwell, and he foresaw pretty good." No sentence like this will, in fact, appear in the final draft, but what White seems to be after here is a kind of aptness. Orwell is a touchstone for the writer's ideas, a way of getting at what he wants to say and finding the words to generalize about his particular situation.

Based on these very rough notes, White typed a first draft, onto which he wrote in further revisions:

which I don't often do but which I
consider a great convenience in
certain circumstances.

My bank, which I have forgotten the name of
in the excitement of the moment, sent me a ~~notice~~ warning the other
day. It ~~read~~ worded: "An important notice to all our checking account
customers." The burden of this communication was ~~this~~ that
~~the Federal Reserve System~~ I would no longer be allowed to
write
~~submit~~ checks that did not bear the special series of
"magnetic ink numbers" along the base. ~~Then~~ My bank said ~~that~~
the Federal Reserve System had notified them that it will not
accept for processing any checks that don't bear these curious   form
numbers. (~~Inxix~~ (I've never been very fond of these numbers, since
For example, I would not be allowed to write a check on a blank
I first laid eyes on them---they look to me kike numbers that
have been ~~run over~~ backed into by a dump truck, or have developed rheumatoid
                                                    that   joints   although the numbers do not
arthritis, and their knuckles have swollen. But, I have kept my
mouth shut, until now.) Now it appears that we are going
to knuckle under to machines, and that I am no longer privilegd
                                                              spooky
to write a check on a blank form, because it lacks these ~~little ones~~
                                                         (or mankind)
little ~~numbers~~ digits. This, I thinkm is a defeat, a surrender. (
It was a clear alternative = whether to accommodate bank customers
I plan to go on ~~wxix~~ instructing ~~bank~~, and I can't think of it
name, to dispense my money in the way I want it dispensed, witjout
any reference to magnetic ink numbers. I will be ~~very~~ interested t
                        by letter, then write blank checks, or whether, to
to see what gappens.   accommodate the Federal Reserve.
            The notice I received says that if I try to
palm off   the check
~~put over~~ a check that lacks the magnetic ink numbers, it cannot
be processed without "delay, extra handling charges, and possible
embarrassment."   I am

2/

rather easily embarrassed---it doesn't take much----and I would like ~~am~~ *of course* *eager*
to ~~know~~ *learn* what form this embarrassment is going to take if I should
decide to write a check using the old blank form that has proved
so convenient for I don't know how many decades, when one is stuck
without one's checkbook or enough lettuce to carry the day.
          The reason given by my bank for this tightening
of its service is ~~that~~ this: "The tremendous increase in the use of
checks made it necessary for the Federal Reserve to establish a
completely computerized operation for processing all checks from all
banks. Their computer can function only when proper magnetic numbers
are used." *Well, I can believe that last* ~~Ixxxxxxxxxxxxxxx~~ part, about the computer requiring
a special diet of funny numbers, ---this I can believe. But I am
suspicious of that first statement, about how the Federal Reserve
would have been unable *had gone over*
cou dn't carry on unless it went over to machines. I think the truth
is ~~itxfxxxxxx~~ the Federal Reserve found *and adventurous* machines handy, and that's
why it went over to them. *But* *we had had, in this country* Suppose there had been a tremendous increase
in the use of checks but *and nobody had got round to inventing the computer* the computer hadn't been invented---what would
h ve happened then? Would ~~banking~~ banks have ~~given up~~ *Wuld the Federal Reserve system have collapsed from exhaustion*
thrown in the sponge? I know banks better than that---they would *and adventure helps*
have cleared those checks ~~if they had to employ retarded children~~ to
Banks love money. and they are not easily deflected from accumulating it.
~~Sxxdavxyxxxxxxvxxxxxxxxxxxxxx~~
Come to think it, I love money, too. I am a lifelong checking account
patron and have had to be ~~txxxxxxx~~ extremely thrifty because of my
refusal to balance my checkbook in the space on the left where you
are supposd to keep track of what you've been spending and depositing.
I've never done that, on the theory that it is a waste of time--also
I don't add good, *n subtract good* and my figures would be *misleading* ~~deceptive~~ because inaccurate.
Instead, I practice thrift and never know my balance until I receive *my*
in the days before machines
statement. Speaking of bank statements, mine used to arrive the first

3

of the month and was legible and decipherable and coherent. Now,
since machines have taken over, it arrives anywhere from the
                                              largely
first of the month to the eighth of the month, and is indecipherable,
except to a man hell bent on deciphering something.

The notice

To get back to the warning from my bank, it ended:
"So remember...be sure to use only your own personal checks with
pre-encoded magnetic ink numbering. It takes both your account
number and your signature for your check to clear properly. Thank you
very much."

This step from notes to first draft is significant: the essay is actually beginning to take shape here. White has used the letter from his bank to provide an opening and conclusion, but you'll note that he hasn't yet discovered the precise design that will allow his finished work to revolve around this letter. In fact, he has to wrench his attention back to the letter in the final paragraph, after a digression about his bank statement and balancing his checkbook. Nor has he quite developed the important image of the bank as a letter writer (although he *has* begun to personify the bank in his opening sentence and later on when he writes, "Banks love money . . ."; and he has also—perhaps for very practical reasons—assumed the pose of not being able to remember his bank's name). The idea about "the danger in a machine culture," which he struggled with in his original notes, appears here in a quite different form—a specific reference to the bank accommodating the Federal Reserve rather than customers—and, consequently, the incident has not yet been fully generalized.

Again, though, White is his own critic. The draft is messy and chewed over, with typed emendations as well as handwritten ones. Some of these changes seem to show White trying to capture fleeting thoughts, slapping them down on paper, as he did in his notes, to save and cull from later on. Others are based on his concern for how an audience will respond (the deletion of the line about banks employing "retarded children" is a good example), while still others are "improvements," revisions of vocabulary and syntax to clarify meaning or create more graceful, forceful expression.

In his second draft, White continues to revise, to tighten his structure and refine his language.

My bank, which I have forgotten the name of in the excitement of the moment, sent me a warning the other day. It was headed: "An important notice to all our checking account customers." The burden of this communication was that I would no longer be allowed to write checks that did not bear the special series of magnetic ink numbers along the base. My bank said the Federal Reserve System had notified them that it will not accept for processing any checks that don't show these knobby little digits. For example, I would no longer be free to write a check on a blank form, because it would lack ~~the~~ a ~~magnetic numbers~~ certain magnetism that computers insist on.

I first encountered these spooky numbers a few years back and took a dislike to them. ~~The~~ They looked like numbers that had been run over by a dump truck, or that had developed rheumatoid arthritis and their joints had swollen. But I kept my mouth shut [about them] as they seemed to be doing me no harm. Now, however, it appears that we are all going to knuckle under to machines ~~and will have to forego~~ that admire these numbers (the must all forego the pleasure and convenience of writing a check on an ordinary, non-magnetic piece of paper. My signature used to be enough to prod my bank into dispatching some of my money to some needy individual or firm, ~~but~~ not any more. This, I think, is a defeat for all---a surrender. In order to accommodate the Federal Reserve system, we are ~~going~~ asked to put ourselves out.

The notice I received says that if I try to

270

2

palm off a check that lacks the magnetic ink numbers, the check cannot be processed without "delay, extra handling charges, and possible embarrassment." I embarrass easy---it doesn't take much, really---and naturally I am eager to learn what form this embarrassment will take if I should decide to write a check using the old blank form that has proved so convenient for I don't know how many decades on those occasions when one is stuck without his checkbook or enough lettuce to carry the day.

"The tremendous increase in the use of checks," writes my bank , warming to its subject, "made it necessary for the Federal Reserve to establish a completely computerized operation for processing all checks from all banks. Their computer can function only when proper magnetic numbers are used." Well, I can believe that last part, about the computer requiring a special diet of ~~deranged numbers~~ malformed numbers; but I am suspicious of that first statement, about how the Federal Reserve would have been unable to carry on unless it went completely over to machines. I suspect that the Federal Reserve simply found machines useful, handy, and ~~sustaining to its ego~~ adventitious. But suppose we had had, in this country, a tremendous increase in the use of checks and nobody had yet got round to inventing the computer---what would have happened then? Am I supposed expected to believe that the Federal Reserve and all their member banks would have thrown in the sponge? I know banks better than that. Banks love money and are not easily deflected from the ~~enchanting~~ delicious business of accumulating it. ~~Somehow they would have found~~ Love would have found a way. Checks would have cleared.

I'm not against machines, as are some people 278

3

who feel that the computer is leading us down the primrose

trail. I ~~kxxxxmxxkixx~~ like machines---particularly the egg

the highest point   *has yet reached*

beater, which is the machine at its finest and most mysterious.

~~But~~ I8m only against machines when the convenience they afford

some   *is considered more important than*

to ~~xomxxtx xxxtxixvxxxxx~~ overshadwos the ~~in~~inconvience they

all x   *50*

cause to ~~xixx xxxx~~. In short, I don't think computers should

wear the pants, or even make the decisions---~~sixxxxdxx~~. They

lack humor, and they are not intuitive--or even aware ofthe

mponderables. I read a poem once written by a computer but,

didn't care much for it. It seemed to me I could write a better.

100

one myself, if I put my mind to it, and my heart in it.

And now I must look around for a blank check.

It's time I found out what form t~~hxxxxmbxxxx~~ my new embarrsment

is going to take. First, thoulg, I!ll have o remember the.

150

name of my bank. It'll come to me, if I sit here long enough.

Oddly enough, the warning notice I received

contained no signature. Imagine a bank

forgetting to sign its name!

≠ 174
278.
270
———
722

The pieces have begun to fall more gracefully into place here. Most important, perhaps, White gets rid of the digression about bank statements at the end of his first draft and replaces it with the more general reflections he has been aiming toward all along. Note how the troublesome sentence from his notes about "the danger in a machine culture" has found its place in the penultimate paragraph of this second draft. (Note, as well, how White has continued to rework and refine it.)

In the handwritten emendations of this draft, we also see White sharpening the wit of his reflections, particularly as he develops his wry personification of his bank and computers in general ("a certain magnetism that computers insist on" and "machines that admire these numbers"). And it is not until now, in his attempt to bring the essay to a satisfactory close, that White adds the final, memorable image of "a bank forgetting to sign its name," an image that eventually grows very naturally out of his process of revising, of focusing and clarifying his ideas in order to make his point most vividly for his audience. Names are no longer important; all that matters now is a magnetic code for computers to read.

Reading White's finished essay as it appeared in the New York Times, we have a hard time realizing that the writer didn't know exactly what he had in mind when he sat down to write. When a piece of writing is successful, we do not see the seams; the words carry us along so that we are not aware of the writer's process. But it is clear from White's notes and his drafts that this graceful, carefully conceived essay required a great deal of work: jotting, scratching out, drafting, rewriting, private questions and decisions, moments of inspiration when the connections began to seem clear, when the work seemed to pay off. What we learn from White's manuscripts is that ideas don't spring full blown from a writer's mind into a clear, coherent form. Rather, ideas may tumble out in unformed, fragmented ways that can be developed, modified, and sharpened draft after draft.

Composition is, then, a process, and the practical implications for student writers are readily apparent. It takes time to put what you have to say, your most personal and immediate responses, into a form that an audience can understand and appreciate, into words that will best express your intentions. Waiting to begin a writing assignment until the night before it is due will not allow this sort of time. Fully developed ideas are the result of revising, of working step by step, and require a series of working sessions over the course of several days or several weeks. Only then can you take full advantage of your reading and writing skills in order to produce a final draft that seems to be ready for an audience. What you end with will very likely come a long way from how you begin.

You've just seen, of course, how E. B. White began. You'll find what he ended with at the beginning of "Reading and Rereading," page 741.

SUGGESTIONS FOR DISCUSSION AND WRITING

1. We have suggested several changes that White made in the course of drafting his essay in order to take into account his readers' attitudes and interests. What other changes like these do you find? What do these changes tell you about the audience White had in mind? How does he encourage the responses he wants from his readers?

2. Compare White's final pattern of organization to the initial notes he made for himself. Do the notes provide any sense of his final pattern?

3. What does White achieve in the course of revising? How has he determined what to keep from earlier drafts and what to delete?

4. Consider some of the words and expressions White chooses that may seem a bit out of the ordinary, either in themselves or in the way they are used. Looking at the words and expressions you have selected, what can you say about White's style, about what gives his essay its particular tone of voice? Look also through the drafts to see the words and expressions which were deleted. In what way do the selected words and expressions best serve White's purpose?

5. Have you ever felt oppressed or victimized by a machine or an institution? Write an essay in which you express your feelings and seek to gain sympathy for your cause or redress for your grievance.

6. If you have recently received any irritating letter, like that from White's bank, jot down your reactions to the content and the tone or approach of the letter. Then, using White's article as a model, write an essay objecting to the letter and its implications.

Suggestions for Writing Across the Disciplines

The following writing suggestions are based on the topical groupings of essays in the Topical Guide to the Contents, p. xxii.

VALUES AND BELIEFS

1. Every piece in this group suggests, either explicitly or implicitly that one thing in life is most important—whether it is faith in God, or reason, or physical love, or knowledge, or beauty. Select several of these discussions and explain in each case why the writer believes in the preeminence of the particular value he or she has chosen. Then indicate the extent to which you share each of these views—and your reasons for agreeing or disagreeing with the writer. Conclude by either making the case for another value entirely as being most important, or by supplying your own reasons for considering one of the values you have already discussed to be the most important.

2. Expressions of value and belief can take many forms, ranging from the most direct statements to ironic or metaphoric figures of speech. Select several of the pieces grouped under this heading and discuss the relationship between the values they express and the form in which they express those values. For instance, one might expect a writer to make the case for reason reasonably or the case for love emotionally, but it is also possible to be passionate about reason and to argue logically that love is the supreme value. Choose poems or essays that display a range of relationships between what they value and how they make the case for so valuing it. Try to discuss the way that a particular form of presentation influences your reception of the case for that particular value.

RACE AND RACISM

3. Using the essays in this grouping, consider the question of racism. What is racism? Why do so many people consider racism to be a great evil? In considering these questions, read essays that present as broad a view as possible of the workings of racism. Consider the scientific arguments of Stephen Jay Gould, the discussions of Nazi racism by Bettelheim and Lifton, and the discussions of

770

racism in America by Douglass, Walker, Angelou, and Momaday. In your essay discuss some of the varieties of racism, the actions resulting from it, and the reasons for its persistence.

4. In a good dictionary examine the definitions of "race" and "culture." Obviously these are not the same thing, but there is much confusion between the two. A number of the essays in this section treat contact between cultures, or the difference between one culture and another (especially the essays by Dinesen, Orwell, and Mead), while others are more concerned with race. Using the essays on foreign cultures as a background, discuss the experience of black and native Americans in the U.S.A. How have race and culture functioned in the experience of these groups within this country? Use specific events drawn from essays by Angelou, Walker, or Douglass to provide a focus for your discussion.

THE STATUS OF WOMEN

5. Using as many as possible of the pieces in this grouping as evidence for your discussion, try to say what it means to be a woman and, in particular, what is means to be a woman at the present point in history. What are the advantages and drawbacks of being a woman now, as opposed to in Voltaire's time, for instance? Should women be content with their present situation or should they work to change it? In answering this question consider some of the specific situations and events mentioned in the essays by Hardy, Fraker, Coward, Miller and Swift. If you are female, how do you feel about it? If you are male, try to imagine how you would feel about these matters if you happened to be female. There is obviously a place in your essay for personal feelings and thoughts, but try to let the situations and events discussed in the essays set the topics for discussion, bringing in personal experiences only if they are relevant.

6. How do men treat women? Looking through this group of essays, what do you consider to be the best example of male behavior toward females? What is the worst? Make a list of examples drawn from various essays, arranged according to your own standards of proper and improper treatment of women by men. Discuss a sequence of examples from your list, making sure to get both extremes of behavior discussed, along with some examples from the middle range. Try to say in each case what aspects of male behavior you approve of and disapprove of, and what your reasons are for this evaluation. If your reasoning is to be coherent, you will need to have worked out some general principles for intersexual behavior.

VIOLENCE AND WAR

7. The essays in this grouping by Hardy, Laurence, and Hersey present very different perspectives on the atomic bombing of two Japanese cities by the U.S.A. at the end of World War II. Write an essay in which you discuss the

771

roles in these historical events played by the major figure of each essay—the ones referred to in each title: "Grandma," "A Flight Member," and "Hatsuyo Nakamura." First describe how each of these individuals was connected to the bombings. Then consider the way each person felt about these events either at the time or afterwards, to the extent that you can do so from the information given in the essays. Conclude by discussing what you have learned from seeing a historical event from these personal perspectives.

8. Let us define violence as a deliberate attempt to injure someone or something. Drawing upon the essays in this grouping, discuss the range of violent behavior in the modern world and various approaches to the limitation or control of violence. Both boxing and nonviolence are ways—however different—of controlling violence. What is war: controlled or uncontrolled violence? Focusing on the essays by King, Bettelheim, and Mead, conclude your essay with a discussion of the extent to which non violence is a viable response to violence.

LIFE AND DEATH

9. The essays in this grouping by Dinesen, Orwell, and Woolf all use the death of a particular animal as the occasion for a discussion of larger questions. Write an essay in which you first discuss what each of those writers learned from their experiences with an iguana, elephant, and moth, and then go on to discuss some experience of your own with observing or encountering or causing a death (preferably in the world of animals, birds, or insects) and what you learned or now understand thinking over that incident.

10. Drawing upon a range of essays from this grouping, write an essay in which you discuss the relationship between life and death in this world. In particular, you should consider the work of Darwin, Tuchman, Kübler-Ross, Dinesen, and Woolf in developing your own essay. You might begin by imagining some features of an alternate world in which no living thing died. Would such a world be better than ours in every respect? What, if anything, might be worse in such a world? Remember to aim at some conclusion about the relationship between life and death. Do not just discuss life and death separately.

HEALTH, DISEASE, AND MEDICINE

11. Medicine is a field that extends from science to human relations. Every physician is both a healer and a scientist. But these two dimensions of medicine are not always in harmony. Consider the range of relationships between science and healing that are to be found in the essays by Thomas, Selzer, and Damasio. Describe and explain several different relationships between the search for med-

ical knowledge and the treatment of individual patients as you find them in these essays. What do you consider the proper or ideal relationship between these two elements of medicine?

12. Suppose the health problems described in the essays of Gold and Brown got really out of hand, creating a disaster on the scale of that described by Tuchman, but here and now. Or suppose the new techniques described by Hubbard led to further developments in bio-genetic technique. Describe our world as it would be after these developments. You may find some guidance in the organization of this kind of essay in Tuchman. Describe what you think might happen as if it had already happened. (Yes, this is a little bit like writing science fiction.)

SCIENTIFIC THINKING

What is a scientist? What are the qualities that distinguish scientific ways of behaving from other ways? In particular, what are the major characteristics of the way scientists think and express their thoughts? Using the essays in this grouping by Hoffman, Guillen, Asimov, Crick, Thomas, and Kuhn (or some other set of comparable weight) develop an essay in which you discuss the key qualities of scientific thought. Remember to consider not only what is said in these essays but also the way in which these scientists put their thoughts into written words.

14. What is a scientific "discovery"? How do scientists extend the range of human knowledge—or is this not what they actually do? Referring to the essays in this grouping by Medawar, Kuhn, Hofstadter, Thomas, and Guillen, develop your own answers to these questions. Try to give adequate summaries of the positions of the writers you discuss, and then either select the one closest to your own and show how you would modify it or develop a different position that expresses your own view of scientific "discovery."

TEACHING, LEARNING, AND SCHOOLING

15. Most of the essays in this grouping bear directly on the matter of schools and schooling. Using the essays by Angelou, Baker, Sizer, Fitzgerald, and Glazer as sources, write an essay in which you discuss the present state of public education in this country—especially secondary or high school education—and recommend any major changes you think should be made. You should feel free to borrow (with appropriate acknowledgment) ideas from the essays you have read, but you should also bring your own experience to bear upon these questions. After all, you've been there.

16. What is a teacher? What is a student, a learner? Using essays in this

section by Angelou, Douglas, Baker, Freud, and Thomas as sources, develop your own view of what it means to learn and to teach. Draw from your reading and from personal experience several examples of the right and wrong way to go about these things. Remember that in this question you are not discussing the formal structure of schools but the personal matter of how a human being should learn and study or help others to learn.

SEARCHING FOR FACTS

17.   The activity of searching for knowledge suggests that behind every fact or set of information there is a story of how the facts were discovered. Often, these stories turn out to be not only fascinating tales, but also factually significant accounts. Indeed, these stories sometimes seem to suggest that a particular method of searching for facts is as important as the facts themselves. What significance do you attach to the various methods by which people search for facts? Write an essay in which you develop and substantiate your view, drawing on the selections by Walker, Wilson, Diamond, and Knightly.

18.   The selections by Fitzgerald, Carr, Gould, and Amundson suggest that searching for facts is less important than interpreting the facts. Indeed, collectively they even seem to imply that a particular fact or set of facts is less important than the method by which it is interpreted. Why do you think they put so much emphasis on interpreting the facts? Do you agree with this emphasis? Write an essay in which you develop and substantiate your view, drawing on whatever selections you wish from this section.

UNDERSTANDING THE PAST

19.   Using the selections by Momaday, Forster, Tuchman, and Gombrich, write an essay in which you explore the nature and influence of "closeness" and "distance" in historical inquiry. In exploring this problem, you might find it useful to think about some of the following questions:
  a. How many kinds of closeness and distance are important for you to consider?
  b. Using you categories, how would you rank these four historians in order of distance from their subject?
  c. How does a distant historian seek to compensate for the disadvantages of distance—and how does a close historian seek to compensate for those of closeness?

20.   Carr, FitzGerald, and Kuhn collectively seem to suggest that the past is far less stable than we ordinarily suppose it to be—that it changes as often as

historians change their ways of understanding the past. Do you agree or disagree with this idea of history? Write an essay in which you take a stand, using as evidence a particular event or set of events from American history.

OBSERVING ANIMALS

21. Examining the selections by Dillard, Mowat, Lawick-Goodall, and Gould, write an essay in which you discuss the problems of observing and understanding animals. Consider such questions as why we look at animals, what methods and tools we use to observe them, and whether they look back. Try to develop a thesis about what we can and cannot learn from animals by observing them. Consider the questions of how the manner of observing influences the creatures under observation and what our attempts to observe animals teach us about ourselves.

22. The selections by Dinesen, Eisely, Gould, and Amundson are concerned in varying degrees and in various ways with problems that arise from misusing animals or misobserving animals for human purposes. Based on your reading of these selections, your own personal experience with animals, and your own ethical convictions, write an essay in which you define what you consider to be the limits in using and observing animals for human purposes.

ON BEING HUMAN

23. Many of the selections in this section are concerned with unusual or bizarre instances of human behavior or experience. In reading about such persons, are you interested in them primarily because of their strangeness or their differences from you? Or does your interest arise and develop out of some connection that you make with their situation that enables you to see them as being in some sense similar to you? Or is there some other reason that sustains your interest in reading about such persons? Write an essay in which you consider your motives for reading about such human beings, referring in particular to the selections by Seabrook, Selzer, Kennedy, Horney, Bettelheim, Milgram, and Lifton.

24. How free are human beings? Consider the essays by Seabrook, Horney, Bettelheim, Kübler-Ross, Lifton, Milgram, and Mead in formulating your response to this question.

PEOPLE

25. Biographical writing, even at the level of sketches, always implies a portrait of the writer, however faintly. Compare Jung's "Sigmund Freud," Walker's "Looking for Zora,' Selzer's "The Discus Thrower," and Bettelheim's "Joey:

A 'Mechanical Boy.'" What signs do you find in those pieces of their authors? Write an essay on two of those four writings, comparing and contrasting the traces of the authors you find in them.

26. Jung, "Sigmund Freud," and Hoffmann, "My Friend, Albert Einstein," wrote of people they knew well. Walker, "Looking for Zora,' Forster, "Voltaire's Laboratory," and Lifton, "What Made This Man? Mengele," wrote of persons at some distance, persons they had different reasons for pursuing. Hersey, "Hatsuyo Nakamura," Selzer, "The Discus Thrower," and Bettelheim, "Joey," wrote of persons they knew in a sense, but not intimately. Drawing on three or four of these essays, write an essay that discusses the ways those authors handle the matter of distance.

CULTURE

27. Several essays in this section focus on specific aspects of culture: Coward's "Let's Have a Meal Together," Minor's "Body Ritual of the Nacirema," Miller and Swift's "Women and Names," Galbraith's "The Technostructure," Ross's "Football Red and Baseball Green," Pascale's "Fitting Employees Into the Company Culture." Compare and contrast two of those essays. What problems and techniques of cultural observation do they demonstrate? What kind of distance do those writers establish in relation to their subjects? Do they convince you of their objectivity and accuracy? Why or why not?

28. Drawing on three or four of the essays in this section, define culture. There are many views of culture, of course, and many of those overlap. What kind of thing does the word "culture" mean to these authors? What notions of culture are defined for their purposes?

ART, SPORT, AND ENTERTAINMENT

29. What are the similarities between art and sport? With reference, perhaps, to Langer's "The Cultural Importance of Art," could you write an essay advancing football, baseball, or boxing as an art (see Ross's "Football Red and Baseball Green" and Oates's "On Boxing")? Or, on the other hand, could you see Wilson's literary pursuits ("The Other Side of the Wall") as a sport? And where would that place the activity White writes of in "The Ring of Time"?

30. Entertainment is another boundary area where, in some cases, popular culture merges with art. Several of the essays here deal with the popular arts. With reference again to Langer's "The Cultural Importance of Art," discuss two or more of the popular arts dealt with in these essays as arts. Try to decide the degree of artfulness you grant them.

ACKNOWLEDGMENTS (*continued*)

David Denby, "The Visionary Gleam," from *New York Magazine*, June 14, 1982. Copyright © 1985 by News America Publishing, Inc. Reprinted with the permission of *New York Magazine*.

Edwin Diamond, "Twelve Days of Terror! The Three-Mile Island Story," from *Sign Off: The Last Days of Television*, 1982, pp. 81–90. Copyright © 1982 by The MIT Press.

Joan Didion, "On Keeping A Notebook," from SLOUCHING TOWARDS BETHLEHEM by Joan Didion. Copyright © 1966, 1968 by Joan Didion. Reprinted by permission of Farrar, Straus and Giroux, Inc.

Annie Dillard, "Lenses," from TEACHING A STONE TO TALK: EXPEDITIONS AND EN-COUNTERS, by Annie Dillard, Copyright © 1982 by Annie Dillard. Reprinted by permission of Harper & Row, Publishers, Inc.

Isak Dinesen, "The Iguana," by permission of Random House, Inc., and the Rungstedlund Foundation. From OUT OF AFRICA by Isak Dinesen. Copyright © 1937 by Random House, Inc., and renewed 1965 by the Rungstedlund Foundation.

Loren Eiseley, "The Bird and the Machine," from THE IMMENSE JOURNEY by Loren Eiseley. Copyright © 1955 by Loren Eiseley. Reprinted by permission of Random House, Inc.

Frances FitzGerald, "America Revised," from AMERICA REVISED by Frances FitzGerald, pp. 7–17. Copyright © 1979 by Frances FitzGerald. Reprinted by permission of Little, Brown and Company, in association with the Atlantic Monthly Press.

E.M. Forster, "Voltaire's Laboratory," from ABINGER HARVEST. Copyright © 1936, 1964 by Edward Morgan Forster. Reprinted by permission of Harcourt Brace Jovanovich, Inc. E.M. Forster, "Voltaire's Laboratory," from ABINGER HARVEST reprinted by permission of Edward Arnold Publishers, Ltd.

Susan Fraker, "Why Women Aren't Getting to the Top," from FORTUNE, April 16, 1984, reprinted by permission of *Fortune* Magazine.

John Kenneth Galbraith, "The Technostructure," from THE NEW INDUSTRIAL STATE, third edition, by John Kenneth Galbraith. Copyright © 1967, 1971, 1978 by John Kenneth Galbraith. Reprinted by permission of Houghton-Mifflin Company.

Lucy Gilbert and Paula Webster, "The Dangers of Femininity," from BOUND BY LOVE by Lucy Gilbert and Paula Webster. Copyright © 1982 by Lucy Gilbert and Paula Webster. Reprinted by permission of Beacon Press.

Nathan Glazer, "Some Very Modest Proposals," from *Daedalus*, Fall 1984, pp. 169–176. Reprinted by permission of *Daedalus*, Journal of the American Academy of Arts and Sciences, Cambridge, Massachusetts.

Michael Gold, "The Cells That Would Not Die," reprinted by permission from the April issue of SCIENCE 81. Copyright © 1981 by The American Association for the Advancement of Science.

E.H. Gombrich, "Art for Eternity," from THE STORY OF ART by E.H. Gombrich, Copyright © 1984, pp. 32–42. Reprinted by permission of Prentice-Hall, Englewood Cliffs, New Jersey.

Stephen Jay Gould, "A Biological Homage to Mickey Mouse," reprinted from THE PANDA'S THUMB: MORE REFLECTIONS IN NATURAL HISTORY by Stephen Jay Gould, by permission of W. W. Norton & Company, Inc. Copyright © 1980 by Stephen Jay Gould.

Stephen Jay Gould, "Evolution as Fact and Theory." Stephen Jay Gould, © 1981 *Discover* Magazine, Time, Inc.

Stephen Jay Gould, "Racist Arguments and IQ," reprinted from EVER SINCE DARWIN: RE-FLECTIONS IN NATURAL HISTORY, by Stephen Jay Gould, by permission of W. W. Norton & Company, Inc. Copyright © 1977 by Stephen Jay Gould. Copyright © 1973, 1974, 1975, 1976, 1977 by The American Museum of Natural History.

Michael Guillen, "Logic and Proof—A Certain Treasure," from BRIDGES TO INFINITY by Michael Guillen. Copyright © 1983 by Michael Guillen. Reprinted by permission of Jeremy P. Tarcher, Inc.

Zoë Tracy Hardy, "What Did You Do in the War, Grandma?" (*Ms.*, August, 1985). Reprinted by permission of the author.

John Hersey, "Hatsuyo Nakamura," from HIROSHIMA: THE AFTERMATH by John Hersey Copyright © 1985 by John Hersey. Reprinted from *Hiroshima* by John Hersey, by permission of Alfred A. Knopf. Originally appeared in *The New Yorker*.

ACKNOWLEDGMENTS

Banesh Hoffman, "My Friend, Albert Einstein," reprinted with permission from the January 1968 READER'S DIGEST. Copyright © 1968 by The Reader's Digest Association, Inc.

Douglas R. Hofstadter, "On the Seeming Paradox of Mechanized Creativity," from METAMAGICAL THEMAS: QUESTING FOR THE ESSENCE OF MIND AND PATTERN by Douglas R. Hofstadter. Copyright © 1985 by Basic Books, Inc., Publishers. Reprinted by permission of the publisher.

Karen Horney, "The Concept of Narcissism," reprinted from NEW WAYS IN PSYCHOANALYSIS by Karen Horney, M.D. by permission of W. W. Norton & Company, Inc. Copyright © 1939 by W. W. Norton & Co., Inc. Copyright renewed 1966 by Renate Mintz, Brigitte Swarzenski, and Marianne von Eckhardt.

Ruth Hubbard, "Test-Tube Babies; Solution or Problem?," reprinted with permission from the March/April 1980 TECHNOLOGY REVIEW, M.I.T. Alumni Association, Copyright © 1980.

James Jeans, "Why the Sky Is Blue," from THE STARS IN THEIR COURSES by James Jeans. Reprinted by permission of Cambridge University Press.

C.G. Jung, "Sigmund Freud," from MEMORIES, REFLECTIONS, DREAMS by C. G. Jung, recorded and edited by Aniela Jaffe, translated by Richard and Clara Winston. Translation Copyright © 1961, 1962, 1963 by Random House, Inc. Reprinted by permission of Pantheon Books, a division of Random House, Inc.

X.J. Kennedy, "Who Killed King Kong?," reprinted by permission of Dissent magazine.

Martin Luther King, Jr., "Pilgrimage to Nonviolence," from STRENGTH TO LOVE, reprinted by permission of Joan Daves. Copyright © 1963 by Martin Luther King, Jr.

Phillip Knightley, "The First Televised War," from THE FIRST CASUALTY, copyright © 1975 by Phillip Knightley. Reprinted by permission of Harcourt Brace Jovanovich, Inc. Phillip Knightley, "The First Televised War," from THE FIRST CASUALTY, reprinted by permission of André Deutsch, Ltd.

Elizabeth Kübler-Ross, "On the Fear of Death," reprinted with permission of Macmillan Publishing Company from ON DEATH AND DYING by Elizabeth Kübler-Ross. Copyright © 1969 by Elizabeth Kübler-Ross.

Susanne K. Langer, "The Cultural Importance of Art," reprinted from PHILOSOPHICAL SKETCHES. Baltimore/London, The Johns Hopkins University Press, 1962.

William Laurence, "Atomic Bombing of Nagasaki Told by Flight Member," Copyright © 1945 by The New York Times Company, Reprinted by permission.

Jane van Lawick-Goodall, "First Observations" pp. 28–37, from IN THE SHADOW OF MAN by Jane van Lawick-Goodall. Copyright © 1971 by Hugo and Jane van Lawick-Goodall. Reprinted by permission of Houghton Mifflin Company.

Ursula Le Guin, "Why Are Americans Afraid of Dragons?" From LANGUAGE OF THE NIGHT. Copyright © 1974 by Ursula Le Guin; reprinted by permission of the author and her agent, Virginia Kidd.

Robert Jay Lifton, "What Made This Man? Mengele," as appeared in The New York Times Magazine, July 21, 1985, "What Made This Man? Mengele" by Robert Jay Lifton, adapted from THE NAZI DOCTORS by Robert Jay Lifton. Copyright © 1986 by Robert Jay Lifton. Reprinted by permission of Basic Books, Inc., Publishers. Copyright © 1985 by The New York Times Company. Reprinted by permission.

Margaret Mead, "A Day in Samoa," from COMING OF AGE IN SAMOA by Margaret Mead. Copyright © 1928, 1955 by Margaret Mead. By permission of William Morrow and Company.

Margaret Mead, "Warfare: An Invention—Not A Biological Necessity," from ANTHROPOLOGY: A HUMAN SCIENCE, pp. 126–134. Reprinted by permission of Wadsworth Publishing Company.

P.B. Medawar, "Can Scientific Discovery Be Premeditated?" (pp. 45–53). From THE LIMITS OF SCIENCE by P.B. Medawar (A Cornelia and Michael Bessie Book). Copyright © 1984 by Peter C. Medawar. Reprinted by permission of Harper & Row, Publishers, Inc.

Stanley Milgram, "Some Conditions of Obedience and Disobedience To Authority," HUMAN RELATIONS, Vol. 18, No. 1, 1965, pp. 57–76. Copyright © 1972 by Stanley Milgram. All rights controlled by Alexandra Milgram, literary executor. Reprinted by permission.

Casey Miller and Kate Swift, "Women and Names," from WORDS AND WOMEN by Casey Miller and Kate Swift. Copyright © 1976 by Casey Miller and Kate Swift. Reprinted by permission of Doubleday and Company, Inc.

778

ACKNOWLEDGMENTS

Horace Miner, "Body Ritual Among the Nacirema," reproduced by permission of The American Anthropological Association from AMERICAN ANTHROPOLOGIST 58:503–507, 1956. Not for further reproduction.

N. Scott Momaday, "The Way to Rainy Mountain," reprinted from THE WAY TO RAINY MOUNTAIN. Copyright © 1969 by The University of New Mexico Press.

Farley Mowat, "Observing Wolves," from NEVER CRY WOLF. Copyright © 1963 by Farley Mowat. By permission of Little, Brown and Company, in association with the Atlantic Monthly Press. Reprinted with permission of the author.

The New York Times, "TWA Flight 514, December 1, 1974," reprinted with permission of AP Newsfeatures.

Joyce Carol Oates, "On Boxing," reprinted by permission of the author and her agent Blanche C. Gregory, Inc. Copyright © 1985 by The New York Times Company. Reprinted by permission.

George Orwell, "Shooting an Elephant," from SHOOTING AN ELEPHANT AND OTHER STORIES by George Orwell, copyright © 1946 by Sonia Brownell Orwell; renewed 1974 by Sonia Orwell. Reprinted by permission of Harcourt Brace Jovanovich, Inc. Reprinted by permission of the estate of the late Sonia Brownell Orwell and Secker & Warburg, Ltd.

Heinz R. Pagels, "The Cosmic Code," copyright © 1982 by Heinz R. Pagels. Reprinted by permission of Simon & Schuster, Inc.

Richard Pascale, "Fitting New Employees Into the Company Culture," from FORTUNE, May 28, 1984. Copyright © 1984 Time, Inc. All rights reserved.

Richard Robinson, "Faith," from AN ATHEIST'S VALUES by Richard Robinson. By permission of Basil Blackwell, Publisher.

Murray Ross, "Football Red and Baseball Green," reprinted by permission of the author.

Bertrand Russell, "Why I Took to Philosophy," from PORTRAITS FROM MEMORY by Bertrand Russell. Copyright © 1951, 1952, 1953, 1956 by Bertrand Russell. Reprinted by permission of Simon & Schuster, Inc.

Jeremy Seabrook, "A Twin Is Only Half a Person," from MOTHER TO SON. Copyright © 1980 by Jeremy Seabrook. Reprinted by permission of Pantheon Books, a division of Random House Inc. Reprinted by permission of Victor Gollancz, Publishers.

Roy Selby, Jr., "A Delicate Operation." Copyright © 1975 by Harper's Magazine. All rights reserved. Reprinted from the December, 1975 issue by special permission.

Richard Selzer, "The Discus Thrower," reprinted by permission of ICM. Originally appeared in Harper's Magazine.

Theodore Sizer, "What High School Is," from HORACE'S COMPROMISE by Theodore R. Sizer. Copyright © 1984 by Theodore R. Sizer. Reprinted by permission of Houghton Mifflin Company.

Richard Taylor, "Faith," reprinted by permission of New York University from RELIGIOUS EXPERIENCE AND TRUTH: A SYMPOSIUM, edited by Sidney Hook. Copyright © 1961 by New York University.

Lewis Thomas, "The Art of Teaching Science," Copyright © 1982 by The New York Times Company. Reprinted by permission.

Lewis Thomas, "1933 Medicine," from THE YOUNGEST SCIENCE by Lewis Thomas. Copyright © 1983 by Lewis Thomas. Reprinted by permission of Viking Penguin, Inc.

Lester Thurow, "The Zero-Sum Game," from THE ZERO-SUM SOCIETY: Distribution and the Possibilities for Economic Change by Lester C. Thurow. Copyright © 1980 by Basic Books, Inc., Publishers. Reprinted by permission of the publisher.

Barbara Tuchman, " 'This Is the End of the World': The Black Death," from A DISTANT MIRROR, by Barbara Tuchman. Copyright © 1979 by Barbara Tuchman. Reprinted by permission of Alfred A. Knopf, Inc. Copyright © 1963 Radcliffe College. Reprinted by permission of the Radcliffe Quarterly.

Alice Walker, "Looking for Zora," reprinted from her volume IN SEARCH OF OUR MOTHERS' GARDENS by permission of Harcourt Brace Jovanovich, Inc.

E.B. White, "The Ring of Time," from ESSAYS OF E.B. WHITE. Copyright © 1956 by E.B. White. Renewed 1984 by E.B. White. Reprinted by permission of Harper & Row, Publishers, Inc.

E.B. White, "Dear Mr. 0214 1063 02 10730 8." Copyright © 1967 by The New York Times Company. Reprinted by permission.

ACKNOWLEDGMENTS

E.B. White, "Drafts," reprinted by permission of Cornell University Library. Copyright © 1967 by The New York Times Company. Reprinted by permission.

George Will, "Well, I Don't Love You, E.T.," as printed in *Newsweek*, Vol. 100, July 19, 1982. Reprinted with permission of The Free Press, a Division of Macmillan, Inc., from THE MORNING AFTER by George Will. Copyright © 1982, 1986 by Washington Post Company.

Douglas Wilson, "The Other Side of the Wall," *The Iowa Review*, v. 10, #1, Winter 1979. Copyright © 1979 by The University of Iowa. Reprinted by permission of the publisher and the author.

Virginia Woolf, "The Death of The Moth," from THE DEATH OF THE MOTH AND OTHER ESSAYS by Virginia Woolf, copyright © 1942 by Harcourt Brace Jovanovich, Inc., renewed 1970 by Marjorie T. Parsons. Reprinted by permission of the publisher. By permission of the author's Literary Estate and the Hogarth Press.

William Butler Yeats, "For Anne Gregory," reprinted with permission of Macmillan Publishing Company from COLLECTED POEMS of William Butler Yeats. Copyright © 1933 by Macmillan Publishing Company, renewed 1961 by Bertha Georgie Yeats.

ART ACKNOWLEDGMENTS

E.H. Gombrich, "Art for Eternity," p. 296: "Portrait Head of Limestone," courtesy of the Kunstlisches Museum von Vienna, p. 298. "Painting of a Pond," reproduced courtesy of the Trustees of The British Museum, p. 300. "Portrait of Hesire," p. 301, reproduced by courtesy of the Egyptian Museum. "King Amenhophis IV," p. 306, reproduced by courtesy of the Staatsmuseum von Berlin. "The Pharoah Tutankhamen and his Wife," p. 307, reproduced courtesy of the Egyptian Museum. "A Dagger from Mycenae," p. 308, reproduced by courtesy of the National Archeological Museum, Athens, Greece. Stephen Jay Gould, "A Biological Homage to Mickey Mouse," p. 500: "Mickey's Evolution," p. 501; "Mortimer Stealing Minnie's Affections from Mickey," p. 506; "Goofy," p. 508; all reprinted courtesy of Walt Disney Productions. Illustration © from Konrad Lorenz: *Über Tierisches Und Menschliches Verhalten*, Vol. II and R. Piper & Co. Verlag, München, 1965. E. B. White, "Drafts," reprinted by permission of Cornell University Library, Copyright © 1967 by The New York Times Company. Reprinted by permission.

Rhetorical Index

ANALOGY

Discussed in "Explaining," p. 259

Exemplified by "The Cosmic Code," pp. 97–107; "Atomic Bombing of Nagasaki Told by Flight Member," pp. 169–175; "Football Red and Baseball Green," pp. 274–283; "On Boxing," pp. 284–295; "A Zero-Sum Game," pp. 361–365; "Joey: A 'Mechanical Boy'," pp. 411–422; "Times and Distances, Large and Small," pp. 487–494; "The Case Against Man," pp. 686–690; "On the Seeming Paradox of Mechanized Creativity," pp. 705–720

ARGUING

Discussed in "Arguing," pp. 543–550

Exemplified by all selections in "Arguing," pp. 550–739

CASE STUDY

Discussed in "Explaining," pp. 259–267

Exemplified by "Love Canal and the Poisoning of America," pp. 223–237; "Two Reports of an Airplane Crash," pp. 238–249; "Joey: A 'Mechanical Boy'," pp. 411–422; "What Made this Man? Mengele," pp. 430–441

CAUSAL ANALYSIS

Discussed in "Explaining," pp. 259–267

Exemplified by "Why I Took to Philosophy," pp. 26–30; "Sigmund Freud," pp. 64–69; "Two Reports of an Airplane Crash," pp. 238–249; "Who Killed King Kong?," pp. 269–273; "Women and Names," pp. 390–402; "Why Women Aren't Getting to the Top," pp. 376–384; "The Concept of Narcissism,"

781

COMPARISON AND CONTRAST

DEFINITION

DESCRIPTION

TOPICAL SUMMATION

Discussed in "Reporting," pp. 121–128

Exemplified by "Two Reports of an Airplane Crash," pp. 238–249; "Some Conditions of Obedience and Disobedience," pp. 442–465; "Tentative Report on the Hudson River Bridge," pp. 509–524; "Two Reports on Prosopagnosia," pp. 525–538